Philosophical Elements of Social Justice

2nd Edition

Ted M. Preston, Ph.D.
Rio Hondo College

A Local Source Textbook™ Company

Philosophical Elements of Social Justice

2nd Edition

Preface to the 2nd Edition

Philosophers have hitherto only interpreted the world in various ways; the point is to change it.[1]

This is a textbook that I hadn't thought I would ever write.

Although I have written several others, and although the subject matter of this book has always been "present" to some degree or another in those books and my courses that use them, it had never occurred to me to focus an entire text and an entire course on the topic of social justice. Then, like many people, I experienced an "awakening" in the eventful year of 2020.

The catalyst for that long-overdue awakening was the killing of George Floyd by police officers on May 25th, 2020. He was certainly not the first Black[2] man to be killed as a result of contact with the police that year, and he wouldn't be the last, but the nature of his killing, captured on camera for approximately nine minutes, and broadcast around the world activated thousands upon thousands of people who, like myself, regrettably, had not prior to that adequately understood, or hadn't been sufficiently motivated.

Thousands upon thousands of people—not only Americans but people from across the globe—started to join with those who had already been struggling for social justice, and we did so in various ways. Some took to the streets to demonstrate, some volunteered for political campaigns, ran for office, or donated to various causes and organizations. Some created or shared content on social media; some organized for change at the local, state, or national levels. One of the things that I did was what I am trained to do: read, research, and reflect. I began to read dozens of books addressing issues of social justice from my own field of philosophy, but also from history, legal studies, political science, and criminal justice. I watched documentaries and joined with colleagues on my campus to participate in campus "conversations." Eventually, I created a new course focusing on the philosophy of social justice, and developed this text to support it.

This text is, and I suspect will always be, a "work in progress." Issues of social justice are countless, as are their interpretations and interventions. Any version of this book will always be inadequate to capture anything better than a fraction of the topics, policies, issues, ideas, and people associated with social justice. Omissions are inevitable, and in no way intended to imply that the topic or thinker is somehow less important, less urgent, or less valuable. In addition, any attempt to be inclusive, including my own, are always imperfect, and are always shaped by the experiences and identities of those involved. In my own case, I am a middle-aged, white, cis-gendered, Christian, married (heterosexual) male, who is highly educated (Ph.D.) and falls in the upper-middle socioeconomic class. I am very much aware that every one of those features places me in a position of relative privilege. Although I like to think I have thought carefully about what I have written in this book, in no way do I deny the potential validity and persuasiveness of

---

[1] Marx, Karl. *Theses on Feuerbach*, #11. The entirely of the (brief) text is available here: https://www.marxists.org/archive/marx/works/1845/theses/

[2] You might notice that, throughout this book, I capitalize Black but not white. You might wonder why. If you're curious, although there remains legitimate debate on this, I agree with the Columbia Journalism Review's justification. They "capitalize *Black*, and not *white*, when referring to groups in racial, ethnic, or cultural terms. For many people, *Black* reflects a shared sense of identity and community. White carries a different set of meanings; capitalizing the word in this context risks following the lead of white supremacists." And, according to CJR's Alexandria Neason, "I view the term *Black* as both a recognition of an ethnic identity in the States that doesn't rely on hyphenated Americanness (and is more accurate than *African American*, which suggests recent ties to the continent) and is also transnational and inclusive of our Caribbean [and] Central/South American siblings. *African American* is not wrong, and some prefer it, but if we are going to capitalize *Asian* and *South Asian* and *Indigenous*, for example, groups that include myriad ethnic identities united by shared race and geography and, to some degree, culture, then we also have to capitalize *Black*." (https://www.cjr.org/analysis/capital-b-black-styleguide.php)

other perspectives, informed by other sorts of experiences.

Although the topic of social justice is very much "present" and practical, this book is presented primarily as a presentation of some of the major philosophical ideas relevant and foundational to social justice. As such, this book will read very much like a philosophy textbook, rather than a work of history, for example. Because copyright laws would require compensation for the inclusion of more recent writers, and because I always strive to keep textbook costs low (which is, itself, something that connects to social justice), this text relies on older resources or my own summaries of more recent ideas. Finally, because contemporary issues concerning social justice are constantly shifting, as are the data that inform them, this book focuses mainly on the more timeless theoretical foundations that inform our approach and response to these issues.

The 2nd edition of this text includes a new chapter on the political thought of Simón Bolívar, a chapter on the political thought of Frederick Douglass, and a chapter on the philosophical foundations of direct-action campaigns, with an appendix focusing on Cesar Chavez. In addition, I have added an appendix to chapter 3 exploring the function of *testimonio*, as well as numerous other additions and attempts at clarification. These changes are the product of the "living laboratory" provided by my students, for whom I am grateful.

Acknowledgments

This book is an expression of some steps from my own walk towards social justice. That walk has been encouraged and aided by many people.

I would like to thank my many colleagues on my campus for their courage and commitment to social justice, not only at our own school but in the broader community. I have especially learned, often silently, from my colleagues in the Behavioral and Social Sciences Division, where passion and commitment combined with expertise in History, Sociology, Psychology, Philosophy, Chicano Studies, and Ethnic, Gender, and Sexuality Studies, to provide a rich source of information and insight.

Special thanks go to my friend and colleague Professor Brian Brutlag, for our countless conversations and "Zoom" meetings during the pandemic of 2020. Every week, he was a sounding board, accountability partner, and source for numerous suggestions of books, films, websites, etc.

On a similar note, I would like to thank my friend, Dr. Kimi Wilson, for his feedback, insight, and encouragement. His work on achieving equity in education is inspiring.[3]

I would (once again) like to thank my colleague Dr. Adam Wetsman for his vision of Gnutext, and his promotion of these books that I write with pleasure.

I would like to thank my wife, Dr. Portia Jackson Preston, for her support of me not only professionally, but personally. As a woman of color, the patience and grace she extended to her white husband who, while well-meaning, sometimes just didn't "get it" as soon as he should have, was both a gift and an inspiration.

Finally, I would be remiss if I did not thank my students, for whom I write. My desire to create affordable and reader-friendly books for *you* is what makes this book, and the others, a reality.

---

[3] https://equation2success.com/

Table of Contents

Introduction

Justice

This is a textbook examining various aspects and foundations of social justice. It seems to make sense, then, to begin this examination with a "simple" question: what is justice?

The answer to this question, within the field of philosophy, is remarkably similar to the answer to many other questions in our field: "philosophers have been debating this issue for thousands of years…"

That answer is not yet the least bit helpful, but it is true. Ancient Western philosophers were very much concerned with the nature of justice, how to achieve it, how it may be applied to various circumstances, etc. This was hardly unique to the ancient Mediterranean Sea, of course. The nature and achievement of justice appears to be a universal concern. In fact, some notion of "justice" appears to even transcend the boundaries of species.

In a now famous research experiment and article by Sarah F. Brosnan and Frans B. M. de Waal, they "demonstrate that a nonhuman primate, the brown capuchin monkey (Cebus apella), responds negatively to unequal reward distribution in exchanges with a human experimenter. Monkeys refused to participate if they witnessed a conspecific obtain a more attractive reward for equal effort, an effect amplified if the partner received such a reward without any effort at all. These reactions support an early evolutionary origin of inequity aversion."[4] In other words, even monkeys seem to have a sense of what is "fair," and get upset when fairness is violated.

Returning to humans, and the ancient Mediterranean Sea, I will begin our examination of justice the way many philosophers do, by referencing the ideas of a vastly more famous philosopher.

Aristotle articulated numerous variations of the concept of justice, seeking to differentiate and understand each of them. "Universal" justice refers to the virtue of a person who is lawful and fair. "Particular" justice concerns "divisible" goods, and our interactions with others. It is itself split into two types: distributive, and rectificatory.

"Distributive" justice concerns distribution of wealth (or "goods") within a community. According to Aristotle the "just" distribution is proportional to merit. "Rectificatory" justice: remedies unequal distributions of gain and loss between two people, such as through crime (hereafter referred to the much easier to say "corrective" justice).

Finally, there is "political" justice," which is based partly on Natural Law, and partly on local legal conventions. Or, in his own words:

> Political justice is of two kinds, one natural, [physikon] the other conventional [nomikon]. A rule of justice is natural that has the same validity everywhere, and does not depend on our accepting it or not. A rule is conventional that in the first instance may be accepted in one way or the other indifferently…[5]

Summarizing Aristotle's list, we have the following types of justice:

- Universal Justice
- Particular Justice
- Distributive Justice
- Corrective Justice
- Political Justice

And, to this list, we may add (still without exhausting all of the options):

- Justice as Equality
- Justice as Fairness

---

[4] https://www.nature.com/articles/nature01963

[5] Aristotle. *Nicomachean Ethics* iii.7

- Justice as Retribution (a variant of corrective justice)
- Justice as Rehabilitation (a variant of corrective justice)
- "Social" Justice

Suffice it to say, "justice" is a versatile concept, admitting of many interpretations, divisions, and articulations. For our purposes, we will focus on political justice, especially with respect to whether justice (and related concepts) are matters of convention or have a foundation in "nature," and distributive, and corrective justice, particularly where they intersect with social justice.

Social Justice

It now seems appropriate to ask "what is *social* justice?" Once again, definitions vary. Jonathan Haidt, for example, describes what he calls "intuitive" notions of justice as the combination of "distributive justice (the perception that people are getting what is deserved) and procedural justice (the perception that the process by which things are distributed and rules are enforced is fair and trustworthy)."[6]

When people, for example, perceive that the police are following fair procedures and treating them and people like them with dignity, they are much more willing to support the police, help them to fight crime, and even accept occasionally being stopped and frisked by the police, whom they see as working to keep their neighborhoods safe. But if people think that the way the police select people to frisk is racially biased and the people like them are treated disrespectfully, with hostility, or even worse, with violence, they will understandably be angry and we'll see the police as the enemy.... Intuitive justice involves perceptions of distributive justice (as given by equity theory) *and* procedural justice. If you want to motivate people to support a new policy or doing a movement in the name of justice, you need to activate in them a clear perception, or intuition, that someone didn't get what he or she deserved (distributive injustice) or that someone was a victim of an unfair process (procedural injustice). If you can't elicit at least one of those feelings, then people are much more likely to be content with the status quo, even if it is one in which some people or groups and up with more resources or more status than others."[7]

In an attempt to capture these various intuitions into a single concept of justice, Haidt defines "*proportional – procedural social justice*" as "the effort to find and fix cases where distributive or procedural justice is denied to people because they were born into poverty or belonged to a socially disadvantaged category."[8] He supports his case for a particular (intuitive) notion of justice by citing developmental psychologists and their studies of very young children.

"Even toddlers seem to recognize the importance of proportionality.... By the age of six, kids show a clear preference for awarding the hard worker in a group, even if equal pay is an option."[9] Research seems to indicate that "humans naturally favors their distributions, not equal ones, and when fairness and equality clash, people prefer fair inequality over unfair equality."[10]

The basic idea here is that (according to Haidt) our intuitive notion of justice does not favor *equal* outcomes but rather *fair* outcomes, where "fair" is understood as an equal ratio for outcomes divided by inputs. In other words, if two people are working on a group project for a class, and one person does 80% of the work, our intuitive notion of justice would favor that person receiving a "more than equal" share of the credit. In fairness, I think Haidt is presenting what is very often a "straw man" counterexample to social justice. The assumption seems to be that social justice demands that undeserving people get to the same "reward" as others, despite the

---

[6] Haidt, Jonathan & Lukianoff, Greg. *The Coddling of the American Mind*. Penguin Books, 2019.p. 217.

[7] ibid., 220.

[8] ibid., 221.

[9] ibid.

[10] Quoted in ibid., 218.

fact that they did less work, were less qualified, etc. This is the classic stereotype of affirmative action, where "unqualified" people get a job, or admitted to a College or University, "just because of their race" (etc.), thereby "taking the spot" of the "more qualified" and "more deserving" (white?) candidate.

While it is possible that that is what some people have in mind when they propose remedies for disparities in education, employment, etc., I find that in the vast majority of cases what is actually being proposed is that equal (or even roughly equal) candidates be given *genuinely* equal *opportunity* – and, given the legacy of discrimination and the reality of implicit bias, that requires a conscious intervention in an attempt to "level the playing field."

Haidt is far from the only person to offer a definition of justice, or social justice, of course.

- "Social justice may be broadly understood as the fair and compassionate distribution of the fruits of economic growth." (United Nations)
- "Social justice is the view that everyone deserves equal economic, political and social rights and opportunities." (National Association of Social Workers)
- "Social justice encompasses economic justice. Social justice is the virtue which guides us in creating those organized human interactions we call institutions. In turn, social institutions, when justly organized, provide us with access to what is good for the person, both individually and in our associations with others. Social justice also imposes on each of us a personal responsibility to work with others to design and continually perfect our institutions as tools for personal and social development." (Center for Economic and Social Justice)

In an attempt to synthesize and summarize, and in the process produce a definition that combines aspects of both distributive and corrective justice, I propose that, ultimately, *social justice means equal rights and equitable opportunities for everyone.*

This textbook will examine some philosophical foundations and other elements of justice, and specifically social justice. The first several chapters are preparatory, and will focus on basic skills and understanding including how to read philosophical sources, what counts as philosophy in general, different interpretations of both knowledge and truth, and how to identify and evaluate arguments and claims. We will then spend a few chapters examining values, starting with an investigation how we actually engage in moral and political reasoning. We will consider different views of human nature (namely, whether we are fundamentally "good" or "bad"). We will then consider the nature of values, such as whether they are objective or subjective, and whether the "ends justify the means," before applying these ideas to some specific cases.

The next section of this textbook will turn to matters of political justice, and examine different interpretations offered by philosophers starting in antiquity all the way up through the twentieth century. We will then consider the concept of "race" from the philosophical perspective, and related issues pertaining to social justice. After considering discrimination and identity politics, we will end the book by considering "action," including philosophical examination of direct action campaigns such as protest movements.

I have provided several comprehension questions at the beginning of each chapter to help readers focus on key elements, vocabulary, and themes. I have also included, in most chapters, a section at the end that tries to highlight the application of the major ideas or themes of that chapter to the specific topic of social justice.

Inserted at various points in each chapter, and sometimes perhaps in longer sections at the end of certain chapters, you will find reading selections pertaining to the main topic of that chapter. These are excerpts from books or dialogues written by some of the finest minds from the history of philosophy, spanning from Antiquity to the present day.

Although I like to think that my own summaries and introductions are illuminating, engaging primary source materials is an essential part of studying philosophy. Engaging the readings yourself, grappling with the arguments, and coming to your own understanding is one of the primary tasks of philosophy.

If you're taking a philosophy course using this book, your instructor will undoubtedly offer assistance along the way, but it's important to meet with these thinkers, your mind to their minds, and participate in the great conversation that we call philosophy. It's also important to remember that we all stand on the shoulders of those who came before us. To remain ignorant of their ideas and achievements, and to attempt to "reinvent the wheel" ourselves, is inefficient at best, and intellectually dishonest and disrespectful, at worst.

Chapter 1: Reading Philosophy

Comprehension questions you should be able to answer after reading this chapter:

1. What are the four steps in the four step process for active reading? Briefly describe each one.
2. What is "flagging?" What is its purpose?

This is a philosophy textbook. It is about philosophy, and it is filled with philosophy. The purpose of this textbook is to provide you with a guided tour of some of the more important philosophical topics from some of the more important philosophers over the last several thousand years. Ideally, you will come to understand the views presented in this book, be able to evaluate them to determine whether you agree or disagree with the arguments that are presented to you, and ultimately to form your own views on these important topics. Before we can do *any* of that though, you have to know how to *read* philosophy.

I am confident that you already know how to read. I am not being the least bit sarcastic. Reading *philosophy*, however, is a somewhat different process than reading other types of materials. It is different from reading works of fiction; it is different from reading history textbooks – and certainly different from reading a math textbook. Due to the particular features of philosophical writings, it is important to learn how to approach reading them so as to promote your understanding and your appreciation of these important works.

Pretty much any work of philosophy is going to attempt to convince you of something – perhaps multiple things. That is to say that the author has a point that they are hoping to present in the most compelling way possible.

There are any number of points that a philosopher may be attempting to get across. Some philosophers will try to convince you that free will is an illusion. Others will try to convince you that morality is culturally relative. Others will try to convince you that morality is best understood as a series of divine commands. Other philosophers will try to claim that knowledge is

impossible. Still other philosophers will try to convince you that knowledge is, in fact, possible. Those are just a handful of countless examples of the things of which a philosopher might try to convince you. Rest assured, however, that the philosophers do indeed have a purpose behind their writings.

The most important thing for you to do as a reader and student of philosophy is to determine what the *point* of a particular philosophical essay or excerpt *is*.

Some philosophers are more reader friendly than others. From my perspective, a good philosopher makes every reasonable effort to be accessible to his or her reader. Presumably, the philosopher wants to be understood, and that means trying to make the writing clear and compelling for the reader. *Very* good philosophical writers will make it *obvious* what their main point is, as well as whatever evidence they are offering to support it. Other philosophers are less friendly, or less skilled as writers. In some cases, the works we are reading were written thousands of years ago, in other languages. There are, literally, translation issues. In some cases, the topics are very complex and unavoidably abstract. While philosophers should not be expected to "dumb down" their work, they do have an obligation, in my opinion, to make a sincere effort to be understandable to the reader.

As a reader, you have an obligation as well. It's not okay to just "give up" simply because the reading is challenging and you don't understand it right away, or because you encounter unfamiliar words. Philosophy is often difficult and challenging, and this is not simply because some philosophers are bad writers, but because the topics they are writing about are deep and important and very often cannot be described in simple and shallow terms.

You will discover that you will probably need to read and reread certain sentences or paragraphs multiple times, slowly and carefully, before they make sense to you. You will discover that you will probably need to use a dictionary when you encounter certain words that you don't understand, and that appear to be important. Later in this chapter, I'm going to offer you some very specific reading strategies that will help you to understand philosophical writing in particular, but that I also believe could be useful for other subjects as well.

Before examining some specific reading tips and strategies, I want to say a little bit more about philosophical writing. In the Western tradition, at least, the vast majority of philosophical essays, or books, that you might read will take the form of "argumentative prose." This simply refers to a style of writing in which the author is attempting to prove a point, and writes in relatively straightforward language – as opposed to poetry, or parables, or writing filled with symbolism and imagery. There are always exceptions, of course, but that description will be true of *most* philosophical writings you will encounter in the West.

Some writings take the form of dialogues. Many of Plato's most famous works are dialogues. In a dialogue, rather than a single voice representing the author, there are multiple characters having a "conversation." The good thing about dialogues is that they are often more enjoyable to read. The challenge of dialogues is that they are also often more difficult to understand, because you have to keep track of various characters and what they represent, and keep in mind that just because a character says something in the dialogue does not mean that the author himself or herself is advocating for that position.

Whether the writing sample is argumentative prose or a dialogue, any good work of philosophy that has stood the test of time is going to offer *arguments* in support of whatever points the author is trying to present. We will discuss arguments in much greater detail in a later chapter. For now, however, just know

that an argument is simply an attempt to prove something by offering evidence in support of it.

As a very trivial example, imagine if someone says "I think it is raining because I remember the weather forecast predicted rain, I just heard thunder, and the person who just came in the room was shaking water off of their clothing and hair." This is not exactly a philosophical argument, but it is an argument nonetheless. The main point (conclusion) is that it is raining. The evidence (premises) offered in support are that the weather forecast predicted rain, the person heard thunder (which is often associated with rain), and they saw someone who was wet (which would make sense if they had just walked in from out of the rain).

Whether or not that is a *good* argument is a separate issue – and one that we will address in general in that later chapter. For now, just recognize that any attempt to prove some point by offering evidence for it is what we mean by an "argument." You will find arguments, or, in some cases, multiple arguments, in *any* work of philosophy.

The distinguishing feature of a work of philosophy is the fact that it is an argument, or at least that it contains them. What you will discover, though, is that a lot more writing occurs within works of philosophy than can be described as an "argument." Philosophers will not only present their main point, and evidence in support of that point, but will also very often provide examples to help illustrate what they mean by various terms or ideas, explain what other people have said about the same topic, anticipate objections to their own point of view and try to demonstrate why those objections fail, and potentially very many other things as well.

One of the challenges of reading philosophy is figuring out what the writer is doing at various places in the text, and why. This is a skill. Please don't be frustrated if you are not "really good" at it right away. It is completely expected and totally normal that you find the experience challenging and even frustrating at first. Like any skill, to get better at it requires practice. It would be unrealistic and unfair to expect yourself to somehow be really good at *any* skill if you are just now starting out.

By way of review, reading philosophical writings is different from reading other sorts of texts. Merely moving your eyes back and forth across some pages or a screen will not be sufficient. In order to identify, understand, and evaluate the position statements being made by the philosophers, you will have to employ "active reading." I will provide some tips and techniques for active reading a little bit later in this chapter.

The good news is that improving the skills necessary for reading philosophy will transfer and be applicable across multiple contexts – basically any situation in which you have to understand the meaning and significance of possibly complex writing. In other words, even if you have no intention of becoming a "professional philosopher," the skills you will develop and improve in your study of philosophy will be useful to you in virtually anything that you choose to do with your life.

With that lengthy preamble behind us, let's get into the actual tips and techniques, starting with what I will call "the basics."

The "Basics"

- Take care of yourself

This might sound trivial, but I actually think it's fairly important. Reading is an activity, and active reading requires effort and concentration. There are things we can do with respect to our environment, and other factors, that will help us to read more effectively.

To begin with, consider your reading environment. Realistically, some of this might be outside of your control. You might have life circumstances such that a secluded quiet library isn't always available to you. You might live in a home with noisy siblings, or next to a home with a barking dog, or any number of other distractions. I don't pretend that I can offer strategies that can somehow neutralize every less-than-ideal aspect of your circumstances and your environment. However, no matter who you are or what your circumstances happen to be, there are probably some concrete things that you can do to make your reading more effective.

As much as is possible, secure a good environment for reading. Distractions are not great for active reading and reading comprehension. To the extent that it's possible, isolate yourself. Find a secluded space, read in the school library, retreat to your bedroom if that is a quieter space in your house, etc.

Make sure that you are not subjecting yourself to your own distractions, by the way! Don't kid yourself: playing around on your phone while you are trying to read will absolutely diminish your efficiency at reading and your understanding of whatever it is you are trying to read. None of us are as skilled at multitasking as we like to think we are. Your mind can only focus on so much at one time, and if you are attempting to read challenging philosophical writings while simultaneously reviewing Instagram, texting any number of friends, etc., your reading comprehension will suffer. Similarly, listening to music might make the reading more pleasant, but you will likely be *distracted* by the music (especially the lyrics).

Also with regard to the reading environment, I propose that you want to be comfortable enough that you're not going to hurt your back or your neck (or suffer any other sort of injury), but not *so* comfortable that you might fall asleep! If you find yourself "drifting off," take a break. When you do take a break, get up and walk around a little bit, maybe do some light stretching – anything that will help restore you and your focus.

Finally, active reading – especially of challenging materials – takes *time*. Give yourself sufficient time to do the reading. If you are trying to cram in an entire chapter worth of reading in fifteen minutes prior to class, or before an assignment is due, it is terribly unlikely that you will be successful in your efforts. Give yourself plenty of time so you don't feel rushed, and so you can take your time on the more difficult passages.

- Interact with the material

As I mentioned above, active reading involves much more than merely moving your eyes back and forth across the page or screen. It would be incredibly convenient if you could just passively absorb material in that way, but it just doesn't work like that.

In order to actually understand and absorb the material, you have to "engage" it. You need to interact with it. One of the ways in which you can interact with the material is by "flagging" the reading, and I will explain that process in much greater detail later in this chapter.

Other ways to engage the material, though, include looking up words or concepts that you don't understand in a dictionary or a philosophical encyclopedia.[11]

You might find it useful to talk to other people (whether other students, friends, family members, etc.) about what you have read. Merely talking about the material will help to reinforce it, and will also reveal gaps in your understanding.

Even if you don't speak with anyone else about the material, you can *imagine* yourself having a conversation with the author, in which you express agreement or disagreement, communicate your confusion, etc. Even if some of those techniques seem silly to you, I suggest that they are at least worth a try.

- Keep reasonable expectations

Reading philosophy is challenging. It is not only possible, but overwhelmingly *likely*, that you will not understand everything you are reading at first. You will likely discover that you will get to the end of the sentence, or paragraph, or page, and realize that you have no idea what it meant.

That is normal.

When that happens, try not to get frustrated. It doesn't mean that you are not intelligent, or that you are ill-suited for philosophy, or that you will never understand the material, or anything similarly dramatic. What it *does* indicate is that you are grappling with challenging material and that, just like every other mere mortal who is participating in the study of philosophy

(including me!), you will often have to re-read something slowly and carefully more than once before you begin to understand it. Extend yourself some compassion, set reasonable expectations of yourself, and give yourself sufficient time and patience to actually do the reading in a way that will help you to understand it.

- "Flag" the reading and take notes.

This is certainly the most "technical" bit of advice that I have for you, and will occupy the remainder of this chapter. I'm going to offer you a multi-part reading process that I'm confident will help you to understand not only the readings in this textbook, but arguably any challenging reading material that you might grapple with in any class, work setting, or context going forward.

Step one: Pre-Read

This might sound unusual, but you should do a little bit of reading before you actually start "reading." This stage of "pre-reading" can include various things.

To begin with, having *context* is very helpful with respect to understanding. By way of analogy, if you walk up to someone in the middle of a conversation, it is much more difficult to "follow" the point of their story than if you had been there from the beginning.

Although this involves "extra work," it will likely improve your understanding if you seek context (when possible) before you "officially" read – especially if you know that the content of that reading is completely new or unfamiliar to you. If, for example, you are about to read a book on virtue ethics, it might be worth the time and effort to do a little bit of preliminary research into "ethics" in general. The previously mentioned online philosophical encyclopedias can be helpful in that regard.

Fortunately, I have written *this* textbook

---

[11] Both the Internet encyclopedia of philosophy (https://www.iep.utm.edu/) and the Stanford encyclopedia of philosophy (https://plato.stanford.edu/) are reliable

resources. They are not, however, necessarily easily accessible though, as the entries are often written at a relatively high level of expertise.

specifically with the "beginner" in mind. Accordingly, I have provided a lot of context for you. As you read the chapters of this book, you will discover that portions of each chapter are dedicated to providing historical context (when appropriate), associations with other issues in philosophy, "real life" examples and applications, explanations of key terms and assumptions, etc. By making sure to read each chapter in *entirety*, you are much more likely to understand the particular arguments offered by the philosophers covered in each chapter.

What does it mean to read each chapter "in entirety?" The simple answer is just to read every page, but certain pages have especially relevant pieces of information for this "pre-reading" process.

The introduction of *this* book, for example, provided an overview of the book, previewed main themes, and explained the structure of the chapters. It provided some insight into what you should expect from the remaining chapters, and how to navigate the book. The table of contents provides a map for where to find the various chapters, and the chapter titles will give an indicator of the subject matter they address.

At the beginning of every chapter, you will find a number of "comprehension questions." Practically speaking, these serve as study guides for quizzes or exams in my classes, but beyond that they are an indicator of what I take to be the most important concepts or issues addressed in that chapter. These are incredibly useful! You should read them during this "pre-read" process so that you already have an idea of what to expect when you read the chapters. By being familiar with these questions, you will know what to look for when you are reading, and you'll be more likely to recognize some of the more important portions of the chapter when you encounter them.

After you have read the chapter, you will want to test your understanding by trying to answer those questions. Even if you only answer them "in your head," they provide a means of self-assessment. If you are able to confidently answer all of the questions, and if you are equally confident that your answers are correct (presumably after having double checked a few of them), then that is a pretty good indicator that you have understood the material. On the other hand, if you have no idea how you would answer those questions, that is a very reliable indicator that you have *not* understood and absorbed the chapter that you have read.

Step two: Fast Read

In step one, you have possibly done a little bit of research to orient yourself to this new material, and you have looked at things like the introduction to this book, and the chapter comprehension questions for the chapter that you are about to read. Now you are ready to "skim" the chapter.

Although this is called a "fast read," that doesn't mean that you're not really paying attention, or that you're not accomplishing anything. The purpose of the fast read is to get an initial sense of the content, structure, and main point (if discernible during the fast read) of that chapter. This is not the final or only time you will read the chapter!

As you are skimming the chapter, pay attention to potentially useful clues. Oftentimes they will be chapter headings or subheadings that will reveal important ideas. Oftentimes you will encounter lists of vocabulary terms, or examples, or other items. This will often be obvious, using "bullet points" or numbered lists as an indicator.

You might also notice that certain words or sentences are emphasized through the use of *italics*, underlining, or **bold** font. Any of these devices indicate that the author thinks that those words or sections are especially important, and the author is trying to draw your attention to them.

During this stage, read the entire chapter (or article, or essay, etc.) fairly quickly. The goal is to develop a basic understanding of the text. You should try to identify the "thesis statement" (main point). Note that you might not be able to do this until you reach the end of the chapter. It's entirely possible that you might initially think that something is the main point, only to change your mind by the time you finish the chapter. That is totally normal.

During this fast read, make notes in the text that will be useful to you during your next (slower) read. Indicate any words that you don't know/understand so you can look them up later. In general, "flag" the reading during this fast read.

"Flagging"

At this point, you might justifiably be wondering what on earth I mean by "flagging." "Flagging" is just a term used in the field of reading comprehension that means "making notes." Flagging refers to a system of notetaking in the book for the sake of improving your understanding.

Despite what anyone might try to sell you, there is no "magic" and perfect system of flagging. The best system is the one that actually works for *you*. I'm going offer some details of a system that I use, and that I think is rather effective, that you should feel free to make any adjustments or improvements from your perspective as you see fit.

The purpose of flagging your text is to make it easier for you the next time you read, and more efficient for you when you are reviewing and studying. Basically, you are providing clues and shortcuts for the sake of your *next* read-through.

Suppose you read a chapter of this book in preparation for a class meeting. Suppose also that three weeks later you will have an exam that covers material from that chapter. Unless you happen to have been blessed with a photographic memory, is terribly unlikely that you will have a perfect recollection of everything that you have read, even if you understood it correctly the first time you read it. In other words, you are going to need to review and refresh your memory in order to prepare for the exam. That is usually called "studying."

If the first time you read that chapter you didn't write any notes in the margins, didn't underline any words, and didn't provide any clues as to which sections of the chapter were especially important and why, when you go to review it to prepare for the exam, you are basically reading it again *as if* for the first time. A much more efficient approach is to have

invested the time and effort during your first reading so that when you are reviewing for the exam you can focus on key terms, main points, formal arguments, etc. "Flagging" is the system that help you to do precisely that.

As I said, flagging just means making marks and notes in the text. For our purposes, I'm going to assume that we are dealing with a good old-fashioned paper book (as opposed to an electronic book, for which different techniques are necessary). These are all recommendations I have for you as you develop your *own* system of flagging.

- Use pencil rather than pen. Pen can bleed through pages, making them difficult to read, and using the pencil allows you to erase your marks if you change your mind about something. For similar reasons I do not recommend the use of highlighters. The ink from highlighters can also bleed through pages, making the opposite side difficult to read. As an alternative, consider making marks along the edge of the paragraphs at the margins.
- Circle "list" words (such as "first" and "second") and underline definitions.
- Write your own thoughts (briefly) in the margins (or on a separate page).
- Use shorthand notes in the margins (such as the following – or whatever makes the most sense for you):
- MP= main point
- EX= example
- C= conclusion
- P= premise
- ?= I don't understand this/this is confusing
- != This is surprising/interesting
- NO!= I disagree with this/this sounds incorrect
- YES!= I agree with this/this sounds correct
- *= this is important
- **= this is really important!

As I mentioned above, none of the particular elements of this approach to flagging is essential. If you prefer to use different marks and symbols, then by all means do so. What matters is that you use a system that *you* understand, and that helps *you* to more easily review and process the information you are reading.

Step three: Careful Read

Once you have read the chapter relatively quickly, making your notes in the margins, indicating what you think to be the main point, supporting details, etc., it is time to read again more slowly and more carefully.

The purpose of this careful read is to develop a more thorough and accurate understanding of the text. To help you in this effort, you should try to do the following:

- Read the entire article/essay very carefully.
- Look at any footnotes or end notes.
- Footnotes or endnotes will generally be one of two types. Some will be citations that provide sources for quotations or data. These will be the most common sort of footnote in this book, as they provide the source of the brief bits of texts that we are studying in the chapters. These notes will require only a very quick glance. Once you determine that they are simply a citation of the source, you can move on. The only exception to that is if you are motivated to do some "fact checking," or additional/independent research. In such cases, it will matter to what the source is so you can do some further investigation.
- One quick note about citations: in addition to fairly standard references that include auth or name, book, title, and page number (or the equivalent), you will also see the term "ibid" used many times in almost every chapter in numerous footnotes. For those not familiar with the term, "ibid." is a Latin abbreviation for "*ibidem*," which means "in the same place." If you see "ibid" in a footnote, it means the source and page is the same as was referenced in the last footnote. You might even see multiple

"ibid" references in a row, which just means you have to glance back through notes until you find a full citation. If you see "ibid" followed by a number, it means the source is the same, but the page number being cited is whatever number appears in that note (as opposed to the same page as before).

- The other sort of footnote or endnote will not provide a citation for source, but will instead provide some additional information, clarification, or an expansion of something in the main body of the chapter. These will have a different format from citation notes, and will probably be a bit longer. Definitely read these, especially if they are convenient footnote at the bottom of the page. Authors use such notes to provide additional information or clarification without "cluttering" the page.[12]
- Correct and add to your previous flagging efforts.
  - Once you have read the chapter more slowly and more carefully, you might have some new or different insights. It is possible that what you thought was the main point during your fast read no longer seems to be the main idea. You might have found additional support for the main point, or other interesting things during this slower and more careful read. Take advantage of the opportunity to add to, correct, or otherwise revise your margin notes. Remember that the entire purpose of making these notes is to benefit *you*. If you don't bother to make any notes, or engage with the text, the only person who will suffer from that is you.

---

[12] This is an example of just such a footnote. I could use it to say a bit more about

"clarification" footnotes without taking up more space in the main body of the text on the page.

- Take lots of notes, in general.
  - o This goes beyond mere "flagging." Don't be afraid to write in the book. It can be a very helpful exercise to try to restate or rephrase what the author is saying in your own words, at key points in the chapter.

Step Four: Summarize & Evaluate

Once you are finished with your slower, more careful read, try to summarize the main points of the article/essay in your own words.

Imagine that you will have to explain the main ideas to someone who hasn't read a single page of the chapter, and you have to do so in thirty seconds or less (if spoken), or two hundred and fifty words or less (if written). You will discover that you really have to have a decent idea of the meaning of what you have read in order to do that.

While summarizing, be sure to practice the "principle of charity." This principle will be discussed in greater detail in another chapter, but it basically means describing the author's point of view in the most favorable way possible (at this stage).

Once you have completed your summary, you are ready for the final (and maybe even the most interesting) step in this process: evaluation. Until you understood what you were reading, you weren't in any position to form any opinions about it. Now, however, it's time to figure out what *you* think.

Having identified the main point/conclusion, do you agree with it? If you do, why? What is so compelling about the argument that you have read?

If you don't agree, why not? Write down some reasons why you disagree with it.

Are you being *charitable*?

How might the author respond to your criticism? To be safe, check to make sure they didn't already anticipate and address your concerns. Good philosophers will often do precisely that.

In theory, if you have completed all of these steps, you have successfully engaged with some philosophical writing. You have carefully read it,

taking notes for your own benefit along the way. You have reviewed and summarized what you have read, and have determined your level of agreement or disagreement (and your reasons why, in either case). Congratulations. You are "doing philosophy!"

That process might seem a bit daunting or intimidating right now. That is an understandable reaction, but it is one that I hope will fade with a little bit of time and practice. Active and careful reading is a skill, and reading philosophy is a specialization of that skill. Like any skill, it takes some time, effort, and practice before you get good at it – but you *will* get good at it! The most effective way to bring about that result is to try. All of the chapters of this book await your efforts.

Appendix: Application to Social Justice

The content of this chapter is subject-neutral. That is, techniques to help you better understand what you read will apply to *anything* that you read. That will certainly be the case with respect to any texts concerning matters of social justice, whether they be books, articles, blogs, etc.

Chapter 2: What *Counts* as Philosophy?

Comprehension questions you should be able to answer after reading this chapter:

1. What is meant by a "family resemblance?" Explain this concept using the example of games.
2. What are the 17 features/characteristics that Santana considers to be relevant to the "family resemblance" for philosophy?

Before *I* say anything in this chapter, I want you to read a few things, and comes to some conclusions on your own. You are about to be presented with several brief selections of texts labeled A, B, C, and D. Read each of these selections and determine which of them, if any, are "philosophical." Which, if any, are examples of philosophy or philosophical writing?

A.

The wise man: a light, a torch, a stout torch that does not smoke.

A perforated mirror, a mirror pierced on both sides.

His are the black and red ink, his are the illuminated manuscripts, he studies the illuminated manuscripts.

He himself is writing and wisdom.

He is the path, the true way for others.

He directs people and things; he is a guide in human affairs.

The wise man is careful (like a physician) and preserves tradition.

He is the handed-down wisdom; he teaches it; he follows the path of truth.

Teacher of truth, he never ceases to admonish.

He makes wise the countenances of others; to them he gives a face; he leads them to develop it.

He opens their ears; he enlightens them.

He is the teacher of guides; he shows in their path.

One depends upon him.

He puts a mirror before others, he makes them prudent, cautious; he causes a face to appear on them.

He attends to things; he regulates their path, he arranges and commands.

He applies his light to the world.

He knows what is above us (and) in the region of the dead.

He is a serious man.

Everyone is comforted by him, corrected, taught.

Thanks to him people humanize their will and receive a strict education.

He comforts the heart, he comforts the people, he helps, gives remedies, heals everyone.

B.

The same thing is both living and dead, waking and sleeping, young and old; for these things transformed are those, and those transformed back again are these.

God is day and night, winter and summer, war and peace, satiety and hunger, but changes, the way [fire] when mingled with perfumes, is named according to the scent of each.

C.

Come now, I will tell thee - and do thou hearken to my saying and carry it away - the only two ways of search that can be thought of. The first, namely, that It is, and that it is impossible for anything not to be, is the way of Conviction, for truth is its companion. The other, namely, that It is not, and that something must needs not be, - that, I tell thee, is a wholly untrustworthy path. For you cannot know what is not - that is impossible - nor utter it; For it is the same thing that can be thought and that can be.

D.

THE MADMAN----Have you not heard of that madman who lit a lantern in the bright morning hours, ran to the market place, and cried incessantly: "I seek God! I seek God!"---As many of those who did not believe in God were standing around just then, he provoked much laughter. Has he got lost? asked one. Did he lose his way like a child? asked another. Or is he hiding? Is he afraid of us? Has he gone on a voyage? emigrated?----Thus they yelled and laughed

The madman jumped into their midst and pierced them with his eyes. "Whither is God?" he cried; "I will tell you. We have killed him---you and I. All of us are his murderers. But how did we do this? How could we drink up the sea? Who gave us the sponge to wipe away the entire horizon? What were we doing when we unchained this earth from its sun? Whither is it moving now? Whither are we moving? Away from all suns? Are we not plunging continually? Backward, sideward, forward, in all directions? Is there still any up or down? Are we not straying, as through an infinite nothing? Do we not feel the breath of empty space? Has it not become colder? Is not night continually closing in on us? Do we not need to light lanterns in the morning? Do we hear nothing as yet of the noise of the gravediggers who are burying God? Do we smell nothing as yet of the divine decomposition? Gods, too, decompose. God is dead. God remains dead. And we have killed him.

"How shall we comfort ourselves, the murderers of all murderers? What was holiest and mightiest of all that the world has yet owned has bled to death under our knives: who will wipe this blood off us? What water is there for us to clean ourselves? What festivals of atonement, what sacred games shall we have to invent? Is not the greatness of this deed too great for us? Must we ourselves not become gods simply to appear worthy of it? There has never been a greater deed; and whoever is born after us---for the sake of this deed he will belong to a higher history than all history hitherto."

Here the madman fell silent and looked again at his listeners; and they, too, were silent and stared at him in astonishment. At last he threw his lantern on the ground, and it broke into pieces and went out. "I have come too early," he said then; "my time is not yet. This tremendous event is still on its way, still wandering; it has not yet reached the ears of men. Lightning and thunder require time; the light of the stars requires time; deeds, though done, still require time to be seen and heard. This deed is still more distant from them than most distant stars---and yet they have done it themselves.

It has been related further that on the same day the madman forced his way into several churches and there struck up his requiem aeternam deo. Led out and called to account, he is said always to have replied nothing but: "What after all are these churches now if they are not the tombs and sepulchers of God?"

Which of those, if any, do you think was an example of philosophy? Why?

Believe it or not, this is a serious question in the context of studying philosophy. In case you are curious, A is a poem from a Nahua song-poet.[13] B is a couple fragments from Heraclitus.[14] C is a couple of selections from a poem by Parmenides.[15] D is a brief excerpt from Nietzsche.[16]

Heraclitus and Parmenides are iconic "pre-Socratic" philosophers, usually taught as antagonists to each other, and very likely to be taught in any ancient philosophy class. Nietzsche is even more famous, and certainly regarded as a philosopher. Whether loved or hated (or more likely, misunderstood), his writings would be entirely appropriate for any number of philosophy courses, whether focusing on Contemporary philosophy, existentialism, post-modernism, or even in an introduction to philosophy course.

Out of all four selections, only A (the poetic contribution from the Aztecs) is "controversial" in philosophical circles with respect to whether it "counts" as philosophy. Ironically enough, the usual explanation for its exclusion is because it is overly "poetic." The other selections have been provided for a reason: they are equally "poetic!" The mere fact that someone has written "poetically" rather than with clear argumentative prose hasn't caused Heraclitus, Parmenides, or Nietzsche to be excluded from philosophical consideration. Why then would the Nahua poem be excluded? An overly simple (but sadly partially accurate) explanation for this is racism and cultural bias, but even in these cases, in the vast majority of cases this is the result of regrettable but understandable ignorance, rather than hostility.

In American philosophy departments, "canonical" philosophy, historically and presently, has consisted almost entirely of philosophers (past and present) who happen to be white, male, and from either Europe or North America. The entirety of all other philosophers and traditions across the globe and throughout history is, in contrast, "non-canonical," and usually either dismissed and rejected as not "real" philosophy, or else relegated to (elective) specialty classes typically found only in graduate programs or as upper division undergraduate courses—and even in such cases, rarely so.

As a demonstration of the status of "non-canonical" philosophers in the West, we needn't confine ourselves to academia, but may look to landmark Supreme Court decisions as well. In the majority decision of *Obergefell v. Hodges*, Justice Kennedy cited both Confucius and Cicero in stressing the significance of marriage:

> *Since the dawn of history, marriage has transformed strangers into relatives, binding families and societies together. Confucius taught that marriage lies at the foundation of government. This wisdom was echoed centuries later and half a world away by Cicero, who wrote, "The first bond of society is marriage; next, children; and then the family.[17]*

In a dissenting opinion footnote, the late Justice Antonin Scalia compared Confucius to a fortune cookie: "The Supreme Court of the United States has descended from the disciplined legal reasoning of John Marshall and Joseph Story to the mystical aphorisms of the fortune cookie."[18]

A philosopher who pre-dated nearly all Western (canonical) philosophers by centuries, and whose influence historically and presently on Chinese culture can hardly be overstated, was

---

[13] *Codice Matritense de la Real Academia*, VIII, fol.118, r.- 118,v. trans. by Leon-Portilla 1963.
[14] Attributed to Heraclitus by pseudo-Plutarch, *Consolation to Apollonius* 106e = 22B88., and attributed to Heraclitus by Hippolytus, *Refutation* 9.10.8 = 22B67, respectively.
[15] *Poem Of Parmenides*, English translation: John

Burnet (1892)
[16] Friedrich Nietzsche, *The Gay Science* (1882, 1887) para. 125; Walter Kaufmann ed. (New York: Vintage, 1974): 181-82.
[17] https://www.supremecourt.gov/opinions /14pdf/14-556_3204.pdf
[18] ibid., footnote #22.

reduced to a "fortune cookie."

At worst, this is simply racism.

At best, it is breathtaking ignorance in its literal sense: lacking information—but this is precisely the problem! An accomplished and respected intellect no less than a Supreme Court Justice dismisses the most prominent thinker of a 4,000 year old civilization as equivalent to fortune cookie aphorisms.

Either way, we can see that even the question of who or what "counts" in the field of philosophy is a matter of social justice.

There is no credible intellectual justification for the exclusion of most of the world from the philosophical curriculum. Even a modest amount of research can demonstrate the existence and quality of philosophical arguments (even given the most stringent definition) across the globe, and throughout history. The continued exclusion of these sources, then, is caused by either ignorance, ethnocentrism, or both.

It is my contention that ignorance is both more plausible and more charitable as an explanation. Simply put, philosophers tend to teach what they were taught. If, for generations, philosophy professors taught exclusively the works of white male philosophers from either Europe or North America, then their students who became the next generation of philosophy professors would be disposed to accept and replicate the same curriculum. This cycle can only be broken by making deliberate efforts to do so. This edition of this book is intended to be just such a deliberate effort.

We shall begin in the manner of a good analytic philosopher: conceptual analysis. We need to ask, in the name of consistency, what *should* count as philosophy, and therefore what should be included as candidates for study in philosophy courses and textbooks.

Alejandro Santana proposes that philosophy is best understood as a "family resemblance" as that concept was developed by Wittgenstein.[19] A family resemblance refers to "a complicated network of similarities overlapping and crisscrossing."[20] An iconic example of this is "games."

Some games involve boards, some involve dice, some involve paper, some involve balls, some involve accumulating points, some require teams, etc. There are a number of features associated with "games." Rather than try to provide a precise definition that perfectly captures every single kind of game, games are better understood as exhibiting a variety of features. Some games exhibit some of those features, but not others. Any game will exhibit some, but perhaps no game will exhibit all—nevertheless, they are all still "games." Anything that exhibits literally none of those features probably won't be regarded as a game at all.

Santana similarly addresses the subject matter, origins, aims, and methods of philosophy in developing his definition of "philosophy."

With respect to *subject matter*, works commonly taken to be philosophical (1) address the generally recognized subcategories of philosophy, such as metaphysics, epistemology, value theory, logic, etc. Additionally, (2) practical approaches to philosophy concern how to live a meaningful life, or to live well.

With respect to *origins*, Santana proposes that philosophy *begins with* (3) wonder, (4) reflection, or (5) the clash between traditional beliefs and the need for justification.

Concerning *aims*, Santana proposes that philosophy *seeks* the following: (6) wisdom, (7) knowledge, (8) a clear, comprehensive, and plausible worldview, (9) elimination of doubt, confusion, or nonsense, (10) intellectual liberation and autonomy.

Finally, concerning *methods*, philosophy (11) formulates and answers fundamental questions, (12) critically examines and evaluates fundamental assumptions, (13) provides justification for its claims, (14) raises and addresses objections, (15) analyzes, (16) clarifies concepts, and (17) synthesizes ideas.

---

[19] Santana, Alejandro. "Did the Aztecs do Philosophy?" *APA newsletters*, volume 8, number 1, Fall, 2008. 2 – 9.

[20] Wittgenstein, Ludwig. *Philosophical Investigations*, #65.

With these criteria in mind, consider the following section from Aristotle's *Nicomachean Ethics*:

BOOK II.
MORAL VIRTUE.
1.
Moral virtue is acquired by the repetition of the corresponding acts.
Excellence, then, being of these two kinds, intellectual and moral intellectual excellence owes its birth and growth mainly to instruction, and so requires time and experience, while moral excellence is the result of habit or custom (ἔθος), and has accordingly in our language received a name formed by a slight change from ἔθος.

From this it is plain that none of the moral excellences or virtues is implanted in us by nature; for that which is by nature cannot be altered by training. For instance, a stone naturally tends to fall downwards, and you could not train it to rise upwards, though you tried to do so by throwing it up ten thousand times, nor could you train fire to move downwards, nor accustom anything which naturally behaves in one way to behave in any other way.

The virtues, then, come neither by nature nor against nature, but nature gives the capacity for acquiring them, and this is developed by training.

There are many reasons why Aristotle is rightfully regarded as an iconic and indisputable philosopher. We can see how many "family resemblance boxes" can be checked in even this short passage.

Subject Matter
- ✓ Addresses a generally recognized **subcategory of philosophy**: ethics (1)
- ✓ Concerns **how to live a meaningful life**, or to live well. (2)

Origins
- ✓ Exhibits **wonder** (3)
- ✓ Exhibits **reflection** (4)
- ✓ **Justifies** a claim in the face of opposing cultural assumptions (about human nature, in this case) (5)

Aims
- ✓ Seeks **wisdom**, specifically exploring how to live well (6)
- ✓ Seeks **knowledge** of how character is acquired (7)
- ✓ Seeks a **clear, comprehensive, and plausible worldview** with respect to how to live well (8)
- ✓ Seeks to **eliminate confusion** concerning character and its acquisition (9)
- ✓ Seeks **intellectual liberation and autonomy**. (Indeed, in the same work he will propose that a life of philosophical contemplation is the most fulfilling and free of possible lifestyles.) (10)

Methods
- ✓ **Formulates and answers fundamental questions** (in this case, about moral character) (11)
- ✓ **Critically examines and evaluates fundamental assumptions** (in this case about the nature and acquisition of moral character) (12)
- ✓ **Provides justification for its claims** (in this section, by way of analogy) (13)
- ✓ **Raises and addresses objections** (in other parts of the same text) (14)
- ✓ **Analyzes** (in this case, the nature and acquisition of moral character) (15)
- ✓ **Clarifies concepts** (in this case, the nature and acquisition of moral character) (16)
- ✓ **Synthesizes ideas** (over the course of the complete text he offers a comprehensive view of moral character, ethical decision making, and even some political implications of these.) (17)

Even if someone disagrees with *some* of these examples, it is undeniable that Aristotle satisfies *enough* of the conditions of family resemblance of "philosopher" that he is unambiguously considered one—and one of the most profound and influential philosophers, at that. Equally unsurprising is the fact that he is taught in countless philosophy courses around the world, at all levels. What can we say, though, about more *ambiguous* texts such as the Nahua poem?

Santana argues that poems such as those certainly address "philosophical issues" mentioned in (1) (e.g., death, knowledge, truth), and they show concern for living well (2).

They also exhibit a sense of wonder (3), involve reflection (4), and justify beliefs rather than appealing solely to authority or divine inspiration (5). They additionally seem to pursue aims 6-10.

It's really only with respect to *methods* where *any* questions as to whether the Nahua texts "count" as philosophy arise.

They *do* attempt to answer fundamental questions (11) by critically examining cultural assumptions (12), but they *don't* give rigorous justification by means of *obvious* arguments (13), raise or address objections (14), analyze (15) or clarify concepts (16), or synthesize ideas (17) in ways typical of commonly recognized Western philosophy.

In other words, that poem shows *some* of the characteristics of philosophy, though not *all*. Something similar can be said for all (or nearly all) "undisputed" works of philosophy. Some contemporary works of analytic philosophy excel at features 11-17, but exhibit little "wonder" (3) or show any concern with living a good life (2). Frege's *Foundation of Arithmetic*, for example, is rigorously analytic in defending its claims, but has nothing to say about living well as a human being whatsoever.

While there is no precise dividing line, there is certainly enough "resemblance" between the Nahua poems, and the collection of traits associated with philosophy, to note the "family resemblance"—and the very same process may be applied to other (currently) non-canonical sources as well. By expanding our notion of who does philosophy, and what counts as philosophy, we not only pay respect to wise persons throughout history and from every inhabited continent who have applied reflection and reason

to the human condition, but we also add many more worthy voices of the great conversation.

Now that we have a rough idea of what counts a philosophical source or resource, we can turn our attention to who is capable of studying and participating in philosophy. Given that philosophy is this deep, difficult, highly cognitive and elite activity, who is worthy of participating in this "great conversation?" Who can actually "do" philosophy? Although we are expanding the conversation to include the entire globe, it is still just a handful of elite experts, right?

Nope.

The short answer is "darn near everyone" can do philosophy. To make this case, I would like to offer the analogy of dancing.

What is a dancer? In some cases it is simply anyone who dances. In other cases, it indicates someone who does so professionally, for a living. This usually implies quite a lot of training and experience.

I would argue that *anyone* can dance. Even people with significant physical disabilities can probably find ways to respond rhythmically to music. This does not mean, of course, that everyone dances with *equal skill*, or in ways that are equally appreciated by observers, but certainly the overwhelming majority of people are capable of doing what we call "dance."

Analogously, everyone can philosophize. Some people do it professionally, and some do it with more skill than others, but everyone (barring *profound* mental disabilities or delays) is capable of philosophizing. Like dancing, it gets better with practice, and more informed through study.

Think of this book as a combination of a "dance class" and "dance manual." I'm confident that if you are reading this text, you are already not only capable of doing philosophy, but that you have actually already done some philosophizing, whether you realize it or not. That does not mean, of course, that you philosophize at the same skill level as a "professional," or that your skill can't be improved. I'm here to help you improve.

To that end, we will be considering the efforts of a number of philosophers throughout history and across the globe who were so good at it that I would consider them "professional." We can learn from their example, just as we can learn to dance better by watching performances of those who are already really good.

Along the way, we will practice some specific skills essential to philosophy, such as careful reading, summarizing, and the crafting of logical arguments to support our own positions that we take on philosophical issues, as well as our interpretations and agreement/disagreement with the arguments offered by other people.

By the end of this book (assuming you "show up" and *try*), you *will* be better at doing philosophy. Although I make no assumptions that any of you intend to go "pro," I'm extraordinarily confident that you will benefit from your "training," no matter what your interests happen to be, or what your professional ambitions are. Practicing philosophy will make you a better thinker, a better reader, a better writer, and a better and more persuasive advocate for the things that matter to *you*.

Let's dance.

Critical Analysis

1. In your opinion, what are the strongest and most compelling points made by the philosopher or philosophers in this chapter? Why do you find those points to be convincing?

2. In your opinion, what are the weakest or least convincing points? Why? Can you anticipate any limitations or objections to their ideas not already addressed in the chapter?

Appendix: Application to Social Justice

As mentioned briefly above, the history of what has "counted" as philosophy has been a history that, like the unfolding of history itself, includes bigotry—not only racism, but sexism, colonialism, etc. In this appendix, I would like to (briefly) address the issue of racism in philosophy.

I had the pleasure and privilege of being awarded a sabbatical year for the academic year 2019-2020. The primary purpose of my sabbatical year was to research non-Western philosophers, from throughout history and across the globe, that are not generally regarded as "canon" in philosophy programs in English-speaking countries. "Canon" refers to a body of books, people, and other texts considered to be the most important and influential of that discipline.

For philosophy taught in such departments as all the ones I've ever been a part of as either a student or professor, that canon included philosophers such as Socrates, Plato, Aristotle, Aquinas, Hobbes, Locke, Hume, Kant, Nietzsche, Sartre, etc.

Conspicuously, virtually every major figure (except for some living, writing philosophy professors today) was white, male, heterosexual, and cis-gendered. Even to be exposed to female philosophers usually required that one take a "feminist philosophy" class. The *entirety* of all other philosophers and traditions across the globe and throughout history were rendered, in contrast, "non-canonical," and usually either dismissed and rejected as not "real" philosophy, or else relegated to (elective) specialty classes typically found only in graduate programs or as upper division undergraduate courses—and even in such cases, rarely so.

Most of us who absorbed this curriculum as students, and went on to teach it to future generations of students ourselves, never thought twice about that.

To be clear, I do **not** think that the content of the canon, and the unreflective transmission of it, was—let alone is—the result of a conscious intent to exclude on the basis of race or gender. I think the most charitable and most accurate explanation of it is literal and understandable ignorance. Simply put, philosophers tend to teach what they were taught. If, for generations, philosophy professors taught exclusively the works of white male philosophers from either Europe or North America, then their students who became the next generation of philosophy professors would be disposed to accept and replicate the same curriculum. This cycle can only be broken by making deliberate efforts to do so.

That was the aim of my sabbatical project: to intentionally and sincerely research and incorporate underrepresented sources into the philosophical canon, one department and one College at a time.

Diversifying the curriculum is a worthy goal, and one to which I'm happy to contribute. However, the history of Western philosophy is problematic given today's standards and understanding not only for what it has *excluded*, but also for what it has *included*.

Like the history of Western civilization itself, and no different from the history of virtually every other academic discipline, the history of philosophy includes both individuals and ideas that most of us, today, would presumably and rightfully condemn as racist, sexist, homophobic, (etc.). This is worthy of repeating and expansion.

The taint of racism is not somehow unique to philosophy, nor especially prominent in philosophy.

Because the history of Western civilization itself has been marked by individuals and policies that would be considered racist by almost any contemporary definition, many philosophers fit that description as well—but no more so than prominent figures in psychology, politics and political science, sociology, anthropology, economics, literature, medicine, history, etc.

If anything, the tendency towards self-reflection in philosophy and philosophers makes our discipline, and those in it, perhaps more likely to acknowledge this history, and to do something about it—as we are doing now. Moreover, philosophy emphasizes ideas rather than the source of ideas. In fact, undue attention on the source is considered a case of a logical fallacy, the genetic fallacy. This focus on ideas might well make philosophy easier to redeem and rehabilitate than other fields.

All that being said, Aristotle and Nietzsche were both blatantly sexist. Hume and Kant were both breathtakingly racist. Additional examples are ample, but I will not dignify them by quoting any of them.

Because of this, some argue that these figures should be "purged" from the curriculum. One academic shared her experience in graduate school, and her recommendation for academia. Please note that in the quotation below she is **not** referring to the field of philosophy, specifically.

> *During graduate school, professors told me, again and again, to hold texts in their historical context. Incessantly, they requested that I give white scholars grace. I was to understand them as victims of their time. This, of course, is bullshit. . . .*
>
> *Why are . . . white writers . . . allowed to be stuck in their time, victims of the very white supremacy that they uphold?*
>
> *You can not be both a supremacist and a victim of the very supremacy that you espouse. . . .*
>
> *Why are our expectations for white scholars with ample access so much lower? Why do white scholars remain canonized even though the insidiousness of their texts are proven not to be rooted in victimhood, but agency? . . .*
>
> *By refusing to reimagine not only the canon but also the theories and methods of every single disciple, academia is choosing to remain complicit in upholding white supremacy as its core value. . . .*
>
> *Destroy it all. Not just the syllabus, the discipline. Your whole discipline needs to be dismantled and reimagined. If you care about Black lives, if you truly meant that long-winded email you sent out to your students, then do not continue to be anti-Black in policy and pedagogy. Now is your time to put your scholarship where your mouth is.[21]*

---

[21]https://medium.com/the-faculty/not-just-the-syllabus-throw-the-whole-discipline-in-the- trash-777d19201cb5

I agree with her in part, though certainly not in full.

Certain works in certain disciplines, such as books advocating for the long discredited "science" of eugenics, probably should just be condemned to the garbage cans of history.

But, while I agree that other historically marginalized voices need to be included and heard, and while I agree that oppressive ideas need to be called out and recognized as such, regardless of whatever was "normal" for the culture and era of the historical figure in question, I *don't* agree that controversial figures from the history of philosophy, specifically, should be expelled from the canon entirely solely because their ideas don't correspond to our current moral values and expectations. Another contemporary philosopher (Julian Baggini) agrees, and I think is worth quoting at length.

> We seem to be caught in a dilemma. We can't just dismiss the unacceptable prejudices of the past as unimportant. But if we think that holding morally objectionable views disqualifies anyone from being considered a great thinker or a political leader, then there's hardly anyone from history left.
>
> The problem does not go away if you exclude dead white establishment males. Racism was common in the women's suffrage movement on both sides of the Atlantic. The American suffragette Carrie Chapman Catt said that: 'White supremacy will be strengthened, not weakened, by women's suffrage.' Emmeline Pankhurst, her British sister in the struggle, became a vociferous supporter of colonialism, denying that it was 'something to decry and something to be ashamed of' and insisting instead that 'it is a great thing to be the inheritors of an empire like ours'. Both sexism and xenophobia have been common in the trade union movement, all in the name of defending the rights of workers – male, non-immigrant workers that is.
>
> However, the idea that racist, sexist or otherwise bigoted views automatically disqualify a historical figure from admiration is misguided. Anyone who cannot bring themselves to admire such a historical figure betrays a profound lack of understanding about just how socially conditioned all our minds are, even the greatest. Because the prejudice seems so self-evidently wrong, they just cannot imagine how anyone could fail to see this without being depraved. . . .
>
> Why do so many find it impossible to believe that any so-called genius could fail to see that their prejudices were irrational and immoral? One reason is that our culture has its own deep-seated and mistaken assumption: that the individual is an autonomous human intellect independent from the social environment. Even a passing acquaintance with psychology, sociology or anthropology should squash that comfortable illusion. The enlightenment ideal that we can and should all think for ourselves should not be confused with the hyper-enlightenment fantasy that we can think all by ourselves. Our thinking is shaped by our environment in profound ways that we often aren't even aware of. Those who refuse to accept that they are as much limited by these forces as anyone else have delusions of intellectual grandeur.
>
> When a person is so deeply embedded in an immoral system, it becomes problematic to attribute individual responsibility. This is troubling because we are wedded to the idea that the locus of moral responsibility is the perfectly autonomous individual. Were we to take the social conditioning of abhorrent beliefs and practices seriously,

the fear is that everyone would be off the hook, and we'd be left with a hopeless moral relativism.

But the worry that we would be unable to condemn what most needs condemnation is baseless. Misogyny and racism are no less repulsive because they are the products of societies as much, if not more, than they are of individuals. To excuse Hume is not to excuse racism; to excuse Aristotle is not to excuse sexism. Racism and sexism were never okay, people simply wrongly believed that they were.

Accepting this does not mean glossing over the prejudices of the past. Becoming aware that even the likes of Kant and Hume were products of their times is a humbling reminder that the greatest minds can still be blind to mistakes and evils, if they are widespread enough. It should also prompt us to question whether the prejudices that rudely erupt to the surface in their most infamous remarks might also be lurking in the background elsewhere in their thinking. A lot of the feminist critique of Dead White Male philosophy is of this kind, arguing that the evident misogyny is just the tip of a much more insidious iceberg. Sometimes that might be true but we should not assume that it is. Many blindspots are remarkably local, leaving the general field of vision perfectly clear.

The classicist Edith Hall's defence of Aristotle's misogyny is a paradigm of how to save a philosopher from his worst self. Rather than judge him by today's standards, she argues that a better test is to ask whether the fundamentals of his way of thinking would lead him to be prejudiced today. Given Aristotle's openness to evidence and experience, there is no question that today he would need no

persuading that women are men's equals. Hume likewise always deferred to experience, and so would not today be apt to suspect anything derogatory about dark-skinned peoples. In short, we don't need to look beyond the fundamentals of their philosophy to see what was wrong in how they applied them.

One reason we might be reluctant to excuse thinkers of the past is because we fear that excusing the dead will entail excusing the living. If we can't blame Hume, Kant or Aristotle for their prejudices, how can we blame the people being called out by the #MeToo movement for acts that they committed in social milieus where they were completely normal? After all, wasn't Harvey Weinstein all too typical of Hollywood's 'casting couch' culture?

But there is a very important difference between the living and the dead. The living can come to see how their actions were wrong, acknowledge that, and show remorse. When their acts were crimes, they can also face justice. We just cannot afford to be as understanding of present prejudices as we are of past ones. Changing society requires making people see that it is possible to overcome the prejudices they were brought up with. We are not responsible for creating the distorted values that shaped us and our society but we can learn to take responsibility for how we deal with them now.

The dead do not have such an opportunity, and so to waste anger chastising them is pointless. We are right to lament the iniquities of the past, but to blame individuals for things they did in less enlightened times using the standards of today is too harsh.[22]

We can shake our heads at Aristotle's

---

[22] https://aeon.co/ideas/why-sexist-and-racist-philosophers-might-still-be-admirable

embarrassing dismissal of the intellectual and moral capacities of women, and *still* study and benefit from his foundational exploration of what would eventually become known as virtue ethics.

David Hume was a brilliant philosopher whose contribution to Western philosophy is almost without peer, thus far. *And*, he held racist beliefs. We can either ignore his commentary on race, or perhaps better yet acknowledge it as an example of how otherwise brilliant people can be shamefully misguided on certain matters. We can condemn his views on race as both factually and morally wrong either way, *and still* appreciate his insights into epistemology. This is where I think Baggini actually states his case poorly, above. He writes: "To excuse Hume is not to excuse racism." But who is *excusing* Hume? To acknowledge his racist ideas, condemn them as such, but still benefit from his numerous non-racist insights is certainly not to excuse either racism in general, or Hume's racism, in particular.

And, maybe Baggini is correct? Perhaps Hume and Aristotle, knowing what we do now, would have advocated very different views if they were writing today? None of that means that their recorded views on certain subjects aren't morally offensive to our contemporary sensibilities, but it could suggest that we proceed with some measure of humility, open to the very real possibility that some of *our own* current views might someday be judged harshly in the future. I'm ashamed of some of the things I believed and endorsed when I was a teenager, and as a young man. I like to think that my worldview, including both beliefs and values, has become more morally mature over time, but I think I would be both hopelessly naïve and viciously arrogant to think that my present values somehow now perfectly align with a timeless righteousness and justice, and that I have no more room for improvement— and I think the same applies to all of us, if we're being honest with ourselves.

I'm confident each one of us has, in our past, believed and done, and, unfortunately, probably will again in the future believe and do, things that are insensitive, inaccurate, unenlightened, oppressive, etc. So did Aristotle, Hume, and probably all the other currently canonical figures in Western philosophy (and presumably most, if not all, of the major figures in every *other* field as well!).

I'm equally confident that the more diverse figures that I have tried to add to the canon are subject to similar human failings.

Nezahualcoyotl was a brilliant Aztec philosopher king, and I am proud that in some of my courses and textbooks I am able to shine a deserved spotlight on him. He brings a valuable voice to the Great Conversation that has long neglected the wisdom of people like him. He was also complicit in the human sacrifice that was "normal" for his culture and time. I think American philosophy students should study him *and* condemn human sacrifice. Confucius was, by his own admission, a conservative philosopher, and one of the traditional values he "conserved" was the *patriarchal* culture of ancient China. Confucius was no more a gender progressive than was Aristotle, but I think he should be *included* (and contextualized), just as I think Aristotle should *not* be *excluded* (and, when included, should be contextualized as well). It's also worth pointing out that both Confucius and Aristotle can be interpreted in ways consistent with more egalitarian views of gender. In other words, their antiquated views on gender aren't somehow indispensable to their otherwise valuable ideas.

Chapter 3: The Love of Wisdom

Comprehension questions you should be able to answer after reading this chapter:

1. What are the features of the "Socratic method?
2. Why was Socrates' death inspirational to so many?
3. Why do you think Socrates claimed that "the unexamined life is not worth living?" Do you agree? Why or why not?
4. What was the cause of Sor Juana's pursuit of education, according to her own testimony? How did she educate herself? What sorts of subjects did she study?
5. When Sor Juana didn't have access to books, how did she continue to learn?
6. What arguments does Sor Juana offer for why women should be educated?

When you think of a "philosopher," what comes to mind? Who does that philosopher look like? What makes that person "philosophical?" Given those standards, do you consider yourself a philosopher? Why or why not?

Depending upon your background, you might have any number of different ideas when it comes to philosophy and philosophers. Some people have in mind a very specific set of "famous" people from the Western philosophical tradition, such as Socrates and Aristotle (among many others). Others may think instead (or in addition) of famous non-Western thinkers such as Confucius (among many others). Others may have in mind less traditionally recognized (but still popular) thinkers such as Alan Watts (among many others). Others will envision people who have degrees in philosophy, even though they might be better known for their work in other fields, such as Angela Davis, Steve Martin, Bruce Lee, and Aung San Suu Kyi (among many others). Still others will generate entirely different lists based upon other criteria.

If you read the chapter on "what counts as philosophy," I hope that one of the things you took from that chapter is that there probably isn't a precise definition of a "philosopher" that will clearly indicate for each person whether they are, or are not. Instead, there is a "family resemblance" of traits associated with philosophy and philosophizing, and as long as someone exhibits some of those traits to sufficient degree a case can be made that they are doing philosophy.

In this chapter, we will consider two famous individuals, one of whom is undoubtedly regarded as a philosopher, and the other of whom (I believe) *should* be.

Socrates

Socrates (470 - 399 BCE), pictured here, is the iconic "philosopher" in the West, but he was also a man. He was a husband and father of three children. He was an itinerant teacher who seemed to rely on the support of his wealthier friends, as he charged nothing to those he "instructed." He served in the military, and his courage in war was recognized. He never wrote anything himself. All we think we know about him comes from the writing of others, most notably Plato, but also Aristophanes and Xenophon. Finally, he was put on trial for atheism and corrupting the youth of Athens. After being convicted and sentenced to death, he drank hemlock and died.

Socrates presents an interpretation problem. As already mentioned, he didn't write philosophical texts or dialogues himself. He is lampooned in Aristophanes' *Clouds*, and presented as a serious philosopher by both Xenophon and Plato. Our greatest source for all things Socrates is his student Plato, but Plato was roughly 45 years younger than Socrates, and was only 25 when Socrates was tried and executed. Plato was only a young child when most of the events and conversations reported in his dialogues could have actually taken place. It's unlikely that a five year old Plato was not only present for all these conversations, but memorized them precisely that he might write them down some decades later. We have, then, *"the problem of Socrates:"* what did Socrates himself really believe and teach and say? How much of Plato's "Socrates" is actually Socrates, and not just Plato wearing a "Socrates" mask? We can't know for sure. What we can know, however, is that Socrates (whatever he said!) was a hugely influential and revered figure for ancient philosophers, as all the philosophical schools to come after him (except for Epicureanism) either traced themselves back to Socrates himself, or at least claimed that Socrates was an embodiment of their ideals.

Socrates is most well-known for the "*Socratic method.*" Socrates, himself (according to legend), claimed to know nothing (and from this it is easy to see the lineage the Skeptics traced back to him), and also claimed to be seeking knowledge from those with whom he spoke. Socrates starts from the position of (alleged) ignorance, all due to a fateful prophecy he received:

> You must have known Chaerephon; he was early a friend of mine, and also a friend of yours, for he shared in the recent exile of the people, and returned with you. Well, Chaerephon, as you know, was very impetuous in all his doings, and he went to Delphi and boldly asked the oracle to tell him whether -- as I was saying, I must beg you not to interrupt -- he asked the oracle

> to tell him whether anyone was wiser than I was, and the Pythian prophetess answered, that there was no man wiser. Chaerephon is dead himself; but his brother, who is in court, will confirm the truth of what I am saying.

> Why do I mention this? Because I am going to explain to you why I have such an evil name. When I heard the answer, I said to myself, What can the god mean? and what is the interpretation of his riddle? for I know that I have no wisdom, small or great. What then can he mean when he says that I am the wisest of men? And yet he is a god, and cannot lie; that would be against his nature. After long consideration, I thought of a method of trying the question. I reflected that if I could only find a man wiser than myself, then I might go to the god with a refutation in my hand. I should say to him, 'Here is a man who is wiser than I am; but you said that I was the wisest.' Accordingly I went to one who had the reputation of wisdom, and observed him -- his name I need not mention; he was a politician whom I selected for examination -- and the result was as follows: When I began to talk with him, I could not help thinking that he was not really wise, although he was thought wise by many, and still wiser by himself; and thereupon I tried to explain to him that he thought himself wise, but was not really wise; and the consequence was that he hated me, and his enmity was shared by several who were present and heard me. So I left him, saying to myself, as I went away: Well, although I do not suppose that either of us knows anything really beautiful and good, I am better off than he is, -- for he knows nothing, and thinks that he knows; I neither know nor think that I know. In this latter particular, then, I seem to have slightly the advantage of him.[23]

---

[23] Plato, *Apology*. Note: all references attributed to Socrates are from this source, unless

Being proclaimed the wisest of all, Socrates sought a counter-example—someone who would prove wiser than he. So, he spoke with all sorts of prominent people, people who claimed to be wise, in an effort to confirm their wisdom. The result was always the same: by virtue of his interrogation, they were revealed to be lacking in wisdom after all. His method was consistent:

- Ask a question concerning an important issue, all while claiming not to have an answer himself.
- Attack whatever answers (often definitions) are provided by identifying logical flaws (e.g., circularity, definition by example, etc.).
- Employ a reductio ad absurdum argument to reveal further flaws, and/or use counter-examples to the same effect.

Consider the following example from the *Apology*:

(Socrates) But still I should like to know, Meletus, in what I am affirmed to corrupt the young. I suppose you mean, as I infer from your indictment, that I teach them not to acknowledge the gods which the state acknowledges, but some other new divinities or spiritual agencies in their stead. These are the lessons by which I corrupt the youth, as you say.

(Meletus) Yes, that I say emphatically.

(Socrates) Then, by the gods, Meletus, of whom we are speaking, tell me and the court, in somewhat plainer terms, what you mean! for I do not as yet understand whether you affirm that I teach other men to acknowledge some gods, and therefore that I do believe in gods, and am not an entire atheist -- this you do not lay to my charge, -- but only you say that they are not the same gods which the city recognizes --

the charge is that they are different gods. Or, do you mean that I am an atheist simply, and a teacher of atheism?
(Meletus) I mean the latter -- that you are a complete atheist.

(Socrates) What an extraordinary statement! Why do you think so, Meletus? Do you mean that I do not believe in the godhead of the sun or moon, like other men?

(Meletus) I assure you, judges, that he does not: for he says that the sun is stone, and the moon earth.

(Socrates) Friend Meletus, you think that you are accusing Anaxagoras: and you have but a bad opinion of the judges, if you fancy them illiterate to such a degree as not to know that these doctrines are found in the books of Anaxagoras the Clazomenian, which are full of them. And so, forsooth, the youth are said to be taught them by Socrates, when there are not unfrequently exhibitions of them at the theatre (Probably in allusion to Aristophanes who caricatured, and to Euripides who borrowed the notions of Anaxagoras, as well as to other dramatic poets.) (price of admission one drachma at the most); and they might pay their money, and laugh at Socrates if he pretends to father these extraordinary views. And so, Meletus, you really think that I do not believe in any god?

(Meletus) I swear by Zeus that you believe absolutely in none at all.

(Socrates) Nobody will believe you, Meletus, and I am pretty sure that you do not believe yourself. I cannot help thinking, men of Athens, that Meletus is reckless and impudent, and that he has written this

---

otherwise indicated.

indictment in a spirit of mere wantonness and youthful bravado. Has he not compounded a riddle, thinking to try me? He said to himself: -- I shall see whether the wise Socrates will discover my facetious contradiction, or whether I shall be able to deceive him and the rest of them. For he certainly does appear to me to contradict himself in the indictment as much as if he said that Socrates is guilty of not believing in the gods, and yet of believing in them -- but this is not like a person who is in earnest.

I should like you, O men of Athens, to join me in examining what I conceive to be his inconsistency; and do you, Meletus, answer. And I must remind the audience of my request that they would not make a disturbance if I speak in my accustomed manner:

Did ever man, Meletus, believe in the existence of human things, and not of human beings?...I wish, men of Athens, that he would answer, and not be always trying to get up an interruption. Did ever any man believe in horsemanship, and not in horses? or in flute-playing, and not in flute-players? No, my friend; I will answer to you and to the court, as you refuse to answer for yourself. There is no man who ever did. But now please to answer the next question: Can a man believe in spiritual and divine agencies, and not in spirits or demigods?

(Meletus) He cannot.

(Socrates) How lucky I am to have extracted that answer, by the assistance of the court! But then you swear in the indictment that I teach and believe in divine or spiritual agencies (new or old, no matter for that); at any rate, I believe in spiritual agencies, -- so you say and swear in the affidavit; and yet if I believe in divine beings, how can I help believing in spirits

or demigods; -- must I not? To be sure I must; and therefore I may assume that your silence gives consent. Now what are spirits or demigods? Are they not either gods or the sons of gods?

(Meletus) Certainly they are.

(Socrates) But this is what I call the facetious riddle invented by you: the demigods or spirits are gods, and you say first that I do not believe in gods, and then again that I do believe in gods; that is, if I believe in demigods. For if the demigods are the illegitimate sons of gods, whether by the nymphs or by any other mothers, of whom they are said to be the sons -- what human being will ever believe that there are no gods if they are the sons of gods? You might as well affirm the existence of mules, and deny that of horses and asses. Such nonsense, Meletus, could only have been intended by you to make trial of me. You have put this into the indictment because you had nothing real of which to accuse me. But no one who has a particle of understanding will ever be convinced by you that the same men can believe in divine and superhuman things, and yet not believe that there are gods and demigods and heroes.

At this point, Meletus already looks ridiculous, given that he has been reduced to the absurd position that although Socrates believes in no gods at all, he nevertheless believes in the offspring of gods! This process will continue until it becomes obvious to any impartial observer that Socrates is not guilty of the charges brought against him—not that it helped him in that case.

There are various ways to interpret his argumentative approach, with the *least* charitable being that Socrates was some sort of bully who preferred clever arguments over fists. If Plato's account of Socrates (especially in the *Apology*) is remotely accurate, Socrates was no bully, but saw himself to be on a divine mission.

And so I go about the world, obedient to the god, and search and make enquiry into the wisdom of any one, whether citizen or stranger, who appears to be wise; and if he is not wise, then in vindication of the oracle I show him that he is not wise; and my occupation quite absorbs me, and I have no time to give either to any public matter of interest or to any concern of my own, but I am in utter poverty by reason of my devotion to the god.

He also saw himself in service to Athens, and believed that his confrontations and interrogations were efforts to improve the very souls of those with whom he spoke.

Men of Athens, I honour and love you; but I shall obey God rather than you, and while I have life and strength I shall never cease from the practice and teaching of philosophy, exhorting any one whom I meet and saying to him after my manner: You, my friend, -- a citizen of the great and mighty and wise city of Athens, -- are you not ashamed of heaping up the greatest amount of money and honour and reputation, and caring so little about wisdom and truth and the greatest improvement of the soul, which you never regard or heed at all? And if the person with whom I am arguing, says: Yes, but I do care; then I do not leave him or let him go at once; but I proceed to interrogate and examine and cross-examine him, and if I think that he has no virtue in him, but only says that he has, I reproach him with undervaluing the greater, and overvaluing the less. And I shall repeat the same words to every one whom I meet, young and old, citizen and alien, but especially to the citizens, inasmuch as they are my brethren. For know that this is the command of God; and I believe that no greater good has ever happened in the state than my service to the God. For I do nothing but go about persuading you all, old and young alike, not to take thought for your persons or
your properties, but first and chiefly to care about the greatest improvement of the soul. I tell you that virtue is not given by money, but that from virtue comes money and every other good of man, public as well as private.

It seems suitable, in an obvious sort of way, to end our brief treatment of Socrates with his death. Despite his superior arguments, Socrates was convicted on the charges brought against him. When given an opportunity to propose his own punishment, he first suggested that his "punishment" be free public meals for the rest of his life! At the urging of Plato and others present, he then suggested a modest fine. He refused to cower and plead for mercy, confident in his own righteousness. When the sentence of death was pronounced, he did not cower then either. Instead, he offered an argument for why death is not a bad thing.

Let us reflect in another way, and we shall see that there is great reason to hope that death is a good; for one of two things -- either death is a state of nothingness and utter unconsciousness, or, as men say, there is a change and migration of the soul from this world to another. Now if you suppose that there is no consciousness, but a sleep like the sleep of him who is undisturbed even by dreams, death will be an unspeakable gain. For if a person were to select the night in which his sleep was undisturbed even by dreams, and were to compare with this the other days and nights of his life, and then were to tell us how many days and nights he had passed in the course of his life better and more pleasantly than this one, I think that any man, I will not say a private man, but even the great king will not find many such days or nights, when compared with the others. Now if death be of such a nature, I say that to die is gain; for eternity is then only a single night. But if death is the journey to another place, and there, as men say, all the dead abide, what good, O my friends and judges, can be greater than this? If indeed when the pilgrim arrives in the world below, he is delivered from the professors of justice in this world, and finds the true judges who are said to give judgment there, . . . Above all, I shall then be able to continue my search into true and false knowledge; as in this world, so also in the next; and I shall find out who is wise, and who pretends to be wise, and is not. What would not a man give, O judges, to be able to examine the leader of the great Trojan expedition; or Odysseus or Sisyphus, or numberless others, men and women too! What infinite delight would there be in conversing with them and asking them questions! In another world they do not put a man to death for asking questions: assuredly not. For besides being happier than we are, they will be immortal, if what is said is true.

Perhaps more important and impressive than his words, were his deeds. In another dialogue written by Plato (the *Crito*), one of Socrates' friends visits him in prison prior to his execution with plans for his escape. Rather than seizing the opportunity to save his own life, Socrates seizes one last opportunity to offer moral instruction. *He demonstrates that it is not life that is to be valued, but a good and just life.* Socrates imagines himself being interrogated by the laws of Athens themselves should he escape.

Consider, Socrates, if this is true, that in your present attempt you are going to do us wrong. For, after having brought you into the world, and nurtured and educated you, and given you and every other citizen a share in every good that we had to give, we further proclaim and give the right to every Athenian, that if he does not like us when he has come of age and has seen the ways of the city, and made our acquaintance, he may go where he pleases and take his goods with him; and none of us laws will forbid him or interfere with him. Any of you who does not like us and

the city, and who wants to go to a colony or to any other city, may go where he likes, and take his goods with him. But he who has experience of the manner in which we order justice and administer the State, and still remains, has entered into an implied contract that he will do as we command him. And he who disobeys us is, as we maintain, thrice wrong: first, because in disobeying us he is disobeying his parents; secondly, because we are the authors of his education; thirdly, because he has made an agreement with us that he will duly obey our commands; and he neither obeys them nor convinces us that our commands are wrong; and we do not rudely impose them, but give him the alternative of obeying or convincing us; that is what we offer and he does neither. These are the sort of accusations to which, as we were saying, you, Socrates, will be exposed if you accomplish your intentions; you, above all other Athenians." Suppose I ask, why is this? they will justly retort upon me that I above all other men have acknowledged the agreement. "There is clear proof," they will say, "Socrates, that we and the city were not displeasing to you. Of all Athenians you have been the most constant resident in the city, which, as you never leave, you may be supposed to love. For you never went out of the city either to see the games, except once when you went to the Isthmus, or to any other place unless when you were on military service; nor did you travel as other men do. Nor had you any curiosity to know other States or their laws: your affections did not go beyond us and our State; we were your especial favorites, and you acquiesced in our government of you; and this is the State in which you begat your children, which is a proof of your satisfaction. Moreover, you might, if you had liked, have fixed the penalty at banishment in the course of the trial-the State which refuses to let you go now would have let you go then. But you pretended that you preferred death to exile, and that you were not grieved at death. And now you have forgotten these fine sentiments, and pay no respect to us, the laws, of whom you are the destroyer; and are doing what only a miserable slave would do, running away and turning your back upon the compacts and agreements which you made as a citizen. And first of all answer this very question: Are we right in saying that you agreed to be governed according to us in deed, and not in word only? Is that true or not?[24]

If Socrates were to escape from his sentence, he would not only violate the laws of his city-State, he would reveal himself to be a fraud. He had long claimed that death was not a bad thing, and that *nothing in life or death could truly harm a virtuous person*. If he were to flee death, his actions would contradict his words. Deeds, not mere words.

In his death, Socrates' philosophy and status as a philosopher is arguably most evident. It is one thing to be clever and gifted in speech. The Sophists could all be described so. A true philosopher, on the other hand, *lives* his (or her) philosophy. Or, in Socrates' case, dies for it.

Pythagoras *might* have been the first to seek "salvation" in philosophy, but Socrates was the first to provide a living (and dying) testimony to how philosophy can transform one's life. Small wonder that nearly every philosophical school to come would point to him as either founder or inspiration.

He exerted obvious influence on his most famous pupil, Plato (and Plato's most famous pupil: Aristotle). When Arcesilaus converted Plato's Academy to Skepticism, they stressed Socrates' own denial of wisdom and his ceaseless questioning. One of Socrates' associates, Antisthenes, contributed to the Cynic school, which emphasized Socrates' simple lifestyle and insistence that virtue is sufficient for happiness. The Cynics then transmitted Socrates to the Stoics, who emphasized Socrates' claim that virtue is the only true good, as well as his call for a life lived in accordance with reason.

Socrates, whether via his words or his example, transcended the death imposed upon him to become the icon of the Western philosopher.

Sor Juana Inés de la Cruz

Currently taught more often in History or Literature courses, than in philosophy courses, Sor Juana Inés de Asbaje y Ramírez de Santillana (de la Cruz) nevertheless had both the heart and mind of a true philosopher.

She was born on November 12, 1648. She was a self-taught scholar of numerous subjects, including philosophy and various sciences. She educated herself by reading books from her grandfather's library, in secret – since this was forbidden for young girls. She was fluent in Spanish and Latin (which she learned at the age of three), and could also write in Nahuatl.[25] She lived during the colonial period of Mexico, and contributed to early Mexican literature.

Juana became *Sor* Juana when she became a nun in 1667 and began writing both poetry and prose dealing with religious topics, as well as the more controversial topics of love and even feminism.

In November of 1690, the bishop of Puebla, Manuel Fernández de Santa Cruz published her critique of a 40-year-old sermon by Father António Vieira. He did so without her permission, and under the pseudonym of "Sor Filotea." He also published his own letter that criticized her comments and claimed that, as a *woman*, she should give up writing and devote herself to prayer.

She did *not* give up her writing at that time, but instead responded with a letter Respuesta a Sor Filotea de la Cruz ("Reply to Sister Philotea"). In this letter, she defended women's right to an education while explaining her own educational journey.

Her outspoken views resulted in her condemnation by the Bishop of Puebla, and she

---

[24] Plato, *Crito.*
[25] Nahuatl is the language of the indigenous

Nahua people, who are discussed in several places in this book.

was eventually forced to sell her personal collection of books in 1694. She died the next year of the plague, on April 17. She contracted the disease while treating her fellow nuns who had been afflicted.

For our purposes, we will consider a handful of excerpts from her "Answer by the poet to the most illustrious Sister Filotea de la Cruz by Sor Juana Inés de la Cruz (1691)." Please note that Sor Juana uses many Latin phrases. I have provided translations in brackets within the selections, since my assumption is that most of you don't read Latin any more than I do!

The pattern for the remainder of this chapter will be as follows: I will provide a short excerpt from the letter for you to read. I encourage you to pause and reflect and come to your own interpretation of that piece of text. I will then offer a brief summary and analysis of my own, before moving on to the next section.

We will begin with her explanation of her pursuit of education and thirst for knowledge.

(6) My writing has never arisen from my own decision, but rather from outside sources. Truthfully, I could say to them: Vos me coegistis [you have compelled me]. What is really true—and I will not deny it (on the one hand because it's well known to everyone, and on the other hand because, even though it might count against me, God graced me with of a gift of an immense love for the truth)—is that since the first light of reason dawned on me my inclination toward letters was so intense and powerful that neither reprimands by others, of which I have had many, nor self-reflection, of which I have done not a little, have been sufficient for me to stop pursuing this natural impulse that God put in me. God Almighty knows why and for what purpose. And he knows I've asked him to snuff out the light of my mind and leave only what's necessary to

keep his commandments. Some would say that any more is too much in a woman, and some even say that it is harmful. The Almighty also knows that, since my request failed, I have tried to bury my intellect along with my name and to sacrifice all this only to the one who gave it to me. For no other reason I entered a religious order even though its duties and fellowship were anathema to the unhindered quietude required by my studious intent. Afterwards, once there, the Lord knows (and outside its walls the single person who ought to have known it knows so) what I undertook to conceal my name. But he forbade me to do so because he said it was a sinful temptation, and it surely was. If I could repay some part of the debt I owe you, my Lady, I think just telling you this fact would be sufficient, for never has a word of this left my mouth except for the ears of the person who had a right to hear it. Having just opened wide the doors to my heart and shared its most buried secrets, I now want you to know that trusting you with this information does not contradict what I owe to both your venerable person and your immense favor.[26]

According to Sor Juana, it was God who gave her the gift of a love of truth and learning that she has been unable to repress. She claims to have prayed for this impulse to be "snuffed out," leaving her only "what's necessary to keep his commandments." Those prayers were unanswered. She even entered a religious order in an attempt to suppress her love of learning and devote herself to worship of God and religious contemplation, but even that proved insufficient.

Here, she shows a kinship with Socrates who also claims that he had been inspired by God (although a very different notion of God, to be sure) to philosophize and to interrogate his fellow citizens, and that he ultimately could not

---

[26] "Answer by the poet to the most illustrious Sister Filotea de la Cruz by Sor Juana Inés de la Cruz." (1691) Note: all references attributed to

Sor Juana are from this letter unless otherwise indicated.

resist God's command even though fulfilling it came at his own personal expense. "I shall obey God rather than you, and while I have life and strength I shall never cease from the practice and teaching of philosophy..."

> *(8) I remember that in those days, because I had the sweet-tooth that is normal at that age, I would abstain from eating cheese because I had heard that it turned people into dunces. The desire to acquire knowledge was stronger in me than the desire to eat, even though the latter desire is so strong in children. Later on, when I was six or seven years old, and already knowing how to read and write along with all the other skills that women learn such as embroidery and sewing, I heard that in Mexico City there was a University and there were Schools where people studied the sciences. As soon as I heard this I began to kill my mother by constantly and naggingly begging her to dress me in boy's clothes and to send me to live with some relatives of hers in Mexico City so that I could study by enrolling in the University. She refused, and she was quite right, but I assuaged my desire by reading many kinds of books belonging to my grandfather, notwithstanding the punishment and scolding intended to stop me. So, when I came to Mexico people were amazed, not so much by my intelligence as by my memory and the facts that I had acquired at an age that seemed hardly enough just to be able to learn to speak.*

Even as a young child, Sor Juana's desire for learning was so strong that she craved it even more than candy, even more than food in general. When she learned of a University in Mexico City, she begged her mother to dress her as a boy so that she could move there and enroll in the school. Not giving up, she educated herself by reading her grandfather's books even though doing so invited punishment.

> *(9) I began to study Latin grammar, and I*

> *think I did not have even twenty lessons. I applied myself so intensely that—since this is true about women, and even more so in the bloom of my youth, that we value so highly the natural look of our hair—I would cut off four to six finger lengths of it, measuring up to where it reached before and imposing a rule on myself that, if I did not know whatever I had planned to learn while it was growing back to its original length, I had to cut it off again to punish my dimwittedness. It happened again and again that it would grow and I would not know whatever I had set as my goal, because my hair grew rapidly and I was learning slowly. So I would cut it off as a penalty for my dimwittedness, for it did not seem reasonable to me that a head so denuded of knowledge—which is a more desirable adornment—should be clothed in long hair.*

While her mother punished her for reading and pursuing education in the first place, Sor Juana would punish *herself* for failing to learn quickly enough! She would cut off significant lengths of her hair if she did not meet the educational goals she had set for herself, claiming that a head that lacked knowledge should not be adorned with long and beautiful hair, when wisdom is the "more desirable adornment."

> *(11) I proceeded in this way, as I've said, always directing the path of my studies toward the summit of holy Theology. In order to reach it, it seemed to me necessary to ascend the ladder of the sciences and the humanities, for how can one who does not first know the ancillary fields possibly understand the queen of the sciences? Without logic, how could I possibly know the general and specific methods by which the Holy Scriptures are written? Without rhetoric, how could I possibly understand its figures, tropes, and phrasing? Without the natural sciences, what about so many questions pertaining to the multiple natures the animals used in biblical*

sacrifices, in which so many symbols have already been explained, with many more unexplained? If Saul was cured by the sound of David's harp, was it by virtue of the natural power of music, or the supernatural power God chose to infuse in David? Without arithmetic could one possibly comprehend the computation of so many years, days, months, hours, and the mysterious seventy weeks like those found in Daniel, and still more, the understanding of which requires knowing the natures, concordances, and properties of numbers? Without geometry, how could one possibly measure the Holy Ark of the Covenant and the holy city of Jerusalem, whose mysterious measurements form a cube in all its dimensions, and in which the proportional distribution of all its parts is so marvelous? Without architecture, what about Salomon's great temple, wherein God himself was the draftsman who gave the designs and the plans, and where that wise king was nothing more than the foreman who oversaw the project? In this construction there was no foundation without its mystery, no column without its symbol, no cornice without its allusion, no architrave without is meaning, and so forth, in such a way that the tiniest listel served not only to complement art itself but also to symbolize greater things. Without a thorough understanding of the laws and periods by which history is made up, how can the bible's historical books be understood? I refer to those summaries in which what in fact happened first often is placed later in the narrative. Without a firm command of both branches of the law, how can one comprehend the books of the Law? Without vast erudition, what about so many things in secular history as mentioned in Holy Scripture; so many customs of the gentiles, so many rituals, so many ways of speaking? Without many precepts and much reading in the holy Fathers, how can one understand the concealed sayings of the Prophets? Well

then, if one is not an expert in music, how do we understand those musical intervals and their beauty that abound in many passages, especially in those petitions Abraham made to God on behalf of the cities, asking if he would spare them if there were fifty just men in them? He reduced this number to forty-five, which is sesquinonal (that is, the interval between re to mi); from here to thirty, a sesquitertia, which is that of a diatessaron; from here to twenty, which is the interval the sesquialtera (that is, the diapente); from here to ten, which is the duple (that is, the diapason). And because there are no more intervals, he went no further. Well then, how can we understand this without music? Back there in the Book of Job, God says to him: Numquid coniungere valebis micantes stellas Pleiadas, aut gyrum Arcturi poteris dissipare? Numquid producis Luciferum in tempore suo, et Vesperum super filios terræ consurgere facis? ["Can you fasten the harness of the Pleiades, or untie Orion's bands? Can you guide the Morning Star season by season and show the Bear and its cubs which way to go?" (From Job 38:31 – 32.)]] which terms are impossible to comprehend without knowledge of astronomy. And not only these noble sciences; nor is there any of the mechanical arts that is not mentioned. In sum, this Book encompasses all books, and this science includes all sciences (all of which are used to fathom the one Book), and, after all of which are mastered (obviously, to do so is neither easy nor, indeed, possible), the great science requires another condition beyond everything I have said above, namely, continual prayer and purity of life to beseech God for the kind of purging of the spirit and illumination of the mind that are necessary for understanding such high matters. For, if this is lacking, then everything else is useless. . . .

(38) There is no doubt that to understand

many passages in our holy texts one must command a lot of history, customs, rituals, proverbs, and even various speech patterns from those remote times when they were written so that we can know their gist and to what some turns of phrase are alluding. *Scindite corda vestra, et non vestimenta vestra* ["rend your hearts, and not your garments" (from Joel 2:13)]: Is this not an allusion to the ritual where the Hebrews would tear their garments as a sign of pain, as the evil pontiff did when he said that Christ had blasphemed? Regarding many of the Apostle's passages about succoring widows, don't they also envision customs of those days? How about that passage about the strong woman, *Nobilis in portis vir eius* ["her husband is known in the city gates" (Proverbs 31:23)], doesn't it allude to the custom of placing the judges' courts at the cities' gates? The phrase *dare terram Deo* [to give the land to God], does it not mean to make some kind of vow? *Hiemantes* [those who spend the winter somewhere], is this not what public sinners were called because they made their penance in the open air, unlike others who made theirs in a doorway? That complaint of Christ's to the Pharisee who neither greeted him with a kiss nor washed his feet, wasn't that based on the custom the Jews observed regarding these things? And an infinite number of other passages not only about sacred works but also secular ones as well. The latter are encountered everywhere, like the phrase *adorate purpuram* [honor the purple], which meant to obey the king; *manumittere eum* [to emancipate him], which means to emancipate him, alluding to the custom and ritual of slapping a slave at the moment of freeing him. And that phrase *intonuit coelom* [the sky thundered] by Virgil that alludes to the omen of hearing thunder to the west, which was held to be good. Then there is Martial's phrase *tu nunquam leporem edisti* [you never ate hare], which not only

shows a clever play on words with *leporem* but also alludes to the properties that the hare was said to have. The age-old proverb, *Maleam legens, quae sunt domi obliviscere* [passing by Malia where home is forgotten], which alludes to the grave danger posed by the promontory of Laconia. The age-old answer by the chaste matron to the bothersome suitor, "No doorframes shall be anointed on my account, nor shall the torches burn," meaning that she didn't want to get married, alluding to the ritual of anointing doorways with lard and lighting nuptial torches at wedding, as if we were saying "Don't waste a dowry on me, neither shall the priest give his blessing." Likewise, there is so much commentary on Virgil and Homer and all other poets and orators.

This lengthy selection is actually a combination of two portions of the letter that occur in different places. They basically offer the same insight into the comprehensive and global nature of knowledge, including specifically with respect to religious studies.

For women and girls in general, and for nuns in particular, studying the Bible was regarded as the *only* culturally acceptable educational practice. However, an *effective* study of the Bible requires knowledge of many *other* disciplines, including logic, rhetoric, natural sciences, arithmetic, geometry, architecture, ancient laws and history, music, and astronomy. She provides numerous specific examples to support her claim, not only offering an impressive defense of her claim that informed Bible study requires knowledge of many other subjects, but also demonstrating logical, philosophical argument at the same time. In her own case, her ability to study was continually challenged, first at home, and then in the convent.

(26) Once they achieved this with a very saintly and unassuming mother superior who thought that study was a matter for the Inquisition, and she ordered me not to study. I obeyed her (for the three months

that her authority lasted) regarding not picking up a book; but as far as not studying absolutely anything at all—which is not in my power to do—I failed completely. That is because, even though I did not study with books, I would study with everything else God created by using all of it as my texts, and for a book I used the entire machine of this universe. I saw nothing uncritically; I heard nothing inattentively, even in the tiniest and minutest things. There is no creature no matter how lowly in which we cannot discover the idea of me fecit Deus [God made me]. There is no one at all who is not stunned by intelligent discovery, provided one reflects as one ought to. Hence, I repeat, I looked at and I marveled at all things in such a way that from the very people with whom I was speaking and from the things they were saying I was deriving a thousand ideas. Where could that diversity of cleverness and acumen spring from, since they all come from the same species? What might be the temperaments and hidden qualities that produced this fact? When I would see a shape, I would spend time combining the proportion of its lines and measuring it with my mind and transforming it in different ways. Sometimes I would stroll along the main façade of our dormitory—which is a very spacious room—and I would be observing that, although the lines of its two sides were parallel and the ceiling was flat, my sight imagined that the two lines were approaching each other and that the ceiling was lower in the distance than close by. From this I inferred that the sight lines run straight but not parallel; rather they stretch out forming a pyramidal shape. And I would hazard a conjecture that this might be why the ancients were forced to wonder if the world was a sphere or not. Because, even though it seems so, it might be a trick of the eye by showing concavities where there were none.

When a "mother superior" told her that studying from books was a matter for the "Inquisition" (a not at all subtle threat!), Sor Juana obeyed (for three months) and did not read books. Her thirst for learning however, with irresistible. Even when she was forbidden books, she still learned by making the *world* her laboratory and observatory.

(28) Well, then, my Lady, what can I tell you, about nature's secrets as I've discovered them while cooking? I see that an egg becomes solid and fries in lard or oil, while, on the other hand, it dissolves in syrup. I see that in order to keep sugar in a liquid state it suffices to add to it a very small part of water mixed with quince or another sour fruit. I see that an egg's yoke and white have such opposite characteristics that when one or the other of them is mixed with sugar each one separately works well, but when they are combined they do not. Because I don't want to bore you with which cold facts I'm mentioning them only to give you a full account of my nature—and I think this probably has made you laugh. Nevertheless, my Lady, what can we women possibly know other than kitchen philosophies? Lupercio Leonardo said it quite well: one can philosophize well while preparing dinner. When I see these trivialities I often say this: if Aristotle had cooked stews he would have written a lot more.

In this brief (and famous) section of the letter, we find a specific example of her use of the world as a laboratory, and her irresistible hunger for knowledge. Hunger is the appropriate term here, given that the example she provides is of knowledge acquired from cooking! In a display of humor she even suggests that Aristotle would have been a more prolific writer if he had spent time in the kitchen and "cooked stews."

(29) If my studies, my Lady, were merits (and I do see them so celebrated in men),

in me they would not be so because I act necessarily. If they are blameworthy, for the same reason I believe that I am faultless. But, withal, I always live so distrustful of myself that neither in this regard nor in anything else do I trust my own judgment. Hence, I entrust the decision to that sovereign talent of yours, and, without objection or aversion, I submit myself forthwith to whatever sentence you may give me, for this has been no more than a simple narration of my inclination to letters.

Here, Sor Juana begins a dangerous and clever argument concerning gender norms. She begins by pointing out that her studies would be considered a "merit" (as opposed to something to be criticized) if she were a man. But, because she claims that her thirst for knowledge is irresistible and supplied by God, she claims that she doesn't deserve either credit or blame, as her desire for knowledge did not arise from herself, nor is it something that is under her control.

(30) I confess also that, because all of the foregoing is so clearly true (as I have already said), I had no need to give case examples; nevertheless, I have not lacked for support in the many examples I have read in both sacred as well as secular writings. For I see a Deborah issuing laws in military matters as well as political affairs while governing a people among whom there were so many learned men. I see the extremely wise Queen of Sheba, so learned that she dares test the wisdom of the greatest of all sages by posing riddles without being chastised for doing to; rather, because she did this she will become the judge of unbelievers. I see so many significant women: some adorned with the gift of prophecy, like Abigail; others with persuasion, like Esther; others, with piety, like Rahab; others with

perseverance, like Hannah, Samuel's mother; and infinitely more with other types of talents and virtues.

(31) If I turn to the Gentiles, the first I encounter are the Sibyls, chosen by God to prophesy the principal mysteries of our faith, and they did so in such learned and elegant poetry that is takes one's breath away. I see a woman like Minerva, who was the daughter of the primary god Jupiter and the mistress of all the wisdom in Athens, worshiped as the goddess of the sciences. I see Pola Argentaria, who helped her husband Lucan write the great Pharsalia Battle. I see the daughter of divine Tiresias, who was more learned than her father. I see a Zenobia, queen of the Palmyrians, as wise as she was courageous. Also, Arete, Aristippus's very learned daughter. Also, Nicostrata, inventor of Latin letters and extremely erudite in Greek letters. And Aspasia Miletia, who taught philosophy and rhetoric, and who was the philosopher Pericles' teacher. And Hypatia, who taught astrology and who lectured for a long time in Alexandria. And the Greek Leontium, who wrote against the philosophy of Theophrastus and who thereby changed him mind. And Jucia, and Corinna, and Cornelia. And, in fine, all the huge throng of those who deserved their fame, be they Greeks or muses or pythonesses; for all of them were nothing less than learned women; indeed, they were respected and celebrated and also venerated as such in Antiquity.

In a sustained effort to provide evidence in support of her case, Sor Juana offers numerous examples, both secular and religious, of women throughout history who were both educated and *celebrated* for their intellect and education.[27] Implicitly, she is posing the question: if

---

[27] For example, St. Catherine of Alexandria was one of the most venerated saints of the medieval period, and is the patron saint of philosophers and scholars! For more than 1.5 millennia her

intelligence and education are "bad" in women, why has the church *celebrated* such women from the Bible, and why are such women from secular sources as well celebrated by historians and scholars of the classics?

> *(36) Oh, how much damage would be avoided in our nation if old women were as educated as Leta and if they knew how to teach as St. Paul and my father St. Jerome command! On the contrary, in lieu of this approach and due to the extreme carelessness with which men have chosen to deal with our poor women, if some parents want to have their daughters educated beyond the basic catechism, necessity and the absence of trained older women force them to turn them over to male teachers to teach them reading, writing, arithmetic, music, and other skills. Not a little damage results from this. Every day we hear lamentable examples of such unevenly-matched pairings. Given close physical proximity and contact over time what was thought to be impossible frequently happens with ease. It follows that many parents choose to keep their daughters uncouth and uneducated rather than expose them to such a notoriously perilous familiarity with men. But all this would be avoided if there were educated elderly women, as St. Paul desires, and if the teaching profession were passed from one generation of women to the next just as what happens with sewing and all other customary skills.*
>
> *(37) Because, what problem is there if an elderly woman, who is trained in letters and of saintly conversation and habits, were to take charge of the education of young women? And not the contrary, by which the latter go astray either due to lack of Christian instruction or to having it given to them by such a dangerous method*

> *as the one by which the teachers are men. For if there were no greater risk than the indecency of having a modest and proper woman—one who blushes even when her own father happens to look directly at her—sit at the side of a completely unrelated man who then treats her with both casual familiarity and straightforward authority, then the standard modesty required in dealing with men and in any conversation with them is sufficient cause for forbidding it. Nor do I find that this manner of men teaching women can help but be perilous, save only in the very strict tribunal of the confessional or in the distance at which teaching takes place from a pulpit or in the acquaintanceship at a remove with books, but not in the groping and touching that happens in close contact. And everyone recognizes that this is true. All things considered, it is permitted only because there are no learned elderly women; therefore, not having them does great harm. Those who are attached to the Mulieres in Ecclesia taceant ["the women should keep silence in the churches" (from 1 Corinthians 14:34)] should stop and reflect on this consideration when they curse it when women learn and teach, as if it weren't the Apostle who said: bene docents [teach]. Moreover, that prohibition applies to the case to which Eusebius refers; that is, in the early Church women would instruct each other in the catechism in their temples. Now, the sound of their voices was a distraction when the apostles were preaching, and that is why they were ordered to be silent. The same thing happens now, for while the preacher is preaching one does not pray out loud.*

In another clever move, Sor Juana is using the cultural demand of modesty and propriety to advocate for the education of women. If only men

---

legendary argumentative prowess in defense of Christianity (that led to her martyrdom) has

been honored by the Catholic Church.

are formally educated and allowed to teach, then young girls can only be taught by older men, to whatever extent they are educated at all. But certainly this introduces the possibility of "improper conduct." If *women* were allowed to be educated and to teach, then older women would be available to teach young girls, and families would have no cause to be concerned about improper conduct.

> *(39)... In another passage, Mulier in silentio discat ["let a woman learn in silence") (1 Timothy 2:11)] —which passage is more for women than against them—women are ordered to learn, and of course women must keep quiet while they are learning. It is also written, Audi Israel, et tace ["hear, O Israel, and be silent"]. Here it speaks with the entire community of men and women, and it orders all of them to be quiet, for it is right for those who hear and learn to pay attention and keep quiet. And if this isn't so, I would like those interpreters and exegetes of St. Paul to explain to me how they understand the passage, Mulieres in Ecclesia taceant ["the women should keep silence in the churches" (from 1 Corinthians 14:34)]. Because either they must understand it in the physical sense of pulpits and professors' chairs, or in the formal sense of the universality of all believers, which is the Catholic Church. If they understand it in the first sense, which is its true meaning, in my view, then we see that, in effect, it is not permissible for women to read or preach in the Church. Then, why do they scold women who study in private? And if they take the latter position and they want the Apostle's prohibition to apply absolutely so that women are neither permitted to study nor to write in private, then how is it that the Church has allowed women like Gertrude or Teresa or Birgitta or the nun of Ágreda or many others to write? And if they tell me that these women were saints, that's so, but that does not go against my argument. First, because St.*

> *Paul's proposition is absolute and it includes all women with no exception for saints. In their own time, Martha and Mary, and Marcella the mother of James, and Salome were also saints, and there were many more in the enthusiasm of the early Church, and St. Paul makes no exception for them. So now we see that the Church permits women who are saints and those who are not saints to write, for the woman from Ágreda and María de la Antigua are not canonized, yet their writings circulate widely. Not even when Santa Teresa and the others wrote were they yet saints. Hence, St. Paul's prohibition only envisions public statements from the pulpit, for if it the Apostle had issued a blanket prohibition against writing, then the Church would not permit it.*

In this final passage we will consider, Sor Juana presents a proper philosophical dilemma, in interpreting the apostle Paul: either women are not to *teach*, or women aren't supposed to study *at all*.

If the proper interpretation of Paul's statement is that women are simply not supposed to *teach*, this is not the same thing as saying that women are not supposed to learn, and private study should be permitted.

On the other hand, if the proper interpretation is that women aren't supposed to *study at all*, then why has the church, throughout its history, allowed women to learn and to write, and even celebrated some women in church history for their intellect?

Sor Juana's basic point, of course, is that she should not be criticized or faulted for her love of learning and her pursuit of education and knowledge. She offers a rigorous and impressive argument in defense of her position, and if her argument is convincing there is certainly no reason to think that it would apply uniquely to herself, but would rather be an argument in favor of the education of women in general.

Socrates was criticized for his teachings, and when put on trial and threatened with death, he was encouraged to beg for exile instead. His response, in the *Apology*, was that he could *not* do so.

> For if I tell you that to do as you say would be a disobedience to the God, and therefore that I cannot hold my tongue, you will not believe that I am serious; and if I say again that daily to discourse about virtue, and of those other things about which you hear me examining myself and others, is the greatest good of man, and that the unexamined life is not worth living, you are still less likely to believe me. Yet I say what is true, although a thing of which it is hard for me to persuade you.

Even when convicted and threatened with death he acknowledged that he could not and would not abandon his *sacred* quest for knowledge and his efforts to bring others to knowledge and self-improvement as well. In the end, his commitment cost him his life.

Similarly, Sor Juana attributes to herself an irresistible thirst for knowledge stretching all the way back to her earliest childhood. Despite punishment and prayer and threat of *more* punishment, she was simply "incapable" of abandoning her quest for education and self-improvement. Like Socrates, her pursuit of wisdom was "worth it," despite the risks.

Although she was not *executed* for her efforts, she was publicly censured and forced to relinquish her books and pursuit of learning by those who had the power to enforce it. Her life did not last long after she was forced to give up her books and study, with her dying of the plague just a year later.

In both Socrates and Sor Juana, we have examples of individuals committed to knowledge, the value of education, and the importance of self-improvement. In both cases, we have individuals who clashed with contemporary cultural norms, and who were willing to "risk everything" in the pursuit of knowledge.

What role does education and learning play in *your* life? How much are *you* willing to sacrifice in its pursuit?

Barring *very* unusual circumstances, there is little risk that your pursuit of knowledge through this book or through my courses (or other College courses) will somehow threaten your life! However, for some of you, your pursuit of education might not be a popular choice within your family, or your community. You might not be supported by friends and family, and you might not have role models who have already established a path for you to follow. If nothing else, your pursuit of education and knowledge will require you to sacrifice time and effort, and to delay gratification, in order to make consistent progress towards your worthwhile goals. I offer both Socrates and Sor Juana as possible sources of inspiration and encouragement to assist and support you in your own educational journey.

Critical Analysis

1. In your opinion, what are the strongest and most compelling points made by the philosopher or philosophers in this chapter? Why do you find those points to be convincing?

2. In your opinion, what are the weakest or least convincing points? Why? Can you anticipate any limitations or objections to their ideas not already addressed in the chapter?

Appendix: *Testimonio*

Sor Juana wrote her "Answer by the poet to the most illustrious Sister Filotea de la Cruz by Sor Juana Inés de la Cruz" in 1691. In it, she shared her own personal experience growing up as a girl with a love of learning in a culture that actively discouraged education for girls to the point of prohibiting it. She shared her thoughts and her struggles, and slyly offered a critique of the oppressive gender norms of her place and time in the process. Roughly 300 years later, women in Latin America sharing their stories of oppression and persecution gave rise to what is now known as "*testimonio.*"

What *is* a *testimonio*? Answers vary. One answer is helpful in that it provides not only key elements, but also hints at an origin:

> *Emerging from Latin America, testimonios consist of life stories usually told by a person from a marginalized group in society, to an interlocutor who can write down and disseminate them. The testimonio has an overtly political intent, which... 'is to inform people outside the community/country of the circumstances and conditions of people's lives' and to impel others to take some form of action.[28]*

As a genre, *Testimonio* emerged in the 20th century and is generally associated with a certain type of interview conducted by survivors of trauma and or systemic abuse in Central or South America. However, as the description above indicates, the meaning of *testimonio* goes far beyond the time and location of the experiences that are shared in the *testimonio*. Consider a small assortment of definitions/descriptions.

> *A storytelling genre for the dispossessed and displaced.[29]*

> *An authentic narrative, told by a witness who is moved to narrate by the urgency of the situation (war, revolution, oppression). Emphasizing popular oral discourse, the witness portrays his or her experience as a representative of a collective memory and identity. Truth is summoned in the cause of denouncing a present situation of exploitation and oppression or exorcising and setting aright official history.[30]*

> *An approach that incorporates political, social, historical, and cultural histories that accompany one's life experiences as a means to bring about change through consciousness–raising. In bridging individuals with collective histories of oppression, a story of marginalization is re-centered to elicit social change.[31]*

> *[A] first-person oral or written account, drawing on experiential, self-conscious, narrative practice to articulate an urgent voicing of something to which one bears witness.[32]*

Across these definitions, or descriptions, we find several common themes, or elements. A *testimonio* is a "storytelling," but by a certain sort of person, in a certain way, for a certain sort of purpose. We can speak of the form of a *testimonio*,

---

[28] Prieto, Linda and Villenas, Sofia A. "Pedagogies from *Nepantla*: *Testimonio*, Chicana/Latina Feminisms and Teacher Education Classrooms," Equity & Excellence in Education, volume 45 (3), 2012: 52 – 53.

[29] Cruz, Cindy. "Making Curriculum from Scratch: *Testimonio* in an Urban Classroom." *Equity & Excellence in Education*, 45(3), 2012: 469.

[30] Quoted in ibid., 461.

[31] Bernal, Dolores Delgado; Burciaga, Rebecca; Carmona, Judith Flores. "Chicana/Latina *Testimonios*: Mapping the Methodological, Pedagogical, and Political." *Equity & Excellence in Education*, 45(3), 2012: 364.

[32] Reyes, Kathryn Blackmer and Rodriguez, Julia E. Curry. "*Testimonio*: Origins, Terms, and Resources," Equity & Excellence in Education, volume 45 (3), 2012: 162.

its purpose or end, and its means or tactics.

Form

In the first place, there is obviously someone providing the *testimonio*—a *testimonialista*. There is also, necessarily, someone who is listening to (or reading) the *testimonio*. Some definitions emphasize the dialogical nature of the *testimonio*, defining it as a *"dialogical confrontation with the global institutions that structure and maintain the dominance of hegemonic discourse."*[33] Indeed, some have described the involvement of an "interlocutor" (a person taking part in a conversation) as essential.

> *Testimonio is a dialogic process, much like an oral history, involving two interlocutors. It is the shared result of the interaction and agendas of two or more interlocutors.*[34]

A *strict* definition of a *testimonio*, therefore, precludes autobiographical writing, as it would (usually) not involve a literal conversation with someone else who was documenting the story. A biography, on the other hand, written by another on the basis of interviews, would presumably satisfy the "form" requirement. The need for an interlocutor is potentially debatable. If we trace *testimonio* to its Latin American roots, the archetypal *testimonio* is a story told by a marginalized person in an oppressed group who effectively required the intervention of someone with some amount of privilege (e.g., a journalist, an academic, etc.) to write, publish, and possibly translate their story. Practically speaking, this meant that the participation of another person was literally indispensable. Outside that context of subordination, we might wonder if someone couldn't simply write or tell their own story, by themselves, without the need of a conversation partner to document the story. Of course, even a looser definition that does not require a literal

conversation partner, will still require a reader or listener in order for the *testimonio* to possibly achieve its purpose.

End

The purpose of a *testimonio* is not merely for someone to share a story, and experience whatever healing or catharsis that might produce – although that, in itself, might be a worthy goal. As traditionally understood, *testimonio* have an overtly political agenda.

> *The objective of the testimonio is to bring to light a wrong, a point of view, or an urgent call for action.*[35]

> *The collective goal of testimonio is to name oppression and to arrest its actions whether as genocide, racism, classism, xenophobia, or any other type of institutionalized marginalization.*[36]

Imagine the following:

- An immigrant from Guatemala shares her story of oppression and poverty within her home country, her harrowing journey North, the predatory behavior of human smugglers, her treatment by ICE officers when she was detained at the U.S. Border, and her experience navigating the asylum application process.
- A trans youth tells his story of being bullied as a child, navigating bathrooms and showers at school, being kicked out of his house by unsympathetic parents, and enduring homelessness.
- A young Black man shares his history of being harassed by police, dismissed as "not a good student" by teachers, struggling to find work, and resisting the current of the school-to-prison pipeline in the United States.

---

[33] Cruz, 461. Emphasis added.
[34] Benmayor, Rina. "Digital *Testimonio* as a Signature Pedagogy for Latin@ Studies," Equity & Excellence in Education, volume 45 (3), 2012: 148.

Emphasis added.
[35] Reyes & Rodriguez, 162.
[36] ibid., 164

What each and all these stories (or countless others) "do," among other things is much more than share an interesting personal tale. They are implicitly, and sometimes explicitly, cries for social justice; justice with respect to international and national economic policies, immigration, women's rights, trans rights, the homeless, persons of color, the unemployed, etc. *Testimonio* seek social justice by soliciting solidarity from the listener/reader "as a first step towards social change."[37]

Means

If the purpose (end) is social change/social justice, it is fair to ask *how* it attempts to do so. As mentioned just above, a key strategy of a *testimonio* is to solicit/produce solidarity from the listener/reader for the listener, and more importantly perhaps, for the group of people the individual *testimonialista* arguably represents.

> *Although a testimonio is technically an account made by one person, it represents the voice of many whose lives have been affected by particular social events, such as totalitarian governments, war violence, displacement, or other types of broad social affronts on humanity.[38]*

In other words, someone's story of the daily toll of discrimination, while their own story, is *also* the story of many other people who have had similar experiences. Someone's story of their struggle with homelessness, while unique, has features in common with many other people who have *also* struggled with homelessness. By drawing attention to the story and experience of one, attention is drawn to the experience of many. A *testimonio* is frequently narrated in the first person but alludes to a "broader collective experience" which functions to "raise awareness to the plight endured by this individual and the members of her or his community in order to engender progressive change in the living conditions, policies, or treatment of those peoples. It is meant to reach those with life experiences far removed from the *testimoniante* in order to evoke empathy, sympathy, and advocacy."[39] And, according to some, the "main feature of the testimonial text is the construction of a discourse of solidarity."[40]

This experience of solidarity is not automatic. It requires something from the listener: *active* listening. Active listening is essential to the process of *testimonio* and is not the same thing as simply "hearing." It requires engagement, and an application of the principle of charity.

> *As a listener, another's testimonio is much like a gift – the listener unwraps the testimonio to reveal the heart of the matter. In doing so, the listener's responsibility is to engage the testimonialista in an effort to understand. In this space of exchange between listener and testimonialista, we are able to open doors into another's world, open hearts and minds and at times, become invited participants – we become ... aligned, next to each other, in solidarity.[41]*

If I *listen* to your deeply personal story about your experience of oppression or struggle, and if I do so not with the intention of questioning details of your story, or preparing a rebuttal, but "simply" with the goal of genuinely listening to you, then several outcomes are possible. One possible outcome is that, if my own personal narrative shares similar elements with yours, I might feel validated by your story, and experience a sense of solidarity with you. Another possible outcome is that, if I can't personally relate to your experience, I will at least have an opportunity for personal growth.

> *If speakers and listeners are open to hearing perspectives that may be different*

---

[37] Bernal, Burciaga, & Carmona; 364

[38] Reyes & Rodriguez, 165.

[39] Aleman, Sonya M. "*Testimonio* as Praxis for a Reimagined Journalism Model and Pedagogy,"

Equity & Excellence in Education, volume 45 (3), 2012: 129

[40] Reyes & Rodriguez, 163.

[41] Bernal, Burciaga, & Carmona; 368.

from ones they have lived, testimonio pedagogy can incite personal growth through a reciprocal process of exchange.[42]

I don't know what it's like to be an immigrant, for example, but I do know what it's like to be a human being who can experience all the range of human emotions, including fear, hope, anger, hopelessness, despair, gratitude, betrayal, etc. Another person's *testimonio* could solicit solidarity from me, connecting us "across social positions, across distances, across language, across space, and across time."[43]

Testimonio are valuable not only because of the truths they might share—truths that are often otherwise left unheard—but also because of their potential to solicit solidarity and provide motivation and inspiration. Solidarity generates allies, and motivation/inspiration generates momentum, and the two can combine to produce activism and, with time, social change.

With all of this in mind, is the autobiographical letter written by Sor Juana Inés de la Cruz an example of *testimonio*? Given a very strict interpretation, probably not. If nothing else, she is writing on her own behalf, and therefore lacks the "interlocutor" component. Moreover, her writing precedes the genre of *testimonio*, as recognized today, by several centuries. However, I would propose that on a less strict interpretation, her letter might qualify. In the first place, there is already contemporary precedent for Latina/Chicana academics writing *testimonio* on their own behalf. While recognizing the difference in privilege, due to their being academics, many such scholars nevertheless argue for the legitimacy of their *testimonios*.

There have been important discussions around the idea that obtaining a privileged status might remove one from

the possibility of writing one's subaltern or marginalized life. We... contend that for most Chicana/Latina scholars and other scholars of color, group marginalization continues to exist in academia even when one holds a relatively privileged status.... Indeed, the testimonios of Latinos in academia... expose experiences of rape, attempted suicide, migrations, chronic health problems, struggles within educational institutions, healthcare access, and the labor of academia.[44]

By this reasoning, the relatively privileged status of Sor Juana as an educated woman capable of writing her own story should not disqualify her story as a *testimonio*. Her letter arguably satisfies the form requirement, but what of the other components of a *testimonio*? With respect to the purpose of her letter, it seems very reasonable to conclude that among the purposes was to argue for the education of women and the legitimacy of their intelligence. Attempting to undermine an oppressive patriarchal system by highlighting the pain and marginalization experienced by those subordinated within it certainly seems consistent with the ends of *testimonio*. As for the means, Sor Juana tells her own story, in deeply personal and confessional detail, and in such a way as to theoretically solicit solidarity from the reader. Certainly, other women from her own time as well as today can relate to her experience of gender discrimination, and readers who are not women can be moved to solidarity to the extent that we actively listen to the story and attempt to relate to her experience. All of this sounds very much like a *testimonio* to me. All that being said, the label is (literally) academic, and her letter is noteworthy and valuable regardless of how we might choose to categorize it.

---

[42] ibid.
[43] ibid.

[44] Bernal, Burciaga, & Carmona; 366.

Chapter 4: Knowledge & Truth

Comprehension questions you should be able to answer after reading this chapter:

1. What is "epistemology?"
2. What is Mozi's "reliabilist" understanding of knowledge, based on making correct distinctions?
3. What are Mozi's 3 Fa ("gauges")?
4. Briefly explain the idea of knowledge as "justified true belief."
5. What is a "claim?" What does it mean to say that a claim has a "truth-value?"
6. What is the difference between "knowing how" and "knowing that?"
7. How does Mozi's understanding of knowledge corresponded to a "knowing how?" How does the JTB understanding correspond to a "knowing that?"
8. How is "truth" understood by epistemic relativism?
9. Explain how Socrates tries to refute epistemic relativism.
10. How is "truth" understood by the correspondence theory?
11. Provide your own example of a claim, and then explain what it would mean for that claim to be "true" according to epistemic relativism, and then according to correspondence theory.

Epistemology, which is the focus of this chapter, is the study of knowledge. Believe it or not, there's some pretty serious debate concerning how best to understand "knowledge." Some, for example, believe that we can *never* possess knowledge. Classical skeptics fit this description. Others believe that "knowledge" is never more than personal perspective. Epistemic relativists such as this will be addressed later in this chapter. Still others believe that knowledge is something objective and "out there" to be discovered. What do you think?

As already mentioned, there are a variety of interpretations of "knowledge." We cannot possibly consider all of them, or even very many of them. For our limited purposes, we will consider two interpretations: Mozi's and Plato's.

> What does it mean to "know" something? If you had to define "knowledge" in one sentence, what would *your* definition be?

Mozi

Mozi lived at roughly around the same time as Socrates (circa 480 – 390 BCE for Mozi, and circa 470 – 399 BC for Socrates), but very little is known about Master Mo (also known as Mozi, or Mo Di). Mozi flourished during the "warring

states period" (475 – 221 BCE), but faded from significance as Confucianism became the State philosophy during the Han Dynasty (206 BCE – 221 CE).

The Confucian standard (which represented the primary rival for Mohism at the time) was *li* (ritual), established by the traditional culture. This was a socially conservative standard, appealing to the authority of ancient Sage Kings and endorsing their prescribed cultural practices with little questioning. The Mohists acknowledged the existence of *multiple* perspectives with respect to cultural values, at roughly the same time Herodotus was doing so in Greece, to demonstrate the *ineffectiveness* of this appeal to (traditional) ritual.

> *Now those who support lavish funerals and prolonged periods of mourning say, "if lavish funerals and prolonged mourning really are not the way of the Sage Kings why is it that the gentlemen of the middle Kingdom continue these practices without interruption and follow them uncritically?"*
>
> *Our teacher Mozi says, "this is just a case of people "following what they are used to and approving of what is customary."" In*

ancient times, east of the state of Yue was the state of Kaishu. When the first son was born to the people of this state they would carve him up and eat him saying it was beneficial to his future younger brothers. When their father died, they would carry their mothers off to some distant place and abandon them there saying, "one cannot live with the wife of a ghost!" These practices were both official policy and the popular custom. They were continued without interruption and followed uncritically. But how can this be the way to realize what is benevolent and right? This is just a case of people "following what they are used to and approving of what is customary."[45]

In other words, the mere fact that a community has been practicing a ritual/custom for some amount of time should not be taken to mean that that practice is *correct*. Instead, the Mohists will seek *objective* standards that transcend individual cultures and rituals, in the form of what they call "*fa*" (models, or standards).

Those in the world who perform a task cannot do without models (fa) and standards. There is no one who can accomplish their task without models and standards. Even officers serving as generals or ministers, they all have models; even the hundred artisans performing their tasks, they too all have models. The hundred artisans make squares with a set square, circles for the compass, straight lines with a string, vertical lines with the plumb line, and flat surfaces with the level. Whether skilled artisans or unskilled artisans, all take these five as models. The skilled are able to conform to them. The

unskilled, though unable to conform to them, by following them in performing their tasks still surpass what they can do by themselves.[46]

Fa represent a fascinating philosophical concept, as they provide not only guidance to behavior, but also the very standard of *correctness* by which to measure both our actions and our judgments. *Fa* are very wide ranging in meaning, including basically *any* criterion or paradigm that helps us to make correct judgments.

The Mohists appeared to have understood judgment (of all kinds) as a process of distinguishing relevantly similar kinds of things from dissimilar things, reliably distinguishing "this" (*shi*) from "not" (*fei*).

Thus our Master Mozi's having Heaven's intent, to give an analogy, is no different from the wheelwright's having a compass or the carpenter's having a set square. Now the wheelwright grasps his compass and uses it to measure the round and not round in the world, saying, "what conforms to my compass, call it "round," what doesn't conform to my compass, call it "not round." Hence round and not round can both be known. What is the reason for this? It's that the fa for "round" is clear.[47]

The Mohists understand knowledge as the ability to reliably make these sorts of proper distinctions. Not quite a "correspondence theory" (which we'll discuss later in this chapter), instead they offer what is known today as a **"reliabilist"** account of knowledge.[48] With respect to *justifying* one's judgments, this also is understood in terms of *fa* - specifically the ability to cite a suitable *fa* when making a distinction/judgment.

---

[45] *Mozi*, Book 25: For Moderation in Funerals. (Note: all references in this section are from the *Mozi*, unless otherwise indicated.)
[46] ibid., Book 4: Models and Standards.
[47] ibid., Book 27: Heaven's Intent.
[48] As a contemporary example, Robert Nozick

(1981) proposed what he called a "tracking" theory. In addition to truth and belief, Nozick's conditions for knowledge were: (1) if P were not true then S would not believe that P, and (2) if P were true, S would believe that P.

Because of their emphasis on the actual (reliable) ability to make distinctions, the Mohist theory of knowledge is practical, more so than theoretical or representational. To "know" something is not a matter of having some sort of concept in one's mind that corresponds to reality, but is rather a stable disposition to correctly *distinguish* certain kinds of things from other things.

> *Our Master Mozi said, "Now the blind say, 'What's bright is white, and what's dark is black.' Even the clear-sighted have no grounds for changing this. But collect white and black things together and make the blind select from among them, and they cannot know. So as to my saying the blind don't know white and black, it's not by their naming, it's by their selecting.*[49]

This is an interesting example. From a certain (correspondence) perspective, a blind person's claim that what is dark is black "corresponds to reality," and is therefore a true statement that might technically count as knowledge. However, a genuinely blind person, despite correctly understanding the concepts/meanings of dark and black, cannot reliably distinguish things that are dark from things that are not, and things that are black, from things that are not. Therefore, they don't actually *know* that what is dark is black, on the Mohist account of knowledge.

It's plausible that someone could correctly *distinguish* in this sort of way, without *understanding* in the way we might normally think of "understanding." Children, for example, can correctly recognize straight lines with the help of a ruler, without being able to articulate just what a "straight" line is—as can you, of course. I'm very confident that you can distinguish the straight line from the not-straight line, given choices A and B below.

A:

B:

Indeed, as a well-educated adult, I am very skilled at recognizing straight lines myself, and distinguishing them from those that are not straight, but I had to look up the actual *definition*: "the set of all points between and extending beyond two points."

Similarly, someone might be able to correctly and reliably distinguish righteousness (*yi*) from unrighteousness without any sort of sophisticated understanding of "righteousness" itself – so long as they have been provided an effective standard (*fa*).

It's important to recognize the work that "reliable" does here. A lucky guess will not count for the Mohists any more than it would count for someone subscribing to a definition of knowledge as "justified true belief" (which we will explore next).

> *Now suppose there is a person here, who, seeing a little black, says "Black," but seeing much black, says "White." Then surely we'd take this person to not know the distinction between white and black.*

---

[49] *Mozi*, Book 47: Valuing Duty.

Tasting a little of something bitter, he says "Bitter," but tasting much of something bitter, he says, "Sweet." Then surely we'd take this person to not know the distinction between sweet and bitter.[50]

The error being exhibited in this example is understood not as a lack of correspondence between the person's belief and reality, but rather as a lack of *skill*. Someone who successfully bakes one cake out of 100 would not be regarded as a skilled baker, and someone who only rarely, in practice, makes correct distinctions (such as between things that are bitter and things that are sweet) should not be regarded as someone who "knows" bitterness and sweetness.

Mohists offer three *fa* by which the distinctions between "this" and "not" (including benefit and harm), can be clearly known.

Our teacher Mozi says, "when one advances claims, one must first establish a standard of assessment. To make claims in the absence of such a standard is like trying to establish on the surface of a spinning potter's wheel where the sun will rise and set. Without a fixed standard, one cannot clearly ascertain what is right and wrong or what is beneficial and harmful. And so, in assessing claims, one must use the three gauges."

What are the "three gauges?"

Our teacher Mozi says, "the gauges of precedent, evidence, and application."

How does one assess a claim's precedents?

Our teacher Mozi says, "one looks up for precedents among the affairs and actions of the ancient Sage Kings."

How does one assess a claim's evidence? Our teacher Mozi says, "one looks down to examine evidence of what the people have heard and seen."

How does one assess a claim's application?

Our teacher Mozi says, "one implements it as state policy and sees whether or not it produces benefit for the state, families, and people. These are what are called the three gauges for assessing claims.[51]

In summary, the three *fa* are as follows:

1. Precedence
2. Evidence
3. Application

First, we will consider *precedence*. This is *historical* precedent (example) provided by moral exemplars who reliably distinguished right from wrong, correct from incorrect, in the past. The Sage Kings are offered as sources of precedent because they were regarded to have been successful and wise rulers. To put it bluntly, they seemed to know what they were doing! Indeed, they are regarded as Sage Kings precisely *because* they taught sound doctrines.

Second, there is *evidence*. Evidence involves confirmation of claims by virtue of our sense testimony – in other words, empirical verification.

Finally, there is *application*, understood as demonstration of benefit.[52] This is a pragmatic test. Does the action or policy, in fact, produce benefit? Or does it produce harm?

It is worth pointing out that these standards appear to be presented not so much as a systematic attempt to provide a pragmatic concept of "truth," in general, but primarily as a pragmatic guide to conduct and policies. Their model of reasoning involves citing one or more *fa*

---

[50] *Mozi*, Book 17: Condemning Aggression.
[51] ibid. Book 35: Condemning Fatalism
[52] Arguably, the third *fa* holds priority, given the Mohists' multiple appeal to benefit throughout

their writings, and the fact that they do not endorse any sort of unthinking appeal to authority.

by which to distinguish "this" from "not," then indicating how a particular example either does or does not conform to the *fa*, and then finally concluding that the example therefore is either "this" or "not."

Plato

Equally "objective," but different in approach, we have an understanding of knowledge as it appears in several of Plato's dialogues.

> *If a man knows things, can he give an account of what he knows or not?*[53]

> *And do you not also give the name dialectician to the man who is able to exact an account of the essence of each thing? And will you not say that the one who is unable to do this, in so far as he is incapable of rendering an account to himself and others, does not possess full reason and intelligence about the matter?*[54]

> *For true beliefs – as long as they stay put – or a beautiful thing, too, and everything they bring about is good. They are willing to stay for long, however, that flee from a person's soul. So they aren't of much value until someone ties them down by reasoning out the explanation.*[55]

> *Are you satisfied, then, and do you state it in this way, that true opinion accompanied by reason is knowledge?*[56]

The common theme in each of these examples is the idea that knowledge is more than merely a true belief, but a true belief for which one can give an "account." The generally accepted paraphrase of this definition is that knowledge is "justified true belief." *That* definition has been the

generally accepted definition of knowledge in the history of *Western* philosophy. For the remainder of this chapter, this understanding of knowledge will be referred to as the JTB standard.

> List 5 things that you think you know, and another 5 that you believe, but that you wouldn't claim to know. What do you think is the difference between the examples in your "know" set, and those in your "belief" set?

The definition of knowledge, according to the JTB standard, has three components: belief, justification, and truth—each of which requires a little bit of explanation. We will consider the nature of belief in this chapter. Both justification and truth will receive similar exploration in this chapter, or others.

Belief

It is generally accepted that in order to know something, one must also believe it. It seems odd to say that I "know" Donald Trump is the current U.S. President, but that I don't *believe* that he is. Note that the reverse is not also true. We are quite comfortable with the idea that someone can believe something without also knowing it. For example, at the moment I'm writing this sentence, I believe my wife is at work, but I wouldn't claim to *know* that she is. It's entirely possible that I'm not remembering her schedule accurately, and that she's at a coffee shop. Or, perhaps she's on an errand? As we can see, to know something, one must also believe it, but one can believe without knowing.

An easy way to think of the relationship between belief and knowledge, in this sense, is with the language of a "promotion." We believe all kinds of things, but some of the things we believe have a special quality to them. These beliefs earn a "promotion," and a new title: *knowledge*. What

---

[53] A rhetorical question posed by Socrates in the *Phaedo*, 76b5.
[54] A rhetorical question posed by Socrates in the *Republic*, 534b.

[55] Socrates in the *Meno*, 98a.
[56] A rhetorical question posed by Socrates in the *Theatetus*, 202c.

is this quality that earns the belief a promotion to knowledge? As it turns out, these qualities are the other two parts of our definition of knowledge: justification, and truth.

Before delving into justification, we'll spend a little more time on belief and complicate matters by asking what a belief *is*. A good chunk of my doctoral dissertation was devoted to just that question, but, once again, that level of analysis and expertise is not needed for our own purposes right now. At the minimum, we can simply talk about what form beliefs take in our language, so that we may easily identify them in speech and writing.

Very simply, beliefs appear in the form of "claims." *Claims* are statements, assertions, or propositions (different terms meaning roughly the same thing), and, due to that fact, have what is called a "*truth-value*." To say that a claim has a truth-value is simply to say that it must be either true or false (if true, then its truth-value is true; if false, then its truth-value is false). Note that we do not need to know *which* truth-value applies to a claim to know that it is a claim. Consider the examples below.

Claims	Not Claims
You are reading this sentence right now.	What time is it?
Donald Trump is the current U.S. president.	Please shut the door.
There is intelligent life elsewhere in the universe.	Ouch.

Remember, a claim is a statement that has to be either true or false (even if we're not sure which it is). You either are, or you are not, reading this book right now. Donald Trump either is, or is not, the current U.S. President.[57] You're probably pretty confident about those two. What about life

elsewhere in the universe? Well, you might not be certain either way. But (and this is the important part), we know that there either *is*, or there is *not*, intelligent life elsewhere in the universe. In other words, that claim has a truth-value, even though we don't know (for sure, right now) if that value is "true" or if it is "false."

Now, consider the other column of examples. What time is it? True or false? You probably had to reread those sentences just now, and my question probably still doesn't make any sense. There's a reason for that. "What time is it?" is not the sort of thing that can be either true or false. Neither is "Please shut the door." Neither is "ouch." None of those has a truth-value, because none is a claim, and therefore none is a belief.

Why does this matter? Because claims are the building blocks of arguments, and arguments form the core of what we study and what we do in philosophy. In our next chapter, we will focus on arguments, and how to evaluate them. However, before beginning that deeper dive, I want to make one more distinction concerning knowledge in hopes that will help us to frame the difference between Mozi and JTB.

In everyday language, when we speak of "knowing" things, we often use the word in different ways. Sometimes, we are referring to what is called "knowing how," and other times we are referring to what is called "knowing that." For the most part, the difference between them is fairly obvious and simple.

"Knowing how" refers to a skill. For example, I know *how* to ride a bike. It is something that I'm able to do. "Knowing that" refers to being in possession of an accurate piece of information. For example, I know *that* Sacramento is the capital of the state of California.

Knowledge in the sense of "knowing that" means having beliefs that are true (e.g., Sacramento really is the capital of the state of California), and having those beliefs for the right reasons (so as to distinguish *knowledge* from a

---

[57] Note: as of the time of this writing, Donald Trump has officially lost his bid for reelection, with 306 Electoral College votes having been cast for Joe Biden. However, President Trump has still refused to concede the election. Whether or not he is the President when you are actually reading this chapter is something that remains to be determined. . . .

lucky guess). Knowledge of this sort is a kind of possession, being in possession of justified true beliefs.

Knowledge in the sense of "knowing how," in contrast, is a kind of performance. Someone who knows how to ride a bike is not in possession of some sort of justified fact – they simply have the ability to do something: in this case, ride a bike.

I think a strong case can be made that Mozi's account of knowledge reduces all knowledge to a "knowing how." According to Mozi, for example, to know that something is a cat is not best understood as being in possession of some sort of justified true belief concerning that creature, but is better understood in terms of being able to reliably distinguish that creature as a cat, as opposed to a dog, or a fox, etc. In other words, knowledge is a demonstrable skill.

The JTB standard, in contrast, while certainly recognizing the existence of skills best understood as a "knowing how" (such as, for example knowing how to sail a ship), also recognizes a kind of knowledge that better corresponds to a "knowing that." Knowledge of that kind involves being in possession of justified beliefs that are true, where truth is understood as "corresponding" to an objective reality.

In numerous places throughout this chapter thus far, I have used the words "true" and "truth" in the context of knowledge, but what does it mean for something to be *true*? Once again, this is a complicated issue. Various candidates for "truth" include (but are not limited to) epistemic relativism, correspondence theory, pragmatism, coherentism, realism and anti-realism, and numerous others. Though there are several ways of understanding truth, we will focus on just a couple for our purposes.

> What is "truth?" When you say that something is "true," what do *you* mean by that?

Epistemic Relativism

Epistemic relativism claims that truth is "relative" to the observer. Truth is a matter of perspective. Truth depends on one's point of view. Several ancient Sophists were known to hold this perspective, including Protagoras who allegedly claimed that "man is the measure of all things."[58]

Now, at a certain level, this is obvious and unobjectionable. Most everyone would agree that there are certain kinds of claims we can make, certain kinds of judgments, which are merely expressions of personal opinion, or personal taste. One's favorite color, or whether or not one likes a band, or whether or not one likes spicy food—all such things seem to be matters of perspective. I like spicy food. My mother doesn't. She's not "wrong" or "mistaken" about spicy food—she just has different taste preferences. I really like the band "Switchfoot." I'm sure some people couldn't bear them (as hard as that is for me to believe). Again, no one is in error over such matters.

We call these sorts of claims "subjective claims." When we're dealing with subjective claims, there is no one right point of view, no single correct answer to the questions involving subjective claims. In cases of disagreement, it's not the case that someone must be wrong. Also, in cases of disagreement, there's little that can be accomplished from debate. I can sing the praises of spicy food for hours, but my mother will never be convinced of the truth of my claims and change her mind. This isn't because she's stubborn, it's because she just doesn't like spicy food! Her opinion on this matter is no better, or worse, than

---

[58] Strictly speaking, he is reported to have said "Of all things the measure is man, of the things that are, that [or "how"] they are, and of things that are not, that [or "how"] they are not." Hermann Diels and Kranz Walther. *Die Fragmente der Vorsokratiker.* Zurich: Weidmann, 1985. DK80b1. More "recently," and perhaps more famously, the character Obi Wan Kenobi implied this view in the film Return of the Jedi. "Luke, you're going to find that many of the truths we cling to depend greatly on our own point of view."

my own. It's just different.

So far, there's nothing terribly interesting or controversial about epistemic relativism. Where epistemic relativism does become controversial, however, is when we realize that the theory claims that *all* truths are relative in the way that subjective claims are.

> Is truth simply a matter of opinion? A matter of perspective? Why would someone believe this to be true? What if my opinion is that 2 + 2 = 5? Does it make sense to say that 2 + 2 = 5 is my "truth?"

If you stop to reflect on that for a moment, you can start to see how extraordinary that claim really is (whether true, or not). If all "truths" are matters of perspective, and if no perspective is inherently any more privileged than any other, then everyone is always "right" about everything.

You believe the Earth is a sphere. I believe it's flat (I don't, really). Assuming each claim represents our own respective opinions, why would your opinion be any more "right" than mine? In a sense, we're both right—even though we're making mutually exclusive claims.

I think George W. Bush is the current U.S. President (I don't believe that either). That's my opinion, and I'm entitled to it, and your opinion isn't any more accurate than mine. "But," you might counter, "no one else shares your opinion, while lots of people share mine." Fine. That just means your opinion is more popular—it doesn't mean it's more accurate.

If all truth is subjective, then all truth is like my taste in music. If 99% of the world population couldn't stand Country music, but I loved it, my opinion that Country music is great would be no less legitimate than the roughly seven billion who disagree—it would just be a lot less popular.

To make matters even more interesting, consider this: "all truth is relative" is a claim. That means it's either true, or it's false. If it's false, then we obviously have no good reason to entertain it any further. If, on the other hand, it's true that all truth is relative, then that very claim is itself only

relatively true. That is, it's just a matter of opinion, a matter of perspective. In that case, if I disagree, then my opinion is no worse, no less correct, than that of those who embrace epistemic relativism.

To sum this up, either "all truth is relative" is a relative truth, or it's not-relative. If it's relative, then it's merely an opinion that is no "more true" than an opposing opinion. If it's not-relative, then not all truth is relative, and the claim refutes itself.

There is something seemingly self-refuting, or internally inconsistent, with epistemic relativism. Since all opinions are equally true, it is simultaneously and equally true that epistemic relativism is, itself, both true and false. That epistemic relativism seems to allow for simultaneously true contradictory statements is seen as a potentially serious possible problem for the theory.

Beyond this conceptual puzzle, a figure no less prominent than Socrates himself points out that we do not, in fact, regard all opinions as equally true.

> *How about horses? Does one man do them harm and all the world good? Is not the exact opposite the truth? One man is able to do them good, or at least not many; -- the trainer of horses, that is to say, does them good, and others who have to do with them rather injure them? Is not that true, Meletus, of horses, or of any other animals?*[59]

Here, Socrates points out that certain people (horse trainers) are experts in that field, whereas the rest of us are not. Simply put, they know more about horses than the rest of us do! Now consider the following examples:

---

[59] Socrates, in Plato's *Apology*.

Subject	Expert
Medicine	Medical Doctor
Nutrition	Nutritionist
Carpentry	Carpenter
Botany	Botanist
Chemistry	Chemist
Physics	Physicist
Philosophy	Philosopher

I'll start with a deeply personal example. If you don't believe that my understanding of philosophy, on the basis of my several degrees (B.A., M.A., and Ph.D.), years of experience (more than 20 years at the time of this writing), and "accolades" (e.g., being a tenured professor, and having published multiple articles and textbooks, etc.), is any more informed than your own, why on Earth are you bothering to read this book, or take my class? What is the point of education, in general, if every student is equally informed as his or her teacher?

Let's make it more absurd. Why bother going to the doctor when you are sick and injured? If all opinions are equal, your own opinion about your medical condition is just as good as that doctor's!

Those astrophysicists who have spent decades studying the universe and who are debating whether or not this universe is situated within a broader multiverse? Their views are no better informed than the random person who has never studied that stuff a day in his or her life. Equally true opinions? Presumably not.

What's more, the basic motivation that inspires epistemic relativism appears to presuppose the *falsity* of epistemic relativism. Consider the following examples and inferences:

- Two people taste the same chocolate cake. One thinks it's overly sweet. The other thinks it could stand to be sweeter. Therefore, the sweetness of the chocolate is merely a matter of individual perspective. There is no "Truth" regarding its sweetness.

- I look at a flower and perceive it to be yellow. A bee looks at the same flower and perceives it to be blue with a red

center. Therefore, the appearance of the flower is a matter of individual perspective. There is no "Truth" regarding the appearance of the flower.

Such common sense differences in perspective seem to suggest that epistemic relativism might be the correct way to understand truth. However, if one considers carefully these examples, it will soon be clear that these examples do *not* imply that "*all* truth is relative"—indeed they presuppose something very different.

Epistemic relativism is driven by the force of the relativity of perception. That is, because it is such a common experience for people to perceive "the same thing" in very different ways, it's easy to conclude that truth is relative. Be careful, though! The relativity of perception, even if true, doesn't imply that *all* truth is relative. Some truths must be held absolute in order for the relativity to make any sense.

Reconsider the chocolate cake. Two people taste the same cake with different results. Therefore, perception is relative. What is not thought relative in this example, however, is the existence of the cake, the tasters, and the world in which both cake and tasters exist. The same sorts of presuppositions apply to the flower example.

The bee and I perceive the flower with different results, but what is *not* thought relative is the existence of the flower itself, the bee, myself, and the reality in which all three of us reside.

In order to even make sense of the relativity of perception, one must presuppose that it is "True" that observers exist, and that a reality exists that may be perceived differently. The commonsense observation that initially gives rise to relativism is that the "real world" exists, that perceivers (such as you, me, and the bee) exist, but that we experience the "real world" in different ways.

Even if it's true that perceptions vary, that perceptions are relative, that certainly doesn't entail that *all truth* is relative. Indeed, it's arguable that it *cannot* entail that conclusion, if one accepts that relativity of perception implies absoluteness of perceivers and the world that is being perceived. Full-fledged epistemic relativism seems, then, to suffer from the threat of internal inconsistency. If epistemic relativism is a problematic way to understand truth, we'll have to consider some alternatives.

Correspondence Theory

Consider the following statements:

- The claim that George W. Bush is the current U.S. President is true if and only if he really is the current U.S. President.
- The claim that there are exactly 457 marbles in the jar is true if and only if there really are exactly that many marbles (457) in the jar.
- The claim that there is life on Mars is true if and only if there really is life on Mars.

Are these statements reasonable? If you think so, you're probably sympathetic to what is known as the correspondence theory of truth.

The correspondence theory is ancient, and we find versions of it in both Aristotle and in Plato's dialogues.

Then that speech which says things as they are is true, and that which says them as they are not is false? (Plato, Cratylus, 385b)

[False sentences] speaks of things that are not as if they were. (Plato, Sophist, 263b)

To say of what is that it is not, or of what is not that it is, is false, while to say of what is that it is, and of what is not that it is not, is true. (Aristotle, Metaphysics, 1011b25)

To say of what is that it is not, or of what is not that it is, is false, while to say of what is that it is, and of what is not that it is not, is true. (Aristotle, Metaphysics, 1011b25)

According to correspondence theory, a claim is true if it "corresponds" to the way things really are in the world, if the claim "matches up" with

reality, if it "maps on" to how the world actually is. This is the most stringent of all the approaches to understanding truth because it claims that there is a way that the universe "really is," and our claims are true, or not, depending on whether they match up with the world. This is the approach implicitly employed by most people, whether they realize it or not.

Imagine that you intercept a fellow student on the way to class, and she tells you that the class has been cancelled. Has she told you the truth? What would you need to know in order to make that assessment? Simply this: you would need to know if the class really had been cancelled. If it had, her statement was true. If it had not, her statement was false. Her claim either "corresponded" to the world, or it didn't.

Obviously, not all of our claims will be so easily verifiable. Some truth claims (unfortunately, probably the ones we tend to care the most about—claims about morality, religion, politics, etc.), might be especially difficult to establish because we might not know how "the world is" concerning that particular subject. Do aliens exist, or not? Hard to say, since we haven't explored the entire universe just yet. Is abortion immoral? Hard to say, since there's so much disagreement, and so many compelling arguments that can be given on both sides.

What correspondence theorists will claim is that even if we're not sure what the answers to some of these difficult questions are, we nevertheless can be confident that there *are* answers—not merely opinions—out there for us to discover.

Critical Analysis

1. In your opinion, what are the strongest and most compelling points made by the philosopher or philosophers in this chapter? Why do you find those points to be convincing?
2. In your opinion, what are the weakest or least convincing points? Why? Can you anticipate any limitations or objections to their ideas not already addressed in the chapter?

Appendix: Application to Social Justice

Much like the chapter on reading philosophy, this chapter is ostensibly "content neutral." Knowledge claims will be just as applicable to matters of social justice as anything else we might think or talk about.

Do we "know" that systemic racism is a feature of the American criminal justice system, or do we merely "believe" that it is (or not)? And, what difference might that make either way?

When someone claims that data showing racially disparate impact on minority communities as a result of specific policing procedures such as "stop and frisk" is evidence of systemic racism, is that claim "true?"

If someone perceives an interaction as a "micro-aggression," is the truth of that claim a matter of personal perspective only? Or is it possible that someone could be mistaken, and they were not, in fact, the recipient of a racist interaction even if they experienced it as such? In other words, does the truth of the interaction pertain to the subject who experienced it, or is it an objective feature of the experience itself?

Finally, consider the phenomenon of implicit bias. There is ample research and evidence that indicates that we are all subject to implicit, unconscious biases, and these biases range over race, color, gender, religion, and various other elements of our identities. They have been shown to impact outcomes in employment, bank loans, every step in the criminal justice system, school discipline, and numerous other experiences and aspects of life. The data suggests the presence of prejudicial beliefs, and yet, by virtue of being *implicit*, the subject is not consciously aware of having such beliefs. Someone might sincerely believe they do not hold any prejudicial views, and yet the research on implicit bias, including tests that such a person could take, suggest otherwise.[60] So, is it *true* that the person is prejudiced, even though they sincerely believe they are not? Is the truth of their prejudice a matter of personal perspective, or is it something objective, that can theoretically be observed and verified (or falsified) by others?

---

[60] You can take a variety of implicit biases tests here: https://implicit.harvard.edu/implicit/ Please note that you do not have to register with the site in order to take the tests, but can take them as a "guest."

Appendix/"Deeper Dive"
Kwasi Wiredu: Truth as Opinion

Comprehension questions you should be able to answer after reading this chapter:

1. Why does Wiredu think that the correspondence theory is mistaken?
2. Why does Wiredu think his own theory is different from epistemic relativism?
3. What is "truth," according to Wiredu?
4. What is the difference between a (mere) opinion and a "fact," according to Wiredu?
5. What does Wiredu mean when he claims that to believe something implies a "commitment" to that claim? In this context, what is the difference between a "truth claim" and a "truth?"
6. Explain how Wiredu thinks that some opinions, though personal, can still be "objective."
7. Why does Wiredu think his theory does not allow for simultaneously true contradictory statements, unlike epistemic relativism?
8. Explain how Wiredu's theory might respond to Socrates "expertise" argument against epistemic relativism.
9. Why does Wiredu think his theory allows for "mistaken belief," unlike epistemic relativism?

This additional section to the chapter is admittedly more challenging than what you have already read, and I have provided it for the sake of that challenge. Some of you might want to "dive deeper" into these ideas, and this will help you do that.

Thus far, we have considered epistemic relativism and numerous seemingly serious problems with that theory. As an alternative, we considered the correspondence theory. As is almost always the case in philosophy, however, things are rarely so "simple." In the spirit of a "deeper dive," we will now consider the work of the contemporary Ghanaian philosopher Kwasi Wiredu ("Kwah-see Way-roo-doo").[61]

Truth as Opinion

Wiredu developed his theory of truth with a starting point that will be explored in much more detail in our later chapter on skepticism and certainty. He acknowledges the distinction between "appearance" and "reality."

> *It is a common fact of experience, surely, that we sometimes believe ourselves to perceive things as having certain properties which they do not, in fact, have. Scientifically, such occurrences are susceptible of fairly straightforward explanations in terms of the position and/or the state of the viewer, physiological or psychological. But the very fact that such explanations are available seems to compel us, even in our ordinary common sense thinking, to institute an abstract and quite speculative distinction between Reality, that is, things as they are in themselves and Appearance, that is, things as they appear to us in our individual transitory, "subjective" states. In confirmation of this, moreover, we are*

---

[61] Ghana is located in West Africa, and is increasingly known for producing philosophers well trained in traditional "Western" philosophy, such as Wiredu, as well as philosophers who draw upon the ancient and indigenous intellectual resources of Ghana, such as Kwami Gyeke.

apt to reflect that things must exist and have their own natures when not being observed. In this way we seem led to the conception that the nature of things is independent of the cognitive relation between the knower and the known; independent, in other words, of the fact that anybody may come to perceive them.[62]

However, while this distinction opens the door to skepticism for some philosophers, Wiredu is not actually a skeptic. This distinction between appearance and reality implies that we can't know things as they "really" are. However, our "common sense" experience is that we often perceive things as having properties they do not, in fact, have. For example, a stick will appear bent when viewed in the water, but we presume that it does not "in fact" have the property of being bent. This implies that we *can* know things as they are (somehow conceived).

To put it differently, we have a very strong and reliable notion that, for example, of the various properties we can ascribe to objects, some of them they clearly don't "really" have. For all the subtleties of skepticism, it would be an insincere stretch to look at an ant near my foot and seriously suppose that it has the property of having the same mass as the planet Earth. When we look at a daisy, we can have a legitimate conversation about the color of that flower, but we can't legitimately prescribe to it the property of being 4,000 feet tall, or the property of being invisible.

Given his rejection of skepticism, Wiredu might appear to be on the road to some sort of objective theory of truth such as correspondence theory. However, although he rejects skepticism, he also rejects such objectivist interpretations of truth like the correspondence theory as well. He begins by reviewing the basic assumptions behind such theories. The assumptions that lead to objectivist interpretations of truth are as

follows.

It is an incontestable fact of common experience that we sometimes know some propositions to be true and at other times make mistakes as to the truth. From this fact common sense is apt to infer that, since our opinions may fall short of the truth, we must draw an absolute distinction between truth and opinion. In philosophical development, this conception becomes an objectivist theory of truth. Truth is then said to be independent of, and categorically different from, opinion.... According to the objectivist theory, it makes sense to say that a man's opinions may change but it is meaningless nonsense to say that the truth itself may change. Once a proposition is true, it is true in itself and forever. Truth, in other words, is timeless, eternal.[63]

Wiredu uses the very same argument that he used against skepticism to undermine this objective notion of truth.

This theory about truth, however, goes aground on an objection which may by now be apparent. It is this: if truth is categorically different from opinion, then truth is, as a matter of logical principle, unknowable. Any given claim to truth is merely an opinion advanced from some specific point of view, and categorically distinct from truth. Hence knowledge of truth as distinct from opinion is a self-contradictory notion. But this consequence contradicts the fact of common experience from which we started, namely, that we sometimes know some propositions to be true. Therefore the objectivist theory must be incorrect.[64]

In an interesting maneuver, Wiredu is actually suggesting that a hard distinction

---

[62] Wiredu, Kwasi. "Truth as Opinion." <u>Philosophy and an African Culture</u>. Cambridge University press, 2009: 112-113.

[63] ibid., 114.
[64] ibid., 115.

between appearance and reality, and the implied distinction between a subjective point of view and the objective "fact" of the matter, if taken seriously, should lend itself to skepticism rather than an objective theory of truth. After all, if all we ever have access to is the "appearance" of something, then we never have access to its "reality," and the "truth" of the matter is something always beyond our grasp.

However, returning once again to the common sense experience that we do, sometimes, actually "know" something to be true, Wiredu thinks that the objectivist approach to understanding truth is ultimately flawed. Moreover, he thinks that attempts to ground truth as objective by appealing to something like timeless and eternal abstract objects (such as we find in Plato's theory of the Forms) is needlessly complicated and mysterious.

> Let me begin with an ontological caveat: there is more than a touch of metaphysical extravagance in the notion,…of a vast, or, rather, an infinite array of mind independent abstract entities called propositions existing, or shall we say subsisting, in a rarefied realm of their own, endowed each with its own truth attribute.[65]

As a final criticism of objective interpretations of truth, he offers an argument connecting such theories with systems of oppression that is strongly analogous to the "argument from tolerance" that is addressed in the chapter on ethical relativism in this book. Basically, there is a connection between notions of absolute or objective truth, and oppressive behavior.

> The concept of absolute truth appears to have a tendency to facilitate dogmatism and fanaticism which lead, in religion and politics, to authoritarianism and, more generally, to oppression. I do not say that

this is a necessary consequence of that conception. Indeed, if human beings were always consistent, the doctrine of absolute truth should, as suggested earlier, lead to total skepticism rather than to dogmatism. Besides, it is not here suggested that all advocates of the idea in question are dogmatic or fanatical. It is a fact, nevertheless, that in matters of truth and falsity, drastic persecution is hardly conceivable without pretensions to absolute truth on the part of the persecutors. It is difficult to think that men could imprison and even kill their fellow men for doctrinal differences with a free conscience if they understood clearly that, in doing so, they were acting simply on their own fallible opinions. It is a totally different thing when people believe that they are in the service of absolute truth, particularly if they imagine that the destiny of a nation, or even, perhaps, of the whole of mankind, is in question. There is no end to the mischief and cruelty of which they are capable. Yet, translated into the terms of my theory, such assertions as "The Truth will prevail"; and "The Truth is on our side", amount to no more than "Our opinions will prevail" or "My opinions are on my side.[66]

If the point of Wiredu's objection is that acknowledging truth to be an opinion rather than some sort of objective "fact" will somehow automatically generate tolerance and respect for different perspectives, then *my own* perspective is that he is optimistically overstating the case.

His own interpretation of truth that we will explore later in this chapter is that "opinion," in the way he normally intends it, means something like a "considered opinion," and that believing something necessarily means being committed to the truth of that thing. While it is possible that there could be some psychological difference in terms of motivation and enthusiasm if one

---

[65] Wiredu, Kwasi. "Truths, a Dialogue." Philosophy and an African Culture. Cambridge

University press, 2009: 190.
[66] Wiredu, "Truth as Opinion," 122.

regards a political or religious view as a "fact" as opposed to a "considered opinion," in either case, the person believes that view to be *true*. It is not obvious to me, at least, that someone whose "considered opinion" is that abortion is equivalent to murder, and that it should be stopped by any means necessary will somehow be less zealous in their opposition to abortion than someone who thinks that it is a "fact" that abortion is equivalent to murder, and that it should be stopped by any means necessary.[67]

Although Wiredu rejects correspondence theory (and other "objectivist" theories), and agrees with the epistemic relativist that truth is not a matter of some sort of "fact," independent of personal perspective, he insists that his view is *not* epistemic relativism. Indeed, he is quite *critical* of that theory.

Truth, as I believe I have stressed more than once, cannot be said to depend on a point of view – that gives the impression of relativism; a truth is a point of view. But reference to a truth is not just a reference to a point of view, for the following reason. Reference to a truth carries a commitment which a mere reference to the point of view does not carry.[68]

The first difference, then, between Wiredu's theory and epistemic relativism is this notion of implicit "commitment." Here, it is useful to clarify what he means by "opinion," as well as what it means to "believe" something.

Oftentimes, we distinguish "opinion" from "fact" in terms of degrees of certainty or confidence. In such cases, to describe something as your opinion indicates a certain modesty or hesitation.

A matter of opinion – "opinion" here being used in the weaker sense – is a matter with regard to which criteria are unclear or even possibly nonexistent or the evidence is scanty and there is, consequently, doubt and uncertainty.... In this sense, the proposition that two plus two equals four is not a matter of opinion. However, in the stronger sense of "opinion," it is still an opinion; it is a taking something to be so. It is still an outcome of a mental effort, the result of the mind's activity of systemization and validation.[69]

This distinction is usually repeated when we discuss believing something as opposed to knowing it. Indeed, I proposed in a previous chapter that (among other things) "knowledge" is something that we believe with so much confidence that it earns a "promotion" and the new job title of "knowledge." While Wiredu acknowledges that use of "opinion," that is not what *he* means by the term. A "fact" is not something fundamentally different from an "opinion." Instead, a "fact" just is an opinion held to be secure, a "considered opinion."[70]

To return to my metaphor, Wiredu would say that a belief/opinion of mine that "earns the promotion" can be *called* a "fact," but it *remains* an opinion. The higher degree of confidence I have that that opinion is true will of course make a difference in how I act with respect to that belief, but it remains an opinion all the same, because *all* claims that someone asserts are opinions. That previously discussed distinction between appearance and reality means that "opinions" are the only kinds of claims possible for us. We can meaningfully talk about some opinions being more "considered" than others, but none of our opinions become something that is *not* an opinion as a result.

Importantly, for Wiredu, opinion is all that is needed for truth anyway. As he puts it, "to be true

---

[67] Additional consideration of the "argument from tolerance" is available in the chapter on ethical relativism, as stated, and I encourage you to review that section if you're interested in this issue.

[68] Wiredu, "Truths, a Dialogue," 203.
[69] Wiredu, Kwasi. "In Defense of Opinion," Philosophy and an African Culture. Cambridge University press, 2009. 174-175.
[70] Wiredu, "Truth as Opinion," 115-116.

is to be opined."[71] This is where a clear understanding of just what Wiredu means by "opinion" is necessary, because, as he tries to make very clear, his view is not that *every* belief is somehow equally true – that is a mistake that he attributes to epistemic relativism.

We can speak of beliefs in the abstract without personally *believing* in them. For example, it at least used to be the case that my youngest nephew believed that the "elf on the shelf" worked for Santa and was basically spying on him in the weeks prior to Christmas. In that example, I am speaking *about* a belief, but it is certainly not the case that I myself *believe* that there really is an army of elves, available for purchase, that conduct surveillance on children on behalf of Santa Claus! Using Wiredu's vocabulary, I would describe my nephew's belief about the elf on the shelf as a "truth claim," but I would not describe it as a *truth* for the very simple reason that *I* do not believe that it is true. While a truth claim is a point of view, a "truth" is a truth claim *plus* a *commitment* to that claim. This notion of commitment is very important for understanding his theory.

> *To talk of a truth is to commit yourself to whatever proposition may be in question. On the other hand, one can talk detachably about a point of view, merely noting its existence, for example. A truth claim is obviously the same as a point of view. We may therefore say that the difference between talking of a truth claim and talking of a truth lies in this, that the former does not necessarily involve commitment while the latter involves a commitment on the part of the one who does the talking.*[72]

The difference here might be subtle. Any "truth" is necessarily a point of view. As he puts it, "Truth, then, is necessarily joined to point of view, or better, truth is a view from some point;

and there are as many truths as there are points of view."[73] However, while every truth is a point of view, not every point of view is a *truth*. The difference lies in personal commitment.

> *My formula is not just "P is true = P is believed" but "P is true = P is believed, provided that the two sides of the equation have the same point of view." Let Tp stand for "P is true" and "Bp" stand for "P is believed." Further, let us use numerical subscripts to identify points of view, the same number when repeated indicating the same point of view. Then my formula is $T_1p = B_1p$ not,... $Tp = Bp$.*[74]

Unlike an epistemic relativist who is seemingly committed to agreeing that *every* belief is *equally* true, Wiredu's theory of truth as opinion allows us to be a bit more discriminating. I can entertain countless beliefs. For example, I can presently entertain the belief that it is raining outside as of the time of my writing this sentence. Even though "it is raining outside right now" is a belief, it is not one that I personally endorse, and therefore I would not regard it as true. And, the mere fact that someone *does* endorse a claim as true doesn't require that anyone else, let alone everyone else, agree.

In addition to the issue of commitment, a second important difference between Wiredu's view and epistemic relativism involves the standards he thinks are available for "objectivity."

> *It is the insistence on the need for belief to be in accordance with the canons of rational investigation which distinguishes my view from relativism. Truth is not relative to point of view. It is, in one sense, a point of view. But it is a point of view born out of rational inquiry, and the canons of rational inquiry have a universal human application.*[75]

---

[71] ibid., 114.
[72] Wiredu, "Truths, a Dialogue," 203.
[73] Wiredu, "Truth as Opinion," 115.

[74] Wiredu, "In Defense of Opinion," 187.
[75] ibid., 176-177.

Despite arguing that truth is opinion, and always represents a point of view, Wiredu thinks that "objectivity" is still possible and still applicable to at least some of our opinions. Accordingly, he rejects the common assumption that all opinions are necessarily subjective, while it is only facts that are objective. To justify this, Wiredu offers his understanding of the standards of objectivity.

> *It seems to me that in the way of opinion, that is objective which is in conformity with the principles of rational inquiry, these in their turn, being susceptible of a naturalistic account.*[76]

These "principles of rational inquiry" are universally shared by all human beings (with a few notable and extreme counterexamples, such as those generated by people with significant developmental disabilities, head injuries, etc.). Indeed, he claims that unless "at least the basic canons of rational thinking were common to men they could not even communicate among themselves."[77]

We all have roughly similar rational capabilities, as well as shared commitments to principles that, for most of us, and for most of our lives, we can't even articulate very clearly.[78] A person doesn't have to be familiar with the works of Aristotle to understand that it is literally nonsense if someone claims that his cat is not a cat, given the standard meaning of those terms. It is equally nonsense if someone claims that he is both married and a bachelor, given the standard meanings of those terms.

Unless people shared certain conventions of language and logic in common, communication would be impossible – but communication obviously *is* possible. I'm communicating with you right now! I trust that even if you have to look up a vocabulary term every once in a while, you have a basic understanding of most, if not all, of

the words that I'm using, and you understand why I am using them in the manner that I am. I also trust that even if you find some of the sentences or paragraphs in this chapter (or others) to be challenging, you don't find them to be literally incoherent and meaningless. As an instructor, I occasionally encounter students who are less proficient at writing than other students, but I have literally never encountered a student whom I could not even understand *at all*.

All of these examples illustrate that there is something "interpersonal," something shared, that we may call "principles of rational inquiry." While we don't need to spell all of these out, they include basic principles like logical laws (identity, non-contradiction, excluded middle), basic rules of inference and deduction (that you could study in great detail in a class on critical thinking or logic), general notions like that it is generally more reasonable to believe something on the basis of evidence than in the absence of evidence, let alone in the presence of evidence to the contrary, and so on. These conditions of rationality just *are* what Wiredu thinks makes something "objective."

> *Something can be both personal and rational, but what is rational is objective. "I maintain that, as a psycho-epistemological fact, a basic sensitivity to the demands of rational inquiry is part of the mental makeup of any creature that can be called a human being. This, as I pointed out already, is why there are interpersonal criteria of rational beliefs. The existence of interpersonal criteria is the test of objectivity. Through this what is personal can also be interpersonal. I hope you can now see that my view that truth is opinion does not imply that truth is a subjective matter.*[79]

A belief or claim is objective when it

---

[76] Wiredu, "Truth as Opinion," 121-122.

[77] Wiredu, "Truths, a Dialogue," 222.

[78] I can't help but point out that studying philosophy, especially critical thinking and logic

helps us to understand and articulate these principles.

[79] Wiredu, "Truths, a Dialogue," 217.

conforms to those interpersonal criteria. In contrast, "something is subjective only if it is connected in an unlawlike manner with the peculiarities of a person."[80] In a different essay, Wiredu explains what he means by this.

> In general, it is a judgment rather than a state that can be said to be subjective. Correspondingly, objectivity consists not in absolute independence of the subject as such but only in independence of the peculiarities of the individual. Human beings have a substantial communality of needs, desires, feelings, capabilities etc., but they also have peculiarities. The former is the basis of objectivity, the latter of subjectivity.[81]

As an example, when I come to accept something as my "considered opinion" on the basis of evidence and other principles of rational inquiry, my belief may be called objective, because the formation of that belief is the result of processes shared by all other human beings (standardly). On the other hand, if I come to believe something on the basis of my own peculiar biases (such as a racist worldview), as opposed to through these principles of rational inquiry, then that belief would be subjective instead.

> Belief, as I have said elsewhere, is, standardly, the outcome of rational inquiry. Whether a belief is rationally supportable or not is an objective issue, that is, an issue whose determination does not depend on the psychological peculiarities of any given person. There are interpersonally specifiable criteria of rationally warranted assertability. The existence of such criteria is made possible by the fact that human beings have certain similarities of basic physiological and

mental makeup. This is what lies at the back of the possibility of human community – the possibility, that is, of the use of language and logic among men, the possibility of agreement and also of disagreement, the possibility of moral relations, and so on. The purpose of arguing when there is disagreement among persons is to bring it about by non-arbitrary means that they are of one opinion, that is to say, one rationally warranted opinion.[82]

Because belief formation is subject to these principles of rational inquiry, the formation of opinions is not a random event, or a matter of choice. "'Belief' as I am using it is not a matter of will but of reason."[83]

It is unreasonable and implausible to think that someone can actually believe that the evidence points to the earth being a sphere, for example, but *sincerely* "will" to believe that it's flat instead, no matter *what* interpretation of "truth" they entertained. As a simple demonstration of this, right now, try to believe that you have six arms.

I'm very confident that you cannot. You can *imagine* yourself with six arms. You can *think*, in your head, "I have six arms." You can *say*, out loud, "I have six arms." None of those is actually the same as *believing* that you have six arms, however.

> The formation of opinion is governed by rules – rules of evidence and of formal logic. A person can choose what problems or fields of inquiry he may turn his mind to, but once faced with a specific problem, he cannot decide just anyhow what conclusion to adopt. This fact is of paramount importance for my view of truth. Truth, according to that view, is nothing but opinion; but opinion is

---

[80] ibid., 216.
[81] Wiredu, Kwasi. "What can Philosophy do for Africa?" Philosophy and an African Culture. Cambridge University press, 2009: 57.

[82] Wiredu, "Truths, a Dialogue," 210-211.
[83] Wiredu, "Truth as Opinion," 117.

normally the outcome of rational inquiry.[84]

These rules of evidence and formal logic are not somehow innately understood and employed (with possible exceptions of an intuitive sense of certain logical laws, once language is acquired, I would think), but are *learned* through education (or not) and practiced and improved (or not). Indeed, one of the most valuable virtues of studying philosophy, in my opinion, is that it improves those very capacities and makes us better thinkers, better reasoners.

In summary, while both epistemic relativism and "truth as opinion" reject the idea of something like absolute/eternal truth independent of any perspective, Wiredu thinks that his theory is importantly *different* from epistemic relativism given his appeal to interpersonal standards of rationality as well as in pointing out the significance of personal commitment to beliefs.

As a result of these two differences, Wiredu thinks that his view is not subject to the same sorts of criticisms usually leveled at epistemic relativism, including the ones we considered earlier this chapter.

For example, according to epistemic relativism all truth is a matter of opinion and what makes something true is simply that someone believes it. As a result, we end up with seemingly counterintuitive consequences like that $2 + 2 = 4$ and $2 + 2 = 5$ are each opinions, each "true," and yet they are mutually contradictory. Therefore, epistemic relativism allows for "true contradictions," which seems problematic to say the least.

According to Wiredu's "truth as opinion" view, however, those claims are only contradictory if "opined" from the *same* point of view, which either won't actually ever happen, or is a sign of a "mental abnormality" (to use his vocabulary).

For example, the seemingly contradictory claims that "the movie is boring" and "the movie is exciting" are only technically contradictory if it is one and the same person who is making those claims about the same movie, at the same time, and in the same respect. It would be very unusual indeed if I told you that a specific movie was simultaneously boring as well as exciting. On the other hand, if *I* am making a claim that the movie is boring, and *you* are making the claim that the same movie is exciting, there is no contradiction there – there is simply *disagreement*, which is not the same thing. Or, to go back to the mathematical example, in order for there to be a genuine contradiction it would have to be the case that it is the same person who believes, at the same time and in the same respect, that $2 + 2 = 4$ and $2 + 2 = 5$. This scenario seems unlikely to ever actually manifest in reality. In fact, we would be likely to assume that there is something cognitively impaired about someone who explicitly endorsed obviously contradictory claims simultaneously.[85] As a result, Wiredu thinks his view does not endorse simultaneously true contradictions, but only recognizes the possibility of disagreement, which is hardly unique to his view, or controversial.

Another related objection to epistemic relativism is that it flies in the face of "common sense." Using that very same example of $2 + 2 = 4$, it just seems to be "common sense" that that is a

---

[84] Wiredu, "In Defense of Opinion," 176.
[85] As a sad but true example of this, back when I worked as a counselor at a locked-placement psychiatric hospital, one of the patients with whom I worked believed that his father was Ronald Reagan. He also believed his father was Fidel Castro. In both cases, he meant "biological" father. He also recognized that you can only have *one* biological father. He further recognized that Ronald Reagan and Fidel Castro were not the same person. Despite the fact that he openly acknowledged that it is only possible to have one biological father, he simultaneously claimed that he had two biological fathers. No matter how many times I pointed out this contradiction to him, it made no difference. This gentleman happened to be very seriously mentally ill, which probably explained his ability to seemingly believe explicitly contradictory things simultaneously.

true statement, and anyone who thinks otherwise is mistaken. However, if all beliefs are equally true, someone who thinks otherwise is not actually "mistaken" – at least not in any strong sense of the term. Wiredu seems to agree.

> *I too am reasonably confident in the belief that 2 + 2 = 4 and that anybody who holds the contrary is mistaken. But I cannot help recognizing that this is simply to affirm my belief and express my disagreement with any contrary beliefs. Neither the fact that I hold a given opinion nor that many reputable people share my opinion can transform it into something of a different category from opinion,...[86]*

In other words, to think that someone is mistaken is just to indicate that *you* believe something different from them. The fact of that disagreement doesn't indicate that your claim has a fundamentally different status (such as being a "fact") than that of the other person. Your disagreement just reveals your *own* point of view.

And yet, someone might ask, isn't it just "obvious" that some points of view are better informed than others? One of the criticisms of epistemic relativism that we considered earlier in this chapter is that that theory implies that every perspective is equally "true." If so, that generates all sorts of counterintuitive consequences.

Socrates pointed out, as you hopefully recall, that in actual practice we don't *really* think that all opinions are equally legitimate because we recognize genuine expertise. On a related note, an objector might propose that if all truth is merely opinion, then the project of education is pointless since the opinion of the teacher is no more "true" than that of the student. Wiredu would actually agree that these are serious concerns, but doesn't think that it indicates that truth is something other than opinion. Instead, he would point out that the mere fact that we recognize "expertise" reveals that, *from our own perspective*, the opinion of the expert and the opinion of the

amateur are not actually *equally* informed.[87]

All claims that "something is the case" are opinions, and are equal *in that* they are opinions, but not all opinions are equally "considered." An honest evaluation would presumably *not* result in concluding that the view of the student is as "equally considered" as that of the teacher. Of course, this too, is a matter of perspective. Whether or not someone counts as an expert, and how seriously one takes their expertise, will themselves be matters of opinion.

A final objection to epistemic relativism is that if truth is simply a matter of personal opinion, then there is technically no such thing as a "false belief," since simply to believe something is to render it "true." This results in the rather fantastic scenario in which no one is ever mistaken about *anything* since anything that someone believes is "true" by virtue of the fact that that person believes it.

Technically, Wiredu will agree that there is no such thing as a "false belief," in the sense that *Wiredu* normally intends by "belief." Remember the component of "commitment" that we discussed previously. To believe something is necessarily, implicitly, to already endorse it as true – otherwise you wouldn't believe it. From the first person perspective, one can't normally speak of a false belief because to do so is to simultaneously affirm a belief (as true) by virtue of believing it, but also to reject the belief as false by labeling it false.

> *Talk of false belief is sensible, then, only when a disparity in point of view is envisaged. Thus one can only say "X believes that P but P is false" where the falsity claim obviously originates from a point of view other than X's.[88]*

> *To say that an opinion is not warranted is to dissociate one's point of view from that opinion. To call an opinion true is to identify one's point of view with it.[89]*

---

[86] Wiredu, "Truth as Opinion," 118.
[87] ibid., 117.

[88] Wiredu, "In Defense of Opinion," 185.
[89] Wiredu, "Truths, a Dialogue, 191.

To offer an opinion is already implicitly to accept it as true. For me to speak of a false belief I must necessarily be speaking of someone *else's* belief – one that I disagree with. Alternatively, I might be speaking of one of my own beliefs, but only in the past. It is entirely possible that I *used to* believe something, but *later* changed my mind such that from my *current* perspective that former belief is now false.

> *To say that a proposition I now believe may be false is simply to withdraw my commitments from it hypothetically, and contemplate, equally hypothetically, a negative issue to the corresponding problem... It is not my beliefs, as my belief, that becomes the object of my hypothetical contemplation; it is only the conceptual residue left after the hypothetical subtraction of my commitment that now becomes the object to which falsity is ascribed.*[90]

It is, therefore, a misunderstanding to think that Wiredu's view rules out ever being mistaken – at least according to him.

> *It is not just that I concede that I may mistakenly believe a false proposition; I have always insisted on the importance of recognizing human fallibility in the theory of truth.*[91]

> *...From the fact that a given person believes a certain proposition, it does not follow that the proposition is true... From the fact that a given person believes a certain proposition it does not follow that others will, or ought to, believe that proposition.*[92]

A belief may be labeled mistaken in several different scenarios. If we are merely speaking abstractly about the possibility of a belief being mistaken, then there is nothing preventing us from imagining that a belief is false and that someone has made a mistake. Additionally, very often when we consider *other* people's beliefs, we consider them to be mistaken. This is always the case whenever we have sincere disagreement. Thirdly, even when restricting beliefs to our *own*, we can still acknowledge mistakes as long as we are thinking about former beliefs. Every one of us undoubtedly has come to regard some of the things that we used to believe as a "mistake." It must be remembered, however, that all of these will be considered "mistakes" only from the current perspective of a particular individual.

As a final note concerning Wiredu, he is keenly aware of (and embraces) one final objection that was leveled at epistemic relativism: self-reference. "That truth is nothing but opinion is itself nothing but an opinion."[93] Of course, I'm confident that he would consider that to be his "considered opinion."

Be honest: did you find Wiredu's theory to be challenging to understand? Me too. Philosophy is often challenging, and at times is necessarily so given the complexity of what philosophy aims to understand and discuss. Even the *attempt* at understanding a difficult idea or theory is rewarding, though, because of the "mental workout" it provides, as well as the opportunity to consider new and interesting points of view.

Here is what *I* get from Wiredu's contributions: because of the distinction between appearance and reality, we can never have unmediated and reliable access to reality "in itself," but only ever have access through our own points of view.

To preserve a meaningful notion of truth, we have to abandon the idea that true claims are those that correspond to reality, since we will never be certain what actually corresponds to that unavailable reality. Anything that anyone ever believes will necessarily be a point of view, so any quest to somehow transcend a particular point of view is doomed to failure. This doesn't mean that we have to be resigned to some sort of epistemic free-for-all, however, in which every

---

[90] ibid., 226.
[91] ibid., 195.

[92] ibid., 223.
[93] Wiredu, "Truth as Opinion," 123.

belief is equally true, no matter how it was formed, or regardless of any other consideration. For these reasons, Wiredu rejects both epistemic relativism and correspondence theory. Even though all beliefs are opinions, and necessarily points of view, he does not think that we must regard them as all being "equal."

Focusing on the shared principles of rationality that make communication between human beings possible in the first place, he considers those opinions that are produced in accordance with those shared principles to be "objective," since those principles are not unique to the individual who formed the opinion. In this way, some opinions can be "objective." Opinions that are formed in other ways, in contrast, are subjective, and should not be regarded as equally warranted. Realistically, you are far more likely to be persuaded by my objective opinions than my subjective opinions, and will regard them as much more credible.

For example, suppose that two different women discover a mysterious lump in one of their breasts. Both of them form the opinion that the lump is not cancer and that their lives are not in danger.

One of them (Yvonne) is of the opinion that her lump is not cancerous because she prefers to think positive thoughts, and thinks that she is "too young" to get cancer.

The other of them (Wanda) is of the opinion that her lump is not cancerous because she met with an oncologist who ran numerous tests, including a biopsy, and those tests indicated that the lump was a benign cyst rather than cancer.

On the assumption that any point of view we might adopt must be an opinion, both of their opinions are equally *opinions* – but you probably wouldn't regard them as equal in other respects. I would like to think that you regard Wanda's opinion as being far more "considered" than Yvonne's.

Wanda formed her opinion as a result of gathering evidence and with the aid of an expert – in other words, by methods that we collectively regard as reliable and generally productive of accurate beliefs.

Yvonne, on the other hand, is operating on wishful thinking and assumptions about who can get cancer (for which counterexamples are easily available).

Both are expressing opinions, and both are making truth claims, but they are not "equally considered," and even if you allow a healthy bit of skepticism, I suspect you are vastly more likely to credit Wanda with a truth claim that is also actually a "truth."

Chapter 5: Arguments

Comprehension questions you should be able to answer after reading this chapter:

1. What is an argument?
2. What is meant by a "relevance-relationship" between premises and a conclusion? What does it mean for a deductive argument to be "valid?"
3. What does it mean for a deductive argument to be "sound?"
4. Why is the soundness of arguments often difficult to establish?
5. What is the principle of charity?

When one thinks of "social justice," the word "argument" probably comes to mind—though probably for the wrong reason! It's an old cliché that one doesn't talk about politics or religion at parties, and social justice issues are often regarded in the same way. For most of us, if you want to start an "argument" at a family dinner, we should bring up either politics or religion or some sort of moral issue. That is not usually, however, what an "argument" means in the context of philosophy.

An **argument** *is an attempt to establish the truth of a claim (the conclusion) by offering evidence (premises) in support of that claim.* No name-calling, no chair-throwing, no raised voices—not even any presumption of disagreement. In a philosophical context, an argument is not a fight, but simply an attempt to make a point, using evidence, and following certain rules of reason.

Although we don't usually encounter arguments in the following format (except in philosophy courses), all arguments at least implicitly have the same general form:

> Premise$_1$
> Premise$_2$
> Conclusion

Please note that we have not yet specified any particular content for that argument. That is because arguments can be about *anything*. Any time you try to persuade someone to believe anything at all, on the basis of some kind of reason/evidence, you are offering an argument.

Also note that although there were two premises in the generic argument above, there is nothing special about that number. You might have only a single premise (piece of evidence), or you might have a hundred premises, or any other number whatsoever. So long as you have at least one piece of evidence, at least one reason to believe that the conclusion is true, you have provided an argument.

Every philosophical essay that you read in this book (or any other) is an argument, or at least contains arguments. What all arguments have in common is that they are attempts to demonstrate that a claim (the conclusion) is true, by offering other claims (premises) as evidence. Note that both the conclusion of an argument and all the premises in an argument, are *claims*. This is not a trivial observation! Every (proper) piece of every argument is a claim.

Claims are statements, assertions, or propositions (different terms meaning roughly the same thing), and, due to that fact, have what is called a "*truth-value.*" To say that a claim has a truth-value is simply to say that it must be either true or false (if true, then its truth-value is true; if false, then its truth-value is false). Therefore, every (proper) piece of every argument has a truth-value—which is what makes argument evaluation possible.

However, although some professional philosophers will sometimes write out their arguments in obvious "premise$_1$, premise$_2$, therefore conclusion" format, most philosophical readings are not so blatantly reader-friendly. Philosophical arguments will be made in the context of paragraphs, essays, chapters, or even entire books. As we read, then, our job is to identify the main point the author seems to be trying to make. This is the conclusion. Then, we must try to identify all of the supporting points the author provides in defense of that conclusion. These are the premises. Once we have identified the conclusion and premises, we are prepared to evaluate the argument.

Please be aware that not all arguments are created equal. Just because you have offered a reason to believe something is true doesn't mean you have provided a *good* reason, or even a relevant one. Consider the following example:

Argument (A)
1.   Egg yolks are high in dietary cholesterol.
2.   High cholesterol is associated with increased risk of heart disease.
3.   Therefore, abortion is morally wrong.

Argument (A) is laughably bad, and I'm sure you realize that, but it's important to recognize *why*. It doesn't take much reflection, or any fancy vocabulary, to describe what's going "wrong" with that argument: the premises don't have anything to do with the conclusion! You might rightfully be wondering what the heck eggs and cholesterol have to do with abortion. Clearly, the premises aren't *relevant* to the conclusion.

Relevance-relationships are an important initial way to evaluate the quality of an argument. In general, if the premises aren't "relevant," then we would say that little (if any) support has been provided for the conclusion—and that doesn't make for a very good argument! One specific example of this relevance relationship occurs with deductive arguments

Deductive arguments are constructed with the intent to provide for the certainty of the conclusion, on the assumption that the premises are true. Such arguments are (generally) evaluated in terms of their validity, and soundness. Both of those words (valid, sound) have specific meaning in the context of argument, and both (especially validity) have different uses in everyday speech. For example, you might hear someone say "that's a valid point." What that

person means is that you have made a good point. In that usage, valid means something like "good," or "apt," or "true." That is not what "valid" means for our purposes, though.

Validity

A deductive argument is <u>valid</u> *if the conclusion necessarily follows (logically) from the premises.* Another way of putting that idea is that an argument is valid when, *if* the premises are true, the conclusion must also be true. Or, an argument is valid if it's impossible for the conclusion to be false, *if* all the premises are true. To repeat: validity indicates the right kind of "relevance-relationship" between the premises and the conclusion.

You might have noticed that I italicized the word "if" in a couple of places in the previous paragraph. There's a good reason for that. When we assess an argument's validity, it's a hypothetical exercise. We're not making any claim that the premises are, in fact, true—we're just asking what would happen *if* the premises are true. Consider the following:

1.   All humans are mortal.
2.   Preston is a human.
3.   Therefore, Preston is mortal.

Is this argument "valid," according to our definition? To find out if it is, ask yourself the following: *if* all the premises are true, must the conclusion also be true? *If* it's true that all humans are mortal, and *if* it's true that Preston is a human, then, must it also be true that Preston is mortal? The answer, of course, is "yes." Therefore, this is a valid argument. This indicates that there is the right kind of logical relationship between the premises and conclusion, there is a relationship of structural relevance between them. We haven't yet established that the premises are, in fact, true (that's a later step), but we have established that *if* they are true, the conclusion is as well. That is very important. Let's reconsider example (A) from before:

Argument (A)
1. Egg yolks are high in dietary cholesterol.
2. High cholesterol is associated with increased risk of heart disease.
3. Therefore, abortion is morally wrong.

Just a few paragraphs ago, we articulated the "badness" of this argument using ordinary language. Presumably, you recognized that eggs, cholesterol, and heart disease risks have nothing to do with whether or not abortion is morally wrong! There isn't the right kind of relationship between those premises, and the conclusion. If we consider this in terms of validity, the problem becomes clear.

Is it possible for it to be true that egg yolks are high in cholesterol, and true that high cholesterol is associated with increased risk of heart disease, and yet for it to be false that abortion is morally wrong? Of course that's possible! So, if, for some weird reason, you try to prove the moral wrongness of abortion by appealing to the cholesterol content of eggs, you will fail in grand, embarrassing fashion. Even if all your evidence is proven to be true, you still will not have proven that your conclusion ("abortion is morally wrong") is true.

Soundness

If validity appeals to the hypothetical truth of the premises, soundness refers to their actual truth. *A deductive argument is "sound" when it is both valid and all its premises are, in fact, true.* Notice that in order for an argument to be sound, it must first already be valid. You can imagine an implicit checklist for argument evaluation:

☐ Is the argument valid?
☐ Is the argument sound?

Only if we can "check the first box" do we bother to consider whether the argument is sound. Let's go back to one of our earlier examples:

1. All humans are mortal.
2. Preston is a human.
3. Therefore, Preston is mortal.

Is the argument valid? Yes, it is (as established above).

✓ Is the argument valid?
☐ Is the argument sound?

Since it's valid, we can now move on to consider its soundness. Are all of the premises, in fact, true? To be honest, the issue of "truth" generates all kinds of new questions. What does "truth" mean? What does it take for something to be true, let alone known to be true? You could spend an entire career as a philosophy professor focusing solely on the concept of "truth," and still have plenty of questions remaining. We will not spend entire careers on the concept of truth, but we will spend some time in another chapter on several different interpretations of what it means for a claim to be true. For now, however, let's set aside the murky notion of "truth" and assume (for the sake of argument) that we know what it means for a claim to be true. Even so, how can we tell if a particular claim is, in fact, true?

Obviously, not all claims will be easily *verifiable* as true. While we might be fairly confident that it is true that egg yolks are high in cholesterol, some truth-values (unfortunately, probably the ones we tend to care the most about—truth-values for claims about morality, religion, politics, etc.), might be especially difficult to establish.

Do aliens exist, or not? Hard to say, since we haven't explored the entire universe just yet. Is abortion immoral? Hard to say, since there's so much disagreement, and so many compelling arguments that can be given on both sides. Does God exist? Hard to say, since there are compelling arguments on both sides of the debate, and legitimate debate as to what does or could count as evidence for God's existence in the first place....

Recognizing that some claims will be difficult to establish, let us return to a relatively easy argument just to complete our discussion of "soundness."

1. All humans are mortal.
2. Preston is a human.
3. Therefore, Preston is mortal.

In order for this argument to be sound, it has to be valid, and all of its premises must be true. We've already established that it's valid. Are its premises, in fact, true? Does the claim that "all humans are mortal" seem to be true? If we interpret "mortal" in its usual sense ("liable or subject to death"), then it does, in fact, appear to be true. That all humans are subject to death seems to be true, like it or not. What about the second premise? Is it, in fact, true that Preston (the author of this book) is a human? Again, if we're assuming the usual sense of "human" ("a member of the genus *Homo* and especially of the species *H. sapiens*"), then it would appear that Preston being human is true as well. Given that both premises are, in fact, true, we have established that the argument is not only valid, but sound.

✓ Is the argument valid?
✓ Is the argument sound?

If you have established that an argument is sound, you have proven that the conclusion is true. It doesn't get any better than that! Unfortunately, whenever we're dealing with serious, important arguments, it's usually pretty challenging to establish that the argument is sound. Consider another argument for the wrongness of abortion:

Argument (B)
1. Murder is morally wrong.
2. Abortion is murder.
3. Therefore, abortion is morally wrong.

You should know the routine by now:

☐ Is the argument valid?
☐ Is the argument sound?

If it's true that murder is morally wrong, and it's also true that abortion is murder, must it also be true that abortion is morally wrong? Yes, this is a valid argument. Is it sound? Perhaps, but this

is far from obvious. Murder, by its usual definition, is the unjustified killing of an innocent person, so I suspect *most* people would agree that premise 1 is true.[94] Premise 2 is going to be much more controversial, though. Is abortion the unjustified killing of an innocent person? People who argue that abortion is (at least sometimes) morally acceptable will usually argue either that the fetus is not a "person," or that the killing is justified (or both). Such persons would not grant the truth of premise 2, and would not recognize the argument as sound, even though it is valid.

Let's take a moment to summarize the ground we've covered so far. An argument is an attempt to prove some point by appealing to reasons that support that point. In order for an argument to be a good argument, it needs to at least be valid, and preferably sound as well. For an argument to be valid, it needs to be the case that if all the premises are true, the conclusion has to be true as well. For it to be sound, all the premises must, in fact, be true.

Some of you might have wondered about one of the sentences in that previous paragraph: "in order for an argument to be a good argument, it needs to at least be valid, and preferably sound as well." Perhaps that sentence made you pause, and ask something like "why only *preferably* sound? Why doesn't the argument have to be both valid and sound in order to be good?" If you wondered about that, good for you!

Ideally, of course, good arguments *will* be *both* valid and sound. But, if we insist that an argument be sound in order to be "good," we might be setting the bar so high that few, if any, arguments are "good." This is because, as we have already seen, soundness can be difficult and controversial to establish. Consider one more argument:

Argument (C)
1. If God does not exist, objective moral values and duties do not exist.
2. Objective moral values and duties do exist.

---

[94] In fairness, there might even be disagreement as to the truth of *this* premise!

3. Therefore, God exists.

This is actually one of the more famous arguments for God's existence known as the "moral argument." For our purposes, though, let's just consider our checklist:

☐ Is the argument valid?
☐ Is the argument sound?

If both premises are true, must the conclusion also be true? Yes—and this shouldn't be surprising. Any of the "major" arguments for God's existence, the arguments that have withstood the test of time (often centuries, if not millennia), are presumably going to be valid—otherwise they would have been abandoned long ago.

✓ Is the argument valid?
☐ Is the argument sound?

Now that we know it's valid, is it sound? Is it, in fact, true that if God does not exist, objective moral values and duties do not exist? Is it, in fact, true that objective moral values and duties do exist? Those who use the moral argument for God's existence will offer reasons to accept both premises as true. If you find those reasons compelling, you will presumably conclude that both premises are, in fact, true—in which case you will conclude that the argument is sound. But, if you think the reasons are not compelling, you will instead conclude that the premises are not true—in which case you will conclude that the argument is not sound. Or, perhaps some of you, even after serious consideration, will come to the honest conclusion that you're just *not sure* if those premises are true—in which case you will conclude that you don't know whether the argument is sound.

✓ Is the argument valid?
? Is the argument sound?

That the soundness of this (or any other of the major arguments for, *or against*, God's existence) is in question should not be surprising.

Remember: if an argument is sound, its conclusion *is, in fact, true*. So, if an argument for God's existence can be shown to be sound, that would mean that it is, in fact, true that God exists—and that this has been proven! Conversely, if an argument against God's existence were shown to be sound, it would mean that God has been proven not to exist. Had either of these events occurred, you probably would have heard about it!

Similarly, if the soundness of various arguments concerning moral issues could be easily established, you would think that there would no longer be any debate about things like abortion, eating meat, the death penalty, etc. The fact that people still passionately debate these issues should tell us something about the difficulty in establishing the soundness of those sorts of arguments. Don't be discouraged, though. Just because it's difficult to establish the soundness of these sorts of arguments doesn't mean that there's no point in evaluating them, nor does it mean that we will be unable to say anything evaluative or interesting about them. Even if we're not *sure* if argument B is sound, it's clearly a better argument for the wrongness of abortion than the one referencing the risks of high cholesterol (argument A)!

It's important to point out that it's not very common, in everyday life, to encounter deductive arguments—let alone ones that are presented in such user-friendly formats as a clearly-indicated series of promises with an easily identifiable conclusion. Most people, most of the time, experience (and offer) arguments in far less formal terms. Accordingly, I think it's important to recognize the importance of concepts like validity and soundness, but not to get fixated on them. Recognize that they are examples of broader concepts of argument evaluation.

When someone is trying to convince you of something, the first thing to ask is whether or not any support is being offered. If the answer is "no," then that person is just making a statement, and we will consider how to evaluate unsupported claims in another chapter. If, however, support is being offered, then you have been presented with an *argument*.

If someone is presenting you with an argument, you need to determine whether that support is relevant to the conclusion. With deductive arguments, this is a question of *validity*—but generally speaking you can just ask whether the premises are "relevant." If they are not relevant, that doesn't mean their conclusion is false, but it does mean their evidence doesn't really count as support, and you should treat the conclusion as an unsupported claim. If the premises are relevant, then the next step is to determine if they are true.

When relevant premises are not actually true, then they don't properly support their conclusion, and you should treat the conclusion as an unsupported claim. If the premises are true, however, then the argument is in pretty good shape. After all, we already determined they were relevant, and now we've determined they're also true! With deductive arguments, that means the argument is *sound*, and the conclusion has been *proven* to be true. Even if the argument isn't deductive, though, there is still probably some very impressive support for the conclusion such that it's at least likely to be true. In that case, you should consider how well that newly-proven conclusion fits with your worldview.

We will discuss worldviews in greater detail in another chapter, but, for now, just know that your worldview is your basic understanding of the world and how it works. When claims fit with our worldview, they don't tend to surprise us, and we usually presume they are true (even though they might not be). When they conflict with our worldviews, however, we tend to be skeptical and presume they are false (even though they might be true). When a conclusion has been *proven* to be true, though, that should make a difference to your worldview. If, for example, my current worldview includes a general skepticism about the existence of aliens, but I then see live footage of an alien spacecraft on every major news network, and I am personally abducted by aliens and experimented upon, you better believe that I will revise my worldview to now include the existence of aliens!

Whatever the content of the argument, and perhaps especially when the conclusion conflicts with our own worldview, we need to be self-aware when we are evaluating it. One important element of (honest) argument evaluation is what's known as the "*principle of charity*." Basically, we want to be "charitable" when evaluating arguments—especially if we're inclined to disagree with them.

It's all too easy to develop a "straw man" interpretation of someone else's position, and then dismiss it as foolish, fallacious, or misguided. The fact of the matter is that people don't tend to view their own arguments as foolish. This doesn't mean they aren't, but in order to perform an honest evaluation of an argument, we need to present it in its best possible light. We must put ourselves in the position of the person who presented the argument, consider the argument in the strongest possible way (given the original author's intentions), and then evaluate the argument, so charitably constructed. This is a good approach to evaluating arguments, in general, but it's especially apt in the context of considering formal philosophical arguments in a book like this one.

The sorts of arguments and theories we will consider have stood the test of time. They're considered in this book for a reason. No matter what your personal views happen to be, it's uncharitable to casually dismiss "the other side" as fools offering lousy arguments. You might well conclude that "their" arguments fail, but to be justified in that conclusion you need to consider those arguments charitably, in their best light.

Critical Analysis

1. In your opinion, what are the strongest and most compelling points made by the philosopher or philosophers in this chapter? Why do you find those points to be convincing?

2. In your opinion, what are the weakest or least convincing points? Why? Can you anticipate any limitations or objections to their ideas not already addressed in the chapter?

Appendix: Application to Social Justice

As was the case with the content of some other chapters, arguments are content neutral—perhaps especially so! Arguments, after all, can be about *anything*. Applications to social justice will occur, very simply, whenever the content of the argument pertains to matters of social justice. But, no matter the content, the basic process by which we evaluate arguments remains the same. We must identify the conclusion, identify any premises, and evaluate whether the premises are relevant. Assuming they are relevant, we can then assess whether the premises are true, or at least likely to be true. Premises that are relevant and at least likely to be true provide support for the truth of the conclusion, though whether that support is decisive might remain to be seen.

Chapter 6: Evaluating Claims

Comprehension questions you should be able to answer after reading this chapter:

1. What are the four conditions under which it is reasonable to accept an unsupported claim as true?
2. What are the ways in which we establish the expertise of sources?
3. What is a "worldview?" What do we usually do (in general) when a claim fits with our worldview? What about when it conflicts with it? If a claim that conflicts with our worldview is proven to be true, what should we do with our worldview?
4. What is "fake news?" What are the different possible interpretations of fake news? How is the allegation of information being "fake news" a threat to legitimate critical thinking? How can we respond to it?
5. When should we suspend judgment concerning the truth or falsity of a claim?

Justification

In a previous chapter, we considered different interpretations of knowledge, and focused on the definition of "justified true belief" for the sake of a deeper dive. In another chapter, we considered beliefs as expressed in the form of claims, and considered how we evaluate claims when they are supported by evidence in the form of an argument. We will now consider how we may evaluate claims that do *not* have any formal support provided.

This is still a consideration of justification. The premises of an argument provide justification for the conclusion of that argument, but it is possible for unsupported claims to have justification as well – indeed this is inevitable since the chain of justification must necessarily come to a stop, and usually does so within arguments in the case of premises. To illustrate this simple but important point, imagine a generic but iconic argument.

> Premise$_1$
> Premise$_2$
> Conclusion

Theoretically, the conclusion is being supported by both of the premises in that argument. Those premises serve as the justification for that conclusion. But what about the premises? In order for them to be supported in the same way, each premise would have to be the conclusion of a separate argument, such as the following.

> Premise$_3$
> Premise$_4$
> Conclusion (Premise$_1$)

> Premise$_5$
> Premise$_6$
> Conclusion (Premise$_2$)

So, in order for Premise$_1$ and Premise$_2$ to be "supported," they each need their own argument with supporting premises. But now what about those new premises? In order for those to be supported, all of them need to be conclusions of their own arguments as well – and this goes on "forever." This is not only impractical, but impossible. Simply put, the chain of justification must come to a stop at some point or another.

When we are considering an argument, such as was our focus in a previous chapter, the justification chain effectively comes to a stop with the premises. In such cases, the premises of an argument are treated as an unsupported claim –

which is the focus of this chapter. What we will explore in this chapter is equally applicable to unsupported claims, in general.

When we are presented with a claim (or any piece of information in general) we have three options available to us. We may:

1. *Accept* the claim as true
2. *Reject* the claim as false
3. *Suspend judgment* if we aren't sure of the truth value of the claim.

Considerations of "justification" is the process by which we attempt to determine whether claims are true, or at least likely to be true, and therefore whether we should accept, reject, or suspend judgment. When these claims are the premises of arguments, this process additionally helps us to determine whether the argument is a good argument, and therefore whether or not we can "know" whether the conclusion of an argument is true. Justification is crucially involved in determining the truth of the premises in arguments (once relevance has been established), and in evaluating the truth of an unsupported claim when no proper argument is present at all.

Justification is probably the most controversial element of our definition of knowledge, primarily because we can bicker over what, exactly, counts as "sufficient" justification. Again, this is a very complicated subject, but this is not an extended treatment of epistemology, so we can get by with a basic understanding of the key ideas.

To say that knowledge requires justification is simply to say that you can only "know" something on the basis of good *reasons*. If I present you with a jar filled with marbles, and you guess there are 457 marbles in the jar (just pulling a number "out of the air," at random), and, with a startled look on my face, I tell you that there are, in fact, 457 marbles in the jar, we wouldn't want to say that you *knew* the number of marbles in the jar at the time you guessed. We call it a guess for a reason! You didn't know, but you took a shot at it, and happened to get lucky. That's not knowledge; it's a lucky guess.

Sometimes, we like to distinguish "believing" from "knowing" by making explicit appeals to how much justification we have for the belief in question. I believe my wife is at work, because I have reason to think that she is. However, if my confidence in those reasons is pretty low, I won't have sufficient *justification* to claim to *know* that she's at work.

As I mentioned, justification can be a thorny issue. How can we tell when we have *enough* justification to claim that we know something, as opposed to merely believing it? As with many questions in philosophy, there's no obvious, uncontroversial answer to that question. We can, however, talk about ways in which our beliefs are justified, and the degree to which our beliefs are supported by evidence.

As stated above, when we are presented with an unsupported claim (including the premises of an argument), our three basic options are to accept it as true, reject it as false, or to suspend judgment because we're not sure either way. How do we know which one of those three options is the right one to exercise?

Generally speaking, it is reasonable to *accept* an unsupported claim if the claim:

1. Does not conflict with our own observations
2. Does not conflict with other credible claims
3. Comes from a credible source that offers us no compelling reason to expect bias
4. Does not conflict with our background information/worldview

1) The Claim does not Conflict with our own Observations

We are justifiably skeptical about claims that directly contradict what we have personally observed! If you're texting with a friend, and he is telling you that he's in his car and on the way to meet you at Starbuck's, but you are personally observing him (in secret), right then and there, standing outside the Apple Store talking to your girlfriend, then either your friend is saying something false or you are hallucinating (or something else equally unlikely). Not surprisingly, in such a case you would be inclined to reject his claim as false. On the other hand, if you just came in from the rain and are shaking off your umbrella, and your friend calls and tells you he's running late because it's raining out, you're probably going to accept his claim as true. After all, you personally witnessed the rain too.

2) The Claim does not Conflict with other Credible Claims

In courtroom settings, one of the best ways for an attorney to undermine the evidence offered by a witness or expert is to provide *another* witness or expert who will contradict that evidence. This is often very successful in creating "reasonable doubt" in jurors. So, for example, if one blood-splatter expert testifies that the spray patterns suggest the killer was at least six feet tall (which is bad news for the 6-foot-tall defendant), that claim is undermined if another, equally respectable, blood splatter expert says the patterns are inconclusive.

In the context of philosophy, this is a notorious experience for philosophy students. One philosopher offers a compelling case that we have no free will, but then another equally impressive philosopher says the opposite. In such cases, we often must suspend judgment, even if we don't outright reject the original claim. If, on the other hand, there is no such conflict, if the claim is not being contradicted by other (credible) claims—let alone if there is consensus from a variety of sources—then we are likely to accept the claim as true.

3) The Claim comes from a Credible Source that Offers Us no Compelling Reason to Expect Bias

This criterion actually has two elements: bias, and credibility. "Bias" is an issue when the person making the claim is suspected to have an ulterior motive. For example, if someone is trying

to sell you their used car, they have a personal incentive for you to buy it, and they might be inclined to be less than completely honest about the condition of the vehicle. This doesn't mean they're automatically lying, of course, but careful car buyers will inspect the vehicle, and even enlist the help of someone who knows a thing or two about cars (e.g., an automotive mechanic) to confirm the car really is in good condition. Similarly, when the Tobacco industry spent decades denying the link between smoking and cancer, a clear case can be made that they had an ulterior motive to make that claim.[95] After all, if they admitted smoking caused cancer, it might reduce the number of people who smoke, and therefore their profits. Similarly, we might be reasonably skeptical when the petroleum industry funds lobbying groups denying the link between automobile emissions and climate change.[96]

The possibility of bias doesn't demonstrate the *falsity* of the claim, of course. To *presume* so would actually be an example of what is called the "genetic fallacy"—denying (or accepting) the truth of a claim *solely* because of its source. However, while a possibly-biased source doesn't necessarily indicate their claim is false, it should inspire us to be especially vigilant when evaluating the evidence (if any) that they provide in support of their claim.

Setting aside issues of bias, we can now turn to credibility. Unless one is a radical epistemic relativist, we recognize that not all sources are equally credible. When evaluating a claim, the source matters—especially if the subject matter is significant or if the claim conflicts with our own worldview. I should hope that you trust the testimony of your medical doctor more than you trust the testimony of your neighbor when it comes to your health—unless of course your neighbor also happens to be a medical doctor!

If someone is especially knowledgeable about a particular topic, we tend to give extra "weight" to their claims made about that topic.

---

[95] http://www.who.int/tobacco/media/en/TobaccoExplained.pdf
[96]https://www.theguardian.com/environment/

2015/jul/15/exxon-mobil-gave-millions-climate-denying-lawmakers

Sometimes, we consider such persons "experts."

We establish expertise, generally, by considering the following criteria:

1) Education
2) Experience
3) Accomplishments

Education is just what you think it is. Generally speaking, the more educated someone is on a topic, the more likely we are to (reasonably) take him or her to be an expert on that topic.

Someone who majored in chemistry as an undergraduate probably knows a lot more about chemistry than someone who majored in something else—let alone someone who has never studied chemistry at all. Someone who has a Master's degree (M.S.) in chemistry probably knows even more, and someone with a doctorate (Ph.D.) probably knows even more than that. To be skeptical of this would require you to be profoundly skeptical of the effectiveness of our education system, in general! Keep in mind, of course, that expertise based on education is limited to the focus of one's education. That Ph.D. in chemistry doesn't mean the chemist is also an expert on criminal law!

Experience is also just what you think it is. While education is terribly valuable, relevant experience is valuable as well. *All else being equal*, a medical doctor who has been in practice for 20 years is probably more knowledgeable than a first-year M.D.

Once again, we have to be careful of relevance. The fact that I have been a philosophy professor for nearly twenty years doesn't mean that I "know better" than a first year lawyer when it comes to legal issues. Despite the fact that President Donald Trump has been a wealthy businessman for decades, his claim that he "knows more about ISIS than the generals" is dubious on its surface.[97] For all his alleged business acumen, and despite his clear mastery of the media, then-candidate Trump had literally *no* experience relevant to ISIS, in contrast to "the Generals" and their combined decades of military experience, including years of recent experience specifically opposing ISIS.

Accomplishments often (though not always) come from education and experience, as well as merit. If a cancer researcher, for example, has won a Nobel Prize for her research, that scientist is probably pretty knowledgeable!

Sometimes, some awards or "achievements" are questionable, and serve primarily to stoke the vanity of their recipients. For example, I get solicitations every year to be an "invited speaker" at a conference called the Oxford Round Table. It is held at the very prestigious Oxford University, and being able to put "invited speaker" on your résumé is usually a respectable achievement, for a professor like myself. However, the Oxford Round Table has no affiliation with Oxford University at all (they just rent space!), "invited speakers" (or their campuses) must *pay* several thousand dollars for the privilege to attend, and whether or not one is invited seems to be much more about whether you're on the email mailing list rather than actual achievements or status on the field. In other words, this conference is largely a scam designed to make money for the organizers of the event.

Today, with the increasing influence of social media, we have to be careful not to confuse "notoriety" with being "accomplished." As of 2019, Ariana Grande has over 65 *million* twitter followers compared to only 43 million for CNN. It would be absurd to think that somehow Ariana Grande is a more credible source of information, however, based solely on her superior popularity.

Putting all these ideas together, we can consider a "real-life" example of two experts.

Richard Dawkins:[98]
Education: BA, Ph.D.: Oxford University
Professor (emeritus) Oxford. Specialization: evolutionary biology
Achievements: numerous awards and publications

---

[97] https://www.youtube.com/watch?v=kul34O_yMLs

[98] https://www.richarddawkins.net/richarddawkins/

William Lane Craig:[99]

Education: BA (Wheaton College), MA Phil of Religion & History of Christian Thought (Trinity Evangelical Divinity School), Ph.D. in PHIL (University of Birmingham), Ph.D. in Theology (University of Munich).

Professor: Trinity Evangelical school and Talbot School of Theology. Specialization: Philosophy of religion & Christian doctrine.

Achievements: numerous awards and publications

A legitimate evaluation of these two scholars recognizes that they are both very well educated and accomplished in their respective fields. Both are undoubtedly intelligent persons who deserve respect. This doesn't mean they are always correct, of course—but it does mean we should take them seriously when they offer claims concerning their areas of expertise.

An interesting application that applies to these two, specifically, is that they are considered "rivals." Craig is an outspoken Christian who debates prominent atheists around the world, trying to demonstrate the rationality of Christian faith. Dawkins, on the other hand, is a notorious critic of religion, and the author of such books as "The God Delusion."

While both men are credible experts, even legitimate experts can be guilty of stepping outside their areas of genuine expertise. Dawkins, for example, while unquestionably one of the finest scholars on evolution living today, is *not* an expert on Western philosophy—let alone the philosophy of religion. Not surprisingly, when he writes a book like "The God Delusion" that deals with philosophy, rather than evolution, his credibility is strained. His critiques of the most famous arguments for God's existence in the Western tradition are undeniably outdated, and rely heavily on the criticisms offered by David

Hume—written some two and a half centuries ago. What's worse, is that what he calls his "central argument" is demonstrably invalid (according to the very standards we have addressed earlier in this chapter). Indeed, Craig has described the argument as "the worst atheistic argument in the history of Western thought."[100] In fairness, Craig should be equally cautious about extending his own expertise into the realm of biology.

4) The Claim does not Conflict with our own Worldview

We each have, at our disposal, what we may call our "background knowledge," or "background information," or our "worldview." Whatever we want to call it, it is that vast collection of everything we have heard, seen, read, and otherwise learned, throughout our lives. This collection is everything we know (or think we know) about the world and how it works. It includes your understanding of hugely important questions such as whether or not God (somehow conceived) exists, to your understanding of human psychology, world history, economics, State capitals, and even sports statistics. If you have learned about it, it is part of your worldview.

When presented with a claim, we all immediately evaluate that claim not only in terms of evidence, source, and our own observations, but also with respect to how well it "fits" with our worldview.

Every time we are confronted with a piece of information, we automatically and instantly evaluate it against our background knowledge. If the new information seems to "fit" with our background knowledge, we're likely to accept it as true. If it does not fit, however, if the claim is surprising to us, we're likely to hesitate and to demand more justification before accepting it as true.

For example, if I were to claim that I drove

---

[99] https://www.reasonablefaith.org/william-lane-craig/

[100] http://www.reasonablefaith.org/dawkins-

delusion

home on the Southbound 605 freeway at 5 PM on a Thursday afternoon, and the freeway was wide open, with hardly any cars on it at all, anyone living in Southern California (that is, anyone for whom the 605 freeway, on a weekday, at 5 PM, is part of their background knowledge/worldview) would immediately doubt what I'm saying. Why? Because her understanding of the world and how it works is that Southern California freeways are jammed at that time of day.

When it comes to justification, then, we'll want to know if the belief is consistent with other things that we know about the world and how it works. If the belief is consistent, so far, so good. If it is not, then we'll naturally be skeptical, and we'll require further evidence before accepting the belief.

We always need to be aware, however, that our own background knowledge can be flawed. For example, it used to be part of most people's worldview that the Sun revolved around the Earth. Now, it's part of our worldview that it's the Earth that moves relative to the Sun.

Background knowledge is subject to revision. So, the mere fact that a piece of information conflicts with your understanding of the world does not automatically mean that the claim is false. It's possible that it's true, and that it's your understanding that needs revision. Whenever you get presented with a claim (including the conclusion of an argument) that conflicts with your worldview, but for which you're confident it's true, the reasonable thing to do is to revise your worldview accordingly. Obviously, the more you know, the better equipped you are to evaluate claims, and to be accurate in your evaluations.

It is also important to be honest about the threat of *bias* posed by our worldviews when evaluating information—a bias that we are *all* subject to.

Thus far, I have casually commented on our tendency to accept claims that fit with our worldview, and to be skeptical of those that clash

with it. This is a well-known and studied psychological tendency known as the "confirmation bias." What makes the confirmation bias dangerous, though, is that it distorts our ability to honestly and objectively evaluate claims. This is not merely some anecdotal complaint about the state of debate today. There is scientific evidence to suggest that our brains are "wired" to be resistant to change with respect to "firmly held beliefs."

A study published in 2016 showed, via neuroimaging, that when subjects were presented with arguments that contradicted their strongly held political views, they experienced "increased activity in the default mode network—a set of interconnected structures associated with self-representation and disengagement from the external world."[101] The default mode network is normally shown to active during such states as daydreaming and mind-wandering. It is labeled "default" because the network activates "by default" when the person is not engaged in a task requiring attention.

This is fascinating, if true! It suggests that when our firmly-held political beliefs are challenged, our brains "check out" in ways analogous to daydreaming. How responsive to evidence and argument are we likely to be if our brains are in a "day-dreaming" state when evidence contrary to our firmly held beliefs is presented?

In the final speech President Obama gave as President, he warned against our increasing tendency to operate within our own ideological "bubbles."

> *For too many of us, it's become safer to retreat into our own bubbles, whether in our neighborhoods or College campuses or places of worship or our social media feeds, surrounded by people who look like us and share the same political outlook and never challenge our assumptions. The rise of*

---

101 Kaplan, J. T. et al. Neural correlates of maintaining one's political beliefs in the face of counterevidence. Sci. Rep. 6, 39589; doi:

10.1038/srep39589 (2016). Available at http://www.nature.com/articles/srep39589

naked partisanship, increasing economic and regional stratification, the splintering of our media into a channel for every taste – all this makes this great sorting seem natural, even inevitable. And increasingly, we become so secure in our bubbles that we accept only information, whether true or not, that fits our opinions, instead of basing our opinions on the evidence that's out there.[102]

This isn't merely some anecdotal cautionary tale about liberals only watching MSNBC and conservatives only watching Fox news. A study published in the *Proceedings of the National Academy of Sciences of the United States of America* concluded that "selective exposure to content is the primary driver of content diffusion and generates the formation of homogeneous clusters, i.e., 'echo chambers.' Indeed, homogeneity appears to be the primary driver for the diffusion of contents and each echo chamber has its own cascade dynamics."[103]

In other words, people on Facebook mostly share news that they already agree with, that is consistent with their worldview, and they don't share information that challenges it. As the researchers put it: "users show a tendency to search for, interpret, and recall information that confirm their pre-existing beliefs."

Combine this tendency with the fact that Facebook has nearly 2 billion users (out of roughly 7 billion people on the planet), and reaches 67% of U.S. adults, and that 62% of Americans get their news mainly from social media sites such as Facebook and Twitter.[104] A majority of Americans get their news primarily from social media, and research confirms the application of the confirmation bias to social

media platforms. It should go without saying that these trends seriously compromise our ability to think critically, and to responsibly accept or reject claims. Unfortunately contributing to this effect is the relatively recent phenomena of so-called "fake news."

As of 2017, "Fake News" has entered into the American vocabulary, initially and specifically in the realm of politics—though the phrase is likely to "trend" and apply to other contexts as well. Initially used by liberals to describe right-wing "conspiracy theories," the phrase expanded in use just as did the frequency of fake news itself. Conservatives then adopted the phrase themselves, and the phrase now gets used to describe multiple, significantly different things. This is where philosophy has a chance to shine, considering the experience philosophers have with conceptual analysis. The primary meanings of "fake news" seems to be the following:

- A work of **fiction**, known to be so by the author, but presented as real/true for personal, political, or financial motives.

This is the *original* meaning of fake news, and all other meanings are a departure from this. Another word to describe this kind of fake news is a "lie." A clear illustration of this kind of fake news is the example of Cameron Harris. As reported in an interview with Harris by the New York Times, he admitted to writing multiple completely fabricated stories that he thought would be effective "click-bait" for Trump supporters.[105] He claimed to have done so for financial reasons, citing that he made $22,000 in ad-revenue from his stories, though it was later revealed that he also worked as an aide to a Maryland Republican lawmaker.[106] Eight of his

---

[102] http://www.latimes.com/politics/la-pol-obama-farewell-speech-transcript-20170110-story.html

[103] http://www.pnas.org/content/113/3/554.full

[104] http://www.journalism.org/2016/05/26/news-use-across-social-media-platforms-2016/?utm_content=bufferae870&utm_medium =social&utm_source=twitter.com&utm_campaign=buffer

[105] https://www.nytimes.com/2017/01/18/us/fake-news-hillary-clinton-cameron-harris.html?_r=0

[106] http://www.inquisitr.com/3901102/cameron-harris-fake-news-writer-bought-christian-times-newspaper-for-5-made-22000-and-got-

fake news stories were popular enough to attract the attention of (and debunking by) Snopes.com.[107] His most "effective" story claimed "Tens of thousands of fraudulent Clinton votes found in Ohio warehouse." By his own admission, he invented an imaginary electrical worker and named him "Randall Prince." He copied and pasted a screen shot of a man standing in front of ballot boxes using a google image search. He also invented the motive for the imaginary ballot-tampering: "the Clinton campaign's likely goal was to slip the fake ballot boxes in with the real ballot boxes when they went to official election judges on November 8th."

The fact that the story was a complete *lie* did nothing to stop it from being shared with 6 million people. The fake news story went sufficiently viral that the Franklin County (Ohio) board of elections was forced to investigate—after which they confirmed the story had no basis in reality.[108]

- **Satire**: while also a work of fiction (and known to be so by the author), the work is presented as fiction for the sake of entertainment or to make a point.

Satire is a long-practiced means of both entertainment and persuasion. "The Onion" is perhaps the most famous satirical website today, and it makes no pretense that its stories are true. When The Onion runs the headline, "Trump Calms Nerves Before Inaugural Address by Reminding Himself He's The Only Person Who Actually Exists," it is presumed that the reader will know that they are only trying to be funny.[109] Similarly, when Jonathan Swift famously argued that a solution to Irish poverty was for Irish parents to sell their children as food to wealthy Englishmen, he wasn't being serious! Despite eating children being presented as his "Modest

Proposal," his *actual* proposals were much more serious:

> *Therefore let no man talk to me of other expedients: Of taxing our absentees at five shillings a pound: Of using neither clothes, nor household furniture, except what is of our own growth and manufacture: Of utterly rejecting the materials and instruments that promote foreign luxury: Of curing the expensiveness of pride, vanity, idleness, and gaming in our women: Of introducing a vein of parsimony, prudence and temperance: . . . Of teaching landlords to have at least one degree of mercy towards their tenants. Lastly, of putting a spirit of honesty, industry, and skill into our shop-keepers, who, if a resolution could now be taken to buy only our native goods, would immediately unite to cheat and exact upon us in the price, the measure, and the goodness, nor could ever yet be brought to make one fair proposal of just dealing, though often and earnestly invited to it.*

Satire is "fake news" in the sense that it is not *real*, but nor is it intended to be—and that is a *significant* difference

- A work thought to be true and intended to be true by the author, but **mistaken** in one or more significant details.

In another words, a mistake. An example of a mistake in reporting that was, nevertheless, denounced as "fake news" occurred on the day Donald Trump was inaugurated as President. A White House pool reporter tweeted that a bust of Martin Luther King Jr. had been removed from the Oval Office.[110] In fact, the bust had simply

---

fired/
[107] http://www.snopes.com/tag/christian-times-newspaper/
[108] http://files.constantcontact.com/b01249ec501/58eeb35a-7d61-4807-b168-765d27ca11cf.pdf

[109] http://www.theonion.com/article/trump-calms-nerves-inaugural-address-reminding-him-55095
[110] https://twitter.com/philipindc/status/822603029950173187

been moved to a different part of the office, and the reporter hadn't seen it—something the reporter later acknowledged and for which he apologized. Nevertheless, the initial report was called "fake news" by detractors all the same.[111]

At the risk of editorializing: honest mistakes, while bad, are not properly "fake news." A relevant indicator of intent is whether or not the person who made the initial claim is willing to admit (and correct) the mistake, and apologize.

- A news story deemed "**irrelevant**," or unimportant, or distracting from "real" news (according to the person making the claim).

An example of this might be when reporters comment on the fashion choices of a politician, rather than the substance of her policies. As another example, when Senator Jeff Sessions was nominated to be U.S. Attorney General by President Trump, some reporters (and Democratic politicians) pointed to allegations of racism from his past as a potential disqualifier for confirmation. This was labeled by some as "fake news"—though it's far from obvious that a history of racist behavior is not relevant with respect to one's qualifications for the top law enforcement position in the Federal Government.[112]

- A news story **disliked** by the reader.

This is perhaps the most disturbing usage of "fake news" of them all, in my opinion. This usage occurs when information is dismissed as "fake" simply because it conflicts with the reader's worldview, or because it would be distressing, if accepted as true. To be blunt: not liking a piece of information doesn't mean that it's false. If your medical doctor tells you that you have cancer, dismissing it as "fake news" is of no help.

The problem with the varied and inconsistent usage of the phrase "fake news" isn't just an issue of conceptual fussiness from overly-picky philosophers. Words have meaning. When President Trump refused to take questions from a CNN reporter, and dismissed the network as "fake news," it's likely that what he really meant is something like "I don't like CNN, and how CNN is reporting on my presidency."[113] However, people who listen to and respect President Trump might take his words to mean that CNN intentionally prints stories they know to be false for ulterior motives, and thereby lose confidence in the network as a reliable news source.

This isn't just bad news for CNN's ratings or profit margins. If confidence in mainstream media sources is undermined, people will retreat even *further* into their ideological bubbles, and their critical thinking skills will be even further compromised. President Trump later again labeled major media sources (viz., the New York Times, NBC, ABC, CBS, and CNN) as "fake news," but went further by denouncing them as the "enemy of the American People."

[111]http://www.thegatewaypundit.com/2017/01/fakenews-media-falsely-reports-trump-removed-mlk-bust-oval-office/

[112] http://eaglerising.com/38617/cnn-fake-

news-story-jeff-sessions-is-a-racist/

[113]http://www.cnn.com/videos/politics/2017/01/11/donald-trump-jim-acosta-cnn-fake-news.cnn

 **Donald J. Trump** ✓
@realDonaldTrump

The FAKE NEWS media (failing @nytimes, @NBCNews, @ABC, @CBS, @CNN) is not my enemy, it is the enemy of the American People!

1:48 PM - 17 Feb 2017

↩ ↻ 45,633   ♥ 142,121

Cognitive linguist George Lakoff finds this strategy to be both intentional and dangerous. The adjective "fake" modifies the function of "news." The primary purpose of "news" is to pass along factual information in service to the public good. If "news" is modified with the term "fake," it implies that the basic function of "news" has been compromised.

> *It is done to serve interests at odds with the public good. It also undermines the credibility of real news sources, that is, the press. Therefore it makes it harder for the press to serve the public good by revealing truths. And it threatens democracy, which requires that the press function to reveal real truths.[114]*

Perhaps we would be better and more accurately served by refraining from using the phrase "fake news" entirely?

When Hillary Clinton claimed in 2008 to have run from sniper fire in Bosnia, and her claim was proven to be false, the best-case scenario is that her memory was "mistaken," and the worst-case is that she intentionally lied for some reason.[115] Why bother calling it "fake news" when a "lie" or "mistake" more accurately conveys what

occurred?

When President Trump's press secretary, Sean Spicer, in his very first press briefing, not only claimed that President Trump's inauguration audience was the largest ever, but also condemned journalists for writing "fake news" downplaying the size of the crowds, several troubling things occurred. For one, his claim about viewership was demonstrably false. President Trump's Nielson television ratings were the fifth highest since President Richard Nixon—lower than President Obama's first inauguration, for example, but higher than the inaugurations of both Presidents Clinton and George W. Bush.[116] It's likely that President Trump and his staff would have liked it if their inauguration attendance and Nielson ratings had been the highest, but that preference doesn't mean that reporters who provide the factual numbers, in contrast, are disseminating "fake news." To suggest that they are is, again, to undermine confidence in the press, in general. It also seems unlikely to be helpful when President Trump's counselor, Kellyanne Conway described Spicer's actions in the following way: "You're saying it's a falsehood, and they're giving- Sean Spicer, our press secretary, gave alternative facts to that."[117]

---

[114]http://www.npr.org/2017/02/17/51563046 7/with-fake-news-trump-moves-from-alternative-facts-to-alternative-language
[115]https://www.washingtonpost.com/news/fact -checker/wp/2016/05/23/recalling-hillary-clintons-claim-of-landing-under-sniper-fire-in-bosnia/?utm_term=.e6222cd61035

[116]http://www.washingtonexaminer.com/trump -inaugurations-nielsen-ratings-fourth-highest-since-nixon/article/2612602
[117]http://time.com/4642689/kellyanne-conway-sean-spicer-donald-trump-alternative-facts/

For the sake of conceptual clarity: facts are objective, and are, by definition, true. An "alternative fact," therefore, is a clever term for something that is false—either a mistake, or a lie.

If it is a fact that 2+2 = 4, it is silly to label 2+2 = 5 as an "alternative fact." In reality, 2+2 = 5 is simply a falsehood. If it is a fact that Donald Trump is the 45th President of the United States, to claim that Bernie Sanders is the 45th President is not to offer an "alternative fact," but is simply to claim something that *is not true*. That President Trump's Nielson ratings for his inauguration were not the highest ever is a *fact*. To assert otherwise is not to provide an "alternative fact," but is simply to be either mistaken, or lying.

If you agree that "fake news" is troubling, and if you are motivated to be a good critical thinker, what can you do to be more wary when it comes to the news stories you accept or reject? The good news is that you have already learned how, earlier in this chapter! All of our previous discussion of justification, and how we should evaluate claims, is directly relevant to discerning whether a claim is "fake news," a lie, a mistake, or just simply true or false.

First of all, is the claim supported by evidence? In other words, is it an argument? Press Secretary Spicer didn't offer any evidence in support of his claim about the inauguration Nielson ratings—he just made an assertion. If he had offered an argument, you could try to determine whether his premises were relevant to the conclusion, and ultimately whether they were true. Had he cited Nielson numbers, you could easily fact-them—probably on your phone!

Don't forget the general process of evaluating unsupported claims. It's generally reasonably to accept an unsupported claim if it:

1. Does not conflict with our own observations
2. Does not conflict with other credible claims
3. Comes from a credible source that offers us no compelling reason to expect bias
4. Does not conflict with our background information/worldview

While it might not always be practical for you to investigate the source, at the very least you can try to be aware of the influence of your own worldview. If you know you are firm Trump supporter, then be aware that you are especially vulnerable to believing negative stories about Hillary Clinton—just as Hillary supporters would be especially vulnerable to believing negative stories about President Trump.

Remember to try to employ the "*principle of charity*" that we discussed in a previous chapter. Before getting indignant and retweeting or sharing an incendiary piece of news, try taking a few moments to carefully reflect on the claims being made, and maybe even do some fact-checking before taking a stance. Snopes.com is as very helpful resource in this regard.

Another very simple tip is to be initially skeptical about any stories riddled with spelling or grammar problems, or that use lots of CAPS or exclamation marks!!! Actual, serious journalists are usually pretty good writers, and poor writing can be a sign of an amateur blogger or internet troll. Keeping all of these different tools in mind can help you to be a good critical thinker, and be more confident when you accept a claim as true, or reject it as false—but it is important to remember that we do have a third option.

Thus far, we've only seriously addressed the conditions under which we accept or reject a claim, but there is a third alternative that requires some attention as well: *suspending judgment*. Basically, to accept a claim means you think it's true, to reject it means you think it's false, and to suspend judgment means you're just not sure either way.

It is OK to suspend judgment.

Let me repeat that: it is OK to suspend judgment.

You certainly don't want to spend your life shrugging your shoulders and pleading ignorance, but nor should you pretend to know the truth value of a claim if you honestly don't. Far too often, people accept or reject claims, and take stances on issues, when they know little, if anything, about the subject in question. Pardon my coarse language, but when people do so they are engaging in "bullshit."

Believe it not, "bullshit" is officially a

philosophical term, thanks to the philosopher Harry Frankfurt. Is his aptly title book, *On Bullshit*, he discusses this tendency in human behavior, and distinguishes it from lying.

> *Bullshit [the word] is unavoidable whenever circumstances require someone to talk without knowing what he is talking about. Thus the production of bullshit is stimulated whenever a person's obligations or opportunities to speak about some topic exceed his [or her] knowledge of the facts that are relevant to the topic. This discrepancy is common in public life, where people are frequently impelled —whether by their own propensities or by the demands of others— to speak extensively about matters of which they are to some degree ignorant. Closely related instances arise from the widespread conviction that is the responsibility of a citizen in a democracy to have opinions about everything, or at least everything that pertains to the conduct of his country's affairs.[118]*

In other words, if you ask me what I think about President Trump's choice for Secretary of the Interior, and I have no idea who that is (or even what he or she does), and instead of admitting "I don't know" I instead say that I don't approve of the choice, I have engaged in some "bullshit."[119] The claim I have made exceeds the relevant knowledge I actually have on that topic.

It's clear, I hope, that the proper thing to do in a situation like that is to suspend judgment. Yet, all kinds of people "bullshit" all the time. Why? As Frankfurt mentioned above, "Closely related instances arise from the widespread conviction that it is the responsibility of a citizen in democracy to have opinions about everything,

or at least everything that pertains to the conduct of his country's affairs."

In other words, there is a perceived social expectation that everyone is supposed to have (and be ready to provide) an opinion about *everything*. When this is combined with a crude presumption of epistemic relativism (according to which all opinions are equally legitimate), then we get an especially troubling situation: everyone feels obliged to opine about everything, and no matter how uninformed they might be, think that somehow their own opinion is just as good as anyone else's, and therefore worth sharing.

An intellectually honest alternative to "bullshitting," and one that, frankly, requires both self-awareness and some courage, is to be willing to suspend judgment if you honestly don't know whether a claim is true or false.

Let us now put all these considerations together by comparing two claims, neither of which is supported by an "argument," but are instead simply unsupported assertions.

- "I believe that, someday, my body will die."

To what extent is the belief supported by good reasons and compelling evidence from reliable sources? To be more specific, does the claim conflict with your own observations, or other credible claims? Does it come from a credible source that offers us no compelling reason to expect bias? To what extent is the belief consistent with your worldview?

I propose that ample evidence is supplied every day, every time someone dies. Obituaries, news stories about deaths, and personal experiences and memories of people (and every other animal on Earth) dying all serve as evidence.

My claim that my body will die someday is

---

[118] Frankfurt, Harry G. *On Bullshit*. Princeton University Press, 2005: 63.

[119] In case you are curious, President Trump's Secretary of the Interior is David Bernhardt (as of the time of this writing), and the Secretary's job is to manage the Department of the Interior,

which is the government department that oversees federal land, natural resources, and the administration of programs relating to Native Americans, Alaskans, and Hawaiians.

certainly consistent with your own observations (at least as far as the eventual and inevitable death of human beings in general is concerned).

I can't imagine that you have any reason to think otherwise, so my claim that I will die someday doesn't conflict with other credible claims. I will leave you to determine my "credibility," but it seems unlikely that I'm advancing some sort of ulterior motive by falsely claiming that my body will die someday.

With respect to worldview, the claim is consistent with the complex web of our beliefs involving the natural sciences. Biology and history both inform our worldviews, and our worldviews certainly includes bodily death, whether we like it or not. In other words, there is nothing surprising or implausible about my claim that my body will die someday, based upon your understanding of the world and how it works.

- "I believe that I will win the lottery this week."

To what extent is the belief supported by good reasons and compelling evidence from reliable sources? To be more specific, does the claim conflict with your own observations, or other credible claims? Does it come from a credible source that offers us no compelling reason to expect bias? To what extent is the belief consistent with your worldview?

I would say that, excluding the possibility of cheating, there is no compelling evidence to indicate I will win. Indeed, it's unclear what could possibly count as evidence of this in the first place.

As far as your own observations are concerned, I would be surprised if you knew anyone who has won the lottery before – at least any sort of significant amount.

You might not be in a position to assess my credibility or bias when it comes to my winning the lottery, so you might have to default to your worldview for a final analysis.

The claim that I will win the Powerball jackpot conflicts (or should conflict) with your understanding of probability in general, and with your experience of lotteries, in particular. For example, the odds of winning the Powerball grand prize are 1 in 292,201,338. To win a million dollars has odds of 1 in 11,688,053.[120] In comparison, the odds of being struck by lightning *twice* in your lifetime are 1 in 9,000,000— something much more likely than being made a millionaire by the lottery![121]

When we compare these two examples, we can detect a sharp contrast. In both cases, you probably (rightfully) think you do not have to suspend judgment, but can actually take a stance. The first claim (concerning bodily death) is so strongly justified that you probably not only accept it as true, but with sufficient justification to constitute knowledge.

If you disagree with this, and deny that you know that your body will die someday, you probably think it's impossible to know *anything*. That's not necessarily a bad thing. There is a respectable and ancient school of thought called "Skepticism" that regards knowledge as impossible to obtain. You'll learn more about skepticism in another chapter.

The second example (me winning the lottery) is so poorly justified as to be little better than wishful thinking—certainly not knowledge.

In fairness, the lottery claim is about the future, and many epistemologists would say that future-indexed claims have an indeterminate truth-value, since they haven't happened yet. For that reason, you might be inclined to suspend judgment-and that is a fair position to take. However, even if you're suspending judgment for that reason, you probably think the claim is very likely to turn out to be false.

In a previous chapter, we briefly considered the nature and different possible interpretations of truth and falsity itself. In closing *this* chapter, however, please understand that the tools we have discussed and that you have practiced are

---

[120] http://www.powerball.com/powerball/pb_prizes.asp

[121] http://wncn.com/2016/01/12/odds-of-winning-powerball-jackpot-less-than-being-hit-by-lightning-twice/

indispensable and will be used not only when you evaluate the claims of every other chapter in this book, but also countless times every day *whenever* you get presented with a new piece of information. One of the wonderful things about the study of philosophy is how it translates outside of its own subject matter and provides an incredibly useful radical thinking skills in every aspect of our lives.

Critical Analysis

1. In your opinion, what are the strongest and most compelling points made by the philosopher or philosophers in this chapter? Why do you find those points to be convincing?
2. In your opinion, what are the weakest or least convincing points? Why? Can you anticipate any limitations or objections to their ideas not already addressed in the chapter?

Appendix: Application to Social Justice

At the risk of being outright repetitive by now, this chapter is also "content neutral." The process by which we evaluate claims is identical, whether the claim concerns matters of social justice or literally any other topic whatsoever. Because of the moral and political dimensions of social justice claims, however, such claims are more likely to be "controversial." And, because the sorts of things that tend to be discussed in conversations about social justice tend to be the sorts of things about which "everyone has an opinion," they are perhaps especially vulnerable to "bullshitting" (in the philosophical sense).

Suggest that we should "defund the police," for example, and most Americans are likely to have an opinion—and many of them will be more than happy to share it, regardless of what they actually know (or don't know) about police practices and responsibilities, or whether they even know what the phrase means.

"Defund the police" is a claim. Implicitly, it means "*we should* defund the police." If someone offers evidence in support of that claim, we have

an argument, and we should evaluate it as we learned in a previous chapter. For example:

1. Police officers killed an unarmed black man.
2. The killing was not justifiable.
3. Unjustified police killings should be eliminated or at least reduced.
4. Defunding the police will eliminate or at least reduce unjustified police killings.
5. Therefore, we should defund the police.

The process we learned in this chapter will help us to evaluate the premises in that argument, or even just evaluate the conclusion itself, when it is offered as an unsupported claim (such as on a protest sign).

Remember, it is generally acceptable to accept an unsupported claim as true if it:

1. Does not conflict with our own observations
2. Does not conflict with other credible claims
3. Comes from a credible source that offers us no compelling reason to expect bias
4. Does not conflict with our background information/worldview

Now things get messy....

The first claim is presumably empirically verifiable, so the mere fact that the police shot someone, and that the person was unarmed, shouldn't conflict with our own observations, other claims (etc.) except under unusual circumstances.

The second claim concerns justifiability, which is an assessment of whether the shooting was "appropriate" given the circumstances—and here many people seem to think of themselves as an "expert" (regardless of actual background and training), and many people are subject to bias (often implicit) that informs their judgment, as well as their evaluation of other people's claims.

I have heard people say that police officers should shoot suspects in the hand, or leg, to wound and disable them rather than shooting them in the chest which is more likely to result in death. Such persons clearly have an understanding of shooting firearms that is informed by action movies rather than actual practice, given how unrealistic that proposal is. I have heard other persons say that all such suspects should have "just obeyed" the police officers, and not done anything "threatening," suggesting a lack of understanding not only of how people, in general, respond under stress, but also of specific details in some cases. The point is that even something so seemingly simple as affirming that killing an unarmed man is not justifiable is subject to the very biases and complications discussed in this chapter, and helps to explain why there is widespread disagreement as to whether police reform is needed, and what form that reform should take.

I would like to think that the third claim is fairly uncontroversial! Presumably everyone would be disposed to agree that unjustified police killings should be eliminated or reduced. Where disagreement is likely concerns what counts as "unjustified" and how that elimination/reduction should be sought.

The fourth claim ("Defunding the police will eliminate or at least reduce unjustified police killings.") is subject to the very same sort of controversy and debate as the second claim. What does "defund the police" even *mean*, for example? Some interpret it as "eliminate the police entirely," while others interpret it as "reduce police funding while increasing funding for various social services, and redistribute suitable agents from those other services to non-violent calls rather than the police." Confusion about the intended meaning of the phrase can inspire disagreement that otherwise might not occur, as claimed by President Obama.

> *If you believe, as I do, that we should be able to reform the criminal justice system so that it's not biased and treats everybody fairly, I guess you can use a snappy slogan, like 'defund the police,' but, you know, you lost a big audience the minute you say it, which makes it a lot less likely that you're*

actually going to get the changes you want done.[122]

Even assuming that we can agree on the meaning of "defund the police," there is still the question as to whether that effort will, in fact, reduce or eliminate unjustified police killings—and with respect to that claim most of us are playing arm-chair social scientists, at best. Most of us aren't criminologists, and are relying on our "intuitions" (to put it generously) when we either accept or reject the claim that defunding the police will have a particular outcome. The potential for "bullshit" (in the philosophical sense) is significant, here.

None of this is to suggest, of course, that we should *not* "defund the police"—or even that we shouldn't have opinions about such important matters. It is to suggest, however, that it's helpful to be aware of just how complicated our assessments of such claims actually are so that we might show some humility when it comes to our own stances, and some charity when it comes to our assessment of others'. As with any important philosophical topic, matters of social justice are complicated *because* they are so important. It's the trivial things that are usually "simple." The difficult things, though, are often the ones most worthy of our time, effort, understanding, and action.

---

[122] https://www.youtube.com/watch?v=Yj-eNGfeG0o&feature=youtu.be

Chapter 7: Moral Psychology & Political Decision Making

Comprehension questions you should be able to answer after reading this chapter:

1. In Jonathan Haidt's "rider and elephant" metaphor, what is the "rider?" What is the "elephant?" What is the power dynamic between them?
2. What is Haidt's first principle of moral psychology?
3. According to Haidt, why is it so difficult to change someone's mind with evidence and arguments?
4. Why does Haidt think that the reason acts more like a lawyer or press secretary than a judge when it comes to moral reasoning?
5. What does research on psychopaths tell us about the possible link between emotion, reason, and moral action?
6. What is the definition of each of these terms, according to Haidt:
   a. moral system
   b. intuition
   c. moral intuition
   d. moral judgment
7. According to Haidt, how does natural selection favor both "selfishness" as well as "groupishness?"
8. Provide Haidt's five modules/foundations, and, for each, briefly explain the adaptive challenge they allegedly evolved to address, their original triggers, current triggers, the characteristic emotion they produce, and the virtues associated with them.
9. Briefly describe Shweder's "three ethics":
   a. ethics of autonomy
   b. ethics of community
   c. ethics of divinity
10. How does the "taste bud" analogy allegedly account for both universal moral intuitions as well as cultural differences?
11. According to Haidt, in what way is morality both innate and socially constructed?
12. According to Haidt, in what way is morality both emotional and rational?
13. Briefly explain each of the three levels of personality:
    a. dispositional traits
    b. characteristic adaptations
    c. life narratives
14. For Haidt's sixth moral foundation/module (liberty/oppression), briefly explain the adaptive challenge it allegedly evolved to address, its original triggers, its current triggers, the characteristic emotion they produce, and the virtues associated with it.
15. Choose one of the six moral foundations/modules, and use it to explain the difference between conservative and liberal political views.
16. What are the two steps we considered from Haidt concerning how we might find "common ground" with people with whom we have political disagreement?

Most people are likely to assume that the reasons we have in support of a belief (including moral judgments or political judgments) are the *causes* of those beliefs. That seems "logical," and a fundamental "article of faith" of the teaching and practice of philosophy is that the use of reason through arguments not only demonstrates the truth of claims, but can and should persuade people to accept such claims. If they don't, then they are somehow being "irrational."

Jonathan Haidt is not like "most people."

Consider the following example: Rica believes that abortion is morally wrong, and that "life" (understood here as morally relevant personhood) begins at conception. One interpretation of the relationship between his moral judgment and his belief about when personhood begins is that he has studied the issue, gathered the relevant information, concluded that personhood begins at conception, and as a result judged that abortion is morally wrong. Another interpretation is that Rica has experienced an intuitive aversion to abortion, and as a result judged that abortion is morally wrong. To justify that judgment to others, his reasoning faculty searches for supporting reasons, and comes to believe that personhood begins at conception. In both interpretations, the beliefs and moral judgments are the same – but the order in which they are generated is very different.

Haidt is convinced that, given our example above, the correct interpretation is the one where Rica experiences his intuitive aversion first, and then generates reasons after the fact to justify what he has already concluded. To illustrate this perhaps surprising view of reason and judgment, he offers a "rider and elephant" metaphor.

Think of the mind as the pairing of an elephant and its rider. Rather obviously, the elephant is bigger and more powerful than the person riding it. If the elephant is trained, and the rider knows what she is doing, the rider can certainly try to exert some influence on the actions of the elephant, but let's be realistic: ultimately, the elephant is going to do what the elephant wants to do!

In the elephant and rider metaphor, the rider represents conscious and controlled thought. The elephant is *everything* else, including emotions,

intuitions, dispositions, etc.[123] Continuing with this metaphor, most of our cognitions are intuitive/automatic (i.e., the elephant), including such cognitions as when "our minds appraise the people we encounter on such features as attractiveness, threat, gender, and status."[124] The conscious component (i.e., the rider) is engaged when we consciously, deliberately consider a problem, evaluate evidence, etc. We will get into the evolutionary explanation of the "elephant and rider" later, but for now we will focus on the basic *process* Haidt thinks occurs when we form judgments.

First, there is some "triggering event." That might sound dramatic, but really it just refers to observing something, hearing something, reading something, experiencing something – in other words, you get presented with a new piece of information to process.

Based upon a variety of factors, including personal predispositions and cultural conditioning (both of which will be discussed in greater detail later), your "elephant" will have an intuitive reaction to the triggering event. Most fundamentally, the intuitive reaction will either be positive, or negative. The elephant will either "lean towards" the trigger, or "lean away." The elephant leans towards the triggering event when its intuitive reaction is positive. The elephant likes what it sees. The elephant leans away when its reaction is aversion. This occurs when the elephant experiences something like fear, discomfort, disgust, hostility, anger, etc. as a result of the triggering event.

Now that the elephant has either leaned towards or leaned away, the rider is deployed, but not in the way most of us usually think of when we think of the role of conscious, deliberate reason. Haidt proposes that the rider is *not* best conceived as some sort of objective judge who carefully weighs evidence, but is better seen as a lawyer, or press secretary, whose job is to justify and defend what the elephant has *already*

---

[123] Haidt, Jonathan. *The Happiness Hypothesis. Finding Modern Truth in Ancient Wisdom*. Basic Books: 2006, 17.

[124] Haidt, Jonathan and Joseph, Craig. "Intuitive

Ethics: How Innately Prepared Intuitions Generate Culturally Variable Virtues." *Daedalus*. Fall (2004): 57.

committed to. This is its primary and most important task in this model, but the rider does have other functions.

The rider can do several useful things. It can see further into the future (because we can examine alternative scenarios in our heads) and therefore it can help the elephant make better decisions in the present. It can learn new skills and master new technologies, which can be deployed to help the elephant reach its goals and sidestep disasters. And, most important, the rider acts as the spokesman for the elephant, even though it doesn't necessarily know what the elephant is really thinking. The rider is skilled at fabricating post hoc explanations for whatever the elephant has just done, and it is good at finding reasons to justify whatever the elephant wants to do next. Once human beings develop language and began to use it to gossip about each other, it became extremely valuable for elephants to carry around on their backs a full-time public relations firm.[125]

This notion that *intuitions come first,* and that *strategic reasoning comes second* is Haidt's <u>First Principle of Moral Psychology</u>.[126] The full model that he will develop around this principle is called the "social intuitionist model."

The central claim of the social intuitionist model is that moral judgment is caused by quick moral intuitions and is followed (when needed) by slow, ex post facto moral reasoning.[127]

This model, if accurate, can help us understand why it is seemingly so difficult to "win" an argument by changing someone's mind, especially when we are dealing with moral or political issues.[128] When two people disagree on such an issue, their feelings have come first, and then their reasons come afterwards. The reasons they offer are *not* the cause of their belief! The belief came first, and the reasons were generated afterwards for support. The elephant has leaned in some direction or another, and the rider functions as a lawyer and press secretary to defend the elephant's inclination.[129]

This view of the relationship between reason and our intuitions/emotions is not original. It's most famous spokesperson in philosophical circles is David Hume.

As reasoning is not the source, whence either disputant derives his tenets; it is in vain to expect, that any logic, which speaks not to the affections, will ever engage him to embrace sounder principles.[130]

To make matters potentially more frustrating, in its role as "Press Secretary," most riders tend to be somewhat lazy. Psychologist David Perkins describes a principle of evidence collection and evaluation as a "makes sense" rule. People take a position on some issue, then look for some evidence to support it. If they find

---

[125] Haidt, Jonathan. *The Righteous Mind. Why Good People are Divided by Politics and Religion.* Vintage Books: 2013, 54.

[126] ibid., 61.

[127] Haidt, Jonathan. "The Emotional Dog and its Rational Tail: a Social Intuitionist Approach to Moral Judgment." *Psychological Review,* volume 108 (4), 2001, 817.

[128] Note that while most of the examples and discussion of this model focus on moral and political arguments (as will be the case with our treatment of it as well), Haidt thinks that this

model of reasoning applies to all of our judgments, not just moral and political judgments.

[129] Haidt, *Happiness Hypothesis*, 21-22.

[130] Hume, David. *An Enquiry Concerning the Principles of Morals*, section I. Of the General Principles of Morals paragraph 133, in *Enquiries Concerning Human Understanding and Concerning the Principles of Morals.* Reprinted from the 1777 addition. Third edition. Edited by L.A. Selby-Bigge. Clarendon press: 1975.

enough evidence so that their position "makes sense," they stop thinking. They don't search for the *best* evidence, the most *conclusive* evidence, the most *objective* evidence, the most *verifiable* and *least controversial* evidence, but rather "just enough" evidence that their initial position "makes sense."

If one of our positions is challenged, we embark upon a cognitive mission to bring back evidence/reasons in support of our position. Because most of us are usually successful in this mission, we believe that we have been objective, and that our position is rationally justifiable.[131]

Unfortunately, we don't tend to extend this same assumption of objectivity to the people with whom we disagree. This assumption that our own reasoning is sincere and objective, while other people's reasoning is somehow flawed or unjustifiable, is known as "naïve realism."

> *Each of us thinks we see the world directly, as it really is. We further believe that the facts as we see them are there for all to see, therefore others should agree with us. If they don't agree, it follows either that they have not yet been exposed to the relevant facts or else that they are blinded by their interests and ideologies. People acknowledge that their own backgrounds have shaped their views, but such experiences are invariably seen as a deepening one's insights; but the background of other people is used to explain their biases and covert motivations;... It just seems plain as day, to the naïve realist, that everyone is influenced by ideology and self-interest. Except for me. I see things as they are.... My group is right because we see things as they are. Those who disagree are obviously biased by their religion, their ideology, or their self-interest.[132]*

In reality, according to Haidt, *all* of us are equally predisposed to judge first, and search for reasons later. Each one of us is prone to being biased in our judgments. Causes of biased judgments include "relatedness motives" and "coherence motives."

Relatedness motives involve our tendency to be more sympathetic to claims/evidence/etc. offered by people we like, and critical of those offered by people we don't like or don't trust.

> *From an evolutionary perspective, it would be strange if our moral judgment machinery was designed principally for accuracy, with no concern for the disastrous effects of periodically siding with our enemies and against our friends.[133]*

The other sort of motive, coherence motives, concerns our aversion to information or judgments that refute or contradict our self-image, worldview, or strongly held beliefs in general.

In addition to these biases, Haidt thinks that we are subject to a couple of related illusions. First, is what he calls the "Wag the dog" illusion. This is the belief that our moral judgment (dog) is driven by our moral reasoning (tail), when in fact it is the other way around.[134] Second, is what he calls the "wag-the-other-dog's-tail" illusion. That is the belief that if we successfully "refute" another person's arguments, it will cause them to change their mind with respect to a moral judgment.[135]

According to the social intuitionist model, our arguments (tail) come after we have already made our moral judgments (dog) based on our intuitions. Our arguments don't even cause our own moral judgments, let alone someone else's. When we offer arguments to refute the reasons given by someone else, is very unlikely that that will cause them to change their mind, since the reasons they offer were not the actual causes of their moral judgment to begin with!

---

[131] Haidt, *Happiness Hypothesis,* 65.
[132] ibid., 71.
[133] Haidt, "Emotional Dog," 821.

[134] ibid., 823.
[135] ibid.

Both sides present what it take to be excellent arguments in support of their positions. Both sides expect the other side to be responsive to such reasons (the wag the other dog's tail illusion). When the other side fails to be affected by such good reasons, each side concludes that the other side must be close minded or insincere.[136]

These biases and illusions, combined with our basic model according to which we have an intuitive reaction first, and then deploy reason not actually to gather evidence, but simply to justify to others what we have already concluded, makes truly objective reasoning both rare and difficult to achieve.

Haidt thinks that objective moral reasoning *is* possible in circumstances when the person has sufficient time and processing capacity, motivation to be accurate in their judgment, no pre-existing judgment to defend or justify, and when no coherence or relatedness motivations are triggered. In real life, this is rarely the case.

However, in real judgment situations, such as when people are gossiping or arguing, relatedness motives are always at work. If more shocking or threatening issues are being judged, such as abortion, euthanasia, or consensual incest, then coherence motives also will be at work. Under these more realistic circumstances, moral reasoning is not left free to search for truth but is likely to be hired out like a lawyer by various motives, employed only to seek confirmation of preordained conclusions.[137]

For example, imagine you are working on a math assignment, the results of which will contribute to your course grade, and you are allowed to work with a partner, and you and your partner are disagreeing about how to solve a math problem. You have a motivation to be accurate in your judgment, since your grade will be impacted. Let's assume that you are not

crunched for time, and have the luxury of spending a good chunk of the class session trying to figure out the answer. Let's also suppose that you are sufficiently rested, not overly distracted, etc. While your pride might provide some motivation for you to "stand your ground" and prove that your approach is the correct one, in this sort of scenario you are probably more motivated to get the answer correct so as to earn a good grade, rather than to win an argument. In this sort of scenario, you and your partner are probably capable of objective reasoning.

But now imagine that you are disagreeing with someone about a moral or political issue about which you care a lot. Suppose that your stance on this moral or political issue is somehow significantly tied to your sense of self, and your worldview (including your values). How realistic is it to think that you will be able to set all of those influences aside, and coolly and calmly evaluate the evidence like some sort of robot, and be perfectly fine with reversing your stance on some significant moral or political issue as a result?

Interestingly, the idea of working with a "partner" hints at one of the possible remedies for our own bias when it comes to reasoning. Individuals are not great at reasoning aimed at truth, but in an ideologically diverse group can correct *each other.*

In the same way, each individual reasoner is really good at one thing: finding evidence to support the position he or she already holds, usually for intuitive reasons. We should not expect individuals to produce good, open-minded, truth seeking reasoning, particularly when self-interest or reputational concerns are in play. But if you put individuals together in the right way, such that some individuals can use the reasoning powers to disconfirm the claims of others, and all individuals feel some common bond or shared fate that allows them to interact civilly, you can create a group that ends up producing good reasoning as an emergent property

---

[136] ibid.

[137] ibid., 822.

of the social system. This is why it's so important to have intellectual and ideological diversity within any group or institution whose goal is to find the truth (such as an intelligence agency or community of scientists) or to produce good public policy (such as a legislature or advisory board).[138]

Whether or not you think objective evaluation is likely will indicate whether you embrace a "rationalist model" of moral judgment, or an "intuitionist" model such as the one offered by Haidt. With respect to moral judgment, rationalist models envision people as judges who "weigh" considerations of harm and benefit, rights and justice and fairness (etc.), in order to "pass judgment" on some moral issue.[139]

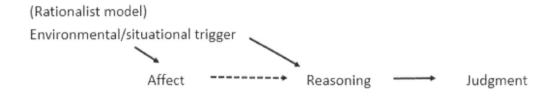

(Rationalist model)

Environmental/situational trigger

Affect ----------→ Reasoning ——→ Judgment

Intuitionist models claim that there are moral truths that are perceived, analogous to sense perception. Such approaches claim that our moral intuitions are triggered first, and then cause us to form moral judgments. A social intuitionist model adds a "social demand for

justification" to the intuitionist model. We still feel the initial intuitive "flash" of like/approval or dislike/aversion, but then reason is recruited like a lawyer (as opposed to a judge) to build a case that justifies our moral judgment to others.[140]

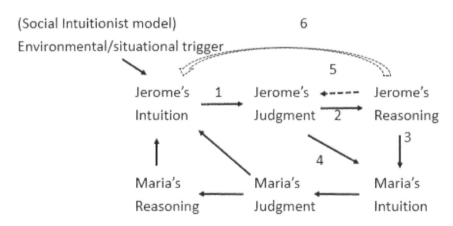

(Social Intuitionist model)   6

Environmental/situational trigger

                                                                                     5

Jerome's   1   Jerome's ←---- Jerome's
Intuition   →   Judgment   2 →   Reasoning

                                                                                     3

                                     4

Maria's   Maria's   Maria's
Reasoning ←   Judgment ←   Intuition

This model might seem a bit overwhelming at first glance, so we will break down each component. First, just like with a rationalist

model, there is some sort of "trigger." This just means that something happens. Using the model above, Jerome observes something, or someone

---

[138] Haidt, *Righteous Mind*, 105.
[139] Adapted from a table in "The Emotional Dog,"

815.
[140] "The Emotional Dog," 814 – 815.

tells Jerome something, or Jerome experiences something, etc. On the basis of Jerome's predispositions (ultimately grounded in his genetic inheritance and life experiences), he has an initial intuitive response that is most basically "positive" or "negative." Everything that follows originates or effects this initial intuitive response.

Link #1 in this model is known as the "intuitive judgment link." Jerome's judgment is an automatic and effortless result of his intuition in this case. Remember, for Haidt, judgment comes first in response to an intuition, and reasoning will come later. If, for example, Jerome is considering abortion, and experiences an intuitive aversion, his moral judgment will be something like "abortion is bad."

Link #2 is the "post hoc reasoning link." After the judgment has already been made, Jerome's "rider" will search for evidence and arguments to support the judgment (after the fact). Using the abortion example, Jerome might identify statistics suggesting a link between abortion and teen suicide, or cite the allegedly racist background of early abortion advocates like Margaret Sanger.[141]

Link #3 is the "reasoned persuasion link." Now we can begin to see the "social" aspect of the social intuitionist model. This link represents how Jerome's reasoning can itself be the "trigger" for someone else's (e.g., Maria's) intuition, which would then branch off into its own chain of intuition, then judgment, then reasoning, etc. If Jerome and Maria are discussing abortion, and he suggests that abortion in the United States has a racist origin, and disproportionately effects "fetuses of color," this might trigger an intuitive response (probably negative) in Maria.

Link #4 is the "social persuasion link." Here we have another example of how Jerome can influence Maria's intuitions, but in this case it is not by direct reasoning, such as the providing of arguments and evidence, but merely by virtue of Jerome having come to his judgment in the first place in such a way that Maria is aware of it. It is

simply a recognition that what other people think can influence our own intuitions, whether by peer pressure, modeling, conformity, or other subtle influences.

> *By seeking out discourse partners who are respected for their wisdom and open-mindedness, and by talking about the evidence, justifications, and mitigating factors involved in a potential moral violation, people can help trigger a variety of conflicting intuitions in each other. If more conflicting intuitions are triggered, the final judgment is likely to be more nuanced and ultimately more reasonable.[142]*

If Maria likes and respects Jerome, his judgment might inspire a "conforming" influence on Maria. If she dislikes and disrespects him, his judgment might well produce the opposite influence.

Link #5 is the "reasoned judgment link." This refers to the (rare?) direct influence of reason and logic on judgment, and includes our ability to override our intuitions. Haidt thinks that this link is not frequently activated, but he does acknowledge that it is possible in some cases for the "rider" to genuinely change the direction of the "elephant." Hypothetically, if Jerome encounters evidence that the alleged link between abortion and teen suicide is fallacious, because the same sort of stressful life experiences that can result in unintended pregnancy for teens can also cause depression (and lead to suicide),[143] and if he reads a compelling article that argues that the allegedly racist origins of the abortion movement are exaggerated or irrelevant, he might form a different intuition—although Haidt would probably think it more likely that he will just search for new evidence instead!

Link #6 is the "private reflection link." This link is also allegedly rarely activated, and represents the process of activating a new

---

[141] https://time.com/4081760/margaret-sanger-history-eugenics/
[142] "The Emotional Dog," 829.

[143] https://www.guttmacher.org/gpr/2006/08/abortion-and-mental-health-myths-and-realities

intuition by means of self-reflection. "Role taking" is an example of how Jerome might generate a new intuition (thereby triggering a new judgment, etc.). Anecdotally, I suspect most of us have had experiences where we felt a certain way about something initially, but then by imagining what it is like in "another person's shoes" we came to feel differently. Jerome might have an initial strongly negative intuition regarding abortion which produces unsympathetic moral judgments when it comes to the idea that women have a "right to choose." But then Jerome takes time and sincerely tries to imagine what it would be like to be a woman facing an unwanted pregnancy, or how we would feel if his sister, or girlfriend were in that situation, and as a result he becomes more sympathetic in his intuition becomes less negative.

For the sake of thoroughness, let's continue exploring this model with another example. Imagine that Jerome and Maria are arguing about the treatment of asylum seekers at the US/Mexico border. Maria thinks that refugees from Central and South American countries should be treated with compassion and respect, while Jerome thinks that immigration law should be enforced and the refugees should be turned away. Over the course of a heated discussion, both of them offer evidence for their position. Maria points out numerous facts concerning the political and economic circumstances of the countries from which the refugees come. Jerome offers a "slippery slope argument" against "open borders."

Not surprisingly, neither Maria nor Jerome seem to be persuaded by each other's arguments. The social intuitionist explanation for this is that arguments and evidence were never the primary cause of their moral judgments in the first place. For whatever reason, based on some combination of personal traits and social influences, Maria is triggered by the thought of the refugees suffering, and is moved to want to prevent harm. For other reasons, also presumably based on some combination of personal traits and social influences, Jerome is triggered by threats to "law and order," and is moved to preserve the integrity and safety of his

community. Each then searches for reasons in support of their respective judgments. When their evidence is attacked, they are more likely to sidestep to other supportive reasons, than to change their minds.

Does this mean that there is no scenario in which their minds might be changed? Not necessarily—but the strategy will likely have to involve triggering intuitions rather than providing compelling arguments.

For example, if Maria can demonstrate that some people that Jerome likes and respects are actually in favor of more compassionate treatment of the refugees, this might trigger a "relatedness motive" in Jerome and inspire him to have a new, more sympathetic, intuition. Or, perhaps Jerome could convince Maria to engage in some "role taking" in which she puts herself in the shoes of someone who has patiently filed for legal immigration, and is still awaiting entry into the United States, while numerous other people gain entry by "cutting in line." Perhaps this would trigger a "fairness" intuition in Maria, and cause her to be more sympathetic to rule following.

Note how often it is a "feeling" that is generating a judgment. Using this model, emotion has a more foundational role to play in moral judgment than does reason. Haidt is far from the first person to suggest this relationship. In fact, he openly acknowledges his debt to David Hume (once again) in this regard.

> *That Faculty, by which we discern Truth and Falshood, and that by which we perceive Vice and Virtue had long been confounded with each other, and all Morality was suppos'd to be built on eternal and immutable Relations, which to every intelligent Mind were equally invariable as any Proposition concerning Quantity or Number. But a late Philosopher has taught us, by the most convincing Arguments, that Morality is nothing in the abstract Nature of Things, but is entirely relative to the Sentiment or mental Taste of each particular Being; in the same Manner as the Distinctions of sweet and bitter, hot and cold, arise from*

the particular Feeling of each Sense or Organ. Moral Perceptions therefore, ought not to be clas'd with the Operations of the Understanding, but with the Tastes or Sentiments.[144]

As evidence of the important link between moral emotion and moral action, studies reveal that people who have abnormal or damaged ventromedial areas of the prefrontal cortex remain quite skilled at reasoning (including reasoning about moral issues) but have greatly diminished capacity for empathy or other morally relevant feelings. Such persons have a logical understanding of actions and consequences, but no emotional attachment to them. This pattern of emotional deficiency combined with intact reasoning is sometimes referred to as "acquired sociopathy" – intentionally invoking an analogy with psychopaths.

Patients with acquired sociopathy do not generally become moral monsters, perhaps because they have a lifetime of normal emotional learning and habit formation behind them. They do, however, become much less concerned with following social norms, and may sometimes show outrageous and antisocial behavior....[145]

Psychopaths are quite capable of reasoning, but lack the emotional capacity for empathy, compassion, and other related intuitions. Psychopaths can reason very effectively, and could presumably follow arguments demonstrating the moral wrongness of murder, but their emotional deficiency prevents them from experiencing the intuitive aversion to harming others, and literal murder results. Hume predicted this sort of outcome centuries ago, when he proposed that a judgment that something is morally wrong, if it is not accompanied by a corresponding *feeling*, will have no effect on behavior.

The end of all moral speculations is to teach us our duty; and, by proper representations of the deformity of vice and beauty of virtue, beget correspondent habits, and engage us to avoid the one, and embrace the other. But is this ever to be expected from inferences and conclusions of the understanding, of themselves have no hold of the affections nor set in motion the active powers of men? They discover truths: but where the truth this which they discover are indifferent, and beget no desire or aversion, they can have no influence on conduct and behavior. What is honorable, what is fair, but is becoming, what is noble, what is generous, takes possession of the heart and animates us to embrace and maintain it. What is intelligible, what is evident, what is probable, what is true, procures only the cool assent of the understanding; and gratifying a speculative curiosity, puts an end to our researches.

Extinguish all the warm feelings and pre-possessions in favor of virtue, and all disgust or aversion to vice: render men totally indifferent towards these distinctions; and morality is no longer a practical study, nor has any tendency to regulate our lives and actions.[146]

In contrast to psychopaths, young children (let alone infants!) couldn't possibly follow and appreciate moral arguments against violence, but because their emotional capacities are intact (unlike in the case of a psychopath) they still *feel* the aversion to harming others. In this way, babies show more moral capacity than adult

---

[144] Hume, David. *Enquiry Concerning Human Understanding*, SECTION I., Of the Different Species of Philosophy., Paragraph 14 originally ended with this note, which appeared only in the 1748 and 1750 editions., E 1.14na.

[145] "The Emotional Dog," 824.

[146] Hume, ibid., *Enquiries Concerning the Principles of Morals, 1.136.*

psychopaths. This fits nicely with the research of Paul Bloom, according to which infants as young as six months of age seem to display intuitive approval or disapproval based on behavior not only directed at them, but at other people. These intuitions are displayed long before the capacity of reasoning and language use manifest. Moral intuitions emerge very early, and appear to be necessary for moral development, but the ability to reason emerges much later in the child.[147]

This account of moral reasoning and judgment, including the role that emotion has to play in that process, is known as a "functionalist" definition of moral systems. As a functionalist definition, morality is being defined by what it *does* as opposed to specifying some specific content. This account, is *descriptive*, rather than *prescriptive*. Like any good philosopher (or, in this case, moral psychologist), Haidt carefully defines his terms before offering his argument.

- **Moral systems:** "interlocking sets of values, virtues, norms, practices, identities, institutions, technologies, and evolved psychological mechanisms that work together to suppress or regulate self-interest and make cooperative societies possible."[148]
- **Intuitions:** "judgments, solutions, and ideas that pop into consciousness without our being aware of the mental processes that lead to them."[149]
- **Moral intuitions:** "subclass of intuitions, in which feelings of approval or disapproval pop into awareness as we see or hear about something someone did, or as we consider choices for ourselves."[150] This is experienced as "the sudden appearance in consciousness of a moral

judgment, including an affective valence (good – bad, like – dislike), without any conscious awareness of having gone through steps of searching, weighing evidence, or inferring a conclusion."[151]
- **Moral judgments:** "evaluations (good versus bad) of the actions or character of a person that are made with respect to a set of virtues held to be obligatory by a culture or subculture."[152]

The most fundamental moral intuition is approval/disapproval towards certain patterns of events. Haidt initially proposes four universal patterns of intuition making use of this foundational approval/disapproval: suffering, hierarchy, reciprocity, and purity.[153] He later expands this into a system of five moral foundations that we will explore below.[154] Their "origin story" is that human beings faced a variety of universal adaptive challenges which, through natural selection, produced corresponding triggers, emotional responses, and virtues (subtly varying by culture).

Haidt's approach to moral psychology is based on an evolutionary understanding of the human mind and the moral judgments it evolved to make on the basis of general environmental challenges early humans experienced. Within the context of ethics, anytime evolution is mentioned, the classic issue of the problem of "selfishness" arises. After all, a caricature of natural selection is that it promotes the survival of the "fittest," and that organisms therefore are somehow hardwired to be selfish. In reality, every evolutionary ethicist whose work I am familiar with argues that it is much more complicated than that. Richard Dawkins offers an argument based upon his understanding of the "selfish

---

[147] Haidt, *The Righteous Mind*, 75.

[148] ibid., 314.

[149] Haidt, Jonathan and Joseph, Craig. "Intuitive Ethics: How Innately Prepared Intuitions Generate Culturally Variable Virtues." *Daedalus.* Fall (2004), 56.

[150] ibid.

[151] "The Emotional Dog," 818.

[152] ibid., 817.

[153] "Intuitive Ethics," 56.

[154] Actually, in his later work, he proposes a sixth foundation – but that foundation is more appropriate for our understanding of political judgment, and will not be considered for the purposes of this chapter.

gene," but offers several adaptations that nevertheless account for altruistic behavior. Haidt, likewise, acknowledges the power of self-interest, but also proposes that natural selection does not favor relentless and uncompromising self-interest.

> I do believe that you can understand most of moral psychology by viewing it as a form of enlightened self-interest, and if it self-interest, then it's easily explained by Darwinian natural selection working at the level of the individual. Genes are selfish, selfish genes create people with various mental modules, and some of these mental modules make us strategically altruistic, not reliably or universally altruistic. Our righteous minds were shaped by kin selection plus reciprocal altruism augmented by gossip and reputation management. . . . that portrait is incomplete. Yes, people are often selfish, and a great deal of our moral, political, and religious behavior can be understood as thinly veiled ways of pursuing self-interest. (Just look at the awful hypocrisy of so many politicians and religious leaders.) But it's also true that people are groupish. We love to join teams, clubs, leagues, and fraternities. We take on group identities and work shoulder to shoulder with strangers toward common goals so enthusiastically that it seems as if our minds were designed for teamwork.... Let me be more precise. When I say that human nature is selfish, I mean that our minds contain a variety of mental mechanisms that make us adept at promoting our own interests, in competition with their peers. When I say that human nature is also groupish, I mean that our minds contain a variety of mental mechanisms that make us adept at promoting our group's interests, in competition with other groups. We are not saints, but we are sometimes good team players.[155]

Haidt's <u>Third Principle of Moral Psychology</u> is that "morality binds and blinds." Natural selection works at *multiple* levels. At the individual level, we're mostly selfish because, at the individual level, in competition with other individuals, selfishness (along with strategic cooperation at times) is rewarded. But, groups also compete with other groups, and natural selection favors those groups who cooperate for the good of the group (even at the expense of the individual).[156]

> Darwin made the case for group selection, raised the principal objection to it, and then proposed a way around the objection: 'When two tribes of primeval man, living in the same country, came into competition, if (other circumstances being equal) the one tribe included a great number of courageous, sympathetic and faithful members, who were always ready to warn each other of danger, to aid and defend each other, this tribe would succeed better and conquer the other. ... The advantage which disciplined soldiers have over undisciplined hordes follows chiefly from the confidence which each man feels in his comrades .... Selfish and contentious people will not cohere, and without coherence nothing can be effected. A tribe rich in the above qualities would spread and be victorious over other tribes.'...
> But in the very next paragraph, Darwin raised the free rider problem, which is still the main objection raised against group selection: "... It is extremely doubtful whether the offspring of the more sympathetic and benevolent parents, or of those who were the most faithful to their comrades, would be reared in greater numbers than the children of selfish and treacherous parents belonging to the same tribe...."

---

[155] Haidt, *The Righteous Mind*, 220 – 221.

[156] ibid., 222.

When groups compete, the cohesive, cooperative group usually wins. But within each group, selfish individuals (free riders) come out ahead. They share in the group's gains while contributing little to its efforts. The bravest army wins, but within the bravest army, the few cowards who hang back are the most likely of all to survive the fight, go home alive, and become fathers...

Darwin proposed a series of 'probable steps' by which humans evolved to the point where there could be groups of team players in the first place.

The first step was the 'social instincts.' In ancient times, loners were more likely to get picked off by predators than were their more gregarious siblings, who felt a strong need to stay close to the group. The second step was reciprocity. People who helped others were more likely to get help when they needed it most.

But the most important "stimulus to the development of the social virtues" was the fact that people are passionately concerned with "the praise and blame of our fellow-men." Darwin, writing in Victorian England, shared Glaucon's view (from aristocratic Athens) that people are obsessed with their reputations. Darwin believed that the emotions that drive this obsession were acquired by natural selection acting at the individual level: those who lacked a sense of shame or a love of glory were less likely to attract friends and mates. Darwin also added a final step: the capacity to treat duties and principles as sacred, which he saw as part of our religious nature.[157]

Unrelenting and unfiltered pursuit of self-interest doesn't actually work out that well for social animals like human beings. As explained above, natural selection would actually favor individuals who pursue self-interest, but who are also capable of and willing to contribute to the survival of the group of which they are a part. The need for both individual and group survival generates multiple "challenges" for which different "solutions" evolved.

In my table below, adapted from a table created by Haidt, we have five foundational moral "modules" at the top of the columns.[158] For each, we can see the original adaptive challenge the module evolved to address, the original triggers that would activate the module (its proper domain), the current extended triggers (its actual domain), the typical emotional "output" produced by the module, and the culturally interpreted virtue associated with that proper emotional output.

---

[157] ibid., 222 – 225.

[158] Adapted from a table in ibid., 146.

Foundation:	Care/ harm	Fairness/ cheating	In group loyalty/ betrayal	Authority/ subversion	Sanctity/ Degradation
Adaptive challenge	Protect and care for children	Benefits of two-way partnerships	Cohesive coalitions; reap the benefits of group cooperation	Relationships within hierarchies, selectively defer to authority	Avoid microbes or parasites
Original triggers	Distress expressed by one's child	Cheating, cooperation, deception, food sharing	Threat or challenge to group	Signs of dominance and submission	Waste (feces, vomit), diseased people
Current triggers	Babies of nearly any species; "baby Yoda"	Faithfulness in relationships, broken or rigged games/machines	Sports teams, nations, ethnic groups, hobbyists	Bosses, respected professionals, political leaders, deities	Taboo ideas (socialism, racism)
Characteristic emotion	Compassion	Anger, gratitude, guilt	Group pride, anger at traitors	Respect/awe, fear/resentment	Disgust
Relevant virtues	Compassion, kindness	Fairness, justice, trustworthiness	Loyalty, patriotism, self-sacrifice	Obedience, deference, loyalty	Temperance, chastity, piety, cleanliness

To truly understand Haidt's description of moral judgment, we need to understand his vision of the mind, in general. His understanding of the mind is not his own unique theory, but rather draws upon the research of numerous other psychologists. A key feature of their understanding of the mind is that most of the mind is composed of hundreds or even thousands of "cognitive modules" that have been designed by means of natural selection to solve specific problems faced by our evolutionary ancestors long ago. An evolved cognitive module, such as

those appearing in each column of this table, is a "processing system that was designed to handle problems or opportunities that presented themselves for many generations in the ancestral environment of the species. Modules are little bits of input – output programming, ways of enabling fast and automatic responses to specific environmental triggers."[159]

These modules provide "programs" for the mind, somewhat analogous to "formulas" that one might create and use in an Excel spreadsheet. Given a certain sort of input, the module produces

---

[159] "Intuitive Ethics," 59 – 60.

a certain sort of output. As Haidt puts it, modules are "little bits of input – output programming, ways of enabling fast and automatic responses to specific environmental triggers."[160] This process was governed by mechanisms of evolutionary theory, most notably natural selection.

> *Human nature is a constellation of loosely organized modules, each designed by natural selection to solve a particular problem in adaptation that, in one way or another, can be traced back to survival and reproduction. Therefore, certain modules may have evolved to address the problem of finding a sexual mate; others may have evolved to assure that offspring are protected and nourished; still others may have evolved to detect cheating and social infractions. Among those adaptations that may distinguish human beings for most of the species are cognitive programs and potentials that enable them, for example, to plan attacks, forge alliances, adjudicate conflicts, predict the intentions of others, develop language, and (taken together) create culture.[161]*

Theoretically, there are a great many modules comprising the mind, addressing a great number of issues and challenges. Perhaps the simplest module to understand is one that addresses the appearance of suffering or distress in one's offspring. From an evolutionary perspective, primate mothers (such as humans) who are predisposed to respond when their infant showed distress (presumably because of hunger, fear, pain, etc.) were more likely to successfully raise their infants than those mothers who were not responsive to distress. The genes, or combination of genes, that resulted in the "offspring stress detection" module were therefore "selected for" by natural selection, and the module bred its way into the human population.

Like any module, the "offspring stress detection" module has a "proper domain," and an "actual domain." The proper domain is the set of scenarios, or the stimuli, that the module evolved to address in its original context. Originally, this module was meant to address indications of distress or fear in one's own child. The *actual* domain now includes many more triggers than that. Women (and men alike) can be triggered by indications of distress/fear in other people's children (including complete strangers, including children on television "on the other side of the world"), in nonhuman animals – especially their young, and even cartoon depictions of young creatures, or "lifelike" robots. Any of you who have ever gotten upset watching commercials raising funds for organizations like the Society for the Prevention of Cruelty to Animals (SPCA), or who have cried when a cartoon character died in a movie, can relate to how much this domain has been extended. In fact, Haidt refers to this module as a general "suffering/compassion" module, indicating that it is no longer aimed exclusively at responding to distress in one's own children.

The connection of this suffering/compassion module to morality might be obvious, at this point. We appear to be hardwired to respond to suffering with compassion and intervention, and the actual domain of this module has extended far beyond its original application so that it can include not just our own family, but complete strangers, and even members of other species. This foundation now (generally) has as its "input" indications of suffering or distress, and has compassion as its output, with a corresponding motivation to act so as to relieve the suffering. From this basic innate capacity, much of our moral framework develops. In addition, because early humans faced many more challenges than just crying babies, many other modules evolved as well—each responding to different problems.

> *The prolonged dependence characteristic of primates, especially humans, made it*

---

[160] ibid.
[161] McAdams, Dan P and Pals, Jennifer L. "A New Big Five. Fundamental Principles for an

Integrative Science of Personality." *American Psychologist,* volume 61 (3), April 2006, 206.

necessary, or at least beneficial, for mothers to detect signs of suffering and distress in her offspring. Mothers who are good at detecting such signals went on to rear more surviving offspring, and over time a communication system developed in which children's stylized distress signals triggered maternal aid. Psychological preparation for hierarchy evolved to help animals living in social groups make the most of the relative abilities to dominate others. Given the unequal distribution of strength, skill, and luck, those individuals who have the right emotional reactions to play along successfully and work their way up through the ranks did better than those who refuse to play a subordinate role or who failed to handle the perks of power gracefully. Similarly, a readiness for reciprocity evolved to help animals, particularly primates, reap the benefits of cooperating with non-kin. Individuals who felt bad when they cheated, and who are motivated to get revenge when they were cheated, were able to engage successfully in more non-zero-sum games with others.[162]

With respect to the fairness/reciprocity foundation, the idea is that certain emotions have evolved that help social organisms benefit from reciprocal altruism with non-kin. This generated interest in, and emotional reaction to, indicators of cheating and cooperation, and with the development of language, generated virtue and vice words related to fairness and reciprocity, and cultural constructs such as rights and justice.[163]

With respect to in-group loyalty, species (including humans) that aggregate into small communities find themselves in competition with other such communities. Natural selection would benefit those groups with individuals that were disposed to be loyal to their group, and to respond with service and loyalty in the event of conflict with other groups. Virtues would develop related to not only loyalty, but heroism and self-sacrifice, and the community would develop aversion to betrayal or free riders.[164]

With respect to dominance/hierarchy, mammals such as humans who are organized into hierarchical groups benefit from being "hardwired" in relation to authority and power. The ability to recognize and respect authority, show deference to those "above" you in the community, and to protect those "beneath" you in the community would be valuable and valued. Virtues concerned with respect and obedience would be developed and encouraged, along with the recognition of abuse of authority (with its many manifestations) as a vice.[165]

The purity module is perhaps the most difficult to understand, particularly in the United States where it does not receive as much emphasis (except, perhaps, in certain religious subcultures), and for that reason we will give it a bit more attention.

Based on our research and that of others, we propose the culturally widespread concerns with purity and pollution can be traced to a purity module evolved to deal with the adaptive challenges of life in a world full of dangerous microbes and parasites. The proper domain of the purity module is the set of things that were associated with these dangers in our evolutionary history, things like rotting corpses, excrement, and scavenger animals. Such things, and people who come into contact with them, trigger a fast, automatic feeling of disgust. Over time, this purity module and its affective output had been elaborated by many cultures into

---

[162] "Intuitive Ethics," 59.

[163] Haidt, Jonathan and Joseph, Craig. "The Moral Mind: How Five Sets of Innate Intuition's Guide the Development of Many Culture – Specific Virtues, and Perhaps even Modules." In P.

Carruthers, S. Lawrence, and S. Stitch (eds.) *The Innate Mind*, vol. 3. New York: Oxford, 2007, 383.

[164] ibid.

[165] ibid., 384

sets of rules, sometimes quite elaborate, regulating a great many bodily functions and practices, including diet and hygiene. Once norms were in place for such practices, violations of those norms produced negative affective flashes, that is, moral intuitions.[166]

For example, vomit is usually an indicator of illness – certainly something dangerous given that illness can spread, and that early humans had very little ability to treat or prevent illness. Even in the modern era, with very effective and sophisticated medical technology available to us, most of us are disgusted if someone is throwing up in our presence. That certainly doesn't mean that we can't (or don't) react with compassion, or that we can't override the disgust, but it's literally a common trope in comedies for one person vomiting to trigger retching and vomiting in other (healthy) people nearby – and I'm pretty confident that any of you would certainly experience an aversive reaction if someone turned towards you and vomited all over your face.

The purity foundation originated as a response to the threat of literal contaminants such as bacteria and disease, but through cultural influence expanded to metaphorically include other culturally specific "pollutants" as well. Initially, it was advantageous for organisms to be careful about what they introduced (literally) into their bodies. Culturally, this developed to include metaphorical "introductions" to the "body" of the community of "impure" or otherwise threatening influences. Virtues concerned with honoring the sacred, promoting temperance, or preserving chastity might develop alongside vices understood in terms of lust, intemperance, and indulgence of sin.[167]

To summarize:

- The Care/harm foundation evolved in response to the adaptive challenge of caring for vulnerable children. It makes us

sensitive to signs of suffering and need; it makes us despise cruelty and want to care for those who are suffering.

- The Fairness/cheating foundation evolved in response to the adaptive challenge of reaping the rewards of cooperation without getting exploited. It makes us sensitive to indications that another person is likely to be a good (or bad) partner for collaboration and reciprocal altruism. It makes us want to shun or punish cheaters.

- The Loyalty/betrayal foundation evolved in response to the adaptive challenge of forming and maintaining coalitions. It makes us sensitive to signs that another person is (or is not) a team player. It makes us trust and reward such people, and it makes us want to hurt, ostracize, or even kill those who betray us or our group.

- The Authority/subversion foundation evolved in response to the adaptive challenge of forging relationships that will benefit us within social hierarchies. It makes us sensitive to signs of rank or status, and to signs that other people are (or are not) behaving properly, given their position.

- The Sanctity/degradation foundation evolved initially in response to the adaptive challenge of the omnivore's dilemma, and then to the broader challenge of living in a world of pathogens and parasites. It includes the behavioral immune system, which can make us wary of a diverse array of symbolic objects and threats. It makes it possible for people to invest objects with irrational and extreme values - both positive and negative - which are important for binding groups together.[168]

One of the appealing features of this "five foundations" model is that it is consistent with the psychological "building blocks" that appear to

---

[166] "Intuitive Ethics," 60.
[167] "The Moral Mind," 384.

[168] The *Righteous Mind*, 178 – 179.

be present with other primates, such as chimpanzees. Additionally, the foundations fit with the "three ethics" hypothesis developed by Richard Shweder. Shweder is a cultural anthropologist who has proposed that cultures tend to exhibit one of three major ethical orientations: autonomy, community, or divinity.

The ethic of autonomy is based on the idea that people are, first and foremost, autonomous individuals with wants, needs, and preferences. People should be free to satisfy these wants, needs, and preferences as they see fit, and so societies develop moral concepts such as rights, liberty, and justice, which allow people to coexist peacefully without interfering too much in each other's projects. . . .

The ethic of community is based on the idea that people are, first and foremost, members of larger entities such as families, teams, armies, companies, tribes, and nations. These larger entities are more than the sum of the people who compose them; they are real, they matter, and they must be protected. People have an obligation to play their assigned roles in these entities. Many societies therefore develop moral concepts such as duty, hierarchy, respect, reputation, and patriotism. In such societies, the Western insistence that people should design their own lives and pursue their own goals seems selfish and dangerous-a sure way to weaken the social fabric and destroy the institutions and collective entities upon which everyone depends. . . .

The ethic of divinity is based on the idea that people are, first and foremost,

temporary vessels within which a divine soul has been implanted. People are not just animals with an extra serving of consciousness; they are children of God and should behave accordingly. The body is a temple, not a playground. Even if it does no harm and violates nobody's rights when a man has sex with a chicken carcass, he still shouldn't do it because it degrades him, dishonors his creator, and violates the sacred order of the universe. ...In such societies, the personal liberty of secular Western nations looks like libertinism, hedonism, and a celebration of humanity's baser instincts.[169]

These three "ethics" express different priorities and orientations of different cultures, but Haidt thinks they can each be explained by appealing to his foundations. The harm and fairness foundations lead to the ethic of autonomy, the in-group and authority foundations lead to the ethic of community, and the purity foundation leads to the ethic of divinity.[170]

The "three ethics" hypothesis and the "moral foundations" theory provide a fascinating intersection of anthropology, psychology, and philosophy, and might help to establish the existence of "universal" moral values while simultaneously allowing for and explaining the existence of sometimes significant cultural variation – the variation that inspires some people to embrace ethical relativism.

Haidt in contrast, insists that he is *not* an ethical relativist. In an endnote, he makes this quite clear. "I am not saying that all moral visions and ideologies are equally good, or equally effective at creating humane and morally ordered societies. I am not a relativist."[171]

So, how do we understand the existence of

---

[169] Haidt acknowledges that the ethic of divinity is "sometimes incompatible with compassion, egalitarianism, and basic human rights (*The Righteous Mind*, 124)."

[170] "The Moral Mind," 385.

[171] *The Righteous Mind*, 398, end note 28. Going

further, Haidt acknowledges that although many well-intentioned people praise diversity, in the context of morality, it is *incoherent* to claim to desire or prefer diversity. If, for example, you sincerely believe that abortion is "murder," you presumably desire that abortion be illegal. What

cultural differences while simultaneously claiming the existence of universal moral intuitions? By way of analogy, humans are capable of a range of sounds that is greater than that used by any existing language. Rather than make use of every existing phoneme, cultures "prune" and develop languages that use only a subset of the available sounds. Infants are born capable of distinguishing and producing all of these sounds, but over time and maturation this ability is focused on the particular subset of sounds used by the child's culture, and the ability to produce the other sounds is diminished. For example, a child born in the United States speaking and hearing only English could take courses in the Chinese language in College, and even move to China and become effectively "fluent" in a Chinese dialect. This person is unlikely to ever sound just like a native Chinese language speaker raised in China, who has spoken Chinese her entire life, however. A native speaker who is paying attention will probably always be able to detect "something" about the American's accent.

The cultural anthropologist Ruth Benedict claimed that there is something analogous for cultures with respect to traits, norms, virtues, etc. Human beings are capable of a range of moral intuitions greater than that which any culture can emphasize. In other words, no culture can value "everything" within a moral context *equally*. "A culture the capitalized even a considerable proportion of these would be as unintelligible as a language that used all the clicks, all the glottal stops, all the labials."[172]

Now consider the framework of ethics of autonomy, community, and divinity.

A child is born prepared to develop moral intuitions in all three ethics, but her local cultural environment generally stresses only one or two of the ethics. Intuitions within culturally supported ethics become sharper and more chronically accessible, whereas intuitions with an unsupported ethics become weaker and less accessible.[173]

How do we account for the obvious variation between cultures with respect to their values and prioritized virtues? *One* way to account for this is by acknowledging that different cultures make relative use of the fundamental modules. Some cultures, for example, especially more fundamentalist cultures, place a high value on purity, whereas the contemporary culture of the United States places very little emphasis on notions of purity (with notable and consistent exceptions for fundamentalist subcultures within the United States).

Another way to account for variation between cultures is to acknowledge that different cultures will interpret fundamental virtues in different ways. Loyalty will be appreciated in every culture, but how loyalty is recognized and encouraged will vary from one culture to the next, possibly corresponding to which fundamental modules are prioritized within a culture. Cultures that emphasize authority and hierarchy, for example, might interpret loyalty in terms of loyalty to those in position of authority, while a culture emphasizing purity might interpret loyalty in terms of loyalty to a deity or church. The virtue of "honor" might be interpreted in terms of sexual chastity in a purity culture, or "chivalry" in a hierarchical/patriarchal culture. "In each of these cases, different moral underpinnings provide the virtue with different eliciting conditions and different appropriate behaviors and responses."[174]

By way of analogy, the brain is like a book. The first draft of that book is written by our genes

---

would it mean to invite "diversity" on this matter? How can abortion be both legal and illegal? Can you possibly think that the views and values of "murderers" are equally valid as your own? As Haidt puts it, "if you prefer diversity on an issue, the issue is not a moral

issue for you; it is a matter of personal taste (*The Happiness Hypothesis*, 178)."
[172] Benedict, Ruth. *Patterns of Culture*. Boston: Houghton Mifflin, 1959, 24
[173] "The Emotional Dog," 827.
[174] "Intuitive Ethics," 64.

as we develop as a fetus. None of the chapters are complete, some are more developed than others, but none of the chapters are completely blank. Chapters address such topics as sexuality, language use, food, morality, and a great many other things.[175] Because each chapter is already initially structured, it is simply not the case that "anything goes" within them on the basis of experience and cultural influence. A culture could not edit a food chapter to make human beings consider dirt and pebbles a tasty treat, let alone a healthy diet. Cultures have to work within the parameters of the rough draft, and in the example of food that is going to include a built in set of taste receptors and a natural preference for sweet tastes. The particular kind of food that satisfies that "sweet tooth" might vary significantly by culture, though. One culture might favor fruit, while another favors processed candies – but no culture is going to satisfy the sweetness taste receptor with vinegar or a lemon. Or, to use a different analogy, playing off the taste example just provided, consider taste buds.

> *The five foundations are, to propose an analogy, the innate "taste buds" of the moral sense. The human tongue has five kinds of receptors, each of which translates a chemical pattern in a substance into an affective experience that is positive (for sweet, salt, and glutamate) or negative (for bitter and, beyond a certain level of intensity, for sour). These taste buds tell us something about how our ancestors lived: They ate fruit and meat, and had a variety of perceptual tools in their tongues (and noses and eyes) that meshed with conceptual tools in their brains to help guide them to fruit and meat. Similarly, the five foundations suggest some things about how our ancestors lived: They were ultrasocial creatures . . . finely tuned for (1) rearing children and helping kin, (2) selectively cooperating with non-kin while remaining vigilant for cheaters, (3)*

> *forming strong in-groups for the purpose of cross-group competition, (4) organizing themselves hierarchically, and (5) attending to each other's physical states, and altering interactions and contacts accordingly. The taste buds on the tongue gather perceptual information (about sugars, acids, etc.), whereas the taste buds of the moral sense respond to more abstract, conceptual patterns (such as cheating, disrespect, or treason). Nonetheless, in both cases, the output is an affectively valenced experience (like, dislike) that guides subsequent decisions about whether to approach or avoid the object/agent in question.[176]*

According to this theory, evolution prepared the human mind to be responsive to certain sorts of threats by building hardwired intuitive responses to triggers. For example, humans are born with a few hardwired fears, but we come prepared to acquire certain fears easily (e.g., of snakes, spiders, mice, open spaces), and cultures vary in the degree to which they reinforce or oppose such fears. A fear of snakes might come naturally to humans because as the human brain evolved over a tremendous span of time from earlier, more primitive, mammalian life, our "ancestors" might very well have been preyed upon by snakes. Early mammals developed a cognitive "module" involving wariness around snake-like things because it was beneficial in the context of natural selection, and some version of that module got passed along all the way down the evolutionary branches, including some version of it that exists within the human brain. This fear can be overridden, of course, given that some people keep snakes as pets, and within some cultures people are conditioned to be less fearful around snakes. What we have not been hard wired for, however, is a fear of lettuce.

Believe it or not (this is a true story!), many years ago I was having lunch with a couple of friends and their young son (approximately seven years old). He was a timid little boy in

---

[175] *The Righteous Mind*, 152 – 153.

[176] "The Moral Mind," 385.

general, but I was honestly dumbfounded when the server brought his food to the table and the boy cringed and started crying. His meal was chicken fingers with French fries served in a basket on a couple pieces of lettuce for garnishment. The boy said "I'm scared," and after several minutes of gentle questioning by his father, the boy pointed to the lettuce in the basket. As I continued to sit, amazed (but with a polite look of concern on my face), his father courageously plucked the lettuce from the basket, hid it under his own napkin, and assured the boy that he was safe now. At the risk of being insensitive: seriously? The boy's distress was certainly real. In other words, he wasn't "faking it"—but I very much believe that his distress was completely unwarranted. Setting aside a very sophisticated anxiety about food poisoning from improperly washed lettuce (which was not his concern, in case any of you are wondering), there is literally no rational basis for fearing lettuce whatsoever. His fear is not the result of innate intuition, but rather a misfiring of his "fear module" as a result of some sort of social conditioning, or chemical imbalance, or the like. As a reminder:

The righteous mind is like a tongue with six taste receptors. In this analogy, morality is like cuisine: it's a cultural construction, influenced by accidents of environment and history, but <u>not so flexible that anything goes</u>. You can't have a cuisine based on tree bark, nor can you have one based primarily on bitter tastes. Cuisines vary, but they all must please tongues equipped with the same five taste receptors. <u>Moral matrices vary, but they all must please righteous minds equipped with the same six social receptors</u>.[177]

Culture provides individuals with an extensive "menu" of stories about how to live. Individuals choose from what is available on the menu. Individual tastes vary, as will selections. Even after the meal arrives, individuals will continue to add their own "seasoning" to reach a flavor uniquely their own. Nevertheless, given that we are all allegedly operating from the same universal moral foundations, we should expect to see some significantly similar themes across cultures, and there does appear to be ample evidence of the existence of cross cultural moral intuitions.

> *It seems that in all human cultures, individuals often react with flashes of feeling linked to certain moral intuitions when they perceive certain events in their social worlds: when they see others (particularly young others) suffering, and others causing suffering; when they see others cheat or fail to repay favors; and when they see others who are disrespectful or who do not behave in a manner befitting their status in the group. With chimpanzees, these reactions occur mostly in the individual that is directly harmed. The hallmark of human morality is third-party concern: person A can get angry at person B for what she did to person C. In fact, people love to exercise their third-party moral intuitions so much that they pay money to see and hear stories about fictional strangers who do bad things to each other.*[178]

For any human, within any culture, a triggering event produces an intuitive "flash." This flash, combined with cultural learning, generates a moral judgment. These flashes are not virtues, but are necessary elements of virtue building. Even the creation of a "vice" arguably requires tapping into a different sort of intuition. For example, it is sadly obvious that human beings are capable of vicious acts of bigotry and violence seemingly in clear violation of what we would expect to be their "suffering/compassion" trigger. How can we explain how Nazis could participate in the mass murder of millions of people while *believing* that they were actually doing a morally good thing? A possible

---

[177] *The Righteous Mind*, 133. Emphasis added.

[178] "Intuitive Ethics," 58.

explanation is that either the "in-group" trigger or the "purity" trigger (or both) were employed to override the "suffering" trigger. It is widely documented how the Nazi party systematically attempted to "dehumanize" their enemies/targets – especially Jews. By portraying Jews as "vermin," the purity trigger could be utilized so as to generate an intuitive response of "disgust" within German citizens in general, and Nazi party members in particular. By portraying Jews as a "foreign threat" who are undermining German society, the in-group trigger could be utilized so as to generate suspicion and hatred of "them" and loyalty among non-Jewish Germans. I hope it's obvious that this was a possible explanation, and *not* a justification of Nazi beliefs and practices. It was intended solely as an example of how the social intuitionist model interprets the formation of moral judgments and associated virtues within a particular culture.

Of course, mature moral functioning does not consist merely in intuitive reactions to triggering events. Feeling nauseated when someone vomits in front of you might well be a manifestation of disgust prompted by a trigger of the "purity module," but merely feeling sick is not itself a moral judgment. Moral judgment also includes the acquisition and use of various moral concepts pertaining to actions, events, and traits (most notably, virtues and vices).

> *Virtues are social skills. To possess the virtue is to have extended and refined one's abilities to perceive morally relevant information so that one is fully responsive to the local sociomoral context, to be kind, for example, is to have a perceptual sensitivity to certain features or situations, including those having to do with the well-being of others, and for one's motivations to be appropriately shaped and affected. To be courageous is to have a different kind of sensitivity; to be patient, still*

another.[179]

Six general virtues, or families of related virtues, appear to be cross-cultural: wisdom, courage, humanity, justice, temperance, and transcendence. These virtues are admittedly vague, which is arguably their strength. Courage might manifest in any number of ways depending upon cultural conditions, but it is unlikely that you will find a culture that prefers cowardice.[180]

A virtuous *person* is one who "has the proper automatic reactions to ethically relevant events and states of affairs, for example, another person's suffering, an unfair distribution of a good, a dangerous but necessary mission."[181]

All of this talk of virtue might suggest that Haidt is building towards a system of virtue ethics, and that is partially correct—but with a disclaimer. Haidt stresses that his social intuitionist model is *descriptive*. That is, it describes how moral judgments are actually made, as opposed to how they *should* be made.[182] In his 2007 article, "The Moral Mind," Haidt claims that he is "not proposing that virtue ethics is the best normative moral theory."[183] He does, nevertheless, claim an affinity for virtue ethics, and suggests several reasons why virtue ethics aligns well with his understanding of moral psychology.

For one, virtue ethics recognizes that moral education is achieved by shaping emotions and intuitions more so than by developing strictly rational decision-making procedures. In addition, virtue approaches traditionally emphasize practice and habit acquisition rather than strict reasoning.[184]

Eventually, in a later work (*The Righteous Mind*), he actually does take a stab at "prescription," recommending some version of rule utilitarianism that aims to produce the greatest total good when it comes to legislation and public policy.[185] When it comes to moral guidance for individuals, however, Haidt *does*

---

[179] "The Moral Mind," 386.
[180] *The Happiness Hypothesis*, 167.
[181] "Intuitive Ethics," 61.
[182] "The Emotional Dog," 815.

[183] "The Moral Mind," 368.
[184] ibid.
[185] *The Righteous Mind*, 316 and end note #70 on page 441.

endorse virtue ethics.[186]

So, is morality innate, or socially constructed? Haidt says "both." Morality is innate by virtue of the fact that it arises from natural, biologically-based, evolution driven "modules." Morality is socially constructed by virtue of the fact that virtues are interpreted, modeled, and taught/trained within specific cultural contexts.

Is morality emotional, or rational? Haidt says "both." Morality is emotional because our moral judgments begin with an emotional response (most basically, "approval/disapproval") generated by an intuition. Morality is rational because we use reasoning to justify and defend our moral judgments (after the fact) that were produced by our intuitions in the first place – and because reason is involved in several of the "links" in the social intuitionist model."[187]

Keeping in mind that Haidt proposes that reason does not play the role most of us think it does with respect to moral or political judgment, it should not come as a surprise to discover that he thinks that most of us hold the *political* positions we do, and our party affiliations, not on the basis of logical arguments and compelling reasons, but rather because of our pre-existing intuitions. From where do these intuitions come? From the same basic sources as our moral intuitions: genetics and cultural conditioning.

> *Whether you end up on the right or the left of the political spectrum turns out to be just as heritable as most other traits: genetics explains between a third and a half of the variability among people on their political attitudes. Being raised in a liberal or conservative household accounts for much less.[188]*

This might seem to be a shocking claim. Whether you voted Democrat or Republican is a matter of genetics? Not exclusively, of course – not even according to Haidt. But, there does appear to be evidence that there are genetic

differences correlating with the political differences. One example of genetic differences between those who self-identify as liberal and those who self-identify as conservative involves genes related to the neurotransmitter dopamine, which is associated with openness to experience – strongly correlated with liberalism. As a result of genetic inheritance, some people have brains that are more or less reactive to threats, and more or less pleased by change and new experiences. Those are the two primary personality factors consistently found to distinguish liberal from conservative personalities.[189]

One's personality, of course, plays a significant role in one's political outlook. Haidt's favored theory of personality proposes that personality consists of three levels:

1. Dispositional traits
2. Characteristic adaptations
3. Life narratives[190]

Dispositional traits include the genetic components. This is the "first draft" of the brain. This first draft is not the final draft, as it undergoes an editing process. This is where characteristic adaptations come in. These are an individual's particular responses to specific environmental features and life events.

It might help to frame dispositional traits as the "nature" component and characteristic adaptations as the "nurture" component. While our genetics provide the first draft (dispositional traits), our childhood experiences, environmental and cultural influences, and the specific events in our lives (and how we respond to them) also supply a significant component to our eventual personality.

Finally, we have the contribution of "life narratives." These are the stories that we tell ourselves to make sense of our own lives and to give it coherence. Using a literary metaphor, we imagine our life as an unfolding story, and we supply various themes, metaphors, symbols, and

---

[186] ibid., end note #68 on page 441.
[187] "Intuitive Ethics," 64.
[188] *The Righteous Mind*, 324.

[189] ibid., 325.
[190] ibid., 325 – 328.

other "literary devices" that help us make sense of ourselves, and the story being told by our life. As an example, perhaps you see yourself as a poorly understood introvert, going through life according to your own standards, and not quite fitting in. Or perhaps you see yourself as the embodiment of the "American dream." It is with life narratives, especially, that cultures provide significant influence, as they will supply the larger pool of available themes, existing life "stories," and meaningful symbols from which an individual may choose.

This is to say that individuals select and appropriate in the making of narrative identity. They choose from competing stories, rejecting many others, and they modify the stories they choose to fit their own unique life, guided by the unique circumstances of their social, political, and economic worlds, by their family backgrounds and educational experiences, and by their dispositional traits and characteristic adaptations. A person constructs a narrative identity by appropriating stories from culture. Self and culture come to terms with each other through narrative."[191]

To summarize the three levels of personality:

1. Dispositional Traits
   a. Definition: broad individual differences in behavior, thought, and feeling that account for general consistencies across situations and over time.
   b. Function: sketch a behavioral "outline."
   c. Relations to culture: similar traits are found across many cultures, but cultures influence how these traits are expressed.
2. Characteristic Adaptations
   a. Definition: specific motivational, cognitive, social, and developmental variables contextualized by situation, and social roles which may change over the course of one's life. Examples include goals, values, coping strategies, relationship patterns, etc.
   b. Function: fill in the details of human individuality
   c. Relations to culture: cultures may differ with respect to their most valued goals, beliefs, and social strategies (e.g., individualism versus collectivism).
3. Integrative Life Narratives
   a. Definition: internalized life stories that integrate past, present, and an imagined future to provide a coherent and meaningful personal identity. Such life stories can change considerably over time, and differ with respect to themes, "tones," "plots," and other "literary devices."
   b. Function: provide meaning for a person's life within the context of their culture.
   c. Relations to culture: cultures provide a "menu" of stories for the individual to appropriate.[192]

This account of personality helps us to understand the particular intuitions an individual might experience, and the resulting judgments they might make. We can now turn to an expanded version of what *should* be a familiar chart to expand Haidt's account of moral judgment into the realm of politics, in an attempt to understand our political differences.[193]

---

[191] "The Big Five," 212.
[192] ibid., 212.
[193] Adapted from Haidt's original table, and integrated with the 6th module, *The Righteous Mind*, 200 – 201.

Foundation:	Care/ harm	Fairness/ cheating	In group loyalty/betrayal	Authority/ subversion	Sanctity/ degradation	Liberty/ Oppression
Adaptive challenge	Protect and care for children	Benefits of two-way partnerships	Cohesive coalitions; reap the benefits of group cooperation	Relationships within hierarchies, selectively defer to authority	Avoid microbes or parasites	Excessive dominance; illegitimate authority
Original triggers	Distress expressed by one's child	Cheating, cooperation, deception, food sharing	Threat or challenge to group	Signs of dominance and submission	Waste (feces, vomit), diseased people	Aggression, controlling behavior
Characteristic emotion	Compassion	Anger, gratitude, guilt	Group pride, anger at traitors	Respect/awe, fear/resentment	Disgust	Righteous anger, reactance
Relevant virtues	Compassion, kindness	Fairness, justice, trustworthiness	Loyalty, patriotism, self-sacrifice	Obedience, deference, loyalty	Temperance, chastity, piety, cleanliness	Courage, justice, independence

Haidt uses the very same moral foundations theory developed to understand the different sorts of moral judgments individuals and cultures favor to understand political differences as well. Basically, we can understand political differences as different responses to the same basic moral foundations. Consider the "fairness" foundation, for example.

"Everyone" cares about "fairness," but conservatives and liberals stereotypically experience and understand fairness in different ways. Liberals tend to understand fairness in terms of equality, while conservatives tend to understand fairness in terms of proportionality (i.e., that people get what they have earned, in proportion to what they have contributed, even though this rarely produces equal outcomes).[194]

Now consider the "authority" foundation. "Everyone" has some investment in "respect for authority," but what will trigger that foundation will vary across cultures and political ideologies. As an example of a possible "trigger" for the "authority foundation" in the United States, we can consider forms of address. There are probably generational differences here, but when I was a child it was considered shocking and presumptuous to refer to *any* adult by their first name. I referred to my parents by "mom" or "dad." Other adults were invariably "Mr. So-and-

so," "Mrs. So-and-so," or something equally suitable like "Coach So-and-so." There were some adults, including parents of other kids sometimes, that would ask me to call them by their first name, but it felt weird, and if I complied I was uncomfortable doing so. As an adult, and specifically as a professor who has earned a doctorate, I will confess that I cringe a little bit inside when a student refers to me as "Ted." To be fair, I honestly don't think that there has *ever* been an example of this where the student was *intending* to be disrespectful. Nevertheless, Haidt would say that my "authority foundation" is triggered by violations of respect for authority when my status in the social hierarchy as an "elder" (Mr.) professional (Professor) who has achieved a culturally respected educational accomplishment (Doctor) is implicitly challenged by the casual use of my first name instead.

What might we say about stereotypical liberals and progressives concerning authority triggers? I personally find that conservatives tend to associate authority with parents, and members of the military or law enforcement. "Disrespecting" one's parents by disobedience or defiance, members of the military by burning flags or "taking a knee" during the national anthem, or members of law enforcement by protesting police tactics or supporting

---

[194] ibid., 160 – 161.

organizations like Black Lives Matter, all seem to trigger aversive reactions from stereotypical conservatives, and all could theoretically be traced to issues of authority.

Stereotypical liberals place far less emphasis on respect for authority in general, and seem to be triggered less often and less easily. Because their worldview tends to be less hierarchical in its political and organizational structures, it is more difficult to trigger a strong reaction concerning authority – but a general aversion to being "disrespected" applies even in a relatively flat social structure.

The "sanctity foundation" is a bit more mysterious in the West compared to the other foundations, and especially so for liberals (which is part of the "problem" for the Democratic Party in the United States according to Haidt). Conservatives, and especially religious conservatives, are much more familiar and comfortable with talking about and valuing the "sacred." A pro-life conservative, for example, might claim that all life is "sacred" – and mean it. Conservatives might be opposed not only to the use of narcotics and alcohol, but even body modification such as tattoos and piercings, because of their belief that the body is a "temple."

Liberals, stereotypically, are not as adept with this vocabulary, and are sometimes even hostile to it, seeing it as language from oppressive religious systems. Even within liberal circles, however, we sometimes find sanctity language used in the context of environmental concerns (e.g., respecting "mother nature"), dietary concerns (e.g., insisting on organic, non-GMO foods), or preserving "safe spaces" free from the polluting and harmful presence of "hateful" language, symbols, or ideas.

The sixth foundation/module that did *not* appear in his original discussion of moral foundations is the liberty/oppression foundation. In the context of politics, the liberty/oppression foundation is triggered differently for conservatives and liberals. This foundation inspires liberals to zealously value and pursue equality, sometimes understood in terms of civil rights, human rights, or social justice. At the policy level, this can translate into higher taxes on the wealthy, comprehensive social safety nets, a guaranteed minimum wage, etc. For more conservative personalities, however, this foundation is triggered by the experience of "tyranny." It is usually not groups that embody tyranny, but the government itself, in the mind of conservatives. This might explain why they tend to favor "limited" government (at least in some respects), a "laissez-faire" economics system with few regulations, and rejection of globalism/multi-nationalism.[195]

Haidt provides a useful summary that not only addresses the foundations as they are experienced by both liberals and conservatives, but also indicates which foundations are more important for each.

> *The various moralities found on the political left tend to rest most strongly on the care/harm and liberty/oppression foundations. These two foundations support ideals of social justice, which emphasized compassion for the poor and a struggle for political equality among the subgroups the comprise society. Social justice movements emphasize solidarity – they call for people to come together to fight the oppression of bullying, domineering elites….*
>
> *Everyone – left, right, and center – cares about care/harm but liberals care more. Across many scales, surveys, and political controversies, liberals turn out to be more disturbed by signs of violence and suffering, compared to conservatives and especially to libertarians.*
>
> *Everyone – left, right, and center – cares about liberty/oppression, but each political faction cares in a different way. In the contemporary United States, liberals are most concerned about the rights of certain vulnerable groups (e.g., racial minorities, children, animals), and they look to government to defend the week*

---

[195] ibid., 204.

against oppression by the strong. Conservatives, in contrast, hold more traditional ideas of liberty as the right to be left alone, and they often resent liberal programs that use government to infringe on their liberties in order to protect groups that liberals care most about. For example, small business owners overwhelmingly support the Republican Party in part because they resent the government telling them how to run their businesses under its banner of protecting workers, minorities, consumers, and the environment. This helps explain why libertarians have sided with Republican Party in recent decades. Libertarians care about liberty almost to the exclusion of all other concerns, and their conception of liberty is the same as that of the Republicans: it is the right to be left alone, free from government interference.

The fairness/cheating foundation is about proportionality and the law of karma. It is about making sure that people get what they deserve, and do not get things they do not deserve. Everyone – left, right, and center – cares about proportionality; everyone gets angry when people take more than they deserve. But conservatives care more, and they rely on the fairness foundation more heavily – once fairness is restricted to proportionality....

The remaining three foundations – loyalty/betrayal, authority/subversion, and sanctity/degradation – show the biggest and most consistent partisan differences. Liberals are ambivalent about these foundations at best, whereas social conservatives embrace them. (Libertarians have little use for them, which is why they tend to support liberal positions on social issues such as gay marriage, drug use, and laws to "protect" the American flag.)...

Liberals have a three-foundation morality,

whereas conservatives use all six. Liberal moral matrices rest on the care/harm, liberty/oppression, and fairness/cheating foundations, although liberals are often willing to trade away fairness (as proportionality) when it conflicts with compassion or with their desire to fight oppression. Conservative morality rests on all six foundations, although conservatives are more willing than liberals to sacrifice care and let some people get hurt in order to achieve their many other moral objectives.[196]

To summarize his analysis of the relative importance of the different foundations, we may say the following of the three major political orientations in the United States:

- Libertarian[197]
    - most "sacred" value: individual liberty
    - most significant foundation: liberty/oppression
    - less significant foundation: fairness/cheating
    - least significant foundations: care/harm, loyalty/betrayal, authority/subversion, sanctity/degradation
- Liberal[198]
    - most "sacred" value: care for victims of oppression
    - most significant foundation: care/harm
    - less significant foundations: liberty/oppression, fairness/cheating
    - least significant foundations: loyalty/betrayal, authority/subversion, sanctity/degradation
- Conservative[199]
    - most "sacred" value: preserve the institutions and traditions that sustain a moral community

---

[196] ibid., 211 – 214.
[197] ibid., 352.

[198] ibid., 351.
[199] ibid., 357.

- most significant foundations: care/harm, liberty/oppression, fairness/cheating, loyalty/betrayal, authority/subversion, sanctity/degradation

To say that a foundation is "less significant" or even "least significant" certainly does not mean that it has no significance whatsoever. Haidt is not claiming that libertarians don't care about issues of care/harm. Instead, he's claiming that the most significant (and likely to be triggered) moral foundation for someone who self-identifies as a libertarian is liberty/oppression. Other foundations are experienced as less significant, and therefore less likely to generate a response. No one is claiming that libertarians are somehow lacking in compassion and literally don't care if people are homeless, but in terms of their political positions and the policies that they tend to support, they are not very likely to support government intervention to help homeless people (because they don't believe that is a proper function for the government), but they are very much likely to support policies that preserve and protect civil liberties.

According to Haidt, liberals place comparatively lesser value on loyalty/betrayal, but this certainly doesn't mean that they place no value on loyalty, including the patriotic variety. Instead, it means that a stereotypical liberal is much more likely to be animated by "social justice" issues understood through the lens of care/harm, or, to a slightly lesser extent, through the lens of liberty/oppression or fairness/cheating, than to be animated by appeals to nationalism.

Recalling our previous (brief) discussion of life narratives, Haidt offers a general "Liberal progress" narrative that he thinks informs the personal life narrative of many self-identified liberals.

Once upon a time, the vast majority of human persons suffered in societies and social institutions that were unjust, unhealthy, repressive, and oppressive. These traditional societies were reprehensible because of their deep-rooted inequality, exploitation, and irrational traditionalism .... But the noble human aspiration for autonomy, equality, and prosperity struggled mightily against the forces of misery and oppression, and eventually succeeded in establishing modern, liberal, democratic, capitalist, welfare societies. While modern social conditions hold the potential to maximize the individual freedom and pleasure of all, there is much work to be done to dismantle the powerful vestiges of inequality, exploitation, and repression. This struggle for the good society in which individuals are equal and free to pursue their self-defined happiness is the one mission truly worth dedicating one's life to achieving."[200]

Using moral foundations theory, Haidt recognizes the care/harm foundation primarily, the liberty/oppression foundation (as both freedom from oppression and freedom to pursue happiness as one defines it), and fairness as political equality. Authority is mentioned only in a negative sense, and there is no mention of either loyalty or sanctity.[201]

Haidt's interpretation of conservatives perhaps requires the most explanation, given that he suggests that they value each foundation equally. This indicates that stereotypical conservatives can be triggered by *any* of the foundations, and have political views corresponding to each, including the lesser-used-in-the-West sanctity/degradation foundation. The conservative narrative will, not surprisingly, be quite different.

Once upon a time, America was a shining beacon. Then liberals came along and erected an enormous federal bureaucracy that handcuffed the invisible hand of the

---

[200] Christian Smith, as quoted in ibid., 331.

[201] ibid., 331 – 332.

free market. They subverted our traditional American values and opposed God and faith at every step of the way .... Instead of requiring that people work for a living, they siphoned money from hardworking Americans and gave it to Cadillac-driving drug addicts and welfare queens. Instead of punishing criminals, they tried to "understand" them. Instead of worrying about the victims of crime, they worried about the rights of criminals .... Instead of adhering to traditional American values of family, fidelity, and personal responsibility, they preached promiscuity, premarital sex, and the gay lifestyle ... and they encouraged a feminist agenda that undermined traditional family roles .... Instead of projecting strength to those who would do evil around the world, they cut military budgets, disrespected our soldiers in uniform, burned our flag, and chose negotiation and multilateralism .... Then Americans decided to take their country back from those who sought to undermine it.[202]

With respect to the moral foundations, Haidt recognizes the presence of liberty (understood as freedom from government constraint), fairness (understood as proportionality, namely, not taking money from hard workers and getting it to "welfare queens"), loyalty (to the flag and military), authority (with respect to the undermining of family and tradition), and sanctity (replacing devotion to God with celebrating promiscuous and "deviant" sexual behavior). Care, so central for the liberal narrative, was only mentioned for victims of crime.[203]

This is an important observation: not only will different political orientations emphasize different foundations, but they will interpret the *same* foundations (e.g. care/harm) in different ways, with liberals (for example) focusing on the care and protection of vulnerable populations (e.g., ethnic minorities, the LGBTQ+ community, people with disabilities, etc.), and conservatives (for example) focusing on the care and protection of victims (and possible victims) of crime.

Conclusion

We have now come to the end of our brief exploration of Haidt's social intuitionist theory of moral judgment, in which he proposes that humans have evolved to experience intuitive/emotional responses to various triggers of their hard wired modules/foundations, and then employ reason only after the fact to justify that intuitive reaction to oneself and others.

If moral judgment is driven by emotions/intuition, and if our elephant's "rider," by its very nature, acts more like a lawyer doggedly defending its case than a judge impartially evaluating evidence, what hope do we have to find common ground when we disagree with others on moral issues? Haidt proposes a couple of practical steps by which we might better get along.

First, we should recognize that all parties to the "debate" are morally motivated. In other words, everyone thinks that they are "right" and everyone thinks that they have good reasons for staking out the position that they do. By recognizing that people on the "other side" are not necessarily immoral, but are *similarly* moral – despite emphasizing different moral foundations—we might be better equipped to understand one another, and even to find some "common ground." Speaking of himself and his liberal colleagues, Haidt confesses:

> *We supported liberal policies because we saw the world clearly and wanted to help people, but they supported conservative policies out of pure self-interest (lower my taxes!) or thinly veiled racism (stop funding welfare programs for minorities!). We never considered the possibility that there were alternative moral worlds in which reducing harm (by helping victims) and increasing fairness (by pursuing group*

---

[202] Christian Smith, as quoted in ibid., 332 – 333.

[203] ibid., 333.

based equality) were not the main goals. And if we could not imagine other moralities, then we could not believe the conservatives were as sincere in their moral beliefs as we were in hours.[204]

Another step he proposes to encourage common ground is to try to frame your position on a moral issue using language that can appeal to a new "trigger" for people who disagree. As an example, if I am involved in an argument with someone about the moral status of same-sex relationships, and whether same-sex relationships should be legally recognized through marriage, and *my* position is that same-sex relationships are morally justified, and that same-sex couples *should* be allowed to benefit from a legal recognition of marriage, and my "conversation partner" disagrees, it might be helpful to frame my position in ways to which my "conversation partner" might be sympathetic.

If he thinks that same-sex relationships are "gross," then it appears that his purity module is being triggered in a way that mine is not. His elephant is leaning away from "same-sex relationships" and his rider will try its best to come up with justifications for that. I could try to convince him that there isn't anything "gross" about same-sex couples, but a more effective strategy might be to shift his attention to a different module and elicit a new intuition.

Perhaps I could point out the real life occurrence of suffering experienced by people in same-sex relationships (prior to the extension of marriage rights nationwide), not merely because their relationship didn't have the same social/legal recognition, but because of the practical consequences of not having that legal recognition, such as not having automatic custody of children in the event that their biological parent dies, or not having access to hospital rooms or medical decision-making authority in the event of a health crisis, or numerous other such differences. Or, perhaps I could try to demonstrate that there is something unfair about consenting adults in heterosexual relationships having a legal right (with numerous benefits) if consenting adults in homosexual relationships do not, thereby triggering his reciprocity module.[205]

In any event, thinking that "they" are just ignorant or immoral is unhelpful, and, if Haidt is correct about how moral and political reasoning really occurs, neither accurate nor charitable as well.

Critical Analysis

1. In your opinion, what are the strongest and most compelling points made by the philosopher or philosophers in this chapter? Why do you find those points to be convincing?

2. In your opinion, what are the weakest or least convincing points? Why? Can you anticipate any limitations or objections to their ideas not already addressed in the chapter?

Appendix: Application to Social Justice

This chapter focuses far less on what justice *is* than on how people *form their beliefs* about justice, and *respond* to arguments and claims concerning justice. I have addressed Jonathan Haidt's particular views on social justice in the appendix to the chapter on "safe spaces," as well as (briefly) in the introduction to this text, so I will not address that issue here. Instead, I address the theme of "strategy."

Presumably, social justice activists not only want to be correct in their views, but *effective* in their advocacy. While there is certainly something valuable about being "right," it is arguably even better to be both "right" *and* to achieve your social justice goals.

If Haidt is correct, and most people don't come to conclusions concerning moral and political claims, including justice claims, on the basis of arguments and evidence, but instead on the basis of their emotions and moral intuitions, then the "winning" strategy for activists will take

---

[204] ibid., 126.

[205] ibid., 65.

that into consideration. Rather than confronting "the other side" with refutation, counter arguments, and data, one might be better served by attempting to find common emotional ground. As just one example, consider calls to "defund the police."

It is both uncharitable and inaccurate (most of the time) to think that people who are opposed to police reforms are opposed simply because they are racist, and are indifferent (or worse) to the systemic racism we find in the criminal justice system. Instead, if Haidt is correct, it is much more likely that their opposition stems from their own experiences and the moral intuitions derived from them. In such a case, accusing them of racism will not only not change their minds, but will almost certainly *harden* their opposition. Even presenting them with data on the disparate outcomes experienced by people of color within the criminal justice system might be ineffective because that strategy presupposes that their conclusion ("police reform is not a good idea") was based upon their evaluation of premises, including data about the criminal justice system.

For more likely, according to Haidt, is that they have a generally positive disposition towards law enforcement. Presumably, they have not had negative experiences with the police, or at the very least have not had racialized negative experiences with the police. This will not be surprising if they are white. They might generally regard the police as heroes and "the good guys" who protect us from "the bad guys." Simply telling them that their heroes are actually villains, and that they are racists if they don't see it that way, is unlikely to change their perspective, to say the least.

What might be more effective? On the assumption that they are conservative, try to tap into their favored moral foundations and/or try to engage the "conservative narrative." According to the conservative narrative, liberals undermine our safety and quality of life by worrying more about criminals than about the victims of crime. It might be productive, therefore, to try to frame police reform in terms of protecting the rights of *innocent* persons. There is ample evidence that police suspect people of color of criminal activity not only at higher rates than white people, but at higher rates than would be proportionate to actual criminal activity by race.

One of the more important moral foundations for conservatives is the liberty/oppression foundation, as well as the fairness/cheating foundation. While liberals might be more motivated by pointing out the "harm" experienced by people of color at the hands of police, conservatives might be more motivated by demonstrating that the liberty of such persons is being diminished by an oppressive police policy, and that fairness is being violated when people of color are disproportionately targeted by police. If conservatives "hold more traditional ideas of liberty as the right to be left alone, and they often resent liberal programs that use government to infringe on their liberties," one might think that their liberty/oppression foundation might be triggered by pointing out how "stop and frisk" policies unquestionably violate the "right to be left alone," and is most certainly a case of the government infringing upon liberties!

The fact that such treatment, and such policies, are evidence of systemic racism might well be true, but, true or not, framing objections to the policy in that way is probably far less likely to be persuasive to conservatives than framing it in terms of violations of liberty.

Chapter 8: Family Models of Politics & Justice

Comprehension questions you should be able to answer after reading this chapter:

1. What is a "conceptual metaphor?"
2. Explain the "strict father" model. What are its main features and assumptions? Be sure to discuss "folk behaviorism," reward and punishment, moral strength, self-discipline, competition, self-interest, and internal and external evils.
3. Explain the "nurturant parent" model. What are its main features and assumptions? Be sure to discuss empathy, attachment, self-care, internal and external evils, and emotional maturity.
4. Using the example of federal student loans, compare and contrast conservative and liberal positions using their respective family models.
5. Describe conservative model citizens, and "demons." Do the same for liberal model citizens and "demons."

Many of the chapters in this book are attempts to describe the philosophical foundations of various political theories, including different visions of the State, the origin and purpose of the State, different visions of human nature, the scope and limit of laws, the nature of law itself, the value (and limits) of tolerance and pluralism, and different conceptions of justice, among other things.

This historical survey, I hope, is interesting—but is it useful? What if contemporary politicians and voters alike do not employ such rational, "philosophical" approaches to political decision-making? What if politics has been divorced from philosophy?

George Lakoff (born May 24th, 1941) is not a philosopher, but rather a "cognitive linguist." He has been a professor of linguistics at U.C. Berkeley since 1972.

I am not a political philosopher and did not begin with any philosophical presuppositions about what I would find. Nor did I use either the intellectual tools or forms of reasoning of political philosophers. These results emerged from empirical study using the tools of a cognitive scientist to study political worldviews. As empirical findings, they have a very different status than theoretical speculations, and so should not be confused with political philosophy—for which, incidentally, I have great respect.[206]

Lakoff was initially motivated by his own personal confusion, his recognition that he literally did not understand why conservatives supported the positions they did. At first glance, liberal and conservative policy stances might seem unusual, or even contradictory, from the outside. Conservatives, after all, tend to be very much opposed to abortion, and yet are also opposed to government programs to provide prenatal care to low-income mothers—programs proven to reduce infant mortality rates. How does this make sense? How can a conservative be so dedicated to the value of the fetus in the womb, but not support government programs that would actually increase the chance of that fetus surviving? And why would they be opposed to government programs that protect and provide for those fetuses after they are born?

On the other hand, how can liberals be in favor of the right to abortion (which kills "children"), but then turn around and support welfare and other government programs that benefit children? Do liberals love children, or think they should be killed? Which is it? How can

---

[206] Lakoff, George. *Moral Politics, How Liberals and Conservatives Think.* University of Chicago Press, 2002: 21-22.

liberals be in favor of government spending on AIDS research and prevention, but then be in favor of things like needle exchange programs (which could be seen as implicitly accepting behavior that increases risk of spreading HIV), as well as condoning the homosexual "lifestyle" which is associated with the spread of HIV in the first place?

Conservatives claim to be in favor of cutting spending and for small government, but then want to increase military spending, and use the government to interfere with people's sex lives. Liberals claim to be for equal opportunity, but then support "reverse discrimination" practices like affirmative action. How can these seemingly inconsistent positions (on both sides) be reconciled?

To account for these seeming contradictions, he develops a view that our political decision-making is not guided by philosophical ideals and arguments, but by *metaphors*. A "conceptual metaphor," to be specific, is "a correspondence between concepts across conceptual domains, allowing forms of reasoning and words from one domain . . . to be used in the other."[207] Metaphors, by definition, are figures of speech in which a word or phrase is applied to an object or action to which it is not literally applicable; a thing regarded as representative or symbolic of something else, especially something abstract. This latter part of the definition is most applicable for what Lakoff has in mind.

When it comes to politics, Lakoff argues that that both "conservatives" and "liberals" experience, understand, and act on political issues by virtue of how they are "framed" as metaphors—with conservatives and liberals employing different metaphors (or at least interpreting the metaphors in importantly different ways).

A non-political example that should be quite familiar to philosophers and students of philosophy is the metaphor of argument as "war" or combat. I have often referred to philosophy conferences as "philosophical blood sport"—and I did not intend the metaphor to be positive.

Arguments are usually seen as a "zero sum" contest, in which one person "wins," and the other, necessarily, "loses." You "defend" your argument, and "attack" others'. We speak of criticisms that are "on target" as opposed to those that "miss the mark." If you search YouTube for footage of debates (especially those between atheists and theists), you can find such video titles as "Professor Lawrence Krauss, Atheist, destroys idiotic Muslim in debate." Arguments are "shot down," "defeated," and "destroyed."

While it's possible that this is all just hyperbole used to express excitement, Lakoff claims that the metaphors we use color the way we experience and interpret things. When it comes to contemporary American politics, Lakoff claims that both liberals and conservatives employ the same basic, central metaphor: the political community as family. However, their respective models of the family are strikingly different, thereby causing liberals and conservatives to interpret political issues in very different ways, and causing them to offer very different solutions to the same "problems."

According to Lakoff's analysis, conservatives employ what he calls a "strict father" model of the family.

The Strict Father Model

A traditional nuclear family with the father having primary responsibility for the well-being of the household. The mother has day-to-day responsibility for the care of the house and details of raising the children. But the father has primary responsibility for setting overall family policy, and the mother's job is to be supportive of the father and to help carry out the father's views on what should be done. Ideally, she respects his views and supports them.

Life is seen as fundamentally difficult and the world as fundamentally dangerous. Evil is conceptualized as a force in the world, and it is the father's job to support

---

[207] ibid., 63.

his family and protect it from evils -- both external and internal. External evils include enemies, hardships, and temptations. Internal evils come in the form of uncontrolled desires and are as threatening as external ones. The father embodies the values needed to make one's way in the world and to support a family: he is morally strong, self-disciplined, frugal, temperate, and restrained. He sets an example by holding himself to high standards. He insists on his moral authority, commands obedience, and when he doesn't get it, metes out retribution as fairly and justly as he knows how. It is his job to protect and support his family, and he believes that safety comes out of strength.

In addition to support and protection, the father's primary duty is tell his children what is right and wrong, punish them when they do wrong, and to bring them up to be self-disciplined and self-reliant. Through self-denial, the children can build strength against internal evils. In this way, he teaches his children to be self-disciplined, industrious, polite, trustworthy, and respectful of authority.

The strict father provides nurturance and expresses his devotion to his family by supporting and protecting them, but just as importantly by setting and enforcing strict moral bounds and by inculcating self-discipline and self-reliance through hard work and self-denial. This builds character. For the strict father, strictness is a form of nurturance and love -- tough love.

The strict father is restrained in showing affection and emotion overtly, and prefers the appearance of strength and calm. He gives to charity as an expression of

compassion for those less fortunate than he and as an expression of gratitude for his own good fortune.

Once his children are grown -- once they have become self-disciplined and self-reliant -- they are on their own and must succeed or fail by themselves; he does not meddle in their lives, just as he doesn't want any external authority meddling in his life.[208]

Let's work through this description, one important piece at a time. First, the very name of the model is important: strict *father*. This is a gendered model, with males being in charge. This model of the family is the "traditional" (patriarchal, hetero-normative) model, with one male and one female, in which the male is the head of the household. The mother has an important role to play as well, of course, but hers is a support role, whereas his is a leadership role.

With leadership comes responsibility. The primary responsibility of the father is to protect and provide for his family—and this is necessary because the world is seen as a dangerous, competitive place with limited resources. Evil is a real force in the universe, and not merely a matter of "misunderstanding" or different perspectives. Given this binary view of good and evil, the world is filled with genuine threats. Some of them are external threats, such as criminals (thieves, rapists, murderers, pedophiles, terrorists, etc.), but other threats are internal: primarily uncontrolled desires and moral weakness.

In order to defend against internal and external threats alike, the father (and mother) must be "strong," and he must teach and train his children to be strong as well, so that they can resist evil and defend their own families when they are adults. Some of this teaching might be literally instructional, such as talking to children about morality and character, but this instruction is primarily in the form of discipline and punishment. Children must learn to obey the

---

[208] Lakoff, George. "Metaphor, Morality, and Politics, Or, Why Conservatives Have Left Liberals in the Dust." 1995. *Social Research* 62(3):177-213

(just) commands of their parents (primarily their father), not only because the commands are issued for a good reason, but also because obedience is itself a necessary trait to acquire in life.

When children disobey, and behave badly, they must be punished so they learn that there are negative consequences for undesirable behavior, and so that they will be trained to behave differently in the future. This punishment is for their own good. Over time, they will internalize the discipline, gain control over themselves, and be able to act properly without the threat of punishment—but it is naïve to think that this will happen all on its own, in the absence of consistent discipline and punishment for violating the rules. It is only by acquiring self-discipline that children can become strong enough to resist "internal" threats as adults.

Once the children have grown, they are adults responsible for their own behavior. The parents will still love them, but will not meddle in their lives, as it is no longer their place to do so. Grown children can be prepared for the challenges of adult life, but they must be allowed to sink, or swim, on their own.

Strict Father Politics

Using Lakoff's interpretation of these family metaphors, he proposes that conservative politics can be understood in terms of the following moral categories:

1. Promoting Strict Father morality in general.
2. Promoting self-discipline, responsibility, and self-reliance.
3. Upholding the Morality of Reward and Punishment
4. Protecting moral people from external evils.
5. Upholding the Moral Order.

First, there is the promotion of the strict father moral worldview, in general. This includes the promotion and reinforcement of metaphors of moral strength, moral boundaries, and moral authority. Remember: the distinction between good and evil is real, grounded in reality, and corresponding to genuine evil (and goodness). It is imperative that one be strong enough to resist and defeat evil. Strict moral boundaries must be maintained, so that evil (people, or ideas) can't infiltrate the community (or mind) and undermine it from within. Just as criminals or terrorists might sneak in through a crack in the defenses, so too can moral weakness creep into one's character by a lapse of self-discipline. For these reasons, the moral rules that identify what is morally right and wrong must be respected and obeyed, and those in authority, whose job it is to teach and enforce these rules, should be obeyed as well.

Not surprisingly, there is an authoritarian strain in strict father politics, and authority figures command respect—as do those who literally protect us from danger, such as the military and police. The strict father model recognizes and reveres legitimate moral authority—but resents illegitimate authority as "meddling." Fathers know what's best for their own families, and don't need the "nanny state" meddling in their homes and interfering, as if the government knows better. By extension, local authorities know better how to deal with local issues (than does the Federal government)—which helps to explain conservatives' emphasis on "State's Rights."

Second, there is the promotion of self-discipline, personal responsibility, and self-reliance. All of these qualities require (and show) moral strength. Only those who are self-disciplined will be strong enough to resist temptations, and be responsible adult citizens. By taking responsibility for one's actions and one's life, the citizen becomes self-reliant, and capable of surviving and succeeding in the dangerous, competitive world. Any actions that promote and reinforce personal responsibility and self-reliance, then, will fit with this model, while those that seem to undermine those qualities will be opposed.

Thirdly, and relatedly, there is the upholding of the morality of reward and punishment. According to the strict father model, all people are governed by "folk behaviorism"—which is just to say that we act for the sake of obtaining rewards and avoiding punishment. "People, left to their own devices, tend simply to satisfy their desires. But, people will make themselves do things they don't want to do in order to get rewards; they will refrain from doing things they do want to do in order to avoid punishment."[209]

Young children will not automatically do the right thing (as they would have no notion of what that is, without first being taught!), nor will they automatically obey their parents (once they have been taught), without some incentive to do so: punishment for disobedience. Adults are no different. When we obtain rewards for certain actions, we are motivated to perform them, and when we are punished for other actions, we are motivated to avoid them. Self-interest is what drives us, in either case.

In the real-world, resources are scarce, and we are in competition with others for those scarce resources. Obtaining those resources is rewarding, and so we are motivated to develop those qualities which will help us obtain those rewards (e.g., self-discipline, a good work ethic, personal responsibility, etc.). If the reward can be obtained without those qualities, the motivation to obtain them dissolves. Giving someone a so-called "free lunch" is ultimately harmful to them, as it undermines the natural system in which rewards only come to those who have earned them by virtue of their talent, hard work, and self-discipline. Rewards given to those who haven't earned them via competition are immoral, and remove the incentive to become self-disciplined and obey authority (and rules, in general). If the recipient never acquires those traits and that self-discipline, they will be unable to compete should their "meal ticket" ever stop with the handouts!

Competition is necessary and good. It creates incentive to develop your talents, and to work hard. Given the scarcity and gritty reality of life, competition prepares us to survive and succeed in the real world. But, even if there was no scarcity, and there were more than enough "things" for everyone, competition would still be a good thing (and necessary) because it promotes the self-discipline needed to make plans, make commitments, and carry them out. Even a basic plan of life for oneself requires the ability to make decisions and then act in pursuit of that plan. All the material resources in the world won't do you any good if you don't have enough focus and willpower to make use of them.

If competition is good, then the outcomes of competition are good as well. In a competition, some people "win," and others "lose." Not everyone can finish first. This means that a hierarchy will emerge, with the most successful competitors at the top. They deserve to be there, and to reap the rewards of winning. "Losers" don't deserve the rewards of "winners"—not if the competition is to retain any meaning.

Everyone is equally motivated by reward and punishment, all equally motivated by the pursuit of self-interest. This pursuit is a good thing, though, since the collective pursuit of individual self-interest is thought to maximize the well-being of all involved. This folk interpretation of Adam Smith explains conservatives' devotion to free-market capitalism. Competition and the pursuit of self-interest is morally good. Systems that interfere with this (such as socialism or communism), are immoral systems in that they interfere with this maximization of well-being, unjustifiably (and presumably ineffectively) meddle in the private pursuit of self-interest by individuals, and undermine the moral values of competition, hard work, and self-discipline.

A particular application of this moral value of upholding the morality of reward and punishment is preventing interference with the pursuit of self-interest by self-disciplined, self-reliant people. Someone who is self-disciplined, and works hard in pursuit of his own self-interest, while playing by the rules of society, is "doing it right." Such persons are behaving as they are supposed to. To put obstacles in their path, or to help other, less-worthy people "win" instead, is to rig the system. That is unfair, immoral, and undermines the whole system of reward and punishment. Not surprisingly, then, conservatives will generally be opposed to

---

[209] *Moral Politics*, 67.

policies which interfere with business (e.g., "excess" regulations), or that "punish" success (e.g., taxes), as well as policies that allows others to "cheat" or provide an "unfair advantage" (e.g., affirmative action).

The idea of the "American Dream" fits perfectly with the strict father worldview. American is a land of opportunity. Anyone with the self-discipline to work hard and follow the rules can, and will, climb the ladder of success and live the American dream. Therefore, anyone who has not succeeded either lacks talent or hasn't worked hard—either way, they don't deserve the success of a hard-working and talented person. If the person hasn't worked hard, then he is lazy, and doesn't deserve success. If he is a hard-worker, but is untalented, then it's only fair that he doesn't enjoy the same success as the more-talented. After all, in a race, you can push yourself as hard as you can, but if someone else is just more athletic than you, that person will win the race, despite your hard work—and they should. At the societal level, then, the poor deserve their poverty (they have "earned" it), and the rich deserve their success and prosperity (as they have earned it). The rich are, therefore, not merely wealthier than others, but morally better than others—at least with regard to the moral virtues of talent and hard work.

The strict father emphasis on strength and self-discipline can help us to understand stereotypically conservative positions on various policies. Why are conservatives (generally) opposed to welfare? Because it gives people something for "nothing," removes their incentive to work—and even does so at the expense of "winners" (i.e., those who do work and pay their taxes). Why are conservatives opposed to giving free condoms to teenagers, even though doing so is proven to reduce teen pregnancy and STD infections? Because teenagers should have (or acquire) the self-discipline to refrain from sex— and if they don't they have to face the consequences. Otherwise, they will never learn their lesson and grow stronger.

Fourthly, we have the morality of protecting moral people from external evils. Since protection from external evils is a fundamental part of strict father morality, protective actions are moral and inhibiting them is immoral. Not surprisingly, conservatives tend to be in favor of large, powerful militaries, and supporters of the police. In addition, they tend to favor gun-rights and gun-ownership.

Finally, we have the moral value of upholding the "moral order" itself. This moral order refers back to the family model, in which there is a clear (gendered) hierarchy, presumed hetero-normativity, and unquestioned obedience on the part of children. "Father knows best," in this model—and with religious (usually Christian) variations of this model, God is placed at the very top of the hierarchy. What this means is that policies or movements that defy or disrupt this order are seen as deviant and dangerous. Feminism, acceptance of homosexuality as a morally legitimate alternative to heterosexuality, atheism/humanism/Islam/religious pluralism, immigrants with different cultural norms and speaking different languages . . . all these things (and others) can be seen as subversive forces from which the family (and community) needs protection.

To summarize:

Conservatives believe in individual responsibility alone, not social responsibility. They don't think government should help its citizens. That is, they don't think citizens should help each other. The part of government they want to cut is not the military (we have over 800 military bases around the world), not government subsidies to corporations, not the aspect of government that fits their worldview. They want to cut the part that helps people. Why? Because that violates individual responsibility.

But where does that view of individual responsibility alone come from? The way to understand the conservative moral system is to consider a strict father family. The father is The Decider, the ultimate moral authority in the family. His authority must not be challenged. His job is to protect the family, to support the family (by winning competitions in the marketplace), and to teach his kids right from wrong by disciplining them physically when they do wrong. The use of force is necessary and required. Only then will children develop the internal discipline to become moral beings. And only with such discipline will they be able to prosper. And what of people who are not prosperous? They don't have discipline, and without discipline they cannot be moral, so they deserve their poverty. The good people are hence the prosperous people. Helping others takes away their discipline, and hence makes them both unable to prosper on their own and function morally.

The market itself is seen in this way. The slogan, "Let the market decide" assumes the market itself is The Decider. The market is seen as both natural (since it is assumed that people naturally seek their self-interest) and moral (if everyone seeks their own profit, the profit of all will be maximized by the invisible hand). As the ultimate moral authority, there should be no power higher than the market that might go against market values. Thus the government can spend money to protect the market and promote market values, but should not rule over it either through (1) regulation, (2) taxation, (3) unions and worker rights, (4) environmental protection or food safety laws, and (5) tort cases. Moreover, government should not do public service. The market has service industries for that. Thus, it would be wrong for the government to provide health care, education, public broadcasting, public parks, and so on. The very idea of these things is at odds with the conservative moral system. No one should be paying for

anyone else. It is individual responsibility in all arenas. Taxation is thus seen as taking money away from those who have earned it and giving it to people who don't deserve it. Taxation cannot be seen as providing the necessities of life, a civilized society, and as necessary for business to prosper.

In conservative family life, the strict father rules. Fathers and husbands should have control over reproduction; hence, parental and spousal notification laws and opposition to abortion. In conservative religion, God is seen as the strict father, the Lord, who rewards and punishes according to individual responsibility in following his Biblical word.

Above all, the authority of conservatism itself must be maintained. The country should be ruled by conservative values, and progressive values are seen as evil. Science should NOT have authority over the market, and so the science of global warming and evolution must be denied. Facts that are inconsistent with the authority of conservatism must be ignored or denied or explained away. To protect and extend conservative values themselves, the devil's own means can be used against conservatism's immoral enemies, whether lies, intimidation, torture, or even death, say, for women's doctors.

Freedom is defined as being your own strict father — with individual not social responsibility, and without any government authority telling you what you can and cannot do. To defend that freedom as an individual, you will of course need a gun.[210]

Liberals, in contrast, while still employing a

---

[210] http://georgelakoff.com/2011/02/19/what-conservatives-really-want/

family metaphor, envision the "nurturant parent" model instead.

The Nurturant Parent Model

The family is of either one or two parents. Two are generally preferable, but not always possible.

The primal experience behind this model is one of being cared for and cared about, having one's desires for loving interactions met, living as happily as possible, and deriving meaning from one's community and from caring for and about others.

People are realized in and through their "secure attachments": through their positive relationships to others, through their contribution to their community, and through the ways in which they develop their potential and find joy in life. Work is a means toward these ends, and it is through work that these forms of meaning are realized. All of this requires strength and self-discipline, which are fostered by the constant support of, and attachment to, those who love and care about you.

Protection is a form of caring, and protection from external dangers takes up a significant part of the nurturant parent's attention. The world is filled with evils that can harm a child, and it is the nurturant parent's duty to be ward them off.

Crime and drugs are, of course, significant, but so are less obvious dangers: cigarettes, cars without seat belts, dangerous toys, inflammable clothing, pollution, asbestos, lead paint, pesticides in food, diseases, unscrupulous businessmen, and so on. Protection of innocent and helpless children from such evils is a major part of a nurturant parent's job.

Children are taught self-discipline in the service of nurturance: to take care of themselves, to deal with existing hardships, to be responsible to others, and to realize their potential. Children are also taught self-nurturance: the intrinsic value of emotional connection with others, of health, of education, of art, of communion with the natural world, and of being able to take care of oneself. In addition to learning the discipline required for responsibility and self-nurturance, it is important that children have a childhood, that they learn to develop their imaginations, and that they just plain have fun.

Through empathizing and interacting positively with their children, parents develop close bonds with children and teach them empathy and responsibility towards others and toward society. Nurturant parents view the family as a community in which children have commitments and responsibilities that grow out of empathy for others. The obedience of children comes out of love and respect for parents, not out of fear of punishment. When children do wrong, nurturant parents choose restitution over retribution whenever possible as a form of justice. Retribution is reserved for those who harm their children.

The pursuit of self-interest is shaped by these values: anything inconsistent with these values is not in one's self-interest. Pursuing self-interest, so understood, is a means for fulfilling the values of the model.[211]

Let's work through this description, one important piece at a time, as well. Once again, the

---

[211] Lakoff, "Metaphor, Morality, and Politics, Or, Why Conservatives Have Left Liberals in the Dust."

name of the model is telling: "nurturant parent" is gender-neutral, and not even hetero-normative. What is essential is merely that the parent be "nurturant," and this could presumably be the case with any combination of male or female parents, singly or in groups.

In contrast to the discipline-focused strict father approach, the nurturant parent model uses nurturance to develop in children both self-nurturance (the ability to care for oneself) as well as the ability to care for others. This model rejects the "folk behaviorism" of the strict father model, and doesn't accept that children (or people in general) learn primarily via rewards and punishment. Instead, the emphasis is on attachment.

If a child develops a secure and loving "attachment" to her parents, they will model that nurturing behavior themselves. From that secure attachment, they will try to anticipate their parents' expectations, and will be motivated to please them—not from fear of punishment, but from a desire to make happy someone you love. By way of analogy, if you are in a deeply loving romantic relationship, you (presumably) want your partner to be happy, and it makes you feel good when your actions are pleasing to them. You try to anticipate what will make them happy (or upset), and you probably do your best to make them happy. This is presumably not merely (or even primarily) because you're afraid they will break up with you if you don't, but because of the empathy you have for them. In a way, their happiness becomes your own. It is true, of course, that if you continually disappoint them, they might leave you, and you might experience that as a "punishment," but, if your actions are truly driven primarily by that fear of punishment, how much do you actually *love* that person?

When parents love and nurture their children, the children develop the capacity to become loving and nurturing themselves. Confident in their own worth, they have self-esteem, and are less likely to act out against others to compensate for their own sense of inadequacy (e.g., the stereotypical interpretation of bullies as lacking in self-esteem, and trying to gain it at the expense of others). Well-nurtured

parents develop self-discipline as well, but not from fear. As children become more capable of caring for themselves and others (requiring self-discipline, of course), this pleases their parents, and the behavior is reinforced

Rather than focusing on strength and discipline, this model focuses on the experiencing of caring and being cared for. This is not to say that strength and self-discipline are unimportant—just that these qualities develop from the experience of unconditional love and consistent care, rather than discipline and the fear of punishment. Children who are well cared for learn to care for themselves, and to be empathetic—and therefore are motivated to care for others as well.

When morality is understood in terms of empathy rather than strength, the strict "good-evil" dichotomy fades away. People with different values are not necessarily "evil," and it is virtuous to be able to empathize with others and see things from their own point of view. Even when people, regrettably, harm others (such as criminal behavior, or even acts of terrorism), it is too simplistic to dismiss such persons as irredeemably "evil." Surely there are causes for hurtful behavior. Mental illness? In that case, we should try to provide better mental health care for that person, and the community in general. Addiction? In that case, we should help people to overcome their addictions, perhaps by providing rehabilitation services. Poverty or oppression? Maybe some criminal acts are symptoms of broader societal problems, and we should try to address those "macro" issues so that fewer people are led to make poor life choices. Even the most despicable acts of terrorism might have roots in poverty and foreign policy issues. This is not to justify the behavior, but to try to understand it so that we are able to prevent such horrible acts rather than merely punishing those who commit them.

With regard to "internal evils," the nurturant parent model doesn't look to temptation and weakness of will as an explanation, but to such traits as selfishness, lack of social responsibility, arrogance, self-righteousness, insensitivity—and other traits associated with a lack of empathy.

Nurturant parents also believe that the world is filled with dangers from which the child needs protecting, but rather than focusing solely on "bad people" (who are often the products of bad childhoods, destructive social and economic circumstances, and a lack of being loved and appreciated) as the source danger in the world, they consider also the dangers of such things as pollution, poverty, second-hand smoke, unsafe food sources or consumer products, and "unscrupulous business practices."

The children of nurturant parents are not considered impertinent for asking questions. Blind obedience to authority is neither expected, nor desired. Children are to be encouraged to ask questions, so that they can understand why some behaviors are loving, and others are not. In this way, their empathy increases with understanding, and their own capacity for nurturance increases as well.

As adults, they are self-confident and emotionally mature. They practice self-care, which enables them to "be there" for others, when needed. As an empathetic person, they will recognize the connections between persons, and the value of all individuals, and seeks to make the community more caring and responsive to the needs of others. Cooperation, rather than competition, is emphasized; as is interdependence over hierarchy. It is not the case that if one person "wins," another must "lose." Sometimes, we can all have our needs met, and be happy.

Although children grow up to become adults, they never cease to be your "child"—and nurturant parents will continue to support and care for their children regardless of their age.

Nurturant Parent Politics

In contrast to the moral categories in the strict father model, we have the following moral categories for liberal politics, according to Lakoff:

1. Empathetic behavior and promoting fairness.
2. Helping those who cannot help themselves.
3. Protecting those who cannot protect themselves.
4. Promoting fulfillment in life.
5. Nurturing and strengthening oneself in order to do the above.

First, we have the moral value of empathy. While strength is the focus of the strict father model, empathy is the focus for the nurturant parent. To care for another one must be able to empathize with them, to be moved and motivated by the other person's fear, pain, or joy. Those who can't empathize at all are considered psychopaths!

Empathy is thought to be essential for notions of fairness and reciprocity. When a child does something unkind to another child, we might ask them how they would feel if that had been done to them, instead. For adults, we might appeal to the Golden Rule, or urge someone not to judge until they have "walked a mile in the other person's shoes." The assumption is that if you can identify with the other person, and imagine their needs, suffering, or happiness as your own, you will motivated for them to be treated fairly—just as you would want to be treated fairly!

The more capable we are of empathy, the more likely we will be to be concerned with others' lives, and to help those in need. This brings us to the *second* moral value: helping those who cannot help themselves.

Parents are naturally moved, by love, to care for their children who, for many years, are not capable of caring for themselves. A loving parent doesn't demand some sort of payment from her infant in exchange for food, protection, affection, and care! Because of our empathy for others, their suffering becomes our own (in a sense), and this can motivate us to help others in need. I could be that homeless person on the street, and I would want someone to take a moment and offer me some kindness, and maybe some food. In different circumstances, I could have been one of those Syrian refugees fleeing from ISIS, and would want my fellow humans to offer me some kindness and care.

The *third* moral value, very much related to the second, is protecting those who cannot protect themselves. Just as a nurturant parent will protect his child from dangers (which include not only "strangers," but also things like lead in paint, unsafe child car seats, climate change, polluted water supplies, etc.), so too should we protect anyone who needs it from dangers, to the extent that we can. If we can empathize with a woman in an abusive relationship, we would want to protect her from that violence, and we would be moved to protect the Syrian refugees, and we would be moved to protect people threatened by a natural disaster, or from crippling poverty, etc.

Fourthly, nurturant parents recognize that being a loving parent isn't only about protecting from danger and providing the necessities of life. A nurturant parent doesn't merely want her child to survive, but to thrive. This means promoting fulfillment in life. If you empathize with others, you recognize that they have hopes and dreams just like we do, they have potential that can be realized (possibly with some help), and an intrinsic worth—just like ourselves. Nurturant parents try to help their children flourish as individuals by promoting their education, enriching hobbies, creative expression, meaningful work, healthy relationships, etc. Adults deserve no less.

Finally, being a nurturing parent requires empathy for oneself as well! To care for others, one must also care for oneself. This means taking action to remain healthy, rested, and cared-for.

The Two Models Applied and Compared

Clearly, these contrasting models reveal two different parenting models. The first emphasizes "tough love," and sees the role of the parent as protector and moral instructor so that the child may grow into a successful adult. The second emphasizes healthy attachment (achieved by continuous nurturance), so that the child may grow into an emotionally mature and empathetic adult, equipped to care for others in return. We can now apply these family models to the State, in an effort to understand the differences between conservative and liberal worldviews, and policy stances. As an example, we will consider federally-funded College loans.

The official Democratic Party platform for the 2016 campaign season says this about student loans (emphasis added):

Making Debt-Free College a Reality

Democrats believe that in America, if you want a higher education, you should always be able to get one: money should never stand in the way. Cost should not be a barrier to getting a degree or credential, and debt should not hold you back after you graduate. Bold new investments by the federal government, coupled with states reinvesting in higher education and Colleges holding the line on costs, will ensure that Americans of all backgrounds will be prepared for the jobs and economy of the future. Democrats are unified in their strong belief that every student should be able to go to College debt-free, and working families should not have to pay any tuition to go to public Colleges and Universities.

We will also make community College free, while ensuring the strength of our Historically Black Colleges and Universities and Minority-Serving Institutions. <u>The federal government will push more Colleges and Universities to take quantifiable, affirmative steps in increasing the percentages of racial and ethnic minority, low-income, and first-generation students they enroll and graduate.</u> Achieving these goals depends on state and federal investment in both students and their teachers. Whether full-time or adjunct, faculty must be supported to make transformative educational experiences possible.

Providing Relief from Crushing Student Debt

As we make College affordable for future students, <u>we will not forget about the millions of borrowers with unsustainable levels of student debt, who need help right now.</u> Democrats will allow those who currently have student debt to refinance *their loans at the lowest rates possible. <u>We will simplify and expand access to income-based repayment so that no student loan borrowers ever have to pay more than they can afford. And we will significantly cut interest rates for future undergraduates because we believe that making College more affordable is more important than the federal government making billions of dollars in profit off those loans.</u> Democrats will also fight for a student borrower bill of rights to ensure borrowers get adequate information about options to avoid or get out of delinquency or default. We will hold lenders and loan servicers to high standards to help borrowers in default rehabilitate and repay their debts. We will continue the important Public Service Loan Forgiveness and loan discharge programs begun by the Obama Administration. Finally, Democrats will restore the prior standard in bankruptcy law to allow borrowers with student loans to be able to discharge their debts in bankruptcy as a measure of last resort. To make progress toward these goals, the government should offer a moratorium on student loan payments to all federal loan borrowers so they have the time and get the resources they need to consolidate their loans, enroll in income-based repayment programs, and take advantage of opportunities to reduce monthly payments and fees.[212]*

The official Republican Party platform for the 2016 campaign season, in contrast, says the following about student loans (emphasis added):

College Costs
The cost of a College education has long been on an unsustainable trajectory, rising year by year far ahead of inflation. Nationwide, student debt now exceeds

credit card debt with average debt levels per student totaling roughly $27,000. Delinquency rates on student loans are now as high as they were on subprime mortgages during the housing crisis. Over half of recent College grads are unemployed or underemployed, working at jobs for which their expensive educations gave them no preparation. We need new systems of learning to compete with traditional four-year schools: Technical institutions, online Universities, life-long learning, and workbased learning in the private sector. Public policy should advance their affordability, innovation, and transparency and should recognize that a four-year degree from a brick-and-mortar institution is not the only path toward a prosperous and fulfilling career. <u>The federal government should not be in the business of originating student loans. In order to bring down College costs and give students access to a multitude of financing options, private sector participation in student financing should be restored. Any regulation that increases College costs must be challenged to balance its worth against its negative economic impact on students and their families.</u>

In order to encourage new modes of higher education delivery to enter the market, accreditation should be decoupled from federal financing, and states should be empowered to allow a wide array of accrediting and credentialing bodies to operate. This model would foster innovation, bring private industry into the credentialing market, and give students the ability to customize their College experience.[213]

Republicans   are   officially   against

---

[212] The entire platform is available as a pdf here: https://democrats.org/where-we-stand/party-platform/

[213] The entire platform is available as a pdf here: https://www.gop.com/platform/

(originating) federal student loans, whereas Democrats support it. What explains this difference? Lakoff thinks he knows the answer.

From a "liberal" perspective, federal student loans are a good and worthy cause. It helps those who can't help themselves (i.e., to pay for College). It promotes fulfillment in life since education is fulfilling in itself, and a higher education allows access to more fulfilling work. It strengthens the community by producing a better-educated citizenry and ultimately bringing in more tax money. It makes access to College more fair since the opportunity to go to College will not be dependent upon the contingencies of birth (i.e., how wealthy is the family into which you were born?). Finally, and perhaps most importantly, it is empathetic behavior. If someone is talented enough to get accepted into a College, and wants to attend, but is being held back by financial struggles, it is simply the nurturing thing to do to help them.

From a "conservative" perspective, however, this is a bad idea. Since loan recipients are dependent upon the loan, federal loan programs create dependency on the government rather than promoting self-reliance. Since not everyone has access to the loans, because they are based on financial need, they are unfair, and interfere with the free market. After all, private lending institutions, like any other commercial interest, will be driven by competition and market demands, so long as they are not interfered with. The government hand-picking some people to receive loans on the basis of their perceived "need" rather than by what the market will bear interferes with what would otherwise be the fair pursuit of self-interest. Moreover, since the loans are subsidized by the government, they are ultimately provided by tax-payer dollars. Since all the risk is borne by the government in the event a student defaults on the loan, it is tax-payer dollars that will be lost, rather than private lending institutions. Private lenders, of course, wary of losing their money, carefully screen to whom they lend money, so as to minimize that risk. "Riskier" clients either don't get loans at all, or else pay higher interest rates to account for their "riskiness." Not so with federal loans. But,

since the program takes money earned by one group and, through taxation, gives it to another group, it is unfair and penalizes the pursuit of self-interest by taking money from someone who has earned it and giving it to someone who hasn't.

Admittedly, the Republic platform doesn't claim that *no* student loans should be available, but that it should be handled by the "private sector." Notice, though, that on this issue the official position of the Republican party is not entirely consistent with the strict father model. It claims that, while the federal government should not be providing student loans, it "should serve as an insurance guarantor for the private sector as they offer loans to students." Perhaps the assumption is that access to College education is a worthy enough goal that private lenders should be encouraged in their lending, by virtue of the government guaranteeing the loans? In any event, this is a nice illustration that neither of the major political parties are presumed to be 100% compliant and consistent with their respective family models.

Moving on to other examples, with regard to social and economic forces, liberals and conservatives tend to have striking different interpretations. Liberals tend to recognize that some people are "trapped" by their circumstances (e.g., poverty, racism, sexism, high crime neighborhoods, lack of resources, poorly funded schools, etc.), and a nurturing parent (or nurturing government) should be motivated by empathy to help those people. If social and economic forces are the problem, the solution must address those forces!

Conservatives, on the other hand, believing in the "American dream" and its meritocracy, deny the strength of economic and social forces. Anyone with sufficient talent and self-discipline can (and will) succeed. The solution is not to provide "handouts" and short-circuit the true path to success, but, instead, to emphasize personal responsibility and hard work.

With the regard abortion, one might wonder how conservatives can be "pro-life" but against providing subsidized pre-natal care, or food assistance to poor parents. There is no necessary inconsistency, if one believes that the fetus is innocent, and abortion is, therefore, murder—and categorically evil. That being said, if someone isn't prepared to deal with the predictable consequences of sex (i.e., pregnancy), that person shouldn't be having sex in the first place. If someone is too poor to care for their children, they shouldn't have them! They should have sufficient will-power to abstain from sex, or at least use reliable birth control. Providing free services to poor parents only subsidizes their weakness and reinforces it.

From the liberal perspective, nurturant parents see the pregnant girl or woman as being "in trouble" and therefore in need of help. The anxiety and possible guilt or shame she is experiencing from the unintended pregnancy is "punishment" enough—she certainly doesn't need to be scolded on top of it. If she is seeking an abortion, she has concluded she isn't ready to be a mother yet, or else doesn't think she can handle a child (or another one). If that is the case, she is in no position to properly care for the child, once it is born, and her self-care would suggest that she not have to endure the pregnancy either.

This sort of comparison and analysis is possible, in principle, with each and every point of political contention in the United States today. The same family models that allow us to predict (and understand) conservative and liberal stances on various policy issues also allows us to generalize and identify, for each, their respective "heroes" and "villains."

Model Citizens and "Demons"

"Conservative" model citizens have conservative values, act to support those values, are self- disciplined and self-reliant, generally uphold the morality of reward and punishment, work to protect moral citizens, and act in support of the moral order. Those who best exemplify those traits are successful, wealthy, law-abiding, conservative businessmen who support a strong military and a strict criminal justice system, and are against government regulation and things like affirmative action.

They are our role-models, the people whom all Americans should emulate. Such people deserve to be rewarded and respected because they succeeded through hard work and have earned whatever they have through their own self-discipline. Therefore, they deserve to *keep* what they have earned.

Through their own success and wealth they create jobs, which they "give" to other citizens. Even simply by investing their money to maximize their earnings, they become philanthropists who "give" jobs to others and thereby "create wealth" for others. Their successful pursuit of self-interest helps many others as well.

If such persons are conservative model citizens, their opposites (whom Lakoff terms conservative "demons") are against conservative values (e.g., Strict Father morality, in general). This includes feminists, gays, and other "deviants" who defy the very assumptions of the Strict Father family. Other "demons" are the advocates of multiculturalism, who reject the primacy of the Strict Father model and who deny American "exceptionalism," postmodern humanists who deny the existence of any absolute values, and progressive "egalitarians" who are against hierarchy, in general.

There are many such "demons" in the United States. They include people whose lack of self-discipline has led to a lack of self-reliance. This would include unwed mothers on welfare, since their lack of sexual self-control has led to their dependence on the state. It also includes unemployed drug users, whose weakness has led to drug addiction, which has itself led to their being unable to support themselves. It additionally includes any able-bodied people on welfare. Such persons can work, but don't. Given this land of opportunity, this means they are lazy and are willing to be a burden to others.

Other sorts of "demons" are the so-called protectors of the "public good." This will include environmentalists, consumer advocates, advocates of affirmative action, and advocates of government-supported universal health care ("Obamacare!")—all of whom want the government to interfere with the pursuit of self-interest and thus constrain the business activities of the conservatives' "model citizens."

Yet another type of "demon" opposes law and

order, and a strong military. This includes antiwar protesters, advocates of prisoners' rights, opponents of police brutality, and those pushing for "gun-control." People who would restrict access to guns are not only trampling on the 2nd Amendment, but are trying to take guns away from those who need them to protect themselves and their families both from criminals and from possible government tyranny. Of all these "demons," abortion doctors might be the worst, since they directly kill the most innocent people of all: unborn babies.

Once again, in sharp contrast, "liberals" have a very different image of a model citizen. Liberal model citizens are those who are empathetic, help the disadvantaged, protect those who need it, promote and exemplify fulfillment in life, and who take proper care of themselves so that they can do all those things!

Such persons are those who live a socially responsible life, such as socially responsible professionals; environmental, consumer, and minority rights advocates, as well as union organizers. Such persons also include doctors, and social workers who devote their lives to helping the poor and the elderly, as well as peace advocates, educators, artists, and those in the healing professions, in general.

Lakoff claims that liberals have their own "demons." Liberal "demons" are mean-spirited, selfish, and unfair people who have no empathy and show no sense of social responsibility. Right at the top of this list are wealthy corporations and business persons who care only about profit, and use their power and political influence to pursue it, at all costs.

Other liberal "demons" are those who ignore, harm, or exploit the disadvantaged. Companies or politicians who "bust" unions are an example of such "demons," as are large agricultural firms that exploit farm workers by exposing them to poor working conditions for low pay. Also included here would be those who oppose

providing health care or other necessary services to the needy.

Another kind of "demon" is one who hurts either people or the environment itself. This will include not only criminals, but also "out-of-control" police who use brutal tactics. It also includes polluters, those who make unsafe products or engage in consumer fraud, and large companies that make extensive profits from government subsidies by contributing to politicians and their campaigns.

Finally, additional liberal "demons" include those who are opposed to publicly supporting education, art, and research, as well as other personal (and culturally) enriching activities.

Conclusion

Lakoff's approach is a sharp departure from everything else we have done and considered in this book. Rather than offering an argument for what the State *should* do, or what sorts of policy stances we should have, he offers an explanation for the opinions we form, and the actions we take, not in terms of philosophical arguments, but contrasting family metaphors.[214]

If Lakoff is right, most of us don't vote from well-considered philosophical positions, nor are we responsive to arguments. Instead, we interpret political situations and "arguments" through the lens of our dominant family model. In that case, a more effective means of political persuasion than rational argument would be an informed and intentional use of metaphor— something Lakoff thinks explains how Ronald Reagan won over so many traditionally democratic voters in the 1980s, ushering in the "Reagan Revolution."

Rather than taking a stance on whether Lakoff's approach, or that of traditional political theorists, is correct, I propose that we attempt to understand both. On the one hand, there is rhetoric, psychology, and an understanding of how emotions are triggered (or even

---

[214] In fairness, at the end of *Moral Politics*, Lakoff does advocate for the superiority of the Nurturant Parent model, and is active in promoting liberal causes and politicians. Most of

his book (and all of our use of it), though, is limited to the descriptive, rather than the prescriptive.

manipulated). On the other hand, there are coherent world views, in which one hopes to construct (or at least operate from) consistent premises that inform political conclusions.

Perhaps these are skill sets belonging to two different kinds of politicians? One is the domain of the charismatic leader (or advisor) who can swing votes and "get things done." The other is the domain of the traditional "statesman," who can conceive of the proper aims and actions of the State in the first place. There is no question that this book has focused more on the latter, than the former.

Hyperlinks to the official party platforms of the two "Major" parties (and their two most credible competitors) are provided below.[215] If you are reading this book in a traditional printed format, though less convenient, the URL can easily be typed into your web browser (or found on your own using a simple search in your favorite web browser).

Democrat Party:
https://www.demconvention.com/wp-content/uploads/2020/08/2020-07-31-Democratic-Party-Platform-For-Distribution.pdf

Green Party: http://www.gp.org/platform

Libertarian Party:
https://www.lp.org/platform/

Republican Party: https://prod-cdn-static.gop.com/docs/Resolution_Platform_2020.pdf?_ga=2.165306300.2055661719.159812463 8-455285808.1584478680

I encourage you to read them with both kinds of lenses in place. With one lens, look for the telltale signs of either the "strict father" or "nurturant parent" models. With the other, look for traces of influence from any of the several substantial political thinkers and their ideas we explore in this book. To what extent are these

ideas used in coherent and consistent fashion? Both approaches should be informative.

Critical Analysis

1. In your opinion, what are the strongest and most compelling points made by the philosopher or philosophers in this chapter? Why do you find those points to be convincing?

2. In your opinion, what are the weakest or least convincing points? Why? Can you anticipate any limitations or objections to their ideas not already addressed in the chapter?

Appendix: Application to Social Justice

Almost every chapter of this book features philosophical ideas that, in some way or another, pertain to social justice. This chapter, and the previous chapter, deviate from that pattern. As mentioned earlier in the chapter, Lakoff is not a philosopher, but a cognitive linguist. His contribution to our exploration is his ability to provide another way to understand why people value what they do, and why people make the political decisions that they do – both of which are relevant to social justice issues.

If Lakoff is correct, and people vote and support or oppose laws and policies not on the basis of data and arguments and evidence but more so on the basis of how those issues are "framed," and how the frame intersects with their preferred family metaphor, then we need to reconsider what is actually taking place when people disagree over social justice issues, as well as reconsidering what strategies to use to overcome those disagreements.

That there is something strategic about the terms we use is obvious. There is a reason why people who are against abortion refer to their position as "pro-life" as opposed to "anti-choice," and a reason why those who are in favor of access

---

[215] As of the publication of this book, the most recent platforms for the Democrat party and the Green party were 2020. The Libertarian made

no changes to their platform since they updated it in 2018. The Republican party made no changes to their 2016 platform.

to abortion refer to their position as "pro-choice" as opposed to "pro-abortion." It is an issue of "messaging," and "tone." All of us employ (and respond to) metaphors when we communicate, and this is no less the case when we are dealing with politics.

> Trump uses metaphors often, mostly as weapons against his enemies. Think "drain the swamp," "rigged system," "deep state" and, most infamously, "build the wall." When he calls Washington a "swamp," he doesn't mean a steamy marsh teeming with alligators. He means a corrupt city full of dirty politicians who need to be removed.[216]

Lakoff has long argued that conservatives are *better* at messaging and framing than progressives.

> . . . Conservatives, especially conservative think tanks, have framed virtually every issue from their perspective. They have put a huge amount of money into creating the language for their worldview and getting it out there. Progressives have done virtually nothing. . . .
>
> Because they've put billions of dollars into it. Over the last 30 years their think tanks have made a heavy investment in ideas and in language. In 1970, [Supreme Court Justice] Lewis Powell wrote a fateful memo to the National Chamber of Commerce saying that all of our best students are becoming anti-business because of the Vietnam War, and that we needed to do something about it. Powell's agenda included getting wealthy conservatives to set up professorships, setting up institutes on and off campus where intellectuals would write books from a conservative business perspective, and setting up think tanks. He outlined the whole thing in 1970. They set up the Heritage Foundation in

> 1973, and the Manhattan Institute after that. [There are many others, including the American Enterprise Institute and the Hoover Institute at Stanford, which date from the 1940s.]
>
> And now, as the New York Times Magazine quoted Paul Weyrich, who started the Heritage Foundation, they have 1,500 conservative radio talk show hosts. They have a huge, very good operation, and they understand their own moral system. They understand what unites conservatives, and they understand how to talk about it, and they are constantly updating their research on how best to express their ideas. . . .
>
> Conservative foundations give large block grants year after year to their think tanks. They say, 'Here's several million dollars, do what you need to do.' And basically, they build infrastructure, they build TV studios, hire intellectuals, set aside money to buy a lot of books to get them on the best-seller lists, hire research assistants for their intellectuals so they do well on TV, and hire agents to put them on TV. They do all of that. Why? Because the conservative moral system, which I analyzed in "Moral Politics," has as its highest value preserving and defending the "strict father" system itself. And that means building infrastructure. As businessmen, they know how to do this very well.
>
> Meanwhile, liberals' conceptual system of the "nurturant parent" has as its highest value helping individuals who need help. The progressive foundations and donors give their money to a variety of grassroots organizations. They say, 'We're giving you $25,000, but don't waste a penny of it. Make sure it all goes to the cause, don't use it for administration, communication, infrastructure, or career development.' So there's actually a structural reason built

---

[216] https://www.sacbee.com/latest-   news/article224572335.html

into the worldviews that explains why conservatives have done better.[217]

As further illustration of his point, we may consider an excerpt from a "briefing book" written by conservative activist Christopher Rufo, one of the leading *anti*-Critical Race Theory activists. The booklet is designed as a field manual to help individuals organize and frame their efforts to discredit (and ban) Critical Race Theory from workplace trainings and school curricula (whether they exist there, or not). The most obviously relevant section is entitled "winning the language war," and in that section he provides specific examples of how to frame the topic and phrase one's position so as to maximize public support.   Here are some relevant "highlights:"[218]

To successfully fight against critical race theory, we must adopt language that is trenchant, persuasive, and resonates with the public. Here are some powerful words and phrases to include in your communications.

Defining critical race theory
o   "Race-based Marxism"
o   "State-sanctioned racism"
o   "Woke racism"
o   "Racial engineering"
o   "Critical race theory divides Americans into oppressor and oppressed based on their skin color."
o   "Critical race theory says the solution to past discrimination is present discrimination. I reject this. Racism is always wrong."
o   "I oppose racism, whether it comes from the Klan or from critical race theory."
o   "Critical race theory teaches that individualism, rationality, and hard work are racist. This is an insult to hard-working American families of all racial

backgrounds."
o   "Critical race theory rejects the idea of equal protection under the law. I believe everyone has the right to equal treatment, no matter where they come from."

Critical race theory in schools
o   "Race reeducation programs"
o   "Political predators" (reference to activist teachers).
o   "Neo-racist theories have no place in public education."
o   "Critical race theory teaches children that they are defined by their race, not as individuals."
o   "Critical race theory teaches children to hate each other and hate their country."
o   "Critical race theorists have the right to express their beliefs as individuals; they do not have the right to use taxpayer money to indoctrinate children."
o   "Critical race theory is not a free speech issue; it's a compelled speech issue. Public schools do not have the right to violate a child's conscience."
o   "We must prioritize excellence, which inspires people from all racial backgrounds to achieve their potential."
o   "Our goal is diversity without division."

Anti-CRT legislation
o   "Neo-racist theories have no place in our public institutions."
o   "Public institutions must reflect the values of the public—not fringe racial theories that seek to divide Americans into oppressor and oppressed."
o   "This bill does not prevent schools

---

[217] https://www.berkeley.edu/news/media/releases/2003/10/27_lakoff.shtml

[218]   https://christopherrufo.com/crt-briefing-book/?fbclid=IwAR11RecFoZMWbkU3VcuRQ5V

WVIoAllRztH1D42qjfDGq_vLHwrr8aiD14Vk

from teaching about racism, slavery, and segregation. It prohibits schools from indoctrinating students into fringe racial theories that claim one race is superior to another or that individuals should be treated differently on the basis of race."

o "This is not a free speech issue; it's a compelled speech issue. The government does not have the right to force individuals to believe in race essentialism, collective guilt, or racial superiority theory."

o "Free speech was designed to protect the individual against the government, not to empower the government to force individuals to believe in fringe racial theories."

o "This legislation is about limited government—public institutions can no longer promote racist theories using taxpayer dollars."

This understanding of the role of conceptual metaphors in decision-making is not the product of armchair philosophizing or mere speculation. Lakoff has conducted his own research, and his conclusions have been supported by other studies as well. One such study revealed that attitudes towards crime as well as attitudes towards responses to crime vary significantly based upon how the crime is "framed."

When the crime is described using the metaphor of a "beast" preying upon a community, subjects were more likely to support an increase in police and putting offenders in prison. But, if the crime is described using the metaphor of a "virus" infecting a city, subjects were more likely to want to treat the problem with social reform.[219]

Although "enforcement" was the preferred response using either frame, the percentage of

support dropped from 71% to 54% simply by describing the crime as a virus rather than a beast. This study detected the political pattern that we might suspect: Republican subjects were more likely to support enforcement strategies than Democrats (by 10%), but the difference was substantially less than the difference triggered by the metaphor. Participants who read that crime was a beast were about 20 percent more likely to suggest an enforcement-based solution than participants who read that crime was a virus, regardless of their political persuasion.[220]

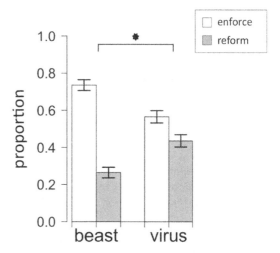

One of the issues where progressives and conservatives differ significantly is their view of the extent (and even existence) of systemic/institutional racism. President Joe Biden repeatedly called out systemic racism throughout his 2020 campaign, and has appointed several experts on systemic racism to his transition team.[221] President Trump, in contrast, has at times denied that systemic racism is a problem, such as is indicated in his reply to the question "does the United States have a broader problem of race:"

I don't believe that at all.[222]

[219] Thibodeau PH, Boroditsky L (2011) Metaphors We Think With: The Role of Metaphor in Reasoning. PLoS ONE 6(2): e16782. https://doi.org/10.1371/journal.pone.0016782
[220] https://news.stanford.edu/news/2011/

february/metaphors-crime-study-022311.html
[221] https://nonprofitquarterly.org/biden-names-systemic-racism-experts-to-transition-teams/
[222] https://www.ft.com/content/3d044bed-f468-42f4-9953-94568860c4f6

But, on another occasion, he seemingly acknowledged the existence of systemic racism while simultaneously diminishing its significance. In response to the question, "Is there systemic racism within police departments and is there any sort of retraining that they need?" he replied "That's always the question. You've got to ask, is there? And I guess there probably is and that's very sad. There is and I think there's not much, or hopefully, there's not much."[223] Vice President Mike pence was more direct, *criticizing* Joe Biden and Kamala Harris for their belief in the existence of systemic racism (*and* implicit bias) in the United States.

> *And I must say this, this presumption that you hear consistently from Joe Biden and Kamala Harris, that America is systemically racist. That as Joe Biden said, that he believes that law enforcement has an implicit bias against minorities, is a great insult to the men and women who serve in law enforcement. And I want everyone to know, who puts on the uniform of law enforcement every day, that President Trump and I stand with you.[224]*

As a partial explanation for this difference in perspective, Lakoff claims that conservatives are much more sympathetic to claims of "direct causation" rather than "systemic causation."

> *Direct causation is dealing with a problem via direct action. Systemic causation recognizes that many problems arise from the system they are in and must be dealt with via systemic causation. Systemic causation has four versions: A chain of direct causes. Interacting direct causes (or chains of direct causes). Feedback loops. And probabilistic causes. . . . Systemic causation has chains of direct causes, interacting causes, feedback loops, and probabilistic causes — often combined.*

> *Direct causation is easy to understand, and appears to be represented in the grammars of all languages around the world. Systemic causation is more complex and is not represented in the grammar of any language. It just has to be learned.*

> *Empirical research has shown that conservatives tend to reason with direct causation and that progressives have a much easier time reasoning with systemic causation. The reason is thought to be that, in the strict father model, the father expects the child or spouse to respond directly to an order and that refusal should be punished as swiftly and directly as possible.*

> *Many of Trump's policy proposals are framed in terms of direct causation.*

> *Immigrants are flooding in from Mexico — build a wall to stop them. For all the immigrants who have entered illegally, just deport them — even if there are 11 million of them working throughout the economy and living throughout the country. The cure for gun violence is to have a gun ready to directly shoot the shooter. To stop jobs from going to Asia where labor costs are lower and cheaper goods flood the market here, the solution is direct: put a huge tariff on those goods so they are more expensive than goods made here. To save money on pharmaceuticals, have the largest consumer — the government — take bids for the lowest prices. If Isis is making money on Iraqi oil, send US troops to Iraq to take control of the oil. Threaten Isis leaders by assassinating their family members (even if this is a war crime). To get information from terrorist suspects, use water-boarding, or even worse torture methods. If a few terrorists might be coming with Muslim refugees, just stop allowing all Muslims into the country. All this makes*

---

[223] https://wjla.com/news/nation-world/at-sinclair-town-hall-trump-admits-systemic-racism-exists-in-policing

[224] https://www.rev.com/blog/transcripts/kamala-harris-mike-pence-2020-vice-presidential-debate-transcript

sense to direct causation thinkers, but not those who see the immense difficulties and dire consequences of such actions due to the complexities of systemic causation.[225]

In other words, the strict father model employed by most conservatives predisposes them to understand outcomes as the effects of the choices of individual agents, in which their action directly causes the effect. If a black man was shot by the police, he presumably *caused* that outcome by engaging in criminal activity, by resisting arrest, by "reaching for something," etc.

Liberals who are more likely to employ the nurturant parent model, in contrast, are more open to explanations involving systemic causation. Rather than frame the police shooting solely, or even primarily, in terms of the discrete actions of individual agents, they are more open to seeing a web of causes all contributing to the outcome. Some of the strands of that web will include the actions of individuals, of course, but will also potentially include "strands" like poverty, police policies that are racially disparate in their application and impact, implicit biases, the "war on drugs," over-policing of communities of color, and any number of other possible contributors.

If this analysis is correct, it might help us to understand why conservatives so quickly either fault the person who was shot, or frame the problem as the matter of a "bad apple," and see no need for any substantial change to the system itself. Liberals, in contrast, are disposed to not only want punishment for the officer, but will also be disposed to want to address the other "strands," seeing that the effect will continue unless the *systemic* causes are addressed.

Lakoff's contribution extends to more than simply *understanding* political beliefs and decision-making. He also provides lessons in *strategy*. Because most (if not all) social justice issues are understood to be "progressive" agendas in the United States, the fact that Lakoff

now focuses primarily on how to help progressives better "frame" their messages is convenient for our purposes. As examples, he proposes several simple substitutions of terms to better appeal to conservative and libertarian Americans.[226]

Old term	New term
Taxpayers	Caring citizens
Taxes	Public revenue
Corrupt business	Ethical business
Regulations	Public protections
Government	Public government of, by, and for the people

Consider some of the examples from the table above. Not many people like paying taxes. Even if you generally support the programs that require taxpayer funding at the local, state, or federal level, it remains nevertheless the case that paying taxes means having less money. To put a more positive "spin" on taxation, Lakoff is proposing that progresses frame it as a matter of shared resources and care. When the government collects taxes, it is actually collecting "public revenue." Thinking of the revenue as "public" already places it in the category of something that rightfully belongs to all of us, as opposed to something "private." Being a taxpayer is reframed as being a "caring citizen," which emphasizes the fact that the revenue is being used for positive purposes and the collective good. It's likely that more of us will feel better about having less money because we are "caring" than having less money because we are subject to a financial obligation.

As one more example from the table, progresses tend to be much more in favor of regulating businesses than are conservatives. To the conservative ear, "regulations" sounds like interference, or restriction. They are things that are opposed to freedom and autonomy. In an effort to secure more "buy-in" from conservatives, Lakoff proposes that progressives

---

[225] https://press.uchicago.edu/books/excerpt/2016/lakoff_trump.html

[226] https://empathysurplus.com/george-lakoff-cognitive-scientist-and-linguistic-expert-for-progressive-speech/

frame their agenda in terms of "public protections" instead. Most of us are inclined to have a positive attitude towards something that protects us. Thinking of regulations as something that protects us rather than restricts us is a potentially helpful reframe.

Another general "tip" he provides is that progressives should stop trying to "win" by offering what they believe to be compelling arguments backed up with evidence, data, facts, etc. This, according to Lakoff, stems from a false view of how people engage in political decision-making. Ironically, attempting to refute someone's position by offering evidence to the contrary simply reinforces the "frame" for that person.

> *Remember not to repeat false conservative claims and then rebut them with the facts. Instead, go positive. Give a positive truthful framing to undermine claims to the contrary. Use the facts to support positively-framed truth. Use repetition.*[227]

On a similar note, he also proposes leading with "values, not policies and facts and numbers."[228] Because he thinks all politics, fundamentally, is moral, it is the underlying values that will have the most impact, and not data.

Finally (for our purposes), and probably most controversially, given the nature of this textbook, he recommends that liberals "give up identity politics."

> *No more women's issues, black issues, Latino issues. Their issues are all real, and need public discussion. But they all fall under freedom issues, human issues. And address poor whites! Appalachian and rust belt whites deserve your attention as much as anyone else. Don't surrender their fate to Trump, who will just increase their*

suffering.[229]

If you find yourself resistant, or even angry, in response, keep in mind that Lakoff is not addressing either the truth or the moral rightness of identity politics. He is addressing strategy. Assuming his understanding of family metaphors is correct, the "strict father" model used by conservatives understands the outcomes of our lives in terms of individual actions and personal responsibility, generally rejecting the significance of group membership as well as social/systemic explanations for outcomes. From within the strict father model, identity politics is a deflection of personal responsibility. While that is certainly subject to debate (and anyone subscribing to the nurturant parent model will almost certainly disagree), if the goal is to secure "buy-in" or "common cause" with conservative voters, reframing issues in ways they will resonate with might be *effective*. This is a strategy to which former President Barack Obama seems sympathetic:

> *If you believe, as I do, that we should be able to reform the criminal justice system so that it's not biased and treats everybody fairly, I guess you can use a snappy slogan like 'Defund The Police,' but, you know, you lost a big audience the minute you say it, which makes it a lot less likely that you're actually going to get the changes you want done. But if you instead say, 'Let's reform the police department so that everybody's being treated fairly, you know, divert young people from getting into crime, and if there was a homeless guy, can maybe we send a mental health worker there instead of an armed unit that could end up resulting in a tragedy?' Suddenly, a whole bunch of folks who might not otherwise listen to you are listening to you.*[230]

---

[227] https://press.uchicago.edu/books/excerpt/2016/lakoff_trump.html
[228] ibid.
[229] ibid.

[230] https://www.cnn.com/2020/12/02/politics/barack-obama-defund-the-police/index.html

Chapter 9: This is not a "Safe Space" (Sort of)

Comprehension questions you should be able to answer after reading this chapter:

1. What are Mill's three regions of human liberty?
2. How does Mill use utilitarianism to justify both freedom of expression and freedom of lifestyle?
3. What are the four advantages/reasons Mill offers in defense of free expression?

I say this with all due respect and care: this textbook is not a "safe space," nor is any class I teach with this text (or any other).

What I *mean* by that is that receiving, considering, and addressing criticism of one's views—even deeply held views—is an essential experience of not only philosophy specifically, but education in general.

To "protect" you from disagreement, criticism, and exposure to other points of view (including ideas and perspectives that you might find to be offensive) would not only be patronizing to you, but would rob of you of the experiences necessary for intellectual and personal growth.

However uncomfortable it might be to consider views different from, and even antithetical to, one's own, there is *wisdom* in engaging in dialogue with "the other side." Supreme Court Justice Sonia Sotomayor says:

Quiet pragmatism, of course, lacks the romance of vocal militancy. But I felt myself more a mediator than a crusader. My strengths were reasoning, crafting compromises, finding the good and the good faith on both sides of an argument, and using that to build a bridge. Always, my first question was, what's the goal? And then, who must be persuaded if it is to be accomplished? A respectful dialogue with one's opponent almost invariably goes further than a harangue outside his or her window. If you want to change someone's mind, you must understand what need shapes his or her opinion. To prevail, you must first listen.[231]

Journalist, progressive activist, and former "Green Jobs" advisor to President Obama, Van Jones, puts it even more forcefully:

I don't like bigots and bullies. I just want to point that out... But I got tough talk for my liberal colleagues on these campuses. They don't tend to like it but I think they like me so I get away with it. I want to push this. There are two ideas about safe spaces: One is a very good idea and one is a terrible idea. The idea of being physically safe on a campus—not being subjected to sexual harassment and physical abuse, or being targeted specifically, personally, for some kind of hate speech—"you are an n-word," or whatever—I am perfectly fine with that. But there's another view that is now I think ascendant, which I think is just a horrible view, which is that "I need to be safe ideologically. I need to be safe emotionally I just need to feel good all the time, and if someone says something that I don't like, that's a problem for everybody else including the administration."

I think that is a terrible idea for the following reason: I don't want you to be safe, ideologically. I don't want you to be safe, emotionally. I want you to be strong.

---

[231] U.S. Supreme Court Justice Sonia Sotomayor, *My Beloved World*

That's different.

I'm not going to pave the jungle for you. Put on some boots, and learn how to deal with adversity. I'm not going to take all the weights out of the gym; that's the whole point of the gym. This is the gym. You can't live on a campus where people say stuff you don't like?! And these people can't fire you, they can't arrest you, they can't beat you up, they can just say stuff you don't like- and you get to say stuff back- and this you cannot bear?!

This is ridiculous BS liberals! My parents, and Monica Elizabeth Peak's parents [points to someone in the audience and greets her] were marched, they dealt with fire hoses! They dealt with dogs! They dealt with beatings! You can't deal with a mean tweet?! You are creating a kind of liberalism that the minute it crosses the street into the real world is not just useless, but obnoxious and dangerous. I want you to be offended every single day on this campus. I want you to be deeply aggrieved and offended and upset, and then to learn how to speak back. Because that is what we need from you in these communities."[232]

John Stuart Mill

Perhaps the most iconic thinker associated with the value of free expression and exchange of ideas, though, is John Stuart Mill. Mill claimed that "utility" is the basis for all his political ideas, and that the only legitimate use of legal coercion is to prevent harm (as opposed to coercion for paternalistic reasons).[233] Mill then lays out the domain of human liberty, as he understands it.

This, then, is the appropriate region of human liberty. It comprises, first, the inward domain of consciousness; demanding liberty of conscience, in the most comprehensive sense; liberty of

thought and feeling; absolute freedom of opinion and sentiment on all subjects, practical or speculative, scientific, moral, or theological. The liberty of expressing and publishing opinions may seem to fall under a different principle, since it belongs to that part of the conduct of an individual which concerns other people; but, being almost of as much importance as the liberty of thought itself, and resting in great part on the same reasons, is practically inseparable from it. Secondly, the principle requires liberty of tastes and pursuits; of framing the plan of our life to suit our own character; of doing as we like, subject to such consequences as may follow: without impediment from our fellow-creatures, so long as what we do does not harm them, even though they should think our conduct foolish, perverse, or wrong. Thirdly, from this liberty of each individual, follows the liberty, within the same limits, of combination among individuals; freedom to unite, for any purpose not involving harm to others: the persons combining being supposed to be of full age, and not forced or deceived.

No society in which these liberties are not, on the whole, respected, is free, whatever may be its form of government; and none is completely free in which they do not exist absolute and unqualified. The only freedom which deserves the name, is that of pursuing our own good in our own way, so long as we do not attempt to deprive others of theirs, or impede their efforts to obtain it. Each is the proper guardian of his own health, whether bodily, or mental and spiritual. Mankind are greater gainers by suffering each other to live as seems good to themselves, than by compelling each to live as seems good to the rest.

---

[232] CLIP: Van Jones on safe spaces on College campuses

[233] Both of those claims are explored and defended in the later chapter on utilitarianism.

Mill lists three regions of human liberty:

1. Conscience (including freedom of expression and opinion)

2. Lifestyle (including freedom of personal taste and life-plan)

3. Association (including freedom to form groups, political parties, etc.)

For our purposes we focus on just the first two regions—but first note the repetition of two key ideas in the last paragraph of the quotation above. He emphasizes personal autonomy when he states that the "only freedom which deserves the name, is that of pursuing our own good in our own way, so long as we do not attempt to deprive others of theirs, or impede their efforts to obtain it." That is, people should be free to live their lives as they see fit, without interference, unless interference is necessary to prevent them from harming others.

Then, he reiterates his utilitarian foundation. "Mankind are greater gainers by suffering each other to live as seems good to themselves, than by compelling each to live as seems good to the rest."

It's important not to gloss over this point.

Why should government intrude minimally in persons' lives? Why should people be allowed to live as they see fit, provided they're not harming others? Because we are "greater gainers" when we do so. In other words, this approach to governing *maximizes utility*.

In fairness, though, if the justification for a "hands off" approach to governing is that it maximizes utility, then it would follow that if that were not true, and a more intrusive approach actually produced more utility, then Mill, in order to be consistent, would have to endorse *that* approach instead. It falls to him, therefore, to justify his utilitarian interpretation of his broadly libertarian approach to governing. We will see how he does so first with regard to freedom of conscience/expression.

---

234 https://www.billofrightsinstitute.org/founding-documents/bill-of-rights/

Freedom of Conscience/Expression

The U.S. Constitution was ratified in 1788. Included in that Constitution is the Bill of Rights. The first amendment states that "Congress shall make no law respecting an establishment of religion, or prohibiting the free exercise thereof; or abridging the freedom of speech, or of the press; or the right of the people peaceably to assemble, and to petition the government for a redress of grievances."[234]

Mill's *On Liberty* was published in 1859, over 80 years later. Clearly, "freedom of expression" was not invented by Mill, nor first recognized by Mill, but had, instead, been part of the philosophical landscape for some time. Mill does offer a valuable contribution, however, by offering a philosophical defense of the value of freedom of conscience and expression in terms of utility.

He starts his defense of freedom of opinion and expression in bold terms. "If all mankind minus one, were of one opinion, and only one person were of the contrary opinion, mankind would be no more justified in silencing that one person, than he, if he had the power, would be justified in silencing mankind."

Suppose that there are seven billion people in the world. If 6,999,999,999 of them all believed the same thing, and only one person out of that seven billion believed otherwise, it would be just as unjustifiable to silence that one person as it would for that one to silence the 6,999,999,999. This is an extraordinary claim! But, Mill doesn't merely assert this out of some sentimental appreciation for the minority opinion, but out of his utilitarian worldview.

Were an opinion a personal possession of no value except to the owner; if to be obstructed in the enjoyment of it were simply a private injury, it would make some difference whether the injury was inflicted only on a few persons or on many. But the peculiar evil of silencing the expression of an opinion is, that it is robbing the human race; posterity as well as the existing generation; those who dissent from the opinion, still more than those who hold it. If the opinion is right, they are deprived of the opportunity of exchanging error for truth: if wrong, they lose, what is almost as great a benefit, the clearer perception and livelier impression of truth, produced by its collision with error.

Mill believes that a *greater good* is served by not silencing any particular point of view, even if there is clear and overwhelming consensus opposing it. Interestingly, he claims the greater harm from silencing that opinion applies to those who *disagree*. With regard to that unpopular opinion, it is either true, or it is false. If it is true, then the majority are "deprived of the opportunity of exchanging error for truth." In other words, we remain *wrong*.

An increasing number of parents in the United States believe that vaccinations are linked to autism in children, and a great many more are unsure. Of Americans surveyed, 6% think vaccines cause autism, 41% think that they do not, and 52% (a majority) are unsure.[235] Even President Trump has contributed to the vaccine-autism link. In 2015 he said "We had so many instances, people that work for me, just the other day, 2 years old, a beautiful child, went to have the vaccine and came back and a week later got a tremendous fever, got very, very sick, now is autistic."[236] Back in 2012, he tweeted "Massive combined inoculations to small children is the cause for big increase in autism."[237] This, despite the fact that only *one* study has ever linked vaccinations to autism, and that solitary study has since been discredited as fraudulent, the article was officially retracted from the science journal in which it was published, and the researcher who wrote it lost his medical license![238] Given the public health dangers of "anti-vaxxers," we might think that promoting the discredited link between vaccines and autism should be prohibited. Mill, however, would presumably disagree.

What if, contrary to all expectations and evidence, the anti-vaxxers are actually *right*?

First: the opinion which it is attempted to suppress by authority may possibly be true. Those who desire to suppress it, of course deny its truth; but they are not infallible. They have no authority to decide the question for all mankind, and exclude every other person from the means of judging. To refuse a hearing to an opinion, because they are sure that it is false, is to assume that their certainty is the same thing as absolute certainty. All silencing of discussion is an assumption of infallibility. Its condemnation may be allowed to rest on this common argument, not the worse for being common.

No one is infallible. Every person is capable of being mistaken, and we can be mistaken as individuals as well as in communities. Medieval communities who believed the bubonic plague was being spread by witches or Jews were *mistaken*. It's possible (however unlikely) that *there really is* a danger posed by vaccinations, in which case the safer course of action is to allow dissent.

To be clear, allowing dissent does not entail putting the dissenting voice on equal footing with the consensus view. To say that people should be allowed to express contrary opinions is just that: they are *allowed* to. It doesn't mean they should be treated as having the same credibility as the majority who disagrees. It might be consistent

[235] http://www.huffingtonpost.com/2015/03/06/gallup-poll-vaccines_n_6818416.html
[236] http://www.standard.net/National/2017/01/10/Trump-asks-vaccine-skeptic-Robert-Kennedy-Jr-to-lead-commission-on-vaccine-safety-1

[237] https://twitter.com/realdonaldtrump/status/238717783007977473?lang=en
[238] http://www.publichealth.org/public-awareness/understanding-vaccines/vaccine-myths-debunked/

with Mill's theory to allow anti-vaxxers to express their perspective, but it certainly doesn't mean that we should pretend that their view has the same standing as the overwhelming majority of every doctor and researcher who has any experience and expertise in this subject.

Some internet "experts" claim that Hillary Clinton is actually an alien reptilian shapeshifter (along with a surprising number of other celebrities and politicians!).[239] Much more "popular"—and seemingly much more dangerous—a shocking number of Americans believe that "a group of Satan-worshipping elites who run a child sex ring are trying to control our politics and media." This core belief of the QAnon conspiracy is believed to be "true" by 17% of Americans, with another 37% being "not sure."[240] There were partisan differences in these beliefs. Among Republicans, only 14% thought that claim was false (i.e., 86% thought it was true or they weren't sure), compared to 46% of Democrats.[241]

It is technically possible that these conspiracy-theorists are right, and a subversive alien invasion is underway, and/or a secret cabal of baby-killing Satan worshippers pull the strings of global governments, and Donald Trump was secretly recruited by top U.S. Generals because only he could save us—but it seems vastly more likely that those initially promoting these claims are either mentally-ill, or gullible, or internet trolls. We certainly shouldn't claim that it is just as likely that our world leaders are aliens as that they are not—but nor should we literally censor the conspiracy theory (according to Mill), no matter how bizarre or implausible it might be.[242]

Thus far, we have considered the value of

allowing free expression out of concern that the minority view might be true. It's entirely possible, though, that the view is false. Even then, Mill thinks there is value in it being expressed. Confidence in the truth of one's own claim requires a clash with opposing points of view.

> *There is the greatest difference between presuming an opinion to be true, because, with every opportunity for contesting it, it has not been refuted, and assuming its truth for the purpose of not permitting its refutation. Complete liberty of contradicting and disproving our opinion, is the very condition which justifies us in assuming its truth for purposes of action; and on no other terms can a being with human faculties have any rational assurance of being right.*

Consider the example of climate change deniers. The overwhelming majority of climate scientists are convinced that human activity contributes (harmfully) to global warming.[243] However, there is a minority view that either denies the extent of human-impact, or that is least unsettled on it. Mill would already think that they should be allowed to express and explore that view, given the possibility that they might be correct, but he would also claim that the existence of this contrary view serves to sharpen and strengthen the majority view.

Those of us who subject ourselves to differing points of view run the risk of actually learning something from the process! Even if we conclude (repeatedly) that the other point of

---

[239] http://alien-uforesearch.com/ researchdiscussion/viewtopic.php?t=3125
[240] https://www.ipsos.com/en-us/news-polls/npr-misinformation-123020
[241] ibid.
[242] Note that this endorsement of the free exchange of ideas is not without any limits whatsoever, even for Mill. The more "dangerous" an idea becomes, the more likely a utilitarian case for suppression of that idea could be made. QAnon, for example, has now been connected to

numerous criminal acts, and QAnon supporters played a prominent role in the January 6th, 2020 attempted insurrection when the Capitol building was temporarily taken over by various groups of Trump supporters. https://www.cnn.com/2021/01/07/us/insurrection-capitol-extremist-groups-invs/index.html
[243] http://www.politifact.com/virginia/ statements/2016/apr/04/don-beyer/don-beyer-says-97-percent-scientists-believe-human/

view is mistaken, the process of examining it and being challenged by it is an intellectual "workout" that strengthens our confidence in our own view and enhances our ability to defend it. Without this contrast, Mill claims our ideas can turn into "dogma."

> *However unwillingly a person who has a strong opinion may admit the possibility that his opinion may be false, he ought to be moved by the consideration that however true it may be, if it is not fully, frequently, and fearlessly discussed, it will be held as a dead dogma, not a living truth.*

As mentioned in an earlier chapter of this book, in the final speech President Obama gave as President, he warned against our increasing tendency to operate within our own ideological "bubbles."

> *For too many of us, it's become safer to retreat into our own bubbles, whether in our neighborhoods or College campuses or places of worship or our social media feeds, surrounded by people who look like us and share the same political outlook and never challenge our assumptions. The rise of naked partisanship, increasing economic and regional stratification, the splintering of our media into a channel for every taste – all this makes this great sorting seem natural, even inevitable. And increasingly, we become so secure in our bubbles that we accept only information, whether true or not, that fits our opinions, instead of basing our opinions on the evidence that's out there.[244]*

This isn't merely some anecdotal cautionary tale about liberals only watching MSNBC and conservatives only watching Fox News. A study published in the "Proceedings of the National Academy of Sciences of the United States of America" concluded that "selective exposure to content is the primary driver of content diffusion and generates the formation of homogeneous clusters, i.e., 'echo chambers.' Indeed, homogeneity appears to be the primary driver for the diffusion of contents and each echo chamber has its own cascade dynamics."[245]

In other words, people on Facebook mostly share news that they already agree with, that is consistent with their worldview, and they don't share information that challenges it. As the researchers put it: "users show a tendency to search for, interpret, and recall information that confirm their pre-existing beliefs."

Combine this tendency with the fact that Facebook has nearly 2 billion users (out of roughly 7 billion people on the planet), and reaches 67% of U.S. adults, and that 62% of Americans get their news mainly from social media sites such as Facebook and Twitter.[246]

A majority of Americans get their news primarily from social media, and research confirms the application of the confirmation bias to social media platforms. It should go without saying that these trends seriously compromise our ability to think critically, and to responsibly accept or reject claims. Mill described this condition with prescience more than 150 years ago.

> *The greatest orator, save one, of antiquity, has left it on record that he always studied his adversary's case with as great, if not with still greater, intensity than even his own. What Cicero practised as the means of forensic success, requires to be imitated by all who study any subject in order to arrive at the truth. He who knows only his own side of the case, knows little of that. His reasons may be good, and no one may*

---

[244] http://www.latimes.com/politics/la-pol-obama-farewell-speech-transcript-20170110-story.html
[245] http://www.pnas.org/content/113/3/554.full

[246] http://www.journalism.org/2016/05/26/news-use-across-social-media-platforms-2016/?utm_content=bufferae870&utm_medium=social&utm_source=twitter.com&utm_campaign=buffer

have been able to refute them. But if he is equally unable to refute the reasons on the opposite side; if he does not so much as know what they are, he has no ground for preferring either opinion. The rational position for him would be suspension of judgment, and unless he contents himself with that, he is either led by authority, or adopts, like the generality of the world, the side to which he feels most inclination. Nor is it enough that he should hear the arguments of adversaries from his own teachers, presented as they state them, and accompanied by what they offer as refutations. That is not the way to do justice to the arguments, or bring them into real contact with his own mind. He must be able to hear them from persons who actually believe them; who defend them in earnest, and do their very utmost for them. He must know them in their most plausible and persuasive form; he must feel the whole force of the difficulty which the true view of the subject has to encounter and dispose of; else he will never really possess himself of the portion of truth which meets and removes that difficulty. Ninety-nine in a hundred of what are called educated men are in this condition; even of those who can argue fluently for their opinions. Their conclusion may be true, but it might be false for anything they know: they have never thrown themselves into the mental position of those who think differently from them, and considered what such persons may have to say; and consequently they do not, in any proper sense of the word, know the doctrine which they themselves profess. They do not know those parts of it which explain and justify the remainder; the considerations which show that a fact which seemingly conflicts with another is reconcilable with it, or that, of two apparently strong reasons, one and not the other ought to be preferred. All that part of the truth which turns the scale, and decides the judgment of a completely informed mind, they are strangers to; nor is it ever really known, but to those who have attended equally and impartially to both sides, and endeavoured to see the reasons of both in the strongest light. So essential is this discipline to a real understanding of moral and human subjects, that if opponents of all important truths do not exist, it is indispensable to imagine them, and supply them with the strongest arguments which the most skilful devil's advocate can conjure up.

In what might come as a shocking claim, Mill suggests that if you only know your own side of a debate, rather than this causing you to be certain of your own opinion, it should instead cause you to suspend judgment! After all, if you don't know what reasons exist that are contrary to your own, how can you be confident that those hypothetical reasons are not better than yours? It's not even sufficient to hear opposing points of view from others, if those others actually agree with you. Pretending to "debate" the issue with like-minded friends isn't good enough. "He must be able to hear them from persons who actually believe them; who defend them in earnest, and do their very utmost for them."

This is what we try to do when we employ the principle of charity when evaluating arguments (as described in chapter one). Indeed, Mill even gestures at this when he says "So essential is this discipline to a real understanding of moral and human subjects, that if opponents of all important truths do not exist, it is indispensable to imagine them, and supply them with the strongest arguments which the most skilful devil's advocate can conjure up." But, there is no comparison between considering "the other side" as best you can, and actually *hearing* (or reading) the other side from people who actually sincerely believe in it.

Practically speaking, this means that if you self-identify as a liberal, you should probably turn off MSNBC and NPR and watch Fox News from time to time. Conversely, if you are conservative, that might mean turning off Rush Limbaugh and listening to Keith Olbermann for a change. If you are a person of faith, actually read some serious, credible arguments for atheism. If you are an atheist, read some serious, scholarly books or articles from people of faith. While it's possible that you might change your mind, this isn't necessarily very likely. Far more likely, but still valuable, is that you *understand* the different perspective, and thereby better understand *your own*.

Thus far, we have consider the value of free expression based on the possibility that the idea might be true, or, that even if it is false there is still value in considering alternatives. Mill reminds us that there is still a third option, as well.

We have hitherto considered only two possibilities: that the received opinion may be false, and some other opinion, consequently, true; or that, the received opinion being true, a conflict with the opposite error is essential to a clear apprehension and deep feeling of its truth. But there is a commoner case than either of these; when the conflicting doctrines, instead of being one true and the other false, share the truth between them; and the nonconforming opinion is needed to supply the remainder of the truth, of which the received doctrine embodies only a part. Popular opinions, on subjects not palpable to sense, are often true, but seldom or never the whole truth. They are a part of the truth; sometimes a greater, sometimes a smaller part, but exaggerated, distorted, and disjoined from the truths by which they ought to be accompanied and limited. Heretical opinions, on the other hand, are generally some of these suppressed and neglected truths, bursting the bonds which kept them down, and either seeking reconciliation with the truth contained in the common opinion, or fronting it as enemies, and setting themselves up, with similar exclusiveness, as the whole truth.

When dealing with simple and uncontroversial claims, truth is pretty binary. 2+2 = 4, and any contrary view is simply mistaken. It's an all-or-nothing situation. 2+2 = 4 is entirely true, and 2+2 = "anything else" is entirely false. In other cases, however—and especially when it comes to politics—it is often the case that "both sides" have something to contribute in a meaningful way. Mill makes this connection to politics explicitly clear.

In politics, again, it is almost a commonplace, that a party of order or stability, and a party of progress or reform, are both necessary elements of a healthy state of political life; until the one or the other shall have so enlarged its mental grasp as to be a party equally of order and of progress, knowing and distinguishing what is fit to be preserved from what ought to be swept away. Each of these modes of thinking derives its utility from the deficiencies of the other; but it is in a great measure the opposition of the other that keeps each within the limits of reason and sanity. Unless opinions favourable to democracy and to aristocracy, to property and to equality, to co-operation and to competition, to luxury and to abstinence, to sociality and individuality, to liberty and discipline, and all the other standing antagonisms of practical life, are expressed with equal freedom, and enforced and defended with equal talent and energy, there is no chance of both elements obtaining their due; one scale is sure to go up and the other down. Truth, in the great practical concerns of life, is so much a question of the reconciling and combining of opposites, that very few have minds sufficiently capacious and impartial to make the adjustment with an approach to correctness, and it has to be made by the rough process of a struggle between combatants fighting under hostile banners. On any of the great open questions just enumerated, if either of the two opinions has a better claim than the other, not merely to be tolerated, but to be encouraged and countenanced, it is the one which happens at the particular time and place to be in a minority. That is the opinion which, for the time being, represents the neglected interests, the side of human well-being which is in danger of obtaining less than its share.

The Affordable Care Act ("Obamacare) was incredibly unpopular among conservatives, and the House of Representatives voted to repeal it (unsuccessfully) dozens of times. President Trump campaigned promising to "repeal and replace" the ACA, and began taking steps to do so within days of his inauguration. Interestingly, though, several of the key components of the ACA actually came from a conservative think tank: the Heritage Foundation.[247] In fact, a bill inspired by the Heritage Foundation report was introduced by Republican Senator John Chafee of Rhode Island in 1993, and that bill was co-sponsored by 18 other Republican Senators, including former Republican Presidential candidate Bob Dole. The bill called for:

- An individual mandate
- Creation of purchasing pools
- Standardized benefits
- Vouchers for the poor to buy insurance
- A ban on denying coverage based on a pre-existing condition[248]

If these ideas sound familiar to you, they should: all of them are found in the ACA, and most of them were originally considered to be "conservative" ideas.

While the idea that health care is a "right" and that certain services, such as birth control, should be provided by all insurance policies might be "liberal" ideas, the notion of personal responsibility behind the individual mandate, and the free-market appeal of "exchanges" are traditionally conservative ideas. Whether the ACA was good and successful policy is subject to honest debate, but Mill is confident that the exchange and combination of ideas often serves the greater good.

If nothing else, opposition parties are valuable in that they limit the "success" of the dominant party at the time. "Each of these modes of thinking derives its utility from the deficiencies of the other; but it is in a great measure the opposition of the other that keeps each within the limits of reason and sanity." We might imagine Mill saying that it serves a greater good that Republicans limit the efforts of Democrats, and vice versa, that the United States is better off when policy reflects a moderated compromise between the wish lists of both parties, rather than an unrestrained embodiment of either party's "perfect" society.

To summarize Mill up to this point, we can appeal to Mill himself, who helpfully reviews his argument thus far:

We have now recognised the necessity to the mental well-being of mankind (on which all their other well-being depends) of freedom of opinion, and freedom of the expression of opinion, on four distinct grounds; which we will now briefly recapitulate.

***First**, if any opinion is compelled to silence, that opinion may, for aught we can certainly know, be true. To deny this is to assume our own infallibility.*

***Secondly**, though the silenced opinion be an error, it may, and very commonly does, contain a portion of truth; and since the general or prevailing opinion on any subject is rarely or never the whole truth, it is only by the collision of adverse opinions, that the remainder of the truth has any chance of being supplied.*

***Thirdly**, even if the received opinion be not only true, but the whole truth; unless it is suffered to be, and actually is, vigorously and earnestly contested, it will, by most of those who receive it, be held in the manner of a prejudice, with little comprehension or feeling of its rational grounds. And not only this, but, **fourthly**, the meaning of the*

---

[247] http://www.heritage.org/research/reports/1989/a-national-health-system-for-america

[248] https://www.congress.gov/bill/103rd-congress/senate-bill/1770

doctrine itself will be in danger of being lost, or enfeebled, and deprived of its vital effect on the character and conduct: the dogma becoming a mere formal profession, inefficacious for good, but cumbering the ground, and preventing the growth of any real and heartfelt conviction, from reason or personal experience.[249]

Freedom of Lifestyle

Having addressed Mill's defense of free opinion and expression, we can now turn to his defense for the freedom to live as one sees fit, to live a lifestyle of one's own choosing, so long as no harm is being inflicted on anyone else. He recognizes, of course, that actions are more subject to proper limitation than are ideas.

No one pretends that actions should be as free as opinions. On the contrary, even opinions lose their immunity, when the circumstances in which they are expressed are such as to constitute their expression a positive instigation to some mischievous act. An opinion that corn-dealers are starvers of the poor, or that private property is robbery, ought to be unmolested when simply circulated through the press, but may justly incur punishment when delivered orally to an excited mob assembled before the house of a corn-dealer, or when handed about among the same mob in the form of a placard. Acts, of whatever kind, which, without justifiable cause, do harm to others, may be, and in the more important cases absolutely require to be, controlled by the unfavourable sentiments, and, when needful, by the active interference of mankind. The liberty of the individual must be thus far limited; he must not make himself a nuisance to other people. But if he refrains from molesting others in what

concerns them, and merely acts according to his own inclination and judgment in things which concern himself, the same reasons which show that opinion should be free, prove also that he should be allowed, without molestation, to carry his opinions into practice at his own cost.

Several points are worth reviewing here. First, not even opinions are entirely immune to restriction. Deliberately using speech to incite a riot, for example, is not a legitimate use of one's freedom to express an opinion.

The U.S. Supreme Court case of *Schenck v. United States* established that "the most stringent protection of free speech would not protect a man falsely shouting fire in a theater and causing a panic. [...] The question in every case is whether the words used are used in such circumstances and are of such a nature as to create a clear and present danger that they will bring about the substantive evils that Congress has a right to prevent."[250]

Decades later, the case of *Brandenburg v. Ohio* refined this ruling by stating that even speech that supports breaking the law, and even violence, is protected by the First Amendment unless it directly encourages people to immediately break the law.[251] We might imagine the difference between someone blogging about overthrowing the government, versus someone speaking to a crowd of people and encouraging them to assault the politician who is giving a speech just a few yards away.

In any event, as free as expression should be for Mill, this freedom is not unlimited, and the freedom of actions even less so. "Acts, of whatever kind, which, without justifiable cause, do harm to others, may be, and in the more important cases absolutely require to be, controlled by the unfavourable sentiments, and, when needful, by the active interference of mankind."

Any action that harms others is subject to

---

[249] I have added my own emphasis to this quotation.
[250] https://supreme.justia.com/cases/federal/

us/249/47/case.html
[251] https://supreme.justia.com/cases/federal/us/395/444/

restriction. Again, obvious cases include rape and murder. But, if someone's actions harm no one at all, or even if they only harm himself or herself, then that person should be left free to "carry his opinions into practice at his own cost."

You might think that someone is wasting their life, squandering their potential, or acting foolishly or sinfully. You might think that someone who smokes marijuana is harming themselves and their life prospects, or that someone who gives a good portion of their money to their church is a fool. You might think that homosexuality is "gross," or that monogamy and marriage are "unnatural."

Mill would say you are free to *judge* other lifestyles however you please, and it's even acceptable for you to try to convince the person to change their ways. What is not acceptable, however, is to use the power of the State to make "them" live more like you.

One more time, Mill offers a utilitarian justification for his endorsement of individuality and being free to live your life as you see fit.

It is not by wearing down into uniformity all that is individual in themselves, but by cultivating it and calling it forth, within the limits imposed by the rights and interests of others, that human beings become a noble and beautiful object of contemplation; and as the works partake the character of those who do them, by the same process human life also becomes rich, diversified, and animating, furnishing more abundant aliment to high thoughts and elevating feelings, and strengthening the tie which binds every individual to the race, by making the race infinitely better worth belonging to. In proportion to the development of his individuality, each person becomes more valuable to himself, and is therefore capable of being more valuable to others. There is a greater fulness of life about his own existence, and when there is more life in the units there is more in the mass which is composed of them. As much compression as is necessary to prevent the stronger specimens of

human nature from encroaching on the rights of others, cannot be dispensed with; but for this there is ample compensation even in the point of view of human development. The means of development which the individual loses by being prevented from gratifying his inclinations to the injury of others, are chiefly obtained at the expense of the development of other people. And even to himself there is a full equivalent in the better development of the social part of his nature, rendered possible by the restraint put upon the selfish part. To be held to rigid rules of justice for the sake of others, develops the feelings and capacities which have the good of others for their object. But to be restrained in things not affecting their good, by their mere displeasure, develops nothing valuable, except such force of character as may unfold itself in resisting the restraint. If acquiesced in, it dulls and blunts the whole nature. To give any fair-play to the nature of each, it is essential that different persons should be allowed to lead different lives.

He describes cultivating individuality as a process that makes a person "noble and beautiful." Cultivating individuality makes life "rich" and makes the human race "infinitely better worth belonging to." It makes life have "greater fullness." "In proportion to the development of his individuality, each person becomes more valuable to himself, and is therefore capable of being more valuable to others." That is, developing my own individuality not only makes my own life more valuable to me, but also more valuable to others—hence the "greater good." Forced conformity, in contrast, "dulls and blunts the whole nature."

So long as we're not harming anyone else, Mill thinks we should be free to experiment with our own vision of the good life. Some of these experiments will turn out well and satisfying, and others of us might learn from those examples and emulate those lifestyles ourselves. Other experiments will turn out poorly, such as a life of opiate-addiction. Sadly, there is utility in that example as well: it might teach the rest of us not to make those same mistakes. In any event, we should be free to pursue our own good, at our own cost, and to our own benefit, so long as we're not harming anyone else in the process.

Critical Analysis

1. In your opinion, what are the strongest and most compelling points made by the philosopher or philosophers in this chapter? Why do you find those points to be convincing?

2. In your opinion, what are the weakest or least convincing points? Why? Can you anticipate any limitations or objections to their ideas not already addressed in the chapter?

Appendix: Application to Social Justice

Jonathan Haidt (an expert in moral psychology who was the focus of an earlier chapter in this book), perhaps controversially, argues that "social justice" is not the proper "*telos*" (goal) for a University (or presumably, by extension, a College).

First, for the record, Jonathan Haidt "considers himself a centrist who sides with the Democratic Party on the great majority of issues, but who has learned a lot from the writings of conservative intellectuals, from Edmund Burke through Thomas Sowell. [He has never]… Voted for a Republican for Congress or the Presidency. [He shares]… most of the desired ends of social justice activism, including full racial equality, an end to sexual harassment and assault, comprehensive gun-control, and responsible stewardship of the environment. [But he believes]… that the way social justice is currently being conceptualized and pursued on campus is causing a variety of problems and engendering resistance and resentment for reasons that some

of its advocates don't seem to recognize."[252]

In other words, Haidt is *not* approaching this topic as someone somehow hostile to "social justice" and its aims. That being established, before evaluating his potentially controversial claim, and identifying its connection to this chapter, it would help to identify what is meant by a "*telos*."

Telos is a Greek word meaning (roughly) goal, end, or purpose. Numerous ancient Greek philosophers such as Plato and Aristotle thought that all human activity was guided by some *telos* or another, and the proper *telos* for that activity was the one best suited to its nature. We get an extended discussion of this idea in Plato's *Republic* when Thrasymachus and Socrates are arguing about the nature of justice.

Thrasymachus claims that justice is simply a pretty label that we attach to the preferences and values of the ruling party (whether individual, as in a king or dictator, or group, as in an oligarchy or democracy). Whoever is in charge, wherever they might be, promote their own interests and call that "justice." When someone else takes over, they do the same thing.

In response to Thrasymachus' position, Socrates begins his predictable line of attack. He first gets Thrasymachus to acknowledge that those in power sometimes make mistakes about what is to their advantage, and that subjects are to obey those laws anyway—and that it is right for them to do so. Accordingly, even though "justice" is defined as the advantage of the stronger, it is nevertheless "just" to do things which are actually to their disadvantage.

Socrates continues by once again making reference to justice as a skill and begins with analogy. Medicine considers the welfare of the body, not the welfare of medicine. In other words, a doctor, when she is practicing medicine, is not aimed at wealth or prestige, but at healing the sick. Also, medicine is for the advantage of the "weaker" party. It serves the patient (the one who is sick), not the doctor (the one who is well).

---

[252] Haidt, Jonathan & Lukianoff, Greg. *The Coddling of the American Mind*. Penguin Books, 2019. P. 216.

By analogy, Socrates claims, rulers, when they practice the craft of ruling, consider not their own welfare, but that of their subjects. Justice, then, is not concerned with the advantage of the stronger (i.e., the ruler), but, if anyone at all, of the weaker (i.e., the ruled).

Thrasymachus immediately offers an analogy of his own: shepherds are indeed concerned with their welfare of their flock, but only so that they can sell or eat them later! Socrates proceeds to attack *this* analogy, claiming that different skills are at work. Medical doctors, for example, are concerned with the success of their practice. However, a *different* skill is employed when the doctor is considering and working on the financial success of her practice. When she is doing *medicine*, her craft focuses on healing the body. Similarly, the shepherd, when acting as a shepherd, is focused on the well-being of the flock. When the shepherd turns his attention to making a profit, a different skill is employed. Socrates suggests that something like "money-making" is this overarching (different) skill that conjoins with every other craft. Carpentry concerns working with wood, but to be a financially successful carpenter requires the skill of "money-making." When working with the wood, though, the skill is carpentry, not money-making. Rulers, *qua* rulers, are not working to their own benefit. When they do, they are exercising a different skill.

With that admittedly lengthy (but important) explanation in place, we can now turn to why Haidt thinks that social justice is not the proper *telos* of the University/College. He gives several examples of different fields, each with their own *telos*.[253]

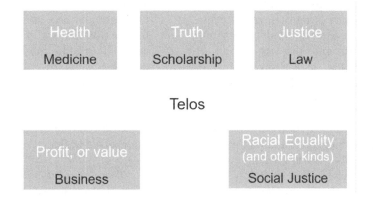

Telos

Respectively, the *telos* of medicine is health, that of scholarship/education is truth, that of law is justice, that of business is profit or value, and that of social justice is racial equality (among other things).

These *teloi* can have what he calls "constructive interactions" with one another, such as when truth in scholarship helps medicine to promote health, or when a profitable business helps to finance social justice causes, etc. In addition, though, they can exhibit "destructive interactions."

When, for example, profit is taken to be the *telos* of medicine, the health of patients might be sacrificed for the sake of greater profits for a health insurance company. In the case of social justice, he thinks this sort of destructive interaction occurs when the *telos* of social justice (racial equality, etc.) is substituted for the proper *telos* of these other fields.

<hr>

[253] https://heterodoxacademy.org/blog/one-telos-truth-or-social-justice-2/ Haidt gives explicit permission for teachers, such as myself, to freely use his images and presentation.

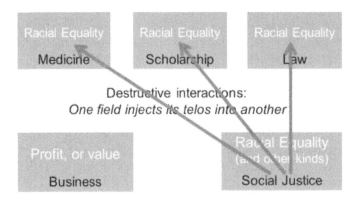

Each *telos* is proper and worthy of pursuit within its own field, but when we substitute the *telos* of one field for the proper *telos* of another, we are engaging in a fundamentally different activity, much as Socrates suggested occurs when a physician is pursuing profit rather than the health of a patient. There is a proper relationship between social justice and scholarship. Certainly the pursuit of truth and the acquisition of education in Colleges and Universities is protected and enhanced when relationships of racial equality (etc.) are honored and achieved in the classroom and on the campus. When students, staff, or faculty are subject to racism, it is not only a moral wrong, but an impediment to their education or work. Haidt would acknowledge that social justice certainly has a role to play on College campuses. However, what he rejects is the idea that social justice is the primary goal, or that it supersedes all other goals – truth, in particular.

"Truth" is, of course, a notoriously "complicated" concept in philosophy. Please see the chapter entitled "Truth" for a more detailed accounting of some different possible interpretations of truth. Of note, the reality of implicit bias reveals that, even if truth is objective, what actually *is* true might not necessarily be what people in positions of privilege assume it to be, even if they have sincere intentions. If nothing else, this indicates the value of having multiple points of view represented in the academy, and elsewhere—something that Haidt is actually arguing for, though not, in his case, in terms of axes of identity.

How might the goals of social justice somehow interfere with the pursuit of truth? Through dogmatism and the silencing of perspectives that are not deemed to be in harmony with the social justice agenda as it is understood on that campus. Given the progressive nature of social justice movements and activists, the most likely way that this will manifest is by the silencing of "conservative" voices, or the banning of viewpoints thought to be offensive to marginalized groups. One of the "dangers" is that those committed to social justice don't necessarily recognize the power that they themselves wield.

There's something missing from the social justice narrative . . .: it doesn't take into account the power and oppression it exerts itself. In a society where social justice advocates are outside the dominant power structure—as was the case when these ideas were originally articulated—this doesn't matter much, since their power is negligible. That's increasingly no longer the case, as social justice advocates have come to exert major influence over central areas of society, and consequently have also gained substantial power over society as a whole. Clearly, an accurate model of societal power must include social justice ideology and its advocates.

If this seems strange, it's because social

justice advocates have created a portrayal of themselves as being outside the flow of power; everyone else is exerting power or being oppressed by it, while they are simply observing it, and any power they do exert is selfless and unoppressive. Oppression is class-based, we've been conditioned to think, or based on race, gender, or sexual orientation. We therefore don't see the power and oppression exerted by social justice advocates, because it's based on none of those things; it's based on values. And there's nothing selfless about it. People exert power to shape the world according to their values, while preventing others from doing the same. In fact, there are close similarities between value oppression and other forms of oppression.
. . .

An analogous claim can be made of a social justice society, it seems to me. This is most obvious in parts of society where social justice ideology is strongest. In those parts of society, values like equality, liberation, and cosmopolitanism aren't just treated as values—organisations of society that different people prefer to different degrees—they're considered moral. Consequently, conflicting values are considered immoral: people who value a more competitive society, or a smaller government, or a stronger national identity, or a tougher culture, or more traditional family structures, or less immigration aren't just regarded as having different values; they're regarded as bad people. . . .

The larger lesson from including value oppression in our societal power analysis is that it reveals the limitations of social justice ideology. We can't simply set as a goal to 'fight oppression' and 'dismantle power structures' because social justice

ideology doesn't just do those things, it simultaneously creates its own power structures and oppression. Social justice advocates don't see this because their power analysis is incomplete; it doesn't include value oppression.

Including values in our power analysis makes it clear there can be no such thing as simply removing power, because it takes power to remove power. Consequently, power doesn't disappear, it redirects. In order to remove what they perceive as oppression—say by class, or race, or gender—social justice advocates have to erect their own power structure. They reshape morality, the culture, the language, and the legal system to make people do what they otherwise wouldn't. And the more they try to eliminate those other forms of oppression, the more tightly they have to oppress people's values. To increase freedom on one dimension, one must remove it on another.[254]

We could see how the suppression of certain ideas would be problematic by appealing to Mill's arguments from earlier in the chapter, even if we only focus on how the suppression of certain points of view might actually undermine the accuracy of one's own, and the successful pursuit of one's own agenda.

Our understanding of the relationship between truth and social justice can be enhanced by C.S. Lewis' essay entitled "First and Second Things." According to Lewis, if you put second things first and first things second, then you lose both, but if you keep first things first and second things second, then you can hold onto both.

Consider running and health. Of these two goods, health must take priority – in Lewis' language, it must be the "first thing." If a

---

[254] https://quillette.com/2018/02/17/thinking-critically-social-justice/

person becomes obsessive about running and prioritizes it above her health, then she may continue to run even if injured. Over time, if she continues to prioritize running over health, she will further damage her body, perhaps resulting in a permanent inability to run. On the other hand, if she prioritizes her health and keeps running in second place, then she will rest when injured and, consequently, will be able to enjoy more running in her life overall. Therefore, if one prioritizes running over health, in the end one will end up with neither, but if one puts health first, one can have both.

Truth and social justice can be viewed as having a similar relationship. If we prioritize social justice over truth we will get neither; whereas if we prioritize truth over social justice, we can get both. Why is this? In short, because acting on an inadequate understanding of what the world is like and how it works won't reliably get you what you want. Not just that, it can actually cause harm. . . .

Since your beliefs about the best solution were based on an inadequate understanding of the world, acting on them would result in harm. In other words, good intentions, kindness, the desire for justice – these aren't enough. If you want to help people, you must first understand what the world is really like.

How does this connect to social justice? To take a single example, on many campuses in the US, there have been calls for increased Diversity, Equity, and Inclusion (DEI) programming. Surely the goal of making members of campus communities that have been historically kept on the margins feel more welcome is a laudable

one. Nevertheless, the calls for increased DEI programming operate under the belief that more DEI programming of the sort that Universities have adopted up until this point will make those who have been on the margins feel more welcome on campus. But will it? I can't answer that question definitively – although the available research suggests, in fact, that standard DEI programming undermines the very goals that it seeks to obtain. My point is only that it matters if that belief is true. If it is false, then continuing to push the current kind of DEI programming may actually lead to the opposite of its stated goals. Effective social justice advocacy relies on properly understanding the world.

The same point would apply to myriad other social justice initiatives: Should we defund the police? Should we replace phonics with the whole word method for learning to read? Should we end the drug war? Should we pay reparations to the American descendants of slavery?

If successful social justice advocacy depends on truth – on accurately understanding how the world works – then it behooves us to do our level best to make sure that we understand the world before we take action. To not do so increases the likelihood that any intervention on behalf of social justice will actually harm the very people that we set out to help, thus hindering and not facilitating human emancipation.[255]

In other words, the relationship between social justice and scholarship can be either constructive or destructive. Presumably, the achievement of social justice depends on truth – not only the truth of the moral claims posed by

---

[255] https://heterodoxacademy.org/blog/truth-and-social-justice-how-Universities-can-embrace-both-of-these-values/

activists, but the truth of data used to formulate strategies, evaluate policies, analyze outcomes, etc. If the goal of "racial equality" *somehow* substantially interferes with the ability of a College or University to pursue and establish the truth, then the very aims of social justice are being undermined.

One example (among many) of how this might occur involves our analysis of disparate outcomes.[256] Haidt proposes that those with the *telos* of social justice in mind will typically interpret any "outcome gap" to be evidence of discrimination—and it very well could be. His concern, though, is that "if you suggest an alternative explanation for the gap, others may take you to be saying that the problem is not as severe as the speaker believes it is – and if anyone in the room is displeased by that suggestion, then you may be accused of committing a micro-aggression (specifically a "micro-invalidation"). If your alternative hypothesis includes the speculation that there could be differences in some underlying factor, some input that is relevant to the outcome…, then you may be violating a serious taboo."[257]

Concern about the social or professional consequences of even raising the possibility that there are other potential explanations for the disparity can produce a "chilling effect" on speech.

If professors and students are hesitant to raise alternative explanations for outcome gaps, then theories about those gaps may harden into orthodoxy. Its ideas may be accepted not because they are true but because the politically dominant group wants them to be true in order to promote its preferred narrative and preferred set of remedies. At that point, backed by the passion and certainty of activists, flawed academic theories may be carried out of the Academy and be applied in high schools, corporations, and other

organizations. Unfortunately, when reformers try to intervene in complex institutions using theories that are based on a flawed or incomplete understanding of the causal forces at work, there reform efforts are unlikely to do any good – and might even make things worse.[258]

Should that occur, not only does it undermine the (proper) *telos* of scholarship (viz., truth), but it even undermines the effective pursuit of the aims of social justice as well. Instead, each field (scholarship and social justice) should pursue its own proper goal, and a constructive relationship with one another.

This, of course, is not the *only* way to see the relationship between social justice and the pursuit of truth. Some argue that the social justice approach, which emphasizes the dynamics of power and oppression, is actually superior to a so-called "disinterested" pursuit of truth, and might even find a model in Socrates himself.

Socrates, the famous Athenian philosopher of the fifth century BCE, is beloved as the paragon of open debate, an example for all teachers to follow. He engaged in vigorous discussion with some of the most influential political and educational figures in Athens, usually to demonstrate that even the wisest figures in society did not know nearly as much as they thought they did.

Socrates's questioning of the powerful made these leaders so uncomfortable that they eventually used trumped-up charges of corrupting the youth to execute him, making him a martyr for free speech and open debate that many exalt today. . . .

Even if Socrates regularly humiliated his sparring partners, his method of dialectic did not consist of mere ridicule or dismissal

---

[256] Disparate outcomes are addressed in much more detail in the chapter on discrimination.
[257] Haidt, *The Coddling of the American Mind*,

228-229.
[258] ibid., 229.

of the opinions of others. Rather, he sought out the most renowned experts on any given topic, took their ideas seriously, and proceeded to show where the ideas were lacking.

Socrates's method benefited his students (and maybe even some of the powerful people whom he challenged) precisely because he didn't just call for an open marketplace of ideas, but deliberately steered the conversation to the point at which true inquiry could begin and true knowledge sought. . . .

Socratic dialectic, then, as practiced by Socrates and those who followed him, is a form of debate in which new ideas can emerge only after the very best ideas of the very best thinkers have been considered and taken seriously. <u>*Socratic dialectic does not, however, give all ideas and opinions equal weight. Rather it encourages experts to engage with one another, and new ideas and perspectives to emerge from their learned disagreements and debates.*</u>

Socrates did not believe in a "disinterested pursuit of truth," and neither should we. Truth depends on different perspectives and lenses, and this is what experts in the humanities — the so-called social justice warriors — bring to education. Critical theories about race, gender and sexuality are not undermining education. Rather, they complicate and expand our understanding of familiar topics. . . .[259]

So, what is the "final word" on this topic? Appropriately enough, I don't think there is a "final word," or at least not one that I am equipped to provide. As is often the case when dealing with values, and specifically competing values, the proper path is not always easily spotted or easily traveled. Undoubtedly, both truth and justice are great goods. Presumably, both can be pursued at Colleges and Universities. The precise boundaries and relationship between them, and to what extent each should be prioritized and in what context, is difficult to establish – but that difficulty should not discourage us from trying to honor both.

---

[259] https://www.washingtonpost.com/news/made-by-history/wp/2018/01/09/why-social-justice-warriors-are-the-true-defenders-of-free-speech-and-open-debate/ Emphases added.

Chapter 10: Human Nature. . . "Good" or "Evil?"

Comprehension questions you should be able to answer after reading this chapter:

1. What did Mengzi believe (in general) about human nature?
2. What explains "bad" behavior according to Mengzi?
3. What is meant by the idea of a "moral sprout?" What are the means by which our sprouts can be nurtured and cultivated?
4. What is the responsibility of the ruler/government with respect to cultivating "moral sprouts?"
5. Explain the basic features of Mengzi's thought experiment concerning a child falling into a well. What is it supposed to illustrate?
6. What did Xunzi believe (in general) about human nature?
7. What explains "bad" behavior according to Xunzi?
8. Explain the basic features of Xunzi's "state of nature" argument. What is it supposed to illustrate?
9. What is the purpose of (Confucian) rituals, for Xunzi?
10. Explain Xunzi's metaphor of "steaming and bending wood." How does it apply to human nature and moral development?

When you think about people, in general, which seems to be true? That people are basically good, "deep down," but can be tempted to do bad things as a result of circumstances? Or that people are basically "bad," and have to be educated and disciplined in order to behave themselves?

This fundamental question of human nature has generated debate across the globe and for thousands of years. It has significance not only with respect to our understanding of human nature, including psychology, but also because of its impact on our understanding of ethics. Depending upon what you think the "true" nature of human beings is, you will likely have different interpretations of our moral obligations as well as different understandings of moral education and training. The political relevance for this exploration is simply this: what you think about human nature does (or *should*) have a heck of a lot to do with what sorts of government you think is necessary or desired (and for what purposes), as well as what sorts of policies should be implemented (and for what purposes).

For our purposes, we will focus on two Confucian philosophers, Mengzi and Xunzi, and then consider an extension of this debate by exploring the theory of psychological egoism.

Mengzi (372 – 298 BCE), also known in the West as Mencius, is a Confucian philosopher who lived in the fourth century BCE. He never met Confucius, let alone studied with him—though he was allegedly trained by Confucius's grandson, Zisi (three generations after Confucius). His most famous work, "The Book of Mengzi," was written in dialogue form – much like many of the works of ancient Mediterranean philosophy. In China, he is generally considered second only to Kongzi/Confucius himself with respect to Confucian thinkers.

Xunzi (313 – 238 BCE), also known as Hsün Tzu, is also a Confucian philosopher from the same time period. He spent most of his career at the Jixia Academy, a "think tank" created by the ruler of Qi to gather intellectuals to study, teach, and devise the State. His most famous work, the self-titled "The Hsün Tzu," addresses ethics, metaphysics, epistemology, philosophy of language, and psychology. Xunzi's thoughts are a clear example of sustained philosophical arguments. Xunzi attempted to defend Confucianism not only against competitors from the outside (e.g. Mohisim) but also from alternative interpretations from the inside (e.g. Mengzi).

Both philosophers believed that implementing the teachings of Confucius was essential to restoring peace and order to the community. They share a basically Confucian ethical perspective, but are famous for their *disagreement* concerning human nature, namely, whether it is good or bad.

Mengzi claimed that human nature is "good." In contrast, Xunzi believes that human nature is primarily egoistic and must be manipulated and given a new "shape" through external forces before we will become virtuous. Although this will not occur unaided, Xunzi thinks that we are all capable of moral cultivation and development given good teachers and regular performance of ritual practices.

A central difference between them is whether moral development is imposed from the outside, or arises naturally if unimpeded. Their chosen metaphors are illustrative. Mengzi appeals to agricultural metaphors in which properly nurtured "sprouts" will develop according to their nature. In contrast, Xunzi uses crafting metaphors involving the alteration of wood or metal.

Both alterations are permanent, but one occurs naturally, and the other will not occur barring outside intervention.

For Mengzi, moral development is a matter of working *with* one's nature. For Xunzi, it is working to *overcome* one's nature A crooked piece of wood will not naturally become straight; it will not straighten out on its own. Such a piece of wood can only be made straight through the application of pressure from an external source.

It is this debate concerning human nature that will be our focus.

Mengzi: Humans are Naturally "Good"

Mengzi claims that humans are naturally good, with an intuitive sense of moral rightness

and wrongness. He is *not* claiming that all humans always act rightly. This is demonstrably false. I'm confident that you, just like me, have done some things that weren't "right" at various times in our lives. Instead, he is claiming that *normally*, given proper development, people delight in "righteousness." This natural disposition can be corrupted, but it is our inborn tendency nevertheless. To argue for this view of human nature, he gives an example of an allegedly spontaneous reaction to a hypothetical scenario.

> *The reason why I say that humans all have hearts that are not unfeeling toward others is this. Suppose someone suddenly saw a child about to fall into a well: everyone in such a situation would have a feeling of alarm and compassion – not because one sought to get in good with the child's parents, not because one wanted fame among their neighbors and friends, and not because one would dislike the sound of the child's cries.*[260]

Some key elements of the thought experiment include the fact that he is concerned with what a person would feel "suddenly." This will indicate their natural/instinctive reaction, before any social conditioning can set in. He also focuses on the person's thoughts and feelings, rather than actions (which might allow for indecision, hesitation, fear, etc.). If the goal is to discern human nature, it makes more sense to focus on the immediate thoughts and feelings a person would have, rather than the actions they might actually take, since there are any number of variables that might account for action or inaction.

Mengzi supposes that *everyone* would react with concern if a child fell into a well (or was otherwise subjected to a sudden harm or danger), and, that if anyone did *not* react in a similar way, we would conclude that there is something (morally) wrong with them! The ultimate point of

---

[260] *Mengzi*, section 2A6. (Note: all references from this section are from the *Mengzi*, unless otherwise indicated.)

the thought experiment is that, at our deepest and most instinctive levels, we would *all* react with concern and compassion. To further reinforce his point, Mengzi offers a *second* thought experiment:

> *Life is something I desire; righteousness is also something I desire. If I cannot have both, I will forsake life and select righteousness.... It is not the case that only the worthy person has this heart. All humans have it. The worthy person simply never loses it. A basket of food and a bowl of soup – if one gets them then one will live; if one doesn't get them then one will die. But if they're given with contempt, then even a homeless person will not accept them. If they're trampled upon, then even a beggar won't take them.*[261]

In this hypothetical scenario, he is imagining someone who needs food (e.g., a homeless person), and who presumably wants food very much. However, if someone offers that person food in a contemptuous, disrespectful manner, they will refuse it. As an extension of this thought experiment, imagine yourself in a difficult financial situation: homeless and hungry perhaps? Are there certain things you still wouldn't do, even in exchange for food and shelter? Are there things that you would still refuse to do, out of pride, or a sense of dignity?

These example reactions from the two thought experiments are meant to reveal "universal" impulses, the seeds/sprouts (*duan*) of righteousness, benevolence, and right conduct. The "heart of compassion" is shown in the well example, and is the "sprout of benevolence." The "heart of disdain" is shown in the beggar example, and is the "spirit of righteousness"

> *Humans all have the heart of compassion. Humans all have the heart of disdain. Humans all have the heart of respect. Humans all have the heart of approval and disapproval. The heart of compassion is benevolence. The heart of disdain is righteousness. The heart of respect is propriety. The heart of approval and disapproval is wisdom. Benevolence, righteousness, propriety and wisdom are not welded to us externally. We inherently have them. It is simply that we do not reflect upon them. Hence it is said, "seek it and you will get it. Abandon it and you will lose it."*[262]

Benevolence involves compassion for others, and obligates us to help others. Righteousness concerns personal integrity that resists doing shameful things even when personal gain/cost is at stake. Examples provided by Mengzi include not accepting a gift given with contempt, begging in order to obtain luxuries, or cheating at a game. This is a negative prohibition to refrain from shameful actions. Wisdom consists in being a good judge of character, skill at prudential reasoning/practical reason, prudence, and understanding and commitment to the other virtues. Finally, there is propriety. This is appropriate respect displayed through ritualized actions (e.g., extending courtesy).

Moral development, for Mengzi, is the result of "cultivating" these natural impulses ("sprouts"). Indeed, what makes us essentially and properly *human* is the presence of these four moral "sprouts," which, under appropriate circumstances, develop into the four Confucian virtues of wisdom (*zhi*), ritual propriety (*li*), righteousness (*yi*), and benevolence (*ren*). While everyone has this potential, there is no *guarantee* that the potential will be actualized.

By way of analogy, under suitable circumstances any acorn will develop into an oak tree, but if individual acorns are not in a suitable environment (e.g. with sufficient soil and water), that potential will never be actualized. Mengzi appeals explicitly to agricultural metaphors such as this.[263]

To say that human nature is good, then,

---

[261] ibid., 6A10.
[262] ibid., 6A6.

[263] ibid., 6A7.

certainly doesn't mean that all humans always behave morally rightly, but merely that our natural dispositions aim at virtue, and will become virtues if properly developed. How do we cultivate the "sprouts?" Mengzi proposes that this involves the responsibility of both rulers (i.e., the government) and individuals. We will begin with personal responsibility.

It is the responsibility of the individual to exert conscious and deliberate practice of benevolence and righteousness. As a Confucian, Mengzi would understand this in terms of practicing ritual. As our "sprouts" develop, we will become wise enough to be discerning in our moral judgments. Reflection allows us to recognize similar cases, to extend our natural inclinations in one case (e.g., loyalty to one's spouse) to similar cases (e.g., loyalty to friends or rulers), and even to recognize when general rules may be *violated* in particular circumstances.

> *To not pull your sister-in-law out when she is drowning is to be a beast. That men and women should not touch in handing something to one another is the ritual, but if your sister-in-law is drowning to pull her out with your hand is discretion.*[264]

An element of Confucian ritual observance is that men and women should refrain from physical contact (with exceptions for spouses, children, etc.). However, to refrain from extending a hand to save the life of your drowning sister-in-law, while consistent with a *strict* interpretation of ritual observance, is not righteous. Someone who has become wise will be able to recognize when "discretion" is needed even at the expense of ritual.

Given that Mengzi claims that human nature is "good," how does he account for evil? In the first place, he qualifies our good nature.

> *As for what they genuinely are, humans can become good. That is what I mean by calling their natures good. As for their*

becoming not good, this is not the fault of their potential.[265]

That is, our innate goodness doesn't mean we are all actually good, but merely that we have natural inclinations to become good, assuming nothing interferes with our moral development—and there are plenty of ways that this development can be sabotaged by external circumstances, such as the corrupting and competitive influence of society, or a lack of education and resources. By way of analogy, plants naturally grow, but not in the absence of proper soil, water, sunlight, etc.

> *The trees of Ox Mountain were once beautiful. But because the mountain bordered on a large state, hatchets and axes besieged it. Could it remain verdant? Due to the respite it got during the day or night, and the moisture of rain and dew, it was not that there were no sprouts or chutes growing there. But oxen and sheep then came and grazed on them. Hence, it was as if it were barren. People seeing it barren, believed that there had never been any timber there. Could this be the nature of the mountain?*

> *When we consider what is present in people, could they truly lack the hearts of benevolence and righteousness? That by which they discard their genuine hearts is simply like the hatchets and axes in relation to the trees. With them besieging it day by day, can they remain beautiful?...Others see someone who is like an animal, and think that there was never any capacity there. Is this what a human genuinely is?*[266]

In this example, there is a mountain which is naturally beautiful and covered in trees, but the trees are cut down by loggers and the ground trampled by livestock until the mountain looked

---

[264] ibid., 4A17.
[265] ibid., 6A6.

[266] ibid., 6A8.

barren. The mountain was not *naturally* barren, but was rendered so because of outside intervention. By way of analogy, humans are naturally disposed to goodness, but our nature can be "trampled" by outside forces as well.

Aside from proper teaching and practice, he also thought that moral development requires the people have their basic needs met (e.g., food, shelter, etc.). It is the responsibility of the *ruler* (the government) to provide safety and basic life necessities.

> To lack a constant livelihood, yet to have a constant heart – only a scholar is capable of this. As for the people, if they lack a constant livelihood, it follows that they will lack a constant heart. And if one simply fails to have a constant heart, dissipation and evil will not be avoided. When they thereupon sink into crime, to go and punish them is to trap the people. When there are benevolent people in positions of authority, how is it possible to trap the people? For this reason, an enlightened ruler, in regulating the people's livelihood, must ensure that it is sufficient, on the one hand, to serve one's father and mother, and on the other hand, to nurture wife and children. In good years, one is always full. In years of famine, one escapes death. Only when the people have a regulated livelihood do they rush toward the good, and thus the people follow the ruler easily.[267]

Also:

> In years of plenty, most young men are gentle; and in years of poverty, most young men are cruel. It is not that the potential that Heaven confers on them varies like this. They are like this because of that by which their hearts are sunk and drowned. Consider barley. Sow the seeds and cover them. The soil is the same and the time of planting is also the same. They grow

> rapidly, and by the time of the summer solstice they have all ripened. Although there are some differences, these are due to the richness of the soil, and to unevenness in the rain and in human effort.[268]

The "social justice" implications here are significant! In the first place, Mengzi is explaining criminal behavior in terms of societal factors such as unemployment and poverty. When people fall into criminal behavior, it is not because they are "evil," but because of oppressive circumstances. Returning to the "Ox Mountain" analogy, we might compare poverty, poor education, unemployment, addiction, discrimination, and other oppressive social factors to the "loggers" and "livestock" that leave the mountain "barren." Beyond offering an explanation for negative behavior, Mengzi is clearly advocating that the ruler (government) should provide basic needs so that our natural "sprouts" may develop.

Xunzi: Human Nature is "Evil"

> People's nature is bad. Their goodness is a matter of deliberate effort. Now people's nature is such that they are born with a fondness for profit. If they follow along with this, then struggling and contention will arise, and yielding in deference will perish therein. They are born with feelings of hate and dislike. If they follow along with these, then cruelty and villainy will arise, and loyalty and trustworthiness will perish therein. They are born with desires of the eyes and ears, a fondness for beautiful sights and sounds. If they follow along with these, then lasciviousness and chaos will arise, and ritual and the standards of righteousness, proper form and good order, will perish therein. Thus, if people follow along with their inborn nature and dispositions, they are sure to come to struggle and contention, turn to disrupting social divisions of disorder, and

---

[267] ibid., 1A7.

[268] ibid., 6A7.

end up in violence.[269]

The point here is pretty straightforward: human nature is "bad." To support this claim, Xunzi offers several arguments, including a "state of nature" argument. The state of nature argument from Xunzi presumes a primarily self-interested human nature.

> *As for the way that the eyes like pretty colors, the ears like beautiful sounds, the mouth likes good flavors, the heart likes what is beneficial, and the bones and flesh like what is comfortable – these are produced from people's inborn dispositions and nature.*[270]

In the state of nature, self-interest and limited resources produce conflict.

> *Liking what is beneficial and desiring gain are people's inborn dispositions and nature. Suppose there were brothers who had some property to divide, and that they followed the fondness for benefit and desire for gain in their inborn dispositions and nature. If they were to do so, then the brothers would conflict and contend with each other for it.*[271]

We are to imagine an environment in which everyone pursues their own (natural) self-interest, without restraint. His assumption is that conflict, even violent conflict, would be inevitable. In the "state of nature" people were/are dangerous.

> *People were deviant, dangerous, and not correct in their behavior, and they were unruly, chaotic, and not well ordered. . . . The strong would harm the weak and take from them. The many would tyrannize the few and shout them down.*[272]

This is an intriguing thought experiment, to be sure. Let us suppose, for the moment, that it is accurate and that it reveals that human nature is fundamentally "bad." This might all seem rather depressing and optimistic. However, in a potentially surprising twist, Xunzi finds some room for *optimism*.

Although conflict and the pursuit of self-interest might be our natural state, we are not condemned to *remain* this way. In fact, it is obvious that human beings are capable of living together in harmony. I assume that *you*, for example, live in "harmony" (for the most part, at least), with most other people! This harmony will not happen on its own, however, according to Xunzi. He makes the solution to this natural conflict clear in the very same paragraph in which he condemns human nature as bad.

> *Thus, if people follow along with their inborn nature and dispositions, they are sure to come to struggling contention, turn to disrupting social divisions and disorder, and end up in violence. So, it is necessary to await the transforming influence of teachers and models and the guidance of ritual and the standards of righteousness, and only then will they come to yielding in deference, turn to culture and order, and end up under control. Looking at this way, it is clear that people's nature is bad, and their goodness is a matter of deliberate effort.*[273]

Consistent with the Confucian emphasis on tradition and ritual, Xunzi claimed that ancient Sage Kings set up laws and rituals to address this conflict.

> *From what did ritual arise? I say: humans are born having desires. When they have desires but do not get the objects of their desires, then they cannot but seek some*

---

[269] *Xunzi*, Chapter 23: Human Nature is Bad. (Note: all references in this section are from the *Xunzi* unless otherwise indicated.)
[270] ibid.

[271] ibid.
[272] ibid.
[273] ibid. Emphasis added.

means of satisfaction. If there is no measure or limit to their seeking, then they cannot help but struggle with each other. If they struggle with each other then there will be chaos, and if there is chaos then they will be impoverished. <u>The former Kings hated such chaos, and so they established rituals and the standards of righteousness in order to allot things to people, to nurture their desires, and to satisfy their seeking.</u> They cause desires never to exhaust material goods, and material goods never to be depleted by desires, so that the two support each other and prosper. This is how ritual arose.[274]

And:

They made clear ritual and the standards of righteousness in order to transform them. They set up laws and standards in order to manage them. They multiplied punishments and fines in order to restrain them. As a result, they caused all under Heaven to become well-ordered and conform to the Way.[275]

In other words, the solution to the chaos and conflict in the state of nature is the imposition of *rules*. Moral rules were invented by the "Sage Kings" to provide the artificial constraints necessary to reshape character for the sake of a proper society.

As a simple example, a very young child, when hungry, will simply grab at any nearby food, but I suspect that you exercise much more restraint when *you* are hungry. Even if you're *very* hungry, you don't just grab food out of a stranger's hand! You probably exercise this kind of restraint not only in cases when your taking of the food would be considered illegal (theft), but even sometimes out of simple politeness. Perhaps you wait until everyone at your table is served before you start eating? Or maybe you wait until someone prays over the food, if you are religious?

Our "natural" disposition when we are hungry is simply to eat without regard for others, but we can overcome this by means of instruction and socialization. This training occurs within the home (probably by parents or guardians), but also out in society in the form of laws, policies, social norms, customs, etc. From a Confucian perspective, this involves adhering to rituals. Rituals and standards of righteousness establish rules concerning property and entitlement.

Ritual is that by which to correct your person. The teacher is that by which to correct your practice of ritual. If you are without ritual, then how do you correct your person? If you are without a teacher, how do you know that your practice of ritual is right?[276]

And:

Someone asks: if people's nature is bad, then from what are ritual and the standards of righteousness produced? I answer: in every case, ritual and the standards of righteousness are produced from the deliberate effort of the Sage; they are not produced from people's nature. Thus, when the Potter mixes clay and makes vessels, the vessels are produced from the deliberate efforts of the craftsman; they are not produced from people's nature. Thus, when the craftsman carves wood and make utensils, utensils are produced from the deliberate efforts of the craftsman; they are not produced from people's nature. The Sage accumulates reflections and deliberations and practices deliberate efforts . . . in order to produce ritual and standards of righteousness and to establish proper models and measures. So, ritual and the standards of righteousness and proper models and measures are produced from the deliberate efforts of the Sage; they are not

---

[274] ibid., Chapter 19: Discourse on Ritual. Emphasis added.

[275] ibid., Chapter 23: Human Nature is Bad.
[276] ibid., Chapter 2: Cultivating Oneself.

produced from people's nature.[277]

Virtue does not arise naturally, but is instead acquired from practice and self-cultivation. This transformation requires effort and training. Similar to Aristotle, who claimed that our character is developed by habit (much as the skill of a harpist is practiced by playing the harp), Xunzi thinks that the (good) character of a "gentleman" can be achieved only by continuous practice in right conduct, by "deliberate effort." "Though the Way is near, if you do not travel along it, you will not reach the end; though the task is small, if it is not acted upon, it will not be completed."[278]

Metaphorically, becoming "good" requires bending/shaping—a metaphor Xunzi invokes multiple times

Through steaming and bending, you can make wood straight as a plumb line into a wheel. And after its curve conforms to the compass, . . it will not become straight again, because the steaming and bending have made a certain way. Likewise, when wood comes under the incline, it become straight, and when metal is brought to the whetstone, it becomes sharp. The gentleman learns broadly and examines himself thrice daily, and then his knowledge is clear and his conduct is without fault.[279]

And:

Thus, crooked wood must await steaming and straightening on the shaping frame, and only then does it become straight. Blunt metal must await honing and grinding, and only then does it becomes sharp. Now since people's nature is bad, it must await teachers and proper models, and only then do they become correct in their behavior. They must obtain ritual and the standards of righteousness, and

only then did they become well ordered. Now without teachers or proper models for people, they will be deviant, dangerous, and incorrect in their behavior. Without ritual and the standards of righteousness, they will be unruly, chaotic, and not well ordered. In ancient times, the Sage Kings saw that because people's nature is bad, they were deviant, dangerous, and not correct in their behavior, and they were unruly, chaotic, and not well ordered. Therefore, for their sake they set up ritual and standards of righteousness, and established proper models and measures. They did this in order to straighten out and beautify people's nature and inborn dispositions and thereby correct them, and in order to train and transform people's nature and inborn dispositions and thereby guide them. And for the first time they were well ordered and conformed to the Way. Among people of today, those who are transformed by teachers and proper models, who accumulate culture and learning, and who make ritual and the standards of righteousness their path become gentleman. Those who give rein to their nature and inborn dispositions, who take comfort in being utterly unrestrained, and who violate ritual and the standards of righteousness become petty men. Looking at it this way, it is clear that people's nature is bad, and their goodness is a matter of deliberate effort.[280]

The metaphor is wonderfully clear: a warped piece of wood will not become straight on its own. In order to become straight, pressure must be exerted on it from an external source. The pressure must be sufficiently strong, and continuous, in order to change the shape of the wood. However, once sufficient pressure has been applied, the wood not only becomes straight, but will *remain* straight (barring further intervention).

---

277 ibid., Chapter 23: Human Nature is Bad.
278 ibid., Chapter 2: Cultivating Oneself.

279 ibid., Chapter 1: An Exhortation to Learning.
280 ibid., Chapter 23: Human Nature is Bad.

According to Xunzi, human nature is "bad" (warped). It will remain so barring outside intervention. However, by the application of sufficiently strong and consistent education and ritual observance ("pressure"), our nature can be transformed ("straightened") so that we act righteously, and in harmony with others. Xunzi states all of this in sharp (direct) contrast to the views of his fellow Confucian, Mengzi.

Mengzi says: people's nature is good. I say: this is not so. In every case, both in ancient times and in the present, what everyone under Heaven calls good is being correct, ordered, peaceful, and controlled. What they call bad is being deviant, dangerous, unruly, and chaotic. This is the division between good and bad. Now does he really think that people's nature is originally correct, ordered, peaceful, and controlled? Then what use would there be for Sage Kings? What use for ritual and the standards of righteousness? Even though there might exist Sage Kings and ritual and the standards of righteousness, whatever could these add to nature's correctness, order, peacefulness, and self-control? Now, such is not the case, because people's nature is bad. Thus, in ancient times the Sage Kings saw that because their nature is bad, people were deviant, dangerous, and not correct in their behavior, and they were unruly, chaotic, and not well ordered. Therefore, for their sake they set up the power of rulers and superiors in order to control them. They made clear ritual and the standards of righteousness in order to transform them. They set up laws and standards in order to manage them. They multiplied punishments and fines in order to restrain them. As a result, they caused all under Heaven to become well-ordered and conform to the Way. This is the order of the Sage Kings, and the transformation from ritual and the standards of righteousness.

Now suppose one were to try doing away with the power of rulers and superiors, try doing without the transformation from ritual and the standards of righteousness, try doing away with the order of laws and standards, try doing without the restraint of punishments and fines. Then stand aside and observe how all the people of the world would treat each other. If it were like this, then the strong would harm the weak and take from them. The many would tyrannize the few and shout them down. One would not have to wait even a moment for all under Heaven to arrive at unruliness and chaos and perish. Looking at it in this way, it is clear that people's nature is bad, and that their goodness is a matter of deliberate effort.[281]

In these passages, we see not only his fundamental disagreement with Mengzi, but also a repetition of his state of nature argument, his view of the origin of ritual, and the necessity of ritual for moral development. Although Xunzi might be regarded as pessimistic, in that he thinks humans are naturally "bad," he is also *optimistic* with respect to our *potential* to be good. He believes that moral development is something of which we are *all* capable.

In general what made Yu Yu was his practice of humanity, morality, the model of law, and rectitude. Since this is so, then each of these four are the rational principles that we can know and which we're capable of putting into practice. That being so, it is clear that the man in the street can become Yu, since it is possible for every man to understand the substance of human, morality, the model of law, and rectitude and the ability to master their instruments.[282]

We are each capable of overcoming our nature and becoming good, provided that we benefit from good instruction and socialization,

---

[281] ibid.

[282] ibid.

just as all babies (under normal circumstances) are capable of eventually learning how to restrain their impulses and not just grab any food in their vicinity whenever they get hungry.

Interestingly enough, research is currently underway concerning babies and moral development, and we have an opportunity to consult that research and see whether it favors Xunzi, or Mengzi.

Research has been conducted for decades in the "Baby Lab" (formally known as the "Infant Cognition Center") at Yale University, with the test subjects being babies under 24 months of age. The purpose of the research has been to gauge how much (if at all) babies understand "good" and "bad" behavior. The details are somewhat complicated, but the basic elements of one of the experiments are not: show a baby a puppet show in which a puppet displays "helping" behavior, and a different puppet engages in "unhelpful" behavior, and then see which puppet the babies prefer. More than 80% of the babies preferred the "nice" puppet (controlling for various other factors that might contribute to the choice)—and the percentage rises to 87% by the age of three.

Paul Bloom (a psychology professor connected to the lab) concludes that the research shows that babies are born with a rudimentary (though admittedly limited) sense of justice. Babies are born with a natural preference for "nice" behavior over "mean" behavior, but it takes development and instruction before they extend these moral notions outside their immediate circle of family.[283]

Bloom's research suggests that humans have innate capacities, presumably the result of evolutionary forces (from his perspective), that include a basic "moral sense" (that allows us to distinguish kind of behavior from cruel behavior, for example), capacity for empathy and compassion, and rudimentary senses of fairness and justice.

These capacities are indeed rudimentary, and limited in the scope of their application (e.g.

babies exhibit sharing behavior initially only to family and friends, and not strangers). In fact, Bloom acknowledges that babies appear to exhibit hostility to strangers in a rudimentary sense of "tribalism." Nevertheless, these moral capacities, rudimentary though they might be, still exist and exist naturally/innately within babies.

Evidence from the baby lab *seems* to support the view of Mengzi over that of Xunzi, suggesting that humans possess innate moral "sprouts" that must be cultivated and nurtured, as opposed to having no natural inclination towards moral behavior at all, and requiring the external imposition of virtue.

Critical Analysis

1. In your opinion, what are the strongest and most compelling points made by the philosopher or philosophers in this chapter? Why do you find those points to be convincing?
2. In your opinion, what are the weakest or least convincing points? Why? Can you anticipate any limitations or objections to their ideas not already addressed in the chapter?

Appendix: Application to Social Justice

With respect to social justice, the relevance of this chapter might not be immediately obvious, but it's significant. To put it bluntly, any issue of social justice presupposes that people are behaving "badly." Whether the issue is discrimination and bigotry, racialized violence, disparities in health or education or treatment in the criminal justice system, or any of the numerous other issues raised in the context of social justice, the "common denominator" is the perception that some persons, either personally, or through the institutions they have created and/or participate in, are doing or allowing things that are unjust. Our understanding of that,

---

[283] According to Bloom, "We are by nature indifferent, even hostile to strangers; we are

prone towards parochialism and bigotry."

as well as our remedies, will (or at least *should*) be informed by our view of human nature.

If, for example, you agree with Xunzi that people are basically "bad" and must be corrected by external forces to behave properly, then you will *expect* injustices to occur, and you will probably see the role of the State as, among other things, providing the necessary corrective measures. You will probably be more likely to think that laws and regulations which "force" people to refrain from discriminatory practices, for example, will be not only appropriate but necessary, given that people simply can't be relied upon to do the right thing by themselves, given our "bad" nature.

On the other hand, if you agree with Mengzi that we are basically "good," but that our natural good development can be prevented due to poor social conditions, then you will probably think of the State more in terms of what it should provide rather than what it should prevent or demand. You will be concerned about whether people are being provided with the basic necessities of life, whether they are safe and secure, and whether they have the resources and support they need in order to develop their "moral sprouts."

Both interpretations lend themselves very well to the causes of social justice. But, given their different views of human nature and the proper role of the State, the causes of violations of social justice, and the proper responses or preventative measures, will likely be a bit different according to each.

Appendix/"Deeper Dive": Psychological Egoism

Comprehension questions you should be able to answer after reading this appendix:

1. What are altruistic motivations?
2. What are egoistic motivations?
3. What is the difference between a descriptive theory and a prescriptive theory?
4. What is psychological egoism? What does it claim about human motivation?
5. Why would psychological egoism, if true, have such a significant impact on our understanding of ethics?
6. Explain the following possible problems for psychological egoism:
   a) "post hoc ergo propter hoc fallacy"
   b) "unfalsifiability"
   c) "defining self-interest."

Some of you might want to "dive deeper" into the ideas we started exploring in this chapter, and this appendix will help you do that.

Earlier we reviewed arguments from Xunzi that included a thought experiment involving his vision of the "state of nature," intended to reveal *human* nature. We can now cross the globe and find a seemingly kindred spirit in the character of Glaucon as depicted in Plato's *Republic*.

Now that those who practise justice do so involuntarily and because they have not

the power to be unjust will best appear if we imagine something of this kind: having given both to the just and the unjust power to do what they will, let us watch and see whither desire will lead them; then we shall discover in the very act the just and unjust man to be proceeding along the same road, following their interest, which all natures deem to be their good, and are only diverted into the path of justice by the force of law. The liberty which we are supposing may be most completely given to them in the form of such a power as is said to have been possessed by Gyges the ancestor of Croesus the Lydian. According to the tradition, Gyges was a shepherd in the service of the king of Lydia; there was a great storm, and an earthquake made an opening in the earth at the place where he was feeding his flock. Amazed at the sight, he descended into the opening, where, among other marvels, he beheld a hollow brazen horse, having doors, at which he stooping and looking in saw a dead body of stature, as appeared to him, more than human, and having nothing on but a gold ring; this he took from the finger of the dead and reascended. Now the shepherds met together, according to custom, that they might send their monthly report about the flocks to the king; into their assembly he came having the ring on his finger, and as he was sitting among them he chanced to turn the collet of the ring inside his hand, when instantly he became invisible to the rest of the company and they began to speak of him as if he were no longer present. He was astonished at this, and again touching the ring he turned the collet outwards and reappeared; he made several trials of the ring, and always with the same result-when he turned the collet inwards he became invisible, when outwards he reappeared. Whereupon he contrived to be chosen one of the messengers who were sent to the court; where as soon as he arrived he seduced the queen, and with her help conspired against the king and slew him, and took the kingdom.[284]

In seeking to explain the nature and origin of justice, Glaucon appeals to the myth of Gyges' ring. According to this myth, a shepherd named Gyges is tending his flock one day, when an earthquake splits the ground. He explores the fissure and discovers a large tomb in the shape of a horse. Inside, he finds the body of a giant. The

dead giant is wearing a ring. Gyges takes the ring. The shepherd-turned-grave robber discovers that this is no ordinary ring. When he manipulates the ring a certain way, he becomes invisible! When he twists it back, he becomes visible once more. After mastering the ring, he arranges to have himself sent as the representative of his village to the royal court. Once there, he uses to power of the ring to murder the king and claim power for himself.

Before we come to any harsh judgments against Gyges, Glaucon recommends a thought experiment.

Suppose now that there were two such magic rings, and the just put on one of them and the unjust the other; no man can be imagined to be of such an iron nature that he would stand fast in justice. No man would keep his hands off what was not his own when he could safely take what he liked out of the market, or go into houses and lie with any one at his pleasure, or kill or release from prison whom he would, and in all respects be like a God among men. Then the actions of the just would be as the actions of the unjust; they would both come at last to the same point. And this we may truly affirm to be a great proof that a man is just, not willingly or because he thinks that justice is any good to him individually, but of necessity, for wherever anyone thinks that he can safely be unjust, there he is unjust. For all men believe in their hearts that injustice is far more profitable to the individual than justice, and he who argues as I have been supposing, will say that they are right. If you could imagine any one obtaining this power of becoming invisible, and never doing any wrong or touching what was another's, he would be thought by the lookers-on to be a most wretched idiot, although they would praise him to one another's faces, and keep up appearances with one another from a fear that they too

---

[284] Plato, *the Republic*, book II.

might suffer injustice.[285]

Imagine there are two such magic rings, each of which renders the wearer invisible. These days, we might need to get a little more sophisticated. Perhaps you suppose that even invisible persons might still leave behind fingerprints, or hair samples, or other means by which a clever forensic investigator could identify a perpetrator. They're magic rings. We can make them do whatever we want! Suppose the rings render the wearer invisible, magically cloaks any heat signatures, erases fingerprints, eliminates DNA evidence, etc.

Now, give one of the two rings to someone whom you regard as tremendously virtuous and just. Give the other to someone quite the opposite: a vicious and unjust jerk. What, do you suppose, each would do with the ring?

Glaucon believes that both the "just" and the "unjust" would come "at last to the same point." That is, they would each, eventually, do the same thing: whatever it is that each wanted.

To make matters more interesting, give yourself one of the rings. What would *you* do? Be honest!

If your answer includes anything you would not already do right now, without the ring, you have confirmed Glaucon's point (and his fear). If you would do something *with* the ring, that you would not do *without* it, it suggests that the reason why you refrain from that action now is not any commitment to moral principles, but fear of getting caught and punished. Remove the fear, and watch out….

They say that to do injustice is, by nature, good; to suffer injustice, evil; but that the evil is greater than the good. And so when men have both done and suffered injustice and have had experience of both, not being able to avoid the one and obtain the other, they think that they had better agree among themselves to have neither; hence there arise laws and mutual covenants; and that which is ordained by law is

termed by them lawful and just. This they affirm to be the origin and nature of justice;--it is a mean or compromise, between the best of all, which is to do injustice and not be punished, and the worst of all, which is to suffer injustice without the power of retaliation; and justice, being at a middle point between the two, is tolerated not as a good, but as the lesser evil, and honoured by reason of the inability of men to do injustice. For no man who is worthy to be called a man would ever submit to such an agreement if he were able to resist; he would be mad if he did. Such is the received account, Socrates, of the nature and origin of justice.[286]

The outcome of Glaucon's thought experiment provides a possible insight into human nature. If it is true that any one of us would ultimately and inevitably abuse the power of Gyges' ring, then the reason why most of us usually obey the rules and "play nice" with one another is fear. Although we would like to be able to do whatever we want, to whomever we want, whenever we want, we recognize that such behavior just isn't possible. None of us is Superman.

However powerful a given individual might be, she isn't bulletproof (to put it bluntly). No matter how wealthy, how powerful, how well-connected, each one of us is all-too-human, and all-too-vulnerable. Realizing that, and wishing to minimize the risk we face from others, we make mutual promises to "play nice." I won't rob you so long as you don't rob me. I won't kill you, so long as you don't kill me. We surrender some of our own power, and our own freedom, when we make those promises, but in exchange for that we gain security.

We behave ourselves because it is in our <u>self-interest</u> to do so. If it were no longer necessary, no *longer* in our self-interest (e.g., if we had Gyges' ring), we would no longer be inclined to "play nice."

---

[285] ibid.

[286] ibid.

Notice that the common theme in both cases is the same: self-interest. When we obey the law, it is because we perceive it is in our self-interest to do so. When we instead break the law, it is because we perceive it is in our self-interest to break it, instead.

These are understandable and even inevitable behaviors, according to psychological egoism. *According to PE, each person always pursues her own self-interest, without exception.* We can't help but do so. We're "wired" to always pursue our own self-interest. To see the ramifications of this, it will be useful to distinguish two basic kinds of motivation: altruistic, and egoistic.

Altruism: acting for the benefit of others; acting for the sake of others; foregoing some benefit for oneself so that another may enjoy a benefit instead

Egoism: acting for self-benefit; acting from self-interest; promoting one's own good (possibly at the expense of another's)

Presumably, the most morally relevant of those two types of motivations is the altruistic variety. After all, it's easy to think of moral obligations that involve acting for the benefit of others. The most obvious examples involve anything charitable. Giving money to help the poor instead of spending on something for yourself, or donating time to work for the good of others (instead of using that time for your own benefit), are both examples of altruistically motivated actions. Whether or not a particular altruistic behavior is morally required of us would, of course, be subject to interpretation and debate, but the mere idea that we are all, at least sometimes, morally obligated to put other people's interests ahead of our own seems uncontroversial.

What if altruistically motivated behavior is impossible, though?

Psychological Egoism

Psychological egoism is a descriptive theory of human nature. That is, rather than making recommendations (as we find in prescriptive theories), it seeks merely to describe the nature of something—in this case, human motivation. As such, it claims to be empirical and scientific.

According to psychological egoism (henceforth referred to as PE), every single human being, without exception, is always driven solely by egoistic motivations. Altruism is an illusion, a myth. Even those actions that we believe to be altruistic in intention actually serve self-interest—otherwise, they would not be performed.

If this is true, it has profound implications for our understanding of moral obligation. The following argument illustrates why.

1. Everyone always acts from self-interest (PE).
2. If one can't do something, one is not obligated to do it ("ought implies can").
3. Altruism requires putting others' interests ahead of our own.
4. Altruism is therefore impossible (from lines 1 and 3).
5. Altruism is therefore never required (from lines 2 and 4).

Notice just how significant this is, if true. Every major ethical system in the world (with the notable exception of ethical egoism) claims that altruism is at least sometimes required of us. I'm confident that no matter what your own approach to ethics is, you believe that at least *sometimes* the morally right thing to do is to put another person's interests ahead of your own.

PE says that to do so is impossible.

You and I are *incapable* of putting other people first. Since it's impossible for us, we are never obligated to put others first. Therefore, we never have a moral obligation to behave altruistically. That means every major ethical system in the world (except for ethical egoism) is mistaken. Unless you happen to be an ethical egoist, you will need to revise your understanding of moral obligation.

If PE is true, it clearly has a profound impact on ethics. But, *is* it true? Should we believe it is? Why would anyone? The most often provided reason is because it appears that PE can provide an egoistic explanation for any action whatsoever, no matter how altruistic it might appear on the surface.

I'm going to pretend to be a psychological egoist, and set the bar very high, right from the beginning: I'm going to prove that Mother Teresa was selfish.[287]

"Mother Teresa was selfish?" you might ask. "Certainly," I reply.

She was a nun, right? That suggests she took her religion pretty seriously. She believed in heaven and hell. As a Roman Catholic, she likely placed even greater emphasis on "works" (as opposed to faith alone) than would Protestants. In her own words: "I heard the call to give up all and follow Christ into the slums to serve Him among the poorest of the poor. It was an order. I was to leave the convent and help the poor while living among them."

On the very reasonable assumption that she believed that her actions in this world would impact her prospects in the next, the cost-benefit analysis is embarrassingly simple: a few decades of service and sacrifice in exchange for an eternity of indescribable bliss. This is easy math! By living "altruistically," Mother Teresa was promoting her own Salvation. Maybe she even didn't even have to wait in line to get into Heaven....

What's more, she was a celebrity, and not merely well-known, but beloved and admired by millions, if not billions, of people. That probably felt pretty good! She actually won the Nobel Peace Prize is 1979. Moreover, she was "beatified" by the Catholic Church in 2003, and Canonized in 2016, which means she is now officially recognized as a "Saint" within the Catholic Church.

Finally, by her own description, she was happy! "Poverty for us is a freedom. It is not mortification, a penance. It is joyful freedom. There is no television here, no this, no that. But we are perfectly happy." She was happy in her life. She was happy being poor. She was happy serving others.

To sum up, by serving the sick and the poor, Mother Teresa became famous and beloved, she made herself happy, and she engineered an eternity of reward for herself. Was she motivated by self-interest? So it would seem! And, if someone like Mother Teresa falls prey to egoistic interpretation, how much more easily do the rest of us? It seems that everyone (even Mother Teresa) is always driven by self-interest.

It appears to be a fact that people do indeed act for the sake of self-interest. That is, it's not difficult to think of examples where it is obvious that people acted for their own benefit, sometimes at the expense of others. It also appears that any action can be explained in terms of self-interest (e.g., Mother Teresa "serving" the poor). PE offers itself as an explanatory theory to account for those facts: all people necessarily (and exclusively) act from self-interest.

We now face the following question: is this explanatory theory (PE) the only, or at least the best, way to understand human behavior? If the answer is "yes," then we would have good reason to accept PE, and consequently accept the serious implications it would have on our understanding of ethics. If the answer is "no," however, then we may reject both PE and its serious implications. We have reviewed reasons to think PE is true, so we will consider some reasons to reject it.

---

[287] For those who aren't familiar with Mother Teresa: she was a globally-recognized Catholic nun who spent most of her life in India. She founded the "Missionaries of Charity" that included over 4,500 nuns and is active in over 130 countries. The organization runs hospices and homes for people with HIV/AIDS, leprosy and tuberculosis. It also operates soup kitchens, dispensaries and mobile clinics, child and family counseling programs, and orphanages and schools. Nuns of the order must take (and adhere to) vows of chastity, poverty and obedience, as well as a fourth vow: to give "wholehearted free service to the poorest of the poor."

Possible Problem for PE #1: the "post hoc ergo propter hoc" fallacy

"Post hoc ergo propter hoc" is a Latin phrase. Roughly translated: "after the fact, therefore because of the fact."

The post hoc fallacy is an abuse of what is otherwise a perfectly legitimate form of causal inference. As I write this sentence, I first tap a key, then a letter appears on the monitor. Therefore, tapping the key causes the letter to appear. Nothing weird or presumptuous about that piece of reasoning! First one thing happens (tapping the key), then another thing happens (a letter appears), therefore the first thing (tapping) causes the second thing (appearing). Try a different example, though. I had some eggs for breakfast. Later in the day, the Dow Jones Industrial Average lost several hundred points. Therefore, my eating eggs caused the Dow to lose hundreds of points. Who would have guessed that my dietary practices exerted so much terrible influence over the U.S. economy?

They don't, of course—and I'm sure you recognize that it's silly to think that just because one thing happened first (eggs for breakfast), and then something else happened later (Dow loss), the two are somehow causally connected. When such a causal connection is hastily drawn, we have an example of the post hoc fallacy.

This kind of fallacious reasoning can occur not just with respect to causes, but also with *reasons*. For example, prior to obtaining full time employment at Rio Hondo College, I taught at several campuses, usually in the same academic terms. Some semesters, I taught at CSU Long Beach, Cal Poly Pomona, *and* UC Riverside. A typical day might involve starting in Long Beach and teaching there, then driving to Riverside and teaching a class there, then driving to Pomona to teach another class, and returning home to Long Beach to collapse from exhaustion, grade exams, prep for the next day, or whatever else seemed most appropriate. As a result of all that commuting, I burned up a lot of gasoline. It would be a mistake, though, to think in the following way:

1. Professor Preston drove to work.
2. As a result, he burned gasoline.
3. Therefore, he drove in order to burn gasoline.

I assure you that burning gas was not my goal. If I could have avoided it, I would have. My goals were many (e.g., to earn a paycheck, to advance my career, to do what I love, etc.), but burning gas was not among them. Just because an action produced a particular outcome (and a predictable one, at that) does not mean that the action was done *for the sake of* that outcome.

How does this apply to PE, you might wonder? Psychological egoists note that Mother Teresa helped the poor. As a consequence, she was made happy, became famous, and possibly earned herself eternal reward. Therefore, she helped the poor *for the sake of* her own happiness, fame, and eternal reward.

This is possibly true, of course, but may we simply *assume* it to be true? Just because helping others made her happy, does that mean she did it *in order* to promote her own happiness? Are we justified in assuming that to be the case, when we weren't justified in assuming that I commuted for the sake of burning gas? Isn't it possible (simply *possible*) that she helped the poor for some other reason (e.g., because it was the right thing to do, or because she thought it was God's will), and, as a result of her actions, she was made happy—but that her own happiness wasn't her goal? Consider (and compare) the following charts:

(A)

Action	Result	(inferred) Goal
Help the poor	Feel happy	Feel happy
Commute	Burn gas	Burn gas

v.

(B)

Action	Result	(actual) Goal
Help the poor	Feel happy	Do the right thing
Commute	Burn gas	Earn a paycheck

PE seems to assume that the egoistic explanation, represented in (A), is the correct explanation—but assuming and proving are two very different things. One might also assume that I commuted in order to burn gas! But, the critic of PE might allege that just as the correct explanation of my commuting is something other than burning gas (e.g., earning a paycheck), so too might the correct explanation of Mother Teresa's behavior be something other than self-interest. In other words, the explanation offered in (B) could be the correct kind of explanation. Unless a reasonable causal connection can be traced and *demonstrated*, it appears that PE is possibly guilty of the post hoc fallacy.

Can such a causal connection be demonstrated? Seemingly not. Consult your own experience. How often do you perform an action with your goal being “to satisfy self-interest?” Isn't it, instead, usually the case that your goal is something else altogether, and that when you achieve *that* goal, your self-interest is (at least sometimes, somehow conceived) served?

For example, suppose you buy your mother a nice present for Mother's Day, and she is visibly happy when you give it to her. You then feel

Example
Helping the poor
Donating to charity
Risking your life for another
Donating a kidney to a friend

On the surface, at least, this might seem like an incredible strength of the theory. No matter what example you provide, a psychological egoist can show how it is motivated by self-interest, even if this requires appealing to subconscious motivations.

You think you helped the poor because it was the “right thing to do,” but really you did it to feel good about yourself. Don't think so? Well, that should come as no surprise. It's in your self-interest to not think of yourself as selfish, and instead to think of yourself as truly generous and charitable. If you were honest with yourself, though, and dug deeply enough into the layers of your motivation, you would eventually uncover your own self-interest. Don't think so? You obviously haven't delved deeply, and honestly

proud and happy, and have a wonderful Mother's Day with her. Presumably, you could not have felt “proud and happy” if you had not desired to make your mother happy with the gift. If you couldn't care less about that, why would her happiness have made you proud and happy yourself? Implicitly, then, your desire was to make your mother happy—*that* is what you were pursuing. To have experienced happiness when your desire was satisfied, you had to have a desire other than your own happiness! If so, this suggests that it is not the case that *all* our actions are motivated by our own happiness, or self-interest. Rather, our actions seem to be motivated by all kinds of other desires, and when those desires are satisfied we often experience happiness or the fulfillment of our self-interest as a *result*.

Possible problem #2: Unfalsifiability

PE is often regarded as very convincing (at least initially) because it seems capable of providing an egoistic explanation for *any and every* action whatsoever.

Egoistic Explanation
Feeling self-righteous
Tax deduction
Avoiding survivor's guilt
Adulation for being a hero

enough, yet. Keep up the soul-searching! When may you stop? When you finally realize that your motivation was self-interested, of course!

Do you sense the problem, yet? Taken to this extreme, PE's explanatory power is quickly revealed to be falsifiable. This is not a virtue for a theory. If there is no possible way to disprove the theory, no possible counter-example that can be provided, the theory is unfalsifiable. This is another way of saying that it is unverifiable, untestable.

This is a not a good thing for a theory of human nature, for a theory that claims to be an explanatory theory, for a theory that cloaks itself in the language of science. In science, if a hypothesis is not testable, it is not scientific. End of discussion.

If the hypothesis that all human acts are egoistic is not testable (because it is not falsifiable), it is not scientific. End of discussion. Proponents of PE may *assume* that all our motivations are egoistic, they may *assert* that all our motivations are egoistic, but assuming and asserting and not at all the same thing as *proving*.

Possible Problem #3: Defining "self-interest"

PE claims that all our motivations are egoistic, that we always act in our own self-interest. By now, you're probably wondering what, exactly, that means. After all, "acting in self-interest" may mean any number of things, some of which being more plausible than others. Let us consider some possible meanings of "self-interest." For each candidate, we will consider both its meaning and whether, if true, it would rule out altruistic motivations.

1.   We always do what is best for us.

Perhaps "self-interest," as understood by PE, means that we always do what is best for ourselves. If this were true, then altruistic motivations would be impossible, given that we always do what is best for ourselves. That rules out putting what is best for another first, if so doing would not be best for you as well. But, does it seem to be true that "we always do what is best for ourselves?"

It's clear that we do *not* always do what is best for ourselves. Sometimes we behave foolishly, recklessly, and dangerously. Sometimes we ruin our lives by making stupid mistakes. Sometimes the damage isn't so dire, but we recognize our errors all the same. Clearly, we do not always do what is best, even for ourselves. So, if this is what PE means by "self-interest," PE would be mistaken.

2.   We always do what we *think* is best for us.

This seems to be a more plausible candidate, as it allows for honest mistakes. Perhaps we always do what *seems* to be best, but it turns out,

in retrospect, that we were wrong. "I thought that cheating on the exam would be best for me, but it turns out I was mistaken. I had no idea the professor was so skilled at catching cheaters...."

This candidate is also a clear threat to altruistic motivations, since (like #1) it rules out ever acting in such a way that benefits another unless you *think* it's also best for yourself.

While this interpretation is more plausible than #1, it still seems false. If you're anything like me, you've had experiences in which you've said to yourself something along the lines of:

"I know I shouldn't do this, but...."
"I know I'm going to regret this...."
"I know this is a bad idea, however...."

It seems to be the case that we sometimes do something while fully aware of the fact that it's not smart, or wise, or healthy, or prudent, or even the least bit a good idea. But, we do it anyway. If so, it would appear that it is not the case that we always do even what we *think* to be best.

3.   We always do what we want most to do, all things considered.

This seems most plausible of all. Perhaps what PE boils down to is that we always do what we most want, and sometimes what we most want is pretty stupid, or harmful, or reckless. For example, a smoker wants to quit, and knows she should, but she continues smoking anyway. How can we understand that? Simply: although she wanted to quit, she wanted another cigarette even more. A person wants to lose weight, but still doesn't begin to exercise or control caloric intake. Explanation? Although he wants to lose weight, he wants to enjoy food and avoid strenuous exercise even more. What about when the smoker finally quits? Simple: at that point, her desire to quit was stronger than her desire to smoke. Whatever it is that we do, it's what we most wanted to do—otherwise, we'd have done something else.

So far, so good. A critic might wonder, however, just how it is that we discern what we most want to do. How can such things be identified? Easily, according to this interpretation of PE. We simply identify the action performed. We can identify what we most want, retroactively, by observing behavior. The mere fact that we perform an action X is evidence that what we most wanted was to do X---otherwise, we'd have done Y (or Z, etc.). Closer inspection, however, reveals this understanding to be problematic—circular, in fact. Consider the following:

1. **We always do what *we most want to do*.**

Now, what is it that we most want to do? What does that phrase mean?

2. **What we most want to do, is *whatever it is that we actually do* (otherwise, we would have done something else).**

So, "what we most want to do" is understood to be "what we actually do." If this is correct, I should be able to substitute "what we actually do" for "what we most want to do" wherever I find it expressed (such as in statement #1 above). Behold.

3. **We always do what we actually do.**

Brilliant! Obviously true. Also trivially true. Meaninglessly true. "We always do what we actually do?" How about simplifying that expression?

4. **We do what we do.**

This is what is called a "tautology." A tautology involves a repetition of meaning, saying (essentially) the same thing, but using different words—especially when the additional words fail to provide additional clarity. Of course it is true that "we do what we do." The problem is that this tells us nothing interesting. It's a safe assumption that all intentional human action is motivated by

some sort of desire, that we perform actions on the basis of *some* sort of motivation. But, does it seem accurate to identify every (and any) desire or motive with "self-interest?"

> *In assessing whether an action is self-interested, the issue is not whether the action is based on a desire; the issue is what kind of desire it is based on. If what you want is to help someone else, then your motive is altruistic, not self-interested.*[288]

PE claims that all actions are motivated by self-interest, that all motivations are egoistic. This seems obviously false, if we understand "self-interest" to mean something like "putting yourself first, at the expense of others." One can immediately begin to generate counter-examples: charitable giving, the life and work of Mother Teresa, sacrificing your own life to save another's, etc. Given the categorical nature of PE, all it takes is a single counter-example to refute the theory. In order to defeat these sorts of counter-examples, PE must be understood in such a way that even examples like those can be understood as egoistically motivated. This requires stretching the meaning of "self-interest" so as to incorporate every possible action whatsoever. Concepts are kind of like gum, though: the more you stretch it, the weaker and more transparent it becomes. Concepts have meaning not only by what they include, but also by what they *exclude*. Stretch a concept so that *nothing* is excluded, and *everything* is included, and the concept ceases to have meaning!

For example, in sports, the "MVP" is literally *the* "most valuable player." "The most" is a superlative term. By definition, only one member of the team can be the MVP. Imagine that a well-intentioned Little League coach is trying to increase the self-esteem of his players, and at the annual awards banquet announces that *every* player is the MVP that year. What does "MVP" now mean? When every player is the MVP, all MVP means (now) is "player." The word has

---

[288] Rachels, James. The *Elements of Moral Philosophy* 7th edition. McGraw Hill, 2012: 68.

literally lost its meaning, by being misapplied—no matter how well-intentioned the gesture might have been.

As another example, pretend you are an anthropologist, and you are visiting a recently discovered tribe of people called "Prestonians," where the inhabitants speak "Prestonian" due to the pervasiveness of the word "Preston" in their language. You are trying to learn this language, and a member of the Preston tribe points to what you call a tree, and says "Preston." He then points to what you call a dog and says "Preston." He points to another tribesman punching someone in the face and says "Preston," then points to a local couple kissing passionately: "Preston." He later points to a woman giving birth and says "Preston," and then to a man who just died of a heart attack: "Preston." After several days, you realize that everything he points to, he calls "Preston," and whenever you attempt to ask him a question in your own language, with the additional use of pointing and hand gestures, he always pauses, seems to reflect, and then answers "Preston."

What does the word Preston mean, in his language? You don't have the slightest clue, do you? *Everything* seemed to be "Preston"—which made it impossible for you to discern what the word *actually means*.

In the same way, psychological egoists point to "everything" and call it "egoistic," or "selfish." Saving a life? Selfish. Taking a life? Selfish. Helping the poor? Selfish. Hurting the poor? Selfish. Going to class? Selfish. Skipping class? Selfish. Given this usage, "selfish" or "self-interested" has no more meaning than does "Preston!" If "Preston" means "everything," it actually means *nothing*. So too with selfishness, or self-interest.

PE has an easy way to fix this problem: tighten up the meaning of self-interest so that "acting from self-interest" ceases to imply a tautology. If PE does this, the "definitional" problem can be resolved—but it is soon replaced by a new problem: it is no longer anything close to obvious that all actions really are motivated by self-interest!

It is possible that even seemingly heroic actions are motivated by self-interest, but is it plausible? Think about what this would mean. On September 11th, 2001, 346 firefighters were killed. They were moving into the World Trade Towers, while everyone else was trying to get out. PE does provide a possible explanation for their seemingly heroic behavior: self-interest. Perhaps they wanted to feel like heroes. Perhaps they didn't want to avoid losing their jobs, or being scorned by their peers for cowardice. In any event, PE claims their motivations must have been self-interested. On September 12th, 2001, USA Today reported that two men (Michael Benfante and John Cerqueira) spent an hour carrying an unnamed woman who used a wheelchair down 68 flights of stairs, at clear and obvious risk to their own life. PE offers an explanation for why they did so: self-interest (somehow conceived). Millions of ordinary citizens donated money, and time, and blood for the relief effort after 9-11. Why did they all do so? Self-interest, according to PE.

When I was a senior in high school, my father lost his job due to "downsizing." He ended up finding another job, but there's a story behind it. My dad had been a broadcast engineer for most of his working life. He had left a position as the Director of Engineering at a television station to take a sales job with a large company. He sold the broadcasting equipment he had used, purchased, and knew so much about in his capacity as an engineer. Much earlier in his career, he had worked for a boss he disliked very much—so much so that he took another job in another State to get away from him. Years later, that same boss became the boss of the television station my dad had left when he took the sales position. Then, he was "downsized" from his sales position, and found himself unemployed, and wondering how he was going to support his family. As I mentioned, he did find another job—an entry level engineer position at his old television station. He was the lowest seniority person in the very same department that he used to manage. He was working beneath the same guys that he used to supervise—and his boss was the *same guy* that inspired him to move across the country just to get away from him. Only as an adult now myself, can I appreciate how humbling that must have been for him: to have to take a job from a man he disliked, and did not respect; to have once been the manager, and to then be the "low man on the totem pole," with the worst shifts and the least seniority. What I found out from him decades later, but had never known before, was that he had been offered *another* job. It would have required us to move, however, and he refused to move during my senior year in high school. He knew how disruptive that would be to me socially, and emotionally, and (more importantly) academically. I was a good student, and was poised to be the first person in our immediate family to go to College, and one of only a handful in our entire extended family. He didn't want to mess things up for me. So, instead, he humbled himself and essentially started over in his career working for a man he despised. It seems to me that he acted *selflessly*, for my sake— certainly not for his own. However, the psychological egoist must interpret his actions as having been motivated by his own self-interest.

It is possible that self-interest is the explanation for all those actions, and for any other you or I might imagine. Since PE is unfalsifiable, we can't, of course, know with certainty whether those actions (or any other) really are motivated by self-interest. So, all you and I can do is try to figure out what seems to make the most sense. If, based on your experience of the world and how it works, it appears to you that PE offers the best explanation of human behavior, including the examples above, then PE is probably a compelling theory to you. On the other hand, if it appears to you that humans are at least sometimes capable of genuine altruism, that not every action is motivated by self-interest, then you will probably reject PE.

Chapter 11: Moral Subjectivism

Comprehension questions you should be able to answer after reading this chapter:

1. What are subjective claims? What are objective claims?
2. How do Subjectivists understand moral claims? What makes a moral claim "true," according to subjectivism?
3. What do subjectivists mean when they say moral claims are neither analytically true nor empirically verifiable? Why would this be an argument for moral claims being subjective, rather than objective?
4. What do subjectivists mean when they say that moral claims are "conventional," rather than objective?
5. If subjectivism is true, can anyone ever be mistaken about a moral value judgment? Why or why not?
6. If subjectivism is true, how would we have to understand a person's moral "progress" (or regress)?
7. If subjectivism is true, how would we have to interpret claims that some people (e.g., Martin Luther King Jr.) were morally better than other people (e.g., Osama Bin Laden)?
8. If subjectivism is true, how must we understand "disagreement" on moral issues? How will moral conflict be resolved?

As I hope you recall from a previous chapter, a "claim" (in the context of philosophy) is simply a statement, an assertion, or a proposition. One of the features of claims is that they have a "truth value." This is just a fancy way of saying that a claim must be either true or false, even if we're not sure which one it is.

For example, "Ted Preston is a philosophy professor" is a claim. That claim is either true, or it isn't. If you have no idea who Ted Preston is (or to which Ted Preston I refer), you might not be sure whether it is a true statement, but you can be confident that it's either true or it's false. If you have enough information, you might be confident as to *which* one of those two truth values is accurate. But, what is it that would *make* the claim true (or false)? How would we know? The answer depends upon the kinds of claims we're talking about.

We may divide claims into two basic categories: objective claims, and subjective claims.

Objective claims concern facts, while subjective claims concern opinion. If a claim is objective, its truth or falsity is independent of whatever *I* believe or desire. It is sometimes said

that "facts don't discriminate." If it is a fact that 2 + 2 = 4, then it is true that 2 + 2 = 4 even if I believe that 2 + 2 = 17, or even if my deepest desire is that 2 + 2 = 17. Bluntly, it doesn't matter what I believe or desire. If it is a fact that 2 + 2 = 4, then the truth of that claim applies equally to every person at every time and at every place. If I disagree, I am just plain mistaken. If a billion people disagree, then a billion people are mistaken.

Error is possible when we're dealing with objective claims. In fact, one of the ways to figure out if a claim is objective is to ask yourself what it would mean if two or more people disagreed about the claim. If their disagreement indicates at least one of the people is mistaken, that's a pretty good sign that the claim is objective. If I think that 2 + 2 = 17, and you think that it equals 4, that's an indicator that one of us mistaken (or maybe both of us are mistaken, and the correct answer is some third option that neither one of us came up with).

Subjective claims, in contrast, concern opinions and personal taste preferences.

Disagreement does *not* indicate error. If I think a meal is delicious, and you think it's too spicy, it's not the case that one of us is "wrong" about the meal. If I love the band "Switchfoot," and you can't bear to listen to them, it's not the case that one of us is in error. Opinions are indexed to particular people, at particular times and places. The truth or falsity of a subjective claim is "up to me" in a meaningful sort of way—unlike the truth or falsity of objective (factual) claims.

One of the kinds of claims we make—indeed, one of the most *important* kinds of claims we can make—are moral claims. Moral claims are simply assertions involving some moral issue. "Eating meat is wrong." "War is never justifiable." "Abortion is wrong." "Premarital sex is morally acceptable." These are all examples of moral claims. What we now have to address is whether

moral claims are subjective, or objective? Are moral claims more like answers to math problems, or more like food preferences?

> What is your favorite flavor of ice cream? Your favorite musical group? Is the death penalty morally justifiable? What about unprotected sex without telling your partner you're HIV positive? Do you think the last few questions are similar to first few questions? Why, or why not?

First, consider a visual representation that applies if moral claims are *objective.*

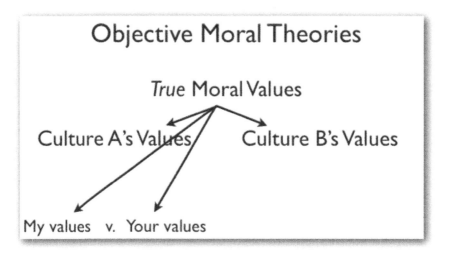

If moral claims are objective, then they appeal to facts (as opposed to opinions). I am going to begin an extended analogy that should resonate with most of you: tests and answer keys.

An answer key for a test is a version of the test that includes all of the correct answers. When a student takes a test for which there is an answer key, the student's answers are compared to the answer key for grading purposes. Consider the following mathematical example.

X + 3 = 5

Solve for X.

My answer: X = 1
Your answer: X = 2
Answer key: X = 2

The correct answer (i.e., the answer found in the answer key) is that X = 2. Your answer was 2. You got it right. My answer was 1. I got it wrong.

As mentioned a few paragraphs ago, before we even looked at the answer key, we had reason to believe at least one of us was wrong. After all, we gave two different answers to the same math problem. It was possible that neither one of us got the correct answer, but what wasn't possible was that *both* of us got the correct answer.

If moral claims are objective, then there are moral *facts*. As facts, they apply equally to all people at all times. These moral facts are our moral "answer key." We can imagine that we are all continually engaged in a process of moral "test-taking." Each day, by virtue of what we do, or fail to do, we are morally tested. As communities, too, we are being "tested" by virtue of the laws, policies, and actions we take (or fail to take) as communities. What determines whether an action taken by either an individual or by a community is morally correct? The "answer key."

If, for example, it is a moral fact that killing innocent people is morally wrong, then if you and I give two different "answers" to that same moral "question," one of us right, and the other wrong (here's a hint: whichever one of us is a murderer, is wrong).

If a particular culture allows, let alone perpetrates, the killing of innocent people, then that culture is *wrong* on that particular issue.

Obviously, there is room for plenty of spirited debate as to just which moral values are "facts" belonging in the universal moral answer key, but what any objective approach to ethics will have in common is the belief that there *is* such an answer key, even if we don't fully agree as to its contents.

Subjectivism

In contrast to such objective approaches, a subjectivist approach to morality holds that moral claims are matters of personal *opinion*. As such, there is no "fact" that validates some opinions, but refutes others. Very simply, if I believe something is morally wrong, then, for me, it *is* morally wrong. If you believe differently, then it's not wrong for *you*. If you and I disagree, it's not the case that one of us is mistaken—we simply have different opinions on the matter.

If subjectivism is true, then moral claims share the same (or at least a similar) status as other claims indicating personal preference or perspective. A comparison of objective and subjective claims might make this clearer, as well as make clear one of the significant implications of subjectivism.

Objective claims
- 2+2 = 4
- Bachelors are unmarried men
- The final two Democratic presidential candidates in 2020 were Joe Biden and Bernie Sanders
- The director of *The Hateful Eight* is Quentin Tarantino
- Bacon is usually made from pork
- Abortion is the intentional termination of a pregnancy.
- Subjective claims
- Math is boring
- It's better to be a bachelor than married
- Bernie Sanders is the better Presidential candidate
- The Hateful Eight was awesome!
- Bacon is delicious.
- Abortion is morally wrong.

One of the observations we can make about these groupings is that all of the examples of objective claims are either "analytic" claims or are empirically verifiable.

An analytic claim is a claim that is true (or false) by definition, by the very meaning of the words it contains. 2 + 2 = 4 is an analytic claim. Given the meaning of two, four, plus, and equals, we know that it is true that 2 + 2 = 4. The same is also true of our second example: bachelors are unmarried men. That is simply the definition of a "bachelor." Assuming you know what the word means, you know that it is true that bachelors are unmarried men, "by definition." The final example from the objective column is also an analytic claim. Abortion just *is* the intentional termination of a pregnancy.

The remaining examples of objective claims are not true by *definition*, but can be *demonstrated* to be true (or false) with a little bit of research and effort. Simply by checking to see which were the final two candidates for the Democratic party in 2020 on primary ballots and in Democratic debates allows us to verify that the claim is true. Similarly, we can check the film credits for *The Hateful Eight* using resources such as "imdb" allows to verify who directed that film.[289] Finally, a survey of bacon production, or even a simple examination at a grocery store, would allow us to verify that most bacon is pork (as opposed to turkey, for example).

Now turn to the examples of subjective claims, and notice a stark contrast: they are neither analytic claims nor empirically verifiable. Starting with the claim that math is boring, regardless of whether *you* find math to be boring, you undoubtedly recognize that there is nothing inherent to our very concept of math that renders it boring (unlike being unmarried being inherent to our concept of a bachelor), nor is there any way to "prove" that math is boring. Even if you survey thousands of people, and discover that most people describe math as boring, all you have proven is that *"most people surveyed describe math as boring,"* not that math *is* boring.

With regard to whether it's better to be married or a bachelor, once again we would all recognize that responses will vary. Some people love being married, others love being single—and neither preference is analytically true nor empirically verifiable as "correct." So, too, with preferring Bernie Sanders to Joe Biden, whether or not *The Hateful Eight* was "awesome," and even whether or not bacon is delicious.

Last, but certainly not least, what about that claim that abortion is morally wrong? This is clearly a moral claim (i.e., a claim concerning a moral issue), and some subjectivists will say that, like those other claims, it is neither analytic nor capable of empirical verification. This leads us to an official argument for moral subjectivism.

Moral claims are not objective because moral claims aren't provable

1. Objective claims must be either analytic claims or empirically verifiable.
2. Moral claims are not analytic claims.
3. Moral claims are not empirically verifiable.
4. Therefore, moral claims are not

objective claims.

5. Therefore, moral claims are subjective claims.

Let us now consider the argument, one line at a time. As with any virtually any claim in philosophy, the first premise is subject to disagreement.[290] However, that objective claims must be either analytic or empirically verifiable is a widely-accepted understanding of objective claims, and will be our working definition, given our limited purposes.

The second and third premises are much more important and interesting. The second premise claims that moral claims are not analytic claims. That is, they are not inherently true or false in the way that "bachelors are unmarried men" is inherently true, and "Ted is a married bachelor" is inherently false.

Consider the moral claim that it is wrong to steal. You might agree with that statement. You might think it is "obviously" true. However, you probably also acknowledge that if someone disagrees, and asserts that it is *not* wrong to steal (perhaps because they have a particular understanding of "property" and "property rights?"), that person has not uttered a literal logical contradiction.

You might think that person is mistaken, but the person hasn't said something literally incoherent—unlike someone who says a bachelor is married. Even in cases of passionate disagreement, such as between "Pro-Life" and "Pro-Choice" camps, there is no notion that the "other side" believes something literally incoherent and logically impossible. If you agree with this reasoning, then this indicates that moral claims are not *analytic* claims, not true (or false) *by definition*.

The third premise claims that moral claims are not empirically verifiable. To return to our example of theft, supporters of this argument would say that there is no way to *prove* that

---

[289]http://www.imdb.com/title/tt3460252/?ref_=nv_sr_1

[290] Indeed, an amusing possible criticism of this claim is that it is, itself, neither analytic nor

empirically verifiable, and therefore not an objective claim, according to its own standards....

stealing is wrong (or disprove it). After all, what test could someone propose that would *prove* the wrongness of stealing?

You could certainly prove the financial impact of stealing, or you could verify what someone (e.g., the thief, or the victim) *said* about stealing, or you could try to document the ownership of the item in question to determine whether a theft actually occurred, or you could verify that the act was indeed a violation of the law simply by consulting the laws in the place where the act occurred—but what verifiable fact or feature of reality corresponds to the *wrongness* of the stealing? Some subjectivists answer that there is no such verifiable fact or feature, and therefore moral claims are not empirically verifiable.

If objective claims must be either analytic, or empirically verifiable, and if moral claims are neither, then it seems to follow from that that moral claims are not objective. If they are not objective, but are, nevertheless, claims, then what remains for them is to be *subjective* claims.

Another argument for subjectivism relies upon the judgment that moral claims are not "natural." That is, they do not come from "Nature," but are rather the product of human conventions, and are therefore arbitrary and subjective, as opposed to objective.

Moral claims aren't objective because they are merely conventional

By way of analogy, consider the game of chess. In chess, there are certain rules that govern the movement of the pieces. Rooks can only move forward and backward, or from side to side. Bishops can only move diagonally. Knights can only move in "L" shapes. If I try to move a Knight one space directly forward, I have broken one of the rules of chess—but the rules themselves are completely conventional and arbitrary. There is nothing "natural" and necessary about chess. Human beings happened to invent a game, and came up with a handful of arbitrary rules that govern it. Unlike the "rules" (i.e., Laws) of Nature,

though, they are optional and arbitrary. Gravity, in contrast, is neither arbitrary, conventional, nor optional.

Some subjectivists will argue that moral "laws" (rules) are far more like the rules of chess than like the Laws of Nature, and for that reason are subjective rather than objective. Or, to put it a bit differently, natural laws are descriptive (i.e., they tell us how things in nature will behave) whereas moral claims are prescriptive (i.e., they tell us how moral agents *should* behave).

1. Natural Laws are descriptive, not prescriptive
2. Moral claims, though, are prescriptive.
3. Therefore, moral claims are not natural/objective but are conventional/subjective.

In support of the first premise, note that we recognize that natural laws don't make recommendations, but instead describe, explain, and predict. For example, Newton's law of Universal Gravitation claims that "any two bodies in the universe attract each other with a force that is directly proportional to the product of their masses and inversely proportional to the square of the distance between them." There is nothing to be recommended here. Newton wasn't suggesting how bodies should behave, but describing how they do behave. There are no value judgments in that description.

Even when we describe the behavior of other living things, we don't imply any sort of value judgments, but merely offer amoral descriptions of their behavior. The behavior of a hawk taking a fish from another hawk and a human stealing a fish from another human are outwardly the same—or at least very similar. Why is one "taking" and the other "stealing?"

Chimpanzees are somewhat notorious among primatologists for killing other (rival) chimps.[291] Most of us, however, would call that behavior "killing" rather than "murder"—and

---

[291] http://www.bbc.com/news/science-environment-29237276

even if we use the word "murder" we would probably acknowledge that we are using the word differently than when we use it with human actions. If, by chance, you think chimps are sufficiently self-conscious that such killing really *is* murder, then switch my example to a black widow spider killing and eating her mate, and now ponder how killing became murder when it reached the chimpanzee.

What, though, justifies our different judgment? Why is it "killing" if a chimpanzee ends the life of another chimpanzee through violence, but "murder" if a human does the same thing to another human? From a purely naturalistic perspective, humans are primates just as are chimpanzees, after all. . . .

At this point, the subjectivist could say that it is clear that Nature does not prohibit killing. In fact, killing (in the form of predation) is a *necessity* for a great many species! Killing fellow humans is "wrong" not because "Nature" says so, but because humans have said so. In effect, we have set up some "rules" for a "game," and one of those more common rules is that we're not (usually) allowed to kill one another. There is, however, nothing "natural" about that rule any more than there is something "natural" about the rules of chess. We can easily imagine different rules for human behavior just as we can imagine different rules for chess. Accordingly, given the difference between moral claims and Natural Laws, we should recognize moral claims as arbitrary, conventional prescriptions rather than objective descriptions.

Consider, now, the implications of this, if true. Given the subjective nature of moral claims, some will focus on the "rules" of the "games" we create as communities, and identify morality in terms of those collective rules. We will consider this interpretation in the form of ethical relativism in a later section.

Others, though, will question the validity of the "game" itself, and emphasize the arbitrary nature of those rules. If the moral rules are "arbitrary," what could make one rule more legitimate than another? There are a lot of different ways to play Poker. In some versions, the Joker is in play, and is "wild"—meaning it can

stand for any card you want. Or, in some versions, it can only stand for specific cards. Or, some people don't include the Joker at all.

Which of those variations is "true" Poker? Who has the authority to make such a judgment? Maybe some people like playing Poker without a Joker, and others like playing with the Joker being wild. Which of those groups is "right?" Does that question even make any sense? How could one style of play somehow be more "correct" than the other, if we acknowledge that the rules of Poker are completely arbitrary and products of human convention to begin with?

Now imagine that we consider moral "rules" (i.e., moral claims) in the same way. There are many different styles of "play," representing many different personal preferences. If you and I disagree about some particular moral issue, neither one of us is "mistaken." For one of us to be mistaken, there would need to be some sort of independent "answer key" against which we could compare our own values.

What or who could provide that "answer key?" Someone else? Why should her opinion count for more than our own? What about majority opinion? Isn't that just popularity?

Just because lots of people enjoy Country Music doesn't mean someone is mistaken for not liking it. Similarly, just because more people like to play Poker without the Joker than with it doesn't mean that those who like playing with the Joker are mistaken—they're just outnumbered.

What about appealing to the law? This sounds like an appeal to the "rules of the game." But, given the arbitrariness of those rules in the first place, no one could be "mistaken" if they prefer, instead, to substitute their own "house rules." Of course, if you're playing Poker at someone else's table, you might be bound to play by their rules, but that doesn't mean your own version of the game is "wrong." It might well be prudent of you to play by the rules of your host, but that is just a practical consideration, and in no way implies that your host's rules are somehow more correct than your own! If the only sources to which we may appeal are other humans, the question remains: why would one human's values be somehow more authoritative, more morally accurate, than another's?

Recall that, if moral claims are subjective, then the truth-value of a moral claim is not a "fact," nor is it "absolute" in any sense, but is, instead, a matter of personal perspective. Musical preferences, favorite colors, and favorite foods are easy and obvious examples of those sorts of claims. But, is my belief that it's wrong to torture babies for fun the same kind of claim as my belief that triple-cream brie is the best kind of cheese? Just a matter of perspective? Merely personal opinion? A matter of taste?

If you and I disagree about spicy food, we tend to think that's not a big deal. I'll eat spicy food, and you won't. Everyone's happy. But, what if I think it's OK for me to steal your identity and charge a bunch of merchandise in your name? I keep all the stuff, and you get stuck with the bill. You find out it was me, and you come complaining:

You: "Hey, Ted! What's wrong with you? Why did you steal my credit card and buy all that stuff for yourself? I just got a huge credit card bill in the mail?"

Me: "Um, I wanted the stuff, and I also didn't want to pay for it myself. Seemed like a pretty good way to handle that particular problem. . . ."

You: "But you can't just steal my credit card because you want something and don't want to have to pay for it! That's wrong!"

Me: "No it's not. . . ."

You: "What are you talking about? Of course it is!"

Me: "I don't think it is—and I would appreciate it if you would drop that self-righteous tone. The way you're speaking to me, it's as if you think your opinion concerning identity theft is somehow better, or more accurate, than mine. How arrogant. . . ."

Subjectivism is the view that has been lurking in the background for this entire section, thus far. According to Subjectivism, moral claims are matters of opinion, rather than fact. They are subjective, rather than objective. Moral claims are indicators of personal preference or taste, and are therefore more similar to a claim concerning whether I liked a movie than to a claim concerning who directed the movie.

According to Subjectivism, being opposed to abortion is more like offering your opinion about a painting than answering a math problem. Because moral claims appeal to opinions rather than facts, there are no "right" answers to our moral questions. Instead, something is morally right or wrong (to me) just to the extent that I *believe* it is, and if you should disagree with me, your opinion is no more (or less) correct than my own.

We will now consider some possible criticism of moral subjectivism so you can decide, for yourself, whether it's the best interpretation of moral claims.

Possible problems for Subjectivism

What most of these possible problems will have in common is that they involve "intuition tests." In a previous chapter, we addressed how we process new pieces of information. As you might recall, we each have, at our disposal, what we may call our "background knowledge," "background information," or our "worldview." Whatever we want to call it, it is that vast collection of everything we have heard, seen, read, and otherwise learned, throughout our lives. This collection is everything we know (or think we know) about the world and how it works.

Every time we are confronted with a piece of information, we automatically and instantly evaluate it against our background knowledge. If the new information seems to "fit" with our background knowledge, we're likely to accept it as true. If it does not fit, however, if the claim is surprising to us, we're likely to hesitate and to demand more justification before accepting it as true.

Each of the possible problems for

subjectivism we will consider involves an implication of subjectivism. In each case the strategy is the same: "if subjectivism is true, then [something else] is also true." That "something else" is being presented as a "possible problem," in the following way: each implication of subjectivism is a new piece of information. It either fits nicely with your worldview, sounding "right"—in which case you are likely to accept it as true, and this indicates that you might well be a subjectivist. On the other hand, this new piece of information might conflict with your worldview, and sound "wrong"—in which case you are likely to reject it as false, or at least be skeptical and demand some convincing evidence before revising your worldview.

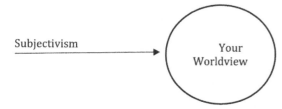

If any of these implications conflicts with your worldview, that doesn't necessarily mean that subjectivism is *false*, of course, but it would indicate that subjectivism *seems* at least unlikely to be true, given your understanding of the world and how it works.

Possible problem #1: Subjectivism is counter-intuitive because no one is ever "mistaken" about moral value judgments

We can now consider a possible (and disturbing) possible problem arising from Subjectivism: no one is ever "wrong"—at least not in any strong sense.

Professor Emeritus Harry Jaffa (from my own Alma Mater, Claremont McKenna College), penned a fictionalized account of a conversation between the serial killer Ted Bundy and one of his victims, "Laura." Jaffa has admitted that it was "composed on the same principle as the speeches in Thucydides' History of the Peloponnesian War,

attributing to each speaker the words that fit his character and the circumstances in which he spoke." In other words, he made it up—but in a way that he thought was at least consistent with the character of Bundy. Though I can't express enough how much I disagree with Professor Jaffa on certain subjects, he has managed to make the crux of a subjectivist understanding of morality clear in this dialogue. A brief excerpt follows:

Bundy: I recognize that your life and your freedom are very valuable to you, but you must recognize that they are not so valuable to me. And if I must sacrifice your life and freedom to mine, why should I not do so? The unexamined life was not worth living to Socrates. And a life without raping and murdering is not worth living to me. What right do you—or does anyone—have, to deny this to me?

Laura: But rape and murder are wrong. The Bible says they are wrong, and the law says they are wrong.

Bundy: What do you mean by wrong? What you call wrong, I call attempts to limit my freedom. The Bible punished both sodomy and murder with death. Sodomy is no longer regarded as a crime, or even as immoral. Why then should murder—or rape? . . .

I want you to know that once upon a time I too believed that God and the moral law prescribed boundaries within which my life had to be lived. That was before I took my first College courses in philosophy. Then it was that I discovered how unsophisticated—nay, primitive—my earlier beliefs had been. Then I learned that all moral judgments are "value judgments," that all value judgments are subjective, and that none can be proved to be either "right" or "wrong." . . . And I quickly discovered that the greatest obstacle to my freedom, the greatest block and limitation to it, consisted in the insupportable "value judgment" that I was bound to respect the rights of others. I asked myself, who were these "others"? Other human beings, with human rights? Why is it more wrong to kill a human animal than any other animal, a pig or a sheep or a steer? Is our life more to you than a hog's life to a hog? Why should I be willing to sacrifice my pleasures more for the one than for the other? Surely, you would not, in this age of scientific enlightenment, declare that God or nature has marked some pleasures as "moral" or "good" and others as "immoral" or "bad?"

Jaffa's point is pretty simple: if moral truth is relative to the individual, then, strictly speaking, Bundy isn't *wrong* (as in, "incorrect") to believe that raping and murdering is a fine form of entertainment.

I disagree with Bundy, of course, and so do you (I hope!). But, if moral claims are subjective, then all that means is that we have a different *opinion* about rape and murder than he does. Our opinion is neither better, nor worse, than Bundy's—in much the same way that someone who dislikes spicy food isn't "wrong" (whatever I might believe about their taste preferences). Similarly, someone who believes it's acceptable to have sex with young children isn't "wrong" according to a subjectivist approach. Such a person's opinion is no doubt quite unpopular, but "unpopular" isn't the same thing as "wrong."

I like garlic. For the most part, you can't put too much garlic in food as far as I'm concerned. Garlic ice cream is a feature at the Gilroy Garlic Festival, and can be purchased at the garlic-themed "Stinking Rose" restaurant in Los Angeles. Despite my love of garlic, I have never been excited about garlic ice cream. To be honest, garlic ice cream doesn't sound very appealing to me at all, though there are clearly some people who *do* like garlic ice cream—after all, the makers wouldn't bother making it if no one bought it!

I don't think those garlic ice cream enthusiasts are mistaken. If they like garlic ice cream, how can they be wrong about that? At the same time, those garlic ice cream fans must recognize that their ice cream preference is not very popular. They shouldn't be surprised when they can't find garlic ice cream in the freezer section of the grocery store, or at Baskin-Robbins. Instead, such venders cater to much more popular taste preferences such as mint chip, cookies and cream, etc. That doesn't mean that those of us who prefer mint chip are "correct" and those who prefer garlic ice cream are "incorrect"—but it does mean that we're in the majority, that our preference is more popular, and that our preference is much more likely to be honored in our community.

If subjectivism is true, then Ted Bundy's preference for rape and murder is like another person's preference for garlic ice cream. He was not "mistaken," but his view was unpopular, and he was outnumbered by those of us who believe rape and murder are wrong. That helps to explain why rape and murder are illegal, and why he was punished (executed!) once he was caught.

None of that indicates that he was *mistaken* about rape and murder, though. If Subjectivism is true, none of us can be "mistaken" about any moral claim, no matter what example we might conjure.

People who like garlic ice cream aren't mistaken. That's just what they like. Is that true of pedophiles as well? Are we willing to think of "I like garlic ice cream" and "I like raping children" as the same kinds of claims?

I'm being intentionally provocative here, because it's essential that we understand what it means if subjectivism is the proper way to understand morality. It's possible that moral truths really are simply matters of personal opinion. I don't personally think that is true, but it's *possible*. If that's the case, "morality," as most of us commonly understand it, doesn't exist—and this is why Subjectivism is presented as a "challenge" to ethics.

Critics of Subjectivism will point out that we do not, in fact, regard all opinions as equally true. This is evident, according to the critic, by the fact that we recognize areas of expertise, and experts whose views are regarded as more credible and authoritative as a result of that expertise.

Consider the following examples:

Subject	Expert
Medicine	Medical Doctor
Nutrition	Nutritionist
Carpentry	Carpenter
Botany	Botanist
Chemistry	Chemist
Physics	Physicist
Philosophy	Philosopher

I'll start with a deeply personal example. If you don't believe that my understanding of philosophy, on the basis of my several degrees (B.A., M.A., and Ph.D.), years of experience (more than 20 years at the time of this writing), and "accolades" (e.g., being a tenured professor, and having published multiple articles and textbooks, etc.), is any more informed than your own, why on Earth are you bothering to read this book, or take my class? What is the point of education, in general, if every student is equally informed as his or her teacher?

Let's make it more absurd. Why bother going to the doctor when you are sick and injured? If all opinions are equal, your own opinion about your medical condition is just as good as that doctor's!

Those astrophysicists who have spent studying the universe and who are debating whether or not this universe is situated within a broader multiverse? Their views are no better informed than the random person who has never studied that stuff a day in his or her life. . . .

You don't accept that as true, of course—and this is the critics point. In actual practice, we don't really believe that "all opinions are equal," but instead recognize that some people know what they're talking about, and others don't. Socrates himself criticized epistemic relativism (and moral subjectivism) thousands of years ago:

Why, that all those mercenary individuals, whom the many call Sophists and whom they deem to be their adversaries, do, in fact, teach nothing but the opinion of the many, that is to say, the opinions of their

assemblies; and this is their wisdom. I might compare them to a man who should study the tempers and desires of a mighty strong beast who is fed by him—he would learn how to approach and handle him, also at what times and from what causes he is dangerous or the reverse, and what is the meaning of his several cries, and by what sounds, when another utters them, he is soothed or infuriated; and you may suppose further, that when, by continually attending upon him, he has become perfect in all this, he calls his knowledge wisdom, and makes of it a system or art, which he proceeds to teach, although he has no real notion of what he means by the principles or passions of which he is speaking, but calls this honourable and that dishonourable, or good or evil, or just or unjust, all in accordance with the tastes and tempers of the great brute. Good he pronounces to be that in which the beast delights and evil to be that which he dislikes; and he can give no other account of them except that the just and noble are the necessary, having never himself seen, and having no power of explaining to others the nature of either, or the difference between them, which is immense.[292]

In other words, these intellectual mercenaries know nothing of good or evil, justice or injustice. Instead, they merely *observe* what actually happens in the world, what people seem to like and dislike, and *proclaim* those things to be good or bad, just or unjust.

If we recognize that this sort of relativism is rife with problems in a non-moral context (e.g., think about what it would mean for it to be "just a matter of opinion" that humans require oxygen to survive), why should we entertain the notion in moral contexts?

The question we must now consider is whether moral claims concern a matter of possible expertise ("morality"), in which case we

---

[292] Plato, *Republic*, 493a-c.

would presumably recognize that some people are better informed than others, and that not all views are equally good. Or, if we reject that, then we are presumably treating moral claims as mere indicators of personal taste. I might recognize that some people might be experts at "baking," and are certainly better informed than I am when it comes to how best to bake a cake, but I don't recognize that anyone else is somehow more informed than I am about what sort of cake I like! If you've gone to culinary school, your understanding of how to bake a red velvet cake is probably better informed than my own, but it makes no sense to suggest that you know better than I do regarding whether or not I *like* red velvet cake.

Herein lies the intuition test: based upon your worldview, is "morality" more like a skill that allows for expertise ("e.g., "baking"), or is it more like a personal taste preference ("red velvet cake is my favorite")?

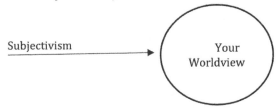

Possible problem #2: subjectivism is counter-intuitive because it doesn't allow for objective moral progress or regress in individuals

Another possible problem with subjectivism is what it does to our notions of moral progress and regress. In actual practice, we speak about people becoming morally better or worse people over time. "He's really turned his life around!" "What happened to Jane? She used to be such a good person?" What would such statements mean from a subjectivist perspective?

Stanley "Tookie" Williams was executed by the State of California in 2005. His impending execution was covered extensively in the California media not only because executions are infrequent in California, but also because Tookie

had become a bit of a celebrity, and had numerous actual celebrities lobbying for a stay of execution. Although several different arguments were offered for why he should not be executed, one particular argument was, by far, employed most often: Tookie had "reformed."

Although he was convicted of several murders from 1979, and although he was a co-founder of the notorious Crips gang, his supporters claimed that he had transformed himself while in prison, and was no longer the man he used to be. He had become a morally better person, and didn't deserve to die (at least not any more).

Twenty-five years ago when I created the Crips youth gang with Raymond Lee Washington in South Central Los Angeles, I never imagined Crips membership would one day spread throughout California, would spread to much of the rest of the nation and to cities in South Africa, where Crips copycat gangs have formed. I also didn't expect the Crips to end up ruining the lives of so many young people, especially young black men who have hurt other young black men.

Raymond was murdered in 1979. But if he were here, I believe he would be as troubled as I am by the Crips legacy.

So today I apologize to you all -- the children of America and South Africa -- who must cope every day with dangerous street gangs. I no longer participate in the so-called gangster lifestyle, and I deeply regret that I ever did.

As a contribution to the struggle to end child-on-child brutality and black-on-black brutality, I have written the Tookie Speaks Out Against Gang Violence children's book series. My goal is to reach as many young minds as possible to warn you about the perils of a gang lifestyle.

I am no longer "dys-educated" (disease

educated). I am no longer part of the problem. Thanks to the Almighty, I am no longer sleepwalking through life.

I pray that one day my apology will be accepted. I also pray that your suffering, caused by gang violence, will soon come to an end as more gang members wake up and stop hurting themselves and others.

I vow to spend the rest of my life working toward solutions.

Amani (Peace),

Stanley "Tookie" Williams, Surviving Crips Co-Founder, April 13, 1997.[293]

What would it mean to say that Tookie was a better person in 2005 than he was in 1979? Better how? By what standard? By *whose* standard? Remember, if moral truths are subjective, his beliefs and values in 1979 were not *wrong* (mistaken). Whatever he believed was right, *really was* right (for him).

In 2005, he allegedly possessed a different set of values. Those values were neither better nor worse than his values from 1979. They were simply different.

If you think he had become a better person, then, according to Subjectivism, that's simply *your* opinion. One can imagine that some of his still-dedicated Crips associates might disagree.

From a subjectivist perspective, to say that Tookie became a better person is to say something like the following:

- *"I* like Tookie a lot more than I used to."
- *"I* wouldn't have wanted to hang out with Tookie in 1979, but I would have in 2005."
- *"I* didn't have much in common with Tookie back in 1979, but now I do."
- "Tookie would have made me uncomfortable back in 1979, but now I feel good about him and his values."

293 http://www.villagevoice.com/news/ tookies-long-goodbye-6401007

Only if morality is *not* simply a matter of opinion, only if there is some non-subjective notion of truth behind it, can we have any strong notion of people becoming better or worse over time. Perhaps progress and regress are merely matters of perspective, but if you disagree and think there is a more powerful sense in which people can become morally better or worse, then you presumably disagree with the claims of subjectivism.

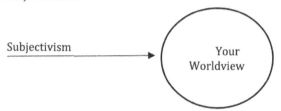

Possible problem #3: subjectivism is counter-intuitive because it doesn't allow for objective moral comparisons between individuals.

We've just seen how subjectivism can't provide strong comparisons of the *same* person over time. Now we can see how it also can't provide for strong comparisons of *different* people at the *same* time.

Consider these two men:

Now consider these two quotations. One is attributed to each man. I'll let you make an educated guess as to who is responsible for each quotation. . . .

The pieces of the bodies of infidels were flying like dust particles. If you would have seen it with your own eyes, you would have been very pleased, and your heart would have been filled with joy.[294]

Nonviolence is the answer to the crucial political and moral questions of our time; the need for mankind to overcome oppression and violence without resorting to oppression and violence. Man must evolve for all human conflict a method which rejects revenge, aggression and retaliation. The foundation of such a method is love.[295]

I'm going to "boldly" proclaim that MLK was morally superior to bin Laden. I'm even going to assume that most of you agree. What would that

mean, though, given a subjectivist framework? It certainly could *not* mean that King was morally better in any "objective sense"—after all, there is no such thing as moral objectivity from the point of view of the subjectivist. Instead, it must mean that my own *personal opinion* (yours too, presumably) is that King was morally superior.

That's just *my* opinion, though, and one that is no more or less correct than that of the most zealous fan of al-Qu'aida or bin Laden. If someone else thinks bin Laden to be the morally superior man, he or she is not "wrong"—we just have different moral taste preferences. To say that MLK is the better man is really just an indicator of my own values, as opposed to any claim about some moral truth—at least not any truth that is more than mere opinion.

One must grant, in all fairness and honesty, that the subjectivists *could* be right. It might be the case that all our moral judgments are simply expressions of personal opinion (or personal feelings), and nothing stronger than that. You must ask yourself, in light of what is *possible*, if it's also *probable* that subjectivism is true. Are we

---

[294] Osama bin Laden speaking about the 17 sailors who died in the suicide bombing of the USS *Cole* off the coast of Yemen, on a video made at the wedding of his son in southern Kandahar (February 2001)

[295] From Martin Luther King's Nobel Peace Prize acceptance speech (1964)
https://www.nobelprize.org/nobel_prizes/peace/laureates/1964/king-acceptance_en.html

incapable of any stronger moral comparison than the expression of our personal tastes? Is proclaiming King to be the morally better man the same kind of claim as pronouncing Switchfoot to be the best contemporary rock band?

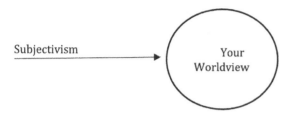

Subjectivism → Your Worldview

Possible problem #4: subjectivism is counter-intuitive because moral conflict must be resolved by appeals to power, rather than truth

One final (potentially disturbing) implication of subjectivism: if all moral judgments are mere expressions of personal opinion, and if no opinion can claim the mantle of truth, then moral disagreements cannot be resolved by appealing to the truth.

If you and I agree disagree on an objective matter, disagreement indicates error. If I claim that Barack Obama was the 42nd President of the United States, and you claim that George W. Bush was the 42nd President of the United States, at least one of us must be mistaken, since only one person could have been the 42nd President.[296] However, if I claim that George W. Bush is handsome and you claim that he is not, it is entirely consistent that both of us can be correct, since we are not actually contradicting each other. Note the comparison:

Objective claims
Barack Obama was the 42nd President
George W Bush was the 42nd President

Subjective claims
I think G.W. Bush is handsome
You think G.W. Bush isn't handsome

The claims in the first column can't be *both* be true at the same time, but the claims in the second can certainly both be true at the same time. This indicates, to subjectivists, that moral disagreement doesn't involve anything like the simultaneous utterance of contradictory claims, but merely the simultaneously different personal attitudes about something experienced by two different people.

If truth can't be used to settle moral conflict and debate, what can? If you and I disagree about some moral issue, and it's impossible (even in principle) for either one of us to establish who is correct (or at least closer to the truth), then what will resolve the conflict? The only thing left: power.

Thrasymachus, in Plato's *Republic*, argued famously that "might makes right."

I declare justice is nothing but the advantage of the stronger.[297]

Rather than viewing morality and justice as anything lofty and noble, a much simpler (and more cynical) interpretation is offered: the people in charge get to make the rules. Whatever they say is right, is, for all practical purposes, "right." One of the perks of being the most powerful person is that you get to enshrine your own personal values into law and custom—at least until someone more powerful comes along with a different set of values.

From the standpoint of subjectivism, those of us who think it abhorrent to have sex with a child don't have "better" values than a pedophile. We're not "right." What we are, is more powerful, if for no other reason than because we are more numerous. It just so happens that the no-sex-with-children crowd gained control at some point in our history, and has remained more populous

---

[296] Actually, in that case both of us would be mistaken, since Bill Clinton was the 42nd President. Congratulations to those of you

paying attention!
[297] Plato, *Republic*, 338c.

and more powerful than the percentage of our population who think it acceptable to have sex with children. We have no (objective) moral advantage over them, but we can force them to follow our values rather than theirs. After all, if they refuse, we'll throw them in jail.

Returning to our abortion example, neither side is "correct" or "incorrect," but in an ostensibly democratic society like the United States of America, whichever side can generate more votes and elect candidates that agree with them will have more power, and will "win."

Once again, the subjectivist could reply that, like it or not, that's just how things are. Moral judgments are all matters of personal opinion (or expressions of feelings), and the values supported by our laws and customs are not superior (in any strong, objective sense) to those values we label deviant.

Moral disagreement *could*, in fact, always be a power struggle, and is only ever resolved by force (social, or physical). That's possible, but does it seem to be true? Is there nothing more to your value judgments than opinion, or feelings? No way to resolve disagreement than by force? Can we only ever hope to be the most powerful, as opposed to the most right? Is it ever possible for someone to have no power, but nevertheless be *right*? If subjectivism is the best way to understand morality, it truly does require a radical revision of our understanding of morality, a revision that many of you might find untenable

Critical Analysis

1. In your opinion, what are the strongest and most compelling points made by the philosopher or philosophers in this chapter? Why do you find those points to be convincing?

2. In your opinion, what are the weakest or least convincing points? Why? Can you anticipate any limitations or objections to their ideas not already addressed in the chapter?

Appendix: Application to Social Justice

Somewhat similar to the chapter on human nature, in which the application to matters of social justice was a matter of how we would interpret those issues in the first place (as well as possible responses), the content of this chapter also presents an interpretive approach.

For any social justice issue, someone will inevitably be making (or evaluating) value judgments. That is, it's profoundly unlikely that anyone is conversing about matters of social justice in a purely disinterested manner, as though they were anthropologists neutrally observing various human behaviors and institutions. Instead, it is much more likely to be the case that when someone is discussing a social justice issue they are criticizing a practice or state of affairs, or else defending them. All of the following are examples of claims that offer value judgments.

- We should "defund the police."
- Police reform shouldn't be pursued since the problem is merely some "bad apples."
- The U.S. Government should offer reparations to the descendants of enslaved persons.
- Current generations should not have to pay for the sins of previous generations.
- Undocumented persons should be offered educational and health care services.
- It's wrong to "reward" illegal activity by providing government services to people in the country illegally.

Each of those statements is a claim, and whether you think that those sorts of claims are objective or subjective is a pretty big deal. The approach to moral value judgments offered in this chapter (viz., Subjectivism) proposes that all such claims are subjective, rather than objective. The truth of any such claim is a matter of personal perspective only, and there is no objective, neutral standpoint from which to evaluate or judge between such claims.

If you agree with the basic elements of subjectivism, you must accept that any and all claims about what is just or unjust, what should or shouldn't be done, are matters of personal opinion only, and are "true" only with respect to the person making the claim. That means that even a claim like "racism is morally wrong" is a matter of personal opinion.

If you think that racism is morally wrong, and that we should act, as a community, to eliminate racist practices and outcomes, and a white supremacist thinks that racism is both natural and good, and that our society should be constructed around and in support of white supremacy, there is no sense (according to subjectivism) in which one of you is "right" and the other is "wrong." In that hypothetical scenario, *I* happen to think that *you* are correct—but that's only my own subjective perspective, which doesn't make the claim any truer.

This is largely just a reminder of one of the various "possible problems" for subjectivism addressed earlier in the chapter. If you found those objections persuasive, then you have probably already rejected subjectivism anyway. Otherwise, it's still possible to endorse subjectivism *and* pursue various social justice causes. In so doing, however, you'll just have to be aware of the fact that the values you are promoting are only subjectively valid, that those with whom you disagree are not (objectively) "mistaken," and that, ultimately, which "side" prevails on that issue will come down to who can exert the most "power."

Chapter 12: Ethical Relativism

Some are uncomfortable with the radical individualism entailed by subjectivism, but nevertheless agree that moral value judgments are matters of opinion, rather than fact. For those that continue to resist what we'll call an "objective" understanding of morality, the most logical alternative to subjectivism is ethical relativism (sometimes called cultural relativism, but because this is easily confused with the anthropologist's usage of that same term, I have elected to use ethical relativism instead).

Ethical Relativism

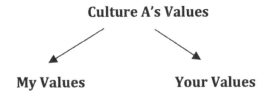

Consider the image above. It represents the kinds of judgments and comparisons possible according to ethical relativism. No such image was provided for subjectivism, in our previous section, since, if subjectivism is true, no comparisons of values are possible anyway—at least not anything other than a "taste test."

Ethical relativism operates on just the same assumptions as subjectivism with one notable difference: whereas subjectivism claims that moral judgments are matters of personal opinion, and gain whatever legitimacy they have from the endorsement of the individual, ethical relativism claims that morality is a matter of *collective* judgment.

What is right and wrong is determined by the prevailing values of a given community. You've probably heard the expression, "when in Rome, do as the Romans do." Assuming this is meant as more than just practical advice, this is an expression of ethical relativism.

> What is your "culture?" Describe it, and its influences, as thoroughly as you're able. Be sure to consider possible cultural elements as race, gender, religion, nationality, sexual orientation, generation, and (dis)ability. Describe specific moral recommendations made by your culture (e.g., prohibiting pre-marital sex). List at least 5. Do you obey these recommendations? Discuss why, or why not. Do you agree with your culture's values? Why, or why not?

According to ethical relativism, what is morally right and morally wrong is established by the dominant values of a given culture. This allows for moral judgments and comparisons concerning individuals—at least within the same community. The standard we would use for such judgments would be the dominant values of the culture in question. Each culture provides its own "answer key" for its own community. For example, in the United States, an adult male marrying a 9 year-old girl would not merely be considered morally wrong, he would be prosecuted for a sex crime! Thus, because the dominant cultural values of the U.S. frown upon such marriages, it is morally wrong to marry 9 year old girls in the U.S. Not so, elsewhere, however.

Tihun, a 9 year old Ethiopian girl, was arranged to marry a 19 year old Orthodox Church deacon by her father. This is not an aberration. According to UN and Ethiopian statistics, in some parts of Ethiopia almost 90 percent of the local girls are married before age 15 (technically, it is against Ethiopian law to marry anyone under the

age of 18, but the punishment is a $12 fine, is rarely enforced, and is generally ignored by the conservative population.). "'In truth, if a girl reaches 13, she is already too old to be married,' declares Nebiyu Melese, 54, Tihun's wiry farmer father. 'I know some people say this is uncivilized. But they don't live here. So how can they judge?'"[298]

"How can they judge?" According to ethical relativism, we can't—at least not with any special credibility. Because ethical relativism claims, like subjectivism, that there is no set of "true" moral values that apply to all people, everywhere, and at all times, there is no *objective* standard (no universal answer key) with which to judge the values of a culture.

From *within* a given culture, one may (and should) employ the values of that culture, and individuals can (and should) be judged according to those standards. In the U.S., if you marry a 9 year old and I don't, I'm a morally superior person than you are (on that one issue, at least) because my values and behavior are more in harmony with those prescribed by our culture. Outside of our own culture, however, we are in no position to judge.

Why would anyone accept this view? There are several reasons, and not all of them are based on mistakes. One that *does* rest on a mistake, however, involves the *observation of cultural differences* throughout the world. This simple observation of differences is "commonsense," and has been made by countless people, including such philosophers as Cicero.

> *Now if any one, carried in the chariot of winged serpents, of which the poet Pacuvius makes mention, could take his flight over all nations and cities, and accurately observe their proceedings, he would see that the sense of justice and right varies in different regions.... If I were to describe the diverse kinds of laws, institutions, manners, and customs, not only as they vary in the numerous nations,*

---

[298] https://www.chicagotribune.com/news/ct-xpm-2004-12-12-0412120359-story.html

but as they vary likewise in single cities, as Rome for example, I should prove that they have had a thousand revolutions.[299]

One need not be especially well-traveled, or cosmopolitan, to know that different cultures have different practices, and (seemingly) different values. Certain examples are obvious. Australian aborigines eat the "witchety grub" and consider it a welcome delicacy. Most Americans would only eat grubs if on a reality TV show. Americans eat meat with reckless abandon (222 pounds per person, in 2018, according to the U.S. Department of Agriculture), but Indian Hindus abstain from eating meat.[300]

It is not only our diets that vary, from one culture to the next. Marriage practices, sexual taboos, notions of masculinity and femininity, notions of "family," clothing practices, funerary practices, and many other activities vary. One need not be a world traveler to know this, just watch PBS or National Geographic.

Some ethical relativists, such as Ruth Benedict, observe these cultural differences, and make something morally significant out of it. Benedict claims that standards of normalcy and deviance vary from one culture to the next.

The above picture shows former President George Herbert Walker Bush walking hand-in-hand with Saudi King Abdullah. In the United States, this is an interesting event, because in the U.S. it isn't "normal" for grown (heterosexual) men to hold hands. That is, when we see two adult men holding hands, we assume they are homosexual, and that their hand-holding means basically the same thing as when straight men and straight women hold each other's hands. Even for straight allies, men holding hands is seen as a sub-cultural practice for homosexuals—there's been little, if any, infiltration of this practice into the (straight) mainstream culture. The practice, and its meaning, however, is quite different in the Saudi culture. Men hold hands as

---

[299] Cicero, *The Republic*, Book 3.

[300] "He who desires to augment his own flesh by eating the flesh of other creatures lives in misery in whatever species he may take his birth." (Mahabharat 115.47—for those unfamiliar, the Mahabharat is one of two major Sanskrit epics of ancient India. It is also an important part of Hindu mythology. Thus, quoting sections and verses from the Mahabarat is analogous to quoting from chapter and verse from the Christian Bible.)

a display of friendship, not as a display of a romantic relationship.

"We" give a "high-five," "they" hold hands.

Americans eat with forks, the Chinese eat with chopsticks.

American men wear pants, traditional Scotsmen wear kilts. Different strokes for different folks....

Most of us are willing to acknowledge that certain practices vary from one culture to the next, and that each is a *legitimate* practice. That is, it's hard to find someone who would claim, in any serious tone, that it's "wrong" to eat with chop-sticks, Chinese or not, and that eating with a fork is the only morally legitimate means to transport food to one's mouth. Benedict goes quite a bit farther than this, though, by claiming not only that "normalcy" varies (legitimately) from one culture to the next, but also that "normal" and "morally good" are synonymous terms. In other words, when we say that something is morally good, what we're really saying is that the practice in question is what we consider "normal," and if we label something to be morally bad, that's just another way of saying it's "weird." A slight bit of logic allows us to see the implication of this.

1. What is considered "normal" varies (legitimately) across cultures.
2. Therefore, there is no single standard of normalcy for humankind.
3. "Normal" and "morally good" are synonymous terms.
4. Therefore, there is no single standard of moral goodness for humankind.

A few points require immediate attention.

1. It is far from *obvious* that "normalcy" and "morality" are, in fact, synonymous terms—at least not across the whole range of practices deemed either normal/deviant, or good/bad.

For example, it's possible that there are practices deemed normal or abnormal that we don't regard as having any moral significance whatsoever. Talking to oneself in public is seen as "weird" in the U.S. culture, and is often assumed to be a sign of mental illness, but it's not obvious that it would also be considered morally wrong. Piercing one's face is still considered "extreme," despite the increasing popularity of body piercings, but it's not easy to find someone who would claim that those who do so have committed a moral offense.

Similarly, it's not obvious that we would all agree that certain practices, deemed immoral, are of the same type as those we also deem "abnormal." Child-rape is certainly considered deviant, and perceived as "weird," but the act seems to be more than *just* "weird." Intentionally urinating on oneself in public is weird. Very weird, in fact. Is raping a child just very, very weird? Very, very, very weird? Or, are some acts *qualitatively different*, such that they no longer fit into our categories or normalcy/deviancy, but require their own (distinct) category: good/evil?

Consider this Venn diagram:

"Normal/abnormal" v. "Moral/immoral"(?)

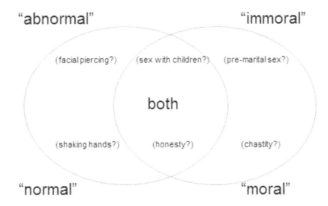

"abnormal" "immoral"

(facial piercing?) (sex with children?) (pre-marital sex?)

both

(shaking hands?) (honesty?) (chastity?)

"normal" "moral"

It seems possible that certain actions (e.g., extensive facial piercings) might be considered "abnormal/deviant" within a community, but *not* considered immoral. In fact, every time I survey my students and ask them if having facial piercings is morally wrong, almost no one ever says "yes"—though nearly everyone acknowledges that it is outside the "norm."

Other actions might be considered "immoral," but are not abnormal in the sense of unusual or atypical. For example, pre-marital sex is the "norm" in the United States. The overwhelming majority of Americans has sex before marriage, across most demographic groups—but many (even if grudgingly) consider pre-marital sex to be (technically) morally wrong. Here we have an example of something "normal" (as in "common") but possibly immoral. Some actions, though, are generally considered to be *both* abnormal *and* immoral. Pedophilia is certainly outside the norm, but also widely regarded as morally wrong.

On the "positive" side, certain actions are "normal" in the United States (e.g., shaking hands as a form of greeting), but without necessarily attributing any moral "goodness" to the act. Other actions are regarded as possibly morally good (e.g., abstaining from pre-marital sex—chastity), but are not the norm. Still other actions might be regarded as both the "norm" as well as being morally good (e.g., honesty).

We can dispute particular examples, but the key question to ask is whether this preceding discussion, in general, seems plausible? If the relationship depicted in the Venn diagram seems plausible, then it would indicate that "normal" and "moral," while related, are *not* synonymous terms.

2. As James Rachels has argued, the mere fact of difference does not mean that there are no values that apply to all people, everywhere. The observation of cultural differences is consistent with *both* ethical relativism *and* objective approaches to ethics. Therefore, the fact of cultural differences is not automatically support for ethical relativism.

In cases of difference, a relativist will conclude that there are no universal values. Someone who believes morality is objective will look at those same differences and conclude that at least one of the cultures is *mistaken*.

Consider an analogy: if two people come up with two different answers to the same math problem, we would be foolish to leap to the conclusion that both of them are correct, or (more foolish still) that there is no "correct" answer at all. Much more plausibly, we would infer that at least one of those persons (and maybe both!) is mistaken and came up with the wrong answer.

Similarly, just because two different cultures come up with two different "answers" to the same (moral) question, that doesn't necessarily mean that both cultures are equally morally correct or that no "correct" answer exists. It's possible that one culture is mistaken. It might be *difficult to discern* who is right, and who is wrong, but there is nothing logically inconsistent with looking at two cultures, one of which prosecutes the rapist when a woman is raped, the other of which stones the woman to death for adultery, noting the different responses, and concluding that one of them is in error. My own vote is against stoning rape survivors. . . . What's the point? Simply this: the fact of cultural differences, by itself, is *not necessarily* an indicator of the truth of ethical relativism.

Cultural differences alone do not require one to accept ethical relativism, but there might well be other reasons to do so. For example, in that same dialogue from Cicero I quoted earlier, the character Philus infers that "universal" moral values don't exist given the existence of such cultural diversity.

> If this justice were natural, innate, and universal, all men would admit the same law and right, and the same men would not enact different laws at different times.[301]

If there is allegedly "one single law for all humanity," why are there so many different opinions, customs, and human laws? How do we explain all the cultural differences, variations in laws across geographic location and time, and all the differences in opinion even within the same community? How do we explain how same-sex marriage can be celebrated by a majority of the population in some countries, today, while homosexuals are being executed in brutal fashion in other parts of the world?

Cicero *himself*, however, did not find this argument persuasive.

> Yet we are confused by the variety and variability of men's opinions; and because the same disagreement does not occur in regard to the senses. We think the senses are reliable by nature whereas we brand as illusory those ideas that vary from one person to another and do not always remain consistent within the same person. This distinction is far from the truth. In the case of our senses, no parent or nurse or teacher or poet or stage-show distorts them, nor does popular opinion lead them astray. For our minds, however, all kinds of traps are laid, either by the people just mentioned, who on receiving young untrained minds stain them and twist them as they please, or else by that power which lurks within, entwined with every one of our senses, namely pleasure, which masquerades as goodness but is in fact the mother of all ills. Seduced by her charms, our minds fail to see clearly enough the things that are naturally good, because those things lack the sweetness and the exciting itch of pleasure.[302]

Think of it this way: most of us are not skeptics of relativists with respect to basic claims about perceptible things. As an example, most people are pretty darn confident that elephants are larger than house flies—and anyone who claims otherwise is either doing something odd with language, or else likely adopting an insincere philosophical pose for the sake of being contrary. Because sense-testimony is generally conducive to agreement, we imagine that empirical matters are factual, objective. However, when it comes to moral judgments, there is a variety of views.

Some people think that abortion is acceptable, and others think it is murder. Some people believe it's wrong to eat meat, and others worship at the altar of bacon. Same-sex marriage is now a constitutional right in the United States, but homosexuals are executed by being thrown

---

[301] Cicero, ibid.

[302] Cicero, *Laws*, 1.47

off of buildings in ISIS-controlled parts of Syria.[303] We are taught one thing by our parents, perhaps another by teachers, perhaps another by friends, still another by our church, and yet another by the media and pop culture. This dizzying influx of contrary moral messages can cause us to conclude that there is no moral "truth" at all—only opinion.

What's more, Cicero points out that we can be "charmed" by pleasure into thinking that certain actions, because they are pleasurable, are also therefore "good"—while our senses generally provide no such ulterior motive.

For all these reasons, Cicero explains how people can come to the *false* conclusion that there is no objective moral law. However, Cicero is confident that there is, that, because we are social beings, unjust acts are contrary to our natural fellowship, and true laws, therefore, are intended to maintain social order and harmony.

Another reason one might think there are no "universal" values is a general skepticism that a universal moral code could ever be *agreed* upon. After all, that there is deep division on numerous moral issues (e.g., abortion, the death penalty, homosexuality, etc.), is obvious. One might think that agreement will never be reached and take that as a sign that no such set of universal values could exist. That might be true, but it's a hasty conclusion.

Even if humanity never does come to consensus on the requirements of morality, that might say far more about our own limitations than about the actual status of moral values. Humans might never fully understand the laws of Nature, or the true origin of the universe, but that doesn't mean that there is no explanation, no right answer—just none that *we* can reach. Moreover, even if it's true that we can never know (with certainty) the truth concerning our moral obligations, that doesn't mean that we can't *make progress* towards the truth, that we can't come ever closer to a full and accurate ethical theory.

An additional reason someone might embrace ethical relativism is a result of rejecting its perceived alternative: objective ethical theories.[304] This approach is presumably well-intentioned, and is rooted in a recognition that, for most of recorded history, "tribes" have usually assumed their own moral superiority over their neighbors.

In the West, we have a long and bloody history of European (and eventually, American) powers taking notice of a group of people, taking note of how different those people are, judging that to be different is to be "wrong" and in need of "correction," and then using that judgment to justify campaigns of invasion, colonization, exploitation, and even genocide.

If "savages" engage in morally inferior practices, then one is doing them a "favor" by "correcting" them. After all, they're being made "better." Since *our* way is the only *right* way, they should be made to dress like us, marry like us, speak like us, worship like us, govern like us, and so on.

Many of us, looking back on history, and even on contemporary policies and practices, are repulsed by the cruelties and atrocities that were perpetrated by virtue of the self-righteous assumption of one's own moral superiority. If the inspiration for such actions is the belief that there is one set of true moral values (undoubtedly, one's own!), then a *rejection* of such an assumption might prevent such actions. Ethical relativism is seen as the tolerance-producing alternative to objective ethics, and is sometimes, for that reason, embraced. This "argument from tolerance" may be formulated as follows:

The Argument from Tolerance

1. If morality is culturally relative, then there is no independent basis for criticizing the moral values of any other culture.
2. If there is no independent way of criticizing any other culture, then we

---

[303] http://www.nydailynews.com/news/ world/isis-militants-throw-gay-man-building-death-article-1.2041416

[304] Cynics might call this the "liberal guilt argument" for ethical relativism.

ought to be tolerant of the moral values of other cultures.

3. Morality is culturally relative.
4. Therefore, we ought to be tolerant of the moral values of other cultures.

If this argument works, then from ethical relativism we may derive that we ought to be tolerant of other cultures.

Tolerance is a good thing, right? Not necessarily! Ask yourself this question: is there any limit as to what should be tolerated? And what does it even mean to be "tolerant?" Does it mean to let people do whatever they want? Does it allow for judgment, but not intervention? Does it just mean we have to be "polite" when judging others? Which of the following should be (or should have been) "tolerated?" What would it mean to "tolerate" such practices?

- South African apartheid.
- Nazi mass-extermination of Jews.
- The Armenian genocide perpetrated by Turkey in the early twentieth century.
- The Cherokee "Trail of Tears."
- The millions of Native Americans murdered or displaced during the "Westward Expansion" of the United States.
- The *thousands* of African-Americans lynched in the American South.[305]
- The internment of Japanese-Americans during WWII.
- Female Genital Mutilation that currently affects approximately 2 million girls each year.
- The harvesting of organs from executed criminals in China.
- Saddam Hussein's gassing of Kurdish villages.
- Beheadings and crucifixion of "infidels" by ISIS.

(If you don't know what some of these examples refer to, look them up!)

A first problem with the argument from tolerance is that it's not at all obvious that tolerance is always a good thing. It certainly seems to be the case that some practices, and some values, should *not* be tolerated. Which values fit into that category will be subject to spirited debate, of course, but it does seem that such a category exists.

A second problem with the argument from tolerance is a problem of internal consistency. Premise 1 seems uncontroversial, but premise 2 requires a close examination.

Premise 2 claims that "we" ought to be tolerant. Two words are significant: "we," and "ought." Notice that "ought" is a value-term. To say that we ought to do something is to make a prescriptive claim. We *should* be tolerant. It's *good* to be tolerant. It's *right* to be tolerant. Who, exactly, are "we" who are being told that "we" *ought* to be tolerant? There are three possibilities:

1. "We" are all of humanity—all people, in all places, at all times.
2. "We" are people from the same culture as the person making the argument.
3. "We" are people from a different culture than that of the person making the argument.

No matter which is intended (1-3), a problem emerges. Let's work backwards. If (3), then we are from a *different* culture than that of the person urging us to be tolerant. Why should we listen to her? Her values might be right for her own people, but they don't apply to us. If ethical relativism is true, we should heed the moral requirements of our own culture, and not hers.

If (2), then she is speaking to us as a peer. Now we must figure out what the values of our (shared) culture happen to be. Is tolerance, in fact, a dominant value in our culture? If so, then we *should*, in fact, be tolerant (whatever that means), but *not because of her argument*. We should be tolerant because that is what our cultural values prescribe. She's merely

---

[305] At least 3,400 from 1882-1968.

"preaching to the choir."

On the other hand, what if our culture is not tolerant? What if we come from an imperialist culture that believes that other cultures' values are savage and wrong? In that case, according to ethical relativism, we should be *in*tolerant! In fact, that tolerance-promoting troublemaker is actively encouraging us to be immoral by going against the values of our culture. This is something no self-aware, self-respecting cultural relativist could prescribe!

If (1), then she is claiming that there is at least one value (tolerance) that applies to all people, everywhere, at all times. That flatly contradicts a central feature of ethical relativism: namely, that there are *no* values that apply to all people, everywhere, at all times. She has contradicted herself and supplied the counter-example to her own theory. How embarrassing for her!

None of this means that a cultural relativist cannot, or will not, be tolerant. Instead, it simply demonstrates that tolerance is not a necessary consequence of ethical relativism. Indeed, anyone who alleges that ethical relativism *does* require, or even recommend, toleration reveals that he simply has not correctly understood ethical relativism!

Consider an analogy: suppose I were to tell you that my favorite thing about soccer (in America, soccer— "football" everywhere else in the world) is the fact that any player, at any time, can pick up the ball with his or her hands and run with it.

If you know anything about soccer, you immediately realize that I do not, given the fact that most players are *not* allowed to use their hands during the game. My comment is no commentary on soccer, but rather on my own *misunderstanding* of soccer.

Similarly, if someone tells me how ethical relativism requires (or even promotes) tolerance or respect for diversity, I immediately realize that this is no commentary on ethical relativism, but rather an indicator of that person's *misunderstanding* of ethical relativism.

According to ethical relativism, you should be tolerant only if that is what your culture

demands, and if a culture is intolerant, that culture is not "wrong" for being so. This indicates a very important feature of ethical relativism: *ethical relativism does not take a stance on any moral issue whatsoever*. Instead, it provides a decision-making procedure with regard to the moral rightness or wrongness of whatever example we might entertain: "ask your culture."

This is simple to illustrate. According to ethical relativism, all moral values are relative to a particular culture. Therefore, ethical relativism (itself) does not indicate that abortion is morally acceptable (or unacceptable). Instead, it claims that the rightness or wrongness of abortion will depend upon the culture in question. In some cultures, abortion is morally wrong, but in others cultures it is acceptable. Similarly, ethical relativism takes no stance on the death penalty. The death penalty will be morally acceptable in some cultures, and unacceptable in others. Slavery is neither morally right nor wrong according to ethical relativism—but it will be morally right (or wrong) in *particular cultures*. So, too, with homosexual sex acts, human sacrifice, eating meat, pre-marital sex, etc.

Toleration and/or respect for diversity are moral values like *any other* just mentioned. Ethical relativism does not endorse, or reject, toleration or respect for diversity. Instead, according to ethical relativism, the rightness or wrongness of toleration will depend upon the culture in question. Ethical relativism does not— and can't—require toleration, though a particular culture *might*.

One final time, the preceding discussion is neither an indictment of ethical relativism, nor of toleration, but is simply meant to illustrate that the idea that ethical relativism somehow requires or promotes toleration is a *myth*. There might well be good reasons to endorse ethical relativism as an ethical theory, but the belief that it requires or promotes tolerance should not be one of them.

We now know that ethical relativism claims that all moral values are relative to particular cultures, and we have considered several reasons why someone might think this interpretation is correct (e.g., a general skepticism concerning universal moral values, a (misguided) association of ethical relativism with tolerance, or Benedict's argument concerning normalcy and morality). We will now consider some reasons to reject ethical relativism, and enable you to make your own assessment.

Ultimately, ethical relativism is potentially vulnerable to the very same criticisms that were leveled against subjectivism, but adjusted to reflect ethical relativism's emphasis on collective values as opposed to personal opinion. Also, just as with subjectivism, most of these possible problems amount to "intuition tests" in which a new piece of information (an implication of ethical relativism) is evaluated against your worldview.

Possible problem #1: ethical relativism allows no objective stance from which to evaluate other cultures' values.

Much as subjectivism does not allow moral comparisons of individuals (beyond expressions of our own personal opinions), ethical relativism is incapable of strong cross-cultural comparisons.

Consider the Taliban. Prior to the U.S. led overthrow of the Taliban (2001), the laws and practices of Afghanistan drew considerable international criticism. Here are a few examples:

- Public executions, including stonings, were common.
- Kite-flying (a "frivolous" activity) was outlawed.
- TV, music, and the internet were banned (to remove "decadent" Western influences).
- Men were *required* to wear beards.
- Girls were forbidden to attend school.
- Women could not be examined by male doctors.

- Women could no longer work *as* doctors (think about what these last two mean for women's health care under the Taliban).
- Women could not leave the home without a male escort.
- "Idolatrous" art was destroyed--such as the giant statues of Buddha (constructed 2nd and 3rd centuries A.D., destroyed in 2001).

Much more recently (and similarly), the practices of ISIS (or ISIL)[306] have drawn international criticism. Public executions, including stonings and crucifixions occurred "daily" in ISIS-controlled parts of Syria, women are lashed if not sufficiently "covered," international journalists are beheaded on camera, and (interestingly enough, given the context of this book) philosophy has been banned as a form of blasphemy.[307]

If ethical relativism is true, then the practices of the Taliban (or ISIS) are neither better nor worse than those of any other culture—just "different." Of course, the U.S. overthrow of the Taliban could not be condemned either, so long as it was consistent with the dominant values of U.S. culture. Moreover, neither the Taliban (or ISIS) nor the U.S.-led overthrow could be judged by other cultures—after all, they have no privileged position from which to judge the U.S. any more than the U.S. has a privileged position from which to judge the Taliban.

Perhaps this is accurate, and no community is ever in a position to judge another. If so, though, we must face a radical revision of our common practices, since we do, in fact, tend to condemn cultures such as Nazi Germany, the Taliban, and apartheid-era South Africa. Many countries condemn the actions of ISIS. Is there *any* behavior, *any* cultural practice, from *any* period in human history that you think is just plain *wrong*, period? Slavery? Human sacrifice? Child rape? Genocide? Anything at all?

If there is even one act, practice, or behavior

---

[306] "Islamic State of Iraq and al-Sham," or the "Islamic State of Iraq and the Levant," respectively.

[307] http://www.cnn.com/2014/09/04/world/meast/isis-inside-look/index.html?hpt=hp_t1

that you think is always morally wrong, regardless of time, place, or opinion, you have an intuitive disagreement with ethical relativism. If you think condemnation that is more than a mere expression of collective taste is possible, then you would have reason to reject ethical relativism.

Possible problem #2: Moral reformers are always morally "wrong."

According to ethical relativism, the right thing to do is, by definition, whatever one's culture tells one to do. Since the dominant values of one's culture are the ultimate arbiter of morality (the "supreme court" of morality, as it were), there is nothing to which one can appeal that is "higher" than one's culture. You can never go "over the head" of your culture in the event that you disagree with its values. So where does that leave reformers?

A reformer, by definition, is trying to change her culture. All reformers detect something about their culture that they think is morally wrong, or unjust, and they try to change it. According to ethical relativism, though, it is not the individual's judgment that establishes what is right and wrong; it is the collective judgment of the entire culture as expressed in its dominant values.

By definition, then, someone who is trying to change the values of the culture is trying to change what is "right." That makes them *wrong*, doesn't it?

Both Martin Luther King Jr. and Rosa Parks were icons of the American Civil Rights era. Both fought against racism and segregation laws. Both were also criminals, by definition, since they deliberately disobeyed segregation laws, and both were arrested for their "offenses." Both believed that the values of their culture, at the time, were wrong, and in need of correction. But who were they to challenge the values of their culture? By offering a set of values different from that of their culture, at the time, weren't they morally in the wrong, by definition? And yet, don't we tend to have precisely the *opposite* view of reformers, at least in retrospect?

When Rosa Parks died in 2005, her body was displayed in the Capitol Rotunda. The tribute, which requires an act of Congress, has taken place only 31 times in this country's history. Those receiving this rare honor include President Abraham Lincoln and several other Presidents, eight members of Congress, and two Capitol police officers slain at their posts, among a handful of others.[308] President Bill Clinton delivered a eulogy for her. In it, he said that she made us a "better people, and a better country."[309]

If ethical relativism is true, what could it mean that she made us "better?" The segregationist values prior to the Civil Rights Movement were not "wrong," after all—just "wrong" given our *current* dominant values.

Much as individuals cannot get morally better or worse, in any strong sense, from a subjectivist perspective, neither can cultures get morally better or worse over time from the perspective of ethical relativism. Cultures become "different," but their former values were not "wrong;" they were "right," at the time. This aspect is especially fascinating considering how often proponents of ethical relativism condemn the "imperialist" practices of their own culture! If ethical relativism is true, on what grounds can they complain about their own culture's values?

In fairness, the advocate of ethical relativism could reply in the following way: "when we complain about our own culture, our complaint is that the practices of our culture are not consistent with its values. So, too, with reformers in general. What reformers do is appeal to the already existing values of their culture that are not being honored, to some extent."

Using the example of the Civil Rights Movement, a relativist could say that King and

---

[308] If you are interested in a full and up-to-date listing, check the following URL:
http://www.aoc.gov/nations-stage/lying-state
[309] The full transcript of his eulogy for her is available here: http://www.washingtonpost.com/wp-dyn/content/article/2005/11/02/AR2005110202154.html

others appealed to the values of equality, brotherhood, freedom, and dignity that were already found in Christianity and in the political philosophy that shaped our government and society.

When King advocated equality, he was not introducing some new, alien value into the culture, but was simply pointing out that U.S. society was not living up to its very own ideals, by virtue of the rampant discrimination at the time. Indeed, the advocate of ethical relativism could argue that had those basic values of equality, freedom, opportunity, and the like not already been present in the culture, the Movement could have never taken hold and been successful.

If that's true, then Civil Rights activists were not "in the wrong," but were, instead, champions of the actual cultural values of the United States. Historians will be better prepared to address this issue, but it seems (to me) overly generous to think that racism and segregationism were not expressions of the dominant values at the time, considering how pervasive and enduring racism, and its legacy, has proven to be. Anti-"race-mixing" laws were not overturned by the Supreme Court until 1967. Lest one think such laws were regional only, found in the deep South alone, bear in mind that California's anti-miscegenation law was not overturned by a California Supreme Court until 1948, a mere seven years prior to the beginning of the Civil Rights Movement.

Let us suppose, however, for the sake of argument, that interpreting successful reform movements (such as the Civil Rights Movement, for example) as cases where reformers were actually appealing to pre-existing cultural values is plausible. This approach nevertheless seems limited, however, in that it would appear that a culture could never undergo a radical transformation from within. Social change would always need to be somehow consistent with already existing and honored values. Any radical change would have to be understood in terms of an "invasion" of a foreign value, and in terms of that initially-"wrong" value "vanquishing" and ultimately replacing the native values, much as a foreign usurper may claim a throne. Small

changes might be understood as a somewhat different application of an already dominant value, while major change must come from the outside. Major changes, at the least, and the advocates of major change, would have to be considered "wrong," at the time.

This produces a potentially counter-intuitive evaluation of moral reformers—at least those advocating "major" change. In trying to change the "right" values of their culture, moral reformers are always "wrong." If they succeed, and their own values become dominant later on, they will be hailed as moral visionaries, in retrospect. But, in their own time, they are moral villains.

Perhaps that's just "how it is." We must acknowledge the possibility that our own perception that a culture (including our own) has gotten morally better or worse over time is just an expression of the bias of our own time and place. *We* think segregation laws are wrong because, in our own time, they are considered wrong. Had we been born (Caucasian, presumably) a half-century ago, though, we would have likely thought differently. Perhaps, at the time, we would have been "right."

On the other hand, if you have any strong intuition that cultures really *do* get morally better or worse over time (e.g., that a culture that abandons slavery has become objectively morally better than it had been), and that such judgments are not mere expressions of current collective opinion, then you presumably have a hard time accepting the implications of ethical relativism. What is certain is that ethical relativism requires a radical revision of our everyday notions of cultural moral progress and regress.

Possible problem #3: "Culture" is a vague concept.

You've perhaps noticed that I've tossed around words like "we" and "our" quite a bit in these past few pages. I've been speaking of U.S. culture, on the reasonably safe assumption that the overwhelming majority of you are Americans, or at least reside in the U.S., but to speak of the U.S. culture as if it were some obvious and monolithic thing is problematic. Just what is a "culture," anyway?

Merriam-Webster defines "culture" as "the customary beliefs, social forms, and material traits of a racial, religious, or social group." This is extraordinarily vague, and maybe even hopelessly so. To see why this is a problem, think of yourself, and your own social context. How do you self-identify, according to the following criteria?

- Race/ethnicity
- National origin
- Gender
- Sexual orientation
- Ability/disability
- Socio-economic status
- Religious affiliation (atheist, agnostic, or secular humanist are each acceptable responses to this)

- Generation (e.g., "baby-boomer," "Gen-X," "Gen-Next.")
- Citizenship status
- State, county, and city of residence
- Group memberships (e.g., fraternal orders, Freemasons, etc.)

This is a partial list, to be sure, but serves to illustrate the possible problem. If you live on a small, remote island in which everyone comes from the same ethnic stock, belongs to the same religious tradition, and shares the same values, the identification of your culture is probably pretty simple. I, however, live in Southern California, and it's hard to imagine a more diverse, pluralistic region than L.A. County. According to the U.S. Census Bureau, the following was true of the people of L.A. County as of 2010:[310]

RACE	People	%
American Indian and Alaska Native	72,828	0.7
Asian	1,346,865	13.7
Filipino	322,110	3.3
Japanese	102,287	1.0
Korean	216,501	2.2
Vietnamese	87,468	0.9
Other Asian [1]	145,842	1.5
Asian Indian	79,169	0.8
Black or African American	856,874	8.7
Chinese	393,488	4.0
Cuban	41,350	0.4
Mexican	3,510,677	35.8
Native Hawaiian and Other Pacific Islander	26,094	0.3
Native Hawaiian	4,013	0.0
Guamanian or Chamorro	3,447	0.0
Samoan	12,115	0.1
Other Pacific Islander	6,519	0.1
Puerto Rican	44,609	0.5
White	4,936,599	50.3
Two or More Races	438,713	4.5

With respect to religion, the Association of Religion Data Archives tracked over 100 different denominations/faith traditions in 2010 within L.A. County, from the American Baptist

---

[310] More detailed (and updated) information is available at the following URL. As of the time of this writing, 2010 is still the most current available data.
https://factfinder.census.gov/faces/nav/jsf/pages/community_facts.xhtml?src=bkmk

Association to Zoroastrians.[311] That's over a hundred different faith traditions in only one county, of one region, of one state, in the United States.

I (and probably you, as well) live in a diverse, pluralistic society. Why does this matter so much? Ethical relativism tells us that what determines moral rightness and wrongness is the dominant values of one's culture—but what is my culture? What is yours? Which values are the dominant ones?

If you're considering the moral permissibility of an abortion, for example, isn't it possible that you might get one answer if you live in Salt Lake City, Utah, and another if you live in San Francisco, California? One answer if you are Catholic, and another if you are Episcopalian? One answer if you live in L.A. County, another if you live in Orange County (both within the State of California)? One answer if your family has just immigrated to the U.S., and another if your ancestors arrived on the Mayflower? One answer if you were born between 1940 and 1960 ("Baby-Boomer"), another if you were born between 1961 and 1981 ("Generation X"), and still another if you were born after 1982 ("Generation Y"/"Generation Next")?

Just how big and influential does a group have to be to count as a culture? As of 1995, the North American Man/Boy Love Association (N.A.M.B.L.A.) boasted a membership of 1,100—though the organization has gone largely dormant these days. Is that enough to constitute a culture (one that advocates what the rest of us call pedophilia and pederasty, but a "culture" nonetheless)? If it is not a culture, why not? How large must a "social group" be to count as a culture? If it is a culture, then, according to ethical relativism, are its values just as legitimate as any others'? How do we handle the fact that the N.A.M.B.L.A. "culture" (or perhaps sub-culture) is found within other, broader cultures in which "man-boy love" is condemned as child rape?

From which group does one get one's values?

[311] More detail information is available here: http://www.thearda.com/rcms2010/r/c/06/rcms2010_06037_county_name_2010.asp

Do we just pick for ourselves which group's values we'll adopt and value? If so, isn't that just subjectivism?

Whatever other challenges ethical relativism faces, a key feature of any ethical theory is its ability to provide a decision-making procedure, a method for resolving what to do when faced with a difficult ethical decision. If ethical relativism fails to provide this decision-making procedure, due to the vagueness of the very concept of "culture," then it fails as an ethical theory.

"Just consult the laws of the land," one might reply. "If it's against the law, then it's morally wrong according to your culture." This is probably too simplistic, though, given the fact that we recognize a distinction between what is legal/illegal and what is right/wrong. Lying, in most contexts, is not illegal, but is nevertheless generally regarded as wrong. African-Americans sitting at certain lunch counters was illegal at one time in the U.S., but most of us would deny that doing so was also morally wrong. Indeed, the very fact that we have a concept of "just" *and* "unjust" laws tells us that legality and morality, while usually overlapping, are not always the same thing. This is just one more challenge for this already besieged approach to ethics, but I'm not done yet!

All other challenges to ethical relativism aside, if one can establish that there are, in fact, at least some values that are found in all societies, at all times, and in all places, then such a finding would lend much credence to the claim that at least *some* moral values are universal, and that ethical relativism is false. James Rachels has attempted to provide a compelling argument that this is so.

"Universal" Moral Values: James Rachels

Rachels proposes that there is more moral "universality" across cultures than we might initially recognize. One reason for this is because cultures might manifest the same underlying value in different ways, given contingent historical, geographical, climatic, and other circumstances.

For example, throughout most of the U.S., the dead are buried below ground, but in New Orleans, they are buried above ground. Why? New Orleans is below sea-level, and has a high water table. Graves fill with water, and caskets float, creating an unhealthy, as well as deeply disturbing, result.[312] This is an example of how geography can influence the *manifestation* (burial below v. above ground) of the *same underlying value* (honor the dead). Other cultures cremate. Ancient Egyptians mummified their dead. All believed it to be morally right to honor the dead, but due to different circumstances, they demonstrated that belief in different ways.

As another example, consider child-rearing. Some cultures adopt the so-called "nuclear family" (mom, dad, and 2.5 kids under the same roof). Others prefer extended families (multiple generations in the same home), and still others embrace communal child-rearing in which responsibility for caring for the young is shared by the larger community, including non-blood relatives.

There are any number of explanations for why one culture might manifest its child-care in one fashion, while a different culture does so in another, but the allegation is that the underlying value is the same, even though the manifestation is different.

The moral value that the young should be cared for is, in fact, one of a handful of values that Rachels claims that all cultures must have, if they are to survive as a culture. It is thus a *universal* (non-relative) value. Consider the alternative.

Try to imagine a culture in which no moral value was placed on caring for the young. There is no stigma, no shame, no pressure, no laws associated with child-rearing. How could such a culture persist? In order to survive, a culture must produce new members who will survive long enough to continue its traditions, and then create the next generation themselves. Although

people care for children in a variety of formats, we struggle to even *imagine* a culture that does not care for them at all.

As another example, Rachels claims that no culture could survive if it did not have some prohibition against murder. Try to imagine what it would be like to live in a society in which no positive value was placed on innocent life, and in which there was nothing wrong with killing innocent people. What an anxiety-filled existence! How could such a culture avoid self-destruction?

As a final example, consider honesty. Rachels claims that all cultures, in order to survive as cultures, must endorse honesty and condemn deception. Why? Consider the alternative. If there was no stigma attached to deception, and no expectation of honesty, under normal circumstances, why would you ever believe what other people tell you? What you read? What you hear? Why would you assume the words you're reading right now are sincere and accurate? Why go to school, if it's just as likely that your instructors are lying as they are not? Why read the newspaper (or, more likely, internet news sources), if it's no worse for it to be filled with lies than the truth? Clearly, without an expectation of honesty, there's no basis for trust. Without trust, there's no basis for cooperation, and without cooperation, there is no society—not even family units can survive without trust-enabled cooperation. Obviously, people can and do lie, but this is the exception, rather than the rule. Imagine trying to get through your day if it was just as likely that everyone you met was lying to you as that they were telling the truth!

If Rachels is correct, then this is a major accomplishment. Though we might bicker as to just *which* moral principles and values are necessary for any society to survive (and are, therefore, "universal"), it would appear that there are some that fit that description. If so, then ethical relativism is wrong with respect to its claim that all values are relative, and that none is universal. That, at the very least, is a very

---

[312] http://www.experienceneworleans.com/deadcity.html

important start for the rest of our process, in that it would allow us to operate on the assumption that (at least some) moral claims are objective.

If at least some moral claims are objective, then it's possible to make strong, meaningful comparisons of individuals, and of entire cultures. What will be the standard by which such comparisons are possible? The set of true moral values that apply to all people, everywhere, at all times.

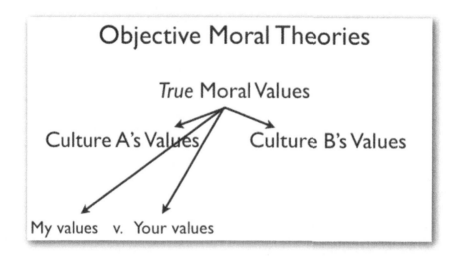

"Universal" Moral Values: C.S. Lewis

Although his reasons are very different from those of James Rachels, C.S. Lewis agrees that there are universal (objective) moral values.

Lewis starts from what he takes to be the universal recognition of objective moral "rights" and "wrongs." This is evident, he thinks, from the fact that we all tend to *judge* the behavior of others (and ourselves). We really do think that some actions are good, and others bad—and morally so, not merely so in terms of what's prudent. We really do think that some actions are virtuous, and others vile, and that some people are heroes, and others villains. Although our particular examples might vary, we all engage in this general behavior. In addition, we have behavioral expectations of others, and we are upset when people violate them. We all think there are certain things that people just shouldn't do, and we get upset with them if they do it anyway.

Spouses shouldn't be unfaithful. Friends shouldn't lie to you. Politicians shouldn't accept (or expect) bribes. Your neighbor shouldn't steal from you. No one should molest your child. And so forth.

We don't merely blithely announce our expectations, and then shrug when they're violated, as though it didn't matter. We are offended, indignant, outraged, betrayed, hurt. . . With respect to our own behavior, when someone else accuses *us* of violating moral norms, we usually try to make excuses for the behavior, if we don't outright confess—thereby implying the need for an explanation in the first place. Compare the following hypothetical exchanges:

You: "Hey! Don't cut in line in front of me."
Me: "My friend has been saving my spot."

You: "Hey! Don't cut in line in front of me."
Me: "I'll do whatever I want!"

While there certainly are some people who flout convention, and are unashamed to do, we tend to judge those people very harshly—sometimes going so far as to label them sociopaths. Most of us play by the rules, try to justify our actions if we're caught "bending" them, get upset with others when they break them, and all the while at least implicitly acknowledge the existence of "the rules" in the first place. The implicit premise here seems to be that we all know that there exist certain (objective) moral principles.

Lewis is aware that not everyone would so readily agree to that claim, and he anticipates (and addresses) several possible objections. A first, obvious, objection is the theory of ethical relativism itself. But, just as Rachels argued that there are fewer differences in values across cultures as there might appear, Lewis makes a similar point.

> *Think of a country where people were admired for running away in battle, or where a man felt proud of double-crossing all the people who had been kindest to him. You might just as well try to imagine a country where two and two made five. Men have differed as regards what people you ought to be unselfish to-whether it was only your own family, or your fellow countrymen, or everyone. But they have always agreed that you ought not to put yourself first. Selfishness has never been admired. Men have differed as to whether you should have one wife or four. But they have always agreed that you must not simply have any woman you liked.*[313]

Indeed, Lewis echoes most of the objections we have thus far considered. With regard to the fact that, if ethical relativism is true, there is no objective stance from which to evaluate or criticize any culture's values or practices, Lewis draws on his own experience of facing the threat of the Nazis in his lifetime. The Nazis were, for him, an example of a people and a cultural program gone *wrong*, and the mere fact that some Nazis might have thought differently doesn't change that fact. "People may be sometimes mistaken about [morals], just as people sometimes get their sums wrong; but they are not

a matter of mere taste and opinion any more than the multiplication table."

A related objection was that, if ethical relativism is true, moral reformers are, paradoxically, always morally wrong. And yet, as Lewis points out, people *do* argue that reform is possible, and desirable.

> *If no set of moral ideas were truer or better than any other, there would be no sense in preferring civilised morality to savage morality, or Christian morality to Nazi morality. In fact, of course, we all do believe that some moralities are better than others. We do believe that some of the people who tried to change the moral ideas of their own age were what we would call Reformers or Pioneers-people who understood morality better than their neighbours did.*[314]

Another objection to the existence of objective moral values, very much in the spirit of ethical relativism, is that "morality" is merely social conditioning produced by our education and upbringing. Lewis, however, replies that *how* something is learned doesn't necessarily indicate its ultimate source or status (e.g., we learn the multiplication tables at school without this implying that math is merely a human convention). "But," the skeptic might wonder, "why think that morality is objective in a way analogous to math?" Because, says Lewis, the "Moral Law" is (generally, at its core) the same across cultures, whereas mere convention (e.g., which side of the road one drives on) is not.

Returning to his arguments against ethical relativism, Lewis reiterates that we do, in actual practice, hold some cultural norms to be "better" or "worse" than others (e.g., Nazis are worse!), and alleged differences in values are often just differences in matters of fact. We have already rehearsed this point about alleged differences in values being just differences in local expressions of those values previously in this chapter, but

---

[313] C.S. Lewis, *Mere Christianity*, Book 1, chapter 1.

[314] ibid., Book 1, chapter 2.

Lewis uses an interesting example that's worth quoting: witch burning.

> *I have met people who exaggerate the differences, because they have not distinguished between differences of morality and differences of belief about facts. For example, one man said to me, 'Three hundred years ago people in England were putting witches to death. Was that what you call the Rule of Human Nature or Right Conduct?' But surely the reason we do not execute witches is that we do not believe there are such things. If we did-if we really thought that there were people going about who had sold themselves to the devil and received supernatural powers from him in return and were using these powers to kill their neighbours or drive them mad or bring bad weather, surely we would all agree that if anyone deserved the death penalty, then these filthy quislings did. There is no difference of moral principle here: the difference is simply about matter of fact. It may be a great advance in knowledge not to believe in witches: there is no moral advance in not executing them when you do not think they are there. You would not call a man humane for ceasing to set mousetraps if he did so because he believed there were no mice in the house.[315]*

A different sort of objection to the claim that morality is objective brings us back to the evolutionary understanding of morality previously considered by our appeals to Dawkins and Rachels. Perhaps "morality" is just our evolution-produced "herd instinct," just one instinctive drive amongst other instinctive drives? Lewis replies that desires are not identical to our sense of obligation with respect to those desires. For example, my awareness that I ought to be forgiving is not at all the same as a desire to be forgiving. Indeed, often our desires are in sharp contrast to our sense of obligation.

Moreover, Lewis thinks that it makes little sense to understand moral prescriptions as impulses or desires amongst others, as he can identify no particular impulses or desires that the "Moral Law" tells us always to restrain or to pursue. Indeed, our sense of moral obligation seems to be a different sort of thing by which we judge between desires and impulses.

> *Supposing you hear a cry for help from a man in danger. You will probably feel two desires-one a desire to give help (due to your herd instinct), the other a desire to keep out of danger (due to the instinct for self-preservation). But you will find inside you, in addition to these two impulses, a third thing which tells you that you ought to follow the impulse to help, and suppress the impulse to run away. Now this thing that judges between two instincts, that decides which should be encouraged, cannot itself be either of them. You might as well say that the sheet of music which tells you, at a given moment, to play one note on the piano and not another, is itself one of the notes on the keyboard. The Moral Law tells us the tune we have to play: our instincts are merely the keys.[316]*

Nor does it seem plausible, according to Lewis, that morally good behavior is merely socially useful behavior (e.g., what's needed for community flourishing, as Rachels might argue). According to Lewis, morally good behavior *is* socially useful, but that doesn't explain its purpose (in a non-circular way), since being "socially useful" *is* one of those behaviors we label "good."

> *If a man asked what was the point of playing football, it would not be much good saying 'in order to score goals,' for trying to score goals is the game itself, not the reason for the game, and you would really only be saying that football was football-which is true, but not worth*

---

[315] ibid.

[316] ibid.

saying. In the same way, if a man asks what is the point of behaving decently, it is no good replying, 'in order to benefit society,' for trying to benefit society, in other words being unselfish (for 'society' after all only means 'other people'), is one of the things decent behaviour consists in; all you are really saying is that decent behaviour is decent behaviour.[317]

While Lewis and Rachels agree, then, on the existence of universal moral values, they very much disagree as the nature of the source and grounding of those values. For Rachels, our objective moral values arise as dispositions to behave that promoted our survival, and are, indeed, necessary for human survival and flourishing in communities. For Lewis, the ultimate source of those moral values is a transcendent, morally perfect God—though his defense of that claim is beyond the scope of this chapter, or even this book.

Although we have seen two critiques of ethical relativism from Rachels and Lewis, it's important to make three concessions:

1. Some differences are probably so significant that they're not best understood as merely different manifestations of the same underlying values.

For example, someone might claim that marriage is one way of expressing the value that human sexuality should be constrained, and Female Genital Mutilation (FGM) is simply another. I, for one, find the practices different enough that I doubt they express the same value at all. This is certainly subject to debate. The point, at this stage, though, is simply to acknowledge that it would be too easy, and too sloppy, to gloss over the genuine and controversial differences between various cultural practices by suggesting that they are just different manifestations of the same value. While there might be more universality than there appears, there's probably also less universality than we might wish were the case.

2. Both subjectivism and ethical relativism have something worthwhile to offer.

There is certainly a category of value judgments that we make that is best understood using the subjectivist model. Our judgments concerning aesthetic preferences, for example, music, art, food, and so on, all very reasonably seem to be nothing more (or less) than expressions of personal opinion. They can, and should, be understood through the subjectivist lens

There is another category of values and behaviors that seem to be based on cultural standards, and is both more than mere personal opinion, and less than a universal moral value. Once again, the exact content of this category is probably difficult to articulate, but things like expectations of behavior in particular settings (e.g., how to behave with respect to greetings, when visiting holy sites, when a guest in someone's home, etc.) are probably examples.

A lesson to be learned from both subjectivism and ethical relativism is to be cautious of hasty assumptions and self-righteousness.

It's all too easy to presume one's own view of the world, and one's own values, are the absolute truth and worthy of promulgation. History is filled with the tragic consequences of such assumptions. Both subjectivism and ethical relativism give us reason to slow down, restrain our arrogant tendencies, and pay careful attention to what other individuals, and other communities, have to say.

Where both go too *far*, however, is in thinking that no truth is possible, that there are no right answers at all, that no meaningful comparisons and judgments are possible, and that no individual (or group) ever does wrong (in any strong sense beyond our own personal or collective opinion).

Indeed, there's a dangerous irony lurking behind both theories: the subjectivist judgment that all values are mere opinions is *itself* a mere opinion (according to its own standards), yet is offered as a rule for all; and the ethical relativism

---

[317] ibid., Book 1, chapter 3.

view that all values are relative to one's culture is also usually (implicitly, and mistakenly) offered as a reason for all people to be accepting, respectful, and tolerant, of other culture's values, even when some cultures clearly value doing just the opposite.

Critical Analysis

1. In your opinion, what are the strongest and most compelling points made by the philosopher or philosophers in this chapter? Why do you find those points to be convincing?

2. In your opinion, what are the weakest or least convincing points? Why? Can you anticipate any limitations or objections to their ideas not already addressed in the chapter?

Appendix: Application to Social Justice

This section mirrors the same section from the subjectivism chapter in the very same way the content of both chapters mirror one another. Both subjectivism and ethical relativism assert that moral claims are subjective rather than objective—they merely differ with respect to which personal opinions "matter." For subjectivists, moral claims (including those pertaining to social justice issues) are matters of *personal* opinion, whereas for ethical relativists they are matters of the dominant values of a particular culture.

Obviously relevant in the context of social justice is how we must interpret cultural progress and reformers. In almost every case, activists making social justice claims are going to be in the cultural *minority*.

Recall our "working definition" of social justice from the Introduction of this text: *social justice means equal rights and equitable opportunities for <u>everyone</u>*.

If someone is raising a social justice issue at all, it means that equal rights and equitable opportunities are *not* presently obtained by everyone. To put it bluntly, if everything was already "good," why would anyone be complaining? Basically, anyone raising social justice issues is occupying the role (to some degree) of a "moral reformer," and is subject to the same assessment of reformers we considered earlier in this chapter.

If the dominant values of your culture revolve around and support white supremacy, then, according to ER, those values are "correct" (for that culture). If you're trying to change that, you're (by definition) morally "wrong."

To evade those charges of being in the wrong, you have a couple of options. One would be to demonstrate that your values actually *are* expressions of the dominant values of the culture, and that the practices or institutions you're protesting are somehow not in harmony with those values. For example, in Dr. Martin Luther King's sermon "The American Dream," he says that he will "preach a sermon in the spirit of the founding fathers of our nation and in the spirit of the Declaration of Independence."[318]

"We hold these truths to be self-evident, that all men are created equal, that they are endowed by God, Creator, with certain inalienable Rights, that among these are Life, Liberty, and the pursuit of Happiness." This is a dream. It's a great dream.

The first saying we notice in this dream is an amazing universalism. It doesn't say "some men," it says "all men." It doesn't say "all white men," it says "all men," which includes black men. It does not say "all Gentiles," it says "all men," which includes Jews. It doesn't say "all Protestants," it says "all men," which includes Catholics. (Yes, sir) It doesn't even say "all theists and

---

[318] The sermon was delivered at Ebenezer Baptist Church, Atlanta, Georgia, on 4 July 1965, and is available here: https://kinginstitute.stanford. edu/king-

papers/publications/knock-midnight-inspiration-great-sermons-reverend-martin-luther-king-jr-4

believers," it says "all men," which includes humanists and agnostics.

Then that dream goes on to say another thing that ultimately distinguishes our nation and our form of government from any totalitarian system in the world. It says that each of us has certain basic rights that are neither derived from or conferred by the state. In order to discover where they came from, it is necessary to move back behind the dim mist of eternity. They are God-given, gifts from His hands. Never before in the history of the world has a sociopolitical document expressed in such profound, eloquent, and unequivocal language the dignity and the worth of human personality. The American dream reminds us, and we should think about it anew on this Independence Day, that every man is an heir of the legacy of dignity and worth.

Now ever since the founding fathers of our nation dreamed this dream in all of its magnificence—to use a big word that the psychiatrists use—America has been something of a schizophrenic personality, tragically divided against herself. On the one hand we have proudly professed the great principles of democracy, but on the other hand we have sadly practiced the very opposite of those principles. . . .

And so it is marvelous and great that we do have a dream, that we have a nation with a dream; and to forever challenge us; to forever give us a sense of urgency; to forever stand in the midst of the "isness" of our terrible injustices; to remind us of the "oughtness" of our noble capacity for justice and love and brotherhood.

This is why we must fight segregation with all of our nonviolent might. (Yes, sir; Make it plain) Segregation is not only inconvenient—that isn't what makes it wrong. Segregation is not only

sociologically untenable—that isn't what makes it wrong. Segregation is not only politically and economically unsound— that is not what makes it wrong. Ultimately, segregation is morally wrong and sinful. To use the words of a great Jewish philosopher that died a few days ago, Martin Buber, "It's wrong because it substitutes an 'I-It' relationship for the 'I-Thou' relationship and relegates persons to the status of things." That's it. (Yes, sir). . .

We have a great dream. (Great dream) It started way back in 1776, and God grant that America will be true to her dream. . . .

So yes, the dream has been shattered, (Amen) and I have had my nightmarish experiences, but I tell you this morning once more that I haven't lost the faith. (No, sir) I still have a dream (A dream, Yes, sir) that one day all of God's children will have food and clothing and material well-being for their bodies, culture and education for their minds, and freedom for their spirits. (Yes)
I still have a dream this morning: (Yes) one day all of God's black children will be respected like his white children. . . .

There are several things worth pointing out from this excerpt from his sermon. MLK is claiming that the moral values and guiding principles that ought to be honored in the United States are those proclaimed in the Declaration of Independence and espoused by the Founders. Referring to these values as the "dream," he portrays segregation and racism as a "nightmare" and a deviation from and betrayal of that "dream." In other words, it's the racists and segregationists who are violating our cultural norms, and it is those advocating for equal treatment under the law and dignity for all persons who are actually honoring our cultural norms.

This is a debatable matter of history, of course. There is ample evidence that the

Founders were not at all egalitarian in their thinking on race (or gender, or class), and it's hard to ignore that slavery was literally written into the Constitution that followed the Declaration, and that white supremacy had been promoted and preserved for nearly two centuries as of the time of King's sermon. It's "charitable," to say the least, that genuine equality was the "true" guiding moral principle of our Nation and that any violations of that were (and are) deviations from the norm. Nevertheless, even if I might personally question the accuracy of King's *historical* claim, he shows the general method by which an ethical relativist might evade the charge that their reform efforts are "immoral."

A second strategy by which an ethical relativist might evade the "immoral reformer" charge is by appealing to the vagueness of "culture," and/or the existence of sub-cultures. For example, there is no question that, for most of American history (at minimum), acceptance (let alone validation) of LGBTQ+ persons and their equal rights was not "mainstream." Consider same-sex marriage, for example.

In 2020, roughly 67% of Americans support the legal recognition of same-sex marriage. In 1996 (when I was in College!), that percentage was only 27%.[319] While a majority of Americans *now* support same-sex marriage, that was not the case even only a generation ago. From the beginning of the United States, until only recently, inclusion and acceptance of LGBTQ+ persons was simply *not* a cultural norm.

However, that paints with a pretty broad brush. Presumably someone could argue that LGBTQ+ acceptance might have been the "norm" within *some* communities, even historically. If the LGBTQ+ *community* is considered a *culture*, then an ethical relativist could acknowledge that LGBTQ+ activism, while considered "wrong" from the perspective of the laws and norms of the USA, in general, was nevertheless "right" according to the norms of the LGBTQ+ culture. Even *today*, that figure of 67% support might benefit from a closer look.

67% of "Americans" support same-sex marriage as of 2020, but that figure varies significantly by political affiliation. 83% of Democrats are supportive, compared to only 49% of Republicans. If we consider party affiliation to be a "culture," then it is presumably the case that various issues concerning the LGBTQ+ community are considered "right" in the "Democrat culture" but "wrong" in the "Republican Culture." Now think of how that might work out regionally.

President Trump won the State of Arkansas in the 2020 Presidential Election 62% to 35%, suggesting that Arkansas is very much a "Republican" State. We might reasonably infer that Arkansas is unlikely to be "gay-friendly," in terms of its values, even if 2/3 of Americans are. But even *that* doesn't tell the whole story. While Trump won Arkansas by a very wide margin, Joe Biden won Pulaski County (where the Capital, Little Rock is located) with 60%. Actually, 8 of the 75 Arkansas counties were "blue" rather than "red."

The pattern for both "red" and "blue" states is remarkably similar: "urban" areas tend to be democratically inclined whereas rural areas tend to be conservatively inclined, regardless of the overall leaning of that State. This might suggest that we reasonably predict that even in Republican States, LGBTQ+ acceptance might still be the norm in the major urban areas, and that even in Democrat States there might be opposition to LGBTQ+ acceptance in rural areas. Even in "deep blue" California, President Trump won 75% of the vote in Lassen County—a much *higher* margin than that by which he won the State of Arkansas.

What's the point of all this analysis? Simply this: from a wide-angle point of view, reformers might be understandably perceived as being morally wrong to the extent they are violating general cultural norms. However, given the complexity of the very concept of culture, and the very real possibility that a more focused view indicates that there are communities within the

---

[319] https://news.gallup.com/poll/311672/support-sex-marriage-matches-record-high.aspx

larger community that might have significantly different norms, it's possible for a reformer to identify herself with one of those communities, according to whose values she is morally right.

Or, the complexity of all this might just reinforce the "culture is a vague concept" concern from earlier in the chapter!

As one final note, I can't resist pointing out that King was *not* in any way an ethical relativist himself, and that is abundantly clear in the sermon above, and in countless other King sources. As King states:

> *...each of us has certain basic rights that are neither derived from or conferred by the state. In order to discover where they came from, it is necessary to move back behind the dim mist of eternity. They are God-given, gifts from His hands.*

The source of our moral value and equal moral standing, according to MLK, is God. We are not equal because the government says so, or because that's what our culture thinks. Instead, we are equal because that's what *God* thinks—and there is nothing culturally relative about that (if true).

King is claiming that the United States has failed to live up to its own moral standards, but it doesn't actually matter whether or not he has accurately understood those standards as a matter of history, as I challenged above. The Founders didn't establish our equality, but, at most, only *recognized* (very much incompletely) what was already objectively the case. And, if King and other Civil Rights activists were, in fact, acting in violation of our cultural norms, so much the worse for those norms! From King's perspective, any cultural practice, law, tradition (etc.) that violates our basic God-given rights is *wrong*, and it is the reformers who are acting rightly.

Appendix/"Deeper Dive"
Alain LeRoy Locke: Positive Pluralism

Comprehension questions you should be able to answer after reading this chapter:

1. Why does Locke reject "absolutism?" Why does he also reject subjectivism?
2. What is the benefit (according to Locke) of focusing on our shared and similar process of "valuing" rather than on our different values?
3. What does Locke mean by "basic/functional equivalence?"
4. What does Locke mean by "functional constancy?"
5. What does Locke mean by the process of becoming "cultured?" How does this happen?

This additional section to the chapter is admittedly more challenging than what you have already read, and I have provided it for the sake of that challenge. Some of you might want to "dive deeper" into these ideas, and this will help you do that. Before delving into the actual theory, I want to begin with some stories/examples.

I have been to several funerals in my life. It seems to be a hazard of aging: the longer you live, the more funerals you attend. Although I am a philosopher by calling and by trade, I occasionally have an opportunity to play "amateur cultural anthropologist." One such occasion is when I attend funerals. First, a very small amount of background information about me.

My wife is African-American. I am Caucasian. In addition to family connections, between the two of us we have (and have had) many friends and associates from a variety of different ethnic and religious backgrounds. While there has not been a tremendous amount of diversity in the funeral services I have personally attended, there has been one consistent and noteworthy pattern, and that is that there seems to be a cultural difference between the "white funerals" and "black funerals."

At this point I would like to pause and acknowledge that I'm attempting to tread very carefully here. At no point in my personal anecdote or in the remainder of this section do I intend any offense. I certainly have no intention of somehow disrespecting either half of my family, whom I love. It is also worth pointing out that stereotyping is potentially dangerous, and not very "philosophical." That being said, if social and cultural patterns were not real in some sense, entire disciplines such as cultural anthropology, sociology, ethnic studies, Chicano studies, Africana studies, etc., would be incoherent and frankly impossible. Disclaimer behind us, allow me to proceed with my anecdotal observations.

Every funeral for a Caucasian friend or family member I have ever attended has been somber, quiet, orderly/predictable, and "dignified." Some of the services have been secular, but many of them have been religious. When religious, the religious components were reserved and focused exclusively on death and mourning. Mourners struggle (sometimes valiantly) to hold back tears and even sometimes simply to maintain a visage of somber resignation. Outbursts are rare, and regarded (though usually with compassion) as a "scene." People quietly enter the church or funeral home, nod solemnly at one another, sit quietly and respectfully through a service and a eulogy or two, and then perhaps depart for a burial/internment that is equally somber, and/or to a reception for food and quiet remembrance of the departed person.

No funeral for a black friend or family member that I have ever attended was even called a "funeral." Instead, every one of them was referred to as a "home going." Officiants (usually pastors) will go out of their way to proclaim that we were there in celebration, that we were *not* there to mourn a death, but to *celebrate* a life. In *every* case, the event was religious in tone, and numerous people would point out that the deceased was now present with the Lord, that their trials and tribulations were at an end, and that the rest of us should rejoice for that. In *every* case, a sermon was given that might or might not have had much of anything to do with death. Sometimes, the sermons turned into an "altar call." Jokes and laughter have been common. Funny stories are shared about the deceased, and occasional raucous laughter is produced. In addition to boisterous laughter, unrestrained weeping has also been a common. In some cases, family members have swooned in the midst of their grief, and had to be held up by others in attendance. Music has been a common component, though usually not hymns, but instead gospel spirituals or modern music. Afterwards, there has inevitably been a "repast," in which a tremendous amount of food is prepared, served, and consumed while many in attendance have *fun*. Music, games, laughter, and pleasant conversation have been the norm. I have commented that if not for the prevalence of people wearing black clothing at the home going celebrations, I would have a hard time distinguishing those events from when I attend family reunions!

Those are just two patterns offered by a very amateur "anthropologist," with a very limited set of experiences. Without question, other communities respond to the death of loved ones still differently. Chinese funerary practices are unique and rich in meaning. *El Dia de Los Muertos* is a fascinating synthesis of ancient Aztec rituals with Catholicism and promotes (in my opinion, at least) a healthy and desirable attitude towards death and the dead.

At the core, we have a single type of event (death) that produces a variety of responses within different communities. What is the best way to understand the existence of this apparent diversity?

One way to interpret these differences is to conclude that they are deep differences, resulting from fundamentally different moral values. Based upon this observation, a couple of sweeping conclusions might be drawn.

One conclusion could be that there is a single morally acceptable response to death, or at least a narrow range of acceptable responses, and that communities that are in harmony with that correct response are morally right, while communities that depart from that response are morally wrong. This sort of interpretation would be consistent with (though not demanded by) ethical theories that are objective.

Another interpretation is likewise to conclude that the apparent differences are deep differences, resulting from fundamentally different moral values, but will *reject* the idea that there is any objective or absolute moral value at the heart of these behaviors. Instead, one could propose that moral values and the moral aspects of actions and traditions, are culturally relative. Under this interpretation, moral claims and moral values are subjective as opposed to objective, and are expressions of dominant values within a particular community. In that case, none of those responses to death were somehow "incorrect," or morally better or worse than the other options. This, of course, would be the view of the ethical relativists that we studied earlier in this chapter.

Yet *another* interpretation might be considered a pragmatic compromise between the other two. According to this interpretation, there are some "universal" moral values that are found in all human communities. However, different communities manifest these values in different (equally legitimate) ways. This interpretation allows that there are some objective moral values or principles, and understands "objective" in this case to mean something like empirically verifiable. However, relativism is preserved with respect to *how* these values are manifested/demonstrated within particular communities. A variety of different practices might all be considered morally good/right despite their differences, because, at their foundational level, we may find a common core value. Although thus far this probably sounds like I'm summarizing the view of James Rachels that

we covered above (and, in fairness, there are significant similarities), the pragmatic compromise that we will consider in the following section actually comes from Alain LeRoy Locke.

Alain LeRoy Locke

Alain LeRoy Locke (1885 – 1954) is generally considered an American pragmatist, alongside John Dewey and William James, and influenced by the idealist Josiah Royce (under whom he studied while attending Harvard University to earn a bachelor's degree – he would later earn a PhD in philosophy from Harvard University as well). In 1907 he was chosen as the first ever African-American Rhodes scholar. While Locke's accolades are many, and his influence on American culture as a prominent gay African-American thinker and cultural innovator, especially through the Harlem Renaissance, is significant, for our purposes we will focus on his promotion of pluralism.

Locke's appreciation of pluralism is arguably at least partially due to the influence of William James. James described absolutism as the "root of most human injustices and cruelty," while endorsing pluralism as "the basis of all our tolerance, social, religious and political."[320]

Before delving into Locke's view on pluralism, we need to understand absolutism, in contrast, and why he found it so threatening.

Absolutism

Absolutism, for our purposes, refers to a point of view, or theoretical stance, that presupposes that there is an "objective reality which it is the function of science to analyze, measure and explain, or monopolistic versions of human nature and experience, which is, similarly, the business of social science to record and describe."[321]

---

[320] James, William. *Talks to Teachers on Psychology, and to Students on Some of Life's Ideals*. Frederick H. Burkhart, Fredson Bowers, and Ignas K. Skrupskesis (eds). Cambridge, MA:

Harvard University Press, 1983. Pp. 150-151.
[321] Locke, "Pluralism and Intellectual Democracy," *The Philosophy of Alain Locke: Harlem Renaissance and Beyond*, edited by

This reality has objective features that are "out there" for humans to discover, study, and understand. Among those objective features are "absolute" moral values. An "absolute," in this sense, is a concept or principle that is thought to apply to all people, everywhere, at all times. In a moral context, this means that there are certain moral values or principles that apply to all people, and are morally binding, regardless of social or historical context. Such absolute moral values, if they exist, exist independently from particular human communities, and their truth exists independently of the endorsement of any particular person or community. From this perspective, moral development is a matter of discovery – discovering the absolute norms and principles that already exist, and recognizing their application to us as human beings.

According to his analysis, "absolutists" are engaged in the project of applying certain value laden "predicates" to actions and things. A predicate is a fancy grammatical term that (roughly) means the same thing as "property" or "quality." A thing (e.g., an apple) will have various properties (e.g., being edible, being red, being a certain size, having a certain mass, etc.). Those properties are also its "predicates."

"Morally good" would be an example of a *value* predicate. The absolutist "discovers" which actions exhibit that predicate, and because those actions have "goodness" as a property, that property is presumed to be in some sense essential for that action. This makes it "universal."

As a specific example, the act of murder might be seen to have a predicate/property of moral "wrongness," and this means that there is something inherently and universally morally "wrong" with murder. If monogamy, for yet another example, has the property/predicate of

"morally good," and polygamy has the property/predicate of "morally bad," then if a different culture has a different view of things, they are simply *mistaken*, much as if they mistakenly thought that fire did not exhibit the property of being hot.

Absolutism leads to discounting differing values as incorrect, or worse. Locke, however rejects the idea that there are some set of values that corresponds to some sort of objective reality. In part, this is inspired by an observation of diversity. "The further we investigate, the more we discover that there is no fixity of content of values, and the more we are bound, then, to infer that their identity as groups must rest on other elements."[322]

At first glance, this, is simply his version of the "observation of cultural differences" discussed previously in this chapter. But, Locke is also motivated by "pragmatic" considerations, inspired, among other things, by a belief in the seeming futility of absolutism.

> But when we consider the odds against the complete community of culture for mankind, and the unlikelihood of any all-inclusive orthodoxy of human values, one is prepared to accept or even to prefer an attainable concorde of understanding and cooperation as over against an unattainable unanimity of institutional beliefs.[323]

Perhaps even more dramatically, Locke states that "absolutism is doomed in the increasing variety of human experience."[324]

Locke seems genuinely skeptical that objective moral values exist, but even if they *did*, they seem beyond the reach of human discovery and knowledge, and the undeniable diversity of

---

Leonard Harris (Philadelphia, PA: Temple University Press, 1989), p.56.
[322] Locke, "Values as Imperatives," *The Philosophy of Alain Locke: Harlem* Renaissance *and Beyond,* edited by Leonard Harris (Philadelphia, PA: Temple University Press, 1989), p. 40.

[323] Locke, "Cultural Relativism and Ideological Peace," *The Philosophy of Alain Locke: Harlem Renaissance and Beyond,* edited by Leonard Harris (Philadelphia, PA: Temple University Press, 1989), p. 71.
[324] Locke, "Values as Imperatives," 48.

human customs and values makes absolutism a *dangerous* point of view. While valuing is a natural and necessary part of the human experience, it also generates a "problem."

> *The common man, in both his individual and group behavior, perpetuates the problem in a very practical way. He sets up personal and private and group norms as standards and principles, and rightly or wrongly hypothesizes them as universals for all conditions, all times and all men. . . Thus our varied absolutes are revealed as largely the rationalization of our preferred values and their imperatives.*[325]

In other words, people take their own personal values and project them onto humanity itself, imagining that they are somehow universal and true, and applicable to all people. A natural extension of that is the belief that anyone who disagrees is mistaken. The "dangerous" extension of that idea is that those who are mistaken need to be "corrected." In order to neutralize that dangerous tendency, Locke proposes that we understand the process by which we acquire our values in the first place.

The Valuing Process

Pluralism (whether religious, cultural, moral, etc.), understood here as the mere *observation* of cultural differences, is a basic and unavoidable feature of the world. Values are equally basic and "unavoidable" in the sense that *all* humans do "value" things.

Values (for Locke) are feelings, attitudes, preferences and beliefs (religious, political, aesthetic, or ethical). Our values organize and direct our experience. They generate "imperatives" (rules and guidelines) which function as guides to behavior.

Because of *differences* in values, they also lead to conflict—but this is because values have not been understood properly (according to Locke). Values pertain to the "valuer" (the one

doing the valuing), not the things *valued*.

> *The effective antidote to value absolutism lies in a systematic and realistic demonstration that values are rooted in attitudes, not in reality, and pertain to ourselves, not to the world.*[326]

In other words, as an admittedly controversial example, a book such as the Bible or the Qur'an is holy and to be respected not because of any features of the book itself, but because some people *ascribe* that sort of value to the book. Because values arise from individuals, as opposed to being independent properties of things, values are not "objective"—at least not in the sense normally intended by objectivists. This does not mean, however, that they are purely subjective or arbitrary. To understand this, we need to better understand Locke's view of the origin of values and the valuing process itself.

Locke's hypothesis is that we first have an "affective experience" (i.e., an experience that triggers a feeling of some sort), and then rationalize that experience by applying seemingly universal predicates to it. Values such as "beauty, goodness, truth (as approval or acceptance) [and] righteousness are known in immediate recognitions of qualitative apprehension."[327]

As an example, someone might have an emotional experience of shock and disgust upon witnessing another person being physically assaulted. This powerful emotional experience produces a negative value judgment concerning physical assault. Reason is then brought in to validate that value judgment by inferring that some predicate such as "morally wrong" or "evil" applies to the act itself. The person then rationalizes their judgment by thinking that they merely *perceived* the inherent wrongness in the act, which *causes* them to have the negative emotional response – rather than the other way around. The other way around, of course, being that the *feeling* causes the idea/judgment of

[325] ibid., 35 & 46.
[326] ibid., 46.
[327] ibid., 39.

"wrongness."[328]

Values begin in individual moments of feelings, and then "trickle up" by blending with *other* people's moments of valuing/feeling until they become *cultural* values (as opposed to merely individual values).

While this process might not sound problematic in the case of assault, the very same sort of emotional response and rationalization could occur in more controversial cases, such as someone from a particular culture *feeling* a sense of outrage if a woman "disobeys" a man, or a feeling of revulsion upon seeing two men kiss.

Rather than recognizing the quite possibly culturally conditioned feeling-response for what it is, someone might project their response onto humanity itself, and conclude that their particular value judgment applies "absolutely" to all the same actions, in all the same circumstances around the world. Using the examples I provided, this could result in moral and legal systems that subordinate women or persecute homosexuals. It's not difficult to see how this kind of thinking could result in judgmental behavior and intolerance. Although Locke rejects this sort of absolutism, he *also* equally rejects subjectivism.

> *In de-throning our absolutes, we must take care not to exile our imperatives, for after all, we live by them. We must realize more fully that values create these imperatives as well as the more formally superimposed absolutes, and that norms control our behavior as well as guide our reasoning.[329]*

Locke is *not* endorsing that we abandon our values in general, or any particular values in particular, but "only" that we modify the manner in which we hold those values. Rather than think of our values as "the truth," and any other (different) values as false (or worse), we should think of our values in terms of their function within communities, and in so doing we can find points of similarity across cultures. Moreover,

given his pragmatist inclinations, there is a sense in which our values can be "true" without them being absolute or objective. "Yet truth may also sometimes be the sustaining of an attitude, the satisfaction of a way of feeling, the corroboration of the value."[330] If we accept this pragmatic understanding of truth as something like "something is true if it works," or "something is true if it is effective over time," then our values can be true (in that sense) without somehow being universal or absolute.

> *What seems most needed is some middle ground between these extremes of subjectivism and objectivism. ... Flesh and blood values may not be as universal or objective as logical truth in schematized judgments, but they are not thereby deprived of some relative objectivity and universality of their own. The basic qualities of values should never have been sought in logical classes, for they pertain to psychological categories. They are not grounded in types of realms of value, but are rooted in modes or kinds of valuing.[331]*

Locke recommends that replacing either subjectivism or absolutism with his own brand of "pluralism" preserves our values and avoids the dangers of absolutism. What, though, does Locke mean by pluralism? On the one hand, pluralism might be merely *descriptive*. In this sense, pluralism simply refers to the *recognition* that there are multiple, different cultures, with varying languages, ethnicities, political systems, economic systems, religions, lifestyles, etc. existing throughout history and currently. This is an "anthropological" observation, and what I have called the "observation of cultural differences."

On the other hand, pluralism can be understood as a *normative* concept, in which the pluralist is not merely recognizing the existence of different cultural systems, but is *endorsing* this

---

[328] Note the similarity to Haidt's understanding of reason and feeling/intuition as explained in the appendix of the chapter on evaluating claims.

[329] ibid., 34.

[330] ibid., 37.

[331] Locke, "Values as Imperatives," 38.

diversity and embracing it as a welcome alternative to "universalist" or "absolutist" alternatives.

Locke clearly promoted pluralism in the *normative* sense, regarding absolutism as a threat to peace and democracy. Locke offers this sort of pluralism as a way to generate agreement and cooperation among conflicting value systems, by recognizing common features of *valuing.*

Embracing value pluralism does result in a loss of status for our values, but exchanges them for the pragmatic value of peace and cooperation. This is not meant to result in the loss of concepts of "right" and value entirely, "but rather that there should be only relative and functional rightness, with no throne or absolute sovereignty in dispute."[332]

It is appropriate, and even desirable, that people should care about the values of their community. What is less desirable, according to Locke, is that people care about these values in ways that presuppose that they are the absolute truth, and that any alternative is false or evil. According to Locke, "the gravest problem of contemporary philosophy is how to ground some normative principle or criterion of objective validity for values without resorting to dogmatism and absolutism on the intellectual plane, and without falling into their corollaries, on the plane of social behavior and action, and intolerance and mass coercion."[333]

In other words, Locke is seeking a way to navigate the twin threats of subjectivist "anarchy" on the one hand, and "dogmatic" absolutism on the other. A pluralist believes that values are created by humans, and are therefore situated in specific historical and cultural contexts. *Functional* values serve as a middle ground between "value anarchy" and absolutism. "Norms of this status will be functional constants and practical sustaining imperatives of their correlated modes of existence; nothing more, but also nothing less."[334]

Basic Equivalence

Since Locke rejects the idea that there are stable *properties* of objects or events that can provide an objective basis for moral value, he instead looks for some objectivity in *valuing* in the form of "functional constants," seeking "objective but neutral common denominators."[335]

Despite his rejection of absolutism, Locke believes that humans share a set of basic human values. These are values that are common to all, or at least many, value systems. Examples of such values could include belief in some sort of divine agencies, respect for human life, valuing community cooperation, etc. These values might manifest in a variety of different ways in terms of content, but their form will be shared and similar.

As you hopefully recall from earlier in this chapter, James Rachels similarly argued that there is more moral "universality" across cultures than we might initially recognize. One reason for this is because cultures might manifest the same underlying value in different ways, given contingent historical, geographical, climatic, and other circumstances. We previously considered the various ways in which different cultures treat their dead. Each believed it to be morally right to honor the dead, but due to different circumstances, they demonstrated that belief in different ways.

In a similar fashion, Locke would propose that most (if not all) cultures have beliefs in the "supernatural" that tend to inspire reverence and devotion. In one community, that form will have as its content "Christianity." In another community, that form will have as its content "ancestor worship." The specific content/manifestation is different, but the basic *form and function* is thought to be the same.

Locke uses the term "basic equivalences" to indicate this equality of form, or type.

Recognizing basic equivalence, recognizing similarity in form even if not of content, is meant to help us recognize that other people value potentially different things, but at least in similar

---

[332] Locke, "Pluralism and Intellectual Democracy," 55.
[333] ibid., 36.

[334] ibid., 47.
[335] Locke, "Cultural Relativism and Ideological Peace," 73.

ways.

> The principle of cultural equivalence, under which we would more wisely press the search for functional similarity in our analyses and comparisons of human cultures; thus offsetting our traditional and excessive emphasis upon cultural differences. Such functional equivalences, which we might term "culture cognates" or "culture – correlates," discovered underneath deceptive but superficial institutional divergence, would provide objective but soundly neutral, denominators for intercultural understanding and cooperation.[336]

Though different cultures might value different things, these values are grounded by common types of *feeling* and common *functional roles*. They manifest in many different ways, but in a generic form exist in most, if not all cultures. Although communities might worship different gods, they nevertheless share in common valuing *worship*. This similarity of form allows us to recognize value expressions as "species" of the same "genus." This provides an overlap of values across communities. Many apparent differences in values "would on deeper inspection turn out to be functionally similar."[337]

As another example, consider a marriage ceremony. Marriage can be valued "religiously" and experienced as spiritual. The same marriage could also be valued aesthetically and experienced as beautiful.[338] This illustrates that different ways of valuing can be applied to the same object or experience by different people, or even by the same person. Similarly, different objects can be valued in the same way. Numerous experiences can generate "religious" value, whether attending a high mass at a grand Cathedral, communing with the divine in a natural setting, consuming hallucinogenic mushrooms, or any number of other possible experiences.

> These culture constants or "culture cognates," as the case might be, would then furnish a base not only for mutual cultural tolerance and appreciation but eventually for effective cultural integration. If discoverable in any large number, they might well constitute a new base for direct educational development of world mindedness, a realistic scientific induction into world citizenship.[339]

Locke proposes a conscious shift from focusing on differences to noticing similarities. This recognition of similarities would potentially generate more global and inclusive beliefs and attitudes about other people. Because of these cultural constants/cognates, a persuasive and objective case can be made that we are similar in our valuing even if we are different in our values. Locke is confident that this approach allows for something resembling scientific validity.

> There would also be as a further possibility of such value relativism a more objective confirmation of many basic human values, and on the basis of proof approximating scientific validity. For if once this broader relativistic approach could discover beneath the expected culture differentials of time and place such functional "universals" as actually may be there, these common denominator values would stand out as pragmatically confirmed by common human experience. Either their observable generality or their comparatively established equivalence would give them status far beyond any "universals" merely asserted by orthodox dogmatisms. And the standard of value justification would then not be so very

---

[336] ibid.

[337] ibid.

[338] Locke hypothesizes different "feeling modes," including both the religious and the aesthetic, to

account for this.

[339] Locke, "Cultural Relativism and Ideological Peace," 77.

different from the accepted scientific criterion of proof – confirmable in variability in concrete human experience. After an apparent downfall and temporary banishment, many of our most prized "universals" would reappear, clothed with a newly acquired vitality and a pragmatic validity of general concurrence.[340]

If Locke is right, we should observe some similarities in moral codes and intuitions, and researchers have indeed found the presence of cross-cultural, trans-religious, and trans-lingual moral "intuitions" that often defy our ability to articulate. In one study, contemporary researchers surveyed cultures that included Confucianism, Taoism, Buddhism, Hinduism, "Athenian" philosophy, Judaism, Islam, and Christianity and found a historical/cross-cultural "convergence" of six core virtues that they identified as courage, justice, humanity, temperance, wisdom, and transcendence.[341]

Using Locke's analysis, overlapping values (such as those virtues), and other such cultural cognates and correlates are "objective" because they are available as *real* features of cultures, discoverable by both members of the culture in question and observers. Indeed, by virtue of being observed across cultures, Locke is confident that such "equivalences" could eventually take on a more stable status than our present "universals" that are grounded in (usually religious) worldviews that are *not* universally recognized.

As an example, take the value of innocent human life. Suppose you think that human life (or at least *innocent* human life) is valuable, and that this entails some sort of right not to be murdered. Suppose also that you think that this is true because you believe in a Creator God who has authority over life and death, and who has commanded that people "shall not murder." You have a basis for your valuing of innocent human

life, but it presupposes a religious worldview that is not shared by everyone. Suppose, on the other hand, that someone like Locke observes that in seemingly *every* culture there is a shared norm that innocent life (somehow defined) is to be respected and protected, and that there is a seemingly universal aversion to murder. Suppose also that someone like Locke points out that different communities justify their version of that value in different ways, whether by appealing to a Creator God, or concerns about reincarnation, or a belief that protecting innocent life maximizes happiness and community stability, etc. We still have a basis for valuing innocent human life, but we potentially have a more stable and cross-cultural basis if we establish it on the existence of similar experiences of valuing innocent life, rather than a specific belief pertaining to a specific worldview that is not necessarily shared by other cultures.

Flesh and blood values may not be as universal or objective as logical truth or schematize judgments, but they are not thereby deprived of some relative objectivity and universality of their own. The basic qualities of values... pertain to psychological categories. They are not grounded in types of realms of value, but are rooted in modes or kinds of valuing.[342]

Functionalism

According to Locke, the primary normative character of our values should be understood in terms of their *functional* role as stereotypes of dispositions to feel and act in certain ways. From a functionalist perspective, value claims do *not* "tell us" something about the "properties" of objects, actions, or events.

From the functionalist's point of view the basic error lies in regarding the formal value as the cause of the evaluation or as

---

[340] Locke, "Pluralism and Intellectual Democracy," 56.

[341] Dahlsgaard, Katherine (et al), "Shared Virtue: The Convergence of Valued Human Strengths

across Culture and History," *Review of General Psychology*. Vol. 9 (3) (2005): 203-213.

[342] Locke, "Values As Imperatives," 38.

an essence of the value object rather than the system value of the mode of valuing, which is sometimes the symbol, sometimes its rationale, but in practice and implementation of the value as apprehended. Of course, to the degree that values are regarded abstractly, they take on a quality of universality and seeming independence, but this is merely a common characteristic of all generalizations. But if we can sufficiently explain the character of value–generals as system norms, functional in value discrimination and comparison, they need not then be unrealistically raised to the status of hypostasized absolutes or perennial essences.[343]

Instead, the value is thought to emerge within a particular context, based on the role that the claim plays in that context, and the behaviors the claim makes appropriate in that context. These dispositions will be culturally conditioned and culturally specific, and therefore contingent rather than absolute.

For example, in a culture with strong notions of "modesty," it might become habitual (i.e., one would have a strong and reliable disposition) to avert your eyes if you accidentally walk in on someone while they are undressed, assuming that person is not your romantic partner, but is, instead, a friend or even a stranger. In a culture with a far more "relaxed" attitude concerning nudity (even among strangers), however, people might develop very different dispositions. The particular dispositions that correspond to our values might vary, but the *functions* (in general) will be similar across cultures, will be constant.

"Functional constancy" refers to the ability of basic equivalent values to operate in a stable manner with respect to our valuing activities. Every value within a community is thought to serve a function. Possible functions include

maintaining group solidarity, protecting individuals, preserving life, etc. Common functions can "bridge the gap" across cultural divides.

We can and must go beyond this somewhat anarchic pluralism and relativism to more systematic relativism. This becomes possible as we are able to discover through objective comparison of basic human values certain basic equivalences among them, which we may warrantably call "functional constants" to take scientifically the place of our outmoded categoricals and our banned arbitrary "universals."[344]

As an example, consider the value placed on "family." Valuing family serves a variety functions within a community. It might promote the survival of the group, it might provide for the stable and orderly transmission of property across generations, or any number of other functions. Undoubtedly, "valuing family" will serve similar (even if not precisely identical) functions in different cultures. What *counts* as a family might vary from one culture to the next, but it's extraordinarily likely that whichever cultures we compare, they will have some notion of "family" and some sort of positive value will be attached to it.

Some cultures adopt the so-called "nuclear family" (mom, dad, and 2.5 kids under the same roof). Others prefer extended families (multiple generations in the same home), and still others embrace communal child-rearing in which responsibility for caring for the young is shared by the larger community, including non-blood relatives.

There is any number of explanations for why one culture might manifest its child-care in one fashion, while a different culture does so in another, but the allegation is that the underlying value is the same, even though the manifestation

---

[343] Locke, "A Functional View of Value Ultimates," *The Philosophy of Alain Locke: Harlem Renaissance and Beyond,* edited by Leonard Harris (Philadelphia, PA: Temple

University Press, 1989), p.86.
[344] Locke, "Pluralism and Intellectual Democracy," 55.

is different. The moral value that the young should be cared for is, in fact, one of a handful of values that James Rachels claimed that all cultures must have, if they are to survive as a culture. It is thus a *universal* (non-relative) value.

It's worth noting that while Rachels and Locke both agree that there are shared values across cultures, their arguments for this are distinct. Rachels argues for this universality from an overtly evolutionary perspective, while Locke makes a "functionalist" case. However, it seems possible (though not necessary) to combine their insights.

Locke claims that certain types of valuing are "universal" because they fulfill similar functions in human communities. Rachels offers an explanation as to how those similar functions arose: natural selection. Because certain types of behavioral dispositions, produced by certain forms of valuing, are conducive to the survival of the community, they are "selected." And, because all human communities are *human* communities (in other words, because all humans are the same *species*), what is adaptive should be pretty similar, in least in generic function, across a diverse array of human communities.

Though we might bicker as to just *which* moral principles and values are necessary for any society to survive (and are, therefore, "universal"), it would appear that there are some that fit that description, and this might generate more tolerance and understanding between cultures.

The principle of cultural reciprocity, which, by a general recognition of the reciprocal character of all contacts between cultures and of the fact that all modern cultures are highly composite ones, would invalidate the lump estimating of cultures in terms of generalized, en bloc assumptions of superiority and inferiority, substituting scientific, point by point comparisons with their correspondingly limited, specific, and objectively verifiable superiorities or inferiorities.[345]

Although Locke thinks that embracing "cultural relativism" (understood as his positive brand of pluralism, and, for that reason, hereafter referred to as Positive Pluralism to avoid confusion) can promote tolerance and peace, he does *not* make the mistake of thinking there is a necessary *logical* connection between the two. Those who *do* make this mistake employ the so-called "argument from tolerance," but in so doing reveal a fundamental misunderstanding of ethical relativism, as I argued previously in this chapter.

If a Positive Pluralist advocated tolerance as an "absolute," they would be engaged in precisely the same objectionable behavior that Locke is trying to overcome. Instead, *his* brand of Positive Pluralism can be seen as a different psychological stance, rooted in practical consideration, and something that could produce (as a *psychological* consequence) less dogmatism, more humility, and more appreciation of other cultures.

In other words, he is not making the mistake of seeing that toleration is the logically entailed effect for which relativism is the cause. Instead, he is proposing that recognizing cultural differences, while focusing on cultural constants and similarly functioning values, will likely cause (psychologically) the practical effect of increased tolerance and respect for diversity.

Even if so, a potentially challenging consequence of adopting Positive Pluralism is that we must necessarily abandon the idea that our own particular value system is somehow uniquely or especially correct and true. Positive Pluralists must "wear group labels and avow cultural loyalties less provocatively."[346]

... Relativistic philosophy nips in the psychological bud the passion for arbitrary unity and conformity.... Relativism, with no arbitrary specifications of unity, no imperious demand for universality, nevertheless

---

[345] Locke, "Cultural Relativism and Ideological Peace," 73.

[346] ibid., 74.

enjoins a beneficent neutrality between divergent positions, and, in the case of the context of cultures, would in due course promote, step by step, from an initial stage of cultural tolerance, mutual respect, reciprocal exchange, some specific communities of agreement and, finally, with sufficient mutual understanding and confidence, commonality of purpose and action.[347]

As an example, while Muslims and Christians disagree about the divinity of Jesus, both are devoted to worship of the divine. Although the *content* of their values are different, the feelings that produced those values are thought to be the same.

As a matter of strategy, Locke is proposing fostering cultural toleration in the hopes that this will lead to mutual respect between cultures. The initial strategy would focus on narrowly defined areas of similarity and agreement. This should eliminate belief of superiority and inferiority since these beliefs are normally bound up with judgments of cultural worth within a particular culture.

For Locke, culture refers not only to the practices, traditions, values, etc. of a group of people, but he also has a sense of becoming "cultured." Becoming "cultured" refers to having "the capacity for understanding the best and most representative forms of human expression, and of expressing oneself."[348] Part of becoming "cultured" in this sense is embracing Positive Pluralism! This means learning to recognize that the particular values of your own culture are contingent, and not the "absolute truth," and learning to see and seek common ground with other communities.

Becoming more tolerant is not an automatic or passive process. Education is essential, to the extent that it introduces the absolutist to other values and cultures. In this way, education can correct ignorant and dangerous stereotypes.

People who are homophobic might find it difficult to maintain that stance if they actually get to know some LGBTQ individuals, and interact with them as individuals rather than as caricatures.

A white supremacist who learns of the extensive achievements of African-American intellectuals should probably find it increasingly difficult to maintain a bigoted view of white intellectual superiority. Indeed, reading Locke himself could correct stereotypical and bigoted assumptions about both African-American *and* gay men!

The intentional inclusion of philosophers from across the globe and from many different ethnic and religious backgrounds in this very book could (and I hope *does*) serve a similar function. In addition, the contributions of cultural anthropology might demonstrate common/shared values across cultures, resulting in the absolutist recognizing some common ground, and minimizing perceived differences.

Possible Problems?

There are, admittedly, some immediate challenges to this strategy. Sometimes, it is *precisely* the content (and not the generic form/function) that sets cultures at odds with each other with respect to values. With respect to religion, for example, it is very presumptuous to think that people of faith regard the specific faith tradition to which they belong as simply one possible "filling" within a "container" that might otherwise be filled with other contents, and clearly *is* filled by other contents in other cultures.

How realistic is it to think that a fundamentalist Christian, and a fundamentalist Muslim, will appreciate the fact that each is sincerely and piously dedicated to "faith," without being concerned about the *particular* faith in question? Is it plausible that their shared "fundamentalism" will generate a respect and mutual appreciation that will somehow

---

[347] ibid., 69, 70 – 71.
[348] Locke, "The Ethics of Culture," *The Philosophy of Alain Locke: Harlem Renaissance and Beyond,*

edited by Leonard Harris (Philadelphia, PA: Temple University Press, 1989), 177.

overpower the very fundamentalist nature of their fundamentalism? This example doesn't presuppose that the people of faith in question are somehow especially unreasonable and fanatical, mind you. Arguably, people are committed to their faith tradition because they believe that that particular tradition is *true* – not merely because it fills some generic "supernatural function" in their community, and in their life. As stated by Terrance Macmullan,

> *the very crux of the problem is that the religious, national, or racial absolutist think his or her views are authoritative and thus has no reason to accept diversity.... The absolutist would see the entire project of cultural pluralism as question begging: 'why should I engage in an attempt to articulate values that are meaningful to all people but my values are the ones that all people should be following?' They see the give-and-take of dialogue and reciprocity as undermining whatever absolute truth they hold.*[349]

Even Locke himself admits that pluralism is not a viable strategy for *all* persons. "We know, of course, that we cannot get tolerance from a fanatic or reciprocity from a fundamentalist of any stripe, religious, philosophical, cultural, political or ideological."[350]

Practically speaking, certain examples of engagement are probably futile. Trying to engage with a dedicated jihadist who fully intends to martyr himself in a war against "the West," will probably not work out very well. Engaging with disaffected youth who might otherwise be recruited to a jihadist cause, *before* they can be successfully recruited, however, seems more viable. In viable cases, Locke proposes that three conditions must be met in order to create the environment in which pluralism can produce peace and harmonious cooperation between cultures and subcultures.

First, everyone involved must be willing to make concessions. No reasonable progress can be expected if certain participants refuse to give any ground and expect that their own preferences will be honored without exception or modification.

Second, whatever concessions are made must be of comparable value and significance. Participants have to feel that there is reciprocity and that they remain among equals. Practically speaking, if one party feels like they are "giving up" much more than another, cooperation is unlikely.

Third, the concessions must be important to the parties involved. What this amounts to is parties being willing to set aside some of their more "absolutist" commitments, on the condition that others do as well.

The absolutist can't be ignored, but must be engaged in dialogue. If the end goal is peace and cooperation, that goal will be difficult to reach if we exclude the very people most in need of increased understanding and least likely to be cooperative in the first place.

The preceding several paragraphs admittedly drifted more towards into political strategy than ethical theory, but this also reveals the pragmatic nature of Locke's agenda. He not only believes that absolute moral values don't exist, but also believes that absolutism is *dangerous*. He not only believes that his brand of Positive Pluralism *could* promote toleration, on the basis of recognizing overlapping values, but that we *should* pursue this attitude of toleration and mutual respect for the sake of peace and an end to oppression. This goal requires not only an understanding of ethics at a theoretical level, but a practical approach to actually producing tolerance among participating communities.

---

[349] Macmullan, Terrance. "Challenges to Cultural Diversity: Absolutism, Democracy, and Alain Locke's Value Relativism. *The Journal of Speculative Philosophy*, volume 19 (2), 2005, p. 130.

[350] Locke, "Pluralism and Intellectual Democracy," 57.

Chapter 13: Utilitarianism

Comprehension questions you should be able to answer after reading this chapter:

1. How do utilitarians (in general) determine what is morally right and morally wrong?
2. Who "counts" in the utilitarian cost-benefit analysis?
3. What is the "principle of utility?" What is the "greatest happiness principle?"
4. What is the difference between "act" utilitarianism and "rule" utilitarianism?
5. What is meant by the criticism of utilitarianism that it is too "artificial" and "unrealistic?" How might a utilitarian respond to this criticism?
6. What is meant by the criticism of utilitarianism that it allows, and even requires, "unjust" actions? How might a utilitarian respond?
7. What is meant by the criticism of utilitarianism that it is a "Swinish doctrine?" How does John Stuart Mill respond?
8. What is meant by the criticism of utilitarianism that it is too difficult to anticipate the consequences of our actions? How might a utilitarian respond?
9. According to Mill, what is the only justification for the use of force/coercion by the government against a person?
10. What is the difference between an act of commission and an act of omission?

At 8:46 a.m., on September 11th, 2001, American Airlines Flight 11 was intentionally crashed into the World Trade Center's North Tower. At 9:03 a.m., it was followed by United Airlines Flight 175. At 9:37 a.m., American Airlines Flight 77 was crashed into the Pentagon. United Airlines Flight 93 is believed to have been headed to either the Capitol Building or the White House, but it never reached its intended target. Passengers on Flight 93 resisted, and the plane crashed instead in a field near Shanksville, Pennsylvania at 10:03 a.m. Had the passengers not acted, and brought the plane down themselves, it is likely that the United States Air Force would have done it for them. Consider the following excerpt from an interview with (then) U.S. Vice-President Dick Cheney.

VICE PRES. CHENEY: Well, the--I suppose the toughest decision was this question of whether or not we would intercept incoming commercial aircraft.

TIM RUSSERT: And you decided?

VICE PRES. CHENEY: We decided to do it. We'd, in effect, put a flying combat air

patrol up over the city; F-16s with an AWACS, which is an airborne radar system, and tanker support so they could stay up a long time...

It doesn't do any good to put up a combat air patrol if you don't give them instructions to act, if, in fact, they feel it's appropriate.

MR. RUSSERT: So if the United States government became aware that a hijacked commercial airline[r] was destined for the White House or the Capitol, we would take the plane down?

VICE PRES. CHENEY: Yes. The president made the decision...that if the plane would not divert...as a last resort, our pilots were authorized to take them out. Now, people say, you know, that's a horrendous decision to make. Well, it is. You've got an airplane full of American citizens, civilians, captured by...terrorists, headed and are you going to, in fact, shoot it down, obviously, and kill all those Americans on board?...[351]

The United States government was prepared to shoot down a commercial passenger jet, with 40 innocent civilians onboard. Why would the government be willing to make this decision? Why, for that matter, did the passengers on Flight 93 resist their hijackers, ultimately resulting in the premature crashing of their plane? The answer, in both cases, is quite possibly the same: "It's for the greater good."

That slogan captures the central idea of utilitarianism. Utilitarianism is usually associated with Jeremy Bentham (1748-1832), James Mill (1773-1836), and his son John Stuart Mill (1806-1873)—though early traces of utilitarian thought can be found in the writings of Epicurus (341 BCE-270 BCE).

Utilitarianism is an <u>objective</u> theory, which is to say that utilitarians believe that the morally right thing to do in a given situation is not merely a matter of opinion, but is a *fact*. What, specifically, will be *the* morally right thing to do brings us back to the appeal to "the greater good."

Although utilitarians will often differ with respect to the particulars of their theories, what they will all have in common is an emphasis on the consequences of our actions. For that reason, utilitarianism is one of several theories called "<u>consequentialist</u>." Utilitarianism is not the only consequentialist theory, but it is the most famous. Consequentialist theories are just what they sound like: they are theories emphasizing the consequences, the outcomes of our decisions and actions. In our everyday evaluation of actions, we will sometimes forgive someone when their actions produce undesirable consequences so long as their "heart is in the right place." Not so with utilitarians. *Intentions do not matter* (morally speaking). The only thing that matters when evaluating the moral goodness or badness of an action are the *consequences* of that action.

Although some utilitarians are interested in

the satisfaction of preferences when considering "consequences," most utilitarians (including both Bentham and Mill) focus instead on "happiness." For such a simple word, happiness is notoriously difficult to define, and utilitarians have bickered over how best to understand "happiness" for centuries. For Bentham, the founder of modern utilitarian thought, happiness was to be understood in terms of pleasure, or at least the absence of pain. Unhappiness, then, would be understood in terms of pain.

With pleasure as our focus, the first formulation of utilitarianism is that the morally right thing to do will be whichever action produces, as a *consequence*, the most happiness (pleasure), or the least unhappiness (pain) for all involved. Bentham labeled this the "principle of utility."

The Principle of Utility

> *By the principle of utility is meant that principle which approves or disapproves of every action whatsoever, according to the tendency which it appears to have to augment or diminish the happiness of the party whose interest is in question: or, what is the same thing in other words, to promote or to oppose that happiness....[352]*

Mill provides a very similar principle, one that he calls the "greatest happiness principle."

The Greatest Happiness Principle

> *The creed which accepts as the foundation of morals utility, or the greatest happiness principle, holds that actions are right in proportion as they tend to promote happiness, wrong as they tend to produce the reverse of happiness. By 'happiness' is intended pleasure, and the absence of pain; by 'unhappiness,' pain, and the privation of pleasure.[353]*

---

[351] NBC, 'Meet the Press' 16 September 2001
[352] Bentham, Jeremy. An *Introduction to the Principles of Morals and Legislation*. 1789. Chapter 1: The Principle of Utility. The entire

text is available here:
https://www.earlymoderntexts.com/assets/pdfs/bentham1780.pdf
[353] John Stuart Mill, John Stuart. *Utilitarianism*.

One of the appeals of this approach is how intuitively powerful—even how obvious—is its basic emphasis on pleasure and pain. We don't need any argument to justify our aversion to pain and our inclinations towards pleasure. They just "are." I like pleasure. So do you. Why? I don't know. Maybe God made me that way. Maybe there's an evolutionary advantage in creatures acquiring sentience. Maybe pleasure and pain are "Nature's" way of guiding us with respect to actions to pursue or avoid. Whatever the ultimate explanation happens to be, we all naturally pursue pleasure, and we all naturally avoid pain. What could be more basic, more fundamental, than the value judgments that pleasure is good and pain is bad? What could be more obvious? And, if so obvious and so universal, doesn't it make sense to think that our notion of "good" and "bad," morally speaking, would have something to do with pleasure and pain? Don't we recognize that it's "good" to promote pleasure/happiness, and "bad" to promote pain/unhappiness? Isn't there an element of pleasure or pain to be found in every act we label morally good or bad?

Consider the following actions usually deemed morally wrong, or at least morally suspect. Identify how each is responsible for increasing the amount of pain/unhappiness in the world. Be creative, and don't restrict yourself to short-term thinking.
- Rape
- Child abuse
- Home invasion robbery
- Smoking crack cocaine
- Politicians "selling" their support to lobbyists
- Murder
- Fraud

If you actually performed the recommended exercise, you might have been surprised to see how easy it was to identify the "pain" associated with those examples. This is certainly one of the more powerful appeals of the utilitarian approach. It just seems *obvious* that we do, in fact, care about the amount of pleasure and pain not just in our own lives, but in the lives of others—indeed, in the world in general. Very often, when we condemn the actions of another (or our own actions), one of the first explanations we can offer for our condemnation involves pain.

"Stop! That *hurts.*"

Most of the time, we treat that explanation as a morally sufficient explanation. If what you are doing is hurting someone, you should stop. If you don't, you're doing something morally bad.

There is room for some sophistication with this approach. For example, we recognize that actual physical pain is not the only sort of "pain" that matters.

"When you did that, it really hurt my feelings."

Usually, this sort of appeal doesn't suggest that actual physical pain resulted (though, sometimes powerful emotions do seem to produce a physical reaction in the body, including feelings of pain in the stomach, head, throat, or chest). Nevertheless, we have a concept of emotional pain that is similarly motivating. Embarrassment, a feeling of betrayal, shame, fear … all of these, while not necessarily physically painful, are nevertheless feelings we prefer to avoid, and we describe them in terms of "hurt." Most utilitarians therefore include "emotional" pain in their considerations as well.

Another layer of sophistication that utilitarianism offers, and needs, is the recognition that we do not always categorically avoid painful experiences, nor do we invariably pursue pleasurable experiences. For example, I don't enjoy going to the dentist. It's usually an uncomfortable experience, and sometimes

---

"Chapter 2—What Utilitarianism Is." 1863. Note: all references to Mill are from this source unless otherwise indicated. The full text of this chapter

is available here:
https://www.utilitarianism.com/mill2.htm

actually painful. But, I go anyway (at least twice each year). I have been told that shooting heroin is an intensely pleasurable experience, but I have no intention of pursuing that pleasure—nor do most other people. So, we have two easy examples of avoiding pleasure and pursuing pain. Doesn't that contradict the basic values-assumptions behind utilitarianism? Not at all. Although going to the dentist can be painful, avoiding the dentist can be more so. I endure a little pain to avoid the greater pain of tooth decay and gum disease. We have our children inoculated against diseases even though the needles hurt them. Are we bad utilitarians? Sadists? No. We recognize that the tiny and fleeting prick of a needle is far less painful than polio. Why do we avoid the pleasure of heroin? Because we wish to avoid the greater pain that follows! Not only is heroin deadly and debilitating, but it is powerfully addictive. No one who has ever known an addict would ever claim that the use of heroin is, on balance and all things considered, a "pleasurable" activity.

What these examples and their analyses indicate is that utilitarian thought can be complicated. When calculating the consequences of our actions, we often have to look beyond the immediate experience and anticipate what the consequences will be in the future. Getting a polio vaccination might be slightly painful the moment one receives it, but it spares you from the threat of a far more painful disease later on. In receiving the shot, you are still pursuing the greater happiness.

The final layer of sophistication we'll consider, before getting into the actual application of this kind of theory, involves sentience. As you know by now, utilitarians focus on pleasure and pain. Pain is to be avoided, pleasure is to be pursued, generally speaking. It is good to promote pleasure, bad to promote pain. What's probably obvious to you is that human beings are not the only creatures capable of pleasure and pain. My cat feels pain. So do dogs, and monkeys, and buffalo, and sparrows, and

cows, and lots of other creatures. Much evidence has been gathered demonstrating that mammals, birds, reptiles and amphibians, fish, and cephalopods (such as the octopus) all have central nervous systems, all have nociceptors ("pain receptors") connected to their central nervous system, and all exhibit response to damaging stimuli similar to that of human responses. Although there is less consensus among researchers, it's at least clear that even invertebrates such as lobsters have rudimentary motor responses in response to "noxious" stimulants (e.g., being dropped in boiling water!), though whether they possess a sophisticated enough nervous system for that response to be an indicator of "pain" remains subject to debate.

Debate aside, because a great many non-human creatures can clearly experience pleasure and pain, they "count" as far as utilitarianism is concerned. If pleasure is to be pursued, and pain is to be avoided, this is so for cats and cows as well as for you and me. To ignore this and to consider only human pain is arbitrary, irrational, and "speciesist" (a phrase popularized by the utilitarian Peter Singer, who intentionally wished to conjure associations with racism and sexism). Therefore, when a utilitarian considers consequences, and seeks to maximize happiness and minimize pain (sometimes referred to simply as maximizing "utility"), she will have to consider the pleasure and pain of *every creature* capable of pleasure and pain, human and non-human alike. What's more, no one counts "more" than anyone else in this calculation. My happiness is not more valuable simply because it's mine, nor is mine more valuable simply because I'm human. Everyone's happiness counts equally, all else being equal.[354]

This has been a lengthy introduction to utilitarianism! Let's see how it actually works, in application. There are two major types of utilitarian theories: <u>act</u>, and <u>rule</u>.

Act Utilitarianism

An "act utilitarian" is a utilitarian who

---

[354] Note that having a lesser capacity for pleasure by virtue of being a fish, for example,

would mean that all else is *not* equal.

believes that utility is/ought to be maximized by performing a "cost-benefit analysis" for each intended action on a case-by-case basis. That is, when trying to determine the right course of action, one ought to consider all the available options, weigh their "costs" (pains) and "benefits" (pleasures) for each sentient being involved, and select the option that produces the greatest overall "utility" (i.e., most overall pleasure or least overall pain). The goal is to bring about the "best" possible consequences, given the available options.

Bentham thought that our cost-benefit analysis should be informed by the following variables. When only one sentient being is to be effected, the utility calculation will consider each of the following with regard to pleasure and pain:

1. Intensity (how pleasurable or painful the experience will be)
2. Duration (how long the pleasure or pain will last)
3. Certainty/uncertainty (how confident we can be as to the actual experiencing of the pleasure or pain)
4. Propinquity/remoteness (how soon in time the pleasure or pain will be experienced)
5. Fecundity (the tendency of the experience to produce more of its kind—more pleasure or more pain)
6. Purity (the absence of its opposite—e.g., some pleasures are mixed with pain, while others produce only pleasure)

In the likely event that more than one creature will be affected, we add one more consideration (7): the extent (number affected).

This just means that if five people are involved, we will have to consider how each of the five will be affected, pleasurably or painfully, when weighing our alternatives.

If we were to adopt Bentham's method, then whenever we find ourselves presented with a number of options, and interested in doing the morally right thing, we ought to consider each option, and calculate the pleasure and pain generated with respect to each of the variables above. After we have done so, we identify the option with the greatest overall utility (i.e., the greatest quantity of pleasure or least quantity of pain), compared to the alternatives, and this will show us the morally right thing to do. Lest we think ourselves finished, please note that Mill would add one more level of complexity to this process: "quality" of the pleasures involved.

It is quite compatible with the principle of utility to recognise the fact, that some kinds of pleasure are more desirable and more valuable than others. It would be absurd that while, in estimating all other things, quality is considered as well as quantity, the estimation of pleasures should be supposed to depend on quantity alone.

If I am asked, what I mean by difference of quality in pleasures, or what makes one pleasure more valuable than another, merely as a pleasure, except its being greater in amount, there is but one possible answer. Of two pleasures, if there be one to which all or almost all who have experience of both give a decided preference, irrespective of any feeling of moral obligation to prefer it, that is the more desirable pleasure. If one of the two is, by those who are competently acquainted with both, placed so far above the other that they prefer it, even though knowing it to be attended with a greater amount of discontent, and would not resign it for any quantity of the other pleasure which their nature is capable of, we are justified in ascribing to the preferred enjoyment a superiority in quality, so far outweighing quantity as to render it, in comparison, of small account.[355]

For Mill, not all pleasures are equal, and

---

[355] Mill, ibid.

"quantity" is not the only relevant measure of pleasure. There are the so-called "lower" pleasures, the pleasures we have in common with many other animals. Such pleasures include the pleasures of eating, drinking, sex, sleep, etc. There are also "higher" pleasures, such as creating and appreciating art, pursuing knowledge, games of skill, etc. "Higher" pleasures are qualitatively superior to lower pleasures, and Mill believes that the mere intensity of a lower pleasure is not necessarily sufficient to make it more desirable than a less intense, but superior higher pleasure. Much has been written on the controversial nature of Mill's hierarchy, and whether or not he can actually justify that qualitative distinction. For our purposes, though, let's just assume that there is *something* legitimate about his appeal to quality, and make it our eighth variable. To recap what must be calculated in order to establish the morally right thing to do:

1. Intensity
2. Duration
3. Certainty
4. Propinquity
5. Fecundity
6. Purity
7. Extent
8. Quality

Honestly, I (personally) find this to be a hopeless and fruitless method—though you are certainly not required to agree with me on this point. Bentham was brilliant, and he was certainly articulating an authentic moral insight with what he offers, but a literal assignment of positive or negative values representing pain and pleasure (often referred to as "utils"—positive when pleasure, negative when pain), somehow modified with respect to duration, certainty, "propinquity," "fecundity," and "purity" is an abominable exercise—and a needless one. Several of the variables are painfully abstract ("purity?"), speculative at best ("certainty"), and potentially arbitrary ("intensity"—not to mention Mill's notoriously subjective "quality").

Rather than create an Excel spreadsheet with a formula in an effort to discern whether the morally right thing to do, for example, is to shoot down a hijacked passenger jet with 40 innocent passengers onboard, let's try some intuition and common sense.

Hijackers had set the precedent for what they were probably going to do with United Airlines Flight 93. Three other jets had already been flown into buildings that very morning, killing everyone onboard, and many at the target sites. There was good reason to believe that the 40 passengers were going to die anyway, as terrible as that would be to admit. Prior to September 11th, that would *not* have been the reasonable assumption to make. Organizations have been hijacking passenger jets for political purposes for over 40 years. In the vast majority of those cases, the planes are forced to land somewhere, and negotiations begin. The passengers are either freed after the demands are met (usually the release of some "political prisoners") or the jet is raided by police or military forces. On many occasions, the hijackers were slain, and a few passengers, crew, or police/military personnel often die as well, but most of the passengers end up free and relatively unharmed. Whether or not it was the right thing to do, it at least made sense to *consider* waiting and negotiating with the hijackers. After the first intentional crashes on 9-11, it was no longer safe to assume that the plane would land, and that it would be possible to free the passengers. What became safe for us to assume is that the jet was going to be used as a weapon, and flown into a high-profile target, killing even more people.

Assuming that to be so, it's not hard to see how the cost-benefit analysis would recommend shooting down the plane. The 40 passengers are presumed to be doomed, so their pain, as well as the pain of their friends and family members appears unavoidable. What does appear to be avoidable is additional death and misery. If the jet is shot down, at least no additional people will die—and perhaps future hijackers will have to consider that they will be unable to strike their intended targets since they will be shot down instead. Maybe this will deter similar hijackings in the future? Is anyone being made "happy?" Probably not. This is one of those examples where the utilitarian is looking merely to minimize unhappiness. It's a terrible dilemma, with no "good" outcome available. The best the utilitarian can hope for is the "least bad" consequence.

Notice how important it was to have a sense of history. Prior to 9-11, hijackers did not have a reputation for flying planes into buildings. Now, they do. As act utilitarians, our calculations have to adjust to reflect this. Twenty years ago, the best course of action might well have been to let the plane land, and then either negotiate or use a special forces team to raid the plane. Circumstances change. Perhaps the "shoot it down" approach only makes sense when the plane has been hijacked by members of al-Qu'aida. The simple point is this: an act utilitarian will make a determination of what will maximize happiness for all involved on a case-by-case basis. Sometimes, the right thing to do is to shoot the plane down. Other times, the right thing to do might be to negotiate. Sometimes, the right thing to do is to tell the truth. Other times, the right thing to do will be to tell a lie. Sometimes, it's wrong to steal. Other times, it might be the right thing to do. Although reliable patterns might emerge, what makes an act utilitarian an *act* utilitarian is that she performs the cost-benefit analysis for each individual situation, and recognizes that as the "input" changes, so too will the "output."

That act utilitarianism is sensitive to circumstances is seen by some to be an asset. However, the time it takes to perform such calculations on a case-by-case basis can be seen as a liability. Some are additionally concerned that subjectivity can easily creep into our calculations. Sometimes lying is wrong, other times, it's acceptable. How interesting that most of the time I conclude that it's acceptable is when *I* am the one doing the lying! Isn't it possible that we might "tip the scales" in our own favor when performing our calculations, inflating the value of our own happiness while underestimating that of others?

Rule Utilitarianism

To address these concerns, and others, some turn to "rule utilitarianism." Like act utilitarianism, rule utilitarianism emphasizes happiness, and maximizing utility. Where it differs is with regard to when and how these calculations are performed. Rule utilitarians believe that we best maximize utility by following rules which themselves maximize utility. That might sound complicated, but it's really quite simple. Far more often than not, killing innocent people causes more pain than pleasure. Therefore, human beings decided, a very long time ago, that there ought to be a rule against killing innocent people. You would find it very challenging to find a community anywhere in the world that does not forbid murder. Rather than have to figure things out on a case-by-case basis, rule utilitarians propose that we just follow rules such as "don't kill innocent people." It's possible that in rare, exceptional cases, it might actually maximize utility to kill an innocent person, but it's a very safe assumption that killing innocent people *usually* brings more pain than pleasure, and when it appears otherwise, there's a very good chance we're skewing our calculation to our own benefit anyway. The safe thing to do (morally speaking) is to refrain from murdering people. Theft, more often than not, inflicts more pain than pleasure. Therefore, we should follow the rule that says we shouldn't steal. So, too, with rape. So, too, with lying. And so on.

The "shortcut" provided by rule utilitarianism serves to address at least some of several well-known criticisms of utilitarianism in general. We'll now consider these criticisms, as well as how utilitarians have been known to respond.

Possible problem #1: Utilitarianism is too "artificial" and unrealistic

The basic concern behind this criticism is the claim that no one "calculates" like Bentham proposes. Morality is not a math problem, and often times we must make judgment calls with very little time in which to perform a complex calculation. Therefore, utilitarianism is an unrealistic approach to moral decision-making.

Utilitarian possible response:

Sometimes we *do* perform overt cost-benefit analyses. How many of you have ever listed (either mentally, or actually on paper, or on a spread sheet) the "pros" and "cons" of the options before you, and used that list to make your decision? Even if you rarely, if ever, do so according to eight specific variables Bentham offers, it's entirely possible that the notion of a cost-benefit analysis is not alien to you. Moreover, there's no reason why many of these calculations couldn't be "unconscious," or performed at an intuitive level "instantly." It does not, for example, require very much time to conclude that choking to death the guy who cuts in front of me in line does not maximize utility! That's "easy math," to say the least.... Besides, utilitarians need not be bound by Bentham's specific calculation method, and could instead adopt a much simpler, more intuitive, less quantitative approach to the cost-benefit analysis which, if adopted, side-steps much of this criticism.

Finally, with regard to the charge that we haven't enough time to calculate utility, the rule utilitarian (specifically) has a simple response.

Again, defenders of utility often find themselves called upon to reply to such objections as this — that there is not time, previous to action, for calculating and weighing the effects of any line of conduct on the general happiness. This is exactly as if any one were to say that it is impossible to guide our conduct by Christianity, because there is not time, on every occasion on which anything has to be done, to read through the Old and New Testaments. The answer to the objection is, that there has been ample time, namely, the whole past duration of the human species. During all that time, mankind have been learning by experience the tendencies of actions; on which experience all the prudence, as well as all the morality of life,

are dependent. People talk as if the commencement of this course of experience had hitherto been put off, and as if, at the moment when some man feels tempted to meddle with the property or life of another, he had to begin considering for the first time whether murder and theft are injurious to human happiness.[356]

Mill says "there is ample time, namely, the whole past duration of the human species." What Mill means by this is that it's not as though humans have to figure out fresh each day what sorts of actions promote utility and which do not. Murder is reliably bad as far as utility is concerned. Humans figured out that whole "murder is bad" thing thousands of years ago. They already "did the math" for us. We no more have to rediscover the badness of murder than we have to rediscover the hotness of fire. Much of the time, the calculations have been done, and our answers are obvious, morally speaking. It is, for most of us, a rare thing when we encounter a true moral quandary, a situation in which it is truly unclear which course of action will promote the most happiness. In those situations, we might have to work out the problem ourselves, but most of the time, no time is needed.

Possible problem #2: Utilitarianism allows, and even demands (on occasion), what we would consider to be immoral actions.

Utilitarianism promotes the greatest good for the greatest number. It is undeniable that the individual's happiness might be outweighed, and even sacrificed, for the happiness of a greater number, or even the greater happiness of another individual. There is no shortage of "nightmare" scenarios and perverse hypothetical examples meant to illustrate that such reasoning can generate powerfully (seemingly) *immoral* outcomes. Consider the following (intentionally disturbing) examples:

---

[356] ibid.

- The tremendous suffering of a rape survivor is morally justifiable so long as it's a gang-rape, and a sufficient number of rapists participate such that their combined pleasure outweighs her pain.
- Executing members of that "new Christian cult" in the Roman Coliseum is morally justifiable so long as the pleasure stemming from the crowd's entertainment outweighs the suffering experienced by the martyrs.
- Framing an innocent homeless person for a crime is morally justifiable so long as the pleasure generated by the public's peace of mind outweighs his suffering.
- Killing a hospital patient (who happens to be listed as an organ donor) and fabricating the cause of death is morally justifiable given the number of lives saved and benefited by the organs now available for transplant.

This counter-intuitiveness triggers an "integrity objection," according to Bernard Williams.

> *It is absurd to demand of such a man, when the sums come in from the utility network which the projects of others have in part determined, that he should just step aside from his own project and decision and acknowledge the decision which utilitarian calculation requires. It is to alienate him in a real sense from his actions and the source of his action in his own convictions....It is thus, in the most literal sense an attack on his integrity.*[357]

If utilitarianism really does allow—let alone recommend—such counter-intuitive outcomes, then to the extent such outcomes violate our moral sensibilities, utilitarianism seems suspect, as a moral theory.

---

[357] Williams, Bernard. *Utilitarianism: For and Against*, with J.J.C. Smart, Cambridge University Press, 1973: 116 – 117.

Utilitarian possible response:

One quick and easy reply available to utilitarians is to point out that the critic begs the question in claiming that such outcomes would be immoral. How so? According to utilitarianism, the morally correct thing to do is whatever action will maximize happiness. If (outrageous as this might sound) a gang-rape really does maximize happiness (unlikely though this would be!), then, *by definition* it is the morally right thing to do. If a critic wants to claim that the action is nevertheless immoral, then the critic is clearly appealing to a standard other than maximizing utility. That's fine. It just means the critic is not a utilitarian, and is defining moral rightness and wrongness in some other way. In that case, the conflict is deep, involving fundamental premises concerning what establishes moral rightness and wrongness.

A more compelling response, however, is to once again appeal to rule utilitarianism. A rule utilitarian would likely claim that all four of the examples above are, in fact, examples of morally wrong actions. Why? Because it's likely that each of the four examples would violate a moral rule which tends to maximize utility. Rape does not maximize happiness, in general. That should go without saying. Not surprisingly, a rule forbidding rape would be adopted by rule utilitarians. Killing "outsiders" for entertainment purposes, in general, probably does much more harm than good to any society that does so. Framing innocent people? Imagine the harm done to the justice system, specifically the public's confidence in it, should such actions ever be revealed. Killing organ donors? I don't know about you, but I would cease to be an organ donor if I ever learned that such things were happening, and the damage done to the trust *necessary* for the medical community would be profound. In summary, rule utilitarians can claim that fantastic hypothetical scenarios are likely to be irrelevant, to the extent that they don't apply to rule utilitarianism.

Possible problem #3: Utilitarianism is a "swinish doctrine"

> *Now, such a theory of life excites in many minds, and among them in some of the most estimable in feeling and purpose, inveterate dislike. To suppose that life has (as they express it) no higher end than pleasure — no better and nobler object of desire and pursuit — they designate as utterly mean and grovelling; as a doctrine worthy only of swine, to whom the followers of Epicurus were, at a very early period, contemptuously likened; and modern holders of the doctrine are occasionally made the subject of equally polite comparisons by its German, French, and English assailants.[358]*

Some think there is something low and hedonistic about such an emphasis on pleasure and pain. Perhaps animals can and should be guided by such drives, but human beings are different. We're special. We're better. To the extent that utilitarianism urges us to follow our baser inclinations, it lowers us to the level of swine. Surely human beings can be, and ought to be, guided by nobler aspirations!

<u>Utilitarian possible response:</u>

This sort of criticism was well known to John Stuart Mill. He defends utilitarianism against these charges by first agreeing with the critic that human beings *are* different from non-human animals, and for that reason the sorts of activities that please us will *not* be identical to those that please swine.

> *When thus attacked, the Epicureans have always answered, that it is not they, but their accusers, who represent human nature in a degrading light; since the accusation supposes human beings to be capable of no pleasures except those of which swine are capable. If this supposition were true, the charge could not be gainsaid, but would then be no longer an imputation; for if the sources of pleasure were precisely the same to human beings and to swine, the rule of life which is good enough for the one would be good enough for the other. The comparison of the Epicurean life to that of beasts is felt as degrading, precisely because a beast's pleasures do not satisfy a human being's conceptions of happiness. Human beings have faculties more elevated than the animal appetites, and when once made conscious of them, do not regard anything as happiness which does not include their gratification. . . .*

> *Now it is an unquestionable fact that those who are equally acquainted with, and equally capable of appreciating and enjoying, both, do give a most marked preference to the manner of existence which employs their higher faculties. Few human creatures would consent to be changed into any of the lower animals, for a promise of the fullest allowance of a beast's pleasures; no intelligent human being would consent to be a fool, no instructed person would be an ignoramus, no person of feeling and conscience would be selfish and base, even though they should be persuaded that the fool, the dunce, or the rascal is better satisfied with his lot than they are with theirs. They would not resign what they possess more than he for the most complete satisfaction of all the desires which they have in common with him. If they ever fancy they would, it is only in cases of unhappiness so extreme, that to escape from it they would exchange their lot for almost any other, however undesirable in their own eyes. A being of higher faculties requires more to make him happy, is capable probably of*

---

[358] Mill, ibid.

more acute suffering, and certainly accessible to it at more points, than one of an inferior type; but in spite of these liabilities, he can never really wish to sink into what he feels to be a lower grade of existence. We may give what explanation we please of this unwillingness; ... but its most appropriate appellation is a sense of dignity, which all human beings possess in one form or other, and in some, though by no means in exact, proportion to their higher faculties, and which is so essential a part of the happiness of those in whom it is strong, that nothing which conflicts with it could be, otherwise than momentarily, an object of desire to them.... It is better to be a human being dissatisfied than a pig satisfied; better to be Socrates dissatisfied than a fool satisfied. And if the fool, or the pig, are of a different opinion, it is because they only know their own side of the question. The other party to the comparison knows both sides.[359]

Recall Mill's distinguishing of higher and lower pleasures from earlier in this chapter. Granted, we share the capacity for lower pleasures with other animals, but, unlike them (presumably), we have a capacity for the higher pleasures as well—and the higher pleasures are qualitatively superior. Mill is confident that the vast majority of us recognize this as a fact, and would never pursue a life consisting solely in experiencing lower pleasures, or even a life consisting primarily in experiencing lower pleasures

But what about *this* guy, and the many like him? Isn't it obvious that lots of people *do* pursue "lower" pleasures, and seem to prefer them? Doesn't it seem true that, given a choice, a great many people would pick "beer and UFC" over Shakespeare in the park?

Mill has an answer to that criticism as well.

It may be objected, that many who are capable of the higher pleasures, occasionally, under the influence of temptation, postpone them to the lower. But this is quite compatible with a full appreciation of the intrinsic superiority of the higher. Men often, from infirmity of character, make their election for the nearer good, though they know it to be the less valuable; and this no less when the choice is between two bodily pleasures, than when it is between bodily and mental. They pursue sensual indulgences to the injury of health, though perfectly aware that health is the greater good. It may be further objected, that many who begin with youthful enthusiasm for everything noble, as they advance in years sink into indolence and selfishness. But I do not believe that those who undergo this very common change, voluntarily choose the lower description of pleasures in preference to the higher. I believe that before they devote themselves exclusively to the one, they have already become incapable of the other. Capacity for the nobler feelings is in most natures a very tender plant, easily killed, not only by hostile influences, but by mere want of sustenance; and in the majority of young persons it speedily dies away if the occupations to which their position in life has devoted them, and the society into which it has thrown them, are not favourable to keeping that higher capacity in exercise. Men lose their high aspirations as they lose their intellectual tastes, because they have not time or opportunity for indulging them; and they addict themselves to inferior pleasures, not because they deliberately prefer them, but

---

[359] ibid.

because they are either the only ones to which they have access, or the only ones which they are any longer capable of enjoying.[360]

In other words, when people seem to prefer lower pleasures to higher (and not just sometimes, but in general) there is probably an explanation rooted in the life circumstances of those persons—and this is not hard to understand. Perhaps you work hard all day and come home tired and "brain-dead." You just don't feel like reading philosophy, so you opt for a cold beer and some relatively mindless diversion from the TV. Maybe you live in a neighborhood without a public theatre, or a library. Maybe the "higher" pleasures have never been modeled for you. Elitist though he might have been, Mill seems to be right about our general preference for activities that are mentally stimulating. In fact, psychological studies have suggested that extended passive pleasures actually become mildly *depressive* over time.[361]

Possible problem #4: It's too difficult to anticipate the consequences of our actions.

This criticism emerges from the fact that utilitarianism (like other consequentialist theories) focuses solely on the actual consequences of our actions. The problem is that it is often difficult to predict, with great accuracy, just what those consequences will be, and our actions often produce unintended consequences. This can produce bizarre and counter-intuitive judgments from utilitarians.

Suppose, for example that someone is a guest attending a party celebrating the 2nd birthday for the son of a wealthy business associate. The birthday boy begins to choke on a piece of food. The guest is the only one present who knows how to perform the Heimlich maneuver. Suppose also that the guest is a utilitarian. It seems like "easy math" to conclude that saving the boy's life will

maximize happiness, so the guest does so, and the boy's life is saved. The year is 1959. The wealthy business associate is Muhammed Awad Bin Laden. The birthday boy is little Osama Bin Laden. By saving the boy's life, the guest has facilitated the unintended consequence of the formation of al-Qu'aida and the deadliest terrorist attack (as of the time of this writing) on U.S. soil. With all those things in mind, it seems clear that it was morally *wrong* to save the little boy from choking.

Some of you are probably thinking to yourself, "but that's not fair! How could the guest have possibly known that the two year old boy would grow up to be an international terrorist? It's unfair to expect the guest to work with information he couldn't possibly have."

<u>Utilitarian possible response:</u>

You're correct. That *would* be unfair, and there are a couple ways we can process that. One way is to reject consequentialist theories entirely. Consequences lie in the future, and the future is not perfectly known to us. Perhaps it makes more sense to focus on something better known, such as intent. The guest "meant well," and maybe that's all that really matters. We'll explore a sophisticated approach similar to this in our later chapter on Kantianism.

However, while it's certainly possible to just reject utilitarianism as a result of this criticism, that's not the only response available—nor is it the most reasonable, I think. Why throw out the baby with the bath water? Rule utilitarianism is useful once more, in the face of this criticism. The plain fact is that most babies *don't* grow up to become the heads of terrorist organizations, nor do they become serial killers, or Hitler! For that matter, most don't grow up to cure cancer either. Most babies grow up to be *ordinary* people, sometimes doing good things, and sometimes doing bad things. It would be unreasonable (even irrational) to perceive a two year old choking to

---

[360] ibid.

[361] Interested readers should investigate the works of Mihaly Csikszentmihalyi, a psychologist

famous for his research on happiness. https://www.cgu.edu/people/mihaly-csikszentmihalyi/

death, infer that he will become a terrorist one day, and for that reason decline to help. It makes much more sense to adhere to a "rule" that says something like "try to save the lives of other people, including children, when you're able to do so." In the vast majority of cases, this will maximize utility. Sometimes, it won't—but how could you possibly know which cases those will be? The best anyone can do, utilitarian or otherwise, is to choose the course of action which she has good reason to believe is the right thing to do. Mistakes are possible no matter which theory we adopt. Neither the fact of nor the fear of mistakes should get in the way of our trying to do the right thing, nor be used to call into question the very project of moral understanding in the first place.

For each of the following examples, use either Act or Rule utilitarian reasoning to determine what the right policy/action would be.
- Requiring all Americans to have health insurance.
- Allowing certain school employees (e.g., those who have passed background checks and who have taken gun safety/use courses) to have guns at schools (including Colleges and Universities).
- Deporting undocumented immigrants.
- Public funding of political campaigns.
- Banning abortion except in cases where the mother's life is in danger from the pregnancy.
- Building a wall along the U.S./Mexico border.
- Allowing the water-boarding (i.e., torture) of suspected terrorists during interrogation.

[362] All quotations in this section are from Mill's *On Liberty*, unless otherwise indicated. Selections of that work appear at the end of this

Politics

Having established the basic elements of utilitarian thought, we will now consider a more sustained and politically practical application of utilitarianism as it occurs in another of John Stuart Mill's works: *On Liberty*. In that book, it becomes obvious that utilitarianism is not merely an ethical theory confined to solving personal moral dilemmas, but a prescriptive model for decision making, in general, that explains the proper role and limits of government as well.

Mill begins *On Liberty* with a review of some of the fundamental assumptions long held about the necessity (and dangers) of the State. Reminiscent of Hobbes, he claims that "to prevent the weaker members of the community from being preyed upon by innumerable vultures, it was needful that there should be an animal of prey stronger than the rest, commissioned to keep them down."[362] For Hobbes, this demonstrated the necessity not only of a "sovereign," but one whose power was absolute. As we saw in our chapter on Locke, however, the sovereign, too, could be considered a threat—something Mill recognizes as well.

> But as the king of the vultures would be no less bent upon preying on the flock than any of the minor harpies, it was indispensable to be in a perpetual attitude of defence against his beak and claws. The aim, therefore, of patriots, was to set limits to the power which the ruler should be suffered to exercise over the community; and this limitation was what they meant by liberty.

Mill describes this attempt to secure liberty in terms of establishing certain political rights against the sovereign as well as the establishment of constitutional checks requiring the consent of the community. He seeks to establish in broader terms, though, just what is meant (or should be meant) by "liberty," and on what basis that liberty

chapter.

is to be justified.

In a very reader-friendly fashion, Mill explicitly states his conclusion for us in no uncertain terms, in a section worth quoting at length.

> *The object of this Essay is to assert one very simple principle, as entitled to govern absolutely the dealings of society with the individual in the way of compulsion and control, whether the means used be physical force in the form of legal penalties, or the moral coercion of public opinion. That principle is, that the sole end for which mankind are warranted, individually or collectively, in interfering with the liberty of action of any of their number, is self-protection. That the only purpose for which power can be rightfully exercised over any member of a civilised community, against his will, is to prevent harm to others. His own good, either physical or moral, is not a sufficient warrant. He cannot rightfully be compelled to do or forbear because it will be better for him to do so, because it will make him happier, because, in the opinions of others, to do so would be wise, or even right. These are good reasons for remonstrating with him, or reasoning with him, or persuading him, or entreating him, but not for compelling him, or visiting him with any evil in case he do otherwise. To justify that, the conduct from which it is desired to deter him must be calculated to produce evil to some one else. The only part of the conduct of any one, for which he is amenable to society, is that which concerns others. In the part which merely concerns himself, his independence is, of right, absolute. Over himself, over his own body and mind, the individual is sovereign.*

Consider (and be prepared to discuss) each of the following laws/policies according to Mill's principle.

- Mandatory seatbelt laws.
- Mandatory motorcycle helmet laws.
- Prohibition of marijuana use.
- Prohibition of making or viewing pornography.
- Banning the sale of sugary drinks (e.g., soda).
- Mandating the purchase of Health Insurance as was the case under "Obamacare."

With regard to the application of "force," where force could include legal compulsion or restriction, the application of fines or other punishments, or even the "moral coercion of public opinion," with regard to any interference with the liberty of a person by either another individual or the community as a whole, the only legitimate justification is "self-protection." That is, it is acceptable to use the force of law to prevent someone from harming another, as in the obvious examples of murder or rape. However, it is not justifiable to use the force of law to compel someone to do something for "his own good."

One's "own good," for Mill, is a sufficient reason to try to *persuade* or encourage someone through the use of reason, but "but not for compelling him, or visiting him with any evil in case he do otherwise." Mill is quick to add, in case it wasn't obvious, that "this doctrine is meant to apply only to human beings in the maturity of their faculties." The most obvious examples of exceptions would be children, who clearly don't (and shouldn't) enjoy the same autonomy as adults, though this reasoning would properly apply to adults as well, if they are somehow mentally incapable of self-determination, as might be the case with persons who have serious mental illness or developmental disabilities.

Mill's "hands-off" approach to the infringement of individual liberty makes him the champion of self-professed libertarians. The contemporary Libertarian party in the United

States claim that "Libertarians strongly oppose any government interference into their personal, family, and business decisions. Essentially, we believe all Americans should be free to live their lives and pursue their interests as they see fit as long as they do no harm to another."[363] The connection to Mill is unmistakable, and his appeal is understandable. How, though, does Mill *justify* his vision of such limited government? Very simply: in the same way he justifies any other action or outcome.

> *I regard utility as the ultimate appeal on all ethical questions; but it must be utility in the largest sense, grounded on the permanent interests of man as a progressive being.*

Remember: this is the same John Stuart Mill from earlier in this chapter who endorsed what we called Rule Utilitarianism. What is right or wrong, good or bad, just or unjust, is to be understood in terms of whether and to what extent those actions (or policies) maximize utility. Rather obviously, acts of violence such as rape or murder don't maximize utility for all involved, so it makes sense that we would have rules against them, and use the law to enforce those rules. That is a perfectly legitimate application of State coercion.

It is not only *preventing* certain actions, such as acts of violence, which are justified by appeals to utility, but also (in some cases) compelling persons *to act*.

> *There are also many positive acts for the benefit of others, which he may rightfully be compelled to perform; such as, to give evidence in a court of justice; to bear his fair share in the common defence, or in any other joint work necessary to the interest of the society of which he enjoys the protection; and to perform certain acts of individual beneficence, such as saving a fellow-creature's life, or interposing to protect the defenceless against ill-usage,*

> *things which whenever it is obviously a man's duty to do, he may rightfully be made responsible to society for not doing. A person may cause evil to others not only by his actions but by his inaction, and in either case he is justly accountable to them for the injury. The latter case, it is true, requires a much more cautious exercise of compulsion than the former.*

Some of this should appear as common sense, but other elements of this paragraph should dispel the illusion that Mill was some sort of radical libertarian who proposed no government coercion whatsoever. It might help to distinguish *acts of commission* from *acts of omission*. The basic difference between them is that acts of commission refer to things that we do, and acts of omission to things that we refrain from doing. Telling a lie is an act of commission. Withholding the truth is an act of omission. Forcing someone's head underwater is an act of commission. Standing by and doing nothing while someone drowns is an act of omission.

The most enthusiastic libertarians might claim that the State only has the right to restrict acts of commission, but not acts of omission. For example, it would be legitimate to criminalize murder, but not legitimate to punish someone for "doing nothing" and allowing someone to die who could have been saved. In plainer terms, it's legitimate for the State to prevent you from hurting your neighbors, but it shouldn't force you to help them.

A clear example of this actually occurred in 2011 during one of the Republican primary debates. The following was the exchange between CNN moderator Wolf Blitzer, and candidate (and self-professed libertarian) Ron Paul.

> *BLITZER: . . . you're a physician, Ron Paul, so you're a doctor. You know something about this subject. Let me ask you this hypothetical question.*

---

[363] https://www.lp.org/about/

A healthy 30-year-old young man has a good job, makes a good living, but decides, you know what? I'm not going to spend $200 or $300 a month for health insurance because I'm healthy, I don't need it. But something terrible happens, all of a sudden he needs it.

Who's going to pay if he goes into a coma, for example? Who pays for that?

PAUL: Well, in a society that you accept welfarism and socialism, he expects the government to take care of him.

BLITZER: Well, what do you want?

PAUL: But what he should do is whatever he wants to do, and assume responsibility for himself. My advice to him would have a major medical policy, but not be forced --

BLITZER: But he doesn't have that. He doesn't have it, and he needs intensive care for six months. Who pays?

PAUL: That's what freedom is all about, taking your own risks. This whole idea that you have to prepare and take care of everybody --

(APPLAUSE)

BLITZER: But Congressman, are you saying that society should just let him die?

PAUL: No. I practiced medicine before we had Medicaid, in the early 1960s, when I got out of medical school. I practiced at Santa Rosa Hospital in San Antonio, and the churches took care of them. We never turned anybody away from the hospitals. (APPLAUSE)

PAUL: And we've given up on this whole

concept that we might take care of ourselves and assume responsibility for ourselves. Our neighbors, our friends, our churches would do it. This whole idea, that's the reason the cost is so high. [364]

Ron Paul was confident that charities might step in to provide health services to those who needed them, but he was adamant that the government should not do so, and was equally adamant that people assume personal responsibility for their own lives and circumstances. "That's what freedom is all about, taking your own risks."

Mill is often credited with endorsing the view that the State should only protect citizens from harm, but this overlooks the clear content of the Mill quotation above. "A person may cause evil to others not only by his actions but by his inaction, and in either case he is justly accountable to them for the injury." Mill's own examples include compelling witnesses to testify in court, compelling people to defend their nation through military service, and even compelling people to save others' lives when possible!

Forcing a citizen to pay taxes is not merely "preventing harm" but positively compelling someone to do good (on the assumption that taxes are needed to fund at least the minimal protections and services offered by the government). Forcing citizens to serve in the military is a profound intrusion into their personal liberty, but might be necessary to preserve the State itself, in times of war. Even mandating "saving a fellow-creature's life," while certainly intrusive, is considered legitimate, by Mill.

Such laws are not merely philosophical hypotheticals, by the way. They are called "duty to rescue" laws, and actually exist in several States, including California. California penal code section 152.3 says that:

152.3. (a) Any person who reasonably believes that he or she has observed the

---

[364] http://transcripts.cnn.com/TRANSCRIPTS/ 1109/12/se.06.html

commission of any of the following offenses where the victim is a child under the age of 14 years shall notify a peace officer, as defined in Chapter 4.5 (commencing with Section 830) of Title 3 of Part 2:

(1) Murder.

(2) Rape.

(3) A violation of paragraph (1) of subdivision (b) of Section 288 of the Penal Code.

(b) This section shall not be construed to affect privileged relationships as provided by law.

(c) The duty to notify a peace officer imposed pursuant to subdivision (a) is satisfied if the notification or an attempt to provide notice is made by telephone or any other means.

(d) Failure to notify as required pursuant to subdivision (a) is a misdemeanor and is punishable by a fine of not more than one thousand five hundred dollars ($1,500), by imprisonment in a county jail for not more than six months, or by both that fine and imprisonment.

(e) The requirements of this section shall not apply to the following:

(1) A person who is related to either the victim or the offender, including a husband, wife, parent, child, brother, sister, grandparent, grandchild, or other person related by consanguinity or affinity.

(2) A person who fails to report based on a reasonable mistake of fact.

(3) A person who fails to report based on a reasonable fear for his or her own safety or

for the safety of his or her family.[365]

Admittedly, there are a lot of "disqualifiers" in that law, but the intent is clear: to compel people to "do the right thing," if they are not sufficiently internally motivated to do so. Such laws are legitimate, to Mill—though he acknowledges that such "positive" laws require "a much more cautious exercise of compulsion."

Conclusion

It's easy to see why Mill has been influential to both libertarians and liberals alike. Libertarians (and some conservatives) appreciate his vision of a small and limited government. Liberals appreciate his endorsement of individuality, and rejection of forcing people to conform to a single vision of what's right. It's important to recall, in either case, that his conclusions are informed by a coherent vision of decision-making that applies to all judgments, both ethical and political: the principle of utility. In this, we have a wonderful example of the application of philosophical theory to political practice.

Mill's defense of the classical liberal ideal of letting people live as they see fit, so long as they're not harming others, facilitates the development of a pluralistic society—one in which numerous worldviews, value systems, and political ideologies coexist.

Critical Analysis

1. In your opinion, what are the strongest and most compelling points made by the philosopher or philosophers in this chapter? Why do you find those points to be convincing?
2. In your opinion, what are the weakest or least convincing points? Why? Can you anticipate any limitations or objections to their ideas not already addressed in the chapter?

---

[365] http://law.onecle.com/california/penal/ 152.3.html

Appendix: Application to Social Justice

Utilitarianism gives us an approach by which to evaluate actions, laws, policies, and anything else that has some sort of moral component to it. The application to social justice issues is fairly simple, at least on the surface. Because all moral matters are understood in terms of "utility," justice itself will be understood in terms of utility. As Jeremy Bentham put it, in his usual terse manner:

> *Justice, in the only sense in which it has a meaning, is an imaginary personage, feigned for the convenience of discourse, whose dictates are the dictates of utility, applied to certain particular cases.*[366]

Most likely, though, it will be *rule* utilitarianism that best lends itself to discussions of social justice. Rule utilitarians (like Mill) will ask which rules will generate the most utility. In fact, Mill claims that the requirements of justice "stand higher in the scale of social utility."[367] This probably just means that Mill believes that those rules which pertain to what we label "justice" tend to be those on which a lot of utility is at stake.

Consider, for example, the sorts of rules that govern what we tend to think of as basic human rights. These would include rules against things as murder and enslavement, but arguably also such things as permitting political participation, equal protection under the law, etc. Whether or not someone can treat you as property, or whether or not you are treated the same as others by the laws of your community, have tremendous potential to either promote or at least preserve your happiness, or to inflict significant unhappiness. It's a simple matter, then, to see how the utilitarian framework can be used to evaluate laws and policies, and to make recommendations, within the context of social justice.

Because utilitarian cost-benefit analyses are complicated, in general, we shouldn't be surprised to discover that they are complicated when it comes to social justice, as well. If we use rule utilitarianism, we're *less* likely to run into scenarios that trigger "possible problem #2: Utilitarianism allows, and even demands (on occasion), what we would consider to be immoral actions." Less likely does not mean impossible, though.

It's possible, for example, that a strong case could be made for reparations for the descendants of enslaved persons, but conclude that the (literal) cost to the economy would be too great to justify it. To provide a sense of scale, estimates of the "diverted income" from slavery, from 1790 to 1860 alone, were calculated (compounded and adjusted for inflation) in 1983. The sum was estimated to be between 2.1 and 4.7 trillion dollars.[368] Adjusted to 2020 dollars, but *without* compounding interest, this value is approximately 5.4-12.1 trillion dollars.

As another example, someone could make a persuasive case that our criminal justice system is so poisoned by systemic racism that it needs to be dismantled and rebuilt from the ground up. After the May 2020 murder of George Floyd by police in Minneapolis, the City Council voted unanimously to eliminate the city's police department and replace it with "a department of community safety and violence prevention, which will have responsibility for public safety services prioritizing a holistic, public health-oriented approach."[369] As of December 2020, however, the Council decided to cut the police

---

[366] Bentham, *The Principles of Morals and Legislation*, pp. 125–6.

[367] Mill, John Stuart, *The Collected Works of John Stuart Mill*. Gen. Ed. John M. Robson. 33 vols. Toronto: University of Toronto Press, 1963-91. 259.

[368] Marketti, James. "Estimated Present Value of Income Diverted during Slavery," in America,

Richard. *The Wealth of Races: The Present Value of Benefits from Past Injustices.* Praeger (2002), 107.

[369] https://www.npr.org/sections/live-updates-protests-for-racial-justice/2020/06/26/884149659/minneapolis-council-moves-to-defund-police-establish-holistic-public-safety-forc

budget by $8 million, but *not* reduce its staff. Although there were bureaucratic reasons for this dramatic change of course, including a veto threat by the city mayor, it's likely that part of the reason behind the much more limited action was push-back from residents of the city who suffered from and feared the increase in criminal activity the city had experienced at least in part due to a "reduction" in policing after more than a hundred police officers quit or retired, or went out on leave citing PTSD (in protest). There were twice as many gunshot victims as of December 2020 compared to the same period the previous year; carjackings were up 333%, and violent crime, in general, was up approximately 25%.[370]

One way to interpret all this would be to lean into the data and conclude that a radical reform of police departments imposes too great a "cost" in terms of increased crime (if nothing else), and therefore the "pros" of the current police system outweigh the "cons" (i.e., persons of color suffering from discriminatory police practices). It's entirely possible that the cost-benefit analysis might churn out a different result, however, if we attempt to calculate the "cost" inflicted on people of color, in some cases daily, by traumatic encounters with police, being profiled, being pulled over for "looking suspicious," being approached by officers with their guns drawn because they "fit the description," etc.

Such calculations are complicated not only because of the question of how many variables to include, but also how to weight them. Just how many negative "utils" does a young Black man experience when subject to "stop and frisk?" On the other hand, even a libertarian-leaning utilitarian like Mill, whom we would rightfully suspect to be critical of invasions of privacy and outright harassment, such as that occurring under "stop and frisk" policies, still claims that government coercion is justified to prevent someone from harming others. The rationale for "stop and frisk" policies is that they catch "dangerous" people before they have a chance to

victimize someone. Needless to say, what exactly a utilitarian analysis would recommend is *complicated*.

Another (dramatic) way to respond to the data is to abandon utilitarianism as the proper framework within which to engage matters of social justice. Arguably, most ethicists and political philosophers of the last century or so regard utilitarianism as a *rival* to social justice accounts that they believe find a more suitable home in deontological (or "rights based") theories, or social contract theories such as that developed by John Rawls.[371]

As a final comment in this necessarily brief appendix, it's worth pointing out that Mill's arguments from *On Liberty* are, if nothing else, a nice illustration that social justice issues are not limited to left-wing liberal political perspectives. Mill offers a broadly libertarian case for what might otherwise be considered "progressive" stances, particularly on "social" issues such as sexuality and gender expression. As I wrote previously, he describes cultivating individuality as a process that makes a person "noble and beautiful." Cultivating individuality makes life "rich" and makes the human race "infinitely better worth belonging to." It makes life have "greater fullness." "In proportion to the development of his individuality, each person becomes more valuable to himself, and is therefore capable of being more valuable to others."

That is, developing my own individuality not only makes my own life more valuable to me, but also more valuable to others—hence the "greater good." Forced conformity, in contrast, "dulls and blunts the whole nature." All of this makes a strong case for rejecting conformity in gender expression and sexuality, and could certainly be used to argue for equal treatment under the law for the LGBTQ+ community, as just one example.

---

[370] https://www.usatoday.com/story/news/nation/2020/12/10/minneapolis-approves-cuts-police-budget/3876127001/

[371] Rawls is explored, in detail, in another chapter of this book.

Chapter 14: Helping the "Less Fortunate"

Comprehension questions you should be able to answer after reading this chapter:

1. From within which major ethical theory is Peter Singer working?
2. Explain the general principle that Singer recommends when it comes to helping others.
3. What do you think Singer means by "comparable moral worth?"
4. Does Singer think that our moral obligations are diminished by how far away the needy person is, or by whether or not we know that person? Explain why or why not.
5. Does Singer think that our moral obligation is diminished by the fact that other people might be available to help as well? Explain why or why not.
6. What does Hardin mean by "lifeboat ethics?" What does he mean by the "tragedy of the commons?"
7. Why does Hardin think that helping the needy (at least in certain cases) actually does more harm than good?
8. What is Singer's response to Hardin's argument?
9. Explain the difference (according to Narveson) between starvation as an active verb, and starvation as a noun. Why does this distinction matter, morally speaking?
10. Explain the difference (according to Narveson) between killing and letting die. Why does this distinction matter, morally speaking?
11. Describe the "liberty" approach used by Jan Narveson.
12. What is the "ethics of the hair shirt," and why does Narveson reject it?

In this chapter we will apply ethical theories and moral decision-making to a particular issue. The focus of this chapter will be the moral status of helping others in need.

It goes without saying that people are more or less advantaged/privileged relative to others. We live in a world in which some people have multiple billions of dollars to their name, and can afford to spend what most of us would consider extraordinary sums of money on what many of us would consider luxury items. For example, a "private collector" purchased a single bottle of the 1947 vintage of Château cheval Blanc for $304,375. That amounts to $7609 per glass of wine.[372] At the same time, it is estimated that one person in the world dies *per second* from malnutrition.[373]

Is there anything morally problematic about individuals spending money on "luxuries," while other people literally *die* from lack of food,

potable water, medicine, shelter, or some combination of all of these?

It's important, before attempting to answer this question, that we acknowledge that it does not apply only to the so-called 1% crowd or those with lavishly expensive taste in wine. I suspect that *every* person reading this chapter spends some amount of money each week, if not each day, on things that less fortunate people would label a "luxury" – even if that so-called luxury item is a cup of Starbucks coffee, a ticket to a movie, or some new clothes (when your "old" clothes still shelter you from the elements).

Having studied numerous ethical theories in previous chapters, you should be able to develop general positions on the moral obligation (if any) to help others in need from within the framework of those theories – and this is a worthy and recommended exercise for you. What we will consider in this chapter, however, is what three

---

[372] https://vinepair.com/articles/five-most-expensive-wines-sold/
[373] http://www.theworldcounts.com/counters/g

lobal_hunger_statistics/how_many_people_die_from_hunger_each_year

particular philosophers have said on the issue. In some cases, their approach should feel quite familiar, and we will make the relevant connections when appropriate.

You see a homeless person on the street, with a sign saying: "Hungry. Anything will help."

1. Are you morally obligated to help that person? Why or why not?
2. Are any other people morally obligated to help that person? Why or why not?
3. If anyone is morally obligated to help, what should that help look like? What form should it take?

There are entire communities of people around the world in desperate need of food, safe drinking water, and medicine.

4. Are you morally obligated to help those people? Why or why not?
5. Are any other people morally obligated to help them? Why or why not?
6. If anyone is morally obligated to help, what should that help look like? What form should it take?
7. Should the U.S. government provide foreign aid to help those people? Why or why not? What conditions, if any, should be attached to the offer of help? Is it morally justifiable for the government to tax people who would prefer not to help in order to fund that foreign aid? Why or why not? What should that help look like? What form should it take?

Peter Singer

Singer self identifies as a utilitarian. Accordingly, he believes that actions are morally right or wrong based upon their consequences: morally right if they maximize happiness for every creature involved and morally wrong if they do not.

Singer takes as a generally uncontroversial starting point the recognition that suffering and death from lack of food, water, shelter, or medicine is therefore "bad." If the suffering resulting from lack of resources is a bad thing, then relieving or preventing that suffering, generally speaking will be a good thing – which is to say the morally right thing. As a general principle, he proposes:

> *if it is in our power to prevent something bad from happening, without thereby sacrificing anything of comparable moral importance, we ought, morally, to do it. By "without sacrificing anything of comparable moral importance" I mean without causing anything else comparably bad to happen, or doing something that is wrong in itself, or failing to promote some moral good, comparable in significance to the bad thing that we can prevent. This principle seems almost as uncontroversial as the last one. It requires us only to prevent what is bad, and to promote what is good, and it requires this of us only when we can do it without sacrificing anything that is, from the moral point of view, comparably important.*[374]

On the surface, this might seem simple. Causing harm is morally wrong according to utilitarianism for the simple reason that it inflicts pain. The only way that causing harm could be morally justifiable is if we could demonstrate that doing so will somehow result in less pain than would otherwise have occurred. By extension,

---

[374] All quotations attributed to Singer in this chapter are from his essay: "Famine, Affluence, and Morality" by Peter Singer. *Philosophy and* *Public Affairs*, vol. 1, no. 1 (Spring 1972): 229-243 [revised edition]. The entire text (along with many other writings by Singer) is available here:

preventing harm is morally obligatory and failing to prevent harm (when we are in a position to prevent it) is only morally justifiable if we could demonstrate that permitting the harm to occur will somehow result in less pain than would otherwise occur if we prevented it. Consistent with the utilitarian cost-benefit analysis, preventing harm is not morally required of us if it would require the sacrifice of "anything of comparable moral importance." This is where the simplicity ends.

"Comparable moral importance" is admittedly a vague term. We might think that some examples are easy. For example if a child is drowning just a few feet from shore, and will clearly suffer from the panic of drowning, the physical pain of drowning, and (debatably) from the loss of all future pleasures, and the only "cost" to you in saving that child's life is the discomfort and inconvenience of wet pant legs, the choice seems clear from a utilitarian perspective: save the child! Dry pant legs are not of "comparable moral importance" to that child's very life.

That being said, examples can become increasingly "complicated." Using the example of spending money to provide necessities (such as food) to those in need, just what other expenditures would be considered of "comparable moral importance?" Using similar reasoning, is a Venti cup of coffee from Starbucks of "comparable moral importance" as the life of children? One organization claims that it can provide lifesaving nutrients to a child for $.20 per day.[375] The three dollars spent on that one Venti cup of coffee (without anything fancy or special, and without a tip) could instead provide food to keep one child alive for 15 days, or 15 children alive for one day. It's hard to argue that that cup of coffee is of greater moral value than the lives of 15 children!

To make his principle even more stringent, Singer does not allow that proximity in space (location) or proximity of relationship makes any meaningful difference in terms of moral

obligation. This principle according to which we are morally obligated to help others in need isn't diminished simply because the person is a stranger, nor because the person is "far away." Indeed, advances in technology have made it profoundly easier to help others even on the other side of the world compared to when Singer first published his essay (1972). One can donate money to disaster relief, for example, in less than a minute on a standard smart phone:

http://www.redcross.org/

Considering that all creatures capable of pleasure and pain count equally (all else being equal) in the utilitarian cost-benefit analysis, the fact that the needy person is a "stranger" doesn't somehow diminish the obligation to help. The fact that I know someone doesn't somehow increase their value in the calculation of the greater good, and "relational proximity" ultimately matters no more than does geographic proximity. Nor is our moral obligation diminished by the number of other people who could conceivably help, whether they in fact help, or not.

There is a social psychological phenomenon sometimes referred to as "diffusion of responsibility." This is a phenomenon whereby a person is less likely to take personal responsibility for acting when others (who might themselves act) are present. In 1964, a New York woman by the name of Kitty Genovese was raped and murdered outside her apartment. Thirty-eight of her neighbors witnessed these crimes and not one of them called the police.[376] Their inaction was explained in terms of diffusion of responsibility. Each had assumed that someone else was probably calling the police, and therefore felt no compelling responsibility to do so.

While it is perfectly fine to acknowledge the existence of the psychological phenomenon, Singer thinks that while it might *explain* inaction

---

https://www.utilitarian.net/singer/by/1972----.htm
[375] http://www.kahbayarea.org/

[376] https://www.history.com/topics/crime/kitty-genovese

it does not *justify* it. According to him, the fact that other people also have a moral obligation to help those in need in no way diminishes one's own moral obligation, and the fact that other people fail to do what is morally right does not somehow excuse one's own failure. He acknowledges that many people don't see things the same way, but he replies that "the way people do in fact judge has nothing to do with the validity of my correlation." In other words, our intuitions, perceptions, and actual practices can be mistaken and morally unjustifiable.

If his general moral principle that we are obligated to help others in need when doing so doesn't require the sacrifice of something of comparable moral importance is correct, the fact that some people disagree, and the fact that lots of people don't comply, does nothing to negate the correctness of that principle.

In response to the objection that helping others is better done by government organizations than through private acts of charity, he states, in effect, that the combination of *both* is probably what is morally required of us.

> *I do not, of course, want to dispute the contention that governments of affluent nations should be giving many times the amount of genuine, no-strings-attached aid that they are giving now. I agree, too, that giving privately is not enough, and that we ought to be campaigning actively for entirely new standards for both public and private contributions to famine relief. Indeed, I would sympathize with someone who thought that campaigning was more important than giving oneself, although I doubt whether preaching what one does not practice would be very effective. Unfortunately, for many people the idea that "it's the government's responsibility" is a reason for not giving which does not appear to entail any political action either.[377]*

One objection that he *does* take seriously in

the revised version of his essay is an objection basically rooted in his own utilitarian framework: that helping the needy, specifically in the case of famine relief, fails to satisfy a utilitarian cost-benefit analysis because it merely postpones starvation and will ultimately *increase* suffering. Before addressing Singer's response to this concern, we will consider what is arguably its most infamous source: the "lifeboat ethics" argument of Garrett Hardin.

Garrett Hardin

In 1974, scientist and activist Garrett Hardin published what would become an infamous essay against providing food relief to starving people, specifically in Ethiopia (which was experiencing a devastating famine at the time). A basic premise with which he defended his position involved a "lifeboat" analogy with respect to natural resources. In terms of households, nations, and even the planet, we can imagine ourselves as passengers in a lifeboat, with limited resources, trying to survive while other people remain in the water, wanting to get on the boat. Without question, if we do nothing, the people in the water will die. However, since the lifeboat is already at capacity, letting any more people in will harm those already on board.

Harsh though it might sound, he claims that we are entirely justified in refusing to allow anyone else onto the boat. For anyone currently in the boat who feels guilty about their privileged position, he recommends that they volunteer to leap into the water and give up their spot to someone who (apparently) doesn't feel that same guilt! The fact of the matter is that there are not enough resources to save everyone, that some people will die, and that those in the fortunate position of survivor are not morally obligated to undermine that position for the sake of those in need.

He continues his metaphor by making it clear that, globally and economically speaking, the people in the boat represent persons from "privileged" nations while those in the water represent people from "underprivileged" nations.

---

[377] ibid.

To make a bad situation worse, he points to the differences in population growth rates between "first world" and "developing" nations – a difference that ensures that disparities in resources and life expectancy will only increase over time.

As a contemporary example, in 2017 Niger had a growth rate of 3.2%. South Sudan had a growth rate of 3.8%. In fact, all 20 of the top 20 growth rate countries were in Africa or the Middle East.[378] The United States, in contrast, grew at a rate of .69%--almost 4.5 times *slower* than the growth rate of Niger. The difference in growth rates is accounted for by many factors, including a decline in infant mortality rates, and high fertility rates in high growth rate countries. For example, Niger had a fertility rate of 7.29 in 2015, averaging 7.29 children per woman.[379] The USA, in contrast, had a fertility rate of 1.84 in 2015--roughly ¼ the rate of Niger.[380]

A country with far fewer resources than the United States has substantially higher population growth rates. Not surprisingly, some of those people experience food insecurity.

Are wealthier countries such as United States morally obligated to provide from their own resources to feed the hungry people in other countries? Hardin says no, and that to do so, would ultimately only make the situation worse. Using his own data from 1974:

Now suppose the U.S. agreed to pool its resources with those seven countries, with everyone receiving an equal share. Initially the ratio of Americans to non-Americans in this model would be one-to-one. But consider what the ratio would be after 87 years, by which time the Americans would have doubled to a population of 420 million. By then, doubling every 21 years, the other group would have swollen to 3.54

billion. Each American would have to share the available resources with more than eight people.

But, one could argue, this discussion assumes that current population trends will continue, and they may not. Quite so. Most likely the rate of population increase will decline much faster in the U.S. than it will in the other countries, and there does not seem to be much we can do about it. In sharing with "each according to his needs," we must recognize that needs are determined by population size, which is determined by the rate of reproduction, which at present is regarded as a sovereign right of every nation, poor or not. This being so, the philanthropic load created by the sharing ethic of the spaceship can only increase.[381]

That is, whatever burden is being placed on the resources of the "lifeboat" at present will only be magnified if the number of people "in the water" continues to increase and outpace the number of people with sufficient resources for themselves (i.e., those already in a "lifeboat"). He ties his notion of "lifeboat ethics" to an older idea of the "tragedy of the commons" (a term originally used by William Forster Lloyd in 1833).

The fundamental error of spaceship ethics, and the sharing it requires, is that it leads to what I call "the tragedy of the commons." Under a system of private property, the men who own property recognize their responsibility to care for it, for if they don't they will eventually suffer... If everyone would restrain himself, all would be well; but it takes only one less than everyone to ruin a system of

[378] https://www.statista.com/statistics/ 264687/ countries-with-the-highest-population-growth-rate/

[379] https://www.statista.com/statistics/ 448648/ fertility-rate-in-niger/

[380] https://www.statista.com/statistics/

269941/ fertility-rate-in-the-us/

[381] All quotations attributed to Hardin are from the following essay: http://www.garretthardinsociety.org/articles/art_lifeboat_ethics_case_against_helping_poor.html

voluntary restraint. In a crowded world of less than perfect human beings, mutual ruin is inevitable if there are no controls. This is the tragedy of the commons.[382]

The idea here is somewhat simple and possibly intuitive: when something is "yours," you are motivated to take care of it much more so than if it belongs to "no one" or "everyone." A simple example of this is a public restroom. I am routinely horrified by the conditions of public restrooms, where it seems obvious that some people are making no effort to avoid making a mess – or possibly even making it a point to do so on purpose. Without going into too much detail, I've lost count of the number of times I've seen toilets where someone has urinated all over the seat and on the floor, and even times when someone has defecated on the seat or on the floor! Although I cannot say this with certainty, I'm very confident that those people treat their own bathrooms at home with much more care. It would truly surprise me if very many of those individuals would pee all over their own bathroom floor and then simply walk away. And yet, such actions are not all that uncommon in public restrooms.

To apply this intuition behind the tragedy of the commons to economic decisions and food resources, the assumption is that when people are responsible for their own resources they are much more motivated to take proper care of them. If, instead, resources are held "in common," and anyone may make a claim on these resources even if they have not taken care of them themselves, then people will exploit these resources, take advantage of the system, and the entire system will suffer as a result. In this scenario, Hardin thinks that "helping" with aid merely postpones (and increases) the suffering and death.

We must ask if such a program would actually do more good than harm, not only momentarily but also in the long run. Those who propose the food bank usually

refer to a current "emergency" or "crisis" in terms of world food supply. But what is an emergency? Although they may be infrequent and sudden, everyone knows that emergencies will occur from time to time. A well-run family, company, organization or country prepares for the likelihood of accidents and emergencies. It expects them, it budgets for them, it saves for them. . . .

What happens if some organizations or countries budget for accidents and others do not? If each country is solely responsible for its own well-being, poorly managed ones will suffer. But they can learn from experience. They may mend their ways, and learn to budget for infrequent but certain emergencies. For example, the weather varies from year to year, and periodic crop failures are certain. A wise and competent government saves out of the production of the good years in anticipation of bad years to come. Joseph taught this policy to Pharaoh in Egypt more than 2,000 years ago. Yet the great majority of the governments in the world today do not follow such a policy. They lack either the wisdom or the competence, or both. Should those nations that do manage to put something aside be forced to come to the rescue each time an emergency occurs among the poor nations?[383]

In other words, harsh though it might sound, at the international level, if other countries "bail out" communities that have too large of a population for their current level of resources, then they will never "learn" and make the appropriate adjustments to their family planning and/or their economy. The outside aid will simply "enable" the poor resource management and prolong the suffering.

'But it isn't their fault!' Some kind-hearted liberals argue. 'How can we blame the poor

---

[382] ibid.

[383] ibid.

people who are caught in an emergency? Why must they suffer for the sins of their governments?' The concept of blame is simply not relevant here. . . . As a result of such solutions to food shortage emergencies, the poor countries will not learn to mend their ways, and will suffer progressively greater emergencies as their populations grow. . . .

If poor countries received no food from the outside, the rate of their population growth would be periodically checked by crop failures and famines. But if they can always draw on a world food bank in time of need, their population can continue to grow unchecked, and so will their "need" for aid. In the short run, a world food bank may diminish that need, but in the long run it actually increases the need without limit.

Without some system of worldwide food sharing, the proportion of people in the rich and poor nations might eventually stabilize. The overpopulated poor countries would decrease in numbers, while the rich countries that had room for more people would increase.[384]

Again, harsh as it might sound, Hardin is actually appealing to an implicitly utilitarian justification for not helping the needy – at least in the context he is describing. By providing aid, the "more fortunate" are simply propping up the circumstances and poor lifestyle choices of individuals or governments (or both). Because there is no need for them to change anything, they are unlikely to do so. The very same conditions that produced the "need" will continue to produce that same need in the future, requiring the more fortunate to continue to provide aid, which will continue to perpetuate the need, etc.

To break this cycle of dependency, the needy must do something different. At a personal level, people might need to make more responsible choices. At a national level, governments might

need to change economic policies, or root out corruption, or abandon expensive military spending, etc. At a cultural level, communities might be forced to reconsider their beliefs and values concerning family planning. A culture with too many mouths to feed but that *also* rejects birth control and abortion might need to rethink that life strategy.

In case it's not obvious, the utilitarian justification for this "tough love" is the assumption that the greater good is served not by providing help, but by those in need making the changes necessary so that the same conditions producing their suffering now will not continue to produce them in the future.

Singer was aware of this criticism of his general principle and replied to it in at least two fashions. The first is that even if those observations are true, it merely changes the *type* of help one should provide.

The conclusion that should be drawn is that the best means of preventing famine, in the long run, is population control. It would then follow from the position reached earlier that one ought to be doing all one can to promote population control (unless one held that all forms of population control were wrong in themselves, or would have significantly bad consequences). Since there are organizations working specifically for population control, one would then support them rather than more orthodox methods of preventing famine.[385]

If the concern is that at the international level the cause of starvation is overpopulation, then in the short run some food aid might be appropriate, but in the long run providing resources for population control would be the "aid" that we are morally obligated to provide.

At a personal level, if the cause of someone being homeless and in need is drug addiction, then in the short run food and shelter might be appropriate, but in the long run our moral

---

[384] ibid.

[385] Singer, ibid.

obligation might be to provide resources to combat drug addiction. The obligation remains, but the form it takes might have to be adjusted.

The second way in which Singer acknowledges this criticism is arguably more substantial. As mentioned earlier in this chapter, in the revised version of this essay, Singer acknowledges the credibility of this objection, up to a point, and makes a concession (of sorts).

> . . . for I now think that there is a serious case for saying that if a country refuses to take any steps to slow the rate of its population growth, we should not give it aid. This is, of course, a very drastic step to take, and the choice it represents is a horrible choice to have to make; but if, after a dispassionate analysis of all the available information, we come to the conclusion that without population control we will not, in the long run, be able to prevent famine or other catastrophes, then it may be more humane in the long run to aid those countries that are prepared to take strong measures to reduce population growth, and to use our aid policy as a means of pressuring other countries to take similar steps.[386]

This is actually a significant concession. Acknowledging a bit of political pragmatism, Singer is recognizing that there might be certain nations where political corruption is so entrenched, or governments with such misguided priorities, that providing aid to those nations will not actually help the problem, but will only prolong it. In those cases, the right thing to do might well be to not provide aid, but perhaps direct resources to political and social change instead.

Thus far, we have heard from two people, both working from within some general utilitarian assumptions. Peter Singer claims that we have a moral obligation to provide for the less fortunate unless and up until the point something of "comparable moral value" is sacrificed. Garrett

Hardin similarly appeals to the "greater good," but comes to a very different conclusion: the greater good is served by not providing aid, not prolonging the suffering, but forcing the needy to recalibrate their choices, or, at the level of entire nations, forcing governments to do the same. In sharp contrast to Peter Singer, and working outside the utilitarian approach, we have the (politically) *libertarian* approach advocated by Jan Narveson.

Jan Narveson

As is typical of good philosophers, Narveson begins by carefully defining his terms and distinguishing different meanings of the same term. For example, "starvation" can be understood either as an "active" or as a "passive" word.

The active form of "starvation" is the verb "to starve." That is something that is inflicted on someone else, and might be the moral equivalent of murder since it is the intentional killing of another person. However, "starvation" in the passive sense is a noun, a state of being. In this sense it is something that happens rather than something that is "inflicted," and is much closer to "letting die" than to murder. This distinction is important according to Narveson. With respect to our moral intuitions, we don't treat killing and letting die as a morally equivalent. Even if we think letting someone die is morally problematic, we wouldn't (presumably) recommend life in prison for letting someone on the other side of the world starve – otherwise, wouldn't this entail that nearly all of us are worthy of life sentences in prison?

> As to the first, the argument for nonidentity of the two is straightforward. When you kill someone, you do an act, x, which brings it about that the person is dead when he would otherwise still be alive. You induce a change (for the worse) in his condition. But when you let someone die, this is not so, for she would have died even if you had, say, been in Australia at

---

[386] ibid.

the time. How can you be said to be the "cause" of something which would have happened if you didn't exist?[387]

This is a clever argument. Narveson is claiming that we can demonstrate that killing and letting die are not the same thing by recognizing the different causal relationship someone might have to each.

When you kill someone, you produce a change (i.e. death) that otherwise would not have occurred. When you let someone die, on the other hand, the change occurs completely independently of you. Theoretically, the death would have occurred if you were in a completely different location (e.g. Australia) or even if you never existed in the first place.

He is proposing that there is something conceptually dubious about claiming that you can somehow be the "cause" of something which would have happened even if you had never been born. If you are not meaningfully the cause of the death, then it seems questionable to say that you are morally responsible for it – or at the least it's a very different sort of responsibility than in the case of murder.

In addition to distinguishing different notions of starvation, he also distinguishes "justice" from "charity." Justice is something that is enforceable, that involves behavior subject to constraint, and is rooted in moral obligation. Justice refers to what is required of us. If we fail to do what justice requires, we have done something morally wrong, and we are justifiably subject to moral condemnation. Charity, on the other hand, he regards as something voluntary, and rooted in "feeling" rather than obligation.

For Narveson, the basic issues are as follows:

1. Is there a basic duty of justice to feed the starving?

2. If not, is there a basic requirement of charity to do so (and how strong is that requirement)?

In short, Narveson's answer to both of those questions appears to be "no." His justification for this is rooted in what he calls the "liberty" approach to these issues – an approach known as Libertarianism in the political realm.

The most plausible answer, I think, is the point of view that allows different people to live their various lives, by forbidding interference with the lives of others. Rather than insisting, with threats to back it up, that I help someone for whose projects and purposes I have no sympathy whatever, let us all agree to respect each other's pursuits. We'll agree to let each person live as that person sees fit, with only our bumpings into each other being subject to public control. To do this, we need to draw a sort of line around each person, and insist that others not cross that line without the permission of the occupant. The rule will be not to forcibly intervene in the lives of others, thus requiring that our relations be mutually agreeable. Enforced feeding of the starving, however, does cross the line, invading the farmer or the merchant, forcing him to part with some of his hard-earned produce and give it without compensation to others. That, says the advocate of liberty, is theft, not charity.[388]

Generally speaking, this libertarian approach recommends that people be allowed to conduct their lives as they see fit so long as they are not harming anyone else. People will be allowed to live their life, and to spend their money, as they choose without interference from others.

Requiring someone to provide food for the

---

[387] All quotations attributed to Narveson are from the following source: Jan Narveson. *Moral Matters*, Broadview Press; 2nd edition (1999). Chapter 7. A copy of the entire chapter is available here: http://www.csus.edu/indiv/g/gaskilld/ethics/feeding%20the%20hungry%20mm%2099.htm

[388] ibid.

hungry against their will is a violation of this liberty approach, an unjustified encroachment into the private life of someone else. Obviously, people should be free to voluntarily donate their money as they see fit, including famine relief. But, since we do not have a moral obligation to keep others alive by paying for their food, we are not violating any moral requirements if we choose not to do so, and we are therefore not subject to forced compliance (e.g. through taxation) if we do not. To put it bluntly, if I never had an obligation to do something, you are not justified in forcing me to do it.

From Narveson's perspective, this approach avoids concerns about utility calculations entirely, since it does not consider utility in the first place. The debate between Singer and Hardin concerning whether feeding the starving maximizes utility or merely postpones (and increases) suffering is neatly sidestepped. In addition, this approach avoids what Narveson derisively calls the "ethics of the hair shirt."

For the sake of context, a "hair shirt" refers to a shirt of hair cloth, formerly worn by penitents and esthetic monks in religious communities. The shirt was intentionally uncomfortable so as to provide "mortification of the flesh." Today, the term also is used as an adjective to refer to austere and self-sacrificing personalities or lifestyles. The way Narveson is using the term, the "ethics of the hair shirt" seems to refer to an understanding of moral obligation that places us in the service of others at the cost of our own enjoyment and personal interests.

> In stark contrast to the liberty-respecting view stands the idea that we are to count the satisfactions of others as equal in value to our own. If I can create a little more pleasure for some stranger by spending my dollar on him than if I would create for myself by spending it on an ice cream cone, I then have a putative obligation to spend it on him. Thus I am to continually defer to others in the organization of my activities, and shall be assailed by guilt whenever I

> am not bending my energies to the relief of those allegedly less fortunate than I. "Benefit others, at the expense of yourself -- and keep doing it until you are as poor and miserable as those whose poverty and misery you are supposed to be relieving!" That is the ethics of the hair shirt. How should we react to this idea? Negatively, I suggest. Doesn't that view really make us the slaves of the (supposedly) less well off?[389]

Ayn Rand famously argued that "altruistic" ethical theories (including, specifically, utilitarianism) were misguided and harmful because they obligate us to the service of others, and require us to sacrifice our own lives and own interests for the sake of anyone else who might have some sort of "need." Like Rand, Narveson is proposing that it is perfectly legitimate to favor your own life and your own interests over those of others, and that you are not morally obligated to sacrifice those interests, even if they are "trivial" or of no "comparable moral importance."

Narveson appeals to what he thinks are common intuitions to reject Singer's claim that his moral principle does not recognize the legitimacy of "proximity."

> Normal people care more about some people than others, and build their very lives around those carings. It is both absurd and arrogant for theorists, talking airily about the equality of all people, to insist on cramming it down our throats - which is how ordinary people do see it.[390]

For example, a parent might honestly care considerably more about celebrating a daughter's *fiesta de quince años* than in saving the life of a hungry child on the other side of the world. Undoubtedly, the money that will be spent celebrating that daughter's birthday could be donated to a charitable organization and possibly literally save the life of another child, at least for a time. Singer and Narveson would draw

---

[389] ibid.

[390] ibid.

profoundly different conclusions concerning this example.

From Singer's perspective, the fiesta is not of comparable moral significance to the life of that hungry child, and for that reason it is morally unjustifiable to dedicate resources for a coming-of-age party when it could be spent to save a person's life instead.

Narveson, on the other hand, doesn't recognize the moral obligation to save that hypothetical child in the first place, and while it might be very nice to donate the money instead, it is both reasonable and justifiable to celebrate the birthday instead.[391] That being said, Narveson does acknowledge that in some circumstances some amount of aid is probably morally appropriate.

> *But the anti-welfarist idea can be taken too far as well. Should people be disposed to assist each other in time of need? Certainly they should. But the appropriate rule for this is not that each person is duty-bound to minister to the poor until he himself is a pauper or near-pauper as well. Rather, the appropriate rule is what the characterization, "in time of need" more nearly suggests. There are indeed emergencies in life when a modest effort by someone will do a great deal for someone else. People who aren't ready to help others when it is comparatively easy to do so are people who deserve to be avoided when they themselves turn to others in time of need.[392]*

By way of analogy, in my capacity as a professor I am sometimes asked to do things that technically fall outside my job description. Sometimes this is as simple as a student asking for directions to find a particular office on campus. I think providing whatever assistance I'm capable of in such circumstances is the decent thing to do, and I don't mind doing it, to be honest. Some sort of extreme stance according to which I refuse to even point a student in the right direction because to do so is making an unjustifiable demand of me seems to be a bit "extra." At the same time, if an endless stream of students came to me asking for directions, and I made a point to help every single one of them, every day, find where they need to go, at a certain point I wouldn't even be able to do my actual job, moral obligations notwithstanding.

Similarly, Narveson suggests that it might be a decent and appropriate thing to occasionally help someone in need when the need is urgent, and it is an "emergency." He rejects, however, the idea that we are obligated to make ourselves *equally needy* by virtue of continuing to help others out of our own resources.

One final issue that Narveson considers is more practical than philosophical – though it does have a connection to determining whether or not helping others in need is appropriate. Narveson points out that starvation is often the result of politics (e.g. corruption, war, etc.) rather than a lack of resources.

For example, from 1994 to 1998, at least a half million people (and possibly as many as a million) died from starvation in North Korea. This was the result of a combination of factors including draught, economic mismanagement, and an autocratic government that focused on military spending rather than food production and famine relief.

More than two billion dollars in international food aid was sent to mitigate the severity of the famine. Decades later, little has changed, with the North Korean government spending roughly 25% of its GDP on the military, while 41% of the population is undernourished.[393] As of 2017, many North Korean bellies remained hungry while the government conducted numerous tests of ICBMs. Meanwhile, Russia provided 5,200 tons

---

[391] This distinction between what would be "nice" and what is "morally required" is reminiscent of Thomson's argument for the moral permissibility of abortion from a previous chapter.

[392] ibid.

[393] http://www.bbc.com/news/world-asia-39349726

of flour in food aid.[394] We can easily imagine Hardin calculating that providing food aid to North Korea merely enables the North Korean government to continue to neglect its own people for the sake of military spending, and will ultimately increase suffering over time. Similarly, from Narveson's perspective, "helping" is not identical to "giving free food" in such cases, and food-relief to North Korea would probably not qualify as a suitable "emergency in life."

In contrast, more legitimate inspiration for charity would be natural disasters which cause short-term (and solvable) problems. For example, consider the 2017 flooding of Houston Texas neighborhoods. "Relief" in that case amounts to *temporary* distributions of food, water, and other necessities; *temporary* lodging in shelters, and (in some cases) Federal aid to help businesses and home owners repair flood damage. For those who choose to help, the need is urgent, and there is an "end in sight" with regard to that need, as opposed to an endless need that will always have to be filled.

Narveson neatly and conveniently summarizes himself as follows:

The basic question . . . is whether the hungry have a positive right to be fed. Of course we have a right to feed them if we wish, and they have a negative right to be fed. But may we forcibly impose a duty on others to feed them? We may not. If the fact that others are starving is not our fault, then we do not need to provide for them as a duty of justice. To think otherwise is to suppose that we are, in effect, slaves to the badly off. And so we can in good conscience spend our money on the opera instead of on the poor. Even so, feeding the hungry and taking care of the miserable is a nice thing to do, and is morally recommended. Charity is a virtue. Moreover, starvation turns out to be almost entirely a function of bad governments, rather than nature's inability to accommodate the burgeoning masses. Our charitable instincts can handle easily the problems that are due to natural disaster. We can feed the starving and go to the opera![395]

The moral status of helping others in need is an issue that is urgent, timely, ever-present, and comprehensive. It reaches into massive political and economic issues such as health care and "entitlement" programs, tax policies, international aid, population control, reproductive choice, and foreign intervention. It touches us at the ballot box when we are voting our conscience, and on street corners when we see someone asking for money. Whether we find ourselves in the "privileged" position of being asked, or as the person in need of help, the issue is effectively impossible to escape (though many find ways to ignore it).

There are a variety of ways we might interpret the issue of helping the needy, and more possible answers as to whether we are morally obligated to do so than could possibly be addressed in this one, modest chapter. For our purposes, we considered Singer's utilitarian answer, Hardin's complication of that answer, and Narveson's libertarian rebuttal. What do *you* think?

Critical Analysis

1. In your opinion, what are the strongest and most compelling points made by the philosopher or philosophers in this chapter? Why do you find those points to be convincing?

2. In your opinion, what are the weakest or least convincing points? Why? Can you anticipate any limitations or objections to their ideas not already addressed in the chapter?

---

[394] http://english.yonhapnews.co.kr/search1/26 03000000.html?cid=AEN20170718011600315

[395] Narveson, ibid.

Appendix: Application to Social Justice

In a sense, this appendix is redundant, given that whether or not those in need should be cared for by those whose needs are met is very clearly already a social justice issue.

It's undeniable that there are people who are food, shelter, and medicine insecure at every level; locally, nationally, and internationally. All sorts of questions arise as to the *causes* of these insecurities, and those questions take us through disciplines such as political science, economics, psychology, and sociology, among others. Economics can further help us assess what sorts of interventions would have what sorts of effects on economies, and political science can tell us what sorts of policies would be required to achieve whatever desired outcome we specify. What none of those disciplines can tell us, however, is anything pertaining to the *moral* dimensions of helping those in need.

Do people with food/housing/medicine insecurities *deserve* to be helped by those whose needs are already met? Even if they don't "deserve" our help, is it nevertheless at least either good or right to help anyway? What sort of help is the (morally) "right" sort to provide? Are there limits? Am I morally obligated to give every bit of resource that I have that goes beyond the bare minimum needed to survive until every need is met, or until I'm only barely more "secure" than those who still need help? Those are the sorts of questions addressed already in this chapter, and the different approaches that we've considered can be easily extrapolated and applied to other, similar issues.

- Do we have a moral obligation to help those in need in our own community?
- What about those in other countries?
- What about people in our community who are undocumented?
- What sorts of things present a genuine need that we are obligated to meet? Surely there are obvious necessities of life, such as food, potable water, shelter, and medicine, but what about education?

- It's obvious that some people are "less fortunate" as a result of being a member of a historically and/or currently marginalized or otherwise oppressed group. If we have identified that we are morally obligated to help the "less fortunate," in general, would that extend to an obligation to dismantle and correct for systemic racism (or other forms of prejudice)?

Those are just a handful of relevant questions, and there are many more that could be added to our list. For any such question, we can try to imagine the sort of response a philosopher we considered would gave based on the general framework they have offered. As a *very* brief paraphrase:

- Singer: As a utilitarian, he proposes that "if it is in our power to prevent something bad from happening, without thereby sacrificing anything of comparable moral importance, we ought, morally, to do it." What will qualify as "comparable value" will be debatable, of course, but Singer consistently asserts that maintaining any standard of living above subsistence is not of "comparable value" to the very lives of people in need. Very generally, then, it's safe to say that Singer would support even very aggressive wealth redistribution if it's necessary to provide at least the basic necessities to those in need.
- Hardin: Hardin's "lifeboat" ethics offers a basically utilitarian view as well, but comes to a very different conclusion. He assumes that there are underlying causes of "need" that won't be eliminated simply by providing the things that are needed to those who need them. In other words, if someone is food insecure, homeless, without medical insurance, etc., there are *reasons* for that. Giving a hungry person food today won't stop them from being hungry *tomorrow* if the underlying cause of their hunger isn't resolved as well. Hardin seems to think that these causes are often

what we might call "poor life choices." Those making poor choices might be those in need themselves, such as if someone who doesn't have enough money to meet their needs is in that predicament because they spend their money on unnecessary things instead, or because of addiction, or because they didn't show personal responsibility and lost their job as a result, or because they dropped out of school and don't qualify for more secure employment, etc. It's also possible that "poor choices" are being made by politicians and, as a result, there is an affordable housing problem in the community, etc. Failing to resolve the underlying poor choices will simply perpetuate the problem, and therefore won't actually promote the "greater good." This doesn't mean that no assistance at all should be provided under any circumstances, but at minimum it means that such assistance should be carefully tailored to resolve the root causes of the problem in the first place.

- Narveson: The libertarian perspective offered by Narveson claims that we are not *obligated* to help others in need so long as we are not personally responsible for their need in the first place. If someone wants to help those in need, despite not being obligated to do so, that's perfectly fine— but he thinks it's morally unjustified to force people to lend assistance if they don't want to. Collecting taxes, for example, to fund public assistance for those in need is "theft" rather than "charity," according to Narveson.

Having been reminded of the basic positions of each of these thinkers, you can now try to imagine how each might evaluate various social justice issues, and the possible responses to them. I also encourage you to try to figure out your own response to their respective positions. With whom do you find yourself most in agreement? With whom do you most disagree? If nothing else, figuring that out will help you to identify and clarify your own moral intuitions, and facilitate your own evaluation of social justice issues, and

how we ought to respond to them.

Chapter 15: The First Ethics Debate?
Bartolomé de Las Casas v. Juan Ginés de Sepúlveda

Comprehension questions you should be able to answer after reading this chapter:

1. In what ways were the accounts of the accomplishments and capacities of the indigenous people of the Americas inconsistent and even contradictory? What might account for these different accounts?
2. What was the purpose of the debate at Vallodolid? Who were the two debaters, and for what position did each argue?
3. Explain Sepúlveda's argument that the Native Americans were "natural slaves."
4. Explain Las Casas' classification of "barbarians," and how he claimed that the Native Americans did not meet the criteria for any of those categories.
5. What was Las Casas' explanation for why some people were describing the Native population as uncivilized and savage?
6. What is Aristotle's definition of a "natural slave?" What are the different interpretations of being "entirely without the faculty of deliberation," as discussed in this chapter? Which interpretation do you think seems most plausible, and why?
7. How have Aristotle's arguments concerning "natural slaves" been used by later generations and cultures?

The Debate in Vallodolid

The "colonial period" spanned from 1492 to 1832 and was a period of unprecedented slaughter in which entire civilizations were wiped out and literally millions of indigenous people were murdered, died from disease, were displaced from their homes, or were enslaved.

Seemingly from any perspective, these events would be considered morally abhorrent to say the least, but the allegedly questionable moral status of the indigenous people allowed the colonizers to rationalize their cruelty. The invasion and conquest of the conquistadors not only resulted in the genocide of millions of people, and the destruction of various cultures, but is also widely regarded as marking the "birth" of modern racism.

Psychologists and historians have long understood the role of dehumanizing groups of people in order to rationalize one's own inhumane treatment of them. To rationalize conquest, imperialism, colonialism, slavery, the removal of indigenous people from their ancestral lands, and numerous other shameful actions, it was necessary to portray the victims as uncivilized, savages, less than human. The debate at Vallodolid gave serious intellectual and academic consideration to the idea that the indigenous people of the Western Hemisphere were not fully human.

Accounts of the indigenous people and their capacities varied tremendously. In 1525, the Dominican Tomás Ortiz said that the Indians "are incapable of learning....They exercise none of the humane arts or industries....The older they get the worst they behave. About the age of ten or twelve years they seem to have some civilization, but later they become like a real brute beast....God has never created a race more full of vice... The Indians are more stupid than asses and refuse to improve in anything."[396]

---

[396] Hanke, Lewis. *All Mankind Is One. A Study of the Disputation Between Bartolomé de Las Casas and Juan Ginés de Sepúlveda on the Religious and Intellectual Capacity of the American Indians.* Northern Illinois University Press, 1974: 11-12

While such racist accounts were all too common, they were not the exclusive perspective among Spaniards in general, or even conquistadors in particular. In contrast, the conquistador Bernal Diaz del Castillo described the capacities of Indians rather differently when he saw the Aztec capital, Tenochtitlán.

Gazing on such wonderful sites we did not know what to say or whether what appeared before us was real; from the one hand there were great cities in the lake ever so many more, and the lake itself was crowded with canoes, and in the causeway were many bridges at intervals, and in front of us to the great city of Mexico, and we… We did not even number four hundred soldiers.[397]

In 1532 and 1533 the "Council of the Indies" convened and concluded that the native population was competent and rational, and capable of self-governance. The Franciscan priest Jocobo de Testera said the following in 1533.

How can anyone say that these people are incapable, when they constructed such impressive buildings, made such subtle creations, were silversmiths, painters, merchants, able in presiding, in speaking, in the exercise of courtesy, in fiestas, marriages, solemn occasions, perceptions of distinguished personages; able to express sorrow, and appreciation, when the occasion requires it and, finally, very ready to be educated in the ethical, political, and economic aspects of life? What cannot we say concerning the people of this land? They sing plainsong and contrapuntally to organ accompaniment, they compose music and teach others how to enjoy religious music, they preach to the people the sermons we teach them; they confessed freely and earnestly in a pure and simple manner.[398]

The basic question before the "Council of the Fourteen" was whether it was morally justifiable to wage war and conquer the Indians of the Americas *before* preaching the Christian faith to them, in order to subjugate them so that they would be more easily converted to the faith later.

In the year 1550, a great debate was organized and executed in the city of Vallodolid in the kingdom of Spain. That city still exists, and is the facto capital of the autonomous community of Castile and León.

For the first (known, recognized, and recorded a) time, a global power organized a formal debate to determine whether its foreign-policy (in this case, colonialism and exploitation of the indigenous people of the Americas) was morally justifiable.

Charles V, the Holy Roman Emperor, and the most powerful ruler in Europe, ordered his overseas conquests to be suspended until it was determined if the cause was just. Sadly, this might also have been the first time (at least in the modern era) that a formal effort was made to identify an entire race of people as naturally inferior. The two participants in this debate were Bartolomé de Las Casas and Juan Ginés de Sepúlveda. Sepúlveda would argue that such actions were justifiable, while Las Casas would argue that they are not.

On the first day of the debate, Sepúlveda spoke for three hours, getting a summary of his previously written treatise that drew heavily upon Aristotle to justify "natural slavery." On the second day, Las Casas began to read his own manuscript word for word. This continued for five straight days. Not surprisingly, the Council requested that one of their members produce a condensed summary of the two arguments!

Las Casas was not officially or professionally a philosopher, theologian, jurist, politician, or bureaucrat. He was, however a very prolific and passionate author and activist who was very well educated and constructed sophisticated and systematic arguments in defense of his position. His argument relied on both scholarly sources as well as his own personal experience in the

---

[397] ibid., 12.

[398] ibid., 14

Americas under Spanish rule.

Sepúlveda, in contrast, had never been to America, but was a respected and politically connected scholar whose writings on law, philosophy, and history were considered important in his time. Among his works were translations of several works of Aristotle, including his Politics. Seventeen years before the famous debate, Sepúlveda wrote a book called "Of the Conformity of the Militia with the Christian Religion" (also referred to as *Democrates Primus*) in which he justified the wars (including religious wars) of Spanish King Charles V.

In 1544, he applied the same structure of justification to the wars against the indigenous people of the Americas, writing "*Of the Just Causes of War against Indians*" (also known as *Democrates Secundus*). Las Casas publicly opposed the publication of that work, and it was actually banned from printing in Spain. Undaunted, Sepúlveda sent it to Rome to be printed instead. It was from this work that he generated his defense of the Spanish activities against the indigenous people of America in 1550.[399]

Interestingly, *both* men claimed victory after the debate – though no records of any official judgment are available to verify either claim. Although no record of the final judgment is available, there are detailed accounts of the arguments made by both men. We will first consider the arguments made by Sepúlveda, and then consider the rebuttal offered by Las Casas.

Sepúlveda's Argument

Sepúlveda argued for his position for a total of three hours, summarizing and commenting on *Democrates Secundus*, and arguing for the general inferiority of the Native Americans. In making his case, he drew explicitly and heavily on Aristotle's

theory of "natural slaves." Sepúlveda had translated Aristotle's *Politics*, and had dedicated the translation to Prince Philip of Spain.

Sepúlveda's general strategy was to attempt to demonstrate that the native people of the Americas were "barbarians" according to Aristotle's concept, and were therefore "natural slaves" who are not only justifiably enslaved, but even improved as a result of their servitude. If they resisted servitude under Spanish rule, it was legitimate for the Spaniards to wage war in order to conquer them and force them into submission.

The indigenous people were humans who were governed by "passion" rather than reason according to Sepúlveda, thereby meeting Aristotle's standard of a barbarian/natural slave. They "being slaves by nature, [the Indians], uncivilized, barbarian and inhuman, refused to accept the rule of those civilized [the Spaniards] and with much more power than them."[400]

Some relevant excerpts follow:

LEOPOLD And who is born under such an unlucky star that nature condemned him to servitude? What difference do you find between having nature force one under the rule of another and being a slave by nature? Do you think that judges, who also pay much attention to natural law in many cases, are joking when they point out that all men since the beginning were born free, and that slavery was introduced contrary to nature and as a law of mere humans?

DEMOCRATES I believe that the jurist speaks with seriousness and great prudence, but this word slavery means quite a different thing for the jurist than for the philosopher. For the former slavery is an accidental thing, born of superior

[399] Parise, Agustin. "The Vallodid Controversy Revisited: Looking Back At The Sixteenth Century Debate On Native Americans While Facing the Current Status Of Human Embryos." *Journal of Civil Law Studies*, Volume 1 (1) Civil Law Workshop, Robert A Pascale Series, Revisiting the Distinction Between Persons and

Things, Article 7. 2008.

[400] Juan Gines de Sepúlveda, *Tratado sobre las Justas Causas de la Guerra contra Los Indios*, translated by Marcelino Menendez y Pelayo and Manuel Garcia-Pelayo (Mexico D.F.: Fondo de Cultura Económica, 1941): 153.

strength and from the laws of peoples, sometimes from civil laws, while philosophers see slavery as inferior intelligence along with inhuman and barbarous customs....

Those who surpass the rest in prudence and talent, although not in physical strength, are by nature the masters. Those, on the other hand, who are retarded or slow to understand, although they may have the physical strength necessary for the fulfillment of all their necessary obligations, are by nature slaves, and it is proper and useful that they be so, for we even see it sanctioned in divine law itself, because it is written in the Book of Proverbs that he who is a fool shall serve the wise.... If they reject such rule, then it can be imposed upon them by means of arms, and such a war will be just according to the laws of nature. Aristotle said, "It seems that war arises in a certain sense from nature, since a part of it is the art of the hunt, which is properly used not only against animals, but also against those men who, having been born to obey, reject servitude: such a war is just according to nature.... "...

LEOPOLD According to your opinion, Democrates, in order for a war to be considered just, a worthy aim and upright conduct are required, but this war against the barbarians, as I understand it, is not even undertaken with good intentions, since those who have started it have no other aim than that of acquiring, by right or wrong, the largest possible amount of gold and silver.... And since the Spanish do not wage this war justly or rationally, but with great cruelty and injury to the barbarians, and in the manner of a theft, there is no doubt that the Spanish are obliged to restore to the barbarians the things which they have seized, no less than must highwaymen what they have robbed from travelers.

DEMOCRATES One who condones the rule of a prince or nation over his or its citizens and subjects, Leopold, must not therefore have it thought that he approves of the sins of all their prefects and ministers.... And indeed it is not certain that everyone has waged war in this fashion if various reports which I have recently read concerning the conquest of New Spain [Mexico] are true....

You can well understand, Leopold, if you know the customs and manners of different peoples, that the Spanish have a perfect right to rule these barbarians of the New World and the adjacent islands, who in prudence, skill, virtues, and humanity are as inferior to the Spanish as children to adults, or women to men, for there exists between the two as great a difference as between savage and cruel races and the most merciful, between the most intemperate and the moderate and temperate and, I might even say, between apes and men. . . .

Compare, then, these gifts of prudence, talent, magnanimity, temperance, humanity, and religion with those possessed by these half-men (homunculi), in whom you will barely find the vestiges of humanity, who not only do not possess any learning at all, but are not even literate or in possession of any monument to their history except for some obscure and vague reminiscences of several things put down in various paintings; nor do they have written laws, but barbarian institutions and customs. Well, then, if we are dealing with virtue, what temperance or mercy can you expect from men who are committed to all types of intemperance and base frivolity, and eat human flesh? And do not believe that before the arrival of the Christians they lived in that pacific kingdom of Saturn which the poets have invented; for, on the contrary, they waged continual and ferocious war upon one another with such fierceness that they did not consider a victory at all worthwhile *unless they sated their monstrous hunger with the flesh of their enemies.... Although some of them show a certain ingenuity for various works of artisanship, this is no proof of human cleverness, for we can observe animals, birds, and spiders making certain structures which no human accomplishment can competently imitate."*[401]

In summary, Sepúlveda is drawing on (his interpretation of) Aristotle to claim that human beings exist along a range of capacities. Some human beings, while technically "human" are closer to "beasts" than to "men." The indigenous people of the Americas just so happen to meet that description, and it is therefore morally justifiable for the (superior) Spaniards to use force to conquer and rule over them.

Las Casas' Rebuttal

Las Casas might have been an unlikely champion for the rights of indigenous people, given that he started out as one of the very people who exploited them! He arrived on the island of Hispaniola in 1502, and by his own admission obtained Indian slaves, and put them to work in mines and on his own prosperous estate. In 1512, he participated in the conquest of the island of Cuba and was given land and an *"encomienda"* as a reward.

An encomienda was a system in which people were given as grants. Somewhat similar to European serfdom, "distinguished" individuals would be given a grant, by the Spanish Crown, of a particular number of natives from a particular community. The particular natives would be determined by the local indigenous community, and would provide labor to their "Lord" in exchange for protection against pirates/bandits/etc. as well as instruction in the Christian faith. This was slavery by another name, and rationalized by a variety of means. Las Casas eventually changed his mind about the legitimacy of this system, and gave up his encomienda in 1515, thereafter spending the rest of his life advocating on behalf of the indigenous people of the Americas.

In systematic fashion, he attempted to demonstrate his opponent was both mistaken about Aristotle, and mistaken in his application of Aristotle to the Indians. "Not all barbarians are irrational or natural slaves or unfit for government. Some barbarians, in accordance with justice in nature, have kingdoms, Royal dignities, jurisdiction, and good laws, and there is among them lawful government."[402]

Las Casas described Aristotle's understanding of "barbarians" (as supplemented by St. Thomas Aquinas) as consisting of several different kinds.

1. Those who are barbarians because of their savage (violent and wicked) behavior.

These are literally "savage" people. Las Casas points out that such barbarians exist everywhere, and are not confined to the Americas. He acknowledged the "savage" behavior of some of the Indigenous cultures (including human sacrifice) but pointed out that not only was such behavior not representative of the indigenous people in general, but that such "savagery" has been known throughout all the world and throughout all history, including "civilized" Christian nations. In fact, he claimed that by virtue of their treatment of the Indians, the Spaniards have "surpassed all other barbarians" in this regard!

2. Those who are barbarians because they lack written language.

The second referred to people without a written language (despite having a spoken language) – in other words, preliterate people. This category of "barbarian," according to Las Casas, not only does not justify the designation of "natural slave" but is also inapplicable to the indigenous people of the Americas given the complexity and rationality of their language.

---

[401] Parise, ibid.

[402] Hanke, 75.

3. Those who are *truly* barbarians (and therefore legitimately natural slaves) "either because of their evil and wicked character or the barrenness of the region in which they live....They lack the reasoning and way of life suited to human beings....They have no laws which they fear or by which all other affairs are regulated... They lead a life very much that of brute animals....Barbarians of this kind (or better, wild men) are rarely found in any part of the world and are few in number when compared with the rest of mankind."[403]

The third category referred to people who had no sense of justice or of community. Such persons are truly barbarians (in that sense) because they "have no laws which they fear or by which all their affairs are regulated . . . they lead a life very much that of brute animals. . . . Barbarians of this kind (or better, wild men) are rarely found in any part of the world and are few in number when compared to the rest of mankind."[404]

Indeed, Las Casas thought the rarity of such persons made the very condition of natural slavery too infrequent and improbably to be useful. "It would be impossible to find one whole race, nation, region, or country anywhere in the world that is slow-witted, moronic, foolish, or stupid, or even not having for the most part sufficient natural knowledge and ability to rule and govern oneself."[405] He certainly thought that this category of barbarian did not apply to the indigenous Americans, as they certainly had both a sense of justice as well as sophisticated

civilizations prior to Spanish contact.

In his *De Unico Vocationis Modo*, Las Casas gives his account of both the treatment and motivation of the Indians by their conquerors.

> *Worldly, ambitious men who sought wealth and pleasure placed their hope in obtaining gold and silver by the labor and sweat, even through very harsh slavery, oppression, and death, of not only innumerable people that of the greater part of humanity; they devise the means to hide their tyranny and injustices and to justify themselves in their own light.*
>
> *This is the way they work it out: to assert falsely that the Indians were so lacking in the reason common to all men that they were not able to govern themselves and thus needed tutors. And the insolence and madness of these men became so great that they did not hesitate to allege that the Indians were beasts or almost beasts, and publicly defamed them. Then they claimed that it was just to subject them to our rule by war, or to hunt them like beasts and then reduce them to slavery. Thus they could make use of the Indians at their pleasure.*
>
> *But the truth is that very many of the Indians were able to govern themselves in monastic, economic, and political life. They could teach us and civilize us, however, and even more, would dominate us by natural reason as of the Philosopher said speaking of Greeks and barbarians.*[406]

In other words, accounts of the indigenous people being mentally and morally incompetent,

---

[403] ibid, 83. There is also, technically, a fourth type of "barbarian" which clearly was not originally found in Aristotle: people who did not acknowledge Christ (i.e., non-Christians). Las Casas claimed that Aristotle's formulation (whether correct or not) simply did not apply to the indigenous Americans. While they were not (yet) Christian, he was confident that as a people they were receptive to the faith and that many

had converted, and even more would have converted, if not for the cruelty of their "Christian" Spanish oppressors.)

[404] Quoted in ibid, 83.

[405] Las Casas, *In Defense of the Indians.* Translated and edited by Stafford Poole, C.M. DeKalb: Northern Illinois University Press, 1974: 38

[406] Hanke, 157.

and uncivilized and incapable of civilizing themselves, were simply not true and were driven by plain old-fashioned greed. This sort of rationalization emerges as a predictable pattern, and would not confined to the Americas. In the sixteenth century, English investors look to Ireland for land and resources, and soon enough propaganda developed according to which the Irish (though Catholic) were not actually "Christian," and were unfit stewards of their own land.

> If [they] themselves were suffered to possess the whole country as their septs have done for many hundred of years past, they would never (to the end of the world) build houses, make townships or villages or manure or improve the land as it ought to be, therefore it stands neither with Christian policy nor conscience to suffer so good and fruitful a country to lie waste like the wilderness.[407]

Las Casas supported his perspective by giving numerous examples of the nature and accomplishments of the Indians.

> [They have] important kingdoms, large numbers of people who live settled lives in a society, great cities, kings, judges and laws, persons who engage in commerce, buying, selling, lending, and the other contracts of the law of nations, will it not stand proved that the Reverend Doctor Sepúlveda has spoken wrongly and viciously against peoples like these, either out of malice or ignorance of Aristotle's teaching, and, therefore, has falsely and perhaps irreparably slander them before the entire world? From the fact that the Indians are barbarians it does not necessarily follow that they are incapable of government and have to be ruled by

> others, except to be taught about the Catholic faith and to be admitted to the holy sacraments. They are not ignorant, inhuman, or bestial. Rather, long before they had heard the word Spaniard, they had properly organized states, widely ordered by excellent laws, religion, and custom. They cultivated friendship and, bound together in common fellowship, lived in populous cities in which they wisely administer the affairs of both peace and war justly and equitably, truly governed by laws which at very many points surpass ours, and could have won the admiration of the sages of Athens, as I will show in the second part of this defense.[408]

> Not only have [the Indians] shown themselves to be very wise peoples and possessed of lively and marked understanding, prudently governing and providing for their nations (as much as they can be nations, without faith in or knowledge of the true God) and making them prosper in justice; but they have equaled many diverse nations of the world, past and present, that have been praised for their governance, politics and customs, and exceed by no small measure the wisest of all these, such as the Greeks and Romans, in adherence to the rules of natural reason.[409]

In summary, with respect to Aristotle's definition of natural slavery, Las Casas argued "it does not apply to the Indians, because they are not stupid, no without sufficient judgment to govern their households, as has been proved. On this subject we have already written in our *Apologia*, written in Spanish, as well as in Latin in our work *De Unico Vocationis Modo*, and in another book in Spanish entitled *Apologetica Historia* in which I describe in detail and at length

---

[407] Quoted in Lyons, Oren R. "The American Indian in the Past," in *Exiled in the Land of the Free. Democracy, Indian Nations, and the U.S. Constitution.* Edited by chief Oren Lyons and

John Mohawk. Clear light publishers, Santa Fe. 1992: 25-26.
[408] Hanke., 75-76.
[409] ibid., 77.

the customs, life, religion, government, and good breeding which all these people have, some more than others as the Bishop stated. Some few have not yet reached the perfection of an ordered government, as was the case with all peoples of the world in the beginning, but this does not mean that they lack the necessary reason to be easily brought to an orderly, domestic, and political life."[410]

Some relevant additional excerpts of his *In Defense of the Indians* follows:

Now if we shall have shown that among our Indians of the western and southern shores (granting that we call them barbarians and that they are barbarians) there are important kingdoms, large numbers of people who live settled lives in a society, great cities, kings, judges and laws, persons who engage in commerce, buying, selling, lending, and the other contracts of the law of nations, will it now stand proved that the Reverend Doctor Sepúlveda has spoken wrongly and viciously against peoples like these, either out of malice or ignorance of Aristotle's teaching, and, therefore, has falsely and perhaps irreparably slandered them before the entire world? From the fact that the Indians are barbarians it does not necessarily follow that they are incapable of government and have to be ruled by others, except to be taught about the Catholic faith and to be admitted to the holy sacraments. They are not ignorant, inhuman, or bestial. Rather, long before they had heard the word Spaniard they had properly organized states, wisely ordered by excellent laws, religion, and custom. They cultivated friendship and, bound together in common fellowship, lived in populous cities in which they wisely administered the affairs of both peace and war justly and equitably, truly governed by laws that at very many points surpass ours,

and could have won the admiration of the sages of Athens, as I will show in the second part of this Defense....

Next, I call the Spaniards who plunder that unhappy people torturers. Do you think that the Romans, once they had subjugated the wild and barbaric peoples of Spain, could with secure right divide all of you among themselves, handing over so many head of both males and females as allotments to individuals? And do you then conclude that the Romans could have stripped your rulers of their authority and consigned all of you, after you had been deprived of your liberty, to wretched labors, especially in searching for gold and silver lodes and mining and refining the metals? And if the Romans finally did that, as is evident from Diodorus, [would you not judge] that you also have the right to defend your freedom, indeed your very life, by war? Sepúlveda, would you have permitted Saint James to evangelize your own people of Córdoba in that way? For God's sake and man's faith in him, is this the way to impose the yoke of Christ on Christian men? Is this the way to remove wild barbarism from the minds of barbarians? Is it not, rather, to act like thieves, cut-throats, and cruel plunderers and to drive the gentlest of people headlong into despair? The Indian race is not that barbaric, nor are they dull witted or stupid, but they are easy to teach and very talented in learning all the liberal arts, and very ready to accept, honor, and observe the Christian religion and correct their sins (as experience has taught) once priests have introduced them to the sacred mysteries and taught them the word of God. They have been endowed with excellent conduct, and before the coming of the Spaniards, as we have said, they had political states that were well founded on beneficial laws.... From this it is clear that

---

[410] ibid., 79.

the basis for Sepúlveda's teaching that these people are uncivilized and ignorant is worse than false. Yet even if we were to grant that this race has no keenness of mind or artistic ability, certainly they are not, in consequence, obliged to submit themselves to those who are more intelligent and to adopt their ways, so that, if they refuse, they may be subdued by having war waged against them and be enslaved, as happens today. For men are obliged by the natural law to do many things they cannot be forced to do against their will. We are bound by the natural law to embrace virtue and imitate the uprightness of good men. No one, however, is punished for being bad unless he is guilty of rebellion. Where the Catholic faith has been preached in a Christian manner and as it ought to be, all men are bound by the natural law to accept it, yet no one is forced to accept the faith of Christ. No one is punished because he is sunk in vice, unless he is rebellious or harms the property and persons of others. No one is forced to embrace virtue and show himself as a good man. One who receives a favor is bound by the natural law to return the favor by what we call antidotal obligation. Yet no one is forced to this, nor is he punished if he omits it, according to the common interpretation of the jurists.[411]

In summary, Las Casas claims that Sepúlveda has misapplied Aristotle's (irrelevant) notion of "barbarian." There is ample evidence that the indigenous people of the Americas are civilized, sophisticated, and morally competent human beings. Although he certainly advocates that they be converted to the Christian faith, he thinks they should be done through kindness and persuasion rather than violent submission. The use of force by the kingdom of Spain is not morally justifiable in the Americas.

We have considered what two 16th-century Spaniards thought of Aristotle's views on slavery, but when possible it is prudent to consider the primary source itself. Fortunately, we have the means to do so, so we will now consider what Aristotle had to say about "natural slaves," and you may decide whether either men possessed an accurate understanding and displayed an accurate application.

Aristotle

While several pages of the *Politics* is dedicated to his discussion of slavery, Aristotle is frustratingly vague in what he says. Aristotle described slaves as "animate property."[412] He holds that there are "natural slaves," and he contrasts this with those who become slaves by convention (law). It is always the "natural slave" that he has in mind when defending slavery. A "natural slave" is described as follows:

1. "anybody who by his nature is not his own man, but another's"
2. "anybody who, being a man, is an article of property"[413]

This is embarrassingly circular, of course, if offered as an argument for what makes someone a natural slave. A natural slave is someone who is another man's property? There is nothing yet "natural" about this, since anyone could be captured and placed into a condition of slavery, thereby making a person a "natural slave," by these standards! Fortunately, more detail can be found, particularly if we consult the *Nicomachean Ethics* in addition to the *Politics*.

The many, the most vulgar, would seem to conceive the good of happiness as pleasure, and hence they also like the life of gratification. In this they appear completely slavish, since the life they

---

[411] Las Casas, ibid. This excerpt is available here: https://woodlawnschool.pbworks.com/f/Excerpt+from+In+Defense+of+the+Indians(1550)Bart olom%C3%A9+de+las+Casas'.pdf
[412] Aristotle, *Politics*, 1253b2.
[413] ibid., 1254a6.

decide on is a life for grazing animals.[414]

Aristotle is here describing not actual slaves, but the "slavish" pursuits and pleasures of the "many." From this we can infer what he believes "natural slaves" to be like. He acknowledges that "natural slaves" are humans, but proposes that they have different sorts of capacities that justify their being treated as living instruments. A naturally "slavish" person is focused exclusively on satisfying his or her non-rational desires, and is therefore similar to "beasts." This pursuit of pleasure is all they want, and all they are capable of. As a result of their narrow focus, they lack self-esteem, and will therefore put up with insults in humiliation in ways that others will not.

> *For people who are not angered by the right things, or in the right way, or at the right times, or toward the right people, all seem to be foolish. For such a person seems to be insensible and feel no pain, and since he is not angered, he does not seem to be the sort to defend himself. Such willingness to accept insults to oneself and to overlook insults to one's family and friends is slavish.*[415]

This description actually brings us back to his seemingly circular account of natural slaves from above, in which he seemingly defines a natural slaves simply as one who is property—but his suggestion is that *only* a "natural slave" would endure being the property of another. Someone who is not a "natural slave" would have too much pride to overlook the insult, and would presumably rebel or even commit suicide. If so, then the only people who actually end up as slaves (for long) would be "natural slaves."

Interestingly, Aristotle either contradicts himself, or at least sows the seeds of his own refutation when he describes agricultural work in

his ideal community. "The class which forms it should ideally, and if we can choose it will, be slaves – but slave is not drawn from a single stock, or from stocks of a spirited temper. This will at once secure the advantage of a good supply of labor and eliminate any danger of revolutionary designs. Failing slaves, the next best class will be one of serfs who are not of Greek origin and whose character is like what has just been described. The farmhands employed on private estates should belong to the owners of those estates; those who are employed on public property should belong to the public. How the slaves who till the soil should be treated, and why it is wise to offer all slaves the eventual reward of emancipation, is a matter which we sell discussed later."[416]

Unfortunately, there is no surviving text in which Aristotle fulfills his promise of explaining why slaves should eventually be offered emancipation. For that reason, we can only guess as to his reasons that he might have offered. However, what sense would it make to offer emancipation to a "natural slave," for whom a state of servitude is the best life they can hope for? If there really are such people as "natural slaves," why would emancipation ever be appropriate for them, given the alleged reason for keeping them in slavery in the first place? On the other hand, if it does make sense to offer the reward of emancipation to slaves in the future, this implies that they are capable of living on their own and functioning on their own, which would imply that they are not "natural slaves!"

Beyond claiming that natural slaves are humans who would endure enslavement in the first place, Aristotle also makes some puzzling claims about the capacities of natural slaves. Aristotle claims that makes a human a natural slave is that he (or she) "is entirely without the faculty of deliberation."[417]

For such humans, "the condition of slavery is

---

[414] Aristotle, *Nicomachean Ethics*, 1095b 20

[415] ibid., 1126a5-10.

[416] *Politics*, 1330a13-14.

[417] ibid., 1260a7. He also claims that women have a form of deliberative faculty which is

"inconclusive"—a claim that supports, of course, his claim that males are the natural rulers of females, and that females are generally incapable of the feats of reason that males can perform—a claim that contemporary Aristotle

both beneficial and just."[418] Apparently, a natural slave is some sort of mentally defective human who is *"entirely without"* the ability to deliberate. There are, of course, some people who, as a result of serious developmental delays or mental disorders, are arguably incapable of deliberating on their own behalf. In the vast majority of cases, such persons are in the care of others, wards of the State, supervised in board-and-care facilities, etc. The problem, of course, is that such persons constitute a tiny fraction of the adult population of the adult community, whereas the slave population Aristotle has in mind is larger than the free citizens! Moreover, such "natural slaves," even if they were numerous, would clearly be incapable of performing all the labor (both skilled and unskilled) needed to maintain the community and homes within the *polis*—due to the very cognitive deficiencies that make them "natural slaves" in the first place! Indeed, the impracticality of this has caused some interpreters to conclude that Aristotle actually didn't endorse slavery at all, and that his arguments concerning slavery were actually a subtle form of criticism against the institution!

According to this interpretation, the standards he establishes for natural masters and natural slaves deny rather than establish the existence of actual natural slavery. Wayne Ambler, for example, claims that Aristotle offers an account of natural slavery that is morally justifiable, but unlikely to *ever* be encountered in *actual* houses or cities – and therefore a moot point. As support for this, he points out that Aristotle explicitly acknowledges that not all actual slavery is natural slavery. The standard he provides, however, would require that the relationship between "barbarian" and Greek be analogous to the relationship between the body and the mind. It is natural and proper for the mind to rule the body. This is the iconic example of a ruler/being ruled relationship that Aristotle

offers.[419]

> *As many as differ as much as do soul from body and man from the beast – and they are disposed in this way whose work [ergon] is the use of the body, and this is what is best from them – these are slaves by nature.*[420]

Ambler thinks it is unlikely, however, that any reasonable case could be made that natural slaves are to non-slaves as the body is to the mind. The standard established for a natural slave seem to be that he be human, but is separated from his master (in quality and capacity) as nonhuman animals are from humans. To whom would this *actually* apply?

This seems, to me, to be an overly generous interpretation of a wealthy and privileged aristocrat—that he was somehow secretly progressive and attempting to undermine the social and economic foundation of his entire society, and from which he and his peer group benefitted. This progressive vision of Aristotle is also problematic given that he seemed confident that natural slaves (in sufficient numbers) existed. Why? Because natural slaves are *needed* for at least some human beings to flourish.

> *Upon these principles it clearly follows that a state with an ideal Constitution – a state which has for its members men who are absolutely just, and not men who are merely just in relation to some particular standards – cannot have it citizens living a life of mechanics or shopkeepers, which is ignoble and inimical to goodness. Nor can it have them engaged in farming: leisure is a necessity, both for growth in goodness and for the pursuit of political activities.*[421]

An ideal state, and the flourishing of at least

---

expert and philosopher Martha Nussbaum capably refutes by both *her* standing in the philosophical community as well as the profundity of *her* many books.
[418] ibid., 1255a.

[419] See Ambler, Wayne. "Aristotle on Nature and Politics: the Case of Slavery." *Political Theory*, volume 15 (3) (August 1987): 390 – 410.
[420] *Politics*, 1254b16-19.
[421] ibid., 1329a1.

some individuals, requires that other individuals perform all of the manual labor necessary for the community so that those privileged few may have the leisure time to devote to virtue and philosophical contemplation. Since "nature makes nothing purposeless or in vain,"[422] it stands to reason that natural slaves have been provided for this purpose.

A less radical (and less optimistic) interpretation of Aristotle offered by Malcolm Heath preserves the (unfortunate) elitism of Aristotle's theory while actually retaining its applicability. According to this interpretation, the deficiency from which natural slaves suffer is not a comprehensive cognitive deficiency, but rather a more specific deficiency in their capacity for practical wisdom.[423]

According to Malcolm Heath, Aristotle explicitly states that natural slaves "are human beings, with a share in reason."[424] In the Nicomachean Ethics he likewise acknowledges the humanity of the natural slave.[425]

That being said, he *also* seems to think that the overwhelming majority of the Earth's population consists of "natural slaves!" This would be absurd if it meant that he thought most of the global population was severely developmentally delayed or cognitively impaired.

While Aristotle does refer to non-Greeks as natural slaves, the word that is translated as non-Greek can also be (and is often) translated as "barbarian." The word in Greek is βάρβαρος (transliterated: "*barbaros*"), or βάρβαροι (transliterated: "*barbaroi*").

While "barbarian" has its own connotation today, in Aristotle's time the term simply referred to someone who was not Greek. Admittedly however, there was plenty of ethnocentric judgment involved at that time as well. Barbarians (which is to say anyone who is not Greek!) were allegedly natural slaves, and fit to be ruled by the Greeks. "This is why our poets have said 'meet is it that barbarous peoples should be governed by the Greeks'-- the assumption being that barbarian and slave are by nature one and the same...."[426] Aristotle refers to "distant foreigners" who are lacking in rationality and live by perception alone, like nonhuman animals.[427]

Despite the fact that some barbarians are like nonhuman animals, most are rational (in a sense) and Aristotle explicitly recognizes the accomplishments of certain other cultures. For example, he recognizes the Egyptians for their invention of mathematics (*Metaphysics* 1.1, 981b13-25) and the Babylonians for their accomplishments in astronomy (*On the Heavens*, 2.12, 292a7-9).

If Aristotle did not think that natural slaves (i.e., pretty much anyone who wasn't Greek!) were completely lacking in reason, but nevertheless somehow deficient in reason, what could he mean?

Aristotle distinguishes between several types of reasoning/rationality. Among them are technical, theoretical, and practical reasoning.

Theoretical reasoning is associated with abstract exercises such as mathematics, but is not the sort of reasoning involved in virtuous decision-making.

Technical reasoning is associated with "production," or art/craft (*techne*). Technical reasoning provides hypothetical/conditional imperatives based upon whatever product you are trying to make Production is only instrumentally valuable, based upon the value of whatever is being produced. The virtuous action made possible by practical reasoning, however, is *intrinsically* valuable.

Practical reasoning is the reasoning associated with wisdom, the acquisition of virtue, and living a good life (flourishing, eudaimonia). It provides guidance for life, and enables knowing how to live well.

According to Aristotle, natural slaves are capable of technical reasoning, which is why they are useful as servants. They can be skilled

---

[422] ibid., 1256b20-1.

[423] See Heath, Malcolm. "Aristotle on Natural Slavery." *Phronesis*, volume 53 (3) (2008): 243 – 270.

[424] *Politics*, 1259 b27-8.

[425] *Nicomachean Ethics*, 1161a32-1161b8.

[426] *Politics*, 1252b5-9.

[427] *Nicomachean Ethics*, 1149a9-11.

carpenters, smiths, and even presumably accountants, medical doctors, etc. What they can't do, is live *well* (flourish). Flourishing requires virtuous activity, which itself requires practical reason – something beyond mere technical rationality. When, therefore, Aristotle says that the natural slave "shares in reason to the extent of understanding it, but does not have any himself," he is referring specifically to *practical* reason.

> *But the end of the state is not mere life; it is, rather, a good quality of life. [If your life for the end], there might be a state of slaves, or even a state of animal; but in the world as we know it any such state is impossible, because slaves and animals do not share in true Felicity [eudaimonia] and free choice [i.e. the attributes of a good quality of life].*[428]

> *The slave is entirely without the faculty of deliberation; . . .*[429]

The natural slave is capable of reasoning, but suffers from a diminished capacity. In this sense, they are analogous both to nonhuman animals as well as human children – comparisons that Aristotle makes explicit. Children start out incapable of reasoning in any meaningful sense, including with respect to practical reasoning. Given proper education and training, however, they developed this capability as adults. Nonhuman animals lack the capacity for practical reasoning altogether. Natural slaves are somewhat in between. While they never require the ability to engage in practical reasoning autonomously, they are capable of following instructions provided by fully functioning "Greek" masters, and are therefore somewhat more capable than nonhuman animals.

A far less controversial example of a similar sort of failure of independent reasoning might arise in a math class. I suspect it is not at all uncommon for students in a math class to be incapable (at the time) of solving certain

problems on their own. Nevertheless, when the instructor solves the problem in their presence, they understand each step, and understand that it is the correct method and even that it is the correct answer. Perhaps mysteriously, although they cannot do it on their own, they understand it and recognize it as correct when it is performed by someone else. This is analogous to what Aristotle has in mind with respect to natural slaves and practical reason. While they are incapable of reasoning correctly to virtuous action and a virtuous plan of life on their own, they are capable of executing orders that are given to them, and participating in the virtuous life of their masters.

In summary, natural slaves have an impairment of *practical* reasoning that affects their capacity for deliberation. Although they may be intelligent and skilled in many respects, they can't reason well about virtue and a good life.

What is Aristotle's explanation for this curious and convenient difference in capacities between Greeks and everyone else? Geography and climate.

> *The peoples of cold countries generally, and particularly those of Europe, are full of spirit, but deficient in skill and intelligence; and this is why they continue to remain comparatively free, but attain no political development and show no capacity for governing others. The peoples of Asia are endowed with skill and intelligence, their deficient in spirit; and this is why they continue to be peoples of subjects and slaves. The Greek stock, intermediate in geographical position, unites the qualities of both sets of peoples. It possesses both spirit and intelligence: the one quality makes it continue free; the other enables it to attain the highest political development, and to show capacity for governing every other people – if only you could once achieve political unity. The same sort of difference is that between Greek and non-*

---

[428] *Politics*, 1280a31-4.

[429] ibid., 1260a12.

Greek peoples may also be traced among Greek peoples themselves. Some of them are of a one-sided nature: others show a happy mixture of spirit and intelligence.[430]

People from the cold or "European" climate are spirited/passionate but less intelligent. People from the warmer "Asiatic" climate are intelligent but lacking in spirit/passion. The Greeks, lucky enough to live in a "Golden mean" with respect to climate, are both intelligent and spirited. The quasi-biological/environmental explanation derives from Aristotle's assumption that "excess" in climate must be offset internally. An excessively cold climate requires an increase in internal "heat" (spirit), while an excessively hot climate suppresses that internal heat (diminishing spirit).

The barbarians to the north of Greece come from a colder climate, and therefore are lacking in intelligence while having an excess of spirit. This excess spirit is useful, but only as a tool that requires guidance. Aristotle describes people with excess spirit in the following way. "It is like over hasty servants who run out before they have heard all their instructions, and then carry them out wrongly, or dogs to bark at any noise at all, before looking to see if it is a friend."[431]

Consider the case of courage. *Genuine* displays of courage require deliberate a choice to face something that is properly a source of fear because it is good to do so. Practical reason establishes what is worthy of pursuit and whether or not it is properly a source of fear. Spirit (*thumos*) is then enlisted as support. "Brave men act because of to *kalon* (the good), but *thumos* (spirit) collaborates with them."[432]

Someone motivated to face danger solely by *thumos* without the guidance of practical reason is not displaying genuine courage.[433] In the absence of the contribution of practical reason, the best someone can hope for is to mimic virtuous behavior – but such a person can never

actually act virtuously.

Aristotle's view of natural slaves is not merely a historical curiosity, but had significant and lamentable application millennia later, not only in the rationalization of Spanish colonialism by people like Juan Ginés de Sepúlveda, but also in the context of the enslavement of Africans.

There is one strong argument in favor of negro slavery over all other slavery: that he, being unfitted for the mechanic arts, for trade, and all skillful pursuits, leaves those pursuits to be carried on by the whites; and does not bring all industry into disrepute, as in Greece and Rome, where the slaves were not only the artists and mechanics, but also the merchants.

Whilst, as a general and abstract question, negro slavery has no other claims over other forms of slavery, except that from inferiority, or rather peculiarity, of race, almost all negroes require masters, whilst only the children, the women, the very weak, poor, and ignorant, &c., among the whites, need some protective and governing relation of this kind. . . .[434]

"Modern" (utilitarian) philosopher, John Stuart Mill, acknowledges this unfortunate philosophical "kinship."

There was a time when the division of mankind into two classes, a small one of masters and a numerous one of slaves, appeared, even to the most cultivated minds, to be a natural, and the only natural, condition of the human race. No less an intellect, and one which contributed no less to the progress of human thought, than Aristotle, held this opinion without doubt or misgiving. . . . But why need I go back to Aristotle? Did not the slave owners of the Southern United States

---

[430] ibid., 1327b18-31
[431] *Nicomachean Ethics*, 1149a27-29.
[432] ibid., 1116b30-2.
[433] ibid., 1116b23-7a9.

[434] Fitzhugh, George. *Cannibals All! Or, Slaves Without Masters*: Electronic Edition (1806 - 1881): 297.

maintain the same doctrine, with all the fanaticism with which men cling to the theories that justify their passions and legitimate their personal interests? Did they not call heaven and earth to witness that the dominion of the white man over the black is natural, that the black race is by nature incapable of freedom, and marked out for slavery? some even going so far as to say that the freedom of manual labourers is an unnatural order of things anywhere.[435]

Even Aristotle's climate-based explanation for the "inferiority" of non-Greeks, which might seem laughably naïve and unscientific, has been resurrected *today* by some white supremacists!

In an essay, entitled "Race: Stalking the Wild Taboo", Spencer explains achievement, wealth, and (apparent) intelligence differences between the races as follows:

Perhaps the most important single environmental difference faced by these early humans was that much of the Eurasian landmass turns cold for several months of the year, and food is scarce during this time. It required intelligence, resourcefulness, foresight, and an ability to delay gratification (that is, impulse control), for ancient hunter-gatherers to survive cold winters. People with these qualities were more successful raising children than those who lacked them, so humans in more northerly areas gradually became more intelligent and future-oriented than those who remained in the tropics. The higher intelligence and lower crime rates of Whites and East Asians as compared with Africans may be due in

large part to the selective pressure of cold winters.[436]

Here, he is drawing on the work of Richard Lynn.[437] The basic idea behind Lynn's theory is that "when early peoples migrated from equatorial East Africa into the more northern latitudes of North Africa, South Asia, Europe and Northeast Asia they encountered progressively more cognitively demanding environments that required greater intelligence, including the need to hunt large animals, build fires and shelters and make clothes. The colder the winter temperatures and, the more northerly the environment, and the higher were the IQs that evolved."[438]

Basically, white people come from colder places than black or brown people, and therefore their ancestors were forced (by evolution) to be "smarter" in order to survive. This theoretical explanation for these alleged differences in IQ is not only controversial (to say the least) among scientists, but also seems challenged by common sense and a cursory understanding of history.[439]

The accepted understanding of the evolution of humanity is that all humans alive today are descendants of African ancestors. "H. heidelbergensis" is thought to be the likely ancestor of both modern humans and Neanderthals, and is thought to have migrated from Africa approximately 500,000 years ago. Still within Africa, Homo sapiens diverged roughly 300,000 years ago, and is thought to have migrated roughly 70,000 years ago. Modern humans are thought to have spread across Europe only 40,000 years ago, with migration to the Americas roughly 20,000 years ago.

According to the "cold-weather" theory, the colder temperatures of Europe should have triggered more intelligent humans while those in

---

[435] Mill, John Stuart. *The Subjugation of Women* (1869), paragraph 1.9.

[436] https://nationalpolicy.institute/2017/10/05/race-stalking-the-wild-taboo/

[437] Lynn, Richard. Race Differences in Intelligence: An Evolutionary Analysis, 2nd Revised Edition, Washington Summit Publishers, 2015.

[438] https://www.amren.com/news/2016/07/richard-lynn-on-race-differences-in-intelligence/

[439] https://www.psychologytoday.com/blog/unique-everybody-else/201211/cold-winters-and-the-evolution-intelligence

the warmer climates of Africa and the Middle East, being less intellectually challenged by their environment, would develop less impressive IQ scores. Oddly enough, when we consider the birth of civilization itself, the communities we associate with the development of politics, religion, mathematics, literacy, early science, philosophy, medicine, etc.; they all come from those conspicuously *warm* climates: Babylonia (1895 BCE–619 BCE). Persian Empire (6th century BCE). Ancient Egypt (3150 BCE – 332 BCE). Ancient Greece (480 – 146 BCE).The Roman Republic and Empire (509 BCE – 395 CE).[440]

Their intellectually "superior" counterparts in northern Europe, despite their allegedly genetically superior IQ and tens of thousands of years' worth of evolutionary advantage, were, comparatively speaking, illiterate barbarians during the same time periods. This, in addition to the fact that the civilization of China (with a wide-ranging climate) had been established in the 21st century BCE!

Needless to say, biological/essentialist accounts of racial superiority are as morally and intellectually problematic today as they were in Aristotle's time. As is evident, though, not all of us have advanced in our understanding yet. An unfortunate legacy of Aristotle's work is that some people throughout history (including to this day!) still take seriously his account of racial superiority, and even his suggestion that slavery is *beneficial* for the slave.

For Aristotle, the benefits of slavery for the *master* are pretty obvious: the leisure to devote himself to things intrinsically good, to virtue, and flourishing. A life of theoretical contemplation is the paradigm of an excellent human life in this sense,[441] but a life of political activity is a decent second-best.[442] What about for the slave, though? Arguably, Aristotle's perspective is that being enslaved is also good for the natural slave. Although they are incapable of flourishing for themselves, they can contribute to the good life of their master, and their own life therefore acquires more value.

This notion that certain people are "better off" enslaved rather than free and left to determine their own lives has not disappeared. The conservative cattle rancher Cliven Bundy, made famous for his refusal to pay the Federal Bureau of Land Management fees for his illegal grazing on Federal land for over 20 years, offered his unsolicited opinions on "Negroes" during a television interview in 2017.

> *I want to tell you one more thing I know about the Negro," Bundy said, describing a North Las Vegas public-housing project he apparently used to drive past, where "the door was usually open" and "at least half a dozen people," adults and kids alike, were always sitting on the porch because "they didn't have nothing to do. . . . And because they were basically on government subsidy, so now what do they do?" he continued. "They abort their young children, they put their young men in jail, because they never learned how to pick cotton. And I've often wondered, are they better off as slaves, picking cotton and having a family and doing things, or are they better off under government subsidy? They didn't get no more freedom. They got less freedom.[443]*

Lest we think such views are confined to eccentric cattle ranchers, Trent Franks, the Republican Representative from Arizona, said in 2010 that "far more of the African-American community is being devastated by the policies of today than were being devastated by policies of slavery."

During the 2011 Republican presidential nomination process, both Michele Bachmann and Rick Santorum signed "The Marriage Vow" that included a line about how much stronger African-American families were during the era of slavery.

---

[440] All dates are approximate and very much subject to debate.
[441] *Nicomachean Ethics*, 1178b33

[442] ibid., 1178a9f.
[443] https://www.thedailybeast.com/these-politicians-praise-slavery

Slavery had a disastrous impact on African-American families, yet sadly a child born into slavery in 1860 was more likely to be raised by his mother and father in a two-parent household than was an African-American baby born after the election of the USA's first African American President.[444]

Conservative commentator, writer, and occasional candidate for President Put Buchannan wrote (in a 2008 essay entitled "A Brief for Whitey") that:

America has been the best country on earth for black folks. . . . It was here that 600,000 black people, brought from Africa in slave ships, grew into a community of 40 million, were introduced to Christian salvation, and reached the greatest levels of freedom and prosperity blacks have ever known.[445]

As one final example, in 2012 Republican state Representative Loy Mauch's pro-slavery letters were revealed during his re-election campaign. In one letter, he mused,

If slavery were so God-awful, why didn't Jesus or Paul condemn it, why was it in the constitution and why wasn't there a war before 1861?[446]

Conclusion

The Debate in Vallodolid is potentially fascinating for a variety of reasons. From a historical perspective, as was mentioned at the beginning of this section, it is arguably a "first" in modern European history: the first time a major world power literally suspended an aspect of its foreign-policy to have a sincere debate as to the moral legitimacy of that policy. It is also, arguably, a prime candidate for the first public applied

ethics debate in modern European history.

From a philosophical perspective, it offers an opportunity to examine and evaluate arguments and to see how the ideas of prominent philosophers have been used (and abused) "in real life" to promote or criticize policies. It is also an opportunity to see how much "flexibility" there can be in interpreting the arguments of certain philosophers, particularly when the arguments are admittedly vague or our sources are lacking in what would be useful clarification.

Finally, this debate offers an opportunity to see how (unfortunately) some ideas and tendencies are not mere historical curiosities, but have their own manifestations even today in the racist ideologies and political agendas of certain individuals and organizations.

Critical Analysis

1. In your opinion, what are the strongest and most compelling points made by the philosopher or philosophers in this chapter? Why do you find those points to be convincing?
2. In your opinion, what are the weakest or least convincing points? Why? Can you anticipate any limitations or objections to their ideas not already addressed in the chapter?

Appendix: Application to Social Justice

History is filled with examples of people being grouped together on the basis of some sort of discernible feature, discriminated against (or worse), with the oppression being rationalized by claiming that there is some sort of morally relevant difference between "those people" and people with full and superior moral standing. A great many social justice issues concern differential treatment in this way. Although it is much less common that certain people are

---

[444] ibid.
[445] https://buchanan.org/blog/pjb-a-brief-for-whitey-969
[446] https://www.thedailybeast.com/these-

politicians-praise-slavery.

literally presented as somehow subhuman these days, there is, sadly, no shortage of examples of attempts to discriminate or withhold certain rights or equal protection under the law to certain groups of people nevertheless.

Obviously, racists still suggest that certain groups of people are inferior or superior on the basis of their so-called racial membership. In addition, LGBTQ+ persons are discriminated against because of their alleged "perversion." People with disabilities are discriminated against because of their alleged physical or intellectual inferiority. Non-citizens are targeted because they are "criminals" or "invaders," when, in a great many cases, the only difference between such persons and official citizens is "timing." And so on. . . .

This chapter largely serves the purpose of a history lesson, and, shamefully, shows how the resources of philosophy can be marshalled for oppressive causes. On the bright side, the debate in Vallodolid *also* shows how philosophy can be marshalled to fight *for* justice, and to *defend* persons against unjustifiable oppression.

I would add that it's also a reminder of human fallibility and an encouragement for some humility. As undeniably brilliant as Aristotle was, he was no more immune to the pull of self-interest and the effect of implicit biases than any of the rest of us. His political and economic privilege (and his desire to preserve and justify it) prevented him from seeing the shared and equal humanity of those he would label natural slaves, and even prevented him from detecting the stunning inconsistencies generated within his own philosophical system as a result.

I would humbly propose that if Aristotle can suffer from "blind spots," so can I—and so you can you. While it's too late for Aristotle to redeem his own unfortunate mistaken judgments, we still have time to sincerely evaluate our own beliefs and values, acknowledge our own biases, and strive to continually improve and correct our worldviews.

Go Right to the Source!

You have already read what Las Casas and Sepúlveda thought of Aristotle with respect to his notion of "natural slaves." You have also been exposed to numerous contemporary interpretations along the way. Whenever possible, it is a valuable exercise to go right to the source and see what *you* think the philosopher is saying. To promote that end, a brief excerpt is supplied below. In this excerpt from the *Politics* (in the provided text, the title is translated as "A Treatise on Government"), we have samples of his controversial treatment of slavery.

A Treatise on Government

Translated From the Greek of Aristotle by William Ellis, A.M.
London &.Toronto Published By J M Dent & Sons Ltd. &. In New York By E. P. Dutton
&. Co
First Issue Of This Edition 1912 Reprinted 1919, 1923, 1928
[http://www.gutenberg.org/ebooks/6762]

...

CHAPTER IV

Since then a subsistence is necessary in every family, the means of procuring it certainly makes up part of the management of a family, for without necessaries it is impossible to live, and to live well. As in all arts which are brought to perfection it is necessary that they should have their proper instruments if they would complete their works, so is it in the art of managing a family: now of instruments some of them are alive, others inanimate; thus with respect to the pilot of the ship, the tiller is without life, the sailor is alive; for a servant is as an instrument in many arts. Thus property is as an instrument to living; an estate is a multitude of instruments; so a slave is an animated instrument, but every one that can minister of himself is more valuable than any other instrument; for if every instrument, at command, or from a preconception of its master's will, could accomplish its work (as the story goes of the statues of Daedalus; or what the poet tells us of the tripods of Vulcan, "that they moved of their own accord into the assembly of the gods "), the shuttle would then weave, and the lyre play of itself; nor would the architect want servants, or the [1254a] master slaves. Now what are generally called instruments are the efficients of something else, but possessions are what we simply use: thus with a shuttle we make something else for our use; but we only use a coat, or a bed: since then making and using differ from each other in species, and they both require their instruments, it is necessary that these should be different from each other. Now life is itself what we use, and not what we employ as the efficient of something else; for which reason the services of a slave are for use. A possession may be considered in the same nature as a part of anything; now a part is not only a part of something, but also is nothing else; so is a possession; therefore a master is only the master of the slave, but no part of him; but the slave is not only the slave of the master, but nothing else but that. This fully explains what is the nature of a slave, and what are his capacities; for that being who by nature is nothing of himself, but totally another's, and is a man, is a slave by nature; and that man who is the property of another, is his mere chattel, though he continues a man; but a chattel is an instrument for use, separate from the body.

CHAPTER V

But whether any person is such by nature, and whether it is advantageous and just for any one to be a slave or no, or whether all slavery is contrary to nature, shall be considered hereafter; not that it is difficult to determine it upon general principles, or to understand it from matters of fact; for that some should govern, and others be governed, is not only necessary but useful, and from the hour of their birth some are marked out for those purposes, and others for the other, and there are many species of both sorts. And the better those are who are governed the better also is the government, as for instance of man, rather than the brute creation: for the more excellent the materials are with which the work is finished, the more excellent certainly is the work; and wherever there is a governor and a governed, there certainly is some work produced; for whatsoever is composed of many parts, which jointly become one, whether conjunct or separate, evidently show the marks of governing and governed; and this is true of every living thing in all nature; nay, even in some things which partake not of life, as in music; but this probably would be a disquisition too foreign to our present purpose. Every living thing in the first place is composed of soul and body, of these the one is by nature the governor, the other the governed; now if we would know what is natural, we ought to search for it in those subjects in which nature appears most perfect, and not in those which are corrupted; we should therefore examine into a man who is most perfectly formed both in soul and body, in whom this is evident, for in the depraved and vicious the body seems [1254b] to rule rather than the soul, on account of their being corrupt and contrary to nature. We may then, as we affirm, perceive in an animal the first principles of herile and political government; for the soul governs the body as the master governs his slave; the mind governs the appetite with a political or a kingly power, which shows that it is both natural and advantageous that the body should be governed by the soul, and the pathetic part by the mind, and that part which is possessed of reason; but to have no ruling power, or an improper one, is hurtful to all; and this holds true not only of man, but of other animals also, for tame animals are naturally better than wild ones, and it is advantageous that both should be under subjection to man; for this is productive of their common safety: so is it naturally with the male and the female; the one is superior, the other inferior; the one governs, the other is governed; and the same rule must necessarily hold good with respect to all mankind. Those men therefore who are as much inferior to others as the body is to the soul, are to be thus disposed of, as the proper use of them is their bodies, in which their excellence consists; and if what I have said be true, they are slaves by nature, and it is advantageous to them to be always under government. He then is by nature formed a slave who is qualified to become the chattel of another person, and on that account is so, and who has just reason enough to know that there is such a faculty, without being indued with the use of it; for other animals have no perception of reason, but are entirely guided by appetite, and indeed they vary very little in their use from each other; for the advantage which we receive, both from slaves and tame animals, arises from their bodily strength administering to our necessities; for it is the intention of nature to make the bodies of slaves and freemen different from each other, that the one should be robust for their necessary purposes, the others erect, useless indeed for what slaves are employed in, but fit for civil life, which is divided into the duties of war and peace; though these rules do not always take place, for slaves have sometimes the bodies of freemen, sometimes the souls; if then it is evident that if some bodies are as much more excellent than others as the statues of the gods excel the human form, every one will allow that the inferior ought to be slaves to the superior; and if this is true with respect to the body, it is still juster to determine in the same manner, when we consider the soul; though it is not so easy to perceive the beauty of [1255a] the soul as it is of the body. Since then some men are slaves by nature, and others are freemen, it is clear that where slavery is advantageous to any one, then it is just to make him a slave.

CHAPTER VI

But it is not difficult to perceive that those who maintain the contrary opinion have some reason on their side; for a man may become a slave two different ways; for he may be so by law also, and this law is a certain compact, by which whatsoever is taken in battle is adjudged to be the property of the conquerors: but many persons who are conversant in law call in question this pretended right, and say that it would be hard that a man should be compelled by violence to be the slave and subject of another who had the power to compel him, and was his superior in strength; and upon this subject, even of those who are wise, some think one way and some another; but the cause of this doubt and variety of opinions arises from hence, that great abilities, when accompanied with proper means, are generally able to succeed by force: for victory is always owing to a superiority in some advantageous circumstances; so that it seems that force never prevails but in consequence of great abilities. But still the dispute concerning the justice of it remains; for some persons think, that justice consists in benevolence, others think it just that the powerful should govern: in the midst of these contrary opinions, there are no reasons sufficient to convince us, that the right of being master and governor ought not to be placed with those who have the greatest abilities. Some persons, entirely resting upon the right which the law gives (for that which is legal is in some respects just), insist upon it that slavery occasioned by war is just, not that they say it is wholly so, for it may happen that the principle upon which the wars were commenced is unjust; moreover no one will say that a man who is unworthily in slavery is therefore a slave; for if so, men of the noblest families might happen to be slaves, and the descendants of slaves, if they should chance to be taken prisoners in war and sold: to avoid this difficulty they say that such persons should not be called slaves, but barbarians only should; but when they say this, they do nothing more than inquire who is a slave by nature, which was what we at first said; for we must acknowledge that there are some persons who, wherever they are, must necessarily be slaves, but others in no situation; thus also it is with those of noble descent: it is not only in their own country that they are Esteemed as such, but everywhere, but the barbarians are respected on this account at home only; as if nobility and freedom were of two sorts, the one universal, the other not so. Thus says the Helen of Theodectes:

"Who dares reproach me with the name of slave? When from the immortal gods, on either side, I draw my lineage."

Those who express sentiments like these, shew only that they distinguish the slave and the freeman, the noble and the ignoble from each other by their virtues and their [1255b] vices; for they think it reasonable, that as a man begets a man, and a beast a beast, so from a good man, a good man should be descended; and this is what nature desires to do, but frequently cannot accomplish it. It is evident then that this doubt has some reason in it, and that these persons are not slaves, and those freemen, by the appointment of nature; and also that in some instances it is sufficiently clear, that it is advantageous to both parties for this man to be a slave, and that to be a master, and that it is right

and just, that some should be governed, and others govern, in the manner that nature intended; of which sort of government is that which a master exercises over a slave. But to govern ill is disadvantageous to both; for the same thing is useful to the part and to the whole, to the body and to the soul; but the slave is as it were a part of the master, as if he were an animated part of his body, though separate. For which reason a mutual utility and friendship may subsist between the master and the slave, I mean when they are placed by nature in that relation to each other, for the contrary takes place amongst those who are reduced to slavery by the law, or by conquest.

Chapter 16: Justice. . . Nature, or Convention?

Comprehension questions you should be able to answer after reading this chapter:

1. Who were the Sophists, and what were the cultural conditions that made them possible?
2. What did Protagoras mean when he said that "man is the measure of all things?"
3. What is the difference between *physis* and *nomos*?
4. Why did Antigone disobey Creon's law?
5. Why does Plato (as Socrates) think epistemic relativism is false?
6. What are the "Forms," and what is their relationship to particular objects?
7. What is the point of the "allegory of the cave?"
8. Why is it that only philosophers have "knowledge?"

It seems reasonable to suppose that for as long as humans have been able to think, some people have had "deep thoughts." It's presumptuous to think that the first "deep thoughts" arose in the ancient Mediterranean region, however, we do have an historical record for this time and region that does reveal a remarkable shift in the way people understood their world and its operations, and we can call this the birth of "philosophy"—at least in the West.

In Greece, specifically, prior to philosophy, intellectual and moral authority was associated with celebrated poets, such as Homer or Hesiod (for both of whom, the dates of their lives are fuzzy, at best—*very* roughly 750-650 BCE). Poets and poems (e.g., The Odyssey, the Illiad, Achilles, Ulysses, etc.) served a variety of functions far beyond entertainment. They were the communities' source for history, "science," religion, and morality. Poets were no ordinary people. They were inspired by the Muses (goddesses of inspiration) in a fashion akin to divine inspiration. They spoke, therefore, with a special authority. Poets provided models of virtue and vice to be emulated or shunned (e.g., Achilles), and they explained the nature and operations of the world through myths. *These myths tried to explain the unfamiliar by appealing to the familiar.* For example, that strange glowing ball that seems to travel across the sky? A fiery chariot driven each day by the god Apollo. Unexpected events, such as natural disasters or diseases, were the outcome of the gods' fickle and changing tempers.

The problem, though, of appealing to gods and spirits to explain all the operations of nature and events that transpired, is that these explanations didn't seem to really explain all that much. "The gods did it" doesn't really provide much more understanding of an event than the event offered by itself. Moreover, the inconsistency observed in the world, when the only explanation was "the will of the gods," was a source of confusion and frustration. To remedy this, some poets placed even the gods under the power of the "Fates." *The Fates represented an implicit, objective ordering principle, a source of "justice," as it were, to which even the gods were subject.*

Having now taken the fateful cultural step of supposing that there is some "larger" principle than the anthropomorphic, all-too-human gods with which to interpret reality, the task now shifted to figuring out just what that larger underlying and ordering principle *is*.

Many individuals came forward to offer their answers. They include Thales, Anaximander, Pythagoras, Xenophenes, Heraclitus, Parmenides, Zeno, and Democritus, among others. The pre-Socratic philosophers are a fascinating group of thinkers, and not merely for the sake of history and trivia. In a meaningful way, they changed the way the (Western) world would think for millennia to come. Their inquiries into Nature created both philosophy and, ultimately, science. Their emphasis on reason and rigorous argumentation became a distinguishing feature of philosophy, in particular, and scholarship more generally. Their insights, while not often accepted as-is by many today, nevertheless left traces in other, later philosophers' systems (e.g., Platonism, Aristotelianism, Epicureanism, Stoicism). And, they created the cultural and intellectual climate ripe for the one to come, the one from whom they would (retroactively) receive their designation: Socrates. Before turning to Socrates, however, we will consider his "rivals," the Sophists.

From a socio-historical perspective, we might consider several possible contributors to the rise of sophistry. Ancient Greece had grown more cosmopolitan, and came into ever greater contact with other cultures and traditions. The rise of democracy meant an increased number of voices that not only were heard, but that asserted an equal claim to be heard. Even among the philosophers there was a dizzying diversity of opinions.

"Reality is water."
"No, it's fire."
"Actually, it's 'apeiron.'"
"What the heck is 'apeiron?' Never mind. Regardless, permanence is an illusion."
"On the contrary, it is change that is the illusion."

To make things more maddening, these contradictory positions were being presented via rigorous argumentation. An interesting and compelling case could be made for each. In sum, the ancient Greek world found itself flooded with, and grappling with, pluralism: a diversity of different ideas and values. Given such a cultural and intellectual backdrop, perhaps it should come as no surprise that some thinkers gave up on the search for The Truth.

The **Sophists**, to use a possibly uncomfortable analogy, were what we might expect if a stereotypical University philosophy professor today mated with an equally stereotypical lawyer. We can imagine the offspring to be a very intelligent person, capable of arguing any and every side of a debate, and focused primarily on "victory" as opposed to truth. Such were the

Sophists. Among the most famous of them were Protagoras, Gorgias, and Thrasymachus. If you read much Plato, you'll encounter these names as characters in his dialogues. Indeed, both Protagoras and Gorgias have entire dialogues named after them. Of course, these Sophists always appeared as the antagonists, doing (ill-fated) intellectual battle with the hero, Socrates.

What Sophists had in common with modern day philosophy professors is that they taught in exchange for money. One account of their "curriculum" is as follows: "That learning consists of good judgement in his own affairs, showing how best to order his own home; and in the affairs of his city, showing how he may have most influence on public affairs both in speech and in action."[447] There was, therefore, a presumed political component to their instruction; their students (generally the male children of aristocratic families) were expected to participate in the life of their *polis* (political community). Then, as now, political participation involved debate, and required rhetorical skills—areas in which the sophists excelled.

What Sophists had in common with (stereotypical) modern day lawyers is that they were (generally) willing to take any side in a debate, or court case, if the price was right.

In their defense, *many Sophists were either skeptics or epistemic relativists*. That is, they either believed that "the truth" was unknowable, or else that truth is a matter of perspective. In either case, there is no (knowable) "right" answer to our deep questions, nor any (knowable) "right" outcome to a lawsuit. If "Truth" could not be the arbiter of such things, then we must default to persuasiveness instead. Rhetoric might be more important than reason, if there is no "Truth" to be discovered. Victory, not accuracy, is the only outcome to be pursued and obtained.

Why come to such (possibly depressing) conclusions? Remember the foundation already laid by the pre-Socratics: the distinction between appearance and reality emphasized by those such as Heraclitus, Parmenides, and Zeno make skepticism not only possible, but compelling. If

---

[447] Plato, *Protagoras*, 318e-319a.

we have no clear access to "reality," and must operate solely by "appearances," and if the world appears differently on the basis of who is making the perception, then perhaps the sensible approach to take is that "truth" is simply a matter of perception.

One notable Sophist, Protagoras (490-420 BCE) is credited with the claim that "man is the measure of all things." By this, he meant that *perception is relative to the individual doing the perceiving*, and therefore any contact with reality is unique to that individual. Since perception is our only contact with the world, "reality" is relative to the individual who perceives it. Values are also relative. There is no Nature (*physis*), objective and independent of human traditions, perceptions, and decisions, out there for us to discover. Instead, such things are a matter of convention (*nomos*) or custom. Morality is subjective, but there is a pragmatic value to adhering to shared social conventions for the sake of peace and order.

This distinction between Nature (*physis*) and custom (*nomos*) is critically important for political philosophy, then, as now. There are certain aspects of human life that are obviously "natural." That we speak is natural—but the particular language we speak is a matter of custom. A central and enduring political question is whether politics a function of nature, or convention? Is there a *natural* norm of justice, or is justice "merely" conventional (*nomos*)? Is there a natural law, against which human laws may be evaluated as just or unjust, or are all laws merely matters of convention? Must governments conform to Nature in order to be good and just governments, or are political systems matters of convention instead?

Such questions arise in the story of Antigone, by Sophocles. Sophocles lived from 496 BCE to 406 BCE. He is one of only 3 Ancient Greek tragic playwrights whose works have survived (the other two were Aeschylus and Euripedes). For almost 50 years, Sophocles was the most-awarded playwright in the dramatic

competitions of the city-state of Athens, Sophocles competed in around 30 competition, winning as many as 24 and never placing lower than second place.

He wrote 123 plays, but only 7 survive in complete form: *Ajax*, *Antigone*, *Trachinian Women*, *Oedipus the King*, *Electra*, *Philoctetes* and *Oedipus at Colonus*. Our focus will be *Antigone*.

What follows is a brief excerpt from the full play.

The Oedipus Trilogy, by Sophocles[448]

ANTIGONE

[Backstory: Oedipus sired several children with his wife/mother Jocasta. Their two daughters were Antigone and Ismene, and their two sons were Eteocles and Polyneices. After Oedipus realized he had killed his father and married his mother, in an improbable fulfillment of prophecy, Jocasta committed suicide, and Oedipus blinded himself before begging to be exiled by his brother, Creon. Eteocles and Polyneices go to war with each other in a dispute over succession, and Polyneices enlists the aid of foreign armies in an attack against their home State of Thebes. Both brothers kill each other in battle. Their uncle Creon, who is now the king, orders Eteocles buried with proper rites, and Polyneices to remain unburied—condemning his spirit to a state of unrest forever, as a result. Creon declares it to be a capital offense, should anyone bury Polyneices, contrary to his order. Antigone finds herself in conflict between her sense of duty towards her brother, and her uncle's commands.]

. . .

ANTIGONE
Ismene, sister of my blood and heart,
See'st thou how Zeus would in our lives fulfill
The world of Oedipus, a world of woes!
For what of pain, affliction, outrage, shame,

[448] http://www.gutenberg.org/cache/epub/31/pg31.txt

Is lacking in our fortunes, thine and mine?
And now this proclamation of today
Made by our Captain-General to the State,
What can its purport be? Didst hear and heed,
Or art thou deaf when friends are banned as
foes?

ISMENE
To me, Antigone, no word of friends
Has come, or glad or grievous, since we twain
Were reft of our two brethren in one day
By double fratricide; and since i' the night
Our Argive leaguers fled, no later news
Has reached me, to inspirit or deject.

ANTIGONE
I know 'twas so, and therefore summoned
thee
Beyond the gates to breathe it in thine ear.

ISMENE
What is it? Some dark secret stirs thy breast.

ANTIGONE
What but the thought of our two brothers
dead,
The one by Creon graced with funeral rites,
The other disappointed? Eteocles
He hath consigned to earth (as fame reports)
With obsequies that use and wont ordain,
So gracing him among the dead below.
But Polyneices, a dishonored corpse,
(So by report the royal edict runs)
No man may bury him or make lament--
Must leave him tombless and unwept, a feast
For kites to scent afar and swoop upon.
Such is the edict (if report speak true)
Of Creon, our most noble Creon, aimed
At thee and me, aye me too; and anon
He will be here to promulgate, for such
As have not heard, his mandate; 'tis in sooth
No passing humor, for the edict says
Whoe'er transgresses shall be stoned to death.
So stands it with us; now 'tis thine to show
If thou art worthy of thy blood or base.

ISMENE
But how, my rash, fond sister, in such case

Can I do anything to make or mar?

ANTIGONE
Say, wilt thou aid me and abet? Decide.

ISMENE
In what bold venture? What is in thy thought?

ANTIGONE
Lend me a hand to bear the corpse away.

ISMENE
What, bury him despite the interdict?

ANTIGONE
My brother, and, though thou deny him, thine
No man shall say that _I_ betrayed a brother.

ISMENE
Wilt thou persist, though Creon has forbid?

ANTIGONE
What right has he to keep me from my own?

ISMENE
Bethink thee, sister, of our father's fate,
Abhorred, dishonored, self-convinced of sin,
Blinded, himself his executioner.
Think of his mother-wife (ill sorted names)
Done by a noose herself had twined to death
And last, our hapless brethren in one day,
Both in a mutual destiny involved,
Self-slaughtered, both the slayer and the slain.
Bethink thee, sister, we are left alone;
Shall we not perish wretchedest of all,
If in defiance of the law we cross
A monarch's will?--weak women, think of that,
Not framed by nature to contend with men.
Remember this too that the stronger rules;
We must obey his orders, these or worse.
Therefore I plead compulsion and entreat
The dead to pardon. I perforce obey
The powers that be. 'Tis foolishness, I ween,
To overstep in aught the golden mean.

ANTIGONE
I urge no more; nay, wert thou willing still,
I would not welcome such a fellowship.

Go thine own way; myself will bury him.
How sweet to die in such employ, to rest,--
Sister and brother linked in love's embrace--
A sinless sinner, banned awhile on earth,
But by the dead commended; and with them
I shall abide for ever. As for thee,
　Scorn, if thou wilt, the eternal laws of Heaven....

[Enter CREON—addressing guards and counselors]

CREON
Elders, the gods have righted one again
Our storm-tossed ship of state, now safe in port.
　But you by special summons I convened
　As my most trusted councilors; first, because
　I knew you loyal to Laius of old;
　Again, when Oedipus restored our State,
　Both while he ruled and when his rule was o'er,
　Ye still were constant to the royal line.
　Now that his two sons perished in one day,
　Brother by brother murderously slain,
　By right of kinship to the Princes dead,
　I claim and hold the throne and sovereignty.
　Yet 'tis no easy matter to discern
　The temper of a man, his mind and will,
　Till he be proved by exercise of power;
　And in my case, if one who reigns supreme
　Swerve from the highest policy, tongue-tied
　By fear of consequence, that man I hold,
　And ever held, the basest of the base.
　And I condemn the man who sets his friend
　Before his country. For myself, I call
　To witness Zeus, whose eyes are everywhere,
　If I perceive some mischievous design
　To sap the State, I will not hold my tongue;
　Nor would I reckon as my private friend
　A public foe, well knowing that the State
　Is the good ship that holds our fortunes all:
　Farewell to friendship, if she suffers wreck.
　Such is the policy by which I seek
　To serve the Commons and conformably
　I have proclaimed an edict as concerns
　The sons of Oedipus; Eteocles
　Who in his country's battle fought and fell,

The foremost champion--duly bury him
With all observances and ceremonies
That are the guerdon of the heroic dead.
But for the miscreant exile who returned
Minded in flames and ashes to blot out
His father's city and his father's gods,
　And glut his vengeance with his kinsmen's blood,
　Or drag them captive at his chariot wheels--
　For Polyneices 'tis ordained that none
　Shall give him burial or make mourn for him,
　But leave his corpse unburied, to be meat
　For dogs and carrion crows, a ghastly sight.
　So am I purposed; never by my will
　Shall miscreants take precedence of true men,
　But all good patriots, alive or dead,
　Shall be by me preferred and honored. . . .

[Creon is informed that the body has been buried anyway, contrary to his orders.]

CREON
O cease, you vex me with your babblement;
I am like to think you dote in your old age.
　Is it not arrant folly to pretend
　That gods would have a thought for this dead man?
　Did they forsooth award him special grace,
　And as some benefactor bury him,
　Who came to fire their hallowed sanctuaries,
　To sack their shrines, to desolate their land,
　And scout their ordinances? Or perchance
　The gods bestow their favors on the bad.
　No! no! I have long noted malcontents
　Who wagged their heads, and kicked against the yoke,
　Misliking these my orders, and my rule.
　'Tis they, I warrant, who suborned my guards
　By bribes. Of evils current upon earth
　The worst is money. Money 'tis that sacks
　Cities, and drives men forth from hearth and home;
　Warps and seduces native innocence,
　And breeds a habit of dishonesty.
　But they who sold themselves shall find their greed
　Out-shot the mark, and rue it soon or late.
　Yea, as I still revere the dread of Zeus,

By Zeus I swear, except ye find and bring
Before my presence here the very man
Who carried out this lawless burial,
Death for your punishment shall not suffice.
Hanged on a cross, alive ye first shall make
Confession of this outrage. This will teach you
What practices are like to serve your turn.
There are some villainies that bring no gain.
For by dishonesty the few may thrive,
The many come to ruin and disgrace....

[After the guards expose the body to the elements again, Antigone is caught burying it a second time. She is arrested and brought before the king.]

CREON
Speak, girl, with head bent low and downcast eyes,
Does thou plead guilty or deny the deed?

ANTIGONE
Guilty. I did it, I deny it not.

CREON (to GUARD)
Sirrah, begone whither thou wilt, and thank
Thy luck that thou hast 'scaped a heavy charge.
(To ANTIGONE)
Now answer this plain question, yes or no,
Wast thou acquainted with the interdict?

ANTIGONE
I knew, all knew; how should I fail to know?

CREON
And yet wert bold enough to break the law?

ANTIGONE
Yea, for these laws were not ordained of Zeus,
And she who sits enthroned with gods below,
Justice, enacted not these human laws.
Nor did I deem that thou, a mortal man,
Could'st by a breath annul and override
The immutable unwritten laws of Heaven.
They were not born today nor yesterday;
They die not; and none knoweth whence they sprang.

I was not like, who feared no mortal's frown,
To disobey these laws and so provoke
The wrath of Heaven. I knew that I must die,
E'en hadst thou not proclaimed it; and if death
Is thereby hastened, I shall count it gain.
For death is gain to him whose life, like mine,
Is full of misery. Thus my lot appears
Not sad, but blissful; for had I endured
To leave my mother's son unburied there,
I should have grieved with reason, but not now.
And if in this thou judgest me a fool,
Methinks the judge of folly's not acquit.

CHORUS
A stubborn daughter of a stubborn sire,
This ill-starred maiden kicks against the pricks.

CREON
Well, let her know the stubbornest of wills
Are soonest bended, as the hardest iron,
O'er-heated in the fire to brittleness,
Flies soonest into fragments, shivered through.
A snaffle curbs the fieriest steed, and he
Who in subjection lives must needs be meek.
But this proud girl, in insolence well-schooled,
First overstepped the established law, and then--
A second and worse act of insolence--
She boasts and glories in her wickedness.
Now if she thus can flout authority
Unpunished, I am woman, she the man.
But though she be my sister's child or nearer
Of kin than all who worship at my hearth,
Nor she nor yet her sister shall escape
The utmost penalty, for both I hold,
As arch-conspirators, of equal guilt.
Bring forth the older; even now I saw her
Within the palace, frenzied and distraught.
The workings of the mind discover oft
Dark deeds in darkness schemed, before the act.
More hateful still the miscreant who seeks
When caught, to make a virtue of a crime....

There is a fundamental point of disagreement between Creon and Antigone that is indicative of our previously mentioned distinction between convention (*nomos*) and "natural" Law (*physis*).

Antigone knowingly violated the law! "I knew, of course I knew. The word was plain." However, she justifies her actions by appealing to the "eternal laws of Heaven."

> *Yea, for these laws were not ordained of Zeus,*
> *And she who sits enthroned with gods below,*
> *Justice, enacted not these human laws.*
> *Nor did I deem that thou, a mortal man,*
> *Could'st by a breath annul and override*
> *The immutable unwritten laws of Heaven.*
> *They were not born today nor yesterday;*
> *They die not; and none knoweth whence they sprang*

In other words, Creon's "law" is not consistent with the Laws of the gods, and no matter how powerful a monarch Creon might be, he has no authority to override the "immutable" laws of "Heaven."

As for Creon, he emphasizes the practical importance of preserving the State, and consistency in the application of its laws. To be lenient to a family member (e.g., his nephew Polyneices, who "betrayed" Thebes by not only contesting rulership but especially by allying with foreign powers, or his niece Antigone who disobeyed his command), would be to set "friend before his country." If Creon were to show leniency, then consistency would require the spread of that leniency. "If I allow disorder in my house I'd surely have to license it abroad."

Creon thinks that the duty of the ruler is to "hold to the best plans of all," to count no friend greater than his own "fatherland." In his own mind, at least, he forbade the burial of Polyneices in order to promote the public good, for the sake of public safety, and to serve as a lesson to others. Creon regards the State as "the good ship that holds our fortunes all." In other words, the State is more important than individual interests or familial obligations. Creon simply does not recognize that there is a "higher" law that can somehow supersede his commands—his "just" commands that he makes for the good of the community. By violating the law and appealing to her "conscience," Antigone has placed herself above the laws of her land, and then tries to make a virtue of her criminality.

> *But this proud girl, in insolence well-schooled,*
> *First overstepped the established law, and then--*
> *A second and worse act of insolence--*
> *She boasts and glories in her wickedness....*
> *More hateful still the miscreant who seeks*
> *When caught, to make a virtue of a crime....*

This tension is not antiquated, but deeply relevant today. Ask yourself, what would be an example of current or historical (possible) conflicts between *personal* morality, and *public* (legal) obligation? Or, to put it differently, a situation in which one's personal moral values are in conflict with the law?

Each of the following statements were made by former Arkansas Governor and 2016 Republican Presidential Candidate Mike Huckabee:

> *I have opponents in this race who do not want to change the Constitution. But I believe it's a lot easier to change the Constitution than it would be to change the word of the living God. And that's what we need to do is amend the Constitution so it's in God's standards rather than trying to change God's standards so it lines up with some contemporary view of how we treat each other and how we treat the family.*[449]

---

[449] Mike Huckabee, 1-14-2008: http://thinkprogress.org/politics/2008/01/15/ 18870/huckabee-amend-the-constitution-to-gods-standards/

And:

The Court created a national right to same-sex marriage that doesn't exist in our Constitution, it hijacked the democratic process, subverting the will of Americans in more than 30 states who voted to protect traditional marriage, and trampling on America's most fundamental right — religious liberty....

Can the Supreme Court "decide" this? They cannot. Under our Constitution, we have three, co-equal branches of government. The courts can interpret law but cannot create it. The ruling still requires congressional funding and executive branch enforcement. The Supreme Court is not the "Supreme Branch," and it is certainly not the Supreme Being. If they can unilaterally make law, and just do whatever they want, then we have judicial tyranny.

Throughout our nation's history, the court has abused its power and delivered morally unconscionable rulings. They have rationalized the destruction of innocent human life, defined African Americans as property and justified Japanese-American internment camps. U.S. presidents, including Abraham Lincoln, Andrew Jackson, and Franklin Delano Roosevelt, ignored Supreme Court rulings, rejecting the notion that the Supreme Court can circumvent the Constitution and "make law."...

No man — and certainly no un-elected judge — has the right to redefine the laws of nature or of nature's God. Government is not God. The purpose of marriage is to socially and biologically unite a man and a woman to create the next generation and

to train the next generation to become their replacements. Marriage is a sacred covenant, not just another social contract.
...[450]

Antigone showcases the tension between the view that morality and justice are matters of convention, and the view that there is a "higher" morality in "Nature" against which our conventions may be compared. The Sophists were often the implicit, if not explicit spokespersons on behalf of convention. Socrates, on the other hand, spoke on behalf of "Nature."

Socrates

Socrates' life has already been described in brief detail in the earlier chapter on "Love of Wisdom," so for our present purposes we will skip directly to his engagement with the Sophists.

If "all truth is relative," as many of the Sophists claimed, then it would appear to be the case that no one person is any more qualified with regard to knowledge than is anyone else. All perspectives are equal. Socrates dismisses this view, however, as absurd on its surface. In another Platonic dialogue (*Theaetetus*), Socrates considers the relativism of the Sophist, Protagoras.

Protagoras, for his part, admitting as he does that everybody's opinion is true, must acknowledge the truth of his opponent's belief about his own belief, where they think he is wrong....That is to say, he would acknowledge his own belief to be false, if he admits that the belief of those who think him wrong is true (171a-b).

---

[450] http://www.usatoday.com/story/opinion/
2015/06/25/supreme-court-obamacare-religious-freedom-huckabee-

column/29175727/

There is something seemingly self-refuting, or internally inconsistent, with epistemic relativism. Since all opinions are equally true, it is simultaneously and equally true that epistemic relativism is, itself, both true and false. Beyond this conceptual puzzle, Socrates points out that we do not, in fact, regard all opinions as equally true. If you are not a medical doctor and you think you are healthy, but a medical doctor tells you that you have cancer, do you really regard your respective opinions as equally true? Don't we recognize legitimate expertise in a great many areas of inquiry? If our subject is Plato's philosophy, do we really believe that each person's position is equally true regarding that philosophical system? The opinions of the physicist who has specialized in string theory and the opinion of the philosopher who has specialized in Plato are equally true with regard to Plato? I think a tiger looks friendly, but a trained animal handler warns me that the tiger is about to rip my face off. Equally true opinions? Presumably not. If we acknowledge that different people have different degrees of expertise with regard to different skills, then it would stand to reason that not all people are equally equipped to rule a community (i.e., be a Guardian), and that not all people are even equally equipped to discuss and identify knowledge itself. If "philosophers" are those best equipped to perceive the Truth of things, then it is they who should lead rather than some popularly elected politician. Truth is not up to a majority vote!

This relativism is even more egregious when the issue at stake is morality itself. Socrates seizes the opportunity to take another shot at his Sophist rivals.

Why, that all those mercenary individuals, whom the many call Sophists and whom they deem to be their adversaries, do, in fact, teach nothing but the opinion of the many, that is to say, the opinions of their assemblies; and this is their wisdom. I might compare them to a man who should study the tempers and desires of a mighty strong beast who is fed by him—he would

learn how to approach and handle him, also at what times and from what causes he is dangerous or the reverse, and what is the meaning of his several cries, and by what sounds, when another utters them, he is soothed or infuriated; and you may suppose further, that when, by continually attending upon him, he has become perfect in all this, he calls his knowledge wisdom, and makes of it a system or art, which he proceeds to teach, although he has no real notion of what he means by the principles or passions of which he is speaking, but calls this honourable and that dishonourable, or good or evil, or just or unjust, all in accordance with the tastes and tempers of the great brute. Good he pronounces to be that in which the beast delights and evil to be that which he dislikes; and he can give no other account of them except that the just and noble are the necessary, having never himself seen, and having no power of explaining to others the nature of either, or the difference between them, which is immense (493a-c).

These intellectual mercenaries know nothing of good or evil, justice or injustice. Instead, they merely observe what actually happens in the world, what people like and dislike, and proclaim those things to be good or bad, just or unjust. They perceive cultural and individual differences in practices and values, and conclude something like moral subjectivism or cultural relativism. Socrates, however, disagrees with the strategy of identifying what is just or unjust with the events of this constantly changing world—and this is a problem not merely with respect to moral knowledge.

One of the problems with recognizing "The Truth" (aside from lack of training and qualification) is that the world we experience is constantly in flux, and insufficiently stable so as to provide for knowledge. Plato, ultimately, rejects sense experience as a means of knowledge, because the senses show us only the world of change, and our perceptions are relative to the perceiver. For example, consider hot coffee. Whether or not it is hot depends not only on when the measurement is taken, but also on who is making the determination. My former father-in-law would literally heat his coffee in the microwave until it boiled. Only then did he consider it sufficiently hot. I, on the other hand, consider that to be an example of coffee that is scalding, rather than "hot." Which one of us is right, and when would we have been right?

It might sound like we're backsliding into epistemic relativism again, or into skepticism. Plato does not intend that outcome, though. Knowledge, he claims, is objective, universal, unchanging, grounded in Reason, and is ultimately unavailable to the senses. Knowledge will not pertain to the particular, constantly changing "things" we experience in the world of the senses, but instead to unchanging universal concepts that inform our understanding of particular things in the first place. What we are now delving into is Plato's theory of the Forms.

The Forms

We encounter all kinds of circles in daily life. There is a mirror on my desk that I'm looking at right now. It's in the shape of a circle. The lid of my coffee cup is a circle. Doughnuts are circles, as are tires, as are wedding rings. What each one of these particular objects has in common (among other things) is that they are circular. We have a concept, an ideal, of a circle, and because each of these objects matches up (to an extent) with that concept, we recognize them as circular. None of those objects is itself a perfect circle, but each one approximates a circle—or else we never would have described it as circular.

This notion is clear from Socrates basic line of inquiry in most of the dialogues. He always seems to seek the "universal" behind the "particular." Consider, for example, his famous investigation of piety in Euthyphro.

And what is piety, and what is impiety?

Piety is doing as I am doing; that is to say, prosecuting any one who is guilty of murder, sacrilege, or of any similar crime-

whether he be your father or mother, or whoever he may be-that makes no difference; and not to prosecute them is impiety. . . .

I dare say; and you shall tell me them at some other time when I have leisure. But just at present I would rather hear from you a more precise answer, which you have not as yet given, my friend, to the question, What is "piety"? When asked, you only replied, Doing as you do, charging your father with murder.

And what I said was true, Socrates.

No doubt, Euthyphro; but you would admit that there are many other pious acts? There are.

Remember that I did not ask you to give me two or three examples of piety, but to explain the general idea which makes all pious things to be pious. Do you not recollect that there was one idea which made the impious, and the pious pious?

I remember.

Tell me what is the nature of this idea, and then I shall have a standard to which I may look, and by which I may measure actions, whether yours or those of any one else, and then I shall be able to say that such and such an action is pious, such another impious.

Socrates is assuming that there is some property of "piety" that manifests in any number of acts. It is not identical to any particular of those acts, but those acts simply are "pious" to the extent that they exemplify that quality of piety. An individual act may be pious, or impious depending on circumstances. I might be pious one moment, but impious the next. Piety itself, however, is unchanging.

Plato suggests that our concepts, not only of piety or circles, but of all sorts of other things:

human, chair, Christmas tree, greeting card, television set, onion ring, etc., are "universals" that are exemplified (to varying degrees) by particular things (e.g., actual onion rings, or chairs). He refers to these ideals, these concepts, as "Forms."

According to this theory, there is a Form of a chair. This is what allows us to recognize objects as chairs. Particular objects are related to their Forms in a variety of ways. Particular things (e.g., the chair I am sitting on at this moment) resemble the Form of a chair (otherwise I'd call it something else!). In a very abstract sort of way Plato claims that Forms cause particulars in the sort of way that a statue causes its shadow. Particulars "participate" in their Forms to varying degrees, and this is the means by which we evaluate them. For example, at dog shows various particular dogs are judged by how well they exemplify their breed. Those that "participate" very well in their breed would be regarded as excellent examples of that breed, whereas a "mutt" wouldn't "participate" well at all. Finally, Forms are what make particulars intelligible to us at all. In that Forms are concepts, they are make thought and speech possible. Try to describe an object (e.g., a chair, a doughnut, a human being, etc.) without appealing to concepts. What could you possibly say? The thing I am sitting on is a chair. Oops. I'm not allowed to say chair. OK, it's a piece of furniture. Oops. I can't appeal to "furniture." It's underneath me. Oops. "Underneath" is a concept too. It's supportive. Oops. Gray. Oops. Etc.

At this point, we could simply understand Forms as concepts, and not have anything too controversial on our hands—but Plato does not avoid controversy. Plato doesn't merely claim that the Forms are concepts, in the sense of universal ideas; he argues that they exist, independently of our thoughts, in another realm of existence distinct from the physical world. The physical world is the one we encounter by sense experience. It is constantly changing, and doesn't permit knowledge to be acquired. This is where Plato honors Heraclitus. The intelligible world, on the other hand, is non-physical, eternal, unchanging, and intelligible to Reason. This is

where Plato honors Parmenides. Parmenides and Heraclitus represented two opposite camps, one of which claiming that everything is in flux and the other claiming that there is no change at all. Plato thinks they were both on to something, but also both incorrect. Heraclitus was right about the physical world of sense experience. Parmenides was right about the mental world of the Forms. The correct view is the one that combines both into a single vision of a dualistic reality.

What does any of this have to do with philosophers, and their being the only people who have knowledge? We're getting there! Consider yet another of Plato's allegories—perhaps his most famous: the allegory of the cave. It is worth quoting at length.

> And now, I said, let me show in a figure how far our nature is enlightened or unenlightened:—Behold! human beings living in a underground den, which has a mouth open towards the light and reaching all along the den; here they have been from their childhood, and have their legs and necks chained so that they cannot move, and can only see before them, being prevented by the chains from turning round their heads. Above and behind them a fire is blazing at a distance, and between the fire and the prisoners there is a raised way; and you will see, if you look, a low wall built along the way, like the screen which marionette players have in front of them, over which they show the puppets.

> I see.

> And do you see, I said, men passing along the wall carrying all sorts of vessels, and statues and figures of animals made of wood and stone and various materials, which appear over the wall? Some of them are talking, others silent.

> You have shown me a strange image, and they are strange prisoners.

Like ourselves, I replied; and they see only their own shadows, or the shadows of one another, which the fire throws on the opposite wall of the cave?

True, he said; how could they see anything but the shadows if they were never allowed to move their heads?

And of the objects which are being carried in like manner they would only see the shadows?

Yes, he said.

And if they were able to converse with one another, would they not suppose that they were naming what was actually before them?

Very true.

And suppose further that the prison had an echo which came from the other side, would they not be sure to fancy when one of the passers-by spoke that the voice which they heard came from the passing shadow?

No question, he replied.

To them, I said, the truth would be literally nothing but the shadows of the images.

That is certain.

And now look again, and see what will naturally follow if the prisoners are released and disabused of their error. At first, when any of them is liberated and compelled suddenly to stand up and turn his neck round and walk and look towards the light, he will suffer sharp pains; the glare will distress him, and he will be unable to see the realities of which in his former state he had seen the shadows; and then conceive some one saying to him, that what he saw before was an illusion, but

that now, when he is approaching nearer to being and his eye is turned towards more real existence, he has a clearer vision,—what will be his reply? And you may further imagine that his instructor is pointing to the objects as they pass and requiring him to name them,—will he not be perplexed? Will he not fancy that the shadows which he formerly saw are truer than the objects which are now shown to him?

Far truer.

And if he is compelled to look straight at the light, will he not have a pain in his eyes which will make him turn away to take refuge in the objects of vision which he can see, and which he will conceive to be in reality clearer than the things which are now being shown to him?

True, he said.

And suppose once more, that he is reluctantly dragged up a steep and rugged ascent, and held fast until he is forced into the presence of the sun himself, is he not likely to be pained and irritated? When he approaches the light his eyes will be dazzled, and he will not be able to see anything at all of what are now called realities.

Not all in a moment, he said.

He will require to grow accustomed to the sight of the upper world. And first he will see the shadows best, next the reflections of men and other objects in the water, and then the objects themselves; then he will gaze upon the light of the moon and the stars and the spangled heaven; and he will see the sky and the stars by night better than the sun or the light of the sun by day?

Certainly.

Last of all he will be able to see the sun, and not mere reflections of him in the water, but he will see him in his own proper place, and not in another; and he will contemplate him as he is.

Certainly.

He will then proceed to argue that this is he who gives the season and the years, and is the guardian of all that is in the visible world, and in a certain way the cause of all things which he and his fellows have been accustomed to behold?

Clearly, he said, he would first see the sun and then reason about him.

And when he remembered his old habitation, and the wisdom of the den and his fellow-prisoners, do you not suppose that he would felicitate himself on the change, and pity them?

Certainly, he would.

And if they were in the habit of conferring honours among themselves on those who were quickest to observe the passing shadows and to remark which of them went before, and which followed after, and which were together; and who were therefore best able to draw conclusions as to the future, do you think that he would care for such honours and glories, or envy the possessors of them? Would he not say with Homer,

'Better to be the poor servant of a poor master,' and to endure anything, rather than think as they do and live after their manner?

Yes, he said, I think that he would rather suffer anything than entertain these false notions and live in this miserable manner.

Imagine once more, I said, such an one

coming suddenly out of the sun to be replaced in his old situation; would he not be certain to have his eyes full of darkness?

To be sure, he said.

And if there were a contest, and he had to compete in measuring the shadows with the prisoners who had never moved out of the den, while his sight was still weak, and before his eyes had become steady (and the time which would be needed to acquire this new habit of sight might be very considerable), would he not be ridiculous? Men would say of him that up he went and down he came without his eyes; and that it was better not even to think of ascending; and if any one tried to loose another and lead him up to the light, let them only catch the offender, and they would put him to death (514a-517a).

This allegory attempts to depict the plight of humanity. The vast majority of us are the prisoners in the cave. What we think is knowledge is just the shadowy reflections of copies of real things, symbolic of the mere opinions taught to us by those in positions of power and influence. The objects from which the shadows are cast still only copies of the real objects as they exist outside the cave. The shadows we see, then, are just copies of copies, at least two steps removed from truth. Those who parade these objects and cast the shadows before us are symbolic of illegitimate rulers. The philosopher is the prisoner who manages to break free, who ascends from the cave to behold things are they really are (i.e., who perceives the "Forms," and, who thereby alone has knowledge). Finally, the sun which illuminates those objects is the Form of the Good itself (to be discussed later). Not surprisingly, if the philosopher returns to the cave to explain things to the rest of the prisoners, he's going to sound "crazy," and will be persecuted—just as Socrates was. Also notice that the philosopher doesn't bring light to the cave, but tries to bring prisoners upward into the light.

Compelling as this allegory might be, we still don't have an explanation (beyond metaphor) as to why the philosopher really does have knowledge while the rest of us have mere opinion. This brings us back to the Forms. Only the Forms provide knowledge. Particulars are those imperfect, temporary, changing copies of the Forms that we experience in the sensory world. In the allegory of the cave, particulars are represented by the shadows cast on the walls. The Forms are represented by the original, "real" objects found on the surface. Only the philosopher gets past the shadows to the real thing, only the philosopher gets a glimpse of the forms (by means of Reason, not sight, of course). Therefore, only the philosopher can acquire knowledge.

Another way to represent this is by means of his "Divided Line" (also worth quoting at length).

You have to imagine, then, that there are two ruling powers, and that one of them is set over the intellectual world, the other over the visible. I do not say heaven, lest you should fancy that I am playing upon the name ('ourhanoz, orhatoz'). May I suppose that you have this distinction of the visible and intelligible fixed in your mind?
I have.

Now take a line which has been cut into two unequal parts, and divide each of them again in the same proportion, and suppose the two main divisions to answer, one to the visible and the other to the intelligible, and then compare the subdivisions in respect of their clearness and want of clearness, and you will find that the first section in the sphere of the visible consists of images. And by images I mean, in the first place, shadows, and in the second place, reflections in water and in solid, smooth and polished bodies and the like: Do you understand?

Yes, I understand.

Imagine, now, the other section, of which this is only the resemblance, to include the animals which we see, and everything that grows or is made.
Very good.

Would you not admit that both the sections of this division have different degrees of truth, and that the copy is to the original as the sphere of opinion is to the sphere of knowledge?

Most undoubtedly.

Next proceed to consider the manner in which the sphere of the intellectual is to be divided.

In what manner?

Thus:—There are two subdivisions, in the lower of which the soul uses the figures given by the former division as images; the enquiry can only be hypothetical, and instead of going upwards to a principle descends to the other end; in the higher of the two, the soul passes out of hypotheses, and goes up to a principle which is above hypotheses, making no use of images as in the former case, but proceeding only in and through the ideas themselves.

I do not quite understand your meaning, he said.

Then I will try again; you will understand me better when I have made some preliminary remarks. You are aware that students of geometry, arithmetic, and the kindred sciences assume the odd and the even and the figures and three kinds of angles and the like in their several branches of science; these are their hypotheses, which they and every body are supposed to know, and therefore they do not deign to give any account of them either to themselves or others; but they begin with them, and go on until they arrive at last, and in a consistent manner, at their conclusion?

Yes, he said, I know.

And do you not know also that although they make use of the visible forms and reason about them, they are thinking not of these, but of the ideals which they resemble; not of the figures which they draw, but of the absolute square and the absolute diameter, and so on—the forms which they draw or make, and which have shadows and reflections in water of their own, are converted by them into images, but they are really seeking to behold the

things themselves, which can only be seen with the eye of the mind?

That is true.

And of this kind I spoke as the intelligible, although in the search after it the soul is compelled to use hypotheses; not ascending to a first principle, because she is unable to rise above the region of hypothesis, but employing the objects of which the shadows below are resemblances in their turn as images, they having in relation to the shadows and reflections of them a greater distinctness, and therefore a higher value (509d-511a).

	Objects of Cognition	Kinds of Cognition	
Intelligible World ↕	The Form of the Good The Forms Mathematical Objects	Direct Intuition Intellection Thought	**Knowledge** ↕
Sensible World	Visible Objects Images	Common Sense Belief Imagination	**Opinion**

On the left side of the line, we are dealing with metaphysics, the nature of reality. The "higher" up one goes, the more "real" something is. On the right side of the line, we are dealing with epistemology. The higher up one goes, the closer one is to knowledge. The upper portion of the figure represents the intelligible world (the world of the Forms), while the lower portion represents the physical world (the world of the senses). Starting with the metaphysical side, at the very bottom we have mere images. These would include shadows, reflections, dreams, mirages, etc. They have some "reality," but are faint copies of other, more real, things. Above images, but still part of the physical world, we have all visible things—the objects we encounter by means of our senses. A statue is "more real"

than its shadow, in this sense.

As we continue to ascend, we go beyond the physical world and enter the world of ideas, the Forms. We encounter mathematical objects, which are not physical, but are "real," and that provide the structure and reality to their physical counterparts. Above mathematical objects are the Forms themselves, our concepts of all the things we encounter in the physical world. At the very peak of reality is the Form of the Good itself, that which gives reality and understanding to everything "beneath" it.

On the right side of the line, we are dealing with epistemology, the nature of belief and knowledge. At the very bottom we have imagining, conjecture, and general ignorance. Above mere conjecture we have common sense beliefs, beliefs for which we are confident and that might even be true. As we continue to ascend we go beyond the world of the senses and enter the intelligible realm. We encounter abstract reasoning, and then finally reach direct intuition (pure "perception") of the Forms. Knowledge.

The ascent up the divided line mirrors the ascent out of the cave. In each case, the "higher" one goes, the more "real" are the things one encounters, and the closer one gets to knowledge. The philosopher is the one who has managed to climb out of the cave, who has moved beyond mere appearances and "common sense" and glimpsed the Forms, including the Form of the Good itself.

The Form of the Good is, well, a bit weird. The Form of the Good is represented by the Sun (507c-509b). The Sun is what the philosopher sees when he has emerged from the cave. It illuminates all the other objects (Forms), and is "higher" than them. Just what the Form of the Good is though is probably not altogether clear. Using our everyday sense of "good" in a moral context, it might be confused with other forms, such as justice, or piety, or generosity. But, if all such traits have their own Forms, what is left over for the Form of the Good itself?

A Form is the universal that gives unity to particulars. "Piety," for example, is the property which all pious acts or persons share in. The Form of piety is the absolute best with regards to piousness, because it is the yardstick against which all pious acts are measured, and that which gives meaning to piety in the first place. Procedurally, we observe many things that we call pious, and then we identify their common feature in order to intuit the Form of piety itself. With regard to the Forms, we observe many things (Form of piety, Form of circularity, etc.) that we call Forms. They appear to have something in common—namely, their "Form-ness." The Form of the Good is, for lack of a better expression, the Form of Form-ness itself. But, because Forms are the "best" of whatever they represent, the Form of Form-ness is the property of being best—the Form of "The Good."

This is, admittedly, an unusual use of the term "good." Later thinkers, such as Plotinus, would make the Form of the Good into a divine principle, and Christian theologians (such as St. Augustine) would claim that what Plato calls the Form of the Good is actually God. Plato himself, though, had no such anthropomorphic vision in mind. The Form of the Good is not a person, but an abstract entity—the Form of Form-ness (best-ness, Good-ness) itself.

Those who "see" the Form of the Good are those who have attained the highest level of philosophical abstraction. If it's impressive to ascend from the "shadows" or mere imaginings and opinion to knowledge of things are they really are (Forms), how much more impressive to have ascended higher still (the highest, in fact), to understand the Form that informs all the other Forms? Philosophers have glimpsed the "highest" degrees of both reality and knowledge, at this point—but it's no wonder that when they return to the cave to tell the rest of the prisoners about it, they're regarded as crazy. . . .

Critical Analysis

1. In your opinion, what are the strongest and most compelling points made by the philosopher or philosophers in this chapter? Why do you find those points to be convincing?
2. In your opinion, what are the weakest or least convincing points? Why? Can you anticipate any limitations or objections to their ideas not already addressed in the chapter?

Appendix: Application to Social Justice

This might seem like rather "abstract" chapter for a textbook about social justice, but the core issue of this chapter has a profound impact on how we understand social justice issues in the first place.

The primary question addressed in this chapter is whether justice is a matter of convention (*nomos*) or nature (*physis*). This same basic question, with slight modification, concerns whether our moral value judgments are subjective, or objective—a question considered in several other chapters of this book.

The implications of how we answer that "convention or nature" question frame our basic understanding of the "justice" aspect of social justice. If justice is a matter of convention only, then we have embraced ethical relativism, and what is "just" is simply identical to the "conventions" of a given community. That means that in a society in which white supremacy and racism is the "norm," laws and policies that reflect that are "just" by definition, and any of us involved in reform efforts have now triggered the "moral reformers are always wrong" issue from our chapter on ethical relativism. In a heteronormative society, it is "just" (by definition) to promote heterosexuality and condemn homosexuality, if justice is simply a matter of convention. And so on.

On the other hand, if justice is a matter of "nature," if there is something objective about justice that transcends subjective individual or communal opinions, then it is possible that the "conventions" of a community are unjust, that some societies have unjust laws, and that those seeking to change the laws and norms of such societies such that they align with "Justice" are actually in service to what is *truly* just and right.

This, of course, is precisely the debate presented by Sophocles thousands of years ago. According to the laws (*nomos*) of the kingdom, Creon was acting justly, but Antigone acted according to what she believed was a "higher" law (*physis*) even as she knowingly and willfully engaged in "unlawful" acts.

Chapter 17: Cosmopolitanism

Comprehension questions you should be able to answer after reading this chapter:

1. According to the Stoics, what sorts of things are "up to us?" What things are not? Why should we focus on the things that are up to us?
2. What do the Stoics mean by each of the following? Representation, judgment, assent.
3. Why do they believe we should not "add to appearances?"
4. What are "externals?" Why is their value "indifferent?" In what way are some "indifferents" nevertheless to be "preferred?"
5. What does it mean to "act under reserve?"
6. What stoic ideas influenced Cicero's own philosophy?
7. Explain the role that Reason plays in Cicero's understanding of the universal "kinship" of humanity
8. What are the moral requirements concerning war, for Cicero?
9. Explain his version of "hegemonic leadership."
10. Explain the relationship between natural law and human laws, according to Cicero.
11. What does Cicero mean by a "Republic" (*res publica*)?
12. Why does Cicero favor a "mixed" constitution?
13. Briefly describe Cicero's influence during the Renaissance and Enlightenment.

In the previous chapter, we considered some political philosophy from the ancient Greek perspective. Greek philosophy did not remain only in Greece, however. Philosophy found its way to the Roman Empire, and one of the persons most responsible for disseminating Greek philosophy to educated Romans was Marcus Tullius Cicero (106 BCE – 43 BCE).

Cicero was not merely a "fan" of Greek philosophy who shared his interests with others. He was a careful thinker and a skilled writer who translated Greek thought into the Roman (Latin) language not only in the literal sense of translation, but also to the extent that he coined new Latin vocabulary to help elucidate difficult philosophical concepts. He helped bring ancient Greek thought to the Romans, and then helped to bring both Greek and Roman philosophy to the rest of Europe, somewhat in the Middle Ages—but especially in the Renaissance.

Cicero was a gifted writer, speaker, and transmitter of ideas, in general, but he was no mere theorist. Cicero was an actual politician in his time, rising to the role of Consul (and helping to put down a *coup d'etat* during his tenure!).

We will spend a bit more attention on Cicero's biographical history than we have (or will) on other philosophers in this book—if for no other reason than Cicero's personal life was so fascinating! After a brief review of some of his major life events and accomplishments, we will consider the philosophical training he received, and the foundations upon which his own musings are built. This will manifest as a brief overview of basic Stoic principles. We will then consider Cicero's own positions on political philosophy, specifically, as built on its stoic foundation. Then, we will conclude with a consideration of Cicero's significant impact on the political philosophy that was to follow him.

Cicero's Life

Cicero was born into the "equestrian" order of Roman society in 106 BCE. Cicero achieved public offices at or near the minimum age for each: quaestor (age 31, 76 BCE), aedile (age 37), praetor (age 40, 66 BCE), and consul (age 43, 63 BCE).

That he rose to become consul (joint head of state) is an even more impressive testimony to his talents, given that the patrician class dominated politics. Nobody without senators in their family lineage had been made a consul in the last 30 years, prior to Cicero. In his capacity as consul, he uncovered and prevented a conspiracy by Cataline, and generated some controversy and trouble for himself later when he ordered the execution of some of the conspirators without a trial.

His oratory skill and political talents caught the eye of Julius Caesar, who (in 60 BCE) invited Cicero to be the 4th member of his "partnership" with Pompey and Marcus Licinius Crassus. Cicero declined the offer to join what would become the First Triumvirate due to his concern that it would undermine the Republic.

Cicero briefly fled into exile in 58 BCE when a political enemy (Publius Clodius, a tribune and supporter of Julius Caesar) sought his execution in response to Cicero's own summary execution of rebels during his consulship. His property was confiscated and his house was destroyed. His exile was overturned by a nearly unanimous vote of the Roman senate just a year later, at the request of Pompey, and he was granted amnesty in exchange for being "persuaded" to collaborate with the Triumvirate.

In 52 BCE, Consular elections were suspended, the Senate house was burned down, and Pompey became the sole (instead of joint) Consul—using the need for security and order to justify his de facto dictatorship. When the partnership between Caesar and Pompey unraveled, Cicero supported Pompey—seeing him as the defender of the traditional Roman republic, but making an enemy of Caesar at the same time.

Even though Cicero had joined Pompey in his military campaign against Caesar, Caesar pardoned him after his defeat of Pompey (48 BCE), and Cicero shifted his strategy to trying to promote the revival of the republic from within Caesar's dictatorship. Caesar, however, was reappointed dictator for an "indefinite period," and then for a period of 10 years in 46 BCE.[451]

Over the next several years, Caesar instituted numerous political changes that increased and reinforced his personal power, including granting himself veto power over the Senate, granting himself the power to personally appoint new senators (always loyal to himself, of course!), and imposing term limits on governors (to reduce the power of other generals who might prove to be potential political rivals). In February, 44 BCE, Caesar was appointed "dictator for life." Roughly a month later, he was assassinated on the Ides of March (March 15th).

Cicero had not, himself, participated in the conspiracy or assassination. However, Marcus Junius Brutus allegedly called out Cicero's name, bloodstained dagger in hand, and asked him to restore the Republic, and Cicero's own endorsement of the assassination was unmistakable.

Yet come one, come all, the Ides of March are a consolation. Our heroes most splendidly and gloriously achieved everything that lay within their power.[452]

How I wish you had invited me to that superb banquet on the Ides of March![453]

For Heaven will bear witness that Rome— that any nation throughout the whole world—has never seen a greater act than theirs. There has never been an achievement more glorious—more greatly deserving of renown for all eternity.[454]

In the political instability that followed the assassination, a power struggle broke out between the assassins (led by Brutus and Cassius) and "loyalists" to Caesar (led by Mark Antony and Octavian). Cicero was a political leader—and found himself in direct opposition to Mark Antony. Cicero was the spokesman for the Senate, and Antony was a consul and the unofficial executor of Caesar's will. Cicero tried to

---

[451] Note that, historically, the term limit for a dictatorship was a mere 6 months!

[452] Letter to Atticus, April 9th or 10th, 44 BCE.

[453] Letter to Gaius Trebonius, February 2nd, 43 BCE

[454] Second Philippic against Antony.

manipulate Octavian into opposing Antony, but ultimately failed.

Cicero wrote and spoke publicly against Antony in a series of speeches called the "Phillipics"—actions and writing that ultimately cost him his life. In 43 BCE, Antony, Octavian, and Lepidus formed the Second Triumvirate. They issued proscriptions against Roman citizens, including Cicero (and his brother and nephew).

Cicero was assassinated on December 7th, 43 BCE. Antony then displayed Cicero's severed head and hands (the ones that wrote the Phillipics) in the Roman Forum in a final act of humiliation.

The Second Triumvirate was short-lived, however, with Antony and Octavian soon turning on each other. Octavian proved victorious, solidifying his power and becoming the first Roman Emperor, Augustus.

Not many philosophers can rival Cicero's world-historic status! Beyond his wisdom and talents, he was an associate, at times, friend, and at other times rival, of some of the most famous and powerful (and notorious) politicians to ever grace the world's stage. Cicero was no mere theoretician, imaging how certain political principles might apply in various hypothetical scenarios. Instead, he spoke of the decay of republicanism and the rise of tyranny as a first hand witness, and wrote of resisting tyranny and affirming the rights of all as someone who was literally doing so—even at the eventual cost of his own life.

With the basic elements of his life story in place, we will now turn to his intellectual history, so as to better situate his political thought.

Cicero's Education

Cicero was exposed to, and educated in, a variety of philosophical schools, making him familiar with every major system at the time. He was familiar with Epicureanism, though he rejected it. He appreciated the Peripatetics (Aristotle's school), and sent his own son to study under that system in Greece. He was heavily influenced by two stoic teachers, Posidonius and Diodotus. The influence of stoicism on Cicero is unmistakable, as we shall see. Despite that influence, however, Cicero did not label himself a stoic, but rather claimed a different affiliation: "I, however, belong to the New Academy, which allows wide latitude to adopt any theory supported by probability."[455]

With regard to the Academy (Plato's school), he studied under both Philo of Larissa (160-80 BCE) and Antiochus of Ascalon (130-68 BCE). These two attempted to blend stoic thought in a harmonious way with the Academy, rejecting the unyielding skepticism of earlier incarnations of the Academy, and replacing it with a moderate skepticism; not total suspension of judgment in all cases, but provisional assent to what seems "probable"—while remaining open to contrary arguments. In this way, stoic principles could be affirmed (so long as they seemed probable), as could good ideas from Aristotle, Epicurus, etc. Because of its undeniable influence on Cicero's political thought, we will focus on Stoicism.

Stoicism was named for a porch.

That's right. The word "stoicism" comes from "stoa," meaning a covered walkway (similar to the *peripatoi* from which Aristotle's followers acquired their name: "*peripatetics*."). Specifically, the "*stoa*" at the Agora in Athens is where the philosophers later to be named "stoics" would loiter and lecture.

Stoicism can be divided into two rough periods: First, there was the (Greek) "theoretical" period of its founder Zeno of Citium in Cyprus (344 –262 BCE, as well as his successors: Cleanthes (330 – 230 BCE), and Chrysippus (279 – 206 BCE)(all dates are approximate). Then, there was the (Roman) "therapeutic" period represented by Seneca (4 BCE–65 CE), Musonius Rufus (20-101 CE[456]), Epictetus (55–135 CE) and the Emperor Marcus Aurelius (121–180 CE).

Early Stoicism was heavily theoretical, abstract, detailed, and painstakingly developed. The Stoic system may be divided into three disciplines: logic, "physics," and "ethics." Although Aristotle is often credited for his development of what we now call "logic," a strong

---

[455] *On Duties*, 2.

[456] These dates are largely speculative.

case can be made that the Stoics were more important and influential in this field. They developed what we now call "propositional logic," tests for validity, and several rules of inference including *modus ponens* and *modus tollens*. They also developed careful analyses of concepts, and language in general—all of which was intended to be put to use in their pursuit of *eudaimonia*.

The second category ("physics") involves the Stoic understanding of the cosmos and how it operates. This can get very complicated, but we will consider just enough detail (I hope) to motivate our understanding of the therapeutic application of Stoicism. The two most central ideas (for our purposes) from this category are the Stoic concepts of Fate and Freedom.

Fate and Freedom

The Stoics believed that "God," or "Zeus" (or Nature, or Fate, depending on which Stoic is writing) is immanent throughout the cosmos. To avoid confusing their concept of the divine with the Judeo-Christian concept, I will hereafter use the term "Fate."

The physical universe is Fate's "body." Fate is identical with the cosmos. This view is often referred to as "pantheism." The universe itself is Fate's body, and matter was thought to be inert. Fate is recognized not only as the "body" (to which the cosmos is identical), but also as the "logos" (eternal Reason) that moves and governs all the operations of the universe and the unfolding of history. All events, therefore, are manifestations of Fate's "will." Moreover, Fate is perfectly rational. As such, all events transpire in accordance with perfect Reason. This assumption allows the Stoics to go from mere determinism, to "Providence." All that happens is fated to happen, but all that happens is for the best, and couldn't have turned out any better way.

Although the transition from this Stoic concept of Fate to the Western theistic (e.g., Christian, Muslim, or Jewish) concept of Providence is an easy transition to make (and an appealing one, for some contemporary Stoics), we must be careful not to impose contemporary views of the divine onto the ancient Stoics.

Fate, unlike the Judeo-Christian God, is identical to creation, not its transcendent Creator. And, while Fate is perfectly rational (and therefore a mind), Fate is not "personal" in the way the Judeo-Christian God is thought to be, nor is Fate responsive to human needs or prayers. All events occur (and will occur) as they *must* occur, according to the perfectly rational will of Fate. Praying that events might turn out a certain way is a futile effort—if your hope is to bring about an event that is contrary to the will of Fate. Instead, the Stoics thought we should attempt to align our own will with Fate (more on that later).

Because *all* events are the manifestation of Fate's will, human events are no exception. All the events in your life, and all the actions you take, are fated to occur exactly as they do, and could not have turned out any other way. Nevertheless, Stoics believed that there is something different and special about human beings, and a sense in which we are "free" and accountable for our actions, even though all events are the product of Fate.

It is generally recognized that the Stoics (specifically, Chrysippus) were the first "compatibilists" with regard to determinism and free will. That is to say that the Stoics believed that all events are determined (fated) to occur exactly as they do, but there is, nevertheless, a sense in which we are "free"—and that freedom (and responsibility) is "compatible" with determinism (Fate).

Contemporary compatibilists identify free actions (i.e., those for which we may rightfully be held responsible) as being the effects of "internal causes." An easier way to think about this is to ask, of any action you take, "did I do it because I wanted to?" If the answer is yes, you acted on an internal cause (i.e., something about *you*). If the answer is no, you likely acted on an external cause (i.e., something "outside" of you).

For an obvious example, consider the difference between murder and suicide. Imagine that a person is standing on a balcony, twenty stories up in a tall building. Imagine that this person falls from that balcony to his death below. Now consider two different versions of that story. In one, the person is seriously depressed and wants to end his life. As a result, he leaps over the balcony. In the other version, he is simply admiring the view when another person (for some reason) rushes up behind him and tosses him over the edge. In the first case, the cause was "internal" (the man's own desire to die). In the second, the cause was "external" (the shove from the murderer).

Note that we interpret these events very differently, even though the physical descriptions are quite similar (i.e., a body falling to its death). The first example is an example of suicide, and we say (with however much sympathy and compassion we might be able to generate) that it is his own fault that he's dead. He's responsible for his actions. The second example is an example of murder, and we do not claim that it's his own fault that he's dead. Instead, the responsibility is found with the person who pushed him. Why? Because the murderer is the one who was acting from an internal cause (in this case, apparently, a desire to kill).

Although the Stoics didn't describe their compatibilism in exactly the same way, their system involves the same basic idea: we are responsible for our actions when those actions stem from something about ourselves, as opposed to something wholly external to ourselves. To use the Stoic vocabulary, "externals" can be "initiating causes" (antecedent causes), but are not "principle causes."

Their most famous example used to illustrate this was that of a cylinder rolling down a hill. To make it a bit more visually appealing, instead of a cylinder, think of a tire. If you are standing atop the hill with that tire, and you give it a shove, you have provided the "initiating cause." However, that tire isn't going to roll down the hill unless it has a shape that is conducive to rolling. The "principle cause," therefore, of the tire rolling down the hill is its own shape. After all, you could provide the same initiating cause to an anvil and that anvil won't roll down the hill. Because not all objects will respond to the initiating cause in the same way, the "responsibility" for the event lies in the primary cause, rather than the initiating cause—though, to be sure, the event wouldn't have taken place if not for that initiating cause.

Now, apply this same kind of reasoning to people, and our own behavior. Events that occur around us serve as initiating causes for events. However, to the extent that our own actions are the result of ourselves (as a principle cause), we are responsible for those actions. Consider your reaction to the image here.

The sight of that model was an initiating cause of whatever reaction you had. Your reaction would not have occurred if not for that initiating cause. However, I'm confident that not every reader responded in exactly the same way. Let's break it down to just one (and perhaps the most obvious) response: attraction (or not). Some of you might have deemed the model to be physically attractive, but others did not. The model is the same initiating cause for both groups of responses, so the difference must be found not in the model but in *you.*

Although the sight of the model was the initiating cause of your response, the principle cause was something about *you* that facilitated attraction, or not. Rather obviously, if you are heterosexual female (or a gay male) you're presumably much more likely to find that model sexually attractive than if you are heterosexual male (or gay female). Even if the sexuality "lines up," there are still matters of personal taste. Perhaps that model just isn't "your type?" The point, of course, is that your response to that model is "up to you" in the sense that your actions stem from something about you, as opposed to something wholly external to you.

As another example, consider two politicians both being offered an identical bribe by the same lobbyist. One politician accepts the bribe, the offer refuses. Both experienced the same initiating cause (the bribe), but their reactions were different. Wherein is to be found the difference? In *them*, of course! There is something about the one that makes him susceptible to bribes, and something about the other that makes him resistant. Their actions, therefore, are attributable to themselves, as principle causes, rather than the bribes, as initiating causes.

Just to be clear, compatibilists (include Stoics) acknowledge that the sort of person we are (i.e., our nature as a principle cause) is also the product of Fate—in other words, the sort of person we are, just like everything else in the cosmos, is the will of Fate, and couldn't have been any other way. Nevertheless, when it comes to personal responsibility, what we seek (according to compatibilists) is *not* some ability to somehow defy Fate (or causal determinism, in less "spiritualized" versions of compatibilism), but simply the ability to be able to trace our actions back to our own character, as opposed to something wholly external to us. We blame someone for having an extra million dollars in her bank account when it's the result of accepting a bribe. We don't blame that person if it was the result of an error in a bank computer. The first example can be traced back to her character, the second cannot.

The Roman Stoic, Epictetus, famously delineates those things that are "up to us" from those that are not in the very first paragraph of the *Enchiridion*.

> *There are things which are within our power, and there are things which are beyond our power. Within our power are opinion, aim, desire, aversion, and, in one word, whatever affairs are our own. Beyond our power are body, property, reputation, office, and, in one word, whatever are not properly our own affairs.*[457]

Notice that those few things "within our power" are all "internal," all mental activities stemming from the sort of person we are: "opinion, aim, desire, aversion." Notice also that

those things described as being "beyond our power" are all "external" to us: body, property, reputation, office. You might immediately wonder how your own body is listed as being beyond your power. After all, it seems obvious that one can control one's body to make it do as we wish. Tell that to someone with cerebral palsy, or a broken leg, or arthritis, or who is suffering from a stroke, or in the midst of a heart attack, or who is pinned underneath the rubble of a collapsed building. You can "will" any number of things, but whether or not those things come to be depends upon the cooperation of things not under your control—including the operations of your own body.

You might wonder how "property" is not under your control. After all, your property is *your* property, to dispose of as you see fit—unless someone *steals* it. Or it's destroyed in an earthquake, or eaten by termites. "But isn't my reputation under my own control?" No. Your reputation is always the product of your actions as interpreted and judged by *others*. Those judgments are not under your control. Your behavior might be interpreted as "confidence" by one person and "arrogance" by another. What if the person judging you is racially biased, or sexist?

While traditional ("orthodox") Stoics believed that all events are fated to occur exactly as they do, some contemporary readers might be uncomfortable with the idea of Fate, or Providence, or even the plainly secular notion of causal determinism. Indeed, some contemporary Stoics offer a revised version of what is "up to us" that doesn't place so much emphasis on Fate.

William Irvine, for example, suggests that we should interpret Epictetus' "dichotomy of control" as a "trichotomy of control," instead.[458] A traditional reading of Epictetus' passage above would delineate those things over which we have complete control (e.g., opinion, desire, goal-setting, etc.), from those over which we do not have complete control (e.g., the outcome of

---

[457] Epictetus, *Enchiridion*, section I. The entire work is available at the end of this chapter.
[458] See William Irvine's book, *A Guide to the Good*

Life—and specifically his chapter entitled "The Dichotomy of Control."

events). Irvine, however, thinks these divisions are not sufficiently subtle (or accurate). Instead, he proposes three categories:

1. Things over which we have complete control (e.g. goal-setting).
2. Things over which we have no control at all (e.g., whether or not the sun will rise tomorrow, or events in the past).
3. Things over which we have some control, but not complete control (e.g., whether we win a competition).

Some things are obviously completely beyond our control, and it seems futile to worry about them. It is in no way "up to me" whether the sun rises tomorrow. Similarly, events that have already occurred are obviously beyond my control. Obsessing over something that happened yesterday, or a few years ago, is a waste (except, perhaps, if all we're talking about is learning a lesson so as to be less likely to repeat a similar mistake in the future). Wringing our hands over what happened in the past is not a good use of time or resources, as nothing can be done to change the past.

Other things are things of which we are in complete control. Although Epictetus includes desires and aversions in this category, Irvine thinks him mistaken, if we assume the common understanding of those terms. In a great many cases, desires and aversions simply occur, rise up within us whether we would want them to, or not. If I am hungry, and see some food, it doesn't seem fully under my control whether or not I desire to eat. Similarly, if I am uncomfortable around spiders (as I am), it doesn't seem fully under my control whether or not I will be startled and uncomfortable (to say the least) should a big spider drop onto my face while I'm sleeping. Irvine thinks that desires and aversions actually belong in the third category (see below). If so, what remains for this category? Irvine's answer

is goal-setting and personal values.

Goal-setting is completely under our control in the sense that although we are not in full control over whether we achieve our goals, we are in control of what goals we set for ourselves in the first place. If my goal is to win a sparring match in a martial arts tournament, I have set for myself a goal that is not fully under my control. After all, my opponent is going to have some say as to the outcome of our match! He might be much more skilled than I. My body might not cooperate. I might twist an ankle, or have a heart attack in the middle of the fight. I can't guarantee that I will win the fight, as "winning the fight" is a goal that exceeds my control. But, if my goal is, instead, to fight as well as I'm able, given the circumstances, it seems I have a set a goal that is within my control. After all, my own effort seems "up to me," even in the compatibilist sense favored by traditional Stoics.

Values are also under my control, according to Irvine. Whether or not I become wealthy is not fully up to me, but whether or not I value wealth is—at least in the compatibilist sense that it stems from my character as a principle cause. To the extent that our values stem from, and define, our character, our own character is fully up to us as well.

What remains are all those things that are "somewhat" up to us—neither wholly beyond our control, nor wholly under our control. Let's return to the sparring match, as it illustrates precisely the sorts of actions Irvine thinks belong to this category. As mentioned, the outcome of the match is not fully under my control, but it's also not wholly outside of my control, according to Irvine. After all, my own preparation and effort surely play some causal role in determining the outcome of the match. Needless to say, if I have trained hard, and if I fight to the best of my ability, I am more likely to win the match than if I hadn't trained at all, or if I half-heartedly compete.[459]

To summarize, (orthodox) Stoics believed

---

[459] I feel it important to point out that this trichotomy is *not* orthodox Stoic thought, but Irvine's own, modified, version. A traditional Stoic would likely counter that the outcome of

that match (for example) is not even partially under my control, as I could get in a car accident on the way to the tournament, or have a heart attack moments before it begins, etc.

that all events are fated to occur exactly as they do by virtue of the perfectly rational will of Fate. Nevertheless, there is a sense in which we are responsible for our actions, and our proper focus should be on those things that are "up to us" rather than those that are not. Even a more contemporary (less "fatalistic") interpretation acknowledges that there are degrees of control we can exercise over various things. Recognizing this, and regulating our mental life on that basis, leads us to the final category of Stoic theory: "ethics."

This final category has a misleading name. Most of us, today, when we think of "ethics," think either of a list of moral commandments ("thou shalts" and "thou shalt nots") or else a formalized study of moral concepts. Stoic ethics didn't so much address moral rules governing our behavior with others (though such things were certainly derived from their system) as it addressed an understanding of how best to achieve *eudaimonia* ("happiness"—understood by the Stoics as "tranquility"). Stoicism was more "self-help" than "ethics" (as most understand the term today).

"Ethics" involved the proper use of what is "up to us"—namely, the judgments we make concerning events as they transpire. According to orthodox Stoicism, given Fate, whatever happens was fated to occur, and could not have turned out any other way. Similarly, whatever *will* happen is also the unavoidable will of Fate. What is up to us is the extent to which we align our will with Fate. What is at stake is our own tranquility.

The Stoics offered what would become a famous analogy to illustrate our relationship to Fate. Imagine a dog leashed to a cart (or, today, a slow-moving car). The dog is being pulled, and will be pulled, in whatever direction the cart (or car) goes. Resistance is futile. The cart (or car) *will* "win." In other words, the dog is going to end up wherever he is taken. Now consider the difference between the dog that is being dragged, and the one that is happily following the cart. Both end up at the same destination, but one has a miserable trip. So too with us, and Fate.

Our lives will transpire however Fate wills them to unfold. There is nothing we can do about

that. What is up to us, however, is whether we align our will with Fate and walk, or get dragged. It makes no difference to Fate, but it makes a lot of difference to us. Needless to say, our lives will be much more pleasant if we avoid getting dragged.

Why is it that so many of us get "dragged" along by Fate? Largely because of an improper use of our faculties of "assent" and "desire." Stoicism claims that most of us suffer from false beliefs (judgments) and improper desires. To understand the process by which we form false judgments, we need to understand how the Stoics thought we formed judgments in the first place. Our minds process information in the following steps:

- Representation: the mind receives the images (impressions) that come through our bodily sensations.
- Judgment: An almost involuntary/unconscious judgment concerning the representation, shaped by the person's dispositions, preconceptions, and mental habits.
- Presentation: Presentation of the impression and judgment to the conscious mind. In effect, the soul tells itself what a given impression *is*.
- Assent: Formation of desires and impulses to action based upon our judgments about a thing. We give "assent" to the representation by acting upon it in a certain way.

Imagine that someone returns to a parking lot to discover her car has been keyed. As might be typical, she gets very upset. What has happened here? First, she received an "impression"—namely, the sight of her car with a scratch across its paint. Then, she has a (presumably quick) "conversation" with herself in which she interprets that impression. Judging from her reaction, it's obvious that she formed some sort of negative judgment in response to that impression. "Someone keyed my car? This sucks!" She then "assents" to that judgment by virtue of her actions (e.g., swearing, physiological responses such as an increased pulse rate or a headache, throwing her purse down, etc.).

One of Epictetus' most famous saying is that people "are disturbed not by things, but by the views which they take of things." In other words, things and events are not good or bad, in themselves. They take on the quality of good or bad by virtue of the judgments that we *add* to them. The controversial rejection of emotion attributed to Stoicism stems from this.

Emotions are thought to be our "assent" to judgments. When we cry in response to an event, we have assented to the judgment that there is something "bad" about what happened. When we fume in anger, that anger *is* our assent to the judgment that some event is worthy of our anger. Traditional Stoics believe that that is simply not true.

If I get angry at the sight of my keyed car, my anger is my assent to the judgment that it's a bad thing that my car has been keyed. Stoics believe that we should not "add" to appearances, but accept them as they are presented to us. As Epictetus says, "Right from the start, get into the habit of saying to every harsh appearance, 'You are an appearance, and not the only way of seeing the thing that appears.' Then examine it and test it by the yardsticks you have."

Being angry that my car was keyed implies that I have added a judgment ("this is bad") to an appearance (the literal sight of my car, now with an irregular line through the paint). There is nothing inherently bad about a car with a line scratched through its paint. What makes it bad is my own belief that it is bad. If I don't add that judgment to the appearance, I won't be angered by the sight of it, and my tranquility will be preserved.

"But it *is* a bad thing that your car got keyed!" you might respond. "Now it is worth less, and it doesn't look as good, and you'll have to pay to get the paint fixed, or at least fix it yourself, and that will be a hassle. Some jerk vandalized your property, and he didn't have that right."

So, I should give him control over my mind, in addition to control over my paint job? According to Stoicism, externals are not up to me. My car is an external. I can't control whether or not it remains in pristine condition. Even accepting Irvine's trichotomy of control, at best the appearance of my car is something over which I have some, but not total, control.

For example, I might make it a point to park it only in "good" areas, with ample lighting, and in so doing try to reduce the risk of vandalism. Even then, the best I can achieve is risk reduction, not risk elimination. In an obvious, common-sense, sort of way, I am not in control of the other 7 billion (or so) people in the world. If someone wants to key my car, there is no way I can guarantee it won't happen unless I don't have a car—in which case the person could just vandalize other of my property instead.

Stoicism holds that externals (my car) are not under my control, but my response to events is (at least in the sense that it's based on my character). A vandal has sufficient power to damage my car, but that vandal doesn't have sufficient power to make me upset. I must give him that power. Again we can appeal to Epictetus: "For another cannot hurt you, unless you please. You will then be hurt when you consent to be hurt." When a vandal damages my car, he damages an external—something that was never under my control to begin with. When I become upset at the vandalism, I have let the vandal damage my virtue. "If a person had delivered up your body to some passer-by, you would certainly be angry. And do you feel no shame in delivering up your own mind to any reviler, to be disconcerted and confounded?"

Remember that the primary function of philosophy, of all these efforts, according to Stoicism, is *eudaimonia*—happiness, understood as a state of tranquility that we can achieve when we live "according to Nature." We live according to Nature when we are governed by Reason, when we employ what is up to us (our judgments) properly, by recognizing what is up to us and what is not, and by aligning our will with that of "Fate" with regard to those things not up to us.

If your goal is something different, their advice and strategies are unlikely to make much sense. If, for example, your goal in life is to maintain a car with an unblemished surface, you will probably not agree with their advice. Good luck with that. Vandals are numerous—as are branches, rocks tossed by other cars, birds, wind and other erosive elements, etc. If your happiness is based on whether or not you can keep your car sufficiently pretty, you are setting yourself up for a lifetime of challenge and frustration. If, on the other hand, you prefer tranquility to an impeccably painted car, then the Stoic strategy might be right for you.

While specific exercises will be addressed in the next section, we can presently outline how Stoics believed we should exercise that which is up to us: our judgments.

In the first place, there is the process of disciplining our assent. Recall that for Stoics, "assent" occurs when we accept an appearance as true. However, most of us, much of the time, do not merely accept the appearance as it is presented to us, but "add" to the appearance (e.g., the mere sight of my now-scratched car transforms into the angrily entertained thought that my car has been scratched—with the anger indicating the addition of the judgment that it's a bad thing for my car to have been scratched). Generally speaking, then, we should resist adding to appearances.

In addition to regulating our assent to appearances, we ought to regulate our desires. Given the Stoic belief in Fate, the proper use of desire is to desire whatever is fated to occur. As Epictetus says, "Demand not that events should happen as you wish; but wish them to happen as they do happen, and you will go on well."

We have already discussed the Stoic notions of freedom and Fate above. If you accept the doctrine of Fate, the Stoic advice seems like common sense. If there is a conflict between your desires, and reality, there are only two ways to resolve that conflict: either change reality, or change your desires. But, given the Stoic doctrine of Fate, it is not within our power to change reality. Events will transpire as they have been fated to transpire. So, the only remedy within my power is to change my desires instead.

What should I desire? Whatever it is that actually transpires! If I "embrace fate" and desire things to happen as they do, in fact, happen, then

my desires will always be satisfied, and I will never be frustrated. Even if one accepts Irvine's modified Stoicism with its trichotomy of control instead, and acknowledge that there are things that are up to us (e.g., judgments), other things not at all up to us (i.e., externals, in general), and other things that are not fully up to us (e.g., externals to which we contribute, such as the outcome of a competition), we can still recognize that there is a way to regulate our desires so as to promote our own tranquility.

Imagine that I am going to participate in a sparring match with another fighter. Suppose my desire is to win the fight. If one believes in Fate, I am either fated to win the fight, or not. If I am not fated to win the fight, and I desire to win, then I desire something not under my control, and am setting myself up for frustration. So, a safer (and more appropriate) desire would be to desire whichever outcome is fated to happen. In that way, I will be satisfied either way.

Even if we are reluctant to accept the doctrine of Fate, there is still a plausible sense in which desiring victory is unwise. Even if the outcome is not fated, it nevertheless remains not fully under my control. Using Irvine's categories, I contribute to the outcome of the fight by virtue of my preparation and performance, but it's not fully under my control by any stretch of the imagination. My opponent will presumably want to win, too.

Desiring to "win" is to desire something beyond my control, but desiring something like "doing my best, under the circumstances" is more realistic. Even if I "lose," I can still satisfy my desire if only I do the best I can. This is similar to the folk wisdom behind encouraging someone to "do your best."

At this point, some of you might rightly be wondering if this strategy doesn't just amount to paralysis in the face of life. "Desire what happens? How does anyone *do* anything, then? It's not as if I can sit back and watch my own sparring match to see its outcome, and then quickly desire that particular outcome. It's not as if, when I get sick, I can just wait to see what happens so I know which outcome (recovery, or death) to desire."

According to Stoicism, "externals" have no

true value. Only that which is up to us (our own virtue) has any value. All other things (all externals) are, strictly speaking, "indifferent." Cars are indifferent, having no value (positive or negative). This is why a proper Stoic will not be disturbed if his car gets scratched. It had no value to begin with! All "things" in our lives (e.g., clothes, furniture, iphones, etc.) are indifferent, in this sense. More controversially, even such things as friends, health, and reputation, in that they are externals, are likewise "indifferent."

That being said, some externals, while being "indifferent," are nevertheless "preferred." Things that are "preferred" are those things that are consistent with our nature as rational animals and that are generally conducive to flourishing (though not necessary for it). Eating, for example, is "preferred" over starving. Being healthy is preferred to being sick. Being financially secure is preferable to desperate poverty. Having good friends is preferable to being lonely. Having a good reputation is preferable to being slandered. With regard to things that are preferred, in this sense, it is appropriate for us to pursue them—though we should recognize that they remain "indifferent," remember that our happiness does not depend on them, and "embrace Fate" with regard to them.

How does a Stoic do this? By acting "under reserve." Stoics, like everyone else, have to make plans, have to make decisions, have to actually live their lives. Yet, Stoics are supposed to desire that things happen as they are fated to happen. A Stoic reconciles these demands by forming conditional desires in the following general form: "I want X, if Fate permits" (where "X" is something to be preferred).

Before delving into this notion in greater detail, please note the obvious similarity between "*acting under reserve*" and the Muslim and Christian notion of "God willing." Muslims will often say, of some future event they intend, "insha'Allah" (God willing)."And never say of anything, 'I shall do such and such thing tomorrow. Except (with the saying): 'If God wills!'"[460] In the Christian New Testament, we

find the same idea: "Now listen, you who say, 'Today or tomorrow we will go to this or that city, spend a year there, carry on business and make money.' Why, you do not even know what will happen tomorrow. What is your life? You are a mist that appears for a little while and then vanishes. Instead, you ought to say, 'If it is the Lord's will, we will live and do this or that.'"[461]

What the Muslim, Christian, and Stoic systems have in common in this respect is that each recognizes a power far greater that controls what transpires, and each recognizes the value of aligning your own will with that power. A Stoic, then, will pursue preferable things, but recognize that those things are not under her control (at least not fully), and will also recognize that not even those things have true value. Health is preferable to sickness, and I will pursue it as such. I will even desire health—if Fate permits (or, God willing). If I find myself sick instead of healthy, I will pursue recovery and desire it—if Fate permits. Whatever happens, sickness or health, recovery or decline, is beyond my control, and none of those outcomes is a prerequisite for the only thing of true value: virtue. I can be virtuous (by regulating my assent, and aligning my will with Nature) whether I am sick or healthy—though it's preferable to be healthy.

So, there is no need to think that Stoics must curl up into a fetal position, awaiting Fate and unsure of what they should desire. They will live and choose in ways outwardly similar to everyone else. They will pursue friendship and health, prosperity and love. When they do so, however, they recognize what is up to them, and what it not, and they regulate their desire so as to desire only what Fate permits. They guard themselves from attachment to "indifferents," and they discipline themselves in ways that preserve and promote their own tranquility in the face of whatever Fate has in store. Admittedly, however, this is easier said, than done. Accordingly, Stoicism had numerous exercises with which to make such a life possible.

Some key stoic ideas from this preceding section that will find prominence in Cicero's

---

[460]Surat Al Kahf (18):23-24.

[461]James 4:13-15.

writing include:

- The "divine spark" of Reason within all persons
- The claim that only virtue has intrinsic worth
- The view that Fate/Providence/Reason governs the cosmos
- The value of disciplining one's judgments and emotions

Cicero's Ideas

I want to begin this section with a brief excerpt from one of Cicero's letters to his friend, Atticus, written on March 12th, 49 BCE:

Should one stay in one's country even if it is under totalitarian rule?

Is it justifiable to use any means to get rid of such rule, even if they endanger the whole fabric of the state? Secondly, do precautions have to be taken to prevent the liberator from becoming an autocrat himself?

If one's country is being tyrannized, what are the arguments in favour of helping it by verbal means and when occasion arises, rather than by war?

Is it statesmanlike, when one's country is under a tyranny, to retire to some other place and remain inactive there, or ought one to brave any danger in order to liberate it? . . .

Ought one, even if not approving of war as a means of abolishing tyranny, to join up with the right-minded party in the struggle

against it?

In this personal letter, Cicero is outlining some of the iconic "problems" of political philosophy that thinkers have grappled with for thousands of years, and that continue to this day. When is rebellion justifiable? When is war (rather than mere speech) warranted? Is it a violation of one's duty to one's country to flee the country and preserve oneself rather than stay, resist, and risk persecution?

These musings of Cicero are all the more powerful when we remember that, for him, they were not merely hypothetical questions! He was writing and thinking about these things before, during, and after the "tyranny" of Julius Caesar, and in the context of his own participation in the power struggle that followed.

Our present treatment of Cicero's thought will begin with his (Stoic) understanding of human nature, and the Law of Nature that accompanies it. We will then see how this feeds into his defense of "republican" forms of government,[462] as well as particular policies.

Cicero (like the stoics) believed that all humans are rational, by Nature. This rational soul is the "divine" and immortal element implanted in us all by "God," the "divine spark" or Reason establishing our kinship with each other and with God.[463] As such, we all belong to the common "family" of Humanity itself.[464] Our shared capacity for reason grants us each the additional capacity for moral judgment, and for the cultivation of virtue. "Virtue is the same in humans and gods, for they partake in moral perfection."[465] These capacities can be corrupted by false beliefs and bad habits, but this means they can also be developed as well. "There is no person of any nation who cannot reach virtue with the aid of a guide."[466]

---

[462] Not to be confused with the contemporary Republican party in the United States!

[463] *Republic*, 3.1a. Make no mistake about it, Cicero certainly did not have the Judeo-Christian God in mind! Indeed, Cicero died several decades before Jesus of Nazareth was even born. The "God" that he has in mind is the Stoic notion of

God, understood as the supremely rational "Logos" that governs all the operations of Nature.

[464] *Laws*, 1.23

[465] ibid., 1.25

[466] ibid., 1.30

This kind of cosmopolitanism might seem commonsensical to modern ears, but it's difficult to overstate just how radical this kind of thinking was, at the time. Greeks thought of anyone "non-Greek" as "barbarians." Aristotle argued that some people are "natural slaves." Even during the time of the Republic (to say nothing of the Empire), Rome had a vast slave population, and a vast non-citizen population with few, if any, rights. People who were "other" by virtue of their ethnicity, language, religion, citizenship, or nationality were generally regarded as inferior. This notion that *all* people, regardless of national origin, ethnicity, language, or culture was part of the same cosmic family, that each person has some baseline level of moral value, and that we each have duties to each other—even to those "others" who live "over there" was a philosophically and politically revolutionary idea.

Although cosmopolitan in theory, this does not prevent loyalty to one's own nation or family. Our personal resources and capabilities are less than the needs of all the people in the world, so obligations will vary based on circumstances and the degree of relationships we have with others.[467] Because of our shared kinship with all persons, we have minimal obligations of "decency" to all of humanity, but greater obligations to our own family and country. Our most primary obligations, understandably, are to our own nation, parents, children, and spouse. A secondary tier of obligations would be the rest of one's family. Finally, all the rest of humanity resides in a third tier of obligation.

What this amounts to is a recognition that it is acceptable to prioritize our own national and personal responsibilities.

That does not mean that we are bound to sacrifice our own vital interests to other people. On the contrary, in so far as we can serve our interests without harming anyone else, we should do so. Chrysippus puts the point with his usual aptness: 'A

man running a race in the stadium ought to try his best and exert himself to the utmost in order to win. In no circumstances, however, should he trip up his competitors or impede them with his hand.' The same applies to the struggle of life. Anyone may fairly seek his own advantage, but no one has a right to do so at another's expense.[468]

That being said, we do, nevertheless have responsibilities that cross international borders, and there are limits to what is permissible in our treatment of other nations. "The same thing is established not only in nature, that is in the law of nations, but also in the laws of individual peoples, through which the political community of individual states is maintained: one is not allowed to harm another for the sake of one's advantage."[469]

Indeed, it is possible to infer what Cicero might have thought of the issue of illegal immigration, in this context. "Wrong is likewise done by those who ban and eject foreigners from their cities, . . . True, non-citizens are not entitled to the same rights as citizens . . . . But the exclusion of aliens from the city's amenities is completely opposed to natural human relations."[470] From Cicero's perspective, we have moral obligations to citizens and non-citizens alike due to our shared humanity. In today's terminology, all persons have moral standing regardless of their legal documentation—though he also acknowledges that it is fair for citizens to have more privileges than non-citizens.

In Cicero's time, Rome was a powerful nation that exerted influence over many other lands—and that fact only became more prominent with the growth of the Roman Empire. Today, the United States wields tremendous political, economic, cultural, and military influence across the globe.

"Hegemonic leadership," traditionally, referred to actions taken by a powerful State (e.g., Sparta, or Rome) out of self-interest, but which

---

[467] *On Duties*, 1.59
[468] ibid., 3.42

[469] ibid., 3.23
[470] ibid., 3.46

provided benefits to other States (e.g., security). Today, hegemony tends to refer to the domination by a single powerful nation (e.g., the United States), from a self-appointed mission to defend "the world" against "rogue nations," to preserve peace and economic stability, etc. Cicero, in the context of Roman hegemony, claimed that fear inspires hate, and hegemony by fear was ultimately self-destructive. "Fear is but a poor safeguard of lasting power; while affection, on the other hand, may be trusted to keep it safe forever."[471]

Cicero recognized that power tends to corrupt, however, and when one State wields immense hegemonic power "it is difficult to preserve the spirit of fairness which is absolutely essential for justice."[472] Seemingly benevolent hegemony can degenerate into international-scale tyranny. But, no power is so strong as to be able to rule, by fear, indefinitely.[473] A lasting and just hegemony must be based not on military power and intimidation, but by moral worth, and moral leadership that will earn the admiration and respect of other states.[474]

This idea, while ancient, is not necessarily outdated. In a speech by President Obama made in June, 2009, he said: "Democracy, rule of law, freedom of speech, freedom of religion - those are not simply principles of the West to be hoisted on these countries, but rather what I believe to be universal principles that they can embrace and affirm as part of their national identity, . . . The United States' job is not to lecture, but to encourage, to lift up what we consider to be the values that ultimately will work not just for our country, but for the - the aspirations of a lot of people."[475]

Cicero and President Obama seem to have a couple points in common on this issue. In the first place, both speak from the perspective of a State that is powerful and influential on the global stage. Secondly, they both speak of universal values, transcending borders—and both believe that their respective nations are best served when they lead by example, rather than merely proclaiming and preaching, let alone bullying.

Sometimes, however, no matter how benevolent and enlightened a nation might try to be, conflict with other nations proves unavoidable, and war results. What moral principles govern the waging and conduct of war?

Cicero is sometimes considered the father of "just war theory." Just war theory is usually divided into two categories: *jus ad bellum* and *jus in bello* [roughly, "right to war" and "right in war" (or "laws in war"), respectively].

Jus ad bellum considerations govern when it is morally permissible to go to war in the first place. According to Cicero (and most just war theorists since him), war (the use of force) is

---

[471]ibid., 2.23. Contrast that idea with Machiavelli's, over a thousand years later: "Upon this a question arises: whether it be better to be loved than feared or feared than loved? It may be answered that one should wish to be both, but, because it is difficult to unite them in one person, is much safer to be feared than loved, when, of the two, either must be dispensed with. Because this is to be asserted in general of men, that they are ungrateful, fickle, false, cowardly, covetous, and as long as you succeed they are yours entirely; they will offer you their blood, property, life and children, as is said above, when the need is far distant; but when it approaches they turn against you. And that prince who, relying entirely on their promises, has neglected other precautions, is ruined;

because friendships that are obtained by payments, and not by greatness or nobility of mind, may indeed be earned, but they are not secured, and in time of need cannot be relied upon; and men have less scruple in offending one who is beloved than one who is feared, for love is preserved by the link of obligation which, owing to the baseness of men, is broken at every opportunity for their advantage; but fear preserves you by a dread of punishment which never fails."—The Prince, Chapter 27.

[472] ibid.,1.64

[473] ibid., 2.25-2.26

[474] ibid., 2.31

[475] http://www.telegraph.co.uk/news/worldnews/barackobama/5426465/Barack-Obama-says-US-must-lead-by-example.html

morally permissible only as a last resort. "We must resort to force only in case we may not avail ourselves of discussion."[476] This is an extension of his moral philosophy, in general, according to which a good man is one who helps all whom he can and harms nobody, unless provoked by wrong.[477] In other words, only wars of self-defense are morally justifiable.

With regard to *jus in bello*, there are moral restraints during the conduct of the war as well. "In undertaking, waging, and ending wars both justice and good faith should be as strong as possible, and there should be official interpreters of them."[478] A formal declaration of war is required. "No war is just, unless it is entered upon after an official demand for satisfaction has been submitted or warning has been given and a formal declaration made."[479] Cruelty is to be limited (*On Duties*, 3.46), promises to enemies are to be kept (*On Duties*, 1.40), and enemies who surrender are to be spared (*On Duties*, 1.35).

In case it's not obvious why Cicero thought that even one's enemies have rights, and are people to whom we have moral obligations, remind yourself of his starting premise: all persons share in reason, all people have some measure of moral value, and a natural law governs all people, regardless of political lines drawn on a map. "There is only one justice which constitutes the bond among humans, and which is established by one law, which is the right reason in commands and prohibitions."[480] This natural law can't be overruled by any human decree, nor any considerations of convenience or self-interest. The natural law is the foundation and judge of all human laws, whether domestic or international.

We can distinguish good from bad laws by the standard of nature.[481]

There is one, single, justice. It binds

together human society and has been established by one, single, law.[482]

Law in the proper sense is right reason in harmony with nature. It is spread through the whole human community, unchanging and eternal, calling people to their duty by its commands and deterring them from wrong-doing by its prohibitions. . . . This law cannot be countermanded, nor can it be in any way amended, nor can it be totally rescinded. We cannot be exempted from this law by any decree of the Senate or the people; nor do we need anyone to else to expound or explain it. There will not be one such law in Rome and another in Athens, one now and another in the future, but all people at all times will be embraced by a single and eternal and unchangeable law; and there will be, as it were, one lord and master of us all—the god who is the author, proposer, and interpreter of that law.[483]

Human laws that fail to conform to the standard provided by natural law are not, properly speaking, "laws" at all!

If ignorant unqualified people prescribe a lethal, instead of a healing, treatment, that treatment cannot properly be called 'medical.' In a community a law of just any kind will not be a law, even if the people (in spite of its harmful character) have accepted it. Therefore law means drawing a distinction between just and unjust, formulated in accordance with that most ancient and important of all things—nature; by her, human laws are guided in punishing the wicked and defending and protecting the good.[484]

---

476 ibid.,, 1.34-1.35
477 ibid., 3.76
478 *Laws*, 2.34
479 *Republic*, 3.35
480 *Laws*, 1.42

481 ibid., 1.44
482 ibid., 1.42
483 *Republic*, 3.33
484 *Laws*, 2.13

Going back to the nature (*physis*) v. custom (*nomos*) debate initiated by the sophists several chapters ago, Cicero clearly comes down on the side of nature—a position that will endear him to Christian "natural law" theorists in the Medieval period to come. And yet, if there is allegedly "one single law for all humanity," why are there so many different opinions, customs, and human laws? How do we explain all the cultural differences, variations in laws across geographic location and time, and all the differences in opinion even within the same community? How do we explain how same-sex marriage can be celebrated by a majority of the population in some countries, today, while homosexuals are being executed in brutal fashion in other parts of the world? Prescient thinker that he was, Cicero had an answer for that conundrum, as well.

> *Yet we are confused by the variety and variability of men's opinions; and because the same disagreement does not occur in regard to the senses. We think the senses are reliable by nature whereas we brand as illusory those ideas that vary from one person to another and do not always remain consistent within the same person. This distinction is far from the truth. In the case of our senses, no parent or nurse or teacher or poet or stage-show distorts them, nor does popular opinion lead them astray. For our minds, however, all kinds of traps are laid, either by the people just mentioned, who on receiving young untrained minds stain them and twist them as they please, or else by that power which lurks within, entwined with every one of our senses, namely pleasure, which masquerades as goodness but is in fact the mother of all ills. Seduced by her charms, our minds fail to see clearly enough the things that are naturally good, because those things lack the sweetness and the exciting itch of pleasure.*[485]

Think of it this way: most of us are not skeptics of relativists with respect to basic claims about perceptible things. As an example, most people are pretty darn confident that elephants are larger than house flies—and anyone who claims otherwise is either doing something odd with language, or else likely adopting an insincere philosophical pose for the sake of being contrary. Because sense-testimony is generally conducive to agreement, we imagine that empirical matters are factual, objective. However, when it comes to moral judgments, there is a variety of views.

Some people think that abortion is acceptable, and others think it is murder. Some people believe it's wrong to eat meat, and others worship at the altar of bacon. Same-sex marriage is now a constitutional right in the United States, but homosexuals are executed by being thrown off of buildings in ISIS-controlled parts of Syria.[486] We are taught one thing by our parents, perhaps another by teachers, perhaps another by friends, still another by our church, and yet another by the media and pop culture. This dizzying influx of contrary moral messages can cause us to conclude that there is no moral "truth" at all— only opinion.

What's more, Cicero points out that we can be "charmed" by pleasure into thinking that certain actions, because they are pleasurable, are also therefore "good"—while our senses generally provide no such ulterior motive.

For all these reasons, Cicero explains how people can come to the *false* conclusion that there is no objective moral law. However, Cicero is confident that there is, that, because we are social beings, unjust acts are contrary to our natural fellowship, and true laws, therefore, are intended to maintain social order and harmony.

Given his views on human nature and natural law, what sort of political system does Cicero recommend? Ultimately, he doesn't travel far from either Plato or Aristotle, in that he, like they, advocates a "polity," or "mixed" constitution. A notable difference, of course, is that while Plato imagines an ideal Republic, and Aristotle likewise

---

[485] *Laws*, 1.47
[486] http://www.nydailynews.com/news/

world/isis-militants-throw-gay-man-building-death-article-1.2041416

envisions a polity built "from scratch" in the *Laws*, Cicero models his own "ideal" state off of the actual Roman Republic that he tried so desperately to preserve and resurrect.

The Republic ("*res publica*") means "commonwealth," or the "common good." Technically, any form of government with a shared sense of justice and common interest could be called a "republic," in a broad sense, but for Cicero, a specifically "republican" form of government is a government of the whole people, by the whole people, and for the benefit of all the people.[487]

Like both Plato and Aristotle, Cicero discusses how the three major types of governments are prone to degeneration (monarchy into tyranny, aristocracy into oligarchy, and democracy into anarchic mob rule), even specifically referencing and summarizing Plato's own account.[488] In theory, mixed (balanced) constitution can prevent concentration (and abuse) of power.[489] The "defects" of each major government type are as follows:

Monarchy: the rest of the population has too small a role in legislation/debate

Aristocracy: the masses have too little liberty

Democracy: "equality" is *unequal* since merit is not recognized and rewarded

The best government will be a harmonious mix of all three of the other types—one in which no faction has "too much" power. As the actual Roman Republic was fading before him, Cicero wrote of the undue influence that wealth can have within a political community.

But they maintain that this ideal state has been ruined by people who cannot think

straight—people who, knowing nothing about worth (which resides in a few, and is discerned and assessed by a few), imagine that aristocrats are those with large fortunes and possessions or those who belong to famous families. When, as a result of this vulgar misconception, a few with money, not worth, have gained control of the state, those leaders seize the name of 'aristocrats' with their teeth, though lacking any right to it in fact. Money, name, and property, if divorced from good sense and skill in living one's life and directing the lives of others, lapse into total degradation and supercilious insolence. And indeed there is no more degenerate kind of state than that in which the richest are supposed to be the best. But what can be more splendid than a state governed by worth, where the man who gives orders to others is not the servant of greed, where the leader himself has embraced all the values which he preaches and recommends to his citizens, where he imposes no laws on the people which he does not obey himself, but rather presents his own life to his fellows as a code of conduct?[490]

Offices should not be assigned based on wealth (nor on mob rule, for that matter!), but (ideally) the "best" persons will be awarded office, and those who obtain them will legislate or rule for the good of all, with each class balanced in power and influence. This intended balance of power is not merely defensive, for the sake of stability, but reflects the normative ideal that all segments of the Republic *should* be represented and cared for. When this fails to be the case, the State ceases to be a "republic" (*res publica*) at all.[491]

---

[487] It is impossible not to hear echoes of this in final line of Abraham Lincoln's famous Gettysburg Address: "that we here highly resolve that these dead shall not have died in vain—that this nation, under God, shall have a new birth of freedom—and that government of the people, by the people, for the people, shall not perish from the earth."

[488] *Republic*, 1.65-1.68

[489] ibid., 1.69

[490] ibid., 1.51-1.53

[491] ibid., 3.43-3.45

As previously intimated, in Cicero's own time, the Republic was one in name only (e.g., there was the dictatorship of Pompey, followed by the dictatorship and proto-imperial rule of Gaius Julius Caesar). Cicero's writings aimed to produce a return to republicanism. In the *Roman Republic*, Consuls (joint heads of state) represent the monarchical element, the Senators represent the aristocratic element, and the Tribunes and popular assemblies represent the democratic element. When each class is virtuous, and performs its function for the good of all, the Republic itself will be virtuous, and politically stable.

His "republican" ideal is not applicable only to the actual Roman Republic, of course. In principle, it can be generalized and applied to any suitably arranged State. W. Julian Korab-Karpowicz usefully outlines several political and moral values that are fundamental to Cicero's "republican" government:[492]

- Legitimacy based on justice and service: the government is a trustee of the people, and its function is to care for the welfare of the people, as opposed to any particular faction of the people. (*On Duties*, 1.85)
- Limited and divided political power: a reasoned balance produces harmony and cooperation among social groups is needed. (*On Duties*, 2.69a)
- Freedom and responsibility: citizens have both the right and the duty to become knowledgeable and skillful so that they can be useful to society, and also free to express their opinion and participate in politics. (*Republic* 1.33 and *Laws* 3.27)
- Justice and cooperation: benefit (both individual and national) shouldn't be pursued if doing so harms others, and the common benefit should be pursued by means of just cooperation. (*On Duties*, 2.18)

- Leadership and loyalty: Leaders should be prudent and just, and this will inspire loyalty from the people and the Republic's allies abroad. (*Republic* 5.5 and *Laws* 3.5)
- Rationality and knowledge: All humans are gifted with reason, and should cultivate it to pursue practical and moral wisdom. Knowledge and wisdom are the result of proper education and training. (*Republic* 1.29)
- Human fellowship: common history, cultural traditions, and bonds of worship create strong bonds of fellowship. (*On Duties*, 1.55)
- Openness to other cultures: All humans are gifted with Reason, creating a common kinship that transcends geographical, national, and ethnic (etc.) barriers. (*On Duties*, 3.47)
- Moderation and peace: the well-being of society can be best served through moderate policies, and promoting and preserving peace. (*Republic* 2.26, *On Duties*, 1.35)

Cicero's Influence

Cicero's defense of "republicanism" was profoundly influential in the medieval period, and into the Renaissance and Enlightenment—inspiring Aquinas, Machiavelli, Montesquieu, and American "Founding Fathers" (e.g., John Adams, Thomas Jefferson, and James Madison). Indeed, traces (or at least analogues) of it can be seen in the U.S. government. The Supreme Court and Senate plausibly represent the "aristocratic" element, the President/executive branch the "monarchical" element, and the House of Representatives the "democratic" element

Aristotle wrote about the *Polis*—a kind of city-state that was already going "extinct" even at the time of his writing. Cicero, too, seemed to be writing of a kind of government (i.e., a Republic) that would make way for Imperial rule, only to be followed by the feudal system that would

---

[492] *On the History of Political Philosophy: Great Thinkers from Thucydides and Locke*, by W. Julian

Korab-Karpowicz. Pearson, 2012.

dominate Europe for centuries more. It wouldn't be until the Renaissance, over a thousand years later, that Cicero would be rediscovered, and discover a resurgence of popularity and influence.

Due in part to Petrarch's enthusiasm, the Italian Renaissance could be said to be a revival of Cicero—and only through him, of classical studies, in general. Cicero's ideal of a well-rounded citizen, skilled in language, responsible to his community, cultivated and refined in taste, became the ideal of the "renaissance man" amongst the Italian upper class.

Cicero's influence peaked in the 18th century, manifesting in such important figures as Locke, Hume, and Montesquieu. Cicero was so influential during the Renaissance that his "*De Officiis*" (*On Duties*) was the first classical work to be printed after the invention of the printing press.[493] Voltaire said of *On Duties:* "No one will ever write anything more wise, more true, or more useful. From now on, those whose ambition it is to give men instruction, to provide them with precepts, will be charlatans if they want to rise above you, or will all be your imitators."[494]

His influence did not end in the Renaissance, however, but continued on into the Enlightenment. As mentioned, he also inspired the "Founding Fathers" of America, with John Adams quoting Cicero numerous times in *his Preface on Government* (1786), and saying of him, "As all the ages of the world have not produced a greater statesman and philosopher united than Cicero, his authority should have great weight."[495] Thomas Jefferson also referenced the *Tuscan Disputations* in his own writings, and found a place in the *Declaration of Independence* for natural law and inalienable rights.

In the Middle Ages, Cicero would not "disappear," but his influence would wane, just as that of Greece and Rome, in general. Christian Europe would inherit *something* from ancient philosophy (Plato, through Augustine, and Aristotle, through Aquinas), but political philosophy would take a decidedly Christian turn for the next thousand years, or so. It is to this period of the history of political philosophy that we turn in our next chapter.

Critical Analysis

1. In your opinion, what are the strongest and most compelling points made by the philosopher or philosophers in this chapter? Why do you find those points to be convincing?
2. In your opinion, what are the weakest or least convincing points? Why? Can you anticipate any limitations or objections to their ideas not already addressed in the chapter?

Appendix: Application to Social Justice

Recall some of the questions posed by Cicero in a letter to one of his friends from earlier in the chapter:

> *Is it justifiable to use any means to get rid of such rule, even if they endanger the whole fabric of the state? Secondly, do precautions have to be taken to prevent the liberator from becoming an autocrat himself?*

> *If one's country is being tyrannized, what are the arguments in favour of helping it by verbal means and when occasion arises, rather than by war?*

> *Is it statesmanlike, when one's country is under a tyranny, to retire to some other place and remain inactive there, or ought one to brave any danger in order to liberate it?...*

---

[493] For comparison, *On Duties* was first published in 1465. The *Gutenberg Bible* was printed in 1455.

[494] "Note to Cicero," 1771.

[495] Selars, Mortimer. *American Republicanism: Roman Ideology in the United States*, NYU Press, 1994.

Ought one, even if not approving of war as a means of abolishing tyranny, to join up with the right-minded party in the struggle against it?

With the merest effort, we can "translate" these questions into more contemporary social justice contexts. Because, ironically enough, both Conservatives and Liberals in the United States seem to think that "the other side" is (or threatens) totalitarianism, I will offer roughly parallel versions for each camp.

Liberal: If Trump refuses to concede the 2020 election, should we demand the military remove him from power?
Conservative: If Biden steals the 2020 election, should Trump declare martial law until elections are secure and fair?

Liberal: Is Antifa right? Do we need to use force to stop American fascists?
Conservative: Were the Trump supporters who invaded the Capitol on January 6th 2021 right? Do we need to use force to stop American socialists?

Liberal: Given what's happening in the United States these days, should I just move to Canada?
Conservative: Given what's happening in California these days, should I just move to Texas?

Liberal: Even though I don't agree with Antifa's methods, should I support them anyway given that we're on the same "side?"
Conservative: Even though I don't agree with the Proud Boy's methods, should I support them anyway given that we're on the same "side?"

Whatever "side" *you* are on (if any), these are authentic questions that many of us grapple with—and neither the process of questioning nor the acquiring of answers is easy. If you are disturbed by the many incidents of racialized violence against persons of color by the police, what should you do? Mind your own business and try to forget about it? "Like" and share suitable posts on social media? Call your elected representatives and demand they try to bring about reforms? Vote for like-minded candidates? Participate in peaceful protests? Participate in rioting and looting? Join an organization that is willing to use violence, as deemed necessary, to bring about desired change?

If you have ever found yourself grappling with such questions on that topic, or any other pertaining to social justice, you're in the good company of Cicero, and countless others.

Beyond the timeless questions posed by Cicero, another idea from this chapter directly relevant to social justice is the "cosmopolitanism" of Stoicism derived from their version of "natural law."

In the West, at least, moral consideration had been historically "tribal." Those with moral "standing," the people who "count" when it comes to moral obligations, were members of your own family, (literal) tribe, and fellow "countrymen." Even within those circles, neither women nor children had equal moral standing to (adult) men. People from other communities and cultures were not "us," and, in some cases, were extended no moral standing at all. Not surprisingly, it was a simple matter to rationalize wars of conquest, looting of resources, capturing "foreigners" as slaves, and outright slaughter, given that "they" didn't have any rights or moral value.

With the Stoics, this mentality started to change. Even among "enlightened" philosophers of the ancient world, the Stoics were the "progressives" of their time. According to the Stoics, what makes someone "count," morally speaking, is their capacity for Reason. Since Reason is a shared capacity across humanity, we are all part of the same extended "family." Theoretically, using Reason as a necessary and sufficient condition for moral standing, *all* of humanity (with the admitted exclusion of persons with severe cognitive disabilities) "counts," regardless of "race," gender, culture, class status, etc. Male or female, emperor or slave, citizen or foreigner—Reason binds us all together with ties of moral obligation.

Although it found very imperfect and self-serving application, these Stoic ideas found expression in the Enlightenment ideas of "freedom," "equality," "natural rights," and other (now) familiar moral and political ideals. As mentioned earlier in the chapter, Cicero, specifically, was a source of inspiration for the Founding Fathers of the United States. The very notion of "natural rights" or "human rights," so central to campaigns of social justice—particularly for marginalized minority groups—can be traced back to the paradigm shifting contributions of the stoics. Even if Stoicism is not explicitly mentioned by very many people acting within the sphere of social justice today, a great many such persons, and the ideas they espouse are standing on Stoic foundations.

Chapter 18: Natural Law

Comprehension questions you should be able to answer after reading this chapter:

1. Why does Augustine reject the "optimism" of ancient political philosophy?
2. Why does Augustine think that it doesn't matter all that much under what political system a citizen or subject lives?
3. What does Augustine mean by the "Two Cities?" What are they, and who are the citizens of each?
4. What are the restraints on human laws and rulers, according to Augustine?
5. What is meant by *jus ad bello* and *jus in bello*? What requirements are associated with each of those two categories?
6. For Aquinas, what is the difference between "felicity" and "beatitude?" How does this difference relate to the proper roles for the Church and the State?
7. What does Aquinas mean by each of the following? Eternal Law, Natural Law, Human Law, Synderesis, Conscience.
8. What is a "conclusion" from the natural law? What is a "determination" from the natural law?
9. What is the "Law of Nations?"
10. Why does Aquinas think that kings should resist becoming tyrants?
11. What are the functions of human laws (and punishment)?
12. Explain Aquinas' position on private property. Are there any (moral) limits on wealth? How is Aquinas' approach to political philosophy different from Augustine's?

Our last chapter ended with Cicero, and, historically, the birth of the Roman Empire once Octavian became "Augustus." As mentioned, the influence of classical political philosophers did not disappear entirely during the Middle Ages. Indeed, the first thinker we will consider mentions Cicero by name numerous times. However, the tone of political philosophy, and the basic assumptions guiding it, changes in a profound way during this period, as illustrated by the "political philosophy" of St. Augustine.

Saint Augustine

Augustine is a very difficult "political philosopher" to explain or study, in part because Augustine would have been unlikely to consider himself as having done "political philosophy!"

Indeed, he has no particular work or essay which especially lends itself to gleaning his vision of politics. Instead, one must hunt for hints and themes throughout his massive theological work, *The City of God*.[496]

Augustine was born in 354 CE in Numidia—a North African province of the Roman Empire. At the age of 19, Augustine read Cicero's *Hortensius* and developed his love of philosophy. This led him to read, among many other things, the Bible—though he was not initially impressed! Instead, he drifted into Manichaeism and was associated with that school of thought for a decade.[497] Over this time, he also studied Skepticism and Neo-Platonism. Eventually, he began to study the Bible again, and was influenced by Bishop Ambrose of Milan. After experiencing a seemingly miraculous event

---

[496] For that reason, I have not included any primary source texts from Augustine, beyond the quotations found throughout the first section of this chapter. For those who would like to read *The City of God*, you may find a public domain version of it at the following URL: http://oll.

libertyfund.org/titles/2053

[497] A religion founded in the 3rd century, CE, by the Persian Mani that offered a thoroughly dualistic understanding of reality, including a vision of an eternal battle between (equal) forces of good and evil, light and darkness.

[hearing what sounded like a child's voice repeating "*tolle lege*" ("pick it up and read it")], he opened the Epistles of Paul to a random page and was drawn to *Romans* 13:13-14 ("Let us walk honestly as in a day, not in revelry and drunkenness, not in debauchery and licentiousness, not in quarreling and jealousy."). He eventually converted to Christianity himself, and was baptized by Bishop Ambrose on Easter in 387.

Upon his conversion, Augustine abandoned his old life for the sake of his new life, breaking with his Manichaean past and ultimately founding a monastery and school in Hippo (North Africa). He was ordained a priest in 391, an auxiliary bishop in 395, and was appointed Bishop of Hippo in 396—a position he would fill until his death, 34 years later.

This was a time of political and theological unrest for the Roman Empire. The Emperor Constantine converted to Christianity in 312 CE, and moved the capital of the Empire to Constantinople (named after himself) in 330. Although Christianity was now the dominant religion of the Empire, there were still many pagans, many of them from influential families. Indeed, it was not until 392, that the Emperor Theodosius commanded that formal public worship of pagan gods (the "gods of Rome") would end.

The Goths invaded and plundered Greece in 395, and then turned to Italy in 401-403. Other barbarian tribes invaded Gaul and Spain. Within the church, heresies were popping up—and Augustine first turned his writings to attack the views of the heretics, including his own former Manichaeism, as well as Pelagianism.[498]

In 410, Rome itself was sacked by the Goth invaders—something that hadn't happened for 800 years. Some of the Roman elite began to suggest that the gods of Rome were punishing the Empire for abandoning them—that the plight of Rome was the fault of Christianity. This allegation inspired the writing of Augustine's hugely influential *City of God*, within which he would not only defend Christianity against that charge, but also offer a withering criticism of the "virtues" of the Roman Republic (a topic we will turn to later).

Augustine died in 430. In 432 Vandals conquered and burned Hippo. After conquering Carthage in 439, they set their sights on Rome. In 476, a Germanic chieftan (Odaecer) toppled the last Roman Emperor (Augustulus Romulus). The "Eternal Empire" was divided amongst barbarian tribes, and the so-called Dark Ages began.

For roughly 500 years after the sack of Rome, various armies of barbarian invaders devastated Europe. With the fall of the Roman Empire, strong national powers (in the West) disappeared, replaced by small kingdoms and local governing. Self-supporting villages, dominated by agriculture, became the foundation for the feudal system in which lords (members of the noble class, including royalty) who typically had some land would offer some of that land (and a pledge of protection) to vassals, in exchange for loyalty, taxes, and service (including military conscription).

In an interesting twist, the barbarian invaders who were responsible for the collapse of the empire and this new geopolitical landscape, ultimately converted to Christianity. Though the barbarians had disrupted the overarching political authority of the Roman Empire, it was eventually replaced with the overarching religious authority of the Christian Church. Across Europe, a new notion of cultural unity developed: "Christendom."

Within the context of the feudal system, a new vision would emerge of Christian society jointly governed by two governments: one secular (King), and one spiritual (Pope). The pope was superior to the king in spiritual matters, while the king was superior to the pope in temporal (lay) matters. The pope and the church needs the support and protection of the king and his resources, but the king needs salvation.

Augustine's lifetime saw the end of the Roman Empire, and the beginning of the new medieval world in Europe. Augustine himself is

---

[498] A "heresy" that, among other things, denied the doctrine of Original Sin.

generally regarded as the first Christian philosopher, and a "bridge" between the ancient and medieval worlds.

Augustine was classically trained and educated, and although he held that Christianity was the one, true faith, and that pagan philosophies were all misguided to varying degrees, he did respect the Platonist school, crediting Plato with, in effect, having the right general idea of God and virtue, but missing the mark due to his lack of access to Revelation. Aristotle, too, conceived of God as the "Unmoved Mover," and the Stoics regarded God as a divine mind governing all of Nature.

As Augustine described them, "They were ignorant of the end to which all these [truths] were to be referred and the standard by which they were to be assessed."[499] There is precedent for giving ancient (pagan) philosophers partial credit for their insights. The Apostle Paul wrote that "They know the truth about God because he has made it obvious to them. For ever since the world was created, people have seen the earth and sky. Through everything God made, they can clearly see his invisible qualities—his eternal power and divine nature."[500]

Although Augustine is considered a "bridge" between the ancient (pagan) and medieval (Christian) worlds, his own approach to politics is also very much a rejection of much that was taken for granted by ancient philosophers.

The tradition of political philosophy as exemplified by such persons as Plato, Aristotle, and Cicero was one in which all parties took for granted that political society is natural for humans, and that we can only fulfill our potential within a political community. Although there was disagreement as to how best to do so, "everyone" agreed that the function of the State was to mold its citizens into the virtuous persons that they potentially are. Without too much exaggeration, politics was a means of "perfecting" (as much as is possible) the members of a community—even if only a small subset of that population (e.g., the "aristocrats") might fully actualize their potential.

The optimism of the Classical tradition is rejected by Augustine as naïve. Because of the Fall of Man, humans are incapable of "perfecting" themselves or even of achieving genuine and lasting happiness without the assistance of God. As a Christian, he accepted the doctrine of original sin, according to which all persons are spiritually depraved and disposed to sinfulness. All persons have fallen away from God and righteousness, and require salvation and God's grace in order to be better and to do better.

Because of our sinful nature, humans are naturally predisposed to misbehave. Left to our own devices, we will pursue our own desires, even at the expense of others. The State (and the threat of punishment) is necessary to restrain our behavior. Rather than being the natural means by which humans can be "perfected" within a community (as had been the vision of Plato, Aristotle, and Cicero), the State, for Augustine, is the necessary consequence of sin, and exists primarily to preserve order.

As we saw in the previous chapter, Cicero offered the historic Roman Republic as a model for a polity, and lamented its decline into what was a "republic" in name only. Augustine denies that a true Republic ever existed at all. Without God, there is no true justice, and instead people will pursue their own desires and possibly cloak it in the mantle of virtue. The shared values and vision of the common good that allegedly bound the members of the Ancient Republic together was really merely a "common agreement on the objects of their love"[501], and therefore, "there never was a Roman commonwealth."[502]

Justice is not truly possible in this world, though some communities come closer to it than others. Justice is not merely "giving to each their due," as was the commonly accepted definition in the ancient world. Instead, Augustine conceives justice as "love serving God only, and therefore ruling well all else." This provides the basis for his criticism of Cicero's idealized Roman Republic. Because the Romans never loved God, they were incapable of ever producing a genuine "republic"

---

[499] Augustine, *City of God*, 18.41
[500] *Romans*, 1.19-1.20

[501] *City of God*, 19.24
[502] ibid., 19.21

or "commonwealth," or ever being truly just. Indeed, without the true justice that starts with the love of God, he dismisses all States (even the Roman Republic) as mere gangs. "And what are kingdoms but gangs of criminals on a large scale? What are criminal gangs but petty kingdoms?"

Though actual earthly States will never be ideal, they do, nevertheless, serve a divine purpose: they maintain order and prevent excessive violence by the threat of punishment. With regard to crime and punishment, Augustine thinks that rulers are always authorized to punish "sins against nature" (e.g., murder), and also justified in punishing "sins against custom" (e.g., punishing tax evaders), so long as those customs do not themselves contradict God's commandments (e.g., punishing someone for worshipping God!).

The idealistic Statecraft of ancient philosophers was misguided, according to Augustine, not only because of the existence of sin, but because it's basic aim is futile. By seeking a kind of "salvation" in this life ("perfecting" citizens within their political community), ancient philosophers neglected the only salvation that exists and matters: eternal salvation. Moreover, against the backdrop of eternity, any human life—and even the life of an entire community, such as Rome, or the United States—is a mere "speck."

Augustine's pessimism (or possibly realism, depending on your perspective) is not to be confused with a different breed of pessimism/realism that would find eloquent voice in later thinkers, such as Hobbes and Machiavelli.

Augustine believes that politics is incapable of "saving" humanity, but his solution is not to eliminate moral considerations from the political sphere altogether, as a result. Instead, he shifts the source of moral improvement and salvation from politics to the God who "gives instructions for the promotion of the highest morality and the reproof of wickedness."[503] To grant such power and authority to political institutions, instead, is a form of idolatry.[504]

Because of his belief that the State (and politics) is incapable of "saving" persons, and that our proper priority should be Eternity, rather than this life, Augustine thought that it mattered little under what sort of political system a citizen of the "City of God" lived. Unlike his predecessors, he didn't advocate for any particular governmental type (e.g., monarchy, oligarchy, democracy, mixed polity, etc.), but thought that Christians should adapt and live according to the values of the Church no matter where they might reside.

This is not to say that he is completely indifferent to earthly laws, nor that there is no limits to what a Christian citizen should accept from their secular rulers. The primary goal of the State is to prevent and resolve conflicts. So long as it does this, there need be no conflict between the Christian and the State. They are free to follow the advice of Jesus himself to "Render therefore unto Caesar the things which are Caesar's; and unto God the things that are God's."[505]

However, what the Christian may not (morally) do is cooperate with any legislation that prevents them from worshipping, nor any that compels them to do impious or immoral things (e.g., a Christian has moral grounds to refuse to worship the Emperor of Rome as a deity).[506] Within such limits, though, the Christian citizen or subject should be obedient.

Let every person be subject to the governing authorities. For there is no authority except from God, and those that exist have been instituted by God. Therefore whoever resists the authorities resists what God has appointed, and those who resist will incur judgment. For rulers are not a terror to good conduct, but to bad. Would you have no fear of the one

---

[503] ibid., 2.25

[504] An interesting article on contemporary political "idolatry" in U.S. politics may be found here: http://www.huffingtonpost.com/jim-wallis/the-idolatry-of-politics_b_1475132.html

[505] *Matthew*, 22.21

[506] *City of God*, 5.17

who is in authority? Then do what is good, and you will receive his approval, for he is God's servant for your good. But if you do wrong, be afraid, for he does not bear the sword in vain. For he is the servant of God, an avenger who carries out God's wrath on the wrongdoer. Therefore one must be in subjection, not only to avoid God's wrath but also for the sake of conscience. For because of this you also pay taxes, for the authorities are ministers of God, attending to this very thing. Pay to all what is owed to them: taxes to whom taxes are owed, revenue to whom revenue is owed, respect to whom respect is owed, honor to whom honor is owed.[507]

Augustine grants to earthly rulers much leeway with regard to their laws and policies. They are free to enact whatever laws they wish, so long as they don't conflict with God's laws, and citizens (including Christian citizens) have a duty to obey those laws (so long as they don't conflict with God's laws), regardless of the moral qualities of their ruler, with no right to rebel or to civil disobedience.

While rejecting the idealistic perfectionism of ancient political philosophy, Augustine offers an alternative (Christian) model based off of his vision of "two cities," governed by two different objects of love. There is "the self-love that reaches the point of contempt for God," and "the love of God carried as far as contempt of self."[508]

The "Earthly City" aims at human glory, while the citizens of the "City of God" aim at glorifying God. The former is focused on the life of the "Flesh;" the latter on things of the "Spirit." In the Earthly City, people focus on the pleasures of earthly life, and the rewards and honors of this life. In the City of God, earthly goods are correctly regarded as being, ultimately, "worthless," and people are unattached to them, viewing themselves as though they were pilgrims journeying through a foreign land.[509]

It is important to note that Augustine is not describing two literal cities, or even two literal *kinds* of cities. Instead, he's describing different ways of life, different worldviews, and different perspectives. Within any actual community (e.g., Rome, Athens, Los Angeles, etc.) residents of both "cities" will be found, often living right next door to each other. Some Romans (or Angelinos) will be residents of the "Earthly City," and others will be residents of the "City of God"—it depends entirely on their faith (or lack thereof), the condition of their soul, and their fundamental value orientation in life.

The "City of God" can be found everywhere, or nowhere. Not even a specifically Christian theocracy would be identical to the City of God. Citizenship in the City of God is determined at the individual level, not at the institutional level—and certainly not established by lines on a map. It is a universal community of believers living in any and all nations who have set their hearts on God, and are "citizens" by God's Grace.

It is because of the non-political, non-geographical nature of the City of God that Augustine is so "hands off" with regard to actual political systems, and laws—with the only limit being that the "laws of man" not clash with the laws of God. There is even a place for war, within this framework.

Although Jesus is called the "Prince of Peace," Augustine was not a strict pacifist. He thought that Christians had a moral duty to seek and promote peace, but did allow that some use of violence (even war) can be justifiable. Acknowledging that it would be a great injustice if an unjust power conquered and ruled over just people, wars of self—defense, to repel an aggressor, are morally justifiable.[510] Christians, however, are morally entitled to refuse to fight in an unjust war.

Since Augustine is credited with being the first Christian philosopher, he is also credited with being the first Christian "just war theorist"—though his ideas are quite similar to those espoused by Cicero, before him.

As described in the previous chapter, just

---

[507] *Romans*, 13:1-7
[508] *City of God*, 14.28

[509] ibid., 19.17
[510] ibid., 4.15

war theory is generally broken down into two components: *jus ad bello* and *jus in bello*. The former refers to the conditions necessary for a morally justifiable war in the first place, and the latter refers to morally justifiable conduct while waging war. With regard to *jus ad bello*, Augustine claims the following conditions must be met:

- Just cause: self-defense against an external invasion, to avenge unjust injuries, to punish nations for failing to make amends for their unjust actions, to come to the defense of allies unjustly attacked, to gain the return of something wrongfully taken, to obey a divine command to go to war (which, practically speaking would be determined and issued by the head of State).

- Right will: intending the restoration of peace, taking no delight in violence, not seeking conquest for its own sake or for its spoils, and seeing war only as a necessity.

- Declared: by a competent authority, publicly, and only as a last resort.

With regard to *jus in bello*:

- Proportional response: with violence constrained by what is necessary, militarily.

- Discriminating: between combatants and non-combatants (e.g., women, children, elderly, clergy, etc.).

- Observing good faith: with the enemy (e.g., honoring promises/treaties, avoiding treachery, etc.).

War, while permissible (and perhaps unavoidable, given humanity's "fallen" nature), is nevertheless subject to moral constraints.

The transition in Europe from paganism to Christianity had significant impact on culture and philosophy, as evidenced by Augustine. However, his voice was not the sole Christian approach to political philosophy in the Middle Ages. Nearly a thousand years later, another Saint and brilliant Christian philosopher would offer a very different approach to political philosophy. Much as Augustine drew upon classical philosophy in the person of Plato, so too would Saint Thomas Aquinas draw upon antiquity as well—but with a preference for Aristotle, and arguing to a very different conclusion.

St. Thomas Aquinas

Saint Thomas Aquinas was born in either 1224 or 1225 CE. His education began at an early age, when, at age 5, he was placed in a Benedictine monastery to receive his elementary and religious education. In 1239, he enrolled at the University of Naples to study Liberal Arts. While there, he was exposed to Aristotle's writings, and came into contact with members of the Dominican Order—an order to which he declared his intention to join at the age of 19.

In what sounds like the plot of a movie, he was actually kidnapped by his own family and held for one year while they tried to dissuade him from joining the order! After his eventual release, he went to Paris and studied under the renowned Scholastic philosopher, St. Albert the Great. He earned his bachelor's degree in 1248, and was ordained a priest at the age of 25.

Aquinas' brilliance was such that he was alleged to be capable of dictating multiple treatises to multiple scribes simultaneously! One of those treatises was begun in 1266, his *Summa Theologica*. His talent and wisdom attracted notice, and he became an advisor to Popes Alexander IV and Urban IV.

Aquinas died on March 7th, 1272, at the age of 50. He was canonized in 1323, and proclaimed "Doctor of the Church" in 1567.

Although Aquinas was a prolific writer, and a comprehensive philosopher and theologian, our focus in this book is political philosophy, and so we must set aside the vast majority of Aquinas' contributions to both philosophy and theology for the sake of that focus. As was the case with Augustine, Aquinas did not produce a particular work, obviously devoted to political philosophy, within which we may find his clearly stated political views. Instead, his political thoughts are dispersed throughout his many written works, especially the *Summa Theologica*.

It is somewhat accurate (though admittedly oversimplified) to state that Aquinas offered an adaptation of the political philosophy of Aristotle that we already covered in a previous chapter, modified and supplemented to fit a Christian worldview. In fairness, it would be both uncharitable and inaccurate to suggest that he *merely* "Christianized" Aristotle. Aquinas draws on other sources of inspiration as well, including Plato, and Cicero—particularly the Stoic notion of natural law. Nevertheless, his debt to Aristotle is undeniable, going so far as to refer to Aristotle simply as "*The* Philosopher!"

Aristotle's works had been "lost" the West since the 6th century CE, but had made their way East to Syria and Persia, where they were translated into Arabic. When the Arab world expanded all the way to Spain, and certainly as a result of the Crusades, Europeans came into contact with Arab learning, and the Arabic translations of Aristotle. They were first translated from Arabic into Latin, and eventually original Greek texts were found and translated straight to Latin without Arabic as an intermediary.

Thanks to Aquinas' heavy, systematic, and sympathetic use of Aristotle, the Catholic Church moved away from Platonism (which had been adopted, in part, due to Augustine's influence) and towards a harmonizing of Aristotle and Christian doctrine. When we delve into the particulars of Aquinas' views, the similarity to Aristotle will be fairly obvious.

This is not to say their views are identical, of course. Where Aquinas differs from Aristotle is obvious: Christianity! Aristotle did not assume that there exists a universal human community with one supreme Lawgiver as its creator and Lord. In addition, Aquinas recognizes an "end" that can't be addressed even by the best possible regime. Politics, while natural for us, is not capable of addressing our *super*natural end.

Humans achieve full perfection only in Heaven (if at all). Our imperfect happiness attainable on Earth he calls "felicity," while our perfect happiness attainable only in the afterlife is called "beatitude." The Church (not the State) is needed to guide us towards *that* end. The State can help, in that good regimes and good laws can help citizens be more virtuous—which can prepare us to be receptive to Grace, and the virtues of Faith, Hope, and (Christian) Charity.

For Aristotle, there was no meaningful distinction between civic life and religious life. Participation in religious observances was not a private matter concerning one's soul, but another aspect of being a good citizen of the *polis*. Aquinas, however, while recognizing the value of both Church and State, tries to separate and protect the authority of each within their own proper sphere. "Just as the leader or ruler has chief authority in the city, so does the Pope in those things which pertain to God."[511]

> *Spiritual and secular power are both derived from the Divine power, and so secular power is subject to spiritual power insofar as this is ordered by God: that is, in those things which pertain to the salvation of the soul. In such matters, then, the spiritual power is to be obeyed before the secular. But in those things which pertain to the civil good, the secular power should be obeyed before the spiritual, according to Matthew 22:21: 'Render to Caesar the things that are Caesar's.'*[512]

The Church holds complete authority over spiritual matters, but is limited in secular authority—except if a secular ruler or law intrudes upon spiritual matters: "The secular power is subject to the spiritual, even as the body is subject to the soul. Consequently the judgment is not usurped if the spiritual authority interferes in those temporal matters that are subject to the spiritual authority or which have been committed

---

[511] Commentary on the Epistle to the Hebrews, V.1

[512] Scripta super libros sententiarum II, Dist.44, quaest.3

to the spiritual by the temporal authority."[513]

Despite his recognition and appreciation of the secular sphere, there is no mistaking the fact that Aquinas places ultimate authority with the church, and that he believes kings, just like everyone else, are equally in need of the guidance and sacraments it offers.

> Now the same judgment is to be formed about the end of society as a whole as about the end of one man. If, therefore, the ultimate end of man were some good that existed in himself, then the ultimate end of the multitude to be governed would likewise be for the multitude to acquire such good, and persevere in its possession. If such an ultimate end either of an individual man or a multitude were a corporeal one, namely, life and health of body, to govern would then be a physician's charge. If that ultimate end were an abundance of wealth, then knowledge of economics would have the last word in the community's government. If the good of the knowledge of truth were of such a kind that the multitude might attain to it, the king would have to be a teacher. It is, however, clear that the end of a multitude gathered together is to live virtuously. For men form a group for the purpose of living well together, a thing which the individual man living alone could not attain, and good life is virtuous life. Therefore, virtuous life is the end for which men gather together....
>
> Yet through virtuous living man is further ordained to a higher end, which consists in the enjoyment of God, as we have said above. Consequently, since society must have the same end as the individual man, it is not the ultimate end of an assembled multitude to live virtuously, but through virtuous living to attain to the possession of God....

> Thus, in order that spiritual things might be distinguished from earthly things, the ministry of this kingdom has been entrusted not to earthly kings but to priests, and most of all to the chief priest, the successor of St. Peter, the Vicar of Christ, the Roman Pontiff. To him all the kings of the Christian People are to be subject as to our Lord Jesus Christ Himself. For those to whom pertains the care of intermediate ends should be subject to him to whom pertains the care of the ultimate end, and be directed by his rule.[514]

Given the focus of *this* book, we shall have to set aside Aquinas' thorough and influential treatment of our "supernatural ends," set our feet firmly on the Earth, and focus on our natural ends, as understood via Aquinas' interpretation of the natural law.

Natural Law

In his discussion of law, we find a rare occasion when Aquinas sounds more like Plato, than Aristotle.

"Law" is a sort of rational pattern analogous to Plato's Forms. In human laws, the idea the ruler has in his mind as to what his subjects should be is "law." God is the supreme Law-Giver. The rational pattern within God's mind supplies the Eternal Law, which "is nothing but the rational pattern of the Divine wisdom considered as directing all actions and motions."[515]

Most things are governed by the Eternal Law without the possibility of disobedience. For example, most things in the universe simply "obey" the laws of nature. Imagine the absurdity of a rock "rebelling" against the pull of gravity, or an acorn defiantly growing into a zebra, rather than an oak tree! Humans, however, complicate the Eternal Law by virtue of our free will.

> Wherefore, since all things subject to Divine providence are ruled and measured

---

[513] *Summa Theologica*, II-II, 6-.6
[514] *De Regimine Principum*, Book 1, chapter 15

[515] *Summa Theologica*, I-II, 93.1.

by the eternal law, as was stated above (Article [1]); it is evident that all things partake somewhat of the eternal law, in so far as, namely, from its being imprinted on them, they derive their respective inclinations to their proper acts and ends. Now among all others, the rational creature is subject to Divine providence in the most excellent way, in so far as it partakes of a share of providence, by being provident both for itself and for others. Wherefore it has a share of the Eternal Reason, whereby it has a natural inclination to its proper act and end: and this participation of the eternal law in the rational creature is called the natural law.[516]

Because human subjection to the Eternal Law is different, Aquinas calls it being under the "Natural Law"—but "The Natural Law is nothing else than the rational creature's participation of the Eternal Law." That is, the natural law is simply the eternal law as it is applied to humans.

The natural law guides humans via natural inclinations toward the natural perfection to which God intends us. This includes, among other things, moral instruction.

Aquinas calls the natural knowledge humans have instructing fundamental moral requirements of our human nature "Synderesis."

Now it is clear that, as the speculative reason argues about speculative things, so that practical reason argues about practical things. Therefore we must have, bestowed on us by nature, not only speculative principles, but also practical principles. Now the first speculative principles bestowed on us by nature do not belong to a special power, but to a special habit, which is called "the understanding of principles," as the Philosopher explains (Ethic. vi, 6). Wherefore the first practical principles, bestowed on us by nature, do

not belong to a special power, but to a special natural habit, which we call "synderesis." Whence "synderesis" is said to incite to good, and to murmur at evil, inasmuch as through first principles we proceed to discover, and judge of what we have discovered.[517]

A more familiar term, "conscience," he defines as an act of applying synderesis to concrete situations.

*For conscience, according to the very nature of the word, implies the relation of knowledge to something: for conscience may be resolved into "cum alio scientia," i.e. knowledge applied to an individual case. . . . Wherefore, properly speaking, conscience denominates an act. But since habit is a principle of act, sometimes the name conscience is given to the first natural habit---namely, 'synderesis': thus Jerome calls 'synderesis' conscience (Gloss. Ezech. 1:6); Basil [*Hom. in princ. Proverb.], the "natural power of judgment," and Damascene [*De Fide Orth. iv. 22] says that it is the "law of our intellect." For it is customary for causes and effects to be called after one another.*[518]

To illustrate: according to Aquinas, by synderesis we understand that adultery is morally wrong, but by conscience we understand that having sex with a particular woman who is not my wife is a case of adultery. Synderesis recognizes general principles, while conscience applies them. Synderesis reveals that stealing is wrong, and conscience tells me that taking office supplies is a case of stealing.

The natural knowledge of our moral requirements as supplied by synderesis is universal, unchangeable, and can't be "abolished from the hearts of men."[519] With this notion of a universal moral code applying to all humans,

---

[516] ibid., I-II, 91.2
[517] ibid., I, 79.12

[518] ibid., I, 79.13
[519] ibid., I-II, 94.4-94.6

regardless of race or nationality, Aquinas is clearly drawing more from Cicero than Aristotle.

Assuming that synderesis supplies basic moral instruction, we may now turn to the specifics of that instruction. According to Aquinas, the first moral precept of the natural law is that "good is to be done and pursued and evils is to be avoided."[520]

Aquinas does not bother to prove this. Instead, he claims that this precept of practical reason is analogous to the law of non-contradiction for speculative reason: neither can be demonstrated (proven), but both are principles without which reasoning to conclusions (logical, or moral, respectively) is impossible.

Think of it this way: how would you even talk about *any* notion, *any* interpretation, of "good" or "evil" at all without presupposing that "good" is *good*, and "evil" is *bad*? And yet, how could you possibly "prove" that "good" is *good*? These notions appear intuitive and unavoidable in the abstract, even if we might disagree as to their specific applications.

If we accept that good is to be pursued, and evil avoided, how do we know what qualifies as good or evil? Aquinas thinks that our natural inclinations provide a rudimentary guide to "natural goods." For example, our natural inclination to self-preservation, avoidance of pain, pursuit of pleasure, reproduction and care of our offspring, living within a community, etc., are indicators of natural goods.

These inclinations are not infallible, of course. They can (and often are) corrupted by sin, so we are not merely to act on any inclination we happen to have! Instead, we need to recognize the "natural purpose" of the inclination, and then act on it only insofar as that purpose is respected. For example, according to Aquinas (and the official Natural Law doctrine of the Catholic Church), our sexual inclination has a "natural purpose" of reproduction. Therefore, the only proper way to act on that inclination is one which "respects" its purpose: reproduction. Not surprisingly, then, Aquinas (and the Catholic Church) are opposed to

homosexual activities, masturbation, oral sex, the use of contraception—and any sexual activity that can't (feasibly) result in conception. Accordingly, Aquinas specifies that all inclinations belong to the natural law only insofar as they are "ruled by reason."[521] We experience inclinations, but must test them with Reason to determine whether it is right to indulge and pursue them.

Although the natural law provides basic moral guidelines for human life, it does not provide specific guidance. For example, it is "natural" that those who commit crimes but should be punished, but what nature does not reveal to us is what exact punishment is appropriate based on the crime. Human law is needed to flesh out the details.

The first function of human law is to provide the details (understandably) left out by natural law. The second function of human law is to enforce the specific interpretation of natural law that is expressed in human law. In some cases, human laws are so close to what is offered by natural law that we find them existing "universally" in all human communities. To use Aquinas' vocabulary, some human laws constitute "conclusions" from natural law. These pertain to matters about which natural law offers clear guidance (e.g., murder is wrong). Aquinas refers to these "conclusions" as the "law of nations," as they are (or ought to be) found in all nations, given that all humans have the same nature, and are subject to the same natural law. Indeed, a human law that opposes natural law is no longer properly "law" at all.

As Augustine says (De Lib. Arb. i, 5) "that which is not just seems to be no law at all": wherefore the force of a law depends on the extent of its justice. Now in human affairs a thing is said to be just, from being right, according to the rule of reason. But the first rule of reason is the law of nature, as is clear from what has been stated above (Q[91], A[2], ad 2). Consequently every human law has just so much of the nature

---

[520] ibid., I-II, 94.2

[521] ibid., I-II, 94.2

of law, as it is derived from the law of nature. But if in any point it deflects from the law of nature, it is no longer a law but a perversion of law.[522]

Other human laws involve much longer chains of reasoning to link them back to natural law, and so might be specific to certain communities only. These laws constitute "determinations" from natural law, and these pertain to the particular details/applications that are based in the conclusions from natural law.

Some things are therefore derived from the general principles of the natural law, by way of conclusions; e.g. that "one must not kill" may be derived as a conclusion from the principle that "one should do harm to no man": while some are derived therefrom by way of determination; e.g. the law of nature has it that the evil-doer should be punished; but that he be punished in this or that way, is a determination of the law of nature.[523]

Aquinas offers his own analogy to try to clarify the relationship between conclusions and determinations of natural law. All houses have certain essential elements (e.g., having a foundation, a roof, etc.), but may have particular details added to them that may vary from house to house (e.g., whether the house is built from brick or wood, whether the roof is tile or shingle, how many windows it has, etc.).

Analogously, human laws are to be based on general natural law principles (e.g., murder is a criminal offense), but may vary with regard to details (e.g., punishing murder with execution as opposed to life imprisonment).

"Conclusions" of natural law give us the basic moral "foundation" for any person or community. The inclusion of "determinations" of natural law allows for diversity of expression, so long as the particular values don't contradict the natural law itself. To reuse an example, we might think that a conclusion from natural law is that murderers

should be punished, but some chains of reasoning ("determinations") might lead some communities to punish with the death penalty, and others with life imprisonment. Either could be consistent with the natural law. A community that did not prohibit murder at all, however, would be contradicting the natural law.

In addition to the guidance offered by both human laws and the natural law, *Divine Law* is needed for several reasons. One reason is because human laws can be made in error. That is, it is possible that a human law is an unjust law (by virtue of contradicting the natural law).

Another reason is because human laws can't direct the soul (the intentions) of the citizen, but only his outward acts. That is, a human law might cause someone to abstain from adultery from the threat of punishment, but that person can still commit adultery "in his heart."

Finally, human law is imperfect in its ability to punish or forbid *all* evil deeds. The Divine Law regulates and punishes us as sinners, not criminals. There might be actions which are not illegal, but are nevertheless "sinful."

Wherefore laws imposed on men should also be in keeping with their condition, for, as Isidore says (Etym. v, 21), law should be "possible both according to nature, and according to the customs of the country." Now possibility or faculty of action is due to an interior habit or disposition: since the same thing is not possible to one who has not a virtuous habit, as is possible to one who has. Thus the same is not possible to a child as to a full-grown man: for which reason the law for children is not the same as for adults, since many things are permitted to children, which in an adult are punished by law or at any rate are open to blame. In like manner many things are permissible to men not perfect in virtue, which would be intolerable in a virtuous man.

Now human law is framed for a number of

---

[522] ibid., I-II, 95.2

[523] ibid., I-II, 95.2

human beings, the majority of whom are not perfect in virtue. Wherefore human laws do not forbid all vices, from which the virtuous abstain, but only the more grievous vices, from which it is possible for the majority to abstain; and chiefly those that are to the hurt of others, without the prohibition of which human society could not be maintained: thus human law prohibits murder, theft and such like.[524]

Law and punishment can prevent wrongdoing, first by fear of punishment, and eventually (possibly) by shaping moral character so that citizens willingly do what is right, not from fear, but from virtue.

> . . . man has a natural aptitude for virtue; but the perfection of virtue must be acquired by man by means of some kind of training. Thus we observe that man is helped by industry in his necessities, for instance, in food and clothing. . . . Now it is difficult to see how man could suffice for himself in the matter of this training: since the perfection of virtue consists chiefly in withdrawing man from undue pleasures, to which above all man is inclined, and especially the young, who are more capable of being trained. Consequently a man needs to receive this training from another, whereby to arrive at the perfection of virtue. And as to those young people who are inclined to acts of virtue, by their good natural disposition, or by custom, or rather by the gift of God, paternal training suffices, which is by admonitions. But since some are found to be depraved, and prone to vice, and not easily amenable to words, it was necessary for such to be restrained from evil by force and fear, in order that, at least, they might desist from evil-doing, and leave others in peace, and that they themselves, by being habituated in this way, might be brought to do willingly what hitherto they did from

fear, and thus become virtuous. Now this kind of training, which compels through fear of punishment, is the discipline of laws. Therefore in order that man might have peace and virtue, it was necessary for laws to be framed: for, as the Philosopher says (Polit. i, 2), "as man is the most noble of animals if he be perfect in virtue, so is he the lowest of all, if he be severed from law and righteousness"; because man can use his reason to devise means of satisfying his lusts and evil passions, which other animals are unable to do.[525]

Human laws therefore serve two important ends: peace/order, and instilling virtue. Aquinas (in agreement with Aristotle) claims that one of the natural goods to which we are all inclined is to live in a community. Being part of a civil society is an aspect of our human nature—not an artificial construct, nor a mere "contract."

The Value of Civil Society

In contrast to the social contract tradition, which finds ultimate authority in the humans who form the contract in the first place, Aquinas (following Aristotle) claims that humans are naturally social/political beings, and therefore the foundation/origin of society is the God who created us in the first place, endowing us with the particular natures we possess. Moreover, authority has its origin in God, rather than "man." This is not to be confused with some sort of endorsement of the "divine right" of kings. Aquinas is not claiming that particular rulers are given their authority by God Himself, but rather that the very existence of authority at all comes from God via the natural law.

Aquinas is a sharp contrast to Augustine. Augustine (like Plato) has his eyes firmly in a transcendent "other" world. This Earthly world is Fallen, sinful, destructive, and temporary. Politics is necessary to restrain the worst excesses of our sinful behavior, but it is not "good." Indeed, Augustine thought that the need for politics runs counter to God's original intentions for humans,

---

[524] ibid., I-II, 96.2

[525] ibid., I-II, 95.1

and is now needed only because of the Fall of Man. "God did not intend that His rational creature, made in His own image, should have lordship over any but irrational creatures: not man over man, but man over the beasts."[526]

Aquinas, though, accepting Aristotle's claim that humans are naturally social and political animals, has a much more positive view of politics. Politics is not a corrective measure necessary because of the Fallen world. He agrees, of course, that our highest good can only be achieved with God in Heaven, but he sees value in the present goods available here on Earth as well. Political rulership ("dominion"), though established by human law, arises from the natural law, and can be perfectly consistent with the divine law.

> *If, then, it is natural for man to live in the society of many, it is necessary that there exist among men some means by which the group may be governed. For where there are many men together and each one is looking after his own interest, the multitude would be broken up and scattered unless there were also an agency to take care of what appertains to the commonweal. In like manner, the body of a man or any other animal would disintegrate unless there were a general ruling force within the body which watches over the common good of all members. With this in mind, Solomon says [Eccl. 4:9]: "Where there is no governor, the people shall fall."[527]*

The achievement of earthly wellbeing requires political community, and government. This government does not exist solely to restrain and coerce by force and fear (as claimed by Augustine), but can and should be something benevolent, serving to fulfill our human nature.

With Aquinas, politics and authority is now associated with the "good" Creation of God, rather than as a consequence of sin, as developed by Augustine. Politics is no longer a necessary evil, but a natural expression of our human nature, and a legitimate means by which we can facilitate virtue and promote the common good. The very purpose of civil authority is to direct its citizens towards the common good. Where Augustine deviated sharply from classical political theory, Aquinas reclaims it—situating it within a Christian worldview.

As previously mentioned, Aquinas (in his *Commentary on the Politics*) reiterates Aristotle's argument that, from our capacity for speech, our political/social nature is demonstrated (since, by means of speech, humans alone can deliberate on the nature of good and evil, justice and injustice, and pursue a common understanding of virtue). In addition to whatever else we are, other roles we adopt, all humans are "naturally" citizens—requiring participation in a political society. Political society not only provides safety and economic benefits, but it enhances the moral and intellectual lives of the humans within it.

Within a community, individual interests can be set aside for the same of the common good. "The common good is the end of each individual member of a community, just as the good of the whole is the end of each part."[528] Living in a political community does not serve merely the negative function of restraining vice, but is intended to serve the positive function of promoting virtue.

> *For an individual man to lead a good life two things are required. The first and most important is to act in a virtuous manner (for virtue is that by which one lives well); the second, which is secondary and instrumental, is a sufficiency of those bodily goods whose use is necessary for virtuous life. Yet the unity of man is brought about by nature, while the unity of multitude, which we call peace, must be procured through the efforts of the ruler. Therefore, to establish virtuous living in a multitude three things are necessary. First*

---

[526] Augustine, *City of God*, 19:15.
[527] Aquinas, *De Regimine Principum*, book 1

chapter 1.
[528] *Summa Theologica*, II-II, 58.9

of all, that the multitude be established in the unity of peace. Second, that the multitude thus united in the bond of peace, be directed to acting well. For just as a man can do nothing well unless unity within his members be presupposed, so a multitude of men lacking the unity of peace will be hindered from virtuous action by the fact that it is fighting against itself. In the third place, it is necessary that there be at hand a sufficient supply of the things required for proper living, procured by the ruler's efforts.[529]

While it is true that the State exists to establish and secure peace, it also exists to direct its members to "acting well." Do not think Aquinas is speaking merely of laws and punishments to inhibit criminal behavior. He also indicates another -function of the State: procuring a "sufficient supply of the things required for proper living."

Aquinas, like Aristotle before him, sees the State as a necessary means by which we can pursue the life proper to a human being. Since we can only fulfill our full human potential as citizens, it not only matters that we live in a State, but what *kind* of State. In contrast to Augustine, who argued that it mattered little (ultimately) what particular form of government under which we lived (since, the "City of God" transcends all national and political boundaries), Aquinas argues that only in the "best regime" can good citizens and good human beings coincide.

Aquinas uses Aristotle's method of classifying types of government based on who rules, and for whose sake—with the same (familiar) six possibilities: Monarchy (Tyranny), Aristocracy (Oligarchy), and Polity/Republic (Democracy).

Among those, Aquinas claims that monarchy is the best of those kinds of State, and tries to demonstrate this by way of analogy, using Nature as a guide. The body is ruled by one agency (the soul), rather than a few, or many—and Nature itself is ruled by one, supreme God.

However, the potential for corruption (leading to tyranny) makes monarchy dangerous. As regards "tyranny," Augustine claimed that all authority (even that of a tyrant) is derived from God, with tyrants serving to punish sinners and test the faith of believers. Christians subject to a tyrant should realize that such is what sinners (such as themselves!) deserve, use it as an opportunity to grow in faith and look to Heaven, and endure as best they can—so long as the tyrant doesn't require the Christian to disobey God (e.g., by worshipping an idol). In that case, the Christian should disobey, and prepare to be a martyr.

Aquinas, though, thinks that kings exist not simply to punish and test, but to promote the common good. Those who promote their own interests at the expense of the public interest are tyrants (following Aristotle's classification). Such a tyrant, far from being an instrument of God's will, is actually betraying the purpose for which God appointed him in the first place.

Aquinas makes a concerted effort to demonstrate that tyranny isn't even in the best interests of the tyrant. The true happiness of a king is not to be found in mere power or earthly riches.

Now it is manifest that all earthly things are beneath the human mind. But happiness is the last perfection and the perfect good of man, which all men desire to reach. Therefore there is no earthly thing which could make man happy, nor is any earthly thing a sufficient reward for a king. For, as Augustine" says, "we do not call Christian princes happy merely because they have reigned a long time, or because after a peaceful death they have left their sons to rule, or because they subdued the enemies of the state, or because they were able to guard against or to suppress citizens who rose up against them. Rather do we call them happy if they rule justly, if they prefer to rule their passions rather than nations, and if they do

---

[529] *De Regimine Principum*, Book 1, chapter 16.

all things not for the love of vainglory but for the love of eternal happiness. Such Christian emperors we say are happy, now in hope, afterwards in very fact when that which we await shall come to pass.[530]

If true happiness can only be supplied by God, should God grant eternal happiness, then the king should be motivated to please God by ruling justly. Even at the earthly level, Aquinas claims that kings (like everyone else in the world) value and desire friendship, but that tyrants have no real friends.

First of all, among all worldly things there is nothing which seems worthy to be preferred to friendship. Friendship unites good men and preserves and promotes virtue. Friendship is needed by all men in whatsoever occupations they engage. In prosperity it does not thrust itself unwanted upon us, nor does it desert us in adversity. It is what brings with it the greatest delight, to such an extent that all that pleases is changed to weariness when friends are absent, and all difficult things are made easy and as nothing by love. There is no tyrant so cruel that friendship does not bring him pleasure.[531]

Moreover, those kings who become tyrants because they think it better secures their rule are just plain mistaken. What follows is a lengthy quotation, worthy of being provided, at length, if for no other reason than the contrast it will provide with Machiavellian thinking in our next chapter.

The consequence of this love is that the government of good kings is stable, because their subjects do not refuse to expose themselves to any danger whatsoever on behalf of such kings. An example of this is to be seen in Julius Caesar who, as Suetonius relates [Divus Iulius 67], loved his soldiers to such an extent that

when he heard that some of them were slaughtered, "he refused to cut either hair or beard until he had taken vengeance." In this way, he made his soldiers most loyal to himself as well as most valiant, so that many, on being taken prisoner, refused to accept their lives when offered them on the condition that they serve against Caesar. Octavianus Augustus, also, who was most moderate in his use of power, was so loved by his subjects that some of them "on their deathbeds provided in their wills a thank-offering to be paid by the immolation of animals, so grateful were they that the emperor's life outlasted their own" [Suetonius, Divus Augustus 59]. Therefore it is no easy task to shake the government of a prince whom the people so unanimously love. This is why Solomon says (Prov 29:14): "The king that judges the poor in justice, his throne shall be established forever."

The government of tyrants, on the other hand, cannot last long because it is hateful to the multitude, and what is against the wishes of the multitude cannot be long preserved. For a man can hardly pass through this present life without suffering some adversities, and in the time of his adversity occasion cannot be lacking to rise against the tyrant; and when there is an opportunity there will not be lacking at least one of the multitude to use it. Then the people will fervently favour the insurgent, and what is attempted with the sympathy of the multitude will not easily fail of its effects. It can thus scarcely come to pass that the government of a tyrant will endure for a long time.

This is very clear, too, if we consider the means by which a tyrannical government is upheld. It is not upheld by love, since there is little or no bond of friendship between the subject multitude and the

---

[530] ibid., Book 1, chapter 9.

[531] ibid., Book 1, chapter 11.

tyrant, as is evident from what we have said. On the other hand, tyrants cannot rely on the loyalty of their subjects, for such a degree of virtue is not found among the generality of men, that they should be restrained by the virtue of fidelity from throwing off the yoke of unmerited servitude, if they are able to do so. Nor would it perhaps be a violation of fidelity at all, according to the opinion of many,' to frustrate the wickedness of tyrants by any means whatsoever. It remains, then, that the government of a tyrant is maintained by fear alone and consequently they strive with all their might to be feared by their subjects. Fear, however, is a weak support. Those who are kept down by fear will rise against their rulers if the opportunity ever occurs when they can hope to do it with impunity, and they will rebel against their rulers all the more furiously the more they have been kept in subjection against their will by fear alone, just as water confined under pressure flows with greater impetus when it finds an outlet. That very fear itself is not without danger, because many become desperate from excessive fear, and despair of safety impels a man boldly to dare anything. Therefore the government of a tyrant cannot be of long duration.[532]

Tyrants will lack friends, and those rulers who rule by fear rather than love will not win the support of their subjects. They might be too cowed by fear to rise up against him, but they will also be reluctant to defend or support him. In addition, should the king meet with any "adversity," they might notice the vulnerability and be quick to seize the opportunity to overthrow him.[533]

If his defense of monarchy (and arguments against tyranny) happens to fall on deaf ears, he

is prepared to concede that, while monarchy might be the "best" regime, in principle, it might not be the best in *practice*. As a practical concession, then, he proposes a mixed government, somewhat similar to Aristotle's proposal, but using ancient Israel as a model.

Moses represents the monarchical element, the council of 72 elders represents the aristocratic element, and the "able men" chosen from "all the people" represents the democratic element.[534] The "ideal" Roman Republic of Cicero (so thoroughly critiqued by Augustine) is replaced with an ideal (similarly) mixed regime rooted in Scripture.

Two points are to be observed concerning the right ordering of rulers in a state or nation. One is that all should take some share in the government: for this form of constitution ensures peace among the people, commends itself to all, and is most enduring, as stated in Polit. ii, 6. The other point is to be observed in respect of the kinds of government, or the different ways in which the constitutions are established. For whereas these differ in kind, as the Philosopher states (Polit. iii, 5), nevertheless the first place is held by the "kingdom," where the power of government is vested in one; and "aristocracy," which signifies government by the best, where the power of government is vested in a few. Accordingly, the best form of government is in a state or kingdom, where one is given the power to preside over all; while under him are others having governing powers: and yet a government of this kind is shared by all, both because all are eligible to govern, and because the rules are chosen by all. For this is the best form of polity, being partly kingdom, since there is one at the head of

---

[532] ibid., Book 1, chapter 11.

[533] Keep Aquinas' arguments here in mind when you encounter Machiavelli, in a later chapter, arguing the opposite: that it is better to be feared than to be loved (if one must choose).

[534] "But select capable men from all the people-- men who fear God, trustworthy men who hate dishonest gain--and appoint them as officials over thousands, hundreds, fifties and tens." (Exodus, 18:21)

all; partly aristocracy, in so far as a number of persons are set in authority; partly democracy, i.e. government by the people, in so far as the rulers can be chosen from the people, and the people have the right to choose their rulers.

Such was the form of government established by the Divine Law. For Moses and his successors governed the people in such a way that each of them was ruler over all; so that there was a kind of kingdom. Moreover, seventy-two men were chosen, who were elders in virtue: for it is written (Dt. 1:15): "I took out of your tribes wise and honorable, and appointed them rulers": so that there was an element of aristocracy. But it was a democratical government in so far as the rulers were chosen from all the people; for it is written (Ex. 18:21): "Provide out of all the people wise [Vulg.: 'able'] men," etc.; and, again, in so far as they were chosen by the people; wherefore it is written (Dt. 1:13): "Let me have from among you wise [Vulg.: 'able'] men," etc. Consequently it is evident that the ordering of the rulers was well provided for by the Law.[535]

As a reminder, Aquinas claimed that the natural law provides various natural inclinations towards natural goods, of which one was living in community with others. Another natural inclination, is self-preservation. Given that we are naturally inclined to self-preservation, earthly happiness, and living within a community, it is appropriate for us to seek to acquire the material means to promote those ends.

For imperfect happiness, such as can be had in this life, external goods are necessary, not as belonging to the essence of happiness, but by serving as instruments to happiness, which consists in an operation of virtue, as stated in Ethic. i, 13. For man needs in this life, the necessaries

of the body, both for the operation of contemplative virtue, and for the operation of active virtue, for which latter he needs also many other things by means of which to perform its operations.

On the other hand, such goods as these are nowise necessary for perfect Happiness, which consists in seeing God. The reason of this is that all suchlike external goods are requisite either for the support of the animal body; or for certain operations which belong to human life, which we perform by means of the animal body: whereas that perfect Happiness which consists in seeing God, will be either in the soul separated from the body, or in the soul united to the body then no longer animal but spiritual. Consequently these external goods are nowise necessary for that Happiness, since they are ordained to the animal life. And since, in this life, the felicity of contemplation, as being more Godlike, approaches nearer than that of action to the likeness of that perfect Happiness, therefore it stands in less need of these goods of the body as stated in Ethic. x, 8.[536]

Property

"Property" is natural for human beings, and based in natural law—though no particular institution of property is dictated by natural law. Nevertheless, Aquinas does advocate for private property for three reasons:

First because every man is more careful to procure what is for himself alone than that which is common to many or to all: since each one would shirk the labor and leave to another that which concerns the community, as happens where there is a great number of servants. Secondly, because human affairs are conducted in more orderly fashion if each man is charged with taking care of some

---

[535] *Summa Theologica*, I-II, 105.1

[536] ibid., I-II, 4.7

particular thing himself, whereas there would be confusion if everyone had to look after any one thing indeterminately. Thirdly, because a more peaceful state is ensured to man if each one is contented with his own. Hence it is to be observed that quarrels arise more frequently where there is no division of the things possessed.[537]

Private property causes us to manage natural resources better, since humans naturally care more for what is their own, rather than what is held in common (e.g., think of how much more "sanitary" most people are in their own bathroom, as opposed to a public bathroom at a gas station, for example). That extra care isn't merely because we are sinful and depraved, but because we are limited in our perspective and capacities. We can't care for all things equally well, and without property laws usage of resources would be ambiguous, and more conflict would occur. There is very much a limit to property, however.

Following Aristotle, Aquinas thinks we (naturally) are entitled to as much property as needed to meet our earthly needs. Anything in excess of that admittedly ambiguous "need" is owed (morally speaking) to the poor—those whose needs are not yet met.[538] Although he endorses private property, he also would endorse something like "progressive taxation" today.

Now according to the natural order established by Divine Providence, inferior things are ordained for the purpose of succoring man's needs by their means. Wherefore the division and appropriation of things which are based on human law, do not preclude the fact that man's needs have to be remedied by means of these very

things. Hence whatever certain people have in superabundance is due, by natural law, to the purpose of succoring the poor. For this reason Ambrose [*Loc. cit., A[2], OBJ[3]] says, and his words are embodied in the Decretals (Dist. xlvii, can. Sicut ii): "It is the hungry man's bread that you withhold, the naked man's cloak that you store away, the money that you bury in the earth is the price of the poor man's ransom and freedom."

Since, however, there are many who are in need, while it is impossible for all to be succored by means of the same thing, each one is entrusted with the stewardship of his own things, so that out of them he may come to the aid of those who are in need. Nevertheless, if the need be so manifest and urgent, that it is evident that the present need must be remedied by whatever means be at hand (for instance when a person is in some imminent danger, and there is no other possible remedy), then it is lawful for a man to succor his own need by means of another's property, by taking it either openly or secretly: nor is this properly speaking theft or robbery.[539]

Note the numerous ideas contained above: private property is acceptable and good, and, practically speaking, each person should be the managers of their own property/wealth. However, wealth in "excess" of one's needs is "naturally" due/owed to the poor—and given desperate enough need, the poor taking excess from the wealthy (should they refuse to donate it) isn't even, properly speaking, "theft!"

In fairness, Aquinas is not describing some sort of "communist" redistribution of wealth until no one has "excess" and everyone has the exact

---

[537] ibid., II-II, 66.2

[538] As an illustration, Aquinas would presumably be against Floyd "Money" Mayweather spending $4.8 million on a single car (the Koenigsegg CCXR Trevita—of which only two exist in the world), when other humans literally starve to

death as a result of their poverty.

http://www.cnn.com/2015/08/27/sport/floyd-mayweather-4-8-million-car/index.html
[539] Summa Theologica, II-II, 66.7

same standard of living. Instead, he's talking about an admittedly ambiguous minimum standard of living needed to prevent someone from being "hungry" or "naked"—and the "redistribution of wealth" requires a need that is "manifest and urgent," an "imminent danger" with "no other possible remedy." Really, what Aquinas seems to be describing is a regulated system of private property in which individuals have the freedom to own property, pursue profit, and acquire wealth, but with the understanding that their property may be "regulated" when the common welfare, the interest of the whole community, is at stake.

Conclusion

The "Fall of Rome" arguably led to the end of an era of political philosophy in the West. The optimism and perfectionism displayed by philosophers as Plato, Aristotle, and Cicero gave way, in the Dark and Middle Ages, to an admittedly more pessimistic (or realistic, depending on one's perspective) approach to politics such as that advanced by Augustine.

The ascendancy of Christianity as a worldview quite understandably led Christian philosophers to place their hope in the "world to come" rather than this "fallen" world.

With Aquinas, however, some of the "optimism" of ancient political philosophy was recovered. By synthesizing Aristotelian and Stoic philosophy with Christian doctrine, Aquinas was able to keep his eyes on "Heaven," while affirming the value of politics as both consistent with our nature, and necessary for the fullest (Earthly) expression of that nature.

Aquinas inspired a variety of political thinkers including Richard Hooker (who influenced John Locke with regard to natural law)—not to mention, of course, the profound influence of Aquinas' development of natural law on the official doctrine of the Catholic Church, resulting in numerous specific policy positions (e.g., opposition to birth control and abortion) even to this day.

While the cultural and intellectual domination of Christianity would continue for several more centuries, the next major period of political philosophy will actually hearken back to Augustine's pessimistic/realistic view of human nature, and the limited role of politics as necessary for restraining our worst (natural) tendencies. Such views will find voice in the infamous Niccolò Machiavelli, and Thomas Hobbes.

Critical Analysis

1. In your opinion, what are the strongest and most compelling points made by the philosopher or philosophers in this chapter? Why do you find those points to be convincing?
2. In your opinion, what are the weakest or least convincing points? Why? Can you anticipate any limitations or objections to their ideas not already addressed in the chapter?

Appendix: Application to Social Justice

In the previous chapter, we saw how certain stoic ideas such as "cosmopolitanism," and our shared capacity for reason, laid a foundation for ideas central to social justice issues and causes. In this chapter, that foundation is built upon in the form of "natural law."

In addition to being both an approach to ethics and a significant interpretive lens through which to view the philosophy of law, natural law theory has a clear application to social justice issues—most obviously with respect to the very concept of an unjust law. Perhaps especially worthy of mention is Martin Luther King Jr., who cited Aquinas' notion of unjust laws being invalid in his "Letter from a Birmingham Jail."

How does one determine whether a law is just or unjust? A just law is a man-made code that squares with the moral law or the law of God. An unjust law is a code that is out of harmony with the moral law. To put it in the terms of St. Thomas Aquinas: An unjust law is a human law that is not rooted in eternal law and natural law. Any law that uplifts human personality is just.

Any law that degrades human personality is unjust. All segregation statutes are unjust because segregation distorts the soul and damages the personality. It gives the segregator a false sense of superiority and the segregated a false sense of inferiority.

It is difficult to overstate the value of the "traction" that natural law can provide a social justice campaign. Social justice efforts are, by their very nature, virtually inevitably "revolutionary" to some degree or another. We can imagine a scenario in which preserving the status quo is framed as a matter of social justice, as we normally understand it, such as an effort to prevent a conservative movement from "rolling back" rights gained by a previously marginalized minority group (e.g., legal recognition of same-sex marriage), but far more likely is it that we will find social justice activists seeking to *change* the status quo.

Activists speak, write, campaign, lobby, and engage in direct action on behalf of women because there are patriarchal elements in our culture, on behalf of people of color because there are racist elements in our culture, on behalf of persons with disabilities because there are able-ist elements in our culture, on behalf of transgender persons because there are gender normative elements in our culture, on behalf of gay and bisexual people because there are heteronormative elements in our culture, on behalf of the poor and working-class people because there are classist elements in our culture, on behalf of immigrants and undocumented persons because there are nativist elements in our culture, and so on.

In each case, our institutions and laws are presently such that there are marginalized groups underserved, subject to disparate and discriminatory impact, or outright oppressed by the current "system" – including the legal system. Appealing to the law, as is, will hardly be helpful if it is a current law that is generating, or at least allowing, the oppression!

While it is possible to advocate for social change, and even achieve it, within the framework of ethical relativism, there is much more psychological, rhetorical, and (if I may offer an editorial opinion) *conceptual* "traction" if activists are able to appeal to something above and outside their own subjective perspective and self-interest.

If it is true that there exists a higher "law" to which all human laws may be compared, and by which all human laws may be judged, then activists may point to that higher (natural) law and, in so doing, potentially substitute the label of "criminal agitator" with the label of "advocate for justice."

It must be acknowledged, of course, that "both sides" can make use of this strategy. Christian conservatives, for example, can (and have) proclaimed that God's law (as they understand it) supersedes any human law, and for that reason any human laws that extend respect and equal rights to LGBTQ+ persons are illegitimate and unjust. That an ethical framework is susceptible to interpretation is hardly unique to natural law, however. Even subjective systems such as ethical relativism are subject to interpretive disagreements, such as when two ethical relativists disagree as to what, in fact, is "right" according to their own (shared) culture.

In addition to the significance of natural law for social justice, a second significant contribution from this chapter is Aquinas' claim (contra Augustine) that the sort of government we are subject to actually *matters*. Recall one of the things Aquinas said on this issue:

For an individual man to lead a good life two things are required. The first and most important is to act in a virtuous manner (for virtue is that by which one lives well); the second, which is secondary and instrumental, is a sufficiency of those bodily goods whose use is necessary for virtuous life. Yet the unity of man is brought about by nature, while the unity of multitude, which we call peace, must be procured through the efforts of the ruler. Therefore, to establish virtuous living in a multitude three things are necessary. First of all, that the multitude be established in the unity of peace. Second, that the multitude thus united in the bond of peace, be directed to acting well. For just as a man can do nothing well unless unity within his members be presupposed, so a multitude of men lacking the unity of peace will be hindered from virtuous action by the fact that it is fighting against itself. In the third place, it is necessary that there be at hand a sufficient supply of the things required for proper living, procured by the ruler's efforts.[540]

For Aquinas, we are naturally social, and will inevitably form communities – and it is right that we do so. The kind of State in which we live, and the nature of the government under which we live, are not trivial matters though. This is because the State not only has the basic function of protecting us, but the more active and positive function of helping us to become more virtuous and to live well. That means that, contrary to the claims of libertarians and certain conservatives, who object to the overreach of the "nanny state," it is very much within the legitimate scope of government to make moral recommendations, and to enact and enforce policies that promote them.

In addition to making and enforcing laws protecting us from each other (including, presumably, from hate crimes, discrimination, etc.), the State also has an obligation to promote a "sufficient supply of the things required for proper living, procured by the ruler's efforts." While we could certainly debate just what things are required for "proper living," and what amount of such things is required, it is clear that Aquinas thinks that it is the proper role and responsibility of the ruler (i.e., government) to "procure" those things for all members of the community in the event that they do not already have access to them. Obvious candidates for such requirements for proper living include food, housing,

education, and healthcare, at minimum.

With Aquinas, we have the foundations for an argument, grounded on Natural Law (a specifically Christian one, at that), that the government is obligated to provide certain basic necessities. We therefore have some philosophical "ammunition" for the battles for State subsidized food, housing, education, and healthcare – all of which feature prominently in social justice campaigns. Indeed, King himself was committed not merely to racial justice, but *economic* justice.

In the last months of his life, MLK was focused on poverty and economic injustice, and was organizing a "Poor People's Campaign" that would result in another march to Washington DC to demand federal funding for full employment, antipoverty programs, housing for the poor, and a guaranteed annual income (now referred to as a universal basic income, or UBI—the central element of Andrew Yang's Presidential campaign platform in 2020, and his continued focus to this day).[541]

Among other "basic necessities of life" King was campaigning for was the right to education and health care. The Poor People's Campaign was "rebooted" in 2017 by Reverends William Barber and Liz Theoharis.[542]

It's hardly a coincidence that a man so obviously and explicitly influenced by Aquinas would advocate that the State provide the very sorts of necessities that Aquinas himself proposed centuries ago, nor a coincidence that King's work would be taken up by other ministers of the same faith decades later. Regardless of whether one is sympathetic to the religious worldview of Aquinas, his arguments for a justice that transcends human convention and that it is the proper obligation of the government to provide that justice, even in the form of providing "life's necessities," are potentially relevant and very useful to contemporary social justice advocates.

---

[540] *De Regimine Principum*, Book 1, chapter 16.
[541] https://www.theatlantic.com/politics/archive/2018/04/mlk-last-march/555953/

[542] https://www.cnn.com/2019/01/20/us/poor-peoples-campaign-mlk-legacy/index.html

Chapter 19: American Political Philosophy
Frederick Douglass: Reformer and Self-made Man

Comprehension questions you should be able to answer after reading this chapter:

1. What did Douglass believe about human nature?
2. What is the role/job of the reformer, according to Douglass?
3. What is meant by "moral ecology," and what were the effects of the slavery moral ecology on beliefs, values, and behavior in slave states?
4. What are some of the fundamental beliefs of classical liberalism? What is the difference between a traditional liberal and a reform liberal?
5. What are some of the basic premises of natural law theory?
6. How does Douglass use natural law theory in his arguments against slavery?
7. Using natural law theory, how does Douglass demonstrate that enslaved persons are *persons*, with equal rights?
8. What is the doctrine of "universal self-ownership?" How does this idea contribute to Douglass' political views?
9. How does Douglass extend his arguments for equality regardless of race to equality regardless of sex/gender?
10. Why does Douglass think government is necessary? What is its primary purpose?
11. What is Douglass' doctrine of "true virtue?"
12. What does Douglass mean by "civic responsibility?" What does it require from us?
13. What did Douglass mean by "fair play?"
14. What did Douglas mean by a "Self-made (Person)?"
15. What are some of Douglass' policy proposals and stances on political issues that might be relevant today?

Biographical information

Frederick Douglass is a world-historic figure. This chapter is not a biography but is rather devoted to political philosophy. However, aside from providing interesting trivia, Douglass' biography provided significant influence on his moral and political views, and for that reason a brief survey of these details provides us with useful insight as well.

He was born Frederick Augustus Washington Bailey, an enslaved person in Maryland. Because he was born enslaved, his precise birth date was not known even to himself, but he claimed February 14th as his birthday because his mother referred to him as her special "valentine. His birth year was either 1817 or 1818. While his mother

(Harriet Bailey) was an enslaved Black person, his (presumed) father was white, and her "master," Aaron Anthony. At the age of 6, Douglass was sent to live and work at the Wye House plantation, where Anthony worked as the overseer of the enslaved persons.

After Anthony died in 1826, the young Douglass was given to Lucretia Auld, the wife of Thomas Auld, who in turn sent him to live with Thomas' brother Hugh Auld in Baltimore. Hugh's wife, Sophia, was initially kind to young Douglass, and started teaching him the alphabet when he was about 12 years old. Her husband eventually discovered this and forbade it, explaining that literacy would only encourage slaves to desire freedom. She not only stopped her lessons, but hid reading materials from him, including her Bible.

Douglass' thirst for education had been activated, though, and he continued to teach himself, in secret. He learned to read from some of the white children in the neighborhood and would read any materials he could get his hands on, including pamphlets, newspapers, and books of any kind.

Covey, who (Douglass said) never tried to beat him again.

In 1837, Douglass met and fell in love with a free Black woman, Anna Murray. With her assistance, he fled to New York as a "fugitive slave." She joined him in New York where they married on September 15th, 1838. To help evade capture, he also changed his name to Douglass (having been inspired by characters of that name from the poem "The Lady of the Lake" by Walter Scott).

Living in New Bedford, Douglass regularly attended abolitionist meetings, and subscribed to *The Liberator*, the weekly newspaper of famed abolitionist William Lloyd Garrison. Douglass was present at a speech given by Garrison in 1841, and, at another meeting, Douglass was unexpectedly invited to address the crowd himself. His performance was so compelling that he quickly became a regular anti-slavery lecturer. In addition to giving countless speeches over the remainder of his life, he also wrote several versions of his autobiography: *The Narrative of the Life of Frederick Douglass, an American Slave* (1845), *My Bondage and My Freedom* (1855). *Life and Times of Frederick Douglass* (1881).

As Douglass' public prominence increased, so too did fear for his well-being given that he was still (legally) a fugitive slave. At the advice of some of his friends, he fled the United States and lived for several years in England, Ireland, and Scotland. While there, some of his British abolitionist supporters raised funds and purchased his (legal) freedom from Thomas Auld so that the most obvious threat to his freedom would be removed.

Douglass returned to the United States and started his own abolitionist newspaper, *The North Star*, in 1847. His abolitionist efforts went beyond writing articles and giving speeches. He and his wife personally supported the

In 1833, Thomas Auld reclaimed Douglass and sent him to work for the notorious "slave-breaker" Edward Covey, where Douglass received frequent whippings. At the age of 16, Douglass risked his very life by daring to fight back and resist a whipping, and prevailed in a fight against

Underground Railroad, providing shelter and resources in their own home for more than 400 escaped enslaved persons.

Douglass' activism extended beyond the obvious self-interest of abolitionism. He was the only Black person to attend the first women's rights convention in the United States, the Seneca Falls Convention of 1848. While there, Douglass gave a speech in support of women's equal rights—the right to vote, in particular.

A true and committed reformer, Douglass and his family supported the abolitionist movement not only with his intellect and resources, but even with his own sons. When Black persons were finally allowed to serve the Union in the Civil War, three of his sons enlisted and served. Charles Douglass joined the famous 54th Massachusetts Infantry Regiment, Lewis Douglass fought at the Battle of Fort Wagner, and Frederick Douglass Jr. served as an Army recruiter.

After the victory of the Union in the Civil War, Douglass continued to be politically active, campaigning in support of Constitutional amendments and for the efforts of Reconstruction in the South. President Rutherford B. Hayes nominated Douglass to be the (first Black) Marshal for the District of Colombia, and he was confirmed to that post by the Senate in 1877. He would later be appointed ambassador to Haiti by President Benjamin Harrison.

On February 20, 1895, Douglass gave a speech at a meeting of the National Council of Women in Washington D.C. He returned home and suffered a massive and fatal heart attack shortly thereafter.

In death, Douglass was given great honor. Thousands of people passed by his coffin to show their respect. Among his pallbearers were U.S. Senators and Supreme Court Justices. A letter from Elizabeth Cady Stanton was read at his funeral, and Susan B. Anthony spoke at the service as well. His coffin was transported to Rochester for burial, where flags were flown at half-mast and children were released from school early to pay their respects.

A gifted and eloquent writer, a skilled and moving orator, and a dedicated, consistent, and sincere champion for equality of *all* persons, Douglass serves as a rich resource for political philosophy. One of the more interesting and compelling aspects of Douglass as a philosopher is that, unlike so many "theorists," Douglass' personal, lived, experience of the horrors of slavery directly informed his philosophical insights and arguments. That personal experience informed his commitment not only to the principle of "self-ownership," but also his views on personal responsibility.

Slavery

There is no question that the greatest animating force for Douglass, for much of his life, was his opposition to slavery. I will not be offering any sort of detailed account of the horrors and depravity of that institution, but will instead start with the simple (and odious) premise that slavery is a system that (1) treats persons as property, (2) provides unlimited power of the "master" over the enslaved person, and (3) extends to domination over not only the body of the enslaved person, but also their mind/"soul" by virtue of controlling access to education, literary, free worship, etc. As Douglass himself described it:

The condition of the slave is simply that of the brute beast. He is a piece of property – a marketable commodity in the language of the law, to be bought or sold at the will and caprice of the master who claims him to be his property; he is spoken of, thought of, and treated as property. His own good, his conscience, his intellect, his affections are all set aside by the master. He is as

much a piece of property as a horse. If he is fed, he is fed because he is property. If he is clothed, it is with a view to the increase of his value as property.[543]

Under the (literally inhumane) system of slavery, enslaved persons are not *persons* at all, but resources to be exploited. Their value is purely instrumental, in the same way that a horse is valued, or a hammer. "Care" for enslaved persons, such as it was, was simple self-interest, much as someone might be motivated to take decent care of their tools.

The very existence and persistence of the institution of slavery was, for Douglass, a manifestation of an unfortunate aspect of human nature.

Human nature

Like many philosophers across time and across the globe, such as Xunzi, Hobbes, and Machiavelli, Douglass had a "pessimistic" (or perhaps "realistic?") view of human nature. Douglass believed that human beings contained within them a universal spirit of *selfishness*. Although human beings are subject to reason, revelation, and stirrings of conscience, this internal spirit of selfishness is capable of blinding human beings (morally speaking) into committing acts of evil that can clearly be known to be wrong. The proof of this selfishness is given evidence by "the facts of human nature, and by the experience of all men in all ages."[544]

From the earliest periods of man's history, we are able to trace manifestations of that spirit of selfishness, which leads one man to prey upon the rights and interests of his fellow man. Love of ease, love of power, a strong desire to control the will of others, lay deep-seated in the human heart. These elements of character, overriding the better promptings of human nature, [have] cursed the world with slavery and kindred

---

[543] Buccola, Nicholas. *The Political Thought of Frederick Douglass. In Pursuit of American Liberty.*

New York: New York University Press (2012), 16.
[544] ibid., 20.

crimes.[545]

The institution of slavery was a manifestation of this selfish tendency, but slavery was hardly the only manifestation. Douglass would later identify the selfishness of economic elites as the cause of the vast disparity between the rich and the poor in his nation at the time. He further connected this spirit of selfishness with the male tendency to oppress women, in the context of his support of the suffrage movement.

Our selfish tendency, along with our ability to overcome it and make morally good choices instead, provides a microcosm of a "war" that takes place in each human heart, and ultimately in our shared lives.

> *Men have their choice in this world. They can be angels, or they can be demons. In the apocalyptic vision, John describes the war in heaven. You have only to strip that vision of its gorgeous Oriental drapery, divest it of its shining and celestial ornaments, clothe it in the simple and familiar language of common sense, and you will have before you the eternal conflict between right and wrong, good and evil, liberty and slavery, truth and falsehood, the glorious light of love, and the appalling darkness of human selfishness and sin. The human heart is a seat of constant war.... Just what takes place in individual human hearts, often takes place between nations, and between individuals of the same nation. Such is the struggle now going on in the United States. The slaveholders had rather reign in hell than serve in heaven.*[546]

Douglass believed that we all faced a moral imperative to participate on the *right* side of this struggle. Within our hearts, this means choosing to act morally rightly. Within our communities, this means fighting against injustice. Leading the charge in this fight is the "reformer."

Reformers

> *Two hostile and irreconcilable tendencies, broad as the world of man, are in the open field; good and evil, truth and error, enlightenment and superstition. Progress and reaction, the ideal and the actual, the spiritual and material, the old and the new, are in perpetual conflict, and the battle must go on till the ideal, the spiritual side of humanity shall gain perfect victory over all that is low and vile in the world. This must be so unless we concede that what is divine is less potent than what is animal; that truth is less powerful than error; that ignorance is mightier than enlightenment, and that progress is less to be desired than reaction, darkness and stagnation.*[547]

This excerpt from a speech not only demonstrates the "battle" vocabulary he uses in the context of reform and reformers, but also reveals his understanding of the relationship of reformers to truth. To put it mildly, Douglass was no moral subjectivist or ethical relativist. For Douglass, the battle between good and evil is not simply a difference in perspectives, but an objective matter about which some people are *right*, and others are *wrong*, both morally and intellectually. He associates injustice with error. Supporters of the institution of slavery, for

---

[545] ibid.

[546] "Substance of a Lecture [on secession and the Civil War]," a speech delivered at Zion Church in Rochester, New York on June 16, 1861, and published in *Douglass's Monthly*, July 1861). Quoted in Douglass, Frederick. *The Essential Douglass. Selected Writings and Speeches*. Edited by Nicholas Buccola. Indianapolis: Hackett Publishing (2016), 158.

[547] "It moves, or the Philosophy of Reform," a speech delivered to the Bethel Literary and Historical Association in Washington DC, on November 20, 1883, and published as a pamphlet. Quoted in Douglass, Frederick. *The Essential Douglass. Selected Writings and Speeches*. Edited by Nicholas Buccola. Indianapolis: Hackett Publishing (2016), 289 – 290.

example, are acting morally wrongly, but they are also literally mistaken about the demands of justice and the morality of that institution.

All reform, whether moral or physical, whether individual or social, is the result of some new truth or of a logical inference from an old and admitted truth.

Strictly speaking, however, it is a misnomer to prefix the word truth with the words new and old. Such qualifying prefixes have no proper application to any truth. Error may be old, or it may be new, for it has a beginning and must have an end. It is a departure from truth and a contradiction to the truth, and must pass away with the progressive enlightenment of the race; but truth knows no beginning and has no end, and can therefore be neither old nor new, but is unchangeable, indestructible and eternal.

Hence all genuine and lasting reforms must involve a renunciation of error which is transient, and the return to truth which is eternal.

The mission of the reformer is to discover truth, or the settled and eternal order of the universe.[548]

We will explore the (Natural Law) basis for his views on the objective nature of moral truths in a later section, but for now we will focus on the roll of the reformer himself or herself in that context. The role of the reformer, according to Douglass, can be described as follows:

1. Remind others of the moral requirements of Natural Law.
2. Call attention to the gaps between the requirements of Natural Law and the existing human laws (including rights, protections, etc.) in the community.

3. Act and agitate to close that gap.

Or, to put it simply, the reformer is called to point out what is right, point out where the community has gone wrong, and call the community to correct its errors. This "call to repentance" is analogous to the role of Old Testament prophets in the Bible, urging ancient Israel to turn from its "wicked ways" and return to the ways of God. As a man of faith, and as a subscriber to a religiously-informed Natural Law theory, Douglass would undoubtedly agree with this comparison. Speaking of the reformer, Douglass said:

His great work on earth is to exemplify, and to illustrate and to engraft those principles upon the living and practical understandings of all men within the reach of his influence. This is his work; long or short his years, many or few his adherents, powerful or weak his instrumentalities, through good report, or through bad report, this is his work. It is to snatch from the bosom of nature the latent facts of each man's individual experience, and with steady hand to hold them up fresh and glowing, enforcing, with all his power, their acknowledgment and practical adoption.[549]

By the very nature of a reformer, they must be critical of their community. In the wildly implausible scenario that someone's community is morally perfect, there would be no need for a reformer or for reform! But, since humans have never yet established a genuine "Heaven on Earth," there is need for individuals to challenge their communities and point out when they have gone wrong, morally speaking.

Then, as now, some people claim that any criticism of one's own country shows a lack of patriotism. Florida Governor (and GOP Presidential-hopeful) Ron Desantis has been a public leader in the effort to ban the teaching of Critical Race Theory (CRT) in his State, saying that it (CRT) is "basically teaching kids to hate our

---

[548] ibid., 298.

[549] Quoted in Buccola, 104.

country and to hate each other based on race."[550] Setting aside the fact that a very specific (Graduate-level) academic theory taught in law school has been conflated with nearly any discussion of race or racism, what of the idea that pointing out racist practices perpetuated by our Nation teaches us to "hate our country," to become unpatriotic? Douglass had a response to this long ago.

> We have heard much of late of the virtue of patriotism, the love of country, and this sentiment, so natural and so strong, has been impiously appealed to, by all the powers of human selfishness, to cherish the viper which is stinging our national life away.... I, too, would invoke the spirit of patriotism; not in a narrow and restricted sense, but I trust, with a broad and manly signification; not to cover up our national sins, but to inspire us with sincere repentance; not to hide our shame from the world's gaze, but utterly to abolish the cause of that shame; not to explain away our gross inconsistencies as a nation, but to remove the hateful, jarring, and incongruous elements from the land; not to sustain an egregious wrong, but unite all our energies in the grand effort to remedy that wrong.[551]

In other words, rather than casting the criticism of the reformer as unpatriotic, Douglass presents the reformer as the *genuine* patriot. Among zealously patriotic Americans, one sometimes hears the slogan, "my country, right or wrong." When expressed in that way, it is a call to unconditional patriotism. Support of one's country no matter what the country has done, is doing, or intends to do. Ironically, the *full* version of that slogan was made famous by an American

Senator who actually intended the opposite! "My country, right or wrong; if right, to be kept right; and if wrong, to be set right."[552] In 1872, Senator Carl Schulz made this statement in the Senate, as a way to criticize what he regarded as imperialistic American foreign policy. Far from a slogan commanding unwavering approval of anything the country does, Schulz, like Douglass, is claiming that such approval is only warranted when the country's policies are *right*. When they are not, this needs to be pointed out so that the nation's moral course can be corrected. Needless to say, the institution of slavery was a moral deviation that Douglass felt compelled to point out.

> Fellow citizens! I will not enlarge further on your national inconsistencies. The existence of slavery in this country brands your Republicanism as a sham, your humanity as a base pretense, and your Christianity as a lie. It destroys your moral power abroad; it corrupts your politicians at home. It saps the foundation of religion; it makes your name a hissing, and a byword to a mocking earth. It is the antagonistic force in your government, the only thing that seriously disturbs and endangers your Union. It fetters your progress; it is the enemy of improvement, the deadly foe of education; it fosters pride, it breeds insolence; it promotes vice; it shelters crime; it is a curse to the earth that supports it; and yet, you cling to it, as if it were the sheet anchor of all your hopes.[553]

Douglass, as a writer, describes the vocation of the reformer—but much more than this, he actually performs that role himself, and dedicated his entire adult life to the causes of justice and equality. Douglass sought to achieve a version of

---

[550] https://www.kcrg.com/2021/05/18/politicians-attack-critical-race-theory-without-understanding-it-experts-say/
[551] ibid., 111.
[552] https://www.bartleby.com/73/1641.html
[553] "What to the Slave is the Fourth of July?" A speech delivered in Rochester, New York on July 5, 1852, and published as a pamphlet. Quoted in Douglass, Frederick. *The Essential Douglass. Selected Writings and Speeches*. Edited by Nicholas Buccola. Indianapolis: Hackett Publishing (2016), 68.

the United States in which each person was genuinely free to be the author of their own lives. Such an outcome could only be achieved when a (limited) government protected the *equal* rights of *all* individuals. More than this, the government must also promote *fairness* in social and economic activities.

Such an outcome, and such a government, will not be achieved on its own. Members of the community must cultivate what he called "true virtue." True virtue is the distinguishing feature and animating force of the reformer.

> *The doctrine of true virtue requires us to do what we can to help those who are being denied the basic promises of liberalism. In other words, if the government is failing to protect a person's rights, provide her with equality before the law, or ensure that she's treated fairly in the social and economic spheres, each of us has a responsibility to use the moral and political means available to us to rectify the situation.*[554]

Slavery/moral ecology

As mentioned in the previous section, Douglass believed that the role of the reformer was to critique his or her community to the extent that it is failing to live up to what is morally required. This is necessary not only to correct for injustice, but also because Douglass believed that individual values and behavior are influenced and shaped by the "moral ecology" in which one lives and was raised. In other words, the values and practices of the community make an impression on the people who live in that community and dispose them to behave in ways consistent with those values. If the community values are morally misguided, it is the community itself that must be corrected. The institution of

slavery created just such a "moral ecology," according to Douglass.

> *The slaveholder, as well as the slave, is the victim of the slave system. A man's character greatly takes its cue and shape from the form and color of things about him. Under the whole heavens there is no relation more unfavorable to the development of honorable character, than that sustained by the slaveholder to the slave. Reason is imprisoned here, and passions run wild.*[555]

According to Douglass, both the slaveholder and the enslaved person are influenced, in their personality and character, by the institution of slavery. White persons who didn't happen to own slaves, but who lived in slave holding States, would be similarly influenced by their community's standards. Not surprisingly, Douglass believed that this influence was vicious. The moral wrongs of slavery included not only specific acts, but also the destructive and corrupting influence it had on the very character of the people living within its influence. Douglass spoke of this influence applying even to people who otherwise seemed kind and loving, such as the white woman he served when he was a child.

> *At first, Mrs. Auld evidently regarded me simply as a child, like any other child; she had not come to regard me as property. This latter thought was a thing of conventional growth. The first was natural and spontaneous. A noble nature, like hers, could not, innocently, be wholly perverted; and it took several years to change the natural sweetness of her temper into fretful bitterness.*[556]

---

[554] Buccola, 158-159.

[555] "Gradual Initiation to the Mysteries of Slavery," Chapter V of *My Bondage and My Freedom*, quoted in Douglass, Frederick. *The Essential Douglass. Selected Writings and Speeches.* Edited by Nicholas Buccola.

Indianapolis: Hackett Publishing (2016), 3.

[556] "Life in Baltimore," chapter X of *My Bondage and My Freedom*, quoted in Douglass, Frederick. *The Essential Douglass. Selected Writings and Speeches.* Edited by Nicholas Buccola. Indianapolis: Hackett Publishing (2016), 9 – 10.

Mrs. Auld, by her uncorrupted human nature, initially saw young Frederick as a child, like any other. She was initially kind to him, and even taught him how to read. Eventually, though, the cultural pressures of slavery corrupted her default kindness and compassion and hardened her heart even against a *child*. The institution of slavery, and the moral ecology it generates, influences not only individuals, but ultimately the basic institutions of the community.

Slavery, like all other gross and powerful forms of wrong which appeal directly to human pride and selfishness, when once admitted into the framework of society, has the ability and tendency to get a character in the whole network of society surrounding it, favorable to its continuance. The very law of his existence is growth and dominion. Natural and harmonious relations easily repose in their own rectitude, while all such as are false and unnatural are conscious of their own weakness, and must seek strength from without. Hence the explanation of the uneasy, restless, eager anxiety of slaveholders…. Slavery is the most stupendous of all lies, and depends for existence upon a favorable adjustment of all its surroundings. Freedom of speech, of the press, of education, of labor, of locomotion, and indeed all kinds of freedom, are felt to be a standing menace to slavery. Hence, the friends of slavery are bound by the necessity of their system to do just what the history of the country shows they have done – that is, to seek to subvert all liberty, and to pervert all the safeguards of human rights. They could not do otherwise. It was the controlling law of their situation.[557]

The perpetuation of slavery requires the

suppression of freedom, not only of the enslaved person, but even of "free" persons as well, as it can't permit the free exchange of ideas that would threaten the institution. As a result, the institution of slavery renders the community increasingly authoritarian and oppressive to *everyone* within its reach—at the expense of the values and rights of liberalism, and the genuine practice of democracy.

It is the task of the reformer to point out the moral failings of the moral ecology of slavery, and to act to replace it with one that is just and fair. The reformer is the first of two ideal types, according to Douglass. The reformer's task is to achieve "liberalism" in his or her society. Once that society has been achieved, Douglass encourages us to aspire to become his second ideal type: the "self-made man."[558] The self-made person exemplifies the good life that is made possible in a liberal society, once fairness and equality are achieved. We will explore both types in greater detail in later sections, but for now we will briefly identity what is meant by a "liberal" society in the first place.

Liberalism

In our current context, "liberalism" does not refer to the contemporary Democratic party in America, or the opposite of American Conservativism. Instead, liberalism refers to Classical Liberalism—political ideas and ideals that developed during the European Enlightenment, and which exhibited powerful and lasting effects on European and American systems of government. Core principles of this classical liberal tradition include:

- A belief in the existence of an individual right to life, liberty, and private property ownership.
- A belief that the Church and the State are (and should be) separate domains of

---

557 "Substance of a Lecture [on Secession and the Civil War]," 162 – 163.

558 Note that there is nothing specifically gendered about this type, and Douglass was

personally a committed feminist, for his time. With the exception of direct quotations, I will use the term "self-made person" in the place of "self-made man" going forward.

influence, but that religious and moral diversity ("pluralism") should be tolerated, or even celebrated.

- A belief that a limited government is the best system by which to protect individual rights.
- A belief that democracy (with limitations on the majority and protections for minorities) is the best form of limited government by which to protect individual rights.

Why democracy, specifically?

From the liberal perspective, democracy is usually seen as the form of government most likely to serve the overriding aim of securing freedom. The democratic commitments to free elections, representative and transparent political institutions, checks and balances, and equality before the law are more compatible with the core commitments of liberalism than any of the alternatives.[559]

Today, liberals (in this sense) can be further divided into traditional (classical) liberals, and "reform" liberals.

Classical liberals believe the conditions are met for the exercise of personal freedom when a limited government protects the rights of individuals to life, liberty, and property. Reform liberals share the classical liberal belief in individual rights, but worry about whether or not genuine freedom can be exercised under conditions of economic and social inequality. Reform liberals contend that true liberty can only be realized in communities that empower individuals to fulfill their potential.[560]

At the risk of oversimplification, classical liberals resemble contemporary libertarians, who seek both limited government and tend to be opposed to providing socio-economic "safety nets." Reform liberals, in contrast, resemble contemporary "progressives" who believe that socio-economic inequities hinder genuine liberty and inhibit the exercise of individual rights and therefore government must take action to address inequities.

Douglass is a nuanced thinker with respect to this vocabulary. He is clearly classically liberal in his zealous defense of individual rights and limited government. He is also, however, a "reform" liberal given what he will have to say about the interventions needed to provide "fair play" to all citizens—especially formerly enslaved persons and their descendants. He *also* promotes a strong sense of mutual responsibility—something that is not typical of classical liberalism, in general, as it tends to be more individualistic in its approach to public life. Finally, Douglass's endorsement of democracy, and his argument in favor of universal suffrage, is rooted in his commitment to Natural Law.

Natural law

Natural Law is an approach to philosophy, particularly moral philosophy, which is generally traced back through St. Thomas Aquinas to Aristotle and the Stoics, including Cicero. By way of a quick "intro to Natural Law," we will consider Cicero very briefly.

Consistent with the Natural Law tradition, in general, Cicero observed that all persons share in Reason, all people have some measure of moral value, and a Natural Law governs all people, regardless of political lines drawn on a map, or other morally irrelevant distinctions.

There is only one justice which constitutes the bond among humans, and which is established by one law, which is the right reason in commands and prohibitions.[561]

This natural law can't be overruled by any human decree, nor any considerations of convenience or self-interest. The natural law is

---

[559] Buccola, 45.
[560] ibid., 6.

[561] Cicero, *Laws*, 1.42

the foundation and judge of all human laws, whether domestic or international.

> We can distinguish good from bad laws by the standard of nature.[562]

> There is one, single, justice. It binds together human society and has been established by one, single, law.[563]

> Law in the proper sense is right reason in harmony with nature. It is spread through the whole human community, unchanging and eternal, calling people to their duty by its commands and deterring them from wrong-doing by its prohibitions. . . . This law cannot be countermanded, nor can it be in any way amended, nor can it be totally rescinded. We cannot be exempted from this law by any decree of the Senate or the people; nor do we need anyone to else to expound or explain it. There will not be one such law in Rome and another in Athens, one now and another in the future, but all people at all times will be embraced by a single and eternal and unchangeable law; and there will be, as it were, one lord and master of us all—the god who is the author, proposer, and interpreter of that law.[564]

Human laws that fail to conform to the standard provided by natural law are not, properly speaking, "laws" at all!

> If ignorant unqualified people prescribe a lethal, instead of a healing, treatment, that treatment cannot properly be called 'medical.' In a community a law of just any kind will not be a law, even if the people (in spite of its harmful character) have accepted it. Therefore law means drawing a distinction between just and unjust, formulated in accordance with that most

ancient and important of all things—nature; by her, human laws are guided in punishing the wicked and defending and protecting the good.[565]

Centuries later, Aquinas added a Christian "spin" to Natural Law. God is the supreme Law-Giver. The rational pattern within God's mind supplies the Eternal Law, which "is nothing but the rational pattern of the Divine wisdom considered as directing all actions and motions."[566]

Most things are governed by the Eternal Law without the possibility of disobedience. For example, most things in the universe simply "obey" the laws of nature. Imagine the absurdity of a rock "rebelling" against the pull of gravity, or an acorn defiantly growing into a zebra, rather than an oak tree! Humans, however, complicate the Eternal Law by virtue of our free will.

> Wherefore, since all things subject to Divine providence are ruled and measured by the eternal law, as was stated above (Article [1]); it is evident that all things partake somewhat of the eternal law, in so far as, namely, from its being imprinted on them, they derive their respective inclinations to their proper acts and ends. Now among all others, the rational creature is subject to Divine providence in the most excellent way, in so far as it partakes of a share of providence, by being provident both for itself and for others. Wherefore it has a share of the Eternal Reason, whereby it has a natural inclination to its proper act and end: and this participation of the eternal law in the rational creature is called the natural law.[567]

Because human subjection to the Eternal Law is different, Aquinas calls it being under the "Natural Law"—but "The Natural Law is nothing

---

[562] ibid., 1.44
[563] ibid., 1.42
[564] Cicero, *Republic*, 3.33

[565] *Laws*, 2.13
[566] Aquinas, *Summa Theologica*, I-II, 93.1.
[567] ibid., I-II, 91.2

else than the rational creature's participation of the Eternal Law." That is, the natural law is simply the eternal law as it is applied to humans. The natural law guides humans via natural inclinations toward the natural perfection to which God intends us. This includes, among other things, moral instruction. Aquinas calls the natural knowledge humans have instructing fundamental moral requirements of our human nature "Synderesis."

> *Now it is clear that, as the speculative reason argues about speculative things, so that practical reason argues about practical things. Therefore we must have, bestowed on us by nature, not only speculative principles, but also practical principles. Now the first speculative principles bestowed on us by nature do not belong to a special power, but to a special habit, which is called "the understanding of principles," as the Philosopher explains (Ethic. vi, 6). Wherefore the first practical principles, bestowed on us by nature, do not belong to a special power, but to a special natural habit, which we call "synderesis." Whence "synderesis" is said to incite to good, and to murmur at evil, inasmuch as through first principles we proceed to discover, and judge of what we have discovered.[568]*

A more familiar term, "conscience," he defines as an act of applying synderesis to concrete situations.

> *For conscience, according to the very nature of the word, implies the relation of knowledge to something: for conscience may be resolved into "cum alio scientia," i.e., knowledge applied to an individual case. . . . Wherefore, properly speaking, conscience denominates an act. But since habit is a principle of act, sometimes the name conscience is given to the first*

*natural habit---namely, 'synderesis': thus Jerome calls 'synderesis' conscience (Gloss. Ezech. 1:6); Basil [*Hom. in princ. Proverb.], the "natural power of judgment," and Damascene [*De Fide Orth. iv. 22] says that it is the "law of our intellect." For it is customary for causes and effects to be called after one another.[569]*

To illustrate: according to Aquinas, by synderesis we understand that adultery is morally wrong, but by conscience we understand that having sex with a particular woman who is not my wife is a case of adultery. Synderesis recognizes general principles, while conscience applies them. Synderesis reveals that stealing is wrong, and conscience tells me that taking office supplies is a case of stealing.

The natural knowledge of our moral requirements as supplied by synderesis is universal, unchangeable, and can't be "abolished from the hearts of men."[570] With this notion of a universal moral code applying to all humans, regardless of race or nationality, Aquinas is clearly drawing more from Cicero than Aristotle.

Assuming that synderesis supplies basic moral instruction, we may now turn to the specifics of that instruction. According to Aquinas, the first moral precept of the natural law is that "good is to be done and pursued and evils is to be avoided."[571] Aquinas does not bother to prove this. Instead, he claims that this precept of practical reason is analogous to the law of non-contradiction for speculative reason: neither can be demonstrated (proven), but both are principles without which reasoning to conclusions (logical, or moral, respectively) is impossible.

Think of it this way: how would you even talk about *any* notion, *any* interpretation, of "good" or "evil" at all without presupposing that "good" is *good*, and "evil" is *bad*? And yet, how could you possibly "prove" that "good" is *good*? These notions appear intuitive and unavoidable in the

---

[568] ibid., I, 79.12
[569] ibid., I, 79.13

[570] ibid., I-II, 94.4-94.6
[571] ibid., I-II, 94.2

abstract, even if we might disagree as to their specific applications.

If we accept that good is to be pursued, and evil avoided, how do we know what qualifies as good or evil? Aquinas thinks that our natural inclinations provide a rudimentary guide to "natural goods." For example, our natural inclination to self-preservation, avoidance of pain, pursuit of pleasure, reproduction and care of our offspring, living within a community, etc., are indicators of natural goods.

These inclinations are not infallible, of course. They can (and often are) corrupted by sin, so we are not merely to act on any inclination we happen to have! Instead, we need to recognize the "natural purpose" of the inclination, and then act on it only insofar as that purpose is respected. For example, according to Aquinas (and the official Natural Law doctrine of the Catholic Church), our sexual inclination has a "natural purpose" of reproduction. Therefore, the only proper way to act on that inclination is one which "respects" its purpose: reproduction. Not surprisingly, then, Aquinas (and the Catholic Church) are opposed to homosexual activities, masturbation, oral sex, the use of contraception—and any sexual activity that can't (feasibly) result in conception. Accordingly, Aquinas specifies that all inclinations belong to the natural law only insofar as they are "ruled by reason."[572] We experience inclinations but must test them with Reason to determine whether it is right to indulge and pursue them.

Although the natural law provides basic moral guidelines for human life, it does not provide specific guidance. For example, it is "natural" that those who commit crimes but should be punished, but what nature does not reveal to us is what exact punishment is appropriate based on the crime. Human law is needed to flesh out the details.

The first function of human law is to provide the details (understandably) left out by natural law. The second function of human law is to enforce the specific interpretation of natural law that is expressed in human law. In some cases,

human laws are so close to what is offered by natural law that we find them existing "universally" in all human communities. To use Aquinas' vocabulary, some human laws constitute "conclusions" from natural law. These pertain to matters about which natural law offers clear guidance (e.g., murder is wrong). Aquinas refers to these "conclusions" as the "law of nations," as they are (or ought to be) found in all nations, given that all humans have the same nature, and are subject to the same natural law. Indeed, a human law that opposes natural law is no longer properly "law" at all.

> *As Augustine says (De Lib. Arb. i, 5) "that which is not just seems to be no law at all": wherefore the force of a law depends on the extent of its justice. Now in human affairs a thing is said to be just, from being right, according to the rule of reason. But the first rule of reason is the law of nature, as is clear from what has been stated above (Q[91], A[2], ad 2). Consequently every human law has just so much of the nature of law, as it is derived from the law of nature. But if in any point it deflects from the law of nature, it is no longer a law but a perversion of law.[573]*

Other human laws involve much longer chains of reasoning to link them back to natural law, and so might be specific to certain communities only. These laws constitute "determinations" from natural law, and these pertain to the particular details/applications that are based in the conclusions from natural law.

> *Some things are therefore derived from the general principles of the natural law, by way of conclusions; e.g. that "one must not kill" may be derived as a conclusion from the principle that "one should do harm to no man": while some are derived therefrom by way of determination; e.g. the law of nature has it that the evil-doer should be punished; but that he be*

---

[572] ibid., I-II, 94.2

[573] ibid., I-II, 95.2

punished in this or that way, is a determination of the law of nature.[574]

Aquinas offers his own analogy to try to clarify the relationship between conclusions and determinations of natural law. All houses have certain essential elements (e.g., having a foundation, a roof, etc.), but may have particular details added to them that may vary from house to house (e.g., whether the house is built from brick or wood, whether the roof is tile or shingle, how many windows it has, etc.). Analogously, human laws are to be based on general natural law principles (e.g., murder is a criminal offense), but may vary with regard to details (e.g., punishing murder with execution as opposed to life imprisonment).

"Conclusions" of natural law give us the basic moral "foundation" for any person or community. The inclusion of "determinations" of natural law allows for diversity of expression, so long as the particular values don't contradict the natural law itself. To reuse an example, we might think that a conclusion from natural law is that murderers should be punished, but some chains of reasoning ("determinations") might lead some communities to punish with the death penalty, and others with life imprisonment. Either could be consistent with the natural law. A community that did not prohibit murder at all, however, would be contradicting the natural law.

Although a lengthy tangent, this explanation of Cicero and Aquinas will make Douglass' own Natural Law foundations more obvious, and his vocabulary and reasoning all the clearer. For example, a central premise of Natural Law theory is that Law (properly speaking) is objective, and that human laws are correct or incorrect (just or unjust) to the extent that they conform to the demands of Natural Law.

> *Rights do not have their source in the will or grace of man. They are not such things as he can grant or withhold according to his sovereign will or pleasure.*[575]

> *Fellow citizens: some things are settled, and settled forever – not by the laws of man, but by the laws of God; by the constitution of mankind; by the relationship of things and by the facts of human experience.*[576]

> *Numbers should not be looked to so much as right. The man who is right is a majority. He who has God and conscience on his side, has a majority against the universe. Though he does not represent the present state, he represents the future state. If he does not represent what we are, he represents what we ought to be.*[577]

If something is forbidden by Natural Law, no human law can justify it. If the majority within a community favor something that violates the requirements of Natural Law, the majority is mistaken—and if only one person disagrees, that one person is in possession of truth compared to the many who possess a falsehood.

> *Error may be new or it may be old, since it is founded in a misapprehension of what*

---

[574] ibid., I-II, 95.2

[575] "I am a Radical Woman Suffrage Man," an address delivered in Boston, Massachusetts, on May 28, 1888, in Blassingame. *The Frederick Douglass Papers*, 5: 383.

[576] "The Kansas – Nebraska bill," a speech delivered in Chicago, Illinois on October 30, 1854, and published in Frederick Douglass's paper, November 24, 1854) quoted in Douglass, Frederick. *The Essential Douglass. Selected Writings and Speeches*. Edited by Nicholas Buccola. Indianapolis: Hackett Publishing (2016), 97.

[577] "The Fugitive Slave Law," a speech delivered to the National Free Soil convention in Pittsburgh, Pennsylvania on August 11, 1852, and published in *Frederick Douglass's Paper*, August 20, 1852). Quoted in Douglass, Frederick. *The Essential Douglass. Selected Writings and Speeches*. Edited by Nicholas Buccola. Indianapolis: Hackett Publishing (2016), 75.

truth is. It has its beginnings and has its endings. But not so with truth. Truth is eternal. Like the great God from whose throne it emanates, it is from everlasting unto everlasting, and can never pass away.[578]

These truths, and the rights Reason will eventually reveal, are *universal*—applicable to all persons by virtue of being persons.

Human rights stand up on a common basis; and by all the reason that they are supported, maintained and defended, for one variety of the human family, they are supported, maintained and defended for all the human family; because all mankind have the same wants, arising out of a common nature.[579]

We are asked if we should turn the slaves all loose. I answer, yes. Why not? They are not wolves nor tigers, but men. They are endowed with reason – can decide upon questions of right and wrong, good and evil, benefits and injuries and are therefore subjects of government precisely as other men are.[580]

The enslaved person is a *person*. Slaves are capable of all the arts and professions of other men, and even while enslaved are put into service in those professions, using those tools, engaged in those crafts, etc. Their personhood is only ever questioned specifically with regard to a justification of keeping enslaved persons as property. They are otherwise implicitly regarded as persons given that they are held accountable for their actions and subject to punishment, as

though they are capable of rational decision-making and knowledge of right as opposed to wrong behavior.

The slaveholders themselves acknowledge it in the enactment of laws for their government. They acknowledge it when they punish disobedience on the part of the slave. There are seventy-two crimes in the state of Virginia, which, if committed by a black man (no matter how ignorant he be) subject him to the punishment of death; while only two of the same crimes will subject a white man to the like punishment. What is this but the acknowledgment that the slave is a moral, intellectual and responsible being.... It is admitted in the fact that Southern statute books are covered with enactments forbidding, under severe fines and penalties, the teaching of the slave to read or to write. When you can point to any such laws, in reference to the beasts of the field, then I may consent to argue the manhood of the slave.[581]

In summary, the enslaved share in the same capacity for Reason as all other (typical) humans. They can reason, know right from wrong, can communicate with as much sophistication as any other human (given access to education), are forced into service in ways that require intelligence and skill and not mere strength, and, importantly, are held legally and morally responsible for their actions—*especially* in slave-holding States. There is literally no consistent, non-hypocritical and self-serving, rational basis for regarding Black persons as somehow less of a person, and less subject to the protections (and

---

[578] "The Kansas – Nebraska bill," 107.

[579] "Claims of the Negro Ethnologically Considered," a speech (commencement address) delivered on July 12, 1854, before the literary societies of Western reserve College in Hudson, Ohio and published as a pamphlet. Quoted in Douglass, Frederick. *The Essential Douglass. Selected Writings and Speeches*. Edited by

Nicholas Buccola. Indianapolis: Hackett Publishing (2016), 88.

[580] "The Black Man's Future in the Southern States," an address delivered in Boston, Massachusetts, on February 5th, 1862, in Blasingame. *The Frederick Douglass Papers*, 3: 505.

[581] "What to the Slave is the Fourth of July?", 58.

obligations) of Natural Law as any other person.

> Would you have me argue that man is entitled to liberty? That he is the rightful owner of his own body? You have already declared it.... There is not a man beneath the canopy of heavens, but does not know that slavery is wrong for him.[582]

Such objective truths, discovered by Reason, are true and remain true regardless of local customs or preferences. One of those truths is a doctrine of "self-ownership," from which we may derive our right to liberty.

Self-ownership

> Whether men should be slave or free, does not depend on the success or failure of freedom in any given instance. Some things have been settled independently of human calculation and human adjudication. One of these things is, that man has by nature a right to his own body, and that to deprive him of that right is a flagrant violation of the will of God. This is settled. And if desolation and ruin, famine and pestilence should threaten, emancipation would still be the same urgent and solemn duty that it ever was. When the God of all the earth ordained the law of freedom, he foresaw all its consequences. Do right though the heavens fall. We have no right to do evil that good may come, nor to refrain from doing right because evil may come.[583]

> [The right to liberty] existed in the very idea of man's creation. It was his even before he comprehended it. He was created in it, endowed with it, and it can never be taken from him. No laws, no statutes, no compacts, no covenants, no compromises, no constitutions, can abrogate or destroy

it. It is beyond the reach of the strongest earthly arm, and smiles at the ravings of tyrants from its hiding place in the bosom of God. Men may hinder its exercise – they may act in disregard of it – they are even permitted to war against it; but they fight against heaven, and their career must be short, for eternal providence will speedily vindicate the right.[584]

> The Supreme Court of the United States is not the only power in this world. It is very great, but the Supreme Court of the Almighty is greater. Judge Taney can do many things, but he cannot perform impossibilities. He cannot bail out the ocean, annihilate the firm old earth, or pluck the silvery star of liberty from our northern sky. He may decide, and decide again; but he cannot reverse the decision of the Most High. He cannot change the essential nature of things – making evil good, and good evil. Happily for the whole human family, their rights have been defined, declared, and decided in a court higher than the Supreme Court.... Your fathers have said that man's right to liberty is self-evident. There is no need of argument to make it clear. The voices of nature, of conscience, of reason, and of revelation, proclaim it as the right of all rights, the foundation of all trust, and of all responsibility. Man was born with it. It was his before he comprehended it. The deed conveying it to him is written in the center of his soul, and is recorded in heaven. The sun in the sky is not more palpable to the sight than man's right to liberty is to the moral vision. To decide against this right in the person of Dred Scott, or the humblest and most whip-scarred bondsman in the land, is to decide against God. It is an open

---

[582] ibid., 59.

[583] "Freedom in the West Indies," an address delivered in Poughkeepsie, New York, on August 2, 1858, in Blassingame, *The Frederick Douglass Papers*, 3: 222-223.

[584] "An Anti-Slavery Tocsin," an address delivered in Rochester, New York, on December 8, 1850, in Blassingame, *The Frederick Douglass Papers*, 2: 161.

*rebellion against God's government. It is
an attempt to undo what God has done, to
blot out the broad distinction instituted by
the All-Wise between men and things, and
to change the image and superscription of
the ever-living God into a speechless piece
of merchandise.*[585]

The doctrine of self-ownership is an essential component of Douglass' understanding of political rights and obligations.

*[There] was one idea, rule or principle, call
it what you will, which entirely took
possession of me, even in childhood, and
which stood out strongly, invincible
against every argument drawn from
nature and Scripture in favor of slavery.
What was the idea, rule, or principle? This
it was: every man is the original, rightful,
and absolute owner of his own body; or in
other words, every man is himself, is his
self, if you please, and belongs to himself,
and can only part from his self-ownership,
by the commission of a crime.*[586]

According to the doctrine of universal self-ownership, every human being is the "original, rightful, and absolute owner of his own body."[587] Douglass appealed to this doctrine in an amazing argument that he offered to his former "master," Thomas Auld, in defense of his own escape from slavery.

*The morality of the act, I dispose as
follows: I am myself; you are yourself: we
are two distinct persons, equal persons.*

*What you are, I am. You are a man, and so
am I. God created us both, and made us
separate beings. I am not by nature bound
to you, or you to me. Nature does not make
your existence depend upon me, or mine
depend upon yours. I cannot walk upon
your legs, or you upon mine. I cannot
breathe for you, or you for me; I must
breathe for myself, and you for yourself.
We are distinct persons, and are each
equally provided with faculties necessary
to our individual existence. In leaving you,
I took nothing but what belonged to me,
and in no way lessened your means for
obtaining an honest living. Your faculties
remain yours, and mine became useful to
their rightful owner.*[588]

Slaves and masters are distinct and separate persons, with unique personalities. Each person is equally a person, established by similar capacities to reason and distinguish right from wrong. Equality of personhood is established by a self-evident and universal desire for freedom. Douglass believed that the shared desires and intellectual and moral capacities of human beings entitles them to an equal case for self-ownership. If we respect this principle of self-ownership, it entails that we refrain from depriving others of their lives, their liberty, their property, their pursuit of education and work, and their ability to (equally) participate in self-governance.

Linking a right to liberty to this Natural Law foundation is significant. According to Natural Law traditions, an individual cannot voluntarily surrender their own self-ownership without violating the Natural Law. In other words,

---

[585] "The Dred Scott Decision," a speech delivered at the anniversary of the American antislavery Society in New York, New York on May 14, 1857, and publish as a pamphlet. Quoted in Douglass, Frederick. *The Essential Douglass. Selected Writings and Speeches.* Edited by Nicholas Buccola. Indianapolis: Hackett Publishing (2016), 123.

[586] "A Friendly Word to Maryland," an address delivered in Baltimore, Maryland, on November

17, 1864, in Blassingame, *The Frederick Douglass Papers*, 4:42.

[587] Buccola, 2.

[588] "Letter to my old Master [Thomas Auld]," published in *The Liberator*, September 22, 1848. Quoted in Douglass, Frederick. *The Essential Douglass. Selected Writings and Speeches.* Edited by Nicholas Buccola. Indianapolis: Hackett Publishing (2016), 29.

surrendering self-ownership would be morally wrong even if particular individuals consented to it. From this right to self-ownership/liberty, we can derive a right to life as well, as well as other rights. That we have a right to life is indicated by our instinctive aversion to violence and even the sight of blood.

The shedding of human blood at first sight, and without explanation is, and must ever be, regarded with horror; and he who takes pleasure in human slaughter is very properly looked upon as a moral monster. Even the killing of animals produces a shudder in sensitive minds, uncalloused by crime; and men are only reconciled to it by being shown, not only its reasonableness, but its necessity. These tender feelings so susceptible to pain, are most wisely designed by the Creator, for the preservation of life. They are, especially, the affirmation of God, speaking through nature, and asserting man's right to live. Contemplated in the light or warmth of these feelings, it is in all cases, a crime to deprive a human being of life: but God has not left us solely to the guidance of our feelings, having endowed us with reason, as well as with feeling, and it is in the light of reason that this question ought to be decided.[589]

It is not easy to reconcile human feeling to the shedding of blood for any purpose, unless indeed in the excitement which the shedding of blood itself occasions. The knife is to feeling always an offense. Even when in the hands of a skillful surgeon, it refuses consent to the operation long after reason has demonstrated its necessity. It

even pleads the cause of the known murderer on the day of his execution, and calls society half criminal when, in cold blood, it takes life as a protection of itself from crime. Let no word be said against this holy feeling; more than to law and government are we indebted to this tender sentiment of regard for human life for the safety with which we walk the streets by day and sleep secure in our beds at night. It is nature's grand police, vigilant and faithful, sentineled in the soul, guarding against violence to peace and life.[590]

Human beings (universally) both want to direct their own lives, and we have the capacities (reason, free will, moral judgment) that make it possible for them to do so. These capacities supply the foundation for a principle of self-ownership, which is itself the principle serving as a foundation for individual rights to life, liberty, political participation, and private property ownership.

If (it is argued) we respect that an individual owns himself or herself, we should not only refrain from interfering with their liberty, but also from taking their life (as it isn't "ours" to "take"). Given that we are alike in our right to liberty and life, we also have a basis to believe that we are (and ought to be) politically *equal*. The doctrine of self-ownership is central to Douglass' thoughts, and versatile—applicable not only to abolitionism, but also women's rights, universal suffrage, religious liberty, and immigrants' rights.

Women

While there is no question that the central focus of Douglass' political activism was the abolition of slavery, and the political, social, and

---

[589] "Is it Right and Wise to Kill a Kidnapper?" An essay published in *Frederick Douglass's Paper*, June 2, 1854) quoted in Douglass, Frederick. *The Essential Douglass. Selected Writings and Speeches.* Edited by Nicholas Buccola. Indianapolis: Hackett Publishing (2016), 76 – 77.

[590] "John Brown," a speech delivered in Harpers Ferry, West Virginia at the 14th anniversary of Storer College on May 30, 1881, quoted in Douglass, Frederick. *The Essential Douglass. Selected Writings and Speeches.* Edited by Nicholas Buccola. Indianapolis: Hackett Publishing (2016), 260.

economic status of Black persons after emancipation, Douglass was also consistent with the extension of his principles to other causes as well, most notably women's rights.

As mentioned in the introduction of this chapter, Douglass was the only Black person to attend the first women's rights convention in the United States, the Seneca Falls Convention of 1848, where he gave a speech in support of women's right to vote. He continued to support gender equality until the literally last day of his life, which he spent giving a speech at a meeting of the National Council of Women in Washington D.C.

His support of women's right to vote, specifically, was a natural extension of his arguments in support of racial equality and the right of Black persons to vote: the doctrine of self-ownership.

> *If men could represent woman, it follows that woman could represent man, but no opponent of woman suffrage will admit that woman could represent him in the government, and in taking that position he would be right; since neither can, in the nature of things, represent the other, for the very obvious reason that neither can be the other. The great facts underlying the claim for universal suffrage is that every man is himself and belongs to himself, and represents his own individuality, not only in form and features, but in thought and feeling. And the same is true of woman. She is herself, and can be nobody else than herself. Her selfhood is as perfect and as absolute as is the selfhood of man. She can no more part with her personality than she can part with her shadow.*[591]

Much as he pointed out the rational and moral capacities that humans share, regardless of race, in his defense of racial equality, he makes the same case for shared capacities with respect to women.

> *The question which should be put to every man and which every man should put to himself is, who and what is woman? Is there really anything in her nature and constitution which necessarily unfits her for the exercise of suffrage? Is she a rational being? Has she knowledge of right and wrong? Can she discern between good and evil? Is she a legitimate subject of government? Is she capable of forming an intelligent opinion of public men and public measures? Has she a will as well as a mind? Is she able to express her thoughts and opinions by word and acts? As a member of society and citizen of the state, has she interests like those of men, which may be promoted or hindered, created or destroyed, by the legislative and judicial action of the government? When these questions are answered according to truth, the right of woman to participate in the government under which she lives, and which she is taxed to support, does not seem absurd.*

> *I hold that there is not one reason, not one consideration of justice and expediency, upon which man can claim the right to vote which does not apply equally to woman. If he knows right from wrong, so does she; if he is a subject of government, so is she; if he has a natural right to vote, so has she; if she has no right to exclude him, he has no right to exclude her. . . . She has all the attributes that fit her for citizenship. Equally with man she is a subject of the law. Equally with man she is bound to honor the law. Equally with man she is bound to obey the law. There is no more escape from its penalties for her than for him. When she violates the law in any way, or commits crime, she is arrested, arraigned, tried, condemned, and punished, like any other criminal. She then*

---

[591] "Who and What is Woman?" an address delivered in Boston, Massachusetts, on May 24, 1886, in Blassingame, *The Frederick Douglass Papers*, 5: 255.

finds in her womanhood neither excuse nor protection. If the law takes no thought of sex when it accuses her of crime, why should it take thought of sex when it bestows its privileges?[592]

Note the clearly parallel and familiar arguments here. One could easily substitute "Black" for "woman" in each occurrence of his argument and the argument would work equally well. By virtue of being a *person*, Black or white, male or female, we have the same capacity for rational decision making, moral and legal accountability, intentional action, discernment of right from wrong, interests that may be promoted or hindered, and so on. In addition to this rights-based argument in defense of women's rights, he also makes a consequentialist argument for women's political participation.

First, as a matter of principle, he claimed it is a violation of the natural dignity of women to exclude them from equal citizenship. This exclusion does positive injury to women because it is a denial of their humanity. Second, the exclusion of women is harmful to society as a whole because they are unable to include their wisdom and virtue in the process of self-government and hence unable to contribute to the common good.[593]

Douglass recognizes not only that denying women the right to participate in self-government harms women and their interests, but also harms the community to the extent that it withholds the positive contributions women

could and would make, were they to be politically involved.

Why is the right to vote so important to Douglass? Why is it imperative that Black persons and women be allowed to vote? Because the United States is a *democracy*.

Again, I want the elective franchise, for one, as a colored man, because ours is a peculiar government, based upon a peculiar idea, and that idea is universal suffrage. If I were in a monarchical government, or an autocratic or aristocratic government, where the few bore rule and the many were subject, there would be no special stigma resting upon me, because I did not exercise the elective franchise. It would do me no great violence. Mingling with the mass I should partake of the strength of the mass; I should be supported by the mass, and I should have the same incentives to endeavor with the mass of my fellow man; it would be no particular burden, no particular deprivation; but here where universal suffrage is the rule, where that is the fundamental idea of the government, to rule us out is to make us an exception, to brand us with the stigma of inferiority, and to invite to our heads the missiles of those about us; therefore, I want the franchise for the black man.[594]

In a democracy, specifically, voting is an indicator of status. Being disenfranchised is equally an indicator of less-than status. Beyond the self-interest that is served by voting, being

---

[592] "Address to the Annual Meeting of the New England Woman Suffrage Association," a speech delivered in Boston, Massachusetts, May 24, 1886, and published as "Frederick Douglass on Woman Suffrage" in the *Boston Women's Journal*, June 5, 1886). Quoted in Douglass, Frederick. *The Essential Douglass. Selected Writings and Speeches.* Edited by Nicholas Buccola. Indianapolis: Hackett Publishing (2016), 305 – 306.

[593] Buccola, 70.
[594] "What the Black Man Wants," a speech delivered at the annual meeting of the Massachusetts antislavery Society in Boston, Massachusetts, January 26, 1865, and published in *The Liberator*, February 10, 1865. Quoted in Douglass, Frederick. *The Essential Douglass. Selected Writings and Speeches.* Edited by Nicholas Buccola. Indianapolis: Hackett Publishing (2016), 192.

denied the vote carries with it the "stigma of inferiority." As a further demonstration of Douglass' progressive vision, he advocated for equality across gender lines, *and* across the Black/white binary, advocating for the rights of Chinese immigrants as well.

> *I have said that the Chinese will come, and even some reasons why we may expect them in very large numbers in no very distant future. Do you ask if I would favor such immigrations? I answer, I would. Would you admit them as witnesses and our courts of law? I would. Would you have them naturalized, and have them invested with all the rights of American citizenship? I would. Would you allow them to vote? I would. Would you allow them to hold office? I would. But are there not reasons against all this? Is there not such a law or principle as that of self-preservation? Does not every race owe something to itself? Should it not attend to the dictates of common sense? Should not a superior race protect itself from contact with the inferior ones? Are not the white people the owners of this continent? Have they not the right to say what kind of people shall be allowed to come here and settle? Is there not such a thing as being more generous than wise? In the effort to promote civilization may we not corrupt and destroy what we have? Is it best to take on board more passengers than the ship will carry?... I submit that this question of Chinese immigration should be settled upon higher principles than those of a cold and selfish expediency. There are such things in the world as human rights. They rest upon no conventional foundation, but are eternal, universal and indestructible.... I want a*

> *home here not only for the Negro, the Mulatto, and the Latin races, but I want the Asiatic to find a home here in the United States, and feel at home here, both for his sake and for ours. Right wrongs no man. If respect is had to majorities, the fact that only one-fifth of the population of the globe is white and the other four-fifths are colored ought to have some weight and influence in disposing of this and similar questions. It would be a sad reflection upon the laws of nature and upon the idea of justice, to say nothing of a common Creator, if four-fifths of mankind were deprived of the rights of migration to make room for the one-fifth. If the white race may exclude all other races from this continent, it may rightfully do the same in respect to all other lands, islands, capes and continents, and thus have all the world to itself, and thus what would seem to belong to the whole would become the property of only a part.[595]*

The beginning of that quotation consists of Douglass asking a series of rhetorical questions, in the imagined voice of someone arguing against immigration and for "secure borders." We can see that the basic elements of that position haven't changed in over 150 years. In Douglass' time, people opposed to Chinese immigration expressed concern that "their" civilization would be corrupted and destroyed. This fear and this phrasing has not disappeared. Conservative Fox News host Tucker Carlson has devoted numerous segments of his popular program to what is known as the "replacement" theory—an argument against immigration from non-European (i.e., non-white) countries.[596] Current GOP Representative Matt Gaetz of Florida has endorsed this theory as well.

---

[595] "Our Composite Nationality," a speech delivered on December 7, 1869, in Boston, Massachusetts and published in *Boston Daily Advertiser*, December 8, 1869. Quoted in Douglass, Frederick. *The Essential Douglass. Selected Writings and Speeches*. Edited by

Nicholas Buccola. Indianapolis: Hackett Publishing (2016), 224-225.
[596] https://www.businessinsider.com/tucker-carlson-again-pushes-white-supremacist-conspiracy-theory-2021-9

Matt Gaetz ✔
@mattgaetz   ...

.@TuckerCarlson is CORRECT about Replacement
Theory as he explains what is happening to America.

The ADL is a racist organization.

theguardian.com
Fresh calls for Fox News to fire Tucker Carlson over 'replacement theory'
Host dismisses Anti-Defamation League after organization urges network to drop
him

GOP Representatives Marjorie Taylor Green and Paul Gosar announced their intention to form a caucus in the House of Representatives to promote and preserve "Anglo-Saxon" values. Referring to immigration, they claimed that the USA is a "a nation with a border, and a culture, strengthened by a common respect for uniquely Anglo-Saxon political traditions," which is "threatened when foreign citizens are imported en-masse."[597] After some pushback from within their own party, they revoked their caucus plans.

Douglass also conjures the argument that immigration results in taking "on board more passengers than the ship will carry." In other words, immigrants create a burden on scarce resources that should be reserved for American citizens.

On May 5th, 2022, Texas Governor Greg Abbott announced his intention that Texas would submit a challenge to the 1982 Supreme Court decision, *Phyler v. Doe*, that ruled that States must provide undocumented children with access to public education. In defense of his desire to prevent undocumented children residing in his State from going to school, he mentioned that "the challenges on [their] public systems is extraordinary," as well as complaining of Texas "having to bear that burden."[598] Even in "liberal" California, a majority of voters passed Proposition 187 in 1984, also called the "Save our State" initiative. That bill denied undocumented persons access to public education, social services, and non-emergency health services. Like Abbot in Texas, the text of Prop 187 claimed Californians were "suffering economic hardship" because of the presence of undocumented immigrants. That bill was ruled to be in violation of *Phyler v. Doe*—the very Court decision Abbot intends to challenge today.

If those views and arguments persist to this day, Douglass arguments *against* them are still relevant today as well. Douglass urges us to look to "higher principles than those of a cold and selfish expediency." He is speaking not only in support of immigration, the rights of immigrants, and the value of what immigrants can offer to the United States, but he is even arguing, well ahead of his time, against the implicit doctrine of white supremacy that informed (and still informs) attitudes towards immigration. Observing that the vast majority of humans on this planet are not white, he claims that it would be a "sad reflection upon the laws of nature and upon the idea of justice" if that minority could effectively claim the planet as theirs and dictate the movements and status of the other four-fifths of the global population who happen to be people of color. Ultimately, and "simply," Douglass is arguing for political *equality* for all persons, regardless of race, nationality, gender, or socio-economic status.

> *For ourselves, it is scarcely necessary to say that we are opposed to all aristocracy, whether of wealth, power, or learning. The*

---

[597] https://www.forbes.com/sites/andrewsolender/2021/04/16/marjorie-taylor-greene-forming-caucus-to-promote-anglo-saxon-political-traditions/?sh=67ecc9c65672

[598] https://www.businessinsider.com/texas-greg-abbott-immigration-children-education-2022-5

beauty and perfection of government in our eyes will be attained when all the people under it, men and women, black and white, shall be conceded the right of equal participation in wielding its power and enjoying its benefits. Equality is even a more important word with us than liberty. Equality before the law... is to the colored man the crowning point of political wisdom.[599]

Equality before the law is, of course, a legal status, requiring the endorsement and enforcement of the government in question. We may now consider Douglass' views on the nature and purpose of government, in general.

Government

Like many other political thinkers, Douglass believed government was necessary because of human nature. We find echoes of this idea in Hobbes, Xunzi, and in the Federalist Papers, among others. Recall that Douglass believed that a tendency towards selfishness was an aspect of human nature. The human heart is a battleground between good and evil, where individuals choose whether to act according to the requirements of morality, or whether to act wrongly and transgress against the natural rights of their neighbors. Unfortunately, and inevitably, some people will choose evil actions over good.

Because there are hardened villains, enemies to themselves and to the well-being of society, who will cheat, steal, rob, burn and murder their fellow creatures, and because these are the exceptions to the mass of humanity, society has the right to protect itself against their depredations

and aggressions upon the commonweal. Society without law, is society with a curse, driving men into isolation and depriving them of one of the greatest blessings of which man is susceptible.[600]

Natural rights are not self-protecting. They must be recognized in the Constitution of a government. In the absence of a constitution, "government is nothing better than a lawless mob."[601] Legally recognized rights are not self-enforcing. Once rights are recognized in the Constitution, or subordinate laws that follow, they must be *supported* by the government. "Pen, ink, and paper liberty are excellent when there is a party behind it to respect and secure its enjoyment. Human laws are not self-executing. To be of any service they must be made vital, active, and certain."[602]

The first and fundamental function of government, then, is to protect the natural rights of those it governs. Everything else that a government is or does is secondary to this fundamental obligation. Similar to John Locke, Douglass claimed that a government which does *not* protect those rights, or, even worse, actually violates them itself, is "arbitrary, despotic, tyrannical, corrupt, unjust, [and] capricious."[603]

A specific example of a government not only failing to protect rights, but actively violating them itself, came in the form of the infamous Fugitive Slave Act of 1850 which not only required that escaped enslaved persons be returned to their "owners," even if they were currently residing in a free State," but also made the Federal Government itself responsible for finding and returning escaped slaves. I have included the entirety of the Act below, for reference.

---

[599] "Politics an Evil to the Negro," an essay published in the *New National Era*, August 24, 1871. Quoted in Douglass, Frederick. *The Essential Douglass. Selected Writings and Speeches.* Edited by Nicholas Buccola. Indianapolis: Hackett Publishing (2016), 233.

[600] "Is Civil Government Right?" An essay published in *Frederick Douglass's Paper*, October 23, 1851. Quoted in Douglass, Frederick. *The Essential Douglass. Selected Writings and Speeches.* Edited by Nicholas Buccola. Indianapolis: Hackett Publishing (2016), 48.

[601] Quoted in Buccola, 74.

[602] Quoted in ibid., 75.

[603] Quoted in ibid., 62.

Section 1

Be it enacted by the Senate and House of Representatives of the United States of America in Congress assembled, That the persons who have been, or may hereafter be, appointed commissioners, in virtue of any act of Congress, by the Circuit Courts of the United States, and Who, in consequence of such appointment, are authorized to exercise the powers that any justice of the peace, or other magistrate of any of the United States, may exercise in respect to offenders for any crime or offense against the United States, by arresting, imprisoning, or bailing the same under and by the virtue of the thirty-third section of the act of the twenty-fourth of September seventeen hundred and eighty-nine, entitled "An Act to establish the judicial courts of the United States" shall be, and are hereby, authorized and required to exercise and discharge all the powers and duties conferred by this act.

Section 2

And be it further enacted, That the Superior Court of each organized Territory of the United States shall have the same power to appoint commissioners to take acknowledgments of bail and affidavits, and to take depositions of witnesses in civil causes, which is now possessed by the Circuit Court of the United States; and all commissioners who shall hereafter be appointed for such purposes by the Superior Court of any organized Territory of the United States, shall possess all the powers, and exercise all the duties, conferred by law upon the commissioners appointed by the Circuit Courts of the United States for similar purposes, and shall moreover exercise and discharge all the powers and duties conferred by this act.

Section 3

And be it further enacted, That the Circuit Courts of the United States shall from time to time enlarge the number of the commissioners, with a view to afford reasonable facilities to reclaim fugitives from labor, and to the prompt discharge of the duties imposed by this act.

Section 4

And be it further enacted, That the commissioners above named shall have concurrent jurisdiction with the judges of the Circuit and District Courts of the United States, in their respective circuits and districts within the several States, and the judges of the Superior Courts of the Territories, severally and collectively, in term-time and vacation; shall grant certificates to such claimants, upon satisfactory proof being made, with authority to take and remove such fugitives from service or labor, under the restrictions herein contained, to the State or Territory from which such persons may have escaped or fled.

Section 5

And be it further enacted, That it shall be the duty of all marshals and deputy marshals to obey and execute all warrants and precepts issued under the provisions of this act, when to them directed; and should any marshal or deputy marshal refuse to receive such warrant, or other process, when tendered, or to use all proper means diligently to execute the same, he shall, on conviction thereof, be fined in the sum of one thousand dollars, to the use of such claimant, on the motion of such claimant, by the Circuit or District Court for the district of such marshal; and after arrest of such fugitive, by such marshal or his deputy, or whilst at any time in his custody under the provisions of this act, should such fugitive escape, whether with or without the assent of such marshal or his deputy, such marshal shall be liable, on his official bond, to be prosecuted for the benefit of such claimant, for the full value of the service or labor of said fugitive in the State, Territory, or District whence he escaped: and the better to enable the said commissioners, when thus appointed, to execute their duties faithfully and efficiently, in conformity with the requirements of the Constitution of the United States and of this act, they are hereby authorized and empowered, within their counties respectively, to appoint, in writing under their hands, any one or more suitable persons, from time to time, to execute all such warrants and other process as may be issued by them in the lawful performance of their respective duties; with authority to such commissioners, or the persons to be appointed by them, to execute process as aforesaid, to summon and call to their aid the bystanders, or posse comitatus of the proper county, when necessary to ensure a faithful observance of the clause of the Constitution referred to, in conformity with the provisions of this act; and all good citizens are hereby commanded to aid and assist in the prompt and efficient execution of this law, whenever their services may be required, as aforesaid, for that purpose; and said warrants shall run, and be executed by said officers, any where in the State within which they are issued.

Section 6

And be it further enacted, That when a person held to service or labor in any State or Territory of the United States, has heretofore or shall hereafter escape into another State or Territory of the United States, the person or persons to whom such service or labor may be due, or his, her, or their agent or attorney, duly authorized, by power of attorney, in writing, acknowledged and certified under the seal of some legal officer or court of the State or Territory in which the same may be executed, may pursue and reclaim such fugitive person, either by procuring a warrant from some one of the courts, judges, or commissioners aforesaid, of the proper circuit, district, or county, for the apprehension of such fugitive from service or labor, or by seizing and arresting such fugitive, where the same can be done without process, and by taking, or causing such person to be taken, forthwith before such court, judge, or commissioner, whose duty it shall be to hear and determine the case of such claimant in a summary manner; and upon satisfactory proof being made, by deposition or affidavit, in writing, to be taken and certified by such court, judge, or commissioner, or by other satisfactory testimony, duly taken and certified by some court, magistrate, justice of the peace, or other legal officer authorized to administer an oath and take depositions under the laws of the State or Territory from which such person owing service or labor may have escaped, with a certificate of such magistracy or other authority, as aforesaid, with the seal of the proper court or officer thereto attached, which seal shall be sufficient to establish the competency of the proof, and with

proof, also by affidavit, of the identity of the person whose service or labor is claimed to be due as aforesaid, that the person so arrested does in fact owe service or labor to the person or persons claiming him or her, in the State or Territory from which such fugitive may have escaped as aforesaid, and that said person escaped, to make out and deliver to such claimant, his or her agent or attorney, a certificate setting forth the substantial facts as to the service or labor due from such fugitive to the claimant, and of his or her escape from the State or Territory in which he or she was arrested, with authority to such claimant, or his or her agent or attorney, to use such reasonable force and restraint as may be necessary, under the circumstances of the case, to take and remove such fugitive person back to the State or Territory whence he or she may have escaped as aforesaid. In no trial or hearing under this act shall the testimony of such alleged fugitive be admitted in evidence; and the certificates in this and the first [fourth] section mentioned, shall be conclusive of the right of the person or persons in whose favor granted, to remove such fugitive to the State or Territory from which he escaped, and shall prevent all molestation of such person or persons by any process issued by any court, judge, magistrate, or other person whomsoever.

Section 7

And be it further enacted, That any person who shall knowingly and willingly obstruct, hinder, or prevent such claimant, his agent or attorney, or any person or persons lawfully assisting him, her, or them, from arresting such a fugitive from service or labor, either with or without process as aforesaid, or shall rescue, or attempt to rescue, such fugitive from service or labor, from the custody of such claimant, his or her agent or attorney, or other person or persons lawfully assisting as aforesaid, when so arrested, pursuant to the authority herein given and declared; or shall aid, abet, or assist such person so owing service or labor as aforesaid, directly or indirectly, to escape from such claimant, his agent or attorney, or other person or persons legally authorized as aforesaid; or shall harbor or conceal such fugitive, so as to prevent the discovery and arrest of such person, after notice or knowledge of the fact that such person was a fugitive from service or labor as aforesaid, shall, for either of said offences, be subject to a fine not exceeding one thousand dollars, and imprisonment not exceeding six months, by indictment and conviction before the District Court of the United States for the district in which such offence may have been committed, or before the proper court of criminal jurisdiction, if committed within any one of the organized Territories of the United States; and shall moreover forfeit and pay, by way of civil damages to the party injured by such illegal conduct, the sum of one thousand dollars for each fugitive so lost as aforesaid, to be recovered by action of debt, in any of the District or Territorial Courts aforesaid, within whose jurisdiction the said offence may have been committed.

Section 8

And be it further enacted, That the marshals, their deputies, and the clerks of the said District and Territorial Courts, shall be paid, for their services, the like fees as may be allowed for similar services in other cases; and where such services are rendered exclusively in the arrest, custody, and delivery of the fugitive to the claimant, his or her agent or attorney, or where such supposed fugitive may be discharged out of custody for the want of sufficient proof as aforesaid, then such fees are to be paid in whole by such claimant, his or her agent or attorney; and in all cases where the proceedings are before a commissioner, he shall be entitled to a fee of ten dollars in full for his services in each case, upon the delivery of the said certificate to the claimant, his agent or attorney; or a fee of five dollars in cases where the proof shall not, in the opinion of such commissioner, warrant such certificate and delivery, inclusive of all services incident to such arrest and examination, to be paid, in either case, by the claimant, his or her agent or attorney. The person or persons authorized to execute the process to be issued by such commissioner for the arrest and detention of fugitives from service or labor as aforesaid, shall also be entitled to a fee of five dollars each for each person he or they may arrest, and take before any commissioner as aforesaid, at the instance and request of such claimant, with such other fees as may be deemed reasonable by such commissioner for such other additional services as may be necessarily performed by him or them; such as attending at the examination, keeping the fugitive in custody, and providing him with food and lodging during his detention, and until the final determination of such commissioners; and, in general, for performing such other duties as may be required by such claimant, his or her attorney or agent, or commissioner in the premises, such fees to be made up in conformity with the fees usually charged by the officers of the courts of justice within the proper district or county, as near as may be practicable, and paid by such claimants, their agents or attorneys, whether such supposed fugitives from service or labor be ordered to be delivered to such claimant by the final determination of such commissioner or not.

Section 9

And be it further enacted, That, upon affidavit made by the claimant of such fugitive, his agent or attorney, after such certificate has been issued, that he has reason to apprehend that such fugitive will he rescued by force from his or their possession before he can be taken beyond the limits of the State in which the arrest is made, it shall be the duty of the officer making the arrest to retain such fugitive in his custody, and to remove him to the State whence he fled, and there to deliver him to said claimant, his agent, or attorney. And to this end, the officer aforesaid is hereby authorized and required to employ so many persons as he may deem necessary to overcome such force, and to retain them in his service so long as circumstances may require. The said officer and his assistants, while so employed, to receive the same compensation, and to be allowed the same expenses, as are now allowed by law for transportation of criminals, to be certified by the judge of the district within which the arrest is made, and paid out of the treasury of the United States.

Section 10

And be it further enacted, That when any person held to service or labor in any State or Territory, or in the District of Columbia, shall escape therefrom, the party to whom such service or labor shall be due, his, her, or their agent or attorney, may apply to any court of record therein, or judge thereof in vacation, and make satisfactory proof to such court, or judge in vacation, of the escape aforesaid, and that the person escaping owed service or labor to such party. Whereupon the court shall cause a record to be made of the matters so proved, and also a general description of the person so escaping, with such convenient certainty as may be; and a transcript of such record, authenticated by the attestation of the clerk and of the seal of the said court, being produced in any other State, Territory, or district in which the person so escaping may be found, and being exhibited to any judge, commissioner, or other office, authorized by the law of the United States to cause persons escaping from service or labor to be delivered up, shall be held and taken to be full and conclusive evidence of the fact of escape, and that the service or labor of the person escaping is due to the party in such record mentioned. And upon the production by the said party of other and further evidence if necessary, either oral or by affidavit, in addition to what is contained in the said record of the identity of the person escaping, he or she shall be delivered up to the claimant, And the said court, commissioner, judge, or other person authorized by this act to grant certificates to claimants or fugitives, shall, upon the production of the record and other evidences aforesaid, grant to such claimant a certificate of his right to take any such person identified and proved to be owing service or labor as aforesaid, which certificate shall authorize such claimant to seize or arrest and transport such person to the State or Territory from which he escaped: Provided, That nothing herein contained shall be construed as requiring the production of a

transcript of such record as evidence as aforesaid. But in its absence the claim shall be heard and determined upon other satisfactory proofs, competent in law.[604]

Douglass' reaction to the passage of this Act was, not surprisingly, an unambiguous and public condemnation.

> *Human government is for the protection of rights; and when government destroys human rights, it ceases to be a government, and becomes a foul and blasting conspiracy; and is entitled to no respect whatever.*[605]

Given Douglass' Natural Law arguments in defense of universal self-ownership, the institution of slavery was profoundly unjust. The fact that the United States government not only allowed slavery, but actively supported and enforced it, rendered the U.S. Government unjust as well. In his role as a reformer, Douglass repeatedly pointed out this injustice and urged the people and politicians of the United States to repent and abolish its unjust laws and institutions.

Interestingly, while the selfish and dangerous side of human nature makes government necessary in the first place, Douglass' optimism concerning human nature inspires his endorsement of a democratic system of government, specifically.

> *Why is this respect to be shown to the majority? Simply because a majority of human hearts and intellects may be presumed, as a general rule, to take a wiser and more comprehensive view of the matters upon which they act than the*

---

[604] https://www.battlefields.org/learn/primary-sources/fugitive-slave-act#:~:text=Passed%20on%20September%2018%2C%201850,returning%2C%20and%20trying%20escaped%20slaves.

[605] "The Fugitive Slave Law," a speech delivered to the National Free Soil convention in Pittsburgh,

Pennsylvania on August 11, 1852, and published in *Frederick Douglass's Paper*, August 20, 1852. Quoted in Douglass, Frederick. *The Essential Douglass. Selected Writings and Speeches.* Edited by Nicholas Buccola. Indianapolis: Hackett Publishing (2016), 73.

minority. It is in accordance with the doctrine that good is the rule, and the evil the exception in the character and constitution of man. If the fact were otherwise, (that is, if men were more disposed to evil than to good), it would, indeed, be dangerous for men to enter into a compact, by which power should be wielded by the mass, for then evil being predominant in man, would predominate in the mass, and innumerable hardships will be inflicted upon the good.[606]

True virtue

So far, we've spent a lot of time on Douglass' doctrine of self-ownership, which was a key premise in his arguments against slavery and for equal rights. In this sense, Douglass is operating squarely in the classical liberal tradition which promotes individual rights and extensive personal liberty, both of which are to be protected by a limited, constitutionally-constrained government. We will now turn to his doctrine of "true virtue," which will demonstrate how Douglass is helpful in bridging the gap between liberal individualism (which sometimes drifts into self-centeredness) and the *mutual responsibility* necessary for a just and stable society. This sense of mutual responsibility will reinforce not only his views about reformers explained previously in this chapter, but also his claims about "self-made men" that will be explored a bit later.

According to the doctrine of true virtue, each individual has (at times, extensive) obligations to advocate for the rights of others.[607] Clearly, this is reflected in the actions of the reformer—but *why* do we have such responsibilities towards one another? Because of our interdependence.

It must in truth be said though it may not accord well with self-conscious individuality and self-conceit, that no

possible native force of character, and no depth or wealth of originality, can lift a man into absolute independence of his fellow man, and no generation of men can be independent of the preceding generation. The brotherhood and interdependence of mankind are guarded and defended at all points. I believe in individuality, but individuals are, to the mass, like waves to the ocean. The highest order of genius is as dependent as is the lowest. It, like the loftiest waves of the sea, derives its power and greatness from the grandeur and vastness of the ocean of which it forms a part. We differ as the waves, but are one as the sea.[608]

Often missing in the more libertarian and "ruggedly individualistic" strains of classical liberalism is a recognition that no one is truly and completely independent of others. We all have depended on others and will continue to do so, and others will have need to depend upon us. A recognition of this mutual interdependence can (and should) inspire both a sense of responsibility towards others ("civic responsibility") and an imperative to make something of one's life so as to be *less* dependent on others and more useful to the community ("self-made men").

Civic responsibility

In this context, civic responsibility refers to obligation we all have, within our community, to promote and pursue justice for all of its members. For Douglass, this meant actively ensuring that the natural rights of all persons are being respected and protected. Rather obviously, In Douglass' time this meant actively campaigning against slavery. It was not enough to simply refrain from participating and profiting from the institution of slavery oneself. Nor would it be sufficient for a Southerner to simply move to a

---

[606] *The Life and Writings of Frederick Douglass*, 5: 210-211.

[607] Buccola, 2.

[608] "Self-Made Men," an address delivered in

Carlisle, Pennsylvania, in March 1894, in Blassingame, *The Frederick Douglass Papers*, 5: 549.

free State in the North, or for any American to expatriate to a country that prohibited slavery. Civic responsibility requires more—it requires that each person (according to their capacities) do what was within their power to *abolish* slavery.

> To leave the slave in his chains, in the hands of cruel masters, who are too strong for him, is not to free ourselves from responsibility. Again: if I were on board of a pirate ship, with the company of men and women whose lives and liberties I had put in jeopardy, I would not clear my soul of their blood by jumping in the longboat, and singing out no union with pirates. My business would be to remain on board, and while I never would perform a single act of piracy again, I should exhaust every means given me by my position, to save the lives and liberties of those against whom I had committed piracy. In like manner, I hold it is our duty to remain inside this union, and use all the power to restore [to the] enslaved millions their precious and God-given rights. The more we have done by our voice and our votes, in times past, to rivet their galling fetters, the more clearly and solemnly comes the sense of duty to remain, to undo what we have done. Where, I ask, could the slave look for release from slavery if the union were dissolved.[609]

A striking parallel today is the distinction between being racist, non-racist, and anti-racist. Ibram X. Kendi defines racism as a "powerful collection of racist policies that lead to racial inequity and are substantiated by racist ideas."[610] He argues that it is not morally sufficient to be not-racist, but that one should be an *anti*-racist, and promote *anti*-racism.

What's the problem with being "not racist?" It is a claim that signifies neutrality: "I am not a racist, but neither am I aggressively against racism." But there is no neutrality in the racism struggle. The opposite of "racist" isn't "not racist." It is "antiracist." What's the difference? One endorses either the idea of a racial hierarchy as a racist, or racial equality as an antiracist. One either believes problems are rooted in groups of people, as a racist, or locates the roots of problems in power and policies, as an antiracist. One either allows racial inequities to persevere, as a racist, or confronts racial inequities, as an antiracist. There is no in between safe space of "not racist." The claim of "not racist" neutrality is a mask for racism.[611]

Much as Kendi argues, today, that we are obligated to be actively *anti*-racist, Douglass, in his time, argued that Americans were obligated to be actively *anti*-slavery. Practically speaking, what did civic responsibility require from Americans, specifically as regards enslaved persons?

First, and most obviously, it required doing whatever was necessary to abolish slavery! Once that monumental task was achieved, civic responsibility required positive steps taken to guarantee equality under the law. Examples of such steps included the adoption of the 13th, 14th, and 15th Amendments to the U.S. Constitution. Recall, though, something that was stated above. Legally recognized rights are not self-enforcing. Once rights are recognized in the Constitution, or subordinate laws that follow, they must be *supported* by the government. "Pen, ink, and paper liberty are excellent when there is a party behind it to respect and secure its enjoyment. Human laws are not self-executing. To be of any service they must be made vital, active, and

---

[609] "The Dred Scott Decision," an address delivered in New York, New York, in May 1857, in Blassingame, *The Frederick Douglas Papers*, 3: 173.

[610] Kendi, Ibram X. *How to Be an Antiracist*. One World, 2019, 20.
[611] ibid., 9.

certain."[612]

The programs of Reconstruction after the Civil War, including the Freedman's Bureau, were efforts in that spirit—and were necessary and morally required. In his 1881 autobiography (*The Life and Times of Frederick Douglass*), he said "Though slavery was abolished, the wrongs of my people were not ended. Though they were slaves, they were not yet quite free. No man can be truly free whose liberty is dependent upon the thoughts, feeling, and actions of others, and who has himself no means in his own hands for guarding, protecting, defending, and maintaining that liberty. Yet the Negro after his emancipation was precisely in this state of destitution. He was free from the individual master but the slave of society. He had neither money, property, nor friends. He was free from the old plantation, but he had nothing but the dusty road under his feet. He was free from the old quarter that once gave him shelter, but a slave to the rains of summer and the frost of winter. He was in a word, literally turned loose, naked, hungry, and destitute to the open sky."

Reconstruction was ended far too soon, as part of a political bargain between Democrats and Republicans, and the Southern States immediately reversed the gains made by formerly enslaved persons through the enactment of "Jim Crow" laws, replacing slavery with a new racial caste system whose legacy endures to this day, despite the achievement of the Civil Rights Era. Then, as now, Douglass argued that what civic responsibility demanded of us was that we create conditions of equality and genuine "fair play."

Fair play

"Simply" put, "fair play" meant that the government was insuring the social and economic rules were not rigged against certain persons and should "level the playing field." It probably comes as no surprise, though, that what exactly Douglass meant by "fair play," and how

others have attempted to appropriate Douglass in contemporary contexts, is far from simple.

At first glance, Douglass' appeal to fair play sounds like a libertarian appeal for mere non-interference, as we see in a speech given in 1865, and echoed in another speech in 1871.

> *What I ask for the Negro is not benevolence, not pity, not sympathy, but simply justice. The American people have always been anxious to know what they shall do with us. [...] Everybody has asked the question, and they learned to ask early of the abolitionists, "what shall we do with the Negro?" I have had one answer from the beginning. Do nothing with us! You're doing with us has already played the mischief with us. Do nothing with us! If the apples will not remain on the tree of their own strength, if they are worm eaten at the core, if they are early ripe and disposed to fall, let them fall! I am not for tying or fastening them on the tree in any way, except by nature's plan, and if they will not stay there, let them fall. And if the Negro cannot stand on his own legs, let him fall also. All I ask, give him a chance to stand on his own legs! Let him alone! If you see him on his way to school, let him alone, don't disturb them! If you see him going to the dinner table at a hotel, let him go! If you see him going to the ballot box, let him alone, don't disturb him! If you see him going into a workshop, just let him alone, – your interference is doing him a positive injury.... Let him fall if he cannot stand alone! If the Negro cannot live by the line of eternal justice... The fault will not be yours, it will be His who made the Negro, and established that line for his government. Let him live or die by that. If you will only untie his hands, and give him a chance, I think he will live. He will work as readily for himself as the white man. [...]*[613]

---

[612] Quoted in Buccola, 75.
[613] "What the Black Man Wants," a speech

delivered at the annual meeting of the Massachusetts antislavery Society in Boston,

Our standing answer in the old time was, "do nothing with the Negro. Give him fair play, and let him alone. If he lives, well. If he dies, equally well." If a man cannot live and flourish where the conditions of life and prosperity are just and equal, his case furnishes the best reason in the world why he ought to die. Of course, the lame, the halt, and the blind, and persons of a like description are exempted from this philosophy. Aside from this, we have absolutely no retraction or modification to make a better answer. The principle that each member of the human family is bound to support and perpetuate his own existence, cannot be suspended in the interest of any class of men, black or white. All that any man has a right to expect, ask, give, or receive in this world, is fair play. When society has secured this to its members, and the humblest citizen of the Republic is put into the undisturbed possession of the natural fruits of his own exertions, there is really very little left for society and government to do. What remains for enlightenment and civilization may be safely left to individual exertion, outside of government machinery."[614]

The libertarian tone here is easily spotted. "Leave him alone" seems to be all that Douglass is requesting for Black persons in the United States—though, in fairness, even "leave him alone" would require, at that time, a *profound* change in behavior from white Americans. Murder, intimidation, and terrorism is not leaving anyone alone. Discriminatory laws that prevent Black persons from working in certain jobs, acquiring an education, or voting or running for office do not leave anyone alone. Even simply to "leave [Black persons] alone" would require genuine equality and protection under the law!

Many contemporary conservatives imagine that such *de jure* equality now exists (at least since the Civil Rights legislation of the 1960s) and cite Douglass as an authority in support of libertarian policy stances, including opposition to things like affirmative action. The conservative Cato Institute, for example, has produced a book entitled "Self-Made Man," portraying Douglass as an ardent free-market capitalist and libertarian.[615] We will examine Douglass' passionate *criticism* of free-market capitalism in a later section, but, presently, we must dispel the myth that Douglass thought that justice for Black persons required merely that they be "left alone." It's easiest to let Douglass speak for himself on this matter.

I have said "give the Negro fair play and let him alone." I meant all that I said and a good deal more than some understand by fair play. It is not fair play to start the Negro out in life, from nothing and with nothing, while others start with the advantage of a thousand years behind them. He should be measured, not by the heights others have obtained, but from the depths from which he has come. For any adjustment of the scale of comparison, fair play demands that to the barbarism from which the Negro started shall be added two hundred years heavy with human bondage. Should the American people put a schoolhouse in every Valley of the South and a church on every hillside and supply the one with teachers and the other with preachers, for a hundred years to come, they would not then have given fair play to the Negro.

The nearest approach to justice to the Negro for the past is to do him justice in the present. Throw open to him the doors of

---

Massachusetts, January 26, 1865, and published in *The Liberator*, February 10, 1865). Quoted in Douglass, Frederick. *The Essential Douglass. Selected Writings and Speeches.* Edited by Nicholas Buccola. Indianapolis: Hackett

Publishing (2016), 196.
[614] "Politics an Evil to the Negro," 233.
[615] https://www.cato.org/policy-report/january/february-2018/self-made-man

the schools, the factories, the workshops, and of all mechanical industries. For his own welfare, give him a chance to do whatever he can do well. If he fails then, let him fail! As a soldier he proved it. He has since proved it by industry and sobriety and by the acquisition of knowledge and property. He is almost the only successful tiller of the soil of the South, and is fast becoming the owner of land formerly owned by his old master and by the old master class. In a thousand instances has he verified my theory of self-made man. He well performed the task of making bricks without straw; now give him straw. Give him all the facilities for honest and successful livelihood, and in all honorable avocations receive him as a man among men.[616]

Douglass is acknowledging the obvious disparities in wealth, education, opportunities, social status, and a great many other things, which existed between white and Black Americans in his time. Douglass personally lived as an enslaved person, escaped, bought his freedom, fought for years as an abolitionist, and lived to see all remaining enslaved persons emancipated and provided with *nothing* with which to start their new lives. If we employ the metaphor of a foot race, it is absurd to suggest that "fair play" means letting every runner try their best when some of the runners have literally only just been released from shackles! As Douglass said above, "it is not fair play to start the Negro out in life, from nothing and with nothing, while others start with the advantage of a thousand years behind them." He provides a vivid description of the conditions liberated Black persons experienced, and the progress they had made despite those circumstances.

Much complaint has been made that the freedmen have shown so little ability to take care of themselves since their emancipation. Men have marveled that they have made so little progress. I question the justice of this complaint. It is neither reasonable, nor in any sense just. To me, the wonder is, not that the freedmen have made so little progress, but, rather, that they have made so much; not that they had been standing still, but that they have been able to stand at all.

We have only to reflect for a moment upon the situation in which these people found themselves when liberated: consider their ignorance, their poverty, their destitution, and their absolute dependence upon the very class by whom they had been held in bondage for centuries, a class whose every sentiment was averse to their freedom, and we should be prepared to marvel that they have under the circumstances done so well.

History does not furnish an example of emancipation under conditions less friendly to the emancipated class, than this American example. Liberty came to the freedmen of the United States, not in mercy but in wrath; not by moral choice, but by military necessity; not by the generous action of the people among whom they were to live, and whose goodwill was essential to the success of the measure, but by strangers, foreigners, invaders, trespassers, aliens, and enemies. The very manner of their emancipation invited to the heads of the freedmen the bitterest hostility of race and class. They were hated because they had been slaves, hated because they were now free, and hated because of those who had freed them. Nothing was to have been expected other than what has happened; and he is a poor student of the human heart who does not see that the old master class would naturally employ every power and means in their reach to make the great measure of emancipation unsuccessful and utterly odious.[617]

---

[616] "Self-Made Men," 341.

[617] "Extract from a speech on the West India

What about today? *If* the United States had truly repented of its sin of slavery and racism, and genuinely restored Black persons to a place of fair and equal political, social, and economic status after the Civil War, then we could be having a very different conversation today. But that didn't happen.

Opposition to Reconstruction was fierce and violent in the South. Racism persisted both there and in the North. Jim Crow laws quickly replaced slavery as a new racial caste system, and openly endured until the late 1960's when, once again, the Federal government had to *force* States to cease overt racial discrimination. Today, decades later, there is still ample evidence of implicit bias, and racially disparate outcomes in housing, education, wealth, health and other aspects of life in America. In other words, "fair play" has *still* not been achieved.

How do we address past injustices, in the spirit of fair play? Douglass told us above: "The nearest approach to justice to the Negro for the past is to do him justice in the present." What does "justice in the present" look like? Back in 1865, Douglas suggested that "should the American people put a schoolhouse in every Valley of the South and a church on every hillside and supply the one with teachers and the other with preachers, for a hundred years to come, they would not then have given fair play to the Negro." Taken seriously, that means that *if* Americans had invested heavily in Black Americans back in 1865, *even as of 1965*, fair play would not have been provided. But that didn't happen. The proper response then, as now, for Douglass is something very different from merely "leaving alone."

They need and ought to have material aid

of both white and colored people of the free states. A million dollars devoted to this purpose would do more for the colored people of the South than the same amount expended in any other way. There is no degradation, no loss of self-respect, in asking this aid, considering the circumstances of these people. The white people of the nation owe them this help and a great deal more. The key-note of the future should not be the concentration, but diffusion [and] distribution. This may not be a remedy for all evils now uncured, but it certainly will be a help in the right direction.[618]

There is nothing vague about this proposal. A little over 20 years after his initial appeal for fair play, Douglass is proposing a million dollars of direct aid. In today's dollars, that would amount to over $31 million dollars, for just one set of projects. Douglass is not proposing this as charity. As he said, "the white people of the nation owe them this help and a great deal more." "Owe" indicates an obligation, a debt to be repaid—and he thinks a "great deal more" than that is owed.

To provide a sense of scale, estimates of the "diverted income" from slavery, from 1790 to 1860 alone, were calculated (compounded and adjusted for inflation) in back in 1983. The sum was estimated to be between 2.1 and 4.7 *trillion* dollars.[619] Adjusted to 2020 dollars, but *without* compounding interest, this value is approximately 5.4-12.1 trillion dollars.

Whether one agrees with the idea of reparations (in whatever form) or not, whether one agrees with Douglass' claim that much needs to be done before fair play is achieved, or not, it is

Emancipation," delivered in Elmira, New York on August 1, 1880, and published as an appendix in *The Life and Times of Frederick Douglass* (Hartford, Connecticut: Park Publishing Company), 1881. Quoted in Douglass, Frederick. *The Essential Douglass. Selected Writings and Speeches.* Edited by Nicholas Buccola. Indianapolis: Hackett Publishing (2016), 255-6.
[618] Douglass, Frederick. "Strong to Suffer, and Yet

Strong to Survive," an address delivered in Washington D.D., on Aril 16, 1886, in Blassingame, *The Frederick Douglass Papers*, 5: 233.
[619] Marketti, James. "Estimated Present Value of Income Diverted during Slavery," in America, Richard. *The Wealth of Races: The Present Value of Benefits from Past Injustices.* Praeger (2002), 107.

certainly *not* the case that Douglass thought that justice for Black persons required nothing more than mere non-interference.

Self-made (Persons)

While it is inaccurate to say that Douglass believed that Black persons should simply be "left alone," as opposed to being beneficiaries of the sorts of social and economic policies necessary to establish fair play, it *is* fair to say that Douglass believed that once a liberal society had been achieved, in which all citizens experienced equality and fair play, individuals had an obligation to make something of their lives through their own efforts and to contribute meaningfully to their community.

> *Douglass's aims were essentially liberal; he sought to achieve a political community in which each individual was free to author his or her own life. He believed this goal could be realized only when limited government was established to protect the rights of all individuals, guarantee equality before the law, and promote fairness in the social and economic spheres. For Douglass, the process of achieving and maintaining this liberal political community was dependent upon the prevalence of a particular set of virtues. What Douglass called "true virtue" was the paramount of these virtues; he used this term to capture the idea that each of us has a moral obligation to combat injustice.... The doctrine of true virtue requires us to do what we can to help those who are being denied the basic promises of liberalism. In other words, if the government is failing to protect a person's rights, provide her with equality before the law, or ensure that she's treated fairly in the social and economic spheres, each of us has a responsibility to use the moral and political means available to us to rectify the situation.*

> *In addition to the doctrine of true virtue, which is essential to achieving and maintaining a just society, Douglass believed the virtues embodied in the self-made man were vital to a flourishing community.... He hoped that once set free from the impediments of injustice, inequality, and unfairness, individuals would devote themselves to soulful hard work so that they would be better able to contribute to the well-being of those around them.*[620]

To summarize, Douglass offers two ideal types of persons. The first, the reformer, is the type of person needed to achieve justice and liberalism in the first place. The second, the self-made man, exemplifies the good life that is made possible in a liberal society, once (classical) liberalism is achieved. The self-made man is the best representative of the capabilities of human nature. "He dignifies his freedom by using it in a virtuous way in order to achieve individual, familial, and community flourishing."[621] Such a person exemplifies the good life that can be pursued and achieved so long as "simple justice" is secured for all individuals.

Just who are these self-made (persons)? Douglass has much to say about them.

> *My theory of self-made man is, then, simply this; that they are men of work. Whether or not such men have acquired material, moral or intellectual excellence, honest labor faithfully, steadily and persistently pursued, is the best, if not the only, explanation of their success.*[622]

> *The self-made men are the men who, under peculiar difficulties and without the ordinary helps of favoring circumstances, have attained knowledge, usefulness, power and position and have learned from themselves the best uses to which life can*

---

[620] Buccola, 158-159.
[621] ibid., 102.

[622] Quoted in ibid., 117-118.

be put in this world, and in the exercises of these uses to build up worthy character. They are the men who owe little or nothing to birth, relationship, friendly surrounding; to wealth inherited or to early approved means of education; who are what they are, without the aid of any of the favoring conditions by which other men usually rise in the world and achieve great results.... They are the men who, in a world of schools, academies, colleges and other institutions of learning, are often compelled by unfriendly circumstances to acquire their education elsewhere and, amid unfavorable conditions, to hew out for themselves a way to success, and thus to become the architects of their own good fortune. They are in a peculiar sense, indebted to themselves for themselves. If they have traveled far, they have made the road on which they traveled. If they have ascended high, they have built their own ladder. From the depths of poverty such as these have often come. From the heartless pavements of large and crowded cities; barefooted, homeless, and friendless, they have come. From hunger, rags and destitution, they have come; motherless and fatherless, they have come, and may come. [623]

These are extreme and inspirational examples, to be sure—but so is the reformer. Both represent ideal types. Few of us will manage to ascend to the virtuous heights of either, but that doesn't mean we can't use those ideals as a target. Not everyone can be a reformer like John Brown or Frederick Douglass, but we can all finds ways to fight for justice in our own way, according to our own capacities. Similarly, not everyone can exemplify a genuine "rags to riches" success story, no matter how hard one might try, but that doesn't mean we can't all find ways in which to make the most of the opportunities and resources we do have available to us, and to find

ways to make ourselves useful to others and to our community, in general.

Everyone is capable of bettering themselves to some degree or another, and everyone is capable of contributing to their community in some way. For Douglass, contributing to society and making a success of one's life was not only virtuous, but politically useful—especially (and perhaps controversially) in the case of Black persons.

> *The world says the black man is unfit to live in a mixed society – to enjoy, and rightly appreciate the blessings of independence – that he must have a master, to govern him, and the lash to stimulate him to labor. Let us be prepared to afford, in our lives and conversation, an example of how grievously we are wronged by such prevailing opinion of our race. Let us prove, by facts, not by theory, that independence belongs to our nature, in common with all mankind, that we have intelligence to use it rightly, when acquired, and capabilities to send to the loftiest elevations of the human mind. Let such examples be given in the mental cultivation, and moral regeneration of our children, as they increase in knowledge, in virtue and in every ennobling principle in man's nature.* [624]

> *Men are not valued in this country, or any country, for what they are; they are valued for what they can do. It is in vain that we talk about being men, if we do not know the work of men. We must show that we can do as well as be.... Society is a hardhearted affair.* [625]

> *We must be respected. And we cannot be respected unless we are either independent or aiming to be.* [626]

Douglass is encouraging Black persons to live

---

[623] "Self-Made Men," 335.
[624] Quoted in Buccola, 94.

[625] Quoted in ibid., 95.
[626] Quoted in ibid.

well, educate themselves, work hard, contribute to society, *earn* respect from others (even their detractors) and prove the racists wrong by means of providing counter-examples to the racist stereotypes. This recommendation, while prudent, is also potentially controversial.

Ibram X. Kendi calls this strategy "uplift suasion" (also known as "respectability politics"). He claims that it is based on the idea what white people could be persuaded away from their racist ideas if only they saw Black people "uplifting" themselves from their "low station in American society." "Positive Black behavior, abolitionist strategists held, undermined racist ideas, and negative Black behavior confirmed them."[627]

Kendi condemns this strategy as both racist and impossible. It is racist because it implies that Black people are partially or completely responsible for the existence and persistence of racist ideas.

> To believe that the negative ways of Black people were responsible for racist ideas was to believe that there was some truth in notions of Black inferiority. To believe that there was some truth in notions of Black inferiority was to hold racist ideas.[628]

The strategy was also impossible to execute because the people involved were/are, contrary to racist thinking, equally *human*.

> Free Blacks were unable to always display positive characteristics for the same reasons poor immigrants and rich planters were unable to do so: free Blacks were human and humanly flawed.[629]

Finally, Kendi condemns the strategy of uplift suasion because it presumes a nonexistent rational and consistent basis for racist beliefs.

> Uplift suasion assumed, moreover, that racist ideas were sensible and could be

undone by appealing to sensibilities. But the common political desire to justify racial inequities produced racist ideas, not logic. Uplift suasion also failed to account for the widespread belief in the extraordinary Negro, which had dominated assimilationist and abolitionist thinking in America for a century. Upwardly mobile Blacks were regularly cast aside as unique and as different from ordinary, inferior Black people. . . . Consumers of racist ideas sometimes changed their viewpoints when exposed to Black people defying stereotypes (and then sometimes changed back when exposed to someone confirming the stereotypes). Then again, upwardly mobile Blacks seemed as likely to produce resentment as admiration. "If you were well-dressed they would insult you for that, and if you were ragged you would surely be insulted for being so," one Black Rhode Island resident complaint in his memoir in the early 1800s. It was the cruel illogic of racism. When Black people rose, racists either violently knocked them down or ignored them as extraordinary. When Black people were down, racists called it their natural or nurtured place, and denied any role in knocking them down in the first place.[630]

The dilemma of respectability politics is that any "failure" reinforces the negative prejudicial beliefs about the group in question. But, any "success" is either explained away or interpreted to be only an "exceptional" case that does nothing to "uplift" the group. In an infamous footnote authored by David Hume, for example, he claims of Black people that "none ever discovered any symptoms of ingenuity," and then dismisses a prominent contemporary counter-example to that sweeping and racist generalization.

> In JAMAICA, indeed, they talk of one negroe

---

[627] Kendi, Ibram X. *Stamped From the Beginning. The Definitive History of Racist Ideas in America.* Bold Type Books, New York, 2016: 124.

[628] ibid.
[629] ibid., 125.
[630] ibid.

as a man of parts and learning; but 'tis likely he is admired for very slender accomplishments, like a parrot, who speaks a few words plainly.[631]

The "parrot-like" person in question was Francis Williams, who, according to Edward Long's *History of Jamaica*, was the son of a free Black couple in Jamaica, and sponsored by the Duke of Montagu as an "experiment" in whether "a negro lad, trained at a grammar school and then at a university would be found equal in literary attainments to a white man."[632] Williams is reported to have attended Cambridge, and returned to Jamaica as a poet, businessman, and teacher of reading, writing, Latin, and mathematics to Black children.

While some of the details of Williams' biography have been debated,[633] Hume did not dispute any particular aspect of his story, but entirely dismissed even the possibility that a Black man could be genuinely intelligent and educated, comparing his achievements to that of a trained parrot instead. This example is worth emphasizing, because it reveals that even a brilliant world-historic philosopher renowned for his insights into *reasoning* on the basis of *evidence* can be "immune" to evidence and reason when it challenges his deeply held racist beliefs. This further demonstrates the futility of respectability politics, setting aside the moral concerns about that strategy. Hume's racism was not "dedicated." It's not as though he specialized in racist research and discourse. Indeed, the most egregious example of racist thought we have from him comes from that footnote cited above, the entirety of which amounts to only a few paragraphs. Hume's racism was "casual" as opposed to "professional." That is not meant to diminish or excuse it, but actually to reinforce the "futility" argument against respectability politics all the more strongly. If even a *casual* racist and professional intellectual, who argued that belief

should be proportioned to evidence, couldn't be "persuaded" by "uplift suasion," why should we imagine that *others* would be?

For our purposes, the core ideas from Douglass we have explored involve the Natural Law foundations of his political thought, in general, his ideal types (i.e., the reformer and the self-made person), and the extension of all those ideas to his arguments against slavery, and for political equality and fair play. Douglass wrote on a great many other matters, though, and while we can't explore many of them, or any of them in great detail, we will conclude this chapter by *briefly* considering just a few more. For the most part, I will let Douglass' words speak for themselves.

Property

I argued earlier in this chapter that it is misleading to suggest that Douglass was a free-market capitalist. This point was made in the context of fair play for Black persons. There is ample evidence that Douglass was "progressive" about economic policy, in general. This is not to say that he rejected capitalism, or private property. In fact, his theory of property is essentially the same as John Locke's—namely, that something becomes personal property when a resource is invested with labor.

> *The theory of property in the soil runs thus: that man has a right to as much soil as is necessary for his existence; and when a human being has incorporated a portion of his own strength and that which belongs to his personality into that soil against the universe.*[634]

Property, however, is a means to an end for Douglass, and not at all the most important thing to value, or right to be protected.

> *The question, whether civilization is*

---

[631] Hume, "Of National Characters," *Essays, Moral and Political*, 2nd Edition, 1742.
[632] https://ecda.northeastern.edu/item/neu:m04109796/

[633] https://www.tandfonline.com/doi/abs/10.1080/0895769X.2019.1652554?needAccess=true&journalCode=vanq20
[634] Quoted in Buccola, 52.

designed primarily for man or for property, can have but one direct answer, whatever may be the methods each may think desirable by which to attain that end. The happiness of man must be the primal condition on which any form of society alone can found a title to existence. The civilization, then, looked at in its material aspect alone, which on the one hand constantly increases its wealth trading capacities and on the other as steadily leaves out the direct benefits thereof to at least seven-tenths of all who live within its influence, cannot have realized the fundamental condition of its continuance. That society is a failure in which the large majority of its members, without any direct fault of their own, would, if any accidental circumstances deprive them for a month of the opportunity of earning regular wages, be dependent upon private or public charity for daily bread. Yet such is the actual condition of even favored American labor.[635]

Note some important phrasing. It is the "happiness of man" that is the "primal condition on which any form of society alone can found a title to existence." Property and wealth, while valuable, are subordinate to both freedom and happiness in Douglass' value hierarchy. Wealth is not worth "more" than freedom or happiness, and any civilization that, while increasing its wealth, "leaves out the direct benefits thereof" to a majority of its population "cannot have realized the fundamental condition of its continuance." Such a community is failing the very mandate of its existence. As a quick means of assessment, Douglass proposes that we ask what would happen to someone if they went for a month without pay through no fault of their own. Would they be forced to rely on charity to survive? If the answer would be "yes" for a large majority of its members, that society is a "failure."

In the United States today, 51% of Americans (a slim majority) have less than three months' worth of emergency savings to get them through tough times. 25% have no emergency savings at all.[636] 56% of Americans couldn't cover $1,000 in costs in the event of an emergency.[637] This is combined with massive (and increasing) wealth and income inequality. In the United States, three individuals (Warren Buffet, Bill Gates. And Jeff Bezos) own as much wealth as the bottom half of all Americans combined—and this isn't even including Elon Musk, the world's richest person as of the time of this writing.[638] This wealth inequality is also a racial inequality, with the racial wealth divide having grown over the last three decades. Black families are twice as likely as white families to have no wealth at all.[639]

While Douglass does not offer specific policy proposals to correct this, we can, at minimum, infer that he would speak out against this inequality and economic vulnerability in his role as a reformer, and we might even be able to infer some general strategies he might promote based on suggestions he made in his own time: direct cash aid and education spending.

Policy reforms

Douglass did offer some very specific suggestions on certain policies, as it turns out. Specifically, he would:

- Limit a President to a single term in office.

---

[635] "The Labor Question," an essay published in the *New National Era*, October 12, 1871. Quoted in Douglass, Frederick. *The Essential Douglass. Selected Writings and Speeches.* Edited by Nicholas Buccola. Indianapolis: Hackett Publishing (2016), 236.
[636] https://www.cnbc.com/2021/07/28/51percent-of-americans-have-less-than-3-months-worth-of-emergency-savings.html
[637] https://www.cnbc.com/2022/01/19/56percent-of-americans-cant-cover-a-1000-emergency-expense-with-savings.html
[638] https://inequality.org/facts/wealth-inequality/
[639] https://inequality.org/facts/wealth-inequality/#racial-wealth-divide

I would abolish, if I had it in my power, the two-term principle. Away with that. While that principle remains in the Constitution, while the president can be his own successor, and is eligible to succeed himself, he will not be warm in his seat in the presidential chair (such as poor human nature), before he will begin to scheme for a second election. It is a standing temptation to him to use the powers of his office in such manner as to promote his own political fortune. The Presidency is too valuable to allow the man who occupies the position the means of perpetuating himself in that office. Another objection to this provision of the Constitution is, that we have a divided man in the presidential chair. The duties of the presidency are such as to require a whole man, the whole will, and the whole work; but the temptation of the president is to make himself the president of a presidential party as well as of the country, and the result is that we are only half served. What we want is the entire service of a man reduced to one term, and then he can bring to the service of his country an undivided man, an undivided sense of duty and devote his energies to the discharge of his office without selfish ends or aims. Blot out of this two-term system.[640]

The reasoning here is consistent with arguments for term limits, in general: it theoretically limits the influence of personal ambition.

- Abolish the office of Vice-President of the United States

Another thing I am in favor of. I am in favor of abolishing the office of the vice president.... We don't need them. There is no more need of electing a vice president at the same time we elect the president then there is need of electing a second wife when we have got one already.... The presidency of the United States, like the crown of the monarchy, is a tempting bobble. It is a very desirable thing. Men are men. Ambition is ambition the world over. History is constantly repeating itself. There is not a single crown in Europe that has not at some time been stained with innocent blood – not one.... For the crown all manner of crimes have been committed. The presidency is equally a tempting bobble in this country. I am not for placing that temptation so near any man as it is placed when we elect the vice president. I am not for electing a man to the presidential chair, and then putting a man behind him with his ambition all leading that way – with his desires, his thoughts, all directed upon that chair, with the knowledge, at the same time, that only the president's life stands between him and the object of his ambition.[641]

This is an interesting proposal that must be understood in context. Conspiracy theorists aside, I don't know how worried most contemporary Americans are that the Vice-President would have the President assassinated so that they could become President themselves. In Douglass' defense, though, President Lincoln, whom Douglass knew personally and with whom he had worked, *had been assassinated*. While there is no reason to think Andrew Johnson had something to do with it, Johnson's presidency was disastrous for Black Americans and with respect to Reconstruction efforts. It had only been two years since Lincoln's assassination when Douglass wrote this suggestion, so the threat was much more realistic for him than it might seem for many of us.

---

[640] "Sources of Danger to the Republic," a speech delivered in St. Louis, Missouri, February 7, 1867, and published in the St. Louis Missouri Democrat, February 8, 1867. Quoted in Douglass, Frederick.

The Essential Douglass. Selected Writings and Speeches. Edited by Nicholas Buccola. Indianapolis: Hackett Publishing (2016), 211.
[641] ibid., 212.

- Abolish the Presidential pardon

Another thing I would abolish – the pardoning power. I should take that right out of the hands of this one man…. A bad president, for instance, has the power to do what? What can he not do? If he wanted to revolutionize this government, he could easily do it with this ponderous power; it would be an auxiliary power. He could cry "havoc, and let slip the dogs of war," and say to the conspirators: "I am with you. If you succeed, all is well. If you fail, I will interpose the shield of my pardon, and you are safe. If your property is taken away from you by Congress, I will pardon and restore your property. Go on and revolutionize the government; I will stand by you."[642]

The power of Presidential pardon has always been controversial. Alexander Hamilton felt the need to justify it in Federalist Paper #74. "[T]here are often critical moments when a well-timed offer of pardon to the insurgents or rebels may restore the tranquility of the commonwealth; and which, if suffered to pass unimproved, it may never be possible afterwards to recall." The vision, here, is that for the sake of healing a politically divided nation, it might be important to offer "forgiveness" to insurgents. The assumption is that the party or power that *was attacked* would be the one to offer the forgiveness. Douglass is warning of the opposite: that the President would be *on the side* of the insurgents and could offer them the promise of a pardon to provide them encouragement. Recent memory provides examples of the very sort of nightmare scenario Douglass described. Referring to the 2024 election, and those being prosecuted for their involvement in the January 6th Insurrection, President Trump said "If I run and if I win we will treat those people from

January 6 fairly. We will treat them fairly. And if it requires pardons, we will give them pardons because they are being treated so unfairly."[643]

Free speech

Douglass spoke of the importance of free speech and a free press specifically in the context of laws passed to suppress abolitionism.

I understand the first purpose of the slave power to be the suppression of all anti-slavery discussion…. First, the right of speech is assailed, and both parties pledged themselves to put it down…. These parties on this presumption, are pledged to put down free discussion by law – to make it an offense against the law to speak, write, and publish against slavery, here in the free states, just as it now is an offense against the law to do so in the slave states. One end of the slave's chain must be fastened to a padlock in the lips of northern freemen, else the slave will himself become free. Now, gentlemen, are you ready for this? – Are you ready to give up the right of speech, and suppress every human and Christ-inspired sentiment, lest the conscience of the guilty be disturbed?[644]

During the period of slavery, it was illegal for enslaved persons to learn to read or write (or for others to teach them to do so), and the motivation behind this was fear that knowledge would inspire rebellion.

Slave-holding States then made it illegal to distribute newspapers or articles (etc.) calling for the abolition of slavery--in clear violation of the 1st Amendment.[645] During the Civil Rights Movement, several Southern States attempted to ban protests against segregation through the use of "breach of peace laws,[646] and activists were

---

[642] ibid., 211-212.
[643] https://www.theguardian.com/us-news/2022/jan/30/trump-pardon-promise-capitol-rioters-dictators-john-dean-nixon
[644] "The Kansas – Nebraska Bill," 99 – 100.

[645]https://www.mtsu.edu/first-amendment/article/2/abolitionists-and-free-speech
[646] https://mtsu.edu/first-amendment/article/1204/breach-of-peace-laws

labelled "agitators"[647]--a label that continues to get used today.

We see a continuation of this trend, this very thing Douglass warned about and spoke against, with the current wave of State laws banning the teaching of what is being called, usually inaccurately, "Critical Race Theory" (CRT), and information about gender and sexuality. As of the time of this writing, seven States had banned the teaching of "CRT" (Arkansas, Florida, Idaho, Iowa, New Hampshire, Oklahoma, and Tennessee), and all the following States were *working* on bans: Georgia, Alabama, Kentucky, Louisiana, Michigan, Missouri, Montana, Ohio, Pennsylvania, Rhode Island, South Carolina, Texas, Utah, Washington, West Virginia, and Wisconsin. Language used in the Florida law is especially relevant: "An individual should not be made to feel discomfort, guilt, anguish, or any other form of psychological distress on account of his or her race."[648]

I'll offer the question Douglass posed above as the final words on this subject, and in this chapter: "Are you ready to give up the right of speech . . . lest the conscience of the guilty be disturbed?"

Critical Analysis

1. In your opinion, what are the strongest and most compelling points made by the philosopher or philosophers in this chapter? Why do you find those points to be convincing?

2. In your opinion, what are the weakest or least convincing points? Why? Can you anticipate any limitations or objections to their ideas not already addressed in the chapter?

Appendix: Application to Social Justice

As has been the case, and will be the case, with several other chapters, the *core* of this chapter addresses social justice considerations in a fundamental and unambiguous manner. No further demonstration of relevance is necessary in this appendix.

---

[647]https://www.nytimes.com/2020/06/08/us/ outside-agitators-history-civil-rights.html
[648] https://www.flsenate.gov/Session/Bill/

Chapter 20: Political "Realism"

Comprehension questions you should be able to answer after reading this chapter:

1. Why does Machiavelli focus on historical examples of politics?
2. What does Machiavelli mean by each of the following terms? *Virtú, Fortuna, Necessitá.*
3. Why does Machiavelli think that a Prince should not always be virtuous/good?
4. What does Machiavelli mean when he says a successful Prince must possess the properties of both the fox and the lion?
5. Why does Machiavelli think it is better to be feared, than to be loved (if one must choose)?
6. What is the "State of Nature," according to Hobbes? What are its features? What is it like?
7. What does it mean to say that Hobbes is a "nominalist" with regard to concepts like "justice" and "(moral) goodness?"
8. What does Hobbes mean by a "law of nature?" What are the first three laws of nature, according to Hobbes?
9. What is a "social contract?" What is the purpose of forming a social contract? Why does Hobbes think the State of Nature would inspire us to want to form a social contract?
10. What is a "sovereign," and why does Hobbes think we need one?
11. Why does Hobbes think the power of the sovereign must be absolute?
12. Why does Hobbes think that it is impossible for the sovereign to act unjustly?

Machiavelli

While previous chapters focused on the shift from classical political theory to medieval (Christian) political thinking, this chapter focuses on the beginning of "modern" political philosophy.

Niccolò di Bernardo dei Machiavelli (henceforth, just Machiavelli) was born in Florence on May 3rd, 1469 –roughly two hundred and twenty five years after the death of Aquinas. Florence had ostensibly been a Republic, but had been ruled by the Medici family (autocratically) since 1434.

Florence was the center of the European Renaissance. A Platonic academy was established in 1462 by Marsilio Ficino, and the city was home to both Michelangelo and Leonardo da Vinci. There flourished a culture of humanism at the time, stressing rationalism and individualism, rejecting much medieval thought, including Augustine's emphasis on our "Fallen" nature. The humanists at the time were optimistic about the human potential for excellence and improvement.

In 1494, there was a regime change in Florence, with the Medici's being expelled. The City was first ruled by a strict Dominican priest named Girolamo Savonarola. Under his leadership, the "Renaissance" was forced to flee to Venice. Savonarola was eventually excommunicated due to his criticism of the Pope, and ultimately arrested and executed.

In 1498, one of Machiavelli's old teachers (Marcello Adriani) was appointed Chancellor of Florence, and Machiavelli was appointed Second Chancellor and Secretary to the Council of Ten for War. This Council was a group of magistrates who were tasked with diplomatic negotiations as well as supervising the military during war. He received this appointment at the ripe old age of 29!

Machiavelli spent 14 years as a diplomat to other Italian city-states, to the Court of Louis XII in France, and the Court of Maximillian I in Germany. He was influenced by his time in France, as well as by his four-month mission to the Court of the Duke of Romagna: Cesara Borgia (also the son of Pope Alexander IV).

The Medici's were eventually restored to power by means of Pope Julius II on September 14th, 1512. Machiavelli was dismissed from office, and falsely accused of conspiring against the Medici's in an attempt to restore Florence to a Republic. He was arrested and tortured for 22 days before being released and ultimately being granted amnesty—but his political career was over at the age of 43.

He turned to writing, and his works include (among others) *The Prince*, and the *Discourses on the First Ten Books of Titus Livy*[649] (hereafter called the *Discourses*), published after his death (June 21st, 1527) in 1531 and 1532, respectively. In 1559, *The Prince* was put on the recently created Index of Prohibited Books by the Vatican, and he was villain-ized in political treatises and by no less a dramatist than William Shakespeare![650]And yet, the inscription on his tomb in Florence reads: "No eulogy would be adequate to praise so great a name."

Just what did this infamous Machiavelli write, that would make him so praiseworthy, but also be called the Apostle of the Devil?

Method

Methodologically, Machiavelli saw himself as breaking with both the ancient and medieval political traditions, focusing on what is realistic rather than idealistic, from what is and what works rather than what ought to be.

> It remains now to see what ought to be the rules of conduct for a prince towards subject and friends. And as I know that many have written on this point, I expect I shall be considered presumptuous in mentioning it again, especially as in discussing it I shall depart from the methods of other people. But, it being my intention to write a thing which shall be

useful to him who apprehends it, it appears to me more appropriate to follow up the real truth of the matter than the imagination of it; for many have pictured republics and principalities which in fact have never been known or seen, because how one lives is so far distant from how one ought to live, that he who neglects what is done for what ought to be done, sooner effects his ruin than his preservation; for a man who wishes to act entirely up to his professions of virtue soon meets with what destroys him among so much that is evil.[651]

Machiavelli is usually considered the first "modern" political philosopher, and sometimes even the first political scientist. Indeed, in the introduction to his Discourses, he says that his intention is "to open a new route which has not yet been followed by anyone." Part of the reason for this sense of "newness" was due to his belief that politics is better understood by studying the history of actual States and rulers than by means of abstract theorizing.[652]

> Prudent men usually say (and not by chance or without merit) that whoever wants to see what is to be, considers what has been; for all the things of the world in every time have had the very resemblance as those of ancient times. This arises because they are done by men who have been, and will always have, the same passions, and of necessity they must result in the same effects.[653]

The *Discourses* is an extended commentary on Roman history and tactics. On the assumption

---

[649] While excerpts from the Prince are found throughout this chapter, the full text of the Prince may be found here:
http://www.gutenberg.org/cache/epub/1232/pg1232.txt
The Discourses may be found at the following URL: https://en.wikisource.org/wiki/Discourses_on_Livy
[650] In the *Merry Wives of Windsor*, a character

asks: "Am I politic? am I subtle? am I a Machiavel?"
[651] Machiavelli, *The Prince*, Chapter 15.
[652] Although Machiavelli has the advantage of much more history to draw upon, his approach is not entirely new; Aristotle, after all, studied 158 existing constitutions in his time to inform his own views on politics.
[653] Machiavelli, *The Discourses*, III, xliii.

that human nature is unchanging, the lessons of history are applicable "today." Therefore, politicians "today" (whether in his own time, or ours) should model the behavior of (historically) great politicians.

Drawing upon ancient political writings, he acknowledges that all states go through the cycles set down by ancient political philosophers: Monarchy turns to Tyranny, Aristocracy to Oligarchy, and Polity to mob rule ("Democracy")—and sometimes back again. Even the best-planned State, with rulers of the best intentions, are subject to these cycles. War is part of the cycle of politics as well. Even "peaceful" nations will be attacked and must be prepared to defend themselves. This means that all successful States must have "good laws and good armies."[654] Pacifism is unrealistic, as other States will see it as weakness

> ...it is impossible that a Republic succeeds in remaining quiet and enjoy its liberty and her limited confines; for even if she does not molest others, she will be molested: and from being molested there will arise the will and desire for conquest: and even if she should not have any outside enemies, she would find some at home, as it appears necessary to occur to all great Cities.[655]

Since war and other calamities are inevitable, a good ruler (hereafter referred to as "The Prince," using Machiavelli's terminology), is one who is prepared to weather whatever storms come his way, keeping both the State, and his rule of it, secure. Such practical consideration is a sharp departure from both the ancient and Christian traditions, by virtue of it separating morality from politics.

For thousands of years, political writings for (or about) rulers had been exhortations to virtue. Indeed, an entire genre of literature developed in antiquity, and flourished in the Middle Ages and Renaissance, called the "Mirror of Princes." The

Roman stoic Seneca wrote one ("On Mercy"), as did Aquinas ("On Kingship: To the King of Cyprus"). In each case, these works encouraged rulers to be virtuous, and to rule in ways consistent with their own high moral standards. Machiavelli will offer very different advice, and even shifts talk from "virtue" to *virtú*.

Virtú & Fortuna

This terminological shift which might initially seem like a mere play on words is actually of great significance. *Virtú* is not to be confused with "virtue," as traditionally conceived. *Virtú* does not refer to moral character, or specific morally-good character traits, but rather to the qualities a leader needs to maintain the state (and his own rule!). These might include such traits as firmness of purpose, foresight, being able to "read" people, fortitude in the face of adversity, etc. If a single word is needed, "vitality" might be our best choice.

Of lesser importance, but still noteworthy, is his notion of *Necessitá*. *Necessitá* refers to the means to compel human beings to "be good." This can be something like an external threat that unites the people under a common cause [e.g., the (temporary) solidarity observed in the USA after 9-11], or it can be the coercive power of laws, as "Laws can make [people] good."[656]

A final key term for Machiavelli is *Fortuna*. Political stability is threatened by both human weakness and corruption, and as well by *Fortuna*.

Fortuna, translated as "Fortune," is understood as unpredictable (usually harmful!) circumstances. He describes her[657] as "one of our destructive rivers which, when it is angry, turns the plains into lakes, throws down the trees and buildings, takes earth from one spot, puts it in another; everyone flees before the flood; everyone yields to its fury and nowhere can repel it."[658]

She is a mysterious and destructive "force of nature" which can be resisted only by the prior development of *virtú*, and its wise application in

---

[654] *The Prince*, Chp. 12.
[655] *Discourses*, II. xix.
[656] ibid., I.iii.

[657] Yes, he thinks of *Fortuna* as female. . .
[658] *The Prince*, chapter 25.

response to whatever challenges *fortuna* brings. *Virtú* supplies the ability to respond to Fortune at any time and in any way that is necessary. *Virtú* is the ability to overcome, and even benefit, from the fickle, shifting *Fortuna*. This also involves what might be considered morally-questionable tactics and strategies.

Machiavelli urges that a successful ruler must know how not to be good. "Hence it is necessary for a prince wishing to hold his own to know how to do wrong, and to make use of it or not according to necessity."[659]

Amoral (or immoral?) Politics

As mentioned previously, in 1559, all of Machiavelli's works were put on the "Index of Prohibited Books"—a list of books banned by the Catholic Church for heresy or immorality. He was posthumously accused of being inspired by the Devil! But, why the "diabolical" reputation? First, consider a few choice quotations (and then we will put them into proper context, and perhaps save Machiavelli's reputation—at least a little):

"Taking everything into account, one will discover that some qualities that appear to be virtue, if the prince pursues them, will end in his destruction; while other qualities that look like vices, if he pursues them, will result in his safety and well-being."

"[The Prince] needs not be concerned [with public opinion] if he acquires a reputation for those vices without which he would be unlikely to save the state."

"It is not necessary for a prince to have all the above-mentioned qualities [viz,. virtues], but it is very necessary for him to appear to have them."

"Injuries must be committed all at once...benefits should be bestowed little by little"

"A prince must have no other objective, no other thought, nor take up any profession but that of war, its methods and its discipline"

"for a man who strives after goodness in all his acts is sure to come to ruin"

"A prince, therefore, must be indifferent to the charge of cruelty"
"Disorders harm the entire citizenry, while executions...harm only a few"

"About the generality of men: they are ungrateful, fickle, dissembling, anxious to flee danger, and covetous of gain"

"Anyone compelled to choose will find greater security in being feared than in being loved"

"Means of law, and by means of force. The first belongs properly to man, the second to animals; but since the first is often insufficient, it is necessary to resort to the second"

"A wise prince cannot and should not keep his pledge when it is against his interest to do so"

"It is often necessary to act against mercy, against faith, against humanity"

"All men are wicked and will act wickedly whenever they have the chance to do so"

While some of those quotations are, indeed, provocative, we must understand that Machiavelli is not advocating evil for evil's sake, nor even in all circumstances. He is, first of all, presupposing that the subjects of the Prince are "bad"—as he thought was the case in his own Florence. "And I will presuppose a City very corrupt, where such difficulties come to rise very fast, as there are found there neither laws or

---

[659] ibid., chapter 15.

institutions that should be enough to check a general corruption."[660] The admittedly ruthless tactics that might be necessary (at times) to control an unstable and corrupted State are not necessarily suitable for a stable Republic with good citizens. "Different institutions and ways of living must be instituted for a bad subject than for a good one."[661]

Machiavelli's guiding norm is self-preservation for the individual (including the ruler), and for the State. Even "immoral" actions can be justifiable for the good of the State. He justifies this by means of a Roman anecdote:

The Consul and the Roman army (as mentioned above) were besieged by the Samnites, who had proposed the most ignominious conditions to the Romans, which were to put them under the yoke, and to send them back to Rome disarmed; the Consuls were astonished and the entire army was in despair because of this; but L. Lentulus, the Roman legate said, that it did not appear he should avoid any procedure in order to save the country, for as the life of Rome depended on the life of that army, it appeared to him it should be saved in whatever way, and that the country is well defended in whatever way it is defended, either with ignominy or with glory; for by saving that army, Rome would in time wipe out that ignominy; but by not saving it, even though they should die most gloriously, Rome and its liberty would be lost. Which thing merits to be noted and observed by any citizen who finds himself counselling his country; for where the entire safety of the country is to be decided, there ought not to exist any consideration of what is just or unjust, nor what is merciful or cruel, nor what is praiseworthy or ignominious; rather, ahead of every other consideration, that proceeding ought to be followed which will save the life of the country and maintain its liberty.[662]

Simply put, this is a case of the ends justifying the means. The "ends" of peace, security, stability, strength, and preserving the State, justify whatever "means" are required to secure those ends, including cruelty, lies, terrorism, treachery, etc. It is not that rulers should embrace "evil," but that their political decisions should not be based on whether their action will be judged good or evil. They should do whatever is necessary, given the circumstances.

In politics, traditional virtues don't serve the same role as they do in private morality. Traditional virtues are admirable, but no ruler can exhibit them all, all of the time, without coming to ruin, "for a man who wishes to act entirely up to his professions of virtue soon meets with what destroys him among so much that is evil."[663]

"Liberality," for example, from a ruler will likely mean higher taxes on his subjects in order to fund his "generosity". But, these higher taxes are likely to breed resentment from the very subjects to whom he is trying to be generous. Paradoxically, then, a "miser" can be "generous" by not taking so much from his subjects. Similarly, "mercy" might result in increased license and criminality in the population, bringing more harm to the community. "Cruelty," perhaps ironically, might be more "merciful" in the long run.

While it is not important for a Prince to possess traditional virtues, it is important for him to *appear* to have them.[664]

Every one admits how praiseworthy it is in a prince to keep faith, and to live with integrity and not with craft. Nevertheless our experience has been that those princes who have done great things have held good faith of little account, and have known how to circumvent the intellect of

---

[660] *Discourses*, I.xviii.
[661] ibid., I,xviii.
[662] ibid., III. xli.

[663] *The Prince*, chapter 15.
[664] A position reminiscent of that offered by Adeimantus in Plato's *Republic*. . .

men by craft, and in the end have overcome those who have relied on their word. You must know there are two ways of contesting, the one by the law, the other by force; the first method is proper to men, the second to beasts; but because the first is frequently not sufficient, it is necessary to have recourse to the second. Therefore it is necessary for a prince to understand how to avail himself of the beast and the man. This has been figuratively taught to princes by ancient writers, who describe how Achilles and many other princes of old were given to the Centaur Chiron to nurse, who brought them up in his discipline; which means solely that, as they had for a teacher one who was half beast and half man, so it is necessary for a prince to know how to make use of both natures, and that one without the other is not durable. A prince, therefore, being compelled knowingly to adopt the beast, ought to choose the fox and the lion; because the lion cannot defend himself against snares and the fox cannot defend himself against wolves. Therefore, it is necessary to be a fox to discover the snares and a lion to terrify the wolves. Those who rely simply on the lion do not understand what they are about. Therefore a wise lord cannot, nor ought he to, keep faith when such observance may be turned against him, and when the reasons that caused him to pledge it exist no longer. If men were entirely good this precept would not hold, but because they are bad, and will not keep faith with you, you too are not bound to observe it with them. Nor will there ever be wanting to a prince legitimate reasons to excuse this non-observance. Of this endless modern examples could be given, showing how many treaties and engagements have been made void and of no effect through the faithlessness of princes; and he who has known best how to employ the fox has succeeded best.[665]

---

[665] *The Prince*, chapter 18.

As he states in the quotation above, there are different ways to compel people to behave in the ways you want them to. Most generally, the two options are law and force. While the rule of law is proper for "men," sometimes law is insufficient, and a Prince must resort to force (the method proper to "beasts"). This means that a successful Prince must be skilled in the use of both methods.

Machiavelli represents the method of "beasts" with both the fox and the lion. The lion is powerful and bold, but not clever. The fox is clever, but not strong. A Prince who is all "lion" will not see "snares" (conspiracies and other political dangers) before it is too late, and a Prince who is all "fox," though able to detect the dangers, won't be sufficiently powerful to defend against them. "Therefore, it is necessary to be a fox to discover the snares and a lion to terrify the wolves."

Fear and Love

The Prince must be able to "terrify the wolves." Among the most famous positions attributed to Machiavelli is that it is better for a Prince to be feared, than loved. The source of this claim is worth quoting at length:

> *. . . I say that every prince ought to desire to be considered clement and not cruel. Nevertheless he ought to take care not to misuse this clemency. Cesare Borgia was considered cruel; notwithstanding, his cruelty reconciled the Romagna, unified it, and restored it to peace and loyalty. And if this be rightly considered, he will be seen to have been much more merciful than the Florentine people, who, to avoid a reputation for cruelty, permitted Pistoia to be destroyed.*

> *Therefore a prince, so long as he keeps his subjects united and loyal, ought not to mind the reproach of cruelty; because with a few examples he will be more merciful than those who, through too much mercy, allow disorders to arise, from which follow*

murders or robberies; for these are wont to injure the whole people, whilst those executions which originate with a prince offend the individual only. . . .

Upon this a question arises: whether it be better to be loved than feared or feared than loved? It may be answered that one should wish to be both, but, because it is difficult to unite them in one person, it is much safer to be feared than loved, when, of the two, either must be dispensed with. Because this is to be asserted in general of men, that they are ungrateful, fickle, false, cowardly, covetous, and as long as you succeed they are yours entirely; they will offer you their blood, property, life, and children, as is said above, when the need is far distant; but when it approaches they turn against you. And that prince who, relying entirely on their promises, has neglected other precautions, is ruined; because friendships that are obtained by payments, and not by greatness or nobility of mind, may indeed be earned, but they are not secured, and in time of need cannot be relied upon; and men have less scruple in offending one who is beloved than one who is feared, for love is preserved by the link of obligation which, owing to the baseness of men, is broken at every opportunity for their advantage; but fear preserves you by a dread of punishment which never fails.

Nevertheless a prince ought to inspire fear in such a way that, if he does not win love, he avoids hatred; because he can endure very well being feared whilst he is not hated, . . .[666]

Machiavelli's actual position here is subtle. He is certainly not suggesting that a Prince be some sort of tyrannical sociopath, instilling terror in the hearts of his subjects! "Cruelty" and violence are tools, just as mercy and clemency are

tools. Each has its own proper use, in the right context. A Prince that is not fearsome enough will "allow disorders to arise, from which follow murders or robberies." Their State will become disordered, and not only will the Prince risk losing control of his State, but the people are likely to suffer more as well. Disorder and criminality "are wont to injure the whole people, whilst those executions which originate with a prince offend the individual only."

Ultimately, he claims that it is best for a Prince to be both feared *and* loved—perhaps analogous to a parent who is loved by his or her child, but whose authority is also respected and not questioned. However, he recognizes that, "because it is difficult to unite them in one person, it is much safer to be feared than loved, when, of the two, either must be dispensed with." This is because of his admittedly low view of most people. "Because this is to be asserted in general of men, that they are ungrateful, fickle, false, cowardly, covetous, and as long as you succeed they are yours entirely; they will offer you their blood, property, life, and children, as is said above, when the need is far distant; but when it approaches they turn against you."

People are fickle, and so are their affections. When times are good, the subjects will love their Prince. But, in the face of adversity or struggle, their love quickly evaporates. A contemporary expression might capture this tendency: "What have you done for me *lately*?"

If a Prince relies solely on love, his rule is bound to be precarious, since love is so fragile and fleeting. Fear, on the other hand, "never fails." That being said, a Prince should not inspire so much fear that he becomes *hated*, for that, too, will result in a precarious reign.

Machiavelli's Influence

Until Machiavelli, politics was part of ethics. Virtue was thought necessary for political life. With the cultural ascendancy of Christianity, this wasn't overturned but synthesized with the Christian worldview. As of Machiavelli, however, a new option for political theory was possible:

---

[666] ibid., chapter 27.

expediency. "Realism." Machiavelli's somewhat mechanistic/scientific, and admittedly pessimistic, view of human nature called for a new approach to the "science" of governing humans. This new approach remains influential to this day, but found its first major influence in the political thought of Thomas Hobbes, to whom we now turn.

Hobbes

If there is a challenger for Machiavelli's title of "Founder of Modern Political Philosophy," that challenger is Thomas Hobbes.[667]

Hobbes was born in Westport England, on April 5th, 1588. He was brilliant, even as a child—learning Latin, Greek, French, and Italian, in addition to his own native English. He translated Euripides' "Medea" from Greek to Latin at the age of fourteen, and then entered Oxford University at the age of fifteen. After receiving his bachelor's degree five years later in 1608, he was invited to join the Cavendish household (headed by William Cavendish, the Earl of Devonshire) as a tutor. He remained connected to the family for decades, often living with them, and remaining a bachelor his entire life.

In addition to his work with the Cavendish family, he also served as a tutor to King Charles II of France, and acted as secretary for Sir Francis Bacon from 1618-1622. Between 1634 and 1637 he met Galileo Galilei, Rene Descartes, and Pierre Gassendi. Hobbes contributed some criticisms of Descartes' work, to which Descartes offered replies. It is said that their relationship was cool, if not outright acrimonious.[668]

The political context in which we must understand Hobbes' life and thought is one of change and anxiety. The Tudor dynasty ended with Queen Elizabeth's death in 1603. Her cousin James became the first "Stuart" ruler, and embraced the notion of the "divine right" of kings. Accordingly, he tried to rule without the approval of parliament. When James died in 1625, his son Charles I soon found himself at war with both France and Spain. To fund these wars, Charles imposed taxes without parliamentary consent. Hobbes, acting as secretary to the Earl of Devonshire, helped collect these taxes. Eventually, the Civil War of 1642-1646 broke out in protest of these taxes (as well as some religious issues). The King lost the civil war, was executed, and the monarchy was abolished. The Republic of Oliver Cromwell was established, and Hobbes (fearing persecution due to the essay he had written in support of the Royalist position) fled from England to France, where he stayed until 1651.

Hobbes eventually returned to England and "made peace" with the Commonwealth by agreeing to take an oath of Loyalty (the "Engagement Oath"). He immediately generated controversy, though, with the publication of his *Leviathan* in that same year.

Amazingly, Hobbes works managed to anger just about every faction in England. He angered Parliament because, even though he technically endorsed the idea that government is made legitimate by the consent of the governed, he also claimed that this consent entails absolute monarchy. He angered the Royalists because, even though he advocated for absolute monarchy, he denied the divine right of kings. He angered the Church by his materialist worldview, and undeniably heretical (if not outright

---

[667] Although Hobbes might rightfully belong to the "Enlightenment" period addressed in our next chapter, rather than the Renaissance, I pair him with Machiavelli for thematic reasons.

[668] Descartes wrote the following about Hobbes in a letter to Marsenne (1641): "Having now had time to read the last piece by Englishman [Hobbes], I find complete confirmation of the opinion of him that I expressed to you two weeks ago. I think it would be best for me to

have nothing more to do with him, and thus to refrain from answering him. If his temperament is what I think it is, it will be hard for us to exchange views without becoming enemies. It's better for us both to leave things where they are. Please don't tell him any more than you have to of what you know of my unpublished views, because I'm pretty sure that this is someone who is looking to acquire a reputation at my expense, and by sharp practice."

atheistic) claims about God, miracles, revelation, and the Bible.[669]

Nevertheless, Hobbes managed to die an old man, at the age of 91, on December 3rd, 1679. His reputation as an alleged atheist followed him even after his death. *Leviathan* was publicly burned at Oxford on June 21st, 1683, and all of his works were placed on the Vatican's Index of Prohibited Books (joining Machiavelli's!) in 1703.

Overall, Hobbes experienced a country that was always insecure, always at the brink of civil war and calamity. Peace and security were constantly in jeopardy, he thought, because of the greater demand from the growing middle class, and even farmers, for liberty and political participation. The cultural trend was to regard the authority of the Bible (and the Church), and even one's own conscience, as being above that of the king and his agents—or at least comparable. The result of all this "liberty" was instability, and the promise of strife and misery.

Method

Like other scholars of his time, Hobbes saw no distinction between philosophy and science, and he drew political implications from the discoveries of science, rejecting the claims and insights of classical political philosophy as unscientific. Such views were not based on deductive reasoning, but merely their own experience.

In these westerne parts of the world, we are made to receive our opinions concerning the Institution, and Rights of Common-wealths, from Aristotle, Cicero, and other men, Greeks and Romanes, that

living under Popular States, derived those Rights, not from the Principles of Nature, but transcribed them into their books, out of the Practice of their own Common-wealths.[670]

Unlike nearly the entire tradition before him, who believed that the State is natural, and that existing States would conform (more, or less, or not at all) to that natural ideal, Hobbes flatly denies any pre-existing "ideal." Hobbes was convinced that political philosophy should be just as scientifically-based as geometry, astronomy, and "natural philosophy." "The science of making and maintaining commonwealths has definite and infallible rules, as does arithmetic and geometry."[671] To that end, Hobbes embraced a radical "nominalism," framing both geometry and political science as disciplines which start from arbitrary/conventional definitions, which then deduce conclusions on the basis of those definitions.[672]

He also rejected any "teleological" accounts of human nature or politics, denying any natural "ends" to which we incline and towards which we should act. Instead, he interprets politics mathematically, and mechanically, in terms of causes and effects. "A final cause has no place but in such things as have sense and will; and this also I shall prove hereafter to be an efficient cause."[673] In the introduction to *Leviathan*, he proposes: "For what is the heart but a spring; and the nerves, but so many strings, and the joints, but so many wheels, giving the motion to the whole body, such as was intended by the artificer?"[674]

Although Hobbes rejected both teleological views of human nature, as well as natural law approaches, in general, this certainly didn't mean

---

[669] For example, not only does he claim that humans are entirely material, but he also insisted that God must be a material (corporeal) being as well, describing God as a "corporeal spirit." As a result of all this, his book was debated by a committee in the House of Commons in 1666 as a possible item of criminal heresy!

[670] Hobbes, Thomas. *Leviathan*, XXI. Full text is available here: http://www.gutenberg.org/

files/3207/3207-h/3207-h.htm

[671] ibid., XX.

[672] For example, we stipulate what a triangle is (e.g., a 3-side plane figure), and then deduce more information by building on that definition (e.g., that the interior angles of a triangle add up to 180 degrees).

[673] Hobbes, *Leviathan*, X.

[674] ibid., Introduction.

that he rejected the idea that humans had a "nature"—he just interpreted this nature in purely mechanical fashion. Like any machine, the human machine requires a source of "animation." The "passions" are that source. While the objects of our passion may vary, the same general passions (e.g., desire, fear, hope) drive all human behavior, in a mechanically-necessary (causally determined) fashion. Pleasure, for example, is "nothing really but motion about the heart, as conception is nothing but motion in the head."[675] These passions will play a critical role in his understanding of the motivational foundations of civil society:

> The Passions that encline men to Peace, are Feare of Death; Desire of such things as are necessary to commodious living; and a Hope by their Industry to obtain them.[676]

Humans are equally driven by passions, but are equal in other important respects as well. Hobbes claimed that we are all (roughly) equal both physically and mentally.

> Nature hath made men so equall, in the faculties of body, and mind; as that though there bee found one man sometimes manifestly stronger in body, or of quicker mind then another; yet when all is reckoned together, the difference between man, and man, is not so considerable, as that one man can thereupon claim to himselfe any benefit, to which another may not pretend, as well as he. For as to the strength of body, the weakest has strength enough to kill the strongest, either by secret machination, or by confederacy with others, that are in the same danger with himselfe.[677]

This is an admittedly ominous sort of equality. In effect, it is an equality of vulnerability, of fear, and of danger. Even though some people are physically stronger than others, even the

strongest among us is still flesh and bone, equally mortal, and can be overcome by physically weaker foes through cleverness or strength of numbers. Therefore, this basic "equality" will be, for Hobbes, a source of tension and conflict. Conflict is the "natural" state for humanity—in the absence of political society.

This absence of political society is a key assumption driving this notion of the "State of Nature."

The State of Nature

The State of Nature is a notion often attributed to Thomas Hobbes (although many other philosophers have used such a thought experiment, including Xunzi, who is explored in another chapter). The State of Nature is a state of anarchy. It may be conceived as either a pre-political environment, or the condition that obtains when a government loses control over its populace.

> It may peradventure be thought, there was never such a time, nor condition of warre as this; and I believe it was never generally so, over all the world: but there are many places, where they live so now. For the savage people in many places of America, except the government of small Families, the concord whereof dependeth on naturall lust, have no government at all; and live at this day in that brutish manner, as I said before. Howsoever, it may be perceived what manner of life there would be, where there were no common Power to feare; by the manner of life, which men that have formerly lived under a peacefull government, use to degenerate into, in a civill Warre."[678]

The State of Nature, then, is the hypothetical state of existence we would experience in the absence of any governing authority. It is a state of literal anarchy, of basic (physical and intellectual) equality, and a state of absolute freedom. There

---

[675] ibid., VI.
[676] ibid., XIII.

[677] ibid.
[678] ibid.

are literally no restrictions on behavior, beyond what is physically impossible for us to achieve. No laws, no rules—not even notions of right or wrong, justice or injustice. In the State of Nature, every person has a right to anything deemed necessary for self-preservation.

> *To this warre of every man against every man, this also is consequent; that nothing can be Unjust. The notions of Right and Wrong, Justice and Injustice have there no place. Where there is no common Power, there is no Law: where no Law, no Injustice. Force, and Fraud, are in warre the two Cardinall vertues. Justice, and Injustice are none of the Faculties neither of the Body, nor Mind. If they were, they might be in a man that were alone in the world, as well as his Senses, and Passions. They are Qualities, that relate to men in Society, not in Solitude. It is consequent also to the same condition, that there be no Propriety, no Dominion, no Mine and Thine distinct; but onely that to be every mans that he can get; and for so long, as he can keep it."[679]*

Similarly, in the next section of *Leviathan*:

> *And because the condition of Man, (as hath been declared in the precedent Chapter) is a condition of Warre of every one against every one; in which case every one is governed by his own Reason; and there is nothing he can make use of, that may not be a help unto him, in preserving his life against his enemyes; It followeth, that in such a condition, every man has a Right to every thing; even to one anothers body. And therefore, as long as this naturall Right of every man to every thing endureth, there can be no security to any man, (how strong or wise soever he be,) of living out the time, which Nature*

ordinarily alloweth men to live.[680]

Hobbes is already painting a rather bleak picture of human nature and our interactions with one another. Note that the Confucian philosopher Xunzi makes a very similar argument, including his own vision of the "state of nature." Just as Xunzi's pessimistic view of human nature was challenged by Mengzi, so too does Hobbes' vision come with criticism.[681] Some of you, for example, might think that Hobbes is being unfair and unkind in his account of human nature. Just because there is no formal government, codified law, or a police force to enforce laws doesn't necessarily mean we will all become sociopaths, absent any sort of conscience. Like a good philosopher, Hobbes has anticipated this sort of complaint.

> *It may seem strange to some man, that has not well weighed these things; that Nature should thus dissociate, and render men apt to invade, and destroy one another: and he may therefore, not trusting to this Inference, made from the Passions, desire perhaps to have the same confirmed by Experience.*

> *Let him therefore consider with himselfe, when taking a journey, he armes himselfe, and seeks to go well accompanied; when going to sleep, he locks his dores; when even in his house he locks his chests; and this when he knows there bee Lawes, and publike Officers, armed, to revenge all injuries shall bee done him; what opinion he has of his fellow subjects, when he rides armed; of his fellow Citizens, when he locks his dores; and of his children, and servants, when he locks his chests. Does he not there as much accuse mankind by his actions, as I do by my words?[682]*

---

[679] ibid.
[680] ibid., XIV.
[681] I encourage you to read the chapter

addressing Xunzi and Mengzi on human nature for more information.
[682] *Leviathan*, XIII.

What sorts of things do you or your family have, or do, for the sake of home security/defense? Do you lock your doors at night? Do you have an alarm system? A dog? Firearms for self-defense? If you have a car, do you lock it when you leave it in the parking lot? What other source of risk reduction strategies do you employ when going about your daily business (in general)? What, if anything, do these actions reveal about what you think about your fellow human beings?

In effect, Hobbes is claiming that by virtue of our behavior, all of us believe roughly the same thing that he does about human nature – he is just courageous enough to admit it. As evidence of this, he points out the fact that (in his own time) people locked their doors at night, and even inside the house locked their chests (where they would keep valuables). When traveling, people engaged in risk reduction strategies such as being armed and traveling in groups. This is certainly still the case today for most of us. What's more, Hobbes points out that we engage in these behaviors and we are not even in the State of Nature! We *do* live in a society where there are laws, and police officers, and an entire criminal justice system in place to not only protect us but to "avenge" us in the event that we are victimized.

How much more concern would we have, and how much more "paranoid" would we be, if we were actually in the State of Nature? These behaviors reveal, according to Hobbes, that we actually agree with his assessment. It's worth pointing out, though, that Hobbes doesn't think he is actually being *critical* of human beings.

But neither of us accuse man's nature in it. The Desires, and other Passions of man, are in themselves no Sin. No more are the

Actions, that proceed from those Passions, till they know a Law that forbids them; which till Lawes be made they cannot know: nor can any Law be made, till they have agreed upon the Person that shall make it.[683]

Stepping back for a moment, Hobbes is what's known as a "nominalist." As a nominalist, Hobbes denies the independent reality of such concepts as "justice."

A name or appellation therefore is the voice of man, arbitrarily imposed, for a mark to bring to his mind some conception concerning the thing on which it is imposed.[684]

When human beings use language to communicate, we make certain sounds that represent specific concepts. For example, look at the nearby image on this page and determine what it represents.[685]

I am confident that most of you determined that it is a "chair." It is also possible, however, that some of you might have determined that it is *"una silla."* Perhaps less likely, but still possible, some of you might conclude that it is *"une chaise."* As I'm sure all of you already understand, there are many additional sounds from many additional languages that can (and are) used to represent the concept of a chair. There is nothing magical about a chair that requires that the specific sound "chair" be used to represent it. Literally any sound could, in principle, be used to represent that same concept.

As a very primitive "origin story" of language, we might imagine that very early in human development, some human being pointed to an

---

683 ibid.
684 Hobbes, *Elements of Law*, 5.2-3

685 Image copyright CoolCLIPS.com.

object (such as a rock, or a fire) and grunted in a certain sort of way, and the grunt "caught on" such that other people in her same community started using the same grunt to refer to the same thing. In different communities, a different grunt was used, and as a result different languages developed.

Fascinating though this account of language might be, the relevance for our current context is that (for Hobbes) just as "chair" is an arbitrary representation of a particular concept, so too are such sounds as "good," "evil," "just," and "unjust."

Good and evil don't exist as properties of objects or actions in nature all by themselves. Instead, good and evil come to exist because human beings *declare* that certain actions are "good" or "evil." Good and evil are mere words, "ever used with relation to the person that useth them: there being nothing simply and absolutely so; nor any common rule of good and evil, to be taken from the nature of the objects themselves."[686] In other words, Hobbes is a subjectivist.[687]

In the State of Nature, as mentioned, "the notions of right and wrong, justice and injustice, have there no place." This is to say that the State of Nature is not *im*moral, but rather *a*moral. In the State of Nature, I can *take* your stuff, but I cannot *steal* your stuff. In the State of Nature, we can *kill*, but we cannot *murder*. Stealing and murder are morally-laden terms that have no meaning within the State of Nature. Those terms acquire meaning only *within* the State, as specified by the Sovereign. What is "just" (as we will see) is determined by the will of the Sovereign (whatever the Sovereign *names* "just"), and is expressed in the laws of his State.

Even the difference between monarchy and so-called tyranny is subjective. Those who dislike monarchy call it tyranny, those who dislike aristocracy call it oligarchy, and those who dislike polity (democracy) call it mob-rule or anarchy.

There be other names of Government, in the Histories, and books of Policy; as Tyranny, and Oligarchy: But they are not the names of other Formes of Government, but of the same Formes misliked. For they that are discontented under Monarchy, call it Tyranny; and they that are displeased with Aristocracy, called it Oligarchy: so also, they which find themselves grieved under a Democracy, call it Anarchy, (which signifies want of Government;) and yet I think no man believes, that want of Government, is any new kind of Government: nor by the same reason ought they to believe, that the Government is of one kind, when they like it, and another, when they mislike it, or are oppressed by the Governours.[688]

If you've read previous chapters in this book, you recognize those familiar categories of governments: monarchy / tyranny, aristocracy / oligarchy, and democracy (or polity)/anarchy.

Hobbes rejects any meaningful distinction between types of government, and also, importantly, rejects the classical idea of man as a naturally political animal –"which axiom, though received by most, is most certainly false."[689]

It is neither from our nature, nor in fulfillment of our nature, that we form political communities. It is self-interest alone that brings us into community with others. For Hobbes, humans are all equally driven by passions, egoistically motivated, lacking any innate notion of right or wrong, and fundamentally anti-social. Humans are power-seekers, and subject to a "perpetual and restless desire of power after power, that ceases only in death."[690] All other goods (e.g., wealth, knowledge, reputation, etc.) are valued because they facilitate acquiring power. Even happiness itself is conceived as a "continual satisfaction of desire, from one object to another." [691] Reason, then, is no longer the

---

[686] *Leviathan*, VI.
[687] I recommend reviewing the chapter on subjectivism for more information on this concept.

[688] *Leviathan*, XIX.
[689] Hobbes, *De Cive*, 1.2
[690] *Leviathan*, XI.
[691] ibid.

instrument by which we determine what is morally right and wrong. It is, instead, the practical instrument by which we determine which specific *course of action* will best satisfy our passions.

The combination of our being driven by our amoral passions, and the anarchy of the environment in the State of Nature, diminishes any hope of cooperation, and promotes conflict. This is why the State of Nature was described as "a war of every man against every man."[692] Our primary, driving motivations are competition, "diffidence" (fear, suspicion), and "glory."[693]

Without external constraints on our behavior, our passions will drive us to "invade" one another for personal gain. Under these perilous conditions, "war" is more advantageous than "peace." Even those who are satisfied with their lot in life are fools to pursue peace in the State of Nature, as they "would not be able, long time, by standing only on their defense, to subsist."[694] Recalling our presupposed basic physical and intellectual equality, Hobbes envisions conflict and insecurity.

From this equality of ability, ariseth equality of hope in the attaining of our Ends. And therefore if any two men desire the same thing, which neverthelesse they cannot both enjoy, they become enemies; and in the way to their End, (which is principally their owne conservation, and sometimes their delectation only,) endeavour to destroy, or subdue one an other. And from hence it comes to passe, that where an Invader hath no more to feare, than an other mans single power; if one plant, sow, build, or possesse a convenient Seat, others may probably be expected to come prepared with forces united, to dispossesse, and deprive him, not only of the fruit of his labour, but also of his life, or liberty. And the Invader again is in the like danger of another....

Whatsoever therefore is consequent to a time of Warre, where every man is Enemy to every man; the same is consequent to the time, wherein men live without other security, than what their own strength, and their own invention shall furnish them withall. In such condition, there is no place for Industry; because the fruit thereof is uncertain; and consequently no Culture of the Earth; no Navigation, nor use of the commodities that may be imported by Sea; no commodious Building; no Instruments of moving, and removing such things as require much force; no Knowledge of the face of the Earth; no account of Time; no Arts; no Letters; no Society; and which is worst of all, continuall feare, and danger of violent death; And the life of man, solitary, poore, nasty, brutish, and short.[695]

If you are continually fearful for your safety, think about how that will impact your behavior. The fruits of civilization, such as education, invention, science, technology, art, and recreation, all require that a certain basic level of security has been achieved. If you are fearful that you might die if you leave your home, you're unlikely to go to school, or take a piano lesson, or play some basketball. If the fruits of your labors aren't secured by property laws and police protection, you'll be unlikely to try to amass much wealth, because anything you can't keep with you at all times is so likely to be stolen as to not be worth the effort it will take to obtain it in the first place.

Imagine that we're in the State of Nature, and I spend the day gathering nuts and berries. You hide in the bushes, watching. At the end of the day, I return home to my shelter that I spent several days building, to enjoy my dinner of nuts and berries. You sneak up behind me, hit me over the head with a branch you collected, and steal my nuts, berries, and shelter. What, exactly, was the point of my investing all that effort in building a shelter, and gathering food? Instead, it would

---

[692] ibid., XII.
[693] ibid., XIII.

[694] ibid.
[695] ibid.

make much more sense for me to live a bare, subsistence kind of life—never bothering to acquire more than I can use at that very moment, and always looking over my shoulder in case you (or anyone else) is plotting against me.

Such a world will have no industries or Universities, no artistic achievements or great accomplishments of humanity. In order to enjoy any of those things, we need to feel safe. In order to feel safe, we need to be protected. Since no one is so powerful as to be able to protect himself against anyone and everyone (in whatever number), we can't manage this alone. Hobbes' mechanistic account of human motivation and behavior leaves no room for moral "choice." To change behavior, the conditions promoting those behaviors must be changed—and that means leaving the State of Nature.

The very same self-interested passions that drive us to war in the State of Nature drive us to civil society. Humans are machines moved by means of two basic drives: desire for power, and fear of death. The desire for power produces our problems in the state of nature. The fear of death inspires the social contract.

> *The Passions that encline men to Peace, are Feare of Death; Desire of such things as are necessary to commodious living; and a Hope by their Industry to obtain them. And Reason suggesteth convenient Articles of Peace, upon which men may be drawn to agreement.*[696]

In addition to these basic drives, Hobbes proposes that there are "Laws of Nature"—though he means something very different by this term, than did those who came before him. By "law of nature" he means some sort of prudential rule, dictated and determined by reason, which promotes self-preservation.

> *A LAW OF NATURE, (Lex Naturalis,) is a Precept, or generall Rule, found out by Reason, by which a man is forbidden to do,*

that, which is destructive of his life, or taketh away the means of preserving the same; and to omit, that, by which he thinketh it may be best preserved.[697]

Specifically, reason prescribes *"That every man, ought to endeavour Peace, as farre as he has hope of obtaining it; and when he cannot obtain it, that he may seek, and use, all helps, and advantages of Warre."*[698] Following from this precept is the first "Law of Nature," to seek peace. *"The first, and Fundamentall Law of Nature; which is, 'To seek Peace, and follow it.'"* The second Law of Nature follows from the first.

> *From this Fundamentall Law of Nature, by which men are commanded to endeavour Peace, is derived this second Law; 'That a man be willing, when others are so too, as farre-forth, as for Peace, and defence of himselfe he shall think it necessary, to lay down this right to all things; and be contented with so much liberty against other men, as he would allow other men against himselfe.'*[699]

This mutual transfer of rights (to "everything") is a *social contract*.

The Social Contract

Contract approaches weren't entirely new even in Hobbes' time. Glaucon, in the *Republic*, offered one well before Hobbes, and both presuppose the same basic motivation: egoism. All such approaches make politics a matter of *nomos* (convention) rather than *physis* (nature). It is conceivable in such theories that humans *not* be in community with each other. Indeed, this hypothetical scenario is precisely what we imagine when we consider the State of Nature.

As parties to the contract, in exchange for the promise of peace and security, we agree amongst ourselves to limit our behavior so long as others will, too. In other words, I will agree not to kill you, so long as you agree not to kill me. I'll agree

---

[696] ibid.
[697] ibid., XIV.

[698] ibid.
[699] ibid.

not to steal your stuff, so long as you agree to the same.

The only right *never* surrendered in this way is our basic right of self-defense. The whole point of surrendering rights in the State of Nature is for the sake of self-preservation. To *surrender* the right to self-preservation for the *sake* of self-preservation would make no sense, of course.

> *Whensoever a man Transferreth his Right, or Renounceth it; it is either in consideration of some Right reciprocally transferred to himselfe; or for some other good he hopeth for thereby. For it is a voluntary act: and of the voluntary acts of every man, the object is some Good To Himselfe. And therefore there be some Rights, which no man can be understood by any words, or other signes, to have abandoned, or transferred. As first a man cannot lay down the right of resisting them, that assault him by force, to take away his life; because he cannot be understood to ayme thereby, at any Good to himselfe.*[700]

With regard to all of the freedom we surrender, and all the promises we make, the third law of nature is that we *honor* whatever contracts we make.

> *From that law of Nature, by which we are obliged to transferre to another, such Rights, as being retained, hinder the peace of Mankind, there followeth a Third; which is this, That Men Performe Their Covenants Made: without which, Covenants are in vain, and but Empty words; and the Right of all men to all things remaining, wee are still in the condition of Warre.*[701]

Self-interest drives us into the social contract, but doesn't guarantee that we'll honor it. For some, short-term advantage will blind them to long-term self-interest, and such foolish contract-breakers risk forcing us all back into the State of Nature. A coercive power (the "Sovereign") is needed to enforce the social contract, since "covenants without the sword are but words."[702]

This is but the natural conclusion to which Reason leads us, according to Hobbes. It is our fear of death that gets us to accept rules in the first place. Only fear of death (as punishment) can get us to *obey* those rules. If we want the peace promised by the rules, we must implicitly will the rules (and their enforcement) as well. The Sovereign must apply enough fear of punishment to overpower any other passion for criminal gain.

The Sovereign

The social contract tradition denies the "divine right" of kings, and claims that the State (and Sovereign) derive their authority from the consent of the governed. Obviously, not every State is formed by the explicit forging of a contract. Some people are conquered and subjected to a Sovereign. For Hobbes, that doesn't matter.

When we form a contract, it is driven by fear of one another. When we submit to a conqueror, we are driven by fear of the conqueror. Either way, the cause is the same, as is the motivation. So long as we "submit," there is at least implicit "consent."[703]

While not divinely ordained, the Sovereign is, nevertheless, absolute, "or else there is no Sovereignty at all."[704] Rights transferred to the Sovereign are henceforth non-transferable, and *unlimited* in application. The Sovereign's purpose

---

[700] ibid.
[701] ibid., XV.
[702] ibid., XVII.

[703] ibid., XX.
[704] ibid.

is to preserve the State and enforce the social contract, and may do "whatever he shall think necessary to be done" for that purpose.[705]

Sovereignty can't be divided. For Hobbes, there is no security in "checks and balances." Given human nature, the power of the Sovereign must be greater than that of any other person, or collection of them. "If there be no power erected, or not great enough for our security, every man will rely, and may lawfully rely, on his own strength and art for caution against all other men."[706]

As power-seekers, all individuals and factions will seek to acquire more power, if granted any at all—thereby chipping away at the strength and effectiveness of the Sovereign. For the same reason, he denies independent authority for the church, and would make the Sovereign the head of both church and State.

This emphasis on undivided Sovereignty is driven by a fear of civil war, which he regarded as more dangerous than even foreign enemies. This fear of factions and emphasis on unity was nothing new. It goes all the back to and through the writings of Cicero, Aristotle, and Plato, as well. In Antiquity, unity was sought and promoted by means of crafting the best kind of State, and instilling virtue in the rulers and citizens. For Hobbes, this is all misguided both in the sense of being ineffective (factionalism is better prevented by concentrating all power in one place!), and in the sense of having misunderstood the true nature of "justice."

As stated, the Sovereign must be absolute. All authority rests with, and ends with, the Sovereign. The liberty of the subject is understood as just whatever is not forbidden by law. Law is simply "the word of him that by right hath command over others," so the law is simply whatever the Sovereign decrees. Nor is there any such thing as an unjust law.

Since therefore it belongs to Kings to discerne betweene good and evill, wicked are those, though usuall sayings, that he onely is a King who does righteously, and that Kings must not be obeyed, unless they command us just things, and many other such like. Before there was any government, just and unjust had no being, their nature onely being relative to some command, and every action in its own nature is indifferent; that it becomes just, or unjust, proceeds from the right of the Magistrate: Legitimate Kings therefore make the things they command, just, by commanding them, and those which they forbid, unjust, by forbidding them; but private men while they assume to themselves the knowledge of good and evil, desire to be even as Kings, which cannot be with the safety of the Common weale.[707]

Given that it is the Sovereign who defines what is morally right or wrong, just or unjust, no one other than the Sovereign has the authority or prerogative to declare any law just or unjust. As far as the rest of us are concerned, any law issued by the Sovereign is just, by definition. If we don't like that law, we might label it "unjust"—but that just means we don't like it, and our complaint has no moral authority behind it. For the Sovereign, on the other hand, to declare a law unjust means either that he has changed his mind (and is replacing one of his old laws with a new one that better represents his current judgment about something), or else is replacing a law issued by a predecessor. In any case, what makes the law just or unjust is the will and declaration of the Sovereign, and not anything about the law itself.

Given the "absoluteness" of his power, and the fact that only the Sovereign has any legitimate moral authority, there is no right to rebel against the Sovereign. The only time subjects are released from their obligation of obedience to the Sovereign is if the Sovereign is literally incapable of fulfilling his enforcement function, either because he has been overthrown (or slain), or because he has abdicated his authority.

---

[705] ibid., XVIII.
[706] ibid., XVII.

[707] Hobbes, *De Cive*, 12.1

Thus far we have considered only the unlimited authority of the Sovereign, but this authority does come with some obligation on the Sovereign's part. The obligations of the ruler are ostensibly simple: "all the duties of the ruler are contained in this one sentence, 'the safety of the people is the supreme law.'"[708] We may derive from this basic obligation four particular themes:

1. Defense of the subjects against foreign threats.
2. Keeping internal peace and security.
3. "Enriching" the public "as much as consistent with public security."
4. Granting "harmless liberties"—harmless because they don't undermine peace or security.

These "harmless liberties" reveal the nature of subjects under their absolute Sovereign. The subjects have surrendered all political power and rights to the Sovereign, and have ceased to be "political." What remains is economic activity: producing, selling, and buying. This might be an early anticipation of the citizen (or subject) as "consumer."

The Sovereign's primary responsibility is to enforce the "social contract" we've created, and he (or she) does so by punishment, and the threat of punishment. We can still choose to break the contract, but if we do, and we get caught, we're going to be punished. Presumably, the threat of that punishment is enough to inspire most of us to obey the contract most of the time. As a result, we enjoy peace, safety, and security (in theory). As a result of that, we can feel more confident in our possessions and work to acquire more wealth and more things, we can bother to pursue education, we can bother with science and technology and art, and we can bother to pursue and enjoy hobbies and recreational activities. Society flourishes, and our own life satisfaction increases.

International Politics

Finally, let us give brief consideration to international politics, as it involves only a basic extension of Hobbes views on the individual State. States are in their own "macro" State of Nature with respect to each other, just as individuals were. There are no international norms, morals, justice or injustice, either. Just as individuals are driven by self-interest and retain the right of self-preservation, so too do sovereigns and States. "Every sovereign hath the same right, in procuring the safety of his people, that any particular man can have, in procuring the safety of his own body."[709]

He in no way, however, glorified or promoted war, since what we all seek is peace. Reason recommends peace for States as well! Nor does he recommend some sort of "one world government" to do for international stability what the Sovereign does for his subjects. The driving motivation isn't the same, in Hobbes' view.

Although States may be suspicious of each other, and even go to war against each other, it doesn't render the lives of their subjects comparable to that they would be in the State of Nature. "Because [the rulers] uphold thereby the industry of their subjects, there does not follow from it that misery which accompanies the misery of individual men."[710]

Critical Analysis

1. In your opinion, what are the strongest and most compelling points made by the philosopher or philosophers in this chapter? Why do you find those points to be convincing?
2. In your opinion, what are the weakest or least convincing points? Why? Can you anticipate any limitations or objections to their ideas not already addressed in the chapter?

---

[708] ibid., 13.2
[709] *Leviathan*, XXX.

[710] ibid., XIII.

Appendix: Application to Social Justice

Although there are numerous potential applications from this chapter to social justice issues, I'm going to focus on the connection between political realism and the "realist" approach to philosophy of law – including, eventually, Critical Race Theory.

In previous chapters, we've seen the development of natural law theory, and its usefulness in framing social justice issues. Natural law is also a major framework within which to understand jurisprudence (i.e., the philosophy of law). We see the clear beginning of this approach in our chapter on the Stoics and Cicero, and it really came into focus in our examination of Aquinas in the chapter on medieval political philosophy. The natural law approach to philosophy of law was the dominant understanding of jurisprudence in the United States until the twentieth century.

Like many philosophical theories proposing the possibility of objective value judgments, natural law theory was always threatened by ethical relativism and all of the other variants of perspectivism. The modern philosopher David Hume also famously argued that we cannot validly derive an "ought" from an "is." In other words, the fact that something *is* the case (naturally) does not entail that something *should* be the case. As an example:

1. All mammals (as a species) procreate.
2. Humans are mammals.
3. Therefore, humans ought to procreate.

According to Hume's reasoning, this is an invalid argument. The mere fact that mammals procreate does not mean that the human animal (in general) is morally obligated to procreate, let alone that any particular human is.

Centuries ago, Machiavelli and Hobbes stripped politics of any romantic "illusions," or any pretense of idealism and objectivity, reducing politics instead to pragmatic calculations, and in so doing deviating sharply from centuries of political idealism that had preceded them. In the twentieth century, this trend would be extended to jurisprudence as well. The increasing skepticism in the objective validity of natural law (or objective values in general), the resurgence of relativistic philosophies, and the renewed application of Hume's argument from above, all combined to create the space for a new trend in jurisprudence: legal positivism.

Legal Positivism

The term "legal positivism" is derived from the Latin "positum," meaning the law as it is posited, or laid down, or set forth. The validity of any law, according to legal positivism, is based on it being established in an objectively verifiable source. Positivists reject the idea that "law" exists somewhere "out there," independently from human law. There is no "Law" that transcends human laws.

As an example of this approach, it is against the law in the State of California to hold a person "liable" for their actions in trying to offer emergency care to someone in need, *because it says so* under California Health and Safety Code Section 1799.102. If you collapse in my classroom, and stopped breathing, and I try to offer medical assistance by performing CPR on you, but in the process crack some of your ribs, you are not allowed to sue me or prosecute me for something like "assault." According to legal positivism, this isn't because there is some sort of "universal law" against prosecuting people who tried to help you in good faith, but simply because there is a very specific statute in existence in the State of California that forbids it.

According to legal positivism, jurisprudence is simply a matter of matching cases to relevant existing laws. Ultimately, questions of legality are not questions of moral rightness or wrongness ("oughts") but simply questions of what *is*, in fact, prohibited or required by existing law. With legal positivism and its adherents having already stripped jurisprudence of its objective stature, the stage was set for critical legal theory.

Critical legal theory, in general, challenges the idea that law and the legal system are objective, neutral systems. Instead, according to critical legal theory, cultural values and individual biases inform both the law and the actions of people within the legal system, such as prosecutors and judges.

The legal system is inevitably vulnerable to bias and personal interpretation because, while a law is general, specific cases and individuals are always particular, and it requires individual human beings to interpret and apply laws to these specific cases. Because of the indeterminate meaning of laws, and the variety of circumstances present in any case, judges can make decisions based on their personal values and beliefs, and then find a legal justification in the ambiguous law or legal precedents. The "Realist" school of jurisprudence claims that:

> "law" – especially in the form of judicial opinions that decide cases and establish binding rules – resulted more from a judge's "hunch" about right and wrong than from a fixed system of mutual rules or objective principles being applied impartially by detached jurists. In this view, judges decide "questions of law" on the basis of their acculturated beliefs about society; they then turn to the rules of law retrospectively to justify their hunch – based decision, and to dress it up in the language and technicalities of the law. Emphasizing empirical studies about law's social effects, the "realist" perspective challenged the established "formalist" viewpoint, which held that "law" was an autonomous science, standing apart from the rest of society and consisting of fixed rules principles that judges "discovered" and applied consistently according to pure "reason" and deductive logic.[711]

Not surprisingly, the manner in which laws are applied is very much a subject to personal discretion, including personal discretion that is biased.

This "realist" approach to jurisprudence became known as critical legal theory, and has spawned numerous variants of itself collectively known as "critical theory."

> The methodology underpinning much of the social justice perspective is known as critical theory, which draws heavily on German philosopher Karl Marx's notion of ideology. Because the bourgeoisie control the means of production in a capitalist society, Marx suggested, they control the culture. Consequently, the laws, beliefs, and morality of society come to reflect their interests. And importantly, workers are unaware this is the case. In other words, capitalism creates a situation where the interests of a particular group of people—those who control society—are made to appear to be necessary truths or universal values, when in fact they are not.

> The founders of critical theory developed this notion. By identifying the distorting effects power had on society's beliefs and values, they believed they could achieve a more accurate picture of the world. And when people saw things as they really were, they would liberate themselves. Theory, they suggested, always serves the interests of certain people; traditional theory, because it is uncritical towards power, automatically serves the powerful, while critical theory, because it unmasks these interests, serves the powerless.[712]

As an indicator of this general framework, critical theory is also now called "outsider critical theory" or "OutCrit."

> Today's OutCrits its belief that social hierarchies are "constructed" and "contingent" rather than "natural" or

---

[711] Valdes, Francisco. "Legal Reform and Social Justice: An Introduction to Latcrit Theory, Praxis and Community." University of Miami school of Law institutional repository, 2005 pp. 149-150.

[712] https://quillette.com/2018/02/17/thinking-critically-social-justice/

"essential" in character. OutCrits likewise believe that bias and prejudice are widespread and endemic – representing structural or systemic social problems, and not simply some random individuals with a "bad" personal intention to practice discrimination. OutCrits believe that racism, nativism, sexism, homophobia and similar kinds of neocolonial ideologies, which serve to explain and seek to justify today's social legal inequalities, have been taught and learned over the generations: "traditional" privileges and prejudices have been "institutionalized" as "culture" through generations of conquest and colonialism.[713]

Specific versions of "OutCrit" theory include, but are not limited to, Feminist Critical Theory, Critical Race Theory, LatCrit, QueerCrit, and DisabilityCrit. For our purposes, we will focus specifically on Critical Race Theory.

Critical Race Theory

Critical Race scholarship varies in many ways, but is united by two common interests:

1. Investigating how the system of white supremacy has existed and been maintained by various institutions and social systems, including the allegedly neutral rule of law and (more recently) "colorblind" equal protection of the law.

2. The desire to not only understand such things, but to change them.

Racial power, in our view, was not simply – or even primarily – a product of biased decision-making on the part of judges, but instead, the sum total of the pervasive ways in which law shapes and is shaped by "race relations" across the social plane. Laws produced racial power not simply

through narrowing the scope of, say, antidiscrimination remedies, nor through racially biased decision-making, but instead, through myriad legal rules, many of them having nothing to do with rules against discrimination, that continued to reproduce the structures and practices of racial domination. In short, we accepted the crit emphasis on how law produces and is the product of social power and we cross cut this theme with an effort to understand this dynamic in the context of race and racism.[714]

According to critical legal theory, in general, "power" is constructed and preserved by and through the legal system. This includes racial power. In the USA, this is the power of white supremacy-- and this relationship between the law and racial power is the focus of Critical Race Theory (hereafter, CRT).

CRT has attracted the attention of no less a figure than President Donald Trump, who, in the first presidential debate of 2020 explained why he ordered his administration to stop and ban any and all anti-bias trainings that rely on CRT or address white privilege.

Chris Wallace: (32:21)
This month, your administration directed federal agencies to end racial sensitivity training that addresses white privilege or critical race theory. Why did you decide to do that, to end racial sensitivity training? And do you believe that there is systemic racism in this country, sir?

President Donald J. Trump: (32:42)
I ended it because it's racist. I ended it because a lot of people were complaining that they were asked to do things that were absolutely insane. That a radical revolution that was taking place in our military, in our schools, all over the place.

---

[713] Valdes, 152.

[714] "Introduction," *Critical Race Theory. The Key Writings that Formed the Movement*, edited by

Kimberlé Crenshaw, Neil Gotanda, Gary Peller, and Kendall Thomas. The New Press, New York, 1995. XXV.

And you know it, and so does everybody else. And he would know it- [crosstalk 00:33:02]

Chris Wallace: (33:02)
What is radical about racial sensitivity training?

President Donald J. Trump: (33:05)
If you were a certain person, you had no status in life. It was sort of a reversal. And if you look at the people, we were paying people hundreds of thousands of dollars to teach very bad ideas and frankly, very sick ideas. And really, they were teaching people to hate our country And I'm not going to do that. I'm not going to allow that to happen. We have to go back to the core values of this country. They were teaching people that our country is a horrible place. It's a racist place. And they were teaching people to hate our country. And I'm not going to allow that to happen.[715]

In addition to denouncing CRT as "racist," and a "very sick idea" that teaches people to "hate our country," he denounced it on another occasion as "toxic propaganda" that will "destroy our country."[716]

CRT has also been described in far less ominous terms, as "calling for a society that is egalitarian, a society that is just, and a society that is inclusive, and in order to get there, we have to name the barriers to achieving a society that is inclusive."[717] Or, as described by Kimberlé Crenshaw (one of the founding scholars of CRT):

[CRT] is a practice—a way of seeing how the fiction of race has been transformed into concrete racial inequities. . . . It's an

approach to grappling with a history of white supremacy that rejects the belief that what's in the past is in the past, and that the laws and systems that grow from that past are detached from it.[718]

One very simple and serious (and timely, as of the time of my writing of this chapter) example is the disparate impact of Covid-19 on minority populations, specifically Black and Latinx communities. It is well-documented that such persons are twice as likely to die from the virus in the United States as white people.[719]

Without any historical, social, or economic context, one might presume that there is something biological or even genetic about Black and Latinx people that makes them less healthy, in general, or especially susceptible to that virus in particular, or especially reckless with their health, etc. Any such assumption would be false, or at least misleading, however.

Examining the impact of Covid-19 using the framework of CRT would investigate how historical racism and its contemporary manifestations have contributed to the observed disparity. This might include things like access to medical care, health insurance, treatment within the medical care system, access to clean air and water, likelihood of working in "essential" jobs as opposed to being able to work from home, likelihood of living in more densely populated homes or apartments which would make social distancing more difficult, etc. Examining this public health crisis in that manner is not a matter of being "woke" or "politically correct," but being a good and thorough critical thinker capable of arriving at a more complete, nuanced, and accurate understanding.

Volumes of books have been written on CRT, including the anthology referenced (again) in the footnote to this sentence.[720] This appendix of this

---

[715] https://www.rev.com/blog/transcripts/donald-trump-joe-biden-1st-presidential-debate-transcript-2020
[716] https://time.com/5889907/trump-patriotic-education/
[717] https://time.com/5891138/critical-race-

theory-explained/
[718] ibid.
[719] https://www.nytimes.com/interactive/2020/07/05/us/coronavirus-latinos-african-americans-cdc-data.html
[720] *Critical Race Theory. The Key Writings that*

chapter is arguably little more than a "shout out" to that influential field, given that this is not a textbook on philosophy of law, nor even a chapter on that topic. Instead, my intention is more humbly to demonstrate the contributions of various philosophers to not only ideas pertaining to social justice, but entire interpretive frameworks such as Critical Race Theory. Although there were many contributing factors culminating in the development of CRT, one of them is a line that can be drawn from CRT, through the realist theory of jurisprudence, back to the realist approach to political philosophy developed by Machiavelli and Hobbes.

"Banning" Critical Race Theory

If the year 2020 was a year of "awakening" to the continued presence and pervasiveness of systemic racism, the year 2021 was arguably a year of backlash, with battles being waged not only to prevent comprehensive police reform, but also to preserve a "preferred" version of history. President Trump was the most prominent figure associated with preserving a "patriotic" version of history, most obviously represented in his short-lived "1776 Commission." That Commission was explicitly ordered to counter the "1619 Project."

Briefly, the 1619 Project is a Pulitzer prize-winning series from the New York Times that "aims to reframe the country's history by placing the consequences of slavery and the contributions of black Americans at the very center of our national narrative." According to the 1776 Commission, that project is an example of "reckless re-education attempts that seek to reframe American history around the idea that the United States is not an exceptional country

but an evil one."[721] Trump himself referred to the Project in the following manner. "The left has warped, distorted and defiled the American story with deceptions, falsehoods, and lies. There is no better example than the New York Times totally discredited 1619 Project."[722]

President Trump, like many people, lumped together the 1619 Project with "critical race theory," and in September of 2020 issued an executive order banning any training for federal employees that included "critical race theory" or "white privilege" – proclaiming such training to be "divisive, anti-American propaganda."[723] Following the lead of President Trump, numerous Republican governors, Republican led legislatures, and local politicians, have either passed legislation banning the teaching of critical race theory in public schools, or are in the process of doing so.

The state of Florida describes the now-banned critical race theory as "the theory that racism is not merely the product of prejudice, but that racism is embedded in American society and its legal systems in order to uphold the supremacy of white persons."[724] Florida Governor Ron DeSantis said that critical race theory would teach children "the country is rotten and that our institutions are illegitimate." The ban also explicitly forbids the use of the 1619 Project in classrooms.

The state of Arkansas has passed a law preventing state agencies from teaching "divisive concepts" during racial and cultural sensitivity training.[725]

The state of Idaho has now prohibited schools and universities from teaching that "any sex, race, ethnicity, religion, color, or national origin is inherently superior or inferior," – an idea

---

Formed the Movement, edited by Kimberlé Crenshaw, Neil Gotanda, Gary Peller, and Kendall Thomas. The New Press, New York, 1995.

[721] https://trumpwhitehouse.archives.gov/ briefings-statements/1776-commission-takes-historic-scholarly-step-restore-understanding-greatness-american-founding/

[722] https://www.washingtonpost.com/lifestyle/ style/1619-project-took-over-2020-inside-

story/2020/10/13/af537092-00df-11eb-897d-3a6201d6643f_story.html

[723] https://www.whitehouse.gov/wp-content/uploads/2020/09/M-20-34.pdf

[724] https://www.newsweek.com/critical-race-theory-banned-these-states-1599712

[725] https://www.newsweek.com/critical-race-theory-banned-these-states-1599712

which the legislation claims is found in critical race theory (thereby banning critical race theory).[726]

The state of Oklahoma prohibits teachers from instructing students in ways that, among other things, make students feel "guilt" or "anguish" on "account of his or her sex or race."[727] Similar legislation is pending in Iowa, which would ban "stereotyping" and "divisive concepts" in diversity training, and (among other things) that anyone should feel "discomfort, guilt, anguish, or any other form of psychological distress" on the basis of issues of race or sex.[728]

As a brief note: these laws, and others like them, are attempting to ban teachers from instructing students about sex or race in ways that make them *feel* "guilt" or "anguish." The obvious danger to such laws, beyond any other consideration of their merits, is that feelings are subjective and beyond the control of teachers. In theory, a sensitive white student might feel "guilt" or "anguish" merely by being presented with the fact of slavery. For that matter, Black students might feel "anguish" when learning about the evils of slavery! Teachers who are concerned about their job security or "merely" about being harassed by parents, professors who are concerned about being denied tenure (or being offered more classes, if they are non-tenured), and principals and other administrators who are worried about losing funding all might decide that the "safer" strategy is to just minimize discussion of race altogether. This chilling effect on teaching the history of race relations in the United States, and contemporary racial issues, is likely the desired outcome for many of those promoting the bans.

As of the time of this writing, similar legislation is being debated by lawmakers in Michigan, Tennessee, Texas, Georgia, North Carolina, South Carolina, Ohio, South Dakota, Arizona, Kentucky, Utah, New Hampshire, Louisiana, Maine, Missouri, Pennsylvania, Rhode Island, Wisconsin, and West Virginia.[729] Many more local-level efforts to either change curriculum in school districts, recall school board members, or both, have taken place, or are taking place, across America.[730]

Congresswoman Marjorie Taylor Greene said that "Congress should immediately outlaw critical race theory—it should be completely against the law. It's racism, it's hate, and it's dividing our children and teaching them something horrible. It should be completely against the law," adding that "we have to be able to fire any teacher on the spot immediately if they are found teaching critical race theory. And I'm that serious about it. . . . So teach traditional values. Or we will have to defund teachers salaries that refuse. Problems are easy to solve once we start firing people."[731] (As a personal note: if Representative Greene had her way, what I am doing right now would presumably be grounds for termination, and even my arrest and prosecution, if Congress made teaching "CRT" "completely against the law.")

As one final example, Alabama state Representative Chris Pringle (R) introduced legislation to ban teaching CRT in his state, and when asked why he so strongly opposed it, he said "It basically teaches that certain children are inherently bad people because of the color of their skin, period." When asked to identify specific critical race theorists who have actually made such a claim, he eventually answered "I'll have to read a lot more." He also referenced an

[726] https://www.newsweek.com/critical-race-theory-banned-these-states-1599712

[727] https://www.newsweek.com/critical-race-theory-banned-these-states-1599712

[728] https://www.insidehighered.com/news/2021/03/18/trumps-diversity-training-ban-finds-new-life-iowa

[729] https://www.newsweek.com/critical-race-theory-banned-these-states-1599712

[730] https://www.nbcnews.com/news/us-news/critical-race-theory-invades-school-boards-help-conservative-groupsn1270794?utm_source=facebook&utm_medium=news_tab&utm_content=algorithm

[731] https://www.newsweek.com/marjorie-taylor-greene-says-crt-should-outlawed-teachers-fired-spot-1608594

article that allegedly claimed white men had been sent to reeducation camps but was unable to provide the source or a link when asked.[732]

It's worth pointing out that college students, themselves, don't support these bans. While a slim majority of Republican-identifying college students think that public schools should *not* teach about systemic racism, specifically (in contrast to the large majorities of democrat and independent students who disagree), 93% of college students overall (including 73% of college

Republicans) say their own high school's curriculum *didn't focus enough* on the impact of racism on U.S. history. And, even in cases where some students don't personally favor teaching about systemic racism, that doesn't necessarily translate into supporting the ability of politicians to ban such teaching in schools. A large majority of all students, regardless of party affiliation, think that state legislations shouldn't "be able to limit how public schools or universities teach history."[733]

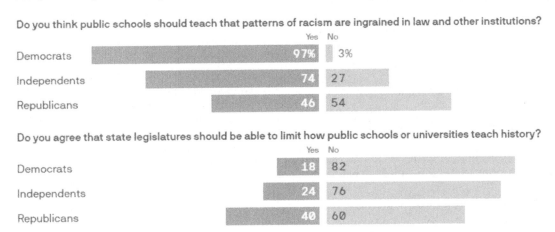

College student attitudes toward action against critical race theory

Among 810 U.S. college students surveyed June 24-28, 2021

Do you think public schools should teach that patterns of racism are ingrained in law and other institutions?

	Yes	No
Democrats	97%	3%
Independents	74	27
Republicans	46	54

Do you agree that state legislatures should be able to limit how public schools or universities teach history?

	Yes	No
Democrats	18	82
Independents	24	76
Republicans	40	60

Data: The Generation Lab; Chart: Danielle Alberti/Axios

I'm extraordinarily confident that the vast majority of Americans who support the banning of critical race theory in public schools (including colleges and universities) are not capable of providing a consistent and accurate definition of the very thing they want to ban. Some knowingly associate CRT with all kinds of topics and concepts that are not actually CRT. "Loudoun

County Public Schools keep saying, 'well, we don't teach Critical Race Theory. Okay, well... it's not like physics or chemistry. It's a theory, right? It's a philosophy of looking at the world and, and equity-based education is the execution of that philosophy."[734] Here, any training or lesson concerning "equity" is regarded as counting as "CRT."

[732] https://www.washingtonpost.com/politics/2021/06/15/scholar-strategy-how-critical-race-theory-alarms-could-convert-racial-anxiety-into-political-energy
[733] https://www.axios.com/critical-race-theory-

polling-college-students-d8b5a7fa-38ac-47b1-b49d-bc3dd1c811e0.html
[734] https://foxbaltimore.com/news/nation-world/states-push-back-against-critical-race-theory-in-education

By way of analogy, imagine that I am proposing that the state of California forbid the teaching of fascism in public schools, including universities. Fascism is "bad," right? Like, Hitler and Mussloni levels of bad. So, it would probably be disconcerting to a lot of people if our public educational institutions were teaching students to be fascists, and it might seem reasonable to prevent that from happening. But now suppose that the examples of fascist teaching that will be banned are things like reciting the pledge of allegiance, playing the Star Bangled Banner or any other "nationalistic" song, teaching anything positive about the U.S. military or military service, or any accounts of U.S. history in which the country is portrayed in a positive light. If you think it requires a serious stretch of the imagination to equate any of those things with fascism, let alone indoctrinating students into becoming fascists, then I think you're correct-- but it's similarly absurd to equate *any* discussion of the history or current impact of racism with "CRT," portray CRT as being *itself* racist or intentionally divisive or hate-inspiring (such that an analogy with something like fascism could be possible in the first place), and then use all those misleading and inaccurate rhetorical devices to justify *censoring* anti-racist ideas from *public* institutions.

Jonathan Chism, an assistant professor of history at University of Houston–Downtown and co-editor of "*Critical Race Studies Across Disciplines*," says that "any anti-racist effort is being labeled as critical race theory. Many that are condemning critical race theory haven't read it or studied it intensely. This is largely predicated on fear: the fear of losing power and influence and privilege. The larger issue that this is all stemming from is a desire to deny the truth about America, about racism."[735]

Media Misinformation

Not understanding what CRT actually is and labeling as CRT *anything* that seems to be a "woke" approach to race, is common. In the vast majority of cases, I believe this is the result of understandable (though culpable) ignorance. Opposition to critical race theory is an overwhelmingly "Republican" stance, and most self-identified Republicans rely on right wing media and social media sources for their information and understanding (much as Democrats usually rely on more left-wing sources). A recent survey shows that, when it comes to political information, 36% of Republicans relied on Fox News, with another 17% using talk radio. The remaining news providers were all under 10%.[736] Roughly a third of GOP voters rely on Fox News as their source for political information—far more than any other news source. As of June 15, 2021, Fox News had mentioned critical race theory nearly 1300 times since March.[737]

---

[735] https://www.nbcnews.com/news/nbcblk/ how- trump-ignited-fight-over-critical-race-theory-schools-n1266701

[736] https://www.forbes.com/sites/bradadgate/ 2021/03/01/in-2020-the-news-sources-for-

republicans-and-democrats-were-very-different/?sh=4fa9d4d34529

[737] https://www.businessinsider.com/fox-news-critical-race-theory-mentions-thousand-study-2021-6

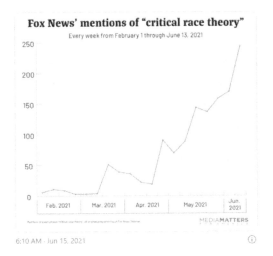

Fox News' mentions of "critical race theory"

Every week from February 1 through June 13, 2021

MEDIAMATTERS

6:10 AM · Jun 15, 2021   ⓘ

Compare the frequency of references to CRT on Fox as opposed to CNN or MSNBC, but also compared to terms like "systemic racism," or "racist."

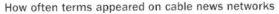

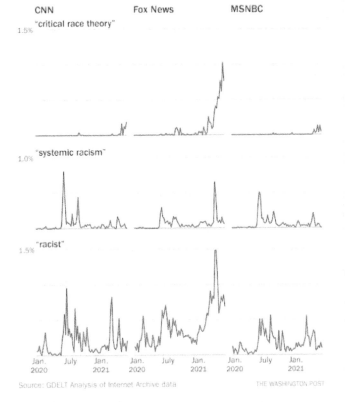

How often terms appeared on cable news networks

Percent of 15-second segments in a week featuring the quoted term.

Source: GDELT Analysis of Internet Archive data   THE WASHINGTON POST

There is a clear correlation between references to CRT on Fox News and references to "racists" or being "racist." This is not a coincidence. One of the (inaccurate) assumptions made about CRT by most who oppose it is that it necessarily and inevitably presents white people as racists. This is not true of CRT if, for no other reason, than because CRT focuses on *systems* and *institutions*, exploring how the legal system (for example) is racist in its application, as distinct from individual participants in the legal system being racists. A signature feature of CRT, in fact, is that it attempts to refocus our understanding of racism *away* from personal attitudes, beliefs, or actions and onto systemic, institutional-level policies and outcomes. Despite that, many people still *presume* that any discussion of racism means personal/attitudinal racism, and therefore that any discussion of white privilege—which simply acknowledges the comparatively beneficial role occupied by white people within our "systems"—means that white people all hold racist beliefs. When defensiveness against being called a racist combines with a belief that it's actually *white* people who are being most discriminated against in America today, such as when 25% of Republicans say that white people experience "a lot" of discrimination (far more than any other racial group!), Republican resistance to CRT is not at all surprising.

There is **a lot** / **some** discrimination against racial group

Democrats/lean   Overall   Republicans/lean

Source: Pew Research Center, March 2021   THE WASHINGTON POST

This, despite the fact that another survey shows that 84% of white Americans claim to have rarely or never experienced discrimination or inequality because of their race or ethnicity, compared to 61% of Black respondents who claim to have often or sometimes encountered racial discrimination.[738]

The popular "Tucker Carlson Tonight" show on Fox featured a prominent anti-CRT activist, Chris Rufo, who proclaimed that "critical race theory has pervaded every institution in the federal government," and that it has become "in essence, the default ideology of the federal bureaucracy and is now being weaponized against the American people."[739]

The even-more-right wing media network Newsmax features articles with titles like "Critical Race Theory Manipulates History,"[740] and in which it is claimed that "CRT proponents view skin color as defining our society. Blacks and other people of color (POC) are defined as powerless and oppressed, whether they know it or not. Whites, solely by virtue of their "whiteness," are privileged oppressors."[741] Another article is entitled "Democrat-Left's Critical Race Theory Preaches Black Failure," and begins by saying "Critical race theory may be the Democrat-Left's filthiest, ugliest Big Lie. It defines America as inherently and irredeemably bigoted, denounces all whites as racial oppressors, and diminishes all Blacks as racially oppressed victims."[742]

In Tennessee, the chief sponsor of a bill to ban CRT, state Rep. John Ragan (R), referred to those who promote CRT as "seditious charlatans [who] would if they could destroy our heritage of ordered, individual liberty under the rule of law, before our very eyes."[743] Sedition refers to incitement to resistance, or insurrection against, lawful authority; an attempt to overthrow the rule of law itself—and this is clearly what Ragan meant by his statement.

Patricia Morgan, a Republican in Rhode Island who proposed that state's "divisive concepts" bill, called critical race theory "a divisive, destructive, poisonous ideology" that encourages people to judge each other by the color of their skin, and that "It makes white males oppressors ... and it makes everyone else the victims."[744]

Such perspectives on CRT are not confined solely to potentially motivated legislators seeking to win the favor of their constituents but have "trickled down" all the way down to average citizens and voters. In an editorial to a local newspaper in New Hampshire, a writer says "CRT is a toxic theory devoid of facts that draws erroneous conclusions based on the opinions of some. CRT declares white people as irredeemable racists. These theorists want to poison the minds of our children by getting them to believe they are racists because of the color of their skin. This toxic theory tells people of color (POC) that white people are racists. So, how can POC be a friend to their fellow students if white students are racist? Parents need to protect their children from this toxic thinking."[745] He continues by defining "equity" as "the code word for one group being better than another"—a definition that I suspect would surprise all of the people I know who work for equity.

These are not isolated perspectives held by extreme outliers. A 2021 survey revealed that 74 percent of respondents are "somewhat or strongly opposed" to white privilege training and to schools communicating that minorities are

---

[738] http://maristpoll.marist.edu/npr-pbs-newshour-marist-poll-race-relations-in-the-united-states/#sthash.hj9T0ZYZ.dpbs

[739] https://www.foxnews.com/politics/chris-rufo-race-theory-cult-federal-government

[740] https://www.newsmax.com/zivadahl/criticalracetheory/2020/10/26/id/993762/

[741] ibid.

[742] https://www.newsmax.com/murdock/critical-race-theory-black/2021/05/26

/id/1022834/

[743] https://thehill.com/homenews/state-watch/551977-gop-legislatures-target-critical-race-theory

[744] https://www.edweek.org/policy-politics/8-states-debate-bills-to-restrict-how-teachers-discuss-racism-sexism/2021/04

[745] https://www.concordmonitor.com/My-Turn-HB-544-embraces-the-values-of-NH-residents-40054309

inherently oppressed.[746] If that is how the questions were worded, that doesn't surprise me all that much, but the same survey showed that just under 70 percent of respondents opposed teaching about systemic racism. At the same time, another survey revealed that 78 percent either had not heard of critical race theory or were unsure whether they had![747] This suggests that a lot of people have very strong opinions about something that most Americans almost certainly couldn't accurately define, given that most Americans hadn't even heard of it. It's also worth pointing out that in the *same* survey in which 74 percent of respondents are "somewhat or strongly opposed" to white privilege training, and just under 70 percent of respondents opposed teaching systemic racism, 49% of respondents claimed that it was very or extremely important to "promote social equity in school."

Clearly, the connection between the many ideas and approaches all lumped together with CRT, and the pursuit of social equity, is not being made by many people—which makes it easier to understand opposition to CRT. If someone doesn't associate CRT, or even equity training and policies, with the achievement of social equity, but instead associates such things with the "toxic" claim that "white people are irredeemable racists," it's not so surprising that a great many people oppose anything even loosely associated with CRT.

While I could not possibly claim to know what every teacher or scholar or trainer says or aims to do in the context of teaching or promoting critical race theory (let alone all of the K-12 teachers who aren't even attempting to teach CRT, but are instead providing lessons on equity,

diversity, and inclusion, but are nevertheless being lumped in with CRT), and while it is certainly (unfortunately) possible that some teachers or trainers use heavy-handed and poorly executed exercises, I can say with a very high degree of confidence that CRT, in general, simply does not match the bogeyman description that is being used to generate support for laws that unambiguously and unapologetically censor certain points of view often while simultaneously openly advocating for what can only be described as propaganda.[748]

As a reminder from earlier in this very chapter, CRT is an approach to scholarship united by two common interests:

1. Investigating how the system of white supremacy has existed and been maintained by various institutions and social systems, including the allegedly neutral rule of law and (more recently) "colorblind" equal protection of the law.

2. The desire to not only understand such things, but to change them.

Additional tenets of CRT include the following, according to Khiara Bridges.

- Recognition that race is not biologically real but is socially constructed and socially significant. It recognizes that science (as demonstrated in the Human Genome Project) refutes the idea of biological racial differences. According to scholars Richard Delgado and Jean Stefancic, race is the product of social

---

[746] https://thefederalist.com/2021/05/11/poll-three-quarters-of-americans-oppose-white-privilege-training/

[747] https://www.theatlantic.com/politics/archive/2021/05/gops-critical-race-theory-fixation-explained/618828/

[748] Propaganda is a strong word, but I think it is justified when no less a figure then President Trump orders the 1776 Commission to develop

"patriotic education" and to promote "pro-American curriculum" that celebrates "the miracle of American history (https://www.washingtonpost.com/education/2021/01/19/trump-patriotic-education-report-slavery-fascists/)." The report of the Commission itself advocates viewing our history with "reverence and love" (ibid. The full report of the 1776 Commission is available at the site as well.).

thought and is not connected to biological reality.

- Acknowledgement that racism is a normal feature of society and is embedded within systems and institutions, like the legal system, that replicate racial inequality. This dismisses the idea that racist incidents are aberrations but instead are manifestations of structural and systemic racism.

- Rejection of popular understandings about racism, such as arguments that confine racism to a few "bad apples." CRT recognizes that racism is codified in law, embedded in structures, and woven into public policy. CRT rejects claims of meritocracy or "colorblindness." CRT recognizes that it is the systemic nature of racism that bears primary responsibility for reproducing racial inequality.

- Recognition of the relevance of people's everyday lives to scholarship. This includes embracing the lived experiences of people of color, including those preserved through storytelling, and rejecting deficit-informed research that excludes the epistemologies of people of color.[749]

First, note that there is no suggestion that white people are all inherently racist, nor even any mention whatsoever of *personal* attitudes or beliefs. All of the focus is on systems and institutions. Admittedly, a key premise of CRT is the recognition of the existence of white supremacy. Anyone who is uncomfortable acknowledging that white people have enjoyed a position of relative privilege throughout the entire history of the United States will probably be dissatisfied with CRT, in general – but is also thoroughly unfamiliar with our actual history.

I propose that there is no honest way to evaluate the history of the United States without acknowledging that, from the very beginning, white persons (and in particular, relatively affluent white males) were relatively advantaged (to varying degrees) compared to all other groups of persons on the continent. Even the most casual examination of the history of how Native Americans were treated by European settlers, the history of slavery, reconstruction, Jim Crow, etc., the struggle for women's rights, the struggle for LGBTQ+ rights, and the history of discrimination against Latinx persons (etc.) demonstrates that the history of the United States has *not* been a history of free and equal participation by *all* persons. That is empirically verifiable and should be so obvious as to be not worth stating.

We can have spirited debates as to how much progress has been made (or not), and we can have spirited debates as to what are the best responses (both personally and politically) to remaining disparities and experiences of discrimination, but that the history of the United States has been, in short, a history of white supremacy is beyond contestation. Or it *should* be beyond contestation. It seems that some opponents of CRT are ostensibly motivated because they honestly believe that neither racism nor any effect of racism exists in the United States today. Missouri state Senator Rick Brattin, who sponsored the Missouri bill, said "What inequities do we deal with today? Everybody has equal opportunity. We're a nation ... of equal opportunity for people to prosper or not prosper. To say that everyone should have equity in property and all things, that's the antithesis of America. That's socialism."

Assuming he is being sincere, Brattin believes that there are no racial inequities today, and denounces CRT as advocating for "equity in property," which he equates to "socialism."[750] In reality, CRT is not even remotely identical to socialism, nor does it necessarily advocate for

---

[749] https://www.americanbar.org/groups/crsj/publications/human_rights_magazine_home/civil-rights-reimagining-policing/a-lesson-on-critical-race-theory/

[750] https://www.edweek.org/policy-politics/8-states-debate-bills-to-restrict-how-teachers-discuss-racism-sexism/2021/04

"equity in property" (though some CRT scholars are fierce critics of American capitalism). CRT certainly does, however, reject the claim that there are no racial inequities in America today. Numerous objective, empirically verifiable studies involving data on incarceration rates, home ownership rates, educational attainment, school suspensions, student loan debt, and even the rates at which doctors will prescribe pain medications, all support the general assumptions of CRT, rather than the personal perspective of Senator Brattin.[751] Ironically enough, his breathtaking ignorance of the actual state of affairs in the United States today (assuming his statements are sincere) is evidence of the importance of an honest assessment of our history, such as that provided by CRT, and how that history has contributed to the present!

Brattin is far from alone, however. A Pew Research Center survey shows that as of September 2020, only 39% of white respondents think that "when it comes to giving Black people equal rights with White people, our country has not gone far enough." 42% thought things were "about right," with nearly 1 in 5 (18%) saying the country has gone *too* far![752] Not surprisingly, there are predictable Party trends as well. Among Democrats, 78% think the country hasn't gone "far enough," while only 17% of Republicans say the same.

---

[751] Lengthier discussions of inequities and disparities can be found in my chapter on Discrimination. Extensive data and analysis are also available at this site, this site, and this site (among others).

[752] https://www.pewresearch.org/social-trends/2020/10/06/amid-national-reckoning-americans-divided-on-whether-increased-focus-on-race-will-lead-to-major-policy-change/

% saying that, when it comes to giving Black people equal rights with White people, our country has ...

	Not gone far enough	Gone too far	Been about right
All adults			
Sept 2020	49	15	34
Jan/Feb 2019	45	15	39
White			
Sept 2020	39	18	42
Jan/Feb 2019	37	19	43
Black			
Sept 2020	86	6	5
Jan/Feb 2019	78	6	14
Hispanic			
Sept 2020	57	13	28
Jan/Feb 2019	48	9	40
Asian*			
Sept 2020	56	15	28

*Asian adults were interviewed in English only.
Note: Share of respondents who didn't offer an answer not shown. White, Black and Asian adults include those who report being only one race and are not Hispanic. Hispanics are of any race. Because this question was only asked of a random half of the sample in 2019, the sample of Asian adults is too small to be shown separately for that survey.
Source: Surveys of U.S. adults conducted Jan. 22-Feb. 5, 2019, and Sept. 8-13, 2020.
"Amid National Reckoning, Americans Divided on Whether Increased Focus on Race Will Lead to Major Policy Change"

PEW RESEARCH CENTER

Within that very modest 17% of GOP respondents who think the country hasn't gone far enough with respect to achieving equal rights, *ignoring* race ("colorblindness") was the preferred approach to reduce inequality by nearly a two-to-one margin, with "accurate history education" to include acknowledging the history of racism in the U.S. being favored by only 16% of Republicans, and policies aimed at addressing "systemic inequality" being favored by even fewer GOP respondents (13%).[753] When only 17% of Republicans believe that there is still work to be done on achieving racial equality in the first place, and when, even among those who think so, the most popular tactic is to not "focus on race," it's no wonder that Republicans tend to have strong opposition to CRT, given that it both claims that there persists racial inequality *and* that to overcome it we must address systemic racism and honestly analyze the history of our

---

[753] https://www.pewresearch.org/social-trends/2020/10/06/amid-national-reckoning-americans-divided-on-whether-increased-focus-on-race-will-lead-to-major-policy-change/

institutions through the lens of race.

For some, examinations of racial discrimination, racism, racial inequities, etc., produce inconvenient truths. It doesn't "feel good" to become aware of, and to attempt to come to terms with, ugly periods in the history of your own country. It is disappointing and even disillusioning to be forced to recognize that the understanding you had of certain historical figures, or even your culture itself, is not as noble as you used to think, or would prefer to believe. It is possible that coming to terms with these things generates feelings of guilt, among other "negative" feelings. That doesn't mean that the *purpose* of CRT specifically, or diversity and equity education/training in general, is to produce feelings of guilt. I know of literally no scholar, activist, educator, or politician who has as an explicit goal making white people feel "guilty," and I similarly know of none that would be satisfied if education and consciousness-raising *only* produced feelings of guilt. Feeling guilty, by itself, accomplishes nothing. Keep in mind that the second common interest of critical race scholarship listed above is *change*, once understanding is attained. The change is not going to happen, however, without understanding.

As just one example, without understanding the long and complex history of how Black persons have been treated since the very beginning of American history, one can't accurately understand current disparities in wealth, education, criminal records, homeownership, and health (among other things). Without understanding that history, it is breathtakingly easy, wholly inaccurate, and morally problematic, to observe the disparities and quickly come to the conclusion that the cause must be something about Black persons, themselves. If Black persons, on average, fare far less well on most measures than white persons in the United States, and if racism is only an artifact of history and is no longer a "problem" today, then it "must" somehow be the fault of Black

Americans that they have less family wealth, lower rates of home ownership, higher rates of incarceration, etc. On the other hand, if someone actually learns about how slavery wasn't just some ugly "episode" in the distant recesses of American history, but produced real, specific, concrete, demonstrable, measurable effects, and various reiterations of our racial caste system (e.g., Jim Crow laws, the "War on Drugs," etc.) that persisted long after slavery was abolished, then the complex causes of *current* disparities can actually be understood—and, once understood, *changed* (assuming there is the will to do so).

Similarly, because CRT emerged as an approach to jurisprudence, much of the actual scholarship done on and with CRT has focused on our legal system. Among the "controversial" claims of CRT with respect to the legal system is that everyone involved in the legal system, including legislators and judges, is a human being, and therefore subject to all the same prejudices as any other human being. The ideal that justice is "blind" is just that: an ideal. Actual "blindness" is not possible, however, for the mere mortals that write laws or make judgments on them.

In the case of *Loving v. Virginia* (1967), the Supreme Court ruled that laws banning interracial marriages were unconstitutional. A Virginia judge had sentenced the Lovings to a suspended sentence of 25 years in prison on the condition that they leave the State and not return for 25 years. In his ruling, he said "Almighty God created the races white, black, yellow, malay and red, and he placed them on separate continents. And but for the interference with his arrangement there would be no cause for such marriages. The fact that he separated the races shows that he did not intend for the races to mix."[754] There is nothing even remotely resembling an impartial "blind" reading of the law in this judgment, as the trial judge was clearly drawing upon his own (prejudiced) "intuitions" about race relations.

The Supreme Court is no more immune to

---

[754] http://law2.umkc.edu/faculty/projects/ftrials/conlaw/loving.html

that tendency than is a local trial judge. In the infamous case of *Dred Scott v. Sandford* (1857), the majority of the Court ruled that Black persons were not citizens, and were "regarded as beings of an inferior order, and altogether unfit to associate with the white race either in social or political relations, and so far inferior that they had no rights which the white man was bound to respect, and that the negro might justly and lawfully be reduced to slavery for his benefit," acknowledging that this "was regarded as an axiom in morals as well as in politics which no one thought of disputing or supposed to be open to dispute, and men in every grade and position in society daily and habitually acted upon it in their private pursuits, as well as in matters of public concern, without doubting for a moment the correctness of this opinion."[755] This reference not only reveals how cultural prejudice informs judicial rulings, but *also* explicitly acknowledges white supremacy as something "no one thought of disputing or supposed to be open to debate." How can it possibly be "controversial," then, to simply acknowledge that the beliefs and values of white supremacy have actually had an impact on things like laws, policies, legal judgments, etc.?

In its essence, that is what CRT is about, and what it does: delve into the role and impact that race (and ultimately other aspects of identity as well) has had on institutions, policies, outcomes, etc., and then, equipped with that understanding, *change* those institutions so that American ideals such as equality before the law, equality of opportunity, liberty, etc., *genuinely* extend to all Americans. You would never think of CRT in such a manner, though, if what you have been told about CRT is that it is a "Big Lie" that is being "weaponized against the American people" to use "divisive concepts" to make white people feel "anguish" and "guilt" and teach people of color that they are "powerless."

Some of the participants in this culture war can't be dismissed as innocently naïve or understandably confused. Some activists are part of coordinated, nationwide efforts, with significant financial and political support. Chris Rufo, mentioned above, bragged on twitter that his efforts were "driving up negative perceptions" of CRT, with the goal that they would "eventually turn it toxic, as [they] put all of the various cultural insanities under that brand category." He also said that "The goal is to have the public read something crazy in the newspaper and immediately think 'critical race theory. We have decodified the term and will recodify it to annex the entire range of cultural constructions that are unpopular with Americans."[756]

---

[755] Dred Scott v. Sandford. Full text available here: http://teachingamericanhistory.org/library/document/dred-scott-v-sandford/

[756] https://web.archive.org/web/20210609235759/https://twitter.com/realchrisrufo/status/1371541044592996352

Christopher F. Rufo ✕ @realchrisrufo · Mar 15
We have successfully frozen their brand—"critical race theory"—into the public conversation and are steadily driving up negative perceptions. We will eventually turn it toxic, as we put all of the various cultural insanities under that brand category.

○ 37   ⟳ 76   ♡ 780

Christopher F. Rufo ✕
@realchrisrufo

Follow

Replying to @realchrisrufo @ConceptualJames

The goal is to have the public read something crazy in the newspaper and immediately think "critical race theory." We have decodified the term and will recodify it to annex the entire range of cultural constructions that are unpopular with Americans.

12:17 PM · 15 Mar 2021

It is both rare and helpful when people make their actual agenda so transparent. Rufo, who is a national spokesperson for the effort to ban CRT across the states and in school districts, openly declared that his goal is to *intentionally* conflate critical race theory with "the entire range of cultural constructions that are unpopular with Americans" and for that association to be triggered whenever someone reads "something crazy in the newspaper." In other words, the attempt to ban CRT isn't actually about critical race theory, as it really is, but a broader attempt to ban teaching, training, or even discussion of virtually anything related to race, prejudice, discrimination, intersectionality, or privilege – including any discussion of history or the legal system that draws upon those things in evaluating policies, institutions, outcomes, etc.

Conclusion

In summary, CRT is a particular academic interpretive approach used across a variety of academic disciplines and topics, such as jurisprudence, criminal justice, education, and public health. It is generally found only in higher education, particularly graduate schools or law schools, although some of the concepts emphasized in CRT, such as implicit bias and systemic racism, have made their way into our broader culture. CRT has specific and documentable premises and interests. Despite all that, "critical race theory" has become the "catch-all" term for virtually *any* discussion of race or identity in education or workplace training, due, in part, to repeated (and misleading) media coverage on Fox news and talk radio, among other sources. This has resulted in widespread public opposition to a straw-man version of CRT, which has been intentionally encouraged and resourced by politically motivated individuals and organizations. All of this has manifested in various legislative acts, in roughly two dozen states as of the time of this writing, that ban the teaching of "critical race theory" (in some manner or another), but which, due to the vague and inaccurate defining of CRT, are far more likely to result in the reduction of teaching or training about race or discrimination, in general, than in the prevention of teaching anything that might accurately be referred to as CRT. These efforts are largely based on misunderstanding and misinformation, and, if successful, serve only to *increase* and *perpetuate* misunderstanding and misinformation.

Appendix/ "Deeper Dive": The Second Amendment

Comprehension questions you should be able to answer after reading this chapter:

1. Explain each of the following approaches to philosophy of law in one sentence:
   a. Natural Law
   b. Legal Positivism
   c. Critical Race Theory (CRT)
2. Briefly explain both the "individual" and "militia" interpretations of the Second Amendment.
3. Briefly explain our natural right to life and self-preservation/self-defense, according to Locke and Natural Law theory.
4. According to Lund, how does the Second Amendment "link" the right of self-defense against criminals and the right of self-defense against tyrannical government?
5. What would justify a right to bear arms according to Legal Positivism?
6. What are the six things we should consider when evaluating the Second Amendment using Legal Positivism, according to Blocher? Briefly explain each.
7. Briefly explain why Heyman thinks that Locke's theory actually does *not* support an *individual* right to bear arms, according to Natural Law theory.
8. How might the wording of Article XVII of the Massachusetts Constitution be helpful and relevant when interpreting the "original intent" of the Second Amendment?
9. What does Heyman mean when he says that the Second Amendment has shifted from an "auxiliary right" to an "archaic right?"
10. Briefly explain the basic function of the Second Amendment as it applied to the following groups, according to Dunbar-Ortiz:
    a. Indigenous (Native) Americans
    b. Black persons
11. What are some examples of how gun control laws have been passed and/or applied in a racist manner?
12. Why is an examination of the history and historical context of the Second Amendment, and gun laws (and Court cases), in general, relevant to Critical Race Theory?

Some of you might want to "dive deeper" into the ideas we started exploring in this chapter, and this appendix will help you do that. In this section, we will take the three interpretive approaches to philosophy of law that we have learned thus far and apply them to a specific and significant legal issue: the Second Amendment of the U.S. Constitution.

As a brief reminder, the **Natural Law** approach to philosophy of law claims that there is a Natural Law that "transcends" human laws, and is the proper foundation by which to establish and evaluate human law. Whether established by God, or Nature, this Natural Law is revealed to us by a proper use of Reason. Because the Natural Law is "higher" than human law, its standards can't be justifiably overridden by "local" standards of justice.

In contrast, the validity of any law, according to **Legal Positivism**, is based on it being established in an objectively verifiable source. Positivists reject the idea that "law" exists somewhere "out there," independently from human law. There is no "Law" that transcends human laws. According to Legal Positivism, jurisprudence is simply a matter of matching cases to relevant existing laws. Ultimately, questions of legality are not questions of moral rightness or wrongness ("oughts") but simply questions of what *is*, in fact, prohibited or required by existing law.

Finally, Critical legal theory, in general,

challenges the idea that law and the legal system are objective, neutral systems. Instead, according to critical legal theory, cultural values and individual biases inform both the law and the actions of people within the legal system, such as prosecutors and judges. The legal system is inevitably vulnerable to bias and personal interpretation because, while a law is general, specific cases and individuals are always particular, and it requires individual human beings to interpret and apply laws to these specific cases. Because of the indeterminate meaning of laws, and the variety of circumstances present in any case, judges can make decisions based on their personal values and beliefs, and then find a legal justification in the ambiguous law or legal precedents. This same bias also applies, of course, to legislators when they are creating laws in the first place. According to critical legal theory, in general, "power" is constructed and preserved by and through the legal system. This includes racial power. In the USA, this is the power of white supremacy-- and this relationship between the law and racial power is the focus of **Critical Race Theory** (CRT).

> [CRT] is a practice—a way of seeing how the fiction of race has been transformed into concrete racial inequities. . . . It's an approach to grappling with a history of white supremacy that rejects the belief that what's in the past is in the past, and that the laws and systems that grow from that past are detached from it.[757]

Natural Law & the Second Amendment

We will begin our application of these theories to the Second Amendment by considering a position statement by the conservative Heritage Foundation.[758] In this article, we find both a (brief) reference to positivism as well as a use of Natural Law to substantiate claims for a "natural right" for both individual and collective self-defense, and consequent right to bear arms under the Second Amendment. In addition, we have a fine example of the use of reason, argument, and philosophical theory to support a policy position.

The basic thesis of the article is that there is a natural right to self-preservation derived "directly from nature and universally acknowledged even by those who contend that political duties arise solely from convention or agreement."[759] In making his case, Lund cites Thomas Hobbes.

> The Right of Nature, which Writers commonly call Jus Naturale, is the Liberty each man hath, to use his own power, as he will himselfe, for the preservation of his own Nature; that is to say, of his own Life; and consequently, of doing any thing, which in his own Judgement, and Reason, hee shall conceive to be the aptest means thereunto.[760]

> For every man is desirous of what is good for him, and shuns what is evil, but chiefly the chiefest of natural evils, which is death; and this he doth by a certain impulsion of nature, no less than that whereby a stone moves downward. It is therefore neither absurd nor reprehensible, neither against the dictates of true reason, for a man to use all his endeavours to preserve and defend his body and the members thereof from death and sorrows. But that which is not contrary to right reason, that all men account to be done justly, and with right. Neither by the word right is anything else signified, than that liberty which every man hath to make use of his natural faculties according to right reason.

---

757 ibid.
758 The full text is available here: https://www.heritage.org/the-constitution/report/the-second-Amendment-and-the-inalienable-right-self-defense
759 Lund, Nelson. "The Right to Arms: an

American Philosophy of Freedom." *First Principles. Foundational Concepts to Guide Politics and Policy.* The Heritage foundation. 62. October 17, 2016, p. 7
760 Hobbes, Thomas. *Leviathan* (Clarendon: Oxford University Press, 1909), chap. 14, ¶ 1.

Therefore the first foundation of natural right is this, that every man as much as in him lies endeavour to protect his life and members.[761]

For Hobbes, a "right" is not derived from something like the Natural Law, but simply indicates the absence of obligations in the state of nature. We have a "right" to self-preservation because, in the state of nature, there are no obligations or restrictions on us, and reason promotes self-preservation. The social contract, according to Hobbes, is a means to protect oneself—a more efficient way to exercise our natural "right" to self-defense. Once we leave the state of nature and submit to a Sovereign, we relinquish all of our liberties/rights we had in the state of nature in exchange for protection and peace.

Although Hobbes acknowledges a type of "natural right" to self-defense, this does not generate a right to bear arms within a society unless the Sovereign says so. The "right" to possess and use weapons, including firearms, in self-defense is not a natural right, but only a contingent legal right once we have formed a social contract and are under the dominion of our government ("sovereign"). In other words, such a (legal) right would exist only if "posited" by the government. For this reason, Lund associates this Hobbesian (Legal Positivism) interpretation with the "modern progressive left" which "ultimately refuses to recognize any principled limits on government power."[762]

Lund finds his justification for a natural rights basis for the Second Amendment not in Hobbes, but in John Locke. Similar to Hobbes, Locke thought all persons were "equal" in the State of Nature—but by this he means that we have similar faculties by virtue of being (equally) God's creations. The State of Nature is a state of equality in that there is no natural superior or inferior therein. The State of Nature can be conceived as a purely hypothetical state, though

Locke described the "inland, vacant places of America" as an example of the State of Nature manifested in reality.[763]

The significance of Locke's assumption that all persons are God's creations shouldn't be underestimated, as it is the basis for several of his key political premises. God created all persons, and we are, in effect, his "property." People are sent into the world,

by his order and about his business, they are his property whose workmanship they are, made to last during his, not another's pleasure: and being furnished with like faculties, sharing all in one community of nature, there cannot be supposed any subordination among us, that may authorize us to destroy one another, as if we were made for one another's uses, as the inferior ranks of creatures are for ours. . . . he has no liberty to destroy himself, or so much as any creature in his possession, yet when some nobler use than its bare possession calls for it.[764]

God creates us all as equals, and intends for us to survive (at least until God wills that we die). Since God intends our survival, God also wills the means necessary for it: life, liberty, health, and property. We, therefore, have natural (God-given) rights to these things, and in the State of Nature we have these rights equally. I have no right to infringe upon another's natural rights, nor does anyone else have the right to infringe upon my own. This conclusion is interpreted as the "law of nature."

The state of nature has a law of nature to govern it, which obliges everyone: and reason which is that law, teaches all mankind who will but consult it, that being all equal and independent, no one ought to harm another in his life, health, liberty or

---

[761] Hobbes, Thomas. *De Cive, in Man and Citizen*, ed. Bernard Gert, (Hackett Publishing, 1972), bk.1, ¶ 7. Emphasis in original.
[762] Lund, 8.

[763] Locke, *Two Treatises on Government*, 2nd Book, 5.36.
[764] ibid. 2.6.

possessions....[765]

Already, we have some important differences between Hobbes' and Locke's visions of the State of Nature. For Hobbes, the state of nature is amoral anarchy. But, for Locke, even in the State of Nature, there is a law of nature, discernible by Reason, which provides moral guidance and moral limits on behavior. The State of Nature is not defined in terms of chaos and violence, but rather by virtue of the lack of a common authority to settle disputes. "Men living according to reason, without a common superior on earth, to judge between them, is properly the state of nature."[766] This is distinct from both civil society (where a government, serving as that common superior, exists) and a state of war, where men don't even abide by the law of reason.

In a clear reference (and critique) of Hobbes, Locke distinguishes between the State of Nature, and a state of war:

> *And here we have the plain difference between the state of nature and the state of war, which however some men have confounded, are as far distant, as a state of peace, good will, mutual assistance and preservation, and a state of enmity, malice, violence and mutual destruction, are one from another. Men living together according to reason, without a common superior on earth, with authority to judge between them, is properly the state of nature. But force, or a declared design of force, upon the person of another, where there is no common superior on earth to appeal to for relief, is the state of war: and it is the want of such an appeal gives a man the right of war even against an aggressor, tho' he be in society and a fellow subject. Thus a thief, whom I cannot harm, but by appeal to the law, for having stolen all that I am worth, I may kill, when he sets on me to rob me but of my horse or coat; because*

> *the law, which was made for my preservation, where it cannot interpose to secure my life from present force, which, if lost, is capable of no reparation, permits me my own defence, and the right of war, a liberty to kill the aggressor, because the aggressor allows not time to appeal to our common judge, nor the decision of the law, for remedy in a case where the mischief may be irreparable. Want of a common judge with authority, puts all men in a state of nature: force without right, upon a man's person, makes a state of war, both where there is, and is not, a common judge.[767]*

This means that the State of Nature is not a "war of all against all," as Hobbes conceived. For Hobbes, people flee the State of Nature out of necessity. For Locke, they do so out of *convenience*. They "unite into a community for their comfortable, safe, and peaceable living one amongst another, in a secure enjoyment of their properties."[768]

An important difference between Hobbes and Locke is that, for Hobbes, people surrender *all* rights and power to the sovereign, who then rules (one hopes!) for their benefit. For Locke, the people form a civil society which is distinct from the State (i.e., the government), and which "retains supreme power."[769]

The State is empowered to act on behalf of the people, but the people never surrender their own power. Legitimate government is constitutionally limited, and exists by the consent of the governed. To remain legitimate, the government must rely on *continuing* consent of the people. The absolute monarchy advocated by Hobbes is *worse* than the State of Nature, according to Locke.

> *To think that men are so foolish that they take care to avoid what mischiefs may be done them by Pole-Cats, or Foxes, but are*

---

[765] ibid., 2.6.
[766] ibid., 2.19.
[767] ibid., 3.19.

[768] ibid., 8.95.
[769] ibid., 13.149.

content, nay think it safety, to be devoured by lions.[770]

In other words, if, in the State of Nature, we are fearful of the power of other individuals, and what they might do with it, given their power-seeking and self-interested nature, how does it make sense to invest *all* that power into a single individual, who is just as power-seeking and self-interested as the rest of us, without retaining any ability to defend ourselves against the very likely abuse of that power? Such a change of state (i.e., from the State of Nature to Hobbes' absolute monarchy) would be irrational.

But though men, when they enter into society, give up the equality, liberty, and executive power they had in the state of nature, into the hands of the society, to be so far disposed of by the legislative, as the good of the society shall require; yet it being only with an intention in every one the better to preserve himself, his liberty and property; (for no rational creature can be supposed to change his condition with an intention to be worse).[771]

In summary, Reason reveals Natural Laws, along with natural rights. Among these rights is a right to self-preservation, and a corresponding duty to refrain from harming others (including taking their life). This duty implies a right not only of self-defense, but also a right for everyone and anyone to *enforce* the Natural Law by punishing those who break it.

He, that, in the state of nature, would take away the freedom that belongs to anyone in that state must necessarily be supposed to have a design to take away everything else, that freedom being the foundation of all the rest; as he that, in a state of society, would take away the freedom belonging to those of that society or commonwealth must be supposed to design to take away

from them everything else, and so be looked on as in a state of war....

Thus a thief, whom I cannot harm but by appeal to the [civil] law for having stolen all that I am worth, I may kill when he sets on me to rob me but of my horse or coat; because the law, which was made for my preservation, where it cannot interpose to secure my life from present force, which, if lost, is capable of no reparation, permits me my own defense and the right of war, a liberty to kill the aggressor, because the aggressor allows not time to appeal to our common judge, nor the decision of the law, for remedy in a case where the mischief may be irreparable.[772]

Using similar reasoning, the right to use even lethal force against personal aggression also demonstrates the right to use force against an unjustly aggressive ruler/government. We have, therefore, a natural right to both individual self-defense against one another, and collective self-defense against tyranny.

The Second Amendment "links the right of self-defense against criminals the right of self-defense against tyranny. The 'right of the people to keep and bear arms' is one that can be exercised by any *individual* to protect his own life and liberty and *collectively* to resist the imposition of despotism. In an echo of Locke's insistence that there are natural duties along with natural rights, the Second Amendment also refers to the well-regulated militia as an institution necessary to the security of a free state. Unlike the armies of the time, which were made up of paid volunteers, the militia tradition entailed a legal duty of able-bodied men to undergo unpaid militia training and to fight when called upon to do so."[773]

The idea that individuals would exercise the right of self-defense personally, or on behalf of others in the community, as opposed to relying on the police to protect the community and

---

[770] ibid., 7.93.
[771] ibid., 9.31.

[772] ibid., 3.18-19.
[773] Lund, 10.

prosecute criminals, might admittedly sound unusual to contemporary ears, but it is important to acknowledge historical context. At the time the Constitution was written, there was no such thing as "the police" as we understand them today.

The original colonies of what would become the United States did not have what we would consider a police force, or police departments. Instead, the colonies followed the policing style in England at the time, which consisted of two types: the communal and informal "watch," and the private security that would be hired by individuals or businesses, analogous to private security services today. The communal watch system consisted of volunteers who were supposed to "keep watch" and warn of any dangers. Boston created such a watch in 1636, New York in 1658, and Philadelphia in 1700.[774]

In addition to the watch system, communities would have "official" law enforcement officers (constables) who were usually paid for any warrant that they served. These constables, in effect, served in an as-needed basis: whenever a crime had occurred, and a warrant for someone's arrest was issued. In many cities, these constables were also responsible for supervising the watch.

Centralized police departments did not emerge until the 1830s, with the first American police force being established in Boston in 1838. Other cities followed, such as New York City in 1845, Chicago in 1851, New Orleans and Cincinnati and 1853, Philadelphia in 1855, Baltimore in 1857, and by the 1880s all major US cities had a municipal police force.[775]

That was the development of law enforcement in *Northern* Colonies and States, at least. The development of law enforcement in the *South* followed a different path. Modern police organizations in the South emerged from slave patrols. The first formal slave patrol was created

in the Carolina colonies in 1704. Such patrols had three primary functions: (1) to chase down, apprehend, and return to their owners, runaway enslaved persons; (2) to provide a form of organized terror to deter slave revolts; and, (3) to maintain a form of discipline for slave-workers who were subject to summary justice, outside of the law, if they violated any plantation rules.[776] After the Civil War, these organizations shifted from vigilante groups to modern Southern police departments, while retaining their original mandate: controlling freed slaves who were now laborers working in an agricultural caste system, and enforcing "Jim Crow" segregation laws, designed to deny freed slaves equal rights and access to the political system.[777]

In summary, according to Lund, the Second Amendment refers both to an individual and collective right to possess and bear arms, and this right emerges from (and is justified by) a Natural Law understanding of our inalienable rights to both life and self-defense. This right functions to allow individuals to operate, as individuals, in self-defense, and also collectively to protect the community from criminals or tyrannical governments.

Although Lund presented Legal Positivism as the framework of liberal progressives who he assumes will be hostile to gun rights, Legal Positivism is simply an interpretive framework that doesn't entail any particular legal judgment. As such, it is possible to arrive at an individual Second Amendment right to bear arms by *that* approach as well, as is evident from the landmark 2008 Supreme Court decision of *District of Columbia v. Heller*.[778]

Legal Positivism & the Second Amendment

The majority opinion in *Heller*, written by the late Justice Scalia, affirmed that the Second

---

[774] Potter, Gary. "The History of Policing in the United States,"
https://plsonline.eku.edu/insidelook/history-policing-united-states-part-1
[775] ibid.
[776] ibid.

[777] ibid. The significance of slave patrols and policing will be addressed more in a later section.
[778] https://supreme.justia.com/cases/federal/us/554/570/#tab-opinion-1962738

Amendment applies to individuals, and not only (or even primarily) to State-run Militias. In that case, The District of Columbia had passed laws that required residents to keep lawfully owned firearms unloaded, disassembled, or bound by a trigger lock when in the resident's home, and prohibited lawful ownership of handguns (though residents could apply for one year licenses to possess handguns). The majority of the Court ruled these regulations to be unconstitutional.

> *The ban on registering handguns and the requirement to keep guns in the home disassembled or nonfunctional with a trigger lock mechanism violate the Second Amendment. Justice Antonin Scalia delivered the opinion for the 5-4 majority. The Court held that the first clause of the Second Amendment that references a "militia" is a prefatory clause that does not limit the operative clause of the Amendment. Additionally, the term "militia" should not be confined to those serving in the military, because at the time the term referred to all able-bodied men who were capable of being called to such service. To read the Amendment as limiting the right to bear arms only to those in a governed military force would be to create exactly the type of state-sponsored force against which the Amendment was meant to protect people. Because the text of the Amendment should be read in the manner that gives greatest effect to the plain meaning it would have had at the time it was written, the operative clause should be read to "guarantee an individual right to possess and carry weapons in case of confrontation." This reading is also in line with legal writing of the time and subsequent scholarship. Therefore, banning handguns, an entire class of arms that is commonly used for protection*

> *purposes, and prohibiting firearms from being kept functional in the home, the area traditionally in need of protection, violates the Second Amendment.[779]*

It should be noted that the Court did not rule out any and all sort of restrictions on gun possession, stating that the ruling should not "be taken to cast doubt on longstanding prohibitions on the possession of firearms by felons and the mentally ill, or laws forbidding the carrying of firearms in sensitive places such as schools and government buildings, or laws imposing conditions and qualifications on the commercial sale of arms."[780]

The Court did offer dissenting opinions in this case as well. Justice Stevens interpreted the Second Amendment as only protecting the right to bear arms within the context of Militia service, writing that "to keep" and "to bear" are not separate rights but one right "to have arms available and ready for military service, and to use them for military purposes when necessary."[781] Justice Breyer wrote a separate dissenting opinion in which he agreed with Stevens ("self-defense alone, detached from any militia-related objective, is not the [Second] Amendment's concern."), but added an "interest-balancing" approach in which the public safety interest in reducing gun violence could outweigh a limited Second Amendment right to possess firearms.

Why have I explained the *Heller* decision in the section considering Legal Positivism? Because Justice Scalia, providing the majority opinion in the *Heller* decision, was operating in the manner of Legal Positivism, and not deriving an individual right to gun ownership in the manner of Natural Law.

> *Non-originalist judges say, 'We agonize a lot.' I don't agonize a lot. Should there be a right to this or that? That's not my job. [Lawyers] are not trained to be moral philosophers, which is what it takes to*

---

[779] https://www.oyez.org/cases/2007/07-290
[780] ibid.

[781] ibid.

determine whether there should be, and hence is, a right to abortion, or homosexual sodomy, assisted suicide, et cetera. And history is a rock-hard science compared to moral philosophy.[782]

In other words, Scalia did not justify his interpretation by appealing to a natural right to self-defense (including the right to firearms), but instead claimed that the "originalist" meaning of the text itself, supported by historical context, simply *posited* that this *legal* (as distinct from moral) right exists.

Scalia's approached to jurisprudence is known as "originalism," or appealing to "original intent." This approach is generally attributed to Robert Bork, an appellate Justice who was nominated to the Supreme Court in 1987, but rejected. In 1989, this "founding father" of originalism made his approach to jurisprudence clear.

If you look at the right to privacy in a rural, rustic society and look at downtown Los Angeles, there cannot be, I think, a rigid idea that is given by some god to our founding fathers that we then follow rigidly today. . . . once you say you don't know what principles they (the framers of the Constitution) were laying down, then you have nothing left to guide you except your own preferences. And you ought not to be making up the law according to your own preferences.[783]

In other words, jurisprudence should follow an approach at least resembling Legal Positivism, rather than attempting to infer the "proper" meaning of law on the basis of higher moral principles such as might be derived under Natural Law theory. Interestingly, specifically with regard to the Second Amendment, Bork seems to have *disagreed* with Scalia on the "original intent" of the Founders. Speaking of the Second Amendment, he said that "its intent was to guarantee the right of States to form militias, not for individuals to bear arms."[784] He also said that "assault weapons could be banned under the Constitution," and, when asked whether his statement would apply to all gun control, he replied "Probably, It doesn't mean it's a great idea. It's probably constitutional."[785]

To take a "positivist" approach to the Second Amendment means that "in the technical, jurisprudential sense . . . the Second Amendment is not natural or God-given, it is not discovered or revealed, it is "positive" – it is law. And there are rules by which American society identifies when something is law and when it is not."[786]

To say that a right exists by a matter of law, as opposed to being a natural or moral right, does not necessarily mean that the scope or exercise of that right is somehow more limited. For example, many (if not most) moral philosophers acknowledge a moral right of self-defense, but impose limits. These limits include the requirement of a sufficient threat that is both imminent and unavoidable, as well as a limit on the amount of force that is acceptable to use in self-defense – generally, an amount that is proportional to the threat. Morally speaking, if someone threatens me with violence by email, my right of self-defense doesn't allow me to drive to their house and shoot them! Not only is the response not proportionate (lethal force versus a mere threat of violence), but the risk was very much distant and even abstract. As another example, if a toddler threatens to "kill me," and begins flailing his tiny little fists against my shins,

---

[782] https://thehill.com/blogs/blog-briefing-room/news/325677-justice-scalia-not-my-job-to-act-as-moral-philosopher

[783] https://www.latimes.com/archives/la-xpm-1989-03-15-me-587-story.html

[784] ibid.

[785] ibid.

[786] Blocher, Joseph & Miller, Darrell A.H. "The Second Amendment as Positive Law." Law & Society Keynote Address. Charleston, South Carolina - February 8, 2019, 108

causing no harm greater than irritation, I have no moral right to shoot and kill this child because, among other things, the threat, while imminent, isn't really much of a threat at all. This is all to say that our moral right to self-defense usually comes with some pretty stringent restrictions. Legally, however, some States in the United States "have expanded these bounds, permitting self-defense when not otherwise necessary or proportional has traditionally understood, for example through the adoption of stand your ground laws."[787]

A Louisiana stand your ground law, for example, reads: "A person who is not engaged in unlawful activity and who is in a place where he or she has a right to be shall have no duty to retreat before using force or violence... and may stand his or her ground and meet force with force."[788]

Variations of such laws exist in numerous States, and are sometimes accompanied (or substituted) by laws enforcing the "castle doctrine," according to which one's home is their "castle," and they have a legal right to defend it, and themselves, using lethal force if necessary, and without a legal requirement to "retreat." Even the State of California has a version of the castle doctrine (Penal Code 198.5 PC). The castle doctrine was invoked in Houston Texas in a case that attracted national media attention.

When Mr. Horn, a 61-year-old retiree living with his daughter and her family in a growing subdivision in this Houston suburb, saw two burglars breaking into the house next door on Nov. 14, he called 911 and grabbed his shotgun. . . . Then there was Mr. Horn's claim of self-defense under the Legislature's reformulation of the "castle doctrine" that, as of September, no longer requires a Texan to retreat before using deadly force at his own "habitation" in the face of a perceived lethal threat. Protecting a neighbor's property, however, is not included.

One vital piece of evidence is certain to be the audiotape of Mr. Horn's 911 calls. In a low, calm and steady voice, he said he saw the men breaking in and asked: "I've got a shotgun; do you want me to stop them?"

The Pasadena emergency operator responded: "Nope. Don't do that. Ain't no property worth shooting somebody over, O.K.?"
Mr. Horn said: "But hurry up, man. Catch these guys will you? Cause, I ain't going to let them go."

Mr. Horn then said he would get his shotgun.

The operator said, "No, no." But Mr. Horn said: "I can't take a chance of getting killed over this, O.K.? I'm going to shoot."

The operator told him not to go out with a gun because officers would be arriving.

"O.K.," Mr. Horn said. "But I have a right to protect myself too, sir," adding, "The laws have been changed in this country since September the first, and you know it."

The operator said, "You're going to get yourself shot." But Mr. Horn replied, "You want to make a bet? I'm going to kill them." Moments later he said, "Well here it goes, buddy. You hear the shotgun clicking and I'm going."

Then he said: "Move, you're dead."

There were two quick explosions, then a third, and the 911 call ended.

"I had no choice," Mr. Horn said when he called 911 back. "They came in the front yard with me, man."

---

[787] ibid., 111.
[788] https://codes.findlaw.com/la/revised-statutes/la-rev-stat-tit-14-sect-20.html

Captain Corbett said that a plainclothes officer had pulled up just in time to see Mr. Horn pointing his shotgun at both men across his front yard, that Mr. Ortiz had at one point started to run in a way that took him closer to Mr. Horn, and that both men "received gunfire from the rear."

That fact, alone, however, was not necessarily conclusive, Captain Corbett said. "It tells an investigator something, but not everything," he added. "They could still have been seen as a threat."

Horn was not arrested the night of the shooting, nor charged by a grand jury with any crime.[789]

While it is possible to justify actions taken under either stand your ground laws or the castle doctrine by appealing to the Natural Law tradition, or natural rights more general, this is not necessary. From a Legal Positivists' perspective, one need only establish that there are, in fact, existing and legitimately passed laws that authorize such behavior—and, in these cases, the permission granted by the laws might well go beyond what might be considered morally permissible from a natural rights perspective.

How, though, in general, would a Legal Positivism approach to the Second Amendment operate? According to Blocher et al., evaluating the Second Amendment as (positive) law to understand its meaning and scope involves six considerations: text, precedent, history, social practice, structure, and prudence.[790] We will consider each (briefly) in turn.

Text

The text of the Second Amendment itself is very brief, and somewhat opaque.

A well regulated Militia, being necessary to the security of a free State, the right of the people to keep and bear Arms shall not be infringed.

Perhaps especially because of the "historical" language used, the text itself is far from clear and obvious. Vigorous debate concerning what is meant by "militia," "the people," and "arms," has lasted decades, if not longer. Does the Second Amendment provide an individual right to bear arms, or only a collective right – and specifically only through membership in a "well regulated" militia? Does a "well regulated militia" specify only a government sanctioned military body, or would it include private militias? Does "the people" refer to individual people, or only the people as a collective? What is included in "arms?" Does that refer only to the firearms available at the time the Second Amendment was adopted? Does it include fully automatic weapons? Nuclear missiles? Clearly, nuance and interpretation are inevitable. Even the most zealous Second Amendment supporter doesn't seem to think that literally everyone has a right to literally any weapon whatsoever. It will be difficult to find someone who thinks that the Constitutional right to bear arms includes convicted felons while they are in prison! Or someone who thinks that nuclear weapons should be legally available at the local gun shop for anyone who could afford them.

Precedent

Precedent refers to rules and principles established by prior cases. This would include, for example, the precedent established by the *Heller* decision. The use of precedent means that the scope and meaning of laws goes beyond the original literal text.

History

Considerations of history take into account historical context concerning when the law was established, including the understanding of law, rights, social conventions, etc., at that time.

---

[789] https://www.nytimes.com/2007/12/13/us/13texas.html

[790] Blocher et al, 112.

Justice Scalia is clearly appealing to history in his opinion in *Heller*, openly referring to the kinds of rights that the Founders would have understood themselves to have. Like text, the use of history requires interpretation as well. Which pieces of evidence from history should be used in determining the scope and meaning of the law? Speaking specifically of gun laws, "some major colonial cities regulated the storage of gunpowder in city limits. Does that provide a historical precedent for safe storage requirements today? Some cities – including famous cow towns like Dodge City and Tombstone – effectively banned handguns within the city limits."[791] And what about overtly *racist* gun laws, several of which will be provided later in this section? Should our contemporary understanding of the Second Amendment be "originalist" in that sense as well, requiring that we exclude racial and ethnic minorities from gun ownership? As a matter of history, it is undeniable that "gun rights" *originally* were meant to apply only to white people.

Social practice

Similar to appealing to history, considerations of social practice involves taking into account how laws function in society today. In the *Heller* decision, the majority ruling extended Second Amendment protection to weapons "in common use." "Common use" was the relevant social practice for that decision. But again, interpretation is necessary. What makes a weapon "common?" Do we consider the number of different kinds of weapons currently owned? But this is question begging. What if certain kinds of weapons have been illegal in most states, and therefore very few people own them, but the ban on these weapons is precisely what is being challenged in a Second Amendment case? In such a case, it would hardly be illuminating to justify maintaining a ban on a weapon because very few people use them, when the reason why very few people use them is because they have been

banned! Which "uses" are relevant? Hunting? Home defense only? What about criminal usage?

Structure

Structure considerations involve the recognition that laws (including laws that address rights) operate in context, interacting with other laws and other rights. The Second Amendment, for example, is not the only Amendment in the Constitution, and the right to bear arms, however interpreted, is certainly not the only right protected by the Constitution. Bearing arms while protesting can very easily be intimidating, and thereby infringe upon other rights, or even the basic operations of democratic governing itself. In 2020, armed protesters in Michigan gathered not only at the State capital to protest Covid-19 restrictions, but later even outside the private residence of the Michigan Secretary of State to protest President Trump losing in that State's general election. The presence of dozens of gun-displaying protesters shouting obscenities through a bullhorn outside one's own home could certainly be experienced as intimidating, and the Michigan Secretary of State interpreted it that way.[792] "The gun debate, in other words, is not simply about a constitutional right on one side and policy considerations on the other; it is often about the accommodation of *multiple* constitutional interests."[793]

Prudence

Also subject to, and demanding, nuance and interpretation, Judges and legal scholars consider issues of prudence when determining the application and scope of the law. For example, Judges, and especially Supreme Court Justices, will often defer to other political branches and/or experts in their respective fields, particularly when legislative bodies are "functioning properly – or at least not imposing burdens on "discrete

---

[791] ibid., 116.
[792] https://www.npr.org/sections/biden-transition-updates/2020/12/07/943820889/

michigan-secretary-of-state-says-armed-protesters-descended-on-her-home-saturday
[793] Blocher et al, 120.

and insular minorities."[794]

As a very recent example, in the 2021 case of *South Bay United Pentecostal Church v. Newsom*, the Supreme Court ruled that California Governor Gavin Newsom's Covid-19 restrictions on indoor church services violated the Constitutional rights of practitioners. In her dissent, Justice Kagan implicitly appealed to prudence and explicitly appealed to expertise.

> *To state the obvious, judges do not know what scientists and public health experts do. I am sure that, in deciding this case, every Justice carefully examined the briefs and read the decisions below. But I cannot imagine that any of us delved into the scientific research on how COVID spreads, or studied the strategies for containing it. So it is alarming that the Court second-guesses the judgments of expert officials, and displaces their conclusions with its own. See Roman Catholic Diocese of Brooklyn v. Cuomo, ante, at 3 (SOTOMAYOR, J., dissenting). In the worst public health crisis in a century, this foray into armchair epidemiology cannot end well.*[795]

Although we've seen how various interpretations of the Second Amendment, including interpretations that are generous with respect to gun rights, are possible under the approach of Legal Positivism, Lund very clearly made his case in the Heritage Foundation position paper using an appeal to the Natural Law tradition. Using that tradition, and especially Locke, Lund argued that we have a natural right to self-defense and a consequent right to bear arms in service to that right, and that these rights are acknowledged and protected by the Second Amendment. It is possible, though, to use the very same tradition, and even the very same philosopher (viz., Locke), and arrive at a *different* conclusion about the Second Amendment.

(More) Natural Law & the Second Amendment

Heyman notes the commonly recognized divide with respect to the Second Amendment. "One position asserts that the Second Amendment was intended to guarantee an individual right to keep and bear arms. The other holds that the right is one that belongs to the people collectively, and that the right is essentially connected with the establishment of "[a] well-regulated militia.""[796] (As a personal editorial note, I would propose that some people actually claim that it supports *both*.)

As stated previously, the language itself is ambiguous. "The people" could be understood collectively, referring to the community as a whole, or individually. Indeed, the ambiguity of the language is why the Positivist approach we just considered relied on so many *other* elements in addition to the text.

Those appealing to the Natural Law tradition claim that there is an inalienable right to defend oneself and others against violence. People gather together by means of a social contract and form governments to better protect themselves. Within society, individuals have a right not only to protect themselves from others in cases of private violence, but also against the government itself should it become tyrannical and oppressive. However, this right to self-defense and self-preservation can't be effectively exercised if the people are denied arms. The Second Amendment, therefore, recognizes and enshrines the right to bear arms as an auxiliary right to a more foundational right of self-defense.

Heyman makes his *opposition* to this interpretation helpfully clear, stating that the object of his article is "to challenge this understanding of the natural rights tradition. While that tradition did hold that individuals in a state of nature had a broad right to use force for self-preservation, that right was not an inalienable one. Instead, when individuals entered into society, they largely gave up this

---

[794] ibid., 122.

[795] https://www.supremecourt.gov/opinions/20pdf/20a136_bq7c.pdf

[796] Heyman, Steven J. "Natural Rights and the Second Amendment," *76 Chi-Kent L. Rev.* 237 (2000), 238

right in return for the protection they obtained under the law. And although the people retain the right to resist tyranny, this was a right to belong to the community as a whole rather than to individuals. For these reasons, the natural rights tradition provides more support for a collective right than for an individualist interpretation of the Second Amendment."[797]

Like Lund, Heyman appeals to Locke—though he comes to a very different conclusion on that basis. We have reviewed Locke above, so only a very brief reminder is warranted.

In the state of nature, everyone has a natural right to life, liberty and property. They also have a right to do whatever is necessary to preserve them, within the limits set by the law of nature. Within the state of nature, people have a right not only to use force in self-defense, but also individually or collectively to punish people who violate the laws of nature and harm others. If one assumes that weapons are useful (let alone necessary) for these purposes, then it would be easy to infer an individual right to bear arms from Locke's theory. In Heyman's view, however, this conclusion is mistaken.

> *For the thrust of Locke's discussion is not to endorse a broad private right to use force, but exactly the opposite: to show why such a right must be radically restricted. . . According to Locke, it is precisely the unrestrained use of force that makes the state of nature intolerable. The problem is that when every individual is a judge in his own case, he is likely to act out of passion and self-interest, pursuing his own advantage at the expense of the rights of others. The lack of a clear, settled law to govern interactions between individuals aggravates the situation. Moreover, even when one is in the right, one may lack sufficient power to protect oneself and one's rights.... The remedy for these evils lies in the social contract, in which individuals agree to form a society for the preservation of their life, liberty, and property. The terms of this*

> *contract have a crucial bearing on our problem. According to Locke, when an individual enters civil society, "he gives up" his "Power... of doing whatsoever he thought fit for the preservation of himself, and the rest of Mankind,... to be regulated by Laws made by the Society, so far forth as the preservation of himself and the rest of that Society shall require; which Laws of the Society in many things can find liberty he had by the Law of Nature."*[798]

In other words, while Locke proposes that there is a natural right to use force for self-defense and self-preservation, this right is not *in*alienable. In fact, it is *alienated* when we enter into the social contract by virtue of surrendering the right to a private pursuit of justice and relying instead on the community for both general protection and the pursuit of justice against offenders.

> *For the very notion of political society is that rights should be determined and disputes resolved not to the "private judgment" of each individual, backed by private force, but rather by the public judgment of the community, as expressed in general laws enacted by the legislature, administered by impartial judges, and enforced by the power of the community as a whole.*[799]

The right to use force in self-defense and for self-preservation is an alienable right, one which individuals give up in the act of forming the social contract. This is in contrast, according to Locke, to the inalienable right to freedom of conscience. It is literally impossible to surrender the freedom to form your own beliefs. We are free to think as we wish regardless of any legal constraints that someone might try to impose on us. This freedom is not subject to separation from the person, unlike the freedom to use force (especially with weapons) which is very much subject to

---

[797] ibid., 241.
[798] ibid., 242-243.

[799] ibid., 243.

separation. Moreover, freedom of conscience, when exercised, doesn't harm others, but the use of force (even when justified) easily and almost inevitably impacts the rights of others. "This point is summed up in Locke's remark that 'though Men uniting into politick societies, have resigned up to the publick the disposing of all their Force, so that they cannot employ it against any Fellow Citizen, any farther than the Law of the Country directs; yet they still retain the power of Thinking' as they like, since that right is an inalienable one."[800]

If individuals truly did have an inalienable right to use force for self-defense, one might reasonably think they also have a right to possess and use weapons (including firearms) for that purpose, but that argument no longer holds if the right to use force is surrendered upon the creation of the social contract. An important exception worth noting is that Locke recognizes that the individual right to self-defense, while generally surrendered over to the community as a whole, is *retained* by the individual should they face an "imminent" attack, such that there is no time or opportunity to appeal to the community for protection. As an example, if someone tackles me from behind and starts violently assaulting me, I am not morally or legally required to refrain from defending myself with force just because I have theoretically "surrendered" my individual right of self-defense over to the community. In that sort of scenario, the police and the criminal justice system, while in existence, couldn't possibly respond sufficiently quickly to protect me, and I therefore have a right to use force on my own behalf. This exception indicates that the right to self-defense is complicated, for Locke. Strictly speaking, that individual right is alienable, but retained under certain dire circumstances. Although this does indicate that we retain an individual right to self-defense (at least under certain circumstances), this does *not* necessarily indicate that we have a corresponding right to possess and use firearms.

When a person is assaulted, he may do anything reasonably necessary to defend himself. This includes not only using his own natural force, but also using anything else in his possession, such as a deadly weapon. It does not follow, however, that the legislature cannot properly make a prospective judgment that citizens would enjoy a higher level security if the possession of such weapons were restricted or even banned.... Under these circumstances, it is an empirical question whether the community would be safer with or without restrictions on guns. And that would seem to be a question for the legislature to decide.[801]

In other words, individual gun rights, if they exist, would exist in the "Positivist" sense of a legal right, as opposed to being derived as a natural right. Such a right, even if it exists, is therefore subject to *change*.

To summarize, Lockean theory holds that when individuals establish a society, they give up the right to use force against others in return for the protection they receive from the community. Immediate self-defense is an exception to this principle, for in that case there is no opportunity to appeal for protection. But one way in which the government can protect its citizens is by regulating the possession and use of weapons. For this reason, such regulation appears to fall on the alienable, not be inalienable, side of the line.... That is not to say, of course, that Locke can be counted as a supporter of gun control laws, for he never addressed the issue. Instead, the point is simply that it is a mistake to assume, as many adherents of the individual right interpretation do, that the issue can be resolved through an appeal to the notion of inalienable rights. Instead, from a Lockean perspective, the matter is one that appears to fall within the legislature's power to regulate for the common good.[802]

---

[800] ibid., 244.
[801] ibid., 244-245.
[802] ibid. 246.

Although Locke recognizes that the individual has a right to resist tyranny in theory, practically speaking, this right will only meaningfully be exercised by the community given how unlikely it is that a single individual, or even a few, would be able to successfully resist the power of their government. Moreover, leaving it up to the judgment of a single person, or a small collection, would make the society vulnerable to capricious rebellions and undermine the stability of the social contract.

After all, the purpose of the social contract is to avoid a state of war by excluding "all private judgment" and private force, and ensuring that disputes are resolved as far as possible by the public judgment of the community.... For all of these reasons, Locke's account strongly focuses on the right of the people as a whole to resist tyranny. . . . When the community determines that the government has become oppressive, it has a collective right to resist the suppression by force, to overthrow the government, and to institute a new one. Implicit in the rights to resistance and revolution is the right to take up arms against a tyrannical government. This too is a right that belongs to the people as a whole, not to individuals as such.[803]

Heyman argues that is a mistake to think that Locke either endorses an individual right to bear arms, or that he clearly opposes it. Although he argues that Locke clearly has a collective right to self-defense in mind, he acknowledges that his theory would allow for a legislature to permit individuals access to firearms. "Whether the path of greater safety lies in retaining a right to arms or not cannot be determined by natural rights theory, i.e., by reason alone, but only by the people themselves when they establish a positive Constitution."[804]

The risk of individuals having access to firearms, of course, is that they might be used "improperly," for either criminal or (unjustified)

political purposes. If that risk could be nullified or at least mitigated, then there could be a basis under a Lockean system for individuals to retain a right to bear arms. Heyman proposes that understanding the Second Amendment as applying to militias rather than individuals can satisfy that condition, "assuming, that is, that citizens were willing to undergo the discipline and burdens incident to bearing arms within this collective context.... [The Second Amendment] can be understood to protect the collective right of the people to have arms, subject to collective discipline and control within the context of "[a] well-regulated Militia.""[805] He thinks this militia-centered interpretation is especially fruitful when we consider the clear influence of the Massachusetts Constitution of 1780 on the eventual wording of the Second Amendment.

The Massachusetts Constitution was drafted by John Adams, a full seven years before the drafting of the U.S. Constitution even began. The language used by the Massachusetts Constitution, and the particular rights enshrined by it, bear an obvious and striking resemblance to the rights and language eventually adopted for the U.S. Constitution, and provide insight into the worldview of the founders, particularly with regard to their understanding of rights and the limitations of government at the time. The Massachusetts Constitution is particularly useful given how carefully it is written with respect to the use of individual or collective terms. It is always abundantly clear whether "people" refers to individuals as individuals, or the community as a whole. While the entire document is interesting, the relevant section is Article XVII.

The people have a right to keep and bear arms for the common defense. And as, in time of peace, armies are dangerous to liberty, they ought not to be maintained without the consent of the legislature; and the military shall always be held in an exact subordination to the civil authority and shall be governed by it.[806]

---

[803] ibid., 248-249. Emphasis in the original.
[804] ibid., 250.

[805] ibid.
[806] ibid., 262.

Consistent with how "the people" is used in every other occurrence in the Massachusetts Constitution, "the people" refers to the community as a whole, and not to individuals as individuals. Moreover, this Article specifically points out that keeping and bearing arms is for the purpose of "common defense." While this would not necessarily preclude individual self-defense, it is obvious that Adams had collective defense, exercised collectively, in mind. Finally, the warning against standing professional armies, and the need for the military to be subordinated to civil authorities, provides further clear evidence that the threat being envisioned is a tyrannical government, not a lone criminal. The proper context for understanding the right to bear arms under Article XVII is collective defense against a tyrannical government. Neither individual self-defense against a home invasion robbery (etc.), nor an individual right to resist "tyranny" is what is being protected by this Article. While it is possible that the Second Amendment of the U.S. Constitution was intended to convey something radically different, that is an argument that would have to be made, and a historical analysis of the progression of language from State constitutions such as this one, and various drafts of the Second Amendment of the U.S. Constitution, actually shows continuity, rather than any sort of meaningful difference in context or intent.

Virginia proposal to amend the Constitution:

> That the people have a right to keep and bear arms; they well-regulated Militia composed of the body of the people trained to arms is the proper, natural and safe defense of a free State. The standing armies in time of peace are dangerous to liberty, and therefore ought to be avoided, as far as the circumstances and protection of the Community will admit; and that in all cases the military should be under strict subordination to and governed by the Civil

power.[807]

This recommendation was endorsed by the ratifying conventions of both North Carolina and New York, and became the starting point of the first draft of the Second Amendment. James Madison introduced his draft in June of 1789.

Madison draft:

> The right of the People to keep and bear arms shall not be infringed; a well armed, and well-regulated militia being the best security of a free country: but no person religiously scrupulous of bearing arms, shall be compelled to render military service in person.[808]

The House of Representatives adopted this version:

> A well regulated militia, composed of the body of the People, being the best security of a free State, the right of the People to keep and bear arms, shall not be infringed, but no one religiously scrupulous of bearing arms, shall be compelled to render military service in person.[809]

The Senate adopted this version (which was the final version):

> A well regulated militia, being necessary to the security of a free State, the right of the people to keep and bear arms, shall not be infringed.[810]

Note that in several of the iterations of what would become the Second Amendment there is an explicit exemption for conscientious objectors. This indicates that "bearing arms" was understood in the context of "rendering military service in person." There would be no need to exempt people for religious reasons if the Second Amendment addressed an individual right to

---

[807] ibid., 274.
[808] ibid.

[809] ibid., 275.
[810] ibid.

bear arms for personal self-defense. Any conscientious objectors could simply choose not to possess weapons, as an individual. It is only in the context of mandatory military service in the local militia that there is any need to even consider the status of conscientious objectors.

The clear implication is that the right to "bear arms" relates to service in the militia. Second, both the Virginia proposal and the House version refer to a militia "composed of the body of the people." This usage suggests that "the people" who have a "right to keep and bear arms" are the same as "the body of the people trained to arms" that constitutes the militia. As in the state's declaration of rights, references to the militia and to the people's right to bear arms appear to be two different ways of saying the same thing.[811]

Most of the State constitutions at the time did not explicitly mention a right to bear arms, but rather spoke of citizen militias. The Virginia Bill of Rights, drafted in 1776, eleven years prior to the drafting of the U.S. Constitution, for example, contains the following:

That a well-regulated militia, composed of the body of the people, trained to arms, is the proper, natural, and safe defense of a free State; that standing armies, in time of peace, should be avoided, as dangerous to liberty; and that in all cases the military should be under strict subordination to, and governed by, the civil power.[812]

The language and context here is essentially the same as in the Massachusetts Constitution: "within the militia, the people had a right to bear arms, and they exercised this right through the militia."[813]

Fearing an overly strong federal government, and especially how it might use the military, it was proposed that the community should rely, as much as possible, on militias rather than regular standing armies. Theoretically, the existence of a well-armed, trained, and disciplined local militia would reduce the need for a standing army in the first place. In addition, in the tragic event that the federal government did become tyrannical, "the people," acting collectively through the militias, would be empowered to resist.[814]

This notion of a citizen militia represented an advance in natural rights theory in two respects. First, whereas Locke tended to view the people as an ultimate but dormant power existing outside the government, liberal Republicanism integrated people into the state through the militia, just as they were also integrated through Republican political institutions. In this way, liberty was made more secure. Second, if a danger of tyranny should arise, the militia provided an effective means through which the people could exercise their collective right to resistance and revolution – rights that were affirmed by many of the state constitutions.[815]

In summary, Heyman claims that in "late-eighteenth-century America,... the right to bear arms was generally understood to be a collective right that was exercised through a citizen militia. This is the right that was secured by the Second Amendment."[816] He claims that a virtue of his interpretation is that it allows the Amendment to be read as a coherent whole, rather than as seeking to accomplish two distinct goals of securing individual rights to arms as well as recognizing the importance of Militias. The "coherent" and focused version holds that the purpose that the Second Amendment was meant to serve was, first, to reaffirm the importance of the militias, and to ensure that the federal government could not disarm it. Simultaneously,

---

[811] ibid.
[812] ibid., 263.
[813] ibid.

[814] ibid., 265.
[815] ibid., 265-266.
[816] ibid., 271.

the Second Amendment aimed to reduce the need for a standing army.[817] This means that individual rights to arms was to be understood in the context of serving in such militias.

Given that historical context, Heyman claims that the status of the Second Amendment is (and should be) different today. We no longer have or rely on citizen Militias in the same sense. The closest thing we have to them are State National Guards. We also have a very large and powerful standing military, against which individual resistance, or even the resistance of State Militias would be futile. However, Heyman claims this is no cause for concern or regret.

> [The] American founders regarded armed revolution as a last resort. It meant the breakdown of the constitutional order and a return to the state of war, in which disputes could be resolved only through force. Instead, the founders sought to prevent tyranny primarily through such institutions as representative government, the separation of powers, an independent judiciary, and constitutional protections for individual rights. These institutions have worked so well that the notion of armed revolution has become anachronistic. This is a sign of strength, not weakness, in our constitutional system. In short, the right to arms has evolved from an "auxiliary right" to an archaic one.[818]

In their own way, both the Natural Law and Legal Positivism approaches have drawn upon history to make their cases. Although Heyman and Lund come to very different conclusions, both of them consult the historical record to determine what they think Locke and the Founders intended with respect to the right to defend oneself, and the Second Amendment. Blocher et al cite history as one of several factors relevant to determining what, exactly, has been "posited" as law according to the standards of Legal Positivism. The final framework we will

employ, Critical Race Theory, will *also* consider historical context, but with a focus on how race has played a role in the understanding of gun rights and gun control in the United States.

Critical Race Theory & the Second Amendment

Though certainly not aligned with the principles or purposes of CRT, even the Heritage Foundation position statement with which we began this section notes (without any commentary) the overtly racist interpretation and application of gun rights in the infancy of the United States.

> Restrictions on the right to arms during the founding period were limited to a few laws directed against distrusted political minorities like Blacks, Indians, and British loyalists, and an occasional safety regulation dealing with such matters as the storage of gunpowder and the discharge of firearms in crowded places.[819]

That is a *very* casual way to acknowledge that, from the very beginning of the United States, gun laws were racialized. Roxanne Dunbar-Ortiz significantly expands upon the racial aspects of the history of gun rights and gun control in the United States, and likewise rejects the interpretation of the Second Amendment according to which the Amendment was meant to apply only to individuals while serving in an official Militia capacity. Instead, she claims that the Second Amendment very specifically enshrines an individual right to possess and bear arms. She defends this interpretation first by claiming that the Militia interpretation would be redundant. Militias, understood as government controlled military units, were authorized and acknowledged by Article 1, Section 8, Clause 15 of the U.S. Constitution "to execute the Laws of the Union, suppress Insurrections and repel Invasion". This section was already in the Constitution prior to the addition of the Bill of Rights, including the Second Amendment. And, in

---

[817] ibid., 277.

[818] ibid., 283.

[819] Lund, 11.

Article 2, Section 2, the President of the United States is designated as commander in chief of the state Militias "when called into the actual Service of the United States." With Militias already established in the Constitution prior to the Bill of Rights, she claims that "the Second Amendment (like the other ten Amendments) enshrined an individual right. The second Amendment's language specifically gave individuals and families the right to form volunteer militias to attack Indians and take their lands."[820]

She also supports her individual interpretation claim by situating the Second Amendment within a historical context of land appropriation and suppression of both Native Americans and Black persons—especially enslaved Black persons.

> *The militias referred to in the Second Amendment were intended as a means for white people to eliminate Indigenous communities in order to take their land, and for slave patrols to control Black people.*[821]

Considering first the appropriation of Native land, she argues that colonists originally established Militias "for the purpose of raiding and razing Indigenous communities and seizing their lands and resources."[822] Colonial laws not only allowed settlers to possess arms, in some cases firearms possession and maintenance was even *required*. In 1658, the colony of Virginia ordered every settler home to have a functioning firearm, and later even provided government loans for those who could not afford to buy a weapon. The colony of New England passed a requirement in 1632 that each (white male) person have a functioning firearm along with two pounds of gunpowder and ten pounds of bullets. Households could be fined for either missing or defective arms or ammunition. She claims that the Second Amendment, ratified in 1791, enshrined these obligations as Constitutional

law.

The second part of her historical thesis concerns slave patrols. While Militias originally formed and were used to seize Native land, and defend against Native resistance, with the development of the plantation economy they "evolved" to be used as slave patrols as well.

> *The 1661 and 1688 slave codes in the British Caribbean colony of Barbados extended the task of controlling enslaved Africans from overseers and slavers to all white settlers, in effect shifting private responsibility to the public. Any enslaved person outside the direct control of the slaver or overseer required passes and was subject to questioning by a slave patrol, as well as by any member of the European population; free Black men were denied such power. This collective racial policing was in addition to the traditional English constabulary that investigated and detained European residents for infractions of laws.*

> *British slavers from Barbados moved in large numbers to the South Carolina colony after 1670, and brought the slave patrol practice with them. By 1704, the South Carolina colonial government had codified slave patrols and embedded them within the already existing volunteer militias, whose principal role was to repel Native Americans whose land they had appropriated. Members of slave patrols were drawn from militia rolls in every locale. The South Carolina structure of slave patrols was adopted in other colonies by the mid-eighteenth century and would remain relatively unchanged until the Civil War.*[823]

By the late seventeenth century, slave codes had been developed in numerous colonies,

---

[820] Dunbar-Ortiz, Roxanne. *Loaded. A Disarming History of the Second Amendment*. City Light Books. San Francisco, 2018, 18

[821] ibid., 37.
[822] ibid., 35.
[823] ibid., 60.

including mandatory slave patrols drawn from existing militias. In 1727, the Virginia colony enacted a law requiring militias to create slave patrols, and imposed fines on white people who refused to serve.[824] Instructions for such a patrol in North Carolina, as outlined in an 1860 text, include the following:

> *The patrol shall visit the Negro houses in their respective districts as often as may be necessary, and may inflict a punishment, not exceeding fifteen lashes, on all slaves they may find off their owner's plantations, without a proper permit or pass, designating the place or places, to which the slaves have leave to go. The patrol shall also visit all suspected places, and suppress all unlawful collections of slaves; shall be diligent in apprehending all runaway Negroes in the respective districts; shall be vigilant and endeavor to detect all thefts, and bring the perpetrators to justice, and also all persons guilty of trading with slaves; and if, upon picking up a slave and chastising him, as herein directed, he shall behave insolently, they may inflict further punishment for his misconduct, not exceeding thirty-nine lashes[825].*

After the Civil War and the official end of slavery, slave patrols were reimagined and rebranded for the period of Reconstruction and Jim Crow.

> *Most ominously, elite white Southerners formed volunteer militias under the guise of private rifle clubs. By 1876, South Carolina had more than 240 such clubs. This allowed thousands of Confederate combat veterans, along with former Confederate guerrillas, to mobilize quickly. Of course, the KKK was the most ominous terrorist organization to emerge from*

> *these efforts, its purpose being to subdue the Freedmen and control Black labor when slavery ended.[826]*

The right to bear arms, according to this historical analysis, must be understood within the context of the promotion and protection of white supremacy. The "flip side" of gun rights, gun control, is *also* susceptible to this context. A partial (chronological) listing of gun control laws based on race, and some related and relevant historical events, includes the following:[827]

1640 Virginia **Race-based total gun and self-defense ban.**
"Prohibiting negroes, slave and free, from carrying weapons including clubs." (*The Los Angeles Times*, " To Fight Crime, Some Blacks Attack Gun Control," January 19, 1992)

1640 Virginia **Race-based total gun ban.**
"That all such free Mulattoes, Negroes and Indians...shall appear without arms." [7 The Statues at Large; Being a Collection of all the Laws of Virginia, from the First Session of the Legislature, in the Year 1619, p. 95 (W.W. Henning ed. 1823).] (*GMU CR LJ*, p. 67)

1712 Virginia **Race-based total gun ban.**
"An Act for Preventing Negroes Insurrections." (Henning, p. 481) (*GMU CR LJ*, p. 70)

1712 South Carolina **Race-based total gun ban.**
"An act for the better ordering and governing of Negroes and slaves." [7 Statutes at Large of South Carolina, p. 353-54 (D.J. McCord ed. 1836-1873).] (*GMU CR LJ*, p. 70)

1791 United States **2nd Amendment to the U.S. Constitution ratified.**

---

824 ibid., 61.
825 Instructions from an 1860 text, *The Practice at law in North Carolina*, quoted in ibid., 63.
826 ibid., 67.

827 This list was compiled by Steve Ekwall, and has been copied verbatim from his text: https://www.sedgwickcounty.org/media/2909 3/the-racist-origins-of-us-gun-control.pdf

Reads: "A well regulated Militia, being necessary to the security of a free State, the right of the people to keep and bear Arms, shall not be infringed."

1792 United States **Blacks excluded from the militia, i.e. law-abiding males thus instilled with the right to own guns.**
Uniform Militia Act of 1792 "called for the enrollment of every free, able-bodied white male citizen between the ages of eighteen and forty-five" to be in the militia, and specified that every militia member was to "provide himself with a musket or firelock, a bayonet, and ammunition." [1 Stat. 271 (*Georgetown Law Journal*, Vol. 80, No. 2, "The Second Amendment: Toward an Afro-Americanist Reconsideration," Robert Cottrol and Raymond Diamond, 1991, p. 331)]

1806 Louisiana **Complete gun and self-defense ban for slaves.**
Black Code, ch. 33, Sec. 19, Laws of La. 150, 160 (1806) provided that a slave was denied the use of firearms and all other offensive weapons. (*GLJ*, p. 337)

1811 Louisiana **Complete gun ban for slaves.**
Act of April 8, 1811, ch. 14, 1811 Laws of La. 50, 53-54, forbade sale or delivery of firearms to slaves. (*Id.*)

1819 South Carolina **Master's permission required for gun possession by slave.**
Act of Dec. 18, 1819, 1819 Acts of S.C. 28, 31, prohibited slaves outside the company of whites or without written permission from their master from using or carrying firearms unless they were hunting or guarding the master's plantation. (*Id.*)

1825 Florida **Slave and free black homes searched for guns for confiscation.**
"An Act to Govern Patrols," 1825 Acts of Fla. 52, 55 - Section 8 provided that white citizen patrols "shall enter into all negro houses and suspected places, and search for arms and other offensive or improper weapons, and may lawfully seize and take away all such arms, weapons, and ammunition...." Section 9 provided that a slave might carry a firearm under this statute either by means of the weekly renewable license or if "in the presence of some white person." (*Id.*)

1828 Florida **Free blacks permitted to carry guns if court approval.**
Act of Nov. 17, 1828 Sec. 9, 1828 Fla. Laws 174, 177;
Act of Jan. 12, 1828, Sec. 9, 1827 Fla. Laws 97, 100 - Florida went back and forth on the question of licenses for free blacks; twice in 1828, Florida enacted provisions providing for free blacks to carry and use firearms upon obtaining a license from a justice of the peace. (*Id.*)

1831 Florida **Race-based total gun ban.**
Act of Jan. 1831, 1831 Fla. Laws 30 - Florida repealed all provision for firearm licenses for free blacks. (*Id.* p. 337-38)

1831 Delaware **Free blacks permitted to carry guns if court approval.**
In the December 1831 legislative session, Delaware required free blacks desiring to carry firearms to obtain a license from a justice of the peace. [[Herbert Aptheker, *Nat Turner's Slave Rebellion*, p. 74-75 (1966).] (*GLJ*, p. 338)

1831 Maryland **Race-based total gun ban.**
In the December 1831 legislative session, Maryland entirely prohibited free blacks from carrying arms. (Aptheker, p. 75) (*Id.*, p. 338)

1831 Virginia **Race-based total gun ban.**
In the December 1831 legislative session, Virginia entirely prohibited free blacks from carrying arms. (Aptheker, p. 81) (*Id.*, p. 338)

1833 Florida **Slave and free black homes searched for guns for confiscation.**

Act of Feb. 17, 1833, ch. 671, Sec. 15, 17, 1833 Fla. Laws 26, 29 authorized white citizen patrols to seize arms found in the homes of slaves and free blacks, and provided that blacks without a proper explanation for the presence of the firearms be summarily punished, without benefit of a judicial tribunal. (*Id.* p. 338)

1833 Georgia **Race-based total gun ban.**
Act of Dec. 23, 1833, Sec. 7, 1833 Ga. Laws 226, 228 declared that "it shall not be lawful for any free person of colour in this state, to own, use, or carry fire arms of any description whatever." (*Id.*)

1840 Florida **Complete gun ban for slaves.**
Act of Feb. 25, 1840, no. 20, Sec. 1, 1840 Acts of Fla. 22-23 made sale or delivery of firearms to slaves forbidden. (*Id.* p. 337)

1840 Texas **Complete gun ban for slaves.**
"An Act Concerning Slaves," Sec. 6, 1840 Laws of Tex. 171, 172, ch. 58 of the Texas Acts of 1850 prohibited slaves from using firearms altogether from 1842-1850. (*Journal of Criminal Law and Criminology*, Northwestern University, Vol. 85, No. 3, "Gun Control and Economic Discrimination: The Melting-Point Case-In-Point," T. Markus Funk, 1995, p. 797)

1844 North Carolina **Race-based gun ban upheld because free blacks "not citizens."**
In *State v. Newsom*, 27 N.C. 250 (1844), the Supreme Court of North Carolina upheld a Slave Code law prohibiting free blacks from carrying firearms on the grounds that they were not citizens. (*GMU CR LJ*, p. 70)

1845 North Carolina **Complete gun ban for slaves.**
Act of Jan. 1, 1845, ch. 87, Sec. 1, 2, 1845 Acts of N.C. 124 made sale or delivery of firearms to slaves forbidden. (*GLJ*, p. 337)

1847 Florida **Slave and free black homes searched for guns for confiscation.**

Act of Jan. 6, 1847, ch. 87 Sec. 11, 1846 Fla. Laws 42, 44 provided that white citizen patrols might search the homes of blacks, both free and slave and confiscate arms held therein. (*Id.* p. 338)

1848 Georgia **Race-based gun ban upheld because free blacks "not citizens."**
In *Cooper v. Savannah*, 4 Ga. 68, 72 (1848), the Georgia Supreme Court ruled "free persons of color have never been recognized here as citizens; they are not entitled to bear arms, vote for members of the legislature, or to hold any civil office." (*GMU CR LJ*, p. 70)

1852 Mississippi **Race-based complete gun ban.**
Act of Mar. 15, 1852, ch. 206, 1852 Laws of Miss. 328 forbade ownership of firearms by both free blacks and slaves. (*JCLC* NWU, p. 797)

1857 United States **High Court upholds slavery since blacks "not citizens."**
In *Dred Scott v. Sandford*, 60 U.S. (19 How.) 393 (1857), Chief Justice Taney argued if members of the African race were "citizens" they would be exempt from the special "police regulations" applicable to them. "It would give to persons of the negro race...full liberty of speech...to hold public meetings upon political affairs, and to keep and carry arms wherever they went." (*Id.* p. 417) U.S. Supreme Court held that descendants of Africans who were imported into this country and sold as slaves were not included nor intended to be included under the word "citizens" in the Constitution, whether emancipated or not, and remained without rights or privileges except such as those which the government might grant them, thereby upholding slavery. Also held that a slave did not become free when taken into a free state; that Congress cannot bar slavery in any territory; and that blacks could not be citizens.

1860 Georgia **Complete gun ban for slaves.**

Act of Dec. 19, 1860, no. 64, Sec. 1, 1860 Acts of Ga. 561 forbade sale or delivery of firearms to slaves. (*GLJ*, p. 337)

1861 United States **Civil War begins.**
1861 Florida **Slave and free black homes searched for guns for confiscation.**
Act of Dec. 17, 1861, ch. 1291, Sec. 11, 1861 Fla. Laws 38, 40 provided once again that white citizen patrols might search the homes of blacks, both free and slave, and confiscate arms held therein. (*Id.* p. 338)

1863 United States **Emancipation Proclamation -- President Lincoln issued proclamation "freeing all slaves in areas still in rebellion."**
1865 Mississippi **Blacks require police approval to own guns, unless in military.**
Mississippi Statute of 1865 prohibited blacks, not in the military "and not licensed so to do by the board of police of his or her county" from keeping or carrying "fire-arms of any kind, or any ammunition, dirk or bowie knife." [reprinted in 1 *Documentary History of Reconstruction: Political, Military, Social, Religious, Educational and Industrial, 1865 to the Present Time*, p. 291, (Walter L. Fleming, ed., 1960.)] (*GLJ*, p. 344)

1865 Louisiana **Blacks require police and employer approval to own guns, unless serving in military.**
Louisiana Statute of 1865 prohibited blacks, not in the military service, from "carrying fire-arms, or any kind of weapons...without the special permission of his employers, approved and indorsed by the nearest and most convenient chief of patrol." (Fleming, p. 280)(*GLJ*, p. 344)

1865 United States **Civil War ends May 26.**
1865 United States **Slavery abolished as of Dec. 18, 1865.**
13th Amendment abolishing slavery was ratified. Reads: "Section 1. Neither slavery nor involuntary servitude, except as a punishment for crime whereof the party shall

have been duly convicted, shall exist within the United States, or in any place subject to their jurisdiction. Section 2. Congress shall have power to enforce this article by appropriate legislation."

1866 Alabama **Race-based total gun ban.**
Black Code of Alabama in January 1866 prohibited blacks to own or carry firearms or other deadly weapons and prohibited "any person to sell, give, or lend fire-arms or ammunition of any description whatever" to any black. [*The Reconstruction Amendments' Debates*, p. 209, (Alfred Avins ed., 1967)] (*GLJ*, p. 345)

1866 North Carolina **Rights of blacks can be changed by legislature.**
North Carolina Black Code, ch. 40, 1866 N.C. Sess. Laws 99 stated "All persons of color who are now inhabitants of this state shall be entitled to the same privileges, and are subject to the same burdens and disabilities, as by the laws of the state were conferred on, or were attached to, free persons of color, prior to the ordinance of emancipation, except as the same may be changed by law." (Avins, p. 291.) (*GLJ*, p. 344)

1866 United States **Civil Rights Act of 1866 enacted.**
CRA of 1866 did away with badges of slavery embodied in the "Black Codes," including those provisions which "prohibit any negro or mulatto from having fire-arms." [CONG. GLOBE, 39th Congress, 1st Session, pt. 1, 474 (29 Jan. 1866)] Senator William Saulsbury (D- Del) added "In my State for many years...there has existed a law...which declares that free negroes shall not have the possession of firearms or ammunition. This bill proposes to take away from the States this police power..." and thus voted against the bill. CRA of 1866 was a precursor to today's 42 USC Sec.1982, a portion of which still reads: "All citizens of the United States shall have the same right, in every state and territory, as is enjoyed by white citizens

thereof to inherit, purchase, lease, sell, hold and convey real and personal property."

1866 United States **Proposed 14th Amendment to U.S. Constitution debated.**
Opponents of the 14th Amendment objected to its adoption because they opposed federal enforcement of the freedoms in the bill of rights. Sen. Thomas A. Hendricks (D-Ind.) said "if this Amendment be adopted we will then carry the title [of citizenship] and enjoy its advantages in common with the negroes, the coolies, and the Indians." [CONG. GLOBE, 39th Congress, 1st Session, pt. 3, 2939 (4 June 1866)]. Sen. Reverdy Johnson, counsel for the slave owner in *Dred Scott*, opposed the Amendment because "it is quite objectionable to provide that 'no State shall make or enforce any law which shall abridge the privileges and immunities of citizens of the United States'." Thus, the 14th Amendment was viewed as necessary to buttress the Civil Rights Act of 1866, especially since the act "is pronounced void by the jurists and courts of the South," e.g. Florida has as "a misdemeanor for colored men to carry weapons...and the punishment...is whipping..." [CONG GLOBE, 39th Con., 1st Session, 504, pt. 4, 3210 (16 June 1866)].

1866 United States **Klu Klux Klan formed.**
Purpose was to terrorize blacks who voted; temporarily disbanded in 1871; reestablished in 1915. In debating what would become 42 USC Sec. 1983, today's federal civil rights statute, Representative Butler explained "This provision seemed to your committee to be necessary, because they had observed that, before these midnight marauders [the KKK] made attacks upon peaceful citizens, there were very many instances in the South where the sheriff of the county had preceded them and taken away the arms of their victims. This was especially noticeable in Union County, where all the negro population were disarmed by the sheriff only a few months ago under the

order of the judge...; and then, the sheriff having disarmed the citizens, the five hundred masked men rode at nights and murdered and otherwise maltreated the ten persons who were in jail in that county." [1464 H.R. REP. No. 37, 41st Cong., 3rd Sess. p. 7-8 (20 Feb. 1871)]

1867 United States **The Special Report of the Anti-Slavery Conference of 1867.**
Report noted with particular emphasis that under the Black Codes, blacks were "forbidden to own or bear firearms, and thus were rendered defenseless against assaults." (Reprinted in H. Hyman, *The Radical Republicans and Reconstruction*, p. 219, 1967.) (*GMU CR LJ*, p. 71)

1868 United States **14th Amendment to the U.S. Constitution adopted, conveying citizenship to blacks.**
Reads, in part: "Section 1. All persons born or naturalized in the United States, and subject to the jurisdiction thereof, are citizens of the United States and of the State wherein they reside. No state shall make or enforce any law which shall abridge the privileges or immunities of citizens of the United States; nor shall any State deprive any person of life, liberty, or property, without due process of law; nor deny to any person within its jurisdiction the equal protection of the laws. "Section 5. The Congress shall have power to enforce, by appropriate legislation, the provisions of this article."

1870 Tennessee **First "Saturday Night Special" economic handgun ban passed.**
In the first legislative session in which they gained control, white supremacists passed "An Act to Preserve the Peace and Prevent Homicide," which banned the sale of all handguns except the expensive "Army and Navy model handgun" which whites already owned or could afford to buy, and blacks could not. ("Gun Control: White Man's Law," William R. Tonso, *Reason*, December 1985) Upheld in *Andrews v. State*, 50 Tenn. (3 Heisk.) 165, 172 (1871) (*GMU CR LJ*, p. 74)

"The cheap revolvers of the late 19th and early 20th centuries were referred to as 'Suicide Specials,' the 'Saturday Night Special' label not becoming widespread until reformers and politicians took up the gun control cause during the 1960s. The source of this recent concern about cheap revolvers, as their new label suggest, has much in common with the concerns of the gun-law initiators of the post-Civil War South. As B. Bruce-Briggs has written in the *Public Interest*, `It is difficult to escape the conclusion that the 'Saturday Night Special' is emphasized because it is cheap and being sold to a particular class of people. The name is sufficient evidence -- the reference is to 'niggertown Saturday night.'" ("Gun Control: White Man's Law," William R. Tonso, *Reason*, December 1985)

1871 United States **Anti-KKK Bill debated in response to race-motivated violence in South.**

A report on violence in the South resulted in an anti-KKK bill that stated "That whoever shall, without due process of law, by violence, intimidation, or threats, take away or deprive any citizen of the United States of any arms or weapons he may have in his house or possession for the defense of his person, family, or property, shall be deemed guilty of a larceny thereof, and be punished as provided in this act for a felony." [1464 H.R. REP. No. 37, 41st Cong., 3rd Sess. p. 7-8 (20 Feb. 1871)]. Since Congress doesn't have jurisdiction over simple larceny, the language was removed from the anti-KKK bill, but this section survives today as 42 USC Sec. 1983: "That any person who, under color of any law,...of any State, shall subject, or cause to be subjected, any person... to the deprivation of any rights, privileges, or immunities to which...he is entitled under the Constitution...shall be liable...in any action at law...for redress...".

1875 United States **High Court rules has no power to stop KKK members from disarming blacks.**

In *United States v. Cruikshank*, 92 U.S. at 548-59 (1875) A member of the KKK, Cruikshank had been charged with violating the rights of two black men to peaceably assemble and to bear arms. The U.S. Supreme Court held that the federal government had no power to protect citizens against private action (not committed by federal or state government authorities) that deprived them of their constitutional rights under the 14th Amendment. The Court held that for protection against private criminal action, individuals are required to look to state governments. "The doctrine in Cruikshank, that blacks would have to look to state government for protection against criminal conspiracies gave the green light to private forces, often with the assistance of state and local governments, that sought to subjugate the former slaves and their descendants... With the protective arm of the federal government withdrawn, protection of black lives and property was left to largely hostile state governments." (*GLJ*, p. 348.)

1879 Tennessee **Second "Saturday Night Special" economic handgun ban passed.**

Tennessee revamped its economic handgun ban nine years later, passing "An Act to Prevent the sale of Pistols," which was upheld in *State v. Burgoyne*, 75 Tenn. 173, 174 (1881). (*GMU CR LJ*, p. 74)

1882 Arkansas **Third "Saturday Night Special" economic handgun ban passed.**

Arkansas followed Tennessee's lead by enacting a virtually identical "Saturday Night Special" law banning the sale of any pistols other than expensive "army or navy" model revolvers, which most whites had or could afford, thereby disarming blacks. Statute was upheld in *Dabbs v. State*, 39 Ark. 353 (1882) (*GMU CR LJ*, p. 74)

1893 Alabama **First all-gun economic ban passed.**
Alabama placed "'extremely heavy business and/or transactional taxes'" on the sale of handguns in an attempt "to put handguns out of the reach of blacks and poor whites." ("Gun Control: White Man's Law," William R. Tonso, *Reason*, December 1985)

1902 South Carolina **First total civilian handgun ban.**
The state banned all pistol sales except to sheriffs and their special deputies, which included the KKK and company strongmen. (Kates, "Toward a History of Handgun Prohibition in the United States" in *Restricting Handguns: The Liberal Skeptics Speak Out*, p. 15, 1979.) (*GMU CR LJ*, p. 76)

1906 Mississippi **Race-based confiscation through record-keeping.**
Mississippi enacted the first registration law for retailers in 1906, requiring them to maintain records of all pistol and pistol ammunition sales, and to make such records available for inspection on demand. (Kates, p. 14) (*GMU CR LJ*, p. 75)

1907 Texas **Fourth "Saturday Night Special" economic handgun ban.**
Placed "'extremely heavy business and/or transactional taxes'" on the sale of handguns in an attempt "to put handguns out of the reach of blacks and poor whites." ("Gun Control: White Man's Law," William R. Tonso, *Reason*, December 1985)

1911 New York **Police choose who can own guns lawfully.**
"Sullivan Law" enacted, requiring police permission, via a permit issued at their discretion, to own a handgun. Unpopular minorities were and are routinely denied permits. ("Gun Control: White Man's Law," William R. Tonso, *Reason*, December 1985)
"(T)here are only about 3,000 permits in New York City, and 25,000 carry permits. If you're a street-corner grocer in Manhattan, good luck getting a gun permit. But among those who have been able to wrangle a precious carry permit out of the city's bureaucracy are Donald Trump, Arthur Ochs Sulzburger, William Buckley, Jr., and David, John, Lawrence and Winthrop Rockefeller. Surprise." (Terrance Moran, "Racism and the Firearms Firestorm," *Legal Times*)

1934 United States **Gun Control Act of 1934 (National Firearms Act) passed.**

1941 Florida **Judge admits gun law passed to disarm black laborers.**
In concurring opinion narrowly construing a Florida gun control law passed in 1893, Justice Buford stated the 1893 law "was passed when there was a great influx of negro laborers in this State....The same condition existed when the Act was amended in 1901 and the Act was passed for the purpose of disarming the negro laborers....The statute was never intended to be applied to the white population and in practice has never been so applied...". *Watson v. Stone*, 148 Fla. 516, 524, 4 So.2d 700, 703 (1941) (*GMU CR LJ*, p. 69)

The list above provides a great many examples of racialized gun laws. For our purposes, we will consider only a couple (more recent) examples.

As can be the case with numerous other issues, not every law or policy that has discriminatory *impact* must have been enacted with conscious discriminatory *intent*. As an example, in the 1990 case of *Richmond Tenants Org. v. Redevelopment and Housing Authority*, the Appeals Court found that a ban of firearms in public housing units was Constitutional, judging the ban to be "rationally calculated to reduce the crime and violence which plague public housing.[828] The Court cited testimony that "tenants are the victims of an extraordinarily high

---

[828] https://casetext.com/case/richmond-   tenants-org-v-redevelopment-and-housing-auth

incidence of crime, much of which is connected to illegal drug traffic. The murder rate in RRHA housing is very high. Tenants are routinely intimidated by gunfire and the presence of youths with guns." They cited further testimony that 1/3 of the annual regional shootings occur in such housing, that for every incident in which a gun is use for self-defense, more than 4 people are killed by a gun accident, that the presence of a gun can make a home more attractive to burglars, that those who acquire guns for self-defense often don't know how to use them properly, and that banning guns can be a "proactive and symbolic step in preventing the escalation of violence.[829] For all these reasons, the Court concluded that the "prohibition on the use and/or possession of various firearms is rationally related to the strong RRHA interest in reducing crime and violence."[830]

For those sympathetic to gun control, this might sound like a reasonable argument drawing upon relevant premises—and perhaps it is. Of note, however, is that the ban on firearm possession is being applied *solely* to public housing tenants. It is well-established that there are racial disparities in poverty rates. Black, Native American, and Latinx households are more likely than white households to be extremely low-income renters - with incomes at or below the poverty level (30% of their area median income). Twenty percent of Black households, 18% of American Indian or Alaska Native (AIAN) households, and 16% of Latinx households are extremely low-income renters, versus only 6% of white non-Hispanic households.[831] Given the correlation between income and use of public housing, a predictable pattern emerges.

Public housing serves black households at a rate substantially greater than their share of the renter population. Forty-eight percent of public housing households are black compared to only 19 percent of all

renter households. . . . Hispanic households are represented in public housing at a rate comparable to their share of renter households (10 percent versus 11 percent). Non-Hispanic white households occupy 39 percent of public housing, considerably less than their share of the total renter population (66 percent).[832]

In other words, there are significant racial disparities in who uses public housing, as a result of other racial disparities in our society. When firearm restrictions are applied specifically to public housing tenants, firearms restrictions are being applied disproportionately to Black persons. Although there might not have been conscious intent to discriminate, and although there might be legitimate reasons to restrict access to firearms, the disparate impact of such a policy situates it uncomfortably within the racialized history of gun rights and gun control in the United States.

The final example we will consider involves the *Republican*-led effort in California to ban open carry of firearms. We should begin with some historical context. It is the 1960s, and among the many social movements and protests of the time, the Black Panther Party emerged. Notable among all the many other organizations, the Black Panthers were conspicuous in their embrace of bearing firearms. The late Stokely Carmichael (to whom the phrase "Black Power" is attributed), described the decision of some African-Americans to arm themselves in the 1960s:

A key phrase in our buffer-zone days was non-violence. For years it has been thought that black people would not literally fight for their lives. Why this has been so is not entirely clear; neither the larger society nor black people are noted for passivity. The notion apparently stems from the years of marches and demonstrations and sit-ins where black people did not strike

---

[829] ibid.

[830] ibid.

[831] https://nlihc.org/resource/racial-disparities-among-extremely-low-income-renters

[832] https://www.huduser.gov/periodicals/ushmc/spring95/spring95.html#foot6

back and the violence always came from white mobs. There are many who still sincerely believe in that approach. From our viewpoint, rampaging white mobs and white night-riders must be made to understand that their days of free head-whipping are over. Black people should and must fight back. Nothing more quickly repels someone bent on destroying you than the unequivocal message: "O.K., fool, make your move, and run the same risk I run-of dying. . . .

Those of us who advocate Black Power are quite clear in our own minds that a "non-violent" approach to civil rights is an approach black people cannot afford and a luxury white people do not deserve. It is crystal clear to us-and it must become so with the white society-that there can be no social order without social justice. White people must be made to understand that they must stop messing with black people, or the blacks will fight back![833]

This might come as a surprise to contemporary readers, but California gun laws at the time allowed for the open carry of firearms. Rifles and shotguns could be carried openly so long as the owner didn't wield them in a threatening manner. Pistols could be carried openly as well, on the outside of clothing. That all changed in 1967.

The Black Panthers had become known for taking advantage of open carry laws while giving recruitment speeches on College and University campuses, and while confronting police officers while on their neighborhood patrols, acting as defenders of minorities stopped by the police. A series of tense altercations between the Panthers and the Oakland Police Department led to State Assemblyman Donald Mulford introducing legislation that would outlaw carrying firearms within city limits. The bill was introduced in April 1967, six weeks after it had been reported that an

armed group of Black Panthers acting as an escort for Malcolm X's widow, Betty Shabazz, were involved in tense, nonviolent confrontations with airport security officers and police in San Francisco. Attorney General Lynch announced that "[t]he time has come.., when we have to legislate against carrying or exhibiting guns in public places."[834]

The Panthers made a public show of opposing the Bill. On the day the Assembly was scheduled to hear it, a group of Black Panthers protested by walking into the Assembly Chamber in Sacramento carrying pistols, rifles, and shotguns. Black Panther Bobby Seale made the following statement before the CA. Assembly:

Statement of the Black Panther Party for Self-Defense calls on the American people in general and the black people in particular to take full note of the racist California legislature aimed at keeping the black people disarmed and powerless at the very same time that racist police agencies throughout the country are intensifying the terror and repression of black people. . . . The enslavement of black people from the very beginning of this country, the genocide practiced on the American Indians and the confining of the survivors on reservations, the savage lynching of thousands of black men and women, the dropping of atomic bombs on Hiroshima and Nagasaki, and now the cowardly massacre in Vietnam, all testify to the fact that towards people of color the racist power structure of America has but one policy: repression, genocide, terror, and the big stick. Black people have begged, prayed, petitioned, demonstrated and everything else to get the racist power structure of America to right the wrongs which have historically been perpetuated against black people. All of these efforts have been answered by more repression,

---

[833] Quoted in Leonardatos, Cynthis Deitle. "California's Attempt to Disarm the Black Panthers" *San Diego Law Review*, Vol 36, 1999:

956
[834] Quoted in ibid. 970.

deceit, and hypocrisy. As the aggression of the racist American Government escalates in Vietnam, the Police Agencies of America escalate the repression of black people throughout the ghettos of America. Vicious police dogs, cattle prods and increased patrols have become familiar sights in black communities. City Hall turns a deaf ear to the pleas of black people for relief from this increasing terror. The Black Panther Party for Self Defense believes that the time has come for black people to arm themselves against this terror before it is too late. The pending Mulford Act brings the hour of doom one step nearer. A people who have suffered so much for so long at the hands of a racist society, must draw the line somewhere. We believe that black communities of America must rise up as one man to halt the progression of a trend that leads inevitably to their total destruction.[835]

Conservative Republican Governor (and future President and GOP icon) Ronald Reagan said the following about public displays of arms, in that context:

There's no reason why on the street today a citizen should be carrying loaded weapons . . . Americans don't go around carrying guns with the idea of using them to influence other Americans.[836]

...The idea in a country like ours that grown men and women think they have got to run around playing cowboys with guns on their belts. They come in and try to impress a legislature. If it wasn't so terribly serious, you'd have to laugh at it, but it is terribly serious.[837]

Mulford vowed to *strengthen* the Bill, in response. On July 26, 1967, the California Senate voted 29-7 in favor of the gun bill after listening to comments related to the Detroit race riots, which had begun three days prior and were still ongoing at the time of the vote.[838] The State Assembly voted unanimously for passage of the law (AB 1591). The Bill, which was approved by Governor Reagan on July 28, 1967, was to take effect immediately. A relevant portion of the new law read as follows:

Act of July 28, 1967, ch. 960, 1967 Cal. Stat. 2459-63. The enacted bill stated in pertinent part:
SECTION 1. Section 12031 is added to the Penal Code, to read:
12031. (a) Except as provided in subdivision (b), every person who carries a loaded firearm on his person or in a vehicle while in any public place or on any public street in an incorporated city or in any public place or on any public street in a prohibited area of unincorporated

---

[835] Quoted in ibid., 971.

[836] Quoted in ibid., 972.

[837] Quoted in ibid., 972, footnote #145.

[838] "On July 23 the mass arrest of blacks at a nightclub selling liquor after the legal closing time detonated six days and nights of epidemic arson and vandalism, six days and nights of black defiance of a system of law and order which seemed so terribly biased against them. Nearly four thousand fires destroyed thirteen hundred buildings. The devastation left five thousand blacks homeless and an equal number jobless. Observing the smoking ruins from a helicopter, the Governor of Michigan remarked that Detroit looked like "a city that had been bombed." Added to the damage caused by burning, looting by tens of thousands of blacks brought the total of lost property to a quarter of a billion dollars. Worse, frightened and untrained National Guardsmen, firing without discipline, accounted for most of the riot's forty three dead and over a thousand wounded. All told, the 1967 summer riots resulted in at least ninety deaths, more than four thousand casualties, and nearly seventeen thousand arrests." (Leonardatos, 977, footnote #179)

territory is guilty of a misdemeanor.[839]

While it might be surprising to contemporary readers that gun control measures were passed in California as a *Republican* effort and signed by a *Republican* Governor, what might be even *more* surprising was that *the N.R.A. supported these efforts*, as indicated by the sponsor of the Bill, Don Mulford.

I am sure you are aware that I am very grateful to the National Rifle Association for its help in making my gun control bill, AB 1591, a workable piece of legislation, yet protecting the Constitutional rights of citizens.[840]

The bill enjoyed the full support of the National Rifle Association.[841]

Sen. John Schmitz, who had tried unsuccessfully to defeat the bill, wrote an editorial holding the N.R.A. directly responsible for its passage, saying: "Members of the National Rifle Association in California should know that their organization, despite its record of opposing gun control bills in the past, favored this bill and that without N.R.A. support it almost certainly would have been defeated."[842]

Although today the N.R.A. is known for its resistance to any attempt to restrict gun ownership, and its zealous defense of gun owners and gun use, this has not always been the case, and even today there are some conspicuous exceptions. Dunbar-Ortiz summarizes the history of the N.R.A., noting its relatively recent shift in focus.

Up to 1975, the N.R.A. had not been opposed to gun regulations and had not made a fetish of the Second Amendment. It had been founded following the Civil War by a group of former Union army officers

in the North to sponsor marksmanship training and competitions. Since the late nineteenth century, target shooting has been a part of the Olympics. In 1934, during the Depression, the N.R.A. testified in favor of the first federal gun legislation that sought to keep machine guns away from outlaws, such as the famous Bonnie and Clyde and Pretty Boy Floyd, and Chicago gangsters. During testimony, a congressman asked the N.R.A. witness if the proposed law would violate the Constitution, the witness said he knew of none. When the N.R.A opened a new headquarters in the late 1950s, its marquee advertised firearms safety education, marksmanship training, and recreational shooting (hunting).

By the time of its 1977 convention, the Second Amendment Foundation and its lobbying arm, the Citizens Committee for the Right to Keep and Bear Arms, founded in Washington State in 1974 seized leadership of the N.R.A. It was then that the N.R.A. centered the Second Amendment as its main concern. Harlon Carter was the primary actor in this "coup" to transform the N.R.A. Carter, following the career path of his father, had been a US Border Patrol Chief with a checkered past. As a youth he killed a fellow teenager, who was Mexican, and was sentenced to three years in prison, which was overturned soon after. As a US Border Patrol Chief, Carter was head of the mid-1950s "Operation Wet Back" program, a violent, corrupt, and a massive roundup and deportation of people who were allegedly undocumented Mexicans."[843]

The N.R.A., as an organization, was not

---

[839] Quoted in Leonardatos, 977, footnote #181.

[840] https://reason.com/wp-content/uploads/assets/db/14030325867418.pdf

[841] https://reason.com/wpcontent/uploads/2014/06/Mulford-Act-letter-2.pdf

[842] https://www.snopes.com/fact-check/nra-california-open-carry-ban/

[843] Dunbar-Ortiz, 124.

focused on the Second Amendment until it came under new leadership in the late 1970s. When the California law was passed a decade prior, the N.R.A. wasn't yet known for obstinate and unwavering resistance to gun restrictions. This new leadership came in the form of someone with "questionable" credentials with respect to race and racism, to put it mildly. Since then, the N.R.A. has become increasingly associated with right-wing militias and white supremacist groups, and has done little to rehabilitate its reputation for racism. Claims that the N.R.A. is less an advocacy group for gun rights and more an advocacy group for gun rights for *white people* acquired more support in 2017 due to the N.R.A.'s response (or lack of response) to the police shooting of Philando Castile.

Castile was a 32 year old Black man and licensed gun owner who was shot in Minnesota by a police officer during a traffic stop for a broken tail light.[844] Video and audio clearly indicate that Castile announced to the officer that he was licensed to carry, and there was a firearm in the vehicle. Officer Yanez told him not to reach for it, but also asked him to retrieve his ID. Castile assured Yanez that he would not reach for it, but Yanez opened fire anyway, shooting Castile numerous times. Castile died from his injuries. Yanez was indicted for manslaughter, and during his trial claimed he had feared for his life because Castile put his hand on his firearm, not his wallet or identification papers, and was pulling the gun from his pocket.[845] A jury acquitted Yanez on all charges.

Given that Castile was a licensed gun owner, legally carrying a firearm, who immediately and calmly informed officers of that fact during his traffic stop, one might assume that the N.R.A. would have expressed outrage that a gun owner was shot to death by police while exercising his Second Amendment Rights. The N.R.A. said literally nothing about the case, though it made

national headlines, for days, until publicly called out for its lack of response. N.R.A. spokeswoman Dana Loesch then finally offered commentary, *blaming* Castile for having had marijuana in his possession, which, according to her, invalidated the "lawful" part of his lawful carrying of a firearm.

Dana Loesch ✓
@DLoesch

Replying to @LauraJanespoon @wert0o and 3 others

He was also in possession of a controlled substance and a firearm simultaneously, which is illegal. Stop lying.

9:53 PM · Aug 9, 2017

♡ 107   ♡ 391   🔗 Copy link to Tweet

Dana Loesch ✓
@DLoesch

Two things: 1. Castile death was awful and avoidable. 2. Carrying firearm w controlled substance is not "lawful carry." Important.

1:43 PM · Aug 10, 2017

♡ 633   ♡ 227   🔗 Copy link to Tweet

Dana Loesch ✓
@DLoesch

Replying to @DLoesch and @EButcher55

Not sure why that didn't occur here. Permit should've been out & hands not moving, LEO should've asked where firearm was located.

5:21 PM · Aug 10, 2017

♡ 1   ♡ 5   🔗 Copy link to Tweet

Dana Loesch ✓
@DLoesch

Replying to @EButcher55

I've been pulled over while carrying and I had out my permit before officer got to the car. There is a reason they teach this in classes.

5:14 PM · Aug 10, 2017

♡ 4   ♡ 26   🔗 Copy link to Tweet

When encouraged to speak out against Black

---

[844] Dashcam video of the encounter is available here: https://www.youtube.com/watch?v=V94Lphx6z6Y Castile's girlfriend streamed live on Facebook, in the immediate aftermath: https://www.youtube.com/watch?v=PEjipYKbO

OU&bpctr=1613851282
[845] https://www.cnn.com/2017/06/30/politics/nra-philando-castile/index.html

gun owners being killed, and to say that "Black lives matter," Loesch replied that "all lives matter."

What is the point of all this history (as opposed to philosophy)? Recall that one of the major themes/aims of Critical Race Theory is investigating how the system of white supremacy has existed and been maintained by various institutions and social systems, including the allegedly neutral rule of law and (more recently) "colorblind" equal protection of the law. This sort of investigation requires not only exercises in jurisprudence, but also an examination of history. The Second Amendment, and the many cases and legal arguments involving it, did not arise nor operate within a conceptual vacuum. The Second Amendment emerged out of an actual historical context that included overt racism and white supremacy, and continues to operate and to be understood within a society still marked by systemic racism.

According to CRT, law is not "neutral," any more than judges or legislators are. If the second aim of CRT (i.e., not only understanding but *changing* systems that support white supremacy) is to be achieved, this racialized history must be revealed and confronted. Examining the history and historical context of gun laws, including the Second Amendment itself, therefore, is not only "interesting," but essential.

Chapter 21: Political Philosophy (Bolívarism)

Comprehension questions you should be able to answer after reading this chapter:

1. What is the "Latin threat" narrative, and how might a study of Latin American political philosophy serve as a response to it?
2. Who were the *criollos?*
3. What were some of Simón Bolívar's complaints against Spanish rule of Latin American colonies?
4. Why does Bolívar think that there is no single form of government (such as democracy) that is suitable for all nations?
5. What is utilitarianism, and how does Bolívar's use of utilitarianism support his position that you described in #4 above? In Bolívar's version of utilitarianism, what is he seeking to "maximize?"
6. Why did Bolívar think that Spanish Americans of his time were "not ready" for full participation in a democratic government?
7. What does history teach us about the success of democracies, according to Bolívar?
8. Why did Bolívar recommend a hereditary Senate?
9. Why did Bolívar recommend that the President serve for life, and appoint his own successor?
10. What was Bolívar's proposed "fourth branch/fourth power" of government, and what was its purpose?
11. What are some ways in which Bolívar was a "pragmatist?"
12. What are some ways in which Bolívar was an "elitist?"
13. What are some ways in which Bolívar was "progressive"?
14. What is meant by "Imperial Republicanism?" What are some ways in which Bolívar could be described as an Imperial Republican?
15. What are some ways in which Bolívar and his political systems were more "progressive" (from a social justice perspective) than those of the United States of America, at the time?
16. Why was there (internal) opposition to the United States participating in the Panama Congress of 1826?

The "Latin Threat"

Perceiving "foreigners" as a threat is as old and enduring as the Republic of the United States of America. Although The USA shares borders with two countries, Canada and Mexico, anxiety about immigration has been focused solely on the Southern border. Obvious candidate explanations for this focus include racism and ethnocentrism, as many Americans perceive Canadians as both racially and ethnically/culturally similar.

This is arguably just the latest iteration of the historical "brown scare" that has been present in the United States for at least one hundred years. In 1913, the *LA Times* ran articles stating that Mexicans were stockpiling weapons along the US-Mexico border in order to raid American communities and would suffer "no pangs of conscience if, drunk with some success, they should mistake and American home or bank for Mexican property or mistake in American miss for a Mexican made."[846]

A Vanderbilt University economics professor testified before the U.S. Congress in 1921 that Mexicans had dangerous core cultural traits. "They seem to be men a few wants, apathetic, without ambition, not concerned for the future. Rarely do they own land. They are improvident and prefer to work intermittently, getting into debt with their employers, who thereby are enabled to hold them to their estates. They are much driven to drinking pulque, an intoxicating liquor."[847]

In fact, claims that immigrants from Latin America are fundamentally "different," and pose a threat to "traditional" American values are made openly and unapologetically *to this day*.

The anti-American left would love to drown traditional, classic Americans with as many people as they can who know nothing of American history, nothing of American tradition, nothing of the rule of law... If you go and look at the radical left, this is their ideal model. It's to get rid of the rest of us because we believe in George Washington, or we believe in the Constitution, and you see this behavior over and over again.[848]

This is an example of what can be termed the "Latin threat narrative." According to this narrative, immigrants from Latin America are a "threat," not *necessarily* because of criminality (though that is often suggested by other, similar threat narratives) but because the United States and Latin American cultures have very different traditions, and very different cultural values. Proponents of this view include Samuel Harrington.[849]

For [Samuel] Huntington, American core culture is defined by its adherence to "the Christian religion, Protestant values and moralism, a work ethic, the English language, British traditions of law, justice, and the limits of government power, and a legacy of European art, literature, philosophy and music." On the other hand, Huntington characterizes Mexican core culture as defined by Catholicism and various "central Hispanic traits" that include "mistrust of people outside of family; lack of initiative, self-reliance, and ambition; low priority for education; [and] acceptance of poverty as a virtue necessary for entrance into heaven.
Not only are the cultures of the two societies irreconcilable, according to Huntington, but Mexican cultural norms actually inhibit the educational, political, and economic success of immigrants and their descendants."[850]

To the extent that Latin American immigrants maintain their values rather than assimilating into the values of the United States, those Latin American values will spread and "undermine" the cultural foundations of the political and economic stability of the United States, according to this narrative.

The continuation of high levels of Mexican and Hispanic immigration plus the low rates of assimilation of these immigrants into American society and culture could eventually change America into a country of two languages, two cultures, and two peoples... There is no Americano dream.

---

[846] Quoted in Orosco, José–Antonio. *Cesar Chavez and the Common Sense of Nonviolence.* Albuquerque: University of New Mexico Press, 2008. P, 18.
[847] ibid.
[848] Interview on 8-4-21 on Fox Business with former GOP House Speaker Newt Gingrich in which he is discussing Latin American immigrants.
https://www.mediamatters.org/media/3960636/embed/embed)
[849] One of Harrington's essays on this topic is available here: https://foreignpolicy.com/2009/10/28/the-hispanic-challenge/
[850] Quoted in Orosco, *Cesar Chavez and the Common Sense of Nonviolence*, 17

There's only the American dream created by Anglo – Protestant society. Mexican-Americans will share in that dream and in that society only if they dream in English.[851]

As one (of several) possible counterpoint(s) to this "Latin threat" narrative, one could argue that there *is* a general "Americano" dream, as opposed to a uniquely "American" dream, by demonstrating that the United States and many countries of Latin America have an identity based on a shared historical struggle for independence and democracy. This struggle did indeed begin in the British colonies that would become the United States in 1776, but the struggle quickly spread to Haiti, and then throughout Spanish America.

North and Latin American nations arose in the eighteenth century as reactions against the power of monarchs and the churches. They routed their protest in the ideas of the Enlightenment, namely the concepts of individual natural rights and an understanding of legitimate government as rooted in the consent of the governed. With this ideological backing, people in the Americas altered their self-understanding from colonial European subjects to sovereign citizens of their own republics.[852]

The following timeline should be used to not only gain an orientation with respect to major revolutionary events in the Americas, but also, eventually, for reference when it comes to our examination of the life and work of "*El Libertador*," Simón Bolívar in the remainder of this chapter.

Timeline

- 1776: U.S. *Declaration of Independence* written, and Revolutionary War begins.
- 1789: U.S. Constitution is ratified. *French Declaration of Rights of Man* and Citizen is written. French Revolution begins.
- 1791: Haitian revolt begins.
- 1804: Independent nation of Haiti is established.
- 1805: Simón Bolívar tours Europe (at age 21), is inspired by liberal movements on the continent, and swears an oath to free American countries from Spanish rule.
- 1808: Napoleon invades Spain and appoints his brother (Joseph) to be the new king of Spain.
- 1811: The colonial government in Venezuela declares independence from Spain on the grounds that Spain is led by an illegitimate French King, initiating a war of independence against Spain that will last for several years.
- 1812: The First Republic of Venezuela collapses. Bolívar writes the "Cartagena Manifesto."
- 1813: Bolívar launches a military campaign to retake control of Venezuela. A second Republic is proclaimed but lasts only a few months before being overthrown by royalist forces.
- 1815: Bolívar flees to the Caribbean, living first in Jamaica and then in Haiti, becoming an associate of President Pétion (the first President of the Republic of Haiti, and one of its founding fathers), and writing the "Jamaica Letter."

---

[851] Huntington, Samuel. *Who We Are: The Challenges to America's National Identity.* New York: Simon & Schuster, 2004. p., 256.
[852] Orosco, José–Antonio. "The Continental Struggle for Democracy. The American Wars of Independence as Experiments in Justice." *Latin American and Latinx Philosophy. A Collaborative Introduction.* Edited by Robert Eli Sanchez Jr. New York: Routledge, 2020, p., 61 – 62.

- 1816: Bolívar returns to Venezuela with support of Haitian soldiers and equipment on the condition that Bolívar frees the slaves of Spanish America (something he accomplishes on June 2 of that year).
- 1817: Bolívar establishes the third Republic of Venezuela.
- 1819: Venezuela and New Granada (present day Columbia, Ecuador, and Panama) unite to form the Republic of Colombia (*Gran Colombia*). Bolívar presents his "Angostura Address."
- 1830: the Republic of Colombia fragments into its original component countries as Bolívar flees in exile and dies of tuberculosis before he can reach Europe.

Historical Context

The American Revolution and the US *Declaration of Independence* can be seen as initiating a "domino effect" in both Europe and Latin America. The United States declared its independence in 1776 and ratified its Constitution in 1789. In that same year, Thomas Jefferson helped the Marquis de Lafayette write the *French Declaration of Rights of Man and Citizen*, paving the way for the French Revolution. Both declarations emphasized notions of equality, freedom, natural rights, and rule by consent of the governed, and appealed to various civil protections and liberties such as freedom of the press and religion, protection against unreasonable arrest, etc.

Just two years later, enslaved persons in Haiti rose up in rebellion and the sovereign nation of Haiti was established in 1804. The first President of Haiti, Toussaint L'Ouverture, defended the revolution and established a government openly indebted to Enlightenment ideals articulated in both the US and French declarations. His *Constitution* acknowledged certain natural rights for all Haitian citizens, including property rights, freedom from unreasonable arrests and searches, and the freedom to petition authorities with complaints. Important differences emerge however, as he made himself governor for life, declared the Catholic Church the official state religion, and it did not emphasize the sovereignty of citizens with respect to the government.

The Haitian revolution was not only significant for the people of Haiti, but directly contributed to other significant events. The cost of fighting (and failing) to maintain its Haitian colony, among other reasons, inspired France to sell its remaining holdings in North America to the United States in the Louisiana Purchase of 1803.

Thomas Jefferson was President at the time, and, being author of the Declaration of Independence, one might assume that he would have great sympathies for the Haitian revolutionaries. Unfortunately, white supremacy proved to be more salient than the ideals of liberty and equality, and the slave owning President not only refused to recognize the new government of Haiti, but even imposed an economic embargo against the new Republic in the hopes that it would fail.

In Europe, the money gained from the Louisiana Purchase helped Napoleon to fund his military efforts on that continent, which included the invasion and occupation of Spain in 1808. This was, unsurprisingly, a significant "distraction" for Spain – and Spanish colonies in Latin America seize the opportunity to liberate themselves.

In the first decade of the nineteenth century there was social unrest and low morale in Spain following its defeat by Britain's Royal Navy at the Battle of Trafalgar (1805). Sensing that this was the time to strike, France's Emperor Napoleon sent his armies to invade Spain. He promptly removed King Ferdinand VII, and placed his own brother, Joseph Bonaparte, on the throne as king of Spain. Although this arrangement did not last long, the news that the French had deposed and replaced Ferdinand VII spread quickly to Spain's American colonies, where anti-royalists then seized their opportunity and established local "juntas" to govern independently, without Spanish authority. In the 1810s came the decisive move to liberation, when anti-royalists in various parts of the viceroyalties refused to recognize authorities loyal to Spain and proceeded to form their own autonomous governments. Meanwhile, in 1813, King Ferdinand VII was restored to power, after which he was determined to support the royalist forces that were trying to put down such insurrections, which had continued to spread in America.

In 1815, he sent an expeditionary force to Venezuela, to intercept pro-independence forces that could gain control of New Granada. But in 1820, a group of liberal Spanish military officers who had been assigned to put down the insurrection in Buenos Aires opposed Ferdinand VII instead. Afflicted by war, poverty, and political upheavals, Spain was too weak to sustain decisive war efforts to regain its lost territories in Latin America. In 1826, the insurgents could claim victory: Spain had lost colonies and almost all Spanish-speaking America except Cuba, whose independence would have to wait until 1898.[853]

Mexico was among the first colony to attempt to break free. José Maria Morelos, a Catholic priest in Mexico, assumed leadership of the revolution and, in 1813, called for a Congress to draft a constitution for a new sovereign nation of Mexico. The outline of this Constitution, *The Sentiments of the Nation*, is reminiscent of both the US and French declarations.

The Fatherland will not be fully free and

our own as long as the government is not reformed by fighting tyranny, [and] establishing liberalism in its place.[854]

Morelos called for a government based on the sovereignty of the people (specifically referring to American-born, as opposed to Iberian born people), rule by consent of the governed, and a federal government divided into three branches, following the model of the United States. Like in Haiti, Catholicism would be the official state religion.

Further south, we come to the example of Simón Bolívar—our focus for this chapter. Although clearly familiar with, and influenced by, various Enlightenment figures such as Locke, Montesquieu, Voltaire, and Rousseau, Bolívar exhibited a "pragmatic" tendency (arguably inspired by Montesquieu) that significantly influenced the form of government he ultimately recommended, and in several cases, *created*, for former colonies of Spain.

Simón Bolívar

Simón Bolívar was a Venezuelan general and statesman, referred to as *el Libertador* (the liberator) for his role in routing Spanish royalist forces in the northern and western regions of Central and South America during the war of independence against Spain.

Bolívar was born in Caracas, Venezuela, in 1783, to a wealthy *criollo*[855] family who owned cacao plantations. He was orphaned at the age of nine, and supported by an uncle, who hired private tutors for him – most notably Simón Rodriguez, who was a disciple of Jean-Jacques Rousseau, and who introduced Bolívar to the ideas of enlightenment philosophers. Bolívar also had opportunities to travel to Europe, where he developed admiration for the liberal values of both the French and American revolutions, and

---

[853] Nuccetelli, Susana. *An Introduction to Latin American Philosophy.* Cambridge University Press, 2020. p., 55.

[854] Morelos, Jose Maria. "Sentiments of the Nation." In *Mexican History*, by Nora Jaffary, Edward Osowski, and Susie Porter. Philadelphia:

Westview Press. 2010, p., 184.

[855] *Criollo* in this context refers to a person of Spanish ancestry born in the Americas. This is not to be confused with the similar sounding French word "*créole*," which usually refers to a person of mixed ancestry.

where he even had an opportunity to personally witness Napoleon Bonaparte crown himself Emperor of France in 1804.

On a visit to Rome in 1805, Bolívar made the dramatic gesture of reading to his tutor (Rodriguez) a pledge that he had written to devote his life to liberating Latin America from Spanish colonial rule – a rather impressive act for a person just 22 years old!

Bolívar returned to Caracas in 1809 to find Venezuela in open rebellion against Spain. Bolívar participated first as a military leader, and then as a politician as well. Over the course of his career, he served as president and dictator of Gran Columbia (a large territory including present-day Columbia, Ecuador, Panama, Venezuela, and parts of northern Peru and Northwestern Brazil), for which he also drafted its constitution. He held a temporary position of leadership in Peru, created an entirely new country (that would be named after him) Bolivia – writing the Constitution for that nation as well. Finally, he attempted to create a pan – national organization of Latin American nations at the Conference in Panama that could both provide unity for those nations as well as creating a geopolitical rival to the United States.

Ultimately, members of his own ruling class (i.e., the *criollos*) rejected several of his proposed reforms, and he was driven into exile after a failed assassination attempt. Before he could make it to Europe, he died of tuberculosis in 1830.

Before examining the specific political ideas espoused and enacted by Bolívar, we will consider some of his sources of influence. First, we will consider Enlightenment philosophy, and then his social status as a *criollo*.

Enlightenment Influence

As mentioned above, among the known philosophical influences on Bolívar we find Hobbes, Spinoza, the Baron d'Holbach, Hume,

Montesquieu, and Rousseau. He was exposed to them in his general education and through his tutor, Simón Rodriguez. In addition, although Bolívar was certainly familiar with the works of Machiavelli, and though some of his themes seem to share an affinity for the author of *The Prince*, Bolívar explicitly *rejected* Machiavelli as an inspiration.

> Bolivar's aide-de-camp recorded a fascinating encounter, interesting in this connection: "a few months before his death, Bolivar visited me in Cartagena, and seeing on my table a volume of a new edition of the works of Machiavelli, observed that I should have better things to do with my time. We discussed the merits of the work, and noticing that Bolivar seemed to know its contents very well, I asked him whether he had read it recently; he responded that he had not read a line of Machiavelli since he left Europe 25 years ago."[856]

The Enlightenment ideas circulating at the time were "disruptive," thought not inherently "revolutionary."

> The belief in natural law led to concepts such as the rights of man and all men are created equal (these are the self-evident truths and unalienable rights in the US Declaration of Independence). It also led to the idea of freedom: of political institutions, religion, and trade, the police in which was then known as liberalism. These concepts were developed over hundreds of years to oppose the notion that God had given the kings or queens the Divine Right to rule over their subject and do with them (or to them) as they desired.[857]

---

[856] Daniel Florencio O'Leary, Memorias (3 vols. Caracas, 1883), Vol. I, pp. 66-7. Quoted in Simon, Joshua. "Simón Bolívar's Republican Imperialism: Another Ideology of American Revolution." In *History of Political Thought*, summer 2012, Vol. 33, No. 2 (Summer 2012), footnote 14.

[857] Velasquez, Francisco H. *Latino/a Thought: Culture, Politics, and Society*. Second Edition. Lanham, MD: Rowan Littlefield, 2009. pp. 35 – 36.

For example, although the rejection of the divine right of kings "disrupted" current understandings of the status of monarchies, this did not entail the overthrow of monarchy in general. Locke, for example, didn't argue for an *end* to monarchy but only for an "executive" that was *constrained* by Natural Law, human rights derived from Natural Law, separation of powers to prevent the abuses of a too-powerful monarch, and an understanding that political rule was by consent of the governed rather than a divine decree. The English monarchy survived the Enlightenment and persisted to this day.

That Enlightenment ideas were not necessarily "revolutionary" is also seen in the fact that many former colonies, once free, did *not* establish new systems of government that completely overturned prior systems of privilege.

The political ideas of the Enlightenment were far from systematic, but a number of characteristic themes can be observed. Human government was by natural rights and social contract. Among the basic rights were liberty and equality. These could be discerned by reason, and reason, as opposed to revelation and tradition, was the source of all human knowledge and action. Intellectual progress should be unhindered by religious dogma, and the Catholic Church was identified as one of the principal obstacles to progress. The object of government was the greatest happiness of the greatest number, happiness being judged to a large extent in terms of material progress. The aim was to increase wealth, though different means were envisaged, some advocating state control of the economy, others a system of laissez-faire. The success of the philosophes in propagating their ideas - and in silencing their opponents - concealed a number of flaws and inconsistencies in their view of the world.

One of the blind spots of the Enlightenment was nationalism, whose embryonic forms it failed to detect and whose demands it did not recognise. Another was social structure and change. The Enlightenment was not essentially an instrument of revolution; it bestowed its blessing on the existing order of society, appealing to an intellectual elite and an aristocracy of merit. While it was hostile to entrenched privilege and to inequality before the law, it had little to say on economic inequalities or on the redistribution of resources within society. It was for this reason that it could appeal to absolutists as well as to conservative democrats, while to those interested in colonial liberation it remained virtually silent.[858]

Arguably, this is consistent with the seemingly paradoxical system of government that Bolivar will later recommend and even implement – namely, one that perpetuates some degree of elitism and inequality. Bolívar, ever the pragmatist with respect to politics, can consistently claim to value the ideal of liberty and equality, while nevertheless not extending it to everyone (once liberated from Spain) for practical reasons. As will be explored later, because of the "passive" tyranny exercised by Spain, Spanish Americans had neither experience with self-government, nor had they developed the necessary "civic virtues" necessary for responsible self-governance. Liberty might be won but can easily be lost if the new government is not suitable for its people. Despite his rejection of Machiavelli, this is the classic Machiavellian challenge for any "new Prince." Having won/established a state, how does one keep it? Machiavelli thought that a people who had been long accustomed to being mere subjects, with no participation in government, would lack the proper character and temperament for stable and responsible participation, if given a chance.

---

[858] Lynch J. (2001) "Simón Bolívar and the Age of Revolution". In: *Latin America between Colony and Nation. Studies of the Americas.* Palgrave Macmillan, London. https://doi.org/10.1057/9780230511729_7

Bolívar's solution to that problem was to not give them the chance! At least not at first.

Bolívar's willingness to perpetuate systems of inequality and privilege is consistent with other statesmen influenced by the Enlightenment, such as the Founding Fathers of the USA, and is also consistent with another significant source of influence on him: his socio-economic status.

Criollo class influences

As mentioned above, Bolívar was born in Caracas, Venezuela into a wealthy *criollo* family who owned cacao plantations. That means that although he was a Spaniard by descent (and would be considered "White Hispanic" for demographic purposes today), the fact that he was born in the Americas meant that he occupied a different social space than Spaniards born in Spain.

For a bit of historical context, in the *past*, *Criollos* had enjoyed significant participation in the administration of the Spanish Empire. However, such administration was accused of rampant corruption and inefficiency, with government posts being literally bought and sold, and settled by incompetent administrators. During the eighteenth century, a series of reforms were passed such that significant military and civilian appointments were no longer available to people born in the Americas but could only be occupied by Spaniards who had been born in Spain. American-born persons of Spanish descent, such as Bolívar, were, in that respect, "second class citizens." Moreover, under the rule of Charles III, economic regulations were tightened and enforced, prohibiting the production of certain goods in the colonies (forcing upon them the relationship of a consumer of products from Spain) as well as prohibiting the exportation of goods that could be deemed competitive to Spanish markets. As was typical of colonial relationships, the Spanish-American colonies were regarded as very much in the service of the economy of Spain itself.

While we will examine the "Jamaica Letter" in

greater detail later, a quick glance at it reveals several political and moral assumptions that guided him: people have natural rights, people have a right to resist being oppressed, and political and economic oppression justifies rebellion.

Similar to the Declaration of Independence, Bolívar begins his Letter with a list of complaints against a "father" country, in his case, Spain. It's worth noting that the "sins" of Spain he lists appear to have been committed primarily against the "*criollos*," by his account, as opposed to the colonists in general.

While, in general, Spanish colonies had been oppressed by the economic policies of Spain according to which the colonies served as a source of labor and a consumer market only, not being allowed to export products in any way that would compete with Spain, Bolívar seemed particularly animated about the lack of access for American-born Spaniards (like himself) to positions of political and administrative authority.

> We were never viceroys or governors, save in the rarest of cases; seldom archbishops or bishops; never diplomats; among the military only subordinates... In brief, we were neither magistrates nor financiers and seldom merchants.[859]

Being denied any opportunity to participate to any meaningful degree in administration of the colonies, the (*criollo*) people of the Americas were kept in a state of "political infancy." Spain's oppressive policies had not only violated the natural rights of its subjects in the Americas and had done so in a way that had stunted the political maturity of Americans, but it had also violated the "social contract" it had enacted with the *criollos* by revoking their ability to participate in governance.

Bolívar denounced Spanish imperialism, but his complaints seem to be less about Spanish absolutism itself than with the exclusion of *criollos* such as himself from the administration

---

[859] Jamaica Letter.

of that empire, as we see again in his later Angostura Address.

> *In absolute governments there are no limits to the authority of public functionaries. The will of the Grand Sultan, the Khan, the Bey, and other despotic sovereigns, is the supreme law, and it is arbitrarily executed by the pashas and inferior governors in Turkey and Persia, where the system of oppression is completely organized, and is submitted to by the people because of the authority from which it emanates. These subordinate officers are entrusted with the civil, military, and political administration, the collection of duties and the protection of religion. But the key difference is this: the governors of Isfahan are Persians, the viziers of the Great Lord in Turkey are Turks, and the sultans of Tartary are Tartars. In China they do not send for their mandarins, military, and literati to the country of Genghis Khan, who conquered them, even though the present race of Chinese are direct descendants of the tribes subjugated by the ancestors of the present Tartars. With us it is quite different. We are controlled by a system which deprives us of the rights to which we are entitled, and leaves us in a sort of permanent infancy with respect to public affairs.[860]*

His status as a *criollo* is relevant because it helps us to understand his personal frustrations with Spain, and how that could have motivated him, but also because it helps us to reconcile his pursuit of liberty and "equality" while simultaneously creating new political systems that, like their neighbors to the North, did *not* grant full political equality to everyone.

Bolívarism

Having explored some historical context and personal influences, we can now begin to consider the main ideas attributed to Bolívar.

It's worth noting that not everything *attributed* to him properly belongs to him. The name of Bolívar, if not his ideas, have been appropriated numerous times in the last couple centuries, most notably by Hugo Chavez (Venezuela) and Nicolás Maduro. Chavez embraced some of the most authoritarian elements of Bolívar's political theory and adopted the "Constitution of the Bolivarian Republic of Venezuela" in 1999, which included a "Republican Moral Council" that bore resemblance to Bolívar's "fourth power/branch (explained later)." The FARC guerrillas in Colombia (also leftist in nature) have also claimed Bolívar as inspiration. For most of the twentieth century, however, Bolívar was more frequently cited as an inspiration for authoritarian *right*-wing military Latin American governments.

While Bolívar did not advocate for anything resembling socialism, there are reasons to associate him with authoritarianism in general—and, given his "pragmatism," it's *possible* that he would have even endorsed socialism for certain nations, given the proper context.

One of his key ideas is that there is no *single* universally valid political system for *all* people, but rather that each nation has to take into account the distinctive characteristics/culture of its own people, as well as their particular historical and geographic circumstances, in order to find the best political arrangement for them. This is somewhat reminiscent of Aristotle, who distinguished several different kinds of State based on who rules, and for what purpose.

---

[860] The Angostura Address.

State	Who rules?	For what purpose?
Tyranny	One person	self-interest
Kingship	One person	collective interest
Oligarchy	A wealthy minority	self-interest
Aristocracy	A virtuous minority	collective interest
Populist democracy	Many (usually poor)	self-interest
Polity	Many	collective interest

Aristotle recognized that all six of those types of State exist (with numerous variations), but believed that only some of them are legitimate, with the rest being deviant or corrupted versions of "proper" government types. All of the "good" constitutions (i.e., kingship, aristocracy, and polity) exhibit justice (in some sense) and promote friendship (harmony) because of their emphasis on the common good.

When one person rules for the common good, that is kingship or monarchy. When the one person rules in his own interests, however, we have a tyranny. When a minority of the population rule for the common good, and when that minority rules because of their virtue and merit, we have an aristocracy; but, when the minority rules for their own interests, and they rule because of their wealth rather than their virtue or merit, we have an oligarchy. Finally, when the "many" rules for the sake of the common good, we have a polity—the system that Aristotle seems to be advocating (despite the fact that a majority of his own population, being slaves and resident aliens, don't seem to count towards this "many!"). But, when the "many" is a mere majority ruling for their own good (e.g., the poor ruling for the sake of the poor), we have a (populist) democracy instead.

The particular names and features of Aristotle's account are far less important than the fact that he, like Bolívar, rejects the idea that there is only *one* type of government that is "good."

For Aristotle, rule by one, a minority, or a majority could each be "good" so long as rule is done for the sake of collective interest. For Bolívar, as we will see, various types of government can be appropriate and justified by appealing to their ability to maximize happiness, safety, and political stability for that community given its current cultural, racial/ethnic, economic, and historical context. In practice, this means that "liberal democracy" is *not* required nor even necessarily *recommended* for all countries. By way of a "formal" argument:

1. "Bolívarism" is a consequentialist theory according to which the moral and political decisions and systems are evaluated on their ability to maximize happiness, political stability, and safety.[861]

2. Because liberal democracy does not automatically and always maximize happiness, political stability, and safety, it is not always to be recommended as a form of government, and other forms of government *are* to be recommended if, given the circumstances they maximize happiness, stability, and safety instead.

3. Because a community's history, and racial and ethnic composition, partially determine what will maximize happiness/stability/safety, those factors must be considered in determining the most suitable form of government for that community.

4. One of the features of a people that establishes whether liberal democracy is a suitable form of government is whether or not they possess sufficient "civic virtue."

5. Because most Latin Americans (at the time) lacked sufficient civic virtue (according to Bolívar), as a result of a

---

[861] Nuccetelli, 60.

long history of Spanish colonial rule, liberal democracy was not suitable for Latin America (at that time).

6. A centralized and non-democratic form of government would better promote happiness/security/stability.

7. Therefore, a centralized, non-democratic form of government is recommended for the people of Latin America (at that time).

We will now consider some of his premises in greater detail, starting with what is arguably his most important premise.

The guiding principle for Bolívar with respect to politics was not religious, nor natural law (usually transmitted through a religious filter in his time), but the *utilitarianism* of Jeremy Bentham and James Mill (son of John Stuart Mill), both of whom he knew personally.

While he does not explicitly reference Bentham and his political speeches, he does explicitly reference appeals to the greatest happiness. He referred to the pursuit of greatest possible happiness as a "universal human instinct," and that this greatest possible happiness is "bound to follow in civil societies founded on the principles of justice, liberty and equality."[862] In other words, justice, liberty, and the quality are a means to an end – the end being the greatest happiness.

In his "Angostura Address," he was even clearer, stating that "the most perfect system of government is that which results in the greatest possible measure of happiness and the maximum of Social Security and political stability."

It is this consequentialist orientation that allows Bolívar to endorse authoritarianism, when doing so is thought to produce the best consequences, even though authoritarianism might seem dissonant with the ideals of a "freedom fighter."

Another of the key premises of Bolívar's political theory is his recognition of the diversity of the people of Latin America, being a mix of European, African, and indigenous people and cultural influences. For Bolívar, this unique mix of people and traits, combined with oppressive and paternalistic Spanish rule, produced a people "not ready" for democracy. We will see this theme recur again and again throughout this chapter.

Bolívar's attitudes about, and commitment to, this "diverse" population is admittedly ambiguous. On the one hand, he was a passionate and consistent abolitionist, who freed enslaved persons when he had opportunities to, and who strongly advocated for the abolition of slavery on numerous occasions. But he also openly acknowledged his anxiety about Afro – Latin Americans wielding political power, perhaps as a result of having witnessed violent racial conflict in the Haitian revolution against the white ruling class (i.e., people who looked like him).

On the one hand, he was ultimately rejected and exiled by his *criollo* peers, arguably because they did not want to share any power with the traditionally marginalized racial and ethnic groups of Latin America. On the other hand, the authoritarian systems that actively maintained the rule of the elite *criollos* and intentionally created numerous barriers to full political participation for anyone else didn't amount to *much* sharing of political power with those historically marginalized groups.

Given the circumstances in Latin America, what will maximize happiness, security, and stability, according to Bolívar, is a form of government that can be referred to as an "authoritarian Republic." Although the details will be explored more later, its features include, among other things, an independent judiciary, a powerful executive that, though elected, will serve for life, and a legislature that includes a hereditary Senate. In the "Angostura Address," he will also propose a fourth branch/power of government, a "moral power" that would be responsible for promoting and maintaining public morals and civic education. We will examine his writing and speeches in order, however, starting with the "Cartagena Manifesto."

---

[862] Quoted in Lynch, 7.

The Cartagena Manifesto

In the Cartagena Manifesto, Bolívar described the causes of the rapid collapse of the first Republic of Venezuela. According to Bolívar: the Constitution of Venezuela was not proper for the people it was meant to govern. It allowed popular elections which resulted in a combination of ignorance and ambition, putting incompetent and immoral men into power, creating division and faction, and ultimately, the collapse of the government. In addition, the federalist structure of the first Republic created a government that was too weak and decentralized to contend with its challenges.

Several themes which will recur over the course of his political career, and speeches/writing, appear for the first time in this Manifesto. To begin with, we find Bolívar's belief that federalism, as a form of government, is not suitable for Venezuela, and probably not for Spanish America in general.

> *But what weakened the Venezuelan government most was the federal form it adopted in keeping with the exaggerated precepts of the rights of man; this form, by authorizing self-government, disrupts social contracts and reduces nations to anarchy. Such was the true state of the Confederation. Each province governed itself independently; and, following this example, each city demanded like powers, based on the practice of the provinces and on the theory that all men and all peoples are entitled to establish arbitrarily the form of government that pleases them.[863]*

In later writings, Bolívar will expand upon his rejection of federalism in greater detail, but at this stage it is sufficient to point out that his complaint is that too much power had shifted to provincial governments, at the expense of a strong centralized government capable of maintaining order. That lack of a strong centralized government was ultimately responsible for the failure of the first Republic of Venezuela. We also see in that same quotation his reference to the "rights of man" as "exaggerated precepts," and a critical statement about "self-government." These indicate his distrust of democracy.

> *The popular elections held by the simple people of the country and by the scheming inhabitants of the city added a further obstacle to our practice of federation, because the former are so ignorant that they cast their votes mechanically and the latter so ambitious that they convert everything into factions. As a result, Venezuela never witnessed a free and proper election and the government was placed in the hands of men who were either inept, immoral, or opposed to the cause of independence. Party spirit determined everything and, consequently, caused us more disorganization than the circumstances themselves. Our division, not Spanish arms, returned us to slavery.*

The first Republic of Venezuela allowed popular elections, and, to put it bluntly, Bolívar thought the people voted "incorrectly." The rural voters were ignorant, and the urban voters were ambitious to the point of factions and division. This concern about factions is shared with *Publius* in the Federalist papers, but, as we will see later, they ultimately offer different means of dealing with factions. For Bolívar, this will not include the federalism modeled by the United States.

In Bolívar's defense, his distrust of popular elections didn't stem from some sort of general contempt of "the people," but from his assessment of the *capacities* of the people at the time.

> *The federal system, although the most perfect and the most capable of providing for human happiness in society, is, nevertheless, the most contrary to the interests of our infant states. Generally*

---

[863] All quotations in this subsection are from the Cartagena Manifesto unless otherwise indicated.

speaking, our fellow-citizens are not yet able to exercise their rights themselves in the fullest measure, because they lack the political virtues that characterize true republicans--virtues that are not acquired under absolute governments, where the rights and duties of the citizen are not recognized.

Spanish Americans, in general, lacked the civic/political virtues necessary for responsible and informed participation in self-government because of their particular historical and cultural circumstances. Spain had not allowed Spanish Americans to participate in their own governance to any significant degree, therefore they had no experience in governing and had never formed the proper sort of character that results from that experience.

This notion of civic virtue can be traced all the way back to Aristotle, at minimum, who argued that civic virtue involved taking turns ruling and being ruled – in other words, some active participation in self-governance. While the particular understanding of civic virtue might vary depending upon the form of government, for a Republic, citizens must be active and engaged to not only promote the public good, but also to protect against government abuses. For a people that, according to Bolívar, had been entirely passive under Spanish rule, they simply were not equipped for the sudden experiment in self-governing.

This recognition that the historical and cultural circumstances of a people can (and should) inform the sort of government that is appropriate for those people is arguably the most significant and lasting point made by Bolívar in this Manifesto.

The codes consulted by our magistrates were not those which could teach them the practical science of government but were those devised by certain benevolent visionaries, who, creating fantastic republics in their imaginations, have sought to attain political perfection, assuming the perfectibility of the human race. Thus we were given philosophers for leaders, philanthropy for legislation, dialectic for tactics, and sophists for soldiers. Through such a distortion of principles, the social order was thoroughly shaken, and from that time on the State made giant strides toward its general dissolution, which, indeed, shortly came to pass. . . .

It is essential that a government mold itself, so to speak, to the nature of the circumstances, the times, and the men that comprise it. If these factors are prosperity and peace, the government should be mild and protecting; but if they are turbulence and disaster, it should be stern and arm itself with a firmness that matches the dangers, without regard for laws or constitutions until happiness and peace have been reestablished.

Criticizing as impractical and idealistic those who create "fantastic republics in their imaginations," Bolívar exhibits a thoroughly pragmatic streak here, claiming that governments must mold themselves to the circumstances, at times, and people in question. There is no single ideal government applicable to all people under all circumstances, but rather, given particular people and particular circumstances, various forms of government – including authoritarian forms of government – will be appropriate. The ideas that we found in the Cartagena Manifesto will reappear in the Jamaica Letter three years later.

The Jamaica Letter

The Jamaica letter was written on September 6, 1815, in Kingston, Jamaica. The entire letter is long and comprised of several parts. We will focus on only a few ideas but will first consider some historical context.

In the Cartagena Manifesto, Bolívar was commenting on the collapse of the first Republic of Venezuela. In the Jamaica Letter, Bolívar is commenting on the fall of the *second* Republic of Venezuela to loyalist forces. Bolívar had been forced to flee Venezuela with his authority questioned even by his own officers. In Jamaica, Bolívar reflected on his experiences of the past few years and engaged in outreach to the British Empire in hopes of obtaining support for his revolutionary efforts. He also observed the outcome of the slave revolt in Haiti, and became acquainted with its new first president, Alexandre Pétion – who, rather than the British, will ultimately provide Bolívar with support.

The Jamaica letter is reminiscent of the United States Declaration of Independence in that it offers a "list of grievances" against the crown (the Spanish Crown, in that case), as well as offering both moral and prudential justification for the revolution.

In that same letter, he also engages in some pragmatic political philosophy reminiscent of Aristotle, in which he rejects the idea that there is a single form of government that is ideal for all the states. Recognizing that Latin Americans are not European nor Indian, but a unique mixture of both, he advocates that Latin Americans devise their own political systems suited to their own national characters. While he admired liberal democracy, he did not recommend it categorically for the emerging nations liberated from Spain.

Bolívar had numerous complaints concerning Spanish rule over its American colonies, though his complaints seem to be less about imperialism in general, than the particular form of imperialism practiced by Spain that denied elite American-born *criollos* (such as himself) the ability to participate in the administration of the colonies.

Bolívar offers two general arguments against the treatment of the Spanish Americans by Spain. One is based on a general appeal to natural law and universal human rights, and the other appeals to a violation of a social contract. His appeals based on the "rights of humanity" would cover all of the people in the Spanish colonies, while his complaints that Spain has violated the "pact" made between the Spanish Crown and the "discoverers, conquerors, and settlers of America" would presumably exclude enslaved Africans and their descendants, as well as indigenous persons, and would presumably apply only to colonists of Spanish descent such as himself.[864] We will now look at several excerpts from the Letter, beginning with those that consist of grievances against Spain.

> *Three centuries ago, you say, "began the atrocities committed by the Spaniards on this great hemisphere of Columbus." Our age has rejected these atrocities as mythical, because they appear to be beyond the human capacity for evil. Modern critics would never credit them were it not for the many and frequent documents testifying to these horrible truths. The humane Bishop of Chiapas, that apostle of America, Las Casas, has left to posterity a brief description of these horrors, extracted from the trial records in Sevilla relating to the cases brought against the conquistadores, and containing the testimony of every respectable person then in the New World, together with the charges, which the tyrants made against each other. All this is attested by the foremost historians of that time. Every impartial person has admitted the zeal, sincerity, and high character of that friend of humanity, who so fervently and so steadfastly denounced to his government and to his contemporaries the most horrible acts of sanguinary frenzy.*[865]

Bolívar draws deep from the well of history to begin his complaints against Spain, not only pointing out that Spanish "atrocities" began

---

[864] Simon, Joshua. "Simón Bolívar's Republican Imperialism: Another Ideology of American Revolution." In *History of Political Thought*, summer 2012, Vol. 33, No. 2 (Summer 2012), pp. 286 – 287.

[865] All quotations in this subsection are from the Jamaica Letter unless otherwise indicated.

centuries ago in the Americas, but also referencing Las Casas as a champion for humanity and justice, and a chronicler of those atrocities.[866]

Success will crown our efforts, because the destiny of America has been irrevocably decided; the tie that bound her to Spain has been severed. Only a concept maintained that tie and kept the parts of that immense monarchy together. That which formerly bound them now divides them. The hatred that the Peninsula has inspired in us is greater than the ocean between us. It would be easier to have the two continents meet than to reconcile the spirits of the two countries. The habit of obedience; a community of interest, of understanding, of religion; mutual goodwill; a tender regard for the birthplace and good name of our forefathers; in short, all that gave rise to our hopes, came to us from Spain. As a result there was born principle of affinity that seemed eternal, notwithstanding the misbehavior of our rulers which weakened that sympathy, or, rather, that bond enforced by the domination of their rule. At present the contrary attitude persists: we are threatened with the fear of death, dishonor, and every harm; there is nothing we have not suffered at the hands of that unnatural stepmother-Spain. The veil has been torn asunder. We have already seen the light, and it is not our desire to be thrust back into darkness. The chains have been broken; we have been freed, and now our enemies seek to enslave us anew. For this reason America fights desperately, and seldom has desperation failed to achieve victory. . . .

The role of the inhabitants of the American hemisphere has for centuries been purely passive. Politically they were nonexistent. We are still in a position lower than slavery, and therefore it is more difficult

for us to rise to the enjoyment of freedom. Permit me these transgressions in order to establish the issue. States are slaves because of either the nature or the misuse of their constitutions; a people is therefore enslaved when the government, by its nature or its vices, infringes on and usurps the rights of the citizen or subject. Applying these principles, we find that America was denied not only its freedom but even an active and effective tyranny. Let me explain. Under absolutism there are no recognized limits to the exercise of governmental powers. The will of the great sultan, khan, bey, and other despotic rulers is the supreme law, carried out more or less arbitrarily by the lesser pashas, khans, and satraps of Turkey and Persia, who have an organized system of oppression in which inferiors participate according to the authority vested in them. To them is entrusted the administration of civil, military, political, religious, and tax matters. But, after all is said and done, the rulers of Ispahan are Persians; the viziers of the Grand Turk are Turks; and the sultans of Tartary are Tartars. China does not bring its military leaders and scholars from the land of Genghis Khan, her conqueror, notwithstanding that the Chinese of today are the lineal descendants of those who were reduced to subjection by the ancestors of the present-day Tartars.

How different is our situation! We have been harassed by a conduct which has not only deprived us of our rights but has kept us in a sort of permanent infancy with regard to public affairs. If we could at least have managed our domestic affairs and our internal administration, we could have acquainted ourselves with the processes and mechanics of public affairs. We should also have enjoyed a personal consideration, thereby commanding a certain unconscious respect from the

---

[866] Las Casas and his arguments are explored in detail in another chapter of this textbook.

people, which is so necessary to preserve amidst revolutions. That is why I say we have even been deprived of an active tyranny, since we have not been permitted to exercise its functions.

Americans today, and perhaps to a greater extent than ever before, who live within the Spanish system occupy a position in society no better than that of serfs destined for labor, or at best they have no more status than that of mere consumers. Yet even this status is surrounded with galling restrictions, such as being forbidden to grow European crops, or to store products which are royal monopolies, or to establish factories of a type the Peninsula itself does not possess. To this add the exclusive trading privileges, even in articles of prime necessity, and the barriers between American provinces, designed to prevent all exchange of trade, traffic, and understanding. In short, do you wish to know what our future held?--simply the cultivation of the fields of indigo, grain, coffee, sugar cane, cacao, and cotton; cattle raising on the broad plains; hunting wild game in the jungles; digging in the earth to mine its gold--but even these limitations could never satisfy the greed of Spain.

So negative was our existence that I can find nothing comparable in any other civilized society, examine as I may the entire history of time and the politics of all nations. Is it not an outrage and a violation of human rights to expect a land so splendidly endowed, so vast, rich, and populous, to remain merely passive?

As I have just explained, we were cut off and, as it were, removed from the world in relation to the science of government and administration of the state. We were never viceroys or governors, save in the rarest of instances; seldom archbishops and bishops; diplomats never; as military men,

only subordinates; as nobles, without royal privileges. In brief, we were neither magistrates nor financiers and seldom merchants--all in flagrant contradiction to our institutions.

Emperor Charles V made a pact with the discoverers, conquerors, and settlers of America, and this, as Guerra puts it, is our social contract. The monarchs of Spain made a solemn agreement with them, to be carried out on their own account and at their own risk, expressly prohibiting them from drawing on the royal treasury. In return, they were made the lords of the land, entitled to organize the public administration and act as the court of last appeal, together with many other exemptions and privileges that are too numerous to mention. The King committed himself never to alienate the American provinces, inasmuch as he had no jurisdiction but that of sovereign domain. Thus, for themselves and their descendants, the conquistadores possessed what were tantamount to feudal holdings. Yet there are explicit laws respecting employment in civil, ecclesiastical, and tax-raising establishments. These laws favor, almost exclusively, the natives of the country who are of Spanish extraction. Thus, by an outright violation of the laws and the existing agreements, those born in America have been despoiled of their constitutional rights as embodied in the code.

This admittedly lengthy excerpt serves two purposes for us. The first is that it provides historical context for Bolívar's complaints and circumstances, as he provides specific details of how Spain has, from his perspective, treated Spanish America unjustly. In this respect, we see a clear analogy with the United States Declaration of Independence which also included a "list of grievances" meant to provide justification for revolution.

The second purpose comes in the form of one

of his specific complaints, namely, that Spanish Americans (or, more specifically, *criollos* like himself) had not been allowed any degree of participation in the government of the Spanish-American territories, thereby leaving Spanish Americans "in a sort of permanent infancy with regard to public affairs."

I emphasize this particular complaint because of the important role it will play with respect to another of Bolívar's significant ideas: that the people of Spanish America are "not ready" for significant self-governance because they lack sufficient "civic virtue." The direct cause of that lack of civic virtue, according to Bolívar, is the fact that Spain, up to that point, had not allowed political participation.

Bolívar move on from this point to engage in some rhetorical gestures, appealing to other nations in Europe to intervene against Spain on behalf of Spanish Americans.

Europe could do Spain a service by dissuading her from her rash obstinacy, thereby at least sparing her the costs she is incurring and the blood she is expending. And if she will fix her attention on her own precincts she can build her prosperity and power upon more solid foundations than doubtful conquests, precarious commerce, and forceful exactions from remote and powerful peoples. Europe herself, as a matter of common sense policy, should have prepared and executed the project of American independence, not alone because the world balance of power so necessitated, but also because this is the legitimate and certain means through which Europe can acquire overseas commercial establishments. A Europe which is not moved by the violent passions of vengeance, ambition, and greed, as is Spain, would seem to be entitled, by all the rules of equity, to make clear to Spain where her best interests lie.

Bolívar suggests that European intervention against Spain is not only morally imperative but is also in the self-interest of Europe and even Spain itself. Despite that, Bolívar laments that, thus far, no help outside Spanish America has been provided.

All of the writers who have treated this matter agree on this point. Consequently, we have had reason to hope that the civilized nations would hasten to our aid in order that we might achieve that which must prove to be advantageous to both hemispheres. How vain has been this hope! Not only the Europeans but even our brothers of the North have been apathetic bystanders in this struggle which, by its very essence, is the most just, and in its consequences the most noble and vital of any which have been raised in ancient or in modern times.

Moving on from his complaints against Spain, and appeals for assistance, Bolívar exhibits what should be a now familiar pragmatic streak, explaining how the particular traits and dispositions of Spanish Americans, as a result of both their multicultural heritage as well as their inability to participate in self-governance, has rendered the people poorly equipped for a Democratic federal system of government.

Events in Costa Firme have proved that institutions which are wholly representative are not suited to our character, customs, and present knowledge. In Caracas party spirit arose in the societies, assemblies, and popular elections; these parties led us back into slavery. Thus, while Venezuela has been the American republic with the most advanced political institutions, she has also been the clearest example of the inefficacy of the democratic and federal system for our new-born states. In New Granada, the large number of excess powers held by the provincial governments and the lack of centralization in the general government have reduced that fair country to her present state. For this reason her foes, though weak, have been able to hold out against all odds. As long as our countrymen do not acquire the abilities and political virtues that distinguish our brothers of the north, wholly popular systems, far from working to our advantage, will, I greatly fear, bring about our downfall. Unfortunately, these traits, to the degree in which they are required, do not appear to be within our reach. On the contrary, we are dominated by the vices that one learns under the rule of a nation like Spain, which has only distinguished itself in ferocity, ambition, vindictiveness, and greed.

It is harder, Montesquieu has written, to release a nation from servitude than to enslave a free nation. This truth is proven by the annals of all times, which reveal that most free nations have been put under the yoke, but very few enslaved nations have recovered their liberty. Despite the convictions of history, South Americans have made efforts to obtain liberal, even perfect, institutions, doubtless out of that instinct to aspire to the greatest possible happiness, which, common to all men, is bound to follow in civil societies founded on the principles of justice, liberty, and equality. But are we capable of maintaining in proper balance the difficult charge of a republic? Is it conceivable that a newly emancipated people can soar to the heights of liberty, and, unlike Icarus, neither have its wings melt nor fall into an abyss? Such a marvel is inconceivable and without precedent. There is no reasonable probability to bolster our hopes.

More than anyone, I desire to see America fashioned into the greatest nation in the world, greatest not so much by virtue of her area and wealth as by her freedom and glory. Although I seek perfection for the government of my country, I cannot persuade myself that the New World can, at the moment, be organized as a great republic. Since it is impossible, I dare not

desire it; yet much less do I desire to have all America a monarchy because this plan is not only impracticable but also impossible. Wrongs now existing could not be righted, and our emancipation would be fruitless. The American states need the care of paternal governments to heal the sores and wounds of despotism and war.

In that section, Bolívar reinforces his claim that Spanish Americans are not ready for democratic participation in a republic, and that a federal system of government is not suitable. His authoritarian tendencies are revealed in his claim that the new American states "need the care of paternal governments to heal the sores and wounds of despotism and war." Despite that, he clearly and explicitly rejects monarchy as a proper form of government, despite it being clearly paternal.

… I do not favor American monarchies. My reasons are these: The well-understood interest of a republic is limited to the matter of its preservation, prosperity, and glory. Republicans, because they do not desire powers which represent a directly contrary viewpoint, have no reason for expanding the boundaries of their nation to the detriment of their own resources, solely for the purpose of having their neighbors share a liberal constitution. They would not acquire rights or secure any advantage by conquering their neighbors, unless they were to make them colonies, conquered territory, or allies, after the example of Rome. But such thought and action are directly contrary to the principles of justice which characterize republican systems; and, what is more, they are in direct opposition to the interests of their citizens, because a state, too large of itself or together with its dependencies, ultimately falls into decay. Its free government becomes a tyranny. The principles that should preserve the government are disregarded, and finally it degenerates into despotism. The

distinctive feature of small republics is permanence: that of large republics varies, but always with a tendency toward empire. Almost all small republics have had long lives. Among the larger republics, only Rome lasted for several centuries, for its capital was a republic. The rest of her dominions were governed by diverse laws and institutions.

The policy of a king is very different. His constant desire is to increase his possessions, wealth, and authority; and with justification, for his power grows with every acquisition, both with respect to his neighbors and his own vassals, who fear him because his power is as formidable as his empire, which he maintains by war and conquest. For these reasons I think that the Americans, being anxious for peace, science, art, commerce, and agriculture, would prefer republics to kingdoms. And, further, it seems to me that these desires conform with the aims of Europe.

Bolívar's rejection of monarchy appears to be not a concern about the authority wielded by a king or queen, but the tendency towards territorial expansion and constant acquisition of power exhibited by monarchs. These tendencies produce conflict and eventually war, as opposed to the aims of "peace, science, art, commerce, and agriculture" that he associates with republics. While Bolívar has a strong preference for republics under ideal circumstances, he does not regard the current situation as ideal.

Among the popular and representative systems, I do not favor the federal system. It is over-perfect, and it demands political virtues and talents far superior to our own. For the same reason I reject a monarchy that is part aristocracy and part democracy, although with such a government England has achieved much fortune and splendor. Since it is not possible for us to select the most perfect and complete form of government, let us

avoid falling into demagogic anarchy or monocratic tyranny. These opposite extremes would only wreck us on similar reefs of misfortune and dishonor; hence, we must seek a mean between them. I say: Do not adopt the best system of government, but the one that is most likely to succeed

Once again referencing the lack of civic virtues among the people, Bolívar makes his pragmatic appeal abundantly clear: "Do not adopt the best system of government, but the one that is most likely to succeed."

Throughout the history of Western philosophy, political theorists have generally been grouped as either belonging to the camp of Plato, associated with idealism, or Aristotle, who is associated with pragmatism. With his rejection of the pursuit of some "best" system of government for the sake of establishing one that will actually succeed, Bolívar clearly belongs on team Aristotle.

Bolívar's views continued to mature and some of them would actually be implemented in constitutions that he would, himself, write. The final source for Bolívarism we will consult is his Angostura Address of 1819.

The Angostura Address

Still in the midst of fighting for independence from Spain, Bolívar summoned a "Congress" of 26 representatives in the city of Angostura (now Ciudad Bolívar, Venezuela) to promote autonomy for the Viceroyalty of New Granada (present-day Colombia, Panama, Venezuela, and parts of Ecuador), and to install the political system that he thought would be best capable of sustaining a new Republic. In his speech, he will attempt to lay the foundation for a (somewhat) democratically governed "Gran Colombia," that, from his perspective, must not be a simple replica of the constitutions of other nations, but must instead be tailored for the specific circumstances and traits of the people it must govern.

Bolívar begins by "graciously" surrendering the dictatorial powers he had been granted, handing authority over to the representatives, and, symbolically, to "the people."

In transferring to the Representatives of the People the Supreme Power with which I have been entrusted, I fulfill the wishes of my own heart, those of my fellow citizens and those of our future generations which expect everything from your wisdom, uprightness and prudence. In discharging this sweet duty, I free myself from the overburdening of immense authority and the unlimited responsibility weighing upon my weak shoulders! Only a compelling necessity coupled with the commanding will of the People could have made me assume the tremendous and dangerous charge of Dictator Supreme Chief of the Republic. But I can breathe easier now in handing back to you that authority, which I have succeeded in maintaining with so much risk, difficulty and hardships amid the most awful tribulations that could ever afflict any social political body.[867]

This was one step in a back-and-forth dance his career had with dictatorships throughout his political career. On the one hand he openly cautioned of the continuation of authority in one person, and the need for frequent elections.

The continuation of authority in the same person has frequently proved the undoing of democratic governments. Repeated elections are essential to the system of popular government, because there is nothing so dangerous as to suffer Power to be vested for a long time in one citizen. The people become accustomed to obeying him, and he becomes accustomed to commanding, hence the origin of usurpation and tyranny. A proper zeal is the guarantee of republican liberty, and

our citizens must very justly fear that the same Magistrate who has governed them for a long time, may continue to rule them forever.

On the other hand, when he wrote a Constitution for Bolivia, and another proposed Constitution for Colombia later on, he proposed that the president hold office for life. He also spoke of the office of the president in rather lofty terms in the Angostura Address itself.

The President of the Republic comes to be in our Constitution, as the Sun that, firm in the center, gives life to the Universe. This supreme authority must be perpetual...

Bolívar goes on to describe an ideal democratic republic which would abolish "monarchy, distinction, nobility, prerogatives, and privileges" while declaring for the "rights of man and freedom of action, thought, speech, and the press." Democracy was necessary for liberty, but democracy, by itself, could not guarantee prosperity and permanence for the state. A Federalist Democratic system, such as that of the United States of America, managed to work in North America, but Bolívar was deeply skeptical that federalism could be successfully transplanted to Spanish Americans.

It has never for a moment entered my mind to compare the position and character of two states as dissimilar as the Anglo-American and the Spanish-American. It would be more difficult to apply to Venezuela the political system of the United States then it would be to apply to Spain that of England.[868]

In principle, he acknowledged that federal forms of government were theoretically desirable, and democratic systems of checks and

---

[867] All quotations in this subsection are from the Angostura Address unless otherwise indicated.
[868] Note: for anyone interested, the Angostura

Address available in Spanish here: http://www.archivodellibertador.gob.ve/escritos/buscador/spip.php?article9987

balances were worthy of pursuit, but in practice he believed that federalism was not suitable for the particular conditions and people of Spanish America. His rejection of federalism is found in both the Cartagena Manifesto (as we saw earlier) and his Angostura Address.

> *The more I admire the excellency of the Federal Constitution of Venezuela, the more am I convinced of the impossibility of applying it to our situation.*

Part of his reasoning for this was an implicit rejection of the Enlightenment idea that there is a shared, universal human nature that would allow for a single "best" form of government. While he thought that federalism might have worked for the United States of America, he did not think that that system could be copied and successfully deployed among his own people.

> *Notwithstanding the fact that that people is a unique model of political virtues and moral education; notwithstanding that it has been cradled in liberty, that it has been reared in freedom and lives on pure liberty, I will say more, although in many respects that people is unique in the history of humanity, it is a prodigy, I repeat, that a system so weak and complicated as the federal system should have served to govern that people in circumstances as difficult and delicate as those which have existed. But, what- ever the case may be, as regards the American Nation, I must say that nothing is further from my mind than to try to assimilate the conditions and character of two nations as different as the Anglo-American and the Spanish-American. Would it not be extremely difficult to apply to Spain the Code of political, civil and religious liberty of England? It would be even more difficult to adapt to Venezuela the laws of North America.*

In fact, in this very passage where Bolívar praises the political system of the United States of America, he does so with a tone of incredulity. It is remarkable to him that "a system as weak and complicated as the federal system" has found success in the United States. In fact, Bolívar claims that the mistake of attempting to copy the political system of North America had already been made once and was responsible for the failure of the first Republic of Venezuela.

> *The first Congress in its federal Constitution took into consideration the spirit of the Provinces rather than the solid idea of creating a republic indivisible and centralized. Our legislators in this instance yielded to the inconsiderate request of those provincials captivated by the dazzling appearance of the happiness of the American people, believing that the blessings they enjoy are solely due to the form of government and not to the character and habits of the citizens. In effect, the example given by the United States, because of their rare prosperity, was too enticing not to be followed. . . . But, no matter how flattering might appear and might be the effect of this splendid federal system, it was not feasible that Venezuelans could enjoy it of a sudden just after having cast off their fetters. We were not prepared for so much good; good as well as evil produces death when it is sudden and excessive. Our moral constitution had not attained yet the necessary consistency to reap the benefits of a government entirely representative and so exalted that it might he adopted to a republic of saintly men.*

Once again referencing the lack of civic virtue in the population, rather than copying the model of other nations, Bolívar advises crafting a system of government that acknowledges the particular circumstances of its people.

> *Does not the Spirit of Laws state that they must be suited to the people for whom they are made; that it is a great coincidence when the laws of one nation*

suit another; that laws must bear relation to the physical features of a country, its climate, its soil, its situation, extension and manner of living of the people; that they must have reference to the degree of liberty that their constitution may be able to provide for the religion of the inhabitants, their inclinations, wealth, number, trade, customs and manners? Such is the Code that we should consult, not that of Washington!

One of those circumstances is the mixed heritage of Spanish Americans.

We do not even preserve the vestiges of what once we were; we are not Europeans, we are not Indians, but an intermediate species between the aborigines and the Spaniards-Americans by birth and Europeans in right, we are placed in the dilemma of disputing with the natives our titles of possession and maintaining ourselves in the country where we were born, against the opposition of the invaders. Thus, ours is a most extraordinary and complicated case.

. . .

We must bear in mind that our population is not the people of Europe, not of North America, that it is rather a composite of Africa and America, which is an offspring of Europe. Spain herself ceases to be European on account of her African blood, her institutions and her temperament. It is impossible to point out with preciseness to what human family we belong. The greater portion of the natives has been annihilated, the European has mixed with the Native American and the African, and this has mixed again with the Indian and the European. All having been born of the same mother, our parents, of different origin and blood, arc foreigners, and all differ visibly in color of skin. This

dissimilarity is a hindrance of the greatest importance.

Another circumstance is the lack of political experience that he first described in the Jamaica Letter.

Moreover, our part has always been a purely passive one; our political existence has always been null, and we find ourselves in greater difficulties in attaining our liberty than we ever had when we lived on a plane lower than servitude, because we had been robbed not only of liberty but also of active and domestic tyranny. . . . America, on the contrary, received all from Spain, which had really deprived her of true enjoyment and exercise of active tyranny, by not permitting us to share in our own domestic affairs and interior administration. This deprivation had made it impossible for us to become acquainted with the course of public affairs: neither did we enjoy that personal consideration which the glamour of power inspires in the eyes of the multitude, so important in the great revolutions. I will say, in short, we were kept in estrangement, absent from the universe and all that relates to the science of government.

The people of America having been held under the triple yoke of ignorance, tyranny and vice, have not been in a position to acquire either knowledge, power or virtue.

Giving "too much" liberty to a people "not ready" for it, would be a recipe for failure, according to Bolívar.

Liberty, says Rousseau, is a succulent food, but difficult to digest. Our feeble fellow-citizens will have to strengthen their mind much before they will be ready to assimilate such wholesome nourishment. Their limbs made numb by their fetters, their eyesight weakened in the darkness of their dungeons and their forces wasted away through their foul servitude, will they be capable of marching with a firm step towards the august temple of Liberty? Will they be capable of coming close to it, and admiring the light it sheds, and of breathing freely its pure air?

Drawing upon examples of history, Bolívar expresses skepticism as to the durability of federalism, but also in democracy itself.

Only democracy, in my opinion, is susceptible of absolute freedom. But where is there a democratic government that has united all at the same time power, prosperity and permanence? Have we not seen, on the contrary, aristocracy, monarchy rearing great and powerful empires for centuries and centuries? What government is there older than that of China? What republic has exceeded in duration that of Sparta, that of Venice? The Roman Empire, did it not conquer the world? Docs not France count fourteen centuries of monarchy? Who is greater than England? These nations, however, have been, or still are, aristocracies and monarchies.

. . .

Athens is the first to give us the most brilliant example of an absolute democracy, and at the same time Athens will offer the most melancholy example of the extreme weakness of such a system of government. The wisest among the legislators of Greece did not see his republic last ten years, and suffered the humiliation of having to acknowledge the inadequacy of absolute democracy to govern any form of society, even the most cultured, moderate and restrained, because it only shines with flashes of liberty.

Democracy might be wonderful as an ideal, but Bolívar claims that the testimony of history does not provide examples of democracies that have actually endured through time.

Let us not lose, then, the benefit of the lessons drawn from experience, and may the schools of Greece, Rome, France, England and America instruct us in the difficult science of creating and maintaining the nations under proper laws, just, legitimate and above all useful. We must never forget that the superiority of a government does not consist in its theories, or in its form, or in its mechanism, but in its being appropriate to the nature and character of the nation for which it has been instituted.

. . .

Indefinite liberty, absolute democracy are the rocks upon which all republican hopes have been wrecked. Cast your eye over the ancient republics, the modern republics, the rising republics; almost all have tried to establish themselves as absolute democracies, and almost all have failed in their just aspirations. They are praise- worthy, undoubtedly, who wish for legitimate institutions and social perfection! But, who has told men that they possess already all the wisdom, that they practice all the virtues uncompromisingly demanded by the union of power and justice. Only angels, not mere men, can exist free, peaceful, and happy, while exercising all the sovereign power.

Here, Bolívar acknowledges the moral limitations of human beings in a manner reminiscent of what *Publius* stated in Federalist Paper 51: "If men were angels, no government would be necessary. If angels were to govern men, neither external nor internal controls on government would be necessary." Since he is proposing governments for humans rather than angels, Bolívar must be "practical." Democracy, therefore, should not be held up as some sort of absolute ideal. Nor should equality be pursued unconditionally, since "equality" admits of various understandings.

That men are all born with equal rights to the benefits of society, has been sanctioned by the majority of the learned; but it has also been sanctioned that not all men are equally capable of attaining every distinction; while all should practise virtue not all do practise it; all should be courageous and all are not courageous; all should possess talents and all do not possess them. Hence the real distinction existing among individuals of the most liberally established society. If the principle of political equality is generally acknowledged, that of physical or moral inequality is also recognized. Nature has made men unequal as regards genius, temperament, strength and characteristics. The laws correct that difference by giving man a place in society so that education, industry, service, virtue may give him a fictitious equality, properly called political and social equality.

While everyone should be considered equal under the law, not everyone is equal in terms of intellect and character, and it is not necessarily the case that everyone should have equal social status, or equal political participation, if the circumstances don't support that. Rather than maximizing equality, liberty, political participation, or some other political ideal, Bolívar proposes that the guiding principle of politics should be utilitarianism.

The most perfect system of government is that which produces the greatest sum of happiness possible, the greatest sum of social security and political stability. Through the laws enacted by the first Congress we have the right to expect that happiness be the lot of Venezuela, and through your laws we must hope that security and stability will perpetuate such happiness.

The best political system, according to Bolívar, is one that maximizes happiness, stability, and security. Depending upon the particular circumstances of the community, various forms of government will be better suited to maximizing those values. While Federalist systems of government, and democratic systems more generally, might maximize happiness/stability/security in some cases, they will not do so in *all* cases – and, specifically, they will not do so for Spanish America, according to Bolívar.

Ironically enough, for all of his talk of not looking to other constitutions as a model to implement, Bolívar ends up proposing that the representatives effectively copy the system of the British government.

Rome and Great Britain are the two nations which have excelled most among ancient and modern peoples. Both were born to rule and to be free, but both were constituted not with dazzling forms of liberty, but built on solid foundations. Hence, I recommend you, Representatives, to study the British Constitution, which is the one that seems destined to do the most possible good to the peoples that adopt it. But no matter how perfect it may be, I am very far from suggesting a servile imitation. When I speak of the British Government, I only refer to whatever it has of the republican system; and truly, could we call a monarchy a system, that recognizes popular sovereignty, the division and balance of power, civil liberty and the liberty of conscience, the freedom of the press and everything which is sublime in politics? Could there be any more liberty in any republic whatsoever? And, could any more be said of social order? I recommend such constitution as the most worthy of being taken as a model by all who yearn for the enjoyment of the rights of men, and all political happiness compatible with our frail nature.

Our fundamental laws would not be

altered in the least should we adopt a legislative power similar to the British Parliament. We have divided, as Americans did, national representation into two Chambers, the Representatives and the Senate. The first is very wisely constituted, enjoys all the functions appertaining to it, and is not susceptible of a radical reform, because it is the Constitution which gave it origin, form and such faculties as the will of the people deemed necessary to be legally and properly represented. If the Senate, instead of being elective were hereditary, it would be, in my opinion, the foundation, the binding tie, the very soul of our republic.

One of the more interesting (and controversial) features of government that Bolívar proposes, drawn from the example of the British House of Lords, is a "hereditary" Senate.

If the Senate, instead of being elective were hereditary, it would be, in my opinion, the foundation, the binding tie, the very soul of our republic. This body would arrest the lightning of government in our political storms, and would break the popular waves. Attached to the government, because of its natural interest of self-preservation, it will always oppose the invasions attempted by the people against the jurisdiction and the authority of its rulers. We must confess it: the generality of men fail to recognize what their real interests are and constantly endeavor to assail them in the hands of their trustees; and the individual struggles against the masses, and the masses against the authorities. It is necessary, therefore, that a neutral body should exist in every government, always siding with the aggrieved party to disarm the offender. This neutral body, to be such, must not owe its origin to the election of the government, nor to the election of the people, so as to enjoy a full measure of freedom, neither fearing nor expecting anything from either

of these two sources of authority. The hereditary Senate, as a part of the people, shares in its interests, in its sentiments, in its spirit. For this reason it is not to be presumed that a hereditary Senate would disregard the popular interests or forget its legislative duties. The Roman Senators and the Lords of London have been the staunchest columns on which the structure of political and civil liberty has been erected.

These Senators would be elected by Congress the first time. The succession to the Senate should engage the first attention of the government, which would educate them in a college especially devoted to instructing these tutors, future legislators of the country. They should learn the arts, sciences and letters, the accomplishments of the mind of public men; from childhood they should know the career to which Providence has destined them, and from a tender age they should temper their soul to the dignity awaiting them.

The creation of a hereditary Senate would be in nowise a violation of political equality; I do not pretend to establish a nobility because, as a famous republican has said, it would be to destroy at the same time equality and liberty. It is a calling for which candidates must be pre-pared; it is an office requiring much knowledge and the proper means to become learned in it. Everything must not be left to chance and fortune in the elections; the people are more easily deceived than Nature perfected by art, and although it is true that these Senators would not spring from the womb of Perfection, it is also true that they would spring from the womb of a learned education. On the other hand, the liberators of Venezuela are entitled to hold, always, a high rank in the republic which owes its existence to them! I believe that posterity would grieve to see the effacement of the illustrious names of their first benefactors. I say, moreover, that it is a matter of public interest, or the gratitude of Venezuela, of national honor, to preserve with glory to the end of posterity a race of men of virtues, prudence and valor, who mastering all obstacles have founded the republic at the cost of the most heroic sacrifices. And if the people of Venezuela do not applaud the elevation of their benefactors, they are unworthy of being a free people, and never will be free.

A hereditary Senate, I repeat, will be the fundamental support of the Legislative Power and, therefore, the basis of the entire government. It will equally serve to counterbalance both the government and the people; it will be an intermediate power that would blunt the shafts those two eternal rivals direct against each other. In all conflicts, the calm reasoning of a third party becomes the means of reconciliation; thus, the Senate of Venezuela will be the keystone of this structure so delicate and so liable to violent shocks; it would be the rainbow which calms the storms and maintains harmony between the members and the head of this political body.

Nothing whatever could corrupt a legislative body vested with the highest honors, self-dependent, having nothing to fear from the people, and nothing to expect from the government; having no other object than the repression of all elements of evil, and the fostering of all elements of good, and having the greatest interest in the existence of a society, in the good or bad results of which it must participate. It has been very justly said that the Upper House of England is invaluable to the nation because it is a bulwark to liberty, and I may add, that the Senate of Venezuela would be not only a bulwark to liberty but a support to make the republic

everlasting.

Bolívar's endorsement of the hereditary Senate seems to be the result of a combination of tremendous confidence in those Senators and a basic distrust of direct election by the people. His confidence is expressed in his glowing description of the traits of these hypothetical Senators who would undoubtedly be "elite," but elite in terms of their education, preparation for public service, and dedication to wise governance on behalf of the people they represent. This is extraordinarily optimistic, to put it mildly.

He claims that the value of a hereditary Senate is that the Senators would share the interests of the people, along with their opinions and "spirit." But it's not at all obvious how an entrenched hereditary elite would somehow automatically share the interests of "the people." Indeed, hierarchical societies throughout human history have suggested exactly the opposite, including to this day.

He also claimed, specifically, that this hereditary Senate is not a violation of "political equality; it is not a nobility I wish to establish." Even though Bolívar explicitly claims that this does not create "nobility," it's difficult to see how it does not – especially when the model inspiring this proposal is the British House of Lords who are, notably, nobility. A hereditary ruling class initially selected from wealthy and politically connected (Spaniard) landowners seems precisely to be the beginning of a "noble" class.

It is also important to point out that there is something undeniably self-serving about this proposal, as this new hereditary class of political leaders would be elected by the very Congress to whom he was speaking, made up of socially and economically privileged *criollos* such as himself. Once this first batch of Senators was elected, the position would automatically be transferred to their children.

In fairness, Bolívar seems sincere in his belief that these hereditary senators would truly be the most capable among the population, raised from birth to be prepared for the responsibility of governing, and motivated to govern wisely and justly. Bolívar seems sincerely to believe that this elite class will be a de facto meritocracy, as future generations of these hereditary senators will be raised with their political destiny in mind and will receive the best education and preparation for their inevitable leadership positions, but this is arguably wildly optimistic faith in the enlightened benevolence and incorruptibility of the (permanent) wealthy and politically connected class.

Bolívar is also hardly the first political theorist to suggest that an "enlightened" elite can better serve the people than the people themselves. The Guardians of Plato's *Republic* immediately come to mind, and Senators in the U.S. Congress were not originally directly elected by their constituents, but were selected by state representatives, and to this day remain very much an "elite" institution – at least with respect to wealth and influence.

Although there are many more intriguing ideas presented in the Angostura Address, our final consideration will be another of his more "controversial" proposals, and arguably the most original: the creation of a "fourth branch" of government.

Popular education should be the paramount care of the paternal love of Congress. Morals and enlightenment are the poles of a republic; morals and enlightenment arc our prime necessities. Let us take from Athens her Areopagus, and the guardians of customs and laws; let us take from Rome her censors and domestic tribunals, and forming a holy alliance of those useful institutions, let us revive on earth the idea of a people which is not contented with being free and strong, but wants also lo be virtuous. Let us take from Sparta her austere institutions, and forming with these three springs a fountain of virtues, let us give our republic a fourth power, having jurisdiction over childhood and the heart of men, public spirit, good customs and republican morals. Let us establish such an Arcopagus to watch over the education of children, over national instruction, that

it may purify whatever is corrupt in the republic; denounce ingratitude, selfishness, coldness of love for the country, idleness, negligence of the citizens; pass judgment upon the origin of corruption, and pernicious examples, applying moral penalties to correct breaches of custom, just as afflictive punishment is applied to atone for a crime and not only whatever is repugnant to customs but that which weakens them as well; not only what may violate the Constitution, hut also whatever should infringe on public respect.

The jurisdiction of such court, a truly holy tribunal, should be effective with respect to education and instruction, and advisory only in what refers to penalties and punishment. Its annals or records, however, where its acts and deliberations are kept, the moral principles and the conduct of the citizens, shall be the hooks of virtue and vice; books that the people will consult for their elections, the executives for their decisions and the judges for their trials. Such an institution, no matter how chimerical it may appear, is infinitely more feasible than others which ancient and modern legislators have established, much less useful to human kind.

While you are probably already familiar with the three traditional branches of government (i.e., legislative, judicial, executives), the existence of a fourth branch quite probably comes as a surprise. This innovative fourth branch, or fourth "power," is described as a "moral power" by Bolívar and exists to promote the very civic education and virtue that he finds lacking in the people. Although the job description is vague, this fourth branch would be responsible for the maintenance and promotion of "public morals."

It is easy (and probably appropriate) to be concerned about the scope of authority for a public institution intended to (literally) police morals, and it is certainly the case that such institutions have been used numerous times throughout history in oppressive ways. For example, the "Committee for the Propagation of Virtue and the Prevention of Vice" has existed in Afghanistan since 1992, expanded by the Taliban when they took control of the country in 1996, and was *continued* by the new government of Afghanistan after the Taliban was overthrown by the United States, where it remained devoted to the "promotion of virtue and prevention of vice."[869]

Much closer (geographically) to Bolívar, Hugo Chavez oversaw the creation of a new constitution for the "Bolivarian Republic of Venezuela" in which he attempted to implement many of Bolívar's recommendations, including a version of the "moral power." The 1999 Constitution of Venezuela created a "citizen power" designated by a "Republican moral counsel" intended to regulate public morality. In practice, this ultimately provided justification for increasing restrictions on basic freedoms (especially freedom of speech) in the decades since.

Even Bolívar himself appealed to reasons of "public morality" when he limited various basic liberties and even outlawed the teaching of Bentham's philosophy (to which he himself subscribed!) when he had (again) assumed full dictatorial powers in 1828.

As undoubtedly authoritarian as this sounds, and is, keep in mind that Bolívar believed that the people of Spanish America were not yet mature enough or possessing of sufficient civic virtue for responsible self-governance.

> No matter how great the wisdom contained in codes, systems and statutes, they are a dead letter having but little influence in society; virtuous men, patriotic men, learned men make the republic.

While this is an obvious justification for depriving the people of political power, and a reliable blueprint for authoritarianism, in his defense, Bolívar wanted to *remedy* that problem in hopes that the people would eventually be capable of genuine self-determination. This required the development of civic virtues and a proper education, so he envisioned an additional branch of government devoted to precisely those things. This, at least, certainly distinguishes Bolívar from others who would keep the people in a state of *perpetual* political alienation. In this way, Bolívar appears both authoritarian and progressive at the same time.

A way in which Bolívar was unqualifiedly progressive was in his condemnation of slavery. To his credit, he used his influence and authority to "implore" that the representatives continue and confirm the abolition of slavery that Bolívar himself implemented, in the name of not only civil and political law, but the laws of nature themselves.

> I would not mention to you the most notable acts of my administration, did they not concern the majority of the Venezuelans. I refer, Gentlemen, to the most important resolutions taken in this last period. Atrocious, godless slavery covered with its sable mantle the land of Venezuela and our skies were overcast with storm clouds threatening a deluge of fire. I implored the protection of the God of Humanity, and Redemption scattered the storm. Slavery broke its chains and Venezuela has found herself surrounded by her new children, grateful children who have turned their instruments of captivity into arms of liberty. Yea, those who were slaves are now free; those who were the enemies of their foster mother are now the defenders of a country. To emphasize the justice, the necessity, the beneficent results of this measure, is superfluous, when you know the history of the Helots, Spartacus

---

[869] As of the time of this writing, the Taliban have *reclaimed* control of Afghanistan, and will undoubtedly preserve this institution.

and Haiti; when you know that one cannot be free and enslaved at the same time, unless in violation of the laws of nature and the civil and political laws. I leave to your sovereign decision the reform or abrogation of all my statutes and decrees; but I implore of you the confirmation of the absolute freedom of the slaves, as I would beg for my life and the life of the Republic.

We have now worked our way through excerpts of three of Bolívar's most significant writings: the Cartagena Manifesto, the Jamaica Letter, and Angostura Address. We can now identify and expand upon a handful of core ideas that emerge from those sources.

Bolívar the "pragmatist"

To say that Bolívar was a pragmatist is not to associate him with the official philosophical movement known as "pragmatism," generally associated with the American philosophers William James, Josiah Royce, Charles Sanders Peirce, and John Dewey. Instead, Bolívar was pragmatic in the colloquial sense of being "practical" as opposed to being "idealistic."

Bolívar's pragmatism revealed itself in his understanding of the practical limits of both liberty and equality. Starting with liberty, he was wary of unrealistic and exaggerated standards of freedom. "Abstract theorists create the pernicious idea of unlimited freedom."[870] Absolute freedom, according to Bolívar, would inevitably deteriorate into absolute power (tyranny), which is the antithesis of freedom. "Complete liberty and absolute democracy are but reefs upon which all Republican hopes have foundered."[871]

Much as he sought to find a mean between anarchy and democracy, he also sought a mean with regard to freedom, pursuing a "practical" or "social" liberty that would be a mean between the needs of society and the rights of the individual. In principle, he thought that a clear and strong

system of justice and law would provide just that balance, with the law protecting the masses and meritocracy rewarding virtue.

Bolívar had a nuanced understanding of equality as well, entertaining both an "absolute" and "relative" concept of equality, depending on context. Between Spain and the Americas, his vision of equality was absolute. The people of the Americas are and ought to be equal with those of Spain. When it came to equality amongst Americans, however, that equality was not exactly "equal." Bolívar acknowledged the obvious differences amongst Americans, recognizing that Americans were a mix of Europeans, Africans, and indigenous persons. Within that mix, there were natural variations. While all humans were born with an equal right to share in the benefits of society, it was clear to Bolívar that not everyone was equal with regard to their physical or mental talents, their education, their virtue, etc. Equality before the law was the essential foundation, and proper laws (and education) could begin to close gaps in social equality. To pursue this end, he imagined free public education provided to all people and reforms specifically targeting the most disadvantaged, such as those without property, and enslaved persons.[872]

Consistent with his pragmatism, Bolívar thought that state constitutions had to conform to their circumstances: the environment, character, history, and resources of the people the Constitution was meant to govern. Spanish America was very different from North America. The people of Spanish America were ethnically different, and thoroughly mixed (unlike the stricter racial segregation and hierarchy in North America), and the people of Spanish America had no prior experience with self-governance. As

---

[870] Quoted in Lynch, 12.
[871] Quoted in Lynch, 13.

[872] Lynch, 12 – 13.

stated in the Jamaica Letter, "do not adopt the best system of government, but the one that is most likely to succeed."

Bolívar the "elitist"

The elitist tendencies of Bolívar are, firstly, exhibited in his writings. As mentioned above, he found inspiration in the undeniably elite institution of the British House of Lords, speaking of it quite favorably.

> *Its aristocracy is immortal, indestructible, tenacious, and as durable as platinum; above all it was useful and active in the service of arms, commerce, scholarship and politics.*[873]

Like the Founding Fathers of the United States of America, Bolívar was a member of the wealthy land owning elite and had not only "confidence" in himself and his peers but also "reservations" about the capabilities of the "people" to govern themselves. Consistent with his pragmatism, he pursued a mean between aristocracy and populist anarchy.

> *I imagine that in Lima the rich will not tolerate democracy, nor will the freed slaves and pardos accept aristocracy. The former will prefer the tyranny of a single man, to avoid the tumult of rebellion and to provide a least a peaceful regime.*[874]

In addition, Bolívar shows some elitism when his elitist ideas were given form in the actual constitutions of new governments that he himself wrote. One such Constitution was the Bolivian Constitution of 1826.

Crafted, not surprisingly, for the new country of Bolivia (named after himself), this Constitution included division of power between legislative, executive, and judicial branches.

The legislative branch was divided into three bodies (as opposed to the more typical two branches): tribunals, senators, and censors – all of whom being elected, and named after their Roman predecessors.

Senators and tribunes had fixed terms, while censors serve for life. The tribunals were responsible for finance and major policies, the Senators were guardians of law and the relationship of the government with the church, and the censors were responsible for the preservation of civil liberties, the Constitution itself, and cultural mores – in other words, this was his "fourth branch" (proposed in his Angostura Address) reconceived as a third chamber of the legislature. Collectively, another key function of the legislature was to name the (first) president and to approve a list of successors that would be submitted by that president, and each president to come.

Regarding elections, he enacted multiple layers of *indirect* elections. Every ten citizens would choose representatives (electors), who would themselves name representatives (as well as nominating majors and judges/justices), who would then take part in the election of national Senators and Tribunes. In other words, there would be three degrees of separation between the people and their "elected" representatives in the legislature: the people vote (1) for a representative, who appoints (2) a representative who votes (3) for Senators and Tribunes who then make legislative decisions.

Note that this is quite similar to how some elections were originally handled in the United States of America, with State populations voting for State legislators, who would then elect Congressional Senators, who would then vote on national policies. Also similar to the United States, only property owners, "intellectuals," and business owners were allowed to vote, at the time.

A point of *dissimilarity*, however, to the United States, is that the Bolivian president would be appointed by the legislature (as opposed to being elected by something like the Electoral College) and serve for *life*. The president would also have the ability to appoint his own successor, with the vice president, serving in the absence of the president, being next in line for the

---

[873] Quoted in Lynch, 5.

[874] Quoted in Lynch, 5-6.

presidency. This complete rejection of electing the executive, and the recommendation of a life term for the executive, is a shocking about-face from Bolívar's stated principles at the address at Angostura: "the continuation of authority in the same individual has frequently meant the end of democratic governments. Repeated elections are essential in proper systems of government."

Bolívar the "progressive"

While there is certainly evidence of elitist elements in Bolívar's ideas and actual statecraft, there are also unquestionably "progressive" elements as well, and this tension between the elitist and progressive strains is found in both the political thought of Bolívar as well as in his North American counterparts.

While both ostensibly shared a dedication to the values of liberal democracy and of the European Enlightenment, the political thinkers of Latin America demonstrated concern for social justice (racial and economic) in ways that their northern counterparts did not, perhaps as a result of significant cultural differences.

In North America, the colonies were basically culturally homogenous, even though they were divided along lines of race, class, and gender. Despite the presence of enslaved Africans and displaced indigenous people, there was no significant attempt to incorporate elements of those cultures. Women, people of color, and men who did not own property were excluded from participation in self-government.

In Latin American societies, in contrast, multiculturalism was already in place due to the mixing of indigenous, European, and African culture. Indeed, even the kingdom of Spain (and the Iberian Peninsula) was a cultural mix of various influences, not only European but African, Jewish, and Muslim.

While the Latin American revolutions would not by any stretch of imagination produce absolute equality amongst its new citizens, there were clear efforts to extend liberty, rights, and political participation (to some degree) to the very sorts of people that remained marginalized in the North-- not to mention the fact that abolition of slavery came to many Latin American nations *decades* before it would be achieved in the United States.

In addition, rather than pursuing a policy of *taking* land from indigenous people, Bolívar had a history of attempting to *restore* land to indigenous persons. He issued a decree in Trujillo (Peru) in 1824 that was designed to promote agricultural production but that also served a social justice function. According to the decree, all state lands were to be offered for sale at one third of their estimated value, not to include lands already in the possession of Indians, who would be declared owners of that land with the right to sell or otherwise dispose of it however they wished. Indian "community lands" were to be distributed to landless occupants who would be made owners of that land, with the vision of creating independent farmers.[875]

Bolívar the "Imperial Republican"

Given both his elitist and progressive elements, we can rightfully say that Bolívar was a man of seeming contradictions.

He was a staunch anti-colonialist when it came to Spanish America; but he had high praises for the Roman imperial ethos, he seemed content with the British imperialism of his day, and he repeated many of the tropes typical of 19th Century colonialist thinking. He was a spirited combatant of monarchies, yet he insisted

---

[875] Lynch, 21. Although well-intentioned, the policies did not have the effects for which Bolívar had hoped. The land that was available for distribution to indigenous people was not the best land, is that had already been acquired by wealthy landowners. Moreover, granting indigenous people land, but without supplying

them with investment resources, including equipment, resulted in many indigenous people having to go into debt to already wealthy landowners in order to begin farming in the first place. When many of them, predictably, could not pay back their debt, they were forced to sell their land to the wealthy anyway.

on being president for life (i.e., a king without a crown). He ardently defended freedoms, yet he believed that South American nations were not fully prepared for liberal systems. He genuinely emancipated slaves, yet was extremely afraid of a takeover by pardos and "all the savage hordes from Africa and America who roam like wild deer in the wilderness of Colombia."[876]

Much as the American Revolution provided example and inspiration for several other revolutions (e.g., French, Haitian, Venezuelan, etc.), so too did these other revolutions occasionally serve as examples for one another.

Bolívar lived in Haiti for a time after its own revolution and was a personal associate of L'Ouverture. While there was much that Bolívar admired in the Haitian revolution, something that made him understandably nervous was the racially motivated violence (arguably to the point of genocide) against the white ruling elite. Himself both elite and white (a Spaniard born in Venezuela), Bolívar was concerned about the possibility of racial factions undermining civic solidarity in Venezuela and other new nations. In this respect, the multiculturalism found in the former Spanish-American colonies was not always regarded as an asset.

To prevent racial factions, Bolívar will ultimately propose a number of admittedly authoritarian features, including a president that would serve for life, a hereditary Senate, a new "branch" of government responsible for maintaining public morality and promoting civic education, and a very indirect method of voting for the population.

He spent his life fighting for liberty but was reluctant to fully extend that liberty to the majority of the population he liberated. This seeming inconsistency between high-minded liberal ideals espoused by revolutionaries and "liberators" and the less-than-liberal

governments they eventually implement was not unique to Bolívar but was found among the Founding Fathers of the United States, and among Enlightenment thinkers in general.

The view sometimes referred to as "liberal imperialism" proclaimed the value of liberty and equality but saw imperialism (which notoriously excluded liberty and equality for the colonized) as a legitimate means to extend liberal enlightenment values to regions of the world "not yet ready for their full implementation."

This 'liberal imperialism' defended 'European imperial rule as a benefit to backward subjects, authorized the abrogation of sovereignty of many indigenous states, and licensed increasingly interventionist policies in colonized societies' systems of education, law, property, and religion.[877]

Joshua Simon proposes the term "Republican imperialism" in an attempt to represent the tensions and seeming inconsistencies exhibited by Bolívar and others of his time. Simon describes it as a paradoxical doctrine that combines ideals of liberty and equality (particularly in the context of overthrowing colonial rule) with elitism and inequality within the newly liberated society.[878]

Bolivar was quite conscious of the elite social makeup of his movement's leadership and of the difficulties this implied for both the prosecution of the revolution itself and creation of an independent state. His writings are haunted by the spectre of 'pure democracy' and its implication, which he termed 'pardocracia': rule the free, mixed-race population that made up a plurality of Venezuela's inhabitants. He struggled with the possibility that this poor underclass, disdaining the 'legal equality' his revolution offered, would demand

---

[876] Andrade, G. and Lugo-Ocando, J., 2018. The Angostura Address 200 Years Later: A Critical Reading. *Iberoamericana – Nordic Journal of Latin*

American and Caribbean Studies, 47(1), p. 82.
[877] Quoted in Simon, 288.
[878] Simon, 282-283.

'absolute equality, both public and private', which would mean the 'extermination the privileged class' to which he himself belonged, and the abandonment of the enlightened projects that he honed to undertake in independent America. Thus, Bolivar led armies of liberation across the continent, forcefully annexing royalist territories and imposing a highly centralized constitution that concentrated authority in an American-born elite, defending these measures as indispensable means of establishing stable republican government in Spanish America.[879]

...

Though, as we have seen, Bolivar defended the Spanish American revolutions by reference to putatively universal republican ideals of independence and self-government, he favoured institutions that would limit the access of particular groups to high office, and repeatedly subjected cities and regions held by his opponents to military conquest and forced annexation. . . . Bolivar's theories of representation, separated powers, territorial expansion and federalism [can be described] as a republican imperialism. 'Republican', because in Bolivar's defence of imperial expansion, a lack of civic virtue, rather than economic and political backwardness, forms the basis of a 'strategy of exclusion' . . . In short, Bolivar's argument will be that because, after years of Spanish domination, Americans 'lack the political virtues that characterize the republican', their newly independent states should adopt constitutions that insulate government from popular control. In service to this end, Bolivar recommended hereditary legislative

chambers, special authorities to control press, education and public morality, a lifetime executive, and other surprising constitutional innovations.[880]

Although the philosophers of the Enlightenment, and the politicians inspired by them, preach to the values of "universal" equality and liberty, and the value of self-determination, their unwillingness to extend these allegedly universal ideals to all people in their midst was conspicuous.

In the United States of America, "universal" did not include women, the poor, or anyone who wasn't white. The leaders of the American Revolution were, generally, wealthy and elite land (and slave) owners who, while desiring greater freedom and self-determination for people like *themselves*, were also motivated to preserve their own privilege.

This theme of distrusting the masses (despite proclaiming to be fighting for freedom and the rights of "the people"), and, once liberated, designing a system of government that privileged the elite and diminished the influence of the larger population, was not unique to North America, and found parallels in the government's conceived and implemented by Bolívar as well.

To rationalize preaching liberty and equality while simultaneously withholding it required "strategies of exclusion." One notable description of this came from John Stuart Mill, who said "liberty, as a principle, has no application to any state of things anterior to the time when mankind has become capable of being improved by free and equal discussion."[881]

Mill's generally libertarian philosophy, which prohibited interference with personal liberty and action (so long as no harm was being inflicted) on utilitarian grounds, explicitly excluded people who he thought were incapable of making rational choices. Most obviously, this applied to children, but this kind of reasoning could also easily be extended to entire groups of adults who

---

[879] Simon, 283.
[880] Simon, 288-289.

[881] Mill, John Stuart. "On Liberty." Available here: https://www.econlib.org/library/Mill/mlLbty.html

were *perceived* as being incapable of making rational choices in their self-interest.

For people such as Bolívar (as well as most if not all of the Founding Fathers of the United States of American), it was a simple matter to dismiss many people as being incapable of rational participation in governance. Likely candidates could include women, Africans (whether enslaved or not), indigenous persons, or simply "poor" people who lacked sufficient education and character to make informed and wise political decisions.

A difference between Bolívar and the Founding Fathers of the United States worth mentioning (again) is that Bolívar understood the lack of civic virtue amongst Spanish Americans as the result of oppressive rule by Spain. This deficit could (and should) be *corrected* by proper education and cultivation of virtue, at which time more participation in government would be justified. In the United States, however, the prevailing opinions, as exemplified in the *Federalist Papers*, were generally pessimistic about human nature. Convinced that factions were inevitable, and that virtue was insufficient to guarantee the preservation of liberty, the U.S. Constitution was designed not only with systems of checks and balances and separations of powers, but to use ambition to counteract ambition.

> *That is to say, they viewed their constitutional innovations as mechanisms for stabilizing republican government by "economizing on virtue," by aligning personal interests with public goods or by balancing personal interests against one another, rather than as an educative regime designed to inculcate virtue in the populace.*[882]

For Bolívar, at least, exclusion was theoretically *temporary*. He consistently rejected monarchy, and favored representative democracy, and although he initially sought to create barriers between "the people" and their ability to directly participate in the government, he offered specific plans and institutions designed to prepare the people for a day when those barriers could be *removed*.

If the justification for denying self-governance to much of the people is that they lack sufficient education and civic virtue, the solution to that problem is to *provide* that education and development of virtue – and his "fourth branch" would be given that task.

Regardless if we agree with Bolívar's lack of confidence in the ability of most Spanish Americans to competently and responsibly participate in government, his exclusions do not appear to be based on any sort of *essentialist* elitism, according to which some people are literally incapable of ever anticipating meaningfully in politics, but is instead based on the *contingent* historical legacy of Spanish rule which, being passively oppressive, did not prepare Americans for their eventual liberation.

As a final (and sobering) point of comparison between Bolívar and his North American contemporaries, we will consider the United States' response to Bolívar's final and most ambitious political effort: the creation of an Inter-American Federation of nations that would include as many of the nations of the Americas as would be willing to join.

Panama Congress Of 1826

Although Bolívar privately thought that Haiti and the United States were too culturally different from other potential members to actually join, they were invited to participate in exploring this possibility at a summit in Panama City. While US President John Quincy Adams thought that sending representatives would be a good way for the United States to advocate for republican forms of government, freedom of religion, and trade opportunities with Latin America, he faced a significant opposition from Southern senators.

Missouri Senator Thomas Hart Benton spent several months in 1826 attempting to derail US participation in the Congress of Panama for

---

[882] Simon, 302-303.

reasons undeniably based on white supremacy and the interests of slave holding states.

One of the topics of conversation scheduled to be discussed at the Congress of Panama was the treatment of Africans in the Americas and the possibility of a "uniform rule of conduct" with regard to the treatment of Africans.

With the notable exception of the United States, delegates to the Congress would be made up of nations that had collectively *abolished* slavery, granted equality to Black citizens, and, in some cases were majority Black and were ruled by Black persons. The threat to slavery and white supremacy in the United States was too great to permit participation in this Congress. Speaking specifically of Haiti, Senator Benton said the following.

We purchase coffee from her and pay her for it; but we interchange no consuls or ministers. We receive no mulatto consuls, or black ambassadors from her. And why? Because the peace of eleven states in this union will not permit the fruits of a successful Negro insurrection to be exhibited among them. It will not permit consuls and ambassadors to establish themselves in our cities, and to parade to our country, and give their fellow black in the United States, proof in hand of the honors which await them, for the like successful effort on their part. It will not permit the fact to be seen, and told, that for the murder of their masters and mistresses, they are to find friends among the white people of these United States.[883]

Speaking of Black equality throughout Latin America, more generally, he said:

Five nations who have already put the

black man upon an equality with the white, not only in their constitutions but in real life; five nations who have at this moment (at least some of them) black generals and their armies and mulatto Senators in their Congresses![884]

Finally, speaking of concerns about the status of slavery in the United States, Benton added:

They say they only go to consult! I say, there are questions not debatable… I would not debate whether my slave is my property; and I would not go to Panama to "determine the rights of Haiti and of Africans" in the United States. Mister President, I do repeat, that this is a question which ought not to be agitated by us, neither at home nor abroad.[885]

Virginia Senator John Rudolph went even further than Benton by "saying the quiet part out loud" when addressing the seeming inconsistency between the ideals of the Declaration of Independence and the inequalities perpetuated by slavery. When it was suggested that the ideals of the South American republics were the same as those espoused in the U.S. Declaration, he *denounced the ideals of the US Declaration of Independence* as a "pernicious falsehood!"

Sir, my only objection is, that these principles, pushed to their extreme consequences – that all men are born free and equal – I can never ascend to, for the best of all reasons, as it is not true – – – even though I find it in the Declaration of Independence.[886]

Rudolph further dismissed the ideals of

---

[883] Fitz, Caitlin. *Our Sister Republics: The United States in an Age of American Revolutions*. New York: WW Norton, 2016. p., 35.

[884] ibid.

[885] ibid.

[886] Quoted in Orosco, José-Antonio. "The Continental Struggle for Democracy. The American Wars of Independence as Experiments in Justice." *Latin American and Latinx Philosophy. A Collaborative Introduction*. Edited by Robert Eli Sanchez Jr. New York: Routledge, 2020. p., 73.

Thomas Jefferson as suggesting "more of a professor of a university than the language of an old statesman," and he referred to the ideals as "metaphysical madness," and the musings of "mathematicians and stargazers."[887]

In other words, equality that extends across racial lines has no place in "real life," but is only a dangerous and abstract ideal.

Ultimately, the United States *did* send a delegation to the Congress of Panama, but the effort was moot, as one delegate died on the way, and the other arrived late, after the Congress had already concluded!

Conclusion

This chapter started by considering the provocative claim that immigrants from Latin America posed a "threat" to the cultural and political values of the United States by virtue of their being "different."

A serious examination of this alleged threat would take us far beyond the boundaries of philosophy, as it would require not only a thorough assessment of current political values of Latin American immigrants who enter the United States, but *also* a thorough assessment of the *actual* current political values of U.S. citizens.

A *charitable* assessment of this threat would overlook the obvious racist and ethnocentric subtext and consider the more "neutral" U.S. values of "the Constitution," "liberal democracy" and "individual rights" referenced at the beginning of this chapter.

If we consider the espoused values of the Founders of the United States, as well as those of the former Spanish colonies that would follow the footsteps of the United States to independence, a strong case can be made that there is, in fact, significant overlap of values, given the undeniable similarities in their Constitutions (e.g., separation of powers, indirect elections, etc.), and in the Enlightenment influences that inspired them.

In fact, where there are points of divergence, they often seem to fall in favor of the "liberalism" of the Latin American governments who, for example, voluntarily abolished slavery decades before Southern States were *compelled* to do so after a long and bloody civil war.

It can certainly be argued that many Latin American countries currently suffer from corruption in their government, and that many of those governments, such as that of Bolívar's own Venezuela, have turned much more authoritarian since their founding, and are oppressive with respect to individual liberties, civil rights, freedom of the press, etc. From a "liberal" perspective, that is an unfortunate degeneration from initially promising origins—but is even that really so "different" from what we observe in the United States today?

With respect to the U.S. Constitution, immigrants who become naturalized citizens must pass an examination that includes numerous questions about the Constitution. One out of three Americans would fail that test.[888] It's not at all obvious that Americans understand our Constitution better than immigrants, or, perhaps more importantly, that they value what is actually in it.

President Trump lavished praise on the Constitution, claiming "I feel very strongly about our Constitution. I'm proud of it, I love it." However, when asked specifically about how he would protect the powers listed in Article 1 (which mostly covers the powers of Congress), he said "I want to protect Article I, Article II, Article XII."[889]

There is no Article XII in the U.S. Constitution.

When participating in a filmed reading of the Constitution for Constitution Day, President Trump struggled to read aloud Article II (which addresses the election and powers of the President, no less), blaming it on the writing

---

[887] ibid.

[888] https://www.coloradoan.com/story/news/2014/03/29/immigrants-know-more-about-america-than-we-do/7017175/

[889] https://www.usatoday.com/story/opinion/2016/09/16/trump-constitution-libel-article-geneva-khan-first-amendment-chilling-column/90378484/ (Editorial note: the author of this article, John Pitney Jr., is a deeply conservative Republican.)

being "like a foreign language." His difficulty didn't suggest illiteracy, but rather *unfamiliarity*—a problem not shared by other (Republican) participants such as Senator Ted Cruz, Vice President Mike Pence, and former Vice President Dick Cheney.[890]

Much more relevant, however, are the actions of President Trump (and some of his supporters) that display a willingness to disregard the Constitution when it's inconvenient to honor it, such as when it comes to respecting free speech and freedom of the press, honoring treaties, and honoring the outcomes of elections, as evident by the efforts of the January 6th 2021 insurrectionists to prevent Congress from certifying the results of the Presidential election.

More generally, 26% of Americans qualify as "highly right wing authoritarian,"[891] and 39% of Republicans agreed that "if elected leaders will not protect America, the people must do it themselves, even if it requires violent actions."[892]

When someone like Newt Gingrich claims that immigrants don't share the American values of "rule of law" or "individual liberty," it needs to be observed that many Americans don't seem to share those values either! And, while there is certainly a left-wing authoritarianism observed today in many Latin American countries, the salient difference with the United States might be that it's "left" and not that it's "authoritarian."

With regard to respecting individual rights, many Americans would understandably ask, "whose rights?" Are the rights of people of color being respected within the criminal justice system, or in any of the other institutions in the United States that show evidence of systemic racism? Are the rights of women being respected when it comes to efforts to restrict reproductive choice, or to block equal pay laws? Are the rights of LGBTQ+ persons being respected?

It seems that the *political* "threat" of Latin immigrants, if any, is rooted more in anxiety that

their values might be "left-leaning" rather than somehow fundamentally un-American. For conservative-minded persons concerned about future elections, this is an understandable anxiety, but it speaks more to a desire to promote a particular brand of *conservative* American political ideology (at best), or just plain white supremacy (at worst).

---

[890] https://www.vanityfair.com/news/2020/01/donald-trump-disastrous-encounter-with-the-constitution-very-stable-genius
[891] https://morningconsult.com/2021/06/28/global-right-wing-authoritarian-test/

[892] https://www.npr.org/2021/02/11/966498544/a-scary-survey-finding-4-in-10-republicans-say-political-violence-may-be-necessa

Chapter 22: Social Contract & Pluralism

Comprehension questions you should be able to answer after reading this chapter:

1. What is Rawls' "Original Position" (OP)?
2. What is the "veil of ignorance" (VOI)? Explain what is meant by "ignorance," in this context. Of what are participants "ignorant?" What is the purpose of this ignorance?
3. What are Rawls' Two Principles of Justice? (POJ)
4. What are the "basic liberties" described in the 1st POJ?
5. What are the "primary goods" in the 2nd POJ? What two conditions must be met to justify an unequal distribution of primary goods? How could an unequal distribution of primary goods be to everyone's advantage?
6. Who are the "least advantaged?" Why should we focus on them, when considering applications of the two Principles of Justice?
7. What does Rawls mean by each of the following? Reasonable pluralism, well-ordered society, overlapping consensus, comprehensive moral doctrine, public reason, stability.
8. What does it mean to be constrained by "public reason" in the context of political debates and activism?
9. According to Rawls, when it is acceptable to "resist" our institutions and laws?
10. What is the difference between a "state," and a "people?" What are the features of "Peoples?"
11. What is the difference between "liberal" people and "decent" people?
12. Why does Rawls reject a global redistribution principle under a "one world government?"
13. What is a "burdened society?" What is the "duty of assistance" to burdened societies? How and when is that duty fulfilled?
14. What is an "outlaw state?" What are Rawls' principles of "just war" with respect to outlaw states?

Having surveyed some thinkers from across a couple thousand years' worth of political philosophy, we will now turn to a decidedly contemporary and American political philosopher: John Rawls.

Rawls was born on February 21st, 1921. Before he died in 2002, he taught at both Harvard and Oxford. He is undeniably a candidate for the most famous and important American philosopher of the 20th century. He was presented with a National Humanities Medal by President Bill Clinton in 1999, in recognition of how Rawls's work "helped a whole generation of learned Americans revive their faith in democracy itself."[893]

His most famous work is *A Theory of Justice*, first published in 1979. This book revolutionized contemporary ethical and political thought, and is now regarded as "one of the primary texts in political philosophy," according to Cambridge Dictionary of Philosophy.

At the heart of Rawls' philosophy is a 20th century version of the social contract approach— sometimes called an "enlightened" social contract. We will consider his approach to the social contract tradition in three stages:

1. His development of a "liberal political conception of justice"
2. His consideration of political stability given the fact of pluralism
3. His extension of stages one and two into

---

[893] *"The National Medal of the Arts and the National Humanities Medal". Clinton4.nara.gov. 1999-09-29.*

the realm of international politics

Stage 1: The Original Position

As mentioned, Rawls is part of the same social contract tradition that we have studied earlier in this chapter; a tradition that includes such theorists as Hobbes, Locke, and Xunzi. In each case, they had their own particular vision of the State of Nature—and Rawls is no different, in that regard.

Central to understanding Rawls' interpretation of the social contract tradition is his idea of the "original position." The "original position" (hereafter referred to as the OP) is another hypothetical situation, another thought-experiment analogous to that of the State of Nature itself. The OP is the hypothetical meeting that Rawls imagines taking place when people collectively decide to leave the State of Nature and create a government under which to live.

So, imagine a meeting of all the people who will be living in that new society. They have gathered together in order to decide upon the most fundamental political questions, such as what kind of government they will have, what sorts of laws, what sorts of rights (if any), how to distribute the resources of their society, and so on. What sort of decision-making procedure could participants employ, in the OP, in order to produce a government and laws that will be just and fair, that will be agreeable to everyone in the society?

To promote fairness, Rawls imagines that participants in the OP must first pass through a "veil of ignorance" (hereafter: VOI). Imagine that everyone must pass under a curtain before entering the meeting hall, and, when they do, this curtain temporarily suppresses all kinds of memories and information—it induces a selective "ignorance." Obviously, this is an imaginary process, but Rawls thinks it gives us insight into the requirements of justice. The image below should look somewhat familiar, as a simpler version of it was used in our previous explanation of Hobbes. There, the idea was that we emerge from the State of Nature to create a social contract, and then appoint a Sovereign to enforce that contract. In the expanded version applicable to Rawls, we emerge from the State of Nature into the OP, where we will decide on the social contract and Sovereign—but a key feature of the OP is that we are behind the VOI.

Behind the veil, participants are "ignorant" as concerns a variety of pieces of demographic information. These include:

- Race and ethnicity
- Gender
- Age
- Physical and mental ability or disability
- Sexual orientation
- Religious affiliation
- Socioeconomic status
- Generation (e.g., "Baby Boomer," "Gen X," "Millennial")
- Vision of the good life (i.e., personal

values)

In other words, the participants become ignorant of anything and everything that tells them who they are within their society. Once behind the VOI, a participant will not know his/her gender, or race, or age; s/he will not know if s/he is a genius or someone with a mental disability, an Olympic class athlete or someone with profound physical disabilities, a devout Christian or a Muslim or an atheist, a billionaire or a homeless person. Participants do not know to what generation they belong (meaning, a generation that has already lived and died, or living now, or one not yet born), or even what they find valuable in life.

Participants are not ignorant of everything, of course. To begin with, they have *concepts* of all of those things (e.g., race, gender, religion, etc.)—they just don't know how those concepts apply to themselves, or other participants.

In addition, in order to make important political decisions, they must have other kinds of basic knowledge intact. In order to decide what sort of government to create, what sorts of tax systems to enact, etc., participants must have a rudimentary understanding of the following:

- Basic economics
- Basic political theory
- Basic science
- Basic social sciences (including psychology and sociology, and that different persons have different worldviews and values)

Note the repetition of the word "basic." No one is suggesting that participants all have a Ph.D. in economics, or are professional psychologists. Instead, they are assumed to have the basic everyday understanding of the world and how it works that you and I already possess. They understand that there are different kinds of political systems (e.g., democracy, monarchy, theocracy, etc.) and have basic understanding of how they work. They have a basic understanding of economics (e.g., supply and demand). They have a basic understanding of human psychology (e.g., motivation, behavioral tendencies, etc.).

This sort of knowledge will allow them to decide between different forms of government, and will allow them to agree upon certain approaches to social and economic policy. The value of what they *do* know is obvious, but what's the value of what they do *not* know (i.e., all that demographic information suppressed by the VOI)? If you haven't figured it out already, you'll probably be stunned by how obvious the answer is.

As Rawls puts it: The purpose of the veil of ignorance is to ensure that principles of justice are chosen such that "no one is advantaged or disadvantaged in the choice of principles by the outcome of natural chance or the contingency of social circumstances." Put another way, if you don't know who you are, you can't use that information when making your decisions. In one word, the purpose of the VOI *is fairness.*

As an example, consider the very basic question of what sort of government ("Sovereign") to create/appoint. A participant in the OP suggests a dictatorship, in which one person wields all power, and everyone else has to submit to that one person's power. Keeping in mind that you don't know who you are when you step out from behind the VOI, would you agree to a dictatorship? Of course not! It's likely that the only way you would agree to a dictatorship is if you knew you were going to be the dictator. But, behind the VOI, you don't know who you are. Maybe you're the dictator, but it's much more likely that you're not.

So, what system would you agree to, then? Probably some form of democracy, since, in a democracy, (almost) everyone (in theory) has a right to participate in the political process. With a democratic political system, it doesn't matter who you are behind the VOI. If you agree to a democracy, you will have a presumably equal right to participate in basic political decision-making no matter who you happen to be.

To continue with the same example, having agreed upon "democracy," you now turn to the question of who will vote. Suppose that someone proposes that only property-owning white males will be allowed to vote. Would you agree to that behind the VOI? Of course not! You don't know whether or not you own property (socioeconomic status), whether or not you're white (race/ethnicity), or whether or not you're male (gender). Suppose you agree to this, then step out from behind the VOI to discover you're an African-American woman. Now you can't vote. Pretty foolish of you, right? If you don't know your own race or ethnicity, you're not going to agree to any law or policy that privileges one race over another. So too with gender. So too with religion.

Would you agree to form a State in which everyone must be Christian, if you had to make this decision behind the VOI? No way. For all you know, you're Muslim, or Hindu, or an atheist. For the very same reason, you would never agree to a social contract in which everyone was bound by Sharia law, nor one in which the exercise of religion (in general) was banned. None of those outcomes would be *fair*.

As previously stated, the primary purpose of the VOI is to ensure fairness. How do we ensure fairness? Recall that Rawls' theory is situated within the Social Contract tradition.

> *Here we face a difficulty for any political conception of justice that uses the idea of a contract, whether social or otherwise. The difficulty is this: we must find some point of view, removed from and not distorted by the particular features and circumstances of the all-encompassing background framework, from which a fair agreement between free and equal persons can be reached. The original position, with the feature I have called 'the veil of ignorance,' is this point of view.*[894]

The participants in the OP are not presumed to be idealists, seeking to create a utopia for all. Much more modestly, they are merely presumed to be self-interested. I want the best social contract for myself. You want the best one for yourself. And so on. How can we take that basic self-interest, and turn it towards fairness? By preventing participants from using certain (presumably politically irrelevant) pieces of information, such as race or gender, in making their decisions.

Perhaps controversially, or perhaps in a display of common-sense, Rawls thinks that the contingencies of birth are morally arbitrary. No one "deserves" to be born into a rich or poor family, into one ethnic group or another, into one sex or gender or sexual orientation, more or less naturally intelligent or physically gifted, etc. These are unearned accidents of birth. Since none of us "deserves" them, none of us is entitled to any benefit we might receive (or penalty we might suffer) due to the contingency of our birth.

Bluntly: things like race, gender, sexual orientation, religious affiliation, socioeconomic status (etc.) shouldn't *matter* in the context of constructing a just and fair social contract, and the just and fair political, legal, and economic institutions that will govern it, or the just and fair laws that should flow from those institutions. Since those things shouldn't matter, we shouldn't take them into consideration—and the VOI attempts to enforce that.

In theory, the only principles, laws, and policies you would agree to behind the VOI are those that you would agree to no matter who you are in society. If you would agree to them, no matter whom you are, that's a pretty good indicator that they're fair. In essence, if I don't know who I will be once I step out from behind the VOI, the contract that's best for "me" will turn out to be the contract that is best for anyone and everyone.

Using this basic approach, we *could* test every single policy proposal, law, and political decision by the standard of "would I agree to this behind the VOI?" However, Rawls offers us a shortcut. Rawls believed that the basic outcome of the OP and decisions made behind the VOI could be summarized by two basic <u>principles of justice</u>:

1. *Each person is to have an equal right to the most extensive scheme of equal basic liberties compatible with a similar scheme of liberties for others.*

2. *Social and economic inequalities are to be arranged so that they are both (a) reasonably expected to be to everyone's advantage and (b) attached to positions and offices open to all.*

The first principle of justice (hereafter referred to as a POJ) deals with basic rights and liberties and applies to the design of the political constitution of the society. The second POJ deals with the just distribution of what Rawls calls

---

[894] Rawls, John. "Justice as Fairness: Political not Metaphysical," *Philosophy and Public Affairs,* 14(3), 1985: 235.

"primary goods" (including wealth), and therefore to the economic institutions and policies of the society.

Basic Liberties

Rawls claims that participants behind the VOI would agree to equal access to, and an equal share of, certain **basic liberties**. If you are a United States citizen, or live in the U.S., or have merely heard of the U.S., you are probably familiar with the sorts of liberties he has in mind:

1. Political liberty (the right to vote and hold public office)
2. Freedom of speech and assembly
3. Liberty of conscience and thought
4. Freedom of the person (e.g., freedom from psychological oppression, physical assault, dismemberment, etc.)
5. The right to hold personal property
6. Freedom from arbitrary arrest and seizure

Certainly the idea that we have the right of free speech and the free exercise of religion is neither original nor unique to Rawls. One of the impressive things about Rawls' philosophy, though, is that he gives us a way to explain *why* we think we all do (or should) have such liberties, and why we think (for the most part), that everyone should have them equally. Moreover, his justification for such a right does not depend upon any particular religious, worldview—unlike Locke, perhaps.

For Locke, our rights, even in the State of Nature, come by virtue of our being equally created by God. What if you are an atheist, and don't believe that anyone is created by God,

equally or otherwise, because God doesn't exist? If, on the other hand, we derive our rights based on what we would (theoretically) agree to behind the VOI, then we have a justification for that right whether your worldview is religious, or naturalistic.

Let's start with the equal right to participate in the political process (i.e., democratic self-governance). *Why* do we think it just that we have such a right, and that is unjust if it is denied us? Think about what you would agree to behind the VOI. Not knowing who you are, it would be foolish of you to deny political participation to anyone on the basis of such things as race, gender, income, etc., because you might unwittingly disenfranchise yourself in the process.

So, what *would* you agree to? Who should be allowed to participate? *Everyone*—or, at least almost everyone, with few and defensible exceptions.[895] In that way, no matter who you are when you step out from behind the VOI, you have a right to self-governance. How much of a right? An equal right. In that way, no matter who you are, you have no less (nor any more) of a right than anyone else. Not only would it be foolish of you to agree to a contract where some people have rights, and others don't (while not knowing into which group you fall!), it would also be foolish of you to agree to a contract in which some people have a greater share of a right than do others (again, while not knowing into which group you fall).

As one more example, let's consider certain civil liberties pertaining to criminal trials. Some people express frustration with the fact that it costs more to execute a condemned criminal in the U.S. than to imprison him for the rest of his life.[896] How is this possible? How could a few

---

[895] Note: Some of you might be thinking that the fact that one must be 18 years old, or older, to vote in the U.S. signifies a violation of Rawls' procedure. After all, you don't know how old you are behind the VOI. However, no matter who you are behind the VOI, you probably recognize that children aren't terribly well equipped (mentally, and in terms of maturity) to vote. You are aware of basic human nature behind the VOI, after all.

Moreover, all one needs do in order to overcome this age discrimination is survive to the age of 18. Unlike denying the vote on the basis of race or gender, which is nothing one can "outgrow," a minimum age requirement is a temporary distinction, and could survive the scrutiny of the VOI.

[896] For example, according to the Death Penalty Information Center, if the Governor of the State

seconds of electricity, or a single bullet, or a dose of poison, be more expensive than room and board for life? Many of you already know the answer: because of the lengthy and expensive appeals process.

It's not as if a criminal is sentenced to death and is then dragged out behind the courthouse and shot. Instead, most condemned criminals spend decades filing appeals to their conviction, and the State must pay for its own attorneys and associated fees every single time—and often must pay for the condemned person's lawyer as well. By the time a couple decades go by, the cost adds up.

"I have the solution!" you exclaim. "Eliminate all those costly appeals! If a judge or jury finds the guy guilty, and sentences him to death, drag him out of the room and shoot him. Problem solved."

And yet, we have all those appeals and "safety nets" in place to protect convicted criminals. Why would we (or should we) have all those protections in place? Go behind the VOI, and you'll find your answer.

Not knowing who you are, you don't know if you're someone who has been, or ever will be, involved in the criminal justice system. It's a possibility though. Not knowing your income level, you don't know if you'll be able to afford an attorney—but you better believe you'd want one! So, behind the VOI, you would agree that everyone should have access to a lawyer, even if they can't afford to pay for one personally.

You'd want other protections in place, too. You'd want for *the State* to have to *prove* that you're guilty, instead of you having to prove that you're innocent. You'd want the State to have to present evidence against you, in public, as opposed to being able to arrest, try, and convict you on evidence unseen (or maybe even on no evidence at all).

What about all those expensive appeals?

You'd want those too. A dirty, ugly, fact is that innocent people have been, and continue to be, convicted of crimes they did not commit. Set aside conspiracy theories and crooked cops, sometimes people just plain make a mistake, and point to the wrong guy in a police lineup, or think they remember seeing someone who they didn't really see. It happens. It happens in death penalty cases as well.

In the year 2000, Illinois Governor George Ryan (a death penalty *supporter*) put an indefinite hold on executions in his state after 13 death row inmates' convictions were overturned. Also in 2000, the most comprehensive study (at that time) of death penalty cases in the U.S. found that 2/3 of all capital sentences that were reviewed were overturned when appealed due to either errors or inappropriate conduct during the trial. Examples of problems included incompetent defense teams, evidence suppressed by police and prosecutors, misinformed jurors, and biased judges.

DNA evidence alone has resulted in the post-conviction exoneration of 329 people (so far)—and 20 of them had been sentenced to death.[897] People awaiting execution on death row have been found innocent, and released, before it was too late. It's reasonable to believe that, sometimes, it was already too late — and an innocent person was put to death.[898] Imagine that you are that innocent person, wrongfully convicted and facing execution. Wouldn't you want a right to an appeal, every reasonable chance to prove that a mistake was made, before it's too late? That's why, behind the VOI, recognizing that someday we might be the person needing those protections, we would agree to them—despite the inconvenience, annoyance, and expense, when we're not the ones having to worry about it.

We could conduct this same exercise with

---

of California "commuted the sentences of those remaining on death row to life without parole, it would result in an immediate savings of $170 million per year, with a savings of $5 billion over the next 20 years."
(http://www.deathpenaltyinfo.org/costs-death-penalty)

[897] http://www.innocenceproject.org
[898] http://www.sfgate.com/crime/article/Judge-says-California-executed-man-who-6300005.php?cmpid=fb-desktop

each of the basic liberties. Put yourself behind the VOI, and ask yourself what you would agree to, and you'll be able to figure out why each of those basic liberties makes the list and, just as importantly, why the first POJ requires that each of us has an equal share of those liberties.

Primary Goods

We now turn to the second POJ. As a reminder, according to the second POJ, "social and economic inequalities are to be arranged so that they are both (a) reasonably expected to be to everyone's advantage and (b) attached to positions and offices open to all."

The second POJ, then, concerns the just distribution of "primary goods." "*Primary good*" is simply a term used to signify those things which nearly all of us want, all things considered, and that we typically would rather have more of, than less. Primary goods are those things which are useful in the pursuit of a wide range of visions of the good life. Examples of primary goods include:

- The basic right and liberties addresses in the 1st POJ
- Freedom to move and choose from among a wide variety of occupations
- Income and wealth
- Access to educational resources
- Access to health care
- The social bases of self-respect that give citizens a sense of dignity and self-worth

It's hard to find someone who doesn't want income, and the opportunity to earn it; who doesn't want access to health care or education, and so on. A harsh fact concerning some of these primary goods, though, is that they are finite. There is not an infinite amount of wealth, or educational access, or health care to go around. A simple illustration is available if you have ever had to sit in the waiting area of an emergency room waiting for medical attention for yourself or a loved one. Many patients with only a few doctors results in a long wait. Because some primary goods are limited, it's inevitable that we come up with some method of distributing them—this is an issue with which every society must contend, and that must be addressed by any social contract.

There are many possible methods of distribution. One person could get everything. Or a few people get most, and the rest fight for the scraps. Or, (as of 2017), the wealthiest 0.1% of Americans could make 188 *times* as much as the bottom 90% *combined*.[899] Or, everyone gets an equal share—or any number of distributions in-between. Which, distribution, though, is *fair* (given Rawls' approach)? Put yourself behind the VOI, and find out.

What would you agree to behind the VOI? We might assume that a participant's default choice of distribution will be "equal" — everyone has an exactly equal share of each primary good. That would mean that we all have an equal educational opportunity, equal access to health care, an equal standard of living, and so on. Why would we agree to that? Because no matter who I am once I step out from behind the VOI, I'm no worse off than anyone else. No one else has better health care, or a better standard of living, etc. However, while this might be our default distribution, Rawls claims that we don't have to stick with the default.

There is a way in which some inequality is permissible and just. An unequal distribution of primary goods is acceptable if and only if everyone is better off by virtue of that unequal distribution than they would have been had the distribution be equal. How is that possible? Consider the following two bar graphs.

---

[899] https://inequality.org/facts/income-inequality/

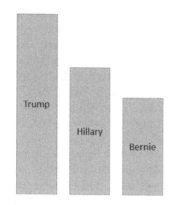

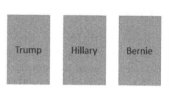

These two graphs represent the distribution of primary goods in two hypothetical communities ("left," and "right"). These are very simple communities, as each contains only three people: Trump, Hillary, and Bernie. Obviously, this is a grossly oversimplified picture, with only three people in each community, but that's all we need to illustrate the point. In the left-side community, there is an unequal distribution of primary goods. Trump has more of those goods (e.g., wealth, income, access to education, etc.) than Hillary and Bernie, and Hillary has more than Bernie. In the right-side community, there is a perfectly even distribution instead. Trump, Hillary, and Bernie each have an exactly equal share of those goods.

Although our default distribution that we would agree to behind the VOI would be the kind we see in the right-side community (i.e., a perfectly equal distribution), Rawls acknowledges that unequal distributions would be agreeable so long as they are "reasonably expected to be to everyone's advantage" and "attached to positions and offices open to all."

To be attached to positions and offices open to all simply means that it must be possible, in principle, for anyone to enjoy the greater share of the distribution. There must be genuine equality of opportunity (though not a guaranteed equality of outcome).

... fair equality of opportunity is said to require not merely that public offices and social positions be open in the formal sense, but that all should have a fair chance to attain them. To specify the idea of fair chance we say: supposing that there is a distribution of native endowments, those who have the same level of talent and ability and the same willingness to use these gifts should have the same prospects of success regardless of their social class of origin, the class into which they are born and develop until the age of reason. In all parts of society there are to be roughly the same prospects of culture and achievement for those similarly motivated and endowed.[900]

If it's possible for some people to become wealthier than others, that possibility must be open to everyone (in theory). Laws or customs that allowed only people of a particular race, or religion, or gender, for example, to attain great wealth, or to attend the best schools, would not satisfy this requirement, and would be considered unjust.

As to the first requirement, that the unequal distribution be to everyone's advantage, we can see how this is possible by comparing the two graphs. Notice that although the distribution is unequal in the left-side community, and some people are better off than others, every member

[900] Rawls, John. *Justice as Fairness: A Restatement.* Erin Kelly, ed. Cambridge: Harvard   University Press 2001: 43-44.

of left-side is better off than she or he would be in right-side. Trump has a greater amount of primary goods in left-side than he does is right-side. So do Hillary and Bernie. This is important. Behind the VOI, I don't know who I am in society (e.g., Trump, Hillary, or Bernie). If I had to choose between left-side and right-side, why would I pick left-side? Because no matter whom I am in left-side, I'm better off. Even if I'm the worst off, comparatively (Bernie), I still have more in left-side than I do in right-side. It makes sense, then, for me to pick left-side, no matter who I might turn out to be.

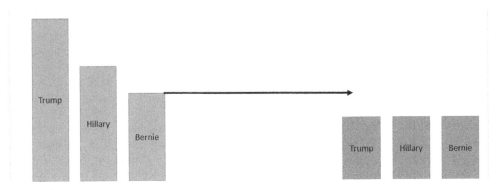

Some of you might be thinking to yourself, "wait a minute! This is an unfair comparison. Each person is comparatively better off in left-side than in right-side because there are more primary goods to distribute in left-side." This is true. If you take the total combined area of each bar in left-side, and compare it to the total combined area of each bar in right-side, left-side does produce a much greater overall area, representing a greater amount of primary goods to distribute.

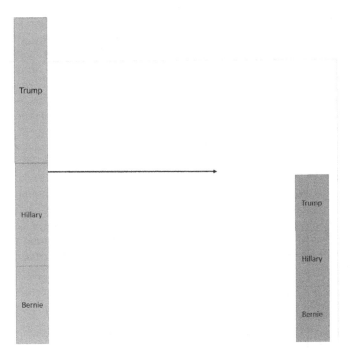

This isn't necessarily cause for suspicion, though — it's the product of a basic promise of capitalism. A key assumption behind capitalism — especially the *laissez-faire* variety — is that by allowing people to pursue wealth and luxury, the economy is stimulated and grows larger than it would be under a more egalitarian system.

If I knew that no matter how hard I worked, and no matter how much I risked, I would never be any better off than my neighbor, I (allegedly) wouldn't have the incentive to work so hard or take those risks — but that hard work and risk-taking is precisely what produces economic growth and improves society. Billionaires are far wealthier than the average citizen, but they don't just swim around in a tank of money; they use it. That use of money creates jobs, and the wealth "trickles down" to others, ultimately making everyone better off than they otherwise would have been — or so the argument goes.[901]

This sort of reasoning explains how the unequal distribution in left-side makes everyone better off compared to the equal distribution found in right-side. By allowing Trump to be so much more fabulously wealthy than Bernie, it makes Bernie better off too (i.e., better off than he would have been in a perfectly equal distribution).

Rawls was profoundly critical of *actual* U.S. economic policy, and thought that our own systems of distribution did not actually satisfy this requirement, but he was open to the possibility, in principle, that unequal distributions could be justified. We need to be careful that these unequal distributions really are to everyone's advantage, though, and one way to do this is by focusing on the "least advantaged," and how they are impacted by the proposed unequal distribution. Who are these least advantaged?

...persons whose family and class origins are more disadvantaged than others,

whose natural endowments (as realized) permit them to fare less well, and whose fortune and luck in the course of life turn out to be less happy, all within the normal range . . . and with the relevant measures based on social primary goods.[902]

Candidates for the "least advantaged" include (but are not limited to) the homeless, the sick, the injured, victims of natural disasters, people with physical or mental disabilities, and people belonging to groups that have traditionally been discriminated against (e.g., on the basis of race, gender, religion, etc.).

"Least advantaged" is not necessarily a permanent classification. If I get hurt at work, that can place me among the "least advantaged" for a time, but if I heal and can return to work and normal life, my relative disadvantage goes away.

If a group of people is discriminated against, its members may be amongst the least advantaged, but *if* circumstances *truly* change and there is no longer any stigma or harm attached to that group membership, people belonging to that group will no longer count as "least advantaged" (for that reason).

Remember, too, that we're talking about a *relative* disadvantage. If I'm blind, it's going to be more difficult for me to succeed in life than if I had use of my eyes—not impossible, but more difficult. If I'm a woman in a society that is somewhat gender biased, it will be more difficult for me to succeed—not impossible, just more difficult.

In an ideal (Rawlsian) world, everyone has an equal chance at a good life. In the real world, we face obstacles that shouldn't be there: discrimination, for example, or even just plain bad luck. Unequal distributions of primary goods are justifiable only if they are to everyone's advantage, and a good way to see if everyone is better off is to check with the least advantaged. If they're better off, it's a good bet that everyone

---

[901] This involves important and complicated economic theories, for which there is great debate. Take an economics class to explore this

further.

[902] Rawls, John. *A Theory of Justice*, revised edition. Harvard University Press, 1999: 83.

else is too.

It's important to remember that society is not obliged to arrange its practices and institutions so as to guarantee a perfectly equal distribution of goods. Instead, the arrangements must be such that at least those actions and policies that result in an unequal distribution of goods bring about a state of affairs in which the least-advantaged are better off than they would have been in the absence of the action or policy.

Stage 2: Pluralism

Having established the basic foundation for Rawls' approach to the social contract tradition in terms of the original position, veil of ignorance, and two principles of justice, we will now turn to the political issue that occupied him in the latter stages of his life and career, and which might seem especially relevant to the current U.S. political climate: the "problem" of reasonable pluralism.

We will first explore the concept of reasonable pluralism itself, consider Rawls' "solution" for it, and then consider how President Barack Obama employed a Rawlsian political philosophy in his own approach to public policy.

Pluralism, in general, merely refers to the fact that a variety of different worldviews exist. Some worldviews are religious (e.g., Christianity, Islam, Hinduism, etc.), and some are purely naturalistic (e.g., atheism, humanism, etc.). Even within these broad categories of religious and naturalistic, there are widely differing worldviews. Anglican Christianity is quite different from Wahabist Islam, for example. Religious and moral values range across a wide spectrum, and these values influence our political beliefs and values as well.

There is a difference, though, between mere pluralism and *reasonable* pluralism. Mere pluralism simply recognizes the plurality of views. Reasonable pluralism refers to the idea that no one worldview has an obvious monopoly on rationality. That is just to say that smart, sincere, reasonable people can be Christian, Muslim, atheists, Buddhists, etc. Such persons can be pro-life, or pro-choice; vegetarian, or omnivores; for or against the death penalty. It is simply not the case that one worldview is "obviously" true, and anyone subscribing to any other is "crazy."

Is the existence of reasonable pluralism in Western democratic societies also the *problem* of reasonable pluralism? Can a "well-ordered society" achieve the "overlapping consensus" of reasonable "comprehensive moral doctrines" needed to achieve "stability?" Before addressing that question, it's important to identify some key vocabulary.

- *Well-ordered society*: a society in which everyone accepts, and knows that everyone else accepts, the basic principles of justice, in which the main social and political institutions of that society satisfy those principles of justice, and in which the citizens regard their basic institutions as just and comply with their demands.

- *Comprehensive moral doctrine*: a "worldview," including views on morality, religion, etc.

- *Overlapping consensus*: when citizens support and obey laws and public policies for reasons internal to their own comprehensive moral doctrines, supporting the same law but for possibly different reasons.

- *Stability*: when citizens willingly obey their society's laws and policies, even in cases of sincere disagreement.

Rawls gives serious consideration to the problem of reasonable pluralism in his book entitled *Political Liberalism*, where one of his foci is to answer the question of how it is possible for a just and stable society of free and equal citizens to exist and endure when its citizens "remain profoundly divided by reasonable religious, philosophical, and moral doctrines."[903]

---

[903] Rawls, John. *Political Liberalism*. New York: Columbia University Press, 1996: xxxix.

Stability is an important issue because laws and policies are *coercive*. Citizens tend to accept coercion when they recognize that the coercion is legitimate, but resist when they think it is not. Laws forbidding murder and laws forbidding African-Americans from eating at lunch counters were, are, and should be received very differently, and afforded very different levels of respect. Acts of civil disobedience for the sake of pedophilia and acts of civil disobedience for the sake of ending segregation are (and should be) regarded with very different degrees of acceptance and respect.

Rawls' goal is to "uncover the conditions of the possibility of a reasonable public basis of justification on fundamental political questions' given the fact of 'reasonable pluralism' in a democratic culture."[904] To this end, he develops a political conception of justice that does not rely on any particular comprehensive moral doctrine for its foundation and that could, in theory, be endorsed by adherents of many different (and even competing) comprehensive moral doctrines. This political conception of justice is intended to be consistent and harmonious with various, competing, comprehensive doctrines so as to achieve the above-mentioned "overlapping consensus." His account of justice as "fairness," involving the ideas of the original position, veil of ignorance (etc.) described earlier in this chapter is an example of just such a political conception of justice. In theory, people from a wide range of worldviews could agree upon the procedures and principles provided by his theory (or so he hoped, at least), resulting in an overlapping consensus and a stable society.

It is important to note that Rawls is asking about stability with respect to a *well-ordered* society. If a society is well-ordered, then it is a society "in which everyone accepts, and knows that everyone else accepts, the very same principles of justice"[905] As well, the main social

and political institutions of that society are believed, with good reason, to satisfy those principles. Finally, the citizens regard the society's basic institutions as just, have a normally effective sense of justice themselves, and so generally comply with their society's basic institutions.

In other words, if you live in a "well-ordered society," everyone in your society has a basic, shared sense of justice and what it requires, your government and laws are themselves just, and, as such, inspire you (and others) to obey those (just) laws and respect those (just) institutions.

The possible "problem" is that some *reasonable* comprehensive doctrines could be so at odds, in certain places, with the principles of justice and the just society that results from them, that an overlapping consensus would not be achieved, and stability would not be achieved either.

Why would pluralism represent a threat to the stability of such a society? Generally, because pluralism entails different (and sometimes competing) views of the demands of morality and what constitutes a good and right way to live— and therefore what sorts of laws and public policies might be necessary and appropriate.

The most obvious possible tensions arise from religiously-based moral doctrines, in which an adherent might believe it morally imperative that one abstain from certain behaviors (or perform others), but such is not the belief of other fellow citizens. For example, the consumption of alcohol is forbidden by Islam on the basis of scripture—but the appeal to the Qur'an will hardly be persuasive to anyone who isn't a Muslim, and who has no other reason to believe drinking alcohol is morally wrong.[906] Unless the Muslim seeking to ban alcohol by means of public policy can somehow demonstrate that the "principles of justice" require the prohibition of alcohol consumption, it is entirely possible

---

904 ibid., xxi.

905 ibid., 35.

906 "You who believe! Intoxicants, gambling, al-ansāb, and al-azlām (arrows for seeking luck or

decision) are an abomination of Shaytān's (Satan's) handiwork. So avoid that in order that you may be successful."
—Qur'an, Surah 5 (al-Ma'idah), ayah 90

(indeed *likely*) that other citizens, who subscribe to other, reasonable, comprehensive moral doctrines (i.e., nearly any other major worldview than Islam), will disagree with and resist the proposed ban on alcohol—and be *reasonable* in so doing.

It's worth taking a moment, here, to make an important point: the *truth* of Islam (or any other comprehensive moral doctrine) is *not* what is up for debate here. Islam might offer a true account of what is right and wrong, or it might not. That is beside the point.

What is at issue here is what is reasonable to do or require within a political context. If everyone within a society was Muslim, and shared the same core values, then it is unlikely that there would be much disagreement as regards alcohol—nor would any ban on alcohol consumption likely be controversial or seem unreasonable. But, in a great many communities (including the United States), it is simply not the case that "everyone" is *anything*: not Muslim, not Christian, not Buddhist, not atheist. Instead, we are a mix of (mostly) reasonable and, at times, competing comprehensive moral doctrines.

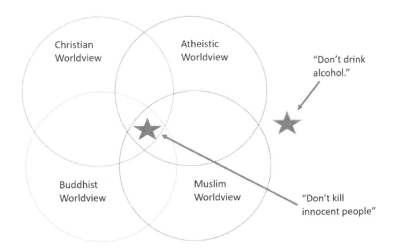

To put it bluntly, if I am a Christian I would probably find it unreasonable to be denied some wine at dinner (let alone at communion!) just because my Muslim neighbor's God (in whom *I* don't believe) forbids it, just as if I were an atheist, I might find it unreasonable for my Christian neighbor to make homosexual activity illegal because his God (in whom I don't believe) thinks it an "abomination."[907]

Given the existence of reasonable pluralism, is it even possible to achieve the overlapping consensus of reasonable comprehensive moral doctrines needed for stability? Even if citizens have deep disagreements on certain issues because of their different worldviews, can there

be enough "buy-in" to achieve a stable, well-ordered society?

To explore this issue of stability in the face of pluralism, we will consider the political hot-button of abortion—considering what (little) Rawls had to say about abortion, and how the moral and political issues surrounding abortion present a "stability" issue.

First, and for the record, what did Rawls say about abortion, himself? We will consider two representative quotations from Rawls (with underlining added for emphasis):

1. Regarding the troubled question of abortion: consider the question in terms

---

[907] Not all Christians believe this, of course. . . .

of these three important political values: the due respect for human life, the ordered reproduction of political society over time, including the family in some form, and finally the equality of women as equal citizens.. . . <u>any reasonable balance of these three values will give a woman a duly qualified right to decide whether or not to end her pregnancy during the first trimester.. . . [A]t this early stage of pregnancy the political value of the equality of women is overriding, and this right is required to give it substance and force</u>.[908]

2. In particular, when hotly disputed questions, such as that of abortion, arise which may lead to a stand-off between different political conceptions, citizens must vote on the question according to their complete ordering of political values. Indeed, this is a normal case: unanimity of views is not to be expected. Reasonable political conceptions of justice do not always lead to the same conclusion; nor do citizens holding the same conception always agree on particular issues. Yet the outcome of the vote, as I said before, is to be seen as legitimate provided all government officials, supported by other reasonable citizens, of a reasonably just constitutional regime sincerely vote in accordance with the idea of public reason. This doesn't mean the outcome is true or correct, but that it is reasonable and legitimate law, binding on citizens by the majority principle.

Some may, of course, reject a legitimate decision, as <u>Roman Catholics may reject a decision to grant a right to abortion. They may present an argument in public reason for denying it and fail to win a majority. But they need not themselves exercise the right to abortion. They can recognize the right as belonging to legitimate law enacted in accordance with legitimate political institutions and public reason, and therefore not resist it with force</u>. Forceful resistance is unreasonable: it would mean attempting to impose by force their own comprehensive doctrine that a majority of other citizens who follow public reason, not unreasonably, do not accept. <u>Certainly Catholics may, in line with public reason, continue to argue against the right to abortion</u>. Reasoning is not closed once and for all in public reason any more than it is closed in any form of reasoning. Moreover, that the Catholic Church's nonpublic reason requires its members to follow its doctrine is perfectly consistent with their also honoring public reason.

I do not discuss the question of abortion in itself since my concern is not with that question but rather to stress that political liberalism does not hold that the ideal of public reason should always lead to a general agreement of views, nor is it a fault that it does not. Citizens learn and profit from debate and argument, and when their arguments follow public reason, they instruct society's political culture and deepen their understanding of one another even when agreement cannot be reached.[909]

In brief, Rawls appears to believe that women have a right to make their own reproductive choices, at least within the first trimester of pregnancy—but far more important than his personal view on abortion, and far more relevant for our purposes in this chapter, is what he says about those who disagree.

---

[908] Rawls, *Political Liberalism*, 243 (footnote 32). Emphasis added.

[909] Rawls, John. "The Idea of Public Reason Revisited," in *The Law of Peoples with "The Idea of Public Reason Revisited."* Harvard University Press, 2002: 169-171. Emphasis added.

...unanimity of views is not to be expected. Reasonable political conceptions of justice do not always lead to the same conclusion; nor do citizens holding the same conception always agree on particular issues. Yet the outcome of the vote, as I said before, is to be seen as legitimate provided all government officials, supported by other reasonable citizens, of a reasonably just constitutional regime sincerely vote in accordance with the idea of public reason. This doesn't mean the outcome is true or correct, but that it is reasonable and legitimate law, binding on citizens by the majority principle.[910]

It is inevitable that citizens will disagree with each other on various laws and policy issues—even important, high-stakes issues like abortion, war, the death penalty, environmental policy, etc. Nevertheless, the policy outcome might still be the result of fair and legitimate political processes (e.g., a majority vote subject to just Constitutional constraints), in which case the law or policy is reasonable and legitimate—even if not "true."[911] The hypothetical Catholics who disagree are certainly free to abstain from abortion themselves, and to continue to vote against abortion access, and preach against it at the pulpit or over the dinner table—but what they may not do is use *force* to impose their will on their fellow citizens.

Forceful resistance is unreasonable: it would mean attempting to impose by force their own comprehensive doctrine that a majority of other citizens who follow public reason, not unreasonably, do not accept.[912]

In fairness, though, just how much force will an appeal to "reasonableness" have? If one believes that "abortion is murder," and one's "just" society not only permits the murder of unborn babies but perhaps even subsidizes and otherwise supports it by means of health care policies, one is likely to be dismayed at the unwillingness of one's public institutions to do the "right" thing. What does this admittedly hard case tell us about pluralism and Rawls' ability to address it?

Whether or not such a scenario indicates a stability problem depends upon whether or not the pro-life activists in question are "reasonable." Rawls defines a person as <u>reasonable</u> when, among equals, "they are ready to propose principles and standards as fair terms of cooperation and to abide by them willingly, given the assurance that others will likewise do so. Those norms they view as reasonable for everyone to accept and therefore as justifiable to them; and they are ready to discuss the fair terms that others propose."[913]

<u>Unreasonable</u> persons, on the other hand, "plan to engage in cooperative schemes but are unwilling to honor, or even to propose, except as a necessary public pretense, any general principles or standards for specifying fair terms of cooperation. They are ready to violate such terms as suits their interests when circumstances allow."[914]

To put this in very simple, non-political terms: imagine that you and a friend both want to play a new video game, and are trying to decide who gets to go first. You agree to flip a coin and the winner of the coin toss will get to play first, and then after one hour the other person gets to play. Your friend then reveals to you the following: "Just so you know, if I win the coin toss, everything will go as planned. But, if I lose, I'm just going to beat you up, and play first anyway—oh, and you won't get a turn at all, let alone the first one." Your friend doesn't sound very reasonable! What's the point of even doing the

---

[910] ibid., 169.

[911] This is just to say that it could, in fact, be *true* that there is a God who forbids abortion, and therefore laws that allow abortion are "false"—but those laws might nevertheless have been the result of just, fair, and reasonable political processes.

[912] ibid., 170.

[913] Rawls, *Political Liberalism*, 49.

[914] ibid., 50.

coin toss at all, if your friend isn't going to abide by the outcome anyway? Similarly, what's the point of an election if one side intends to assassinate the opposing candidate and impose a military coup if they should happen to lose? Democracy is great, so long as "we" win—but if we lose, to hell with voting? For Rawls, "reasonable" people intend to abide by the rules, even if they "lose." "Unreasonable" people are willing to cheat and ignore the rules if they should "lose."

Returning to the example of abortion, certain sorts of responses from our activist in question would be indicative of unreasonableness. Obvious examples would be things like bombing abortion clinics, murdering abortion providers, violent overthrow of the government or an election result, etc. Far less dramatic than any of those things is an unwillingness to honor "public reason."

Public Reason

The idea of public reason limits political discussion and deliberation primarily (and at the least) done by judges and justices, government officials (especially legislators and executives), and political candidates and their campaign spokespersons. *Ideally*, it applies to ordinary citizens as well whenever they personally deliberate upon, endorse or reject, and ultimately vote on a given policy.

> *A democratic government should justify its policies solely in terms of values that every reasonable citizen can endorse, at least when matters of basic justice are at stake. And, since the policies of a democratic government are ultimately the policies of the people, ordinary citizens should, in voting or in public advocacy, also support only those positions on matters of basic justice that can be justified in this way.*[915]

Or, as Rawls states in "The Idea of Public Reason Revisited":

> *Our exercise of political power is proper only when we sincerely believe that the reasons we offer for our political actions— were we to state them as government officials—are sufficient, and we also think that other citizens might reasonably accept those reasons.*[916]

The central claim of **public reason** is that, when dealing with the scope of basic liberty and other matters of basic justice, citizens should take only those positions that are defendable from some liberal political conception of justice, independently of any wider comprehensive moral doctrine.

According to Rawls, if a policy addresses "fundamental issues," it must be supported by the political values of public reason. "Since the exercise of political power must be legitimate, the ideal of citizenship imposes a moral, not a legal, duty—the duty of civility—to be able to explain to one another on those fundamental questions how the principles and policies they advocate and vote for can be supported by the political values of public reason."[917]

In other words, while it is (of course) not *illegal* (in the United States) to invoke religious reasons for opposition to abortion, and, if you do, you certainly do not violate any *legal* obligations of citizenship, it is, nevertheless, a "duty of civility" to offer reasons that are not unique to any particular worldview (e.g., Christian), but that instead draw on "public reason."

The point of invoking public reasons is a recognition that we have a duty to justify our policy decisions to one another by appealing to public values and public standards, principles of reasoning and pieces of evidence that all citizens could reasonably endorse and that do not rely on controversial theories, metaphysical assumptions, or controversial evidence.

To use an admittedly extreme example,

---

[915] de Marneffe, Peter. "Rawls' Idea of Public Reason," Pacific Philosophical Quarterly, 1994, 75 (3/4): 233.

[916] Rawls, "The Idea of Public Reason Revisited," 578.

[917] Rawls, *Political Liberalism*, 217.

imagine a small but wealthy organization of citizens lobbies to end (and ban) all vaccination of children, and their reason for this is that they have received telepathic communications from an alien mothership warning that only unvaccinated children will be allowed to "beam up" when the ship comes to claim us and take us to our new home in another galaxy. Needless to say, very few of us will be persuaded by appeals to telepathic messages from aliens.

Similarly, if People for the Ethical Treatment of Animals (PETA) lobbied to ban all animal experimentation and meat consumption because their members all claim to have been animals in one of their many past lives, they would find no allies among the majority of citizens who do not believe in reincarnation. Perhaps wisely, PETA focuses on the far less controversial claim that animals experience pain—something that we can all acknowledge, and something which (could) appeal to any and all of us.

The moral/civil "demands" of public reason do not apply to everything and every context. Rawls claims that, at minimum, public reasons should be invoked when deep, fundamental issues of justice are at stake, such as "constitutional essentials" and matters of basic justice. When political decisions concern things like who gets to vote (or whether to impose voter-ID laws), which religions are to be tolerated (or whether to provide public financial support to private church charities), who can own property, who should be assured equality of opportunity—basically, anything involving the basic liberties described earlier in this chapter—then public reasons should be provided so that, in theory, people from across a wide variety of comprehensive moral doctrines could understand, and agree to, the reasons provided for one's policy stance.

Even when dealing with constitutional essentials and basic liberties, the demand of public reason is merely that public reasons be provided, not that non-public reasons be excluded. Citizens may offer *nonpublic reasons* as support for their views so long as the public reasons are themselves sufficient to render their answer to a political question "reasonable." A sufficient reason is one that is "good enough, standing on its own, to justify the position taken in public political debate."[918]

> *Reasonable comprehensive doctrines, religious or non-religious, may be introduced in public political discourse at any time, provided that in due course proper political reasons—and not reasons given solely by comprehensive doctrines—are presented that are sufficient to support whatever the comprehensive doctrines introduced are said to support. This injunction to present proper political reasons I refer to as the proviso, and it specifies public political culture as distinct from the background culture.[919]*

Thus, groups are not entirely prevented from appealing to the values from their comprehensive doctrines when promoting policies concerning fundamental issues, but they are obliged to use such values as *supplements* to their already sufficient argument that has been made under the restrictions set by the idea of public reason. A policy issue that isn't so "fundamental" (i.e., doesn't pertain to basic justice or constitutional essentials, such as how much public funding to provide for State parks) need not be justified by public reason at all, but Rawls says that it is nevertheless "usually highly desirable to settle political questions by invoking the values of public reason."[920] That is, while it is not required that non-essential issues be justified by public reason, it's a good and desirable thing if they are.

Why would citizens, individually or collectively, agree to abide by the limits of public reason? Rawls thinks that this is because they might recognize that it is the reasonable and morally civil thing to do. This is so because "except by endorsing a reasonable constitutional

---

[918] de Marneffe, "Rawls' Idea of Public Reason," 230 (note 12).
[919] Rawls, "The Idea of Public Reason Revisited,"

591.
[920] Rawls, *Political Liberalism*, 215.

democracy, there is no other way fairly to ensure the liberty of its adherents consistent with the equal liberties of other reasonable free and equal citizens."[921]

That is, a reasonable comprehensive moral doctrine will recognize that *reasonable* political judgments cannot be overridden according to the dictates of a particular comprehensive doctrine without trampling on the rights of other free, equal, and reasonable citizens.

Those who wish to override their fellow citizens when the reasonable judgments of the majority are at odds with the values of their own doctrine are *un*reasonable because they refuse to honor the reasonable judgments arrived at by their fellow citizens through legitimate majoritarian political procedures. What could this be other than an attempt to *coerce* others into accepting one's own beliefs? In the case of our hypothetical pro-life activist, *she* believes that abortion is murder. Clearly, not everyone else does!

What might our pro-lifer do in such a situation? One option would be to attempt to coerce others into compliance through acts of sabotage, intimidation, or civil disobedience. As an extreme example, Dr. George Tiller was shot and killed by Scott Roeder in 2009. Dr. Tiller was one of only a few doctors willing to perform late-term abortions, and Roeder publicly confessed to the killing, offering the following as his justification: "preborn children's lives were in imminent danger."[922]

However, according to Rawls, "Forceful resistance is unreasonable: it would mean attempting to impose by force their own comprehensive doctrine that a majority of other citizens who follow public reason, not unreasonably, do not accept."[923] If our pro-lifer is "reasonable," she must honor the policies and laws of her society—though she is free to use *legitimate* means to alter policies. For example, she might support Operation Rescue financially, educate herself on the merits of the pro-life position, sponsor and participate in "speak-outs" and consciousness-raising events, wear and distribute pro-life t-shirts and caps, lobby her elected representatives, and otherwise attempt to persuade her fellow citizens that abortion is wrong.

A Christian pro-lifer who adheres to the constraints of public reason will recognize that not all her fellow citizens share her theological worldview—nor even do all her fellow *Christian* citizens share her political stance on abortion. Recognizing that other (reasonable) citizens subscribe to other (reasonable) worldviews, she will not base her public opposition to abortion solely on a reference to a Bible verse—a reference that many of her fellow citizens (e.g., atheists, Hindus, Buddhists, etc.) will not accept as authoritative.[924] Instead, she will attempt to offer reasons to oppose abortion that could, in theory, be agreeable regardless of one's particular worldview.

Given that most of us, for example, agree that someone taking our own life (in most cases) would be a bad thing, perhaps the pro-lifer could offer an argument demonstrating the basic similarity between a fetus and an adult with respect to the default value of life itself, and propose that just as (generally speaking) it would be wrong to deprive an adult of his or her life without proper justification, so too is it wrong (in general) to deprive a fetus of its life (without proper justification).[925]

This strategy does not require that the pro-lifer accept that other worldviews are equally true, nor that she abandon her own faith and convictions. It merely acknowledges that, in the

---

[921] Rawls, "The Idea of Public Reason Revisited," 590.

[922] AP: Man admits killing Kansas abortion doctor". *MSNBC*. Associated Press. November 9, 2009.

[923] Rawls, "The Idea of Public Reason Revisited," 606.

[924] For example, Job 31:15: "Did not he that made me in the womb make him? and did not one fashion us in the womb?"

[925] Please don't assume that this is my advocacy against abortion access, nor that this is the best (let alone only) way to formulate such a strategy. This example is just that: an example.

public political sphere, it is "reasonable" to advocate for or against policy positions without relying solely on potentially controversial (and not universally recognized) values and beliefs.

Depending on what sorts of expectations she has, and on what sorts of activities in which she's

willing to engage, our pro-lifer is either reasonable or unreasonable. If *unreasonable*, then, surprisingly enough, there is no "stability" problem. This is so because of the way Rawls defines the stability issue to begin with.

Recall that our focus is on a well-ordered society. Rawls claims a well-ordered democratic society can be well-ordered by a political conception of justice so long as two conditions are met. The first is that citizens from *reasonable* comprehensive doctrines (at least) belong to the overlapping consensus. That is, they generally endorse that conception of justice. The second condition is that "unreasonable comprehensive doctrines do not gain enough currency to undermine society's essential justice."[926]

The overlapping consensus is built from *reasonable* comprehensive doctrines. If our pro-lifer's comprehensive moral doctrine is unreasonable in the ways described above, then she is not part of the overlapping consensus in the first place. Accordingly, she is not a threat to *stability*—though she might well be a threat to the well-orderedness of the society if her comprehensive moral doctrine is both unreasonable and gains sufficient "currency."

To step away from our pro-lifer for a moment, consider the example of ISIS (or ISIL). The particular Salafist version of Islam espoused by this organization is an example of a comprehensive moral doctrine. Using Rawls'

vocabulary, it is also undeniably an "unreasonable" comprehensive moral doctrine because, among other things, it opposes democracy!

Adherents to this worldview believe that their views are "the truth," that all opposing views are heretical or blasphemous, and that even voting itself is morally wrong. Clearly, sincere members of ISIS would not abide by the outcome of a fair election that doesn't go their way, if they are opposed to elections in the first place! Anywhere where ISIS has gained "sufficient currency" (e.g., ISIS-controlled portions of Syria or Iraq) are simply not "well-ordered" societies governed by a liberal political conception of justice. The stability concern does not arise here because there is no well-ordered society to be stable, or unstable, in the first place.

The United States, however, is not ISIS-controlled Syria or Iraq, and a case could be made that U.S. society is well-ordered.[927] Here, though, the same as "there," well-orderedness can be threatened by "unreasonable" groups who grow too large or too influential—and this is precisely the worry behind the possible problem of pluralism. Though the analogy with ISIS might be

---

[926]Rawls, *Political Liberalism*, 39.

[927] A claim subject to debate, of course. . . .

uncomfortable and overly provocative, it's not difficult to see how the analogy can be made.

Why should we assume that a sincere pro-lifer would be persuaded by the appeal to reasonableness? Why assume that she would acknowledge that it is unreasonable to expect others to comply with the demands of *her* comprehensive moral doctrine (forcibly, if necessary) given the reality of reasonable pluralism? If our pro-lifer believes her doctrine to be *true*, what force does an appeal to "reasonableness" have on her? Michael Huemer, using the example of a religious fundamentalist, argues that appeals to reasonableness will be effective only insofar as the dissident values reasonableness more than his "truth."

> *If a view which entails that I should do act A is true, whereas another view which entails that I should not do A is, while false, more 'reasonable' than the first, then what must I do? Ex hypothesi, I should do act A— that is, act in accordance with the first view.*[928]

His general point is that any value (such as "reasonableness") brought to bear on a comprehensive doctrine will be *evaluated from the viewpoint of that doctrine*. We might imagine our pro-lifer scoffing at appeals to reasonableness, if reasonableness demands that she tolerate the "murder" of unborn children. Indeed, the aforementioned Roeder posted a comment on the Operation Rescue website, claiming that Dr. "Tiller is the concentration camp 'Mengele' of our day and needs to be stopped before he and those who protect him bring judgment upon our nation."[929]

Needless to say, urging someone like Roeder to be "reasonable" might be unpersuasive, much as urging members of ISIS to be "reasonable" might be. This is *not* to suggest that people opposed to abortion are "just like members of

ISIS!" This is only to point out that appeals to "reasonableness" will only be persuasive to the extent that one values reasonableness, and it's not difficult to imagine any number of comprehensive moral doctrines in which "reasonableness" is less important that "truth," or "God's will."

Be that as it may, Rawls claims that the zeal to embody the whole truth in politics is incompatible with an idea of public reason belonging to democratic citizenship. In other words, if a citizen believes that policy should conform to the dictates of her comprehensive doctrine *regardless* of what the majority of her fellow citizens (reasonably) believe because the "truth" of her doctrine trumps the demand for "reasonableness" in political deliberation, this citizen is herself unreasonable. "When there is a plurality of reasonable doctrines, it is unreasonable or worse to want to use the sanctions of state power to correct, or to punish, those who disagree with us."[930] Such persons certainly exist, maybe even in a hypothetical well-ordered society, but in such a society, as unreasonable, they are not part of the overlapping consensus of reasonable comprehensive moral doctrines anyway.

Does this mean that it could *never* be reasonable, from a Rawlsian perspective, for a pro-lifer (or adherents to any other comprehensive moral doctrine) to insist that her values be enforced? That it is never justifiable to "act up" in defense of one's values? As it turns out, resistance is, sometimes, justifiable.

Under the principle of fairness, a person is required to "do his part as defined by the rules of an institution" given two conditions:

1.   The institution is itself just (i.e., satisfies the principles of justice).
2.   The person has voluntarily accepted the benefits provided by the institution.

[928] Huemer, Michael. "Rawls' Problem of Stability," *Social Theory and Practice*, 22(3): 383.
[929] "Shooter In Kansas Physician Killing Held Extreme Beliefs". Anti-Defamation League. June

2, 2009. Archived from the original on June 8, 2009.
[930] Rawls, *Political Liberalism*, 138.

That is, someone who benefits from a just institution is obligated to fulfill her obligations as defined by the institution. On the other hand, "it is not possible to be bound to unjust institutions, or at least to institutions which exceed the limits of tolerable injustice."[931]

We are morally bound to *just* institutions, but *not* to those that are intolerably unjust. A society with an inadequate political conception of justice, or one in which the public institutions are not themselves just (or permit gross injustice to occur) is not one with respect to which one must necessarily be tolerant. As examples, Rawls appeals to both the abolitionist and civil rights movements.

Both slavery and racial discrimination violate the principles of justice. That such things were not only permitted, but even legislated and enforced by the political institutions of the country at the time, is indicative that our public institutions, at least with respect to those issues, were *unjust*. Both abolitionists and leaders of the civil rights movement extensively appealed to their comprehensive moral doctrines (typically, religiously-based) to provide arguments against those practices—though they certainly also appealed to the *public* (shared) values of freedom and equality. Rawls supposes that such activists "could have seen their actions as the best way to bring about a well-ordered and just society in which the ideal of public reason could eventually be honored. . . . Given those historical conditions, it was not unreasonable of them to act as they did for the sake of the ideal of public reason itself."[932]

Exactly *when* civil disobedience, inspired by our comprehensive moral doctrines, is justified is a complicated question, and beyond the scope of this chapter. With certain issues, and in certain scenarios, however, justice might not only allow, but *depend upon*, an activist doing more than simply attempting to persuade others, through the use of public reasons, to change the problematic policies. By definition, such a society is not a well-ordered society, and so our focus will have shifted from stability issues to the justice of civil disobedience, but this is nevertheless one scenario in which more aggressive measures might be appropriate.

Stage 3: International Politics

Keep in mind everything that you have learned in the previous two stages: some of it is about to get recycled.

John Rawls offers an interpretation of the social contract tradition that attempts to not only establish the bases of a just and fair constitution and political institutions, but also define the basic principles of justice that will determine the legitimacy of our laws and policies, and establish our basic liberties. This conception of justice as fairness is an example of a political conception of justice that is not dependent upon any particular comprehensive moral doctrine, but is intended to be consistent with a wide variety of them. In this way, Rawls offers an example of how an overlapping consensus of reasonable comprehensive moral doctrines can be achieved.

By justifying our policy positions within the limits of public reason, we promote and preserve the legitimacy of those policies such that, even when we "lose," we still respect the legitimacy of that outcome, and will honor the results, despite our disagreement. In this way, the well-ordered society becomes and remains stable, despite the existence of reasonable pluralism with respect to worldviews.

We will now consider what Rawls had to say about the extension of his theory into the realm of international politics. Although it might be overly simple, for our purposes I think an instructive way to understand this third stage is simply as a combination of the first two.

In the first stage, Rawls employs the idea of the original position to identify the principles of justice that he thinks individuals would agree to when constructing their society and its political institutions. At this third stage, a second "original position" will be employed with the notable exception being that instead of individuals being the participants, it will be entire "peoples."

In the second stage, Rawls considered how the pluralism of comprehensive worldviews held

---

[931] Rawls, *A Theory of Justice. Revised Edition*, 96.

[932] Rawls, *Political Liberalism*, 250-251.

by different individuals could be accommodated in a way that achieves political stability within their shared society. At this third stage, Rawls considers how the pluralism of dominant comprehensive worldviews held by different societies can be accommodated in a way that achieves political stability within our shared global community.

Before delving into the synthesis of these two stages however, I want to introduce a little bit of vocabulary, much as I did in the previous section.

- "States:"
  o A group of persons moved by desires to enlarge territory, or to convert other societies to its religion, or to gain power over others, or to increase its own relative economic strength resources.
  o Not to be confused with "peoples"
- "Peoples:"
  o A group of persons who have (sufficiently) in common traits such as culture, history, tradition, or sentiment.
  o They are presumed to be ruled by a common government, and attached to a common conception of what is right and what is just.
  o In most cases, this will usually correspond to the term "nation." However, this is not necessarily always the case.
  o They see themselves as free, politically independent, and equally deserving of respect.
  o They are "reasonable" to the extent they honor fair terms of cooperation with other peoples, and are willing to abide by them even at the expense of their own interests, so long as other peoples are willing to do the same.
  o They are unwilling to impose by force their own political or social ideals on other reasonable peoples.
  o Peoples may be subdivided into two types:
    ▪ Liberal peoples: peoples

governed by liberal principles of justice identical to, or at least similar to, those developed in *A Theory of Justice*. ("Stage 1" of this chapter)

- Decent peoples: peoples who are *not* "just" according to the standards of liberal principles of justice.
  - The basic institutions of their society do *not* recognize reasonable pluralism, nor do they have "liberal" equality with regard to their citizens or subjects.
  - Their public institutions might be organized around a single comprehensive doctrine, probably religious in nature, and their political system might not be democratic. However, they are sufficiently well-ordered to merit equal membership in the international society.
  - They do not have aggressive foreign policies.
  - Although they are not liberal societies (in the sense of political conceptions of justice), they do secure and honor a core list of human rights, and their government, even if not a democracy, does make a sincere effort to consult with representatives of all social groups.
  - They also allow for protest, and for their citizens to immigrate to other countries.

Whereas stages one and two of our exploration of Rawls concerns individual human beings within one domestic political community, stage three will concern "peoples," within one global political community.

The (global) Original Position

For those of you paying attention, you might recall that in a footnote earlier in this chapter I mentioned that although Rawls thinks participants would be ignorant of contingent "accidents of birth" such as race, gender, ability, sexual orientation, etc. (among other traits), he did not think that nationality or citizenship status should be included among those traits of which participants are ignorant. This is a significant omission that produces significant consequences. For example, because participants at the first original position are ignorant of their socioeconomic status, they are motivated to agree to principles of justice that include restrictions on inequality with regard to primary goods. The second principle of justice, as you might recall, only allows unequal distributions if these unequal distributions are open to everyone and improve the circumstances of everyone involved more so than would have an equal distribution.

One could easily imagine, and some critics of Rawls' international theory have in fact imagined, that representatives of societies at the second original position might make similar demands, thereby introducing a global redistribution principle. Much like the second principle of justice only allows for unequal distributions of primary goods between individuals within a particular society if those unequal distributions are to everyone's advantage, someone might suppose that at this second original position representatives of societies would only agree upon unequal distributions of primary goods between entire societies if those unequal distributions were to the advantage of *all* societies.

Just as at the level of the first original position this mentality produces redistribution of wealth and a fairly robust system of social safety nets, we would anticipate that a similar approach at the global level would likewise result in substantial redistributions of wealth between nations – and yet, Rawls *rejects* this outcome.

Although Rawls does use the idea of the original position a second time to develop his international notions of justice, and although participants are "ignorant" of the relative wealth, prosperity, and power of the nation they represent, he thinks that participants would not operate as they did at the first original position—demanding that inequalities be addressed through redistribution of primary goods, if necessary. Specifically, they will not demand that national resources be redistributed to improve the lives of the least well-off nations. Although there will likely be in some cases large differences in wealth between individuals of different countries, and between countries themselves, Rawls thinks that this is not in itself objectionable. At this point, we can offer his explanation as to why.

Rawls' account that he develops in the *Law of Peoples* is constrained, by his own admission, by the need to describe a "realistic utopia." Essential to this constraint, and his claim that the principles of justice developed in the original position do not apply on a global scale, is his belief that a "world state" proposed at a global-level original position is unworkable for a variety of reasons, including cultural and communication difficulties. He claims that a world government "would either be a global despotism or else will rule over a fragile Empire torn by frequent civil strife as various regions and peoples tried to gain their political freedom and autonomy."[933]

In other words, a so-called "one world government" (within which resources might be redistributed according to some global principle of justice analogous to the second principle of justice in the first original position) is not a feasible option.[934] Beyond that though, Rawls

---

[933] John Rawls, *The Law of Peoples*, Harvard University press, 1999. p. 36.

[934] His rejection of the feasibility of a so-called "one world government" has an impact on immigration policy as well. Just as Rawls does not exclude nationality behind the veil of ignorance, nor does he (to a point at least) exclude citizenship status. This is just to say that he thinks it is reasonable (and probably inevitable) that a society would keep track of

seems to think that even if such a system was possible, global redistribution of primary goods would not be desirable or fair.

> *If a global principle of distributive justice for the Law of Peoples is meant to apply to our world as it is with its extreme injustices, crippling poverty, and inequalities, its appeal is understandable. But if it is meant to apply continuously without end – without a target, as one might say – and the hypothetical world arrived at after the duty of assistance is fully satisfied, its appeal is questionable. In the latter hypothetical world a global principle gives what we would, I think, regard as unacceptable results.*[935]

This is not to say that Rawls will claim that nations have no responsibility to assist other, less advantaged communities. Under the Law of Peoples, there is a "duty of assistance" to "burdened societies." Burdened societies "lack the political and cultural traditions, human capital, and know-how, and, often, the material and technological resources needed to be well-ordered."[936]   The "duty of assistance" is structurally *dis*similar to the difference principle developed in the (original) OP, however, for a variety of reasons.

For one, the difference principle in the first original position applies continuously. Policies are to be continuously adjusted and applied to make sure that unequal distributions of primary goods are to everyone's advantage. The duty of assistance agreed to at the second original position, however, is fulfilled once the burdened society is well-ordered.

Another point of difference is that the difference principle is specifically about primary goods, while the duty of assistance might not actually involve much actual wealth. If the burdened society is not well-ordered because of technological limitations, or institutional deficiencies, then the assistance provided might more appropriately be information, technology, training, etc.

In effect, Rawls promotes a two-tiered approach to distributive justice: at the first level, which is a domestic context, there is a demand for a roughly egalitarian distribution of primary goods – with exceptions being justifiable only if they meet both conditions set out in the second principle of justice. In the international context, however, equality just requires that each person finds themselves in a well-ordered "people," and that "people" be respected within international society.

This strong distinction between domestic and international demands of justice is justified by Rawls by his claim that limitations on distributive justice are consequences of tolerating and respecting the decisions, including the economic decisions, of peoples. On the assumption that these peoples are well-ordered, they have made autonomous decisions concerning their economic policies, savings rates, population policies, etc. These decisions have

---

(and regulate) immigration. John Rawls argues that although national boundaries are arbitrary from a historical point of view, an important role of government is to be the "effective agent of a people as they take responsibility for their territory and the size of the population, as well as for maintaining the lands environmental integrity. Unless a definite agent is given responsibility for maintaining an asset and bears the responsibility and loss for not doing so, that asset tends to deteriorate." (*Law of Peoples*, 8) Moreover, of the numerous causes of immigration, Rawls thinks that several would

disappear in the ideal society of liberal and decent peoples. One cause is the persecution of religious and ethnic minorities. Another is a denial of human rights. Another is political oppression. Yet another is fleeing from starvation or desperate poverty. If genuine freedom and equal justice were established, in ways consistent with or at least similar to those prescribed by the principles of justice, he thinks that than many of the causes of immigration would be eliminated. (*Law of Peoples*, 9)

[935] ibid., 117.
[936] ibid., 106.

consequences. He thinks it would be disrespectful of decisions made by peoples, presumably adopted for what those peoples took to be good reasons, to require one people to compensate another.

> *I believe that the causes of the wealth of a people and the forms it takes lie in their political culture and in the religious, philosophical, and moral traditions that support the basic structure of their political and social institutions, as well as in the industriousness and cooperative talents of its members, all supported by their political virtues.... The crucial elements that make the difference are the political culture, the political virtues and civic society of the country, its members' probity and industriousness, their capacity for innovation, and much else. Crucial also is the country's population policy: it must take care that it does not overburden its lands and economy with a larger population than it can sustain.... What must be realized is that merely dispensing funds will not suffice to rectify basic political and social injustices (though money is often essential). But an emphasis on human rights may work to change ineffective regimes and the conduct of the rulers who have been callous about the well-being of their own people.[937]*

The duty of assistance requires well-ordered peoples to help burdened societies eventually become members of the society of well-ordered peoples. Achieving membership is the goal. Once it is achieved, additional assistance is not required, even though the newly well-ordered society might still be economically (relatively) poor.[938]

> *One reason for reducing inequalities with a domestic society is to relieve the suffering and hardships of the poor. Yet this does not require that all persons be equal in wealth. In itself, it doesn't matter how great the gap between rich and poor may be. What matters are the consequences. In a liberal domestic society that gap cannot be wider than the criterion of reciprocity allows, so that the least advantaged (as the third liberal principle requires) have sufficient all-purpose means to make intelligent and effective use of their freedoms and live reasonable and worthwhile lives. If that situation exists, there is no further need to narrow the gap. Similarly in the basic structure of the Society of Peoples, once the duty of assistance is satisfied and all the peoples have a working liberal or decent government, there is again no reason to narrow the gap between the average wealth of different peoples.[939]*

Rawls gives an example of two liberal (or at least "decent") peoples with roughly the same level of wealth in terms of primary goods and roughly the same population size. The first decides to industrialize and increase its rate of saving, and the second does not. The second is content with its current condition, and enjoys a more leisurely society. Decades later, the first society is twice as wealthy as the second. On the assumption that both societies are liberal or decent, and that their peoples are free, responsible, and able to make (and have made) their own decisions, should the first country be taxed to increase the wealth of the second? According to the duty of assistance, the answer is no. According to a global egalitarian principle without a target, the answer would be yes. Rawls thinks that this is unacceptable.[940]

At this point, we have only considered what

---

[937] ibid., 108-109.

[938] ibid., 111.

[939] ibid., 114.

[940] ibid.,117. Editorial Note: it seems that this line of reasoning could work backwards, and

against the basic assumptions behind *A Theory of Justice*, as well, operating as a criticism of Rawls. One could argue that a significant contributing factor to differences in wealth and prosperity for *individuals* is individual choice,

Rawls is denying at the global stage. It's time to backtrack and develop what he is supplying as well. With regard to international political philosophy, Rawls begins within the social contract tradition and adds to it his thought experiment of the original position (and veil of ignorance). He will extend this thought experiment by introducing a second "original position," in which representatives of "liberal peoples" make agreements with other such peoples.

At the second veil of ignorance, participants do not know the size of their territorial population, the relative strength of the people whose interests they represent, the extent of the resources, the level of their economic development, or other such information.[941] Rawls makes the connection between the original position and the issues he addressed in *Political Liberalism* clear:

> *Putting people's comprehensive doctrines behind the veil of ignorance enables us to find a political conception of justice that can be the focus of an overlapping consensus and thereby serve as a public basis of justification in a society marked by the fact of reasonable pluralism.*[942]

Participants at this second original position are largely and strategically "ignorant," as in the first OP—but just like in the first OP, they retain some information as well. What they *do* know is that they come from reasonably favorable conditions such that a constitutional democracy is possible for their politically liberal society. It is also the case that their basic needs are met, though they are not necessarily "cheerful and happy."[943] In addition, such peoples have an interest in a proper sort of self-respect, as a people. This is not mere nationalism or patriotism, though there is undoubtedly some overlap. What distinguishes peoples from states in this regard is that peoples are prepared to grant the same respect and recognition to other peoples as they desire for themselves.[944]

In the first OP, Rawls thinks participants would agree (among other things) to the Two Principles of Justice. At the second OP, he comes up with a similar (lengthier) set of principles on an international scale:

1. Peoples are free and independent, and their freedom and independence are to be respected by other peoples.
2. Peoples are to observe treaties and undertakings.
3. Peoples are equal and are parties to the agreements that bind them.
4. Peoples are to observe a duty of nonintervention.
5. Peoples have the right of self-defense but no right to instigate war for reasons other than self-defense.
6. Peoples are to honor human rights.
7. Peoples are to observe certain specified restrictions in the conduct of war.
8. Peoples have a duty to assist other peoples living under unfavorable conditions that prevent their having a just or decent political and social

---

personal responsibility, management of money and savings habits, etc. Couldn't one argue that it is unfair and unreasonable to expect other individuals to make up for the deficiencies of less responsible individuals in order to secure more equal distributions of wealth and prosperity? A critic of Rawls could generate a parallel example involving *individuals* who make informed and autonomous decisions that result in significant differences in their share of primary goods within the community. On the assumption that these different outcomes result from those actual decisions, as opposed to the contingencies of birth that are excluded behind the veil of ignorance, is it fair to redistribute primary goods to benefit the lesser advantaged in this case, if Rawls is opposed to it at an international level?

[941] ibid., 34 – 35.
[942] ibid., 32.
[943] ibid., 47.
[944] ibid., 35.

regime.[945]

Having established the international equivalent of the "principles of justice" (and having done so using basically the same method as employed in *A Theory of Justice*), we can now turn to the international equivalent of the issue of pluralism.

Global Pluralism

After the first OP, even after a liberal political conception of justice had been worked out, there remained the task of figuring out how people subscribing to a variety of different world views could achieve a stable, overlapping consensus. That was the work of *Political Liberalism*. In *Political Liberalism*, Rawls addresses the fact of reasonable pluralism and tries to articulate ways in which the fact of reasonable pluralism need not become the *problem* of reasonable pluralism. The *international* equivalent of this is the fact of diversity with respect to culture, religion, tradition, etc.

At neither the domestic nor international level is it reasonable to try to force policies on those who disagree by means of force itself. The political conception of justice includes an idea of toleration that operates at both the domestic and international level. We may paraphrase Rawls' argument in defense of this notion of reasonable tolerance as follows:

1. Not all reasonable persons affirm the same comprehensive doctrine.
2. Of the many reasonable comprehensive doctrines that are affirmed, not all of them can be true (as judged from within any one comprehensive doctrine).
3. It is not unreasonable of someone to affirm a reasonable comprehensive doctrine.
4. Those who affirm reasonable comprehensive doctrines that are different from our own are reasonable, just as we are reasonable in affirming

our own reasonable comprehensive doctrine.
5. It is unreasonable to use political power to repress comprehensive doctrines that are reasonable yet different from your own.[946]

There is a direct and intended parallel between *Political Liberalism* and the "society of peoples" he develops in the *Law of Peoples*. In *Political Liberalism*, the proposal is that in a constitutional democratic system, comprehensive moral doctrines of "truth," or of "right," are to be replaced (in political discourse) by the idea of the "politically reasonable" addressed from one citizen to another. This involves adhering to the limits of "public reason."

In the society of peoples, public reason is likewise invoked and its principles are addressed from one peoples to another. The comprehensive moral doctrines which might be persuasive within a particular society are replaced by public reasons which could be shared by a variety of different peoples.[947]

Within a politically liberal constitutional democracy, the ideal of public reason is idealized by government officials whenever they (in their speech and conduct) follow public reason. Citizens follow public reason when they vote and act *as* if they were legislators.

At the level of peoples, the ideal of public reason is realized when executives and legislators of those peoples likewise follow the principles of the Law of Peoples and explain their reasons to other peoples in ways that could theoretically be shared. Analogously, at this level, private citizens should simply aspire in their voting and actions to act as though they were these legislators.[948]

The importance of adhering to public reason cannot be overstated as far as Rawls is concerned. His endorsement of the urgency and necessity of public reason seems especially prescient given the current climate of political discourse in the United States.

---

[945] ibid., 37.
[946] Paraphrased from ibid., 16, footnote 8.

[947] ibid., 55.
[948] ibid., 56.

Without citizens' allegiance to public reason and their honoring the duty of civility, divisions and hostilities between doctrines are bound in time to assert themselves, should they not already exist. Harmony and concord among doctrines and a people's affirming public reason are unhappily not a permanent condition of social life. Rather, harmony and concord depend on the vitality of the public political culture and on citizens' being devoted to and realizing the ideal of public reason. Citizens could easily fall into bitterness and resentment, once they no longer see the point of affirming an ideal of public reason and come to ignore it.[949]

In *Political Liberalism*, the goal was to generate an overlapping consensus between reasonable people from across a variety of comprehensive doctrines for the sake of establishing a stable and well-ordered society. Only "reasonable" persons could be candidates for the overlapping consensus because only reasonable persons would agree to the principle of reciprocity, according to which it is agreed that it is unreasonable to use force to exert one's political will. Now that we have shifted to international politics, it remains to be seen who Rawls thinks can be a part of the society of peoples.

Rawls does *not* limit the society of peoples only to liberal constitutional democracies, such as those he presupposes in *Political Liberalism*. Instead, he claims that liberal societies are required to cooperate with all peoples in "good standing." To require that all societies be liberal would be to violate the requirement of

appropriate toleration found in *Political Liberalism* itself.

So long as a non-liberal society's basic institutions meet certain minimum requirements, then those peoples are "decent," though not "liberal."[950] Rawls breaks up societal types into several categories, including "reasonable liberal peoples," "decent peoples" (a variety of which will be discussed below), and "burdened societies" (for whom the "duty of assistance" was discussed above). Recall that a burdened society is one whose "historical, social, and economic circumstances make their achieving a well-ordered regime, whether liberal or decent, difficult if not impossible."[951] In addition, there are "outlaw states" (who will be discussed at the end of this section).

An example of an alternative to liberal political constitutional democracies that is, nevertheless, "decent" is a "decent hierarchical society." As a hypothetical example of such a society, Rawls imagines an imaginary Muslim theocracy that he calls "Kazanistan."[952]

What makes a decent hierarchical society "decent," is that it satisfies several criteria. First, it is not aggressive, and recognizes the necessity of diplomacy and trade as opposed to war. Although its particular comprehensive moral doctrine (religious or otherwise) has significant influence on government and its policies, it respects the political and social values of other societies.[953]

Second, its system of law secures human rights for all of its members. These rights include the right to life (and the means of subsistence and security), liberty (including freedom from slavery, serfdom, and forced occupation, property (specifically *personal* property), and

---

[949] ibid., 175. It seems clear to me that the sort of cynicism and resentment that Rawls is concerned with could arise not only within the sphere of national politics, but international politics as well. It is not difficult to notice dissatisfaction among citizens with their own governments, as well as the international community, such as the United Nations.
[950] ibid., 59-60.

[951] ibid., 90.
[952] It is important to note that Rawls does not assume that any "decent hierarchical societies" actually exist, any more than he assumes that any genuine liberal political constitutional democracies actually exist. In both cases, ideals are presented.
[953] ibid., 64.

formal equality before the law.[954]

In addition, the system of law imposes moral duties and obligations that are recognized and respected by its people and which operates through political and social cooperation.

Finally, there must be a sincere and reasonable belief on the part of judges and other administrators of the legal system that the law is actually guided by a "common good" idea of justice, assigns human rights to all its members, and is upheld in good faith.[955]

An important limitation to decent hierarchical societies is that although they might have a state religion which is the ultimate authority within their own society, that authority may not be extended to relations with *other* societies. In addition, there must be a "sufficient measure of liberty of conscience and freedom of religion and thought, even if these freedoms are not as extensive nor as equal for all members of the decent society as they are in liberal societies. Although the established religion may have various privileges, is essential to the societies being decent that no religion be persecuted, or denied civic and social conditions permitting its practice in peace and without fear."[956]

Rawls allows that "reasonableness" exists along a spectrum, and is not simply binary. With regard to freedom of religion, a genuinely liberal society allows for full and equal freedom of religion, and is thus fully reasonable in that regard. A fully unreasonable society, in contrast, denies it entirely. A decent hierarchical society would be somewhere in between: allowing for some of freedom of conscience, but not full and equal expression of it.[957]

Liberal and decent peoples alike are to be respected, and can cooperate to form the overlapping consensus that generates the society of peoples, but "outlaw states" are a different matter. Outlaw states do not meet the standards of either liberal or decent societies, and as such are aggressive and dangerous. Outlaw states are the equivalent of "unreasonable" individuals with "unreasonable" comprehensive moral doctrines with regard to stability and an overlapping consensus in a particular society.

Outlaw states are likewise "unreasonable," and Rawls claims that liberal and decent societies have a right to intervene against outlaw states, when necessary.[958] This generates one of the *rare* circumstances in which Rawls thinks that war is justifiable.

According to Rawls' version of just war theory, no state has a right to go to war in pursuit of its rational, as opposed to reasonable, interests. For example, it might be in the rational interest of a society to invade a vulnerable neighbor in order to seize its wealth and resources. However, to do so is not "reasonable." Only wars of self-defense are justifiable. Such wars are waged in order to protect the basic freedom of citizens and political institutions, as opposed to in order to gain the wealth, power, territory, etc.[959] The official principles that make up his just war doctrine with regard to *jus in bello* (the conduct of war) are as follows:

(I)   The aim of a just war is just and lasting peace among peoples.

(II)   Well-Ordered peoples don't wage war against each other, but only against non-well-ordered states who threaten them.

(III)   Well-Ordered peoples distinguish between the leaders of an outlaw state, its soldiers, and its civilian population. Because the outlaw state is not well-ordered, its civilian population is not responsible for the aggressive acts of their leaders. Aside from the upper ranks of officers, soldiers are also not responsible.

(IV)   During the conduct of war, a well-ordered people should indicate the kind of peace and relationships they seek to obtain.

(V)   War plans and strategies must be

---

[954] ibid., 65.
[955] ibid., 66 – 67.
[956] ibid., 74.
[957] ibid., 74.
[958] ibid., 81.
[959] ibid., 91

limited by the preceding principles.[960]

Application: President Barack Obama and John Rawls

In this application section, I would like to offer an example of where political philosophy has concrete policy implications. Far from being a "merely theoretical" exercise, political theories can, and do, influence politicians and policies alike, in this case, the policies and strategies of President Barack Obama being influenced by the theories of John Rawls.

There is reason to believe that President Obama is familiar with the work of John Rawls. For one, his Columbia College roommate says so!

Mr. Boerner recalls Mr. Obama wrapping himself in a green sleeping bag (seen in this photo Mr. Boerner took) to keep warm when they studied at home. They listened to reggae. Bob Marley. Peter Tosh. Talked philosophy. Theories of justice and John Rawls. Mr. Boerner recalled Mr. Obama joking that he would rather be spending his time pondering Lou Rawls, the singer.[961]

Far more compelling than an appeal to his roommate's memory, though, is a comparison of some excerpts of one of President Obama's speeches with statements written by Rawls himself.[962] For example, both Rawls and Obama are concerned with the "problem" of reasonable pluralism.

How it is possible for a just and stable society of free and equal citizens to exist and endure when its citizens 'remain profoundly divided by reasonable religious, philosophical, and moral doctrines? (Rawls)

I answered with what has come to be the

typically liberal response in such debates - namely, I said that we live in a pluralistic society, that I can't impose my own religious views on another, . . .(Obama)

Both see the value of, and need for, and "overlapping consensus" of comprehensive moral doctrines.

<u>Overlapping consensus</u>: wide-spread agreement on core issues involving various (and even competing) comprehensive moral doctrines—necessary for a stable, well-ordered society. (Paraphrase of **Rawls**)

Moreover, if we progressives shed some of these biases, we might recognize some <u>overlapping values</u> that both religious and secular people share when it comes to the moral and material direction of our country. (**Obama**—emphasis added)

Both recognize the importance of being able to articulate one's policy positions by appealing to shared values, and reasons that could, in principle, be endorsed by a wide variety of people—even though who do not agree with one's own comprehensive moral doctrine.

Our exercise of political power is proper only when we sincerely believe that the reasons we offer for our political actions— were we to state them as government officials—are sufficient, and we also think that other citizens might reasonably accept those reasons. (Rawls)

Whatever we once were, we are no longer just a Christian nation; we are also a Jewish nation, a Muslim nation, a Buddhist nation, a Hindu nation, and a nation of nonbelievers.

---

[960] ibid., 94 – 96.

[961] http://cityroom.blogs.nytimes.com/2009/01/20/recollections-of-obamas-ex-roommate/comment-page-2/

[962] The full transcript of this speech is available here: http://www.nytimes.com/2006/06/28/us/politics/2006obamaspeech.html?_r=0

And even if we did have only Christians in our midst, if we expelled every non-Christian from the United States of America, whose Christianity would we teach in the schools? Would we go with James Dobson's, or Al Sharpton's? Which passages of Scripture should guide our public policy?...

This brings me to my second point. Democracy demands that the religiously motivated translate their concerns into universal, rather than religion-specific, values. It requires that their proposals be subject to argument, and amenable to reason. I may be opposed to abortion for religious reasons, but if I seek to pass a law banning the practice, I cannot simply point to the teachings of my church or evoke God's will. I have to explain why abortion violates some principle that is accessible to people of all faiths, including those with no faith at all.

Now this is going to be difficult for some who believe in the inerrancy of the Bible, as many evangelicals do. But in a pluralistic democracy, we have no choice. Politics depends on our ability to persuade each other of common aims based on a common reality. It involves the compromise, the art of what's possible. At some fundamental level, religion does not allow for compromise. It's the art of the impossible. If God has spoken, then followers are expected to live up to God's edicts, regardless of the consequences. To base one's life on such uncompromising commitments may be sublime, but to base our policy making on such commitments would be a dangerous thing. And if you doubt that, let me give you an example.

We all know the story of Abraham and Isaac. Abraham is ordered by God to offer up his only son, and without argument, he takes Isaac to the mountaintop, binds him to an altar, and raises his knife, prepared

to act as God has commanded.

Of course, in the end God sends down an angel to intercede at the very last minute, and Abraham passes God's test of devotion.

*But it's fair to say that if any of us leaving this church saw Abraham on a roof of a building raising his knife, we would, at the very least, call the police and expect the Department of Children and Family Services to take Isaac away from Abraham. We would do so because <u>we do not hear what Abraham hears, do not see what Abraham sees, true as those experiences may be. So the best we can do is act in accordance with those things that we all see, and that we all hear, be it common laws or basic reason</u>. (**Obama**, with emphasis added)*

While Rawls thinks that we have a moral and civil duty to one another to advocate for our policy positions by appealing to reasons subject to the limits of public reason, he also recognizes that non-public reasons may be invoked as well, as a supplement (as does Obama).

*Reasonable comprehensive doctrines, religious or non-religious, may be introduced in public political discourse at any time, provided that in due course proper political reasons—and not reasons given solely by comprehensive doctrines—are presented that are sufficient to support whatever the comprehensive doctrines introduced are said to support. (**Rawls**)*

But what I am suggesting is this secularists are wrong when they ask believers to leave their religion at the door before entering into the public square. Frederick Douglas, Abraham Lincoln, Williams Jennings Bryant, Dorothy Day, Martin Luther King - indeed, the majority of great reformers in American history - were not only motivated by faith, but repeatedly used religious language to argue for their cause.

So to say that men and women should not inject their "personal morality" into public policy debates is a practical absurdity. (Obama, with emphasis added)

Perhaps more forcefully than Rawls, President Obama recognizes the importance and value of one's comprehensive moral doctrine. However, he also clearly recognizes the importance of being able to "translate" those values into shared, overlapping values.

Democracy demands that the religiously motivated translate their concerns into universal, rather than religion-specific, values. It requires that their proposals be subject to argument, and amenable to reason. I may be opposed to abortion for religious reasons, but if I seek to pass a law banning the practice, I cannot simply point to the teachings of my church or evoke God's will. I have to explain why abortion violates some principle that is accessible to people of all faiths, including those with no faith at all. (Obama)

None of the preceding is meant to suggest that President Obama was exclusively, or even primarily, "Rawlsian" in his political theory or practice. It is, however, a clear example of where theory meets practice, and when a political philosopher can influence the decisions and strategies of actual political leaders.

However "theoretical" political philosophy might be, we should always remember that the *point* of these theories is to ultimately find application in the actual political institutions, policies, and lives of real people.

Critical Analysis

1. In your opinion, what are the strongest and most compelling points made by the philosopher or philosophers in this chapter? Why do you find those points to be convincing?
2. In your opinion, what are the weakest or least convincing points? Why? Can you anticipate any limitations or objections

to their ideas not already addressed in the chapter?

Appendix: Application to Social Justice

The "enlightened" social contract approach developed by John Rawls is widely regarded as the most significant contribution to political philosophy from the twentieth century, and even to this day. His impact on the field can't be overstated. With respect to social justice, applications are obvious, especially from the earlier stages of his career.

The veil of ignorance is a powerful device that allows us to "strip away" aspects of identity that contribute to tribalism and bigotry. It is especially valuable that the idea is so simple. If I don't know my own race, it violates self-interest to agree to a system of justice that allows for racism. If I don't know my own gender, it violates self-interest to agree to a system of justice that allows for gender discrimination. If I don't know my own religious values (if any), it violates self-interest to agree to a system of justice that allows for discrimination on the basis of religion, and so forth. The two principles of justice also provide "simple" guidelines that help us to make sure that our system of justice, and all that the institutions and policies that supported, are just and fair.

With a mere surface examination, we can see that virtually all (if not all) of the "questionable" (from the social justice perspective) campaigns, policies, and laws from our own history all the way up through the present moment violate one or both principles of justice, or, at minimum, aren't something that people would have agreed to from behind the veil of ignorance. As a series of rhetorical questions, would politicians, military leaders, bureaucrats, or even private citizens have agreed to any of the following if their own identity with respect to race, ethnicity, gender, sexuality, religion, etc. were unknown to them at the time?

- Genocide of Native Americans.
- Forced relocation of Native Americans to reservations.
- Race based slavery.

- Jim Crow racial segregation laws.
- Racially motivated lynching.
- Withholding citizenship to only white persons.
- Withholding the right to vote to only property owning white males.
- Racially motivated voter suppression.
- Banning Muslims from entering the United States.

Additional examples are endless, but I suspect the point is already made: Rawls has provided a thought experiment in a philosophical system that allows those of us working within and for social justice a philosophical framework with which to justify our claims.

This is not to say that Rawls' approach is ideal, or that he is without his critics. Indeed, our next chapter will be dedicated to a sustained criticism of Rawls by Charles Mills, according to which he claims that Rawls' theory is inadequate to address existing racial injustice. In addition to offering that criticism, though, Mills offers a way to modify and "rehabilitate" Rawls so that the (modified) framework can still be put to good use.

Chapter 23: The Racial Contract

Comprehension questions you should be able to answer after reading this chapter:

1. What are some of the ideas and principles associated with (traditional) Liberalism?
2. Why does Mills think that Rawls' theory of justice does *not* apply to the United States' political system?
3. What is the difference between ideal theory and non-ideal theory?
4. What are the differences between societies that are in the "I-zone" and those that are outside of the "I-zone?"
5. What is the difference between a society with racism, and a racist society, according to Mills?
6. What is the "basic structure" of a society according to Rawls? What does it include?
7. What is it about the basic structure of the United States that makes Mills think that we are a racist society as opposed to being a society with racism?
8. What changes to the original position and the veil of ignorance does Mills think we need to make in order for it to be applicable to a non-ideal (racist) society like the United States?
9. What are the three principles of corrective racial justice that Mills proposes? What is meant by each of the three?

Charles Mills is a Caribbean philosopher from Jamaica known for his work in social and political philosophy, particularly in oppositional political theory as centered on class, gender, and race. Within philosophical circles, he is most well-known for his sustained criticism of the social contract developed by Rawls as being inadequate to address contemporary social justice issues, particularly pertaining to race and racism. Mills' critique actually begins much earlier in the history of philosophy than Rawls. He begins with Liberalism – the tradition of which Rawls is a part.

Liberalism

Liberalism in this sense is not to be confused with the left wing of the Democratic Party in the United States, but instead refers to the political ideology developed from the 1600s through the 1800s in contrast to "traditional" doctrines involving monarchies and other inherited class status such as aristocracy, feudalism, etc.

Liberalism of this sort is associated with significant philosophical and political figures such as John Locke, David Hume, Adam Smith, Immanuel Kant, Thomas Paine, Thomas Jefferson, Jeremy Bentham, John Stuart Mill, and others. Among the key themes developed by and attributed to Liberalism are rule of law, limited government, rule by consent, participatory government, and equality among individuals (including equal rights). For all of Liberalism's celebrated principles, however, Mill points out that the *actual* history of liberal societies has been, in fact, quite "illiberal."

> *Far from being in principled combat from the start against anti-egalitarian beliefs and systems of ascriptive hierarchy of all kinds, Liberalism has been complicit with many of them until comparatively recently. (And some critics would say, it is in effect, if no longer overtly, still thus complicit today.) Liberalism as ideal turns out to be illiberalism in actuality.*[963]

The gap between what Liberalism preaches and what it actually practices in specific so-called liberal societies creates an opportunity for the

---

[963] Mills, Charles W. 2020 Tanner Lecture on Human Values - Theorizing Racial Justice:

https://www.youtube.com/watch?v=78wzAfQu9Mw&t=5306s

development of a number of critiques focusing on specific failures of liberalism to live up to its principles. In the United States, for example, the "social democratic critique" targets "bourgeois" Liberalism and classism. Originally in the United States, only white male property owners could vote. Now, there remain vast economic disparities (e.g., the "1%").

The "feminist critique" targets "patriarchal" Liberalism and male power. Originally in the United States, women couldn't vote until 1920. Now, there still remains a gender gap ("glass ceiling") in income and professional opportunity.

As a final example, the "racial critique" targets "racist" Liberalism and racist (white supremacist) power. Originally in the United States, we had slavery, the 3/5 compromise, and then Jim Crow laws. Now, we still have racial disparities in virtually "everything." Where is this celebrated equality among individuals and equal rights?

The Limits of Rawls

As a reminder, the fundamental "output" of Rawls' thought experiment are the principles of justice that will govern the "basic structure" of a society. The elements of a basic structure include its Constitution, legal system, economy, and family. In addition, the veil of ignorance is designed to channel self-interest to produce fairness. Because one does not know who they will be with respect to race, gender, etc., outside the veil, prudence dictates agreeing to a basic structure that is equally advantageous and fair regardless of those things.

Although, on its surface, this philosophical framework might seem very well suited to prevent injustice and promote equality and other virtues of social justice, Mills had what he described as an "epiphany" regarding the limitations of Rawls' theory: "Rawls's theory of justice does not apply to the United States."

This is, admittedly, a shocking statement for him to make – claiming that the most significant and celebrated *American* political philosopher of

the twentieth century and beyond has produced a philosophical theory that is inapplicable to his own country. Nevertheless, Mills offers a sophisticated and formal argument to defend his claim. He offers the following premises regarding the scope and applicability of Rawls' theory to the United States political system.

- TJ(R&~R): Rawls's theory of justice applies both to racist and non-racist (Western liberal) societies.
- TJ(~R): Rawls's theory of justice only applies to non-racist (Western liberal) societies.
- USA(~R): The United States is not a racist (Western liberal) society.
- USA(R): The United States is a racist (Western liberal) society.

While they might seem confusing now, set these premises aside for the moment and we will return to them and see their significance a bit later.

The basic point that Mills is attempting to make is that Rawls has developed a system that does not apply to racist societies, and given that the United States *is* a racist society, it therefore does *not* apply to the United States. He claims that Rawls's own words support that "TJ(~R): Rawls's theory of justice only applies to non-racist (Western liberal) societies." In Rawls' last published work, *Justice as Fairness*, he states the following:

> *Justice as fairness is a political conception of justice for the special case of the basic structure of a modern democratic society. . . . From the start, then, we view a democratic society as a political society that excludes a confessional or an aristocratic state, not to mention a caste, slave, or a racist one.*[964]

A "confessional state" refers to a theocracy. A theocracy, along with all of the other types of

---

[964] Rawls, John. Justice as Fairness: A Restatement. Bellknap Press, 2001. section 7.3.

states mentioned in the quotation, all have in common a fundamental inequality among persons. States that exhibit fundamental inequality are states to which his theory does not apply. At this point, it is fair of you to wonder why Rawls would develop a theory that is limited in application in the first place, let alone limited by its inapplicability to so many actual existing states. The answer to that question is found in the distinction between "ideal" theory and "non-ideal" theory.

Ideal theory presupposes a "perfect" State and system of justice given a certain set of standards. As an ideal, it is (admittedly) almost certain to never be realized in real life. Non-ideal theory will apply to any State and system of justice that fails to satisfy the ideal. Note that this dichotomy goes all the way back to at least Plato and Aristotle. In the *Republic*, Plato devised an "ideal" State which included elements and an origin story that made it utterly implausible even

to the characters within Plato's own dialogue! Plato's most famous student, Aristotle, in contrast, developed his treatise on *Politics* after an empirical examination of nearly 150 existing State constitutions. Both idealism and realism have their virtues and their drawbacks, and the tension between these approaches has persisted for literally thousands of years.

Returning to Rawls: because the description of non-ideal theory will include virtually every society that exists or ever has existed, it represents a very wide range! Some systems of justice will be much closer to the ideal than others. Mills refers to a narrow band within the "I-Zone" ("Ideal Zone") as including societies that are sufficiently well ordered and just as to fall within the scope of Rawls' theory. All other societies outside of this range are too imperfect to be addressed by ideal theory. This is illustrated by the image below.[965]

DIFFERENTIATING THE NON-IDEAL

So, while there are certainly some limitations with respect to which societies are subject to

Rawls's theory of justice, it is at least not the case that they must be literally "perfect." Instead, they

---

[965] https://tannerlectures.utah.edu/ MILLSTANNERLECTURE.pdf

must be "close enough" to the "I-Zone." In his own language, Rawls usually referenced this "close enough" with expressions like "reasonably just" or "nearly just" or "more or less just," as we can see from the selection of statements below spanning all four of his major works, with emphases added.

From *A Theory of Justice*

"the special case of a nearly just society, one that is well-ordered for the most part but in which some serious violations of justice nevertheless do occur"

"a (more or less) just democratic regime."

From *Political Liberalism*

"a nearly just democratic society"
"a more or less just constitutional regime."

From *The Law of Peoples*

"a reasonably just domestic society"

"a reasonably just constitutional democratic society (hereafter sometimes referred to simply as a liberal society)"

"a reasonably just constitutional democratic government"

"a reasonably just (though not necessarily a fully just) constitutional democratic government."

From *Justice as Fairness*

"a reasonably just, though not perfect, democratic regime"

How do we determine whether a society is "close enough," though? With respect to racism, Mills proposes that this will be the difference between societies *with* racism versus a *racist*

society.

To begin with, Rawls defines a society as a "cooperative venture for mutual advantage." Mills defines a **society with racism** as a basically just society that happens to have some individuals with racist views and behaviors, that, despite occurrences of racism and discrimination, retains a just and fair basic structure.

In contrast, a **racist society** is a society in which racism has significantly shaped its basic structure. Rawls' ideal theory excludes racist societies because they don't even satisfy the definition of a "society," given that they are not organized for mutual advantage. In addition, the contamination of racism in their basic structure puts them outside of the "I-Zone" for ideal theory.

Why, then, would Rawls have never bothered to mention, over a career spanning decades, that his celebrated system of justice doesn't apply to his own country? Because, Mills supposes that Rawls simply did not regard the United States as a racist society.

So, for Rawls TJ(~R) was true but USA(R) was false. Any non-ideal "principles for meeting injustice" potentially derivable from his ideal principles would, by his tacit stipulation, be restricted to liberal states in the "nearly just" I-zone, whose injustices were at worst mild ones.[966]

In regard to this, Mills thinks that Rawls was simply mistaken. To determine whether the United States qualifies as a racist society, we need to know whether the basic structure of the United States is significantly impacted by race and racism. As a reminder, the basic structure consists of the "main political and social institutions" of a society. According to Rawls, it includes the following:

The political constitution with an independent judiciary, the legally recognized forms of property, and the structure of the economy . . . as well as the

---

[966] Mills, Tanner Lecture, ibid.

family in some form, . . .[967]

We may now ask whether the basic structure of the United States has been significantly affected by race and racism. As only a partial answer to this question we may consider the following:

- Race–based Slavery, and a slave economy
- Slavery included in the U.S. Constitution
- 3/5 compromise
- Jim Crow
- Anti-miscegenation laws
- "Separate but equal" (*Plessy v. Ferguson*)
- Extralegal murder (lynching)
- Educational and residential segregation
- Disenfranchisement and voter suppression
- Racially disparate impact: wealth, education, policing, punishment, healthcare, housing

Given all the evidence just listed above (and more) Mills is confident in offering the following short and simple argument:

1. USA(R)
2. TJ(~R)
3. Therefore, Rawls's theory of justice does not apply to the United States.

If you are in need of a quick translation or reminder of the meaning of those symbolized premises, according to the first premise it is true that the United States is a racist society. The second premise claims that the theory of justice does not apply to racist societies. Therefore, Rawls's theory of justice does not apply to the United States.

Rehabilitating Rawls to Reform the Racial Contract

If the only thing Mills had to offer was a

critique of Rawls, it might be philosophically interesting, but what makes his efforts even more interesting and fruitful is that he also offers a way to "rehabilitate" Rawls so that his theory of justice is applicable even to racist societies such as our own. According to Mills, Rawls' theory could theoretically be used to generate corrective principles for non-oppressive societies, but not oppressive societies like the United States.

Rawls's theory of justice only applies to Western societies in the I-zone, not racist Western societies beyond the I-zone, such as the United States. Here it is not a matter of a "deviation" from a "basic structure" that is essentially sound, but rather a basic structure that is itself racialized, unfairly privileging the dominant race, call them the R1s, at the expense of the subordinate race or races, call them the R2s. Obviously, then, this is not a society to be conceived of as a "cooperative venture for mutual advantage," since there is no reason why the R2s would have voluntarily signed on to such an agreement in the first place. Rather, it is a society that needs to be understood as an "exploitative venture for R1/white advantage."[968]

To explain his effort at rehabilitation requires us to get "fancy" again, and delve into more symbolic language. A "simple" way of depicting Rawls's two principles of justice is by the following formula, where the arrows indicate lexical ordering:[969]

$$BL \rightarrow (FEO \rightarrow DP)$$

BL refers to "Basic liberties," including such things as the right to vote, run for office, have freedom of speech, liberty of conscience, the right to hold personal property, etc.).

FEO refers to "Fair Equality of Opportunity." This is a formal equality of opportunity, including

---

[967] Rawls, *Justice as Fairness*, p. 10.

[968] Mills, Tanner Lecture, ibid.

[969] "Lexical" refers to a system of ordering in which the order matters. As an example, the

order of entries in a dictionary depends on their first letter unless these are the same in which case it is the second which decides, and so on

prohibition against discrimination, as well as resources to equalize for class disadvantage.

DP refers to Rawls' "Difference principle," according to which socio-economic inequalities are to be arranged for the greatest benefit of the least advantaged.

Putting them all together, as Mills puts it:

The first principle of justice, the guarantee of the equal basic liberties, is lexically dominant (must be satisfied first) over the second principle, in which, in a subordinate lexical ordering, fair equality of opportunity is lexically dominant over the difference principle.[970]

Because these are principles for an ideal well-ordered society, I, their actual scope is highly restricted:

$$PDJ [BL \rightarrow (FEO \rightarrow DP)]I$$

For non-ideal societies (such as United States) we will need principles of corrective justice:

$$PCJ \sim I$$

Remember though, that not all non-ideal societies are equally far from the ideal (the "I-Zone"). To distinguish between them, Mills will symbolize principles of corrective justice for both non-oppressive ($\sim O$), but not ideal ($\sim I$) societies, and non-ideal ($\sim I$) societies that are also oppressive (O)(i.e., whose basic structure is oppressive).

$$PCJ [PCJ1*PCJ2*PCJ3]\sim I(\sim O)$$
$$PCJ [PCJ4*PCJ5*PCJ6]\sim I(O)$$

Or, in a possibly more helpful illustration created by Mills himself:[971]

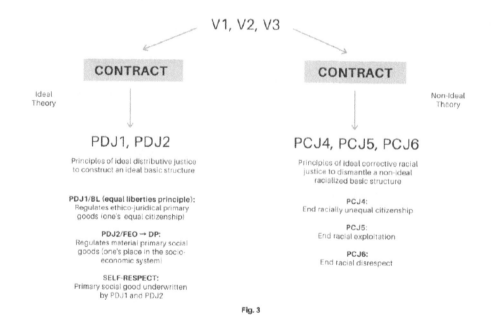

Fig. 3

---

[970] Mills, Tanner Lecture ibid.
[971] https://tannerlectures.utah.edu/
MILLSTANNERLECTURE.pdf

Translation?

For "ideal" societies, the principles of distributive justice are just those that are expressed by the two principles of justice explored in the Rawls chapter, as the first principle covers basic liberties, and the second principle provides fair equality of opportunity and the difference principle.

For non-ideal societies that are "close enough," they will need some additional principles of (corrective) justice, which would need to be specified, to "fix" the imperfections.

Non-ideal societies that are not "close enough" and are outright oppressive, however, will require *different* (and presumably more substantial) principles of corrective justice to fix the even more serious imperfections.

What might those corrective principles look like? To identify them we must return to the Liberalism that we first discussed at the beginning of the chapter.

Mills describes Liberalism as exhibiting certain core features, including "a characteristic set of value-commitments" and a "certain social ontology." The "characteristic set of value-commitments" includes equality, freedom, and self-realization of individuals. However, in actual liberal societies such as the United States, only *some* people were or are given *genuine* opportunity for self-realization, and *lack* of equality and unequal freedom have often been the norm for many people, including in ways officially enshrined by law and in the Constitution itself.

The "certain social ontology" refers to the sorts of beings which "exist," politically and socially. Liberalism, historically, focuses only on individuals, and fails to recognize the identity of groups and the reality of the political and economic consequences of group membership, particularly with respect to race. The traditional liberal "map" of sociopolitical relationships has presumed free and equal participants, but if the map is to be accurate for actual countries like the United States, white supremacy must be officially acknowledged. Clearly, the actual history of a society contributes to its current basic structure, and this history must be acknowledged, including the history and legacy of oppression and discrimination.

While Liberalism traditionally provides a "schedule of rights, protections, and freedoms for individuals, these rights, protections, and freedoms must be responsive to all of the adjustments required by acknowledging the actual history of the society, the sociopolitical "map" that has described (and continues to describe) its members, etc. In other words, to be useful, Liberalism can't be purely an exercise in abstraction, but must contend with real history and actual people.

In pursuit of rehabilitating Rawls, Mills thinks we must recognize that the social contract of the United States is a "racial contract," one with an oppressive basic structure. We have to consider:

1. A certain social ontology of individuals as racial group members, R1s and R2s, whites and nonwhites, in relations of domination and subordination.
2. A conceptual cartography of the sociopolitical in terms of an R1-dominant, white supremacist American polity, with all the consequent ramifications for its constituent social institutions; and a historical account.
3. An account of the history that has led up to the present that has brought such a polity into existence, requiring attention to the dynamics of European settler colonialism and Atlantic slave societies standardly ignored in the political philosophy literature.[972]

Only by accurately considering 1-3 can we correctly establish a "schedule of rights, protections, and freedoms for (racialized) individuals" such that they can actually achieve a "characteristic set of value-commitments" (Equality, freedom, and self-realization of individuals).

---

[972] Mills, Tanner Lecture, ibid.

What would a version of Rawls' Theory of Justice, with these modifications in mind, look like? It begins all the way back at the original position. To make an adjustment for use in a non-ideal society, we must describe the participants as "choosing principles of justice for a racially oppressive, ill-ordered, R1-supremacist society, in which the R1s dominate the R2s, as modeled by the racial domination contract."[973] In other words, one of things participants "know" behind the veil is that they come from a racist society in which some people (R1s) dominate others (R2s).

The veil of ignorance is similarly modified in that the veil will now admit knowledge of the historically R1-supremacist nature of the society, while blocking knowledge of R1/R2 demographic proportions. In other words, participants know that R1s stand in a relation of racial domination to R2s, but they don't know whether they are an R1 or an R2.

Participants' motivation remains the same: prudence and maximizing self-interest. As a result of the modifications, though, the general outcome is different.

> *Worried that we might turn out to be R2s in an R1-dominant order basically unchanged or only mildly reformed, or R1s in an R2-dominant order where long-standing R2 racial ressentiment can at last find its vindictive expression, we will make sure that rights, freedoms, and protections are in place to produce a racially equitable order for us whatever we are.[974]*

Put simply, participants wouldn't want to be oppressed by virtue of being an R2, or subject to vengeance if they happen to be an R1, so they would choose corrective measures to address the injustice and inequality. Mills proposes the following as principles of corrective racial justice we would choose behind the veil:

- PCJ4: End racially unequal citizenship
- PCJ5: End racial exploitation
- PCJ6: End racial disrespect

What might these principles look like in actual practice? He provides the following (very incomplete) examples for each:

Ending racially unequal citizenship (PCJ4)
- Rethinking the "strict scrutiny" standard established by the Supreme Court
- Rescinding 2013 *Shelby County v Holder* Supreme Court decision
- Ending felony disenfranchisement because of its racially disparate impact
- Ending voter suppression, including redrawing racially gerrymandered districts
- Examining the role of representation in the electoral College and the Senate in perpetuating white majoritarianism
- Increased funding for antidiscrimination laws
- Structural reform of the criminal justice system
- Dismantling the "urban ghetto"
- Restructuring the American educational system to eliminate racially disparate outcomes

Ending racial exploitation (PCJ5)
- Prohibiting unequal pay for equal work
- Initiating nationwide affirmative action programs
- Address and compensate for the racial wealth gap resulting from discrimination and unpaid slave labor
- Address and compensate for the racial wealth gap resulting from discrimination in housing, employment, lending, and education

Ending racial disrespect (PCJ6)
- Removing public racist imagery (Native American team names and mascots, Confederate flag, Civil War monuments)
- Federal apologies for overtly racist policies
- Rewriting textbooks to acknowledge white supremacy and systemic racism
- Devising early childhood educational

---

[973] ibid.

[974] ibid.

programs to combat the development of implicit bias

Clearly, dismantling centuries of racial oppression and injustice would and will take quite a lot of effort! However, it's what he thinks we would agree to "behind the veil"—once all the needed adjustments to the veil are made, at least. Finally, although Mills' emphasis is on the treatment of Black Americans, he thinks that his modified version of Rawls' theory is easily applicable to all relevant racial groups.

The R2 category, being just the negation of R1 ("nonwhite"), will include different racial groups, with different histories and different claims to justice. Recent work in critical race theory has warned of the dangers of trying to squeeze all racial relations into the "black-white binary." Anti-Latinx, anti-Asian/Asian-American, and anti-Native American racism have historically taken different forms, with different dikailogical remedies arguably being called for. In the case of Native Americans in particular, demands for, say, land and sovereignty are quite different from African American demands for affirmative action or reparations. My hope is that the principles are articulated at a sufficiently high level of abstraction that these differences can be accommodated once the particular racial histories are taken into account.[975]

Critical Analysis

1. In your opinion, what are the strongest and most compelling points made by the philosopher or philosophers in this chapter? Why do you find those points to be convincing?

2. In your opinion, what are the weakest or least convincing points? Why? Can you anticipate any limitations or

objections to their ideas not already addressed in the chapter?

Appendix: Application to Social Justice

Social Justice is at the heart of this chapter in terms of both content and motivation. It provides an example of a philosopher (who is, perhaps conspicuously, both a person of color and an immigrant) who perceived a glaring "void" that had gone largely unnoticed and not-addressed throughout nearly 50 years of Rawls scholarship.

Justice is central to social justice, obviously, but even "Liberal" attempts to provide principles of justice will come up short if they fail to grapple with the unfortunate reality of oppression and its history (and legacy) in "real life." A theory might be "ideal" in the sense that it is sketching out a "perfect" version of a society, but it is hardly *ideal* if it can't actually be used in many (if any) actually existing communities.

To his credit, Mills has attempted not only to point out the deficiencies of an iconic and influential theory of justice, but also to demonstrate how it could be modified such that it can be used, in powerful and helpful ways, to conceptualize not only the nature of racist injustice, but also the interventions, both general and specific, that are needed to *correct* for that injustice. In this way, Mills serves not only as a model of scholarship in philosophy, but has provided a potentially compelling framework within which to understand justice in a racialized and racist society, and by which to justify corrective measures.

---

[975] ibid. Note: "dikailogical" is a needlessly fancy term referring to justice, as in justice being served.

Chapter 24: Philosophy of "Race"

Comprehension questions you should be able to answer after reading this chapter:

1. Explain how Supreme Court decisions such as *Dred Scott*, *Ozawa*, and *Thind* can be used as evidence for the social-construction of race.
2. What is the difference between "racialism" and "racism?" What do they have in common?
3. What is the "popular account" of race?
4. What is the difference between a "race" and a "racialized group," as described by Blum?

Before reading anything in this chapter, consider the following exercise.

> Imagine that someone wants to know who you are. Complete the following sentence. Be thorough!
> "I am … "

Although you might have been abstract enough to describe yourself as a "person" or "human," you *probably* described yourself, instead, in terms of your age (generation), race or ethnicity, sexual orientation, relationship status, profession, socioeconomic status, political affiliation, ideology, disability, gender, and possibly some reference to your pets or hobbies! Whether they should or should not, clearly such things are considered to be part (and perhaps constitutive) of who we are, as persons.[976]

For all of these possible "anchors" or "foundations" for identity (i.e., race, gender, sexual orientation, etc.), not merely entire chapters, but entire books could be (and have been) written. We can't possibly hope to be so ambitious, and so will focus on just one such foundation: race/ethnicity.

If someone were to ask you your race, the answer probably comes to your mind instantly. "White" (or Caucasian). "Black" (or perhaps African-American). Latino. Chicano. Hispanic. Asian. Chinese. Indian. Native American. Mixed….

We think and speak as though these terms are fixed and clear, when that is, in fact, far from the case. We will begin by considering some important vocabulary, both as they are commonly used, as well as in more philosophically "precise" terms. We will also consider a variety of perspectives, for the sake of balance.

Let us begin, then, with the "everyday" meanings of race and ethnicity. In common usage, these are often muddled, or treated as though interchangeable. Indeed, we can try to dodge our own confusion as to the exact meaning of those terms by the use of the combined term "race/ethnicity!"

Although interpretations vary, for our purposes we will say that "*race*," as the term is *commonly* used, refers to a biological type of human being (e.g., the "white race," the "black race," etc.), whereas "*ethnicity*" refers to learned

---

[976] In this regard, I am a middle-aged, white, cis-gendered male, Christian, married (heterosexual) man, who is highly educated (Ph.D.) and falls in the upper-middle socioeconomic class. That is not intended as boasting, but as a confession: I am very much aware that every one of those features places me in a position of relative privilege. Although I will devote a good portion of this chapter discussing race and racial identity, I am very much aware that I have never personally experienced what it is like to be a member of a marginalized group, and I undoubtedly have numerous "blind spots" as a result. Although I think I have good reasons for the positions I advance in this chapter, in no way do I deny the potential validity and persuasiveness of other perspectives, informed by other sorts of experiences.

cultural behaviors that are often *associated* with a certain ancestry and physical appearance.

Race has been presumed to be biologically transmitted, whereas ethnicity is thought to be culturally transmitted. In use, both "Irish" and "Scottish" people might be considered members of the "white race," though of different ancestry and cultural heritage. Similarly, in common usage, anyone with a Spanish surname and descended from a Spanish-speaking people might be considered ethnically Hispanic, including Spaniards—though Spaniards would not be "Latinos," since they don't come from "Latin America." To further complicate matters, there is also the consideration of nationality, since Hispanic/Latino people from Mexico are distinct from those hailing from El Salvador.

Rather than trying to parse the nuances of various ethnic distinctions, I would like to address a more foundational (and possibly more controversial) issue: the nature of race itself. Although the view I'm about to present has become increasingly accepted, especially among biologists, anthropologists, and sociologists, it might nevertheless come as a surprise to some of you: "race," as a biological concept, is a *fiction*—a "*social construct*" created and perpetuated in cultures but not existing in nature. The evidence for this "socially constructed" interpretation of race is both ample, and, I think, compelling. Let's begin with some history.

Race?

The history of the meaning of "race" reveals just how mercurial the concept has been. In ancient Greece and Rome, race referred to group membership in terms of one's ancestral place and culture. The Greeks, for example, were a "race." The Greeks recognized physical differences amongst people (e.g., the darker skin of Africans, the lighter skin of Northern Europeans, etc.), but did not presume superiority or inferiority on such bases (though they did regard their own *culture* (Greece) as superior!).

In the Middle Ages, race referred more to one's "lineage," as in personal family ancestry, or a people of common origin and history. For example, there was the Anglo-Saxon "race" (i.e.,

"Germanic" people who came to inhabit what is now England and Wales), the Norman "race" (i.e., the descendants of Viking raiders who populated the region of Normandy in what is now France), and the Teutons (i.e., descendants of "Germanic" tribes).

When European powers turned to conquest, colonization, and slavery, racial thinking began to develop as a rationale for these actions—though race was *still* not a biological concept. As of the 17th century, race referred more to a culture or civilization in a particular area. The French, for example, would have been considered a "race."

The 18th century saw race in terms of religious and cultural divisions. Throughout these centuries, for example, Native Americans and Africans were regarded first as "heathens" (and therefore "inferior"—but because they weren't Christians, not because of their biology). Then, they became "savages" (and therefore "inferior," but because they were "uncivilized," not because of their biology).

With the spread of slavery, neither religion nor culture was sufficient to justify differential treatment, since both could be overcome by conversion or education. An educated, Christian African would no longer be a "heathen" or a "savage." What could justify his continued enslavement? To remain viable, differential treatment (including enslavement) had to be founded on something permanent and unchangeable.

The focus on Africans for the slave population was practical, rather than rooted in racial ideology (at least initially). Of the various groups of people who had been used for cheap (or slave) labor in the "New World," Africans proved most suitable. Poor Europeans were insufficient in number, and could easily blend in with the population of free persons if they escaped slavery. Native Americans could escape and seek refuge with other (free) tribes, and were vulnerable to European diseases anyway. Africans, in contrast, were easily identifiable thanks to their skin color, stood out amongst European settlers, were accustomed to the heat prevalent in the Southern American colonies and Caribbean (unlike European workers, for example), had no local groups to which they could escape (unlike Native Americans), and were generally unfamiliar with the territory.

Africans would need to be classified as a distinct (and "inferior") race to justify their enslavement, and to allow the pretense of consistency when the United States of America emerged from the Declaration of Independence and the Constitutional Convention. The highest legal authority in the United States shamefully sealed the status of "Blacks" in the *Dred Scott v. Sandford* of 1857.

. . It is difficult at this day to realize the state of public opinion in relation to that unfortunate race which prevailed in the civilized and enlightened portions of the world at the time of the Declaration of Independence and when the Constitution of the United States was framed and adopted. But the public history of every European nation displays it in a manner too plain to be mistaken.

They had for more than a century before been regarded as beings of an inferior order, and altogether unfit to associate with the white race either in social or political relations, and so far inferior that they had no rights which the white man was bound to respect, and that the negro might justly and lawfully be reduced to slavery for his benefit. He was bought and sold, and treated as an ordinary article of merchandise and traffic whenever a profit could be made by it. This opinion was at that time fixed and universal in the civilized portion of the white race. It was regarded as an axiom in morals as well as in politics which no one thought of disputing or supposed to be open to dispute, and men in every grade and position in society daily and habitually acted upon it in their private pursuits, as well as in matters of public concern,

without doubting for a moment the correctness of this opinion.[977]

Note that while the ruling ostensibly applies only to slaves and their descendants, the rationale for the ruling refers to the "unfortunate race" (i.e., "Blacks") who are "so far inferior that they had no rights which the white man was bound to respect."

The Dred Scott case not only established that escaped slaves had no rights of citizens, but that the very "race" of people of whom those slaves belong are inherently inferior and without any rights at all! This was not the last time the Supreme Court validated unmistakably racist ideas, nor even the last time the Supreme Court helped to define race itself, as we shall see a little later in this section.

By the late 18th and early 19th centuries, race had emerged as a biological concept, alongside the development of modern biological science and classification methods. Linnaeus (1701-1778) was the founder of modern taxonomy, and applied his thinking to humans as well as other animals. He identified four distinct kinds of humans, and believed them to have been created distinctly/differently by God: Asiaticus, Europaeus, Africanus, and Americanus. These four groups were "natural kinds" by which all actual humans could be sorted and understood.

Despite the obvious ability to interbreed with members of the other "kinds," Linnaeus thought of these kinds as "species-like"—implying natural, permanent, and important differences between them. His typological descriptions of each included not only physical traits, but mental and personality traits as well. According to his stereotypes, Asiaticus is ruled by emotion and ritual, whereas Europaeus is ruled by laws and intelligence; Americanus is ruled by custom and superstition, whereas Africanus is ruled by caprice and whim. Conveniently enough, it was his *own* "kind" that was governed by reason and law, whereas all other "races" were naturally governed by mere opinion and whatever passing fancy caught their attention.

---

[977] *Dred Scott v. Sandford*. Full text available here: http://teachingamericanhistory .org/library/document/dred-scott-v-sandford/

An alternative to Linnaeus developed even in his own time. Louis Leclerc developed a classification system that didn't claim inherent (and inherited) natural differences, but instead focused on different cultural conditions. "Those marks which distinguish men who inhabit different regions of the Earth are not original, but purely superficial."[978]

Linnaeus' approach prevailed, though, and its legacy included a biological basis for race, assuming significant and immutable differences, as well as the confusion of cultural factors for innate (biological) factors to account for differences in communities.

By the mid-19th century, race was firmly accepted in terms of biological groupings of human beings (e.g., "Negroid," "Caucasoid," "Mongoloid") who shared inherited physical, mental, and moral traits that are different from those of other races.

It can't be overlooked that race, as a biological concept, was developed by American scientists during the periods of both slavery and segregation, and was instrumental in the justification of both practices. Racial classification made a big difference in one's legal status in the United States. In 1790, Congress' first act was to restrict naturalized citizenship to "free white persons" only. Blacks were included in 1870 (after the Civil War, of course), but East Asians and Filipinos had to wait until 1952! Considerations of the naturalness and immutability of race found also their way into interpretations of law, as the Supreme Court once again offered its "enlightened" opinions on the issue.

Takao Ozawa was born in Japan in 1875, but moved to California in 1894, where he attended UC Berkeley. He moved to what was then the "territory" of Hawaii, and applied for naturalization in 1914. The U.S. District Attorney of Hawaii opposed his application on the grounds that Ozawa was of the Japanese race, and therefore not a white person. Ozawa fought this judgment for eight years, with his case ultimately reaching the Supreme Court. Among several arguments he offered, one was literal: his skin color was "white."

Although he was of Japanese ancestry, his skin color was literally the same pinkish color as that of "white" people. Therefore, he was a white person. The Court rejected his logic.

Manifestly, the test [of race] afforded by the mere color of the skin of each individual is impracticable as that differs greatly among persons of the same race, even among Anglo-Saxons, ranging by imperceptible gradations from the fair blond to the swarthy brunette, the latter being darker than many of the lighter hued persons of the brown or yellow races.[979]

Here, the Court accepts and asserts that skin color does *not* reliably correlate with racial identity. However, rather than rejecting racial classification in biological terms, the "experts," anthropologists, and scientists of the time resorted to continually shifting standards to maintain their racial groupings. So would the Court.

Rejecting Ozawa's claim based on skin color, the Court ruled that "the words 'white person' are synonymous with the words 'a person of the Caucasian race.'" However, just three months later, the Court rejected its very own equivalence of "white" and "Caucasian" in *United States v. Thind*.

Bhagat Singh Thind came to the United States from India on July 4th, 1913. Importantly, anthropologists of that era had classified Asian Indians as "Caucasians" rather than "Mongolians." Thind seized on this and applied for naturalization on the grounds that he was Caucasian, and therefore a "white person."

The Ninth Circuit Court of Appeals asked, "Is a high caste Hindu of full Indian blood, born at Amrit Sar, Punjab, India, a white person?" Note already the conflation of religion (Hindu) with "race," the assumption that "race" is something

---

[978] Smedley, Audrey. *Race in North America: Origin and Evolution of a Worldview*. 2nd ed.

1993: 165.
[979] Ozawa v. United States.

carried by blood, and even that something like place of birth is somehow relevant to whether someone is "white."

The Court accepted that Thind was Caucasian. "It may be true that the blond Scandinavian and the brown Hindu have a common ancestor in the dim reaches of antiquity, but the average man knows perfectly well that there are unmistakable and profound differences between them today." The Court then argued that the word "Caucasian" is "at best a conventional term." "What we now hold is that the words 'free white persons' are words of common speech, to be interpreted in accordance with the understanding of the common man, synonymous with the word 'Caucasian' only as that word is popularly understood."

In *Ozawa*, the Court rejected literal "whiteness" in the sense of pinkish skin, in favor of a "scientific" classification, in order to exclude a person of Japanese ancestry from being considered "white." In *Thind*, just three months later, the *same Court* abandoned "science" altogether, appealing to the "understanding of the common man" to exclude someone from India from being considered "white."

The mental gymnastics performed by the Justices to preserve racial preferences is breathtaking, but we can't ignore the fact that these decisions had profound life-impacting results. Neither East Asians nor Asian Indians, nor, indeed, anyone who wasn't "white"—as understood by the "common man"—could be or could become citizens. Not only did this ostracize and limit the rights of such persons, these decisions even *stripped away* the citizenship of at least 65 Asian Indians to whom it had previously been granted. One such person was Vaisho Das Bagai.

Vaisho had renounced his British citizenship to become an American. With his American citizenship stripped away, he became a citizen of no country at all. Because he was not a citizen (any longer), he was no longer allowed to own

property in California, and was forced to sell his home and general store. The U.S. Government even refused to grant him a passport to visit his family in India. He committed suicide in 1928, and sent one of his suicide notes to the San Francisco Examiner:

I came to America thinking, dreaming and hoping to make this land my home. Sold my properties and brought more than twenty-five thousand dollars (gold) to this country, established myself and tried my very best to give my children the best American education.

In year 1921 the Federal court at San Francisco accepted me as a naturalized citizen of the United States and issued to my name the final certificate, giving therein the name and description of my wife and three sons. In last 12 or 13 years we all made ourselves as much Americanized as possible.

But they now come to me and say, I am no longer an American citizen. They will not permit me to buy my home and, lo, they even shall not issue me a passport to go back to India. Now what am I? What have I made of myself and my children?

We cannot exercise our rights, we cannot leave this country. Humility and insults, who is responsible for all this? Myself and American government.

I do not choose to live the life of an interned person; yes, I am in a free country and can move about where and when I wish inside the country. Is life worth living in a gilded cage? Obstacles this way, blockades that way, and the bridges burnt behind.[980]

Although both the effect of, and very

---

980 http://www.aiisf.org/stories-by-author /876-bridges-burnt-behind-the-story-of-vaishno-das-bagai

probably the intent behind, the Court decisions was racist, that racism was predicated on deeply held (and arguably *false*) premises. Those premises, however, were (and are) *widely believed.*

The "popular account" of race, for the last 150 years or so, is that races are real, naturally occurring, and more stable/real/natural than contingent human groupings such as nationality or religion. Many would agree, for example, that "France" is a contingent historical artifact that didn't always exist, didn't have to exist, and could cease to exist (e.g., if Hitler had won the Second World War).

So too with religion. Scientology hasn't always existed, and very few people (if any) still worship the ancient Egyptian pantheon (e.g., Isis and Osiris). Races, on the other hand, are generally regarded as older, inevitable, immutable, and more "natural."

The racial assumptions that emerged from the 18th and 19th centuries included profound (and damaging) ideas:

- All humans fall into one, and only one, distinct, natural, fixed race.[981]
- These races are presumed to differ (essentially) in significant physical, mental, and moral qualities.

- Every member of a race is thought to possess their races "essence," and this essence is transmitted to one's children.
- There are physical indicators that allegedly correlate with race membership, and that provide mental "shortcuts." For example, dark skin and curly hair indicates that someone is "Black," which also means (according to *racist stereotypes*) that that person is "lazy."
- A natural hierarchy is thought to exist based on the "natural superiority" of some races over others. Although the precise number of races and their relative placement varies, in the United States it has always been the assumption that "whites" were at the top and "blacks" were at the bottom.

The belief that there are distinct, natural races, and that each race has its own particular "essence" that is transmitted by biological means, is known as "racialism."[982] This is not to be confused with racism! Racism certainly includes racialist beliefs, but *adds* to them notions of superiority/inferiority, negative stereotypes, and moral judgments. In other words, racism is value-laden, whereas racialism is value-neutral.

Racialism: beliefs and actions presupposing the

---

[981] The racism inherent to racial essentialism (originally, at least) is evident in the "one drop rule." Historically, in the United States, one was "white" if they had no "black" ancestry anywhere in the family lineage. Even "one drop" of "black" meant that you were not "white." The assumptions lurking behind the "one-drop" rule are hardly ancient history, by the way. In March of 2016, a 6-year old girl was taken from her ("white") foster parents in Santa Clarita, California, after having lived with them for four years. Her biological parents had lost custody of her after a child abuse investigation. Her mother also had substance abuse issues, and her father had a criminal record. She was removed from foster care, though, because she is "1.5% Choctaw," and a 1978 federal law was invoked (The Indian Child Welfare Act, designed to

prevent large numbers of native American children to be adopted away from their tribal heritage and placed in non-Native American households). Although this child had never actually been exposed to any Native American culture, the mere "fact" that she was 1.5% Choctaw meant she was "Native American" under federal law, and therefore subject to the Indian Child Welfare Act. http://m.nydailynews.com/news/national/girl-6-foster-family-native-american-law-article-1.2572704

[982] Note: this term is used by different people in different ways. I offer a specific definition of this term in this section, and it is that specific definition that is presupposed for the remainder of this chapter.

existence of *biologically-transmitted racial "essences."*[983]

Racism: *negative* value judgments and actions based on racialist assumptions.[984]

Arguably, most Americans are "racialists," whether they realize it or not, and whether or not they are additionally *racists*. This is so despite the clear evidence for the social construction of race (as seen by our survey of history and Supreme Court rulings above), and despite the lack of evidence for *biologically-based* races or racial essentialism.

To put it plainly, there is no genetic basis for racial classification. There are no general racial characteristics that are shared by all members of the same "race," nor any genes shared by all such members. 85.4% of genetic differences between humans occur *within* a population ("race"), with roughly 85% of all human genetic variation found in a random sample of two people from the *same* tribal/ethnic group, from the same region. Genetic differences between people of different "races" are only marginally greater than that of two people from the same "race." Even the study of diseases that are more prevalent in certain "races" (e.g., sickle cell anemia in "Blacks") is based on *social definitions of race*. Nor is there any "race" found in or transmitted by blood. Although we might say that someone has "Native American blood" in them, there are only four major blood types (A, B, AB, and O), that can be additionally "positive" or "negative"—but none of these correspond to racial membership.

It's worth noting that only some patterns of physical features have acquired any racial significance. We don't regard height (e.g., "over

seven feet tall," or "under five feet tall") as a signifier of racial membership, nor do we regard being a "redhead" as indicative of one's race. Not even skin color reliably picks out a particular group of people (e.g., some Australian Aborigines are darker in complexion than many African-Americans, but are not regarded as "black"—at least not by Americans).

Simply put, which physical differences or similarities "count" has been historically arbitrary. Again and again, the pattern was the same: "races" were first defined based on socio-cultural conventions, and then physical means of classification were selected based on their usefulness in discriminating between the already-created socially constructed groups.

Finally, if race were truly and merely a matter of physical features, there could be no distinction between "looking white" (for example) and actually *being* white. To "appear white" just would mean that one *is* white, if personal appearance were all that mattered. And yet, for centuries there has been a meaningful notion of "passing" in the United States. . . .

Although it might seem like I'm belaboring the point, establishing the lack of a genetic basis for race is *important* because, without genetic carriers, racial traits can't be biologically *inherited*.

Children might model behavior exhibited by their parents, but this doesn't entail anything resembling genetic destiny. "Lazy" parents might inspire laziness in *any* child, including an adopted child from another "race." Moreover, such learned behaviors could include a fondness for cloth napkins as much as "laziness"—neither of which is biological nor essentialist.

---

[983] This is not to be confused with ethnicism or ethnocentrism, both of which concern ethnicity, which refers to *learned* cultural *behaviors and norms*, as distinct from biologically-transmitted traits.

[984] There is also what is known as "institutional racism," which, in general, is racism expressed and practiced by social and political institutions, as distinct from racism by individuals. Institutional racism can be conscious and

intentional, such as segregation laws, or unconscious and racist in its effects, rather than intentions, such as disparate minimum prison sentences for crack and powder cocaine. Institutional racism can be both a product and a source of embedded racist cultural practices within our social structure. This then creates barriers and privileges based on race through socio-political institutions.

Although races seemingly don't exist as biological entities, there are certainly what Lawrence Blum calls *"racialized groups."* Blum describes *"racialization"* as the:

> *treating of groups as if there were inherent and immutable differences between them; as if certain somatic characteristics marked the presence of significant characteristics of mind, emotion, and character; and as if some were of greater worth than others.*[985]

Racialized groups can shift over time. The "Irish" used to be a "race," but are now an "ethnicity." To say that races are "social constructions," that there are not "races" in the sense of biological kinds but that instead there are "racialized" groups, is *not* to deny "race" any kind of existence at all! Nations are "social constructions," as is the State of California, but both are "real." Neither the USA nor California, however, have existed or will exist "naturally" and immutably throughout time. Nor is it the case that someone born in California necessarily and immutably inherits any particular physical, intellectual, social, or moral traits as a result of the particular State in which they are born!

Analogously, "races," as biological groupings, don't exist as natural artifacts—but racialized groups are real, treated as real, and *experienced* as real by their members. Members of racialized groups are often treated in similar ways, and thus often share similar experiences (e.g., being followed in stores, being asked if they speak English, being asked "where are you from?", etc.). This shared experience can contribute to someone adopting a group identity, and this self-identification can further contribute to the members' "racialization."

Finally, it's important to note that racialized thinking (racialism) can result not just in negative racist stereotyping (or worse), but also more well-meaning agendas such as using race to create diversity at Colleges and Universities.

Critical Analysis

1. In your opinion, what are the strongest and most compelling points made by the philosopher or philosophers in this chapter? Why do you find those points to be convincing?
2. In your opinion, what are the weakest or least convincing points? Why? Can you anticipate any limitations or objections to their ideas not already addressed in the chapter?

Appendix: Application to Social Justice

Racism is, obviously, a significant point of focus with respect to social justice. Merriam Webster *now* includes the following as definitions of racism:

1. A belief that race is a fundamental determinant of human traits and capacities and that racial differences produce an inherent superiority of a particular race.
2. The systemic oppression of a racial group to the social, economic, and political advantage of another.

We will briefly consider each.

According to the first definition, racism is a belief. We may expand our notion of "belief" to include, more generally, attitudes, perceptions, dispositions, inclinations, etc. It is, admittedly, debatable whether this does or should include "implicit" or "unconscious" beliefs and attitudes as well. According to this definition, to be a racist is to hold beliefs (somehow understood) involving (a) race–realism (discussed previously in this chapter) and (b) racial hierarchy (according to which some races are "superior" to

---

[985] Blum, Lawrence. *I'm not a Racist, But. . . The Moral Quandary of Race.* Cornell University Press, 2002: 147.

others). If you entertain such beliefs, you are racist. If you do not, you are not racist.

One of the main points of this chapter was to demonstrate that "race" is a social construct and does not refer to any biological essence or genetically transmitted cluster of morally relevant properties. Ideally, if one could simply present the mountain of evidence for race as a social construct to people who are racists according to that first definition, we could "cure" racism by correcting their false beliefs. It's not even necessary to address the racial hierarchy component if we have falsified the race-realism component.

That strategy, even while well-intentioned, is certainly a case of wishful thinking for at least two reasons. The first reason is because of how "resilient" racist beliefs can be. The earlier chapter on moral psychology addresses our stubbornness in much greater detail. The second reason, though, is because even if we are successful in our effort to "cure" racist beliefs, that will not address the second definition of racism: the systemic oppression of a racial group to the social, economic, and political advantage of another.

According to the second definition, racism is a feature of *systems*. Racism of this sort does not require any particular person to hold racist beliefs. The system itself "does the work." The systemic oppression does not have to be deliberate/intentional. Policies and systems can produce disparate outcomes along racial lines without explicitly *intending* those outcomes. For example, it is well-documented that medical doctors in the United States exhibit racial bias in their assessment and treatment of pain in their patients. A meta-analysis of twenty years' worth of studies found that black patients were 22% less likely than white patients to receive pain medication from their doctors.[986] This disparity in outcome is presumably the result of, among

other things, the fact that 40% of first and second year medical school students believe "black people's skin is thicker than white people's."[987] Healthcare professionals are just as subject to implicit bias as the rest of us.[988] Such implicit biases produce disparate outcomes within a racist system without requiring that any of the doctors involved consciously hold beliefs about racial superiority or harbor any negative feelings or intentions about people of color at all.

When dealing with this second type of racism, the problem isn't a false belief that may be corrected. Proving that "race doesn't exist" won't reform a systemically racist system that doesn't require conscious beliefs about race in the first place.

Ibram X. Kendi offers a useful third definition of racism that seems to combine the individual attitude component of the first definition, and the systemic element of the second definition. According to Kendi, racism is a "powerful collection of racist policies that lead to racial inequity and are substantiated by racist ideas."[989]

To clarify some of his terms, "racist policy" is defined as any measure that produces or sustains racial inequity between racial groups,[990] and "racist idea" is defined as any idea that suggests one racial group is inferior or superior to another racial group in any way.[991]

Racist policies account for the systemic oppression, and racist ideas provide rationalization for the policies.

According to the first definition from above, remember that as long as you do not consciously hold racist beliefs, you are not a racist. Not being a racist according to the second definition is much more challenging, given that no conscious beliefs are required, and it is entirely possible to be a beneficiary of a systemically racist system even if you don't consciously want the "privilege." Kendi forcefully rejects the adequacy of being "not racist," in any sense, however. Instead, he

---

[986] https://pubmed.ncbi.nlm.nih.gov/22239747/

[987] https://www.aamc.org/news-insights/how-we-fail-black-patients-pain

[988]

https://pubmed.ncbi.nlm.nih.gov/28249596/
[989] Kendi, Ibram X. *How to Be an Antiracist*. One world, 2019, 20.
[990] ibid., 18.
[991] ibid., 20.

offers that one should be an *anti*-racist, and promote *anti*-racism.

> *What's the problem with being "not racist?" It is a claim that signifies neutrality: "I am not a racist, but neither am I aggressively against racism." But there is no neutrality in the racism struggle. The opposite of "racist" isn't "not racist." It is "antiracist." What's the difference? One endorses either the idea of a racial hierarchy as a racist, or racial equality as an antiracist. One either believes problems are rooted in groups of people, as a racist, or locates the roots of problems in power and policies, as an antiracist. One either allows racial inequities to persevere, as a racist, or confronts racial inequities, as an antiracist. There is no in between safe space of "not racist." The claim of "not racist" neutrality is a mask for racism.*[992]

According to Kendi, racist and anti-racist are not permanent properties of people or systems, but are constantly in flux.

> *A racist is someone who is supporting a racist policy by their actions or inaction or expressing a racist idea. An antiracist is someone who is supporting an antiracist policy by their actions or expressing an antiracist idea. "Racist" and "antiracist" are like peelable nametags that are placed and replaced based on what someone is doing or not doing, supporting or expressing in each moment. These are not permanent tattoos. No one becomes a racist or antiracist. We can only strive to be one or the other. We can unknowingly strive to be a racist. We can unknowingly strive to be an antiracist. Like fighting an addiction, being an antiracist requires persistent self-awareness, constant self-criticism, and regular self-examination.*[993]

Some of the concepts from earlier in the chapter receive a "rebranding" under Kendi's definitions. A "race-realist," for example, is labeled a "biological racist," and is understood as someone "who is expressing the idea that the races are meaningfully different in their biology and that these differences create a hierarchy of value."[994] A biological antiracist, in contrast, is "one who is expressing the idea that the races are meaningfully the same in their biology and there are no genetic racial differences."[995]

Racism operates at both the individual and systemic level, and Kendi offers some (basic) guidelines for those seeking to be anti-racist individually, and who want their institutions to be anti-racist as well.

Individual

- Stop using the "I'm not a racist" or "I can't be racist" defense of denial.
- Admit the definition of racist (someone who is supporting racist policies were expressing racist ideas).
- Confess the racist policies you support and racist ideas you express.
- Accept their source (one's upbringing inside a nation making us racist).
- Acknowledge the definition of antiracist (someone who is supporting antiracist policies or expressing antiracist ideas).
- Struggle for antiracist power and policy in your spaces. (Examples include seizing a policymaking position. Joining an antiracist organization or protest. Publicly donating time or privately donating funds to antiracist policy makers, organizations, and protests fixated on changing power and policy.)
- Struggle to remain at the antiracist intersections where racism is mixed with other bigotries. (Examples include eliminating racial distinctions in biology and behavior. Equalizing racial distinctions

---

[992] ibid., 9.
[993] ibid., 22-23.

[994] ibid., 44.
[995] ibid.

in ethnicities, bodies, cultures, colors, classes, spaces, genders, and sexualities.)

- Struggle to think with antiracist ideas. (Examples include seeing racist policy in racial inequity. Leveling group differences. Not being fooled into generalizing individual negativity. Not being fooled by misleading statistics or theories that blame people for racial inequity.)[996]

Groups

- Admit racial inequity is a problem of bad policy, not bad people.
- Identify racial inequity in all its intersections and manifestations.
- Investigate and uncover the racist policies causing racial inequity.
- Invent or find antiracist policy that can eliminate racial inequity.
- Figure out who or what group has the power to institute antiracist policy.
- Disseminate and educate about the uncovered racist policy in antiracist policy correctives.
- Work with sympathetic antiracist policy makers to institute the antiracist policy.
- Deploy antiracist power to compel or drive from power the unsympathetic racist policymakers in order to institute the antiracist policy.
- Monitor closely to ensure the antiracist policy produces and eliminates racial inequity.
- When policies fail, do not blame the people. Start over and seek out new and more effective antiracist treatments until they work.
- Monitor closely to prevent new racist policies from being instituted.[997]

Counterpoint: "Woke Racism?"

Ibram X. Kendi has rocketed out of academia and into mainstream consciousness with his *How to be Antiracist*, becoming a New York Times bestselling author and, in many cases, a

household name. Not all households speak favorably of him though—and it would be presumptuous and false to assume that any that don't are populated with racists. One of Kendi's most vocal critics is John McWhorter, another Black scholar, who teaches at Columbia University and specializes in linguistics. McWhorter claims that the contemporary antiracism movement as represented by Kendi, and others such as Ta-Nehisi Coates and Robin DiAngelo, is misguided and even harmful to people of color (especially Black persons).

McWhorter refers to contemporary antiracism as "3rd Wave" Antiracism—an intentional reference to the history of feminism. Feminism has traditionally been broken into at least three (and possibly four) major phases, described as "waves." The first wave is associated with the women's suffrage movement as well as abolitionism. It began in the late 19th century and ended in the mid-20th century. The goals of this wave included the achievement of basic political equality, such as women achieving the right to vote. The second wave began in the 1960s and 70s and was inspired by the Civil Rights Movement and Vietnam War protests. It focused on institutional reform, such as reducing gender discrimination, and promoting workforce equality. The third wave is generally regarded as beginning in the 1990s and is associated with deconstructing norms of gender and sexuality. The third wave was much more aware of the intersection of aspects of identity, such as race. In fact, this is the time in which the term "intersectionality" was developed. Scholars debate whether we are presently in a fourth wave, or simply a continuation and expansion of the third wave. To the extent that there is a fourth wave, it is associated with responding to the backlash against feminist gains, expanding trans rights, and forcing a societal reckoning over sexual harassment and sex crimes, as exemplified by the #MeToo movement.

McWhorter frames anti-racism in this same fashion, proposing that there have likewise been three waves. He associates the first wave with

---

[996] Paraphrased from ibid., 226.

[997] ibid., 231-232.

attempts to secure basic political equality, such as the abolitionist movement against slavery, and the Civil Rights Movement against legalized segregation. McWhorter associates the second wave with attempts in the 1970s and 1980s to battle racist attitudes and cultural traditions. He considers the third wave to have begun in the 2010s and continuing into today. This third wave is focused on systemic racism and dismantling white privilege.[998]

One of McWhorter's observations of 3rd Wave Antiracism is that it makes a series of seemingly contradictory claims/demands that might seem confusing or frustrating to those attempting to understand and follow them.[999] These allegedly contradictory tenets are arranged as pairs in the following chart.

1.	When black people say you have insulted them, apologized with profound sincerity and guilt.	1. Don't put black people in a position where you expect them to forgive you. They have dealt with too much to be expected to.
2.	Don't assume that all, or even most, black people like hip hop, are good dancers, and so on. Black people are a conglomeration of desperate individuals. "Black culture" is code for "pathological, primitive ghetto people."	2. Don't expect black people to assimilate to "white" social norms, because black people have a culture of their own.
3.	Silence about racism is violence.	3. Elevate the voices of the oppressed over your own.
4.	You must strive eternally to understand the experiences of black people.	4. You can never understand what it is to be black, and if you think you do, you're a racist.
5.	Show interest in multiculturalism.	5. Do not culturally appropriate. What is not your culture is not for you, and you may not try it or do it.
6.	Support black people in creating their own spaces and stay out of them.	6. Seek to have black friends. If you don't have any, you're racist. And if you claim any, they'd better be *good* friends—albeit occupying their private spaces that you aren't allowed in.
7.	When whites move away from black neighborhoods, it's white flight.	7. When whites move into black neighborhoods, it's gentrification, even when they pay black residents generously for their houses.
8.	If you are white and date only white people, you're a racist.	8. If you're a white and a black person, you are, If only deep down, "exotifying" an "other."
9.	Black people cannot be held accountable for everything every black person does.	9. All whites must acknowledge their personal complicitness in the perfidy of "whiteness" throughout history.
10.	Black students must be admitted to schools via adjusted grade and test score standards to ensure a representative number of them and foster a diversity of views in classrooms.	10. It is racist to assume a black student was admitted to a school via racial preferences, and racist to expect them to represent the "diverse" view in classroom discussions.

---

[998] McWhorter, John. *Woke Racism, How a New Religion has Betrayed Black America.* Portfolio, 2021: 4-5.

[999] ibid., 8-9. Note: although I capitalize Black throughout this book, McWhorter does not, so any direct quotations from him will not follow that convention.

Logically, these pairs *appear* to be contradictory. On the surface (and at face value), it seems difficult to reconcile how white persons should "elevate the voices of the oppressed (i.e., people of color) over [their] own" *and* that (white) "silence is violence," or that white persons should show interest in other cultures *but* that doing so is cultural appropriation and must be avoided. However, McWhorter has an answer: 3rd Wave antiracism functions as a "religion."

Within various religions, seeming contradictions in doctrine are allowed, and followers are supposed to take certain things on "faith." For example, the Christian doctrine of the Trinity simultaneously holds that God is one, but also three, in person. The Catechism of the Catholic Church, specifically, speaks of the Trinity as one of the "mysteries that are hidden in God, which can never be known unless they are revealed by God" 'and declares that "the mystery of the Most Holy Trinity is the central mystery of Christian faith and life."[1000]

McWhorter claims that 3rd Wave Antiracism is itself (functionally) a religion. As a religion, it has several features in common with other religions. The proponents of this "religion," The Elect:

- **Have certain doctrines or articles of faith that aren't to be questioned**. For certain sorts of Christians, for example, the infallibility of the Bible is something that is taken on faith, and seeming errors or contradictions found within the Bible are not to be entertained as challenges to the faith. For 3rd wave antiracists, the existence and pervasiveness of racism is not to be questioned, nor is the testimony of any person of color who claims to have been a victim of racism (including microaggressions). Racial disparities can only be the result of racism. Questioning the internal logic of the central tents (e.g., that students of color should be admitted to schools to provide a "diverse" perspective, but that asking that student to provide that perspective is racist) indicates that one still doesn't "get it."

- **Have clergy**. Christian churches have priests or pastors who are sometimes considered "anointed," and whose sermons are received as inspired. McWhorter claims that the writings of Ibram X. Kendi (*How to be Antiracist*), Ta-Nehisi Coates ("The Case for Reparations"), and Robin DiAngelo (*White Fragility*) are treated with a similar reverence—to the point that some white persons post pictures of themselves reading these works on social media as evidence that they are "doing the work."

- **Have original sin**. In Christianity, the doctrine of original sin is a theological doctrine that claims that all human beings are born sinful and require redemption from a Savior (Jesus). The original sin of 3rd wave antiracism is white privilege—something that every white person is born with and from which every white person benefits to some degree. White persons should continually "confess" their privilege while recognizing that they can never be absolved of it.

- **Evangelize**. Christians are commanded to spread the "good news" of the Gospel throughout the Earth and convert unbelievers. Antiracists are similarly called upon to convert the uninitiated through social media posts, workshops, diversity training, and public shaming (if necessary).

[1000] *Catechism of the Catholic Church,*

[237] Archived March 3, 2013, at the Wayback Machine.

- **Are Apocalyptic**. Christianity envisions an "end time" when Jesus will return to Earth and usher in a new era (though this is interpreted differently by different denominations). 3rd wave antiracists envision a "judgment day" when America finally atones for racism (despite the fact that what would count as sufficient atonement, and who could determine such a thing, is unclear).
- **Ban heretics**. Christian denominations throughout history have expelled heretics from their community (or worse!). Catholics, for example, can be excommunicated. Similarly, racist persons, or even insufficiently antiracist persons (e.g., white persons who are insufficiently engaged in the fight against racism, or who question the scope of their privilege) are to be called out and sometimes "banned" from communities (e.g., being fired from their job).[1001]

This comparison is *not* intended to be favorable. Because 3rd Wave Antiracism functions as a religion, and its supporters, therefore, function like members of a "faith," both its doctrines and followers are, to some extent, beyond the reach and appeal of reason.

My goal is not to venture a misty statement that today's hyper wokesters need to understand the diversity of opinions is crucial to a healthy society. Citing John Stuart Mill at them serves no purpose; our current conversations with massive amounts of energy by missing the futility of "dialogue" with them. Of 100 fundamentalist Christians, how many do you suppose could be convinced by argument to become atheists? There is no reason that the number of people who can be talked out of this religion should be any higher.[1002]

Comparing "The Elect" to fundamentalists, McWhorter believes that they are "immune" to dialogue, debate, and even evidence. This might be problematic enough, but he also believes that The Elect offer a version of antiracism that is useless, and even harmful.

3rd Wave Antiracism is "useless," according to McWhorter, because it is "performative" rather than productive.

Kids build forts because they like building forts. As often as not, after they built one, they don't really spend much time in it. People claiming that the "work" of white privilege consciousness raising is a prelude to political action are like kids pretending their forts are for protection. It feels good to say that all of this rhetoric and dismissal is necessary for changing "structures." But the real reason they are engaging in this suspiciously lengthy prelude is that there is a joy almost all of us take in hostility. Most who aren't up for wielding it themselves don't mind watching it slung. . . .

If Elect philosophy were really about changing the world, its parishioners would be ever champing at the bit to get out and do the changing, like . . . Dr. King.

It would be a problem among their flock: persuading adherents to sit tight and engage in the navel gazing, set jawed, hermetic reprogramming exercises rather than going out to do real things for real people in need. The gloomy performance art's fuzzy connection to relieving the ills of those people in the real world would feel trivial. It would elicit disgust and dismissal from those initially attracted to something promoted as being devoted to change, until they realized it was only devoted to self-gratification.[1003]

While he has acknowledged in numerous interviews and articles that he does not think that

---

[1001] McWhorter, 25-45.
[1002] ibid., xii-xiii.

[1003] ibid., 74-75.

"The Elect" are *consciously* promoting a movement that reduces to mere virtue signaling, at best, he nevertheless thinks that any assumptions that their favored activities (in his view) actually make a positive difference to race relations or the status of persons of color is delusional. Forcing white employees to "confess" their privilege at mandatory workplace trainings, teaching children to sort one another into categories of oppressed and oppressor, and posting photos of oneself on social media reading *White Fragility* (#doingthework), is analogous to a parishioner swooning and waving her hand at Church: it accomplishes nothing for anyone other than the person performing the act—and for that person it functions primarily to show others how "faithful" they are. In this sense, the "activism" of 3rd Wave Antiracists is performative. In addition, though, McWhorter claims their activities are actually *harmful*.

The alleged harm of 3rd Wave Antiracism comes in at least two forms. First, harm is done to "heretics." "Heretics," in this sense, can include anyone who challenges the basic claims of 3rd Wave Antiracism, or even those who are insufficiently enthusiastic in their support.

> *Battling power relations and their discriminatory effects must be the central focus of all human endeavor, be it intellectual, moral, civic, or artistic. Those who resist this focus, or even evidence insufficient adherence to it, must be sharply condemned, deprived of influence, and ostracized.*[1004]

Labeled "woke" culture or "cancel culture" in the media (and especially by right-wing media), examples include protests to prevent invited speakers from making speeches on college campuses, campaigns to have people fired from their jobs or entire shows or movies cancelled, and, most simply, attaching the socially disastrous label of "racist" to people who "sin" or who refuse to show sufficient faith. These sorts of behaviors tun "The Elect" into dangerous "crusaders."

> *But as most of us can see, there is a difference between being antiracist and being antiracist in a hostile way, where one is to pillory people for what, as recently as ten years ago, would have been thought of as petty torts or even as nothing at all, to espouse policies that hurt black people as long as supporting them makes you seem aware that racism exists, and to pretend that America never makes any real progress on racism and privately almost hope that it doesn't, because it would deprive you of a sense of purpose.*[1005]

Here, McWhorter makes clear a couple of important points. One is that he is not somehow opposed to antiracism efforts, but only "hostile" antiracists that he finds in the 3rd Wave. He has expressed admiration, approval, and appreciation for 1st and 2nd Wave Antiracist efforts. Second, he thinks that the harm of 3rd Wave Antiracism is not limited to the white people at risk of being "cancelled," but that it extends to Black people as well. He claims that it does so in the following ways (at minimum):

> You are to turn a blind eye to black kids getting jumped by other ones in school.
> You are to turn a blind eye to black undergraduates cast into schools where they are in over their heads, and into law schools and capable of adjusting to their level of preparation in a way that will allow them to pass the bar exam.
> You are to turn a blind eye to the willful dimness of condemning dead people for moral lapses normal in their time, as if they were still alive.
> You are to turn a blind eye to the folly in the idea of black "identity" as all about what whites think rather than about what black people themselves think.
> You are to turn a blind eye to lapses in black intellectuals' work, because black people lack white privilege.
> You are to turn a blind eye to the fact that social history is complex, and instead pretend

---

[1004] ibid., 11.

[1005] ibid., 21-22.

that those who tell you that all racial discrepancies are a result of racism are evidencing brilliance.

> *You are to turn a blind eye to innocent children, taught to think in these ways practically before they can hold a pencil.*[1006]

Focusing on just one of his examples, we will consider school discipline. It is well documented that Black children (especially boys) get suspended and expelled from schools at a higher rate than students of other races or ethnicities. One study showed that Black students lost 103 days per 100 students enrolled due to suspensions—82 more days than the 21 days their white peers lost due to out-of-school suspensions.[1007] An obvious potential explanation for this disparity is racism.

> *Black Boys get suspended and expelled from schools and more than other kids. According to elect ideology, this must be because they are discriminated against. Specifically, we are told to think that the reason these boys get disciplined more than other kids is because teachers hold biases against them. The white*

kid acting up is scamp; the black kid acting up as a thug. [1008]

McWhorter also questions the 3rd Wave Antiracist assumption that *any* disparity in outcomes is explained by racism.

> *The nut of the issue has always been that if we don't trace the problems to racism, then the only other possibility must be that black people are inherently deficient somehow. Given how vastly unlikely that seems, we must point to racism.*[1009]

Though this is not *his* point, there might very well be something to that explanation, at least with respect to the school discipline data. Another study finds a strong correlation between faculty implicit bias and suspensions for Black students, and the predicted differences in disparities emerge "even after accounting for several context-varying factors that contribute to achievement or opportunity gaps, including individual-based factors (e.g., poverty) and school-based factors (e.g., racial segregation)."[1010]

[1006] ibid., 97-98.

[1007] https://www.usnews.com/news/education-news/articles/2020-10-13/school-suspension-data-shows-glaring-disparities-in-discipline-by-race

[1008] McWhorter, 98.

[1009] ibid., 120.

[1010] https://www.brookings.edu/blog/brown-center-chalkboard/2020/07/20/educator-bias-is-associated-with-racial-disparities-in-student-achievement-and-discipline/

Figure 2: County-level white-Black disciplinary differences by bias

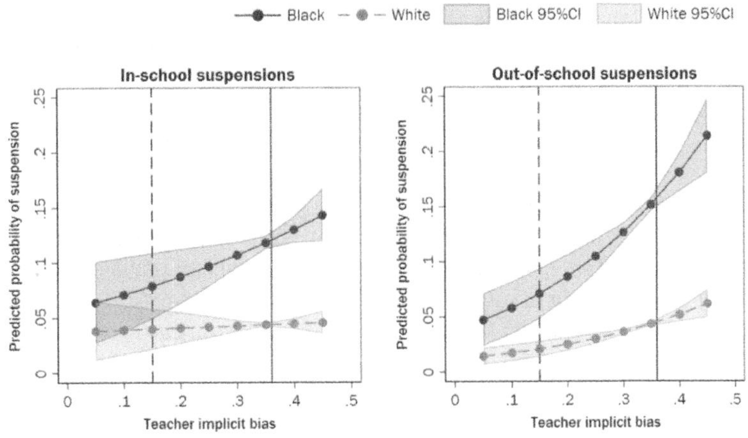

Source: Chin, M. J., Quinn, D., Dhaliwal, T. K., & Lovison. V. (forthcoming). Bias in the air: A nationwide exploration of teachers' implicit racial attitudes, aggregate bias, and student outcomes. Educational Researcher.

McWhorter, though, points to a different explanation.

The National Center for Education Statistics found that in 2015, 12.6% of Black Kids surveyed nationwide had had a fight on school grounds, while only 5.6% of white kids had…. In 2013, The numbers were 12.8% versus 6.4. In other words, black kids were more than twice as likely to engage in violence at school as white kids. A Fordham Institute study showed the same thing in 2019. It surveyed 1200 black and white elementary and high school teachers nationwide and found that teachers in high poverty schools were twice as likely as those in other schools to say that verbal disrespect was a daily occurrence in their classrooms, six times as likely to say that physical fighting was a daily or weekly occurrence, and three times as likely to report being personally assaulted by a student.[1011]

In other words, the reason Black boys are being suspended or expelled at higher rates than other groups of children is because they are committing acts of violence at a higher rate than other groups of children. The disparate outcome isn't the result of racism by the teachers, but because of disparate rates of discipline-worthy behaviors. What's more, 3rd Wave attempts to eliminate the "racism" in school discipline by reducing the amount of discipline doled is not desired by *Black* teachers.

Reports from a New York City initiative have even more explicitly located and a special problem with school violence among black boys. The initiative sought to reduce suspensions of black boys in response to the reports claiming that the suspensions were driven by racism. Teachers reported less order and discipline in their classrooms, particularly in black and Latino, dominated secondary schools. Many black teachers said the suspensions and similar kinds of discipline should be used more often, despite the fact that black teachers were slightly more likely to believe also that school discipline could be racially biased. In the high poverty schools, 60% of African American teachers--slightly more than the 57% of white teachers--said that issues with student behavior made

---

[1011] McWhorter, 100.

learning difficult.[1012]

In addition, attempting to reduce racial disparities in discipline by reducing discipline applied to Black students results in more acts of violence (i.e., harm) inflicted on *other* Black students.

> *But the simple fact is this: black boys do commit more violent offenses in public schools than other kids. Period. The Elect earnestly decried that most black kids go to school with only other black kids, because it fits into their agenda to point out "segregation." But that "segregation" also entails that the black boys they think should be allowed to beat up other kids in school are handing out the beatings to other black kids. This means that if we follow these prophets' advice and go easier on black boys, we hinder the education of other black students.*[1013]

McWhorter grants that racism has *something* to do with Black students having lower high school graduation rates but thinks that the spotlight aimed by 3rd Wave Antiracists is shining in the wrong place. He cites an experiment done in Philadelphia in 1987 that he thinks illustrates that the "problem" is not racist teachers or a lack of resources at mostly minority schools because of racist administrators or local politicians.

In this experiment, a rich donor "adopted" 112 Black 6th graders and guaranteed them a fully funded education all the way through college so long as they didn't do drugs, commit crimes, or have any children before getting married. In addition to this promise, he provided tutors, workshops, after school programs, summer programs and supplied counselors for when they encountered any sort of difficulties. Of the 112 children, 45 didn't finish high school. Among the boys, 19 of the 67 had become felons. Among the girls, more than half had a child before turning 18, and, 12 years later, the 45 girls from the study had a total of 63 children.[1014]

These outcomes suggest to McWhorter that the problem is not a lack of resources or opportunity, but rather some cultural differences regarding what is considered "normal" for Black kids as opposed to white kids. McWhorter identifies the culprit as a cultural acceptance (resignation) of not finishing school, teen pregnancy, and criminal behavior, and a lesser value (even to the point of rejection) attached to education. McWhorter *does* acknowledge the role that racism plays in these cultural differences.

> *Those cultural factors can certainly be traced to racism. In the past, such as dehumanization, leading to people to see themselves as separate from the norms of their surrounding society. . . . it means that through no fault of their own, it was not resources, but those unconsciously internalized norms . . . that kept those kids from being able to take advantage of what they were being offered. . . . The reason for this was nothing pathological about the kids, but it wasn't a "racism" that anyone could simply "eliminate," either. The racism in question had been threaded subtly through the endless currents and eddies of decades of social history, leading to that moment. . . . Many have argued that this is because of an idea among black teens that to embrace school is "acting white.*[1015]

McWhorter points to the social backlash and abuse Black kids faced in the aftermath of school desegregation. Many white parents, students, and teachers were unwelcoming at best, and openly hostile at worst, creating an unpleasant, unwelcoming environment at school. "School" was associated with white hostility, and Black students understandably were less engaged and motivated, in addition to their education being actively undermined at times by racist teachers.

> *That kind of rejection can make a person disidentify from a whole environment, and one result was a sense. This school was for white*

[1012] ibid., 101.
[1013] ibid, 98-99.

[1014] ibid., 122.
[1015] ibid., 122-125.

kids, something outside of the authentic black experience. This, to be sure, was because of racism. But overtime, open white resistance to black kids in these schools preceded as attitudes on race changed. Nonetheless, a cultural meme casting school as "white" had set in, and it has become self perpetuating since. . . . The "acting white" charge is one of those cultural traits that has lasted beyond what created it. Black students may level the charge, even in extravagantly funded schools, where nonwhite teachers are as exquisitely sensitized about racism as humans can be, quite unlike the nasty, dismissive teachers that black kids encountered decades ago.[1016]

Cultural memes, such as the idea that Black children who are serious about their education are "acting white," can last far beyond their initial causes. The infamous Tuskegee experiment in which Black men were intentionally left untreated for syphilis and deceived about this fact (allowing not only their disease to progress, but also their unwittingly spreading it to their partners!) generated intense distrust of the medical community among many Black persons—a distrust that continues (for some) to this day, more than 50 years after the experiment ended. Similarly, McWhorter thinks that *current* racial disparities in educational achievement are not best explained by *current* racism within schools, systemic, or otherwise.

Is the reason black kids often think of school as white that white people today don't like them, or that the system is somehow set against black kids learning? No: that analysis makes no sense, period. Only a heedless, numb kind of fealty, a quiet refusal to engage the actual individuals we are talking about, would insist that "racism closed code is why a black kid, decades after 1966, gives a black nerd trouble for studying hard. Racism sparked this problem. Originally, to be sure, but the solution today cannot be to wave a magic wand and "eliminate racism," because the teachers who

exerted racism upon black kids three generations ago are now mostly dead.[1017]

As a brief editorial note: this analysis doesn't acknowledge the potential existence of existing implicit bias among teachers, administrators, school counselors, and other school staff. Cultural attitudes about education could be the result of past practices but could also be the result of a combination of that *in addition* to a recognition of *current* unequal treatment.

For all of his criticism, McWhorter does attempt to provide a *constructive alternative* to the current antiracist agenda. Instead of looking to white people to confess their privilege and atone for racism, he proposes that the "war on drugs" be ended, that the "phonics" method of reading be used in school rather than the current "whole word" method, and that alternatives to four-year degrees be made available and celebrated.

These three "simple" interventions would make a tangible improvement in the lives of many people of color as literacy rates would rise (potentially inspiring a greater interest in school and an appreciation of education), fewer people of color would be in jail over drug charges or killed over disputes in the black market, and more people of color would have satisfying and well-paying jobs (that are often highly skilled as well) that require "only" vocational training or a degree or certificate from a community college. As just one very local example, Rio Hondo College has dozens of degrees and certificates for "vocational" programs such as automotive repair, welding, electric vehicle and fuel cell technology, engineering design drafting, architectural drafting, accounting, income tax preparation, small business management, hospitality management, nursing, yoga instruction, child development, and drug studies—among many others.

Notably absent among his recommendations is any attempt to reform the criminal justice system (aside from ending the war on drugs). What about "defunding the police," or some sort

---

[1016] ibid., 126.

[1017] ibid., 128-129.

of attempt to reduce racially disparate rates of police contact, and especially police violence?

> *I heartily espouse police reform, but consider it unlikely that anything can be done to stop cops from firing their weapons lethally in tight or even risky situations. I know this partly because, even in the wake of George Floyd's murder, throughout 2020, cops continued killing or maiming people, despite all eyes upon them, with no real consequences. . . . The key is that changing the cops will take eons; changing black lives should take less time than that. However, with no war on drugs, encounters between black men and the cops will be rarer. No cops will be sent to poor neighborhoods to sniff out people selling or carrying drugs or to break up a drug selling rings, nor will cops be assigned to sit roadside waiting to stop people for drug possession. Furthermore, better educated people with solid jobs, raised more often by two parents able to focus their full attention upon them, will be that much less likely to end up in ugly encounters with the police.[1018]*

This is one final (for our purposes) practical gesture by McWhorter. He doesn't deny that people of color experience harm from the criminal justice system, but he's not optimistic about the chances of any meaningful reform of the system. Given the unlikelihood of success, energy spent on protests demanding that communities "defund the police" is a waste, and might often be merely performative, like other activities of 3rd Wave Antiracists.

[1018] ibid., 146-147.

Chapter 25: White Nationalism

Comprehension questions you should be able to answer after reading this chapter:

1. What is "white nationalism?
2. What is a "race realist?"
3. What is an "ethno-state?"
4. What are some of the political goals of contemporary white nationalists such as Richard Spencer and Jared Taylor?
5. According to Hitler, what is the proper relationship between "race" and the State?
6. What are some of the educational reforms proposed by Hitler? What ultimate purpose do these reforms (and government in general) serve?
7. What is the difference between "racialism" and "racism?" What do they have in common?
8. What is the "popular account" of race?
9. Explain why it would be relevant in the context of a white nationalism if "race" were a social construct (as opposed to a biological "essence")?
10. What does Nietzsche mean by the *Übermensch*? Explain why this is not necessarily a reference to the Aryan "master race".
11. What is the "artistic" interpretation of the "will to power"? How can it be seen as a refutation of the "Nazi" totalitarian/political interpretation of the will to power?

I did not enjoy researching or writing this chapter. The subject matter is "ugly."

Just to put all cards on the table: I'm "white."[1019] I am *not*, however, anything resembling a white supremacist or a white nationalist. I generally try to refrain from editorializing in my chapters, but this chapter will be an exception to that general rule.

I am opposed to white supremacist/white nationalist ideologies (and, frankly, any *other* race-based ideologies as well) for both moral reasons as well as epistemic reasons. That is to say that I think such ideologies are both morally misguided and intellectually bankrupt. What they are not, however, are mere historical curiosities—just one more relic in a pile of bad and dangerous ideas.

Unfortunately, white supremacy/nationalism has been rebranded and is enjoying a resurgence and relevance. It has found a home in the "alt-right" movement, and spokespersons for, and sympathizers of, this movement have become increasing accepted into

"mainstream" political consideration and discourse.

While this iteration of their ideology is new, the ideology itself is not. It can be traced back rather easily to the worldview of the Nazi party, and the words of none other than Adolf Hitler. What was true about this ideology then is equally true now: it is based on multiple mistakes. For our purposes we will consider only two of those mistakes:

1. A mistaken understanding of Nietzsche.
2. A mistaken understanding of race.

We will begin this chapter with a brief treatment of contemporary white nationalism as expressed by some of its more prominent spokespersons (Jared Taylor and Richard Spencer). We will then trace those ideas back to the "philosophy" of Hitler. We will consider the alleged contributions of Nietzsche to the Nazi ideology as well as their assumptions about race. We will conclude by demonstrating that

---

[1019] Although, exactly that *means* is complicated – as I hope was evident from the earlier chapter on the philosophy of race.

Nietzsche (for all his merits and flaws) was demonstrably opposed to race-based notions of supremacy and openly critical of German nationalism, and that the basic assumptions about race that are fundamental to this ideology have no grounding in science.

White Nationalism

"White nationalism" can, with some controversy, be taken as a euphemism for white supremacy. The basic position of white supremacy is, I suspect, self-explanatory: the belief that there is such a thing as the "white" race, and that that race is superior to other (non-white) races.

Traditionally, white supremacy has been associated with Nazism, neo-Nazis, the Ku Klux Klan, and various other hate groups. Today, some people associated with white nationalism use other terms to describe themselves: "alt-right," "identitarians," or "race realists."

Whatever the name, the political goal is basically the same: the establishment of a white "ethno-state," where "white culture" is celebrated, and the "perils" of multiculturalism are avoided by virtue of segregation.

White nationalism has manifested in increasing numbers of rallies and protests, including the "Unite the Right" rally that occurred in August, 2017 in Charlottesville, Virginia. The protest was ostensibly over the pending removal of a statue of Robert E Lee from Emancipation Park. As the Confederate general, Lee is a symbol for white supremacists/nationalists and the removal of his statue was seen as another example of the attack on "white culture." One of the organizers of the event, Nathan Damigo, said that one of the purposes of the rally was to unify the white nationalist movement in the United States.[1020] Protesters consisted of a mix of white supremacists, white nationalists, neo-Nazis, militia members, and Klansmen. They displayed Confederate flags, swastikas, semi-automatic rifles, and some chanted racist and anti-Semitic slogans during their march. The rally was

especially controversial due to the violent confrontation between the protesters, and counter protesters. Dozens of people were injured, and one woman was killed, when one of the white supremacists intentionally rammed his car into a crowd of counter protesters. Further controversy was generated when President Trump commented on the rally:

I think there is blame on both sides. You look at both sides. I think there is blame on both sides. I have no doubt about it. You don't have doubt about it either. If you reported it accurately, you would say that the neo-Nazis started this thing. They showed up in Charlottesville. Excuse me. They didn't put themselves down as neo-Nazis. You had some very bad people in that group. You also had some very fine people on both sides. You had people in that group -- excuse me, excuse me. I saw the same pictures as you did. You had people in that group that were there to protest the taking down, of to them, a very, very important statue and the renaming of a park from Robert E. Lee to another name.

George Washington was a slave owner. Was George Washington a slave owner? So will George Washington now lose his status? Are we going to take down -- excuse me. Are we going to take down statues to George Washington? How about Thomas Jefferson? What do you think of Thomas Jefferson? You like him. Good. Are we going to take down his statue? He was a major slave owner. Are we going to take down his statue? It is fine. You are changing history and culture.

You had people and I'm not talking about the neo-Nazis and the white nationalists. They should be condemned totally. You had many people in that group other than neo-Nazis and white nationalists. The

---

[1020] http://www.modbee.com/news/article167213427.html

press has treated them absolutely unfairly. Now, in the other group also, you had some fine people but you also had troublemakers and you see them come with the black outfits and with the helmets and with the baseball bats. You had a lot of bad people in the other group too.[1021]

In President Trump's defense, he does attempt to make a distinction between white nationalists and some "very fine people" that were involved (on the same side) of the same protest. *However*, his defense of the cultural value of the Robert E Lee statue, his analogy to George Washington and Thomas Jefferson, and his statement about "changing history and culture" seem to suggest a solidarity with those who are

claiming that "white culture" is under attack. It is certainly the case that some of the more prominent members of the white supremacists/nationalist movement interpreted his words to be very favorable to their cause.[1022]

David Duke
@DrDavidDuke

Follow

Thank you President Trump for your honesty & courage to tell the truth about #Charlottesville & condemn the leftist terrorists in BLM/Antifa

NBC News @NBCNews
President Trump: "George Washington was a slave owner... Are we gonna take down statues to George Washington? How about Thomas Jefferson?"

1:45 PM - 15 Aug 2017

Richard Spencer
@RichardBSpencer

Follow

Trump's statement was fair and down to earth. #Charlottesville could have been peaceful, if police did its job.

Trump: You had very fine people, on both sides
President Donald Trump answers questions at a press briefing on infrastructure at Trump Tower in New York.
cnbc.com

2:33 PM - 15 Aug 2017

For a variety of reasons, the white nationalist movement (or alt-right) has made its way into

representative of the white supremacist movement, and Richard Spencer is a leader of the "alt – right" and will be featured in greater detail later in this chapter.

[1021] https://www.vox.com/2017/8/15/16154028/trump-press-conference-transcript-charlottesville

[1022] David Duke is the former "grand Wizard" of the Ku Klux Klan and a globally recognized

mainstream media coverage and political discourse. Although it is far from being a mainstream political movement, it cannot and should not be ignored. To put it bluntly: we have seen this sort of thing before, historically speaking. Then, as now, such ideas were dangerous.

The *Turner Diaries* was written over 40 years ago by William Luther Pierce. It is a work of dystopian fiction depicting a white nationalist revolution (fictionally begun on 9-16-1991) in the United States, and culminating in an overthrow of the government, a campaign of global genocide against non-white people, and the institution of a white supremacist State. The revolutionary work is carried out by an organization of loose "cells" called The Order. One of the more chilling and memorable portions of the revolution is called the "day of rope."

Today has been the Day of the Rope — a grim and bloody day, but an unavoidable one. Tonight, from tens of thousands of lampposts, power poles, and trees throughout this vast metropolitan area the grisly forms hang. Even the street signs at intersections have been pressed into service, and at practically every street corner I passed this evening on my way to HQ there was a dangling corpse, four at every intersection. Hanging from a single overpass only about a mile from here is a group of about 30, each with an identical placard around its neck bearing the printed legend, "I betrayed my race."

Two or three of that group had been decked out in academic robes before they were strung up, and the whole batch are apparently faculty members from the nearby UCLA campus. ...The first thing I saw in the moonlight was the placard with its legend in large, block letters: "I defiled my race." Above the placard leered the horribly bloated, purplish face of a young woman, her eyes wide open and bulging, her mouth agape.

Finally I could make out the thin, vertical line of rope disappearing into the branches above. I shuddered and quickly went on my way. There are many thousands of hanging female corpses like that in this city tonight, all wearing identical placards around their necks. They are the White women who were married to or living with Blacks, with Jews, or with other non-White males. There are also a number of men wearing the I-defiled-my-race placard, but the women easily outnumber them seven or eight to one. On the other hand, about ninety per cent of the corpses with the I-betrayed-my-race placards are men, and overall the sexes seem to be roughly balanced.

Those wearing the latter placards are the politicians, the lawyers, the businessmen, the TV newscasters, the newspaper reporters and editors, the judges, the teachers, the school officials, the "civic leaders", the bureaucrats, the preachers, and all the others who, for reasons of career or status or votes or whatever, helped promote or implement the System's racial program.[1023]

The problem with the *Turner Diaries* is that it's not just a case of troubling fiction: it has had real-world consequences, inspiring dozens of armed robberies and more than 200 murders in the decades since its publication.[1024] Oklahoma City Bomber Timothy McVeigh was inspired by the book. Indeed, characters in the book blow up a federal building using a truck filled with explosives and fertilizer!

[1023] The fact that I wrote this chapter, not to mention that I am married to an African-American woman, would certainly qualify me as a "race traitor," in this scenario.

[1024] https://www.theatlantic.com/politics/archive/2016/09/how-the-turner-diaries-changed-white-nationalism/500039/

An actual white nationalist gang calling itself "The Order," in direct reference to the novel, murdered three people and committed robberies back in 1983. Some members referred to the Diaries as their "bible." One member of this gang (David Lane) became a writer himself (while in prison). One of his works is entitled the "White Genocide Manifesto." The manifesto equates "integration" with white genocide. He later condensed his views into a slogan now known in white supremacist/nationalist circles as "The 14 Words:" "We must secure the existence of our people and a future for white children." Other contemporary white nationalists have continued this theme of framing "race-mixing" and multiculturalism as "white genocide."

Even the imagery of the "day of the rope" has found recent and disturbing manifestation when, on January 6th 2020, Trump supporters invaded and occupied the Capitol building in Washington D.C. in an attempt to stop the certification of the election results and preserve the Trump presidency. Some of them actually built a scaffold with a noose outside the building, and others fashioned a noose from camera cords after destroying some media equipment.[1025] These can't be taken to be merely symbolic displays produced by frustrated protestors, given that large crowds were captured on video chanting "hang Mike Pence" (Trump's own Vice President).[1026]A day before these events, a disgruntled citizen of Shasta County California, in a public statement before the city council, said "When the ballot box is gone, there is only the cartridge box. You have made bullets expensive. But luckily for you, ropes are reusable."[1027]

In the remainder of this section, I will provide a brief overview of two of the more prominent figures of the *contemporary* white nationalist movement, Richard Spencer and Jared Taylor, before considering their more infamous predecessor.

Richard Spencer[1028]

Richard Spencer (May 11, 1978 --) is the president of the National Policy Institute, which is widely regarded as a white supremacists think tank.[1029] Spencer rejects that label and calls himself an "identitarian" instead. The problem with this rejection is that his words demonstrate a pattern in which he clearly *does* think that "white" peoples are superior to non-white peoples. Consider, for example, when President Trump stirred up controversy by referring disparagingly to Haiti, El Salvador, and African countries (in general).

Why are we having all these people from shithole countries come here?[1030]

It is worth pointing out that, at the same time, President Trump proposed immigrants from Norway as a preferable alternative. Norway is 83% Norwegian, and 8.3% (other) European,

---

[1028] In the spirit of transparency, Spencer's current values and political affiliation are ambiguous compared to when this chapter was first written. Although he does not appear to have relented on his white nationalist beliefs, he claims to have withdrawn his support of the Republican Party due to their foreign interventionism and incompetence (). In response, Joe Biden's campaign manager said "What you stand for is absolutely repugnant. Your support is 10,000% unwelcome here (ibid.)."

leaving just less than 9% of its population "non-European."[1031]   In   fairness,   Norway   is consistently ranked among the top 5 "happiest" countries,[1032] and scores considerably better than the United States with respect to crime rates,[1033] so there are legitimately "good" things to say about Norwegians that ostensibly have nothing to do with race. In context, however, suggesting that the USA recruit more Norwegian immigrants immediately after calling "black" (Haiti; all of Africa) and brown (El Salvador) countries "shit holes" certainly raises the idea that   race   is   a   factor—and   Spencer enthusiastically agreed.

I must come to the defense of #Haiti! It's a potentially beautiful and productive country. The problem is that it's filled with shithole people. If the French dominated, they could make it great again. #MakeHaitiGreatAgain

8:14 PM - 11 Jan 2018

While Twitter is hardly the vehicle for nuanced philosophical discourse, the basic point here is obvious. Haitians (who are black) are "shithole people." The French (who are white—at least "traditionally," and in all the ways that count according to Spencer) would make Haiti "great again." It's impossible to *not* detect the supremacist tone here. When countries are ruled by white people, they are great. When they are ruled by non-white people (or, at least, specifically, black people), they are "shitholes."

Spencer claims to have created the term "alt-right" to represent a movement about "white identity." While he had been known in various corners of the Internet for years, he achieved national mainstream prominence when a video of him speaking at a National Policy Institute conference just after 2016 election of President Trump went viral. Most noteworthy was him proclaiming "hail Trump, hail our people, hail victory!" In response, several members of the audience gave the Nazi salute.[1034]

It's hard to believe that the specific use of the word "hail," in the phrase "hail Trump" (rather close to "*heil* Hitler"), and the Nazi salute in response show no connection to Hitler and the Nazis. Indeed, like many white nationalists, Spencer embraces the notion of an essential culture/"spirit" of a people that is quite similar to the notion of a "Volk" that we find in Hitler.

The political outcome that Spencer and his followers seek is the creation of a distinct and separate "white Christian ethno-state," with distinct geographic borders, populated with people of European descent (as understood to be fair skinned people who populated Europe several hundred years ago). The process by which this outcome is to be achieved is the cultivation of ethnic pride for white people and the promotion of government policies that promote and protect that new white racial consciousness.

Practically speaking, this will mean the mainstream acceptance of "white pride," the dismantling of programs that allegedly promote the welfare and success of non-white persons in the United States over those of white people, a radical change in immigration policies to favor immigrants from predominately white countries and to exclude (or even deport) non-white immigrants, etc.

In an essay, entitled "Race: Stalking the Wild Taboo", Spencer explains achievement, wealth, and (apparent) intelligence differences between the races as follows:

> *Perhaps the most important single environmental difference faced by these early humans was that much of the Eurasian landmass turns cold for several months of the year, and food is scarce during this time. It required intelligence, resourcefulness, foresight, and an ability to delay gratification (that is, impulse control), for ancient hunter-gatherers to*

[1031] https://www.indexmundi.com/norway/demographics_profile.html
[1032] http://worldhappiness.report/ed/2018/
[1033] http://www.nationmaster.com/country-info/compare/Norway/United-States/Crime
[1034] Bradner, Eric (November 22, 2016). "Alt-right leader: 'Hail Trump! Hail our people! Hail victory!'". CNN

survive cold winters. People with these qualities were more successful raising children than those who lacked them, so humans in more northerly areas gradually became more intelligent and future-oriented than those who remained in the tropics. The higher intelligence and lower crime rates of Whites and East Asians as compared with Africans may be due in large part to the selective pressure of cold winters.[1035]

Here, he is drawing on the work of Richard Lynn.[1036] The basic idea behind Lynn's theory is that "when early peoples migrated from equatorial East Africa into the more northern latitudes of North Africa, South Asia, Europe and Northeast Asia they encountered progressively more cognitively demanding environments that required greater intelligence, including the need to hunt large animals, build fires and shelters and make clothes. The colder the winter temperatures and the more northerly the environment, the higher were the IQs that evolved."[1037]

Basically, white people come from colder places than black or brown people, and therefore their ancestors were forced (by evolution) to be "smarter" in order to survive. This theoretical explanation for these alleged differences in IQ is not only controversial among scientists, but also seems challenged by common sense and a cursory understanding of history.[1038]

The accepted understanding of the evolution of humanity is that all humans alive today are descendants of African ancestors. "H. heidelbergensis" is thought to be the likely ancestor of both modern humans and Neanderthals, and is thought to have migrated from Africa approximately 500,000 years ago. Still within Africa, Homo sapiens diverged roughly 300,000 years ago, and is thought to have migrated roughly 70,000 years ago. Modern humans are thought to have spread across Europe only 40,000 years ago, with migration to the Americas roughly 20,000 years ago.

According to the "cold-weather" theory, the colder temperatures of Europe should have triggered more intelligent humans while those in the warmer climates of Africa and the Middle East, being less intellectually challenged by their environment, would develop less impressive IQ scores. Oddly enough, when we consider the birth of civilization itself, the communities we associate with the development of politics, religion, mathematics, literacy, early science, philosophy, medicine, etc.; they all come from those conspicuously *warm* climates: Babylonia (1895 BCE–619 BCE). Persian Empire (6th century BCE). Ancient Egypt (3150 BCE – 332 BCE). Ancient Greece (480 – 146 BCE).The Roman Republic and Empire (509 BCE – 395 CE).[1039]

Their intellectually "superior" counterparts in northern Europe, despite their allegedly genetically superior IQ and tens of thousands of years' worth of evolutionary advantage, were, comparatively speaking, illiterate barbarians during the same time periods. This, in addition to the fact that the civilization of China (with a wide-ranging climate) had been established in the 21st century BCE!

Spencer draws upon another contemporary white nationalist, Jared Taylor, in his echoing of the claim that it is "natural" to prefer members of the same race, citing him specifically in an essay sub-section entitled "The Preference for One's Own."[1040] We will now turn to Taylor himself.

[1035] https://nationalpolicy.institute/2017/10/05/race-stalking-the-wild-taboo/

[1036] Richard. *Race Differences in Intelligence: An Evolutionary Analysis*, 2nd Revised Edition, Washington Summit Publishers, 2015.

[1037] https://www.amren.com/news/2016/07/richard-lynn-on-race-differences-in-intelligence/

[1038] https://www.psychologytoday.com/blog/unique-everybody-else/201211/cold-winters-and-the-evolution-intelligence

[1039] All dates are approximate and very much subject to debate.

[1040] https://nationalpolicy.institute/2017/10/05/race-stalking-the-wild-taboo/

Jared Taylor

Samuel Jared Taylor (September 15, 1951 –) is another white nationalist/supremacist. He is the founder and editor of a white supremacist magazine entitled "American Renaissance."[1041] He is an author and publisher, and the former director of the National Policy Institute (a white nationalist "think tank" based in Virginia, now run by the aforementioned Richard Spencer). A key premise in Taylor's worldview is the idea of "race realism."

What we call race realism is what was considered common sense until perhaps the 1950s. It is a body of views that was so taken for granted it had no name, but it can be summarized as follows: That race is an important aspect of individual and group identity, that different races build different societies that reflect their natures, and that it is entirely normal for whites (or for people of any other race) to want to be the majority race in their own homeland.[1042]

Taylor believes in and argues for an essentialist notion of race, according to which real, meaningful, and enduring differences between peoples is accounted for by their race. He claims that recognition of these "facts" was, until relatively recently, accepted as obvious and common sense by all people, and is presently accepted and promoted by all people with the notable exception of "whites."

People of all races generally prefer the company of people like themselves. Racial diversity is a source of conflict, not strength. Non-whites, especially blacks and Hispanics, nurture a strong sense of racial pride and solidarity. Whites have little sense of racial solidarity, and most whites strongly condemn any signs of it.[1043]

He further argues that the recognition of distinct races, and preferring one's own, is natural, inevitable, and entirely appropriate.

Racial identity comes naturally to all non-white groups. It comes naturally because it is good, normal, and healthy to feel kinship for people like oneself. Despite the fashionable view that race is a socially created illusion, race is a biological reality. All people of the same race are more closely related genetically than they are to anyone of a different race, and this helps explain racial solidarity.

Families are close for the same reason. Parents love their children, not because they are the smartest, best-looking, most talented children on earth. They love them because they are genetically close to them. They love them because they are a family.

Most people have similar feelings about race. Their race is the largest extended family to which they feel an instinctive kinship. Like members of a family, members of a race do not need objective reasons to prefer their own group; they prefer it because it is theirs (though they may well imagine themselves as having many fine, partly imaginary qualities).

These mystic preferences need not imply hostility towards others. Parents may have great affection for the children of others, but their own children come first. Likewise, affection often crosses racial lines, but the deeper loyalties of most people are to their own group—their extended family.[1044]

Notice that Taylor explicitly claims that race is "reality" and it is biological rather than socially constructed—a point I will attempt to refute later in this chapter. In addition, he claims that racial

---

[1041] https://www.amren.com/

[1042] https://www.amren.com/about/issues/

[1043] Jared Taylor, *White Identity. Racial*

Consciousness in the 21st Century. New Century Foundation. 2011, 201.

[1044] ibid., 204.

preferences need not imply hostility towards other races, it is natural/normal/healthy/good to prefer people of one's own race.

Despite making it a point to say that these preferences need not imply hostility, there is ample hostility throughout Taylor's writings. I have provided a replica of the table of contents from his book, *White Identity. Racial Consciousness in the 21st Century*. I do this so that you may see the themes and subcategories he addresses in the book.

Chapters 1 – 4 attempt to argue for the natural and objective reality of segregation and racial preference and for the failure of attempts to integrate and to ignore this "reality." Chapters 5 – 7 offer his account of how non-whites embrace their own racial identity and consciousness, and advocate for "their own kind." Chapter 8 provides a thorough (and not terribly surprising) demonstration of the rampant racist assumptions that many white people (including presidents, politicians, and business leaders) exhibited and expressed for most of the history of the United States. He provides this history presumably in an attempt to demonstrate the "naturalness" of racial bias. In the final chapter (chapter 9) he offers a painstaking account of the "crisis" that is developing as a result of multiculturalism and increasing numbers of non-white people living in the United States.

Again, despite his claim that racial preference "need not imply hostility" towards other races, it's difficult to see how the depiction of a "crisis" for white people and white culture brought about by other races would not engender hostility, particularly when the crisis is described in terms of increasing national poverty rates (caused by non-white people), a deteriorating public school system (caused by non-white people), the loss of jobs for white people (caused by non-white people), increased crime and violence (caused by non-white people), the deterioration of our medical system (caused by non-white people), increased political corruption (caused by non-white people), and the loss of a distinctive and valued "white culture" (caused by non-white people).

Here is a very small sample from the many statistics and anecdotes that Taylor cites:

Fourteen-year-old James Tokarski was one of a handful of whites attending Bailly Middle School in Gary, Indiana, in 2006. Black students called him "whitey" and "white trash" and repeatedly beat him up. They knocked him unconscious twice. The school offered James a "lunch buddy," to be with him whenever he was not in class, but his parents took him out of Bailly. The mother of another white student said it was typical for whites to be called "whitey" or "white boy," and to get passes to eat lunch in the library rather than face hostile blacks in the lunch room.[1045]

Some people claim that all population groups commit crimes at the same rates, and that racial differences in incarceration rates reflect police and justice system bias.

This view is wrong. The US Department of Justice carefully tracks murder, which is the violent crime for which racial data on victim and perpetrator are most complete. In 2005, the department noted that blacks were six times more likely than whites to be victims of murder and seven times more likely to commit murder. . . There are practically no crimes blacks and Hispanics do not commit at higher rates than whites, whether it is larceny, car theft, drug offenses, burglary, rape, or alcohol offenses. Even for white collar crimes— fraud, racketeering, bribery/conflict of interest, embezzlement—blacks are incarcerated at three to five times the white rate, and Hispanics at about twice the white rate.[1046]

It is sobering to visit the websites for the FBI and various state police agencies and look at the photographs of the "most wanted" criminals. There is a huge preponderance of blacks and Hispanics, and sometimes not a single picture of a white criminal.[1047]

Small towns south of Los Angeles, such as South Gate, Lynwood, Bell Gardens, Maywood, Huntington Park, and Vernon were once white suburbs but have become largely Hispanic. They have also become notorious for thieving, bribe-taking politicians. Mayors, city council members, and treasurers have paraded off to jail.[1048]

The United States is now a nation that can produce headlines such as these: Baby Dies in Bucket of Mom's Vomit; 99-Year-Old Woman Among Rapist's Victims; Mom Allegedly Microwaves Baby; Town Stunned As 8-Year-Old Charged in Two Killings; Woman Accused of Using Infant as Car Down Payment; L.A. Police Say Killing of 3-Year-Old in Gang Attack Was Intentional;

[1045] ibid., 179.
[1046] ibid., 181 – 182.

[1047] ibid., 184.
[1048] ibid., 186.

North Dade Baby Shower Turns Deadly as Gunfight Breaks Out; Mother, Daughter and Granddaughter Teamed Up for Attack; Boston Police Say 7-Year-Old Shot 8-Year-Old Dead; Florida Woman Starves Children and Throws Dead Baby into Garbage Can; Parents Fight Over Which Gang Toddler Should Join; Mayhem Erupts Throughout City After Appeal to End Violence.

The people in these stories are about evenly split between blacks and Hispanics. As America's population changes, headlines like these will become more common.[1049]

His point is not subtle: the differences between the white race and other races amount to differences between what is good and what is bad, what is superior and what is inferior. No one could possibly think that he is not projecting some sort of negative judgment on non-white people when he paints such a vivid picture of crime, violence, corruption, moral decay, and an "otherness" that is building to a "crisis" for white people. Indeed, one of his explicit goals is to "awaken" white people to racial consciousness so that they can actively fight against such dire trends as those he points out.

All other groups take it for granted that they have a right to speak out in their own interests. Only whites have lost this conviction.[1050]
If whites permit themselves to become a minority population, they will lose their civilization, their heritage, and even their existence as a distinct people.[1051]

The number of Hispanics is growing very quickly in this country, and Hispanics are ecstatic about this. It means their language, their culture, their physical type, their heritage, their aspirations are all

gaining ground and could eventually dominate the United States. Hispanics want this very much, and they consistently try to change laws and policies to increase their numbers, and benefit their people. This is considered a sign of healthy collective pride.

But if whites tried to delay their dispossession, if whites proposed steps to maintain their majority status, that would be hate and bigotry. Why? The processes are perfectly symmetrical. The percentage of Hispanics increases as the percentage of whites decreases. Why is it right for Hispanics to celebrate their gains but wrong for whites to regret their losses?

I make no secret of my view on this. My ancestors have been white for tens of thousands of years. My children are white and I want my grandchildren to be white. I like the culture of Europe, I prefer the society that whites create. What's wrong with that?[1052]

At what point would it be legitimate for whites to act in their own group interests? When they become a minority? When they are no more than 30 percent of the population? Ten percent? Or must they never be allowed to take any action to ensure that the land in which they live reflects their values, their culture, their manners, their traditions, and honors the achievements of their ancestors? If whites do not cherish and defend these things, no one else will do it for them. If whites do not rekindle some sense of their collective interests they will be pushed aside by people who have a very clear sense of their interests. Eventually, whites will come to understand that to dismantle and even demonize white racial consciousness while other races cultivate racial consciousness is a fatal form of

---

[1049] ibid., 200.
[1050] https://www.amren.com/about/issues/
[1051] https://www.amren.com/about/issues/

[1052] https://www.amren.com/features/2015/04/white-survival-beyond-left-and-right/

unilateral disarmament.

For their very survival as a distinct people with a distinct culture, whites must recognize something all others take for granted: that race is a fundamental part of individual and group identity. Any society based on the assumption that race can be wished or legislated away ensures for itself an endless agony of pretense, conflict, and failure. For 60 years, we have wished and legislated in vain. In so doing, by opening the United States to peoples from every corner of the world, we have created agonizing problems for future generations. As surely as the Communists were mistaken in their hopes of remaking human nature, so have been the proponents of diversity and multi-culturalism.[1053]

Given the "crisis" and "agonizing problems" produced by multiculturalism and growing populations of non-white people, Taylor advocates a variety of specific political policies in response:

End immigration ("it is not in the interests of whites to be displaced by others.")
Recognize that "when whites prefer to live, work, and go to school with people of their own race that it is no different from anyone else wanting to do these things. Whites—and others—should have legal

means to preserve local majorities if that is their preference." This, presumably, amounts to a demand for the reintroduction of legal segregation on the basis of race as well as the right to discriminate on the basis of race, in housing, the workplace, and education – in other words, the undoing of the Civil Rights Movement of the 1960s.

"End the current propaganda about the advantages of diversity, for it only justifies [white] dispossession."[1054]

In addition, while he does not appear to advocate for any laws specifically forbidding "miscegenation," he does describe it as the means by which to eliminate "whites." Indeed, interracial relationships (that include white people) are sometimes literally described as "white genocide."

[1053] Taylor, 205.

[1054] ibid., 205.

Cultural Combat @CulturalCombat · 17 Sep 2016
Damn you, #OldNavy! We thought you had learned!

#miscegenation #WhiteGenocide

Old Navy Official
@OldNavy
Fashion for the people. Be inspired, get some nice things, start the conversation.
#oldnavystyle Questions? Tweet @ONCustSe or call 1-800-OLD-NAVY
San Francisco, CA OldNavy.com

For most of American history, miscegenation was the ultimate nightmare for whites. . . . Of course, widespread miscegenation would not eliminate race; it would eliminate whites. Whites are no more than 17 percent of the world's population and are having perhaps seven percent of the world's children. No one is proposing large-scale intermarriage for Africa or Asia. Nor would mixing eliminate discrimination. Blacks, South Americans, and Asians discriminate among themselves on the basis of skin tone even when they are the same race. . . . The revolution in thinking among today's whites leaves no grounds to argue against their own displacement through immigration or disappearance through intermarriage. . . . All non-whites celebrate their growing numbers and influence—just as whites once did. Whites—not only in America but around the world —cheerfully contemplate their disappearance as a distinct people.[1055]

While the intensity and tone of someone like Taylor (and his sympathizers) might be "elevated," the basic themes and concerns have penetrated to mainstream media coverage. In 2018, *National Geographic* dedicated an entire issue to matters of race (calling it literally "The Race Issue"). One of their articles was entitled "As America Changes, Some Anxious Whites Feel Left Behind."[1056]

While always a part of American politics, race seemed to have an enhanced prominence in the 2016 presidential election. "The biggest difference between the two parties is the urban-rural divide. That gap widened. Politically, that translates into race and identity as the main political dividing line. Rural and exurban America is very white, and generally inward-looking. Urban America is very diverse and cosmopolitan. . . . In 1992, a majority of the voters in both parties were white Christian. Today, the GOP has essentially become a party of white Christians, while Democrats rely on a coalition of religiously, racially and ethnically diverse voters."[1057]

Clearly, the phenomenon of white nationalism raises many issues, including epistemological, moral, and political. The policies advocated by white nationalists such as Spencer and Taylor are, quite frankly, frightening. These policies, however, do not emerge from a vacuum.

[1055] ibid., 151 – 165.
[1056] https://www.nationalgeographic.com/magazine/2018/04/race-rising-anxiety-white-america/

[1057] https://www.nbcnews.com/politics/white-house/how-2016-election-exposed-america-s-racial-cultural-divides-n682306

Instead, they emerge from a worldview that presupposes certain key premises. Among these are "race realism," the dependency relationship between race and culture, and the critique of certain cultures/races in terms of degeneration and superiority/inferiority.

I will first demonstrate the philosophical foundations of their movement as it is found in the writings of Hitler.[1058] Then, in the remainder of the chapter, I will attempt to demonstrate that the white nationalist worldview rests upon a very shaky foundation. I will do this primarily by demonstrating that their understanding of race (and Hitler's as well) is simply misinformed. I will also attempt to demonstrate that the appreciation for Nietzsche shared by both the Nazis and contemporary white nationalists is equally misinformed.

Hitler

Adolf Hitler (20 April 1889 – 30 April 1945) was an Austrian-born German politician and the leader of the National Socialist German Workers Party (Nazi party). He was the totalitarian leader of Germany from 1933 to 1945. He gained popular support by promoting German nationalism, anti-Semitism, anti-capitalism, and anti-communism. Under his rule, Nazi forces engaged in the systematic murder of as many as 17 million civilians, an estimated six million of whom were Jews.

There should have been nothing surprising about the policies Hitler pursued once he acquired power. He had made no secret of his values, beliefs, and ambitions – detailing them a decade prior to taking power in his lengthy book, *Mein Kampf* ("my struggle"). In that work, he details his understanding of race, culture, and the

proper role and purpose of the state.

Hitler (like many from his time, and even today) believed that "race" was real. The current name for this is "race realism." He states that, among the most "patent principles of Nature's rule" is "the inner segregation of the species of all living beings on this earth."[1059] Moreover, in addition to being real, race is relevant—indeed, it is the *most* relevant aspect of a person. As you presumably already know, Hitler also believed that the various races of humanity were not equal. At the apex of humanity (according to Hitler) is the Aryan race.

> *Everything we admire on this earth today – science and art, technology and inventions – is only the creative product of a few peoples and originally perhaps of one race. On them depends the existence of this whole culture. If they perish, the beauty of this earth will sink into the grave with them.*

> *All the human culture, all the results of art, science, and technology that we see before us today, are almost exclusively the creative product of the Aryan. This very fact admits of the not unfounded inference that he alone was the founder of all higher humanity, therefore representing the prototype of all that we understand by the word 'man.' . . . Exclude him – and perhaps after a few thousand years darkness will again ascend on the earth, human culture will pass, and the world turned to a desert.*[1060]

With his assumptions of the existence of

[1058] To be clear, I'm not claiming that there is a direct link between the writings of Hitler and the ideas of Richard Spencer and Jared Taylor specifically, as though they sat down one day, read "*Mein Kampf*" and then developed their worldviews in direct response. It is entirely possible that independent ideas informed both Hitler and contemporary white nationalists. Do not think of this section as intellectual

biography. But what I think can be demonstrated, however, is the similarity and overlap of ideas.

[1059] *Mein Kampf,* volume 1, chapter XI: nation and race. All references from this section of the chapter are from this book, unless otherwise indicated.

[1060] ibid.

distinct races, and a natural hierarchy among those races, he vehemently opposed any sort of "race-mixing."

> *Any crossing of two beings not exactly the same level produces a medium between the level of the two parents. This means: the offspring will probably stand higher than the racially lower parent, but not as high as the higher one. Consequently, it will later succumb in the struggle against the higher level. Such mating is contrary to the will of Nature for a higher breeding of all life. The precondition for this does not lie in associating superior and inferior, but in a total victory of the former. The stronger must dominate not blend with the weaker, thus sacrificing his own greatness. Only the born weakling condemn this as cruel, but he after all is only a weak and limited man; for if this law did not prevail, any conceivable higher development of organic living beings would be unthinkable.[1061]*

He not only proposed keeping the races "pure" by avoiding race mixture, but an active and deliberate "breeding program" was an essential element of his political program, as we will see in a later section. For Hitler, race and politics are and *must* be connected. Indeed, he claimed that race was the very foundation of the (proper) state!

> *If we try to penetrate to the inner meaning of the word völkisch we arrive at the following conclusions: the current political conception of the world is that the State, though it possesses a creative force which can build up civilizations, has nothing in common with the concept of race as the foundation of the State. The State is considered rather as something which has resulted from economic necessity, or, at best, the natural outcome of the play of*

political forces and impulses. Such a conception of the foundations of the State, together with all its logical consequences, not only ignores the primordial racial forces that underlie the State, but it also leads to a policy in which the importance of the individual is minimized. If it be denied that races differ from one another in their powers of cultural creativeness, then the same erroneous notion must necessarily influence our estimation of the value of the individual. The assumption that all races are alike leads to the assumption that nations and individuals are equal to one another.[1062]

In contrast to his race-based concept of the State, he distinguishes several other (flawed and misguided) variants.

> *Those who hold that the State is a more or less voluntary association of men who have agreed to set up and obey a ruling authority.[1063]*

This is a generic "social contract" model of the State—the very type considered in several other chapters of this book, and promoted by political theorists such as Hobbes, Locke, Rousseau, and Rawls, among others.

> *Those who hold that "the State exists to promote the good of its subjects....Moreover, in this view the first duty laid upon the State is to guarantee the economic well-being of the individual citizens.[1064]*

This second category is even more general than his depiction of the social contract tradition. It could include anything from utilitarian justifications of the State, to more communitarian models such as Aristotle's *Polis*, and others. It seems that the States in this category have in common that they are thought to exist to promote

---

1061 ibid.

1062 Volume 2, Chapter I: Philosophy and Party.

1063 ibid.

1064 ibid.

the "good" of those subject to them, and Hitler assumes that some sort of economic good is the foremost good to be pursued.

Hitler thinks both these models are getting it wrong. The "correct" justification for the State is "a means for the realization of tendencies that arise from a policy of power, on the part of a people who are ethnically homogenous and speak the same language."[1065]

In contemporary alt-Right vocabulary, he is promoting the idea of an "ethno-state." An ethno-state is simply a political entity populated by, and run in the interest of, a particular ethnic group. For contemporary white nationalists like Richard Spencer and Jared Taylor, the ethno-state they long for is a "white Eurocentric" ethno-state. For Hitler, it was a State by and for the German *volk.*

The State is only a means to an end. Its end and its purpose is to preserve and promote a community of human beings who are physically as well as spiritually kindred. Above all, it must preserve the existence of the race, thereby providing the indispensable condition for the free development of all the forces dormant in this race. A great part of these faculties will always have to be employed in the first place to maintain the physical existence of the race, and only a small portion will be free to work in the field of intellectual progress. But, as a matter of fact, the one is always the necessary counterpart to the other.

Those States which do not serve this purpose have no justification for their existence. They are monstrosities. The fact they do exist is no more of a justification than the successful raids carried out by band of pirates can be considered a justification of piracy....

The State is only the vessel and the race is what it contains. The vessel can have a meaning only if it preserves and

safeguards the contents. Otherwise it is worthless.

Hence the supreme purpose of the folkish State is to guard and preserve those original racial elements which, through their work in the cultural field, create that beauty and dignity which are characteristics of a higher mankind. We, as Aryans, can consider the State only as a living organism of a people, an organism which does not merely maintain the existence of a people, but functions in such a way as to lead people to a position of supreme liberty by the progressive development of the intellectual and cultural faculties.[1066]

This "*volkstadt*" is not identical to a culture, and he insisted that the two notions not be confused. The point (for Hitler) is not to have "people" speaking German, listening to Wagner, dancing polkas, and eating schnitzel. Not just any "people" will do, and the fact that non-German people might adopt and emulate German cultural traditions signified nothing.

What they mostly meant by Germanization was a process of forcing other people to speak the German language. But it is almost inconceivable how such a mistake could be made as to think that a Negro or Chinaman will become a German because he has learned the German language and is willing to speak German for the future, and even to cast his vote for a German political party. Our bourgeois nationalists could never clearly see that such a process of Germanization is in reality de-Germanization; for even if all the outstanding and visible differences between the various peoples could be bridged over and finally wiped out by the use of a common language, that would produce a process of bastardization which in this case would not signify Germanization but the annihilation of the

---

[1065] ibid.

[1066] ibid.

German element. In the course of history does happen only too often that a conquering race succeeded by external force in compelling the people whom they subjected to speak the tongue of the conqueror and that after 1000 years their language was spoken by another people and thus the conqueror finally turned out to be the conquered.

What makes a people, to be more correct, a race, is not language but blood. Therefore it would be justifiable to speak of Germanization only if that process could change the blood of the people who would be subjected to it, which is obviously impossible. A change would be possible only by a mixture of blood, but in this case the quality of the superior race would be debased. The final result of such a mixture would be that precisely those qualities would be destroyed which had enabled the conquering race to achieve victory over and inferior people. It is especially the cultural creativeness which disappears when the superior race center mixes with an inferior one, even though the resultant mongrel race should excel a thousandfold in speaking the language of the race that once had been superior.

A profound truth is that the capacity for creating cultural values is essentially based on the racial element and that, in accordance with this fact, the paramount purpose of the State is to preserve and improve the race; for this is an indispensable condition of all progress in human civilization.[1067]

Every aspect of the State will be governed by an appeal to race, its promotion, and its preservation. This is nowhere as obvious as in Hitler's views on public education.

If we consider it the first duty of the State to serve and promote the general welfare of the people, by preserving and encouraging the development of the best racial elements, the logical consequences of this task not be limited to measures concerning the birth of the infant members of the race and nation but that the State will also have to adopt educational means for making each citizen a worthy factor in the further propagation of the racial stock.

Just as, in general, the racial quality is the preliminary condition for the mental efficiency of any given human material, the training of the individual will first of all have to be directed towards the development of sound bodily health. For the general rule is that a strong and healthy mind is found only in a strong and healthy body. The fact that men of genius or sometimes not robust in health and stature, or even a basically healthy constitution, is no proof against the principle I have enunciated. These cases are only exceptions which, as everywhere else, prove the rule. But when the bulk of a nation is composed of physical degenerates it is rare for a great spirit to arise from such a miserable motley. . . .

The State that is grounded on the racial principle and is alive to the significance of this truth will first of all have to base its educational work not on the mere imparting of knowledge but rather on physical training and development of healthy bodies. The cultivation of the intellectual facilities comes only in the second place. And here again is character which has to be developed first of all, strength of will and decision. And the educational system ought to foster the spirit of readiness to accept responsibilities gladly. Formal instruction in the sciences must be considered last in importance. Accordingly the State which is

---

[1067] ibid.

grounded on the racial idea must start with the principle that a person whose formal education in the sciences is relatively small but was physically sound and robust, of a steadfast and honest character, ready and able to make decisions and endowed with strength of will, is a more useful member of the national community than a weakling who was scholarly and refined. A nation composed of learned men who are physical weaklings, hesitant about decisions of the will, and timid pacifists, is not capable of assuring even its own existence on this earth. In the bitter struggle which decides the destiny of man it is very rare that an individual has succumbed because he lacked learning. Those who fail are they who try to ignore these consequences and are too fainthearted about putting them into effect. There must be a certain balance between mind and body. An ill-kept body is not made a more beautiful sight by the indwelling of a radiant spirit. We should not be acting justly if we were to bestow the highest intellectual training on those who are physically deformed and crippled, who lack decision and are weak willed and cowardly. What has made the Greek ideal of beauty immortal is the wonderful union of a splendid physical beauty with nobility of mind and spirit.[1068]

Note the heightened emphasis on physical fitness, and the proposed reduction in the curriculum of science. Formal instruction in the sciences "must be considered last in importance." This is far removed from our contemporary emphasis on STEM (Science, Technology, Engineering, and Math) training, and the trend of reducing or even eliminating physical education requirements.

Under Hitler's vision, "character" is developed "first of all," and he states this in terms of strength of will.

Loyalty, self-sacrifice and discretion are virtues which a great nation must possess. And the teaching and development of these in the school is a more important matter than many other things now included in the curriculum. To make the children give up habits of complaining and whining and howling when they are hurt, etc., also belongs to this part of the training. If the educational system fails to teach the child at an early age to endure pain and injury without complaining we cannot be surprised if at a later age, when the boy has grown to be the man and is, for example, in the trenches, the Postal Service is used for nothing else than to send home letters of weeping and complaint. If our youths, during their years in the primary schools, had had their minds crammed with a little less knowledge, and if instead they had been better taught how to be masters of themselves, it would have served us well during the years 1914 – 1918.[1069]

Character training occurs in the context of physical training, including mandatory boxing and rigorous fitness training. This increased emphasis on physical training comes at the expense of more traditional academic subjects— all of which will be instituted and run by the State.

The formal imparting of knowledge, which constitutes the chief work of our educational system today, will be taken over by the People's State with only few modifications. These modifications must be made in three branches.

First of all, the brains of the young people must not generally be burdened with subjects of which 95% are useless to them and are therefore forgotten again. The curriculum of the primary and secondary schools presents an odd mixture at the present time. In many branches of study the subject matter to be learned has

---

[1068] ibid.

[1069] ibid.

become so enormous that only a very small fraction of it can be remembered later on, and indeed only a very small fraction of this whole mass of knowledge can be used. On the other hand, what is learned is insufficient for anybody who wishes to specialize in any certain branch for the purpose of earning his daily bread. Take, for example, the average civil servant who is passed through the Gymnasium or High School, and ask them at the age of 30 or 40 how much he has retained the knowledge that was crammed into him with so much pains....[1070]

All along, the central focus of this new education program is race.

The whole organization of education and training which the People's State is to build up must take as its crowning task the work of instilling into the hearts and brains of the youth entrusted to it the racial instinct and understanding of the racial idea. No boy or girl must leave school without having obtained a clear insight into the meaning of racial purity and the importance of maintaining the racial blood unadulterated. Thus the first indispensable condition for the preservation of our race will have been established and thus the future cultural progress of our people will be assured."[1071]

Even with regard to particular subjects, such as history, race takes center stage.

It is the business of the People's State to arrange for the writing of a world history in which the race problem will occupy a dominant position.[1072]

The training of boys does not end once they complete their primary education. He also envisions mandatory military service for all boys,

unless they are physically unfit to serve. Already physically fit and "strong in character" from their school days, their training could focus specifically on military skills and matters. After a man completes military training, will be given two certifications:

1. Diploma of citizenship, permitting participation in public affairs.
2. Certification of fitness for marriage (based on physical health)

Note the significance of this: in order to be "certified" to participate in politics, and even to marry and have children, a man must have served in the military to the satisfaction of the State. As for girls, "in the education of the girl the final goal always to be kept in mind is that she is one day to be a mother."[1073]

One final core principle governing Hitler's ideal State (for the purposes of our focus) is found in the lengthy quotation below (and worth quoting at length, with emphasis added). You might find it hauntingly familiar, if you have read previous chapters of this book.

It will be the task of the People's State so to organize and administer its educational system that the existing intellectual class will be constantly furnished with supply of fresh blood from beneath. From the bulk of the nation the State must sift out with careful scrutiny those persons who are endowed with natural talents and see that they are employed in the service of the community. For neither the State itself nor the various departments of State exist to furnish revenues for members of a special class, but to fulfill the tasks allotted to them. This will be possible, however, only if the State trains individuals specially for these offices. Such individuals must have the necessary fundamental capabilities and willpower. The principal does not hold true only in regard to the civil service but

---

[1070] ibid.
[1071] ibid.

[1072] ibid.
[1073] ibid.

also in regard to all those who are to take part in the intellectual and moral leadership of the people, no matter in what sphere they may be employed. The greatness of a people is partly dependent on the condition that it must succeed in training the best brains for those branches of the public service for which they show a special natural aptitude and in placing them in the offices where they can do their best work for the good of the community. If two nations of equal strength and quality engage in a mutual conflict that nation will come up us which has entrusted its intellectual and moral leadership to its best talents and that nation will go under whose government represents only a common food trough for privilege groups or classes and where the inner talents of its individual members are not availed of.

Of course such a reform seems impossible in the world as it is today. The objection will at once be raised that it is too much to expect from the favorite son of a highly placed civil servant, for instance, the he shall work with his hands simply because somebody else whose parents belong to the working class seems more capable for a job in the civil service. That argument may be valid as long as manual work is looked upon in the same way as it is looked upon today. Hence the People's State will have to take up an attitude towards the appreciation of manual labor which will be fundamentally different from that which now exists. If necessary, it will have to organize a persistent system of teaching which will aim at abolishing the present day stupid habit of looking down on physical labor as an occupation to be ashamed of.

The individual will have to be valued, not by the class of work he does but by the way in which he does it and by its usefulness to the community.... On the ideal or abstract plans all workmen become equal the

moment each strives to do his best in his own field, no matter what that field may be. It is on this that a man's value must be estimated, and not on the amount of recompense received.

In a reasonably directed State care must be taken that each individual is given the kind of work which corresponds to his capabilities. In other words, people will be trained for the positions indicated by their natural endowments: but these endowments are faculties are innate and cannot be acquired by any amount of training, being a gift from Nature and not merited by men. Therefore, the way in which men are generally esteemed by their fellow citizens must not be according to the kind of work they do, because that has been more or less assigned to the individual. Seeing that the kind of work in which the individual is employed is to be accounted to his inborn gifts and resultant training which has received from the community, it will have to be judged by the way in which he performs this work entrusted to him by the community. For the work which the individual performs is not the purpose of his existence, but only a means. His real purpose in life is to better himself and raise himself to a higher level as a human being; but this he can only do in and through the community whose cultural life he shares. And this community must always exist on the foundations on which the State is based. He ought to contribute to the conservation of those foundations. Nature determines the form of this contribution. It is the duty of the individual to return to the community, zealously and honestly, what the community has given him. He who does this deserves the highest respect and esteem. . . .

The present epoch is working out its own ruin. It introduces universal suffrage, chatters about equal rights but can find no *foundation for this equality. It considers the material wage as the expression of a man's value and thus destroys the basis of the noblest kind of equality that can exist. For equality cannot and does not depend on the work a man does, but only on the manner in which each one does the particular work allotted to him. Thus alone will mere natural chance be set aside in determining the work of a man and thus only does the individual become the artificer of his own social worth.*[1074]

One basic theme here is that the community takes priority over the individual. Another is that individuals are "naturally" suited to fulfill different functions within a community, and the community is best served if persons fulfill the role for which they are best suited—even if their personal preference would be to do something else. Moreover, there is honor to be found in any occupation/role, so long as one performs at his or her best, in service to the community. If you have studied Plato's *Republic* (especially with me), this might sound familiar, as it sounds very much like the "principle of specialization."

This is a "totalitarian" vision, no doubt, but, in a gesture that makes me admittedly uncomfortable, I want to highlight an idea from Hitler that is not in any obvious way evil or horrifying: valuing honest labor, of any kind, and not being "elitist" about certain kinds of work. In his proposed system, horrifying though it would be in other respects, one goal is to change cultural norms so that "blue collar" jobs, including manual labor, are no longer looked down upon as somehow inferior, degrading, worthy only of "stupid" people, etc. Another goal is the simultaneous dismantling of the prestige that comes merely from occupying a conventionally "respected" role such as scientist, doctor, lawyer, etc. People will be esteemed based on how hard and capably they work, regardless of the particular kind of work. In theory, someone who works hard and well at mowing lawns would be just as esteemed as a similarly hard working

lawyer, and *more* esteemed than a lawyer who "phones it in."

Not to overdo the comparison, but Hitler's similarity to Plato does not end with the Principle of Specialization. They also share in common a rejection of democracy.

Hence the People's State must mercilessly expurgate from all the leading circles in the government of the country the parliamentarian principle, according to which decisive power through the majority vote is invested in the multitude. . . . There are no decisions made by the majority vote, but only by responsible persons. And the word 'council' is once more restored to its original meaning. Every man in a position of responsibility will have councillors at his side, but the decision is made by that individual person alone. . . . No vote will be taken in the chambers or Senate. They are to be organizations for work and not voting machines. The individual members will have consultive votes but no right of decision will be attached thereto. The right of decision belongs exclusively to the president, who must be entirely responsible for the matter under discussion.[1075]

In summary, Hitler advances a political philosophy that rejects democracy in favor of the totalitarian rule of a "charismatic" individual. He advocates significant educational and social reform, and all of this for the sake of the only legitimate purpose of the State (in his estimation): the preservation and promotion of the ("Master") race.

Obviously, a key premise for any ideology promoting racial supremacy, whether Hitler's or that of contemporary white nationalism, is the existence of race itself. Indeed, as stated, for Hitler, the preservation and promotion of race was the fundamental purpose of the State. Moreover, not just any concept of race will do. Within these ideologies, race has to do quite a lot

---

[1074] ibid.

[1075] ibid.

of "work." It has to be something that is biologically real, and transmitted across generations through reproduction. Otherwise, Hitler's obsession with eugenics and racial purity, and contemporary white nationalists' anxiety about "white genocide," makes little sense. Race has to be something that is not identical to culture; race and ethnicity must signify fundamentally different things. Moreover, race has to not only be an aspect of one's identity, but an *essential* aspect. That is, one's race must be not only something "real," but among the most important elements of who you are – if not *the* most important element. As it turns out, however, "race" isn't so simple and "genetic" as racial supremacists might believe.[1076]

The "*popular account*" of race, for the last 150 years or so, is that races are real, naturally occurring, and more stable/real/natural than contingent human groupings such as nationality or religion. Many would agree, for example, that "France" is a contingent historical artifact that didn't always exist, didn't have to exist, and could cease to exist (e.g., if Hitler had won the Second World War).

So too with religion. Scientology hasn't always existed, and very few people (if any) still worship the ancient Egyptian pantheon (e.g., Isis and Osiris). Races, on the other hand, are generally regarded as older, inevitable, immutable, and more "natural."

The racial assumptions that emerged from the 18th and 19th centuries, which were adopted by people like Hitler, and which continue to be employed by contemporary white nationalists such as Spencer and Taylor, included profound (and damaging) ideas:

- All humans fall into one, and only one, distinct, natural, fixed race.[1077]
- These races are presumed to differ (essentially) in significant physical, mental, and moral qualities.
- Every member of a race is thought to possess their races "essence," and this essence is transmitted to one's children.
- There are physical indicators that allegedly correlate with race membership, and that provide mental "shortcuts." For example, dark skin and curly hair indicates that someone is "Black," which also means (according to *racist stereotypes*) that that person is lazy.
- A natural hierarchy is thought to exist based on the "natural superiority" of some races over others. Although the precise number of races and their relative placement varies, in the United States it has

---

[1076] Note that some of this section is the same material as appears in the earlier chapter on the philosophy of race. If you have already read that chapter, this material will serve as a review. If you have not read that chapter, please consult it for a sustained treatment of this concept.

[1077] The racism inherent to racial essentialism (originally, at least) is evident in the "one drop rule." Historically, in the United States, one was "white" if they had no "black" ancestry anywhere in the family lineage. Even "one drop" of "black" meant that you were not "white." The assumptions lurking behind the "one-drop" rule are hardly ancient history, by the way. In March of 2016, a 6-year old girl was taken from her ("white") foster parents in Santa Clarita, California, after having lived with them for four years. Her biological parents had lost custody of

her after a child abuse investigation. Her mother also had substance abuse issues, and her father had a criminal record. She was removed from foster care, though, because she is "1.5% Choctaw," and a 1978 federal law was invoked (The Indian Child Welfare Act, designed to prevent large numbers of native American children to be adopted away from their tribal heritage and placed in non-Native American households). Although this child had never actually been exposed to any Native American culture, the mere "fact" that she was 1.5% Choctaw meant she was "Native American" under federal law, and therefore subject to the Indian Child Welfare Act.
http://m.nydailynews.com/news/national/girl-6-foster-family-native-american-law-article-1.2572704

always been the assumption that "whites" were at the top and "blacks" were at the bottom.

The belief that there are distinct, natural races, and that each race has its own particular "essence" that is transmitted by biological means, is known as "racialism."[1078] This is not to be confused with racism! Racism certainly includes racialist beliefs, but adds to them notions of superiority/ inferiority, negative stereotypes, and moral judgments. In other words, racism is value-laden, whereas racialism is value-neutral.

Racialism: beliefs and actions presupposing the existence of *biologically-transmitted racial "essence*s."[1079]

Racism: *negative* value judgments and actions based on racialist assumptions.[1080]

White nationalists are necessarily racialists, in that they explicitly espouse "race realism," but they also tend overwhelmingly to be racist as well, given their obvious disdain for "non-whites." Arguably, *most* Americans today are "racialists," whether they realize it or not, and whether or not they are additionally *racists*. This is so despite the clear evidence for the social construction of race (as seen by our survey of history and Supreme Court rulings above), and despite the lack of evidence for *biologically-based*

races or racial essentialism.[1081]

To the extent that any worldview requires "race realism" in this biological sense, that worldview is unwarranted. In other words, when it comes to race, both Hitler and contemporary white nationalists are simply mistaken. Another shared error involves the belief that Nietzsche was somehow a philosophical forefather and source of intellectual support for such worldviews.

Nietzsche

I know my fate. One day my name will be associated with the memory of something tremendous—a crisis without equal on earth, the most profound collision of conscience, a decision that was conjured against everything that had been believed, demanded, hallowed so far. I am no man, I am dynamite.[1082]

Friedrich Wilhelm Nietzsche (15 October 1844 – 25 August 1900) was a German philosopher notorious for what he wrote, for what people *think* he wrote, for the influence he has had on philosophy, and for the (often unjustified) influence he has had on various cultural and political movements.

He was born in the small German town of Röcken bei Lützen, located in a rural farmland area southwest of Leipzig, on October 15, 1844.

[1078] Note: this term is used by different people in different ways. I offer a specific definition of this term in this section, and it is that specific definition that is presupposed for the remainder of this chapter.

[1079] This is not to be confused with ethnicism or ethnocentrism, both of which concern ethnicity, which refers to *learned cultural behaviors and norms*, as distinct from biologically-transmitted traits.

[1080] There is also what is known as "institutional racism," which, in general, is racism expressed and practices by social and political institutions, as distinct from racism by individuals. Institutional racism can be conscious and intentional, such as segregation laws, or

unconscious and racist in its effects, rather than intentions, such as disparate minimum prison sentences for crack and powder cocaine. Institutional racism can be both a product and a source of embedded racist cultural practices within our social structure. This then creates barriers and privileges based on race through socio-political institutions.

[1081] Again, see the chapter on the philosophy of race for a sustained argument in support of this claim.

[1082] Nietzsche, Friedrich. "*Ecce Homo,*" in *The Portable Nietzsche*. Edited and Translated by Walter Kaufmann. New York. Penguin Books, 1982. "Why I am a Destiny," section 1.

His father was the town minister, and his grandfathers were also Lutheran ministers. When Nietzsche was 4 years old, his father died from a "brain ailment," and Nietzsche's infant brother died just a few months later.

Nietzsche entered the University of Bonn in 1864 as a theology and philology student. He attended lectures by the classics scholar Friedrich Wilhelm Ritschl (1806-1876). Ritschl was clearly impressed by the young Nietzsche, eventually writing a glowing recommendation of Nietzsche for a position on the classical philology faculty at the University of Basel.

However many young talents I have seen develop under my eyes for thirty-nine years now, never yet have I known a young man, or tried to help one along in my field as best I could, who was so mature as early and as young as this Nietzsche. His Museum articles he wrote in the second and third year of his triennium. He is the first from whom I have ever accepted any contribution at all while he was still a student. If--God grant--he lives long enough, I prophesy that he will one day stand in the front rank of German philology. He is now twenty-four years old: strong, vigorous, healthy, courageous physically and morally, so constituted as to impress those of a similar nature. On top of that, he possesses the enviable gift of presenting ideas, talking freely, as calmly as he speaks skillfully and clearly. He is the idol and, without wishing it, the leader of the whole younger generation of philologists here in Leipzig who--and they are rather numerous--cannot wait to hear him as a lecturer. You will say, I describe a phenomenon. Well, that is just what he is-- and at the same time pleasant and modest. Also a gifted musician, which is irrelevant here.[1083]

Nietzsche was offered the position and he began teaching there in May, 1869, at the modest age of 24! His writings, over the span of his career, covered a wide variety of topics: art, philology, history, religion, tragedy, culture, and science. He is known for his "perspectivism," his "genealogical" critique of both religion and Christian moral values, his theory of "master" and "slave" morality, his existentialist response to the alleged "death of God," his idea of the "eternal recurrence," and the "*übermensch*," and the "will to power" (among other things).

Nietzsche served as a hospital attendant during the Franco-Prussian War (1870-71). He witnessed the horrors of war, contracted diphtheria and dysentery, and would suffer from a variety of health problems for the rest of his life. Migraine headaches, vision problems, and vomited precipitated his resignation from his teaching position in June, 1879.

In Turin (Italy), on the morning of January 3, 1889, Nietzsche experienced a mental breakdown which would leave him mentally incompetent for the rest of his life. One theory is that this was the result of syphilis;[1084] another is that it was an effect of his use of chloral hydrate as a sedative; and yet another is that he suffered from a genetic disorder inherited from his father.

After a brief stay in a "sanatorium," his mother took him home and cared for him for the next seven years. After his mother died in 1897, his care was taken over by his sister, Elizabeth. She and her husband Bernhard Förster had been working to establish an Aryan, anti-Semitic German colony in Paraguay called "New Germany" ("Nueva Germania").

Having spent over a decade in a mentally incapacitated state, Nietzsche died on August 25, 1900, prior to his 56th birthday, from pneumonia in combination with a stroke.

After his death, his sister Elizabeth became the curator and editor of his manuscripts. She edited and reframed his unpublished writings to fit her own German nationalist ideology, despite

---

[1083] Nietzsche's recommendation letter from Ritschl.

[1084] Though this theory is now largely thought to

be discredited:
http://www.leonardsax.com/Nietzsche.pdf

the fact that his actual views were explicitly and undeniably opposed to both anti-Semitism and nationalism. Due to her efforts, his work became associated with fascism and Nazism.

Why does Nietzsche matter, in a chapter about white nationalism?

Although I think the connection is misguided and unfair, it is undeniable that the Nazis considered Nietzsche a sympathetic fore-runner, and there is direct evidence that Hitler himself was both familiar with Nietzsche's work, and had a very high regard for him.

> *In the Great Hall of the Linz Library are the busts of Kant, Schopenhauer and Nietzsche, the greatest of our thinkers, in comparison with whom the British, the French and the Americans have nothing to offer. His complete refutation of the teachings which were a heritage from the Middle Ages, and of the dogmatic philosophy of the Church, is the greatest of the services which Kant has rendered to us. It is on the foundation of Kant's theory of knowledge that Schopenhauer built the edifice of his philosophy, and it is Schopenhauer who annihilated the pragmatism of Hegel. I carried Schopenhauer's works with me throughout the whole of the First World War. From him I learned a great deal. Schopenhauer's pessimism, which springs partly, I think, from his own line of philosophical thought and partly from subjective feeling and the experiences of his own personal life, has been far surpassed by Nietzsche.[1085]*

Nietzsche's sister went out of her way to encourage Hitler and the Nazis to appropriate her brother's work, not only by her selective and misleading editing of his notes, and outright forgeries of passages he never wrote, but by direct contact. There is a famous photograph from 1934 depicting her welcoming Hitler when he came to visit the Nietzsche archives. She later gave him Nietzsche's personal walking stick as a gift.[1086]

This association was reinforced by hostile sources as well. In some writings, Nietzsche was nearly (personally) blamed for the occurrence of World War II itself!

> *The Second World War was a war of insanity. Such a catastrophe can of course not develop solely out of the writings of one disturbed philosopher.... But the formulas employed by the perpetrators of the war, and the moral and philosophical justifications which they employed—these were given the "Powers of Darkness" by the lonely thinker of Sils-Maria and Turin.[1087]*

This (hyperbolic) association is not merely a *historical* curiosity. *Contemporary* white supremacists/nationalists continue to point to Nietzsche as an inspiration.[1088] In an interview from 2017, Richard Spencer explicitly credits

---

[1085] H.R. Trevor-Roper, *Hitler's Table Talk 1941-1944, His Private Conversations*, Enigma Books, 2000, pp. 546-547. From a conversation recorded May 16, 1944.

[1086] http://sauer-thompson.com/conversations/archives/elis1933.jpg

[1087] Lange-Eichbaum W. Nietzsche: *Krankheit und Wirkung*. Hamburg: Lettenbauer, 1947. p. 89.

[1088] https://www.nationalaffairs.com/publications/detail/answering-the-alt-right

Nietzsche for his intellectual "awakening." "You could say I was red-pilled by Nietzsche."[1089]

Specifically citing Nietzsche's "On the Genealogy of Morals," Spencer claims that his moral universe was "shattered" by Nietzsche's systematic dismantling of taken for granted moral and religious truths. This undermining of traditional values helps to explain the difficulty of placing Spencer into contemporary conservative "boxes." Unlike many conservatives, he is not bothered by gay marriage or abortion – in fact he favors abortion to the extent that it reduces the number of ethnic minorities that are born. "Smart people are not using abortion as birth control … It is the unintelligent and blacks and Hispanics who use abortion as birth control. . . This can be something that can be a great boon for our people, our race."[1090]

The original Nazis embraced Nietzsche because they (mistakenly) thought he endorsed their anti-Semitism, nationalism, and supremacist ideology. Contemporary white nationalists embrace Nietzsche in part through sharing some ideological "ancestry" with the Nazis, but also because they think Nietzsche's critique of "herd morality" and advocacy for a "master morality" applies to them and their causes. We will now consider (very briefly) Nietzsche's *actual* views, based on the works he wrote, edited, and published himself.

"Was Nietzsche a proto-Nazi/national Socialist?"

Far from it. He explicitly rejects German nationalism, and describes both nationalism and "race hatred" in scathing terms.

…we are not nearly "German" enough, in the sense in which the word "German" is constantly being used nowadays, to advocate nationalism and race hatred and to be able to take pleasure in the national scabies of the heart and blood poisoning that now leads the nations of Europe to delimit and barricade themselves against each other as if it were a matter of quarantine. For that we are too openminded, too malicious, too spoiled, also too well informed, too "traveled": we far prefer to live on mountains, apart, "untimely," in past or future centuries, merely in order to keep ourselves from experiencing the silent rage to which we know we should be condemned as eyewitnesses of politics that are desolating the German spirit by making it vain and that is, moreover, petty politics: to keep its own creation from immediately falling apart again, is it not finding it necessary to plant it between two deadly hatreds? must it not desire the eternalization of the European system of a lot of petty states?[1091]

He could not have been more explicit with respect to his views of *German* nationalism, specifically:

One pays heavily for coming to power: power makes stupid. The Germans, once called the people of thinkers – do they still think it all today? The Germans are now bored with the spirit, the Germans now mistrust the spirit….Deutschland, Deutschland über alles, I fear that was the end of German philosophy.[1092]

[1089] https://www.theatlantic.com/magazine/archive/2017/06/his-kampf/524505/ Note: "red pill" is a slang term derived from a reference to the film "The Matrix." It refers to being awakened to reality, and abandoning a world of illusions.

[1090] https://www.theatlantic.com/magazine/archive/2017/06/his-kampf/524505/

[1091] Nietzsche, Friedrich. *The Gay Science.* Translated by Walter Kaufmannn. Vintage Books, 1974. Section 377.

[1092] Nietzsche, Friedrich. "Twilight of the Idols," in *The Portable Nietzsche.* Edited and Translated by Walter Kaufmann. New York. Penguin Books, 1982. "What the Germans Lack," 1.

"Was Nietzsche an anti-Semite?"

Not at all.

Although he did offer an intense criticism of what we would consider "Judeo-Christian" values, he was not an anti-Semite. There is ample evidence for this. For example, the composer Richard Wagner was a one-time idol for Nietzsche, but he eventually broke with him in dramatic and public fashion precisely because of Wagner's anti-Semitism. In fact, Nietzsche devoted a lengthy essay ("Nietzsche contra Wagner"), and an entire book ("The Case of Wagner"), to his disillusionment with his former friend.

With regard to his sister, their relationship was strained to say the least. A significant source of his eventual contempt for her was her choice of husbands: Bernhard Förster, a prominent leader of the German anti-Semitic movement. Bernhard immigrated to Paraguay after a public scandal involving his abuse of Jewish streetcar passengers. He founded a "Teutonic" colony that he named Nueva Germania. This activity, and her involvement in it, infuriated Nietzsche.

One of the greatest stupidities you have committed – for yourself and for me! Your association with an anti-Semitic chief expresses a foreignness to my whole way of life which fills me ever again with ire or melancholy. . . . It is a matter of honor to me to be absolutely clean and unequivocal regarding anti-Semitism, namely opposed, as I am in my writings. I have been persecuted in recent times with letters and anti-Semitic correspondence sheets; my disgust with this party (which would like all too well the advantage of my name!) is as outspoken as possible, but the relation to Förster, as well as the aftereffect of my former anti-Semitic publisher Schmeitzner, always brings the adherence of this disagreeable party back to the idea that I must after all belong to them . . .

Above all it arouses mistrust against my character, as if I publicly condemned something which I favored secretly – and that I am unable to do anything against it, that the name of Zarathustra is used in every anti-Semitic correspondence sheets, has almost made me almost sick several times.[1093]

You have gone over to my antipodes . . I will not conceal that I consider this engagement an insult – or a stupidity which will harm you as much as me.[1094]

I have not yet laid eyes on my brother-in-law Herr Dr. Förster . . . That suited me excellently just that way.[1095]

In reference to anti-Semites, generally, Nietzsche wrote: "you see, because of this species of men I could not go to Paraguay: I'm so happy that they voluntarily exiled themselves from Europe. For even if I should be a bad German – in any case I'm a *very good European*."[1096]

Even in his own time, anti-Semites had begun to claim him as a kindred spirit, and this was something he found "laughable"—not laughable in that it was somehow insignificant to him, but laughable in that he could have been so thoroughly misunderstood.

I have somehow something like 'influence.'. . . In the anti-Semitic correspondence. . . My name is mentioned almost in every issue. Zarathustra, 'the divine man,' has charmed the anti-Semites; there is a special anti-Semitic interpretation of it which made me laugh very much.[1097]

There is ample evidence that Nietzsche was not anti-Semitic, and none (taken in appropriate context) to indicate that he was. Even if he wasn't an anti-Semite, he could still have been a white supremacist, of course. The contemporary white

---

[1093] Nietzsche, Friedrich. *Gesammelte Briefe* ("notes"), V, 1909. #479. (Letter to his sister.)
[1094] ibid., Letter #377.

[1095] ibid., #418.
[1096] ibid., #443.
[1097] ibid., #460.

supremacist Jared Taylor, for example, is conspicuously *not* anti-Semitic. "I don't think that Jews are the enemy in the way that some people do."[1098] Although white supremacy and anti-Semitism offer come as a package deal, this need not necessarily be the case.

Having established that Nietzsche was not an anti-Semite, we will now (independently) establish that he was not a white supremacist either.

"Was Nietzsche a white (Aryan) supremacist?"

Once again, no.

The most often quoted (out of context) writing from Nietzsche in support of an Aryan interpretation is his reference to the "blonde beast." The "Aryan" reading of this quotation becomes far more challenging, however, given a fuller and more representative context.

> How much respect a noble man has for his enemies! – and a respect of that sort is a bridge to love . . . For he insists on having his enemy to himself, as a mark of distinction, indeed he will tolerate as enemies none other than such as have nothing to be despised and a great deal to be honoured! Against this, imagine 'the enemy' as conceived of by the man of ressentiment – and here we have his deed, his creation: he has conceived of the 'evil enemy', 'the evil one' as a basic idea to which he now thinks up a copy and counterpart, the 'good one' – himself! . . .
>
> Exactly the opposite is true of the noble one who conceives of the basic idea 'good' by himself, in advance and spontaneously, and only then creates a notion of 'bad'! This 'bad' of noble origin and that 'evil' from the cauldron of unassuaged hatred – the first is an afterthought, an aside, a complementary colour, whilst the other is the original, the beginning, the actual deed

in the conception of slave morality – how different are the two words 'bad' and 'evil', although both seem to be the opposite for the same concept, 'good'! But it is not the same concept 'good'; on the contrary, one should ask who is actually evil in the sense of the morality of ressentiment. The stern reply is: precisely the 'good' person of the other morality, the noble, powerful, dominating one, but re-touched, re-interpreted and reviewed through the poisonous eye of ressentiment. Here there is one point we would be the last to deny: anyone who came to know these 'good men' as enemies came to know nothing but 'evil enemies', and the same people who are so strongly held in check by custom, respect, habit, gratitude and even more through spying on one another and through peer group jealousy, who, on the other hand, behave towards one another by showing such resourcefulness in consideration, self-control, delicacy, loyalty, pride and friendship, – they are not much better than uncaged beasts of prey in the world outside where the strange, the foreign, begin. There they enjoy freedom from every social constraint, in the wilderness they compensate for the tension which is caused by being closed in and fenced in by the peace of the community for so long, they return to the innocent conscience of the wild beast, as exultant monsters, who perhaps go away having committed a hideous succession of murder, arson, rape and torture, in a mood of bravado and spiritual equilibrium as though they had simply played a student's prank, convinced that poets will now have something to sing about and celebrate for quite some time. At the centre of _all_ these noble _races_ we cannot fail to see the beast of prey, the magnificent blond beast avidly prowling round for spoil and victory; this hidden centre needs release from time to

---

[1098] https://www.splcenter.org/fightinghate/intelligence-report/2006/schism-over-anti-

semitism-divides-key-white-nationalist-group-american-renaissance

time, the beast must out again, must return to the wild: – <u>Roman, Arabian</u>, Germanic, <u>Japanese nobility, Homeric heroes</u>, Scandinavian Vikings – <u>in this requirement they are all alike</u>.[1099]

It is a curious interpretation indeed to think that Nietzsche is referring specifically to so-called Aryans, when he explicitly points to non-Aryan people (e.g. Roman, Arabian, and Japanese), refers to noble races in the plural, and says of them with respect to this quality that they are "all alike."

In other words, he did not endorse "Aryans" as a "master race," and he certainly did not believe in German supremacy.

The Poles I considered the most gifted and gallant among the Slavic people; and the giftedness of the Slavs seem greater to me than that of the Germans – yes, I thought that the Germans it entered the line of gifted nations only through a strong mixture with Slavic blood.[1100]

Far from endorsing the pursuit of racial "purity," he explicitly advocated for *mixing* the races.

Maxim: to have intercourse with nobody who has any share in the mendacious race swindle.[1101]

Where races are mixed, there is the source of great cultures.[1102]

Yet another quotation that advocates the blending of races simultaneously negates the anti-Semitic interpretation of Nietzsche—a convenient "two for the price of one" rebuttal.

The whole problem of the Jews exists only in nation states, for here their energy and higher intelligence, their accumulated capital of spirit and will, gathered from generation to generation through a long schooling and suffering, it's become so preponderant as to arouse mass envy and hatred. In almost all contemporary nations, therefore – in direct proportion to the degree to which they act up nationalistically—the literary obscenity of leading the Jews to slaughter as scapegoats of every conceivable public and internal misfortune is spreading. As soon it is no longer a matter of preserving nations, but of producing the strongest possible European mixed-race, the Jew is just as useful and desirable an ingredient as any other national remnant.[1103]

In the quest for "the strongest possible European mixed-race," Jews are "just as useful and desirable an ingredient." Not exactly the words of someone in favor of separation and racial purity, nor of someone who thought Jewish people were somehow lesser.

This is not to say that Nietzsche somehow possessed an accurate and progression notion of race. Nietzsche believed in the "Lamarckian" interpretation of evolution according to which offspring inherit the characteristics (including acquired characteristics) of their parents. According to this model, qualities acquired by parents over their lives can actually be passed down, biologically, to their children.

One cannot erase out of the soul of a man what his ancestors have done most easily and often. . . . It is not at all possible that a man should not have in his body the qualities and preferences of his parents

---

[1099] Nietzsche, Friedrich. *On the Genealogy of Morals.* Translated by Douglas Smith. Oxford. Oxford University Press, 1996. First essay, sections 10 and 11. Emphasis added.
[1100] Nietzsche, *Gesammelte Werke*, volume XI, p. 300.

[1101] ibid., volume XVI, p. 374.
[1102] ibid., p. 373.
[1103] Nietzsche, Friedrich. *Human, All Too Human. A Book for Free Spirits*, translated by RJ Hollingdale (Cambridge: Cambridge University Press, 1996), section I, 475.

and ancestors—whatever appearances may say against this. This is the problem of race.[1104]

As a simple example, this model would suggest that if a parent lifted weights and became very strong and fit, their children would be born stronger and fit as well. We now know that this model isn't accurate, and genetic inheritance just doesn't work that way—but this view does help to explain his stance on the value of "race mixing." He advocated "mixed races" so as to cultivate the most diverse and advantageous mix of characteristics.

Importantly, although he seemed to think that characteristics would be transmitted biologically, he was not advocating some sort of eugenics program, in which people of exceptional physical traits breed with each other to produce "superior" babies. Instead, his focus was on culture. His understanding of a people (*Volk*) is based not on race/blood but on shared experience. "When men have lived together for a long time under similar conditions (of climate, soil, danger, needs, and work), then there *comes to be . . .* a people."[1105] With this cultural emphasis, the elevation of humankind, for Nietzsche, was to be found in art, religion, and philosophy – not "race."

We have seen that Nietzsche did not actually advocate anti-Semitism, Nationalism, or (Aryan) racial supremacy. He did write extensively about the "will to power," however, as well as the *Übermensch*. These certainly sound like macho appeals to strength/power, and the so-called "superman" or "overman" certainly seems ripe for placement into an ideology of "supremacy." In the remainder of this section, therefore, we will consider what Nietzsche meant by the will to power, how it applies to the *Übermensch*, and the

sort of "mastery" he had in mind.

"What is the 'will to power?'"

You should become master over yourself, master also over your virtues. Formerly they were your masters; but they must be only your instruments besides other instruments.[1106]

The will to power (hereafter abbreviated as WTP) is not mentioned by name in any officially published work until it is proclaimed by his signature creation, "Zarathustra." Prior to *Thus Spoke Zarathustra*, Nietzsche mentions the WTP in unpublished notes of the late 1870s.

In his early notes and works, Nietzsche considers the WTP to be one of two primary psychological drives (the second drive being fear). From this and other discussions, it becomes clear that Nietzsche's *initial* conception of the power sought by the WTP was political or physical – achieved via social success, making friends, being influential, etc.[1107] What's more, Nietzsche's early discussions of power were often *critical* of this drive. "Who among you would renounce power, knowing and having learned that power is evil?"[1108]

Power is denounced as "evil" because the pursuit of it – still considered the pursuit of worldly power – comes at the expense of personal integrity and individual autonomy. Nietzsche had not yet expanded his conception of power into the all-encompassing drive it would later become

With *Human, All Too Human*, Nietzsche's efforts become clearly focused on psychological forces. One example lies in human knowledge acquisition. Humans do not merely passively receive information from their environment. We might argue over the degree of participation

---

[1104] Nietzsche, Friedrich. *Beyond Good and Evil*. Translated by Walter Kaufmann. New York. Vintage Books, 1989. # 264.
[1105] ibid., # 268.
[1106] *Human, All Too Human*, preface, #6.
[1107] Kaufmann, Walter. *Nietzsche: Philosopher, Psychologist, Antichrist*, fourth edition.

(Princeton: Princeton University Press, 1974), 180.
[1108] Nietzsche, "Richard Wagner in Bayreuth" in *Untimely Meditations*, translated by RJ Hollingdale (Cambridge: Cambridge University Press, 1983), section 11.

humans have, but the notion that humans *do* participate in the learning process seems indisputable.

Humans gather and organize sense data. Out of a chaotic stream of impressions, we construct (or at least filter) a comprehensible (diluted) set of data within which we can operate. We inevitably attempt to make sense of our environment, to give form to it, to impose structures, and, most tellingly, to conform it to our needs.[1109] In this way, Nietzsche argues that philosophers especially exhibit strong WTP. Hitler attempted to conquer the world with his army, but Hegel attempted to subdue the entire cosmos with his philosophical system. To proclaim that the course of history has culminated in one's own theory is a transparent flexing of one's "muscle!"

The gathering, structuring, and production of knowledge, is but one example of the expression of WTP. As has been stated, Nietzsche attempted to explain *all* human behavior as such expressions. As Kaufman notes, an important development in Nietzsche's thought occurs in *Daybreak*, where he recognizes that the Greeks "value the feeling for power more highly than any kind of utility or good name."[1110] His acknowledgment that the people for whom he had great respect also pursued power helped him to develop his idea that not only do *all* people pursue power, but that power can be pursued in different – and praiseworthy – ways. Among the most praiseworthy is the development of *self*-mastery. Consider the first published mention of the WTP in *Thus Spoke Zarathustra*.

A tablet of good hangs over every people.

Behold it is the table of their overcomings; behold, it is the voice of their will to power. Praiseworthy is whatever seems difficult to a people; whatever seems indispensable and difficult is called good; and whatever liberates even out of the deepest need, the rarest, the most difficult – that they call holy.[1111]

It is important to note that in this first official public proclamation of the WTP, it is already conceived in terms of self-overcoming. Through their "overcomings" a people inspire the "awe and envy of their neighbors."[1112]

Interpreters differ on how power should be measured. Kaufmann argues that Nietzsche measures WTP quantitatively. "The quantitative degree of power is the measure of value."[1113] That is, there is some identifiable "quanta" of power and the more one has, the more powerful one is. Unfortunately, all the warrior imagery Nietzsche employs may mislead his readers. Alexander Nehamas has researched *Beyond Good and Evil* and, of the hundred plus names that appear within, 90% are "writers and artists, not *führers* and Homeric heroes."[1114] Kaufmann argues that Nietzsche's condemnation of tyrannical power is explicit, that "tyranny over others is not part of Nietzsche's vision."[1115] Even prior to Zarathustra, Nietzsche envisions a scale of power with a barbarian at the bottom and an ascetic, who triumphs "over himself," at the top.[1116]

We are still on our knees before strength – after the ancient custom of slaves – and yet

---

[1109] Magnus, Bernd. *Nietzsche's Existential Imperative* (Bloomington: Indiana University Press, 1978), 25.

[1110] Nietzsche, *Daybreak*, translated by RJ Hollingdale. Ed. Maudemarie Clark and Brian Leiter (Cambridge: Cambridge University Press, 1997), section 360.

[1111] Nietzsche, "Thus Spoke Zarathustra," in *The Portable Nietzsche*, translated and edited by Walter Kaufmann (New York: Penguin Books,

1976), section 15, p. 170.

[1112] ibid. section 15, p. 170

[1113] Kaufman, 199.

[1114] Solomon, Robert C. "Introduction: Reading Nietzsche," in *Reading Nietzsche*, edited by Robert Solomon and Kathleen Marie Higgins (Oxford: Oxford University Press, 1988): 6.

[1115] Kaufman, 316.

[1116] *Daybreak*, section 113, p. 113.

when the degree of worthiness to be revered is fixed, only the degree of rationality and strength is decisive: we must assess to what extent precisely strength has been overcome by something higher, and the service of which it now stands as means an instrument![1117]

In contrast to Kaufmann, Golomb argues that Nietzsche is better interpreted as promoting *qualitative* measures of power. That is, the kind of power employed by the artist (positive power) is qualitatively different (and more viable) than that exhibited by a thug (negative power). The distinction is that obtained between constructive and destructive power. It is a common theory within the psychological community that domestic batterers attempt to dominate their partners because they feel a lack of power over their own lives and situations. This frustration is given direct and primitive release through violence. This is "negative power" – a power to oppress/destroy. Contrast this behavior with that of a similarly frustrated artist. Rage wells up within him as well. However, rather than releasing these energies in a violent outburst, he takes hold of that energy, transforms it, and *uses* it for something desirable and productive: a work of art. His passions are channeled into artistic expression. He has mastered his drives and, in so doing, achieved a level of mastery over himself. This is "positive" power – a power to transform/create. The difference between these two is not simply a difference of degree but is also a difference in kind. Some manifestations of power are "higher" than others. Mastering (overcoming) oneself is perhaps the greatest of all displays of power and an essential aspect of the present interpretation of the WTP.

This is not to say that Nietzsche claimed that WTP is expressed *solely* as a drive to overcome oneself. The striving for power is more fundamental than its target. "Where I found the living, there I found will to power, and even in the will of those who serve I found the will to be master."[1118] The WTP is in all of us with variance arising only in its expression – and we can already see what expressions Nietzsche favors: self-mastery and authenticity. The person that best expresses power, that is most truly powerful, is the person who looks inward and disciplines herself to greatness. This kind of person is one of Nietzsche's "superior men." Ideally, this kind of person would be the *Übermensch* (Overman).

"What is the Übermensch?"

The Overman is the symbol of what someone will become when he conquers himself.[1119] How does this kind of powerful person arise? The use of reason is indispensable. The powerful person is the rational person who subjects even her most cherished beliefs to scrutiny and he will surrender them if they can't withstand it.[1120] This emphasis on reason gives further support for the position that the kind of powerful character that interested Nietzsche was not a thug or a warlord but was someone with a great mind capable of exerting much power (over himself).

> *Rationality,... Gives men mastery over himself;... Reason is the "highest" manifestation of the will to power, in the distinct sense that through rationality it can realize its objective most fully.... In human affairs too, Nietzsche points out, reason gives men greater power than sheer bodily strength. Foresight and patience, and above all, "great self – mastery"....[1121]*

> *... If his reason is strong enough, he will naturally control his passions. He is, without being ostentatious, an ascetic – insofar as he does not yield to his impulses*

[1117] ibid., section 548, p. 549.
[1118] *Thus Spoke Zarathustra*, section II. 12, p. 226.
[1119] Jaspers, Karl. *Nietzsche: An Introduction to the Understanding of His Philosophical Activity*, translated by Charles F Wallraff and Frederick J

Schmitz (Baltimore: Johns Hopkins *University Press, 1997), p. 128.*
[1120] Kaufman, 244.
[1121] ibid., 230

– but instead of extirpating them he masters and employs them.[1122]

The self-knowledge necessary for this self–overcoming is not easy to come by. "Everybody is farthest away – from himself; all who try the reins know this to their chagrin and the maxim 'know thyself!' Addressed to human beings by a god, is almost malicious."[1123] Self-knowledge is not only difficult, but unsettling – and perhaps not suited for everyone. It appears that some people "must look at themselves only from a distance in order to find themselves at all tolerable or attractive and invigorating. Self-knowledge is strictly inadvisable for them."[1124]

Rejecting both "Platonism" and Christianity alike, Nietzsche believed that because not all people are fundamentally the same, it is absurd to suppose that the same values (or models for life) are appropriate for all people. There are no absolute moral rules or standards, no single blueprint for humanity to which we should all aspire.

This is not to say that Nietzsche was some sort of amoral anarchist, let alone some sort of immoral sociopath. It is not "morality" that he wants to challenge so much as the belief that moralities have an unconditioned, universal validity. Although there is no one set of behaviors valid for all persons, there are moralities that are *conditionally* valid. They are validated on the basis of their ability to "enhance life," given a certain person's own particular constitution—and we do not all have equally "robust" constitutions, according to Nietzsche.

In contrast to "herd morality" and mediocrity, Nietzsche encourages the capable few, the elite, to overcome and master themselves, to achieve their potential and to become the "justification" for mankind. Such a genuinely original and creative person "transvalues" traditional morals, and adopts her own "good" and "evil."

For Nietzsche, the "good" or noble person is someone whose "will to power" is channeled creatively, someone who looks at herself as an artwork in progress, who takes control of herself and masters herself. This artistic metaphor is pervasive in Nietzsche's writings.

It is only as an aesthetic phenomenon that existence and the world are eternally justified.[1125]

To 'give style' to one's character--a great and rare art! It is practiced by those who survey all the strengths and weaknesses of their nature and fit them into an artistic plan until every one of them appears as art and reason and even weaknesses delight the eye.[1126]

Nietzsche's "heroes" and role-models tended to be artists, rather than warrior or politicians. In references to the writer, Goethe, he says:

He did not retire from life but put himself in the midst of it; he was not fainthearted but took as much as possible upon himself, over himself, into himself. What he wanted was totality; . . . he disciplined himself to wholeness, he created himself.[1127]

What makes great persons *great* is their power to channel and transform their own inner drive (their "will to power').

Once you suffered passions and called them evil. But now you have only your virtues left: they grew out of your passions. . . . Once you had wild dogs in your cellar, but in the end they turned into birds and lovely singers.[1128]

The lovely and poetic imagery Nietzsche uses here portrays someone transforming their inner drive and passions, something they once

---

[1122] ibid., 234.

[1123] *The Gay Science*, section 335.

[1124] ibid., section 15.

[1125] Nietzsche, *The Birth of Tragedy*, section 5.

[1126] Nietzsche, *The Gay Science*, section 290.

[1127] Nietzsche, *Twilight of the Idols*, section 49.

[1128] Nietzsche, *Thus Spoke Zarathustra*, section I:5.

regarded as "evil," into something beautiful: "birds and lovely singers."

For Nietzsche, part of what it is to be "good" (according to his own taste, of course!) is to not take life for granted, to not simply go along with the "herd," and to make of yourself a work of art. For those up to the challenge, *authenticity* should be one's goal—not that he believes very many are capable of this achievement! Most of us allow ourselves to be defined by others, and unthinkingly play out that assigned role.

Authenticity comes in two general stages, for those up to the task. The first is when we liberate ourselves from conditioning, rationalizations, illusions, and masks. This is a "negative" stage where one "hammers" one's "idols." It is important to note, though, that hammers are used for both destruction *and* construction; they destroy, but they also build.

After having broken our "tablets" of value, we freely assimilate values and norms consistent with our own nature in the second stage. This is the "positive" stage where we rebuild ourselves, and in which Nietzsche encourages those who can, the few, the "free spirits," to "become who we are."

Be yourself! All you are now doing,

thinking, desiring is not you yourself. . . . We are responsible to ourselves for our own existence; consequently, we want to be the true helmsman of this existence and refuse to allow our existence to resemble a mindless act of chance. One has to take a somewhat bold and dangerous line with this existence: especially as, whatever happens, we are bound to lose it. . . . There exists in the world a single path along which no one can go except you: whither does it lead? Do not ask, go along it.[1129]

The greatest and rarest of such "free spirits" could be considered the *Übermensch*. This "Superman" ("Overman" is a more accurate translation—and one that doesn't conjure up images of spandex and capes!) would be the pinnacle of self-mastery, strong, confident, free—even a replacement for "God" (since Nietzsche believed that "God is dead.").

Despite the fact that the overwhelming number of his admirers think that Nietzsche is writing to "them," in reality, he was writing to a tiny, terribly select few—an elite group into which most of us just would not qualify. Want to find out if you qualify?

[1129] Nietzsche, Friedrich. "*Untimely Meditations.* Translated by R.J. Hollingdale. Cambridge University Press, 1983. "Schopenhauer as Educator," section 1.

Respond to the following statements using the following scale:
>   1 = Strongly Disagree/Very non-Descriptive
>   2 = Disagree/non-Descriptive
>   3 = Agree/Descriptive
>   4 = Strongly Agree/Very Descriptive

1) I feel guilty about what I've done in the past or what sort of person I am.
2) I feel angry about the wrongs I've suffered in the past.
3) I would make a lot of changes if I had my life to live over again.
4) I often have strong desires to do things I don't really want to do, and so I must resist my desires.
5) I don't have many highs or lows. Sometimes it seems like nothing matters much.
6) There is so much world suffering that it would be better if the world had never existed.
7) I need favorable feedback from others in order to feel good about myself.
8) One of the best things about doing nice things for others is the gratitude. Absent that gratitude, I wish I could take it back.

After answering the questions, and adding up your score, consult this footnote to check your result.[1]

The "Overman" is also someone mentally strong enough to affirm the "Eternal Recurrence" of the same.

> *The greatest weight.-- What, if some day or night a demon were to steal after you into your loneliest loneliness and say to you: "This life as you now live it and have lived it, you will have to live once more and innumerable times more; and there will be nothing new in it, but every pain and every joy and every thought and sigh and everything unutterably small or great in your life will have to return to you, all in the same succession and sequence - even this spider and this moonlight between the trees, and even this moment and I myself. The eternal hourglass of existence is turned upside down again and again, and you with it, speck of dust!"*
>
> *Would you not throw yourself down and gnash your teeth and curse the demon who spoke thus?... Or how well disposed would you have to become to yourself and to life to crave nothing more fervently than this ultimate eternal confirmation and seal?[1130]*

The idea of the eternal recurrence is actually an ancient idea, finding a home in Stoic cosmology, for example. Nietzsche's version, however, is best interpreted as an "existential imperative" rather than a cosmological hypothesis.

The question is simply this: given a chance, would you do <u>everything</u> in your life, all over again, exactly the same—all the pains, frustrations, and losses, as well as the triumphs and happy moments—and would you will to do so <u>forever.</u> Finally, could you will that this be so, and be *joyful* in the willing? To do so is to truly "embrace Fate"—what Nietzsche called "*Amor Fati.*" The ability to do so is also, he thought, a profoundly *rare* thing, and anyone capable of doing so has truly executed a beautiful work-of-art self.

A person, in self – overcoming, is self – creating. For Nietzsche, *if* a particular person has risen "above" the animals, it is because that person has cultivated her nature. We are all suspended between two worlds and two selves. On the one hand, we have the world as it is given to us; on the other, there is the world as we create it. On the one hand, we have our empirical self, shaped and molded by prevailing social forces

---

[1130] *The Gay Science*, section 341.

and customs; on the other, we have the self that we create for ourselves. "In man, *creature* and *creator* are united."[1131] Also, "man is a rope, tied between beast and Overman – a rope over an abyss."[1132] The suggested ethic is one of self – realization, posed within a full awareness and acceptance that the majority persons never do realize themselves and are ever resigned to exist in the "herd." "We, however, *want to become those we are* – human beings who are new, unique, incomparable, who give themselves laws, who create themselves."[1133]

> *If will to power is formed – giving, shaping, articulation, then the Übermensch forms and shapes the will to power which he himself is. It is not a question of mastering others, of overcoming the herd by overpowering it. The herd to be overcome is the herd in ourselves. Mastery and overcoming are to be understood as self – mastery and self – overcoming primarily....And since giving form to one's life in this instance cannot be a question of conforming to the format given by others, the Übermensch is self-forming...[1134]*

Conclusion

There is no question that Nietzsche was a radical and provocative philosopher. His writing style is challenging, and this invites numerous interpretations – and misinterpretations. Among the most pernicious of those misinterpretations is that Nietzsche was somehow the intellectual grandfather of Nazi ideology. This is demonstrably false, as I hope has been shown in this chapter. Nietzsche explicitly rejected anti-Semitism, German Nationalism, and notions of racial purity. The *Übermensch*, in his estimation, is far better expressed as a self-mastering free spirit than a totalitarian regime.

Critical Analysis

1. In your opinion, what are the strongest and most compelling points made by the philosopher or philosophers in this chapter? Why do you find those points to be convincing?
2. In your opinion, what are the weakest or least convincing points? Why? Can you anticipate any limitations or objections to their ideas not already addressed in the chapter?

Appendix: Application to Social Justice

The application to social justice here is probably obvious. White nationalism is a movement whose very foundation is racism, and which usually includes anti-Semitism, misogyny, hostility to the LGBTQ+ community, and religious bigotry against non-Christians as well. Each of those represents an area of concern within social justice circles.

While white nationalism might be dismissed as a fringe movement, it should be considered, understood, and philosophically resisted. Their threat can be framed in language that should be familiar if you have read the chapter on Rawls in this book. Fringe groups are not part of a well ordered society, and they represent a threat to stability if they grow large enough, and influential enough.

The White Nationalist movement stepped away from the fringes and towards "mainstream" politics thanks to sustained help from President Donald Trump, whose history of "flirtation" (to put it euphemistically) with white nationalism has been unprecedented for a major party politician in modern times—let alone for a U.S. President.

His former senior advisor, Stephen Miller, has documented ties to the white nationalist movement. An analysis of over 900 emails Miller

---

[1131] Nietzsche, *Beyond Good and Evil*. Section 225, p. 154.
[1132] Nietzsche, "Thus Spoke Zarathustra," section I:4, p. 126.

[1133] Nietzsche, *The Gay Science*, section 335, p. 266
[1134] Magnus, 34.

sent to the alt-right Breitbart organization in 2015 included "links to white nationalist articles, while others included white nationalist slang. Miller also promoted The Camp of the Saints, a white supremacist book that casts immigrants of color as savages who subsist on feces, as well as praise for the nativist, hard-line immigration policies of the 1920s."[1135]

The former CEO of Breitbart, Steve Bannon, also has ties to White Nationalism and served as Trump's Chief Strategist and campaign CEO. The Southern Poverty Law Center called Bannon the "main driver behind Breitbart becoming a white ethno-nationalist propaganda mill."[1136] Regarding Bannon's role in the Trump White House, the Anti-Defamation League said, "It is a sad day when a man who presided over the premier website of the 'alt-right' — a loose-knit group of white nationalists and unabashed anti-Semites and racists — is slated to be a senior staff member in the 'people's house.'"[1137] Breitbart News used to have an entire section called "Black Crime," and two weeks after a white supremacist (who posted pictures of himself with the confederate flag on social media) murdered nine

Black people at church after attending a prayer meeting with them, as their *guest*, Breitbart ran an article praising the "glorious heritage" of that flag.[1138]

As mentioned earlier in this chapter, President Trump infamously proclaimed that there were "very fine people, on both sides" in comments on the violence that took place between "Unite the Right" protesters and counter-protesters.[1139] While not explicitly endorsing the overt white supremacist groups who organized the event, he implied that the "very fine people" were those who were *merely* protesting the planned removal of a stature of Robert E. Lee—the General who led the Confederate States in the Civil War as they attempted to retain slavery.

As recently as late-December, 2020, he refused to sign a defense bill (with so much bipartisan support that it was veto-proof) that mandated the renaming of military bases that had been named for Confederate generals.[1140] He had threatened to do just that months prior, in a tweet that also referred to Senator Elizabeth Warren by the racially offensive term "Pocahontas."

Donald J. Trump
@realDonaldTrump

I will Veto the Defense Authorization Bill if the Elizabeth "Pocahontas" Warren (of all people!) Amendment, which will lead to the renaming (plus other bad things!) of Fort Bragg, Fort Robert E. Lee, and many other Military Bases from which we won Two World Wars, is in the Bill!

8:58 PM · Jun 30, 2020

146K   83.6K people are Tweeting about this

In 2018 he was recorded referring to immigrants from Haiti and Africa as coming from "shithole countries," and expressing a preference for more people from Norway.

[1135] https://www.vox.com/21313021/trump-white-nationalism-supremacy-miller-bannon-immigration
[1136] https://www.buzzfeednews.com/article/tasneemnashrulla/here-are-some-of-the-most-controversial-stories-published-by
[1137] ibid.
[1138] https://www.breitbart.com/politics/2015/

07/01/hoist-it-high-and-proud-the-confederate-flag-proclaims-a-glorious-heritage/
[1139] https://www.whitehouse.gov/briefings-statements/remarks-president-trump-infrastructure/
[1140] https://www.npr.org/2020/12/23/949586964/trump-vetoes-defense-bill-setting-up-congressional-vote-to-override-him

The White House released a statement, in response, which notably *did not deny* the comments were made.

In June of 2020 President Trump shared a video in which a man driving a golf cart with Trump campaign posters is seen chanting "white power,"[1141] and in July he referred to "Black Lives Matter" as a "symbol of hate."[1142]

One of the Trump campaign's official ads during the 2020 campaign, that even included a voiceover from Vice President Mike Pence, featured footage of flaming police cars, protesters

confronting law enforcement personnel and explosions. It ends with slow-motion footage of former Vice President Biden kneeling in a Black church in front of a row of Black leaders, followed by words appearing on the screen: "stop Joe Biden and his rioters." Mike Pence then declares "you won't be safe in Joe Biden's America."[1143]

During one of the 2020 Presidential debates, Trump refused to clearly condemn white

---

[1141] https://www.cnn.com/2020/06/28/politics/trump-tweet-supporters-man-chants-white-power/index.html
[1142] https://www.cnn.com/2020/07/01/politics/donald-trump-black-lives-matter-

confederate-race/index.html
[1143] https://religionnews.com/2020/09/10/trump-campaign-ad-shows-biden-kneeling-in-black-church-to-argue-americans-wont-be-safe/

supremacy during this exchange with the moderator, Chris Wallace from Fox News.[1144]

Chris Wallace: (41:33)
You have repeatedly criticized the vice president for not specifically calling out Antifa and other left wing extremist groups. But are you willing tonight to condemn white supremacists and militia group and to say that they need to stand down and not add to the violence in a number of these cities as we saw in Kenosha and as we've seen in Portland.

President Donald J. Trump: (41:57)
Sure, I'm will to do that.

Chris Wallace: (41:59)
Are you prepared specifically to do it.

President Donald J. Trump: (42:00)
I would say almost everything I see is from the left wing not from the right wing.

Chris Wallace: (42:04)
But what are you saying?

President Donald J. Trump: (42:06)
I'm willing to do anything. I want to see peace.

Chris Wallace: (42:08)
Well, do it, sir.

Vice President Joe Biden: (42:09)
Say it, do it say it.

President Donald J. Trump: (42:10)

What do you want to call them? Give me a name, give me a name, go ahead who do you want me to condemn.

Chris Wallace: (42:14)
White supremacist and right-wing militia.

Vice President Joe Biden: (42:14)
Proud Boys.

President Donald J. Trump: (42:18)
Proud Boys, stand back and stand by. But I'll tell you what somebody's got to do something about Antifa and the left because this is not a right wing problem this is a left wing...[1145]

Even after losing reelection (though still not conceding that loss as of the time of the writing of this chapter), he continued to subtly support the white nationalist cause by appointing two men with well-documented ties to white nationalism to government positions. Darren J. Beattie served as a White House speechwriter until he was fired in 2018 after it was revealed he had spoken at a white nationalist conference. After the election in 2020, President Trump appointed him to the Commission for the Preservation of America's Heritage Abroad.[1146] Around the same time, he appointed Jason Richwine to a senior position at the National Institute of Standards and Technology (NIST). Richwine is known for, among other things, being a policy analyst that was pushed out of a conservative think tank (The Heritage Foundation) for writing that Mexican and other Latino immigrants have lower IQs than white people.[1147]

It would be quite uncharitable to suggest that

[1144] https://www.rev.com/blog/transcripts/donald-trump-joe-biden-1st-presidential-debate-transcript-2020

[1145] The Anti-Defamation League describes the Proud Boys ideology as: "Misogynistic, Islamophobic, transphobic and anti-immigration. Some members espouse white supremacist and anti-Semitic ideologies and/or engage with white supremacist groups." The

Proud Boys have frequently been involved in street violence, and a former Proud Boys member helped organize the "Unite the Right" rally that prompted deadly violence in Charlottesville, Virginia, in August 2017.

[1146] https://www.huffpost.com/entry/trump-appoints-white-nationalists-darren-beattie-jason-richwine_n_5fb6eedbc5b67f34cb398973

[1147] https://www.sciencemag.org/news/2020/

the Trump victory of 2016 was the result of white nationalism, that the Trump Presidency has been centered on white nationalism, or even that President Trump himself is personally sympathetic to white nationalism—though there is certainly evidence in support of each of those claims, to some degree or another.

However, the conspicuous pattern of support from white nationalists, and at least implicit support of white nationalist causes, certainly at least raises the *possibility* that the 45th American President's personal and/or political agendas overlapped with those of white nationalism. Moreover, issues raised by white nationalist groups, and anxieties they express, have *undoubtedly* worked their way into the political process and had an impact on recent elections. A 2017 study of white working-class voters revealed the following trends:

- Nearly two-thirds (65%) of white working-class Americans believe American culture and way of life has deteriorated since the 1950s.
- Nearly half (48%) of white working-class Americans say, "things have changed so much that I often feel like a stranger in my own country."
- Nearly seven in ten (68%) white working-class Americans believe the American way of life needs to be protected from foreign influence.
- Nearly seven in ten (68%) white working-class Americans—along with a majority (55%) of the public overall—believe the U.S. is in danger of losing its culture and identity.
- More than six in ten (62%) white working-

class Americans believe the growing number of newcomers from other countries threatens American culture.
- More than half (52%) of white working-class Americans believe discrimination against whites has become as big a problem as discrimination against blacks and other minorities. Nearly six in ten (59%) white working-class seniors (age 65 and older) believe it is.
- Six in ten (60%) white working-class Americans say because things have gotten so far off track, we need a strong leader who is willing to break the rules.
- Nearly two-thirds (64%) of white working-class Americans have an authoritarian orientation, including 37% who are classified as "high authoritarian."[1148]

Consider those numbers and now place them in the context of some other demographic trends. For the 2016 presidential election, white working-class voters are estimated to have been 44.8% of those who voted.[1149] It is predicted that the United States will become "minority white" as of 2045.[1150] Supposing that that is true, there are still decades remaining in which the white working-class will make up a sizable percentage of voters, and it seems reasonable to predict that if a significant percentage of them are already feeling anxiety about changing demographic and cultural trends, that anxiety will increase as their "minority status" ceases to be paranoia and becomes reality.

The fears and complaints currently marinating and amplifying in the white nationalist movement could certainly become more widespread, and the threat to stability and a well-ordered society would increase as a result.

11/proponent-using-iq-tests-screen-immigrants-named-senior-nist-post?utm_campaign=NewsfromScience&utm_source=JHubbard&utm_medium=Twitter
[1148] Jones, Robert P., Daniel Cox, and Rachel Lienesch. "Beyond Economics: Fears of Cultural Displacement Pushed the White Working Class to Trump | PRRI/*The Atlantic* Report." PRRI. 2017. Available at:

https://www.prri.org/research/ white-working-class-attitudes-economy-trade-immigration-election-donald-trump/
[1149] https://www.americanprogress.org/issues/democracy/reports/2017/11/01/441926/voter-trends-in-2016/
[1150] https://www.brookings.edu/blog/the-avenue/2018/03/14/the-us-will-become-minority-white-in-2045-census-projects/

Indeed, the tragic events of the attempted insurrection of January 6th 2020 were the clearest signs, so far, of significant instability. Given the fact that a clear majority of white working-class voters *currently* exhibit authoritarian traits and think we need a "strong leader who is willing to break the rules," the inclusion of Hitler in this chapter might be disturbingly apt.

Chapter 26: Discrimination

Discrimination and Prejudice

The main topic of this chapter is discrimination, although, as you will see, this actually ranges over a number of different ideas. At times, this chapter might feel like it belongs in an "introduction to legal studies" textbook instead, but we will begin with something that should feel properly philosophical: conceptual analysis.

Although the two terms are often used as though they are interchangeable, discrimination and prejudice actually have distinct meanings.

Prejudice is an unjustified or incorrect attitude (that is usually negative) towards an individual based solely on the individual's membership of a social group. I say "usually" negative, because it is possible that someone might hold a stereotypical view of someone based on their group membership that might be considered a "positive." For example, part of the "model minority" stereotype of Asians in the United States is that Asians are smart and good at math. Although being stereotyped, and having one's individuality be buried under assumptions based on group membership, is unfair and might be experienced as hurtful, it has to be said that "smart" and "good at math," when taken at face value, would not be considered "negative" attributions. All that being said, most of the time, and certainly those times when we tend most to care, the prejudice involves a negative attitude.

Depending on the nature of the prejudice, we have a variety of potential "isms." Racism occurs when someone harbors racial prejudice, sexism occurs when they're prejudiced on the basis of gender, heterosexism is prejudice on the basis of normative heterosexuality, ableism involves prejudice on the basis of disability, classism is prejudice on the basis of socio-economic status, ethnocentrism is prejudice on the basis of cultural membership, etc.

The definition of prejudice that I offered above describes unjustified or incorrect attitudes towards individuals based on their membership. As philosophers, we want to be precise with language use, so it will be beneficial to take a moment to dissect what is meant by unjustified or incorrect *attitude*.

To begin with, we are talking about an attitude as distinct from a belief. A belief, as you hopefully recall from one of the earliest chapters in this book, is expressed as a claim: a statement that has a truth value (either true, or false). An attitude is a settled and stable way of thinking or feeling about someone or something that is typically reflected in behavior. A belief can be isolated, distinct, and possibly have no impact on behavior in some cases. An attitude, in contrast, describes not only the sorts of things that we believe, but also and necessarily how we *feel* and *act*.

Not all attitudes are prejudicial, of course. I have an attitude of "caution" whenever I am working on the roof of my two-story house. I think my beliefs about the danger of falling off a second-floor roof are accurate, and I think my caution is warranted (although the *degree* of anxiety I sometimes experience is probably unwarranted). I don't think my beliefs, feelings, and actions revolving around cautious roof work is "prejudice." What makes an attitude prejudice is that it is *unjustified*.

"Unjustified" could mean either morally unjustified, or rationally unjustified, but I propose that what we normally have in mind in standard cases of prejudice is *both*.

The attitude would be *rationally* unjustified if it is based on a logical fallacy or false information (or both). For example, stereotyping generally involves assuming that a trait found in some, or even many, members of a group is shared by all members of that group. It is fallacious, for example, to assume that an individual Latino is an undocumented Mexican immigrant just because there are many such persons in the United States – nearly 5 million as of 2017.[1151] This is sloppy reasoning for a variety of reasons, obviously. To begin with, for any person of Mexican ancestry in the United States, it is much more likely that they were born in the United States, and are U.S. citizens. Of the over 36 million persons of Mexican ancestry in the United States as of 2017, only 31% were *not* born in the United States[1152] – and even among that 31%, some will have become naturalized citizens, some will have Visas

or will be otherwise legally permitted to be in the United States, etc. In addition, not all Latinos have Mexican ancestry. Someone could be accurately described as Latino so long as they have roots in literally any country in Central or South America. While it is *possible* that a particular person might, in fact, be undocumented and come from Mexico, the potential truth of that claim does not warrant the *assumption*. If a person has negative feelings (e.g., resentment) or engages in behavior (e.g. using hateful language, calling the police to report an "illegal"), on the basis of that faulty reasoning, it would qualify as a case of prejudice.

The other way in which the attitude can be unjustified is if it is *morally* unjustified. It's conceivable that someone could have an unjustified negative attitude that doesn't generate the same sort of disapproval that prejudice in the normal usage of the term does. For an admittedly strange example, someone might have an abiding dislike of cats, and be extremely prejudicial in favor of dogs. Their beliefs about cats might be unjustified, and their attitude might be quite negative, but unless such a person actually *abuses* a cat, we're unlikely to regard their prejudice as the sort of prejudice that *matters*. When a prejudicial attitude causes harm, in some sense, to a person, in contrast, we have a clear candidate for the sort of prejudice that is morally problematic, and the type that we normally have in mind.

The most obvious way in which an attitude might be considered morally unjustified and problematic is if it involves value judgments based on beliefs that should not be considered relevant to the value judgment. For example, the degree to which you assign moral value to a person is a value judgment, as is the moral worth or esteem/respect you extend to them. I submit that race membership is not relevant when it comes to a person's moral value. If someone thinks that a person is morally inferior, or somehow "less than" simply by virtue of their race, that person is using morally irrelevant criteria to make their value judgment. This goes

---

[1151] https://www.pewresearch.org/hispanic/2020/08/20/facts-on-u-s-immigrants/

[1152] ibid.

beyond an intellectual failing and moves into the realm of a moral failing. This is why prejudice is often considered to be both intellectually and morally shameful. Someone who is prejudiced is not only making a "mistake" in their thinking, but a moral mistake as well. It is not only their cognitive faculties at fault, but their moral character in addition.

Like prejudice, discrimination is also a term that requires some "unpacking." To begin with, at face value, there is nothing wrong with discrimination or discriminating. Generically and traditionally understood, discrimination simply refers to the recognition and understanding of the difference between one thing and another. When I go grocery shopping, I "discriminate" in the produce section when I'm selecting fruit on the basis of ripeness. You might "discriminate" in your selection of friends in the sense that you choose people that you enjoy hanging around with rather than people who annoy you. I "discriminate" every time I grade an assignment when I differentiate "A-quality" work from "B-quality" work, etc. None of this is morally questionable. In fact, in some cases "discrimination" is morally demanded from us, such as when we discriminate between the guilty and the innocent within the criminal justice system!

However, "dictionary definition" notwithstanding, in common usage what most of us mean by **discrimination** is something like the unjust or prejudicial treatment of different categories of people or things, especially on the basis of their group membership.

As we saw above, prejudice concerns our attitudes (which themselves impact our thinking and acting), but discrimination necessarily concerns our actions. It is possible to be prejudiced without discriminating. It is also possible (although probably a lot less likely) to discriminate without being prejudiced. Given the *usual* usage of discrimination, what is it about discrimination that makes it *wrong*?

The wrongness of discrimination can be understood in terms of morality or legality. Morally speaking, it might be (and often is) considered morally wrong to discriminate

according to a variety of ethical systems. This is not an ethics textbook, and we will not consider the numerous approaches to understanding our moral obligations, the vast majority of which agree that discrimination on the basis of prejudice is morally wrong. Instead, for the purposes of this chapter, will consider the *legal* "wrongness" of discrimination.

Illegal Discrimination

Discrimination that is illegal does not cover every discrimination that is immoral. For example, there is no legal requirement that we do not discriminate with respect to our friendships and romantic relationships on the basis of race. In other words, you are not breaking any laws if you only date people from your own race, or if all of your friends are of your same race. However, it's entirely possible that there is something morally questionable about those patterns if they are the result of an intentional preference or active dislike of people from other races, as opposed to being the contingent result of living in a community where there were no realistic prospects of intermingling with people of other races, for example.

When discrimination is illegal is (obviously) when its occurrence is in violation of some law. In the United States, certain groups of people belong to "protected classes" as a result of historical oppression and current vulnerability. Presently, protected classes include:

- Race
- National origin
- Religion
- Age
- Gender (including LGBTQ+)
- Disability

Members of these groups are specifically protected from discrimination in a variety of contexts. For the purposes of this section, we will focus specifically on employment discrimination. Several laws and court rulings have specified what sorts of discrimination in employment are illegal in the United States.

- The Civil Rights Act, the Age Discrimination in Employment Act, and the Americans with Disabilities Act prohibit discrimination in employment on the basis of race, color, sex, ethnic origin, age and disabilities.

- Title VII of the Civil Rights Act of 1964 covers the full spectrum of employment decisions, including recruitment, selections, terminations, and other decisions concerning terms and conditions of employment.

- The Supreme Court ruling in *Bostock v. Clayton County, Georgia* and *R.G. & G.R. Harris Funeral Homes Inc. v. Equal Employment Opportunity Commission* (2020), forbids LGBT employment discrimination in the United States under Title VII of the Civil Rights Act of 1964 (as sexual orientation or gender identity is now considered encompassed by the law's prohibition of employment discrimination

If someone believes themselves to have been the victim of employment discrimination, the legal remedy involves filing a lawsuit. The most common legal strategies are filing discrimination lawsuits under either section 1981 of the Civil Rights Act of 1866, or Title VII of the Civil Rights Act of 1964.

Section 1981 of the Civil Rights Act of 1866 is a federal law prohibiting discrimination on the basis of race, color, and ethnicity when "making and enforcing contracts." Section 1981 specifically grants all individuals within the jurisdiction of the United States the same rights and benefits as "enjoyed by white citizens" regarding contractual relationships.[1153] Section 1981 also prohibits retaliation for filing a complaint of discrimination. Section 1981 does *not* prohibit discrimination on the basis of any *other* protected class (such as gender, religious affiliation, etc.). Section 1981 applies to all private employers and labor organizations, but does *not* apply to discrimination by the US federal government as an employer. It also does *not* apply to state or local government employers.

Title VII of the Civil Rights Act of 1964, as amended, protects employees and job applicants from employment discrimination based on race, color, religion, sex, and national origin. It covers the "full spectrum" of employment decisions, including recruitment, selections, terminations, and other decisions concerning terms and conditions of employment.

Although employment discrimination on the basis of membership in a protected class is clearly prohibited, *proving* that you have been the victim of discrimination is (literally) a legal challenge. It is not an exaggeration to say that entire courses in law school are dedicated to the subtleties of discrimination law—not to mention the fact that the legal landscape is constantly changing every year with new laws and court decisions! This one chapter in this introductory textbook will not even pretend to do justice to all of the complexity of this subject. Instead, I will attempt to present (in admittedly broad brush strokes) some of the basic elements of the legal process, and the challenge plaintiffs face in trying to prove that they have been the victim of discrimination.

As of *Comcast Corp. v. National Association of African American-Owned Media* (2020), a plaintiff who sues for racial discrimination in contracting under 42 U.S.C. § 1981 (i.e., section 1981) bears the burden of showing that race was a "but-for" cause of the plaintiff's injury, and that burden remains constant over the life of the lawsuit. That is, the "injury" (e.g., not getting hired, getting fired, not getting the promotion, etc.) would not have occurred "but for" discrimination—there exists no other non-discriminatory explanation or plausible motive. This makes it very difficult to prove that one has been the victim of discrimination when suing under section 1981. Just think about how difficult it would be to rule out *any* other plausible explanation or motive for the outcome. Unless a plaintiff is fortunate enough to have evidence of an explicit demonstration of racist motivation, such as emails, or video or audio recordings, or testimony demonstrating explicit racist language, a confession of racial discrimination in that very

---

[1153] 42 U.S.C. § 1981(a).

case, etc., motive is going to be difficult (if not impossible) to prove.

To begin with, it's unlikely that someone who discriminates on the basis of race is going to want to admit to that when they are being sued! They will, of course, claim that any number of other motives were at work. They didn't discriminate on the basis of race, it was simply the case that someone else was "more qualified." A different candidate got the promotion because they had more "merit." The plaintiff didn't get the job because they just didn't seem to "fit in" with the other staff members. None of those motivations would count as racial discrimination, and any of them could be a plausible explanation for the outcome.

To make it even more complicated, if we allow for the existence of implicit bias, the defendant might not even themselves be aware that they were discriminating on the basis of race – which would make it all the less likely that they would acknowledge racial discrimination as part of their decision process.

For all of these reasons, suing for discrimination under section 1981 constitutes an uphill battle. Why not sue under Title VII then? For one, section 1981 broadly applies to all private employers, whereas Title VII applies to private employers with at least 15 employees. That means that small businesses are excluded under Title VII. In addition, Section 1981 claims have a longer statute of limitations than the Title VII claims, and section 1981 claims cap the damages the plaintiffs can recover. Finally, plaintiffs can also bypass the Equal Employment Opportunity Commission's administrative process, which is required for Title VII claims. This means that Section 1981 lawsuits are subject to less bureaucracy and could proceed more quickly.

This is not to say that there are no advantages of filing a discrimination lawsuit under Title VII. Title VII is broader, as it also covers employment claims based on sex and religion, and also allows for claims of unintentional bias – whereas Section 1981 only applies to claims of intentional discrimination.

As a "deeper dive," we will now engage in a brief exploration of the process of proving discrimination under Title VII. Proving Discrimination under Title VII occurs over three stages:

1. Making a *"Prima Facie"* Case Under Title VII
2. The Employer's Burden
3. The Employee's Rebuttal: Pretext

First, the plaintiff must make a *"prima facie"* case of discrimination. *"Prima facie"* means (roughly) "on the face of it." At this stage, the plaintiff has to demonstrate something that could reasonably be taken to be an example of discrimination has occurred. Part of making this case involves several requirements, some of which might seem painfully obvious. First, the plaintiff must be an employee or applicant (etc.) who is a member of a legally protected class. In other words, they must be alleging that the discrimination was on the basis of something like race, gender, etc. Second, the plaintiffs must have been "qualified" for whatever they claim to have been denied. If it is a job, the plaintiff must meet the minimum qualifications for the job. It is a promotion, they must have been an eligible employee, etc. Finally, the plaintiff must have been denied whatever benefit they are referencing, and in an apparently discriminatory manner. Obviously, if someone never even applied for a job in the first place, it would be a stretch to say that they didn't get the job because of discrimination. Similarly, it would make no sense to claim discrimination if they actually got the job they had applied for (or the promotion, etc.). In summary, the plaintiff must be a qualified candidate who was denied some benefit on the basis of their membership in a protected class.

If the plaintiff is able to make this *prima facie* case, the next stage in the process shifts to the employer. The employer must now present some evidence of a legitimate, nondiscriminatory motive for the challenged action or decision. For example, if they are being sued by someone who claims they were not hired for a job because of their race, the employer must offer some *other* reason for why they were not hired, such as being less competitive than other applicants. Realistically, this is unlikely to be a difficult challenge for the employer given that any number of explanations other than discrimination could plausibly account for their decisions.

The final stage of the process gives the plaintiff an opportunity to offer a rebuttal of the justification offered by the employer. The basic strategy here for the plaintiff is to try to prove that the employer's explanation is a mere "pretext" masking their true discriminatory motive. For example, anyone can *say* that they made their employment decision on the basis of qualifications, but if the plaintiff can establish that the defendant has a long history of similar discrimination, a judge might determine that their true motivation was discrimination, instead. After Congress passed some amendments to Title VII in 1991 (Section 2000e-2), a plaintiff could prevail by proving that race, color, religion, sex or national origin was "a motivating factor" for some adverse employment action—which is a lower standard than the "but for" standard discussed above.

Ultimately, the employee in a discrimination lawsuit has the burden of proof. The employer doesn't have to prove that it did not discriminate; it only has to present some evidence of a legitimate (nondiscriminatory) motive. Even the lower standard of discrimination being a "motivating factor," can be difficult to *prove*.

One of the ways someone might try to prove discriminatory intent, even in the absence of *explicit* evidence (such as racist language), is by pointing to "disparate impact" or "disparate outcomes."

In general, disparate impact occurs when policies, practices, rules, or other systems that appear to be neutral result in a disproportionate impact on a protected group. Prejudice and/or discriminatory intent might not be apparent, and might not even be present – but the effect of the policy (etc.) nevertheless produces an unjustifiably discriminatory result. Evidence for disparate impact has been observed and documented in education, medical care, health, housing, employment, and the criminal justice system, among others.

When it comes to discrimination lawsuits, it is *sometimes* possible to make a discrimination claim under a disparate impact standard, though that standard is difficult to prove. A violation of Title VII of the 1964 Civil Rights Act may be proven by showing that an employment practice or policy has a disproportionately adverse effect on members of the protected class as compared with non-members of the protected class. The disparate impact theory under Title VII prohibits employers "from using a facially neutral employment practice that has an unjustified adverse impact on members of a protected class." A facially neutral employment practice is one that does not appear to be discriminatory on its face; rather it is one that is discriminatory in its application or effect. Disparate impact only becomes illegal if the employer cannot justify the employment practice causing the adverse impact as a "job related for the position in question and consistent with business necessity." This is what is known as the "Business Necessity" defense.

A hugely important Supreme Court case with respect to the use of disparate impact in discrimination cases is *Griggs v. Duke Power Co.* (1971). The ruling in this case provided the first recognition of disparate impact discrimination. As detailed in this case, prior to the Civil Rights Act, the company had permitted black employees to work only in its low-paying Labor department, while white employees were hired or promoted into its higher-paying Maintenance, Operations and Laboratory departments. After the Civil Rights Act, Duke Power Co. began requiring Labor employees who wanted to transfer to another department to have a high school diploma and pass two aptitude tests. A disproportionate number of white employees were able to meet these requirements as compared to black employees. The Supreme Court ruled that the company's requirements had a discriminatory adverse effect on black workers by preventing them from advancing within the company. Duke Power also failed to prove that these requirements reflected an employee's ability to perform the job. Although the practice appeared to be nondiscriminatory, it was illegal because of its discriminatory consequences. This case established what is now known as the "Griggs Standard." The "**Griggs Standard**" established a three-step model as a precedent for establishing discrimination by using disparate impact as evidence.

1. The plaintiff must first prove that a specific employment practice adversely affects employment opportunities of Title VII protected classes. If the plaintiff can establish a disparate impact, then:

2. The employer must demonstrate that the challenged practice is justified by "business necessity" or that the practice is "manifestly related" to job duties. If the employer does not meet the burdens of production and persuasion in proving business necessity, the plaintiff prevails. If the employer does meet these burdens, then:

3. The plaintiff must demonstrate that alternative practices exist that would meet the business needs of the employer yet would not have a discriminatory effect.

Not quite twenty years later, another Supreme Court case (*Wards Cove Packing Co. v. Atonio* (1989)) weakened the disparate impact standards by shifting the burden of proof to the *employees* to demonstrate how a specific employment practice resulted in a discriminatory outcome. In addition, the court lightened the burden on the employer by requiring proof of "business justification," or sufficient reason, rather than business *necessity*. In response, Congress passed the Civil Rights Act of 1991 with the express purpose of overturning the Wards Cove decision:

> *"The purposes of this Act are--*
> *(1) to provide appropriate remedies for intentional discrimination and unlawful harassment in the workplace;*
> *(2) to codify the concepts of 'business*

> *necessity' and 'job related' enunciated by the Supreme Court in Griggs v. Duke Power Co., 401 U.S. 424 (1971), and in the other Supreme Court decisions prior to Wards Cove Packing Co. v. Atonio, 490 U.S. 642 (1989);*
> *(3) to confirm statutory authority and provide statutory guidelines for the adjudication of disparate impact suits under title VII of the Civil Rights Act of 1964 (42 U.S.C. 2000e et seq.); and*
> *(4) to respond to recent decisions of the Supreme Court by expanding the scope of relevant civil rights statutes in order to provide adequate protection to victims of discrimination."*

The amendment included as a provision the three-step process as laid out in the *Griggs* decision and placed the burden back on employers to establish the business necessity of a practice causing disparate impact.

This standard has been employed, revisited, and reconsidered countless times—sometimes with controversial results. In the case of *EEOC v. FREEMAN* (2015. 4th Circuit Court of Appeals), the plaintiff alleged that using criminal background checks and credit checks is discriminatory because racial minorities in the United States are more likely to have criminal records and poor credit histories than white applicants. The 4th Circuit Court rejected this argument:

> *By bringing actions of this nature, the EEOC has placed many employers in the "Hobson's choice" of ignoring criminal history and credit background, thus exposing themselves to potential liability for criminal and fraudulent acts committed by employees, on the one hand, or incurring the wrath of the EEOC for having utilized information deemed fundamental by most employers. Something more... must be utilized to justify a disparate impact claim based upon criminal history and credit checks. To require less, would be to condemn the use of common sense, and this is simply not*

what the laws of this country require.[1154]

At the heart of the Court's rejection of the disparate impact claim is the idea that disparate impact alone does not necessarily indicate unjustifiable discrimination. In this specific example, the Court claims that an employer's *legitimate* interest in knowing whether or not job applicants have a criminal record or poor credit history takes priority over disparate impact claims—unlike, for example, if an employer required employees have addresses in certain neighborhoods that "just so happen" to have very few racial minority residents.

Wealth Gaps

When we observe disparate outcomes by race in things like family wealth, home ownership, educational attainment, incarceration rates, etc., there are generally two broad explanations available: either there is something about our systems and institutions within our society that is producing these disparities (e.g., systemic racism), or there is something about the people themselves that is causing the disparity.

To make this crystal clear, I do **not**, for a moment, think that the explanation for racial disparities is that there is something biologically or culturally "flawed" or "inferior" when it comes to certain races or ethnicities. That is, however, a logically possible explanation. It is certainly the explanation endorsed by racists, and it is even the explanation endorsed (perhaps uncomfortably) by people who don't believe that systemic racism exists or presents much of an obstacle to people of color, even if it does.

As it turns out, it is possible to demonstrate that *systemic racism is the best explanation for disparities*, and we will attempt to do so using just one example: disparities in family wealth

between white and Black households.

Wealth is not the same thing as income, or even "money" in general. One definition of wealth is the value of what you own minus the value of what you owe. Someone might have a job, and earn $5,000 each month, but, by itself, that is not "wealth." Imagine that this person has bills amounting to $6,000 each month. That person goes deeper into debt each month and is not accumulating any wealth. Or imagine someone who drives a very expensive car, but they don't actually own it because they are either leasing it or are making car payments on it. They might appear "wealthy," but until they own the vehicle outright (at which point its value has probably diminished quite a bit!), it doesn't add to their wealth. As another example, imagine a lawyer who brings home $100,000 each year, and, after living expenses, has $2,000 left over each month. But that lawyer accumulated $75,000 in student loan debt. Only after paying off that debt (and any other debt), can we begin to see "wealth" for that person. Mostly capturing the same idea, another way to understand wealth is the resources available to a household at any given point in time. Income is a resource, and debt is a drain on resources—but things like home ownership and retirement accounts count as resources as well. With this understanding of wealth in place, we can focus on the wealth gap by race.

As of 2019 (so, not even considering the racially disparate impact of the Covid-19 pandemic), there is a clear and significant wealth gap between white households and households of people of color. White families have the highest level of both median and mean family wealth: $188,200 and $983,400; Black families' median and mean wealth is less than 15 percent that of white families, at $24,100 and $142,500, respectively; Hispanic families' median and mean wealth is $36,100 and $165,500, respectively.[1155]

[1154] https://www.ca4.uscourts.gov/opinions/published/132365.p.pdf

[1155] Bhutta, Neil, Andrew C. Chang, Lisa J. Dettling, and Joanne W. Hsu (2020). "Disparities in Wealth by Race and Ethnicity in the 2019 Survey of Consumer Finances," FEDS Notes. Washington: Board of Governors of the Federal Reserve System, September 28, 2020, https://doi.org/10.17016/2380-7172.2797 .

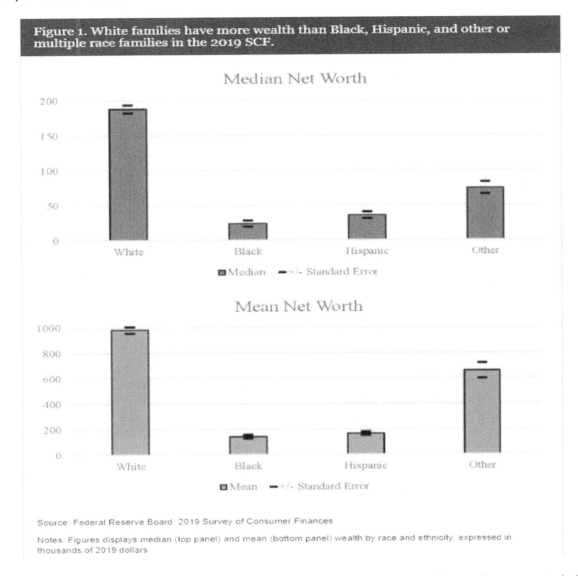

Figure 1. White families have more wealth than Black, Hispanic, and other or multiple race families in the 2019 SCF.

Source: Federal Reserve Board. 2019 Survey of Consumer Finances.

Notes: Figures displays median (top panel) and mean (bottom panel) wealth by race and ethnicity, expressed in thousands of 2019 dollars.

Thus far, all we know is that average wealth varies by race, but we don't yet know why. It helps to first understand how it is that wealth is acquired in the first place?

Among other factors, inter-generational transfers, homeownership opportunities, access to tax-sheltered savings plans, and individuals' savings and investment decisions contribute to wealth accumulation and families' financial security.[1156]

Inter-generational transfers can include inheritance, but also gifts or other forms of support from parents, grandparents, etc. Homeownership is just what it sounds like, and investment and savings decisions refer to personal savings, but also retirement accounts like IRA and 401K. With respect to any measure of "resources" that contribute to wealth, we find racial disparities.[1157]

[1156] Bhutta et al.

[1157] ibid.

	White	Black	Hispanic	Other
Received an Inheritance (Percent)	29.9	10.1	7.2	17.8
Conditional Median Inheritance (Thousands of 2019 dollars)	88.5	85.8	52.2	59.4
Expect an Inheritance (Percent)	17.1	6.0	4.2	14.7
Conditional Median Expected Inheritance (Thousands of 2019 dollars)	195.5	100.0	150.0	100.0
Could get $3,000 from family or friends (Percent)	71.9	40.9	57.8	63.4
Parent(s) have a College Degree (Percent)	34.4	24.8	15.2	40.0

Source: Federal Reserve Board, 2019 Survey of Consumer Finances.

Notes: Table displays inheritances and gifts received, expected inheritances, and other indicators of family support, by race and ethnicity, expressed in either Percent or Thousands of 2019 dollars. Parent(s) with a college degree refers to the parents of the reference person.

White people are more likely to receive an inheritance (which adds to wealth), receive more of an inheritance if they receive one, and are more likely to be able to receive financial assistance from friends or family if they need it. This can take the form of emergency (interest free) loans or outright gifts, down payments on cars or houses (or outright gifts of such things!), paying for college, etc.[1158]

Homeownership is both an *indicator* of wealth, since significant resources are usually needed for down payments and closing costs, as well as a *builder* of wealth due to the traditionally good rate of appreciation in home values over time. While home ownership increases by age for all races or ethnicities, the racial gap in home ownership persists across all age groups.

[1158] I personally know several white parents who purchased cars (an asset) for their children, paid for all their college, provided the down payment for their first home, or even purchased the "starter home" for their adult child, and allowed them to make interest free payments to them rather than paying off a loan to a bank (which would involve large amounts of interest).

Figure 3. Homeownership rises with age regardless of race or ethnicity, though there are significant differences in homeownership between White and non-White families throughout the life-cycle.

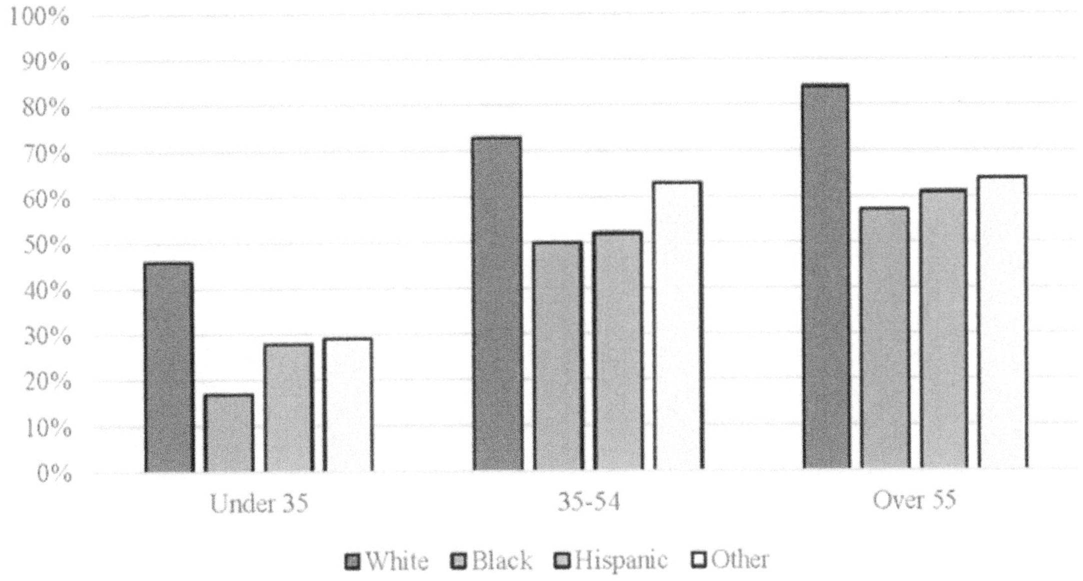

■White ■Black ■Hispanic □Other

Source: Federal Reserve Board, 2019 Survey of Consumer Finances.

Notes: Figure displays homeownership rates by age group and by race and ethnicity. Race categories are displayed in order from left to right.

We observe disparities not only in rates of ownership, but also in the average value of owned homes, with the average value of a white house being $230,000 and the average value of Black and Hispanic homes being $150,000 and $200,000 respectively.[1159] This difference in value produces a difference in wealth, of course, and is explainable in terms of differences in housing appreciation (due to white homes being more likely to be in "good" neighborhoods—which is itself a legacy of residential segregation), amount of down payments, and age of the home owner when purchased (which is later for people of color, allowing for less time to pay down the balance, and for the home to appreciate in value). In addition, homes can be costly to maintain, with inevitable expenses like roof replacement, water heater replacement, and pipe repair. For families with little savings or liquid assets, such repairs have to be either postponed or purchased with debt—which reduces family wealth either through added debt or decline in home value. We also see similar disparities in the possession of retirement accounts, which are another source of wealth.

[1159] Bhutta et al. We will focus more on home ownership later.

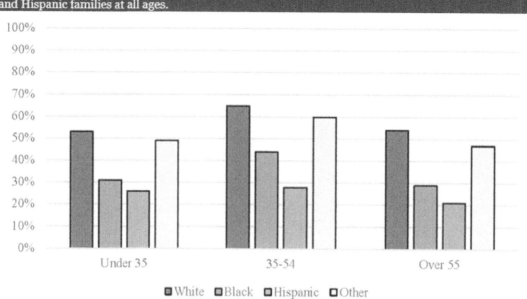

Figure 4. Retirement account ownership peaks at middle age, though ownership is less likely for Black and Hispanic families at all ages.

Source: Federal Reserve Board, 2019 Survey of Consumer Finances.

Notes: Figure displays the percent of families that own a retirement account (IRA or DC plan) with a net positive balance by age group and by race and ethnicity. Race categories are displayed in order from left to right.

Not only are there disparities in participation in retire accounts, but there are also predictable disparities in the *amount* contributed. Among those who have retirement accounts in the first place, the typical White family has about $50,000 saved, compared to $20,000 for typical Black or Hispanic families.

Difference in balances likely reflect a combination of factors including differences in returns from the funds that contributions are invested in, differences families' lifetime contributions to retirement accounts, and differences in employer matching to [defined contribution] plans. For example, the differences in access to employer-sponsored plans . . . imply that fewer Black or Hispanic families are eligible for a plan with an employer match.[1160]

Please note that these measures are objective. We are dealing with facts. There is room for debate as to how best to *interpret* these

facts, but it remains an indisputable **fact** that white households, on average, have much greater wealth, and are advantaged with respect to all those things correlating with and contributing to wealth, such as home ownership and retirement savings. It might not be obvious why these matters, but it *does*, and here is why:

All of this matters because wealth confers benefits that go beyond those that come with family income. Wealth is a safety net that keeps a life from being derailed by temporary setbacks and the loss of income. This safety net allows people to take career risks knowing that they have a buffer when success is not immediately achieved. Family wealth allows people (especially young adults who have recently entered the labor force) to access housing in safe neighborhoods with good schools, thereby enhancing the prospects of their own children. Wealth affords people opportunities to be

---

[1160] ibid.

entrepreneurs and inventors. And the income from wealth is taxed at much lower rates than income from work, which means that wealth begets more wealth.[1161]

In other words, wealth isn't valuable and valued simply for its own sake, but also because of what wealth does, the doors that it opens, the safety and security it provides, the options it makes available, etc. When families have wealth, they are better able to afford higher education (which increases wealth even more) and to do so with less debt; they are better able to purchase a home (which increases wealth), and in "better" neighborhoods—which grants access to "better" schools, which in turn makes it more likely that children will go to college, and have access to "better" colleges, which increases wealth, etc.

One stark (and scary) example of the wealth gap between Black and white homes is found in access to "liquid" assets. A liquid asset is something like money in a savings or checking account. It can be used immediately, as needed. Non-liquid assets are things like houses, cars, stocks and bonds, retirement accounts, etc. They have to be "liquidated" by selling them or cashing them out (sometimes with significant penalties) before they can provide ready-to-use money. Liquid assets are very important to have in the event of some sort of financial crisis, such as a medical expense, car problems, or other unexpected expense. When it comes to liquid assets available in a crisis, there is a huge gap between white and Black households, with most Black families having *no more than $25* in non-retirement liquid wealth, whereas white families typically have over 100 times that amount ($3,000).[1162] A typical Black household has $25 for emergencies. Obviously, any unexpected expense is unlikely to be covered by $25, so such households are likely to acquire debt—which further diminishes their wealth.

FIGURE 1

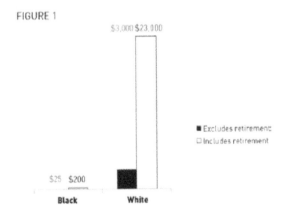

Blacks Have Virtually No Wealth to Draw Upon in Times of Financial Crisis

Liquid wealth by race, SIPP 2011

[1161] https://www.brookings.edu/blog/up-front/2020/02/27/examining-the-black-white-wealth-gap/

[1162] https://gallery.mailchimp.com/bf2b9b3cf3fdd8861943fca2f/files/Umbrellas_Dont_Make_It_Rain8.pdf, p. 5

The wealth gap having been established, what is the best explanation for it? As mentioned above, logically, the two available explanations are either that some degree of systemic racism produces these disparities, or else it is the fault of the people themselves (e.g., people of color don't work as hard, value education less, etc.)

Right away, we can begin to dismiss "personal" explanations for these group disparities. With respect to education, Black families whose heads graduated from college have about 33 percent *less* wealth than white families whose heads dropped out of high school.[1163] You read that correctly. A white family where the head of household dropped out of high school still has 33% *more* wealth than a Black family where the head of household has a college

degree. White families whose head completed some college (such as an AA degree from a college like Rio Hondo), but did not earn a four-year degree, still have slightly *more* wealth than black families with a head that earned a graduate or professional degree.[1164] A graduate or professional degree would be an M.A. or M.S., a Ph.D., a J.D., an M.B.A, an M.D., etc. That means that, on average, a white family whose head of household earned an AA degree still has more wealth than a Black family headed by a medical doctor, lawyer, professor, etc. To put it bluntly, when it comes to the Black/white race gap in wealth, education simply can't explain the difference. Even when a Black household is headed by someone with an advanced degree, that *still* can't compensate for the racial gap.

FIGURE 2

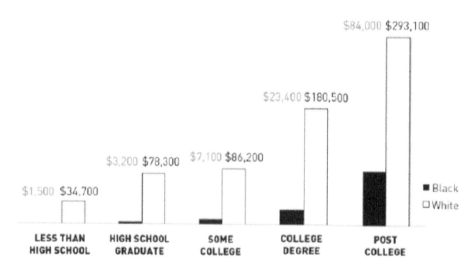

Education is not the Great Equalizer

Median wealth by educational level and race, SIPP 2011

In fact, the relationship between education and wealth is even worse than has been presented thus far. College education is seen as a wealth builder, and this is generally true, but

(unfortunately) with the usual racial disclaimers. White college graduates do generally increase their wealth, but black college graduates can actually see a *decrease* in their wealth. Why?

[1163] ibid., 3.

[1164] ibid., 5.

Because of differences in peer groups and family networks.

One possible explanation for this non-intuitive finding lies in studies showing that extended kin networks are important avenues for wealth transmission in the Black community; that is, Blacks who have "made it" into the middle class are still tied to family members struggling to get by and provide loans and other monetary support to them (Chiteji and Hamilton, 2005). O'Brien (2012) tested this hypothesis and found that middle- class Blacks are indeed more likely to provide informal financial assistance to extended networks, depleting their own wealth accumulation capacity through "negative social capital"....

White college-educated household were significantly more likely to report having received financial support from their parents in 2012. The average transfer received was three times higher at the mean and twice as high at the median than that reported by Black college educated households. Further, these White households were close to twice as likely to have received financial assistance from their parents for education and more than three times as likely for purchasing a home. White college-educated parents were also significantly more likely to financially support adult children's education and home purchase. Not only were these white parents more likely to provide financial assistance to their young adult children, they also were able to give significantly higher amounts. Most notable is the difference for college payments. These White parents contributed close to $73,500, on average, to their children's education, compared with just over $16,000 that Black college-educated parents were able to provide. While such financial gaps may be filled by scholarships, some will also require student loans, launching students on very different economic trajectories into adulthood.

The trends of providing family financial support largely reverse on payments to parents. Proportionately, close to three times as many college-educated Black households than White college-educated houses provided financial support to their parents. Those White households that did support their parents, however, provided more money on average than the Black households did: $1,800 versus $1,200.

In sum, White college-educated households are significantly more likely to receive financial transfers from their parents, whereas Black college-educated households are significantly more likely to provide financial support to their parents.[1165]

Black college graduates are more likely to be the most successful person in their family network, compared to white graduates who are likely to be roughly equally successful as their family network members. This is due simply to higher percentages of white people graduating with college degrees, pre-existing racial disparities in wealth, etc. This means that Black graduates are more likely to be asked for financial assistance, and to give it. This is not a wealth building transfer usually (such as helping someone buy a home or funding college education), but a stopgap measure against financial needs. This doesn't create wealth in the person receiving the financial assistance but reduces wealth for the black college graduate.

If educational differences can't explain the wealth gap, what about work? Maybe people of color have less wealth because they're less likely to work than white people? While there are racial disparities in unemployment rates (which are themselves best explained by systemic racism), the wealth gap persists regardless of work status. White families with a head that is *unemployed* have nearly *twice* the median wealth of Black families with a head that is *working full-time* ($21,892 versus $11,649).[1166]

[1165] "Family Achievements?": How a College Degree Accumulates Wealth for Whites and Not for Blacks Tatjana Meschede, Joanna Taylor, Alexis Mann, and Thomas Shapiro Federal Reserve Bank of St. Louis Review, First Quarter

2017, 99(1), pp. 125-131.
[1166] https://gallery.mailchimp.com/bf2b9b3cf3fdd8861943fca2f/files/Umbrellas_Dont_Make_It_Rain8.pdf, 6-7.

FIGURE 3

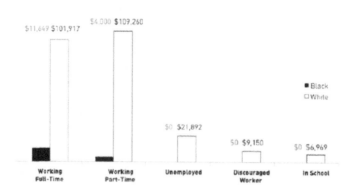

Employment is Not the Great Equalizer

Median wealth by employment/labor force status and race, SIPP 2011

So, maybe the wealth gap is explained by the *kind* of work people do, and the compensation they receive for it? Maybe Black people generally work at lower paying jobs? If so, that should raise some serious questions as well! What accounts for that wage gap? But, as it turns out, we don't need to address that question for our purposes because the wealth gap persists even when incomes are the same. At the "bottom" of the socio-economic ladder we see disparities. The typical Black family in the poorest 20 percent of

the income distribution (i.e., incomes under $18,480 annually) has almost no wealth at all, while a similar white family has nearly $15,000 in wealth—which is actually a higher median wealth than middle-income Blacks with incomes ranging between $36,000 and $54,000! This trend continues as we go up income, with white households making more than $93,000 each year having more than double the family wealth of Black families with the same income.[1167]

FIGURE 4

Family Income is Not the Great Equalizer

Median wealth by income quintiles and race , SIPP 2011

Maybe people of color just don't manage their money as well? Perhaps they spend more on

consumer products, and *that* produces disproportionate debt and a corresponding

---

[1167] ibid., 7.

disparity in wealth? Maybe, but it doesn't appear to be a good explanation for the wealth gap, since white people spend more on virtually *everything*, including alcohol and tobacco—with the notable exception for "apparel and services," for which Black and Asian people spend slightly more.[1168] One possible explanation for part of that, if necessary, is the expensive maintenance required for Black hair—particular when Black persons are discriminated against in schools or work places if they have "natural" hairstyles. But, even if Black people *do* spend conspicuously more on apparel and related services, that alone couldn't possibly account for the vast differences observed in family wealth up and down the socio-economic scale, and down through the generations.

Characteristic	White and all other races	Asian	Black
Housing	21012.00	24694.00	17176.00
Transportation	11070.00	11378.00	8509.00
Food	8425.00	9620.00	5983.00
Personal insurance and pensions	7347.00	10407.00	4894.00
Healthcare	5521.00	4700.00	3354.00
Entertainment	3335.00	3101.00	1548.00
Cash contributions*	2123.00	2207.00	1139.00
Apparel and services	1864.00	1968.00	1971.00
Education	1442.00	3085.00	862.00
Miscellaneous**	951.00	924.00	568.00
Personal care products and services	798.00	738.00	727.00
Alcoholic beverages	647.00	400.00	213.00
Tobacco products and smoking supplies	345.00	133.00	232.00

Maybe Black people spend conspicuously more money on drugs, compared to white people? That's not true either. Despite much higher arrest and incarceration rates for drug offenses, Black drug usage rates are, on average, actually *less* than white drug usage

---

[1168] https://www.statista.com/statistics/694716/consumer-expenditure-by-race-us/

FIGURE 6A.

Rates of Drug Use and Sales, by Race

FIGURE 6B.

Rates of Drug-Related Criminal Justice Measures, by Race

At the state level, blacks are about 6.5 times as likely as whites to be incarcerated for drug-related crimes.

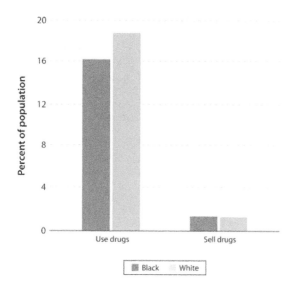

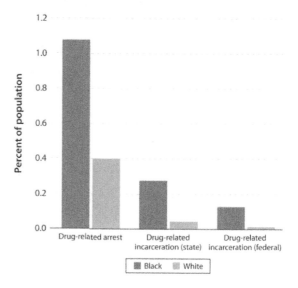

Source: BLS n.d.c; Carson 2015; Census Bureau n.d.; FBI 2015; authors' calculations.

We could continue to seek for some way to blame the individuals for group disparities, in increasingly desperate ways, but the much more plausible explanation is that systemic racism has something to do with the observed differences. Using just one example, the relationship between home ownership and the wealth gap between Black and white families in America, we can see how an honest understanding of history provides the answers.

In the earliest stages of the history of what would become the United States, there was a tremendous property disparity between Black and white persons given that so many Black persons were themselves considered "property!" Indeed, by 1863, enslaved persons were worth $3 billion (adjusted to 2018 dollars).[1169]

[1169] Explained: The Racial Wealth Gap. Episode aired May 23, 2018. Full episode is available here: https://www.youtube.com/watch?v=Mqrhn8khGLM.

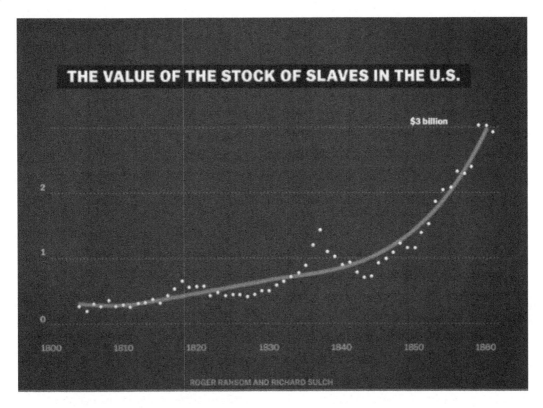

THE VALUE OF THE STOCK OF SLAVES IN THE U.S.

$3 billion

ROGER RANSOM AND RICHARD SULCH

At the end of the Civil War, enslaved Black persons were liberated, and plans were made under Special Field Order 15 to provide freed slaves not more than 40 acres of land, setting aside hundreds of thousands of acres of land in the South.[1170] President Lincoln signed a bill making the plan official, was assassinated a few weeks later, and was succeeded by Andrew Johnson – a notorious racist – who suspended order 15 and returned the appropriated land to the previous white (Confederate) owners. The wealth created by enslaved Black persons for their white owners for 246 years was retained by those white owners, however—cementing the racial wealth gap that persists to this day.

From 1619-1865, Black people were considered property. From 1865-1968, discrimination against Black persons was *legal*, preventing wealth building for people of color in general, and Black people specifically, in a variety of ways, including employment discrimination, education discrimination, and home ownership. For our purposes, we will focus specifically on home ownership.

Home ownership is essential for wealth building for middle class families, or for working class families to rise to the middle class. Home equity accounts for a full two thirds of the wealth of middle-class families.[1171]

[1170] https://www.georgiaencyclopedia.org/articles/history-archaeology/shermans-field-

order-no-15
[1171] Explained: The Racial Wealth Gap.

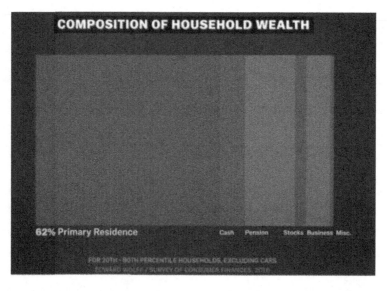

Access to home ownership, then, greatly contributes to wealth, while barriers to home ownership make wealth accumulation virtually impossible. From the birth of the United States all the way until 1968, it was both common and *legal* to discriminate on the basis of race with respect to home buying, and home loans. While home ownership was not always easily accessible for anyone, especially after the Great Depression, government efforts to promote ownership were not extended equally to people of color. Part of Franklin Delano Roosevelt's New Deal was to provide federally insured mortgages to make it easier for people to acquire home loans. The Federal Housing Administration (FHA), however, did not insure homes equally with respect to race. People of color were seen as a threat to property values, because of racism, so communities with any significant number of people of color were "redlined" and considered ineligible for insured loans, not only denying access to loans to such persons, but depressing home values in those areas as well.[1172]

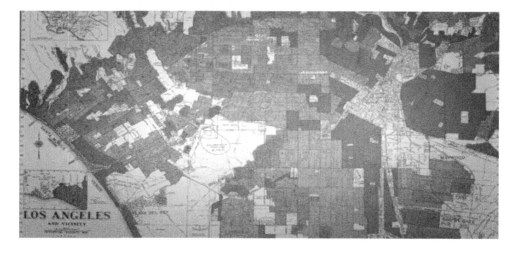

[1172] ibid.

Conjoin this overt discrimination with other (legal) discrimination in education and employment, and there is nothing surprising about the persistence of the wealth gap from slavery through most of the 20th century. Discrimination in housing wasn't outlawed until 1968 by the Fair Housing Act.[1173] Subtler forms of discrimination still took place (and take place) of course, but at least overt discrimination was no longer legally permissible. Nevertheless, centuries of damage had already been dead, resulting in a significant home ownership gap by that time.[1174]

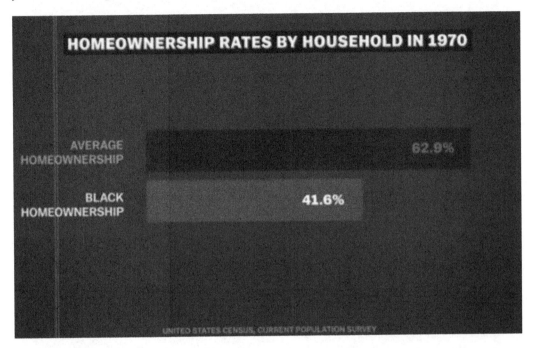

In the 1990s, banks saw an opportunity to "help" (and to increase their own profits) by providing more accessible loans in the form of "subprime mortgages."

'Subprime' refers to the below-average credit score of the individual taking out the mortgage, indicating that they might be a credit risk. The interest rate associated with a subprime mortgage is usually high to compensate lenders for taking the risk that the borrower will default on the loan. These borrowers typically have credit scores below 640 along with other negative information in their credit reports.[1175]

In theory, the existence of subprime mortgages seems like a means to facilitate home ownership for people who would otherwise struggle to qualify for a loan, particularly since they could be obtained without a down payment. However, in actual practice, the issuing of these loans was both predatory and racially biased. Black people were twice as likely to be offered such loans versus white applicants. Despite the fact that subprime mortgages were specifically intended for low-credit applicants, 20% of Black applicants with *good* credit scores were steered into subprime loans.[1176]

[1173] https://www.hud.gov/program_offices/ fair_housing_equal_opp/aboutfheo/history
[1174] Explained: The Racial Wealth Gap.

[1175] https://www.investopedia.com/terms/s/ subprime_mortgage.asp
[1176] Explained: The Racial Wealth Gap.

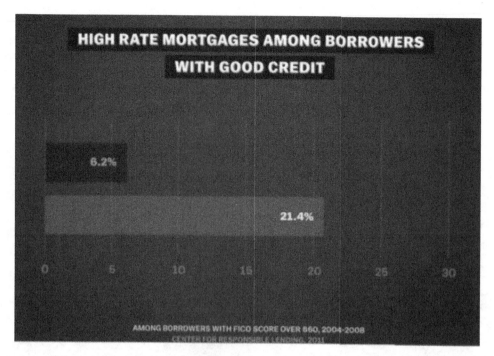

Despite having equally good credit scores as white applicants, 1/5 of Black applicants were still deemed "risky," and offered only subprime mortgages. In addition, subprime mortgages were offered to applicants who genuinely could not afford the homes they were buying—especially given the fact that such loans became increasingly expensive over time, as their interest rates increased.

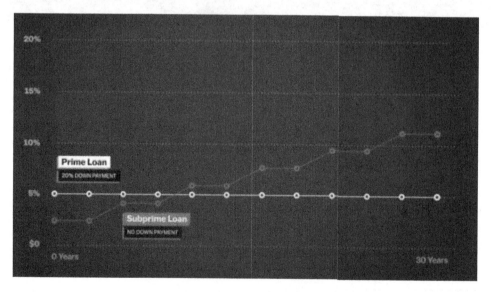

The combination of unqualified borrowers, and the Great Recession and financial crisis of 2008, caused the housing market to collapse. Although the banks themselves received a "bail out," many individual homeowners lost their homes and their wealth—but not equally, with

Black families losing 53% of their wealth compared to 13% for white families. Wells Fargo, as just one example, settled a suit filed by the Justice Department, and was forced to pay $175 million because Black and Hispanic borrowers who qualified for loans were charged higher fees, or rates, or were improperly placed into subprime loans.[1177] That happened in 2012. Not exactly ancient history—but this just this *one* example does show the importance of knowing our history. When people complain about systemic racism, they are not refusing to "let go" of slavery, as is sometimes claimed. Systemic racism was most obvious in the institution of slavery, but continues to this day in various forms, even just with respect to home ownership. Given the essential relationship between home ownership and wealth for middle class families, systemic racism is clearly implicated in the racial wealth gap.

The Criminal Justice System

The use of evidence of disparate impact goes far beyond wealth gaps and employment discrimination cases. As mentioned earlier, there is evidence of racial disparities in education, healthcare, wealth, housing, and numerous other sectors of our society. This section will focus on disparities within the criminal justice system. The Criminal Justice System (hereafter, the CJS) refers to the *entire* system concerning laws, policing, prosecution, trial, sentencing, and punishment. It includes three major components:

1. Law Enforcement
2. Courts
3. Corrections

There is evidence of racial bias (including implicit bias) and discrimination (including disparate impact) in all 3 components. According to The Sentencing Project's "Report of The Sentencing Project to the United Nations Special

Rapporteur on Contemporary Forms of Racism, Racial Discrimination, Xenophobia, and Related Intolerance: Regarding Racial Disparities in the United States Criminal Justice System:" [1178]

- African Americans are more likely than white Americans to be arrested.
- Once arrested, they are more likely to be convicted.
- Once convicted, and they are more likely to experience lengthy prison sentences.
- African-American adults are 5.9 times as likely to be incarcerated than whites.
- Hispanics are 3.1 times as likely to be incarcerated than whites.
- As of 2001, one of every three black boys born in that year could expect to go to prison in his lifetime, as could one of every six Latinos—compared to one of every seventeen white boys.
- Racial and ethnic disparities among women are less substantial than among men but remain prevalent.

Those were just general examples. We will now delve a bit deeper into each of the three components of the CJS, one at a time.

Law Enforcement

Law enforcement refers, primarily, to the police. For our purposes, we will focus *only* on implicit bias and/or disparate impact cases (not explicit, conscious racism). First, some data. In 2016, Black Americans comprised 27% of all individuals arrested in the United States—double their share of the total population. Black youth accounted for 15% of all U.S. children, yet accounted for 35% of juvenile arrests in that year.

Clearly, there is some "disparate impact" at work here. One possible explanation is that there is an unfortunate correlation between race and criminal behavior. But, the trends are better explained as a correlation between *urban poverty*

[1177] https://www.justice.gov/opa/pr/justice-department-reaches-settlement-wells-fargo-resulting-more-175-million-relief

[1178] https://www.sentencingproject.org/publications/un-report-on-racial-disparities/ All data in this section comes from this source, unless otherwise indicated.

and crime (and poverty shows racially disparate outcomes as well).

Similarly, more than one in four people arrested for drug law violations in 2015 was Black, although drug use rates do not differ substantially by race and ethnicity and drug users generally purchase drugs from people of the same race or ethnicity. As a specific example, the ACLU found that Blacks were 3.7 times more likely to be arrested for marijuana possession than whites in 2010, even though their rate of marijuana usage was comparable.

If drug usage rates do not differ substantially by race, what accounts for the higher arrest rates of Black people? Simply put, there are disproportionate levels of "police contact" with African Americans. Police are "efficiently" deployed to "higher crime risk" neighborhoods, resulting in more police contact with people of color, and therefore disproportionate stop and arrest rates.[1179] New York City, in particular, employed two policies that exemplified this tactic.

The "stop and frisk" program broadly targeted male residents of neighborhoods populated by low-income people of color to uncover drugs and weapons. It was shown to be ineffective, and this assessment was further validated when New York City continued its crime *decline* after scaling *back* Stop and Frisk.

The "Broken Windows Policing" is a public safety approach that relies on clamping down on petty offenses and neighborhood disorder. Between 2001 and 2013, 51% of the city's population over age 16 was Black or Hispanic. During that period, 82% of those arrested for misdemeanors were Black or Hispanic, as were 81% of those who received summonses for violations of the administrative code (including such behaviors as public consumption of alcohol, disorderly conduct, and bicycling on the sidewalk.). Research shows that order-maintenance strategies have had only a modest

impact on serious crime rates, but cause damage to communities of color, and expose people of color to a greater risk of being killed during a police encounter.

In general, police are more likely to stop Black and Hispanic drivers for discretionary reasons—for "investigatory stops" (proactive stops used to investigate drivers deemed suspicious) rather than "traffic-safety stops" (reactive stops used to enforce traffic laws or vehicle codes). Once pulled over, Black and Hispanic drivers were three times as likely as whites to be searched (6% and 7% versus 2%). Even though police officers generally actually have a lower "contraband hit rate" when they search Black versus white drivers, Blacks were twice as likely as whites to be arrested.

The Courts

Having been arrested, one will likely find themselves eventually inside a courtroom. The Courts includes all the policies of, and participants in, the prosecution and trial phase of someone's interaction with the CJS. This includes prosecutors, defense attorneys, jurors, and judges. Again, focusing *only* on implicit bias and/or disparate impact cases (not explicit, conscious racism), we find disparate impact at every stage in the Court process.

Once someone is arrested and charged with a crime, they are in the "pretrial" phase. Pretrial detention has been shown to increase the odds of conviction, and people who are detained awaiting trial are also more likely to accept less favorable plea deals, to be sentenced to prison, and to receive longer sentences. Seventy percent of pretrial releases require money bond. Low-income defendants, who are disproportionately people of color, are less able to make bond. Blacks and Latinos are more likely than whites to be denied bail, to have a higher money bond set, and to be detained because they cannot pay their bond.[1180] Persons of color are often assessed to be

---

[1179] The racially disparate persecution and prosecution of racial minorities, and Black people in particular, is thoroughly documented by Michelle Alexander in *The New Jim Crow*, The

New Press, 2020.

[1180] In 2020, CA Prop 25 would have eliminated cash bail, but was voted against (56%).

higher safety and flight risks because they are more likely to experience socioeconomic disadvantage and to have criminal records. Implicit bias also contributes to people of color faring worse than comparable whites in bail determinations.

When a defendant goes on trial, it will matter tremendously to them with what crimes they are charged. Prosecutors are more likely to charge people of color with crimes that carry heavier sentences than whites. Federal prosecutors are twice as likely to charge African Americans with offenses that carry a mandatory minimum sentence than similarly situated whites. State prosecutors are also more likely to charge Black rather than similar white defendants under habitual offender laws.

Setting aside the discrimination, whether conscious or implicit, that may occur *during* the trial, once someone has been convicted even more disparities emerge at the sentencing stage. Although Blacks and Latinos comprise 29% of the U.S. population, they make up 57% of the U.S. prison population. This results in imprisonment rates for Black and Hispanic adults that are 5.9 and 3.1 times the rate for white adults, respectively—and at far higher levels in some states. Of the 277,000 people imprisoned nationwide for a drug offense, over half (56%) are Black or Latino. Nearly half (48%) of the 206,000 people serving life and "virtual life" prison sentences are Black and another 15% are Latino. Among youth, Blacks are 4.1 times as likely to be committed to secure placements as whites, American Indians are 3.1 times as likely, and Hispanics are 1.5 times as likely.

Contributing to these disparities in sentencing are a number of seemingly "race-neutral" policies. Drug-free school zone laws mandate sentencing enhancements for people caught selling drugs in designated school zones. These disproportionately affect residents of urban areas, and particularly those in high-poverty areas – who are largely people of color. As an example, legislators in New Jersey scaled back their state law after a study found that 96% of persons subject to these enhancements were Black or Latino.

As another example, most jurisdictions inadequately fund their public defender programs. Many low-income persons are represented by public defenders with excessively high caseloads, or by assigned counsel with limited experience in criminal defense. Because poverty is disproportionately correlated with race, this means that more people of color rely on these public defenders.

After running the gauntlet of disparities in police contact, prosecution, and sentencing, there are further disparities at the corrections phase.

Corrections

Corrections includes all employees of prisons, as well as parole board members, probation officers, and parole officers. Focusing *only* on implicit bias and/or disparate impact cases (not explicit, conscious racism), we know that parole boards are subject to implicit bias (just like anyone). Based on an analysis of almost 60,000 disciplinary cases from New York state prisons, reporters found that disparities in discipline were greatest for infractions that gave discretion to guards, such as disobeying a direct order. In-prison conduct records are a major determinant of parole decisions.

Once paroled, parole and probation officers are more likely to revoke probation from people of color than whites for comparable behavior. The Urban Institute's examination of probation revocation rates in Dallas County, Texas; Iowa's Sixth Judicial District; Multnomah County, Oregon; and New York City revealed that black probationers were revoked at disproportionate rates in all study sites.

Even if a person of color, convicted of a crime and released on parole, manages to evade all of the higher probability of being sent back to prison, they face a shocking variety of obstacles that prevent them from successfully reintegrating into society.

To begin with the most basic need, convicts face *legal* discrimination when it comes to housing. People with criminal convictions face discrimination in the private rental market and those with felony drug convictions face restrictions in accessing government-assisted housing. Of course, to afford to pay rent, convicted persons will need to find a job.

With respect to employment, nearly one-third of U.S. workers hold jobs that require an occupational license, a requirement which sometimes bars and often poses cumbersome obstacles for people with criminal records. In sectors that do not require licensing, employers are 50% less likely to call back *white* job applicants with incarceration histories than comparable applicants without prison records. Black job applicants, who are less likely to receive callbacks than whites to begin with, experience an even *more* pronounced discrimination related to a criminal record. Whites *with* criminal records receive more favorable treatment than Blacks *without* criminal records.

For those struggling to find a job, the social safety net offers little assistance. The Welfare Reform Act of 1996 imposed a lifetime denial of cash assistance and food stamps to people convicted in State or Federal courts of felony drug offenses, unless States opt out of the ban. By 2018, 24 States had fully opted out of the food stamp ban, 21 others had only done so in part, and five States continued to fully enforce the ban. An even larger number of States continue to impose a partial or full ban on cash assistance for people with felony drug convictions.

For people with criminal records who find themselves frustrated by all of these policies, and who would seek to use the political process to try to change them, they face yet another obstacle: there's a good chance they're not allowed to vote.

6.1 million Americans were forbidden from voting because of their felony record in 2016. Felony disenfranchisement rates for voting age Blacks reached 7.4% in 2016—four times the rate of non-Blacks (1.8%). In three States, more than one in five voting-age Blacks is disenfranchised: Florida, Kentucky, and Tennessee. The majority of disenfranchised Americans are living in their communities, having fully completed their sentences or remaining supervised while on probation or parole.

For anyone troubled by these statistics or these policies, The Sentencing Project has a number of recommendations for how to reduce these disparities.

First of all, they recommend ending the "war on drugs." Nearly 80% of people in Federal prison and almost 60% of people in State prison for drug offenses are Black or Latino.

In addition, they recommend the elimination of "mandatory minimum" sentences. Research shows that prosecutors are twice as likely to pursue a mandatory minimum sentence for Black people as for white people charged with the same offense. Among people who received a mandatory minimum sentence in 2011, 38% were Latino and 31% were Black. Mandatory minimum sentencing does not eliminate discretion in the courtroom, but only shifts it from judges to prosecutors, reducing transparency in decision making.

Prior to sentencing, during the trial phase, they recommend increased funding for public defenders, and the development and implementation of racial bias training. At the pretrial phase, they recommend a reduction in the use of cash bail, and substituting a transparent risk-assessment instrument instead.

Finally, to address the "collateral consequences" of conviction after a person has been released, they recommend that government officials should revise policies that serve no public safety function but impose collateral consequences on people with criminal convictions—such as in the realms of voting, employment, education, housing, and in the social safety net—and encourage similar reforms in the private sector.

Critical Analysis

1. In your opinion, what are the strongest and most compelling points made by the philosopher or philosophers in this chapter? Why do you find those points to be convincing?

2. In your opinion, what are the weakest or least convincing points? Why? Can you anticipate any limitations or objections to their ideas not already addressed in the chapter?

Appendix: Application to Social Justice

Awareness of the disparate impact of policies, laws, etc. on various populations provides a useful insight into some of the less obvious and sometimes "hidden" manifestations of discrimination in our society. However, as good philosophers and critical thinkers, we should be careful about what conclusions we draw on the basis of such data. First and foremost, we must keep in mind that demonstrations of disparate impact reveal *correlations*. When presented with a correlation, there are any number of available interpretations, and a causal relationship is only *one* of those possible interpretations.

> *All social scientists know the correlation does not imply causation. If A and B seem to be linked – that is, they changed together over time or are found together in a population at levels higher than chance would predict – then it is certainly possible that A caused B. But it's also possible that B caused A (reverse causation) or that a third variable, C, caused both A and B and there is no direct relationship between A and B. (It's also possible,... that it's a "spurious correlation" – that there is no link between A and B and the correlation is a coincidence.)*[1181]

When we observe "gaps" for certain groups of people in things like educational outcomes, healthcare outcomes, wages or income, home ownership, etc. what we are observing is an example of a correlation. Membership in that group correlates with a lower probability of being a homeowner (etc.). It is easy to infer that membership in that group *caused* that gap, and within the context of social justice, that is going to look suspiciously like discrimination and/or prejudice – and certainly sometimes that is an accurate inference. However, to be a good critical thinker requires that we consider other

possibilities, or even if discrimination/prejudice is the explanation, our understanding of the precise way in which that produced the outcome might be misinformed.

As an example, I have been personally present at multiple meetings or conversations in which the topic of "representation" in faculty has come up. The basic idea is both simple and compelling: racial and ethnic minorities have been and continue to be underrepresented among College and University faculty. This would be the example of an "outcome gap."

There is something valuable about students "seeing themselves" among the faculty. Therefore, Colleges and Universities should make a dedicated and intentional effort to increase their diversity. As matters of general principle, I absolutely agree with that.

When we get into specifics, however, things get more complicated. One of the specific proposals that I have heard made with respect to my own campus, and about representation on campuses in general, is that the demographics of the employees (specifically faculty and administration) should reflect or "mirror" that of the population we serve. This is an example of what Haidt refers to as "equal-outcomes social justice."

> *More generally, equal – outcomes of social justice activists seem to believe that all institutions and occupations should mirror the overall US population: 50% female, roughly 15% African-American, 15% Latino, and so on. Any departure from those numbers mean that a group is "underrepresented,"   and underrepresentation is often taken to be direct evidence of systemic bias or injustice.*[1182]

Before evaluating the merits of the claim that institutions should mirror the overall population, we need to look at some data, and, as is often the case from a philosophical perspective, it is useful

---

[1181] Haidt, Jonathan & Lukianoff, Greg. *The Coddling of the American Mind*. Penguin Books, 2019. Pp. 227-228.

[1182] ibid., 225.

to begin with some conceptual analysis.

The word "diversity" has a couple of meanings in usage. One meaning is the literal meaning, according to which "diversity" means something like "the practice or quality of including or involving people from a range of different social and ethnic backgrounds and of different genders, sexual orientations, etc." Another meaning of "diversity," undoubtedly evolving from the first meaning, within contexts where persons within institutions were majority white, is simply "non-white."

My campus is diverse in one sense, but not at all diverse in the other. The College is "diverse" if diversity just means *not* majority white. But if diversity refers to something like significant representation across a wide range of different racial and ethnic backgrounds (etc.), then my campus is *not* very diverse, because it is very much ethnically homogenous.

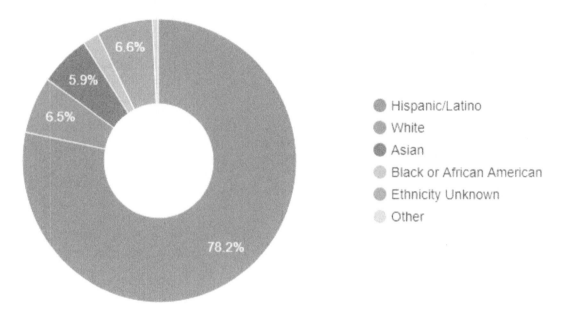

Nearly 80% of the students at my campus are classified as Hispanic/Latino. Asian students make up a little over 6%, white students a little under 6%, and Black students make up such a small percentage that their number doesn't even appear on the chart.[1183] One must look elsewhere to find that Black students are approximately 2% of the student population.[1184]

Already, something like an "equal-outcomes" approach to representation generates a question. Should the faculty mirror the U.S. population, or the population of the Rio Hondo College district? We will get very different goals according to which we select as our goal.

If the faculty should mirror the U.S. population, then 60.1% of our faculty should be white, 12.2% should be Black, 18.5% should be Latinx/Hispanic, 5.6% should be Asian, .7% should be American Indian, and .2% should be Native Hawaiian/API.[1185]

On the other hand, if we embrace the idea that faculty and administration demographics

---

[1183] https://www.Collegefactual.com/Colleges/rio-hondo-College/student-life/diversity/chart-ethnic-diversity.html

[1184] https://scorecard.cccco.edu/oneyear.aspx?CollegeID=881

[1185] https://www.kff.org/other/state-indicator/distribution-by-raceethnicity/?currentTimeframe=0&sortModel=%7B%22colId%22:%22Location%22,%22sort%22:%22asc%22%7D

should mirror that of the population we *serve* (i.e., our students) that would mean that the percentage of faculty/administrators of various racial and ethnic backgrounds (and genders) should mirror that of our student population. That would call for 6.5% of our faculty to be white, 2% to be Black, 78.2% to be Latinx/Hispanic, 5.9% to

be Asian, and, realistically, none should be American Indian or Native Hawaiian/API.

As should be obvious, we are presented with two very different goals depending on which population we attempt to mirror. In either case, the calls for more "diversity" in hiring implies that that mirroring is not occurring.

Although these claims of underrepresentation and the need for more diversity are being made at my own campus, my College actually ranks #21 out of 614 public Colleges or Universities in the United States with regard to diverse faculty.

Rank	Institution	Diversity index	Total full-time instructional faculty members	Nonresident alien	American Indian or Alaska Native
21	Rio Hondo College	65.6[1186]	200	0.50%	2.00%

Asian	Black	Hispanic	Native Hawaiian or Pacific Islander	White	2 or more races	Race unknown
11.70%	3.60%	36.20%	0.00%	44.40%	1.50%	2.00%

Out of 200 full-time professors, just under 11% are Asian, 3.6% are Black, 36.2% are Hispanic, and 44.4% are white. Another source has slightly different (though generally similar) numbers.[1187]

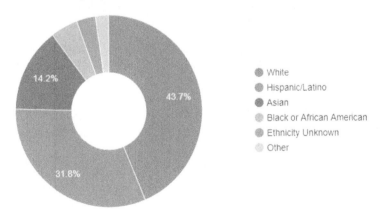

14.2%   43.7%   31.8%

- White
- Hispanic/Latino
- Asian
- Black or African American
- Ethnicity Unknown
- Other

[1186] The "diversity index" indicates on a scale of 1 to 100 the probability that any two full-time instructional faculty members at an institution are from different racial or ethnic groups.

[1187] https://www.Collegefactual.com/Colleges/rio-hondo-College/student-life/diversity/chart-faculty-ethnic-diversity.html

In a recent advertisement for a job in the human resources department posted by the College itself, it was advertised that "Río Hondo College employs approximately 55% tenured track faculty of color; 60% part-time faculty of color; 85% classified staff of color; and 50% administrators of color."[1188]

If we compare student and faculty representation, we get the following:

Race/Ethnicity	U.S. %	Student %	Faculty %
Asian	5.6	6	11
Black	12	2	3.6
Hispanic/Latino	18.5	80	36
White	60	6	44

If the goal is to have roughly equal percentages of faculty corresponding to the U.S. population, then we are "*over*-represented" in Latinx/Hispanic faculty by roughly 100%, and nearly equally "*over*-represented" in our Asian faculty. These numbers suggest we are significantly "*under*-represented," though, in Black and white faculty, and should triple our Black faculty and increase our white faculty by nearly 50%.

If the goal is to have roughly equal percentages of faculty corresponding to the student population, though, coming from our district community, then my campus clearly does not have enough Latinx/Hispanic faculty, and conversely has "too many" white faculty – but *also* "too many" Asian and Black faculty members. Setting aside the legality of the proposal, it would seem that a "hiring freeze" on anyone other than Latinx faculty members would be recommended—male faculty members, to be even more precise, as my campus has "too many" female faculty given our student population.

Gender[1189]	Student %[1190]	Faculty %[1191]
Male	56.8	47.6
Female	43.2	52.4

Setting aside the very important and even more contentious issue as to whether that policy is a *good* one (or legal one), we should consider what the disparities in faculty representation indicate. One interpretation is that, like many other examples of disparities, it is evidence of discrimination. But, if so, "where" and "when" is that discrimination taking place, and perpetrated by whom?

Consider the discipline of Philosophy, for example. While the numbers have been increasing over the past several years, in 2019, only 34.2% of philosophy Ph.D.'s were awarded to women.[1192] Departments will struggle to hire female philosophy professors if few or none *apply*. This indicates that the problem arises much earlier in the "pipeline," and if we are going to be accurate and strategic about addressing it, we need to focus on understanding why female students are less likely to major in philosophy,

---

[1188] (https://www.higheredjobs.com/admin/details.cfm?JobCode=177378521)

[1189] Note: no data is available for students or faculty who identify as non-binary, or anything other than male or female.

[1190] https://www.Collegefactual.com/Colleges/rio-hondo-College/student-life/diversity/chart-gender-diversity.html

[1191] https://www.Collegefactual.com/Colleges/rio-hondo-College/student-life/diversity/chart-faculty-gender-diversity.html

[1192] https://dailynous.com/2020/12/07/race-gender-u-s-philosophy-phds-trends-since-1973-guest-post/

and to pursue it at the graduate level, than to assume discrimination in hiring is occurring, and trying to address the problem at that stage. I propose that something similar is occurring with respect to race and ethnicity.

Much as people with philosophy graduate degrees are overwhelmingly male, they are overwhelmingly white. As of 2019, 81% of philosophy Ph.D.'s were awarded to white people. Hispanic or Latino students received only 6.5% of philosophy Ph.D.'s, with Asian students earning 5.4%, and Black students earning

approximately 4%. Disparities are much worse when we consider Native American students, who earned only .2% of philosophy Ph.D.'s in 2019.[1193]

It is important to point out that many of these numbers are *improvements*. While the percentage of Native American and Black Ph.D.'s has remained stable (and stagnant), the number of Ph.D.'s awarded to Asian and Hispanic/Latino students has actually significantly increased over the past couple decades.

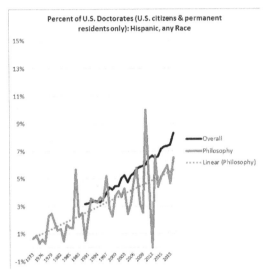

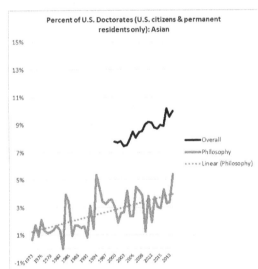

I propose that there are several possible explanations for a relative lack of diversity among College faculty in general (and certainly with respect to philosophy faculty), and that discrimination at the hiring stage (although some of that undoubtedly occurs at times), is not the obvious explanation, nor even the most plausible. Instead, there are recruitment and "pipeline" issues which, if the cause of the disparities, require different sorts of interventions. Trying to solve the lack of minority representation in our profession requires a combination of short term and long term efforts, with corresponding short and long term goals.

In the short term, intentional efforts to

increase outreach in communities underrepresented in our field might mean things like advertising job openings not only in the "usual" places, such as "Jobs for Philosophers" and at the Chronicle of Higher Education, but also places like the Facebook page for the Society of Young Black Philosophers (SYBP).[1194] I didn't even know that group existed until a Black colleague mentioned his membership in it—and if I was not aware of its existence, as a philosophy professor, it's unlikely that Human Resources staff members at my campus did, and were advertising jobs there. The American Philosophical Association has similar groups for philosophers of color, philosophes with

---

1193 ibid.

1194 https://www.facebook.com/groups/

SYBP2010 Society of Young Black Philosophers

disabilities, female philosophers, and philosophers who are Veterans—but membership to these groups requires membership in the APA, and this costs anywhere from $35 annually for Graduate students, to up to $500 annually depending on income. Setting aside the cost, not every philosopher or aspiring philosopher is a member. I let my own membership lapse over 15 years ago—and I only became a member when, as a graduate student, I was encouraged to do so by a faculty mentor. In the short-term, then, among the various interventions that might help would be active outreach to relevant Minority Serving Institutions (MSIs) known to have underrepresented populations, such as Historically Black Colleges and Universities (HBCUs), but also more "modern" efforts such as advertising in Facebook groups like the SYBP.

In the longer term, the "pipeline" issue needs to be addressed. Among the relevant things to consider is the "recruitment" stage during undergraduate years. We know that there are racial disparities in College enrollment and degree attainment, in general.[1195]

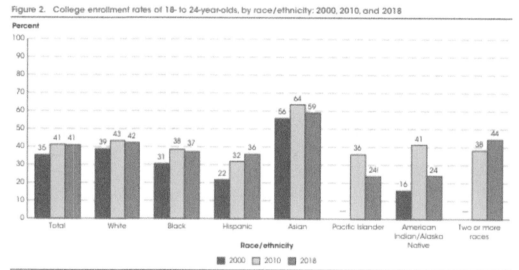

Figure 2. College enrollment rates of 18- to 24-year-olds, by race/ethnicity: 2000, 2010, and 2018

— Not available.
! Interpret data with caution. The coefficient of variation (CV) for this estimate is between 30 and 50 percent.
NOTE: Data are based on sample surveys of the civilian noninstitutionalized population. Separate data for 18- to 24-year-olds who were Pacific Islander and of Two or more races were not available in 2000. In 2000, respondents of Two or more races were required to select a single race category. Prior to 2003, data for Asian 18- to 24-year-olds include Pacific Islander 18- to 24-year-olds. Race categories exclude persons of Hispanic ethnicity. Although rounded numbers are displayed, the figures are based on unrounded data.
SOURCE: U.S. Department of Commerce, Census Bureau, Current Population Survey (CPS), October Supplement, 2000, 2010, and 2018. See Digest of Education Statistics 2019, table 302.60.

While College enrollment has been generally increasing for *nearly* all groups, we still see gaps. As of 2018, 59% of Asian American people age 18-24 were enrolling in college, versus 42% of white youths, 37% of Black youths, and 36% of Hispanic youths. There are even greater gaps when it comes to College completion *rates*.[1196]

[1195] https://nces.ed.gov/programs/coe/pdf/coe_cpb.pdf
[1196] https://edtrust.org/resource/graduation-rates-dont-tell-the-full-story-racial-gaps-in-college-success-are-larger-than-we-think/ Note: unfortunately, this study did not include completion rates for Asian-American students.

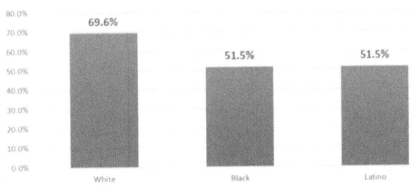

Figure 1: 6-year Graduation Rate by Race/Ethnicity

Note: The six-year graduation rates are for students who 1) started at a public or private, nonprofit four-year institution, 2) initially enrolled full time seeking to earn a bachelor's degree, and 3) and received federal loans in 2003/04.

Source: Authors' analysis of U.S. Department of Education, National Center for Education Statistics, 2003-04 Beginning Postsecondary Students Longitudinal Study, Second Follow-Up (BPS:04/09).

Nearly 70% of white students who enrolled in a 4 year College or University finish within six years, compared to roughly half of either Black or Latino students. So, Black and Latino students are less likely to enroll in College in the first place, and of those who do, they are less likely to finish their 4 year degree. Even this doesn't come close to telling the whole story, though. Now consider the respective rates of student loan default.[1197]

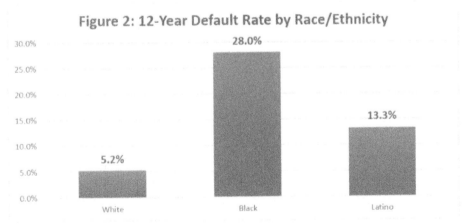

Figure 2: 12-Year Default Rate by Race/Ethnicity

Notes: The 12-year default rates are for graduates who 1) started and completed at a public or private, nonprofit four-year institution, 2) initially enrolled full time seeking to earn a bachelor's degree, and 3) and received federal loans in 2003/04.

Of those students who successfully earned their degree, Latino students are twice as likely as white students to be unable to pay back their student loans, and Black students are nearly six

---

[1197] ibid.

times more likely. These disparate default rates are likely caused by racial disparities in employment opportunities tied to students' majors, institutional reputation (selectivity), and the financial assistance students receive from family to pay back loans.[1198] The consequences of defaulting on a student loan are not trivial.

- The entire unpaid balance of your loan and any interest you owe becomes immediately due (this is called "acceleration").
- You can no longer receive deferment or forbearance, and you lose eligibility for other benefits, such as the ability to choose a repayment plan.
- You lose eligibility for additional federal student aid.
- The default is reported to credit bureaus, damaging your credit rating and affecting your ability to buy a car or house or to get a credit card.
- It may take years to reestablish a good credit record.
- You may not be able to purchase or sell assets such as real estate.
- Your tax refunds and federal benefit payments may be withheld and applied toward repayment of your defaulted loan (this is called "Treasury offset").
- Your wages may be garnished. This means your employer may be required to withhold a portion of your pay and send it to your loan holder to repay your defaulted loan.
- Your loan holder can take you to court.
- You may be charged court costs, collection fees, attorney's fees, and other costs associated with the collection process.
- Your school may withhold your academic transcript until your defaulted student loan is satisfied. The academic transcript is the property of the school, and it is the school's decision—not the

U.S. Department of Education's or your loan holder's—whether to release the transcript to you.[1199]

Why would we want to consider rates of loan default? Because although one measure of "success" for Colleges and Universities is the rate at which they dispense degrees, another, and perhaps more important measure, from a social justice perspective, is the rate at which they prepare students for success in life, including financial success. Looking at just the Black student population, slightly more than 1/3 enroll in College to begin with. Of those, roughly ½ finish. Of that "successful" ½, nearly 1/3 find themselves in financial situations such that they can't repay their student loans—and find themselves subject to all the debilitating consequences listed above.

This might seem like quite a tangent from our original consideration of racial disparities in faculty representation in academic departments! But, the degree to which we have explored further and deeper than might have been originally anticipated is part of the point. Consider just one (final) thing: the possible connection between loan default rates and racial disparities in employment opportunities tied to students' majors. If there is something accurate in this connection, it would also suggest that white privilege includes not only greater wealth and financial stability, but also the "privilege" of entertaining less "practical" majors!

Given that people of color are more likely to experience or come from poverty, it would be understandable if they pursued majors more likely to provide reliable income. It might be (literally) more "costly" for students of color to pursue majors like philosophy. If they believe that, they might understandably be less likely to pursue such majors. Or, perhaps more likely, if family members or College counselors believe that, they might actively discourage students of color from majoring in subjects like philosophy, and steer them towards "safer" and more

---

[1198] ibid.
[1199] https://studentaid.gov/manage-

loans/default

conventionally lucrative majors such as STEM. In either case, we would have racially disparate pursuits of a Bachelor's degree in philosophy, which would contribute to similar (if not greater) disparities in pursuit of a graduate degree in philosophy, which would contribute to a similar (if not greater) disparity in philosophy graduate degree-holders seeking employment as philosophy professors—which brings us back to our starting point. If *that* is the explanation, then to address it we need to address disparities in income and wealth *much* earlier in the pipeline.

In other words, disparities in outcomes, even when caused by discrimination, might be the effect of a discriminatory cause *much earlier in the causal chain* than might be apparent. Trying to solve the problem at the level of the faculty hiring committee might be completely ineffective, or at least far *less* effective than trying to solve the problem where it actually arises. Implicit bias training for search committee members might be a legitimately worthwhile exercise, but if the root cause of the outcome gap occurs much earlier in the pipeline, all the implicit bias training in the world won't produce the degree–holding candidates to apply for the jobs in the first place. Much work needs to be done to achieve equity in education and employment, but to do *effective* work requires careful and critical thinking.

Appendix/"Deeper Dive": The New Jim Crow

Comprehension questions you should be able to answer after reading this chapter:

1. What is the thesis of Michelle Alexander's *The New Jim Crow*?
2. What is the system of mass incarceration? What does it include?
3. What is a racial caste system?
4. What are the three historic racial caste systems observed in the United States, so far, according to Alexander?
5. For each of the 5 parts of the cyclical model explaining our system of mass incarceration, briefly explain each, and provide examples for each part.
   a. Disparate economic conditions
   b. Criminal behavior
   c. Biased policing
   d. Incarceration & criminal record
   e. Civil penalties
6. Why does the model portray a *recurring* cycle?
7. How does the current system of mass incarceration function as a racial caste system analogous to the previous Jim Crow system, according to Alexander?
8. How does the "war on drugs" fit into the cycle, and how does it promote the racial caste system?

Some of you might want to "dive deeper" into the ideas we started exploring in this chapter, and this appendix will help you do that. The focus of this appendix will be Michelle Alexander's *The New Jim Crow. Mass Incarceration in the Age of Colorblindness.* Alexander presents the thesis of her book in unambiguous, reader friendly terms.

This book argues that mass incarceration is, metaphorically, the New Jim Crow and that all those who care about social justice should fully commit themselves to dismantling this new racial caste system. Mass incarceration, not attacks on affirmative action or lax civil rights enforcement – is the most damaging manifestation of the backlash against the civil rights movement.[1200]

Breaking down her thesis, we will need to examine the concept of mass incarceration, determine what she means by a "racial caste system," and establish why the system of mass incarceration functions as the latest iteration of a racial caste system in the United States.

Mass incarceration

To begin with, mass incarceration is just what it sounds like. Lots of people are caught up in the criminal justice system in the United States. In fact, in the United States, 2.3 million people are in prison, a higher rate of incarceration than any other country in the world. Another million people are on probation or parole. Over 20% of the *entire* US population (seventy million people), the vast majority of whom are poor and disproportionately people of color, have criminal records and are subject to legal discrimination for the remainder of their life.[1201] The United States imprisons a larger percentage of its *Black* population than South Africa did during the height of apartheid.[1202]

Alexander's point is not merely that a lot of people are in prison or on probation or parole in the United States.[1203] Clearly, there is a racial component to the incarceration rates, and the disproportionately high number of Black and brown people imprisoned in the United States can be at least partially explained by how the United States has waged its "war on drugs." Alexander summarizes the system of mass incarceration in a helpful manner, and we will use

her summary to launch our examination of certain key elements.

This, in brief is how the system works: the war on drugs is a vehicle through which extraordinary numbers of black men are forced into the cage. The entrapment occurs in three distinct phases, each of which has been explored earlier, but a brief review is useful here. The first stage is the Roundup. Vast numbers of people are swept into the criminal justice system by the police, who conduct drug operations primarily in poor communities of color. They are rewarded in cash – through drug forfeiture laws and federal grant programs – rounding up as many people as possible, and they operate unconstrained by constitutional rules of procedure that once were considered inviolate. Police can stop, interrogate, and search anyone they choose for drug investigations, provided they get "consent." Because there is no meaningful check on the exercise of police discretion, racial biases are granted free rein. In fact, police are allowed to rely on race as a factor in selecting whom to stop and search (even though people of color are no more likely to be guilty of drug crimes than whites) – effectively guaranteeing that those who are swept into the system are primarily black and brown.

The conviction marks the beginning of the second phase: the period of formal control. Once arrested, defendants are generally denied meaningful legal representation and pressured to plead guilty whether they are or not. Prosecutors are free to "load

---

[1200] Alexander, Michelle. *The New Jim Crow. Mass Incarceration in the Age of Colorblindness.* Tenth Anniversary Edition. New York: The New Press, 2020, 14.

[1201] ibid., xxix.

[1202] ibid., 8.

[1203] A period of probation is generally either part

of the original sentence, or served instead of a period of incarceration. Parole, in contrast, is an effective reduction in time served in prison that may be granted at the recommendation of a parole board. For more detailed distinctions, see this summary: https://www.bjs.gov/index.cfm?ty=qa&iid=324

up" defendants with extra charges, and their decisions cannot be challenged for racial bias. Once convicted, due to the drug wars harsh sentencing laws, people convicted of drug offenses in the United States spend more time under the criminal justice systems formal control – in jail or prison, on probation or parole – than people anywhere else in the world. While under formal control, virtually every aspect of one's life is regulated and monitored by the system, and any form of resistance or disobedience is subject to sanction. This period of control may last a lifetime, even for those convicted of extremely minor, nonviolent offenses, but the vast majority of those swept into the system are eventually released. They are transferred from their prison cells to a much larger, invisible cage.

The final stage has been dubbed by some advocates as the "period of invisible punishment." This term, first coined by Jeremy Travis, is meant to describe the unique set of criminal sanctions that are imposed on individuals after they step outside the prison gates, a form of punishment that operates largely outside of public view and takes effect outside the traditional sentencing framework. These sanctions are imposed by operation of law rather than decisions of the sentencing judge, yet they often have a greater impact on one's life course than the months or years one actually stands behind bars. These laws operate collectively to ensure that the vast majority of people convicted of crimes will never integrate into mainstream, white society. They will be discriminated against, legally, for the rest of their lives – denied employment, housing, education, and public benefits. Unable to surmount these obstacles, most will eventually return to prison and then be released again, caught in a closed circuit of perpetual marginality.[1204]

With a general understanding of what is meant by mass incarceration, we can now turn to the concept of a "racial caste system," and see how the system of mass incarceration functions as one, before examining concepts in greater detail, one at a time.

I use the term racial caste in this book the way it is used in common parlance to denote a stigmatized racial group locked into an inferior position by law and custom. Jim Crow and slavery were caste systems. So is our current system of mass incarceration. It may be helpful, in attempting to understand the basic nature of the new caste system, to think the criminal justice system – the entire collection of institutions and practices that comprise it – not as an independent system but rather as a gateway into a much larger system of racial stigmatization and permanent marginalization. This larger system, referred to here as mass incarceration, is a system that locks people not only behind actual bars and actual prisons, but also behind virtual bars and virtual walls – walls that are invisible to the naked eye but function nearly as effectively as Jim Crow laws once did locking people of color into a permanent second class citizenship. The term mass incarceration refers not only to the criminal justice system but also to the larger web of laws, rules, policies, and customs that control those labeled criminals both in and out of prison. Once released from prison, people enter a hidden underworld of legalized discrimination and permanent social exclusion. They are members of America's new undercaste."[1205]

Racial caste systems

There have been several racial caste systems in United States history. The first and most obvious was slavery, where Black persons were not even recognized as *persons*, and were regarded instead as property with which white owners (and white people in general) could treat as they wished. After the Civil War, and during the period of Reconstruction, not merely the "Southern way of life," but the nationwide system of white supremacy was challenged. A new racial caste system developed in the form of "Black codes" and what became known as "Jim Crow."

Among the new laws developed during this time were laws segregating schools and seats on public transportation (among other things), and even more nefarious than these were vagrancy laws and the use of prisoners as labor. In nine southern states, "vagrancy" laws were adopted that made it illegal to be unemployed. You read that correctly. It was a crime to not have a job, despite the fact that having a job, for most of us, even in the best of circumstances, is contingent upon *someone else* hiring us. These vagrancy laws were applied selectively against Black persons, because they were never genuinely about unemployment, but were instead a means of controlling the Black population in the South. Eight of those nine states also enacted "convict laws" that allowed the state to hire out people in County prisons to private companies and plantation owners, where the inmates would work for little or even no pay. One vagrancy law even specifically demanded that "all free Negroes and mulattos over the age of eighteen" have a written proof of a job at the beginning of each year, and those who did not would be judged vagrant and convicted."[1206]

The purpose and effect of these laws were not at all subtle. Aside from maintaining white supremacy and the racial caste system, these laws made it possible to re-create slavery by another name. Black people who could not prove to white police that they had a job could be charged and convicted of "vagrancy." Such "convicts," while not technically slaves, were nevertheless disproportionately and conspicuously Black, and sentenced to forced (often unpaid) labor under deplorable and dangerous conditions.

Throughout all the different manifestations of the racial caste system, police power has been used to create and reinforce the system and the white supremacy it supports. In addition to vagrancy laws being used to create a new forced labor population, additional laws were developed criminalizing such things as "mischief," and "insulting gestures" – inevitably applied selectively against Black persons. Convict labor became a profitable operation, with auctions providing labor to the highest bidder. Tens of thousands of Black Americans were arrested during this time arbitrarily and for trivial offenses, and then subject to various fines and court costs which had to be paid off, in addition to whatever sentence they might have received for their original crime. Typically impoverished, such persons had no way to pay off their "debt" and were therefore sold as forced labor to various corporations, lumber camps, railroads, farms, brickyards, and plantations.[1207] Unlike slave-owners, who had made a substantial investment in their slave population, and therefore had at least some economic self-interest at stake, inspiring them to want to treat their enslaved laborers at least decently enough to survive and continue to work, the private contractors under Jim Crow had no such interest. Conditions were brutal, whippings were common, and those who collapsed from exhaustion or injury were often left to die, and could simply be replaced by another convict.[1208]

There was not even an attempt to deny that convicts were essentially the new population of slaves. While the Thirteenth Amendment to the Constitution abolished slavery, forced servitude was still permitted as punishment for a crime. The Virginia Supreme Court in the case of *Ruffin v Commonwealth* made this status explicit.

[1206] ibid., 35.
[1207] ibid., 39.

[1208] ibid.

For a time, during his service in the penitentiary, he is in a state of penal servitude to the state. He has, as a consequence of his crime, not only forfeited liberty, but all his personal rights except those which the law in its humanity accords to him. He is for the time being a slave of the state. He is civiliter mortus; and his estate, if he has any, is administered like that of a dead man.[1209]

The Jim Crow era ostensibly came to an end as a result of the Civil Rights Movement, culminating in the Civil Rights Act of 1964 and the Voting Rights Act of 1965. While the positive effects of these laws would take some time to manifest, they were nevertheless significant. For example, between 1964 and 1969, the percentage of Black adults registered to vote in the South increased at a staggering rate. In Alabama, it went from 19.3% to 61.3%; from 27.4% to 60.4% in Georgia; from 31.6% to 60.8% in Louisiana; and from 6.7% to 66.5% in Louisiana.[1210]

There can be no question that in the period immediately following the passage of the Civil Rights Act and the Voting Rights Act, demonstrable improvements in the rights, lives, and general conditions of Black persons in the United States occurred. However, as has been the case with every period of disruption of the racial caste system, a period of backlash followed in which the caste system was re-imposed in a different form. Alexander proposes that the current system of mass incarceration is the new case of the racial caste system, effectively, the new "Jim Crow."

To support this claim, we need to see whether and how the system of mass incarceration somehow specifically and disproportionately harms Black persons so as to qualify as a new manifestation of the racial caste system. I propose that the following model can both explain and support that claim.

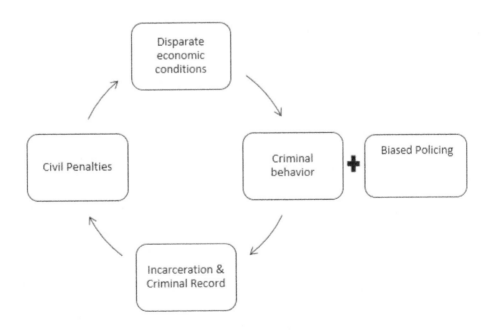

[1209] https://caselaw.findlaw.com/va-court-of-appeals/1339908.html

[1210] Alexander, 47.

Each component of the model will be explained in varying degrees of detail in upcoming sections, but by way of a very brief summary, the model proposes that there exists a number of disparate economic conditions disproportionately impacting people of color in general, and Black persons in particular. These conditions contribute to some (though not all) criminal behavior. This criminal behavior, when combined with biased policing practices throughout the criminal justice system, produces racially disparate rates of incarceration and criminal records. The criminal record, especially the label of being a "felon," results in a wide range of "civil penalties" going far beyond the official punishment for whatever crime was committed (or allegedly committed). As a result of the civil penalties, the formerly incarcerated are far more likely to be unemployed, housing insecure, in debt, and otherwise financially unstable – bringing us back to the starting point of disparate economic conditions. When and if the cycle repeats itself, we have "recidivism," resulting in some persons locked in an endless cycle of economic desperation and incarceration.

Disparate economic conditions

Disparate economic conditions refers to any number of factors resulting in economic instability and conditions of relative disadvantage within American society. Such conditions include poverty, housing, generational wealth, degree attainment, unemployment, poor funding for schools in "urban" school districts, predatory lending practices, and others. While far beyond the scope of this section of this chapter, there is ample evidence of racial disparities for each of these, and more. In other words, people of color are more likely to struggle financially, to be unemployed, to attend schools that are poorly funded, and to lack access to traditional bank loans with favorable interest rates and therefore have to rely on high interest "payday loans," etc. When we consider how the "war on drugs" has contributed to the current system of mass

incarceration, we can gain even more insight by considering the economic conditions of Black Americans at the time the "war" began.

Black Americans were especially hard hit by the economic downturn of the 1970s, which resulted in (and was caused by) globalization and deindustrialization. More than 70% of all Black persons working in metropolitan areas held blue-collar jobs – jobs especially hard-hit by the recession. In the 1970s, the majority of African-Americans attended racially segregated and underfunded schools, and lacked college educations. The new economy left them poorly equipped and far more likely to be unemployed in the changing workforce.[1211]

Unemployment is the best predictor and explanation for criminal behavior, including violent crime in poor Black communities. When researchers control for joblessness, differences in violent crime rates between young Black men and young white men disappear.[1212] That final point is terribly important. Once unemployment rates are taken out of the "equation," there is no statistically significant difference in violent crime rates between young Black men and young white men. Differences in such crime rates are *not* attributable to race, but to *economic* circumstances. Because there are racial disparities in unemployment rates, there are racial disparities in crime rates.

There was, in fact, an increase in crime during the period leading up to the declaration of the "war on drugs." Street crime increased significantly, and the homicide rate doubled. The best general explanation for this increase is both demographic and economic.

The "baby boom" generation became young adults (15 to 24) at this time, and young men are historically most responsible for most crimes. At the same time, there was a surge in unemployment, particularly for Black men, as mentioned above. In addition, there were race riots in 1964 and following the assassination of Martin Luther King Jr. in 1968. Media coverage of these riots reinforced a racialized association of

---

[1211] ibid., 64.

[1212] Wilson, William Julius. *When Work*

Disappears: the World of the New Urban Poor. New York: Vintage Books, 1997. P. 22.

crime/lawlessness and Black men.[1213] *Perception* of criminal behavior, and how it is filtered by, and contributes to, racialized understandings of crime, will be explored in more detail later.

One final (for our purposes) aspect of disparate socio-economic circumstances worth mentioning is how poverty not only contributes to crime, but also the quality of defense one receives if arrested and charged with a crime. Roughly 80% of criminal defendants can't afford to hire an attorney, and therefore make use of public defenders. These public defenders are notoriously overburdened by their number of clients and cases. These attorneys are also often very poorly compensated by the state. Virginia, for example, caps fees paid to court appointed attorneys representing anyone charged with a felony carrying a sentence of less than twenty years at $428. The *most* a public defender can make from serving such a client, regardless of how much time and effort they actually dedicate, is $428. In Wisconsin, anyone earning more than $3,000 per year isn't even eligible for a public defender because that is considered sufficient income to be able to afford an attorney on one's own.[1214] Combined, these anecdotes portray a system in which those "poor enough" to qualify for a public defender really are desperately poor, and in which those public defenders are themselves overworked and undercompensated.

Criminal behavior

While criminal behavior technically refers to all crimes a person might commit, Alexander focuses on drug crimes because the prosecution of these crimes, according to her research and analysis, has had the most significant impact on the growth of the system of mass incarceration and the racially disproportionate aspects of it that qualify it as a new version of the racial caste system.

The overwhelming majority of people in the mass incarceration system are charged with drug offenses and nonviolent crimes. In 2019, of the ten million arrests, only 5% were for violent offenses. Eight out of ten people on probation, and two thirds of people on parole have been convicted of nonviolent crimes.[1215] This is important to point out because it disrupts the commonly held perception that all (or at least most) people in prison are violent and dangerous persons.

Excluding people who have been wrongfully imprisoned and are in fact innocent, everyone in prison has technically committed a crime, and is therefore a "criminal," but for many of those criminals their only offense is possessing or selling a substance that was declared illegal (despite, in some cases, such as marijuana, being less dangerous and less of a contributor to death or crime than the legally available substance of alcohol).

So, why was a "war on drugs" declared in the early 1980s? The common perception is that the "war on drugs" was launched in response to a drug crisis in America, particularly the crack epidemic in "inner cities." In actuality, President Ronald Reagan officially launched the drug war in 1982, several years *before* crack cocaine became a crisis in urban centers and a focus for the media. The Reagan administration used the developing crack problem to publicize and promote its *already existing* campaign against drugs.[1216] When President Reagan officially announced the "war on drugs" in October of 1982, less than 2% of Americans regarded drugs as the most important issue facing the country.[1217] Despite the lack of public concern, and despite the lack of an actual "crisis" (yet), funding for the "war" was immediate and substantial.

Between 1980 and 1984, FBI funding for antidrug efforts increased from $8 million to $95 million, and the Department of Defense anti-drug funding increased from $33 million in 1981 to over a billion dollars in 1991. During that same time, DEA anti-drug budgets grew from $86 million to over a billion dollars. Meanwhile, funding for drug treatment, education, and

---

1213 Alexander, 52.
1214 ibid., 107.
1215 ibid., XIV.

1216 ibid., 6.
1217 ibid., 62.

prevention was actually slashed. The budget for the National Institute on Drug Abuse was reduced from $274 million to $57 million between 1981 and 1984, and anti-drug funds for the Department of Education were cut from $14 million to $3 million.[1218] Budgets reveal strategy, priorities, and values. In cutting funding for education and treatment, while vastly increasing funding for prosecution, the Federal government was sending a very clear message that drug users were not sick, but "bad," and needed to be locked up rather than treated.

Regardless of intentions, the massive funding increase was for a "war" without a terribly threatening enemy (at the time). Remember, the mobilization for "war" occurred before anything resembling a drug crisis or epidemic had manifested. But, if *not* in response to a genuine epidemic, why would an ostensibly unnecessary "war" be declared, and why would so much money be allocated for this unnecessary war? Alexander thinks that the answer can be found by recognizing that the system of mass incarceration is the latest manifestation of the American racial caste system, though this time stripped of *explicit* mentions of race and instead emphasizing public safety and "law and order."

The political slogan "law and order" has always had a racial subtext. The conservative backlash against the civil rights movement framed the behavior of activists as "criminal" and "lawless." In 1965, FBI Director J. Edgar Hoover said, "I am greatly concerned that certain racial leaders are ... suggesting that citizens need only obey the laws with which they agree. Such an attitude breeds disrespect for the law and even civil disorder and rioting."[1219] This sentiment was echoed when the presidential campaign of

Richard Nixon officially referred to him as the "law and order" candidate, and he implied a link between increased crime rates and the civil rights movement, thanks to the "spread of the corrosive doctrine that every citizen possesses an inherent right to decide for himself which laws to obey and when to disobey them."[1220] Nixon also pitted civil rights against safety by saying the "first civil right" was the "right to be free from violence."[1221]

Although Nixon and other conservative politicians publicly avoided using overt racial language, their supporters understood what was meant. A 1968 Time magazine article quoted a supporter of George Wallace: "Y'all know about law and order. It's spelled n-*-*-*-*-*-*."[1222]

Many Americans have little sympathy for criminals, have great concern for public safety, and think that it is necessary to be "tough on crime." As it turns out, *racial attitudes*, as opposed to crime rates or likelihood of victimization, are better predictors of (white) support for both "tough on crime" and anti-welfare measures.

There is a strong correlation between attitudes on crime and on race. Those with the highest degree of concern about crime also tend to oppose racial reform, and their attitudes about crime (as mentioned above) are *unrelated* to their likelihood of victimization.[1223] Despite the fact that Black Americans are much more likely to be victims of crime, white Americans are more punitive – with rural white Americans being the *most* punitive, and the *least* likely to actually be the victims of crime.[1224] To repeat: the people *least* likely to be affected by crime had the *most* punitive positions on crime and punishment. Their attitudes were not driven primarily by actual crime rates, or any sort of personal connection to victimization, but instead by

---

[1218] ibid., 63.

[1219] https://www.themarshallproject.org/2020/10/07/what-trump-really-means-when-he-tweets-law-order

[1220] President Nixon as quoted in ibid., 51. President Trump also referred to himself as a "law and order" candidate and President, publicly using the phrase nearly 100 times in 2020 alone.

(https://www.themarshallproject.org/2020/10/07/what-trump-really-means-when-he-tweets-law-order)

[1221] https://www.themarshallproject.org/2020/10/07/what-trump-really-means-when-he-tweets-law-order

[1222] ibid. I have censored the offensive racial slur.

[1223] ibid., 68.

[1224] ibid., 69.

perception of crime and criminal behavior, which correlated strongly with their attitudes on race. There is an interesting parallel here with attitudes on immigrants and immigration.

48% of people living with a "high concentration of immigrants" in their area think that immigrants strengthen the country, while 47% believe they are a burden. In a curious and seemingly ironic twist, people living in areas with the *lowest* concentration of immigrants are the most likely to perceive immigrants as a "burden" to the country (66%), to be "taking jobs" from Americans, etc. Only 27% of such persons saw immigrants as strengthening the country.[1225] In other words, those most likely to have "harsh" attitudes towards immigrants and their contributions to society are *not* those who have somehow been directly harmed by immigrants, but rather those least likely to have any contact with an actual immigrant at all. In the case of both immigration attitudes and attitudes towards crime and punishment, it is not actual experience and insight driving those attitudes so much as racial biases.

This brings us back to the war on drugs. There is a pervasive implicit bias associating drugs and people of color. A survey conducted in 1995 asked participants "would you close your eyes for a second, envision a drug user, and describe that person to me?" 95% of respondents pictured a Black drug user, and 5% imagined someone from *any other* racial group. Statistically, Black Americans represent only 15% of drug users.[1226] Perception (95%) doesn't even remotely correspond to reality (15%).

There is no good reason to think that police officers, prosecutors, judges, and jurors are somehow profoundly different from the sample in that study, indicating that people in general, *including* agents of the criminal justice system, are prone to implicit bias which associates drug

use and drug crimes with Black persons at a vastly disproportionate rate.

Although often framed as an issue that is especially prominent in communities of color, studies show that drug use and sales occur at similar rates across race. Despite the statistically similar rates of use and sales, some states admit Black men to prison on drug charges at rates 20 to 50 times greater than white men, and in some major cities targeted by the drug war as many as 80% of young Black men now have criminal records.[1227]

Both drug use and the selling of drugs can be explained by appealing to economic desperation. The surge in violence was the result of an unstable street drug market. Eventually, there was indeed a "drug problem" in urban areas, and given the intentional concentration of people of color in urban environments, the drug problem took on a racialized appearance.

There were any number of ways the nation *could have* responded to the drug crisis in poor urban neighborhoods. We could have invested in drug treatment, education, prevention, or economic investment in general. Instead, we invested in "war" and mass incarceration.[1228] The hypothesis that the punitive response to the drug crisis of the 1980s was at least in part driven by a racialized understanding of who the drug users were is supported by the very *different* response to the opioid epidemic that currently affects white Americans at much higher rates today. Rather than suggesting that people "just say no" and getting "tough" on drug users, (white) opioid addicts are regarded as victims, and treated with compassion. Favorite policy responses to the opioid drug crisis include increased prevention, education, and treatment – a very different response than mandatory minimum sentences for crack cocaine.[1229]

[1225] https://www.pewresearch.org/hispanic/2006/03/30/iii-concerns-about-immigrants/

[1226] Betty Watson Burston, Dionne Jones, and Pat Robertson – Saunders, "Drug Use and African-Americans: Myth Versus Reality," *Journal of Alcohol and Drug Abuse* 40 (Winter 1995): 19.

Note: this very closely corresponds to the percentage of Americans who are Black (roughly 13.5%).

[1227] Alexander, 8.

[1228] ibid., 65.

[1229] https://www.vox.com/identities/2017/4/

Biased policing

Bias in policing is a comprehensive term for our purposes, referring to both explicit and conscious racial prejudice, as well as the probably more likely occurrences of implicit bias. In addition, "policing" refers not only to the conduct of police officers, but to all of the agents within the criminal justice system. The Criminal Justice System (hereafter, the CJS) refers to the entire system concerning laws, policing, prosecution, trial, sentencing, and punishment.[1230] It includes three major components:

1. Law Enforcement
2. Courts
3. Corrections

There is evidence of racial bias (including implicit bias) and discrimination (including disparate impact) in all 3 components. According to The Sentencing Project's "Report of The Sentencing Project to the United Nations Special Rapporteur on Contemporary Forms of Racism, Racial Discrimination, Xenophobia, and Related Intolerance: Regarding Racial Disparities in the United States Criminal Justice System:"[1231]

- African Americans are more likely than white Americans to be arrested.
- Once arrested, they are more likely to be convicted.
- Once convicted, and they are more likely to receive lengthy prison sentences.
- African-American adults are 5.9 times more likely to be incarcerated than whites.
- Hispanics are 3.1 times more likely to be incarcerated than whites.
- As of 2001, one of every three Black boys born in that year could expect to go to prison in his lifetime, as could one of every six Latinos—compared to one of every seventeen white boys.
- Racial and ethnic disparities among women are less substantial than among men but remain prevalent.

Those were just general examples. We will delve a bit deeper into each of the three components of the CJS, one at a time, throughout the remainder of this chapter.

Law Enforcement

Law enforcement refers, primarily, to the police. For our purposes, we will focus *only* on implicit bias and/or disparate impact cases (not explicit, conscious racism). First, some data. In 2016, Black Americans comprised 27% of all individuals arrested in the United States—double their share of the total population. Black youth accounted for 15% of all U.S. children, yet accounted for 35% of juvenile arrests in that year.

Similarly, more than one in four people arrested for drug law violations in 2015 was Black, although drug use rates do *not* differ substantially by race and ethnicity and drug users generally purchase drugs from people of the same race or ethnicity. As a specific example, the ACLU found that Blacks were 3.7 times more likely to be arrested for marijuana possession than whites in 2010, even though their rate of marijuana usage was comparable.

If drug usage rates do not differ substantially by race, what accounts for the higher arrest rates of Black people? Simply put, there are disproportionate levels of "police contact" with African Americans. Police are "efficiently" deployed to "higher crime risk" neighborhoods, resulting in more police contact with people of color, and therefore disproportionate stop and arrest rates.

4/15098746/opioid-heroin-epidemic-race
[1230] Some of the content of the next several paragraphs is repeated from earlier in this chapter, and is presented for review purposes. If you are already familiar with that content, feel free to "skim" until you reach new material.
[1231] https://www.sentencingproject.org/publications/un-report-on-racial-disparities/ All data in this section comes from this source, unless otherwise indicated.

As an example, "Broken Windows Policing" is a public safety approach that relies on clamping down on petty offenses and neighborhood disorder. Between 2001 and 2013, 51% of the city's population over age 16 was Black or Hispanic. During that period, 82% of those arrested for misdemeanors were Black or Hispanic, as were 81% of those who received summonses for violations of the administrative code (including such behaviors as public consumption of alcohol, disorderly conduct, and bicycling on the sidewalk.). Research shows that order-maintenance strategies have had only a modest impact on serious crime rates, but cause damage to communities of color, and expose people of color to a greater risk of being killed during a police encounter.

As another example, there is ample evidence of bias with respect to which drivers get stopped and investigated by the police. In one study in New Jersey, data showed that only 15% of all drivers on the New Jersey Turnpike were racial minorities, but 42% of all stops and 73% of all arrests were of Black motorists, even though Black and white drivers violated traffic laws at almost exactly the same rate. A study in Maryland produced similar results, where Black drivers were only 17% of drivers along a particular stretch of highway outside Baltimore, but were 70% of those stopped and searched.[1232] Ironically, both studies revealed that white drivers were actually *more* likely to be carrying illegal drugs or contraband in their vehicles.

In the New Jersey study, white drivers were almost twice as likely to have illegal drugs or contraband as Black drivers, and five times more likely than Latino drivers. Despite being far more likely to have illegal items in their vehicles, white drivers were far *less* likely to be regarded as suspicious, and therefore less likely to be stopped and searched.[1233]

Similar patterns emerge for Latino drivers. A study of more than one thousand highway stops conducted by State troopers in Florida revealed that only 5% of drivers were Black or Latino, but more than 80% of those stopped and searched were minorities. In Illinois, a drug interdiction program targeted Latino minorities who comprised less than 8% of the population, and took less than 3% of personal vehicle trips in Illinois. Nevertheless, they were roughly 30% of those stopped by drug interdiction officers for "discretionary offenses," like failing to signal when changing lanes.[1234]

In general, police are more likely to stop Black and Hispanic drivers for discretionary reasons—for "investigatory stops" (proactive stops used to investigate drivers deemed suspicious) rather than "traffic-safety stops" (reactive stops used to enforce traffic laws or vehicle codes). Once pulled over, Black and Hispanic drivers were three times as likely as whites to be searched (6% and 7% versus 2%). Even though police officers generally actually have a lower "contraband hit rate" when they search Black versus white drivers, Blacks were twice as likely as whites to be arrested.

Once again, there is significant difference between perception and reality, and when people of color are *perceived* as more likely to be criminal, they will be profiled by police, come into contact with police more often, and therefore be "caught" violating some law or another and arrested at disparate rates—reinforcing the biased and inaccurate perception.

The Courts

Having been arrested, one will likely find themselves eventually inside a courtroom, even if only to accept a plea bargain. The Courts includes all the policies of, and participants in, the prosecution and trial phase of someone's interaction with the CJS. This includes prosecutors, defense attorneys, jurors, and judges. Again, focusing *only* on implicit bias and/or disparate impact cases (not explicit, conscious racism), we find disparate impact at every stage in the Court process.

Once someone is arrested and charged with a crime, they are in the "pretrial" phase. Pretrial

---

[1232] Alexander, 167.
[1233] ibid.

[1234] ibid., 168.

detention has been shown to increase the odds of conviction, and people who are detained awaiting trial are also more likely to accept less favorable plea deals, to be sentenced to prison, and to receive longer sentences. Seventy percent of pretrial releases require money bond. Low-income defendants, who are disproportionately people of color, are less able to make bond. Blacks and Latinos are more likely than whites to be denied bail, to have a higher money bond set, and to be detained because they cannot pay their bond.[1235] Persons of color are often assessed to be higher safety and flight risks because they are more likely to experience socioeconomic disadvantage and to have criminal records. Implicit bias also contributes to people of color faring worse than comparable whites in bail determinations.

When a defendant goes on trial, it will matter tremendously to them with what crimes they are charged. Prosecutors are more likely to charge people of color with crimes that carry heavier sentences than whites. Federal prosecutors are twice as likely to charge African Americans with offenses that carry a mandatory minimum sentence than similar white defendants. State prosecutors are also more likely to charge Black rather than similar white defendants under habitual offender laws.

Most jurisdictions inadequately fund their public defender programs. Many low-income persons are represented by public defenders with excessively high caseloads, or by assigned counsel with limited experience in criminal defense. Because poverty is disproportionately correlated with race, this means that more people of color rely on these public defenders.

Setting aside the discrimination, whether conscious or implicit, that may occur *during* the trial, once someone has been convicted even *more* disparities emerge at the sentencing stage.

Although Blacks and Latinos comprise 29% of the U.S. population, they make up 57% of the U.S. prison population. This results in imprisonment rates for Black and Hispanic adults that are 5.9 and 3.1 times the rate for white

adults, respectively—and at far higher levels in some states. Of the 277,000 people imprisoned nationwide for a drug offense, over half (56%) are Black or Latino. Nearly half (48%) of the 206,000 people serving life and "virtual life" prison sentences are Black and another 15% are Latino. Among youth, Blacks are 4.1 times as likely to be committed to secure placements as whites, American Indians are 3.1 times as likely, and Hispanics are 1.5 times as likely.

Contributing to these disparities in sentencing are a number of seemingly "race-neutral" policies. Drug-free school zone laws mandate sentencing enhancements for people caught selling drugs in designated school zones. These disproportionately affect residents of urban areas, and particularly those in high-poverty areas – who are largely people of color. As an example, legislators in New Jersey scaled back their State law after a study found that 96% of persons subject to these enhancements were Black or Latino.

The racialized persecution of anti-drug operations such as these, and the war on drugs in general, is likely largely explained in terms of the implicit biases most (if not all) Americans are subject to, and which inform their perceptions of criminality. If people believe (contrary to fact) that racial and ethnic minorities are more likely to be using and selling drugs, then it would seem only "rational" to focus police attention on those communities. The biased policing in such cases, while biased, is not necessarily the result of any *explicit* racial animus, but is instead the unfortunate consequence of a systemically racist society that subjects all of us to a relentless stream of images associating people of color, and especially Black men, with criminality. Given the circumstances, there is nothing terribly surprising that many people would come to believe that Black men are more likely to engage in criminal behavior. And, if the only images of drug use and drug users someone ever sees on television or in other media sources are of Black people in the "inner city," it should not be surprising if people make those same

---

[1235] In 2020, CA Prop 25 would have eliminated cash bail, but was voted against (56%).

associations with respect to drugs. In addition to bias (implicit and otherwise), however, Alexander thinks that there is something more overtly "political" and self-interested in how the war on drugs has been waged.

From the outset, the drug war could have been waged primarily in overwhelmingly white suburbs or on college campuses. SWAT teams could've rappelled from helicopters in gated suburban communities and raided the homes of high school lacrosse players known for hosting cocaine and ecstasy parties after their games. The police could have seized televisions, furniture, and cash from fraternity houses based on an anonymous tip that a few joints or a stash of cocaine could be found hidden in someone's dresser drawer. Suburban homemakers could have been placed under surveillance and subjected to undercover operations designed to catch them violating laws regulating the use and sale of prescription "uppers." All of this could have happened as a matter of routine in white communities, but it did not. Instead, when please go looking for drugs, they look in the 'hood. Tactics that would be political suicide in an upscale white suburb are not even newsworthy in poor Black and brown communities. So long as mass drug arrests are concentrated in impoverished urban areas, police chiefs have little reason to fear a political backlash, no matter how aggressive and warlike the efforts may be. And so long as the number of drug arrests increases or at least remains high, federal dollars continue to flow in and fill the department's coffers. As one former prosecutor put it, "it a lot easier to go out to the 'hood, so to speak, and pick somebody than to put your resources in an undercover [operation in a] community where there are potentially politically powerful people.[1236]

This brings us back to the beginning of the model, of course. Because people of color are disproportionately likely to be low income, unemployed, lack generational wealth, live in under-served neighborhoods, and lack political connections and influence, they are easy targets. A military style drug raid by police on a wealthy white neighborhood would be guaranteed to generate lawsuits, phone calls to "important people" to get charges thrown out and individual police officers and/or police chiefs to be fired, and an outrage campaign in the media and circles of powerful individuals. Targeting racial and ethnic minorities in working-class or impoverished neighborhoods generates no such risks.

Corrections

After running the gauntlet of disparities in police contact, prosecution, and sentencing, there are further disparities at the corrections phase. Corrections includes all employees of prisons, as well as parole board members, probation officers, and parole officers. Focusing *only* on implicit bias and/or disparate impact cases (not explicit, conscious racism), we know that parole boards are subject to implicit bias (just like anyone). Based on an analysis of almost 60,000 disciplinary cases from New York state prisons, reporters found that disparities in discipline were greatest for infractions that gave discretion to guards, such as disobeying a direct order. In-prison conduct records are a major determinant of parole decisions.

Once paroled, parole and probation officers are more likely to revoke probation from people of color than whites for comparable behavior. The Urban Institute's examination of probation revocation rates in Dallas County, Texas; Iowa's Sixth Judicial District; Multnomah County, Oregon; and New York City revealed that Black probationers were revoked at disproportionate rates in all study sites.

The criminal justice system supports a "revolving door" experience for those who have

---

[1236] Alexander, 155-156.

been convicted and incarcerated. In 1980, only 1% of prison admissions were for parole violation. Twenty years later, that rate had increased to 35%. Of those, only one third were returned to prison for a *new* conviction, whereas two thirds were sent back to prison for a technical violation such as missing an appointment with the parole officer, failing to secure employment, or failing a drug test.[1237]

Civil Penalties

Even if a person of color, convicted of a crime and released on parole, manages to evade all of the higher probability of being sent back to prison, they face a shocking variety of obstacles that prevent them from successfully reintegrating into society. In addition to the official punishment for drug offenses (e.g., prison sentences), there are a great many "civil penalties" for people convicted of drug crimes.

Once released from prison on parole, "convicts" are "barred from public housing by law, discriminated against by private landlords, ineligible for food stamps, forced to "check the box" indicating a felony conviction on employment applications for nearly every job, and denied licenses for a wide range of professions, people whose only crime is drug addiction or possession of small a lot of drugs for recreational use find themselves locked out of the mainstream society and economy – permanently."[1238]

> *The offender may be sentenced to a term of probation, community service, and court costs. Unbeknownst to the offender, and perhaps any other actor in the sentencing process, as a result of his conviction he may be ineligible for many federally funded health and welfare benefits, food stamps, public housing, and federal educational assistance. His driver's license may be automatically suspended, and he may no longer qualify for certain employment and professional licenses. If he is convicted of another crime he may be subject to imprisonment as a repeat offender. He will not be permitted to enlist in the military, or possess a firearm, or obtain a federal security clearance. If a citizen, he may lose the right to vote; if not, he becomes immediately the portable.[1239]*

To begin with the most basic need, convicts face *legal* discrimination when it comes to housing. People with criminal convictions face discrimination in the private rental market and those with felony drug convictions face restrictions in accessing government-assisted housing.

> *The Anti-Drug Abuse Act of 1988 authorized public housing authorities to evict any tenant who allows any form of drug-related criminal activity to occur on or near public housing premises and eliminated many federal benefits, including student loans, for anyone convicted of a drug offense. The act also expanded use of the death penalty for serious drug-related offenses and imposed new mandatory minimums for drug offenses, including a five year mandatory minimum for simple possession of cocaine base – with no evidence of intent to sell.[1240]*

Of course, to afford to pay rent, convicted persons will need to find a job. With respect to employment, nearly one-third of U.S. workers hold jobs that require an occupational license, a requirement which sometimes bars and often poses cumbersome obstacles for people with criminal records. In sectors that do not require licensing, employers are 50% less likely to call back *white* job applicants with incarceration histories than comparable applicants without prison records. Black job applicants, who are less likely to receive callbacks than whites to begin with, experience even *more* pronounced

---

[1237] ibid., 119.
[1238] ibid., 118.
[1239] A task force of the American Bar Association

quoted in ibid., 178.
[1240] Alexander, 68.

discrimination related to a criminal record. Whites *with* criminal records receive more favorable treatment than Blacks *without* criminal records.

For those struggling to find a job, the social safety net offers little assistance, and it would be unfair to frame the war on drugs and punitive approaches to drug crimes solely as a conservative/Republican stance. President Bill Clinton contributed to the war on drugs as well, including harsh civil penalties. In 1996, he signed the Personal Responsibility and Work Opportunity Reconciliation Act which replaced Aid to Families with Dependent Children (AFDC) with a block grant for states called Temporary Assistance to Needy Families (TANF). TANF not only imposed a lifetime limit of five years on welfare assistance, but also a permanent lifetime ban on eligibility for food stamps and welfare for anyone convicted of a felony drug offense, to include simple possession of marijuana.[1241] States may opt out of that ban, but by 2018, 24 States had fully opted out of the food stamp ban, 21 others had only done so in part, and 5 States continued to fully enforce the ban. An even larger number of States continue to impose a partial or full ban on just cash assistance for people with felony drug convictions.

"Crime doesn't pay" is an understatement. In fact, it can be very (literally) expensive. There are many "hidden fees" associated with the criminal justice system. Each State has its own rules and regulations concerning these fees, and results may vary tremendously based upon the State in which someone is charged with a crime. Examples of "pre-conviction service fees" include "jail booking fees levied at the time of arrest, jail per-diems assessed to cover the cost of pretrial detention, public defender application fees charged when someone applies for court appointed counsel, and the bail investigations he imposed when the court determines the likelihood of the accused appearing at trial. Post-conviction fees include presentence report fees, public defender recoupment fees, and fees levied

on people convicted of crimes and placed in a residential or work-release program. Upon release, even more fees may attach, including parole or probation service sees. Such fees are typically charged on a monthly basis during the period of supervision."[1242] In addition, probation officers in most states can require that a parolee set aside 35% of income for the payment of any fines, fees, and restitution charged by various agencies.[1243]

In summary, then, persons convicted of a crime, including specifically a drug offense, are subject not only to the official punishment handed down in court, such as imprisonment of varying length, fines, mandatory rehabilitation, restitution, etc., but also any number of unpublicized and additional penalties that are often more severe, in terms of life prospects, once the official punishment has "ended." These penalties include legally sanctioned discrimination in employment and housing, lack of access to the social safety net with respect to housing subsidies and food stamps, social stigma, likelihood of debt combined with an inability to repay it, and, in most states, disenfranchisement for a varying period of time.

That final penalty, disenfranchisement, might be a special case of "twisting the knife." For people with criminal records who find themselves frustrated by all of these policies, and who would seek to use the political process to try to change them, they face yet another obstacle: there's a good chance they're not allowed to vote. Because felons no longer have the right to vote, they don't even have the ability to vote for political candidates, propositions, or laws that directly impact *themselves*. Convicted felons have no legal ability to directly influence the laws of the nation or even their own community with respect to policing, sentencing, probation, etc. The people most affected by such laws are denied the right to participate in the process by which those laws are established, amended, or abolished.

6.1 million Americans were forbidden from

[1241] ibid., 72.
[1242] ibid., 193-194.

[1243] ibid., 194.

voting because of their felony record in 2016. Felony disenfranchisement rates for voting age Blacks reached 7.4% in 2016—four times the rate of non-Blacks (1.8%). In three states, more than one in five voting-age Blacks is disenfranchised: Florida, Kentucky, and Tennessee. The majority of these disenfranchised Americans are living in their communities, having fully completed their sentences or remaining supervised while on probation or parole.

Back to the beginning: disparate economic conditions

The convicted felon, even if paroled and able to remain free, is burdened not only by the stigma of the felon label, but the many layers of legally sanctioned discrimination that make the formerly incarcerated far more likely to be unemployed, far less eligible for public assistance, for more likely to be housing insecure, and, even if they have friends or family *willing* to provide them shelter, those very same civil penalties targeting felonies can be used to strip social welfare benefits from well-meaning friends and family simply for "sheltering" that person in their home, should they happen to re-offend.

If poverty and joblessness are our best predictors for criminal behavior, should we be surprised when the formerly incarcerated commit crimes again, once released? Recidivism is simply a second and predictable lap around the model, from underprivileged economic conditions, through crime and incarceration and civil penalties, and back again.

While the process and experiences explained by the model might be morally troubling in themselves, what makes the system of mass incarceration a candidate for today's iteration of a racial caste system is the racial component, allowing the comparison with the previous racial caste system of Jim Crow. Alexander makes the parallels clear, and we will consider only some of her points of comparison.

Mass Incarceration v. Jim Crow

- Political motivation

Segregation laws were proposed as part of a deliberate and strategic effort to deflect anger and hostility that had been brewing against the white elite away from *them* and *toward* African-Americans. The birth of mass incarceration can be traced to a similar political dynamic. Conservatives in the 1970s and 1980s sought to appeal to the racial biases and economic vulnerabilities of poor and working-class whites through racially coded rhetoric on crime and welfare.[1244]

- Legal discrimination

Jim Crow laws were overtly discriminatory with respect to employment, housing, education, etc. Many of the very same forms of legal discrimination exist today so long as the person in question has been labeled a felon.[1245]

- Disenfranchisement

During the Jim Crow era, Black Americans were denied their right to vote by means of literacy tests, grandfather clauses, poll taxes, and felon disenfranchisement laws. In our period of mass incarceration, felony disenfranchisement remains, targeting the same population.

Felon disenfranchisement laws have been more effective in eliminating Black voters in the age of mass incarceration than they were during Jim Crow. Less than two decades after the war on drugs began, one in seven Black men nationally had lost the right to vote, and as many as one in four in the states with the highest African-American disenfranchisement rate.[1246]

[1244] ibid., 237.
[1245] ibid., 238.

[1246] ibid., 239.

- Representation

The parallel here is to the era of slavery rather than Jim Crow, but it's worth pointing out all the same. During the period of slavery, enslaved persons counted as 3/5 of a person with respect to determining representation for States in Congress. Although the enslaved persons were not citizens, and of course could not vote, they counted as 3/5 of a person in order to benefit slaveholding states when it came to representation in Congress. Today, most felons likewise cannot vote, but still "count" when it comes to determining representation in Congress. As it happens, most prisons are built in rural areas, which tend to be otherwise sparsely populated and conservative.[1247] Although rural counties contain only 20% of the US population, such counties are the location of 60% of new prison construction.[1248] Incarcerated persons, while not able to participate in the democratic process themselves, nevertheless "count" for the rural communities in which they are incarcerated – but as a *full* person rather than merely 3/5 of a person.

- Segregation

Jim Crow laws mandated racial segregation in housing, businesses, employment, etc. Mass incarceration functions differently, but achieves a similar result.

> It achieves racial segregation by segregating people in prison – the majority of whom are Black and brown – from mainstream society. They are kept behind bars, typically more than 100 miles from home.... Because the drug war has been waged almost exclusively in poor communities of color, when people convicted of drug crimes are released, they are generally returned to racially segregated ghetto communities – the places they call home.[1249]

- Production of race and stigma

Both slavery and Jim Crow served to define race, defining Blackness in terms of slavery, or in terms of an inferior "other" segregated from "normal" (white) people. Because of the media portrayal of criminality along racial lines, and pervasive implicit bias, the system of mass incarceration serves to define Blackness (especially male Blackness) in terms of criminality.

> In this way, the stigma of race has become the stigma of criminality. Throughout the criminal justice system, as well as in our schools and public spaces, young + black + male is equated with reasonable suspicion, justifying the arrest, interrogation, search, and detention of thousands of African-Americans every year, as well as their exclusion from employment and housing and the denial of educational opportunity. Because Black youths are viewed as criminals, they face severe employment discrimination and are also "pushed out" of schools through racially biased school discipline policies.[1250]

Indeed, although nothing can compare to the horror and injustice of slavery, in a certain (very qualified) sense, things are "worse" for Black men today. There are actually *more* Black men subject to the system of mass incarceration today than were enslaved in 1850, just a decade before the beginning of the Civil War. This is a major contributor to the fact that a Black child born today is even less likely to be raised by both parents than a Black child that was born during slavery. And, more Black men are disenfranchised *today* than they were in 1870 – the year the Fifteenth Amendment to the Constitution was ratified that explicitly prohibited disenfranchisement on the basis of

---

[1247] ibid., 240.
[1248] ibid., 242.

[1249] ibid., 242-243.
[1250] ibid., 247-248.

race.[1251]

Critical Analysis

1. In your opinion, what are the strongest and most compelling points made by the philosopher or philosophers in this chapter? Why do you find those points to be convincing?

2. In your opinion, what are the weakest or least convincing points? Why? Can you anticipate any limitations or objections to their ideas not already addressed in the chapter?

[1251] ibid., 224.

Chapter 27: Intersectionality and Identity Politics

Comprehension questions you should be able to answer after reading this chapter:

1. What is meant by "intersectionality?" Provide an example of some possible intersections of identity.
2. Why is a recognition of intersectionality relevant for matters of social justice?
3. What is meant by "identity politics?"
4. What is the difference between "racialism" and "racism?" What do they have in common?
5. How do identity-politics movements attempt to combat/address racism? In what ways might these same movements be "racialist," though not racist?
6. What is "respectability politics" or "uplift suasion?" What are they intended to achieve, and how?
7. What are some possible objections to the strategy of respectability politics?

Intersectionality

Although the term has been vilified in certain conservative corners of the Internet and media, "intersectionality," in its simplest statement, is just the recognition that people can be subject to multiple, overlapping aspects of identity by virtue of their membership to different social groups.

I am male, but also specifically cis-gendered, and also heterosexual. I'm also white, and a natural born citizen of the United States who is a native speaker of English. I have no criminal record, no mental or physical disabilities, and I have earned multiple College degrees. Each one of those contributes something to my identity and my experience as I navigate life in the United States. So too with you, and everyone else, although the particular aspects of our identities will probably vary from each other in all kinds of interesting ways.

I confess that I experience confusion when I see videos on YouTube with titles like "Jordan Peterson debunks intersectionality."[1252] I honestly have no idea how someone could think

that something so patently obvious that the idea that someone who is male will have different experiences than someone who is female, and someone who is a Black male will have experiences different from someone who is a white male, and someone who is a Black female with the disability will have different experiences than a Black female without a disability, and so on.

What is there to "debunk?" That is somewhat of a rhetorical question, because what is usually "debunked" is a strawman caricature of intersectionality that claims that it is all about collecting victimhood badges and that the more aspects of your identity that are "oppressed," the more value your opinion brings to the table, etc. Like any strawman, that caricature is easy to attack – but it's also not what intersectionality actually means.

Although many people have written about intersectionality by now, the concept is generally credited to Kimberlé Williams Crenshaw, from her paper "Mapping the Margins: Intersectionality, Identity Politics, and Violence against Women of Color."[1253] In the paper,

---

[1252] https://www.youtube.com/watch?v=EmNUbf1OHes
[1253] Crenshaw, Kimberlé Williams. "Mapping the Margins: Intersectionality, Identity Politics, and Violence against Women of Color." In, *Critical Race Theory. The Key Writings that Formed the*

Movement, edited by Kimberlé Crenshaw, Neil Gotanda, Gary Peller, and Kendall Thomas. The New Press, New York, 1995 All references in this section refer to that source, unless otherwise indicated. That paper, in its entirety, may also be viewed here: https://pdfs.semanticscholar.org/

Crenshaw acknowledges "failures" within both the feminist movement and the antiracist movement, and claims that these failures are the result of failing to recognize the intersections of race and gender.

> *Racism as experienced by people of color who are of a particular gender – male – tends to determine the parameters of antiracist strategies, just as sexism as experienced by women who are of a particular race – white – tends to ground the women's movement. . . . The failure of feminism to interrogate race means that feminism's resistance strategies will often replicate and reinforce the subordination of people of color; likewise, the failure of antiracism to interrogate patriarchy means that antiracism will frequently reproduce the subordination of women.*"[1254]

To put it simply, focusing exclusively on race doesn't capture the experience of gender. Focusing exclusively on gender doesn't capture the experience of race. Or, in her own words:

> *My focus on the intersections of race and gender only highlights the need to count for multiple grounds of identity when considering how the social world is constructed.*

To illustrate this now (almost) taken for granted understanding, she uses a case study in domestic violence policy and how it intersects with immigration status. In 1990 Congress amended the marriage fraud provisions of the Immigration and Nationality Act to protect women who are victims of domestic violence by US citizens when the perpetrator was a person the women immigrated to the United States to marry. Rather than risk deportation, some immigrant women continued to live with their abusers. The amendment of the marriage fraud rules allow for a hardship waiver caused by domestic violence.

However, many immigrant women, particularly women of color, remained vulnerable because of their inability to meet the conditions necessary for the waiver. The evidence required for the waiver "can include, but is not limited to, reports and affidavits from police, medical personnel, psychologists, school officials, and social service agencies."[1255]

Immigrant women often have difficulty accessing those resources, and overcoming cultural barriers to reporting. Such women are also often dependent upon their American citizen husbands for information about their legal status and rights, and even for translation when language is a barrier.

To summarize, the amendment to the marriage fraud provision, while presumably well intended, didn't consider other dimensions of identity beyond gender. It established requirements that "on paper" are neutral and treat everyone equally, but are not equitable, because they fail to consider that some immigrant women have barriers blocking them from meeting those requirements stemming from their identity not only as immigrants who happen to be women, but especially when they are immigrant women of color.

Additional examples are endless, and generating them can be virtually effortless. As just one exercise, imagine a person has been robbed. Someone suggests they call the police and report the crime. How might their decision and experience of doing so be impacted by the following?

- Their race
- Their ethnicity
- Their citizenship status
- Their gender and gender identity
- Their sexual orientation
- Their income/wealth

734f/8b582b7d7bb375415d2975cb783c839e5 e3c.pdf?_ga=2.183517795.41681160.16098145 72-966915824.1609814572

[1254] Crenshaw, 360.
[1255] ibid., 359.

- Their educational level
- Their relative physical or mental ability or disability
- Their language competency
- Their age
- Their appearance
- Their criminal record (if any)
- etc.

With only a little bit of mental effort, we can easily see how each one of those aspects of someone's identity (as well as others not listed) could influence someone's experience with the police, their beliefs about the police, their confidence in the effectiveness of contacting the police, their fear (if any) of the police, etc.

For anyone interested in crafting public policy, including social justice activists who are seeking to address societal problems, it is imperative to be conscious of the intersection of various aspects of identity so as to avoid unintentional "blind spots," or worse. One of the places where intersectionality is perhaps most likely to appear, and one of the places where it is most important to acknowledge, is within the realm of "identity politics."

Identity Politics

Identity politics in the United States involves stigmatized groups transforming their sense of self by rejecting and/or rewriting negative "scripts" that have been offered by the dominant group within the larger community. Whether on the basis of race, gender, sexual orientation, disability, or religious affiliation, the basic idea is that some groups of people have been marginalized on those bases, and have been told a story about themselves that is negative. Identity politics seek to transform that group membership from a "negative" into a "positive" through political activism, "consciousness-raising," reframing, and other activities.

The implicit assumption behind identity politics is that people can internalize oppressive messages from the dominant group. As examples,

some Black people value lighter skin, or describe some women as having "good" hair (i.e., straight hair), etc. In addition, women inherit the norms of "female" (as defined and transmitted by males!), LGBT persons inherit an identity in contrast to heteronormativity, etc. Identity politics seeks to correct and reframe those messages.

In 2015, student protests ignited across numerous American College and University campuses, including Ithaca College, Smith College, the University of Missouri, Yale, Harvard, Princeton, and my own alma mater, Claremont McKenna College (among others). Students were generally protesting campus conditions for students of color, citing a lack of diversity and cultural sensitivity, and an abundance of "micro-aggressions."

At Claremont McKenna College, Dean of Students Mary Spellman was compelled to resign after protests, and a hunger strike by a student. "Students of Color" issued a letter of their complaints and demands to CMC President Chodosh on April 9th, 2015. It included the creation of a Diversity Chair in the Dean of Students Office, funding for multicultural clubs, a resource center for students of color, greater diversity in faculty and staff, a mentoring program for first year students of color, mandatory and periodic racial sensitivity trainings for all professors, and improved mental health services to cater to the "unique and diverse needs of students of color," among other things.[1256]

The Black Student Union at Oberlin College also issued a list of demands to their College President. In their own words: "these are not polite requests, but concrete and unmalleable demands. Failure to meet them will result in a full and forceful response from the community you fail to support."

The demands included: a 4% increase in Black student enrollment per year (reaching a

---

[1256] The full letter is available here: https://docs.google.com/document/d/19BRi1es J4rlzBLHAQEBHSl7e0wrEiUtLsF5eRdl90No/edit ?pref=2&pli=1

40% increase by 2022[1257]), an increase in specifically Black female instrumentalists in the Jazz department; more Black administrators in the Offices of Financial Aid, Student Health, Student Accounts, the President, Disabilities, the Dean, and Residential Education; that "all Black prospective students be interviewed by admissions officers that are trained in race consciousness practices for undergraduate admissions;" financial aid workshops for Black students by Black financial aid officers; a change in graduation requirements to include an "Intro to the Black Experience" (or similar) course; the recruiting of Black faculty in all of the following departments: politics, philosophy, economics, theater, dance sociology, neuroscience, chemistry, biology, history, classics, physics, creative writing, psychology, athletics, art, anthropology, computer science, cinema studies, comparative American studies, geology, environmental studies, math, religion, rhetoric and composition, and gender sexuality and feminist studies; an increase in the number of black psychologists in the Counseling Center; the creation of designated safe spaces for "Africana identifying students" in several buildings including the library and science center; the immediate promotion to tenure or tenure track for 17 specifically-named faculty; that a Black woman be hired as the head of the Jazz vocal department; that the Black student leaders (who developed these demands, presumably) be provided an $8.20/hour stipend for the organizing efforts; and that eight specifically-named administrators and professors be fired immediately—among numerous other demands.[1258]

My point is *not* to invalidate or question any of the particular example demands, nor to question the lived experiences of the students who made them. Indeed, there are many

legitimate, well-documented disparities and additional obstacles experienced by ethnic minorities in Academia, the workplace, and American society, in general. Minority students, for example, have higher attrition rates in College than do their white peers. This is *not* because of absurd biologically-essentialist reasons, but because of a variety of other reasons, including the fact that attrition rates are *lower* at "highly selective" institutions, where minority students are still underrepresented; and because there is a correlation between completion rates and the time spent pursuing a degree. Minority students are more likely to be part-time students (because of work or family responsibilities), to have to take remedial classes (because of a higher chance of coming from "underperforming" high schools), and to start off in community College (for a variety of reasons, including socio-economic reasons)—all of which correlate to longer times for degree completion, and therefore higher attrition rates.[1259] Given these lower College completion rates for minority students, it's both understandable and appropriate that impacted students would be motivated to advocate for support systems that could help to bridge that gap, including staff and faculty that are sensitive to their needs and particular experiences and backgrounds.

To the extent that these students have grown up in a culture, and sub-cultures, in which their experience has been "racialized," it is likely that their racialist assumptions are inherited and absorbed as part of their basic worldview, as opposed to some sort of contingent belief that could easily be cast aside in the face of a counter-argument. If their life experience, including experiences of racism and marginalization, has *taught* them that they are irreversibly "other," then it should come as no surprise that their self-advocacy relies on that same premise, however

---

[1257] This was not a demand that 40% of the students be black, of course, but rather that the black student population be 40% larger than its current number.

[1258] The full documentation of their demands is available here: https://www.scribd.com/doc/

293326897/Oberlin-College-Black-Student-Union-Institutional-Demands

[1259] http://fivethirtyeight.com/features/race-gap-narrows-in-College-enrollment-but-not-in-graduation/

much they are trying to "flip the script." I want to stress once again that my point is *not* to diminish (let alone deny) the significance or tenacity of their experiences, but rather, in the role of a philosopher, to challenge the racialist (and sometimes plainly *racist*) premises that drive their oppressive experiences, as well as the racialist (as *distinct* from racist) premises that drive (some of) their own responses.

As an example, CMC student activists declare that students of color have "unique" mental health needs. Both CMC and Oberlin activists demand more "diverse" faculty—with Oberlin students demanding specifically black, and, in some cases, specifically black female faculty (as well as black administrators in various offices, and black financial aid counselors).

What assumptions might be being made here? Perhaps that *any* black person hired has the same "essence" as the black students, and will therefore be sensitive to the unique needs and concerns that *only* black students have (which, again, implies racial essentialism). Of course, such an assumption is patently *false*. What if Oberlin College hired black faculty and administrators for every single position demanded by those students—but hired black candidates who *disagreed* with the students' general position and demands? Clearly, not every black person (academic or otherwise) believes and values exactly the same things! There is a big political difference, for example, between Doctor Cornel West[1260] and Doctor Ben Carson.[1261] Would Ben Carson be a satisfying hire for the neuroscience program at Oberlin, or is he the "wrong kind" of black person?

Ironically enough, Ben Carson himself raised such issues in the context of his 2016 Presidential bid. Referring to President Obama, he said "He's an 'African' American. He was, you know, raised white. Many of his formative years were spent in Indonesia. So, for him to, you know, claim that, you know, he identifies with the experience of black Americans, I think, is a bit of a stretch. . .

Like most Americans, I was proud that we broke the color barrier when he was elected, but I also recognize that his experience and my experience are night-and-day different. He didn't grow up like I grew up by any stretch of the imagination, not even close." In reference to his own experiences, he said that most of the racism he experiences comes from "progressives." "I think the way that I'm treated, you know, by the left is racism. Because they assume because you're black, you have to think a certain way. And if you don't think that way, you're 'Uncle Tom,' you're worthy of every horrible epithet they can come up with; whereas, if I weren't black, then I would just be a Republican."[1262]

This gets us to the "normalizing" aspect of racialism. The very notion that there is a "wrong kind" of black person suggests a core of not merely traits, but also beliefs and values that every member of that "race" *should* emulate. A variety of terms, usually meant to be derogatory, are used to express this very notion: "Oreo." "Banana." "Coconut." In each case, the suggestion is the same: although the person is "black" (or "yellow"/Asian, or "brown"/Latino) on the "outside," that person is "white" on the "inside."

By this line of thinking, racial group members are *supposed* to believe and value certain things, and behave and comport themselves in various ways, by virtue of their group membership. Others are *supposed* to recognize (and respect) those things about that group. In some cases, this appears just to be another instance of racial stereotyping.

Many years ago, all of the professors on my campus took part in "diversity training"—one of the more common demands of student activists. The point of this training was to help us all to be conscious of racist stereotyping, to avoid it, and to be sensitive and respectful to students (and faculty) of color—all of which are worthwhile goals. A close paraphrase of the advice that the "expert diversity trainer" provided is as follows.

[1260] http://www.cornelwest.com/
[1261] https://www.bencarson.com/
[1262] http://www.cnn.com/2016/02/23/politics/

ben-carson-barack-obama-raised-white/index.html

We must avoid racist stereotypes, and we must be sensitive to different cultures and their values and practices. For example, African-Americans are more loud, demonstrative, and participatory in conversations...

As the expert continued her presentation, many of my peers looked around at each other uncomfortably. It seemed that the presenter was invoking *racialist* stereotypes in the very attempt to dispel *racist* stereotypes—with the only difference being that she was presenting these generalizations about different races without any tone of negativity—which is what made them racialist, as opposed to racist.

Nevertheless, she was suggesting that we see every student we encounter first through the lens of what we presume their race to be, then to recall a handful of generalizations about that race, and then finally to tailor our treatment of that student on the basis of those generalizations. "Angela is Black, so she is accustomed to animated conversations and expects to be interrupted while speaking, much as I should expect her to interrupt me. Maria, on the other hand, is Latina, and is therefore probably very family-oriented. I should keep in mind that she might have less time to do homework since she probably has to help around the house. Chan, though, is probably Chinese, so he will likely be very studious and respectful, even if very quiet in class—so I shouldn't expect him to participate much...."

Although undoubtedly well-intentioned, it's difficult not to sense that something eerily similar is lurking behind both this kind of diversity training as well as overtly racist beliefs. That eerie similarity is racialism—the idea that there are distinct biological "kinds" corresponding to our categories of race, and that these "kinds" reliably indicate not only physical, but also intellectual and moral, traits.

When seen in such lights, we see the paradox of racial identity politics: it can invoke the very (essentialist) constructs that were/are oppressive in the first place, and is prone to the same racialism (racial essentialism) that informs racism. That is, different groups of people (i.e., different "races") have certain qualities by virtue of their racial "essence." This kind of essentialist thinking suggests that there is a single axis of identity that is discrete and separable, and that should be prioritized.

In fairness, someone might object that while biologically-based racial essentialism is false, what is being invoked is not race, but culture. Rather than claiming that there is some sort of Black "gene" or "essence" transmitted biologically, there is a Black *culture* that is transmitted via the usual means of enculturation/socialization (e.g., the influence of parents, peers, mass media, pop-culture, and other sources of cultural competency). In this way, concerns about "race" being unscientific are moot, since socialization is understood via the social "sciences" (such as sociology) rather than biology or genetics. Using this approach, our "race" vocabulary should properly shift to speaking solely in terms of ethnicity. If so, someone would be "black" in the same sort of way that someone would be "Irish."

Thinking in terms of ethnicity makes racial identity a matter of culture, rather than biology. "Culture," generally, refers to shared, socially constructed aspects of the social environment, including laws, language, educational systems and other social institutions, marriage (and other relationship institutions and norms), as well as all the unspoken "rules" and norms that establish the "ethos" ("character") of the community.

At first glance, this shift is a clear improvement. Racism, after all, seems to presuppose a biologically based racial essence (racialism). Only if certain persons are *inherently* "inferior" by virtue of their inalienable racial membership could it make sense to discriminate on the basis of race. But, if races are replaced with culturally-transmitted ethnicities, no one is "inherently" anything! Certain behaviors and traits might be acquired via socialization, but this is neither genetic destiny nor unalterable. If "those people" have a "poor work ethic," or have "too many children outside of marriage," this is a product of culture, not biology—and cultures can be changed, or escaped. But should they?

Respectability Politics

The (now) controversial comedian Bill Cosby sparked both enthusiastic agreement and equally enthusiastic outrage when he gave the infamous "pound cake" speech in 2004 to commemorate the 50th anniversary of *the Brown v. Board of Education* Supreme Court decision. In that speech, Cosby said the following:

I can't even talk the way these people talk. People with their hat on backwards, pants down around the crack. Isn't that a sign of something, or are you waiting for Jesus to pull his pants up. Those people are not Africans, they don't know a damned thing about Africa. With names like Shaniqua, Shaligua, Mohammed and all that crap and all of them are in jail. The city and all these people have to pick up the tab on them [poor African Americans] because they don't want to accept that they have to study to get an education. I'm talking about these people who cry when their son is standing there in an orange suit. Where were you when he was two? Where were you when he was twelve? Where were you when he was eighteen, and how come you don't know he had a pistol? All this child knows is 'gimme, gimme, gimme.' These people want to buy the friendship of a child and the child couldn't care less and these people are not parenting. They're buying things for the kid. $500 sneakers, for what? And they won't spend $250 on Hooked on Phonics. I don't know who these people [poor African Americans] are. They're [poor African Americans] just hanging out in the same place, five or six generations sitting in the projects when you're just supposed to stay there long enough to get

a job and move out. God is tired of you. You can't land a plane with 'why you ain't.' You can't be a doctor with that kind of crap coming out of your mouth. Where did these people get the idea that they're moving ahead on this? [1263]

While in recent years, Cosby has been a controversial person mainly due to the increased and increasingly detailed coverage of his numerous sexual assault allegations (and convictions), he has long-been controversial for his statements critical of the Black community, and certain aspects of Black culture.[1264]

Critics of Cosby accuse him of elitism and for failing to grasp the impact of institutional racism and other social forces on the well-documented problems faced by the Black community: unemployment, poverty, teen pregnancy, incarceration, addiction, etc. Supporters of Cosby agree with his emphasis on personal responsibility as the solution to a host of self-created (or at least self-perpetuated) problems. Whether one is critical or sympathetic, Cosby provides an example of what is known as "respectability politics."

CNN anchor Don Lemon offered his version of respectability politics in 2013, saying that Conservative commentator Bill O'Reilly "doesn't go far enough" when O'Reilly said that "the reason there is so much violence and chaos in the black precincts is the disintegration of the African- American family. Raised without much structure, young black men often reject education and gravitate towards the street culture, drugs, hustling, gangs. Nobody forces them to do that, again, it is a personal decision." Lemon then proceeded to offer "five things" that Black people should do if "you really want to fix the problem." The list included (starting at #5) "pull up your

---

[1263] The full transcript of Cosby's speech may be accessed here:
http://www.rci.rutgers.edu/~schochet/101/Cosby_Speech.htm

[1264] For the benefit of any reader who struggles to take Cosby seriously due to the deeply troubling sexual assault allegations against Bill

Cosby, please consider that Cosby's views are expressed in the 2007 book *Come on People: On the Path from Victims to Victors*, co-authored by Dr. Alvin Poussaint. If it will help, imagine the views come from Dr. Poussaint alone, and evaluate them solely based on content rather than source.

pants," the use of the "n-word," "respect where you live" (no littering), "finish school," and "probably the most important, just because you can have a baby, it doesn't mean you should. Especially without planning for one or getting married first."[1265]

The idea that Black persons are responsible for their own bleak conditions, and that the key to overcoming those conditions, and even racism itself, is self-improvement, can be traced all the way back to the beginning years of the United States. The American Convention for Promoting the Abolition of Slavery, and Improving the Condition of the African Race was an abolitionist organization that would publish and distribute "advice" for free Blacks.

Abolitionists urged free Blacks to attend church regularly, acquire English literacy, learn math, adopt trades, avoid voice, legally marry and maintain marriages, evade lawsuits, avoid expensive delights, abstain from noisy and disorderly conduct, always act in a civil and respectable manner, and develop habits of industry, sobriety, and frugality. If Black people behaved admirably, abolitionists reasoned, they would be undermining justifications for slavery and proving that notions of their inferiority were wrong.[1266]

At around the same time, we find the example of Maria W. Stewart. Stewart was born the child of free Black parents in Connecticut in 1803. When she was five years old, both of her parents died and she was sent to live with a minister and his family. She worked as a servant and at home until the age of 15. Up to that point, she had not received any formal education. From the age of 15 until the age of 20, she attended Sabbath

School before church service on Sundays. Despite her early lack of education, despite being a woman, and despite being (specifically) a Black woman living in the 19th century, she became a teacher, journalist, lecturer, activist, and abolitionist. She is the first (known) American woman to speak to an audience that consisted of both men and women, white people and black people – and is the first Black woman to make public lectures (period). She lectured on women's rights, in favor of abolition, and for the importance of religion and social justice.

While protesting against the social conditions that Black Americans were forced to endure, she advocated social and moral advancement to Black audiences. She was convinced that the Black community could and should "help itself" by turning to religion and virtue and education even while seeking political and social change. In this way, she provides an early example of what might be considered "respectability politics" or "uplift suasion," but, to the extent that she recognizes unjust social conditions that oppress Black Americans, she does not place the burden of improvement *solely* on the shoulders of those same Black Americans. The following is an excerpt from a speech given to the First African Baptist Church and Society in the city of Boston in October 1831, thirty years before the beginning of the Civil War.

All the nations of the earth are crying out for Liberty and Equality. Away, away with tyranny and oppression! And shall Afric's sons be silent any longer? Far be it from me to recommend to you, either to kill, burn, or destroy. But I would strongly recommend to you, to improve your talents; let not one lie buried in the earth. Show forth your powers of mind. Prove to

---

[1265] https://www.realclearpolitics.com/video/2013/07/27/cnns_don_lemon_bill_oreillys_critic ism_of_black_community_doesnt_go_far_enough. html
[1266] Kendi, Ibram X. *Stamped From the Beginning. The Definitive History of Racist Ideas in America.* Bold Type Books, New York, 2016, 124. A pdf

copy of the original minutes of one of their meetings is available online, and includes a call for establishment of Sunday school education for Black children, as "the first day of the week is too frequently spent in dissipation [self-indulgence] https://www.loc.gov/resource/lcrbmrp.t1502/?sp=21."

the world, that

Though black your skins as shades of night,
Your hearts are pure, your souls are white.

This is the land of freedom. The press is at liberty. Every man has a right to express his opinion. Many thinks, because your skins are tinged with a sable hue, that you are an inferior race of beings; but God does not consider you as such. He hath formed and fashioned you in his own glorious image, and hath bestowed upon you reason and strong powers of intellect. He hath made you to have dominion over the beasts of the field, the fowls of the air, and the fish of the sea. He hath crowned you with glory and honor; hath made you but a little lower than the angels; and, according to the Constitution of these United States, he hath made all men free and equal. Then why should one worm say to another, "Keep you down there, while I sit up yonder; for I am better than thou ?" It is not the color of the skin that makes the man, but it is the principles formed within the soul. . . .[1267]

In this speech, she unambiguously asserts racial equality, appealing to God's considerations and claiming that God has created all humans equal. She also points out that, glaring legal contradictions such as the existence of slavery notwithstanding, that same equality is declared by the U.S. Constitution. In a phrase foreshadowing Dr. Martin Luther King's dream of people being judged not by the color of their skin, but by the content of their character, she asserts that "it is not the color of the skin that makes the man, but it is the principles formed within the

soul."

In another speech, she confronts white America with its injustice and hypocrisy, and does so in the manner of a philosopher, by means of a simple thought experiment and intuition test.

Did every gentleman in America realize, as one, that they had got to become bondmen, and their wives, their sons, and their daughters, servants forever, to Great Britain, their very joints would become loosened, and tremblingly would smite one against another; their countenance would be filled with horror, every nerve and muscle would be forced into action, their souls would recoil at the very thought, their hearts would die within them, and death would be far more preferable. Then why have not Africa's sons a right to feel the same? Are not their wives, their sons, and their daughters, as dear to them as those of the white man's? Certainly, God has not deprived them of the divine influences of his Holy Spirit, which is the greatest of all blessings, if they ask him. Then why should man any longer deprive his fellow-man of equal rights and privileges?[1268]

The thought experiment is as simple as can be: white Americans should imagine that they themselves, and all their families and children, are forever "servants" to Great Britain. In other words, imagine that they and their families were slaves. She predicts that they would prefer even death to that fate. "Then why have not Africa's sons a right to feel the same? Are not their wives, their sons, and their daughters, as dear to them as those of the white man's?" In a simple test of consistency, if such a condition would be

---

[1267] Stewart, Maria W. "Preface," *Meditations from the Pen of Mrs. Maria W. Stewart.* Washington: Enterprise Publishing, 1879. https://digital.library.upenn.edu/women/stewart-maria/meditations/meditations.html Emphasis added.
[1268] Stewart, "Introduction to Religion and the

Pure Principles of Morality, the Sure Foundation on Which We Must Build," *Meditations from the Pen of Mrs. Maria W. Stewart.* Washington: Enterprise Publishing, 1879. https://digital.library.upenn.edu/women/stewart-maria/meditations/meditations.html

unacceptable for white people, why is it acceptable for Black people, given that both are equally Children of God? And, if no such justification for different treatment is available, then "why should man any longer deprive his fellow-man of equal rights and privileges?" Stewart continues casting blame on America and its laws and injustice.

> Oh, America, America, foul and indelible is thy stain! Dark and dismal is the cloud that hangs over thee, for thy cruel wrongs and injuries to the fallen sons of Africa. The blood of her murdered ones cries to heaven for vengeance against thee. Thou art almost become drunken with the blood of her slain; thou hast enriched thyself through her toils and labors; and now thou refuseth to make even a small return.[1269]

America is stained by its sins against the "sons of Africa," to include kidnapping, enslavement, theft of labor, and murder. For all the wrongs and injuries perpetrated by America, it refuses "to make even a small return," namely, *freeing* those still enslaved. Stewart clearly thinks that American laws and practices must change, and that America must repent for its many grievous sins.

And what should Black people do, in response to this oppression and injustice? "Far be it from me to recommend to you, either to kill, burn, or destroy." Instead, she recommends that Black persons "improve [their] talents" and "prove to the world that "though black [their] skins as shades of night, [their] hearts are pure, [their] souls are white." Elsewhere, she amplifies this tone of "encouragement."

> O, ye daughters of Africa, awake! awake! arise! no longer sleep nor slumber, but distinguish yourselves. Show forth to the world that ye are endowed with noble and exalted faculties. O, ye daughters of Africa! what have ye done to immortalize your

names beyond the grave? What examples have ye set before the rising generation? What foundation have ye laid for generation yet unborn? . . . Where is the maiden who will blush at vulgarity and where is the youth who has written upon his manly brow a thirst for knowledge; whose ambition mind soars above trifles, and longs for the time to come, when he shall redress the wrongs of his father, and plead the cause of his brethren? Did the daughters of our land possess a delicacy of manners, combined with gentleness and dignity; did their pure minds hold vice in abhorrence and contempt, did they frown when their ears were polluted with its vile accents, would not their influence become powerful? Would not our brethren fall in love with their virtues? Their souls would become fired with a holy zeal for freedom's cause. They would become ambitious to distinguish themselves. They would become proud to display their talents. Able advocates would arise in our defence. Knowledge would begin to flow, and the chains of slavery and ignorance would melt like wax before the flames.[1270]

Not only is Stewart explicitly encouraging the development and display of virtue in young Black men and women, but is also explicitly proposing that if "the daughters of our land" abhorred vice and possessed manners (among other virtues), "able advocates would arise in our defense" and "the chains of slavery and ignorance would melt like wax before the flames."

While there is surely something valuable about the pursuit of virtue in *anyone*, Stewart's linking of Black cultivation of personal virtue with able (white) advocates arising and the chains of slavery melting away, implies not only that Black virtue has the power to end white racism, but even (worse) that white racism exists and persists because of an insufficient display of Black virtue.[1271]

1269 ibid.
1270 ibid., Emphasis added.

1271 For an analysis of the historical contribution of Black female intellectuals that engages

Kendi calls this strategy "uplift suasion" (also known as respectability politics). He claims that it is based on the idea what white people could be persuaded away from their racist ideas if only they saw Black people "uplifting" themselves from their "low station in American society." "Positive Black behavior, abolitionist strategists held, undermined racist ideas, and negative Black behavior confirmed them."[1272]

Kendi condemns this strategy as both racist and impossible. It is racist because it implies that Black people are partially or completely responsible for the existence and persistence of racist ideas. "To believe that the negative ways of Black people were responsible for racist ideas was to believe that there was some truth in notions of Black inferiority. To believe that there was some truth in notions of Black inferiority was to hold racist ideas."[1273] The strategy was also impossible to execute because the people involved were/are, contrary to racist thinking, equally *human*. "Free Blacks were unable to always display positive characteristics for the same reasons poor immigrants and rich planters were unable to do so: free Blacks were human and humanly flawed."[1274] Finally, Kendi condemns the strategy of uplift suasion because it presumes a nonexistent rational and consistent basis for racist beliefs.

Uplift suasion assumed, moreover, that racist ideas were sensible and could be undone by appealing to sensibilities. But the common political desire to justify racial inequities produced racist ideas, not logic. Uplift suasion also failed to account for the widespread belief in the extraordinary Negro, which had dominated assimilationist and abolitionist thinking in America for a century. Upwardly mobile Blacks were regularly

cast aside as unique and as different from ordinary, inferior Black people. . . . Consumers of racist ideas sometimes changed their viewpoints when exposed to Black people defying stereotypes (and then sometimes changed back when exposed to someone confirming the stereotypes). Then again, upwardly mobile Blacks seemed as likely to produce resentment as admiration. "If you were well-dressed they would insult you for that, and if you were ragged you would surely be insulted for being so," one Black Rhode Island resident complaint in his memoir in the early 1800s. It was the cruel illogic of racism. When Black people rose, racists either violently knocked them down or ignored them as extraordinary. When Black people were down, racists called it their natural or nurtured place, and denied any role in knocking them down in the first place."[1275]

The dilemma of respectability politics is that any "failure" reinforces the negative prejudicial beliefs about the group in question. But, any "success" is either explained away or interpreted to be only an "exceptional" case that does nothing to "uplift" the group. In an infamous footnote authored by David Hume, for example, he claims of Black people that "none ever discovered any symptoms of ingenuity," and then dismisses a prominent contemporary counter-example to that sweeping and racist generalization.

In JAMAICA, indeed, they talk of one negroe as a man of parts and learning; but 'tis likely he is admired for very slender accomplishments, like a parrot, who speaks a few words plainly.[1276]

The "parrot-like" person in question was

---

respectability politics, along with the production of racial knowledge, see Cooper, Brittany. *Beyond Respectability: The Intellectual Thought of Race Women* (Women, Gender, and Sexuality in American History). University of Illinois Press; Illustrated edition (May 3, 2017).

[1272] Kendi, 124.
[1273] ibid.
[1274] ibid., 125.
[1275] ibid.
[1276] Hume, "Of National Characters," *Essays, Moral and Political*, 2nd Edition, 1742.

Francis Williams, who, according to Edward Long's *History of Jamaica*, was the son of a free Black couple in Jamaica, and sponsored by the Duke of Montagu as an "experiment" in whether "a negro lad, trained at a grammar school and then at a university would be found equal in literary attainments to a white man."[1277] Williams is reported to have attended Cambridge, and returned to Jamaica as a poet, businessman, and teacher of reading, writing, Latin, and mathematics to Black children.

While some of the details of Williams' biography have been debated,[1278] Hume did not dispute any particular aspect of his story, but entirely dismissed even the possibility that a Black man could be genuinely intelligent and educated, comparing his achievements to that of a trained parrot instead. This example is worth emphasizing, because it reveals that even a brilliant world-historic philosopher renowned for his insights into *reasoning* on the basis of *evidence* can be "immune" to evidence and reason when it challenges his deeply held racist beliefs. This further demonstrates the futility of respectability politics, setting aside the moral concerns about that strategy. Hume's racism was not "dedicated." It's not as though he specialized in racist research and discourse. Indeed, the most egregious example of racist thought we have from him comes from that footnote cited above, the entirety of which amounts to only a few paragraphs. Hume's racism was "casual" as opposed to "professional." That is not meant to diminish or excuse it, but actually to reinforce the "futility" argument against respectability politics all the more strongly. If even a *casual* racist and professional intellectual, who argued that belief should be proportioned to evidence, couldn't be "persuaded" by "uplift suasion," why should we imagine that *others* would be?

This idea that persecuted minorities are somehow responsible for their oppression, and could liberate themselves from discrimination (and worse) if only they showed white people how "good" and "normal" they are is not limited to Black persons, of course. When members of the LGBTQ+ community are encouraged not to "flaunt themselves" in public, it presupposes that bigotry against that community is caused by certain behaviors, and that ceasing such behaviors would ultimately eliminate the bigotry. There is no evidence that prejudice operates in such a rational and calculating manner, though, and there is an increasing amount of evidence that it does not. The research of Jonathan Haidt, for example, as discussed elsewhere in this book, suggests that we do not arrive at conclusions (including prejudicial ones) after having objectively examined premises, but instead start with our conclusion, produced by an intuitive emotional response, and then search for premises that will rationalize the conclusion we have already adopted. If that general view is correct, then if a member of a minority group presents as "respectable" to a prejudicial person, it is far more likely that they will be perceived as anomalous or somehow "extraordinary" (as described by Kendi above), or simply ignored, than that they will serve as persuasive counter-evidence to the prejudicial belief.

The pressure of respectability politics, long established for the Black community, manifests in obvious and public ways for other communities as well. Fountain connects this history of respectability politics to the Latinx community in the United States, and even demonstrates how it has been used to perpetuate a division between Black and Brown communities, especially in regard to issues of police brutality.

> *The politics of respectability have long suppressed the concerns of the poor and working-class. As New York University anthropologist Arlene Dávila notes in her book Latino Spin, since the late 1980s, middle- and upper-middle class Latinx professionals have promoted marketable images of Latinxs by characterizing the*

[1277] https://ecda.northeastern.edu/item/neu:m04109796/

[1278] https://www.tandfonline.com/doi/abs/

10.1080/0895769X.2019.1652554?needAccess=true&journalCode=vanq20

group as upwardly mobile, hardworking, family oriented, entrepreneurial, law abiding, and inherently conservative. Latinx and non-Latinx, conservatives and liberals alike, have supported these depictions to show that Latinxs are not a social liability for society. Stories about police brutality, however, obscure these narratives. . . . Paul Andow, president of the League of United Latin American Citizens (1963-65), drew a distinction between African Americans' struggles for civil rights and Latinxs. "We have not sought solutions to problems by marching to Washington, sit-in's or picketing or other outward manifestations," he began, "we have always gone to the source of the problem and discussed it intelligently in a calm and collected manner." Decades later, amidst the nascent Black Lives Matter movement, writer Héctor Tobar in a New York Times op-ed echoed a similar sentiment when he declared "we Latinos suffer from a rage deficit." He went onto claim that the Latinx students he spoke to at California State University, Los Angeles, "resist oppression in a low-key, goal-oriented way." They strived for good grades, he claimed, worked while obtaining a degree, and desired to become breadwinners to give back to their communities. Both statements juxtaposed Latinxs as naturally humble and implicitly portrayed African Americans as more militant. On the other hand, they both minimized contemporary and nascent political activism within Latinx communities. . . . After the uprising against police brutality in Newark, New Jersey's Puerto Rican community in September 1974, the Star Ledger quoted one resident named Carmen Conway who claimed, "Puerto Ricans are very quiet as far as rioting is concerned...when they explode,

something extraordinary has happened." Exactly ten years later, MIT professor Yohel Camayd-Freixas made a similar statement after a violent clash between Latinx and White residents in Lawrence, Massachusetts in 1984. "Riots among Hispanics are highly unusual," he insisted. "Things have got to be extremely serious when rioting breaks out among Hispanics." "Extraordinary" and "extremely serious" designated that only in unprecedented situations could a group deemed as passive resort to rioting. Both statements overlooked the numerous urban uprisings among Mexican Americans and Puerto Ricans that had occurred on the mainland since the mid-1960s. . . . SUNY Old Westbury American Studies Professor Llana Barber noted in her book Latino City, these [respectability] narratives erase the stories of the incarcerated, jobless, welfare-recipient, political radicals and, yes, even rioters. All these groups form the collective experiences of Latinxs in the United States. Knowing these stories will better inform people about the dynamics of Latinxs' interactions with law enforcement and the criminal justice system[1279].

Latinx respectability narratives not only undermine Latinx agency and obscure the full history of activism and advocacy within the Latinx community, they also pit Black and Brown communities against each other by portraying the Latinx community as low-key, humble, and seeking intelligent solutions in contrast to the allegedly easily agitated and prone to violence Black community.

The Asian American community is not immune to respectability pressures either—indeed, the "model minority" label is an especially obvious example of precisely such pressures. Like other minority groups, playing the respectability

---

[1279] Fountain, Aaron G. Jr. "Latinx Narratives on Police Brutality, Respectability Politics, and Historical Erasure."

https://www.latinxproject.nyu.edu/intervenxions/latinx-narratives-on-police-brutality-respectability-politics-and-historical-erasure

game is no guarantee for Asian Americans either. Amidst the spread of Covid-19, reports of racist incidents against Asian Americans have spiked, reaching over 500 per week in March 2020 alone. One strategy proposed (by no less a figure than former Presidential candidate and Democratic Party rising star Andrew Yang) to reduce incidents of hate crimes has been for Asian Americans to demonstrate their "Americanness" by visibly engaging in efforts against the virus' spread.[1280]

> *At its heart, this approach to combating racism is merely a resurrection and repackaging of respectability politics. The intuition is that, by highlighting socially-lauded activities or adopting the dominant group's social norms, the group being targeted by racism will be viewed more positively, becoming less of a target for racism.*[1281]

Plouffe attacks this strategy, specifically in the context of the Asian American community, by pointing out, first of all, that it has never worked. He reminds us that Japanese Americans, "who could have been considered an assimilation success story, were subjected to internment camps during World War II, even though some served in the US military with great distinction."[1282] Chinese Americans, too, have endured centuries of discrimination and worse, including Acts of Congress such as the Page Act of 1875 and the Chinese Exclusion Act of 1882. Despite a general strategy of assimilation,

cultural acceptance still hasn't been achieved, and Chinese Americans continue to be targeted by hate crimes due to being wrongfully associated with the spread of Covid-19 in the United States. Setting aside the historical ineffectiveness of respectability politics, Plouffe argues, in harmony with Kendi, that such a strategy is morally problematic as well.

> *The fundamental assumption of respectability politics is that the target group is somehow inherently unworthy of equal treatment or respect. This notion runs counter to the fundamentally American ideal in which all people are regarded as equals. If this implicit underlying inferiority is repeated not only by out-group members but also by prominent in-group members, it is likely to significantly increase the mental-health toll of those targeted by racist abuse.*[1283]

Respectability politics not only contradicts American assumptions of equality, according to Plouffe, but research indicates that the "vigilance" required by respectability strategies imposes a variety of health costs on those called to "perform." Research by Lee and Hicken connect this vigilance to chronic anticipatory stress, which, "as other forms of chronic stress, results in dysfunction of the stress response system and then poor mental and physical health."[1284] Such vigilance behaviors have also been linked to poor sleep,[1285] and high blood pressure.[1286]

Moreover, Plouffe points out that this

[1280]https://www.washingtonpost.com/opinions/ 2020/04/01/andrew-yang-coronavirus-discrimination/

[1281] Plouffe, Michael. "Respectability Politics and Asian America." https://michaelplouffe.net/respectability-politics-and-asian-america/

[1282] ibid.

[1283] ibid.

[1284] Lee Hedwig, Hicken Margaret Takako. "Death by a thousand cuts: The health implications of black respectability." Souls. 2016; 18(2-4): 421–445.

https://www.ncbi.nlm.nih.gov/pmc/articles/PMC5703418/

[1285] Hicken Margaret T, Lee Hedwig, Ailshire Jennifer, Burgard Sarah A, Williams David R. "Every shut eye ain't sleep: The role of racism-related vigilance in racial/ethnic disparities in sleep difficulty." *Race and Social Problems.* 2013;5:100–12. https://www.ncbi.nlm.nih.gov/pmc/articles/PMC3722054/

[1286] Hicken Margaret T, Lee Hedwig, Morenoff Jeffrey, House James S, Williams David R. "Racial/ethnic disparities in hypertension

strategy is morally misguided, as it places the burden of social change on the shoulders of the victims rather than the perpetrators.

> *For Asian Americans, behavioral reform by the victims has often necessitated the giving up of valuable aspects of cultural heritage, something that has never been demanded of the perpetrators. If anything, the perpetrators of racial attacks should be made to bear the burden of responsibility for their antisocial activities; this load should not be foisted upon the victims.*[1287]

Pause for a moment and think about what "respectability" looks like, or demands from, each of the following groups.

- Black persons
- Latino/a/x persons
- Asian American persons
- Transgender persons
- LGBQ+ persons
- "Poor"/working class persons

Whether sympathetic to the strategy of respectability politics, or deeply critical of it, note that *neither* stance relies in any obvious way, upon any notion of "race" as a biological concept at all. Cosby (or Lemon, or Stewart) isn't concerned that young Black men are somehow genetically predisposed to violence (or any other similarly absurd notion). He's concerned about the *socializing* influence of "gangsta rap." "What do record producers think when they churn out that gangsta rap with antisocial, women-hating messages?, Do they think that black male youth won't act out what they have repeated since they

were old enough to listen?"[1288]

Nor is Kendi (etc.) appealing to anything remotely biological in his own critique. Indeed, he explicitly rejects what he calls "biological racism," and instead points to the socializing influence of institutionalized racism, and social determinants of health, prosperity, upward mobility, etc.

Whether one is "conservative" or "progressive," perhaps the obvious solution to the conceptual clumsiness of "race" is to think of "race" as a reference to ethnicity and/or culture, instead. If one does so on the assumption that, in so doing, racism—or even its more well-intentioned relative, racialism—will fade away, then I think one is probably mistaken.

Replace racism with ethnocentrism. "The 'white race' might not be superior, but 'white culture'" *is*, says the racist-with-a-new-title. "Black men aren't biologically prone to criminal behavior, but black culture *socializes* them into criminality nevertheless," says the ethnocentrist (who sounds a heck of a lot like a racist. . . .).

Even the normalizing aspect of racialism discussed above finds a new form with ethnicity. Ethnic minorities who "act white" aren't failing to live up to their biologically inherited racial essence—they're just failing to honor and express their *culture*. The question immediately arises, of course, as to *who* gets to *define* that culture, and its acceptable expressions, and why it's imperative for someone who *looks like* they're a member of that ethnicity or culture to emulate its norms.

To put it bluntly, what is "Black culture?" The hip-hop lifestyle celebrated by "Young Money" artists like Lil Wayne and Drake? Does that speak to the experience of Black men and women who grew up in View Park-Windsor Hills?[1289] Should the son of two medical doctors who grew up

---

prevalence: Reconsidering the role of chronic stress." *American Journal of Public Health.* 2014;104:117–123. https://www.ncbi.nlm.nih.gov/pmc/articles/PMC3910029/

[1287] Plouffe, ibid.

[1288] http://www.nbcnews.com/id/21279731/print/1/displaymode/1098/

[1289] This is an unincorporated part of Los

Angeles County nicknamed "Black Beverly Hills." The population is 84.8% African-American, with an average income of $90,000—tens of thousands of dollars above the county average for white families, and more than double the median income of L.A. County black families. http://www.latimes.com/local/la-me-adv-view-park-20150719-story.html#page=1

living next door to the actress Loretta Divine (an actual View Park resident), in a 5,000 square foot home, feel obliged to get a gold "grill?" Should the son of a single-mother growing up on public assistance in a small apartment in Inglewood do so? Or, should he emulate the lifestyle and values of the wealthy medical doctor instead? Which of these rather distinct lifestyles is a proper representative of "the" Black culture? And who gets to make this determination? What counts as a "culture?" Are all cultures equally good? Should all cultures be respected, or are some worthy of revision?[1290] Shifting our talk from race as a biological concept, to race as a cultural concept (i.e., ethnicity), solves some problems, but generates some of its own. . . .

An honest assessment of identity politics, I think, reveals that, like most things that are important, "it's complicated." On the one hand, there is undoubtedly something valuable and empowering about claiming group membership as a source of strength and solidarity rather than a site for oppression and discrimination. There is no question that significant and moral and legal gains have been made precisely because motivated people have organized around various axes of their identity to lobby, protest, vote, etc. For all of these reasons, and more, identity politics is a good thing. That doesn't mean that identity politics is without challenges or not subject to any nuanced examination.

As already mentioned, there are some conceptual issues. Most of the issues and arguments raised in the context of race or ethnicity apply to other (intersectional) axes of identity as well: gender, sexual orientation, socio-economic status, religion, etc. In each case, some property or group membership is being identified as somehow "essential" with regard to *who you are*. In the case of race, despite it being

the case that the "racialization" people experience is very much real, it is helpful to remember that race is, nevertheless, a social construction.[1291] Even within the movement of Critical Race Theory, there has been spirited debate as to whether the better social justice strategy is to challenge the construct or the system that employs that construct.

> *To say that a category such as race or gender is socially constructed is not to say that that category has no significance in our world. On the contrary, a large and continuing project for subordinated people – and indeed, one of the projects for which postmodern theories have been very helpful – is thinking about the way in which power has clustered around certain categories and is exercised against them. . . . We can look at debates over racial subordination throughout history and see that, in each instance, there was a possibility of challenging either the construction of identity or the system of subordination based on that identity –... In evaluating various resistance strategies today, it is useful to ask which of Plessy's challenges would've been best for him to have won – the challenge against the coherence of the racial categorization system or the challenge to the practice of segregation?[1292]*

Critical Analysis

1. In your opinion, what are the strongest and most compelling points made by the philosopher or philosophers in this chapter? Why do you find those points to be convincing?

2. In your opinion, what are the weakest or

[1290] We consider basic issues of culture, as well as ethical relativism, in the ethics chapter of this book.

[1291] Arguments supporting the idea that race is a social construction are found in much greater detail in the chapter on the philosophy of race in this textbook.

[1292] Crenshaw, Kimberlé Williams. "Mapping the Margins: Intersectionality, Identity Politics, and Violence against Women of Color." ," *Critical Race Theory. The Key Writings that Formed the Movement*, edited by Kimberlé Crenshaw, Neil Gotanda, Gary Peller, and Kendall Thomas. The New Press, New York, 1995. 375-376.

least convincing points? Why? Can you anticipate any limitations or objections to their ideas not already addressed in the chapter?

Appendix: Application to Social Justice

As has been the case, and will be the case, with several other chapters, the *core* of this chapter addresses social justice considerations in a fundamental and unambiguous manner. No further demonstration of relevance is necessary in this appendix.

Chapter 28: Philosophical Foundations of Protests: Human Nature, the Limits of Reason, and Direct Action

Comprehension questions you should be able to answer after reading this chapter:

1. Why do protests and other forms of "direct action" need (or at least benefit from) a justification in their defense? What are some of the "concerns?"
2. What, in general, is a "white moderate," according to King, and why did he find them to be a disappointment and "stumbling block" to progress?
3. What is King's response to charges that direct action violates the law? Be sure to discuss his concept of an unjust law.
4. What are the 4 criteria of justice we considered from the King? List and briefly describe each one.
5. What is "direct action?"
6. When is direct action necessary, and what purposes does it serve?
7. Explain why Niebuhr thinks privileged groups are unlikely to be persuaded by reason/evidence/education alone to relinquish power.
8. Why does Niebuhr think the idea of "original sin" is helpful in a political context?
9. Explain Niebuhr's claim that groups are more immoral than individuals.
10. How do the "illusions" of democracy and meritocracy help those in power rationalize their privilege, according to Niebuhr?
11. What does it mean to say that "reason is the servant of impulse before it is its master?" Why does this matter in the context of using direct action?
12. Why does Niebuhr think that there is no clear line of legitimacy between violent and nonviolent methods of coercion?
13. Why does Niebuhr nevertheless recommend nonviolent methods, especially for minority groups? What are the advantages of nonviolent methods?
14. What/who are the "children of light" and "children of darkness?" Why does Niebuhr recommend a pragmatic middle ground between the two?
15. What does Niebuhr mean by "man's capacity for justice makes democracy possible, but man's inclination to injustice makes democracy necessary?"

The killing of George Floyd by police on May 25, 2020 triggered a massive response, with several polls suggesting that between 15 million and 26 million people in the United States had participated in some form of public demonstration as of June. On June 6th alone, half a million people demonstrated in nearly 550 locations in the United States. Overall, demonstrations of various sizes have taken place in roughly 2,500 towns and cities of equally various sizes across the Nation. Of note: over 40% of counties in the U.S. have had a protest, and 95% of those counties are majority *white*.[1293] These numbers make the 2020 Black Lives Matter demonstrations the largest "protest movement" (in terms of participants) in American history. In comparison, even the historic Civil Rights marches of the 1960's, when *all added together*, would amount a hundreds of thousands of participants—but not millions.

[1293] https://www.nytimes.com/interactive/2020/07/03/us/george-floyd-protests-crowd-size.html

At the same time, coverage of rare cases of looting (which occurred only in the first few days of protests, and, in a few cities in July, arguably due to the insertion of federal agents to suppress protests) dominated news coverage of protests. Note that in some cases, violent "protestors" have actually been revealed to be white supremacists infiltrating the demonstration, acting violently, and intentionally seeking to create civil unrest and generate a backlash against BLM.[1294] Nevertheless, various pundits, editorialists, journalists, and amateur bloggers and social media contributors expressed varying degrees of angst about the civil unrest.

Finally, while 55% of Americans see protests and demonstrations as at least "somewhat effective" tactics for groups to help bring about racial equality, only 19% think such tactics are "very effective." In contrast, 68% suggest that working to get more African Americans elected to public office would be somewhat effective, and 82% think that "working directly with Black[1295] people to solve problems in their local communities" would be somewhat effective. Confidence in the effectiveness of protests seems to vary by party affiliation, with 67% of Republicans thinking that protests/rallies are not too (or not at all) effective in bringing about equality, while only 23% of Democrats believe the same.[1296]

So, given other options, including the "simple" option of voting (for which we must take into consideration historic and current attempts at voter suppression), are protests, rallies, and other forms of demonstration worthwhile? Given the "bad press" of (rare) cases of civil unrest, and the relatively lower confidence in success compared to other possible methods, what justification, if any, do they have?

I propose there are both tactical and philosophical justifications for social action, but that this justification relies upon certain important premises, particularly concerning human nature.

Resistance to Protests

Previously, I mentioned some statistics concerning confidence that demonstrations as effective at bringing about racial equality. I also noted how this confidence varies by political party affiliation. It also varies by race. While 34% of Black Americans see protests as a "very effective" tactic to bring about equality, only 14% of white Americans thought so.[1297]

While there might be (and probably are) numerous reasons for this difference, one difference that must be entertained is that white Americans (in general) have a history of being uncomfortable with protests and other forms of direct social action that sought racial equality for Black Americans. During the Civil Rights Movement, this discomfort was worthy of mention by Martin Luther King, Jr.

MLK

Martin Luther King, Jr. (1-15-1929—4-4-1968) attended segregated schools in Georgia. He graduated high school at the age of fifteen, then earned his BA from Morehouse College (a historically Black College in Atlanta). After attending seminary in Pennsylvania, he earned his doctorate in 1955,[1298] a year after he became

---

[1294] https://www.bbc.com/news/world-us-canada-53579099

[1295] Throughout this paper, you will notice that "Black" is capitalized, whereas "white" is not. This convention has been much debated in recent years. My short explanation is that Black indicates the shared cultural experience of descendants of (often enslaved) Africans in the United States, and their disconnection from their original cultural/ethnic traditions. White doesn't have those same connotations. https://www.cjr.org/analysis/capital-b-Black-styleguide.php

[1296] https://www.pewsocialtrends.org/2020/06/12/amid-protests-majorities-across-racial-and-ethnic-groups-express-support-for-the-Black-lives-matter-movement

[1297]1297 ibid.

[1298] The history of philosophy is filled with some uncomfortable truths. Some of them, coming

pastor of the Dexter Avenue Baptist Church in Montgomery Alabama. Already a member of the executive committee of the National Association for the Advancement of Colored People (NAACP), he led the first Black nonviolent mass demonstration in contemporary U.S. history: the 382 day Montgomery bus boycott. During that time he was arrested, and his home was bombed. He later was elected President of the Southern Christian Leadership Conference, and spent the next eleven years putting into practice his synthesis of Christian ideals and Gandhian tactics of nonviolence. While jailed during a massive protest in Birmingham, Alabama, he wrote the now iconic "Letter from a Birmingham Jail," quoted numerous times below. His accolades included being named *Time* magazine's Man of the Year in 1963, and being awarded the Nobel Peace Prize at the age of thirty-five—the youngest recipient in history, at that time.[1299] He was assassinated on April 4th, 1968, at the age of thirty-nine.

Although King wrote numerous books, letters, and essays, and gave over 2,500 speeches, we will focus primarily on the aforementioned "Letter from a Birmingham Jail." While he was jailed, an ally smuggled in a newspaper which included a "Call for Unity" statement issued by eight white Alabama ministers, condemning King and his methods. King was inspired to write a response.

Begun on the margins of the newspaper in which the statement appeared while I was in jail, the letter was continued on scraps of writing paper supplied by a friendly

Black trusty, and concluded on a pad my attorneys were eventually permitted to leave me.[1300]

Among the many themes King addresses in the Letter is his response to criticisms from those who should theoretically have been his sympathetic allies.

I must make two honest confessions to you, my Christian and Jewish brothers. First, I must confess that over the past few years I have been gravely disappointed with the white moderate. I have almost reached the regrettable conclusion that the Negro's great stumbling block in his stride toward freedom is not the White Citizen's Counciler or the Ku Klux Klanner, but the white moderate, who is more devoted to "order" than to justice; who prefers a negative peace which is the absence of tension to a positive peace which is the presence of justice; who constantly says: "I agree with you in the goal you seek, but I cannot agree with your methods of direct action"; who paternalistically believes he can set the timetable for another man's freedom; who lives by a mythical concept of time and who constantly advises the Negro to wait for a "more convenient season." Shallow understanding from people of good will is more frustrating than absolute misunderstanding from people of ill will. Lukewarm acceptance is much more bewildering than outright rejection.[1301]

---

more to light these days, is the unfortunate and appalling racism of some iconic philosophers, such as David Hume and Immanuel Kant. While reckoning with painful truths, it would be disingenuous to avoid more beloved figures, such as MLK. That King engaged in plagiarism in several of his writings and speeches is now well documented, although the circumstances of his use of others' words are more complicated than mere "copying and pasting."
https://www.washingtonpost.com/archive/opi

nions/1990/11/18/how-king-borrowed/d6fcf0f9-60a1-4b6a-86aa-137075f401e9/

[1299] That distinction now belongs to Malala Yousafzai, who received the award in 2014 at the age of 17.
https://www.nobelprize.org/prizes/lists/nobel-laureates-by-age

[1300] King, Martin Luther, Jr. (1964). *Why We Can't Wait*. New York: Signet Classic (2000), 64.

[1301] Emphasis added. All quotations attributed to

Here, the "white moderate" is identified as a theoretical ally, but source of "disappointment," and, probably worse, a "stumbling block" that is even more of an obstacle than members of the Ku Klux Klan. Even in King's time (and certainly in our own), there are undoubtedly fewer explicit and unapologetic white supremacists than there are moderate-to-liberal-inclined white Americans, who, while benefitting from structural racism, nevertheless don't consciously hold supremacist beliefs or antipathy towards people of color. The problem is that then, as now, such persons tend to be "more devoted to 'order' than to justice." Then, and now, such persons could say "I agree with you in the goal you seek, but I cannot agree with your methods of direct action." Such persons presumably regard racial equality as a worthy goal, but reject the use of protests, sit-ins, or other forms of demonstration as a means to achieve it. They bemoan the civil unrest, the anarchy, the looting or rioting that they imagine might result (and sometimes, though rarely, does), and the general disruption to their sense of routine.[1302]

This issue of "concerned" citizens worrying about demonstrations and their effects seemingly more so than the underlying issues of social justice that prompted the demonstrations in the first place, is hardly new, as King acknowledges.

You deplore the demonstrations taking place in Birmingham. But your statement, I am sorry to say, fails to express a similar concern for the conditions that brought about the demonstrations. I am sure that none of you would want to rest content with the superficial kind of social analysis that deals merely with effects and does not grapple with underlying causes. It is unfortunate that demonstrations are taking place in Birmingham, but it is even more unfortunate that the city's white power structure left the Negro community with no alternative.

Today, one might similarly say that it is "unfortunate" that demonstrations involving millions of Americans have (momentarily) disrupted certain streets or parts of towns, but even more unfortunate that so many Black men are killed by police, disproportionately given their share of the population, that such demonstrations are needed.

In the first couple days of the 2020 BLM protests, some looting occurred. Over the next several weeks of protests, there many more incidents of violence, but they were notably *by police* against protestors. Given the omnipresence of smart phone cameras, live footage of

---

King are from his "Letter from a Birmingham Jail," unless otherwise indicated. The full letter is available here: https://kinginstitute. stanford.edu/king-papers/documents/letter-birmingham-jail

[1302] Anecdotally, I participated in a Black Lives Matter march that effectively stopped traffic at an intersection while the marchers passed through. This was a completely peaceful protest, and the progress of the march was monitored and secured by the local sheriff's department. These sheriffs were also directing traffic so that the marchers could safely pass through the intersection. The entire delay for motorists at that intersection lasted approximately 10 minutes. I personally observed a white woman who was waiting to turn left at that intersection roll down her window, and even step out of her

truck for a moment, to yell at protestors, and hurl profanities at them, for making her "late" in getting her kids home for their dinner. In response to the default chant of that BLM march, she quipped that "my kids' lives matter!" I have no idea what political views she holds, what her particular circumstances were, or whether and to what extent she supported the BLM movement. However, it was evident that a 10 minute delay so that thousands of people demonstrating for police reform aimed at stopping the disproportionate killing of Black men by police officers could pass through an intersection was "too much." *If* she does self-identify as an "ally," I think she would satisfy King's concept of the "white moderate," privileging her convenience over addressing injustice.

protestors being pushed, shot with non-lethal munitions, gassed, and pepper-sprayed was broadcast across the internet.[1303] These incidents of "civil unrest" inspired some commentators and arm-chair pundits to condemn the protests, without which there would have been no violence. Similar comments were made during the Civil Rights Movement, and for similar reasons. King addressed that complaint in his "Letter" as well.

> In your statement you assert that our actions, even though peaceful, must be condemned because they precipitate violence. But is this a logical assertion? Isn't this like condemning a robbed man because his possession of money precipitated the evil act of robbery? Isn't this like condemning Socrates because his unswerving commitment to truth and his philosophical inquiries precipitated the act by the misguided populace in which they made him drink hemlock? Isn't this like condemning Jesus because his unique God consciousness and never ceasing devotion to God's will precipitated the evil act of crucifixion? We must come to see that, as the federal courts have consistently affirmed, it is wrong to urge an individual to cease his efforts to gain his basic constitutional rights because the quest may precipitate violence. Society must protect the robbed and punish the robber.

In a classic *reductio ad absurdum*, King shows the absurdity of such complaints. It is the protestors who have been wronged, and, so long as they are demonstrating nonviolently, it is just as wrongheaded to condemn them for any ensuing violence against *them* as it would be to condemn a victim of robbery for being robbed.

It is also relevant, of course, that whatever is being protested actually be an injustice. What makes the analogy of the robbery compelling is that one accept that Black Americans are the victims of injustice as is the victim of a robbery. Where this gets complicated is when the protest or demonstration either violates a law (as was the case with sit-ins at segregated lunch counters, for example), or is a demonstration against the agents of law (i.e., the police) themselves. To say that the law (or its enforcement) is unjust requires one to commit to an understanding of justice that transcends the dominant values of a particular community. As King points out:

> We should never forget that everything Adolf Hitler did in Germany was "legal" and everything the Hungarian freedom fighters did in Hungary was "illegal." It was "illegal" to aid and comfort a Jew in Hitler's Germany. Even so, I am sure that, had I lived in Germany at the time, I would have aided and comforted my Jewish brothers. If today I lived in a Communist country where certain principles dear to the Christian faith are suppressed, I would openly advocate disobeying that country's antireligious laws.

This understanding presupposes (contrary to ethical relativism, for example), that there exists an objective standard of goodness and justice. This is the first philosophical presupposition of protests we will consider. King himself raises this distinction between just and unjust laws, and appeals to Saint Augustine in his explanation.[1304]

[1303] https://www.cnn.com/2020/06/06/us/police-excessive-force-us-protests/index.html

[1304] As a general comment, Augustine is only one of many philosophers King references throughout his works. In one short section of his "Pilgrimage to Nonviolence" speech given on April 13, 1960, King referenced no less than seven philosophers: Kierkegaard, Nietzsche, Jaspers, Heidegger, Sartre, Hegel, and Tillich. The point of mentioning this is simply to acknowledge his knowledge of philosophy, and its influence on him. Because he was not a "professional" philosophers, he is sometimes not recognized as being a philosopher—though he

There are two types of laws: just and unjust. I would be the first to advocate obeying just laws. One has not only a legal but a moral responsibility to obey just laws. Conversely, one has a moral responsibility to disobey unjust laws. I would agree with St. Augustine that "an unjust law is no law at all."

Now, what is the difference between the two? How does one determine whether a law is just or unjust? A just law is a man made code that squares with the moral law or the law of God. An unjust law is a code that is out of harmony with the moral law. To put it in the terms of St. Thomas Aquinas: An unjust law is a human law that is not rooted in eternal law and natural law. Any law that uplifts human personality is just. Any law that degrades human personality is unjust. All segregation statutes are unjust because segregation distorts the soul and damages the personality. It gives the segregator a false sense of superiority and the segregated a false sense of inferiority. Segregation, to use the terminology of the Jewish philosopher Martin Buber, substitutes an "I it" relationship for an "I thou" relationship and ends up relegating persons to the status of things.

King actually offers numerous criteria of justice (i.e., ways to distinguish just laws from unjust laws) in this passage.

1. Whether a law "squares" with the moral law or law of God (meaning the same thing for King).
2. Whether a law "uplifts" or "degrades" human personality.

3. Whether a law issued by a majority makes demands of the minority that the majority are not themselves subject to.
4. Whether a minority had a role in creating or enacting the law to which it is subject.

We can quickly apply these standards to see how they operate. Consider the extreme example of chattel slavery, which operated in the United States from the early 16th century until officially abolished in 1863, at which time an estimated *4 million* enslaved persons were freed.[1305] Slavery was enshrined in law throughout this period, and it was not only illegal for an enslaved person to escape, but also illegal for free persons to assist them. Slavery was legal, and resisting slavery was illegal. Needless to say, King would claim that slavery was an unjust system, and any laws supporting it and enforcing it were likewise unjust. This can be demonstrated by appealing to any of his 4 criteria.

1. Slavery does not "square" with the moral law or law of God, according to King's understanding, at least. Although arguments were made for centuries to rationalize slavery and proclaim its moral legitimacy, and even its endorsement by Christianity, if nothing else an appeal to the "Golden Rule"—something a child in a Sunday school class could accomplish—would indicate otherwise.
2. Although his appeal to "human personality" is vague, King means something like the inherent dignity of personhood. Slavery clearly does not "uplift," though it does "degrade," human personality, in that sense.

---

certainly was.

[1305] This number does not include, of course, all of the enslaved persons who had either died or been liberated prior to that, nor those enslaved in other countries, nor those who died during the trans-Atlantic voyage. Estimates of the total number of Africans killed by the slave trade *before* their period of enslavement in America range from 30-60 *million*, as reported by Stannard, David. *American Holocaust. The Conquest of the New World.* Oxford University Press (1993), 317-318.

3. Slavery most certainly makes demands of a minority which the majority were not subject to.

4. Enslaved persons most certainly did *not* have a role in creating or enacting the law to which they were subject.

Similar arguments would need to be made (and, I think, could be made) with respect to the laws and practices being protested during the Civil Rights Movement, and the contemporary example of excessive and discriminatory police practices against Black Americans. Nonviolent resistance to such unjust laws and practices, far from demonstrating a disregard for law or justice, actually does the opposite, according to King. Breaking an unjust law, knowingly, openly, lovingly, and with a willingness to accept the penalty is actually expressing the "highest respect" for the law.

> I hope you are able to see the distinction I am trying to point out. In no sense do I advocate evading or defying the law, as would the rabid segregationist. That would lead to anarchy. One who breaks an unjust law must do so openly, lovingly, and with a willingness to accept the penalty. I submit that an individual who breaks a law that conscience tells him is unjust, and who willingly accepts the penalty of imprisonment in order to arouse the conscience of the community over its injustice, is in reality expressing the highest respect for law.

And,

> ...we feel that there are moral laws in the universe just as valid and as basic as man-made laws, and whenever a man-made law is in conflict with what we consider the law of God, or the moral law of the universe, then we feel that we have a moral

> obligation to protest. . . . when the law of our nation stands in conflict with the higher moral law and when a local law stands in conflict with the federal law, then we must resist that law in order to dignify and give meaning in the full outpour of the federal law and the moral law.[1306]

Whether the example is abolition, or the Civil Rights Movement, or the BLM movement, in no case are activists seeking the abolition of law itself, but rather the abolition of *unjust* laws and unjust and discriminatory exercise of policing. Even given that context, though, for each example there have been those who, while not diametrically opposed to the "cause," did not support it either, and expressed "concern" about the timing of the activism, or the pace at which it sought change, or methods (even when nonviolent) by which it pursued those changes.

Concerning those who neither opposed nor supported, but who remained silent and uninvolved, King said the following:

> We will have to repent in this generation not merely for the hateful words and actions of the bad people but for the appalling silence of the good people. Human progress never rolls in on wheels of inevitability; it comes through the tireless efforts of men willing to be co workers with God, and without this hard work, time itself becomes an ally of the forces of social stagnation.

With respect to those who had concerns about the timing or pace:

> Frankly, I have yet to engage in a direct action campaign that was "well timed" in the view of those who have not suffered unduly from the disease of segregation. For years now I have heard the word "Wait!" It rings in the ear of every Negro with

---

[1306] Interview with Martin Luther King, Jr., on "Meet the Press," April 17, 1960. The full transcript is available here:

http://okra.stanford.edu/transcription/docume nt_images/Vol05Scans/17Apr1960_Interviewon MeetthePress.pdf

piercing familiarity. This "Wait" has almost always meant "Never." We must come to see, with one of our distinguished jurists, that "justice too long delayed is justice denied."

We must use time creatively, in the knowledge that the time is always ripe to do right. Now is the time to make real the promise of democracy and transform our pending national elegy into a creative psalm of brotherhood. Now is the time to lift our national policy from the quicksand of racial injustice to the solid rock of human dignity.

And, in general response to all of the "concerns" expressed by "white moderates," King explains his support of direct action (which includes protests, among other things) by way of expressing his "hopes."

I had hoped that the white moderate would understand that law and order exist for the purpose of establishing justice and that when they fail in this purpose they become the dangerously structured dams that block the flow of social progress. I had hoped that the white moderate would understand that the present tension in the South is a necessary phase of the transition from an obnoxious negative peace, in which the Negro passively accepted his unjust plight, to a substantive and positive peace, in which all men will respect the dignity and worth of human personality. Actually, we who engage in nonviolent direct action are not the creators of tension. We merely bring to the surface the hidden tension that is already alive. We bring it out in the open, where it can be seen and dealt with. Like a boil that can never be cured so long as it is covered up but must be opened with all its ugliness to the natural medicines of air and light,

injustice must be exposed, with all the tension its exposure creates, to the light of human conscience and the air of national opinion before it can be cured.

"Direct action" refers to "actions taken when the opponent is unwilling to enter into, or remain in, discussion/negotiation."[1307] Direct action could include protests, boycotts, sit-ins, and other demonstrations, among other things. Direct action is necessary when "law and order" aren't actually equally serving justice. These actions attempt to force persons in positions of power and authority to take some sort of action, whether it be negotiating workplace conditions, abolishing discriminatory laws and practices, integrating schools, etc. Direct action was deemed warranted (and necessary) for two reasons that might seem like statements of the obvious:

1. The desired outcome didn't already exist.
2. Those in a position to grant that outcome were unwilling to do so.

This is where direct action as a tactic comes in. Direct action brings the problem "out in the open." It serves to expose injustice "to the light of human conscience." The point of this, of course, is not *merely* to reveal a fact, but to *solve* a problem. Once revealed, it can be "dealt with." Like a disease, it can be "cured"—but only once the sickness has been discovered and diagnosed.

During the Civil Rights Movement, police brutality against nonviolent protestors shocked the Nation, with many people witnessing on television, for the first time, the level of racism and violence that Black Americans had experienced since before the birth of American itself. Arguably, images of the brutal murder of Emmett Till in 1955 gave further motivation for the Civil Rights Movement, allegedly inspiring Rosa Parks in the context of the Montgomery Bus Boycott.[1308] Televised footage of peaceful

---

[1307] https://thekingcenter.org/king-philosophy/

[1308] Jesse Jackson said, "Rosa said she thought

about going to the back of the bus. But then she thought about Emmett Till and she couldn't do

protestors being assaulted on "Bloody Sunday" arguably resulted in the passage of the Voting Rights Act of 1965.[1309] Easily available footage of the nearly 9 minute choking-to-death of George Floyd in 2020 triggered protests not merely around the country, but even internationally, with events occurring (at minimum) in Sweden, England, Japan, Brazil, Spain, Senegal, Denmark, Scotland, South Korea, Belgium, Hungary, Italy, Australia, Poland, Turkey, France, Switzerland, Portugal, Canada, and Germany.[1310]

Protests such as these not only "shine a light" on an existing injustice, but also serve the practical function of generating "movement" that otherwise would not occur.

You may well ask: "Why direct action? Why sit ins, marches and so forth? Isn't negotiation a better path?" You are quite right in calling for negotiation. Indeed, this is the very purpose of direct action. Nonviolent direct action seeks to create such a crisis and foster such a tension that a community which has constantly refused to negotiate is forced to confront the issue. It seeks so to dramatize the issue that it can no longer be ignored. My citing the creation of tension as part of the work of the nonviolent resister may sound rather shocking. But I must confess that I am not afraid of the word "tension." I have earnestly opposed violent tension, but there is a type of constructive, nonviolent tension which is necessary for growth. Just as Socrates felt that it was necessary to create a tension in the mind so that individuals could rise from the bondage of myths and half truths to the unfettered realm of creative analysis and objective appraisal, so must we see the need for

nonviolent gadflies to create the kind of tension in society that will help men rise from the dark depths of prejudice and racism to the majestic heights of understanding and brotherhood. The purpose of our direct action program is to create a situation so crisis packed that it will inevitably open the door to negotiation. I therefore concur with you in your call for negotiation. Too long has our beloved Southland been bogged down in a tragic effort to live in monologue rather than dialogue.

Recall the assumptions from above concerning when direct action was needed.

1. The desired outcome didn't already exist.
2. Those in a position to grant that outcome were unwilling to do so.

For every protest and reform movement, the desired outcome didn't already exist, and would not be achieved if not for some "nudging." Why would anyone assume that slavery would have just somehow ended on its own, as white slave owners felt increasingly guilty and collectively decided to relinquish the engine of their economy? And how long were enslaved people supposed to wait for that enlightenment to occur? Estimates of the "diverted income" from slavery, from 1790 to 1860 alone, was calculated (compounded and adjusted for inflation) in 1983. The sum was estimated to be between 2.1 and 4.7 trillion dollars.[1311] Adjusted to 2020 dollars, but without compounding interest, this value is approximately 5.4-12.1 trillion dollars.

Why would anyone think that desegregation and the unraveling of Jim Crow laws throughout

---

it." (https://nmaahc.si.edu/blog-post/emmett-tills-death-inspired-movement)

[1309] https://www.clarionledger.com/story/news/local/journeytojustice/2018/03/06/week-civil-rights-history-march-5-march-11/396895002/

[1310] https://www.theatlantic.com/photo/2020/

06/images-worldwide-protest-movement/612811/

[1311] Marketti, James. "Estimated Present Value of Income Diverted during Slavery," in America, Richard. *The Wealth of Races: The Present Value of Benefits from Past Injustices.* Praeger (2002), 107.

the U.S. (but particularly in the South) would have naturally occurred by virtue of the evolving consciences of white supremacists? To the contrary, when the Supreme Court nullified a key section of the Voting Rights Act of 1965 in the 2013 case of *Shelby v. Holder*, a wave of documentable tactics of voter suppression targeting Black communities occurred (and continues to occur), primarily in former Confederate States.[1312] As the most contemporary example, as of the time of this writing, several specific changes have already been produced in direct response to these BLM protests. The Los Angeles Police Department budget was cut by $150 million.[1313] The city of Minneapolis (where Floyd was killed) pledged to "dismantle" and restructure its police force.[1314] The State of New York banned police chokeholds.[1315] The State of Mississippi voted to remove the "rebel" confederate flag from its State flag,[1316] and even NASCAR banned confederate flags at its tracks.[1317]

While none of those satisfies the policy demands of BLM in terms of breadth or depth of policy changes, they are policy achievements nonetheless. In addition, the Black Lives Matter movement is now something that 67% of Americans "support."[1318] Is it at all plausible that we, as a society, would have (or will be) making these changes if *not* for the demonstrations? Is it at all plausible that police budgets in major cities like Los Angeles and New York would be cut if not for the demonstrations? Is it at all plausible that "defund the police" (when understood not as "abolishing" the police, but as shifting funds from armed policing to social services such as mental health intervention, homeless intervention, and drug treatment) would be supported by 72% of Americans, as of June 2020, without the demonstrations? [1319] Would such an idea even have been on our collective minds?

I think the answer to those admittedly rhetorical questions is a resounding "no" in each case.

If that is accurate, it reveals a key function of direct action: "forcing" action on an existing injustice that would otherwise not be acted upon. King was confident that those in power would not voluntarily relinquish power and privilege unless *compelled* to do so, and he was convinced of this due to the influence of the 20th century philosopher and Christian theologian, Reinhold Niebuhr.

Niebuhr

Karl Niebuhr (1892-1971) was a theologian, ethicist, political theorist, and Professor at Union Theological Seminary. He was a widely recognized "public intellectual" throughout much of the mid-twentieth century in the United States, and was awarded the Presidential Medal of Freedom in 1964. He wrote numerous books and essays on theology, ethics, and politics, with the most influential being *Moral Man and Immoral Society*, and *The Nature and Destiny of Man*.

His own political ideology evolved significantly over the course of his life and career. Starting as a pacifist and a socialist, he later developed the ideology known as "Christian Realism." Pointing out the faults of both liberalism and authoritarianism, he ultimately settled on a pragmatic endorsement of

[1312] https://www.theguardian.com/us-news/2020/jun/25/shelby-county-anniversary-voting-rights-act-consequences

[1313] https://www.latimes.com/california/story/2020-07-01/lapd-budget-cuts-protesters-police-brutality

[1314] https://www.nytimes.com/2020/06/07/us/minneapolis-police-abolish.html

[1315] https://www.nytimes.com/2020/06/12/nyregion/50a-repeal-police-floyd.html

[1316] https://www.nytimes.com/2020/06/28/us/mississippi-flag-confederacy.html

[1317] https://www.nytimes.com/2020/06/10/sports/autoracing/nascar-confederate-flags.html

[1318] https://www.pewsocialtrends.org/2020/06/12/amid-protests-majorities-across-racial-and-ethnic-groups-express-support-for-the-Black-lives-matter-movement/

[1319] https://www.vox.com/2020/6/23/21299118/defunding-the-police-minneapolis-budget-george-floyd

democracy, but consistently warned of the perils of inequality, especially with regard to race and class.

Niebuhr's intellectual and cultural influence was considerable. Perhaps best known among those openly influenced by him is Martin Luther King, Jr., but numerous politicians known to have cited him as an influence include Hillary Clinton, James Comey, Madeleine Albright, John McCain, President Jimmy Carter, and President Barack Obama. Indeed, in a 2007 interview, Obama said the following of Niebuhr:

I love him. He's one of my favorite philosophers. . . . I take away [from Niebuhr] the compelling idea that there's serious evil in the world, and hardship and pain. And we should be humble and modest in our belief we can eliminate those things. But we shouldn't use that as an excuse for cynicism and inaction. I take away ... the sense we have to make these efforts knowing they are hard, and not swinging from naïve idealism to bitter realism.[1320]

Returning to Niebuhr's influence on *King*:

My friends, I must say to you that we have not made a single gain in civil rights without determined legal and nonviolent pressure. Lamentably, it is an historical fact that privileged groups seldom give up their privileges voluntarily. Individuals may see the moral light and voluntarily give up their unjust posture; but, as Reinhold Niebuhr has reminded us, groups tend to be more immoral than individuals. We know through painful experience that freedom is never voluntarily given by the oppressor; it must be demanded by the oppressed.

Here, King derives two important ideas from Niebuhr, both of which will be explored in this chapter.

1. Privileged groups seldom give up power voluntarily.
2. Groups are more immoral than individuals.

With respect to privileged groups refusing to relinquish power voluntarily, Niebuhr was explicit. First, Niebuhr proposes that this relinquishing cannot be achieved by persuasion alone, but always requires the use of power, or "coercion," as he will often call it.

When collective power, whether in the form of imperialism or class domination, exploit weakness, it can never be dislodged unless power is raised against it. If conscience and reason can be insinuated into the resulting struggle it can only qualify but not abolish it.[1321]

Power (or coercion), in this case, doesn't refer to violence (although he will have more to say on that later), but includes the coercive power of demonstrations, strikes, boycotts, etc. The need for the imposition of this sort of power is all the greater for minority groups. Although he acknowledges that dialogue and compromise might be effective in some cases, these gentler and more cerebral tactics will not suffice when it is a minority group seeking concessions from a more-powerful majority.

If two parties are in a conflict, let them, by conferring together, moderate their demands and arrive at a modus vivendi.... Undoubtedly there are innumerable conflicts which must be resolved in this fashion. But will a disinherited group, such

---

[1320] https://www.nytimes.com/2007/04/26/opinion/26brooks.html As an additional bit of trivia, Niebuhr is also credited with having created the "Serenity Prayer," now used extensively in 12-Step programs.

[1321] Niebuhr, Reinhold. *Moral Man and Immoral Society. A Study in Ethics and Politics.* Second edition. Westminster John Knox Press, Louisville (1932), xxx.

as the Negroes for instance, ever win full justice in society in this fashion? What might even its most minimum demands seem exorbitant to the dominant whites, among whom only a very small minority will regard the interracial problems from the perspective of objective justice?[1322]

As he mentions, and as seems unfortunately equally relevant today, Black Americans are especially vulnerable to the power of the white majority, and are especially needful of direct action to secure any desired changes.

However large the number of individual white men who do and who will identify themselves completely with the Negro cause, the white race in America will not admit the Negro to equal rights if it is not forced to do so. Upon that point one may speak with a dogmatism which all history justifies.[1323]

Appealing to history to support his case, Niebuhr points out that "all history" justifies his claim that equal rights will not be granted voluntarily. Slavery was not ended voluntarily. Indeed, it took a Civil War and a recently-upgraded estimate of approximately 750,000 deaths.[1324] Segregation was not ended until years of boycotts, demonstrations, marches, sit-ins, and martyrdom forced the various Civil Rights Acts of the 60's, and supporting Supreme Court rulings. In fact, a careful (and depressing) study of U.S. history reveals that for every "advance" in the status and rights of Black Americans, a "backlash" occurred (legislatively, violently, or both).[1325] With history as our guide, what reason would King have to think white Americans in positions of power would give up privilege without being "coerced" into doing so? What reason would contemporary BLM activists have to think that police reform will occur without similar coercion?

To understand why both Niebuhr and King would likely have answered "none" to all those questions, we need to understand why Niebuhr would have also done so, given his influence on King. To do that, we need to unpack some key elements (sometimes shared, sometimes overlapping) of their worldviews. Among them was King's eventual rejection of the twin "extremes" of optimism and pessimism.

The more I observed the tragedies of history and man's shameful inclination to choose the low road, the more I came to see the depths and strength of sin. My reading of the works of Reinhold Niebuhr made me aware of the complexity of human motives and the reality of sin on every level of man's existence. Moreover, I came to recognize the complexity of man's social involvement and the glaring reality of collective evil. I came to feel that liberalism had been all too sentimental concerning human nature and that it leaned toward a false idealism.

I also came to see that liberalism's superficial optimism concerning human nature caused it to overlook the fact that reason is darkened by sin. The more I thought about human nature the more I saw how our tragic inclination for sin causes us to use our minds to rationalize our actions. Liberalism failed to see that reason by itself is little more than an instrument to justify man's defensive ways of thinking. Reason, devoid of the purifying power of faith, can never free itself from

---

[1322] ibid., xxxii. Note: while the use of the word "Negro" might well be unsettling to our contemporary ears, this was the respectable terminology of the time, and can't be avoided when quoting Niebuhr directly.
[1323] ibid., 253.
[1324] https://www.history.com/news/civil-war-

deadlier-than-previously-thought. Note: by percentage of the U.S. population, *today* that death toll would be more than 6 *million*.
[1325] This is thoroughly documented by Carol Anderson in *White Rage: The Unspoken Truth of our Racial Divide*. Bloomsbury (2017).

distortions and rationalizations.

In spite of the fact that I had to reject some aspects of liberalism, I never came to an all-out acceptance of neo-orthodoxy. While I saw neo-orthodoxy as a helpful corrective for a liberalism that had become all too sentimental, I never felt that it provided an adequate answer to the basic questions. If liberalism was too optimistic concerning human nature, neo-orthodoxy was too pessimistic.[1326]

What was needed was a synthesis of both.

An adequate understanding of man is found neither in the thesis of liberalism nor in the antithesis of neo-orthodoxy, but in a synthesis which reconciles the truths of both.[1327]

King's rejection of the optimism of liberalism and the pessimism of what he calls "neo-orthodoxy," and the need for a synthesis that reconciles the two, was directly inherited from Niebuhr, as King himself acknowledges above.

Niebuhr began his philosophical life amidst the historical backdrop of optimism. At the beginning of the 20th century, a widely shared perception in the United States and Europe was that societies and people were making "progress," becoming more just, better educated, and more enlightened. Even the slaughter of the First World War was interpreted in that context. Surely the world had learned its lesson and would "never again" devolve into such violence. . . However, by the end of the decade in which Niebuhr had written *Moral Man and Immoral Society* (i.e., the 1930's), the world would be plunged into World War II, and education, science, technology, and all of the gears of government would be used for genocide, slaughter, and the spread of fascist

totalitarianism. Niebuhr had predicted those developments, and cautioned against them in his writings. Such outcomes were inevitable, he thought, given human nature, unless societies enacted radical egalitarian reforms.

For our purposes, we will consider four key elements of (and stemming from) Niebuhr's interpretation of human nature.

1. Self-interest and "original sin"
2. Groups are more immoral than individuals
3. The necessity of "coercion"
4. The tension between the "children of light" and the "children of darkness"

Self-interest and Original Sin

To begin with, like many other philosophers, such as Xunzi, Hobbes, Machiavelli, and Bentham, Niebuhr believed that humans had a natural impulse towards selfish behavior. In fairness, he believed that humans are "endowed" with both selfish and unselfish impulses. So, we are not exclusively selfish—but selfishness is a powerful predisposition for all of us.[1328] This impulse of self-interest leads to seeking power, wealth, status, and security. Because humans are more sophisticated in our desires compared to other animals, our survival instinct, our will to live, gets transformed into a "will to self-realization." We are interested not only in mere survival, but also "prestige and social approval."[1329] The possession of power and prestige necessarily causes one to come into conflict with the similar conditions of others, and the conflict (and the cruelty that the conflict produces) is magnified at the level of groups, whether ethnic, religious, national, etc. Humans are not only driven by self-interest, but also by anxiety. This anxiety prompts the quest for security, which degenerates into a (biblical) notion of "idolatry."

[1326] King, Martin Luther. "Pilgrimage to Nonviolence" delivered 13 April 1960. Chicago, Illinois.
[1327] ibid.
[1328] Niebuhr, *Moral Man*, 25.

[1329] Niebuhr Reinhold. *The Children of Light and the Children of Darkness. A Vindication of Democracy and the Critique of Its Traditional Defense.* University of Chicago Press, Chicago (1944), 20.

Goaded by anxiety, people seek to secure themselves against these threats. They make themselves the center of their world, as if they were that center. Anxiety grounds self-interest. In biblical language, they practice "idolatry;" that is, they replace God with themselves, or take the place of God. Or, as Niebuhr also puts this, they exhibit "pride." And in the process, they are violent, cruel, and destructive towards others. Pride begets self-concern, and self-centeredness breeds injustice; the cycle of sin, violence, and destruction begins.... We claim that our values, and so our moral judgments, are absolute, in effect God's judgments. Incidentally, such judgments always declare us to be righteous and our opponents wrong – as most personal altercations and all international ones show. Finally, the most serious and of all, we claim our spirits to represent the divine, and our religion to be God's religion. The ultimate sin, therefore, is to claim to be or to represent directly God, the claim religion has illustrated throughout history.... Such pride or idolatry defies God and results in injustice. Here for Niebuhr is the true source of history's tragedy, suffering and despair at best despite the evident development of institutions, legal codes, and moral norms in history; this sin in all its forms of power, intelligence, morals, and religion remains as a most significant dynamic force in history, the major cause of injustice.[1330]

The "religious" vocabulary is unmistakable here, and is hardly surprising given that Niebuhr was both a Christian theologian as well as a philosopher. Indeed, for both Niebuhr and King, their Christian worldview provided essential premises for their conclusions about political action. One of those key premises is the doctrine of "original sin."

Although it admits of many interpretations, the Christian doctrine of original sin generally refers to the belief that human nature is "fallen" from its original exalted state, and for that reason all human beings, by virtue of their very nature, are prone to sinful behavior. Niebuhr, while certainly a Christian, entertained a "symbolic" interpretation of the "fall of man" and original sin, rejecting a literal understanding of historical Adam and Eve, the Garden of Eden, etc. The symbol of original sin expresses this fundamental self-centeredness, and proneness to oppression. This understanding of a "fallen" human nature is important not only theologically, but *politically*.

...it is necessary to point out that the doctrine [of Original Sin] makes an important contribution to any adequate social and political theory the lack of which has robbed bourgeois theory of real wisdom; for it emphasizes a fact which every page of human history attests. Through it one may understand that no matter how wide the perspectives which the human mind may reach, how broad the loyalties which the human imagination may conceive, how universal the community which human statecraft may organize, or how pure the aspirations of the saintliest idealists may be, there is no level of human moral or social achievement in which there is not some corruption of inordinate self-love.[1331]

Original sin offers a way to understand (and respond to) human behavior given the reality of our nature. Other historical attempts to "perfect" humanity and eliminate crime and violence have all failed because they have failed to recognize the origin, the root cause of our bad behavior. Attempts to explain toxic self-interest have focused on various causes for bad behavior: education (or lack thereof), economic systems and inequalities, political systems and oppression. The assumption is that one or more of these corrupt otherwise good people.[1332] "But

---

[1330] Langdon B. Gilkey, in *Moral Man*, xxii-xxiii.

[1331] Niebuhr, *The Children of Light*, 16 – 17.

[1332] This appeal to social forces is common among philosophers with an optimistic view of

no school [of thought] asks how it is that an essentially good man could have produced corrupting and tyrannical political organizations or exploiting economic organizations, or fanatical and superstitious religious organizations."[1333] In other words, if people are essentially good, and it is only "bad" institutions and societal arrangements that corrupt them, why would "good" people have created "bad" institutions in the first place? The better explanation for selfishness, according to Niebuhr, is to look *inward*.

This is not to say that societal structures and institutions have no corrupting role to play. In fact, a second key premise for Niebuhr is that, for all the damage original sin produces, the immorality *increases* once we form into groups.

Groups are more immoral than individuals

Niebuhr believed that our impulse of self-interest prompted us to behave selfishly, and even engage in the idolatry of making ourselves the "center" of the universe. However, it is psychologically challenging to make *oneself* "the center," in this way. There are constant external checks on our ego, and it takes an impressive level of narcissism to consistently act in such a way. But, this is far less difficult on behalf of a *group*.

> We make the interests of our relevant groups central to our thought and action, and hence we give ourselves with all our loyalty and power to our group, to its security and success, and to its conquest and domination of competing groups. Thus result the social, group sins of historical life: sins of class, race, religion, nation, and gender.[1334]

This is an important difference between the moral behavior of individuals and of groups. Groups can justify behavior and policies that individuals often can't or won't. Because the responsibility fades into the group, individuals can rationalize their contributions or complacency, and see themselves (and be seen) as a "good person" even within an unjust or oppressive system.[1335] As an example, individual patriotism is esteemed and respected as altruistic and heroic self-sacrifice, even if the actions of the nation are questionable (or worse).[1336]

> As individuals, men believe that they ought to love and serve each other and establish justice between each other. As racial, economic and national groups they take for themselves, whatever their power can command.[1337]

This difference between the immoral tendencies of individuals and groups was identified by Niebuhr, in the preface to the 1960 addition of *Moral Man and Immoral Society*, as his "central thesis."

> The central thesis was, and is, that the liberal movement both religious and secular seem to be unconscious of the basic difference between the morality of individuals and the morality of collectives, whether races, classes or nations.[1338]

Again, in the introduction to *Moral Man and Immoral Society*, Niebuhr tells us his thesis in very helpful fashion.

> The thesis to be elaborated in these pages is that a sharp distinction must be drawn between the moral and social behavior of individuals and of social groups, national, racial, and economic; and that this distinction justifies and necessitates

---

human nature, such as Mengzi.

[1333] Niebuhr, *The Children of Light*, 17.

[1334] Gilkey, in *Moral Man*, xxiii.

[1335] Niebuhr, *Moral Man*, xix.

[1336] Ironically, Niebuhr proposes that the highest

level of altruism and self-sacrifice is righteous opposition to one's group (using the examples of Jesus and Socrates). ibid., xix.

[1337] ibid., 9.

[1338] ibid., xxvii.

political policies which a purely individualistic ethic must always find embarrassing.[1339]

In other words, to develop effective social and political policy requires that one understand the difference between individuals and groups, and why interventions for one are inappropriate for the other. This misunderstanding allows for several "illusions" specific, though presumably not unique, to the United States (where Niebuhr lived, worked, and advocated).

One of our fundamental illusions, as Americans, according to Niebuhr, is that democracy, unlike dictatorships, monarchies, etc., facilitates cooperation amongst equals, rather than the coercion of the less powerful by the more powerful.

The democratic method of resolving social conflict, which some romanticists hail as a triumph of the ethical over the coercive factor, is really much more coercive than at first seems apparent. The majority has its way, not because the minority believes that the majority is right (few minorities are willing to grant the majority the moral prestige of such a concession), but because the votes of the majority are a symbol of its social strength. Whenever a minority believes that it has some strategic advantage which outweighs the power of numbers, and whenever it is sufficiently intent upon its ends, or desperate enough about its position in society, it refuses to accept the dictates of the majority.[1340]

The present-day increase in tribalism might make this claim seem less shocking than it might have been a few decades ago. Rather than painting a picture of individuals happily accepting outcomes of elections, even when things don't go their way, Niebuhr offers

resentful citizens chafing under the policies forced upon them. Rather than imagining gracious majority party victors crafting policy in ways that consider the interests of the minority, Niebuhr offers triumphant "winners" imposing their will on the "losers." When we consider how both Democrats and Republicans have resorted to unilateral policy-making, without any bipartisan support in recent years, this view is not difficult to entertain.

Just as democracy is illusory, in some respects, so too is our belief that we live in a "meritocracy." Among other things, this "illusion" manifests when privileged persons and groups assume that their privileged status is an indicator of their actual superiority in some meaningful respect.

The educational advantages which privilege buys, and the opportunities for the exercise of authority which come with privileged social position, develop capacities which are easily attributed to innate endowment. The presence of able men among the privileged is allowed to obscure the number of instances in which hereditary privilege is associated with knavery and incompetence. On the other hand it has always been the habit of privileged groups to deny the oppressed classes every opportunity for the cultivation of innate capacities and then to accuse them of lacking what they have been denied the right to acquire.[1341]

As a simple (hypothetical) demonstration: a person is born into privilege by virtue of being born white, male, cis-gendered, heterosexual, and with no disabilities.[1342] The family into which he is born is comfortably middle class, or above. Both parents attended College, and fully expect the child to do as well. They live in a "good" neighborhood, attend well-funded schools with

---

[1339] ibid., xxix.

[1340] ibid., 4.

[1341] ibid., 118.

[1342] I'm not picking on anyone. So far, that

describes *me* – although the rest of the example deviates from my own case in several significant ways.

ample extra-curricular activities, available tutoring, invested and attentive school counselors, etc. He is encouraged to take the PSAT, and SAT, and enroll in AP classes. His parents hire tutors to help him prepare for these exams, and as a result he does reasonably well, improving his chance of acceptance to "good" Colleges. Because the family has been able to accumulate generational wealth, they are able to afford College, and their good credit scores and home ownership qualifies them for low-interest loans in the event they are necessary. Well-prepared, the child does well in College, and uses the alumni connections from that prestigious school to land a respectable job. Looking back, he is proud of his accomplishments, and shakes his head at those whose poor work ethic, laziness, or inability prevented them from achieving the same success as himself. Satisfied with the "rightness" of his superior status, he votes for politicians and policies that reward people like himself, and perhaps even punish the "lazy" people, in hopes that some "tough love" might help them finally find the will to improve their lot in life. Such a person might even come to identify his own values and interests with that of society itself, and think that when he promotes his own interest, it's not actually self-interest at all.

The moral attitudes of dominant and privileged groups are characterised by universal self-deception and hypocrisy. The unconscious and conscious identification of their special interests with general interests and universal values, which we have noted in analysing national attitudes, is equally obvious in the attitude of classes. The reason why privileged classes are more hypocritical than underprivileged ones is that special privilege can be defended in terms of the rational ideal of equal justice only, by proving that it contributes something to the good of the whole. Since inequalities of privilege are greater than could possibly be defended rationally, the intelligence of

privileged groups is usually applied to the task of inventing specious proofs for the theory that universal values spring from, and that general interests are served by, the special privileges which they hold.[1343]

1960's era segregationists weren't protecting "white privilege;" they were protecting "State's rights," the "Southern way of life," "traditional values, "law and order," etc.

Privileged groups have other persistent methods of justifying their special interests in terms of general interest. The assumption that they possess unique intellectual gifts and moral excellencies which redound to the general good, is only one of them. Perhaps a more favorite method is to identify the particular organisation of society, of which they are the beneficiaries, with the peace and order of society in general and to appoint themselves the apostles of law and order. Since every society has an instinctive desire for harmony and avoidance of strife, this is a very potent instrument of maintaining the unjust status quo. No society has ever achieved peace without incorporating injustice into its harmony. Those who would eliminate the injustice are therefore always placed at the moral disadvantage of imperiling its peace. The privileged groups will place them under that moral disadvantage even if the efforts toward justice are made in the most pacific terms. They will claim that it is dangerous to disturb a precarious equilibrium and will feign to fear anarchy as the consequence of the effort. This passion for peace need not always be consciously dishonest. Since those who hold special privileges in society are naturally inclined to regard their privileges as their rights and to be unmindful of the effects of inequality upon the underprivileged, they will have a natural complacence toward injustice.

[1343] ibid., 117.

Every effort to disturb the peace, which incorporates the injustice, will therefore seem to them to spring from unjustified malcontent. They will furthermore be only partly conscious of the violence and coercion by which their privileges are preserved and will therefore be particularly censorious of the use of force or the threat of violence by those who oppose them. The force they use is either the covert force of economic power or it is the police power of the state, seemingly sanctified by the supposedly impartial objectives of the government which wields it, but nevertheless amenable to their interests. They are thus able in perfect good faith to express abhorrence of the violence of a strike by workers and to call upon the state in the same breath to use violence in putting down the strike. The unvarying reaction of capitalist newspapers to outbreaks of violence in labor disputes is to express pious abhorrence of the use of violent methods and then to call upon the state to use the militia in suppressing the exasperated workers.[1344]

In the context of 2020 BLM protests, attempts to fundamentally restructure policing so as to eliminate discriminatory practices that, at times, literally cost Black Americans their lives, are dismissed as "communist," or "anarchist." They are associated with "Antifa."[1345] They are framed as threats to "law and order." BLM has been described as a "terrorist group."[1346] President Trump Tweeted a letter written by his former lawyer (John Dowd) describing protestors as "phony" and "terrorists using idle

hate filled students to burn and destroy."[1347] This was in sharp contrast to the testimony, before Congress, of a National Guard Major, who was on scene in an advisory role, who claimed that those same protestors were "behaving peacefully" and that it was his "observation that the use of force against demonstrators in the clearing operation was an unnecessary escalation of the use of force," that "those demonstrators - our fellow American citizens - were engaged in the peaceful expression of their First Amendment rights."[1348] The mere slogan "Black Lives Matter," was called a "symbol of hate" by President Trump. All of these attributions run counter, of course, to the supposed values of America, the American way of life, etc. By implication, resistance to these demonstrations and their demands is not a sign of racism, or an attempt to retain privilege, but is instead resistance to a threat to America itself. Rejection of BLM can be rationalized as patriotism. And, to the extent that "white moderates" don't truly understand the grievances of the demonstrators, they are prone to be more interested in preserving "peace" than in promoting "justice."

Nor is he likely to understand the desire to break the peace, because he does not fully recognise the injustices which it hides. They are not easily recognised, because they consist in inequalities, which history sanctifies and tradition justifies. Even the most rational moralist underestimates them, if he does not actually suffer from them. A too uncritical glorification of co-operation and mutuality therefore results in the acceptance of traditional injustices and the preference of the subtler types of coercion to the more overt types.[1349]

[1344] ibid., 129 – 130.

[1345] Antifa is short for "anti-fascist." This group is known for its staunch opposition to right-wing groups (especially white supremacists), but also for their aggressive and sometimes violent tactics. https://www.adl.org/resources/backgrounders/who-are-antifa

[1346] https://www.officer.com/command-

hq/news/12215638/minneapolis-police-union-head-calls-Black-lives-matter-terrorist-group

[1347] https://www.politico.com/news/2020/06/04/trump-lawyer-protesters-terrorist-letter-302552

[1348] https://www.bbc.com/news/world-us-canada-53559501

[1349] Niebuhr, *Moral Man*, 233.

While "peace" and "stability" are certainly worthwhile, Niebuhr does not think that they are always the *most* morally imperative of available goals. For Niebuhr, *equality* is more valuable than peace.

The conclusion which has been forced upon us again and again in these pages is that equality, or to be a little more qualified, that equal justice is the most rational ultimate objective for society. If this conclusion is correct, a social conflict which aims at greater equality has a moral justification which must be denied to efforts which aim at the perpetuation of privilege. A war for the emancipation of a nation, a race or a class is thus placed in a different moral category from the use of power for the perpetuation of imperial rule or class dominance. The oppressed, whether they be the Indians in the British Empire, or the Negroes in our own country or the industrial workers in every nation, have a higher moral right to challenge their oppressors than these have to maintain their rule by force. Violent conflict may not be the best means to attain freedom or equality, but that is a question which must be deferred for a moment. It is important to insist, first of all, that equality is a higher social goal than peace.[1350]

Not surprisingly, groups who hold power tend to be reluctant to relinquish (or share) power, not only because of the lowest common denominator of self-interest, but because, within their group, they can rationalize their privilege and their resistance to the demands of oppressed minorities. At least up to a point, the "powers that be" are more likely to use the power they have, in the form of force, to *suppress* direct action campaigns rather than sincerely listen to the complaints, and honestly consider change.

Incidentally it has been an unvarying tendency among governments, and the ruling classes which manipulate government, when anarchy is actually threatened, to re-establish peace by the use of force rather than by eliminating the causes of disaffection.[1351]

In the 1960's, rather than desegregate businesses and schools, demonstrators were arrested, beaten, attacked by police dogs, doused with fire hoses, harassed, threatened, and even murdered. Rather than eliminate the unjust Jim Crow barriers to Black Americans exercising their Constitutional right to vote, "freedom riders" were similarly attacked and again, in some cases, even murdered.[1352] In the Spring of 2020, although some local governments began to consider changes to policing as described above, there were also hundreds of incidents of police using violence against nonviolent protestors and journalists. Amnesty International documented 125 incidents in 40 different States as of June 23rd, 2020.[1353] Their Senior Crisis Advisor on Arms and Military Operations summarized their investigation.

The analysis is clear: when activists and supporters of the Black Lives Matter movement took to the streets in cities and towns across the USA to peacefully demand an end to systemic racism and police violence, they were overwhelmingly met with a militarized response and more police violence.[1354]

Even when concessions *are* made by those in power, it tends to be a tactically minimal gesture, seemingly optimized to retain as much privilege as possible, while mollifying enough demonstrators (and their sympathizers) so as to

---

[1350] ibid., 234 – 235.
[1351] ibid., 137.
[1352] https://www.history.com/this-day-in-history/the-kkk-kills-three-civil-rights-activists

[1353] https://www.amnesty.org/en/latest/news/2020/06/usa-end-unlawful-police-violence-against-Black-lives-matter-protests/
[1354] ibid.

neutralize the "movement."

> *Dominant classes are always slowest to yield power because it is the source of privilege. As long as they hold it, they may dispense and share privilege, enjoying the moral pleasure of giving what does not belong to them and the practical advantage of withholding enough to preserve their eminence and superiority in society.[1355]*

In response to millions of Americans nationwide taking to the streets, every day for weeks, demanding an end to racially disproportionate police violence, Quaker Oats volunteered to get rid of the "Aunt Jemima" brand.[1356] NASCAR gave up the flying of confederate flags at its events, as mentioned above. In so doing, they can feel *good* for having done the "right thing," and "white moderates" (as described by King) can relax, confident that progress has been made. More substantially, Los Angeles proposed to cut the LAPD budget by $150 million, also as mentioned above, but as of the time of this writing no *systemic* changes have been offered.

Even mass demonstrations must overcome a tremendous amount of social and political inertia to effect change, as history reveals. Reason and persuasion are far *less* effective, in that regard. Niebuhr believed that groups will never give up power and privilege by persuasion and reason alone. "Reason is the servant of impulse before it is its master."[1357] Power is necessary, whether political, economic, or even military, to produce change and concessions.

What does it mean to say that "Reason is the servant of impulse before it is its master?" This is actually an essential premise with respect to Niebuhr's (and therefore King's) confidence that direct action is necessary if any social change is to be produced. That Niebuhr believed the use of reason alone is insufficient to generate social change is clear, as he explicitly states so numerous times throughout his writings.

> *Since reason is always, to some degree, the servant of interest in a social situation, social injustice cannot be resolved by moral and rational suasion alone, as the educator or and social scientist usually beliefs. Conflict is inevitable, and in this conflict power must be challenged by power.[1358]*

A key assumption here is that reason is not "objective" in the way that most of us think that it is, nor do we reason objectively in the way that most of us think we do. Rather than being a neutral arbiter of information, reason is more often "deployed" in service to whatever one already believes. This tendency is explained by contemporary moral psychologist Jonathan Haidt by means of a metaphor.[1359]

Think of the mind as the pairing of an elephant and its rider. Rather obviously, the elephant is bigger and more powerful than the person riding it. If the elephant is trained, and the rider knows what she is doing, the rider can certainly try to exert some influence on the actions of the elephant, but let's be realistic: ultimately, the elephant is going to do what the elephant wants to do!

In the elephant and rider metaphor, the rider represents conscious and controlled thought. The elephant is *everything* else, including emotions, intuitions, dispositions, etc.[1360] Continuing with this metaphor, most of our cognitions are intuitive/automatic (i.e., the elephant), including such cognitions as when "our minds appraise the people we encounter on such features as

---

[1355] Niebuhr, *Moral Man*, 121.
[1356] https://www.nbcnews.com/news/us-news/aunt-jemima-brand-will-change-name-remove-image-quaker-says-n1231260
[1357] Niebuhr, *Moral Man*, xviii.
[1358] ibid., xxxi.

[1359] The next several paragraphs are repeated from the chapter on moral psychology in this book.
[1360] Haidt, Jonathan. *The Happiness Hypothesis. Finding Modern Truth in Ancient Wisdom*. Basic Books (2006), 17.

attractiveness, threat, gender, and status."[1361] The conscious component (i.e., the rider) is engaged when we consciously, deliberately consider a problem, evaluate evidence, etc.

First, there is some "triggering event." That might sound dramatic, but really it just refers to observing something, hearing something, reading something, experiencing something – in other words, you get presented with a new piece of information to process.

Based upon a variety of factors, including personal predispositions and cultural conditioning, your "elephant" will have an intuitive reaction to the triggering event. Most fundamentally, the intuitive reaction will either be positive, or negative. The elephant will either "lean towards" the trigger, or "lean away." The elephant leans towards the triggering event when its intuitive reaction is positive. The elephant likes what it sees. The elephant leans away when its reaction is aversion. This occurs when the elephant experiences something like fear, discomfort, disgust, hostility, anger, etc. as a result of the triggering event.

Now that the elephant has either leaned towards or leaned away, the rider is deployed, but not in the way most of us usually think of when we think of the role of conscious, deliberate reason. Haidt proposes that the rider is *not* best conceived as some sort of objective judge who carefully weighs evidence, but is better seen as a lawyer, or press secretary, whose job is to justify and defend what the elephant has *already* committed to. This is its primary and most important task in this model, but the rider does have other functions.

The rider can do several useful things. It can see further into the future (because we can examine alternative scenarios in our heads) and therefore it can help the elephant make better decisions in the present. It can learn new skills and master new technologies, which can be deployed to help the elephant reach its goals and sidestep disasters. And, most important, the rider acts as the spokesman for the elephant, even though it doesn't necessarily know what the elephant is really thinking. The rider is skilled at fabricating post hoc explanations for whatever the elephant has just done, and it is good at finding reasons to justify whatever the elephant wants to do next. Once human beings develop language and began to use it to gossip about each other, it became extremely valuable for elephants to carry around on their backs a full-time public relations firm.[1362]

This notion that *intuitions come first*, and that *strategic reasoning comes second* is Haidt's First Principle of Moral Psychology.[1363] The full model that he will develop around this principle is called the "social intuitionist model."

The central claim of the social intuitionist model is that moral judgment is caused by quick moral intuitions and is followed (when needed) by slow, ex post facto moral reasoning.[1364]

This model, if accurate, can help us understand why it is seemingly so difficult to "win" an argument by changing someone's mind, especially when we are dealing with moral or political issues.[1365] When two people disagree on such an issue, their feelings have come first, and

---

[1361] Haidt, Jonathan and Joseph, Craig. "Intuitive Ethics: How Innately Prepared Intuitions Generate Culturally Variable Virtues." *Daedalus.* Fall (2004): 57.

[1362] Haidt, Jonathan. *The Righteous Mind. Why Good People are Divided by Politics and Religion.* Vintage Books (2013), 54.

[1363] ibid., 61.

[1364] Haidt, Jonathan. "The Emotional Dog and its Rational Tail: a Social Intuitionist Approach to Moral Judgment." *Psychological Review*, volume 108 (4), 200: 817.

[1365] Note that while most of the examples and discussion of this model focus on moral and political arguments, Haidt thinks that this model of reasoning applies to all of our judgments, not

then their reasons come afterwards. The reasons they offer are *not* the cause of their belief! The belief came first, and the reasons were generated afterwards for support. The elephant has leaned in some direction or another, and the rider functions as a lawyer and press secretary to defend the elephant's inclination.[1366]

This view of the relationship between reason and our intuitions/emotions is not original. It's most famous spokesperson in philosophical circles is David Hume.

> As reasoning is not the source, whence either disputant derives his tenets; it is in vain to expect, that any logic, which speaks not to the affections, will ever engage him to embrace sounder principles.[1367]

The common theme we find in Hume, Haidt, and Niebuhr is a rejection of the model of Reason as an impartial, objective, dispassionate judge that will necessarily be swayed by evidence and argument so long as the argument is sound. Haidt claims that the judgment (e.g., "segregation is right") actually comes first, and the "reasons" are developed and deployed to rationalize that already-made judgment. Niebuhr made a similar point nearly a hundred years prior.

> Politics are given their general direction by the pressure of interest of the groups which control them; the expert is quite capable of giving any previously determined tendency both rational justification and efficient detailed application. Such is the inclination of the

human mind for beginning with assumptions which have been determined by other than rational considerations, and building a superstructure of rationally acceptable judgments upon them, that all this can be done without any conscious dishonesty.[1368]

In an individual human mind, reason is deployed like an "attorney" to defend a "client" (e.g., a particular belief or value). Analogously, within groups, including political parties, "experts" can be recruited to lend credibility to whatever position or policy the group has already endorsed. Given Niebuhr's view of the difference between groups and individuals, however little confidence we might have that reason can persuade another human being to change their minds about a deeply held political belief or value is even further diminished if it is a group we are trying to persuade instead.

> It may be possible, though it is never easy, to establish just relations between individuals within a group purely by moral and rational suasion and accommodation. In intergroup relations this is practically an impossibility. The relations between groups must therefore always be predominantly political rather than ethical, that is, they will be determined by the proportion of power which each group possesses at least as much as by any rational and moral appraisal of the comparative needs and claims of each group.[1369]

---

just moral and political judgments.

[1366] Haidt, *Happiness Hypothesis*, 21-22.
[1367] Hume, David. *An Enquiry Concerning the Principles of Morals*, section I. Of the General Principles of Morals paragraph 133, in *Enquiries Concerning Human Understanding and Concerning the Principles of Morals*. Reprinted from the 1777 addition. Third edition. Edited by L.A. Selby-Bigge. Clarendon press: 1975. An interesting, and unfortunate aspect of Hume's personal history is his racism – all the more

disappointing because it is so obviously inconsistent with his official philosophy. That Hume himself was racist, while his philosophical system was not, is capably established by Andrew Valls in "A Lousy Empirical Scientist. Reconsidering Hume's Racism," in *Race and Racism in Modern Philosophy*. Edited by Andrew Valls. Cornell University, 2005.
[1368] Niebuhr, *Moral Man*, 214. Emphasis added.
[1369] ibid., xxxv.

As a simple thought experiment, think of a political issue over which the two major U.S. political parties have deep disagreement in the last 10 years. Now think of how often one party has convinced the other party that they are in any way mistaken about that issue. Now think of how often the two parties have come to a mutually satisfying compromise on that issue. Accordingly, Niebuhr was confident that reason and persuasion alone would not be sufficient to bring about concessions from the dominant group, or substantial social change. Even something like beliefs in racial supremacy, and the inequitable policies that correlate with them, which might seem obviously vulnerable to the use of reason and education, has a certain "immunity" to reason which education is usually not powerful enough to overcome.

> *Our anthropologists rightly insisted that there were no biological roots of inequality between races; and they wrongly drew the conclusion from this fact that racial prejudice is a form of ignorance which could be progressively dispelled by enlightenment.*

> *Racial prejudice is indeed a form of irrationality; but it is not as capricious as modern universalists assume. Racial prejudice, the contempt of the other group, is an inevitable concomitant of racial pride; and racial pride is an inevitable concomitant of the ethnic will to live. Wherever life becomes collectively integrated it generates a collective, as well as an individual, survival impulse. But, as previously observed in dealing with individual life, human life is never content with mere physical survival. There are spiritual elements in every human survival impulse; and the corruption of these elements is pride and the will-to-power. This corruption is deeper and more universal than is understood in our liberal culture.[1370]*

Today, scientists of all kinds, including anthropologists, are almost unanimous in their claim that "race" does not exist as a biological category, but is instead a social construct. Even at the time of Niebuhr's writing (the 1930's), "anthropologists rightly insisted that there were no biological roots of inequality between races." The evidence against an essentialist, biological notion of race is overwhelming. The view of race as a social construct is dominant in the field of science, and is taught in countless classrooms and found in countless books—and yet there is racialism and racism, racial supremacy and racist violence, today just as there was in Niebuhr's time.

"Education" was insufficient to eradicate racial prejudice in the 1930's. It was still insufficient during King's efforts in the 1960's. It seems *still* to be insufficient today, despite almost a hundred years more of education and evidence. What can explain the stubbornness of racism? For Niebuhr, the explanation is that racial prejudice is not an effect caused by mistaken beliefs (such that they could be corrected by a replacement with correct beliefs), but rather the effect of an affective or spiritual cause, understood in terms of our previously discussed self-interested impulses and original sin. That "fallen" nature and self-interest, when "elevated" to the level of groups (such as racial or ethnic groups) becomes tribalism, which can result in discrimination, bigotry, oppression, etc.—all of which being subject to rationalization by our obedient faculty of reason, allowing the members of the dominant group, in many cases, to *sincerely* not even recognize that they are doing anything morally questionable.

Given his lack of confidence that education and moral and political "suasion" could produce racial equity and justice, Niebuhr proposed policies going far beyond educational campaigns.

> *A democratic society must use every stratagem of education and every resource of religion to generate appreciation of the virtues and good intentions of minority*

[1370] Niebuhr, *The Children of Light*, 138 – 139.

groups, which diverge from the type of the majority, and to prompt humility and charity in the life of the majority. It must seek to establish contacts between the groups and prevent the aggravation of prejudice through segregation. It must uncover the peculiar hazards to right judgment which reveal themselves in inter-group relations.[1371]

In the United States, it was simply never the case that segregated communities and schools would have integrated themselves if only the right speech was heard, or book read, or lesson taught. Instead, the communities had to be forcibly integrated, resulting in actual human-to-human contact between white and Black Americans, theoretically resulting in evitable challenges to stereotypes that break down once one is no longer reflecting on an abstract "other." Note that the key element here is that the desired change was not offered voluntarily. To wait for the dominant group to "come around" on its own and decide to give up privilege is a futile strategy, for Niebuhr. To appeal to those in authority is equally futile, given that "those in authority" can be, and usually are, the very dominant group in question!

Government is never completely under the control of a total community. There is always some class, whether economic overlords or political bureaucrats, who may use the organs of government for their special advantages. This is true of both nations and the community of nations. Powerful classes dominate the administration of justice in the one, and powerful nations in the other. Even if this were not the case there is in every community as such, an instinctive avoidance of social conflict and such a superficiality in dealing with the roots of social disaffection, that there is always the possibility of the unjust use of the police power of the state against individuals and

groups who break its peace, no matter how justified their grievance. A community may be impartial in using coercion against two disputants, whose dispute offers no peril to the life and prestige of the community. But wherever such a dispute affects the order or the prestige of the community, its impartiality evaporates.[1372]

There is a "conservative" tendency, then, to "keep the peace" and maintain the status quo, out of deference to order and stability and as an exercise in privilege (even if unconscious). Oppressed minority groups seeking justice, then, can't rely on reason and persuasion, the graciousness of the privileged, or the institutions and mechanisms of government, to secure equality and justice. Instead, such groups must take *action*. They must "coerce" the dominant group to make changes.

The Necessity of "Coercion"

Admittedly controversial, and unlike King, Niebuhr thinks that there is no clear line between "legitimate" nonviolent methods and "illegitimate" violent methods. Niebuhr rejects the idea that violence and revolution are intrinsically immoral. If we accept that "coercion" is necessary to effect social change between groups, it remains to be seen whether violent or nonviolent coercion is morally preferable. Examples of ostensibly nonviolent coercion include boycotts, blockades, trade embargoes, economic sanctions, etc. All of these, however, cause "harm" – including and sometimes especially to innocent persons.

Nor can it be maintained that it isolates the guilty from the innocent more successfully than violent coercion. The innocent are involved with the guilty in conflicts between groups, not because of any particular type of coercion used in the conflict but by the very group character of the conflict. No community can be

---

[1371] ibid., 143 – 144.

[1372] Niebuhr, *Moral Man*, 239.

disciplined without affecting all its members who are dependent upon, even though they are not responsible for, its policies.[1373]

Trade embargoes by the United States against countries with dictatorships (or otherwise "unacceptable" governments) inflicts harm mostly on the citizens or subjects of those countries who, because it is a dictatorship, usually have little to say about the actions of their dictators. The current embargo against Cuba has been in place since 1962. The *implicit* goal of such trade embargoes is to make the people so miserable as a result, that they will rise up in revolution and overthrow the dictator, replacing him with someone more amenable to US foreign policy. There has been no "regime change" despite an embargo lasting nearly 60 years thus far. However, an investigation performed in 1992 by the American Association for World Health determined that "the U.S. embargo of Cuba has dramatically harmed the health and nutrition of large numbers of ordinary Cuban citizens...It is our expert medical opinion that the U.S. embargo has caused a significant rise in suffering-and even deaths- in Cuba."[1374] A trade embargo is "nonviolent," but it causes harm, including deadly harm, all the same.

Boycotting a business because of the racist comments of its CEO, operates in similar fashion. It harms the employees, shareholders (if a publicly traded corporation), and even the customers who would otherwise benefit from the business. The goal is to inflict so much "harm" (mostly on "innocent" people) that they will "rise up" and "overthrow" the CEO. Even something like a Black Lives Matter protest that occupies a freeway, effectively shutting it down, in order to raise awareness about systemic racism and police violence, can result not merely in "inconveniencing" innocent people, but even in their direct harm. It is possible, for example, that

the traffic stoppage could prevent someone with a medical emergency from reaching a hospital in time for life saving interventions. In fact, a 2014 protest in Berkeley, California over police violence (triggered by the killing of Michael Brown in Ferguson, Missouri) allegedly resulted in the death of a man for just that reason.

"Nobody could get to him," a city staffer said, of the man on Kittredge Street, who is believed to have had a heart attack. "Fire couldn't get in without protection, and everyone was tied up. [Paramedics] were able to revive him to get him to the hospital, but it took 35 minutes to get [to Kittredge] because protesters were in the area and no one could go in safely."[1375]

None of this is to suggest that nonviolent methods are illegitimate, nor that violent methods are somehow preferable. Niebuhr's point is that it is simply false to think that the one causes "harm" and the other does not. Either type of method is coercive, and either *does* cause harm.

Once we admit the factor of coercion as ethically justified, though we concede that it is always morally dangerous, we cannot draw any absolute line of demarcation between violent and nonviolent coercion. We may argue that the immediate consequences of violence are such that they frustrate the ultimate purpose by which it is justified. If that is true, it is certainly not self-evident; and violence can therefore not be ruled out on a priori grounds. It is all the more difficult to do this if we consider that the immediate consequences of violence cannot be differentiated as sharply from those of nonviolence, as is sometimes supposed. The difference between them is not an absolute one, even though there may be important

---

[1373] ibid., 241.
[1374] https://www.ncbfaa.org/Scripts/
4Disapi.dll/4DCGI/cms/review.html?Action=CM
S_Document&DocID=17727&MenuKey=pubs

[1375] https://www.berkeleyside.com/2014/12/
19/exclusive-man-died-after-berkeley-protests-
delayed-help

distinctions, which must be carefully weighed. Gandhi's boycott of British cotton results in the undernourishment of children in Manchester, and the blockade of the Allies in war-time caused the death of German children. It is impossible to coerce a group without damaging both life and property and without imperiling the interests of the innocent with those of the guilty.[1376]

This is not to say that there are no differences between violent and nonviolent methods. Certainly, there is a possible morally relevant difference in intent. Violent methods intentionally inflict harm, whereas that is not necessarily the intent of nonviolent action, where the harm is more like "collateral damage."

The distinguishing marks of violent coercion and conflict are usually held to be its intent to destroy either life or property. This distinction is correct if consequences are not confused with intent. Nonviolent conflict and coercion may also result in the destruction of life or property and they usually do. The difference is that destruction is not the intended but the inevitable consequence of nonviolent coercion. The chief difference between violence and nonviolence is not in the degree of destruction which they cause, though the difference is usually considerable, but in the aggressive character of the one and the negative character of the other.[1377]

This is not a trivial distinction. The value of nonviolent methods, for just this reason, will be explored more later. But, unlike King, Niebuhr is at least open to the possibility that violent methods might be justifiable, assuming a sufficiently just cause.

If a season of violence can establish a just social system and can create the possibilities of its preservation, there is no purely ethical ground upon which violence and revolution can be ruled out. . . . The real question is: what are the political possibilities of establishing justice through violence?[1378]

This is now a practical question: assuming violent methods are justified, how likely is it that such methods will actually be successful? Presumably, if the odds are poor, then the violence is not morally justifiable. If the odds are good, though . . . . Even then, Niebuhr thinks the use of violence must be limited and tactical.

If violence can be justified at all, its terror must have the tempo of a surgeon's skill and healing must follow quickly upon its wounds.[1379]

Despite entertaining the use of violent methods, Niebuhr proposes that nonviolent coercion is more advantageous, for several reasons. The first is that nonviolent methods limit the resentment generated in, and retained by, the dominant group forced to make concessions, the organization targeted by demonstrations, etc.

The advantage of nonviolence as a method of expressing moral goodwill lies in the fact, that it protects the agent against the resentments which violent conflict always creates in both parties to a conflict, and that it proves this freedom of resentment and ill-will to the contending party in the dispute by enduring more suffering than it causes. If nonviolent resistance causes pain and suffering to the opposition, it mitigates the resentment, which such suffering usually creates, by enduring more pain than it inflicts.[1380]

[1376] Niebuhr, *Moral Man*, 172.
[1377] ibid., 240.
[1378] ibid., 179.

[1379] ibid., 220.
[1380] ibid., 247.

Note the interesting point in the last sentence: "by enduring more pain than it inflicts." Demonstrations are likely to produce resentment in those being protested, and in those who have a "stake" in the organization, institution, or way of life being protested. If such persons are violently harmed, that resentment will understandably increase. If, however, the demonstrators use nonviolent methods, exercising self-restraint, even though they are *themselves* being harmed, whether through arrest, violent dispersing by the police, or being the victims of violence themselves, as is frequently the case even when employing nonviolent methods, it can be argued that the demonstrators have endured more pain than they have inflicted.

One of the "turning points" of the Civil Rights Movement was in 1965 on "Bloody Sunday," when video footage was captured of completely nonviolent men, women, and children being attacked while walking across the Edmund Pettus Bridge. Local Sheriff Jim Clark had previously ordered all white males in Dallas County over the age of twenty-one to report to the courthouse that morning to be deputized. They joined the police and State troopers in the assault, and were captured on film waving confederate flags and cheering as the nonviolent marchers were charged from horseback, targeted with tear gas, and beaten with clubs, batons, whips, and rubber tubing wrapped in barbed wire.[1381] Dozens of marchers were injured, and 17 had to be hospitalized. Without question, the nonviolent marchers suffered far more harm than they "inflicted," and for that reason they not only stirred sympathy among those viewing the footage, but also made it harder for those in privilege to amass resentment at their actions. Nonviolent methods might even make it more likely that those in power will come to perceive their privilege, and acknowledge injustice.

In every social conflict each party is so obsessed with the wrongs which the other party commits against it, that it is unable to see its own wrongdoing. A nonviolent temper reduces these animosities to a minimum and therefore preserves a certain objectivity in analyzing the issues of the dispute.[1382]

Or, as King put it:

I think at first, the first reaction of the oppressor, when oppressed people rise up against the system of injustice, is an attitude of bitterness. But I do believe that if the nonviolent resisters continue to follow the way of nonviolence they eventually get over to the hearts and souls of the former oppressors, and I think it eventually brings about that redemption that we dream of.[1383]

The image of peaceful protestors being victims of violence by the very agents of "law and order" that they are protesting, whether on the march from Selma to Montgomery, or whether around the nation in the Spring of 2020, also makes it harder for those in power to claim the banner of "law and order" for themselves.

Both the temper and the method of nonviolence yield another very important advantage in social conflict. They rob the opponent of the moral conceit by which he identifies his interests with the peace and order of society. This is the most important of all the imponderables in a social struggle. It is the one which gives an entrenched and dominant group the clearest and the least justified advantage over those who are attacking the status quo. The latter are placed in the category of enemies of public order, of criminals and inciters to violence and the neutral community is invariably arrayed against them. The temper and the method of nonviolence destroys the plausibility of this moral conceit of the entrenched interests.

[1381] https://www.history.com/news/selma-bloody-sunday-attack-civil-rights-movement

[1382] ibid., 248
[1383] King, "Meet the Press" interview.

If the nonviolent campaign actually threatens and imperils existing arrangements the charge of treason and violence will be made against it none-the-less. But it will not confuse the neutral elements in a community so easily.[1384]

It's much harder to dismiss demonstrators as criminals and "thugs," as President Trump referred to protestors outside his political rally in Tulsa, when even the Tulsa police department tweeted that "There are multiple groups of demonstrators with varying viewpoints in the area adjacent to the rally. . . Overwhelmingly these encounters have been peaceful with everyone attempting to share their views." [1385] It's hard to frame Sheriff Jim Clark as the symbol of law, order, and peace, when he and his operatives are seemingly out of control, and wantonly inflicting violence on nonviolent demonstrators who, though being actively victimized, seem very much in command of themselves. Contrast that to a scenario in which protestors *are* violent, in which they loot, riot, destroy public property, or attack other people. In such cases, those in power are much more capable of casting the demonstrators as dangerous criminals, as unreasonable and violent threats to public safety. Whether the violence was warranted or not, the protestors who employ violence provide their opposition with a weapon to be used against them. When the demonstration is by, and on behalf of, a literal minority group, this is all the more dangerous, as King himself warned. Violent methods "intensify the fears of the white majority, and leave them less ashamed of their prejudices towards Negroes," whereas nonviolent direct action can make "an indifferent and unconcerned nation rise from lethargy and... struggle with a newly aroused conscience."[1386] According to Niebuhr:

This means that nonviolence is a particularly strategic instrument for an oppressed group which is hopelessly in the minority and has no possibility of developing sufficient power to set against its oppressors. The emancipation of the Negro race in America probably waits upon the adequate development of this kind of social and political strategy. It is hopeless for the Negro to expect complete emancipation from the menial social and economic position into which the white man has forced him, merely by trusting in the moral sense of the white race. It is equally hopeless to attempt emancipation through violent rebellion.[1387]

To put it bluntly, Black Americans constitute only 13.4% of the U.S. population.[1388] Without "allies," and without tactics that create allies (and avoid creating new "enemies"), efforts to secure equality and justice are doomed to fail. Coalitions of sympathetic persons of numerous races and ethnicities are necessary, and this is much more likely if nonviolent methods are used.

Given Niebuhr's view of human nature, made even worse once people form into groups, it would be understanding to assume that he was a pessimist in general, and perhaps deeply cynical about American democracy. In actuality, he tried to navigate a pragmatic middle ground between the mentalities of those he labeled "children of light" and "children of darkness."

Children of Light and Children of Darkness

The "children of light" generally believe that the conflict between the collective good and self-interest can be resolved, and include not only modern American liberals, but also their political "ancestors" Locke, Smith, Rousseau, Bentham, and Marx (among others). "Children of darkness"

1384 Niebuhr, *Moral Man*, 250.
1385 https://www.cnn.com/2020/06/20/us/nationwide-protests-saturday/index.html
1386 King, Martin Luther. *Where Do We Go from Here: Chaos or Community?* Boston: Beacon press

(2010), 63, 17.
1387 Niebuhr, *Moral Man*, 252.
1388 https://www.census.gov/quickfacts/fact/table/US/PST045219

refers to moral cynics who are "realists" about the ability to overcome self-interest, and include most notably Hobbes and Machiavelli.

Children of darkness "know no law beyond their will and interest."[1389] Children of light, in contrast, are those who believe that "self-interest should be brought under the discipline of a higher law,"[1390] and "in harmony with a more universal good."[1391] The children of darkness are "evil," but "wise," while the children of light are "virtuous," but "foolish."[1392]

Niebuhr claims that the children of light are "foolish" not only because they tend to underestimate the power of self-interest, in general, but specifically because they underestimate this power among themselves, making them naïve and self-deceived.

They [i.e. the children of light] did not fear the power, ambition or collective egotism of the community because they associated undue political restraints upon the individual with the particular form of such restraints which they had known in a feudal economic order on a monarchical political order. They thought they had reduced the power of the community to minimal proportions by the constitutional principles of democratic government, according to which government had only negative powers and was limited to the adjudication of disputes or to the role of a traffic policeman, maintaining minimal order.[1393]

In the United States, specifically, ostensibly with a democratically elected representative government, a Constitution with the guarantee of various rights, and a carefully crafted system of government designed with checks and balances to limit the power of factions, the children of light tend to not see the threat of despotism. However, according to Niebuhr the threat of despotism is always present, alongside its twin threat of anarchy.

So difficult is it to avoid the Scylla of despotism and the Charybdis of anarchy that it is safe to hazard the prophecy that the dream of perpetual peace and brotherhood for human society is one which will never be fully realised. It is a vision prompted by the conscience and insight of individual man, but incapable of fulfillment by collective man. It is like all true religious visions, possible of approximation but not of realisation in actual history.[1394]

Note that Scylla and Charybdis were two "sea monsters" in ancient Greek mythology. They were nearby to each other, so sailors would have to carefully (almost impossibly) navigate between them to avoid a disaster. Niebuhr is describing his "realistic" understanding of politics. Society is always oscillating between the extremes of "despotism" and "anarchy." The tendency for one to go to the extremes in opposition to the other means that we must remain perpetually on guard against *both*.[1395]

1389 Niebuhr, *The Children of Light*, 9.

1390 ibid., 9.

1391 ibid., 10.

1392 ibid., 11.

1393 ibid., 43.

1394 Niebuhr, *Moral Man*, 21 – 22.

1395 Recall that in John Stuart Mill's "On Liberty," he proclaims the value of having "both sides" represented in not only government but policy. "In politics, again, it is almost a commonplace, that a party of order or stability, and a party of progress or reform, are both necessary elements

of a healthy state of political life; until the one or the other shall have so enlarged its mental grasp as to be a party equally of order and of progress, knowing and distinguishing what is fit to be preserved from what ought to be swept away. Each of these modes of thinking derives its utility from the deficiencies of the other; but it is in a great measure the opposition of the other that keeps each within the limits of reason and sanity. Unless opinions favourable to democracy and to aristocracy, to property and to equality, to co-operation and to competition, to luxury

The children of light are optimistic, but probably overly optimistic. The children of darkness are pessimistic, but probably overly pessimistic. The optimism of the children of light, at its worst, manifests as naïveté, rendering the community vulnerable by virtue of ignoring the power of self interest in human nature. The pessimism of the children of darkness, at its worst, manifests itself as despotism, constricting communities to the point that freedom is squeezed out, out of excessive fear of that same human nature. While Niebuhr acknowledges that the threat of our self-interested predispositions and Original Sin is real, and must be addressed in the political context, he also argues that optimism is necessary for social progress.

> The inertia of society is so stubborn that no one will move against it, if he cannot believe that it can be more easily overcome than is actually the case. And no one will suffer the perils and pains involved in the process of radical social change, if he cannot believe in the possibility of a purer and fairer society than will ever be established. These illusions are dangerous because they justify fanaticism; but their abandonment is perilous because it inclines to inertia.[1396]

If someone has no hope that change is possible, that the improvement of institutions is possible, the reduction of injustice is possible, what could motivate them to try to do anything

about it? Without some degree of optimism, demonstrations reduce to riots, angry and frustrated venting. Even with all of the legitimate and long built-up anger and frustration fueling the BLM movement, the demonstrations are each and all aimed at producing specific and tangible policy changes. This presupposes at least some degree of optimism that those policy changes are possible. While praising optimism for the motivation it provides, Niebuhr acknowledges that a society is best served when it manages to incorporate both optimism and pessimism. In the forward to the 1960 edition of "The Children of Light...," Niebuhr states his own view of the "central thesis" of his book:

> A free society prospers best in a cultural, religious and moral atmosphere which encourages neither a too pessimistic nor too optimistic view of human nature. Both moral sentimentality in politics and moral pessimism encourage totalitarian regimes, the one because it encourages the opinion that it is not necessary to check the power of government, and the second because it believes that only absolute political authority can restrain the anarchy, created by conflicting and competitive interests.[1397]

And, in the forward to the first edition of this book, he similarly states,

> A free society requires some confidence in

---

and to abstinence, to sociality and individuality, to liberty and discipline, and all the other standing antagonisms of practical life, are expressed with equal freedom, and enforced and defended with equal talent and energy, there is no chance of both elements obtaining their due; one scale is sure to go up and the other down. Truth, in the great practical concerns of life, is so much a question of the reconciling and combining of opposites, that very few have minds sufficiently capacious and impartial to make the adjustment with an approach to correctness, and it has to be made by the rough

process of a struggle between combatants fighting under hostile banners. On any of the great open questions just enumerated, if either of the two opinions has a better claim than the other, not merely to be tolerated, but to be encouraged and countenanced, it is the one which happens at the particular time and place to be in a minority. That is the opinion which, for the time being, represents the neglected interests, the side of human well-being which is in danger of obtaining less than its share."
[1396] Niebuhr, *Moral Man*, 221.
[1397] Niebuhr, *The Children of Light*, xxvii.

the ability of men to reach tentative intolerable adjustments between the competing interests and to arrive at some common notions of justice which transcend all partial interests. A consistent pessimism in regard to man's rational capacity for justice invariably leads to absolutistic political theories; for they prompt the conviction that only preponderant power can coerce the various vitalities of the community into a working harmony. But the too consistent optimism in regard to man's ability and inclination to grant justice to his fellows obscures the perils of chaos which perennially confront every society, including a free society.[1398]

Practically speaking, what will this "Golden mean" between the "extremes" of optimism and pessimism look like? For one, it will look like democracy. In one of the most famous sentences Niebuhr wrote, "Man's capacity for justice makes democracy possible; but man's inclination to injustice makes democracy necessary."[1399] The optimism that allows us to hope for improvement both in ourselves and in our communities is what allows us to trust in "the people" to participate in governance in the first place. However, our somber recognition of human nature recommends that restraints be placed on the government, including "the people."

The democratic techniques of a free society place checks upon the power of the ruler and administrator and thus prevent it from becoming vexatious. The perils of uncontrolled power are perennial reminders of the virtues of a democratic society; particularly if a society should become inclined to impatience with the dangers of freedom and should be tempted to choose the advantages of coerced unity at the price of freedom.[1400]

We can see here some harmony between Niebuhr's pragmatic approach and one of the central themes of the *Federalist Papers*: the need to limit the power of "factions" and to protect the minority from the coercive power of the majority. Both Niebuhr and "Publius" rejected the idea that moral or religious considerations by themselves, or hope in "enlightened" politicians, could sufficiently protect minorities from oppression at the hands of majorities. Within the *Federalist Papers*, that motivated the development of a large Republic, with numerous "checks" on the power of factions. For Niebuhr, an element of this pragmatic approach (in addition to endorsing democracy), is his (ultimate) endorsement of nonviolent methods of coercion when employing direct action.

An adequate political morality must do justice to the insights of both moralists and political realists. It will recognise that human society will probably never escape social conflict, even though it extends the areas of social co-operation. It will try to save society from being involved in endless cycles of futile conflict, not by an effort to abolish coercion in the life of collective man, but by reducing it to a minimum, by counseling the use of such types of coercion as are most compatible with the moral and rational factors in human society and by discriminating between the purposes and ends for which coercion is used.[1401]

As one final note, still pertaining to optimism, while simultaneously bringing us back full circle to Martin Luther King Jr., Niebuhr recognized the particular value of religion in maintaining optimism and in the pursuit of justice and equality. For King, a pastor as well as a practical philosopher, the incorporation of his Christianity was as valuable as it was inevitable-- although this incorporation required some nuance. King thought that a "turn the other cheek" philosophy applies in the context of *individuals*, but when the

---

[1398] ibid., xxxi-xxxii.
[1399] ibid., xxxii.

[1400] ibid., xxxiii.
[1401] Niebuhr, *Moral Man*, 233 – 234.

context is between *groups* (such as racial, or national groups) "a more realistic approach is necessary." This more realistic approach (of nonviolent resistance/activism) will involve a blending of Niebuhr's "Christian realism," the Christian doctrine of love, and Gandhi's teachings on nonviolent resistance. "Christ furnished the spirit and motivation while Gandhi furnished the method."[1402] Although for the purposes of this chapter we cannot go into greater detail, King explicitly advocated for the necessity of *love* in the midst of direct action campaigns. Volunteers would be required to undergo training in nonviolent resistance, and to undergo a "purification" process in an attempt to give them an orientation of love, even for those who are actively oppressing and seeking to harm them. Niebuhr, likewise, recognized the valuable contribution of religion to campaigns of nonviolent resistance.

> *There is no problem of political life to which religious imagination can make a larger contribution than this problem of developing nonviolent resistance. The discovery of elements of common human frailty in the foe and, concomitantly, the appreciation of all human life as possessing transcendent worth, creates attitudes which transcend social conflict and thus mitigate its cruelties. It binds human beings together by reminding them of the common roots and similar character of both their vices and their virtues. These attitudes of repentance which recognise that the evil in the foe is also in the self, and these impulses of love which claim kinship with all men in spite of social conflict, are the peculiar gifts of religion to the human spirit. Secular imagination is not capable of producing them; for they require a sublime madness which disregards immediate appearances and emphasises profound and ultimate unities.*[1403]

On its surface, this claim that a religious worldview is especially well-suited to the optimism needed to motivate social justice campaigns in the first place, and the nonviolent self-restraint needed for those campaigns to be effective, might seem common sense. The intimate connection between the Church and the Civil Rights Movement of the 1960's would certainly lend support to that perception. It is, and should be, difficult to separate that Movement from the explicit appeals to God's justice, Christian brotherhood, redemption and salvation, and other theologically laden terms, especially as expressed by the Movement's most celebrated spokesperson, the *Reverend* Doctor Martin Luther King Jr. However, in fairness, this association of the church with both optimism and direct action needs to be more carefully considered.

To begin with, during the 1960's it would be overly generous to say that "the church" was supportive of equal rights for Black Americans. It is safe to say that the *"Black"* church was supportive, but it is undeniable that countless "white" churches were either not involved, or even openly supported segregation, including within its own congregation!

> *I think it is one of the tragedies of our nation, one of the shameful tragedies, that eleven o'clock on Sunday morning is one of the most segregated hours, if not the most segregated hours, in Christian America. I definitely think the Christian church should be integrated, and any church that stands against integration and that has a segregated body is standing against the spirit and the teachings of Jesus Christ, and it fails to be a true witness.*[1404]

Clearly, being "religious" is no guarantee that one will be on the side of justice and equality, let alone that will be motivated to act and make sacrifices on their behalf. In addition, while the relationship between the church (Black or

---

[1402] King, "Pilgrimage to Nonviolence."
[1403] Niebuhr, *Moral Man*, 254 – 255.

[1404] King, "Meet the Press."

otherwise) was undeniable during the Civil Rights Movement of the 1960s, it is far from obvious that the church is playing a similar role with the contemporary efforts of BLM. While it is certainly the case that many people of faith support BLM, and actively participate in demonstrations, these demonstrations are generally "secular" with respect to their vocabulary and their activities. In fact, the notable absence of church support (specifically the Black church) has inspired papers and articles to be written in an attempt to account for it.[1405] Some explanations suggest that BLM has more affinity to the Black Power movement of the 60's, than to King's organizations and campaigns. Others suggest that the inclusion of LGBTQ+ interests and participants in BLM is alienating to traditionally socially conservative Black churches. Still others suggest that BLM is primarily driven by young organizers, and young people in the United States, in general, are less religiously affiliated than their predecessors. Whether an explanation is needed, and whatever explanation is best, is beyond the scope of this chapter. Suffice to say, although there is certainly merit in Niebuhr's claim that a religious worldview is useful in the pursuit of social justice, it appears to be less obvious that it is *necessary*.

Conclusion

Philosophy is often regarded as potentially "interesting," but far less often is it regarded as useful—perhaps especially when contending with more pressing matters like inequality, injustice, and deadly and racially disproportionate policing practices. However, whether recognized or not, philosophy is present, and has a role to play, even in street level demonstrations.

The decision to put one's reputation, freedom, livelihood, and even body at risk by demonstrating in the streets, and confronting police and security personnel who are sometimes quick to use violence even against nonviolent and peaceful protestors, is a serious one, to say the least, and ideally one's convictions can be emboldened and steadied by a philosophical justification not only of the cause, but of the *methods* being used. The efficacy of direct action, and specifically nonviolent direct action, as compared to other methods such as mere engagement with available democratic methods (e.g., voting), or even the use of violence, is not necessarily obvious. In this chapter, however, we have seen how an argument can be generated, based on certain assumptions concerning human nature and the psychology and behavior of groups in the political sphere, that direct action is *necessary* for social change, and that *nonviolent methods* of direct action are the most tactically sound.

Critical Analysis

1. In your opinion, what are the strongest and most compelling points made by the philosopher or philosophers in this chapter? Why do you find those points to be convincing?
2. In your opinion, what are the weakest or least convincing points? Why? Can you anticipate any limitations or objections to their ideas not already addressed in the chapter?

Appendix: Application to Social Justice

This entire chapter was explicitly focused on social justice, so, unlike most of the chapters that preceded it, nothing additional will be provided in this appendix.

[1405]
https://religionunplugged.com/news/2017/7/25/the-church-and-Black-lives-matter

https://www.christianitytoday.com/ct/2020/june-web-only/Black-church-Black-lives-matter-police-brutality.html

Appendix/"Deeper Dive"
Cesar Chavez: Community Intellectual

Comprehension questions you should be able to answer after reading this section:

1. What is a "community intellectual?" How are they recognized and what do they do?
2. What was *La Causa*? What was it trying to accomplish?
3. What were some of the Mexican cultural influences on *La Causa*?
4. Explain the role and significance of the "personal transformation" of activists for Chavez. How does it occur, and why is it so important?
5. What are his reasons for rejecting violent methods and accepting only non-violent methods in his direct-action campaigns? (There are several.)
6. In what way does Chavez recognize systemic racism (for his time)?
7. Explain why Chavez rejects constructing his direct-action campaigns along narrow ethnic lines (e.g., Mexican/Mexican American).
8. In what way does Chavez recognize "intersectionality" (for his time)?
9. What are his concerns about "machismo?" What vision of masculinity does he offer in its place?

Some of you might want to "dive deeper" into the ideas presented in this chapter, and this section will help you do that. "Everyone" knows (or at least *should* know—particularly in California) that Cesar Chavez was an activist who campaigned for improved working conditions of farm workers. Similar to Gandhi and Martin Luther King Jr., he organized non-violent direct-action campaigns that sometimes included personal fasts (that sometimes lasted for weeks) in the pursuit of social justice for the (generally) Latino agricultural laborers who were exploited by their employers and taken for granted in their broader society. What a lot of people do not know is that "Chavez worked all his life to establish a deeply democratic society in which ordinary people have the ability to influence the decision-making processes that affect their lives in the political, as well as economic and social, spheres. It is also a society in which the ideal of justice is concerned not merely with the fair distribution of political rights, economic resources, and relations of production but also with giving proper recognition and respect to historically

subordinated or marginalized groups."[1406] In other words, Chavez engaged in moral and political philosophy.

Biography

Cesar Chavez was born in 1927 in Yuma Arizona. He spent most of his childhood working alongside his family in the agricultural fields of California's Central Valley, where he experienced first-hand the racial hierarchy and discrimination experienced by Mexicans and Mexican Americans. He stopped attending school after the eighth grade due to the necessity of him working in order to help support his family. He joined the Navy at the age of seventeen in 1944, serving for two years in the Pacific before returning to farm work. He married his childhood sweetheart, Helen Fabela, in 1948 and they lived together in Delano California, picking grapes and cotton together for several years until they moved to San Jose. In San Jose, he met Father Donald McDonnell (a priest and labor organizer), who introduced Chavez to the teachings of the Catholic Church on

---

[1406] Orosco, Jose-Antonio. *Cesar Chavez and the Common Sense of Nonviolence.* University of New Mexico Press: *Albuquerque.* 2008. Pp 4-5.

labor as well as the philosophy of Gandhi. He also met Fred Ross; a community organizer committed to mobilizing poor people through grassroots organizing. Chavez was recruited by Ross as an organizer and he worked for him for several years until 1962, when Chavez resigned and moved his family back to Delano. Chavez then used his income, savings, and unemployment insurance money to build his own organization devoted entirely to farm workers and their issues. Just two years later, this union had grown to one thousand members.[1407]

In 1965, the leader of the agricultural workers organizing committee (AWOC) asked Chavez's union to participate in a solidarity strike in support of Filipino workers by going on strike against grape growers in Delano. His union voted to go on strike, and to publicize it Chavez organized a protest march through the San Joaquin Valley ending at the state Capitol of Sacramento. Participants marched over 300 miles in one week, arriving on Easter Sunday in 1966. This activism on behalf of farmworkers spread over the next several years, creating a consumer boycott against grape buying. When some of the farmworkers suggested escalating from nonviolence to property damage Chavez initiated a twenty-five day fast to remind his own activists about the value of "penitential suffering for a greater social good."[1408]

The State of California passed the "California Agricultural Labor Relations Act" in 1975, granting farmworkers, for the first time, significant bargaining rights. By the 1980s, Chavez was reimagining the scope and purpose of "La Causa," evolving it into a social movement reaching beyond improving the lives of farmworkers.

It doesn't matter whether we have a hundred thousand members or five hundred thousand members. In truth, hundreds of thousands of farmworkers in California – and in other states – are better off today because of our work. And

Hispanics across California and the nation, who don't work in agriculture, are better off today because what the farmworkers taught people – about organization, about pride and strength, about seizing control over their own lives.[1409]

In the final years of his life, Chavez promoted his "Wrath of Grapes" campaign, in which he attempted to connect the lives of farmworkers to those of ordinary people, forging a sense of community and speaking against an exclusively profit driven motivation for corporations, particularly with respect to the use of pesticides in large-scale agribusiness. He died on April 23, 1993, in Arizona.

Community intellectual

Chavez should not be considered a "general theorist" who developed a detailed theory of justice, in the fashion of John Rawls, or some other famous philosopher, but is rather an example of what is known as a "community intellectual."

A community intellectual is a figure that does not hold an occupation typical of a traditional intellectual but is, nonetheless, involved in the production of knowledge. A community intellectual develops social theory through reflection on her own activism and organizing, such as political meetings, marches, demonstrations, and picket lines within a given group or ethnic community. However, this kind of theory is not meant simply to provide an understanding of the community. It is intended to refine principles and concepts that will help guide political action by a community. Thus, a community intellectual is not a disinterested, objective researcher; she is an activist within the community, trying to find ways to articulate its needs and interests and to construct tactics for achieving those

---

[1407] ibid., 7-8.
[1408] ibid., 9.

[1409] Quoted in ibid., 10.

ends.[1410]

In general, and in summary, community intellectuals:

1. Try to articulate the community's sense of historical agency.
2. Impart to the community the importance of organizing to bring about social change.
3. Instill optimism and belief in the possibility of social change despite setbacks.[1411]

Possessing an eighth-grade education, and not being a professor, writer, or academic in general, he *nevertheless* was a sophisticated thinker who contributed to public discourse on social justice not only by the content of his speeches, but also the example of his activism.

Although Chavez does not have a social theorist's complete understanding of these systematic oppressions, it is clear that he develops, as a community intellectual, a revolutionary outlook that sees injustice and suffering as the result of historic structural imbalances of power within international political and economic institutions and was trying to develop ways of organizing to resist and dismantle their ability to dominate.[1412]

La Causa

Chavez' activism is generally and collectively referred to as *"La Causa."* This was a movement to organize farmworkers to lobby and embark upon campaigns of direct action for the sake of securing better working conditions and treatment. As mentioned above, this campaign ultimately resulted in the passage of the California Agricultural Labor Relations Act, but Chavez had a vision of the value of activism that extended far beyond particular legal or material gains.

Regardless of what the future holds for the [United farmworkers] – regardless of what the future holds for farmworkers – our accomplishments cannot be undone! "La Causa" – our cause – doesn't have to be experienced twice. The consciousness and pride that were raised by our union are alive and thriving inside millions of young Hispanics who will never work on a farm. . . . Once social change begins, it cannot be reversed. You cannot un-educate the person who has learned to read. You cannot humiliate the person who feels pride. You cannot oppress the people who are not afraid anymore.[1413]

We will address Chavez' vision of personal and cultural transformation a bit later, but before looking ahead, we will look back and consider some of the influences that shaped his ideas and his vision for activism.

Chavez openly acknowledged that *La Causa* had moral foundations drawn from Mexican cultural and religious traditions. He credited his mother with introducing him to the value of nonviolence in his childhood, through the use of Mexican folk sayings (*dichos*) concerning conflict resolution.

She taught her children to reject that part of a culture which too often tells its young men that you're not a man if you don't fight back. She would say "no, it's best to turn the other cheek. God gave you senses like eyes and mind and tongue and you can get out of anything. It takes two to fight and one can't do it alone."[1414]

His mother also taught him the value of sacrifice and service. Despite working long and difficult hours doing farm work, she would have

---

[1410] ibid., 5-6.
[1411] ibid., 6.
[1412] ibid., 30-31.

[1413] Quoted in ibid., 22,23.
[1414] Quoted in ibid., 24.

her children help other farmworkers with errands, and she led the family in celebrating the Saints Day of Saint Eduvigis (patron saint of charity) each year, providing assistance to the poor and needy.[1415]

One of the manifestations of the influence of his cultural heritage is his framing of the farm worker march to Sacramento as a religious pilgrimage, modeled after the common and popular pilgrimages performed in Mexico, such as to the Basilica of our Lady of Guadalupe in Mexico City. For many of the Mexican and Mexican American participants in this March, the idea of a pilgrimage was familiar and resonating. Marchers carried flags of the Virgin of Guadalupe, and mass was said at the end of each day. Along the way, political education was offered, with a farmworker's theater group putting on brief skits to teach the farmworkers about activism and labor issues.[1416]

Beyond evoking the idea of a pilgrimage, the March to Sacramento was also designed to evoke the idea of the Lenten penitential procession which takes place in many Mexican and Mexican American communities prior to Easter. For the marchers to Sacramento, penitence would be modeled through the fatigue, hunger, and thirst experienced along the way – ideally inspiring self-reflection and purifying participants of feelings such as anger or resentment. "Similarly, the Sacramento march was to give the farmworker activists the opportunity to reflect on and imagine how to achieve a just resolution to their plight through nonviolence and the experience of sacrificial suffering."[1417] We will now briefly consider the practice of penitence and fasting in this context.

Chavez's strategy of penitential suffering affirms the ancient Mexican value of sacrificing for a greater good and created a way for people to join in solidarity with farmworkers. Thus, not only are these practices deeply in accordance with the cultural self-understandings of Mexicans; penitential suffering would more likely work as an effective political strategy than property destruction and hunger striking in creating a base of widespread public support and solidarity among non-Latinos for the farmworker movement.[1418]

The practice of penitence, in general, was intended to produce personal transformation in the practitioners, as well as cultural change in the community—both of which we will consider a bit later. Chavez practiced *penitence* himself, in addition to promoting it. On multiple occasions, when farmworkers grew frustrated and some of them proposed departures from the purely nonviolent methods they had been employing, Chavez initiated a personal fast, the first of which beginning in February of 1968 and lasting for twenty-five days. He made it clear that this fast was not meant to pressure growers into complying with the demands of the farmworkers but was rather an act of personal penance by which he hoped to gain clarity and focus, and to remind the farmworkers of the virtue of nonviolence and the value of self-sacrifice.[1419]

His own fasts inspired others, including average non-Latino consumers, to join him in their own "mini fasts," creating a sense of solidarity, sympathy, and participation. "When somebody stops eating for a week or ten days, people... want to be part of that experience."[1420]

Going beyond sympathy fasts, those so moved might *also* be inspired to participate in *other* organizing and activism, including participation in consumer boycotts, petitioning growers and grocery store chains to honor the demands of farmworkers, etc. There was something intentionally "manipulative" about Chavez' tactics, but (importantly), not coercive—let alone violent.

The purpose of Chavez's penitential suffering, then, was not to coerce others to

---

[1415] ibid., 24.

[1416] ibid., 26.

[1417] ibid., 27.

[1418] ibid., 29.

[1419] ibid., 27.

[1420] Quoted in ibid., 29.

act. There was no demand attached to it. In fact, he made it clear that the audience for his three famous fasts was not the growers with which the union was seeking negotiation or the supermarkets that sold nonunion produce. Instead, the self-inflicted suffering . . . was meant to accentuate the injustice experienced by the farmworkers and prick the conscience of the public, so that they would "see" the injustice in a new way and be moved to action on behalf of the farmworkers.[1421]

Chavez was hoping to inspire a "revolution," of sorts. This, too, draws upon familiar aspects of Mexican cultural heritage: the idea and experience of revolution. "The revolutions of Mexico were primarily uprisings of the poor, fighting for bread and for dignity. The Mexican American is also a child of revolution."[1422]

Chavez read *"El Plan de Delano"* at each stop of the Sacramento march, arguing that La Causa is a continuation of the ideals of the Mexican revolution of 1910, with the obvious difference being the use of nonviolence as opposed to armed revolution. "Our revolution will not be armed, but we want the existing social order to dissolve; we want a new social order."[1423]

Even the *name* of the manifesto (*El Plan de Delano*) was meant to evoke association with the Mexican Revolution, due to its intentional similarity to Emiliano Zapata's *"El Plan de Ayala,"* which called for land reform, the abolition of indentured servitude, and assistance to the indigenous poor. Similar in scope, *El Plan de Delano* asked, "all political groups and the protection of the government" to end the oppressive practices and experiences of "starvation wages, contractors, day hauls, forced migration, sickness, illiteracy, camps and subhuman living conditions."[1424]

A few paragraphs ago, I claimed that Chavez was hoping to inspire a "revolution, of sorts." This is because of the fact that, although Chavez had a vision of profound personal and societal change towards social justice, he did not seek to somehow tear down existing political and economic structures to their foundation, as other "revolutionaries" had.

> *Chavez's overall political strategy may be reformist; he does not call for the overthrow of the American government or the abolition of capitalism. However, he did have hopes that La Causa would instigate a revolutionary cultural change. First, he believes that training in nonviolent resistance and direct action will transform the farmworkers into Democratic agents who have the skills and abilities to participate, deliberate, and make American liberal democracy more responsive to the needs and interests of the public and not just wealthy corporate interests.*[1425]

Note the subtle distinction here. Chavez did indeed seek profound personal and societal change, but not by massive political and economic upheaval. Instead, he hoped that a campaign of non-violent direct action would transform the hearts and characters of the participants themselves, and then transform those who witness the activists. These personal transformations would then ripple up and through the culture itself, including the economy. Essential to this strategy was the willingness of the activists to lead by example, and to be willing to sacrifice for their cause.

> *So long as we are willing to sacrifice for that cause, so long as we persist in nonviolence and work to spread the message of our struggle, then millions of people around the world will respond from their hearts, will support our efforts, and in the end we will overcome."*[1426]

Also essential to his strategy was a

[1421] ibid., 28-29.
[1422] Quoted in ibid., 29.
[1423] Quoted in ibid., 30.

[1424] Quoted in ibid., 30.
[1425] ibid., 31.
[1426] Quoted in ibid., 29.

commitment to non-violence.

Non-Violence

Chavez favors non-violent direct action and opposes violent methods for several reasons. *One* reason is that those who espouse violent methods often do so from a position of privilege.

> *Examine history. Who gets killed in the case of violent revolution? The poor, the workers. The people of the land are the ones who give their bodies and don't really gain that much for it.... Those who espouse violence exploit people. To commit to arms with many promises, to ask them to give up their lives for a cause and then not produce for them afterwards, is the most vicious type of oppression.*[1427]

While exceptions are undoubtedly possible, and undoubtedly have existed, oftentimes the most enthusiastic proponents of a "by any means necessary" approach to activism are found in the background, or in front of a classroom, or behind a podium, or on a social media platform, safely removed from the consequences of such activism.

In Chavez's time, he consistently insisted that it is those directly affected by policies that should be guiding direct action campaigns. When he was challenged by a group of Chicano activists and their professors at UC Santa Barbara for being "out of touch" with the "*Movimiento,*" he reminded them that one of the essential principles of La Causa was to get the farmworkers themselves to take responsibility for their own organizing. "You've already made it. You've already decided that you don't want to be a farmworker. But that's not a choice we have. You want to become something else, and that's good. But that makes you incapable or unfit to come in and vote with us and have an equal voice in deciding what it is we need and want."[1428]

A *second* mistake involves a misunderstanding of authority. Those who advocate for violent methods seem to assume that effective use of authority requires violence, when "authority" is an alternative means to the same end. Assuming that violence is the only way to exercise authority causes one to fixate on "military ideals and strategies for achieving their goals."[1429] Ironically, when the State exercises violence for the sake of authority, it suggests a *loss* of authority – "it no longer has the authority to bring people together and cooperate of their own free will."[1430] When the police (or other agents of the State) crush protests, disrupt sit-ins, disperse peaceful crowds with tear gas and rubber bullets, etc., they are revealing that they *lack* the authority to inspire obedience and cooperation, and the fact that they must ultimately resort to force and violence reveals a lack of moral justification and authority for the State's position.

If activists resorted to similar methods, they would be making a similar confession. In contrast to nonviolent direct action, the use of violent methods requires protesters to successfully justify their actions to a presumably skeptical public. This can create scenarios in which the protesters must justify themselves to the authorities they are targeting with their methods, State authorities (such as police or politicians – assuming they are not the authorities being targeted), and public observers. "The power structure loves nothing better than to put you behind the eight ball, nothing better than to have you defending yourself instead of defending your people."[1431] Think of how quickly the narrative changes, and media coverage changes, when contemporary marches and other protests degenerate into violence, looting, damage of public property, etc. Footage of protesters throwing rocks at police or smashing windows and looting from stores, even though usually rare and not at all representative of protests, in general, nevertheless take control of the narrative and either prevent witnesses from feeling empathy towards the cause, or even

---

[1427] Quoted in ibid., 61-62.
[1428] Quoted in ibid., 79.
[1429] ibid., 38.

[1430] ibid., 40.
[1431] Quoted in ibid. 42.

alienate some who had already been empathetic. Even if the violence is directed "only" at property, and not persons, it is far more likely to generate resentment, and rather than producing lasting change, it is likely that those in positions of power would seek to undermine whatever concessions (if any) were granted to the workers, at the earliest possible opportunity. "The important thing is that for poor people to be able to get a clean victory is something you don't often see. If we get it through violence, then the employers will just wait long enough until they can get even with you – and then the workers will respond, and then..."[1432]

A *third* mistake made by those who advocate violent methods is in assuming that the use of nonviolent methods of direct action are "passive." Nonviolent methods can be versatile, allowing a variety of tactics and strategies in the pursuit of different goals. Some tactics can be labeled "coercive mechanisms of nonviolence," and are "tactics meant to take away the ability of those with power to maintain the status quo by withholding labor or money."[1433] Examples include work stoppages, consumer boycotts, etc. Such tactics seek to force authorities to change their policies in order to avoid suffering and economic loss.

Other tactics may be called "mechanisms of conversion or persuasion." Such tactics are meant to change the perspective or values of those in positions of authority such that they align with those of the nonviolent protesters. While these tactics don't presume to be able to bring about substantial changes in basic beliefs, at minimum, they might facilitate authorities' understanding the perspective of those protesting and taking them seriously. This goes beyond forced compliance or grudging compromise. Examples of *these* tactics include "penitential pilgrimages" and fasts, such as those undertaken by Chavez himself.

A *fourth* mistake made by those who espouse violent methods, according to Chavez, is in thinking that revolution is simply a matter of

"overturning the State." Or, more simply, the mistake is in thinking that the goal goes no deeper than a specific change in policy or practice. Chavez recognizes that unjust practices and outcomes are rooted not just in specific policies, but social systems, and even cultural norms. "Chavez hope that *La Causa* would create lasting and enduring change by fostering a culture of peace, that is, by affecting cultural attitudes towards peace, violence, and democracy in such a way that people would come to demand more radical social transformations through nonviolence."[1434]

The intended scope of the desired change is vast, but the entry point is very "small"—it is the individual activist himself or herself. Cultural change is the aggregated result of individuals being personally transformed as a result of activism, and witness to activism. In this sense, non-violent direct action is a form of training, that, when repeated, can cause personal transformation.

> *Following the tradition of Aristotelian ethical theory, Chavez thinks that a person repeatedly engaged in certain moral behavior will be more likely to develop that moral virtue as a stable character trait. He designed the tactics of the farmworker struggle not only so that people would be engaged in strategic action to win a labor dispute but also so that individuals would cultivate, in the very performance of the action, the virtues of sacrifice, care, and solidarity with one another... For instance, the union picket lines that surrounded growers' fields during the first great strike were meant as public displays of discontent with the farmworkers' working conditions. Yet Chavez consider them to also be opportunities for the cultivation of activist virtue.[1435]*

This training and character development aims at the acquisition and strengthening or

---

[1432] Quoted in ibid., 61.
[1433] ibid., 41.

[1434] ibid., 44.
[1435] ibid., 51.

moral virtues, such as courage, generosity, justice, etc., but also other valuable traits such as self-confidence, and even eloquence.

> *The picket line is where a man makes his commitment, and it is irrevocable; the longer he's on the picket line, the stronger the commitment. The workers on the ranch committees who don't know how to speak, or who never speak – after five days on the picket lines they speak right out, and they speak better.... [The] picket line is a beautiful thing, because it does something to a human being.[1436]*

This is worth emphasizing. Chavez is claiming, by virtue of his own witness, the transformative effect of righteous activism on the individual participants. While "success" is desired, of course, there is something personally valuable about this sort of activism regardless if the stated political/economic objectives are achieved.

> *Chavez envisions nonviolent direct action not only as an arsenal for overturning unjust institutions but also as the learning tool for the kinds of skills and moral demeanors needed to build and sustain a just society. In walking a picket line, staffing an information table, conducting contract negotiations, or engaging in a fast, a person could begin to understand the nature of planning, group deliberation, and compromise, as well as the importance of service, patience, and sacrifice. These are the organizing skills that allow people to cooperate with one another, to build power – with one another, and to nurture future generations of leaders who can continue to uphold these values and open up new opportunities for freedom.[1437]*

Indeed, so valuable and so primary is this personal transformation, for Chavez, that he is unwilling to compromise it even for the sake of obtaining the stated goals of the direct-action campaign.

> *If I we're to tell the workers: "all right, we're going to be violent; going to burn the sheds and we're going to dynamite the growers' homes and we're going to burn the vineyards," provided we can get away with it, the growers would sign a contract. But you see that that victory came at the expense of violence; it came at the expense of injuring. I think once that happens it would have a tremendous impact on us. We would lose our perspective and we would lose the regard we have for human beings – and then the struggle would become a mechanical thing.[1438]*

One of the problems of how owners/growers treated their workers/employees is that they were being treated as parts of the machine, as replaceable and disposable means to an end. Chavez did not want *La Causa* to resort to the same mentality, and it would do so if it adopted violent methods. In 1971, Chavez gave a speech against the Vietnam War, in which he described *La Causa* as a nonviolent social movement intended to counter the influences of corporate greed and militarism. Going far beyond the struggles of, and injustices experienced by, farmworkers, he campaigned against violence and greed itself, denouncing violence and promoting peace and nonviolence.

> *If we provide alternatives for our young people out of the way we use the energies and resources of our own lives, perhaps fewer and fewer of them will seek their manhood in affluence and war. Perhaps we can bring the day when children will learn from their earliest days that being fully man and fully woman means to give one's life to the liberation of the brother who suffers.[1439]*

[1436] Quoted in ibid., 51-52.
[1437] ibid., 52.

[1438] Quoted in ibid., 59.
[1439] Quoted in ibid., 23-24.

If the goal is to make people morally better, that can't be achieved through the use of violence. To do so would, at minimum, inhibit the positive personal transformation activists might otherwise experience. This personal transformation has value not only for the individual, but also for the community. Individual personal "revolutions" inspire change in others, which eventually, collectively, result in *cultural change*.

> As for the nation as a whole, it doesn't matter to me how our government structure, or what type of political party one may have. The real change comes about when men really want it. In a small way, we try to change ourselves if we try to change those with whom we come into contact.... We must acquaint people with peace – not because capitalism is better or communism is better, but because we as men are better.... We need a cultural revolution.[1440]

In addition to embracing non-violent methods out of principle, and for the sake of the pursuit of the positive personal transformation experienced by the activists, Chavez also believed that there was a strategic advantage to non-violence, related to the avoidance of backlash already mentioned above.

> Chavez thought the strategy more effective than armed struggle because it is more likely that the public will come to the aid of a nonviolent movement that makes an explicit point to respect human life and individual dignity. It is also more likely that the targeted institution can consider grievances, reconsider its policies and actions, and think about the real interests involved in the dispute if it does not feel as though someone is seeking to pull it up by the roots.[1441]

The multiple strategies of nonviolent direct action employed by Chavez results in a "two-handed" theory of nonviolent direct action. The first-hand "shakes up" the system, and the second hand "calms" the target of the direct action through the display of respect and self-restraint. The target is challenged to change but reassured that the goal is not his destruction or harm, but simply justice.

As an editorial note: contrast this with the often-merciless tactics of "cancel culture" which seeks to ruin the lives and careers of individuals for their mistakes (sometimes singular mistakes), and sometimes made years or even decades in the past, with no pretense of an offer of redemption, the ability to make amends, etc. When a person is harmed by being "canceled" in this way, it seems that they would be far less likely to engage in sincere self-reflection, let alone change, given that they have not been provided the incentive, or even an opportunity, to do so.

It should also be noted that if activists not only refrain from violent methods but continue to be non-violent even when they are victims of violent suppression themselves, there is even more potential for the generation of empathy and support. "If, for every violent act committed against us we respond with nonviolence, we attract people's support. We can gather the support of millions who have a conscience and would rather see a nonviolent resolution to problems."[1442] Chavez was explicitly seeking to build coalitions with potential allies.

Intersectionality and Allies

While the vocabulary of intersectionality did not yet exist at this time, Chavez reveals an understanding of intersectionality, nonetheless. While many students and academics interested in supporting *La Causa* shared with the workers an ethnic heritage, they were overlooking, according to Chavez, *differences* in socio-economic class and education. Their shared status as Latino/a/x did not gloss over other relevant differences of privilege. Chavez was also "ahead of his time" in

---

[1440] Quoted in ibid., 44.
[1441] ibid., 51.

[1442] Quoted in ibid., 42.

his recognition that racial prejudice did not operate merely, or even primarily, at the level of individual belief and behavior, but was, relevantly, in operation at the level of systems and organization. Today, we refer to that as systemic racism.

> *Chavez also observed that there is an institutional nexus among agribusiness, politicians, research universities, and consumers that relies on cheap farm labor for production but ignores the death and diseases among farmworkers needed to sustain it. He knew, then, that confronting the system of exploitation would involve more than just altering racist beliefs. Even though they deeply nurtured the structural violence of the industry, a campaign to eliminate prejudice would not, by itself, necessarily transform the relations of production and consumption needed to eliminate exploitation in the fields. Narrow Chicano nationalism that emphasized Chicano ethnic solidarity against white society, in Chavez's view, simply did not have the resources to explain and unpack the interlocking structural and cultural violence enshrined within California agribusiness.*[1443]

Here, we see not only Chavez' understanding that our identities are shaped along various axes (e.g., race and ethnicity, but also gender, also socioeconomic status, also educational attainment, etc.), but also his recognition that if the goal is to produce system-level change, *La Causa* (and presumably other movements as well) shouldn't be constructed as a narrow "ethnic" movement. Chavez was particularly "revolutionary" in that *El Plan de Delano* saw beyond the particular needs and issues of Mexican or Mexican American farmworkers, or even California farmworkers in general.

> *We know that the poverty of the Mexican*

> *or Filipino worker in California is the same as that of all farmworkers across the country, the Negroes and poor whites, the Puerto Ricans, Japanese and Arabians, in short all of the races the comprise the oppressed minorities of the United States.*[1444]

La Causa was not confined to a single race or ethnic group but was meant to address systemic conditions and injustice that serve to oppress people from a *variety* of backgrounds. Chavez's resistance to campaigns to emphasize Chicano ethnic solidarity would almost certainly be controversial in certain circles today.

> *I hear about la raza more and more. Some people don't look at it as racism, but when you say la raza, you are saying an anti-gringo thing and our fear is that it won't stop there. Today it's anti-gringo, tomorrow it will be anti-Negro and the day after it will be anti-Filipino, anti-Puerto Rican. And then it will be anti-poor Mexican, and anti-darker skinned Mexican.*[1445]

While there is no doubt that Chavez was proud of his heritage, and equally no doubt that he drew upon Mexican cultural traditions to inspire workers, and, more so, thought that these cultural values could serve as a model for a morally improved version of the United States, he was *likewise* careful to prevent the movement from being narrowly defined along ethnic lines.

> *We know that the poverty of the Mexican or Filipino worker in California is the same as that of all farmworkers across the country, the Negroes and poor whites, the Puerto Ricans, Japanese, and Arabians, in short all of the races that comprise the oppressed minorities of the United States. The majority of the people on our Pilgrimage are of Mexican descent, but the*

[1443] ibid., 80-81.
[1444] Quoted in ibid., 30.

[1445] Quoted in ibid., 81-82.

triumph of our race depends on a national Association of all farmworkers. . . . If it were nothing but farmworkers in the union now, just Mexican farmworkers, we only have about 30 percent of all the ideas that we have. There would be no cross-fertilization, no growing. It's beautiful to work with other groups, other ideas, and other customs. It's like the wood is laminated.[1446]

Coalition building and ally recruitment was consistent with his principled approach to activism, but also served an obvious practical purpose as well. People in positions of power have used the strategy of "divide and conquer" for as long as there have been people to divide and conquer. Changing the system itself requires collaboration and the recruitment of allies. If *La Causa* was understood as a purely "Mexican" movement, its ability to recruit supporters from other marginalized groups, or even sympathetic members of privilege groups would be lessened, and thereby significantly reduce its potential for success.

In addition to his progressive (at the time) recognition of what we term intersectionality today, Chavez was also "ahead of his time" with respect to his views on gender, *machismo*, and what is now called "toxic masculinity." Chavez understood *machismo* as a form of cultural violence. Aggressive masculinity, or what might be termed today "toxic" masculinity, nurtured violence and violent responses to conflict, and also hindered the effectiveness of *La Causa* to the extent that men prevented women from participating, or ignored the female perspective, or gave inadequate attention to the possible contributions of women. In 1968, Chavez ended his first fast (over twenty-five days) with a speech. He was seated next to Senator Robert Kennedy and was so weak from hunger that he couldn't read the speech himself, and it was read aloud by Minister James Drake.

When we are really honest with ourselves we must admit that our lives are all that really belong to us. So it is how we use our lives that determines what kind of men we are. It is my deepest belief that only by giving our lives do we find life. I am convinced that the truest act of courage, the strongest act of manliness is to sacrifice ourselves for others in a totally nonviolent struggle for justice. To be a man is to suffer for others. God help us to be men![1447]

This portion of his speech reveals that concepts of masculinity, and his desire to provide a new model of masculinity, were not some sort of afterthought for Chavez, but was among his core values. In this remarkable passage, Chavez proposes that genuine courage and "manliness" is displayed *not* in acts of violence or bravado, but in nonviolent acts of self-sacrifice. Care and sacrifice rather than aggression and violence are what makes someone a "man." "For Chavez, as for some feminists, nonviolent theory and practice are mainly about men *un*learning patriarchal notions of gender and learning modes of suffering and other regarding feelings."[1448]

Chavez spoke out against oppression on the axis of gender, condemning "machismo" and concepts of masculinity that were violent and oppressive to women. Chavez understood the role of cultural conditioning in the generation of gender. He credited his own mother with offering an *alternative* to the existing norm. "She taught her children to reject that part of a culture which too often tells its young men that you're not a man if you don't fight back."[1449]

Masculinity as exemplified by "machismo" understands and celebrates power as "power over." Power is measured by the ability one has to make others do what one wants. As such, power is a limited resource. The more power I have, the less you have. By its very nature, then, power involves conflict in which some "win" and others "lose." This is referred to as a "zero sum

---

[1446] Quoted in ibid., 83-84.
[1447] Quoted in ibid., 91.

[1448] ibid., 92.
[1449] Quoted in ibid., 89.

game." The only way I can "win" is if you "lose."

An alternative vision of power is "power with." This understanding of power involves the ability to generate change through "communication, dialogue, mutual attention, and communal identification with one another's aims and interests."[1450] In this understanding of power, power is not a resource to be held by individuals in a "more than" or "less than" relationship to others. Instead, power is generated by, and exercised by, *groups*. The group's ability to *cooperate harmoniously* is the measure of its power, but that power is not held by any particular member of that group.

> *Chavez... Emphasizes the need for nonviolent direct action to help build a community of Democratic deliberation and leadership that seeks to foster skills of self-determination in others. Nonviolence seeks to create ties of solidarity and common purpose so that a group can work together more effectively; in other words, nonviolent direct action seeks to generate "power with." Members are open and vulnerable to one another so that they may care for each other and are willing to suffer and sacrifice.[1451]*

Conclusion

We began this examination of Cesar Chavez by recognizing what "everyone" knows about him, and by now I hope it is clear that his ideas and his contributions to society are even more significant. In addition to being a front-line activist for social justice, which is itself significant and praiseworthy, Chavez also understood and grappled with concepts that, though taken for granted by some today, were quite "revolutionary" in his time: intersectionality, toxic masculinity, systemic racism, and the necessity of coalition-building.

> *Chavez recognizes that people of color in the United States suffer structural violence but also that these institutional inequalities are supported by racist ideas and opinions. He criticizes the narrow view of race he believes is found in Chicano nationalism for being a contributor to cultural violence and for not making a strong connection between race and economic class. In the place of narrow ethnic nationalism, Chavez offers a perspective of radical democracy that tends to envision racial difference and material equality as mutually informative social categories, linking a politics of recognition with a politics of economic redistribution. He also finds within Chicano nationalism an emphasis on machismo that, like the narrow construction of Chicano/a identity, operates as a form of cultural violence, oppressing women and inhibiting the struggle to eliminate structural violence. In the place of machismo, Chavez offers an alternative conception of masculinity that he believes will further the emergence of a culture of peace by undergirding new forms of leadership and decision-making, as well as helping to improve lives and the relationships between men and women.[1452]*

While not usually recognized as an "intellectual," and certainly not an "academic," Chavez nevertheless revealed a depth and sophistication of thought that found expression in his direct-action campaigns. As such, Chavez was clearly a "community intellectual" and serves as a compelling example of the need to reconsider what counts as "philosophy," and who counts as a "philosopher."

[1450] ibid., 93.
[1451] ibid., 94.

[1452] ibid., 96.

NOTES

NOTES

NOTES

NOTES

NOTES